The New York Times
PRACTICAL GUIDE
TO PRACTICALLY
EVERYTHING

The Essential Companion for Everyday Life

edited by

AMY D. BERNSTEIN & PETER W. BERNSTEIN

St. Martin's Press
New York

ACKNOWLEDGMENTS

First, a very special thanks to Christopher Ma, co-creator of the original Practical Guides and trusted friend and adviser.

Janice Olson, who designed, produced and made numerous helpful suggestions on every page, and Anna Isgro, who edited some of the chapters in this book, made invaluable contributions and were indispensable at every turn.

We're fortunate to have friends, acquaintances and relatives, all experts in their respective fields, who were able to pitch in with practical advice and help at a moment's notice. Thanks to Richard Alexander, Robert Ascheim, Helen Bernstein, Robert Bernstein, Dorothy Berwin, Vartan Gregorian, Jane Grossman, Louella Hill, Alexa Hirschfeld, James Hirschfeld, Richard Peña, Gerry Roche, June Schneider and James Stourton. And we benefited from research help from Allison Bernstein, Layla Nemazee and Ceciley Slocum.

In addition, our thanks to Lisa Senz at St. Martin's Press, who put all the pieces together to make this book possible, and Tom Mercer, also at St. Martin's Press, a meticulous, thoughtful and intelligent editor; Alex Ward at the New York Times, who offered acute editorial comments and did yeoman's service in corralling original contributions from many Times reporters and critics; Tomi Murata, Phyllis Collazo and Sheryl Leder, also at the New York Times, smoothed our way.

ISBN-13: 978-0-312-35388-9
ISBN-10: 0-312-35388-X

In the preparation of this book, every effort has been made to offer current, correct and clearly expressed information. Nonetheless, inadvertent errors can occur and information can change. The information in the text is intended to afford general guidelines on matters of interest. Accordingly, the information in this book is not intended to serve as legal, accounting, tax or medical advice. Readers are encouraged to consult with professional advisers concerning specific matter before making any decision and the editors and publisher disclaim any responsibility for positions taken by readers in individual cases or for any misunderstanding on the part of readers.

CONTENTS

Introduction   xiii
Contributors   xiv

CHAPTER 1:

HEALTH & FITNESS

Getting Fit

LOSING WEIGHT: Getting and Staying Trim   3
  Does Your Weight Fit You?   4
  Cyber-Trim and Cyber-Fit   5
  Let's Go to the Tape Measure   6
  Should You Pop a Diet Pill?   6
  Overweight? Check Your Body Mass Index   7
EXERCISE: No Gym, No Fees, No Strangers   9
  Start with 12 Minutes a Day   9
  Workout Benefits at a Glance   10
  Exercise For the Time-Challenged   12
BODY SCULPTING: Cardio Machines   13
  To Sculpt a Trophy Body   15
  Advice Worth Its Weight in Gold   16
  Exercise to Your Heart's Content   17
  Sweating Your Way to Serenity   17
AVOIDING INJURIES: Staying Off the Bench   18
  The Children's Hour   19
  A Cure for Couch Potatoes   20
  The Right Exercise Shoes   21
  Protecting Feet and Joints   21
  Signs That You Are Overdoing It   22

Looking Great

SKIN DAMAGE: The Aging Wars   23
  The New Anti-Aging Makeup   24
  Moles That Turn Deadly   25
  Protecting Yourself From the Sun   26
  January is the Cruelest Month   26
BEAUTY AIDS: A Magic Moisturizer?   27
  The Foundation of Everything   28
  Tips From a Top Makeup Artist   29
  Do-It-Yourself Facial Peels   30
  Adding That Youthful Glow   30
ENHANCEMENTS: A New Kind of Beauty   31
  Six Injections and What They Do   32
  Hand-to-Hand Combat   33

HAIR: An Embarrassment of Baldness   33
  Tender Loving Care for Delicate Hair   34
TEETH: Beyond the Pale   35

Sexuality

HORMONES: Hormones Are Everything   36
  Sex Effects   37
CONTRACEPTION: Better Safe Than Dismayed   38
MENOPAUSE: When Menopause Comes   38
  How Sex Life Changes   40
DYSFUNCTION: When the Pump Won't Work   41
SEXUAL DISEASES: STD's   42
  Protecting Yourself From AIDS   44
  The Search for an AIDS Vaccine   45
ABORTION: Facts and Figures   46
  Options for the Morning After   47

Doctors & Medicine

DOCTORS: Where to Find a Good One   48
  Docs Who Make House Calls   48
  The Doctor Is Online   49
  The Better Off You Are   50
  Talking With Your Doctor   50
HEART DISEASE: Men, Women & Disease   52
  When Seconds Count   52
  Every Stroke Matters   53
  Handicapping Your Mini-Stroke   53
  Acetaminophen: Too Much of a Good Thing 54
  Statins: The New Miracle Drug?   54
  Let the Patient Beware   55
DIABETES: The Diabetes Epidemic   55
BREAST CANCER: A Primer   57
  Performing a Breast Self-Examination   57
  Mammograms   58
PROSTATE CANCER: The Quandary   60
  Watch Your Waist—and Prostrate   60
MENTAL HEALTH: Minding Your Mental Health   61
  Holiday Depression   62
  The Real Nature of Depression   63
ALTERNATIVE MEDICINE: Other Treatments   64
  Hypnosis   64
  Five Alternative Approaches   66
  Well-Kneaded Respites   67
  Exercising Away Back Pain   68

SLEEP: Snoring, From A to Zzzzz   68
Think Before You Sleep   69

Having Children

CONCEPTION: Before You're Pregnant   70
The Best Day to Try Your Luck   70
PREGNANCY: Medical Checks in the Womb   72
Having a Safe Pregnancy   72
How to Figure Your Due Date   73
Some Drugs That Can Cause Problems   74
Avoiding Another Miscarriage   76
Fertilization: Learning the Lingo   77
New Ways to Start a Family   77
When Morning Sickness Comes   78
Quick Delivery? Try Exercise   79
Growth of the Fetus From 8 to 40 Weeks   79
Baby Makes More Than Three   80
Less Pain? Deliver in the Afternoon   80
ADOPTION: Adopting a Baby or Child   80
Resources for Adoptive Parents   82
CHILD DEVELOPMENT & PARENTING: Colic   83
Toxins in Your Breast Milk   84
Serious Face Time With Baby   84
Who's Bringing Up Baby?   85
Watch Them Grow ... and Grow   86
Hello, Mama. Hello, Papa   87
Body Mass Index for Children   88
Have Your Children Had All Their Shots?   89
The Knotty Problem of ADHD   90
The Real Risks to Children   91
How to Raise a Moral Child   93

First Aid & Survival

FIRST AID: The ABC's of CPR   94
A Primer on Rescue Breathing   95
Taking Shock Seriously   96
Controlling Bleeding From an Open Wound   96
Saving a Choking Victim   97
Getting Burned   98
What's Dangerous for Babies   98
When Someone Is Poisoned   99
Treating Insect Bites   99
If a Snake Strikes and Bites   100
How to Alleviate Heatstroke   100
The First Step: A First-Aid Kit   101
DISASTERS: When the Earth Shakes   101
Surviving a Deluge   103
Riding Out a Thunderstorm   104
Preparing for a Hurricane   104
When a Twister Is Approaching   105

Disaster Info   106
Safety for Swimmers and Surfers   107
SELF-DEFENSE: If You're Mugged   107
Basic Moves in Your Own Defense   108
SURVIVAL STRATEGIES: Airplane Crash   109
Before It All Goes Up in Smoke   110
What to Do If Confronted by a Bear   110
Lions and Tigers and Rhinos, Oh My   111
Biological and Chemical Attacks   111

CHAPTER 2:

FOOD & DRINK

Diet & Nutrition

NUTRITION: You Are What You Eat   114
U.S.D.A. Food Guide   115
Calorie Requirements   116
FAT: The Lowdown on Low-Fat Diets   117
The Skinny on Fat   117
Fat Attack   118
VITAMINS: The Home Vitamin Shelf   118
Don't Like the Newest Diet? Wait Awhile   119
More May Be Too Many   122
MINERALS: The Mineral Minder   123
Questions About Calcium   124
HEALTHY EATING: The Food Label   125
How Fish Can Help Your Heart   127
Fish Oil: From Herring to Flounder   127
Oil That's Really Good for You   128
The Almighty Yogurt   129

In the Kitchen

RECIPES & UTENSILS: Evaluate a Recipe   130
A Bare-Bones Kitchen   131
Casting Call for Pots and Pans   131
The Sticky Issues of Teflon   132
FRESH PRODUCE & INGREDIENTS: 133
Ripe for the Picking   133
Hurry Up and Ripen   134
Some Really Delicious Apples   134
Where the Pesticides Are   135
Think Globally, but Eat Locally   136
How Green Is Your Kitchen?   136
COOKING BASICS: Cooking by the Book   138
Germ Warfare   138
How to Carve a Turkey   139
How to Clean a Fish   140
The Catch of the Day   141
How to Grill a Fish   142

And Now, the Perfect Sauce 142
GOURMET DINING: Chillin' With Nigella 143
The Children's Menu 143
Vegetarian Chili With Corn Bread Topping 144
The Many Nuances of Chocolate 144
Cooking With a Foreign Accent 145
Why French Women Don't Get Fat 146
Meeting the Cordon Bleu Test 147
Crème Renversée au Caramel 147

Wine, etc.

WINES: Starting a Wine Collection 148
Wine by the Numbers 148
A Worldwide Wine Sampler 149
Savoring a Good Wine 149
Wine by the Book 150
Ranking the French Elite 151
Wines Have Temperatures, Too 152
For Summer, Think Pink 153
Matches Made in Heaven 154
Plonk Ain't What It Used to Be 155
Champagne on the Cheap 156
BEER: Beyond the Basic Six-Pack 157
The Dos and Don'ts of Drinking 158
SPIRITS: Mixology 101: Classic Cocktails 159
How to Cure a Hangover 159
Stocking the Liquor Cabinet 161
Whiskey-Sipping Secrets 161
Not Just Any Old Mint Julep 162
COFFEE & TEA: The Perfect Cup of Espresso 163
Java Jolts to Start You Up 164
A World Tour of Teas 164

CHAPTER 3:

MONEY

Personal Finance

BUDGETING: You, Inc. 166
Figuring Your Budget 167
Calculating Your Net Worth 167
SAVING: The Best Way to Save 168
The Risks of Online Banking 168
How to Save $100 or More This Year 169
How to Get a Swiss Bank Account 170
Want to Get Rich Quick? 172
Your Chances of (Not) Winning the Lottery 173
CHILDREN: What It Costs to Raise a Child 173
Can I Have an Allowance? 174
Teaching Kids to Use Plastic 174
Reining in Teenage Spending 175
Rules for Boomerang Kids 176
CREDIT: Credit Cards That Reward 177
Checking Up on Your Credit Rating 178
DEBT: Beyond Get-Out-of-Debt Clichés 178
Going Bankrupt Is Harder to Do 179
Choosing a Credit Counselor 180
Filing for Bankruptcy 180

Investing

STOCKS & BONDS: Where to Put Your Money 181
What a Difference 10 Days Make 182
Pick the Stock or the Moment? 183
The Bulls Are Beating the Bears 183
As January Goes, So Goes the Year 184
How Amateurs Might Beat Pros 185
Does Real Estate Beat Stocks? 185
Staying Ahead of the Yield Curve 187
Advice From the Oracle of Omaha 187
Forecasting the Future 189
MUTUAL FUNDS: How to Pick a Fund 190
Why You Can't Beat the Market 191
Reading a Balance Sheet 192
Words to Watch on Wall Street 194
How to Estimate Total Return 195
Does Big Mean Bad for Funds? 196
Beware of Mutual Fund Taxes 197
FINANCIAL ADVISERS: Finding a Broker 197
A Broker by Any Other Name 198
RETIREMENT: Nurturing Your 401(k) 199
Calculating Retirement Needs 200

Real Estate

HOME BUYING: The Long View on Real Estate 202
America's Last True Bargains 204
Better to Buy or Rent? 204
MORTGAGES: The Mortgage Minefield 207
What Lenders Want to Know 208
Which Mortgage Is for You? 210
Terms to Learn Before Closing 212
Figuring Your Monthly Payments 212
Playing the Refinancing Game 213
Beware of the Reverse Mortgage 214
SECOND HOMES: A Cottage in the Country 215
The Priciest Vacation Havens 216
Sick of the Suburbs? 218
OPPORTUNITIES: Houses on the Cheap 220
Bargains Beyond the Borders 221
When You Are Homesick at 64 223
Beyond Houses 224

Insurance & Taxes

BUYERS GUIDE: Policies to Keep You Covered   226
   Life Insurance   226
   Health Insurance   228
   Disability Insurance   229
   Homeowner's Insurance   230
   Automobile Insurance   233
   Filing an Auto Insurance Claim   233
   Why Bet on Long-Term Care Insurance?   234
   Coverage You May Not Need   235
   Know Your Insurance Terms   235
TAX PLANNING: Overlooked Deductions   237
   Preparing Tax Returns Right the First Time   237
   Six Year-End Tax-Saving Tips   239
   Estate Planning: A Trust With Pros and Cons   239
   The Giving Circle   240
   The Give-and-Take of Charitable Giving   241
   What to Show Your Accountant   242
   Picking an Accountant   242
AUDITS: How Does the I.R.S. Pick Audits?   243
   If the I.R.S. Comes Knocking   244

CHAPTER 4:

SPENDING & SAVING

Consumer Advice

SHOPPING ONLINE: The Online Bazaar   246
   Comparison Shopping Made Easy   246
   Sites for Savvy Shoppers   247
STRATEGIES: If You've Got It, Flaunt It   248
   When to Take Out Your Wallet   249
   Tipping: How Much?   250
   Don't Forget the Hotel Maid   250
   Buying Old Is New Again   251
   Worthless Warranties?   252
   The Bargains in Your Post Office   253
IDENTITY THEFT: Protecting Your Data   254
   Who's Vulnerable to Identity Theft?   255
EMERGENCIES: Preparing for a Quick Getaway   256
   In Case I Get Hit by a Bus   257
   Going Out Feetfirst   258
   The Truth About Embalming   259

Autos

BUYING: What Dealers Won't Tell You   260
   Alternatives to Kicking the Tires   261
   New Ways to Buy Used Cars   261
   The Car of the Future?   262
   Cars Across the Land   263
   Beyond Gasoline   264
DRIVING: A Racer on Driving Defensively   265
   What It Takes to Stop in Time   265
   For Safety, First Buckle Up   266
   Holding Your Liquor   267
   The Meaning of Tipsy   267
   Helping Your Child Drive Safely   268
   Choosing a Driving School   269
   When to Hang Up the Keys   270
   Help When You're Stranded   271
MAINTENANCE: The Manual or the Mechanic?   272
   Gas Misers   273
   Drinking Soda and Driving   274
   Gas-Saving Strategies   274
CYCLES & RV'S: 275
   Taking a Cycle for a Spin   275
   Make Room for Scooters   277
   Condos on Wheels   277
   On the Horizon: Off-Road RV's   278
   Stopping Auto Rustlers   279

Home Technology

COMPUTERS: Networking Your Home   280
   Many Computers, Many Choices   283
   A Basic Computer Just for E-Mail   284
   Secrets to Hard-Drive Hygiene   284
   Moving Data to a New Computer   285
   Making Old Files New Again   286
   E.R. for Hard Drives   287
   The Lifespan of a Diskette   288
   Backing Up While On the Go   288
   How Never to Miss an E-mail   289
ONLINE: A Bounty of Browsers   290
   Serene Behind a Firewall   290
SERVICE & ENERGY: Computer Docs   291
   I Vant to Drink Your Vatts   292
AUDIO & VIDEO: Finding Podcasts   292
   Satellite Radio That Follows You Home   293
   TV: Where the World Is Really Flat   294
   Big Screen on a Small Budget   294
PHONES: Making Calls Without a Phone   296
   Should Your PC Be Your Phone?   297
   Choosing a Cellphone Plan   298
CAMERAS: Have Digital, Will Travel   298

Collecting

ART: A Guide for the Artless   300
   When Beauty and Value Merge   302
   What to Look for in a Painting   303

ANTIQUES: How to Spot a Real Antique 303

How to Recognize Famous-Name Antiques 305

What's Your Collection Worth? 306

Going on the Antiques Roadshow 307

AUCTIONS: Hot Bids, Cold Sweats 307

Culling the Junk From the Collectibles 308

Bargains at Charity Auctions 309

Demystifying eBay 310

Shopping in Uncle Sam's Attic 310

Sniffing Out a Fake 311

GEMS, ETC.: Diamonds: What's in a Rock? 312

Pearls: Only the Oyster Knows for Sure 313

The Price of Sparkle in Your Life 314

Silver: Look for a Lion or a King 314

Virtual Stamp Collecting 315

Profiting From Botched-Up Stamps 315

Wine: A Consumable Asset 316

Oriental Rugs: On a Magic Carpet Ride 317

Guitars With a Real Twang 318

CHAPTER 5:

EDUCATION
Pre-K Through 12

PRE-SCHOOL: Lighten Up, Parents 320

How Children Really Learn 321

Identifying a Gifted Child 321

Acquiring a Second Tongue 322

STRATEGIES: Does Music Make You Smarter? 323

Chess Check-up 324

How to Succeed in Science 324

Physical Education Is Getting Fitter 325

TESTING: Public vs. Private School 326

The Child Who Does Too Much 326

Cures for Text Anxiety 327

Homework: A Helping Hand at Day's End 328

TEACHING TECHNIQUES: Single-Sex Schools 329

Goodbye, Class. See You in the Fall 330

Inside the Teenage Mind 330

READING: Summer Reading 332

The Best Books for Kids, 2001-2005 333

College & Beyond

GETTING IN: Translating the "New" SAT 336

SAT Scores: "Will I Get In?" 336

Prepping for the SAT's 337

The Truth About College Rankings 338

Campus Reality Tour 339

The Admissions Game 341

Factors in Admissions Decisions 341

College Athletics: From Field to Dorm 343

Do A.P. Courses Help? 343

Getting Credit Before You Go 345

ARTS EDUCATION: What Would Picasso Do? 346

Dancing Around the Subject 347

FINANCIAL AID: Coping With the Cost 348

College Grants You Don't Have to Repay 350

COURSES OF STUDY: Life 101 350

The Two-Year Option 351

The Student's Life 351

Getting a College Degree Abroad 352

U.S. Exchange Programs 354

Harvard at a Bargain Price 355

The New Face of Facebooks 355

How to Win a Rhodes Scholarship 356

Other Roads to Study Abroad 357

GRAD SCHOOL: Let Abe Lincoln Guide You 358

Psst! Apply to Law School 359

Are You a Master of the Universe? 359

Beyond Law School Rankings 360

If You're Thinking of Med School 361

Is B-School Worth the Big Bucks? 363

THE REAL WORLD: Free Advice 364

CHAPTER 6:

CAREERS
Getting Started

PICKING A PROFESSION: Personality Tests 366

What's Your Type? 367

JOB HUNTING: Networking Online 367

Remember Your SAT Scores? 368

Best Web Sites for Job Seekers 369

Honing Your Skills for the Hunt 370

GETTING HIRED: Job Interviews 371

20 Terms to Avoid on a Résumé 372

A Résumé That Works 373

Now, Let's Go to the Videotape 373

STRATEGIES: Want a Job, Get an Internship 374

Majors With a Pragmatic Bent 374

OCCUPATIONAL OUTLOOK: 375

Where the Best Jobs Will Be 375

Go West, Job Seeker 376

The 30 Fastest-Growing Professions 377

SALARIES: What Legends Get Paid 378

What 100 Jobs Pay 379

Smart Moves

LEADERSHIP: Who Gets to the Corner Office? 382
The Changing Profile of Chief Executives 382
Management by the Book 383
Who Makes It in Washington? 384
OFFICE POLITICS: Bully Bosses 385
A Spotter's Guide to Brutal Bosses 386
Disagreeing With the Boss 387
How to Shush the Office Magpie 388
JOB TRANSFERS: A Year Abroad as a Career Move 388
What to Know Before You Go Abroad 389
STRESS MANAGEMENT: Beat Burnout 390
Commuting: The Long Road to Work 390
Stressful and Stressless Jobs 391
The E-Mail Menace 392
MOVING UP: How to Get Your Next Raise 392
Don't Ask, Don't Tell 393
When You Get a Better Offer 394
How to Get Your Head Hunted 395
MOVING ON: When to Jump Ship 396
If Your Company Is Sold 396
You're Fired: The Art of the Comeback 397
I Quit!!! 397
The Womenless Workforce 399
SECOND CAREERS: What Is Your New Career? 400
Where Career Switchers Go 402
They'd Rather Switch 403
Want to Be Your Own Boss? 404
A Chair Fit for a Chairman 405
Your New "Retirement" Plan 406

CHAPTER 7:

HOUSE & GARDEN

Around the House

REMODELING: How to Pick a Contractor 408
Smaller Families = Bigger Houses? 408
Just in Case Things Go Wrong 410
The Emotional Roller Coaster 411
If I Had a Hammer 411
How Long Is a Lifetime? 412
DECORATING: Antique Hardware 413
How to Stencil a Floor 413
Taming Monster Spaces 414
Living Large in Small Rooms 414
The Secret World of Decorators 415
Ready-to-Eat Kitchens 416
My Stove Is Bigger Than Your Stove 417
Concrete Is Oh-So Decorative 418

Behind Closet Doors 419
Where to Stash a Flat-Screen TV 419
Shelves That Last a Lifetime 420
The Luminous Life of Paint 421
Not All Paints Are Created Equal 422
Fixing the Light Fantastic 423
The Right Shade for the Right Lamp 424
Track Lighting That Disappears 424
The Right Bulb for the Right Light 425
Frame the World Around You 425
FURNISHINGS: A Grandfather Clock to Go 427
Beds You Won't Lose Sleep On 427
A Little Pillow Talk 428
Put Some Spring in Your Sofa 429
What's Hidden Under the Rug? 430
Out, Out, Damn Spot 430
Looking Behind the Curtains 431
MAINTENANCE: Cut Your Heating Bills 431
Potential Savings From a New Furnace 432
When to Fix It, When to Junk It 434
Protecting Your Castle From Time 434
What to Look For on a Leaky Roof 435
Help for a Leaking Toilet 436
If a House Is a Hot Zone 437
When You Fire the Handyman 438

In the Garden

PLANTING: Figments That Turn Into Flowers 440
Where Green Thumbs Shop 440
Where the Growing Zones Fall 441
A Sower's Guide to Soil 442
Tipping the pH Scales 444
Dig and You Shall Reap 445
Good Gardeners' Secret Weapon 445
FLOWERS: A Bulb Lover's Choices 446
We Promise You a Rose Garden 447
Out, Out Black Spot 448
10 (Comparatively) Easy Roses 449
The Scent of a Garden 450
How to Train a Rose 450
10 (Absolutely) Scented Roses 451
Perfect Plants for Tough Places 452
The 60-Second Gardener 453
VEGETABLES: Late-Season Vegetables 454
What Makes Them Heirlooms? 455
A Vegetable for Every Pot 456
Feed Your Plants 458
Herbs for All Spaces 459
PESTS & PRUNING: Doing Battle With Blight 460
How to Attract Butterflies 462

To Lure a Hummingbird 462
Even Plants Need a Haircut 463
How to Delay Blooming 463
Pruners and Spades to Die For 464
TREES & LAWNS: From Root to Branch 465
Trees You Can Adopt 465
Pruning Trees 466
The Mighty Quince 467
The Perfect Lawn 467
The Grass Is Always Greener 469
INDOORS & OUT: Houseplants 470
Location, Location, Location 471
Books: Gardening From A to Z 472
10 Terrific Public Gardens 473
Beautiful Gardens That Gather Moss 473

Pets

DOGS & CATS: Picking a Canine Companion 474
Fair Weather Friends 474
Congenital Defects in Dogs 475
Buying a Pedigree Pup 476
That Doggie in the Pop-up Window 477
Adopting From an Animal Shelter 477
Smelling Like a Wet Dog 477
How to De-Skunk Your Dog 478
Dieting—A Dog's Life 478
All the Cat's Meows 479
Pet Photos: Smile and Say "Arf" 480
Jumpy? Try DogCatRadio 481
VETS: When Your Pet Gets Sick 482
Boosting Your Pet's Well-Being 484
A New Age in Pet Care 485
Finding a Boarding Kennel 486
BIRDS, GERBILS & MORE:
Choosing a Bird Feeder 486
This Recipe Is for the Birds 487
Caged Birds That Sing 488
Thinking of Getting a Gerbil? 488
Bringing Up the Other Baby 489
You Can't Take Them With You 490

CHAPTER 8:

TRAVEL

Getting There

FLYING: Finding Air-Fare Bargains Online 492
Online Travel Sites Worth a Visit 493
All's Fair in the Fare Wars 494
Two Ways to Fly for Peanuts 494

How to Get an Even Cheaper Fare 495
Vacation Packages: A Deal for You 496
Taking the Fear out of Flying 497
A Cure for Jet Lag? 498
Are You on the Safest Airplane? 498
...And in the Safest Seat? 499
If You Are Bumped From a Flight 499
No-Fly Frequent Flier Miles 500
Making the Best of a Long Layover 500
SAILS & RAILS: Tall Ships Sailing 501
If Shuffleboard Isn't Your Thing 501
Deck by Deck 502
Cruising the World 502
Riding the Rails 503
Distances Between Major U.S. Cities 504
LODGING: The World's Most Charming Inns 504
Where the Well-Heeled Stay 506
Taking a Bite of the Big Apple 507
Hush-Hush Hotels 508
Palaces That Could Be Yours 510
Swapping Castles 511
Get Thee to a Monastery 512
INCIDENTALS: It's a Wireless World 512
Getting an 11th-Hour Passport 513
Calling Home for Less 514
The Case for Trip Insurance 515
Travelers' Illnesses 515
A Short Guide to Travel Guides 516
Blogs: Need Even More Travel Advice? 517
Essential Reading 518

Hot Spots

ASIA: Southeast Asia's Tourist Meccas 519
Angkor Wat: Temples & Terror 520
Chowing Down in Shanghai 521
Beyond the Taj Mahal 523
ISLANDS: The Caribbean's Hidden Gems 523
The Next St. Bart's 525
Treasures Beneath the Sea 526
Cuba: You Can't There From Here 527
The Pearl of the Atlantic Regains Its Luster 527
Beyond Hawaii's Big Island 528
Greece: So Many Islands, So Little Time 530
FAMILY TRAVEL: Beyond Disney World 533
Perfect Meals in London and Paris 534
Monaco: Not Just for Adults 536

Natural Treasures

NATIONAL PARKS: America's Crown Jewels 538
Sure Ways to Beat the Crowds 541

The Best Park Guides 545
Where the Crowds Aren't 546
Pick a Park, Any Park 549
Lodges: Places to Hang Your Hiking Boots 551
Paths Across the Nation 552
WILDLIFE: Catch a Glimpse of a Bighorn 554
Where to Watch the Whales 555
WAY SOUTH: Galápagos Unbound 556
A Birdwatcher's Best Friend 557
Rain Forests: Wet and Wild 558
Butterflies Are Free 559
The Pyramids Next Door 559
ON SAFARI: Into the Heart of Africa 561
Where the Wild Things Roam 563

Adventure

TREKKING: A Heck of a Trek 564
G.P.S. Devices: Lost and Found 565
Life Is Better in Bhutan 567
Hiking All Day, Pampered at Night 568
BIKING: Your Personal Tour de France 572
RIVER TRIPS: Slow Boats Through Europe 573
Renting a Canal Cruiser 574
White Water Runs Through It 574
The Ultimate River-Rafting Trip 576
PRISTINE PLACES: Sites for the Intrepid Traveler 577
Follow the Silk Road to the 'Stans 579

CHAPTER 9:

SPORTS & GAMES

A Fan's Guide

BASEBALL: Take Me Out to the Ballgame 582
Baseball's Winter Games 584
Following the Boys of Summer in the Spring 587
TICKETS: Nothing Beats Being There 588
FOOTBALL: Reading the Football Ref's Arms 589
Scalper's Guide: Snagging a Seat 590
Get Ready for the Kickoff 591
BASKETBALL: A Short History of B-ball 592
A Who's Who of Pro Hoop Teams 593
The Odds of Winning the Office Pool 594
HOCKEY: The Fastest Game on Ice 594
Where to Watch the Puck Fly 595
AUTO RACING: Following the Racing Flags 596
LEGENDS: How to Get to the Hall of Fame 597
Must-See Sites for Sports Junkies 598

An Athelete's Guide

GOLF: Get a Grip on Your Golf Game 599
How Handicapping Works 601
Playing Golf Like a Billionaire 602
The Power Game 603
GAME PLANS: How to Play Smart Tennis 604
Basketball: The Home Court Advantage 604
Picking a Tennis Racket 605
Growing Squash 606
Hitting the Softball Every Time 606
From Little Leaguer to All-Star 607
Should Kids Play Football? 608
Sports for a Summer Day 609
How to Ride a Raging Bull 612
Rodeos With a Twist 613
OUTDOORS: Bicycles: Deals on Wheels 614
Beyond the Basic Bike 615
How to Swim Like a Fish 616
Snorkeling: A Mask and the Deep Blue 617
Fishing: Finding Bigger, Meaner Fish 618
Flies That Never Fail 619
A Little Night Fishing 620
Rare Books for an Angler's Soul 621
The Call of the Hunt 621
Dick Cheney's Hunting Lessons 623
Falconry: A Sport of Sultans 624
Rock Climbing: Clinging to the Crags 625
WINTER GAMES: Polar Chills and Thrills 627
Fitting a Snowshoe 627
The Dangers of Thin Air 628
Snowboarding: Catching Some Air 630
Skiing: It's All Downhill From Here 632
Cross-Country Skiing 632
The Best of the West and East 633
How Long Should Your Skis Be? 634
Face-Saving Lessons From the North Pole 635
Igloos: Living Like the Inuit 636
Hitch Rover and Go Skijoring 637
Gear for Warm Toes and Safe Wrists 637
Adventures in Wild Skating 638
Figure-Skating: Making It on the Ice 638
Anatomy of an Ice Skate 640
EXTREME SPORTS: Radical Races 640
Waivers: The Fine Print 641

Parlor Games

POOL: Taking Cues From a Shark 642
Pool Rules 643
ONLINE GAMING: Rules for Multiplayer Newbies 644
BOARD GAMES: Secrets of a Monopoly Champ 645

The Most Landed-on Monopolies 646
A-D-V-I-C-E From a Scrabble Master 647
Go Directly to Go 648
Bored? Looking for Board Games 648
Mah-Jongg: Joining the Tile-High Club 649
Where Kings and Queens Reign 650
CARD GAMES: Poker: Cut the Deck, Please 653
What Beats What 654
Be Prepared to Bet the Ranch 655
A Guide to Poker-Table Manners 657
A Full House With Harry or Johnny 657
Poker Can Make You Rich ... or President 658
The Rest: From Bridge to Solitaire 658
Seduced by Sudoku 664

CHAPTER 10:

ARTS & ENTERTAINMENT
Movies & TV
CLASSICS: The Very Best "Best Movies" List 666
Who Is Oscar, Anyway? 666
FAN FUN: Online Sites for Movie and TV fans 671
PARTIES: Just in Case You Get Invited 672
HOME VIDEO: Best DVD's You Haven't Seen 673
Films for a Very Rainy Day 676
FESTIVALS: Film Festivals Worth the Journey 677
How to Get on a Reality TV Show 678
CHILDREN: The Best 100 Movies for Kids 679

Music
CRITICS' PICKS: Picks for a Desert Island 681
Where Classical Music Thrives 682
What Jazzes Wynton Marsalis 685
POP & ROCK: Rock & Roll Royalty 686
OPERA & BALLET: Cecilia Bartoli Airs Her Arias 689
Opera–Wherever You May Be 690
Ballet at Its Best 691
INDIE MUSIC & JAZZ: The Earliest Recordings 691
For R&B and Jazz Lovers 692
A Who's Who of Music Lists 692
Sites From the Underground 693
FESTIVALS: The Best Summer Festivals 694
The Battle of the Bands 695
The World's Most Remote Music Festival 696

Museums & Books
ART: The World's Great Modern Museums 697
Can't Get to the Louvre? Try This 698

Small European Gems 699
Whistler's Mother Unseated 700
ARCHITECTURE: Sites for Your Eyes 701
GREAT BOOKS: Best Books of the 21st Century 702
Libraries: Getting Lost in the Stacks 708
Beloved American Novels 708

CHAPTER 11:

EVERYDAY SCIENCE
Weather & Geology
FORECASTING: Crickets as Thermometers 710
When to Believe the Weatherman 710
What Weather Maps Say 711
Weather Watching Around the U.S. 712
Know Which Way the Wind Blows 713
Be Your Own Forecaster 714
Why Windchill Matters 715
Hurricanes: Stormy Weather Ahead 715
Avoiding Hypothermia 716
Looking Beyond the Clouds 717
EARTH SCIENCE: How to Read Rocks 717
Common Minerals and Their Uses 718
Predicting Earthquakes 719
Earthquake-Prone Zones 721
The Magnitude of Tremors 721

Stars & Tides
THE STARS & PLANETS: With the Naked Eye 722
The Night Sky: Month by Month 723
Stars and Constellations 724
Our Closest Stellar Neighbors 725
A Portrait of the Planets 726
What's a Planet, Anyway? 728
The Question of Comets 729
Computer-Assisted Telescopes 730
THE SUN & MOON: Solar Eclipses 731
Shadows of the Moon 732
Mountains on the Moon 733
The Phases of the Moon 734
STAR TALK: How to Talk Like an Astronomer 736
Internet Travel: To the Moon, Alice 736
Astrology: What the Stars Say About You 739
The Stars They Are A-Changin' 741
THE TIDES: A Beachgoer's Guide to the Tides 742

Times & Dates
ABOUT TIME: A Very Brief History of Time 744
A Quick Glance at the Clock 744

How to Tell Time Like a Sailor 745
TIME ZONES: Daylight Saving Time 746
International Time Zones 747
CALENDAR DATES: The Perpetual Calendar 748
Holidays Around the World 749
Why Are There Leap Years? 756
How to Keep Your New Year's Resolutions 758
ANCIENT TIMES: The Chinese Zodiac 759
How to Tell Geologic Time 761

Figures & Formulas

WEIGHTS & MEASURES: Measuring Everything 762
Making Do Without a Ruler 762
U.S. Customary Units 763
Temperature Conversions 763
Metric Units 764
The Long and Short of Clothing Sizes 765
Converting U.S. Units to Metric 765
How Far Is That in Miles? 766
Bits, Bytes & Beyond 767
Special Weights & Measures 767
Common Household Measures 768
CHEMISTRY & MATH: Chemistry 769
The Periodic Table of Elements 769
Placing Math on a Timeline 770
Algebra 770
Reading the Signs 770
Roman Numerals 771
Fractions and Their Decimal Equivalents 772
GEOMETRY: Angles and Triangles 772
Quadrilaterals and Other Polygons 773
The Right Way to View Right Triangles 773
Solids 774

CHAPTER 12:

LAW & MORES
Legal Guide

CITIZENSHIP: How to Become a U.S. Ciitizen 776
Registering to Vote 777
How the Electoral College Works 777
How a Bill Becomes a Law 778
Getting a Passport 778
Obtaining a Social Security Number 779
How to Register for the Draft 780
How to Make a Campaign Contribution 780
Deciphering an Opinion Poll 781
How to Join AmeriCorps 782
LEGALITIES: Jury Duty: The Whole Truth 783

Having Your Day in Small Claims Court 784
Where to Go When the Stakes Are Low 785
How to Read Your F.B.I. File 786
Divorce on the Cheap 787
How to Change Your Name 788
When a Child Needs a Guardian 788
Do You Need a Will? 789
LIVING WILLS: Whose Life Is It Anyway? 790

Manners & Miscellany

ETIQUETTE: 21st-Century Manners 791
If the Queen Drops By 792
If You Only Knew What to Do 793
Entertaining With Children 794
Flummoxed by Finger Bowls 795
Putting the "R" back in R.S.V.P. 796
The Lost Art of Letter Writing 796
The Art of the Thank-You Note 797
Minding Multicultural Manners 797
WEDDINGS: Weddings Ring a New Bell 798
Looking for Mr. Right 799
Raising a Glass 800
All the Nuptials Fit to Print 801
What to Say If You Get Cold Feet 801
Ways to Remember a Big Day 802
Stepping Out on the Dance Floor 803
GENEALOGY: Tracing Your Family Tree 803
Finding Grandma, the DNA Way 804
WORDS: *New York Times* Crossword Puzzles 804
Grammar in a Jiffy 805
RESEARCH: Your Personal Reference Desk 806

Signs & Symbols

VISUAL AIDS: Negotiating Highways & Byways 807
Map Symbols 807
International Road Signs 807
CODES: If You Are Lost in the Woods 808
Symbols of Distress 808
Tracking Codes 808
Secrets in Code 809
The Semaphore Code 809
The Morse Code 809
WITHOUT WORDS: Musical Notations 810
Proofreader's Marks 811
Second That Emoticon 811
How to Sign 812
American Sign Language Alphabet 812
The Braille System 812

Index

813

INTRODUCTION

These days, when a Google search takes a nanosecond and gigabytes of data are a click away, who needs a practical guide to everyday life? The answer is practically everyone. Despite the abundance of information at every turn, sorting the salient from the silly, the sensible from the useless and the reliable from the reckless is still a time-consuming and often dissatisfying chore.

That's why we created *The New York Times Practical Guide to Practically Everything*. It's designed to be an all-in-one, do-it-yourself resource, packed with all the information necessary to help you live a rich and well-considered life. Think of it as life's big instruction book, a user's manual for everyday living.

Some books tell you a lot—often too much—about just one thing, like how to play the harmonica, strengthen your abs or plant perfect peas. But for most of us there aren't enough hours in the day to read at length about all the things that interest us. The goal of this book is to offer concise, authoritative—and sometimes entertaining—tips and strategies to serve as reassuring signposts as you navigate the twists and turns of life in the 21st century.

How did we go about it? First of all, we chose key areas—Health, Food & Drink, Money, Spending & Saving, Education, Careers, House & Garden, Travel, Sports & Games, Arts & Entertainment, Everyday Science and Law & Mores. Then we zeroed in on important topics, researching and selecting the most useful advice and strategies. We wanted readers to be able to reach for this book with complete confidence, knowing that they will find high-quality information that will stand the test of time.

To meet those high standards, we relied on *New York Times* writers, reporters and critics who are respected voices in their own fields, from money to health, gardening to home tech, art to music.

They, in turn, sought out the opinions and expertise of doctors, lawyers, academicians, scientists, cooks, and musicians, to name a few. The result is hundreds of expert opinions from *Times* writers and the people they interviewed. David Leonhardt on money matters; Mark Bittman and Marian Burros on food; Tom Kraeutler on home remodeling; *Times* critics Michael Kimmelman and Nicolai Ouroussoff on museums and architecture; Jane E. Brody on health; Cecilia Bartoli and Wynton Marsalis on music; Eric Asimov and Frank J. Prial on wine; Anne Raver, Leslie Land and Ken Druse on gardening; R. W. Apple Jr. and Matt Gross on the pleasures of travel and many, many more.

One of the most interesting lessons we learned as editors was that as fast as the world seems to be moving, some of the chief delights of living well remain enduring and unchanged—from getting the best rate on a mortgage to planting a scented garden, dancing the tango, stocking a wine cellar or finding a puppy. This is as true in the world of manners or in dealing with your money and your health. Handwritten thank-you notes may be losing out to e-mail, but the gesture still rewards both writer and recipient. Stocks go up and down every day and fortunes are made and lost, but the most successful long-term investors, like Warren Buffett, still swear by value investing. Weight-loss fads come and go, but a balanced diet and regular exercise still are the linchpins for enduring health. There still is a world of difference between doing something and doing it well, which is the moral to be drawn from all that you read here. In that respect, we are emulating Benjamin Franklin—a practical philosopher if ever there was one—who claimed, "He that lives well is learned enough."

—*Amy and Peter Bernstein*

The New York Times
PRACTICAL GUIDE TO PRACTICALLY EVERYTHING

Editors: Amy D. Bernstein and Peter W. Bernstein
Contributing Editor: Anna Isgro
Editorial Design: Janice Olson
Copy Editor: Gray Cutler
Illustrations: Steve Noble, Steve McCracken
Cover Designer: David Rotstein
Indexing: Doric Wilson

FEATURED WRITERS • Jennifer Alsever • Lizette Alvarez • R.W. Apple Jr. • Eric Asimov • Ian Austen • Nicholas Bakalar • Lisa Belkin • J. D. Biersdorfer • Mark Bittman • Sandra Blakeslee • Jane E. Brody • Marian Burros • Sean Captain • Hillary Chura • Marjorie Connelly • Ray Cormier • Damon Darlin • Christian DeBenedetti • Chris Dixon • Ken Druse • M. P. Dunleavey • Mark Ellwood • Alan Finder • Deborah Franklin • Jonathan D. Glater • Denise Grady • Tim Gray • Matt Gross • Danny Hakim • William L. Hamilton • Michelle Higgins • Peter Jaret • David A. Kelly • Gina Kolata • Alan B. Krueger • Leslie Land • Denny Lee • Christine Lennon • David Leonhardt • Tamar Lewin • Paul J. Lim • Jane Margolies • Vivian Marino • Patrick McGeehan • Richard J. Meislin • James McManus • Abigail Sullivan Moore • Bonnie Rothman Morris • Maryann Mott • Kate Murphy • Anahad O'Connor • Mitchell Owens • Jon Pareles • Marco Pasanella • Bill Pennington • Frank J. Prial • Anne Raver • Motoko Rich • Stephanie Rosenbloom • Melena Z. Ryzik • Sandra Salmans • Kelefa Sanneh • Liesl Schillinger • Joe Sharkey • Seth Sherwood • Cecilia Capuzzi Simon • Natasha Singer • Michelle Slatalla • Christopher Solomon • Samantha Stainburn • Susan Stellin • Kimberly Stevens • Eric A. Taub • Bob Tedeschi • Stephen Treffinger • Bonnie Tsui • Alina Tugend • Matt Villano • Elizabeth Weil • Gisela Williams • Michael Winerip

CONTRIBUTORS • Conrad de Aenlle • Brian Alexander • Norm Alster • Natalie Angier • Suzy Bales • Ernest Beck • Pam Belluck • Aimée Berg • Leslie Berger • Anna Bernasek • Julie Besonen • Fred Bierman • Julie Bosman • Mary C. Bounds • Michael Brick • Eryn Brown • Janelle Brown • Bill Bryson • Nelson Bryant • Dale Buss • Coeli Carr • Jon Cohen • Jennifer Conlin • Barbara Crossette • Diane Daniel • Eric Dash • Dale DeGroff • Claudia H. Deutsch • Shannon Donnelly • Mary Duenwald • Christopher Elliott • Blake Eskin • Susan Enfield Esrey • Barry Estabrook • Florence Fabricant • Geraldine Fabrikant • Warren Farrell • Susan Ferraro • Adam Fisher • Thomas J. Fitzgerald • Glenn Fleishman • Henry Fountain • Jill Andresky Fraser • Milt Freudenheim • Jonathan Fuerbringer • Alice Gabriel • Debra Galant • Susan B. Garland • Laurel Naversen Geraghty • Anne Glusker • Tim Gnatek • Howard G. Goldberg • Victoria Goldman • Amy Goldwasser • Abby Goodnough • Daniel Grant • Tim Gray • Beth Greenfield • Jane Gross • Lisa Guernsey • Katie Hafner • Suzanne Hamlin • Gardiner Harris • Nancy Hass • Elizabeth Hayt • Patrick O'Gilfoil Healy • Matthew Healey • Martica Heaner • Hubert B. Herring • Robert D. Hershey Jr. • Dennis Hevesi • Louella Hill • Alexa Hirschfeld • James Hirschfeld • Stephen Holden • Ann Hulbert • Harry Hurt III • Julie V. Iovine • Sara Ivry • Stefani Jackenthal • Andrew Jacobs • Caryn James • Scott Jaschik • David Cay Johnston • Sandeep Junnarkar • Andrea Kannapell • Jodi Kantor • Randy Kennedy • Michael Kimmelman • Erika Kinetz • David L. Kirp • Debra A. Klein • N. R. Kleinfield • Brendan I. Koerner • Allan Kozinn • Louise Kramer • Peter D. Kramer • Nicholas D. Kristof • Anne Krueger • Luke Jerod Kummer • Nigella Lawson • Warren E. Leary • Michelle Leder • Yishane Lee • Jeff Leeds • John Leland • Joel Lovell • Sarah Lyall • Nick Lyons • David L. Marcus • Michel Marriott • Dylan Loeb McClain • Charles McGrath • Jesse McKinley • Tara Baukus Mello • Anne Midgette • Lia Miller • Bob Morris • Christine Muhlke • Adam Nagourney • Eric Nagourney • Tim Neville • Andrew Adam Newman • Peter M. Nichols • Elizabeth Olson • John O'Neil • Nicolai Ouroussoff • Dennis Overbye • Alexandra Peers • Richard Peña • Jeanne B. Pinder • David Pogue • Ilana Polyak • Eduardo Porter • Virginia Postrel • Roni Rabin • Ben Ratliff • Julia Reed • Hope Reeves • Stephen Regenold • Lee Reich • Andrew C. Revkin • Alan Riding • Selena Roberts • John Rockwell • Marianne Rohrlich • Donna Rosato • Ellen Rosen • Jody Rosen • Wilson Rothman • Sam Hooper Samuels • Diana Jean Schemo • Seth Schiesel • June Schneider • A. O. Scott • Janny Scott • Kim Severson • Kristina Shevory • Will Shortz • Dinitia Smith • Jennifer Steinhauer • Jane Stern • Michael Stern • Christopher S. Stewart • Florence Stickney • James Stourton • Robert Strauss • Camille Sweeney • Maia Szalavitz • Mary Tannen • Laurie Tarkan • J. Alex Tarquinio • Anthony Tommasini • Luisita Lopez Torregrosa • David Tuller • Ian Urbina • Carol Vogel • Joyce Wadler • Sally Wadyka • Matthew L. Wald • Peter Wayner • Allison Hope Weiner • Alex Wellen • Alex Williams • Florence Williams • Claire Wilson • Alex Witchel • Jennie Yabroff • J. Peder Zane • Marc B. Zawel • Katherine Zoepf • Abigail Zuger

FOR THE NEW YORK TIMES
Administration: *Cristian L. Edwards, President, News Services; Nancy Lee, Vice President, Business Development; Alex Ward, Editorial Director*

HEALTH & FITNESS

Getting Fit   1

LOSING WEIGHT·3: *Getting and staying trim* • *Let's go to the tape measure* • *Should you pop a diet pill?* **EXERCISE·9:** *No gym, no fees, no strangers* • *Start with 12 minutes a day* • *Workout benefits at a glance* • *For the time-challenged, integrative exercise* **BODY SCULPTING·13:** *Best machines in the gym* • *How to sculpt a trophy body* • *Advice worth its weight in gold* • *Sweating your way to serenity* **AVOIDING INJURIES·18:** *How to stay off the bench* • *The right exercise shoes* • *Signs that you are overdoing it*

Looking Great   23

SKIN DAMAGE·23: *Lessons from the aging wars* • *Moles that turn deadly* • *Protect yourself from the sun* **BEAUTY AIDS·27:** *Is there a magic moisturizer?* • *The foundation of everything* • *Tips from a top makeup artist* • *Do-it-yourself facial peels* • *Adding that youthful glow* **ENHANCEMENTS·31:** *A new kind of beauty* • *Six injections and what they do* • *Hand-to-hand combat* **HAIR·33:** *An embarrassment of baldness* • *Tender loving care for delicate hair* **TEETH·35:** *Beyond the pale*

Sexuality   36

HORMONES·36: *Hormones are everything* **CONTRACEPTION·38** *Better safe than dismayed* • **MENOPAUSE·38:** *When menopause comes* **ERECTILE DYSFUNCTION·41:** *When the pump won't work* **DISEASES·42:** *It happened one night: STD's* • *Protecting yourself from AIDS* • *The search for an AIDS vaccine* **ABORTION·46:** *Facts and figures* • *Options for the morning after*

CHAPTER **1. HEALTH & FITNESS**

Doctors & Medicine   48

DOCTORS·48: *Where to find a good doctor* • *The doctor is online* • *Talking with your doctor* **HEART DISEASE·52:** *Men, women & heart disease* • *Every stroke matters* • *Acetaminophen: too much of a good thing* • *Statins:the new miracle drug* **DIABETES·55:** *The diabetes epidemic* **BREAST CANCER·57:** *A primer on breast cancer* **PROSTATE CANCER·60:** *The prostate cancer quandary* **MENTAL HEALTH·61:** *Minding your mental health* • *The real nature of depression* **ALTERNATIVE MEDICINE·64:** *Consider the alternatives* • *Exercising away back pain* **SLEEP·68:** *Snoring, from A to Zzzzz* • *Think before you sleep*

Having Children   70

CONCEPTION·70: *Before you're pregnant* **PREGNANCY·72:** *Having a safe pregnancy* • *Medical checks in the womb* • *Some drugs that can cause problems during pregnancy* • *Avoiding another miscarriage* **ASSISTED CONCEPTION·77:** *Fertilization: learning the lingo* • *New ways to start a family* • *When morning sickness comes* **DELIVERY·79:** *Try exercise for a quick delivery* • *More than three in the delivery room* **ADOPTION·80:** *Adopting a baby or child* **PARENTING·83:** *The answer to colic* • *Serious face time with baby* • *Who's bringing up baby?* **DEVELOPMENT·86:** *Watch them grow and grow* • *Hello, Mama. Hello, Papa* • *Have your children had their shots?* •*The knotty problem of ADHD* • *The real risks to children* • *How to raise a moral child*

First Aid & Survival   94

FIRST AID·94: *The ABC's of CPR* • *Taking shock seriously* • *Saving a choking victim* • *Getting burned* • *When someone is poisoned* • *How to alleviate heatstroke* **DISASTERS·101:** *When the earth shakes* • *Assembling a first-aid kit* • *Surviving a deluge* • *Riding out a thunderstorm* • *Preparing for a hurricane* • *When a twister is approaching* **SELF-DEFENSE·107:** *What to do if you're mugged* • *Basic moves in your own defense* **SURVIVAL STRATEGIES·109:** *Walking away from a crash* • *Before it all goes up in smoke* • *What to do if confronted by a bear* • *A post-9/11 survival kit*

Getting Fit

Getting and Staying Trim
It's a combination of diet and exercise

For many Americans, the battle of the bulge is a way of life, and for some it begins as early as childhood. According to the U.S.D.A., the percentage of children who are overweight has doubled since 1980, and the percentage of adolescents who are overweight has nearly tripled. About nine million young Americans, or more than 15 percent of all children, are overweight. This is particularly troubling , since many of the behaviors that lead to adult obesity are established during childhood.

And even those who manage to stay trim during their youth and into adulthood have difficulty staying trim as they age. A 2005 study published in the *Annals of Internal Medicine* says that 9 out of 10 men and 7 out of 10 women, and half of those who had reached adulthood without a weight problem ultimately became overweight. A third of those women and quarter of the men became obese.

Obesity is reaching epidemic proportions in the United States, bringing with it a host of related diseases. Diagnosed cases of Type 2 diabetes, a major consequence of obesity, have risen dramatically. Just 10 years ago, Type 2 diabetes was virtually unknown among children; now it accounts for almost 50 percent of new cases of pediatric diabetes in some communities.

It is therefore never too early to start paying attention to fitness, which, any expert will tell you, must be a combination of diet and daily exercise, because neither is effective without the other. And it is not a short-lived endeavor. Fitness is for life, a long-term commitment to healthy eating, which necessitates the avoidance of overly protein-rich, fat-laden foods and carving out enough time for daily, vigorous activity.

The reason most people fail to lose weight permanently when they turn to weight-loss programs, liquid diets, or diet pills is that they are seeking rapid, short-term results and abandon the regime once they have achieved their goal. In some cases, it is in fact inadvisable to stay on a particular diet or diet pill for more than a short time. In many cases, the diets and pills (see following article) do not help shed more than a limited number of pounds, can cost quite a lot and cannot guarantee that you will be able to keep the weight off. The result is that Americans spend billions on weight-loss programs and products and they are fatter than ever.

Here, then, are some ideas on how to get fit without spending a lot of money. This advice comes from fitness and diet experts, writers at the *New York Times* and U.S. government sources, such as the U.S.D.A. and the National Institutes of Health:

FORGET QUICK FIXES. Gimmicks don't work. Losing weight and keeping it off requires changing your lifestyle and your mindset—not an easy undertaking. Before throwing away money on programs that don't match your lifestyle, do some research. There are many inexpensive ways to gather information: sign up for free educational classes, nutritional counseling or introductory weight-loss programs given by a local hospital or H.M.O.; buy a good nutrition or exercise book or borrow one from the library.

INSIDE INFO

Does Your Weight Fit You?

The latest guidelines, which apply to both men and women regardless of age, prescribe acceptable ranges rather than specific weights, because people of the same height may have different amounts of muscle and bone. The further you are above the healthy weight range for your height, the higher are your risks of developing weight-related health problems.

○ **GENERAL HEIGHT AND WEIGHT CHART FOR MEN AND WOMEN**

HEIGHT	WEIGHT (lb.) Ages 19 to 34	WEIGHT (lb.) Ages 35 and up
5'0	97-128	108-138
5'1"	101-132	111-143
5'2"	104-137	115-148
5'3"	107-141	119-152
5'4"	111-146	122-157
5'5"	114-150	126-162
5'6"	118-155	130-167
5'7"	121-160	134-172
5'8"	125-164	138-178
5'9"	129-169	142-183
5'10"	132-174	146-188
5'11"	136-179	151-194
6'0	140-184	155-199
6'1"	144-189	159-205
6'2"	148-195	164-210
6'3"	152-200	168-216
6'4"	156-205	173-222
6'5"	160-211	177-228

SOURCES: U.S. Department of Agriculture; U.S. Department of Health and Human Services

CUSTOMIZE YOUR DIET PLAN. Many dieters pay top dollar for commercial weight-loss programs and either don't complete the program or soon regain the weight they lost. The key to permanent weight loss is finding a program that fits your food preferences and lifestyle, says Anne Fletcher, a registered dietitian and diet book author. "Even though something worked for a celebrity or your mother or brother, it may not work for you," she says. The dieters chronicled in Fletcher's book, *Eating Thin for Life: Food Secrets and Recipes From People Who Have Lost Weight & Kept It Off,* lost an average of 63 pounds and kept it off for at least three years. While many failed at weight-loss programs, they learned to piece together different parts of programs that worked for them. "Instead of saying I blew it with Weight Watchers or Jenny Craig, go back and look at what worked in those programs," suggests Fletcher. If eating four grapefruits or bowls of cabbage soup a day didn't work, but packing your lunch every day did, then incorporate that lesson into your weight-reduction plan.

GET TO WORK IN THE KITCHEN. Many weight-loss programs involve using prepackaged foods, prepared by a diet center or purchased at the supermarket. Prepared foods can help in teaching how to control portions, but they cost two to three times as much as the raw ingredients required to make the meal from scratch. "Some of the foods labeled diet are automatically marked up, but if you buy regular products and eat less of them, you save money," advises Dr. Denise Bruner, a weight-loss specialist in Arlington, Va. "If you spend a few extra minutes in the kitchen putting a piece of chicken in the microwave and steaming vegetables, for example, you'd have a less expensive and more nutritious meal," she says.

FIND COST-EFFECTIVE WORKOUTS. Exercise is the other major component of weight loss. But high-priced spa memberships or fancy training equipment aren't needed to reap the benefits of exercise. Invest in a good pair of walking shoes. For results, it's the best and cheapest thing you can do. Other inexpensive and effective exercise tools include elastic bands, an exercise ball, and aerobic and yoga videotapes. More sophisticated home exercise equipment can be worth the cost—if it's not lying idle.

Make a schedule of exercise times and develop a realistic goal of how many hours you can devote each week, and push yourself to meet those goals. Team up with a compatible family member or friend who shares your motivation, and work out together, or at least keep track of each other's hours. If you find exercise boring, do it in front of a TV or with music. If you have children, get them to participate as well.

If you need the motivation of a health club, shop for one that gives you punch for your dollar. Staff credentials are important. Before joining a club, have a staff member perform a fitness evaluation and draw up an exercise plan for you. Consistent use of the club will help justify the cost. Engaging a personal trainer can be expensive but can also make workouts more effective. To defray the cost, meet with the trainer less frequently or train with a partner.

BE FOCUSED. Losing weight on your own is, of course, the best money-saver. Half of the dieters in Fletcher's book lost weight by using no-cost strategies, such as accepting weight loss as a permanent lifestyle change and devising ways to nip small weight gains in the bud.

But the most important lesson they learned is that money can't buy motivation and commitment—the real secret to weight loss. Explains Fletcher, "Successful dieters want to lose weight and stay at the new weight more than they want to engage in behavior that keeps them overweight."

Take advantage of all the free advice and information now available on Web sites, or try paying for one of the low-cost online dieting sites. For some ideas, see opposite.

✔ **TIMELY TIPS**

Cyber-Trim and Cyber-Fit
Web sites to get started and stay on track

✔ **ChaseFreedom** (www.chasefreedom.com) Posts free diet reviews and information "regarding every known diet, pill, and weight-loss program." Reviews come from past visitors and the editorial staff.

✔ **CyberDiet** (www. cyberdiet.com) A subscription to information on how to figure your daily caloric requirements, and customize your diet.

✔ **DietTalk** (www.diettalk.com) A free forum for diet discussion.

✔ **eDiets** (www.ediets.com) A paying site with information on diet programs and advice on nutrition and fitness.

✔ **FreeDieting** (www.freedieting.com) An abundance of free information on diets and fitness.

✔ **My Food Diary** (www.myfooddiary.com) An interactive, paying Web site that allows you to keep a diary of everything you eat, and gives you feedback on the nutritional components of your daily meals and calories burned. Also offers an exercise log, charts and reports, a body log and a discussion forum.

✔ **PeerTrainer** (www.peertrainer.com) This free site offers users anonymity and provides a structured means for organizing participants into groups of four. It uses open diet and exercise logs and provides online channels for members to give feedback, even posting articles, recipes and other tips.

✔ **SparkPeople** (www.sparkpeople.com) This free Web site allows you to personalize your exercise program, and create your own meal plans, as well as share your experiences and trials with others.

SOURCE: Michel Marriott

Let's Go to the Tape Measure

Weight around the belly is more dangerous than around the hips

How your weight is distributed may be even more important than how much weight you have in the first place, at least when it comes to determining risks to your health. If you are carrying too much weight around your waist, your health is at far greater risk than if you are carrying extra weight around your hips, buttocks and thighs. All of that excessive fat around the belly has been found by researchers to be associated with an increased risk of breast and uterine cancer, heart disease and diabetes, as well as a host of other ailments.

To assess whether your weight distribution puts you at higher risk for disease, ask yourself whether your body more closely resembles the shape of an apple or of a pear. "Apples" are often bigger at the waist than in the hips—traits found more often in men than in women. "Pears," on the other hand, carry their weight low. Their waists are smaller than their hips and they are usually women.

Researchers at the University of Glasgow have suggested an easy way to gauge your health risks from carrying too much weight in the wrong places. Their study found significantly higher health risks among women whose waists measure more than 34.5 inches, and for men whose waists exceed 40 inches. Their advice: to ward off health problems, keep your waist size to 31.5 inches if you are a woman, and to 37 inches for a man.

Another study, reported in the November 5, 2005, issue of *Lancet*, the medical journal, has found that waist-to-hip ratio is a better predictor of heart attack than body mass index (BMI), the most common way of determining who is obese. A waist-to-hip ratio (waist measurement divided by hip measurement) below 0.85 in women or 0.9 in men is average. Anything above that is a risk for heart disease.

A body mass index greater than 28.2 in women or 28.6 in men did indicate an increased risk of heart attack, but the relationship disappeared after adjusting for age, sex, geographic region and tobacco use. Waist-to-hip ratio, on the other hand, showed a continuous relationship to heart attack risk even after adjusting for other risk factors. Those in the highest fifth were 2.52 times as likely to have a heart attack as those in the lowest fifth. Waist-to-hip ratio was a predictor of heart attack even in people regarded as very lean, those with body mass indexes under 20. Also, there was no evidence of a threshold where the risk would level off: the higher the waist-to-hip ratio, the higher the risk of a heart attack.

—Nicholas Bakalar

Should You Pop a Diet Pill?

New medications are here, and more are on the way. But experts are skeptical

You may recall the many desperate souls who years ago sought to curb their appetites with amphetamines, drugs that caused extreme nervousness, insomnia and addiction. Among other diet drug fiascos were thyroid hormone, which caused hyperthyroidism; fenfluramine, linked to heart valve abnormalities; and ephedra and phenylpropanolamine, associated with heart problems.

Now a host of other medications, several already on the market and others in the pharmaceutical pipeline, are being cited as safer alternatives. However, these, too, have limitations, so before you ask your physician for a prescription or try to buy the drugs online, you should know just how effective and safe they really are.

Are You Overweight? Check Your Body Mass Index

Your body mass index (BMI) is an important calculation for judging fitness, though it is not a 100 percent accurate indicator, since muscle weighs more than fat. Very muscled bodies will have a higher body mass index, and older people with little muscle will usually have less. The Centers for Disease Control and Prevention suggest that you use it as just one of many factors in judging whether you are in good shape. The formula:

$$BMI = \frac{(Weight\ in\ pounds)}{(Height\ in\ inches) \times (Height\ in\ inches)} \times 703$$

BODY MASS INDEX (BMI) TABLE

Use this table to estimate your BMI. Find height in inches in the first column. Then move across to the right and choose the weight in pounds nearest to yours. Your BMI can be found at the bottom of that column.

HEIGHT	WEIGHT (in pounds)																
4'10" (58")	91	96	100	105	110	115	119	124	129	134	138	143	148	153	158	162	167
4'11" (59")	94	99	104	109	114	119	124	128	133	138	143	148	153	158	163	168	173
5'0" (60")	97	102	107	112	118	123	128	133	138	143	148	153	158	163	168	174	179
5'1" (61")	100	106	111	116	122	127	132	137	143	148	153	158	164	169	174	180	185
5'2" (62")	104	109	115	120	126	131	136	142	147	153	158	164	169	175	180	186	191
5'3" (63")	107	113	118	124	130	135	141	146	152	158	163	169	175	180	186	191	197
5'4" (64")	110	116	122	128	134	140	145	151	157	163	169	174	180	186	192	197	204
5'5" (65")	114	120	126	132	138	144	150	156	162	168	174	180	186	192	198	204	210
5'6" (66")	118	124	130	136	142	148	155	161	167	173	179	186	192	198	204	210	216
5'7" (67")	121	127	134	140	146	153	159	166	172	178	185	191	198	204	211	217	223
5'8" (68")	125	131	138	144	151	158	164	171	177	184	190	197	203	210	216	223	230
5'9" (69")	128	135	142	149	155	162	169	176	182	189	196	203	209	216	223	230	236
5'10" (70")	132	139	146	153	160	167	174	181	188	195	202	209	216	222	229	236	243
5'11" (71")	136	143	150	157	165	172	179	186	193	200	208	215	222	229	236	243	250
6'0 (72")	140	147	154	162	169	177	184	191	199	206	213	221	228	235	242	250	258
6'1" (73")	144	151	159	166	174	182	189	197	204	212	219	227	235	242	250	257	265
6'2" (74")	148	155	163	171	179	186	194	202	210	218	225	233	241	249	256	264	272
6'3" (75")	152	160	168	176	184	192	200	208	216	224	232	240	248	256	264	272	279
BMI	**19**	**20**	**21**	**22**	**23**	**24**	**25**	**26**	**27**	**28**	**29**	**30**	**31**	**32**	**33**	**34**	**35**

RISK OF ASSOCIATED DISEASE ACCORDING TO BMI AND WAIST SIZE

BMI values between 18.5 and 24.9 are considered "normal" or "healthy" weight. BMI's above 25 are unhealthy and have been shown to increase the risk of certain chronic diseases. BMI's under 18.5 are considered "underweight."

BMI		Waist less than or equal to 40 in. (men) or 35 in. (women)	Waist greater than 40 in. (men) or 35 in. (women)
18.5 or less	UNDERWEIGHT	—	N/A
18.5–24.9	NORMAL	–	N/A
25.0–29.9	OVERWEIGHT	Increased	High
30.0–34.9	OBESE	High	Very High
35.0–39.9	OBESE	Very High	Very High
40 or greater	EXTREMELY OBESE	Extremely High	Extremely High

SOURCE: National Institutes of Health

In the June 2005 issue of the *Journal of the American Dietetic Association*, Susan B. Moyers of the University of South Florida College of Medicine reviewed drugs that had been studied as weight-loss aids. Here's Moyers's bottom line: "Whereas the evidence may support the use of medications to enhance weight loss, medication alone without diet/lifestyle change is not effective."

In other words, there is no drug currently available or likely to be available soon that facilitates weight loss without also cutting back on calories consumed. And there is no drug that can help people maintain a weight loss unless they continue to limit calories or increase exercise. Furthermore, there is as yet no drug that enables the morbidly obese, even with a reduced-calorie diet, to lose 100 or more pounds. Typical losses average 5 to 10 percent of initial weight, which can significantly improve health, but won't turn the obese into normal-weight individuals.

The two leading prescription weight-loss aids are Meridia (sibutramine) and Xenical (orlistat). Meridia acts on the brain to reduce hunger and enhance satiety. It reduces between-meal snacking and limits the drop in metabolic rate that accompanies weight loss. Typical weight losses of 5 to 10 percent (10 to 14 pounds in six months) have been reported. The drug should not be used by those with a history of heart disease or stroke, or people who take antidepressants called MAO inhibitors or SSRI's.

Xenical interferes with the enzyme that digests fat and can reduce by a third the amount of dietary fat a person absorbs. In a large four-year study, one quarter of patients who stayed on the drug kept off 10 percent of their initial body weight (about 13 pounds in a year), compared with 16 percent of patients on a placebo. Xenical is not a drug for fat lovers. If more than 20 grams of fat a day are consumed, the drug can cause oily stools, flatus with discharge and fecal urgency. It also interferes with the absorption of fat-soluble vitamins.

Another group of diet drugs are appetite suppressants that result in losses of about one pound a week. Phentride and Ionamin (phentermine); Tenuate (diethylpropion); Didrex (benzphetamine); and Obezine, Bontril and Adipost (phendimetrazine) are all relatives of amphetamines and approved only for short-term use, which precludes their use in treating a chronic disorder like obesity. Tolerance to these drugs develops within a few weeks, and side effects are common, including nervousness, insomnia, rapid heart rate, anxiety and high blood pressure. Another appetite-suppressing drug, Mazanor and Sanorex (mazindol) is sold only online (lack of medical supervision is considered risky) and must not be taken with MAO inhibitors or SSRI's.

Several other drugs approved for other uses are sometimes prescribed "off-label" for weight control. They include Glucophage (metformin), Precose (acarbose) and Glyset (miglitol), which are approved to control blood sugar in people with Type 2 diabetes; the anti-seizure drugs Topamax (topiramate) and Zonegran (zonisamide); and the antidepressants Prozac (fluoxetine) and Wellbutrin (bupropion). All have an array of side effects, though millions of people with the disorders the drugs were licensed to treat have managed to stay on them for years. Their effectiveness as weight-loss aids is somewhat less than that of drugs designed for that purpose.

So what's the bottom line? For the foreseeable future, drugs are not likely to be the solution to obesity, at least not by themselves. As Moyers puts it, "There is no quick fix for a complex problem, and there is no evidence that drug therapy helps to re-educate faulty exercise and eating habits. However," she adds, "evidence does seem to support a hybrid approach consisting of behavior modification and pharmacotherapy in some patients. There must be a strategy to maintain the loss over many years, and such a strategy requires nutrition and physical activity as its anchors."

—Jane E. Brody

No Gym, No Fees, No Strangers

A mat, weights, a resistance band and stability ball may be all you need to work out at home

Not a fan of the crowded, expensive local gym? Who needs it, when you can make your own version of a home gym with a few modular, easily stashable pieces of equipment. More than nine million Americans have decided, for reasons of convenience, flexibility, privacy or cost, to exercise at home. With just a few simple, inexpensive pieces—a set of weights, a mat, a stability ball and a resistance band—anybody can get toned as well at home as at the gym. Here are some low-tech ways of strength-training at home:

Use an exercise band to work shoulders, as follows: Step on the center of a band with one or both feet. Then, with your palms facing forward and elbows bent, grasp the ends of the band and extend your arms above your head. Different bands provide more or less resistance, just as a machine would.

Create circuits within your house. Though some trainers recommend investing in an aerobic workout tape or a treadmill, stationary bike or elliptical machine for cardiovascular exercise, ingenuity can often take the place of technology; doing squats and marching in place and then going up and down the stairs, for example. Running up a flight of stairs is the low-tech version of the treadmill.

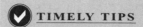 **TIMELY TIPS**

Start with 12 Minutes a Day

That's just the beginning for minimum physical fitness. The President's Council on Physical Fitness and Sports recommends the following schedule:

✔ **Daily: 10 to 12 minutes**
STRETCHING. Stretching exercises should be performed slowly, without any bouncing motion.

✔ **Twice weekly: 20-minute sessions**
MUSCULAR STRENGTH. Exercise all of the major muscle groups. Lifting weights is the most effective means of doing so.

✔ **Three times or more per week: 30-minute workouts**
MUSCULAR ENDURANCE. Exercise all of the major muscle groups. Calisthenics, push-ups, sit-ups, pull-ups and weight training are most effective.

✔ **20-minute programs**
CARDIORESPIRATORY ENDURANCE. Engage in continuous aerobic activity that puts your heart and lungs through the paces. Brisk walking, jogging, swimming, cycling, rope-jumping, cross-country skiing and continuous-action games like racketball and handball fit the bill.

✔ **Every workout: 5 to 10 minutes**
WARM UP. Exercises such as walking, slow jogging, knee lifts, arm circles or trunk rotations are effective.
COOL DOWN. Slow walking, or other low-level exercise, and stretching keep muscles loose.

Use a stability ball to work abdominals. Pull it between your legs during sit-ups, and it works as a resistance device. An old tie can substitute for a yoga strap. Chairs can stand in for weight benches. Use them for tricep dips, seated bicep curls or step-ups.

—Melena Ryzik

HEALTH

WORKOUT BENEFITS AT A GLANCE

From puttering around to Olympic skiing, the estimated calories burned during 30 minutes of activity depends on body weight and intensity of effort.

ACTIVITY		WEIGHT 105	120	135	150	165	180	195
DAILY ACTIVITY	Work, sedentary office	36	41	46	51	56	61	66
	Cooking	60	68	77	85	94	102	111
	Cleaning (heavy)	107	123	138	153	169	184	199
AEROBICS	Low-impact dance	119	136	153	170	188	205	222
	High-impact dance	167	191	215	239	263	286	310
	Water	95	109	122	136	150	163	177
ALPINE	Moderate (recreational)	119	136	153	170	188	205	222
SKIING	Vigorous (steep slope)	167	191	215	239	263	286	310
BASEBALL		119	136	153	170	188	205	222
BASKETBALL	Half-court	143	164	184	205	225	245	266
	Full-court (slow)	191	218	245	273	300	327	355
	Full-court (fast break)	315	360	405	450	495	540	585
BICYCLING	10–12 m.p.h.	143	164	184	205	225	245	266
	12–14 m.p.h.	191	218	245	273	300	327	355
	14–16 m.p.h.	239	273	307	341	375	409	443
BOWLING		72	82	92	102	113	123	133
CALISTHENICS	Light	107	123	138	153	169	184	199
	Heavy	191	218	245	273	300	327	355
CROSS-COUNTRY	2.5 m.p.h.	167	191	215	239	263	286	310
SKIING	4–5 m.p.h.	191	218	245	273	300	327	355
FISHING	Sitting	60	68	77	85	94	102	111
	Standing	84	95	107	119	131	143	155
FOOTBALL	Playing catch	60	68	77	85	94	102	111
	Touch or flag	191	218	245	273	300	327	355
GARDENING		95	109	123	136	150	164	177
GOLF	Pulling cart	119	136	153	170	188	205	222
	Carrying clubs	131	150	169	187	206	225	244
HIKING AND	Cross-country hiking	143	164	184	205	225	245	266
CLIMBING	Mountain trek	191	218	245	273	300	327	355
	Rock climb (vigorous)	253	289	325	361	398	434	470
HORSEBACK	Leisure riding	95	109	123	136	150	164	177
RIDING	Posting to trot	143	164	184	205	225	245	266
	Galloping	188	215	242	269	296	323	350

HEALTH

ACTIVITY		WEIGHT						
		105	120	135	150	165	180	195
ICE OR ROLLER SKATING/BLADING	Sustained moderate	167	191	215	239	263	286	310
	Vigorous (9+ m.p.h.)	215	245	276	307	338	368	399
JOGGING AND RUNNING	12 min./mile pace	191	218	245	273	300	327	355
	10 min./mile pace	239	273	307	341	375	409	443
	8 min./mile pace	298	341	384	426	469	511	554
	6 min./mile pace	382	436	491	545	600	655	709
JUMPING ROPE	Slow	191	218	245	273	300	327	355
	Moderate	239	273	307	341	375	409	443
	Fast	286	327	368	409	450	491	532
MARTIAL ARTS	Tae kwon do, karate, judo	239	273	307	341	375	409	443
	Tai chi	95	109	123	136	150	164	177
RACKET AND COURT GAMES	Racketball (social)	167	191	215	239	263	286	310
	Racketball (competitive)	239	273	307	341	375	409	443
	Handball and squash	286	327	368	409	450	491	532
ROWING AND CANOEING	Leisurely	84	95	107	119	131	143	155
	Vigorous sustained	167	191	215	239	263	286	310
	Very vigorous	286	327	368	409	450	491	532
SAILING	Leisurely	72	82	92	102	113	123	133
	Racing	109	136	153	170	188	205	222
SOCCER	Casual	167	191	215	239	263	286	310
	Competitive	239	273	307	341	375	409	443
SWIMMING	Laps freestyle (moderate)	191	218	245	273	300	327	355
	Laps freestyle (fast)	239	273	307	341	375	409	443
TENNIS	Social doubles	119	136	153	170	188	205	222
	Social singles	157	180	202	225	248	270	293
	Competitive doubles	172	196	221	245	270	295	319
	Competitive singles	227	259	291	324	356	389	421
VOLLEYBALL	Leisurely	74	85	96	106	117	128	138
	Competitve	167	191	215	239	263	286	310
WALKING	24 min./mile pace	72	82	92	102	113	123	133
	20 min./mile pace	84	95	107	119	131	143	155
	17min./mile pace	95	109	123	136	150	164	177
	15 min./mile pace	107	123	138	153	169	184	194
	12 min./mile pace	119	136	153	170	188	205	222
WEIGHT TRAINING	Free weights or machines	143	164	184	205	225	245	266
	Circuit weight training	191	218	245	273	300	327	355

SOURCE: Dr. David R. Stutz, *Forty-Plus Guide to Fitness: A Physicians's Exercise and Sports Program*, Consumer Reports, 1994.

For the Time-Challenged

Integrative exercise may be the answer

For at least a decade, fitness professionals have been trying to persuade Americans to engage in integrative exercise—incorporating exercise into their day rather than accepting the commonplace that you have to change clothes before working out.

Many have heeded this advice in expected ways: by taking the stairs instead of the elevator and wearing pedometers to encourage themselves to walk as much as possible. But some enthusiasts have become more creative about integrative exercise. They are combining fitness with daily chores: getting their pulse rate up while cleaning the house, for example, or hoisting the children to build muscle. And they are proving the experts right: 8 minutes here and 15 minutes there do add up to a good day's exercise.

Some research suggests that going to the gym isn't the best way to increase your overall activity level. Klaas Westerterp, a biologist at Maastricht University in the Netherlands, found in his studies of healthy non-obese adults that people who spent more time doing moderate exercise actually burned more calories over all than those who got moving for short, intense periods. Why? After a tough workout, people typically limited their activity in any given day, Westerterp's study found.

The benefits of moving throughout the day were also demonstrated in a 2004 study about fidgeting. A report by researchers at the Mayo Clinic linked fidgeting to leanness, and the lack of it to being overweight. Just being restless—standing, pacing, toe tapping—can burn about 350 calories a day, the study said. That can add up to 30 or 40 pounds per year. "Plenty of evidence now suggests you can accumulate your physical activity," says Walter Thompson, a professor of kinesiology and health at Georgia State University. Still, he cautions, "a lot of people don't believe it."

The novel ways that people fit exercise into their lives tend to be convenient, as well as slimming. A writer in San Francisco not only jogs between errands, but does yoga in the shower. A big-wave surfer shoveled gravel alongside the workers he paid to build his home in Maui, because the hard labor helped increase upper-body strength. Then there are the lusty and fabled few who have sex as a workout. In what she describes as "a sleepy East Coast university town," a woman in her mid-30's, who wished to remain anonymous, had a yearlong affair that involved physical relations two to four hours a day. She continued to take a few yoga classes a week, but during the relationship, she says, "I didn't have to watch what I ate, I lost a bunch of weight, and suddenly I was fit."

The possibilities are nearly endless. The Centers for Disease Control and Prevention and the American College of Sports Medicine produced a chart categorizing roughly 200 physical activities into two levels of intensity to help people gauge how much exercise they get. In the garden shovel-

---

 **TIMELY TIPS**

Weights With Pizazz

✔ **WHAT THEY ARE:** Smart Bells, part sculpture and part exercise equipment, are the heart of a low-impact exercise program that draws on yoga, dance and martial arts. Smart Bells come in three weights and a variety of colors.

✔ **HOW TO USE THEM:** Each comes with instructional DVD's and a wall chart showing a core routine of 10 exercises.

✔ **INFORMATION:** 800-485-0967 or www.think-fit.com

—Sam Hooper Samuels

ing less than 10 pounds of dirt per minute is classified as moderate activity, while shoveling more than 10 pounds a minute is considered vigorous. Playing a guitar or drums in a band is moderate. Hand-sawing hardwoods is vigorous.

—Elizabeth Weil

Best in Gym

Which cardio machine does the most for you?

Take a peek into most gyms, and it is obvious which cardio machines are the favorites. Quite often rows of treadmills are parked on prime real estate in front of the televisions. Close by, stationary bikes also crowd the floor. And rightly so; these have been the two most popular machines for a cardiovascular workout at health clubs. Lately, their dominance has been challenged by a newcomer, the elliptical motion trainer, a machine that aims to replicate running without the stress on joints.

But of all the machines at health clubs, which one is really the best, the latest fads aside? To help gym-goers make an informed choice, the *New York Times* asked 10 experts—physiologists, researchers, doctors and personal trainers—to rate the five most popular cardio machines according to overall muscle conditioning, and how enjoyable it is to use each one.

The winner, by a solid margin, is the elliptical trainer. Our 10 experts thought it had many virtues, chiefly that it allows a low-impact, high-energy workout that is fun. Used correctly, an elliptical trainer works the muscles of the central core as well as the lower body, although some experts think research is needed to determine how hard a workout its users really get.

"These devices are not always effective in providing much resistance to movement," says Edward F. Coyle, the director of the Human Performance Laboratory at the University of Texas at Austin. "People seem to be able to move effortlessly." But for the most part the panel of experts felt that the elliptical was the best all-around choice.

The rowing machine, which has plummeted in popularity in the last 15 years, ranked a surprising second, tied with the treadmill.

Several panelists argue that rowing machines are highly underrated; when used properly they offer a thorough workout of the major muscle groups, including the back, hips, arms and legs. But despite their advantages, rowing machines demand an intensity of effort that many exercisers find too challenging.

"WHAT DO YOU ENJOY DOING?"

The New York Times *asked 10 fitness experts to give five gym machines ratings of 1 to 10 in five categories, with 10 being the highest score. The highest overall score went to the machine with the least wear and tear on the joints and the highest enjoyment factor.*

	CARDIO BENEFIT:	CALORIES BURNED:	MUSCLES USED:	WEAR AND TEAR:	MONOTONY FACTOR:	GRAND TOTALS:
ELLIPTICAL MACHINE	80	76	78	76	59	369
TREADMILL	88	86	68	49	49	340
ROWING MACHINE	78	71	83	68	40	340
STAIR CLIMBER	79	77	69	59	50	334
STATIONARY BIKE	75	69	61	59	49	313

HEALTH

Whatever machine might become the next big thing, the experts caution that no one of them is right for everyone at all times. Instead, gym-goers should rotate among machines at least once a week. Cross-training, as this is called, addresses a variety of muscles and will help to avoid injuries from overuse. "People are always asking me, 'What is the best exercise?'" says Dr. Paul D. Thompson, a cardiologist at Hartford Hospital. "My answer always is, 'What do you enjoy doing?'"

The best exercise machine, the experts agree, is the one that gets you moving each day. Here are the pros and cons of each machine:

ELLIPTICAL TRAINER

PROS: Joggers, especially those with knee and back problems, use elliptical machines to limit wear and tear on their bodies. Because standing tall on an elliptical requires balance, users could potentially work their core muscles and their heart, and have just as rigorous a workout as when jogging or biking.

CONS: It is easier to coast on an elliptical machine than on a treadmill. The jury is still out on the machine's overall physiological effects, so users should progress slowly. Anyone with balance problems should be especially careful.

STAIR CLIMBER

PROS: Stair climbers get high marks in terms of cardiovascular benefit and calories burned. And they aren't hard for beginners to figure out.

CONS: It's hard work. Climbing stairs leaves one wiped out and not anxious to jump back on. And even when a participant uses the full range of motion, it still only targets a limited amount of muscles.

> **People are always asking me "What is the best exercise?" My answer always is, "What do you enjoy doing?"**

• • •

STATIONARY BIKE

PROS: People with knee or ankle problems may be more comfortable using a bike than running. Stationary bikes come in three styles: upright, recumbent and those for spinning classes led by an instructor. Some models offer a ton of feedback. Spinning bikes are mostly used in a class setting, so the intensity tends to be higher and monotony lower.

CONS: Indoor bikes that offer little pedal resistance are far removed from the outdoor experience and can be boring. Cycling, because of its constant identical motion, can lead to tendonitis.

ROWING MACHINE

PROS: Unlike the other machines, a rowing machine works the upper body and is an excellent all-around calorie-burning device.

CONS: Most people struggle to figure out how to use a rowing machine correctly, so it tends to appeal only to a small but avid following of rowers and self-taught exercisers who want a full-body cardio workout. Another disadvantage: rowing machines tend to place the exerciser low to the ground, where it's more difficult to watch TV.

TREADMILL

PROS: The treadmill retains its popularity, because running is one of the best ways to get into shape and burn calories. Running surfaces of treadmills have improved in recent years to better absorb impact. Jogging while watching TV is easy to do, so workouts pass more quickly.

CONS: Running puts quite a lot of stress on joints. Also keep in mind that treadmill running does not burn as many calories as running outdoors.

—Christian DeBenedetti

To Sculpt a Trophy Body

A program to give muscles tone and definition

Aerobic exercises improve cardiovascular fitness and endurance and can help you lose weight, but they don't necessarily tone or sculpt your muscles. Even if you're an avid jogger, swimmer or cyclist and can run, paddle or pedal forever, your muscles still may not be as toned as you'd like them to be. The only way to achieve muscle definition is to lift weights or do strength training, or anaerobic, exercises that use the body's weight as resistance.

The American College of Sports Medicine recommends including aerobic and anaerobic exercise in any balanced physical fitness program—as does the President's Council on Physical Fitness and Sports (see "Start with 12 Minutes a Day," page 9). Women, in particular, may reap benefits from a program of weight training: strength training improves the muscle and bone strength of women in their 40's, and boosts body image and self-esteem.

Designing a training regimen starts by taking into account your current physique. A rule of thumb: how much weight you lift depends on whether you want to build muscle mass or merely tone and shape your muscles. If you carry more weight and body fat than you are happy with in a certain area, you'll want to go with lighter weights and higher repetitions, 25 to 30, to help burn fat. Don't use too much weight in areas you want to slim down, because you'll end up building up that area. If you're trying to put on weight in specific areas, go with heavier weights and do fewer reps, about 8 to 10.

The key to achieving maximum results is proper form. For starters, don't just lift up and down. Rather, contract your muscles from the moment you start an exercise until you're finished. It's not so much about how much weight you lift, but how hard you squeeze. Also, be sure to extend your muscle entirely with each repetition; that is, use the full range of motion.

Even if you don't have access to a gym, you can invest in inexpensive equipment, such as small free weights, that will help you slim down or build up specific muscle groups. Here are some exercises to help you tone and shape common trouble spots.

DUMBELL FLIES

Tone the pectoral chest muscles without making you look like a bodybuilder.

Lie on your back on a bench with a small dumbbell in each hand. Hold your arms out to the side with your arms bent and your wrists turned toward each other. Lift up toward the ceiling, then bring both arms back down to the side. If you raise the bench so it's on an incline, you'll work muscles higher in your chest. If you lower the bench so your head is below your torso, you'll work the lower chest muscles.

BICEP CURLS

Tone and shape the biceps; build muscles if more weight is used.

Hold a dumbbell in each hand and stand with your arms at your side and your palms facing forward. Curl the dumbbell up toward your chest and turn your wrist out when you are at the end of the curl. Lower the weight slowly, because you're resisting weight and strengthening your muscles as you go down, too. Do 15 to 20 repetitions, alternating arms or lifting both at the same time.

LUNGES

Trim and tone the quadriceps in the legs and gluteal muscles in the buttocks. Using dumbbells adds resistance and helps build muscle rather than slimming you down.

With a dumbbell in each hand, stand with your hands on your hips and take a big step forward with your right foot, bending your knee to form a 90-degree angle. Keep your body straight and be sure your right knee doesn't extend beyond your right toe. Step forward with your left foot, and continue lunging across the room. Repeat 20 to 25 times.

LEG RAISES

The best way to tone the lower abdomen.

To begin, hang from a bar and lift your legs straight in front of you as high as possible, at least at a 90-degree angle. Eventually, work up to 15 to 20 leg raises, but try not to swing. It's a difficult maneuver, so beginners should start by lifting their knees up while someone helps balance them.

STEP-UPS

A simple exercise, yet far more effective at trimming and toning the buttocks than the step machine.

Step up onto a bench or high step, then step down, squeezing your muscles with each step. Do 15 to 20 repetitions on each leg. The higher the bench, the harder the workout.

Advice Worth Its Weight in Gold
To lose weight, don't try weight lifting

Personal trainers, fitness instructors, magazines and books have sold a double-barreled promise that any strength training builds muscle and that having more muscle dramatically speeds metabolism, increasing the calories a person burns while at rest. With all that calorie burning, the story goes, excess weight comes off effortlessly.

The story is wrong in two ways, researchers say. First, muscle is not such an amazing calorie burner. "Even if weight training increases muscle and metabolism, there is little evidence showing that it is enough to cause weight loss," says Joseph Donnelly, the director of the Energy Balance Laboratory at the University of Kansas, who has extensively reviewed studies on the link between resistance training and weight loss.

And, second, many who try weight training—especially women—fail to do what it actually takes to build more muscle. They lift too light a weight, or they neglect to progress to heavier weights as they grow stronger. And often, women who take up weight lifting also diet. In fact, it is nearly impossible to increase muscle while cutting calories.

Regular resistance training, done correctly, has many benefits. It can prevent some of the muscle loss that occurs with weight loss. It can also lower body fat levels and even help preserve bone mass. But the idea that it can magically increase calorie burning is "a very big stretch," says Edward Melanson, an assistant professor in the division of endocrinology, diabetes and metabolism at the University of Colorado Health Sciences Center in Denver.

Proponents of the theory that weight lifting leads to weight loss argue that it is the long-term effect of gaining more muscle, which burns more calories at rest that causes weight loss. Still, that has never been proven in studies which show, rather, that even women who do what it takes to get stronger develop only two to four pounds of muscle after six months of progressive lifting. Given that one pound of muscle burns between 7

ⓘ **INSIDE INFO**

Exercise to Your Heart's Content

○ Checking your pulse rate is one of the best ways to gauge whether you're exercising hard enough to improve your heart and lungs. The American Heart Association advises that you push your heartbeat during exercise to between 50 percent and 70 percent of your maximum heart rate (calculated by subtracting your age from 220).

○ Anything lower than 50 percent does little for your heart's conditioning; anything higher than 75 percent can cause problems unless you're in superb shape. When you're just starting an exercise program, cardiologists recommend aiming for the lower part of the target heart zone and gradually stepping up your pace.

Age	Target heart rate beats per minute	Maximum heart rate
20	100–150	200
25	98–146	195
30	95–142	190
35	93–138	185
40	90–135	180
45	88–131	175
50	85–127	170
55	83–123	165
60	80–120	160
65	78–116	155
70	75–113	150

○ IMPORTANT NOTE: A few high blood pressure medicines lower the maximum heart rate and thus the target zone rate. If you are taking high blood pressure medications, call your physician to find out if your exercise program needs to be adjusted.

---

to 13 calories a day (as determined by studies that measured oxygen and blood flow to tissues), that means the average boost in metabolism is only 14 to 52 calories a day, says Dympna Gallagher, the director of the body composition unit at the New York Obesity Research Center in Manhattan.

The effect of weight lifting "on metabolism is minor and certainly not the savior of dieters," says William Kraemer, a professor of physiology and neurobiology at the University of Connecticut. When people lift light weights and fail to progressively increase the load, they only increase endurance, he noted.

Genetics may also help determine the impact that weight lifting can have on muscle development and metabolism. Researchers at the University of Massachusetts at Amherst looked at almost 600 men and women who did a strenuous, progressive resistance routine for three months, according to a study published in 2005 in *Medicine & Science in Sports & Exercise.* Three percent were "high responders," some of whom doubled their strength. One percent were "low responders," who became only 1 percent stronger than they were when they started. The majority of men and women increased muscle size 15 to 25 percent; most men improved their muscle strength 40 percent, while women increased theirs 65 percent.

—Martica Heaner

Sweating Your Way to Serenity?

Mind-body workouts stretch exercising to a new extreme

Workouts that fuse high-intensity aerobics with a focus on awareness traditionally associated with low-impact practices, like yoga and tai chi, are hitting the trendiest of gyms. By sprinkling classes with Buddhist parables, yoga sutras, chanted affirmations and meditation techniques, fitness instructors hope to take advantage of the yoga craze, while giving students a workout that makes them sweat.

"As people lead increasingly stressful lives, they want their workouts to have more meaning," says David Bluman, director of personal training for ECA World Fitness, an organization that certifies trainers. He recently started incorporating yoga-based breathing and visualization techniques into his own spinning workouts.

While the packaging might be new, the mind-body concept is hardly revolutionary. Yoga and tai chi, which provide the philosophical blueprints for many classes, date back thousands of years. And

coaches have long used mind-body techniques to motivate professional athletes. For example, basketball coach Phil Jackson, a Buddhist, wrote about using Zen meditation with the Chicago Bulls in his 1995 book, *Sacred Hoops: Spiritual Lessons of a Hardwood Warrior.*

Some fitness professionals say it makes little sense, however, to preach mindfulness as students go for the burn. If you look at the essence of yoga as a spiritual practice, the ultimate goal is not to have a tight backside, says David Moreno, the yoga director at Yoga Mandala Studio in Berkeley, Calif., but "to develop the essential nature that goes beyond the confines of your body." Yoga masters in India, he notes, are "not skinny blond aerobics bunnies." Moreover, says Roger Cole, a physiologist who teaches Iyengar yoga at Yoga Del Mar in California, it takes an exceptional instructor to make mindfulness work well in an exercise class. "Teaching cardio is pretty straightforward as long as you raise the heart rate and aren't doing something dangerous," whereas "making it mindful is an art."

The mixed bag of Eastern and Western influences make it hard to gauge what message, if any, is getting through to class members. Some have been known to roll their eyes when instructed to chant while doing crunches. Still, mind-body cardio classes continue to proliferate and to win converts.

—Jennie Yabroff

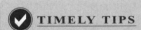 **TIMELY TIPS**

Exercise With a Twist

A small sampling of mind-body cardio classes available on DVD or video:

✔ **Budokon:** A combination karate, yoga and meditation class developed by Cameron Shayne, a Los Angeles trainer. By "organizing the way a person moves," this workout aims to help "organize the way that person thinks and lives," according to www.budokon.com, Shayne's Web site.

✔ **Yoga Groove:** A combination of vinyasa-style yoga and "heart expanding" dance movements set to live tribal drumming. Videos are available at www.mistytripoli.com.

✔ **BodyFlow:** This aerobic dance class borrows movements from tai chi, yoga, and Pilates, plus strength and conditioning exercises, and ends with a 10-minute meditative relaxation on the floor. At Gold's Gyms, among others nationwide. Information on classes is at www.lesmillsusa.com.

—Jennie Yabroff

How to Stay off the Bench

The New York Knicks' doc on avoiding injuries and healing quickly

There's little difference between the injuries sustained by recreational and professional athletes, says Dr. W. Norman Scott, director of the Insall Scott Kelly Institute for Orthopaedics and Sports Medicine, as well as a professor at

HEALTH

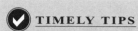 **TIMELY TIPS**

The Children's Hour

Getting your kids started down the fitness track with sit-ups

Starting from when they are very little, make time for an exercise period every day with your children. Turn on some music in the family room, or wherever there is enough space, and let the little ones pick out some of their favorite songs. Walk briskly in place or dance to the music, moving your arms up and down for 5 or 10 minutes so you get your heart pumping, for a good cardiovascular workout.

✔ **Make it fun.** After you cool down, do some stretching for about 10 minutes. Get the children to touch their toes, and reach their arms over their heads while bending sideways. Incorporate some yoga moves, such as standing on one leg, to improve balance. Do it just enough to show them how good it feels.

✔ **Choose exercises your children like,** such as jumping rope and doing sit-ups on a bouncy exercise ball. All the things your children like to do naturally, when they are playing outside, like leapfrog and cartwheels and handstands, are part of a good gymnastic workout. Make the exercise a game, and build up the repetitions slowly, so they can feel a sense of accomplishment when they have increased their endurance.

✔ **Begin slowly, with three sets of 5 or 10 reps.** If they start doing 5 push-ups and get tired, rest, come back, and do it again. If you have a pull-up bar, get them to start with one pullup and slowly help them increase the number they can do. Don't push them and make them too sore. Let them suggest the exercise so they will feel important and engaged.

Einstein College of Medicine and longtime team physician for the New York Knicks basketball team. The only dissimilarity is that pros are more likely to suffer serious injuries, because they play with more force. Below, Scott helps explain what causes some common athletic injuries, how to avoid them and what to do if you get laid up:

NECK: *Serious neck injuries are rare among athletes other than those who participate in contact sports like football and rugby. However, weight lifting, wrestling, even racket sports like tennis can cause chronic aches and pains, especially flare-ups along the nerve route.*

CAUSES: Neck injuries in older amateur athletes are usually a sign of arthritic changes (joint inflammation), which are often totally asymptomatic. Strenuous neck movements often result in an inflammation that is associated with pain running down the arm into the fingers.

PREVENTION: Better overall conditioning is the best way to prevent neck injuries.

TREATMENT: If discomfort is acute, avoid exercise, and don't stretch the muscle. Apply ice immediately, and don't apply heat until 48 to 72 hours after the injury occurs. If necessary, take nonsteroidal anti-inflammatory medications like Motrin, Advil or Aleve (the same is true of all minor injuries).

BACK: *Almost any sport that requires trunk rotations, as in golf or racket sports like tennis.*

CAUSES: Most back injuries are muscular in origin, but, depending on your age, back pain can also be due to arthritic changes like osteoarthritis.

PREVENTION: The best way to prevent back pain is through good overall conditioning and following a good stretching program to increase flexibility.

TREATMENT: Apply ice early on, then apply heat after 72 hours. Water therapy like swimming helps decrease spasms. Try gentle stretching exercises, including an abdominal-strengthening workout.

INSIDE INFO

Cure for Couch Potatoes

○ A Scottish study of teenage schoolchildren demonstrates that those who walk to school in the morning are more active during the rest of the day than their peers who arrive by car, bus or train. The results were published online by the *British Medical Journal*.

○ Why walking to school encourages greater physical activity is not clear, but the authors speculate that a morning walk may stimulate further social interaction and lead to more exercise.

○ By every measurement, the teenagers who walked to school exercised more than those who rode. Those who walked both to and from school got 25 percent more exercise than riders over the entire weekday, 8.9 percent more during school hours, 4.2 percent more while on morning break, 18.4 percent more during lunch break and 17 percent more exercise outside school.

—Nicholas Bakalar

SHOULDER: *Pitching, racket sports, golf, lifting weights and other activities where you put your arm in an overhead position.*

CAUSES: The most common cause is bursitis, an inflammation of a normal structure called the bursa. Shoulder injuries are much more common as a person gets older due to muscle atrophy. Damage to the rotator cuff, a group of tendons that allows you to raise your arm up and down, is usually caused by repetitive motions like pitching a baseball.

PREVENTION: A program for stretching and strengthening muscles can reduce your chances of getting a shoulder injury.

TREATMENT: Continue to move the shoulder; if you don't, it can freeze up very quickly. Rotate your arms and shoulder, moving your hand in front of your body, then backwards, and up and down; also, try to stretch from side to side, bringing your right hand over to touch your left shoulder.

KNEE: *Any sport that requires a pivoting motion, like tennis and basketball; runners are also prone to knee injuries.*

CAUSES: The knee is a joint that's especially susceptible to injuries, usually caused by sudden rotational movements.

PREVENTION: Develop very strong leg muscles by biking, lifting weights and using step machines.

TREATMENT: Follow the RICE principle: Rest (but don't completely immobilize it), Ice, Compression (wrap the knee to reduce swelling) and Elevation. Apply ice for 48 hours, then progress to strengthening exercises. Sprained ligaments will need 3 to 12 weeks of rehabilitative exercise, but a torn ligament or cartilage may need surgery.

ANKLE: *Ankle injuries are common in any sport that requires a lot of running, such as jogging, racket sports, baseball and football.*

CAUSES: Sprains and strains are common injuries that occur when the joint or ligaments connecting bones are overstretched or twisted.

PREVENTION: Make sure you warm up—and your sneakers aren't untied.

TREATMENT: Again, follow the RICE principle, applying ice immediately. If the swelling is slight, you can exercise the following day, but keep your ankle wrapped or wear high-top sneakers. Try strengthening exercises a couple of days after swelling and pain subside.

ELBOW: *Besides tennis, you can develop tennis elbow from any sport that requires you rotate your hand up and down repeatedly, as when you swing a golf club incorrectly.*

CAUSES: Tennis elbow (pain in the forearm and wrist) is a common injury caused by too much tension on the tendons around the elbow.

PREVENTION: Strengthening exercises, like squeezing a rubber ball, build muscles in your forearm.

TREATMENT: Apply ice. If necessary, take anti-inflammatory medications.

The Right Exercise Shoes

Fact vs. fiction in the shoe department

The adage "If the shoe fits, wear it" may be good advice in most situations, but it's no guarantee that your next pair of exercise shoes will fit properly when you get them home from the store. That's because foot sizes vary depending on the time of day, the temperature of your feet and what you've been doing with them. A long jog in warm weather, for example, can expand a runner's feet as much as half a size. Foot specialists advise that the best time of day to shop for shoes is at the end of the day, when your foot is largest. Beyond that, forget fancy designs and high-tech gizmos. Here's what you really need to consider:

The running shoe: This shoe is not only a suitable choice for running, but also good for walking and other lower-impact activities that do not involve repetitive lateral motion. But if you are looking for a shoe to participate in the kind of activities that do involve a lot of repetitive lateral motion, like basketball, tennis and squash, or activities with excessive jumping, such as aerobics—watch out. Wearing running shoes for any of these activities practically invites injury, because they lack adequate support around the ankles.

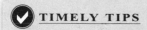 TIMELY TIPS

Protect Feet and Joints

Runners and joggers can keep their feet happy by using a little common sense

1. Buy new running shoes every 250 to 450 miles. Buy new walking shoes after every 400 hours of use. That translates into ten hours of walking weekly for 40 weeks.

2. Remember that your feet aren't identical. Fit the larger one when buying shoes.

3. Always test new shoes before you buy them. Ask the salesperson if you can jog around the block first. Good shoes should feel comfortable right away, not after they've been "broken in."

4. Wear clean, dry socks. You can get blisters otherwise.

5. Avoid running on sidewalks and sand. When your foot hits sand, it keeps going because the sand gives. This can stretch the achilles tendon painfully. Concrete doesn't give at all. It transmits shock through your legs, knees and back.

6. Never begin a workout without first stretching. Gentle, regular stretching greatly reduces the risk of injury.

7. Follow the 10 percent rule. Runners should increase their mileage by 10 percent a week, but level off every third week.

Working out in excess of three to five days a week strains limbs and joints and can cause heel problems, shin splints, ankle twists and stress fractures.

8. Don't be a weekend warrior. Busy weeks leave little time, but it is dangerous to cram a week's worth of exercise into a weekend.

9. Stop exercising at the first signs of pain. Follow the mnemonic RICE—which stands for Rest, Ice, Compression and Elevation—to ease the discomfort.

10. See a doctor if the pain persists. It is difficult to tell if a foot bone is broken.

SOURCE: Dr. Stephen Pribut, podiatrist, Washington, D.C.

TIMELY TIPS

Signs That You Are Overdoing It

Excessive exercise can damage tendons, ligaments, bones, cartilage, joints and muscles and not give minor injuries a chance to heal. Instead of building muscle, too much exercise can lead to muscle breakdown. Girls and young women may stop menstruating and start losing bone, as if they were in menopause. Excessive exercise can also release loads of free radicals, which can cause mutations and may increase cancer risk.

But it is not so much the amount of activity that defines the obligatory exerciser as it is its effects. Some people's bodies can handle more physical stress than others. While there is no clear definition of obligatory exercise, there are telltale signs that exercise is becoming too important to a person and creating undue physical and psychological stress. These indicators were outlined by Molly Kimball, dietitian at the Ochsner Clinic Foundation:

✔ Continuing to train even when ill or injured.

✔ Experiencing anxiety when a workout is missed.

✔ Constantly talking about their sport, training schedule and diet.

✔ Neglecting other important areas of life.

✔ Justifying excessive exercise as necessary to their sport.

✔ Having friends and family notice a loss of perspective.

—Jane E. Brody

Basketball and tennis shoes: They should be judged on whether they offer good traction, good ankle support and firm cushioning. The extra money you spend for shoes that fit these criteria will pay off in the medical bills good shoes help you avoid. Some models that boast flared soles to enhance ankle support also help to prevent the kind of ankle rollovers that result in painful torn ligaments and sprained or broken ankles.

The cross-trainer: Designed for maximum versatility, cross-trainers can be worn for running, walking, racket sports and aerobics, as well as some indoor-court sports, such as basketball and volleyball. Though cross-trainers are versatile, serious runners are best off wearing real running shoes, because cross-trainers lack the sufficient amount of cushioning and ankle support required for regular jogging.

The walking shoe: These are designed for the serious race-walker. They are a needless and expensive investment for those who jog as well as walk for exercise, though. The majority of running shoes are better for your feet than most walking shoes anyway, because running shoes provide more wiggle room for your toes.

Shoes with air-cushioned soles: Air-cushioning sounds high-tech and therefore helpful, but it can cause more problems than it can prevent. Although air-cushioned athletic shoes provide helpful shock absorption, they lack a firm shank below the back of the foot. A firm shank and a slight heel lift prevent the arch of the foot from dropping down too far when the foot moves. If the foot drops too far, it can cause a shift of bones and the development of a variety of podiatric deformities.

SOURCE: Dr. Stephen Pribut, podiatrist, Washington, D.C.

Looking Great

Lessons From the Aging Wars

You can't erase genetic makeup, but you can avoid damage from the sun

Everyone wants to look like Annette Bening at 40, Meryl Streep at 50 or Susan Sarandon at 60, but few people take the preventive measures necessary to maintain youthful-looking skin.

Two factors are critical in determining how your skin ages: genetics and sun exposure. To some extent, your skin's appearance is predetermined by genetic traits inherited from your parents. In addition, fair-skinned people are more likely than the more dark-complexioned to age prematurely, or to develop skin cancer from sun exposure. That's because the fairer-skinned have less pigment to protect them from the sun's rays and are more susceptible to the process known as photoaging, which comes from the cumulative exposure a person receives to the sun.

Photoaging actually plays a bigger role in your skin's appearance than your chronological age. Skin can age as a result of getting too much sun over a short period of time, as well as from the gradual damage of long-term exposure. But most damage occurs by the time you reach age 18. "If you were dealt a bad hand genetically, and you want to make sure you don't get advanced signs of aging, the best thing you can do is avoid the sun," explains Dr. Cherie Ditre, a prominent Philadelphia dermatologist and researcher. Below is a guide to what you can expect of your skin from your 20's

> ❝
>
> **Two factors are critical in determining how your skin ages: genetics and sun exposure.**
>
> • • •

through your 50's, and what you can do to combat the toll of time:

The Twenties. "No one is as gorgeous as a woman in her early 20's. This is the best you're ever going to look," says Dr. Wilma Bergfeld, head of clinical research for the department of dermatology at the Cleveland Clinic Foundation and past president of the American Academy of Dermatology. By the time you reach the late 20's, fine lines will probably develop around the mouth and eyes and be noticeable when you wear makeup. If you become pregnant, you may develop brown spots on your face, either now or later; sun exposure exacerbates the problem.

But how fast your skin ages depends on whether you stay out of the sun and use sunscreen religiously. Other skin-saving strategies include not smoking, controlling your weight and maintaining good health. "It's like anything else—if you wait until the damage is done, it's pretty hard to turn it around," says Bergfeld.

The Thirties. The first real signs of aging usually become apparent after age 30. That's when you'll start to notice more fine wrinkles, see the skin on your eyelids begin to droop, and find the circles under your eyes becoming darker and maybe even puffy. Smokers will develop even more lines around their eyes and mouth.

For many women, the discovery of those first few wrinkles is enough to send them directly to the cosmetics counter. Happily, some products show promise in counteracting the damaging effects of the sun. There's no doubt, says Bergfeld, that simply moisturizing can reduce fine wrinkling up to about 16 percent.

If you're looking for something more potent, moisturizers containing alpha hydroxy acids (AHA's) derived from fruit, sugar cane or lactic acid exfoliate can shed the upper layer of skin, exposing newer skin. Research by Ditre has demonstrated that using AHA's can even reverse some of the signs of photoaging. In a study of 17 adults with severely sun-damaged skin, a lotion with a 25 percent concentration of AHA thickened the outer layers of the skin, increased its elasticity and lightened age spots. There is no evidence, however, that you can prevent wrinkles or turn back the aging clock with AHA's, even in the higher concentrations found in prescription-only formulas. AHA's, says Ditre, are "not a facelift in a jar."

The Forties. Between ages 40 and 50, your skin loses its collagen and elastin (tissues that keep skin firm and plump), which means wrinkles get bigger and deeper, and your skin begins to sag. In addition, your skin gets drier and appears more sallow, pores get larger, eyelids droop more, frown lines show themselves and flat brown spots called liver or age spots appear.

At this stage, says Bergfeld, you should routinely inspect your face and body for potentially cancerous lesions and investigate any suspicious moles or growths, because you're more susceptible to developing skin cancer.

If you already have extensive wrinkling, you may be a candidate for Retin-A at this age. Renova, the acne cream derived from Vitamin A, has long been prescribed to fight wrinkles, and can be used to treat sun-damaged skin and lighten and smooth skin that has turned brown or rough. Renova cannot increase elasticity, eliminate deep wrinkles, or rejuvenate dull or sallow skin, however. "It can't turn a woman who's never taken care of her skin into a youthful 20-year-old," says Bergfeld, "but it can bring about an impressive skin change that people notice."

Drawbacks shouldn't be ignored, however. Most people who use it experience temporary redness, dryness, itching, peeling and a slight burning sensation. For pregnant women and nursing mothers, the medication is entirely off-limits. Moreover, the cream has no lasting benefits if you stop using it.

 TIMELY TIPS

The New Anti-Aging Makeup

Is it a gimmick, or the fountain of youth?

✔ Some dermatologists question whether the ingredients in anti-aging makeup, when added to makeup formulas, are concentrated enough to be effective. It is difficult to tell how much—or how little—of the ingredients the new cosmetics contain, because most labels list their components only by name, not by amount.

✔ "Makeup could have a tiny bit of hydroxy acids, a bit of soy and a tiny amount of peptides and call itself an anti-aging foundation," says Amy B. Lewis, a dermatologist in New York. "But there wouldn't be enough of each active ingredient to be doing anything for you."

✔ She prefers that her patients simply put on a thick layer of moisturizer before applying makeup. "After you put on your moisturizer, if you want to add an anti-aging foundation that contains antioxidants or Retinol, it's not going to hurt you," Lewis says. "But if you are relying on anti-aging makeup to be your skin's sole moisturizer and rejuvenator, you're going to be cheating yourself."

—Natasha Singer

Moles That Turn Deadly

How to check for melanomas

Everyone has moles, an average of 10 to 40 a person, and new ones can develop at any time. Most are smaller than a pencil eraser. If they stay that way, without changing shape, color, size or surface, there is nothing to worry about. But in some cases an overdose of sun can transform innocent moles into potentially deadly cancers. That having been said, most serious cases of melanoma and most melanoma deaths can be prevented. All it takes is regular body vigilance and, most important, a great respect for the damage that can be caused by spending too much time in the sun without adequate protection. "A person who has a history of severe sunburns as a child or teenager is at an especially high risk for the development of melanoma," says Catherine M. Poole, author with Dr. DuPont Guerry IV of *Melanoma,* and herself a melanoma survivor. "Even just one or two bad sunburns can increase the risk of melanoma in later life."

Since 1985, dermatologists have relied on an ABCD criteria: A for asymmetry, B for border irregularity, C for color variations, and D for diameter greater than six millimeters (about a quarter of an inch). Dermatologists at New York University School of Medicine and Royal Prince Albert Hospital in Sydney, Australia, have recently suggested a revised mnemonic device for helping people recognize trouble signs in a mole. In the *Journal of the American Medical Association,* the New York and Sydney physicians suggested adding an E, for evolving, signifying changes in size; shape; symptoms, like itching or tenderness; surface, especially bleeding; and shades of color.

But you won't know if a mole has changed unless you know where all of them are and what they look like. Dr. Howard L. Kaufman, co-director of the Columbia University Melanoma Center and author of *The Melanoma Book,* suggests making a map of all your moles and noting what each looks like, while standing naked in front of a full-length mirror and using a hand-held mirror to see your back. In addition to the most obvious areas of skin, be sure to examine your scalp (part your hair in sections), ears, under your breasts and armpits, under your fingernails and toenails, the palms of your hands and the soles of your feet. As you go, record what you find on a front and rear map of your body. A once-a-month repetition of this examination is advised. If you cannot do this on your own, have a close relative or friend help you, and perhaps return the favor.

If anything unusual is found, either in a new mole or old one, see a dermatologist without delay. If melanoma is caught and treated while it's still a flat lesion, the cure rate is 100 percent. Usually, the treatment is simple outpatient surgery. But the cure rate drops to 70 percent once the cancer has invaded underlying tissue or reached a nearby lymph node, and survival is less than 15 percent once the disease has spread elsewhere in the body.

—Jane E. Brody

The Fifties. The changes that began two decades ago evolve still more—deeper wrinkles, especially around the eyes and mouth; sagging, dry skin; and age spots. By now, your wrinkles are clearly noticeable if you've spent a lot of time tanning yourself over the years, or if you smoke. You're also more likely to see wrinkles if your weight has fluctuated significantly. "It's like stretching a balloon," says Bergfeld. "If it collapses after a while, the skin is really wrinkled and the wrinkles are exaggerated." Aesthetically, it's better to keep on a few extra pounds because they act as a filler, giving you a better-looking face.

Protect Yourself From the Sun

The battle against skin cancer starts at birth

Everyone in the family should be using sunscreen with a sun protection factor (SPF) of at least 15 on exposed skin all year long. Babies should always be kept out of the sun, and toddlers, older children and adults should be well protected with hats and clothing or sunscreen. Be sure to protect your skin on cloudy days, too, since clouds do not filter out UV-A radiation.

It should take an ounce of lotion to cover an adult in a bathing suit. Sunscreen should be applied about 20 to 30 minutes before going out, and reapplied on dry skin after swimming ("waterproof" screens are helpful, but not enough once you're out of the water).

Look for sunscreens that protect against both UV-A and UV-B rays. All sunscreens contain substances that block the UV-B rays that cause sunburn (the SPF rating refers only to these agents). The most effective protection against skin-damaging, cancer-causing UV-A rays comes from zinc oxide, Parsol 1789 (avobenzone) and Eusolex 8020. Some UV-A protection is afforded by titanium oxide, oxybenzone and dioxybenzone.

Melanomas can also develop on the scalp and in the eyes, so don't forget a hat and sunglasses, and on the lips, which should be protected by sunblocking lip balm or lipstick. Too much sun can also increase the risk of developing premature cataracts or degeneration of the retina. Now there are contact lenses that can absorb the sun's harmful rays. A study by Dr. Nadia-Marie Quesnel of the University of Montreal College of Optometry found that contact lenses with a built-in UV filter provide

January Is the Cruelest Month

Protecting your skin against winter's ravages

Simple moisturizing products are best at keeping skin from getting dry, flaky and irritated, because they are denser and more durable than expensive creams and therefore can provide greater and longer-lasting protection. It is not the cold itself, but the dryness it brings to the air, that parches the skin, breaking down its natural protective layer of dead cells. Made of both proteins and fats, this layer, called the stratum corneum, forms an oily coating that usually helps to keep moisture in the skin. When it dries out, the skin is more vulnerable to the elements, slower to heal from injuries, and more prone to flaking and cracking.

To help retain moisture, dermatologists also recommend avoiding scalding showers and harsh soaps, which can strip away the oily layer. "Using moisturizing agents like Dove or Olay or Nivea may be enough to keep your skin in shape for the winter," says Dr. Jerome M. Garden, a dermatologist in Chicago. The idea is to keep bacteria and other irritants out of the skin and hold water in, he says, "keeping cells as plump and protected as possible."

Dr. Brian D. Zelickson, a dermatologist in Minneapolis, recommends adding a little fragrance-free oil to bath water for increased hydration. After a bath or shower, he says, it is better to gently pat yourself dry than to rub and buff the skin with the towel. Then, he says, "while you still have water droplets on your skin, you can coat yourself with a humectant to seal the moisture in." Basic moisturizers like Aveeno or Purpose work well, he says, "but you could also use a little olive oil or Crisco."

Lips, too, are vulnerable to dry air. When windburn and cold winter air cause the corners of the lips to crack and split, Zelickson recommends covering them with A+D Original Ointment, a diaper rash cream made with lanolin that helps treat irritated skin.

—Natasha Singer

better protection against UV rays than regular contacts. However, warns Quesnel, UV-blocking lenses don't eliminate the need for sunglasses.

For more information, a helpful book is *Sun Protection for Life* by Mary Mills Barrow and John F. Barrow.

BEYOND SUNSCREENS

Online sites like Solumbra.com, Coolibar.com and Sungrubbies.com have sprung up to sell clothing designed to block ultraviolet rays. Features to look for are an opaque fabric and a dense weave. Hold clothing up to the light; any pinpricks of light you see are evidence that the sun can penetrate. The effectiveness of clothing is measured by an ultraviolet protective factor (UPF) scale that calculates how well ultraviolet rays are blocked.

"For instance, a light-colored fabric lightly woven, like a white cotton T-shirt, only has a UPF factor of 7," Dr. Susan H. Weinkle, a Florida dermatologist and a spokeswoman for the American Academy of Dermatology, says. "A dark T-shirt has a factor of 10 to 12. But if you took a denim shirt, which is dark and tightly woven, it can give you a sun protective factor as high as 1,700."

Look for sites that publish ratings, like Sun-Clothingetc.com, where the Sunday Afternoons Essential Sun Shirt has a UPF of 40; and Solar-Eclipse.com, where the women's All-Sport Pants have a UPF of 49. Coolibar.com, of St. Louis Park, Minn., guarantees a UPF higher than 50. Among the countries the company imports fabrics from is Australia, where high rates of skin cancer prompted the government to test fabrics for ultraviolet protection.

Another option is a laundry additive called Sun Guard from Rit. The product, available from Sunguardsunprotection.com, provides washable clothes with temporary sun protection without damaging fabrics.

—Jane E. Brody and Michelle Slatalla

Is There a Magic Moisturizer?

The labels just get ever more complicated

When you're trying to decide between, say, L'Oréal Dermo-Expertise RevitaLift Double-Lifting intense retightening gel and anti-wrinkle treatment with protensium and nanosomes of pro-Retinol A ORK-immediate action and Shu Uemura's ACE b-G Signs Preventing Essence with skin-strengthening b-glucan, antioxidant-rich vitamins A, C, E and jasmine extract, are you sure you're qualified to make your purchase?

A hundred years ago, the promises were vaguer, notes Kathy Peiss in *Hope in a Jar*, a history of cosmetics. "Do you yearn for a clear complexion?" asked an advertisement for fancy soap in 1922, while in 1928 Elizabeth Arden's Venetia Cleansing Cream boasted that its "melting purity penetrates every least little pore." But back then cold creams, tonics and lotions were still concocted from a mixture of guesswork and folk wisdom, using ingredients that sometimes worked, sometimes didn't, including glycerine, kohl, aloe and witch hazel on the safe side and arsenic, mercury and bleach on the downright dangerous side.

A great leap in skin care was made in the 1960's and 70's, when Dr. Albert Kligman, a dermatologist at the University of Pennsylvania, discovered that retinoic acid, a vitamin A derivative, could be used in the treatment of acne. Johnson & Johnson soon developed a cream called Retin-A to deploy it. In the 80's Kligman found that Retin-A had a further use: it could fight wrinkles and reverse signs of photoaging in the skin. Retin-A and products like Avage and Renova, which use retinoids (also derived from vitamin A), can be obtained by prescription only. But retinol, a less potent vitamin A offshoot, soon began to appear in over-the-counter preparations.

The Foundation of Everything

You'll move, but your makeup will stay in place

It seems logical enough: in order to keep your makeup from disappearing, you need to give it something to hold on to. That's the premise behind products known as foundation primers.

Primers have been a staple in makeup artists' lines—including those of Laura Mercier, Sue Devitt, Vincent Longo and Nars—for several years. But now specialty lines like Tarte and E.I. Solutions have introduced primers; Estée Lauder has Prime FX; and the products have reached the mass market with the introduction of CoverGirl Outlast, a two-compartment tube that holds a primer in one side and foundation in the other. But is this something women need? Why take the time or spend the money on these products, which generally cost $25 to $40?

Where once there was only a foundation layer for the face, now there are anti-aging serums, day moisturizers and sunscreens meant to go on first. Primers are the newest layer, made necessary, makeup experts say, by ever lighter and sheerer foundations. "Back when we used super-matte, opaque foundation that just covered everything, you didn't need primer," says Jose Parron, the director of the Image Studio at Barneys New York. It is no coincidence that these products share a name with what is put on the walls—or that an artist puts on the canvas—before starting to paint. "Walls and canvas, like the skin, have texture to them," Parron says. Using primer smoothes out that texture so that it doesn't interfere with what the artist wants to create. On the face that means filling in oversize pores, creases and fine lines that can make even the best foundation look less than smooth.

Yet not all women will bother with primer, nor does everyone need to. An oil-free sunscreen can double as primer for problem skin, as can a rich moisturizer for very dry skin.

—Sally Wadyka

In recent years, alpha hydroxy acids and antioxidants (like vitamin C) joined the mix. Some recent breakthroughs include peptides (proteins that seem to prompt the skin to make more collagen), topical muscle relaxants like GABA (gamma amino butyric acid, which stuns wrinkles into tautness) and vasodilators (which can make the lips look fuller and pinker by enlarging blood vessels). Combining cosmetics with medical knowledge, these beauty preparations are often called cosmeceuticals, a term Kligman coined in 1980.

The 1938 Food, Drug and Cosmetic Act defines a drug as something meant to "treat a disease or affect the structure or function of the body." For a cosmeceutical to squeak past that ruling, it cannot alter the structure or function of the skin. And yet, if you're paying $100 or more for half an ounce of a rejuvenating serum that is claiming to change your skin's texture or to "lift" your skin without surgery, are you being cheated?

Not quite. Dr. Jeffrey Dover, who practices at SkinCare Physicians in the Boston area and is an associate clinical professor of dermatology at Yale School of Medicine, created a line of cosmeceuticals for CVS drugstores called Skin Effects. He offered to help decode the labels. "Technically, the over-the-counter products can't claim to actually change the skin," he says. "But the ads are brilliant. If you read them carefully, you'll find that nowhere does it say, 'makes wrinkles go away.' Nowhere does it say, 'brown spots are gone.' They'll say the skin's appearance changes."

—Liesl Schillinger

Tips From a Top Makeup Artist

What makes a woman beautiful

Are you unhappy with your looks? Plagued by freckles or a prominent nose? Do you think your lips are too small or too big? Well, take heart in the fact that even supermodels like Kate Moss struggle with beauty crises and skin care woes, according to Bobbi Brown, who has been makeup artist to these beauties. Brown believes the problem lies not with women, but with conventional notions of beauty.

The key to being perceived as pretty, says Brown, author of *Bobbi Brown Beauty: The Ultimate Beauty Resource,* is to exude self-confidence, by being satisfied with your looks and developing an individual beauty style. "My crusade is to make women comfortable in their own skin," says Brown, founder of Bobbi Brown Essentials, a line of cosmetic and skin care products. We asked Brown how cosmetics can help you achieve a face you can love. Here, Brown offers her expertise.

Don't fix it, enhance it. First of all, things like a small mouth and big nose are traits, not flaws. Sadly, women who have these features have been taught not to like them. The challenge is to reverse this way of thinking. For me, the question is not how do you fix it? It's taking the features that make you who you are, and making the most of them. Accept the features you have, learn to feel good about them and start playing them up.

Use the right foundation. Flaws like uneven skin colorations and dark circles under the eyes should be concealed. But it has to be done naturally. A bad concealer looks worse than dark circles. It's important to use a yellow-toned concealer. Using the right foundation for your skin is key. I only apply oil-free foundation on oily skin because most women need some moisture. The trick to finding the right foundation is to apply it on the side of

your face. If it disappears, then it's the right one.

Don't cover up wrinkles. The closest thing I've found to a miracle in skin care is alpha hydroxy acid, which gives the skin a smoother look. Don't try to cover up wrinkles. Instead, apply a brighter blush on the cheeks or line the eyes to make them more prominent.

Diet and exercise to rescue lackluster skin. I've found that the more you exercise and feel healthy, the younger and fresher you look. If I eat well, I look good. Drinking a lot of water also works for me, both by staving off my appetite and giving my skin a clearer, plumped-up appearance.

Change your makeup seasonally. In the summer, wear less makeup, more pastel colors and a bronzer instead of foundation. In the fall, wear moisturizer and foundation and richer lipstick colors like plums and burgundies. Changing the color of your lipstick is not an absolute necessity every season. I wear nude lipstick year-round, and a lot of women who wear red lipstick do the same thing. But the easiest and quickest way to change your look is by changing lipstick color.

Don't take trends too far. Makeup that works for the runway isn't necessarily meant to be worn on the streets. Don't take trends too literally. For example, if a model is wearing black lipstick on the runway, you might want to go for a darker tone than you normally wear. If the look is lots of shine, use shimmer on select spots, not everywhere. It's what works on you that matters.

Make makeup last. The trick to having makeup last for hours is to layer creamy and dry textures. A concealer, for example, is moist and will stay on only if you layer it with a dry powder. Also, lipstick will stay on longer if you apply color with a lip pencil over it. And using moistened eyeshadow to line your eyes instead of a pencil will result in longer-wearing eye liner.

Expect bad beauty days. Most women tend to put more makeup on when they're having a bad day, but that only makes matters worse. If you're not looking your best, skip the foundation that day. Use a tinted moisturizer and blush instead. And drink lots of water. On a bad day, I wear a baseball cap and sunglasses.

Do-It-Yourself Facial Peels
They are cheaper and safe

The facial peel is hardly a new idea. Cleopatra, before 30 B.C., soaked her face in sour milk, which is high in lactic acid, to remove the top layer of dead cells gently, revealing the smoother skin beneath. Over the next 2,000 years, women tried remedies as varied as old wine and sandpaper to do the same thing.

But now there is a new level of do-it-yourself exfoliation: the at-home peel kit, a personal chemistry set meant to mimic the professional peels performed by doctors and spa technicians, but with less irritation. Recently, beauty brands in every price range have introduced some version of it, from L'Oréal to Chanel. All these kits are supposed to diminish wrinkles, spots and blemishes. Kits for microdermabrasion, another form of exfoliation done at doctors' offices and spas, are also available: the Classic Personal MicroDermabrasion System from Dermanew, for example, and Neutrogena's At Home MicroDermabrasion System.

At-home microdermabrasion is gentler, but less effective than the office kind. In professional microdermabrasion, tiny aluminum oxide crystals are sprayed onto the skin at high pressure and quickly vacuumed away. The do-it-yourself method involves using a battery-operated scrubber to apply thick, gritty creams. The abrasion

---

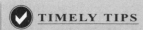 **TIMELY TIPS**

Adding That Youthful Glow
Is it new love, yoga or skin luminizers?

Famous women glow, don't they? Celebrity interviews suggest that their radiance comes from within via Kabbalah, Scientology, new motherhood, new love, yoga, fasting or a humanitarian trip to Africa. But their makeup artists say the radiance comes from skin luminizers, mica and other minerals ground into fine particles to form a veil of delicate sparkle.

By reflecting light, luminizers can balance the appearance of uneven skin tone. "When it's used strategically, it makes everyone look a lot younger, and it adds vibrancy to dull skin," says Patti Dubroff, a makeup artist whose clients include the actresses Jennifer Connelly and Naomi Watts.

To avoid spreading glitter over the entire face, some makeup artists recommend adding only a touch of shine to the cheeks with a creamy blush or a powder. Apply it to the apples of the cheeks and blend it across the cheekbones, says April Greaves, a makeup artist in Los Angeles. Then put a touch only over the brow bones. "On the forehead and nose it can look like oil," Greaves says. "Don't apply it around the eyes, to avoid the wrinkles." She also recommends avoiding pearly white or light gold colors. "Rosy, bronze or fleshy color pigment makes it more realistic."

When applied with a sparing hand, shimmering makeup should merely illuminate the face a little. "Without it, people look noticeably less vibrant," Dubroff says. "It can make anyone look brighter and happier, cleaner and well rested. What could be wrong with that?"

—Christine Lennon

is effective, but what is missing, doctors say, is the vacuum component, which clears pores and is thought to stimulate the production of collagen in the skin. But some users say they're willing to settle for a milder peel in exchange for being able to do it themselves.

The steps involved in chemical peel kits typically include cleaning the face to remove oils, applying an acid solution (with a wide flat brush), removing the product after 5 to 10 minutes and applying a moisturizer. Chemical peel kits come with a warning, recommended by the Food and Drug Administration, that the chemicals make the skin more sensitive to sunlight, so users should wear sunscreen. Some mild redness or stinging is to be expected, but unless the products are left on too long or used too often, nothing worse should result.

—Christine Lennon

A New Kind of Beauty
Surgical procedures and nonsurgical alternatives

Until very recently, the facelift was the most-elected cosmetic surgical procedure to combat the effects of aging skin. Now, however, multi-injection procedures, or filler facelifts, represent a kinder, gentler alternative to surgical facelifts, a way of plumping up rather than cutting away and hoisting sagging tissue. The rising popularity of these techniques is part of a marked national trend. In 2005, for the first time in six years, surgical facelifts did not even make the list of the top five surgical procedures, the American Society of Plastic Surgeons reports.

As opposed to the five- to ten-year effect of a surgical facelift, injections offer only temporary results—lasting six months to two years, depending on which materials are used—but they are far cheaper and less invasive. They also require less recovery time. And though their results are not as dramatic as a facelift, injection cocktails, say doctors who offer them, are sufficient for patients in their 30's, 40's and 50's who do not have a lot of loose skin to cut away.

Side effects like bruising and skin irritation can occur even when only one filler is used. Cosmetic treatments sometimes have adverse aesthetic side effects, which is why potential patients are often advised to take care that the doctor they choose shares their sense of how much work is too much.

Beyond injections, there are other minimally invasive procedures that are currently very popular. Chemical peels and microdermabrasion for the skin surface, to smooth and even it out and remove fine wrinkles; laser hair removal for the entire body and schlerotherapy (injection of blood vessels to remove varicose veins) primarily for the face and legs.

But when it comes to some aspects of the beauty quotient, there is no better choice than to go under the knife to achieve optimum results. Here are a few of the most-elected surgical procedures.

Liposuction. Exercise-resistant fat deposits are removed by a vacuum device. Areas commonly addressed are the abdomen, buttocks, calves, chin, cheeks, neck, thighs and upper arms. Typically an outpatient procedure, liposuction can improve body shape. Permanent if a sensible diet is followed, combined with exercise.

Nose reshaping. A procedure to change the shape of the bridge or tip of the nose or narrow the width of the nostrils, or some of all of the above. Sometimes the reshaping is necessary to alleviate a breathing problem. The procedure is usually outpatient. Recovery time is one to two weeks, but it may take as much as a year before the nose's permanent appearance is fully determined.

Breast enlargement. Implants filled with saline solution are inserted between the breast tissue and

● TIMELY TIPS

Six Injections and What They Do

All of the following have been approved as safe by the Food and Drug Administration, though not necessarily for treating wrinkles.

✔ **BOTOX** smoothes frown lines (those vertical furrows between the eyebrows) by paralyzing the muscles that cause them. The F.D.A. has approved its cosmetic use for this part of the face only, but some doctors also use it on horizontal forehead wrinkles, crows'-feet, neck bands (vertical cords than run below the chin) and the area under the nose to stretch out lines above the lip. If injected incorrectly, Botox can temporarily make the eyelids or lips droop. Treatments last up to four months.

✔ **FAT,** harvested via liposuction, can be purified and safely injected into cheeks, lips or temples, because patients are never allergic to their own fat. Treatments last from six months to several years.

✔ **COLLAGEN** is a fibrous protein that is used to fill wrinkles and acne scars as well as plump lips. Zyderm and Zyplast, made of bovine collagen, can cause itching, swelling and other allergic reactions, so doctors test potential patients to see if they are sensitive. Cosmo-Derm and CosmoPlast, made of human collagen, usually do not cause such reactions. Treatments last three to six months.

✔ **RADIESSE** (formerly known as Radiance) is approved by the F.D.A. to strengthen vocal cords, but a few cosmetic doctors have been using it experimentally to fill in cheeks, chins and deep wrinkles. Made of microscopic calcium particles suspended in a gel, it may cause tiny lumps or bumps, doctors say. The effects are expected to last one to three years.

✔ **RESTYLANE,** a spongy gel made of hyaluronic acid, is used to fill moderate to deep facial folds or off label, to plump lips. Restylane often causes bruising and swelling for a few days. Treatments last up to six months. Hylaform and Captique, other hyaluronic acids, cause less swelling, but doctors say they last only four to five months.

✔ **SCULPTRA** is a synthetic compound that has been approved by the F.D.A. to treat facial wasting in AIDS patients. Some doctors use Sculptra off label to fill hollow cheeks associated with ordinary weight loss or aging, but others question whether it might cause inflammation in people with healthy immune systems. Treatments last up to two years.

—Natasha Singer

the muscles of the chest wall. It is usually outpatient, with general, or local anesthesia with sedation. Recovery may take a few days, and healing a year or more. The results are variable; for some people, replacement or removal is sometimes necessary.

Eyelid surgery. Removes excess fat or drooping flesh from the upper eyelid or under the eyes to reverse the signs of aging, as well as for aesthetic improvement at any time. Usually outpatient, with general anesthesia. Healing takes several weeks.

Tummy tuck. Involves a surgical tightening of the abdominal wall and removing excess fat and skin to obtain a flatter stomach and more waist definition. A general or local (with sedation) anesthetic is used. Two to four weeks' recovery is necessary, and healing takes two to four weeks.

All of these procedures have their own risks and side effects. For more information, visit the American Society of Plastic Surgeons site at www.plasticsurgery.org.

—Natasha Singer

Hand-to-Hand Combat

A few ways to battle the aging appearance of hands

In the battle against aging, the hands matter, too. You can spend all the time you want getting your face treatments and facelifts and creams, but your hands will betray your age every time. The most common problem is dryness. Because hands do not have as many oil glands as other areas of the body, and because they so often are washed in soap (or worse, detergents) and exposed to air and sun, the protective top layer of skin cells is easily stripped away. Here are a few ways to counteract dryness.

Moisturizing creams and lotions contain humectants, like glycerin or hyaluronic acid, which attract moisture from the air and from the deeper layers of skin, and emollients—like petroleum jelly, mineral oil, lanolin or shea butter—soften the skin and provide a protective coating. Prices vary wildly, from a few dollars for drugstore brands to close to $100 for some creams. Is there a difference? Many dermatologists say no. "Read any cream label," says Dr. Marinos Petratos, a dermatologist in New York City. "There will be emollients, lubricating agents and preservatives." Three inexpensive drugstore moisturizers doctors often recommend are Aquaphor, Vaseline Intensive Care lotion and Cutemol cream.

Doctors advise applying moisturizer when the hands are still damp from washing, so that it can trap the water in. Another trick, recommended by Dr. Frederic Brandt, a dermatologist based in New York and Miami, is to apply moisturizer to the hands before bedtime and then wear a pair of cotton gloves overnight to increase penetration.

In addition to dryness, hands suffer from overexposure to sunlight and from aging. Symptoms include wrinkles, brown spots and an increasingly leathery texture. To address this damage, hand creams now include a variety of special ingredients—alpha hydroxy acids (to exfoliate), vitamins A, C and E (to reduce oxidative damage), amino acids and fatty acids (to block moisture loss), retinoids (to stimulate the production of collagen, which makes skin firm) and skin lighteners (to fade brown spots).

Microdermabrasion, chemical peels and laser resurfacing can make skin smoother, even out its color, promote the growth of collagen and get rid of rough patches, dark spots and shallow wrinkles.

Wrinkle fillers used on the face, including Restylane and Sculptra, can also plump up the skin on the backs of the hands. One of the most natural-looking injectables is the patient's own fat, removed via liposuction from, say, the stomach or the inner thighs. Sclerotherapy can reduce the appearance of veins on the backs of the hands. The treatment involves injecting a chemical solution into the blood vessels that causes them to contract.

By far the best way to have beautiful hands is to prevent damage in the first place. Keep them out of hot water whenever possible. And remember that nothing short of gloves beats the daily use of a high-SPF sunscreen.

—Elizabeth Hayt

An Embarrassment of Baldness

Men and women both can suffer from it

When it comes to hair loss, men are often as vain as women. As many as one in two men lose their hair by the age of 50. Women are not immune from balding, either, and just as anxious about it. An estimated 30 million women—about one in five—suffer from female pattern hair loss though for them it is rarely as obvious as men's bald crowns; women's hair thins noticeably over

☑ TIMELY TIPS

Tender Loving Care for Delicate Hair

Suffering from fragile or thinning hair? Here's a list of things to avoid to help preserve your "crowning glory."

✔ **DO NOT ignore the problem.** Early treatment offers the best chance to preserve and thicken the hair that remains. "Like brain cells, once hair cells are destroyed or programmed to destroy, they cannot be regenerated," says Dr. Susan C. Taylor, a Philadelphia dermatologist.

✔ **DO NOT treat hair with heat or harsh chemicals.** Relaxers, peroxide, hot combs, flat irons and even blow-dryers can leave hair brittle and prone to break. "Probably blow-drying with a hot hair dryer is the most damaging thing that women do on a daily basis," says Dr. Janet L. Roberts, a clinical professor of dermatology at Oregon Health &

Science University, in Portland.

✔ **DO NOT crash diet.** Sudden weight fluctuations are a prime culprit for hair loss among young women. Gradual losses of one to two pounds a week may help avoid it.

✔ **DO NOT skimp on protein or iron.** The body needs both to grow healthy hair. "Get some form of protein for breakfast, lunch and dinner," Dr. Roberts says.

✔ **DO NOT style too tightly.** Over time tight braids, cornrows and ponytails may place stress on the hair and the follicle, leading to temporary breakage or even permanent hair loss, Dr. Taylor says.

✔ **DO NOT wash with drying or clarifying shampoos.** Gentle formulas or those labeled "body building" that don't strip the hair of moisture are best for thin, delicate strands.

✔ **DO NOT skip conditioner.** This helps prevent damage to thin or delicate hair by "minimizing

friction between the strands," Dr. Roberts says.

✔ **DO NOT handle hair roughly.** Vigorous towel drying, teasing and scratching may be damaging to the hair and scalp.

✔ **DO NOT brush frequently.** The old adage about brushing 100 strokes a day for healthy hair is actually a recipe for breakage, according to Dr. Roberts. A wide-tooth comb is least damaging of all.

—Laurel Naversen Geraghty

AND HOW NOT TO PICK A HAIRPIECE

✔ **Don't** choose one with too much hair.

✔ **Don't** pick an unrealistic hairline. A 40-year-old, for example, shouldn't have bangs.

✔ **Don't** try to cover up gray hair with a hairpiece. If you have some gray, match the piece with it.

SOURCE: American Hair Loss Council

the entire head. However, female pattern hair loss is usually permanent.

Balding men today have a number of treatment options. They can choose hair-loss therapies to strengthen remaining follicles and prevent further loss. This is somewhat easier in men than in women, because in men the hormone that triggers hair loss—dihydrotestosterone—is known. Doctors can counteract its effect by prescribing Propecia for men. "We have this silver bullet that

puts the freeze, if you will, on male pattern baldness," says Dr. Alan J. Bauman, a hair transplant surgeon in Boca Raton, Fla. "We don't have a treatment like that for women."

Rogaine (the brand name of the drug minoxidil) is the only medicine known to slow hair loss in both men and women. Women's Rogaine is less potent than men's—a 2 percent strength, rather than 5 percent as in men's—but many dermatologists recommend the 5 percent solution for women, too.

It is meant to be dripped onto the scalp twice daily. Because it has not been studied in pregnant women, patients are advised to talk to their doctors if they are expecting or thinking of becoming pregnant. Also, Rogaine is not suitable for people with some medical conditions, such as high blood pressure.

Other drugs target specific causes of hair loss. Those who have abnormally high levels of male hormones, for instance, may be prescribed birth-control pills containing estrogen or may take spironolactone, a drug that blocks the metabolism of male hormones. Those who have alopecia areata, which results from an autoimmune disorder, may be given cortisone shots in the scalp or a topical cream. Some doctors give patients a series of treatments with low-intensity laser light.

For those who are really determined to regain a head of natural hair, there is hair transplantation micrograft surgery, which implants hair follicles taken from the back of the head, two or three at a time. The best candidates for transplants are men with typical male pattern baldness and most women, who tend to lose hair all over. Men and women should consider undergoing transplant surgery as soon as they start to lose hair, says Dr. Barry Resnik, a private practitioner in Aventura, Fla. "When you have enough hair, it looks imperceptible."

—Laurel Naversen Geraghty

Beyond the Pale

Tooth whitening can sometimes go too far

A fondness for pearly white teeth is ancient. In the Bible, Jacob hopes that his son Judah will have "teeth white with milk." But never in history have paper-white teeth been as popular or easy to obtain as they are now.

Whitening treatments in which teeth are coated in a high-strength bleaching gel and then put under an ultraviolet or visible light for three 15- to 20-minute sessions are said to be the fastest method of tooth whitening. Three treatments can lighten teeth as much as using a dentist-dispensed bleaching tray for 10 nights or wearing over-the-counter whitening strips for 16 days, according to a study published this year in the journal *Operative Dentistry.* But many people have found that the initial brilliance begins to fade in a matter of weeks.

"If my daughter were getting married tomorrow and needed quick bleaching, I would recommend an in-office light treatment," says Dr. Bruce A. Matis of the Indiana University School of Dentistry in Indianapolis. "But for those who have time and prefer longer-lasting whitening, I recommend using a dentist-dispensed bleaching tray." But some dentists say that when people routinely use high-strength bleaches, or use whitening products in every step of their oral-care routine, it may add up to a level of exposure to bleaching agents that goes beyond what has been studied.

American products are much more powerful and getting stronger all the time, raising the risk of overexposure to bleach. Fifteen years ago the first trays dispensed by dentists used gels that were 10 percent carbamide peroxide, equivalent to about $3^{1}/_{3}$ percent hydrogen peroxide. Today, some products contain as much as 22 percent carbamide peroxide whitener. And the strongest bleaching strips sold by dentists now contain 14 percent hydrogen peroxide gels. "Once you get above 15 percent carbamide, you are pushing the envelope," says Dr. Van B. Haywood, a professor at the School of Dentistry at the Medical College of Georgia in Augusta. Because of the unknown risks of high peroxide exposure, some dentists advise pregnant women as well as cancer patients and smokers (who are at risk of developing cancer) to avoid tooth whitening altogether.

—Natasha Singer

Sexuality

Hormones Are Everything

When it comes to our sex drive, at least

In the almost fifty years since Masters and Johnson began groundbreaking research on the sex lives of Americans, it has become increasingly clear that the relationship between hormones and sex drive is complex and intimate. Hormones regulate every aspect of our sex lives, and to a large degree, our behaviors as well.

According to Dr. Theresa Crenshaw, a sexual medicine specialist and author of *The Alchemy of Love and Lust*, the difference between men and women lies in how their hormones behave. She calls the mix of hormones and their interactions a "sex soup." As the ingredients interact, so do

 INSIDE INFO

Fertility by the Numbers

Ever since researcher Alfred Kinsey published his famous statistical portrait of male sexual behavior in 1948, Americans have sought to quantify information about sexual and reproductive activity. Here are a few facts:

○ **Sperm Story:** The average male produces sperm at the rate of 500 million per day. Between 120 million and 600 million sperm are released during one ejaculation.

○ **Eggs Aplenty:** A woman is born with 200,000 to 400,000 eggs in her ovaries, all that will ever be available to her. But she will only experience about 500 menstrual cycles during her lifetime, so her egg supply is more than ample for any reproductive needs.

predominant human sexual patterns, and many other attitude-related behaviors. Testosterone, the principal male sex hormone, has circadian rhythms that change during the course of the day, influencing male behavior, chiefly in a man's desire for orgasm. The production of testosterone, like that of estrogen, is governed by the brain's pituitary gland, which secretes hormones that in women stimulate the ovaries to produce estrogen, and in men prompt the testes to generate testosterone.

Women have many more hormones (including testosterone), which have a more complex rhythm and interaction, and in turn make their sex drive more complicated, and subject to variability. Testosterone provokes an interest in sexual fantasies and genital sex in both sexes. "Lust is associated primarily with testosterone in both men and women," says Helen Fisher, an anthropologist and author, most recently of *Why We Love*. Although the neuroanatomical path of testosterone can be mapped, its underlying behavioral mechanism is not known. German researchers, writing in the *Journal of Endocrinology* in 2001, posited the following: "Testosterone might have direct effects on cognitive behavior, e.g., influence the awareness of sexual cues, but it is also suggested that testosterone may act peripherally to enhance sexual pleasure and thereby increase sexual desire and even sexual activity, circumstances and partner permitting." In other words, a tincture of testosterone for a woman having sex could mean the difference between making a mental grocery list or hearing Beethoven's Ninth.

Romantic love is linked with the natural stimulant dopamine and perhaps norepinethrine and serotonin. Feelings of attachment are produced primarily by the hormones oxytocin and vasopressin, which at elevated levels can actually suppress the circuits for lust," says Fisher. Just as male hormones are subject to daily, even hourly fluctuations, female hormone levels rise and fall, though they follow the rhythm of the monthly cycle. When estrogen is predominant, Crenshaw says, "It's the Marilyn Monroe in us." It makes a woman ready and receptive for a man. It may also impair a woman's judgment slightly, and cause her to be less selective. Once she has ovulated, a woman "enters the proceptive or seductive nature of her sex drive."

It is normal, Crenshaw adds, for people to have different sex drives and different rhythms. One partner could be a morning person and the other could be an afternoon person, or they might feel desire on different days of the week. Unless a couple learns to handle, negotiate and make the best of different sex drives early on in their relationship, they're destined for problems. Sexual incompatibility is cited as a top reason for divorce in the United States.

HORMONES AND AGING

Endocrinologists, who study the delicate balance of hormones, emphasize that there is no true male equivalent of menopause. While women's levels of the female hormone estrogen plunge sharply over a relatively short period of time, falling to vestigial amounts, men almost never undergo as precipitous a change in concentrations of the male hormone testosterone.

Nevertheless, a number of recent studies have suggested that male testosterone levels do slump gradually with age, perhaps by as much as 30 to 40 percent between the ages of 48 and 70.

Most studies indicate that the testes, rather than the brain, are to blame for any testosterone decline with age, and that for unknown reasons the testicular tissue becomes gradually less responsive to the tweak of pituitary hormones. As a result, sex drive

INSIDE INFO

Sex Effects

○ **Morning High:** Testosterone levels are highest in the early morning and lowest in the late afternoon and evening. October is the high point of the year for testosterone levels. February is the nadir.

○ **Bigger Breasts:** During intercourse, a woman's breast size may increase as much as 25 percent, and the nipples by one centimeter.

○ **Night Moves:** Average erections per night by age:

Adolescence:	4
Age 30-39:	3
Age 40-69:	2+
Age 70+:	1.7

○ **Peak Time:** Men reach their sexual peak at age 17 and slowly decline from there. Women are at their most receptive around age 40.

HEALTH

diminishes and all the hormones and mechanisms that make erections predictably available become unpredictably available. The frequency of sex goes down, and some men are not able to have sex at all. For those for whom this becomes a problem, testosterone has been used to treat hypogonadism, low testosterone levels in men, but, as with the research on female hormones, the benefits and potential risks of male hormone therapy have yet to be thoroughly studied.

Almost all women can begin menopause as early as 40 and finish in their late 50's. The average age of women at menopause today is 51.4 years. Estrogen levels decrease and almost disappear after menopause. But testosterone, still present in small amounts in the female hormonal mix, may become a more dominant presence than it was before, relative to the ratio of other hormones that

Better Safe Than Dismayed

The ins and outs of birth control

Birth control techniques don't work unless they're practiced consistently and correctly. The following efficacy rates are published by the Guttmacher Institute, a nonprofit corporation for reproductive health research, policy analysis and public education, and Planned Parenthood Federation of America. Understandably, when it comes to sexual intercourse, the stakes are high, because pregnancy is always a risk. Without contraception, some 85 percent of sexually active women would most likely become pregnant within a year. Here's a list of the most popular contraceptives, listed in descending order. (STD is an acronym for sexually transmitted disease.)

ORAL CONTRACEPTIVES: *92 to 97 percent effective*

USE: Pill must be taken on daily schedule, regardless of the frequency of intercourse. Prescription.

RISKS: Water retention, weight gain, bleeding, breast tenderness, hypertension, mood change and nausea. In rare cases, blood clots, heart attacks, strokes. Not usually recommended for women who smoke, especially over age 35.

STD PROTECTION: Confers some protection against pelvic inflammatory disease.

TUBAL LIGATION (women): *95 percent effective*

USE: A onetime procedure performed in an operating room. It requires the use of general anesthesia. Procedure is considered permanent but can sometimes be reversed.

RISKS: Pain, infection and, for tubal ligation, possible surgical complications and bleeding.

STD PROTECTION: None.

MALE CONDOM: *85 to 98 percent effective*

USE: Applied immediately before intercourse; used only once and discarded. Effectiveness largely depends on proper, consistent use. Nonprescription.

---

previously dominated. That's why some women, as they age, develop mustaches and their voices get lower. The good aspect of the continued presence of female testosterone, however is that it allows a woman to retain her sex drive, "I'm not so sure that sex drive diminishes when most people believe it does," says Fisher. "Show me a middle-aged woman who says she's lost her sex drive, and I'll bet if she got a new partner, who excited her, her neurochemical levels for lust and romantic love would shoot back up." For women who complain of low or no libido, prescriptions for testosterone creams, gels and other transdermal treatments have become the means of treatment. Such prescriptions have risen eightfold between 1999 and 2004.

—Camille Sweeney and Natalie Angier

When Menopause Comes

Hormone therapy or not? It's still not clear

The year 2002 may well be remembered as the year of the Great Hormone Panic. After five years, researchers concluded that women who were taking hormones to relieve the symptoms of menopause were at increased risk for breast cancer, stroke and blood clots; furthermore, they were not protected from heart disease. Because of their findings, they halted one of the largest randomized controlled clinical trials of hormone treatment. The Women's Health Initiative trials were under the auspices of the National Heart, Lung and Blood Institute and the National Institutes of Health. The aborted trial included 16,608 postmenopausal women from 50 to 79 who were taking a combina-

RISKS: Rare irritation and allergic reactions.

STD PROTECTION: Latex condoms help protect against all sexually transmitted diseases, including herpes and HIV.

VASECTOMY (for men): *85 to 99 percent effective*

USE: A one-time procedure usually performed in a doctor's office under local anesthesia. Procedure is considered permanent but can sometimes be reversed.

RISKS: Pain, infection and, as with tubal ligation, possible surgical complications and bleeding.

STD PROTECTION: None.

INJECTION : *97 percent effective*

USE: One injection every three months. Prescription.

RISKS: Amenorrhea, headache, nausea, weight gain.

STD PROTECTION: None.

WITHDRAWAL: *73 to 96 percent effective*

USE: Withdrawal of penis before ejaculation.

STD PROTECTION: None

COPPER T IUD; MIRENA IUD: *92 to 94 percent; 99 percent effective, respectively*

USE: After insertion, stays in until physician removes it. Can remain in place for 1 to 10 years, depending on the type. The IUD should only be used by women in monogamous relationships, because multiple partners may increase the risk of developing or aggravating pelvic inflammatory disease. Prescription.

RISKS: Cramps, bleeding, pelvic inflammatory disease.

STD PROTECTION: None.

PERIODIC ABSTINENCE *75 to 91 percent effective, depending on method*

USE: Requires the woman to frequently monitor her body's functions and periods of abstinence; effectiveness depends on accurately predicting when ovulation will occur. Can be used in conjunction with barrier methods to increase effectiveness.

RISKS: None.

STD PROTECTION: None.

---

tion of estrogen and progestin, a synthetic form of progesterone, or a placebo pill.

In February 2004, researchers stopped another trial that included 10,739 women who had had hysterectomies and who were taking estrogen alone or a placebo. Researchers concluded that the therapy increased the risk of stroke and clots in the leg and did not curb heart disease. Women in the study who took estrogen alone actually developed fewer cases of heart disease and breast cancer. But the researchers said the differences were so slight that they might have been because of chance. The women on estrogen also benefited from fewer hip fractures.

The Women's Health Initiative findings challenged the entrenched belief that estrogen protected postmenopausal women from heart disease. The findings also contradicted the results of the Nurses' Health Study, which has followed more than 120,000 female nurses for several decades and which years ago found a correlation between estrogen treatment and a drastically reduced incidence of coronary heart disease.

Still, in 2006, many women continue to turn to hormones for relief, and many gynecologists continue to prescribe them as a first-line therapy for severe menopausal symptoms. And some researchers are testing a new theory, that hormone therapy is beneficial for the heart when it is initiated early, during a narrow "window of opportunity" around the time of menopause and before women develop an excessive buildup of atherosclerotic plaque.

A paper published in the *Journal of Women's Health* in January 2006 added credence to that idea. It reported that women who started therapy soon after menopause reduced the risk of coronary heart disease 30 percent, but that the benefit appeared to diminish the longer women waited to initiate treatment. The paper, based on data from the earlier Nurses' Health Study, suggested that timing the therapy was critical.

Despite the wealth of information about the risks and benefits of hormone therapy, women face difficult choices when contemplating treatment.

Hormone therapy continues to be considered the most effective treatment to relieve hot flashes, insomnia, night sweats and vaginal dryness. There is no one-size-fits-all answer, doctors say. Ultimately, each woman must make her own risk-benefit assessment, taking into account the severity of menopausal symptoms, general health and the potential long-term risks of treatment. Many gynecologists point out that the increased risk to a relatively healthy woman from hormones is slight, though it accumulates over time.

Current recommendations call for using the lowest dose of hormones for the shortest duration of time, and many doctors now prescribe products that contain significantly less estrogen (or estrogen and progesterone) than the doses found harmful in the Women's Health Initiative.

Many alternatives to oral hormones are on the market. One is the transdermal patch, which delivers hormones through the skin. Many doctors think it may reduce clotting risks associated with estrogen.

For patients whose chief complaint is vaginal dryness, which makes intercourse painful, a variety of estrogen-releasing vaginal creams, vaginal rings and vaginal tablets are available.

ⓘ INSIDE INFO

How Sex Life Changes

A widely cited study by Edward O. Laumann, a University of Chicago sociology professor, and others, found that:

○ **By age 30** three-quarters of Americans are either married or living with someone, but they are starting to have "partnered sex" less often than people in their 20's.

○ **During their 30's** more people are having sex with a partner a few times a month, and fewer are having sex a few times a week.

○ **By their 40's** this disparity more than doubles for both men and women.

○ **All ages:** Forty-three percent of women reported some sexual dysfunction, the most prevalent being loss of libido.

—Camille Sweeney

Some physicians prescribe so-called bioidentical hormones, taken orally. Compounding pharmacies that create custom formulations say they use hormones identical in chemical structure to the natural hormones. Consumer advocates say there is no scientific proof that these formulations are safer than commercial ones.

Women have also tried alternative treatments like soy products or herbs (like black cohosh) that contain estrogenlike compounds. They are loosely regulated. Simple changes like more exercise or drinking milk before bed may help with mild symptoms.

If a woman has a history of breast cancer, many doctors recommend a class of antidepressants proved to relieve menopausal symptoms in lieu of hormones.

—Roni Rabin

When the Pump Won't Work

What causes erectile dysfunction and how to treat it

In the past decades, there has been a revolution in the treatment of erectile dysfunction, the inability of the penis to develop and maintain an erection for satisfactory sexual intercourse or activity. Estimates of the prevalence of this dysfunction vary, ranging from about 5 percent of men in their 40's to over 50 percent in their 70's, depending in part on how the disorder is defined. An estimated 15 million to 30 million Americans have erectile problems. But a majority of men afflicted by them have never received a medical diagnosis of erectile dysfunction, and only a small fraction are being treated, experts report. Many men are too embarrassed to mention the problem to their doctors, and many doctors are equally reluctant to ask patients about it.

A man's ability to perform sexually can be impaired by a host of usually interrelated factors, including disorders that affect nerves, blood vessels or hormonal output; certain medications (both prescription and over the counter); diseases like diabetes, stroke, multiple sclerosis or epilepsy; aging; psychological problems like depression and performance anxiety; pelvic trauma, radiation or certain operations; and, of course, a loss of interest in one's sexual partner.

Risk factors for cardiovascular disease—hypertension, abnormal blood lipids, smoking and diabetes—are associated with an increased prevalence of erectile dysfunction, strongly suggesting that men seeking treatment first be evaluated for heart and blood vessel disease. This is best done with a full medical history, measurement of blood pressure, blood sugar and blood lipids, and possibly a treadmill test. A cardiovascular assessment is especially important for men of middle age and older, since resumption of sexual activity after treatment can result in a heart attack in those unaccustomed to the exertion.

Insufficient testosterone is an uncommon cause of erectile dysfunction, affecting about 6 percent of men with this problem. Although giving testosterone to someone with a deficiency may not in itself correct the erectile problem, testosterone is the libido hormone for both men and women, and is an important stimulant of sexual desire.

To appreciate the value of the new drugs, it helps to understand how a normal erection occurs. It is important for men and their partners to understand that these drugs by themselves do not cause an erection or affect libido. They work only as a result of sexual stimulation. With sexual arousal, the penis must fill with blood, causing it to enlarge and become rigid. For as long as arousal persists, fibrous tissue in the penis preserves the erection by creating a cinch to prevent blood from leaving.

In addition to a receptive state of mind, adequate levels of testosterone and healthy blood vessels and nerves, an erection requires the chemical messenger nitric oxide. It plays two critical roles, transmitting arousal impulses between nerves, and relaxing the smooth muscles in arteries, allowing them to expand and fill with blood.

Nitric oxide signals production within artery cells of a chemical called cyclic guanosine monophosphate (cGMP), which increases blood flow to the penis. This chemical is broken down by another, phosphodiesterase-5 (PDE-5), to end the erection. The new drugs all work by inhibiting PDE-5, allowing cGMP to produce and sustain an erection. The erectile drugs come in various dosages, and if a low dose is not effective, a higher can often be tried. In men over 65, however, only the lowest dosages are recommended.

IT HAPPENED ONE NIGHT

Every year, approximately 15 million people contract a bacterial sexually transmitted disease, such as syphilis or gonorrhea, or a viral sexually transmitted disease (STD), like herpes. Following are descriptions of the most common STD's, along with some possible symptoms and treatments.

DISEASE		
HOW SPREAD	SYMPTOMS	TREATMENT
BACTERIAL VAGINOSIS Sexual intercourse, multiple partners, douching, using an IUD	Grayish vaginal discharge	Metronidazole, clindamycin
CHLAMYDIA Vaginal, oral, anal sex; mother to child during birth	Vaginal discharge, vaginal bleeding; burning during urination, discharge in men	Azithromycin, doxycycline, erythromycin (for pregnant women), chlortetracycline (for eyes)
CRABS Contact with infected person, using his/her clothes, towels or bedding	Intolerable itching in genital or other areas	Kwell lotion; clean clothes, towels and bedding
HUMAN PAPILLOMA VIRUS (HPV) Sexual intercourse, oral sex	Women: small, painless warts in labia, vulva, cervix or anus Men: warts on penis or scrotum	Laser beam; podophyllin, trichloracetic acid
GONORRHEA Sexual intercourse, oral sex; mother to child during birth; hand-to-eye contact	Thick, milky discharge; burning, painful urination; pain in lower abdomen, vomiting, rash, chills; fever, pain in wrists and extremities. (almost all men show symptoms; women may be asymptomatic)	Ceftriaxone, Ciprofloxacin

A MAN'S CHOICES

The new drugs for erectile dysfunction are revolutionary, because earlier treatments were more complicated. Here are some options:

Alprostadil. Must be administered directly into the urethra or injected into the penis. The injections, which are more effective, can help men with a variety of underlying causes, both psychological and physical. In one study, more than 80 percent of men and their partners reported satisfactory results.

Vacuum constrictor devices. Use vacuum pressure to promote blood flow into the penis and a constricting ring to keep the blood from escaping. Though it works in about two-thirds of cases, it does prevent ejaculation.

Prosthesis implantation. One kind is a semirigid rod that, in effect, creates a permanent erection, and the other is an inflatable device that can readily pump up the penis when sexual activity is desired.

Drugs such as Viagra, Cialis and Levitra. The three drugs are about equally effective, but there are differences in their actions. In general, the drugs should be taken about an hour before expected sexual activity, and none should be used more than once

DISEASE			
HOW SPREAD		**SYMPTOMS**	**TREATMENT**
GENITAL HERPES			
Sexual intercourse, oral sex		Tingling, itching in genital area, legs, buttocks; painful genital sores	Keep sores clean and dry; xylocaine, ethyl chloride may ease pain
HIV/AIDS			
Sexual intercourse, anal sex, blood transfusions, infected needles		Fatigue, weight loss, swollen glands, fever, night sweats, bronchial infections, sores, loss of appetite, trouble swallowing, recurrent yeast infections (women)	Protease inhibitors in combination with AZT and other drugs
NONGONOCOCCAL URETHRITIS			
Sexual intercourse		Often none; discharge from penis and inflamed urethra	Doxycycline, erythromycin
PELVIC INFLAMMATORY DISEASE (PID)			
Generalized infection of uterus from an STD		Fever, vaginal discharge, painful intercourse, painful urination	Antibiotics to treat specific infection
SCABIES			
Sexual contact, towels		Intense itching, red bumps on torso or hands	Permethrin, eurax
SYPHILIS			
Sexual or skin contact, mother to child at birth		Painless genital sore, rash, sore throat, swollen joints, aching bones, hair loss	Penicillin; tetracycline doxycycline
TRICHOMONIASIS			
Sexual contact		Women: yellow-green frothy discharge with strong odor, discomfort during intercourse, irritation and itching of genitals Men: mild discharge or slight burning after urination or ejaculation	One dose of metronidazole

a day. Viagra is best taken on an empty stomach (dietary fat delays its effect by about an hour). Levitra and Cialis are not affected by food, but the blood level of Levitra is reduced by high-fat meals. None of the drugs should be taken with alcohol, though only Cialis is said to cause dizziness when combined with normal amounts of alcohol.

Viagra and Levitra are effective for about four hours; Cialis, for up to 36 hours. Viagra is most effective after an hour. Levitra may work within 20 minutes and Cialis within 45.

Side effects from these drugs are as follows: headache in 10 to 30 percent of patients; flushing in 10 to 20 percent; heartburn in 3 to 16 percent; runny nose in 1 to 11 percent; changes in color perception in 2 to 10 percent; muscle aches and back pain in up to 10 percent; and dizziness in up to 5 percent. There have also been more than three dozen cases of blindness reported in men taking Viagra and four cases in men taking Cialis. Likewise, deaths and nonfatal heart attacks have been reported in users, but no cause-and-effect evidence in either case has been shown. There are also possible serious interactions with other medications, like nitrates (including nitroglycerin pills, patches and pastes); alpha blockers for hypertension; protease inhibitors used in AIDS treatment; the antifungals ketoconazole and itraconazole; and the acid reducer cimetidine.

Several other drugs, including rifampin, carbamazepine and phenytoin, may decrease the effectiveness of the erectile drugs. In addition, patients should not take Levitra if they have a heart problem called prolonged QT syndrome.

—Jane E. Brody

 INSIDE INFO

The AIDS Toll in the U.S.

○ Despite the significant medical advances in the treatments available, people are still getting sick with HIV/AIDS, and too many are still dying.

○ Listed below are the cumulative estimated numbers of diagnosed AIDS cases since the beginning of the epidemic in 1981, as well as the estimated number of diagnosed cases in the U.S. in 2004. The numbers are distributed according to the person's age at time of diagnosis.

AGE	Estimated # of AIDS Cases in 2004	Cumulative estimated # of AIDS Cases, through 2004*
Under 13:	48	9,443
Ages 13 to 14:	60	959
Ages 15 to 19:	326	4,936
Ages 20 to 24:	1,788	34,164
Ages 25 to 29:	3,576	114,642
Ages 30 to 34:	5,786	195,404
Ages 35 to 39:	8,031	208,199
Ages 40 to 44:	8,747	161,964
Ages 45 to 49:	6,245	99,644
Ages 50 to 54:	3,932	54,869
Ages 55 to 59:	2,079	29,553
Ages 60 to 64:	996	16,119
Ages 65 or older:	901	14,410

*Includes persons with a diagnosis of AIDS from the beginning of the epidemic through 2004.

SOURCE: Centers for Disease Control and Prevention

Protecting Yourself From AIDS

There's still no cure for the disease, but much can be done to avoid contracting it

Acquired immune deficiency disease (AIDS) is caused by human immunodeficiency virus (HIV). It is spread through contact with infected body fluids such as blood and semen. Infected people may harbor the virus within their bodies for several years or even longer before developing symptoms of AIDS. Though symptomless, they can still infect others. Worldwide, most HIV transmission occurs during sexual relations between heterosexual partners. In the United States, the majority of transmission has been between homosexual partners. Transmission among drug addicts who share infected needles is another significant route of transmission in many countries.

The surest way to avoid any risk of getting HIV/AIDS is to eschew sexual intercourse and never take intravenous drugs. HIV is spread primarily by sexual contact with an infected person, by sharing needles and/or syringes with someone who is infected or through transfusions of infected blood or blood clotting factors. Babies born to HIV-infected women may also become infected in the womb or through breastfeeding. The Centers for Disease Control provides some guidelines to prevent exposure:

HOW IT IS–AND ISN'T–TRANSMITTED

Kissing. Casual contact through closed-mouth or "social" kissing is not a risk for transmission of HIV. Because of the potential for contact with blood during "French" or open-mouth kissing, the C.D.C. recommends against engaging in this activity with a person known to be infected. However, the risk of acquiring HIV during open-mouth kissing is believed to be very low.

Biting. In 1997, the C.D.C. published findings from

The Search for an AIDS Vaccine

Researchers have made progress in treating patients who already have HIV, developing powerful drug cocktails that can stave off disease. But when it comes to preventing the virus's spread, success is spotty. One of the few effective interventions involves the use of anti-HIV drugs to keep a mother from infecting her baby.

If anti-HIV drugs can help uninfected babies dodge the virus, might the same approach work for uninfected adults? Could the sexually active take antiretrovirals to avoid contracting HIV in the first place? Intrigued by the prospects, some gay men already have experimented with what's known as "pre-exposure prophylaxis" or PrEP; a 2005 survey conducted by the U.S. Centers for Disease Control and Prevention at gay-pride events in four U.S. cities found that 7 percent of those interviewed said they had tried it.

A half-dozen studies are now under way that will determine whether these men are onto something. The trials all focus on tenofovir (marketed under the brand name Viread), a drug that appears safer than the other AIDS medications on the market. Placebo-controlled trials are enrolling 5,000 people on four continents who are in high-risk groups, including gay and bisexual men, sex workers and injecting drug users. All told, the experiments will cost more than $40 million, which is being paid for by the C.D.C. and the National Institutes of Health, as well as the Bill and Melinda Gates Foundation.

Optimistic mathematical models show that if tenofovir PrEP is effective 90 percent of the time and is used by 90 percent of the people who are at highest risk of becoming infected, it could cut new HIV infections in a community by more than 80 percent in a few years. Even if it works spectacularly well, tenofovir PrEP will not substitute for an AIDS vaccine, the holy grail of prevention research. With a vaccine, a few shots can train an immune system to ward off a disease for decades. But tenofovir PrEP would work only if people take the drug repeatedly. Then again, no AIDS vaccine is on the near horizon. Tenofovir PrEP, in contrast, could prove its worth by 2008.

—Jon Cohen

a state health department investigation of an incident that suggested blood-to-blood transmission of HIV by a human bite. There have been other reports in the medical literature in which HIV appeared to have been transmitted by a bite. Severe trauma with extensive tissue tearing and damage and presence of blood were reported in each of these instances. Biting is not a common way of transmitting HIV. In fact, there are numerous reports of bites that did not result in HIV infection.

Saliva, tears and sweat. HIV has been found in saliva and tears in very low quantities from some AIDS patients. Finding a small amount of HIV in a body fluid, however, does not necessarily mean that HIV can be transmitted by that body fluid. HIV has not been recovered from the sweat of HIV-infected persons. Contact with saliva, tears or sweat has never been shown to result in transmission of HIV.

Insects. From the onset of the HIV epidemic, there has been concern about transmission of the virus by biting and bloodsucking insects. However, studies conducted by researchers at C.D.C. and elsewhere have shown no evidence of HIV transmission through insects—even in areas where there are many cases of AIDS and large populations of insects such as mosquitoes.

WHAT YOU CAN DO

Condoms. The proper and consistent use of latex or polyurethane (a type of plastic) condoms when engaging in sexual intercourse—vaginal, anal or oral—can greatly reduce a person's risk of acquiring or transmitting sexually transmitted diseases, including HIV infection.

There are many different types and brands of condoms available—however, only latex or polyurethane condoms provide a highly effective mechanical barrier to HIV. When condoms are used reliably, they have been shown to prevent pregnancy up to 98 percent of the time among couples using them as their only method of contraception. Similarly, numerous studies among sexually active people have demonstrated that a properly used latex condom provides a high degree of protection against a variety of sexually transmitted diseases, including HIV infection.

In businesses and other settings. Instruments that are intended to penetrate the skin (such as tattooing and acupuncture needles, and ear piercing devices) should be used once and disposed of or thoroughly cleaned and sterilized.

Instruments not intended to penetrate the skin but which may become contaminated with blood (for example, razors) should be used for only one person and disposed of, or thoroughly cleaned and disinfected after each use.

If there is someone with an HIV infection in your house. Gloves should be worn during contact with blood or other body fluids that could possibly contain visible blood, such as urine, feces or vomit.

Cuts, sores or breaks on both the caregiver's and patient's exposed skin should be covered with bandages. Hands and other parts of the body should be washed immediately after contact with blood or other body fluids, and surfaces soiled with blood should be disinfected appropriately.

Practices that increase the likelihood of blood contact, such as sharing of razors and toothbrushes, should be avoided.

Needles and other sharp instruments should be used only when medically necessary and handled according to recommendations for health care settings. (Do not put caps back on needles by hand or remove needles from syringes. Dispose of needles in puncture-proof containers.

SOURCE: Centers for Disease Control and Prevention

Abortion: Facts and Figures
Despite the restrictions on obtaining one, they are easier to have than ever before

More than 25 million Americans have had abortions since the Supreme Court handed down Roe v. Wade, the 1973 decision that made abortion legal. Often kept secret, even from close friends or family, abortion cuts across all income levels, religions, races, lifestyles, political parties and marital circumstances. Despite its quiet occurrence, abortion remains one of the most common surgical procedures for women in America. More than one in five pregnancies ends in abortion.

Since 1992, when the Supreme Court recognized states' authority to restrict abortion as long as they did not create an "undue burden," states have enacted 487 laws restricting patients or providers, in many cases calling for mandatory counseling, waiting periods and parental consent for minors, according to Naral Pro-Choice America. The result is a patchwork of laws and regulations that vary from state to state, some of which may yet come before the U.S. Supreme Court. In surveys, Americans largely support these restrictions, even if they say abortion should be legal.

The tide is slowly turning, however. In March 2006, Gov. Michael Rounds of South Dakota

Options for the Morning After

How to avoid pregnancy after unprotected sex

In the best of all possible worlds, there is no such thing as a sexual slip-up, but the fact is, to err is very human, especially when it comes to sexual intercourse. There are currently two types of emergency contraception for unprotected sex: pills and an emergency IUD. These are for emergencies only, and are not recommended as an alternative form of birth control

PILLS, OR ECP'S: *75 (combination) to 89 (progestin only) percent effective if started within 72 hours after unprotected vaginal intercourse.*

USE: Some ECP's are combination pills, with estrogen and progestin; others are progestin only. Taken by mouth in one (progestin only) or two doses (combination of estrogen and progestin, 12 hours apart) after unprotected sex, these drugs stop the release of an egg from an ovary, may prevent the union of sperm and egg and may prevent a fertilized egg from attaching to the womb. Prescription.

RISKS: Nausea, vomiting and cramping.

EMERGENCY IUD INSERTION: *99.9 percent effective within five days of unprotected intercourse*

USE: Insertion of IUD by a clinician to prevent implantation of any egg that may have been fertilized.

RISKS: Same as those from using IUD's for ongoing contraception.

Source: Planned Parenthood Federation of America, Inc.

signed into law the nation's most sweeping state abortion ban, an intentionally direct legal challenge to Roe v. Wade. The law makes it a felony to perform any abortion, except in a case of a pregnant woman's life being in jeopardy.

As laws have become more restrictive, technology has gone the other way, making abortions possible both earlier and later in pregnancy, and by pill or surgery. Doctors can perform abortions as early as eight days after conception, and 59 percent of women having abortions do so within eight weeks, according to data from the Centers for Disease Control and Prevention.

Through the first 56 days of pregnancy, there are two options for ending a pregnancy: medication abortion or abortion by vacuum aspiration. After 56 days, vacuum aspiration is the only abortion option through the end of the first trimester.

Fewer than 1 percent of women have abortions after 20 weeks. A late-term procedure called intact dilation and extraction, sometimes known as "partial-birth" abortion, accounted for less than two-tenths of 1 percent of all abortions in 2000, according to the Guttmacher Institute, which provides statistics on reproductive matters such as birth control and abortion.

Since September 2000, when the Food and Drug Administration approved the drug mifepristone, sold as Mifeprex, and sometimes called RU-486, for early abortion, many women have chosen this option, according to the manufacturer's data. Mifepristone is given in conjunction with a second pill, misoprostol, usually over two or three days, and requires a follow-up exam with a doctor.

Recently, there has been serious concern because a number of women have taken Mifeprex and subsequently died of a systemic infection from a virulent form of bacteria, *Clostridium sordellii*. These bacteria infect the bloodstream, and produce a toxin that causes something akin to toxic shock syndrome.

—John Leland

Doctors & Medicine

Where to Find a Good Doctor

The best place to search is online

Now that millions of consumers are surfing the Web to research their own medical symptoms, many are taking the next step: comparison-shopping online for hospitals and doctors.

So far, the various consumer databases, many available only to individuals enrolled in insurance plans, have some gaps. At this point, there is much more quality-of-care information available about hospitals than about individual doctors, except in nine states including Florida, Pennsylvania and Wisconsin that make statistics available on the numbers of procedures that surgeons perform. And pricing information still tends to be scarce. But the databases can grow only more robust, now that the full weight of the health insurance industry is behind the trend and the federal government is beginning to wield its influence.

Anyone, insured or not, can now log on to the federal Department of Health and Human Services' Web site, called Hospital Compare (hospitalcompare.hhs.gov), which uses Medicare and Medicaid data to assess the track records of more than 4,000 hospitals around the country. Want to know which hospitals in your city to go to for treating heart attacks or pneumonia? Log on to Hospital Compare, plug in the step-by-step particulars and judge for yourself, based on criteria that include whether the hospitals provide appropriate medicines when patients are admitted and discharged. The government also plans to begin reporting on complications after surgery, and whether doctors and nurses make clear to patients how to take care of themselves after a hospital stay.

Private health plans typically provide more comparative data than the federal Web site. Wellpoint, the nation's largest commercial health insurer, allows its 28 million members to log on to an expanded list of health care information services, which includes software to help members compare their own potential costs under various health plans. Besides Wellpoint and Humana, most of the big insurance companies—including United Healthcare, Aetna and Cigna, as well as many state and regional Blue Cross and Blue Shield insurers—provide this type of information.

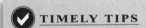 **TIMELY TIPS**

Docs Who Make House Calls

These days, if you are willing to pay the money, you can procure the services of a new breed, the "concierge" or "boutique" doctors, who lavish time, phone calls and attention on patients, using the latest in electronic communications to streamline their care.

✔ These doctors charge fees as high as $10,000 a year, depending on the services promised. The majority charge $1,500 to $2,000.

✔ Basic services consist of same-day or next-day appointments and 24-hour telephone access to the doctor. The most expensive may also promise the doctor will make home visits, deliver medications and accompany patients on visits to other doctors.

—Abigail Zuger

THE DOCTOR IS ONLINE

Here's a selective list of some of the best health and medical information Web sites. In addition to what is listed here, there are gender-specific health links organized by disease categories at the bottom of the page at www.nytimes.com/library/ national/science/health/health-navigator.html.

HEALTH AND MEDICAL GUIDES

• **Achoo** Directory-style guide to health information, with search engine: www.achoo.com

• **Aegis** Comprehensive collection of AIDS information and resources, including HIV Infoweb: www.aidsinfo.org/do/home

• **America's Doctor** Info on trials: www.americasdoctor.com

• **Association of Online Cancer Resources** Tracks cancer developments: www.acor.org

• **University of Wisconsin Comprehensive Cancer Center:** www.uwhealth.org/

• **CDC National Prevention Information Network** HIV, STD and TB information from the Centers for Disease Control: www.cdcnpin.org

• **Columbia University's Complete Home Medical Guide:** www.cumc.columbia.edu/health/index.html

• **Go Ask Alice** Questions & answers from Columbia University: www.goaskalice.columbia.edu

• **Hardin Meta Directory of Internet Health Sources:** www.lib.uiowa.edu/hardin/md/index.html

• **Health Touch** Consumer health information, much of it collected from specialized health organizations: www.healthtouch.com

• **Intelihealth** Features Harvard Medical School's consumer health information: www.intelihealth.com

• **Mayo Clinic:** www.mayoclinic.com

• **Medem** Medical information from many U.S. medical societies: www.medem.com/

• **Medical Matrix** Medical search engine: www.medmatrix.org

• **Medicine.net** Info provided by doctors: www.medicinenet.com

• **Medscape** Up-to-date medical news for doctors and patients: www.medscape.com

• **MedWeb** Search engine from Emory University: www.medweb.emory.edu/MedWeb

• **Multiple Sclerosis Foundation**: www.msfacts.org

• **National Alliance of Breast Cancer Organizations**: www.nabco.org

• **Oncolink** Cancer information from the University of Pennsylvania Cancer Center: www.oncolink.com

• **OnHealth** Health information from traditional and alternative sources: www.onhealth.com

• **Pregnancy and Parenting iVillage** Health info oriented toward parents and children parenting: www.ivillage.com

• **PDR Net** From the publisher of the drug guide (registration required): www.pdr.net

• **WebMD**: www.webmd.com

• **Yahoo Health**: www.yahoo.com/Health

REFERENCE

• **Innerbody.com** Interactive guide to human anatomy: www.innerbody.com

• **Martindale's Health Science Guide** Links to scientific and medical sources: www.martindalecenter.com

• **National Library of Medicine** From the National Institutes of Health: www.nlm.nih.gov

• **Nutrient database from the U.S.D.A.:** www.nal.usda.gov/fnic/foodcomp/search

• **Pubmed** Medline and other journal searches: www.ncbi.nlm.nih.gov/entrez/query.fcgi?DB=pubmed

• **RxList: The Internet Drug Index** Extensive information on prescription and over-the-counter drugs: www.rxlist.com

—Richard J. Meislin

The Better Off You Are

○ The more education and income people have, the less likely they are to have and die of heart disease, strokes, diabetes and many types of cancer.

○ Upper-middle-class Americans live longer and in better health than middle-class Americans, who live longer and better than those at the bottom. And the gaps are widening, say people who have researched social factors in health.

○ As advances in medicine and disease prevention have increased life expectancy in the United States, the benefits have disproportionately gone to people with education, money, good jobs and connections. They are almost invariably in the best position to learn new information early, modify their behavior, take advantage of the latest treatments and have the cost covered by insurance.

○ Smoking has dropped sharply among the better educated, but not among the less.

○ Physical inactivity is more than twice as common among high school dropouts as among college graduates. Lower-income women are more likely than other women to be overweight, though the pattern among men may be the opposite.

○ Some researchers now believe that the stress involved in so-called high-demand, low-control jobs further down the occupational scale is more harmful than the stress of professional jobs that come with greater autonomy and control.

○ The risk factors for a heart attack—smoking, poor diet, inactivity, obesity, hypertension, high cholesterol and stress—are all more common among the less educated and less affluent, the same group that is less likely to receive cardiopulmonary resuscitation, to get emergency room care or to adhere to lifestyle changes after heart attacks.   —Janny Scott

The raw material for the information on the Web systems is typically assembled from data that include medical payment claims, hospitals' reports to Medicare and health care information from employers. Companies that collect and organize the information include Subimo, a privately held company that supplies data for Wellpoint and Michigan Blue Cross, among other insurers; HealthShare Technology, which was acquired by WebMD; and Health Grades, based in Golden, Colo.

—Milt Freudenheim

Talking With Your Doctor
How to get the best care from your physician

During the years he served as Surgeon General, C. Everett Koop became a household name and something of a media star as he made health issues a national topic. After leaving Washington, he founded the C. Everett Koop Institute at Dartmouth College, which develops programs to teach young people about health issues. In this conversation, held in the late 1990's he offers timeless advice about how to go about finding a good doctor.

How should patients choose a doctor?

With a large percentage of the country now in managed care, most people don't have much choice. But if you do have a choice of doctors, one of the things people find most helpful is getting referrals from patients who are satisfied with their doctor. If a doctor doesn't listen to you or doesn't communicate, that's not a doctor to seek out unless there's something very special about him and his knowledge.

How can patients determine whether their doctor is qualified to treat their condition, or whether they need to see a specialist?

INSIDE INFO

The Doctor Is In–for the Moment

○ Patients, on average, have 18 seconds to talk to a doctor before they are interrupted. Women doctors interrupt at the same rate as men.

○ Dr. Richard Frankel, a professor of medicine and geriatrics at Indiana University, recommends that patients decide ahead of time what they want to convey and to defloot interruptions to say it. He also suggests that patients take a list of their complaints and ask the doctor to staple it to their chart. That way, Dr. Frankel says, the doctor almost always addresses them.

○ The Web site RateMDs.com, allows patients to rate their doctors and to read about what experiences others have had.

—Gina Kolata

It depends on your confidence in your doctor. You don't have to know everything to be able to do the right thing. It's those tricky situations where a difference of opinion can make a real difference in the patient's quality of life, or even life itself. Sometimes people understand by attitude, innuendo and body language what their doctor's comfort level is with what he's telling them, and whether he is qualified to treat them in that instance.

● What if you do need a specialist?

If your primary care physician thinks you should see a specialist, ask whether this person has board certification—which means he has passed an exam recognizing his expertise in a particular field of medicine. If you visit the doctor you've been referred to and he says, "You ought to have X, Y, and Z done," you say, "Are there other options?" When he answers, ask, "How often have you done X, Y, and Z, and what are the results?" The more

that patients ask, the more honesty they're going to get from physicians.

● Is there any statistically reliable way to gauge a physician's skill?

In many places now, the batting average of doctors and hospitals in the management of certain problems is being made available. In several states, doctors who do open heart surgery are not only listed with their mortality rate overall, but also their mortality rate in different hospitals where they work. You have pretty good objective evidence, all based on the same kind of statistics. Say your cardiologist says that there are three surgeons to consider in your town, and you can see that one has a 95 percent success rate, one a 92 percent rate and one 89 percent. That gives you a place to go. You then can talk to the doctor with the lowest rating and he may say, "I'm different than the other two because I take every patient that comes my way, and sometimes I take very high-risk patients, and of course they tend to have more problems than the others, while my competitor only takes patients that he knows he's going to succeed with." There are ways you can ferret out the answers you want, but it takes digging.

● When do you advise getting a second opinion?

Second opinions are very important for surgical procedures, especially those that even the laity knows are not always successful, like operations for lower back pain. Then there are the situations where one doctor says you need your gallbladder out and "I can do that through three little incisions with a laparoscope and you'll be out the next day." Another doctor says, "You need an old-fashioned surgical procedure." Then another opinion is necessary. Insurance companies are willing to pay for second opinions, because if the second opinion is not to have surgery and the patient believes it, they save money.

● **What questions should patients ask before undergoing surgery?**

Ask about your particular situation and why it's absolutely necessary to have surgery. Then ask about the risk versus the benefit, and whether you have something that is premalignant or just a nuisance. If you ask questions like this, you can weigh whether the surgery's risk is relatively small and is worth the benefit. I don't think patients should think about the economics of it if it's at all possible to do so.

● **Should patients in an H.M.O. question a decision not to treat their condition?**

They have every right to. One of the sad things about managed care is that in some systems the physician gets docked for doing too much—if he has too many referrals, if his prescriptions are too expensive, if he is seeing too many patients for 20 minutes instead of 15. It's the same thing for a test. If a doctor says, "You ought to have a stress test," you should say, "Doctor, talk to me about why you think it's important that I should have the test." But that demands a frankness with doctors that patients are frequently loath to show.

Men, Women & Heart Disease
The symptoms are different for men and women

Heart disease, strokes and other cardiovascular diseases are the leading causes of death in the United States and other developed countries. They killed 910,600 people in the United States in 2003, the most recent year for which data are available; more than half the deaths, 484,000, were among women. But scientists have only recently started to explore the differences in heart disease between men and women. Among them:

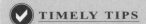

TIMELY TIPS

When Seconds Count

✔ Heart attack victims are less likely to die in hospitals where angioplasty is the usual emergency treatment rather than clot-destroying drugs, according to a large study, reported in *Circulation* in January 2006.

✔ Dr. Harlan M. Krumholz, the senior author on the report and a professor of medicine at Yale, says that if he lived 10 minutes from a hospital that provided angioplasty and 10 minutes from one that provided only the drug treatment, he would "choose the one that did the invasive procedure every time." Still, Dr. Krumholz emphasizes that practical limits must be considered.

● Women with heart disease tend to be sicker than men by the time it is diagnosed.

● Women tend to benefit less from bypass surgery and to have more severe symptoms when they develop heart failure. Some of the difference is because women are older and frailer when they develop heart disease.

● Symptoms of heart attack tend to differ between men and women. Men report crushing pain in the chest, while women are more likely to feel dizzy, sick, short of breath and sweaty.

● Women are more likely than men to have a hidden type of coronary disease in which their heart muscle is starved for oxygen, even though their coronary arteries look clear and free of blockages on X-rays. The condition, which may affect three million American women, greatly increases the risk of a heart attack. Its main symptom is chest pain or discomfort. In many women, the pain occurs, but nothing shows up on an angiogram, a test in which dye is injected into the coronary arteries and they are X-rayed in a search for blockages, so doctors conclude that no treatment is needed.

- Overall death rates from coronary disease have declined in the past few decades, but most of the improvements have been in men's rates.

—Denise Grady

Every Stroke Matters

Paying attention to early warning signs could save your life

If you have a T.I.A.—a transient ischemic attack, commonly called a mini-stroke—a brief episode when blood is cut off to your brain, you should take it seriously. Although the blockage is brief and no detectable brain damage or symptoms persist, such attacks are often the warning sign for a major stroke. Most of these attacks occur in people over 60, and some of them may incorrectly dismiss the short-lived symptoms as merely another sign of age. As a result, it is critically important for someone with such an attack to get prompt medical attention and treatment to prevent a far more serious blockage to the brain.

SYMPTOMS

- Confusion, slurred or garbled speech or difficulty understanding
- Numbness, weakness or paralysis in the face, arm or leg, especially on one side of the body
- Blindness in one or both eyes or double vision
- Trouble walking, dizziness, loss of balance or coordination
- Severe headache with no known cause

DIAGNOSIS

Among the tests that can help in diagnosis are a sonogram of the carotid arteries to look for narrowing or clogging of these crucial blood vessels; C.T. scan or M.R.I. of the brain; C.T. angiogram or M.R.I. angiogram to evaluate the arteries in the neck and brain; and possibly a transesophageal echocardiogram to obtain detailed images of the heart to look for things like blood clots.

 **TIMELY TIPS**

Handicapping Your Mini-Stroke

Oxford and Edinburgh university researchers reporting in the journal *Lancet* recommend this scoring system—called ABCD—that can help predict the risk of a stroke within a week of a transient ischemic attack (T.I.A.):

✔ **A for age 60 or older,** 1 point.

✔ **B for blood pressure,** systolic (the top number) greater than 140 millimeters of mercury, diastolic equal to or greater than 90 millimeters or both, 1 point.

✔ **C for clinical features,** weakness on one side, 2 points; speech disturbance without weakness, 1 point.

✔ **D for duration of symptoms** in minutes, 60 or more, 2 points; 10 to 59, 1 point.

The risk of suffering a stroke within seven days of a T.I.A. was 0.4 percent among patients scoring fewer than 5 points; 12.1 percent for those who scored 5 points; and 31.4 percent for those who scored 6 points.

The early risk of stroke of about 30 percent in T.I.A. patients with an ABCD score of 6 necessitates not only emergency investigation and treatment, but also admission to a hospital.

TREATMENT

Most commonly, patients are prescribed one of two types of medication—anti-platelet drugs or anti-coagulants—to prevent excessive clotting of the blood.

The most common anti-platelet medication is aspirin, usually one 325-milligram tablet a day. Another is clopidogrel (trade name Plavix), which may be used in combination with aspirin.

Anti-coagulants are trickier and require careful monitoring to be sure that the clotting potential is not excessively reduced—a reaction that can cause hemorrhaging. The two anti-coagulants commonly used are warfarin (Coumadin) and heparin.

If one or both carotid arteries are found to be seriously narrowed, surgical removal of the plaque or insertion of a stent to expand the arterial opening may be the recommended therapy.

Researchers point out that even if preventive measures fail to head off a stroke in such patients, the fact that they are in the hospital means that immediate treatment can dissolve the blood clot in the brain and stem the extent and the residual effects of a stroke.

—Jane E. Brody

Too Much of a Good Thing

A popular pain killer can damage your liver

The drug acetaminophen is best known under the brand name Tylenol. But many consumers don't realize that it is also found in widely varying doses in several hundred common cold remedies and combination pain relievers. These compounds include Excedrin, Midol Teen Formula, Theraflu, Alka-Seltzer Plus Cold Medicine, and NyQuil Cold and Flu, as well as other over-the-counter drugs and many prescription narcotics, like Vicodin and Percocet.

The combination of acetaminophen's quiet ubiquity in over-the-counter remedies and its pairing with narcotics in potentially addictive drugs can make it too easy for some patients to swallow much more than the maximum recommended dose inadvertently, according to a study appearing in the December 2005 issue of *Hepatology*. "It's extremely frustrating to see people come into the hospital who felt fine several days ago, but now need a new liver," says Dr. Tim Davern, one of the authors and a gastroenterologist with the liver transplant program of the University of California at San Francisco. The numbers of poisonings, however, are still tiny in comparison with the millions of people who use over-the-counter and prescription drugs with acetaminophen.

—Deborah Franklin

The New Miracle Drug?

Statins may be helpful for a wide range of ailments

Among cardiologists, it has become a running joke: Maybe the powerful drugs known as statins should be added to the water supply. Not only do statins greatly reduce cholesterol and lower mortality in people at risk for heart attacks, but some studies also suggest that they might help to prevent or treat a wide range of ailments, including Alzheimer's disease, multiple sclerosis, bone fractures, some types of cancer, macular degeneration and glaucoma.

In July 2005, the National Institutes of Health, in conjunction with the American Heart Association and the American College of Cardiology, endorsed sharply lowering the desired levels of harmful cholesterol for people at moderate-to-high risk for heart disease. The recommendations were based on clinical trials involving more than 50,000 people.

Yet some experts say statins are more complex than people realize, and that they can have side effects that are in some cases potentially serious, and note that whether the drugs produce any long-term toxicity over 20 or 30 years remains unknown.

Six statins are currently on the market: Lipitor by Pfizer; Zocor by Merck; Crestor by AstraZeneca; Pravachol by Bristol-Myers Squibb; Lescol by Reliant Pharmaceuticals; and Mevacor, also by Merck. The drugs cost $500 to $1,000 or more for a year's supply, depending on the brand and the dosage. Statins slow the production of cholesterol in the body and increase the liver's ability to remove L.D.L., the type of cholesterol linked to heart disease, from the blood.

In the vast majority of patients, doctors say, statins appear to produce few or no side effects. But in clinical trials some patients reported gastrointestinal problems, headaches and nausea. It was unclear if these problems were caused by the medications, because subjects who were taking placebos reported similar side effects. About 1 percent of people on the drugs, clinical trials indicate, develop elevated liver enzymes, and one in 1,000 have drug-related muscle pain and other problems, according to a review by the National Institutes of Health.

Publicity about the benefits of lowering cholesterol through statin treatment, doctors worry, may lead people to think that even those at low risk for heart disease should take the drugs, despite the fact that clinical trials have not yet demonstrated any benefits for such people. In addition, some researchers fear that the findings could lead doctors and patients to ignore the fundamental importance of lifestyle factors, like diet and exercise, to cardiovascular health. "A lot of people think, 'Hey, I'm on statins, I'm protected; I'll have the Big Mac or the foie gras or the crème brûlée,'" says Dr. Eric Topol, former chairman of the cardiovascular department at the Cleveland Clinic in Ohio. "And most doctors give up on lifestyle changes, because it takes an investment of time from both patient and physician.

ⓘ INSIDE INFO

Let the Patient Beware

○ The authors of the guidelines widely used to establish standards for prescribing medicines are often paid by the drug companies whose products they discuss.

○ A 2005 study by the journal *Nature* found that more than one-third of the guideline authors acknowledged some financial interest in the drugs they recommended.

○ In half of the more than 200 guidelines examined, at least one author had received research financing from a relevant company, and 43 percent had at least one author who had been a paid speaker for the company.

○ Thirty-four percent of guidelines explicitly stated that their authors had no conflicts of interest at all. Almost half the published guidelines included no information about potential conflicts.

—Nicholas Bakalar

It's easier to write a prescription for a statin."

Doctors, researchers and other statin experts caution that any patient taking a statin drug should be monitored regularly, not only for cholesterol levels, but for any signs of adverse responses.

—David Tuller

The Diabetes Epidemic

It's incurable, but there are ways to prevent and control it

Nearly 21 million Americans are believed to be diabetic, according to the Centers for Disease Control, and 41 million more are prediabetic; their blood sugar is high, and could reach the diabetic level if they do not alter their living habits. Here are some facts and figures:

What diabetes is. Type 1 and Type 2 diabetes are diseases in which the amount of sugar in the blood rises to dangerous levels. Neither is truly curable. Type 2 is more prevalent, representing more than 90 percent of all cases. In Type 1, a gland, the pancreas, no longer produces insulin because the immune system has destroyed the cells that make it. Thus sugar builds up in the blood, causing internal damage, while cells starve. In Type 2, the body can generally produce insulin, but the diabetic's cells cannot properly use it. In some Type 2 cases, insulin production is insufficient. (A third type, gestational diabetes, afflicts a small number of pregnant women. It usually vanishes after the birth, though it increases the woman's risk of developing Type 2.)

How people get it and how it's treated. The cause of diabetes remains unclear. Type 1 typically surfaces in childhood and is believed to stem from genetic factors activated by an environmental trigger, like a virus. Type 1 diabetics require daily insulin injections to live. Traditionally, Type 2 appears in people over 40. Its onset is also tied to genetics, but is linked to obesity and inactivity as well. Researchers agree that in many cases, the disease can be delayed, and possibly prevented, through exercise and weight loss. However, people typically have Type 2 for 7 to 10 years before it is diagnosed, by which time its untreated presence will often have led to complications. Type 2 diabetics typically take medicines that improve responsiveness to insulin and stimulate the pancreas to make more of it.

Who gets diabetes. African-Americans and Latinos, particularly Mexican-Americans and Puerto Ricans, incur diabetes at close to twice the rate of whites. Some Asian-Americans and Pacific Islanders also appear more prone, and they can develop the disease at much lower weights.

The velocity of new cases among all races has accelerated significantly from just a few decades ago. Genetics cannot explain this surge, because the human gene pool does not change that fast. Instead, the culprit is thought to be behavior: faulty diet and inactivity.

Why doctors are worried. So-called Type 2 diabetes, the predominant form, is becoming a childhood disease, almost unheard of two decades ago.

- One in three children born in the United States five years ago is expected to become diabetic in his/her lifetime, according to a projection by the Centers for Disease Control and Prevention. The forecast is even bleaker for Latinos: one in every two.

- The American Diabetes Association says the disease could actually lower the average life expectancy of Americans for the first time in more than a century.

- Even among Americans who know they have the disease, about two-thirds are not doing enough to treat it.

- Diabetics are two to four times more likely than others to develop heart disease or have a stroke, and three times more likely to die of complications from flu or pneumonia, according to the Centers for Disease Control.

- Most diabetics suffer nervous-system damage and poor circulation, which can lead to amputations of toes, feet and entire legs. According to the federal Agency for Healthcare Research and Quality, some 70 percent of lower-limb amputations in 2003 were performed on diabetics. Studies suggest that as many as 70 percent of amputees die within five years.

- Women with diabetes are at higher risk for complications in pregnancy, including miscarriages and birth defects. Men with diabetes run a higher risk of impotence. Diabetes is the principal reason adults go blind. Young adults with diabetes have twice the chance of getting gum disease and losing teeth.

—N. R. Kleinfield

A Primer on Breast Cancer

Knowing the risk factors will cut your risk of being a victim

After lung cancer, breast cancer is the second largest cause of cancer death in women aged 40 to 55. According to the American Cancer Society, in 2006, an estimated 212,920 cases of invasive breast cancer will be diagnosed, as well as 61, 980 additional cases of in situ breast cancer, and an estimated 40,970 women will die of the disease. Also, approximately 1,720

men in the United States will be diagnosed with breast cancer in 2006, with an estimated 460 men dying of the disease. Marilyn Leitch, professor of surgical oncology and medical director of the Southwestern Center for Breast Care, explains the risks, the precautions that should be followed and the treatment options that are available:

Q **What are the symptoms of the disease?**

The most common symptom is a painless mass found during a breast self-exam. Less common signs are nipple discharge, a change in the appearance of the skin on the breast, such as redness or nipple dimpling, or a lump or swelling under the arm.

Q **Who is most at risk of breast cancer?**

All women are at risk of breast cancer. Breast cancer rarely occurs in men. Advancing age is the most important risk factor—the older a woman gets, the more likely she is to get breast cancer. Roughly

PERFORMING A BREAST SELF-EXAMINATION

1. *Once a month, after your period, examine your breasts. Get to know their shape and texture, and be alert to changes. Raise each arm above your head and turn from side to side, looking for changes in appearance.*

2. *Squeeze the nipple to check for discharge. Check surface for peculiarities. Orange-peel texture could indicate a lump.*

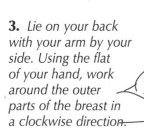

3. *Lie on your back with your arm by your side. Using the flat of your hand, work around the outer parts of the breast in a clockwise direction.*

4. *Raise arm over head. Check inner parts of the breast, along collarbone and into armpit. Stretching the skin makes detection easier.*

77 percent of women diagnosed with breast cancer in a given year are over age 50.

Are there other factors that predispose a woman to developing breast cancer?

They include a prior personal diagnosis of breast cancer or a family history of breast cancer (the closer the relative is, the greater the risk). Having a breast biopsy in the past which shows abnormal changes in the breast's fibrocystic tissue such as atypia, menstruating at an early age or having a late menopause, never having a baby, or getting pregnant for the first time after age 30 are also risk factors.

What can one do to detect a breast cancer early?

Detecting breast cancer involves a three-pronged approach. The most important emphasis is placed on having mammograms, since a mammogram can find the smallest of breast cancers.

 INSIDE INFO

Mammograms

○ Film mammography, a filmed image produced by very low dosage X-rays, is not perfect. A recent study showed that 10 to 20 percent of breast cancers detected by a physical exam were missed by a film mammogram. Yet none of the alternatives have yet been as thoroughly vetted in terms of lives saved.

○ Digital mammograms were found to be better than film mammograms at detecting cancer among three groups of women: those with very dense breasts, as determined by their doctors; women under 50, whatever their breast density; and women of any age who were premenopausal or who had had at least one menstrual period within 12 months of the last mammogram, in a study by the National Cancer Institute

—Deborah Franklin

However, women often find the cancer by self-exam. All women—with or without risk factors—should be aware of their breasts so that they can recognize a lump. Performing breast self-exams every month beginning at age 20 is a good way to become familiar with what is normal for you. It's ideal to do the exam about five to seven days after the menstrual period starts, when breasts are the least tender or full. Postmenopausal women should perform self-exams at the same time each month. Statistically, most women aren't going to detect any abnormalities, but if something seems out of the ordinary, you'll be able to detect it because you'll be familiar with how the breast tissue feels. Examination by a health care professional can also help detect breast cancer. An exam should be performed at least every three years starting at age 20, and every year starting at age 40. A clinical breast exam may be recommended more frequently if you have a strong family history of breast cancer.

What is a mammogram? Is the procedure safe?

A mammogram is an X-ray of the breast that can detect smaller tumors before they can be felt in physical exams. The theoretic risk of radiation is extremely low compared to the risk of getting breast cancer. Today, the technical aspects of doing mammograms have become very rigorous, and women are only exposed to very low doses of radiation. In addition, the Mammography Quality Standards Act, which requires mammography facilities to be certified by the Food and Drug Administration, ensures that high-quality equipment and technicians are used.

How much do mammograms cost?

A diagnostic mammogram costs more than a screening mammogram, because it requires more work on the part of the technician and the radiologist. Costs of mammograms vary by the technique, whether it is digital or analog and whether computer-aided detection (CAD) is added to the radiologist's reading. A screening digital mammogram with CAD costs around $300, and a diagnostic digital mammogram may cost around $350, although the price varies, depending on where you are in the country. Mammograms performed on analog machines with standard X-ray films and without CAD are significantly less expensive, $125 to 150.

What does it mean if a woman finds a lump during a self-exam?

Sometimes a lump is just a thickening in the breast tissue that does not need further treatment. But all women who find a lump should have it checked by their primary care doctor to determine whether it's a dominant mass. If it is, women should have a mammogram and/ or an ultrasound to evaluate the lump. If it is a fluid-filled cyst, the fluid can be removed with a needle, and the lump goes away. If it is a solid lump, a needle biopsy can be done and the cells examined under a microscope to determine if the lump is benign or malignant.

What are the treatment options once you're diagnosed with breast cancer?

Most women with breast cancer are candidates for a breast-saving surgery called lumpectomy, which involves removing the cancerous tumor in the breast, then getting radiation treatment to the breast. The other option for treatment is a mastectomy, which involves removing the entire breast. Breast reconstruction can often be performed immediately, if the woman chooses. With both procedures, the lymph nodes under the arm must be checked to see if cancer has spread to the lymph nodes. In recent years, this is being done with a minimally invasive technique called sentinel node biopsy. This more limited surgery has fewer long-term side effects

Breast cancer is more common in countries where there's a high fat content in the diet, like the U.S., and is quite low in countries that have a lower fat content, like Japan.

• • •

than complete removal of the lymph nodes under the arm.

What are the chances of beating the disease through various treatments?

It depends on the stage of disease when patients are treated. When the breast cancer is confined to the breast, the survival at five years is 98 percent. If it is spread to the lymph nodes, the five year survival is about 80 percent. The good news is that breast cancer death rates have been declining at a rate of 2.3 percent for more than decade. This is due to early detection with mammograms and better chemotherapy and anti-hormonal treatments.

Can a low-fat diet or exercise reduce your risk of breast cancer?

It seems there is some relationship between obesity, a high-fat diet and the development of breast cancer. Breast cancer is more common in countries where there's a high fat content in the diet, like the U.S., and is quite low in countries that have a lower fat content, like Japan. The decreased risk may be related to reducing the level of estrogen in the body. Younger women who are very athletic and women who have multiple pregnancies have fewer menstrual periods, which may have a protective effect, because fewer hormones are produced, than in women who are overweight and tend to produce more estrogen. One study suggests that women who exercise when they're first menstruating and who continue through their reproductive years can greatly reduce their risk of premenopausal cancer, possibly because it can reduce the number of menstrual cycles. A couple of studies have suggested that reduction of weight and fat in the diet improves outcome even after a woman develops breast cancer.

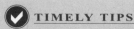

TIMELY TIPS

Watch Your Waist—and Prostate

The correlation between fitness and prostate cancer

✔ Men who gain weight rapidly from age 25 to 40 are twice as likely to have a recurrence of prostate cancer even after surgery as those who do not, according to a report that appeared in the Oct. 1, 2005 issue of *Clinical Cancer Research*. Being overweight at the time of the surgery also appears to increase the risk of recurrence, the study found.

✔ The men at greatest risk had gained an average of three and a half pounds a year from age 25 to 40. Weight gain remained a significant risk factor, even when controlling for clinical characteristics, family history, physical activity, smoking and other factors.

—Nicholas Bakalar

The Prostate Cancer Quandary

Diagnosis is tricky, and there's a debate about treatment

Prostate cancer is the second biggest cancer killer among men, after lung cancer. In 2005 the American Cancer Society estimated there were 30,000 deaths from the disease and 232,000 diagnoses. Fortunately, this form of cancer doesn't have to be fatal, and, especially if caught early, can be treated effectively. Nevertheless, prostate cancer is a tricky disease.

There are two tests used to detect the presence of prostate cancer. The prostate-specific antigen test measures proteins that are produced by the prostate. The P.S.A. test does have limitations: It will yield positive results in two-thirds of the men who take it, but only 30 to 40 percent of those with high P.S.A. levels will actually have prostate cancer. P.S.A. levels are also elevated in men with an enlarged prostate, a noncancerous condition known as benign prostatic hyperplasia, or B.P.H. The second test is the digital rectal exam, where the doctor probes the rectum to check the size of the prostate gland.

Both of these tests have been shown to have limited effectiveness in reducing mortality. The reason? Prostate cancer can progress slowly or very quickly and is unpredictable in its behavior. Unfortunately, it's difficult to determine accurately which cancers will advance quickly and spread, and which might not progress for as long as a decade or more. There are no symptoms in the disease's early stages, but there will be urinary difficulties and some pain as it progresses.

Most doctors agree that not all prostate cancers need to be treated, but it remains unclear which patients with localized prostate cancer will benefit from treatment, and which should be left alone. Prostate cancer is typically found in men 50 years and older, and more often than not, it grows slowly. Some doctors adopt a "surveillance" approach, examining the patient periodically to determine if the disease is spreading. Other doctors treat most cases by either removing the prostate with a procedure called radical prostatectomy, often now done robotically, or administering radiation therapy that kills the cancer cells.

To help clarify the treatment options, the American Urological Association offers guidelines for both doctors and patients that spell out factors to consider when choosing a treatment:

Consider the stage and grade of a tumor. That means estimating the size of the tumor and the extent to which it has spread to other parts of the body. A grade is assigned to a tumor based on the results of an ultrasound test and biopsy, procedures that help determine how aggressive the tumor is, or how quickly it's expected to grow. Patients with small, low-grade tumors fare better than patients with high-grade tumors, regardless of the type of treatment. Some patients with low-grade tumors diagnosed at an early stage may choose surveillance as a treatment option.

Take into account a patient's age, health and life expectancy. Because it's difficult to accurately determine the grade and stage of the cancer, doctors also rely on a patient's age, health and life expectancy at the time of diagnosis to determine whether he's a good candidate for treatment. According to the guidelines, a man's life expectancy should be at least 10 years to be considered a candidate for treatment, because that's how long it usually takes prostate cancer to spread and become fatal.

The younger a man is the more likely he will benefit from treatment, because the disease will probably progress during his lifetime if left untreated. Regardless of the size and grade of the tumor,

> **Because the best treatment for prostate cancer remains unclear, patients need to be involved in making decisions.**
>
> • • •

prostate cancer needs to be treated in someone age 50 or younger.

Understand the side effects of treatment. Some patients are reluctant to undergo prostate surgery, because it may result in impotence and pain. But removal of the entire prostate greatly reduces the likelihood, though does not guarantee, that the cancer will recur. With radiation therapy, the risk of impotence and incontinence is somewhat less, but the cancer may recur because the prostate remains in place. Because the best treatment for prostate cancer remains unclear, patients need to be involved in making decisions, particularly if their case is borderline.

Finally, the American Cancer Society and the American Urological Association recommend that all men age 50 and older who have at least a 10-year life expectancy have both an annual D.R.E. and a P.S.A. test. African American men and those with a family history of early prostate cancer should have an annual P.S.A. and D.R.E. test beginning at age 45. Men at even higher risk (because they have several first-degree relatives who had prostate cancer at an early age) should begin testing at age 40.

 INSIDE INFO

A Tomato a Day

A study by Harvard University researchers suggests that tomatoes in the diet can help ward off prostate cancer.

○ Men who ate at least 10 servings a week of tomato-based products had a 45 percent less chance of getting prostate cancer; men who ate at least 4 servings lowered their risk by 20 percent.

○ The reduced risk may be derived from the antioxidant lycopene, abundant in tomatoes.

Minding Your Mental Health
Substantial relief for depression and anxiety

Depression and anxiety are closely related mental illnesses that are among the most common psychiatric problems suffered by Americans. In recent years, there have been a number of advances in treating mental disorders with psychoactive drugs, but each medication has its drawbacks. Following is a guide to help under-stand depression and anxiety, and the medications available to treat the disorders:

DEPRESSION

Almost 15 million American adults will suffer a bout of depression this year alone, according to the National Institute of Mental Health. Women are more likely to be afflicted than men. The telltale symptoms include persistent feelings of sadness or irritability, changes in weight or appetite, impaired sleep or concentration, fatigue, restlessness, thoughts of death or suicide and loss of interest in sex.

Even though the disorder is very common, nearly two-thirds of depressed people don't get treatment because they don't seek it or their symptoms aren't recognized, according to N.I.M.H. Primary care physicians are the health care providers most likely to see depressed patients, and they should do a thorough physi-cal examination to discover underlying causes. Untreated, prolonged depression is associated with higher rates of heart attack and stroke, espe-cially in older people. Further, it's estimated that at least half of all people who commit suicide are severely depressed.

Yet depression is a very treatable illness. According to N.I.M.H., 80 to 90 percent of those with serious depression can improve significantly, restoring normal function. The most common treat-ments for depression are psychotherapy and antide-pressant medications, often used in combination.

ANXIETY

Experiencing anxiety at some point in life is normal, but for people who suffer anxiety disor-ders, it becomes overwhelming and completely disrupts a person's life. Anxiety disorders encom-pass several distinct disorders:

- Panic disorders occur when a person experiences recurrent panic attacks, which are overwhelming, immobilizing fears with no apparent cause.

- Generalized anxiety disorders are characterized by unrealistic, persistent fears or concerns that something bad is going to happen.

- Phobias occur when people dread a situation or object and go to great lengths to avoid it. Examples include fear of heights (acrophobia) and agoraphobia (fear of being trapped).

- Obsessive-compulsive disorders result in persis-tent irrational thoughts, such as fear of contami-

 INSIDE INFO

Holiday Depression

Psychiatrists have long argued that the holiday season can also be fraught with stress, expecta-tions that go unfulfilled, depression and, for some, loneliness. But studies over the years have found little evidence that depression rates actually climb around Christmas, Hanukkah and New Year's Eve.

○ One of the largest studies, published in the *Archives of General Psychiatry* in the 1980's, found that psychiatric visits tended to dip in the weeks before Christmas and then rise afterward.

○ As for suicides, most studies, including one by the Mayo Clinic that looked at a 35-year period, have found that there is virtually no relationship between the holidays and sui-cides. If anything, studies have found, suicide rates are at their lowest in December, possi-bly because those with depression have more family and friends around to help them cope.

○ One form of depression, seasonal affective dis-order, is tightly linked with winter. But the treat-able condition has more to do with the short, dark winter days than with holiday stress.

—Anahad O'Connor

The Real Nature of Depression

The author of Listening to Prozac *explains*

Depression is poor company. It destroys families. It ruins careers. It ages patients prematurely. Recent research has made the fight against depression especially compelling. Depression is associated with brain disorganization and nerve-cell atrophy. Depression appears to be progressive—the longer the episode, the greater the anatomical disorder. To work with depression is to combat a disease that harms patients' nerve pathways day by day. Nor is the damage merely to mind and brain. Depression has been linked with harm to the heart, to endocrine glands, to bones. Depressives die young—not only of suicide, but also of heart attacks and strokes. Depression is a multisystem disease, one we would consider dangerous to health even if we lacked the concept "mental illness."

This 19th-century belief that depression reveals essence to those brave enough to face it. Van Gogh ... suffered severe depression. His illness, they thought, conferred special vision. In a short story, Edgar Allan Poe likens "an utter depression of soul" to "the hideous dropping off of the veil." By this account, depression is more than a disease—it has a sacred aspect.

Asked whether we are content to eradicate arthritis, no one says, "Well, the end-stage deformation, yes, but let's hang on to tennis elbow, housemaid's knee and the early stages of rheuma-

toid disease." Multiple sclerosis, acne, schizophrenia, psoriasis, bulimia, malaria—there is no other disease we consider preserving. But eradicating depression calls out the caveats.

We idealize depression, associating it with perceptiveness, interpersonal sensitivity and other virtues. Like tuberculosis in its day, depression is a form of vulnerability that even contains a measure of erotic appeal. But the aspect of the romanticization of depression that seems to me to call for special attention is the notion that depression spawns creativity. Objective evidence for that effect is weak. The benefits of major depression, taken as a single disease, have been hard to demonstrate. Depression is not a perspective. It is a disease.

There are circumstances, like the Holocaust, in which depression might seem justified for every victim or observer. Awareness of the ubiquity of horror is the modern condition, our condition. But then, depression is not universal, even in terrible times. To see the worst things a person can see is one experience; to suffer mood disorder is another ... Beset by great evil, a person can be wise, observant and disillusioned and yet not depressed. Resilience confers its own measure of insight. We should have no trouble admiring what we do admire—depth, complexity, aesthetic brilliance—and standing foursquare against depression.

—Peter D. Kramer

Peter D. Kramer is a clinical professor of psychiatry at Brown University and the author of *Listening to Prozac*. This excerpt is adapted from his book *Against Depression*.

nation, that are relieved by repeating routine acts, like washing your hands.

- Post-traumatic stress disorder afflicts survivors of extraordinary trauma, such as war or violent crime.

Although anxiety disorders are more common than depression, people who suffer depression are more likely to seek treatment than those with anxiety disorders. According to the Anxiety Dis-

orders Association of America, only 23 percent of those who suffer an anxiety disorder will undergo treatment. Untreated, anxiety disorders can lead to depression, suicide, substance abuse and an increased risk of heart attack.

Both anti-anxiety medications and cognitive behavioral therapy, which teaches patients how to allay their fears and modify anxiety-producing behaviors, can relieve the symptoms of all types of anxiety disorders. Receiving both treatments simultaneously appears more effective than either one alone, says Dr. Jack Gorman, professor of clinical psychiatry at the Columbia University College of Physicians and Surgeons.

It is also common to be afflicted with two distinct anxiety disorders, or to experience symptoms of both depression and anxiety at the same time. Gorman estimates that 50 percent of people with anxiety disorders will ultimately develop depression: "All of the anxiety disorders are frequently complicated by depression, and when they are, it's a good idea to use medications."

Consider the Alternatives

Biofeedback, visual imagery and yoga, among others, enter the mainstream

Homeopathy? Acupuncture? Massage therapy? Alternative and complementary approaches to medicine are now being recognized as potentially beneficial and valuable by the mainstream medical profession. Complementary medicine, an alternative therapy used as a complement to

---

ⓘ INSIDE INFO

Hypnosis

○ Even with little understanding of how it works, hypnosis has been used in medicine since the 1950's to treat pain and, more recently, as a treatment for anxiety, depression, trauma, irritable bowel syndrome and eating disorders.

○ According to decades of research, 10 to 15 percent of adults are highly hypnotizable.

○ One adult in five is flat out resistant to hypnosis. The rest are in between.

○ Up to age 12, 80 to 85 percent of children are highly hypnotizable.

---

conventional medicine, is now practiced by many doctors. An example of this would be the use of aromatherapy to help mitigate a patient's pain after surgery.

The National Center for Complementary and Alternative Medicine at the National Institutes of Health defines alternative medicine as "a group of diverse medical and health care systems, practices and products that are not presently considered to be part of conventional medicine." But, as Dr. J. Edward Hill, president of the American Medical Association says, although some alternative therapies are unproven, or may ultimately be proven to be ineffective, others may become the scientifically tested therapies of tomorrow. "The key," he says, "is to know the difference. Only good research gives us that knowledge." N.C.C.A.M. is the government's research arm for the rigorous scientific study of complementary and alternative healing practices. Integrative medicine combines those scientifically proven alternative therapies with mainstream medical practices.

Dr. James Gordon, founder and director of the Washington, D.C.-based Center for Mind-Body Medicine, and Chair of the White House Commission on Complementary and Alternative Medicine Policy, discusses the use of some alternative therapies:

◎ What is alternative medicine and how does it differ from holistic or mind-body medicine?

Alternative medicine is basically everything your physician didn't learn in medical school. It uses the techniques of other healing systems, cultures and approaches as an integral part of medical care. Holistic medicine, which comes from the Greek word *holos*, meaning whole, was developed in the 1970's to describe medicine that understood the whole person in his or her total environment and appreciated that a human being was different from and greater than the sum of his or her parts. Mind-body medicine refers to the effects of the mind on the body, and the reciprocal effects of the body on the mind. It emphasizes the largely untapped power we all have to affect our health simply by using our minds through biofeedback, visual imagery, meditation and relaxation. Some physical exercises, like yoga and tai chi, can also profoundly affect mental and emotional function.

● How does alternative medicine differ from conventional medicine in its approach to treating illness?

The understanding that dominates our health care is that if somebody has a disease, we have to go in and find out what the biological basis is, and develop something to solve the biological problem. When you focus on a specific biological reaction and develop a drug for that, like antibiotics, you destroy the bacteria you want to destroy. But in the process you may wipe out all the other bacteria and affect the immune system negatively. A more holistic approach might be to ask, "What can people do for themselves to strengthen their immune system so they don't get infections?" Instead of attacking the disease process as if it were the offender, you strengthen the whole human being, so the disease process no longer has a place.

● Which alternative treatments are best-established?

The best evidence shows that we can use our minds to change in a positive direction many physiological functions that were believed to be beyond our voluntary control 30 years ago. For example, you can lower blood pressure, relieve pain and improve functioning in asthma patients. There's a good deal of evidence that relaxation therapies like biofeedback, hypnosis and guided imagery are effective for treating insomnia and pain. There are also very good studies on acupuncture and herbal therapies; many of them have been done in Asia and Europe.

Other research focuses on the use of chiropractic techniques to treat lower back pain, and on the

> **ⓘ INSIDE INFO**
>
> ## Lighten Up
>
> ○ Exposure to bright artificial light can relieve some cases of depression as effectively as psychotherapy or antidepressant medication, new research suggests.
>
> ○ Strong evidence that exposure to artificial broad-spectrum light was a good treatment not only for seasonal affective disorder, in which people become more depressed in the darker days of winter, but also for the more common nonseasonal depression, was found in a statistical review of 20 rigorously designed studies.
>
> ○ Light therapy usually involves sitting in front of white fluorescent lights with eyes open but not looking directly at the light source.
>
> ○ Treatment time varies from 15 minutes to 90 minutes a day. Symptoms can start to diminish within weeks.
>
> —Nicholas Bakalar

effectiveness of homeopathic remedies for a variety of conditions, including hay fever in children and arthritis. Studies of therapeutic touch show that when people trained as healers bring their hands close to other people, it relaxes them and improves their physiological functioning.

● How do nutrition and exercise fit in?

They are sometimes considered alternative therapies, because they're not ordinarily a part of physicians' practices, although there is an increasing understanding of how nutrition, particularly the Mediterranean diet, can help prevent cardiovascular disease. The same with exercise. Most doctors know a bit about the benefits of aerobic exercise, but most know little about yoga or tai chi, which are enormously helpful in treating many chronic conditions. For example, there are many studies done in India where people have used yoga as part

Five Alternative Approaches

Alternative and complementary approaches to medicine (CAM) are now being recognized as potentially beneficial and valuable by the mainstream medical profession. They come in five types:

1. ALTERNATIVE MEDICAL SYSTEMS are built upon complete systems of theory and practice. Some have developed in Western cultures, such as homeopathic and naturopathic medicine. Non-Western medical systems are those such as traditional Chinese medicine and Ayurveda.

2. MIND-BODY INTERVENTIONS. Mind-body medicine uses a variety of techniques designed to enhance the mind's capacity to affect bodily function and symptoms:

• patient support groups

• cognitive-behavioral therapy

• meditation, prayer, mental healing

• art, music or dance used as therapy

3. BIOLOGICALLY BASED THERAPIES include dietary supplements, herbal products and the use of other so-called natural, but as yet scientifically unproven therapies.

4. MANIPULATIVE AND BODY-BASED METHODS such as chiropractic or osteopathic manipulation, and massage.

5. ENERGY THERAPIES

• Qi gong, Reiki and Therapeutic Touch; these all claim to affect the energy fields surrounding the body.

• Bioelectromagnetic-based therapies; use of electromagnetic fields, such as pulsed fields, magnetic fields or alternating-current or direct-current fields.

SOURCE: National Center for Complementary and Alternative Medicine, National Institutes of Health

of the treatment for asthma, arthritis, hypertension, anxiety and depression—with good results.

Q What should patients look for in a physician who practices alternative medicine?

At a minimum, every physician using alternative approaches should know about relaxation therapies, self-awareness, meditation, nutrition and exercise. Beyond that, it's hard to know which system will be most effective. Sometimes you'll have a sense of which techniques are most important to you. For example, if you have a bad back or musculoskeletal problems, it's best to go to someone who knows manipulation (an M.D. or osteopathic physician) in addition to conventional medicine. If you have food allergies, clearly you want somebody who knows about nutrition. If you have chronic pain, acupuncture is a good bet. It's important to work with someone who knows at least one approach well, but won't beat you over the head with it whether it works or not.

Q How does the relationship between alternative practitioners and their patients differ from the typical doctor-patient relationship?

It involves a teaching relationship—which is not primarily the kind of relationship conventional doctors have with patients. What you want are people who are going to help you learn how to take care of yourself, not people who are going to make you dependent on them. Alternative medicine practitioners sometime use groups as a way of maximizing therapeutic work, because we've found that people can help each other make real changes not only in psychology, but in basic biological processes, simply by sharing their experiences.

A striking study was done at Stanford University, where one group of women with breast cancer received the conventional medical treatment—surgery, chemotherapy and sometimes radiation—and another group, in addition, met together with a

HEALTH

WELL-KNEADED RESPITES

The lure of the foot massage isn't difficult to understand. What else confers so much pleasure? What's more, there's evidence that a therapeutic foot massage technique known as reflexology not only relieves stress and tension, but improves circulation, alleviates minor aches and pains brought on by stress, and promotes healing.

Step 1: *Warm the foot and knead it a little to get the circulation going. Rub a little lotion or aromatic oil on your hands to make it easier to massage.*

Step 2: *Start at the top of the foot with the big toe and work down to the heel, using your thumb or knuckle to gently push each point. If you push gently and hold a reflex point, it will send a message to sedate the corresponding body part, but if you "pulse" the point by pushing in and out, it will stimulate the connecting part. Never pump or*

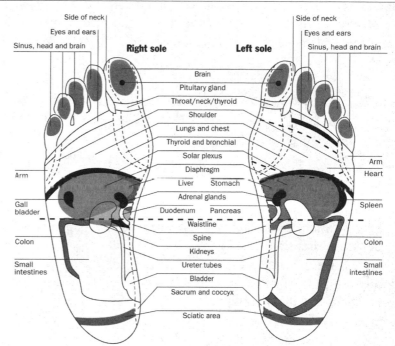

pulse the adrenal points or the intestine (see graphic), just push in and hold them.

Step 3: *Gently rub the sensitive areas and hard spots to help break up calcium deposits. If you hit a point that hurts,*

you've found a trouble spot. For example, if someone has a stomachache, when you massage the corresponding reflex point, it's going to hurt. When that happens, push gently and hold the points, but don't pump them.

---

psychiatrist once a week for an hour and a half for a year. Women in the support group lived on average 18 months longer than women not in the support group. This increased life span has not been found in several other studies, but they are consistent in showing significant improvements in quality of life.

● Does insurance cover alternative therapies?

A lot of things are considered part of general medical treatment—so if I'm a doctor and I do homeopathy or nutritional counseling, that's covered. Most plans also cover chiropractic, and in some states acupuncture. But that's not the case for

many of the services by practitioners who are not medical doctors.

● What should a patient do if his doctor is reluctant to discuss alternative therapies?

Roughly 70 percent of patients receiving alternative therapies don't discuss it with their doctor, because they fear their doctors will not only not be sympathetic, they will be angry. That has to change. Part of being a scientist is keeping an open mind and waiting until all the evidence is in. If patients find doctors irritated with them, or condescending, for being interested in alternative therapies, it's time to say, "That's unacceptable; take a look at the evidence. I need you to help me and not make uninformed judgments."

Exercising Away Back Pain
Pilates, water aerobics and elliptical machines may be the way to cure it

The question of whether to exercise during back pain has confused doctors and patients for years. Research has shown that movement can help heal backs, and within the last several years the medical consensus has shifted away from bed rest and toward exercise, even for people who are not used to daily workouts. Many back specialists now write prescriptions for Pilates, elliptical machines and water aerobics.

But in counseling patients to take the medicine, they are confronting an unexpected hurdle: fear. They are finding that the fear of exercise—and the inactivity that results—can turn what could be short-term back pain into a lifetime of trouble."People are afraid of the spine," says Dr. James N. Weinstein, an orthopedic surgeon and back researcher at Dartmouth Medical School. "There's a fear that they could really do damage to themselves."

In an age of M.R.I. scans and spinal fusion surgery, a treatment as low-tech as exercise can seem to some patients rudimentary or even dangerously illogical. But cardiovascular exercise can increase mobility and help circulation, while strengthening the core muscles closest to the spine can protect against future pain.

Which types of exercise are best for back pain? That depends a little on which doctor you ask. The consensus is that if you do not have shooting leg pain or problems with bowel function, any type of activity—like gardening or dog walking—can speed recovery. Dr. Weinstein strongly advocates

aerobic activity, urging patients to continue cycling or jogging to increase blood flow to the back. But other doctors consider running iffy, because they say it puts a lot of stress on the spine. Almost all encourage walking.

Exercises to strengthen the core—the deep muscles of the abdomen—are generally considered beneficial. "My million-dollar solution for all low back pain, acute and chronic, is core stability," says Dr. Francis O'Connor, a general practitioner specializing in sports medicine at the Uniformed Services University of the Health Sciences in Bethesda, Md. But beware: sit-ups are passé, and the jury is still out on crunches. "We're targeting muscles better now," says Anthony Delitto, a professor of physical therapy at the University of Pittsburgh—with back extensions (like the Superman, in which you lie facedown on the floor and lift the head and chest), and moves that work the oblique muscles of the abdomen.

Dr. James Rainville, the chief of physical medicine and rehabilitation at the New England Baptist Hospital in Boston, focuses on strengthening the back itself, training patients to pick up weights from the floor while keeping the legs straight, so the back bears the brunt of the movement. Dr. Lyle J. Micheli, the director of sports medicine at Children's Hospital in Boston and a doctor for the Boston Ballet, sends people to posture training, water aerobics classes and Pilates.

—Melena Z. Ryzik

Snoring, From A to Zzzzz
A little night music that you'd rather not hear

Snoring is rampant, with some statistics showing that as much as 20 percent of the population snores. And there is no question that men snore a lot more than women; some experts say they are

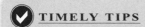

TIMELY TIPS

Think Before You Sleep

Cognitive behavior therapy can help insomnia

A form of talk therapy has been shown to be more effective than sleeping pills at reducing insomnia, and its effects are longer lasting, a 2004 study has found.

Published in the *Archives of Internal Medicine,* the study compared zolpidem tartrate, sold as Ambien, the most widely used sleeping pill, with cognitive behavior therapy. In cognitive behavior therapy, a patient is taught to recognize and change patterns of thought and behavior that contribute to problems.

The patients in the therapy group received five 30-minute sessions over six weeks. The patients were given daily exercises to "recognize, challenge and change stress-inducing" thoughts, and they were taught techniques like delaying bedtime or getting up to read if they were unable to fall asleep within 20 minutes.

The patients who were given Ambien took a full dose for a month and then were weaned off the drug over the course of another month. Long-term use of sleeping pills is not recommended, because dependence can result, the study said.

✔ Two weeks after all treatment had ended, the gap had widened. The patients receiving the therapy fell asleep in half the time it had taken before the study, while the decrease for patients taking sleeping pills was only 17 percent.

—John O'Neil

eight times more likely to than women.

In large part that has to do with men's thicker neck muscles, since snoring results when air passes over relaxed tissue in the throat, causing a full-throttle vibration. Indulging in too many cocktails makes snoring worse for the simple reason that it overrelaxes the body. Growing older, and less toned, exacerbates the problem. Sometimes genes are to blame; some people are just born with a flabby or narrow airway.

Weight gain, too, worsens snoring, because the neck grows thicker. As America has gotten fatter, it also appears to have gotten louder, at least during sleep hours.

Beyond the sleeplessness it inevitably brings for those who must bed down with snorers, snoring can cause serious health problems. More than 12 million Americans suffer from sleep apnea—in which the soft tissue at the back of the throat repeatedly collapses during sleep and blocks off air—and a large number of these people find themselves sleepy at work or behind the wheel, irritable and unable to concentrate. In the most serious cases, apnea can lead to high blood pressure, and less commonly to stroke or heart attack as the body struggles for oxygen.

In response to a need for treatment of snoring and sleep apnea, sleep centers are sprouting in just about every city and major hospital. According to the American Academy of Sleep Medicine, the number of accredited centers in 2005 was 883, up from 297 a decade earlier.

Patients at sleep centers are asked to stay overnight, so their snoring can be monitored and the cause pinpointed. One company, SleepQuest, now sells a sleep-monitoring kit that people can use at home. Depending on the diagnosis, doctors (typically ear, nose and throat specialists) recommend weight loss or some form of mechanical treatment. Patients may be given air pressure machines, which continuously pump air through a mask while the patient sleeps. Or the patient's adenoids, tonsils or uvula (that bell at the back of the throat) can be removed to minimize vibration.

—Lizette Alvarez

Having Children

Before You're Pregnant

The right time to take care of your baby is before you conceive

Once a woman learns she's pregnant, she's likely to revamp her lifestyle by eating balanced meals, and avoiding cigarettes and alcohol. What many women may not realize is that fetal development begins soon after conception, and well before a woman is aware that she is pregnant. Since more than half of all pregnancies are unplanned, many women miss a critical period of time during which they could maximize their chances of delivering a healthy baby.

ⓘ INSIDE INFO

The Best Day to Try Your Luck

A study conducted by researchers at the National Institute of Environmental Health Sciences, and published in the *New England Journal of Medicine*, concluded that:

○ A woman's chances of becoming pregnant are greatest if she has sexual intercourse on the day of ovulation (when the egg is released from the ovary), or in the five days before she ovulates.

○ The finding challenges the conventional wisdom that a woman is fertile from about three days prior to ovulation to about three days afterward.

○ Most surprising was the finding that a woman's chances of conceiving after ovulation are virtually nil.

"We have to change the outdated paradigm that the time to take care of yourself is when you look pregnant," says Merry-K. Moos, a research professor in the Department of Obstetrics and Gynecology at the University of North Carolina at Chapel Hill. Any woman with the potential of becoming pregnant should consider preconceptional counseling, says Dr. Moos. In reality, most women consult a doctor about six to eight weeks after conceiving.

A preconceptional visit involves a series of tests, including screening for existing medical conditions and for any family history of genetic defects. The visit can prevent a lot of potential problems for mother and child. Studies suggest that adopting a healthy lifestyle before conceiving can increase the chances of having a healthy baby. While nothing can guarantee a perfect birth every time, the following advice can raise the odds.

Take folic acid and eat a well-balanced diet. Studies show that a daily dose of folic acid in the very early stages of pregnancy reduces by 50 to 70 percent the likelihood of having a baby with a neural tube defect, such as spina bifida and anencephaly (the absence of a brain). The F.D.A. recommends that all women of childbearing age consume at least 400 micrograms of folic acid each day in addition to the recommended daily amount they should take in from food sources. Folic acid is found in some foods, such as dark leafy greens, like spinach, and whole wheat or enriched bread. The surest way for a woman to get enough folic acid is to take a daily vitamin.

Avoid all undercooked or raw fish, shellfish, egg dishes, red meats and poultry, and all sausages.

Raw, unpasteurized milk, yogurt and cheeses should not be consumed, nor any unpasteurized juices. Carefully wash all vegetables. Raw vegetable sprouts should be avoided.

Put on just enough weight. Many women gain 40 to 50 pounds while pregnant, putting them at an increased risk for complications, including diabetes, high blood pressure, and an increased likelihood of birth by cesarean section. On the other hand, being underweight can lead to low-birth-weight babies. The ideal weight gain for a woman of normal weight, according to the Institute of Medicine, is 25 to 35 pounds. Women should not try to lose weight during pregnancy, but those who are overweight beforehand should try to get within a normal weight range before becoming pregnant.

Exercise. There's ample evidence that moderate to vigorous exercise can be good for both the mother and her fetus. Exercise can boost energy and ease discomforts associated with pregnancy, such as backache, constipation and varicose veins. A 1998 study published in the *American Journal of Public Health* claims that women who exercise throughout their pregnancy have more full-term pregnancies than those who do not. Of course, some sports, like downhill skiing, rock climbing and horseback riding, which can harm the fetus, are off limits. Research also suggests that exercise may prevent gestational diabetes, especially in women with a body mass index greater than 33.

Consult your doctor. Before you become pregnant, you should ask about any prescription drugs you are taking. If possible, you should avoid all drugs during pregnancy, including over-the-counter drugs and herbal medicines and teas. Make sure your immunizations are up to date well before you become pregnant. Ask your doctor before you take any vitamins. Vitamin A, for instance, if taken in

 INSIDE INFO

Fertile Facts

- Each woman is born with millions of immature eggs.
- Normally only one egg is released at each ovulation.
- A menstrual period can occur even if ovulation has not occurred.
- Ovulation can occur even if a menstrual period has not occurred.
- Ovulation can be affected by stress, illness or disruption of normal routines.
- Some women may experience some light blood spotting during ovulation.
- Some women can feel a bit of pain or aching near the ovaries during ovulation called mittelschmerz, which means "middle pain" in German.
- An egg lives 12 to 24 hours after leaving the ovary.
- Implantation of a fertilized egg normally takes place 6 to 12 days after ovulation.
- If an egg is not fertilized, it disintegrates and is absorbed into the uterine lining.

SOURCE: American Pregnancy Association

large doses, can cause birth defects.

Don't smoke or drink. After drug abuse, smoking cigarettes has the most harmful effect on a developing fetus. Studies show that smoking doubles a woman's risk of having an ectopic pregnancy (a pregnancy outside the uterus). It also increases the chances of miscarriage and of delivering a low-birth-weight baby, as well as a baby with a higher risk of having an attention deficit hyperactivity disorder.

Excessive alcohol consumption during pregnancy is a leading cause of preventable mental retardation, learning disabilities and fetal alcohol

HEALTH

syndrome. As it is unclear how much alcohol causes harm, the only way to be entirely safe is to refrain from drinking alcohol while pregnant.

Avoid exposure to all toxic substances. These include such things as paints and other solvents, pesticides, mercury and lead.

Avoid dyeing your hair. This should be avoided, particularly during the first trimester of pregnancy.

Leave cat litter care to others. There is a danger of exposure to parasites from animal feces, which causes toxoplasmosis. Rodents and their droppings carry lymphocytic choriomeningitis virus, which can cause severe abnormalities or loss of the pregnancy.

Limit your intake of caffeine.

Do not take hot baths or use saunas or hot tubs. Hyperthermia can put severe stress on the fetus.

✔ **TIMELY TIPS**

Having a Safe Pregnancy

✔ The March of Dimes has an excellent online Web site with advice on pregnancy, and an interactive component where you can submit questions: www.marchofdimes.com/pnhec.

✔ Other Web sites that cover the subject of substances harmful to the fetus: www.merck. com; Motherisk Program (www.motherisk. org); Center for the Evaluation of Risks to Human Reproduction (cerhr.niehs.nih.gov/); National Center on Birth Defects and Developmental Disabilities (www.cdc.gov/ncbddd/); National Women's Health Information Center (www.4woman.gov/); Organization of Teratology Information Services (www.otispregnancy.org).

Medical Checks in the Womb

Today's tests for genetic defects make far more information available

About 150,000 babies are born with birth defects each year in the United States, according to the March of Dimes. The American College of Obstetricians and Gynecologists says that out of every 100 babies born, three have some kind of major birth defect. The shortlist of the most common birth defects includes:

- **Congenital heart defects** (approximately 1 out of every 125 births)

- **Down syndrome** (approximately 1 in 1,250 children born to women in their 20's; 1 in 400 by age 35; and 1 in 100 at age 40)

- **Cleft lip and palate** (approximately 1 in every 1,000 births)

- **Neural tube defects such as spina bifida (a damaged spinal cord) and anencephaly (the absence of a part of the brain)**(1 of every 2000 live births)

These days, however, there is an increasing number of genetic tests that offer women a chance to learn before, or very early in pregnancy, the likelihood of whether their baby will have a serious birth defect caused by genetic abnormalities. These tests are being administered more frequently, as childbearing couples are now better screened prenatally and, when necessary, counseled to seek more information through diagnostic testing.

At the same time, scientific breakthroughs are providing an increasing number of ways to ensure the development of a healthy fetus. Here is a description of some of the tests that have been used to date and are commonly available:

HEALTH

"It's a Boy!" ... Finally

○ A study of 5,283 Dutch women, which appeared in the *British Medical Journal,* revealed that 57.6 percent of those who took longer than 12 months to become pregnant had boys, compared with 51.1 percent boys among those who became pregnant in less than a year.

○ Maternal age, body mass index and smoking or alcohol use made no difference in the findings.

○ The authors calculated that for each additional year of trying to get pregnant, a couple had a 4 percent increased probability of having a boy.

—Nicholas Bakalar

CARRIER SCREENING TESTS

When the family of a couple has been identified as having inherited disorders, a carrier screen is done to search for the presence of the defective gene, since such disorders may recur in their baby. The test involves taking a sample of saliva or blood to screen for diseases such as cystic fibrosis, Tay-Sachs, sickle cell anemia, and a number of other diseases. This test is done ideally before a woman becomes pregnant, but may be done before, during and after pregnancy.

SCREENING ONCE YOU'RE PREGNANT

It's important to understand the difference between screening tests like AFP, a blood test that measures a chemical called alpha-fetoprotein and helps detect spina bifida and anencephaly, and ultrasound and diagnostic tests, like amniocentesis or chorionic villus sampling (CVS). A screening test doesn't give you a yes or no answer; it just tells you if your risk is average or above or below average. A normal result on a screening test doesn't guarantee you a healthy pregnancy, but your chances of developing certain problems are lower than most. Conversely, if you have an abnormal result from a screening test, you may still have a healthy pregnancy, but you should have a diagnostic test.

THE AFP AND ASSOCIATED BLOOD TESTS

The AFP Plus, or triple test, was developed in the 1980's, when researchers established that certain blood tests in the second trimester could predict the risk of Down syndrome in the fetus and thus enable many women to avoid having amniocentesis. These tests measure a chemical called alpha-fetoprotein (AFP), which is produced by the fetus; a hormone called unconjugated estriol, produced by both the fetus and the placenta; and HCG, human chorionic gonadotropin, a hormone produced within the placenta, in a woman's blood. Later, a fourth blood test for inhibin A improved the ability to predict the presence of the syndrome. Taken together, the results of these tests provide a risk estimate that could be higher or lower, often much lower, than that based solely on a woman's age.

The test, which is normally offered to all

 TIMELY TIPS

How to Figure Your Due Date

This simple mathematical equation was devised by a 19th-century German obstetrician named Franz Karl Naegele, based on the idea that a woman's pregnancy normally lasts 280 days.

✔ Subtract three months from the first day of your last menstrual period, and add seven days to that date, or 280 days from your last menstrual period. If you know your date of conception, you can add 38 weeks or 266 days, and come up with the same date.

SOME DRUGS THAT CAN CAUSE PROBLEMS DURING PREGNANCY

Unless absolutely necessary, drugs should not be used during pregnancy. However, drugs are sometimes essential for the health of the pregnant woman and the fetus. In such cases, a woman should talk with her health care practitioner about the risks and benefits of taking the drugs.

TYPE	EXAMPLES	PROBLEM
Antianxiety drug	**Diazepam**	• When the drug is taken late in pregnancy, depression, irritability, shaking and exaggerated reflexes in the newborn
Antibiotics	**Chloramphenicol**	• Gray baby syndrome • In women or fetuses with glucose-6-phosphate dehydrogenase (G6PD) deficiency, the breakdown of red blood cells
	Ciprofloxacin	• Possibility of joint abnormalities (seen only in animals)
	Kanamycin	• Damage to the fetus's ear, resulting in deafness
	Nitrofurantoin	• In women or fetuses with G6PD deficiency, the breakdown of red blood cells
	Streptomycin	• Damage to the fetus's ear, resulting in deafness
	Sulfonamides	• Jaundice, possibly brain damage in the newborn (much less likely with sulfasalazine) • In women or fetuses with G6PD deficiency, the breakdown of red blood cells
	Tetracycline	• Slowed bone growth, permanent yellowing of teeth and increased susceptibility to dental cavities in the baby • Occasionally, liver failure in the pregnant woman
Anticoagulants	**Heparin**	• When the drug is taken for a long time, osteoporosis and a decrease in the number of platelets (which help blood clot) in the pregnant woman
	Warfarin	• Birth defects; bleeding problems in the fetus and the pregnant woman
Anticonvulsants	**Carbamazepine Phenobarbital Phenytoin**	• Some risk of birth defects • Bleeding problems in the newborn, which can be prevented if pregnant women take vitamin K by mouth every day for a month before delivery, or if the newborn is given an injection of vitamin K soon after birth
	Trimethadione Valproate	• Increased risk of miscarriage in the woman • Increased risk of birth defects in the fetus, including a cleft palate and abnormalities of the heart, face, skull, hands or abdominal organs (the risk is 70 percent with trimethadione and 1 percent with valproate)
Antihypertensives	**Angiotensin-converting enzyme** (ACE) inhibitors	• When the drugs are taken late in pregnancy, kidney damage in the fetus, a reduction in the amount of fluid around the developing fetus (amniotic fluid) and deformities of the face, limbs and lungs
	Thiazide diuretics	• A decrease in the levels of oxygen and potassium and the number of platelets in the fetus's blood

pregnant women, is most accurate at detecting spina bifida and anencephaly, which are suspected when there's an elevated AFP level, but it can also help detect Down syndrome. The AFP Plus test detects 80 to 85 percent of cases of spina bifida and about 65 percent of Down syndrome, which still means that almost one in three cases would not show up.

ULTRASOUND

An ultrasound test is usually offered only when there's another risk factor for a genetic disorder or birth defect, like the mother's age, family history or an abnormal AFP test. Ultrasound uses sound waves that emit from a transducer (a reverse microphone) and bounce off structures. It allows doctors to look at the physical develop-

HEALTH

TYPE	EXAMPLES	PROBLEM
Chemotherapy drugs	**Busulfan Chlorambucil Cyclophosphamide Mercaptopurine Methotrexate**	• Birth defects such as less than expected growth before birth, underdevelopment of the lower jaw, cleft palate, abnormal development of the skull bones, spinal defects, ear defects and clubfoot
Mood-stabilizing drug	**Lithium**	• Birth defects (mainly of the heart), lethargy, reduced muscle tone, poor feeding, under activity of the thyroid gland and nephrogenic diabetes insipidus in the newborn
Nonsteroidal anti-inflammatory drugs (NSAIDs)	**Aspirin Other salicylates**	• When the drugs are taken in large doses, a delay in the start of labor, premature closing of the connection between the aorta and artery to the lungs (ductus arterio sus), jaundice, and (occasionally) brain damage in the fetus and bleeding problems in the woman during and after delivery and in the newborn • When the drugs are taken late in pregnancy, a reduction in the amount of fluid around the developing fetus
Oral hypo-glycemic drugs	**Chlorpropamide Tolbutamide**	• A very low level of sugar in the blood of the newborn • Inadequate control of diabetes in the pregnant woman
Sex hormones	**Danazol Synthetic progestins** (but not the low doses used in oral contraceptives)	• Masculinization of a female fetus's genitals, sometimes requiring surgery to correct
	Diethylstilbestrol (DES)	• Abnormalities of the uterus, menstrual problems, and an increased risk of vaginal cancer and complications during pregnancy in daughters • Abnormalities of the penis in sons
Skin treatments	**Etretinate Isotretinoin**	• Birth defects, such as heart defects, small ears and hydrocephalus (sometimes called water on the brain)
Thyroid drugs	**Methimazole Propylthiouracil Radioactive iodine**	• An overactive and enlarged thyroid gland in the fetus • An underactive thyroid gland in the fetus
Vaccines	**Live-virus vaccines** (measles, mumps, rubella (German measles) polio, chickenpox and yellow fever)	• With rubella vaccine, potential infection of the placenta and developing fetus; • With other vaccines, potential but unknown risks

SOURCE: From the *Merck Manual of Medical Information*—Second Home Edition, pp. 1460-1461, edited by Mark H. Beer. Copyright 2003 by Merck & Co, Inc., Whitehouse Station, N.J.

ment of the baby and get a general picture of the legs, arms and body. The denser the structure, such as bone, the brighter the image. For example, a birth defect like anencephaly is very accurately picked up on ultrasound, because you can see the part of the skull that's not formed. When ultrasound is done after 18 weeks, it will detect most serious heart defects and more than 50 percent of neural tube defects, and it's even more likely to detect major physical problems.

DIAGNOSTIC TESTS

These tests are usually offered only to women age 35 or older at the time their baby is due, unless there's another indication, such as if a woman has already had a baby with a chromosomal abnormality or there's another hereditary risk, or a screening test indicates a problem. Diagnostic tests almost always give you a yes or no answer. Both amniocentesis and CVS have greater than 99 percent accuracy in detecting chromosomal abnormalities. Amniocentesis may also be offered to women at least 14 weeks pregnant because of an AFP or ultrasound finding, but the window of opportunity has closed by that time to perform CVS, which is done between 10 and 13 weeks of pregnancy.

What factors should a couple consider in deciding whether to have a diagnostic test? Couples should consider whether the information the test provides has a real benefit, such as peace of mind or being able to make a decision about the pregnancy. Some decide to have the test because they feel that any risk of an abnormality would justify finding out. Others decide to have the test not based on the statistics, but on fear of the unknown.

AMNIOCENTESIS

Amniocentesis is a procedure done from 14 to 18 weeks of gestation, in which a small sample of amniotic fluid surrounding the fetus is removed by a thin needle inserted through the woman's abdomen. Fetal cells in the fluid are then analyzed for a possible chromosomal abnormality, a process that takes up to two weeks. Amniocentesis can also detect neural tube defects. The risk of miscarriage associated with amniocentesis is one in 200 to 400. Developed in the 1970's, this test was all that was available for prenatal screening. If an abnormality is found, the woman can choose to have a second-trimester abortion, which is physically and emotionally more traumatic than one performed earlier in pregnancy.

CHORIONIC VILLUS SAMPLING (CVS)

CVS involves removing a small amount of cells called the chorionic villi that form the placenta by inserting either a catheter into the cervix or a needle into the mother's abdomen. Then genetic tests are performed on the cells. CVS is performed most often in order to identify chromosomal abnormalities. It is usually performed if a woman desires results early in her pregnancy, if a woman has had a previous pregnancy with chromosomal abnormalities or if the couple is at risk of having a child with a genetic disease. The risk of miscarriage associated with CVS is one in 100 to 200.

SOURCE: National Institutes of Health; March of Dimes

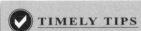 **TIMELY TIPS**

Avoiding Another Miscarriage

A new procedure may increase your odds of having a healthy child

A procedure called preimplantation genetic diagnosis, referred to as PGD, can screen out the abnormal embryos that cause miscarriages. It is an increasingly popular way to ensure a healthy pregnancy for women who have had multiple miscarriages, those having in-vitro fertilization treatment and couples who are carriers of a genetic disorder.

Only healthy, disease-free embryos are implanted into the uterus, increasing the odds of having a successful pregnancy and a healthy child. However, the test is no guarantee that a miscarriage can be avoided, because many factors can interrupt the normal course of a pregnancy.

PGD has also been used by parents who want to have a child who is a tissue match for a sibling with a devastating disease. These so-called save-your-siblings can provide umbilical cord cells to the other child, in some cases saving the sibling's life.   —Laurie Tarkan

Fertilization: Learning the Lingo

As the options for conceiving a child have increased, so have the terms and the acronyms:

Cryopreservation: A technique to preserve embryos or sperm through freezing.

Embryo. The fertilized egg. (Pre-embryo is a term used for the fertilized egg until 15 days after fertilization.)

Embryo Transfer (ET): Placing an embryo into the uterus.

Gamete: A reproductive cell, either a sperm or an egg.

Gamete Intrafallopian Transfer (GIFT): Planting an egg and sperm in the fallopian tubes during a laparoscopy. Fertilization is not documented.

Host Uterus: Also called surrogate IVF or gestational carrier. In these cases a woman takes ovulatory stimulating drugs. The eggs are removed from her ovaries and fertilized with her husband's sperm. The embryo(s) is then transferred into another woman, the gestational carrier (host uterus).

Intra cytoplasmic sperm injections (ICSI). A technique in which a single sperm is injected into a single egg.

In Vitro Fertilization (IVF): Usually done in conjunction with ovarian stimulation. One or more eggs and sperm are put into a petri dish. Fertilization takes place in the laboratory and therefore can be documented.

Laparoscopy: A surgical procedure in which a small incision is made near the navel, so that a tiny fiber-optic instrument can peer into the pelvis.

Micromanipulation: A variety of procedures done in the lab during IVF. Sperm are allowed access into the inner aspect of the mature egg, thereby increasing chances for fertilization. Examples: partial zona drilling, subzonal insemination, intracytoplasmic sperm injection.

Ovum (plural, Ova): The egg.

Ovarian stimulation: A series of drugs used to stimulate the ovary to develop follicles and release eggs.

Progesterone: The hormone secreted by the corpus leteum on the ovary in the second half of the menstrual cycle. It is responsible for the thickening of the uterine lining in preparation for embryo implantation.

Transvaginal Ultrasound: An ultrasound technique using a small vaginal probe. It allows for improved visualization of the ovaries and is usually used to monitor follicular development and for egg release.

Zygote: The cell formed by the union of the male and female cells. Also called fertilized egg.

Zygote Intrafallopian Transfer (ZIFT): Fertilized eggs are transferred into the woman's fallopian tube during a laparoscopy.

New Ways to Start a Family

Options for couples having trouble conceiving are greatly expanded

What causes infertility? Late marriages and biological clocks are frequent factors. Environmental toxins, scarring from infections or previous surgery, and declining sperm counts may also play a role. The age of the mother is one of the biggest factors that influences the ability to conceive, because as women age, they are less likely to ovulate.

The procedures used to correct these problems vary. Sometimes couples just need to adjust their schedules, undergo minor surgery to correct problems in their reproductive organs or take prescription medications to conceive. Certain women who don't release enough eggs can

✔ TIMELY TIPS

For the Over-35 Set

For women over 35, noninvasive screening is fast becoming standard care in gynecological practices. And these days, it's more reliable and less invasive.

✔ It now appears that such screening can be completed with great accuracy in the first trimester, according to a study published in the November 2005 issue of the *New England Journal of Medicine.* The report found that a combination of three noninvasive tests conducted at 11 to 13 weeks of gestation was 87 percent accurate in predicting the presence of Down syndrome.

✔ The screening tests used were an ultrasound evaluation of the thickness of the fetal neck, called nuchal translucency, and two blood tests, pregnancy-associated plasma protein A, or PAPP-A, and beta human chorionic gonadotropin, or HCG Adding a second ultrasound of the fetal nasal bone may push the accuracy of these tests even higher.

—Jane E. Brody

be treated with a fertility drug such as Clomid or Serophene).

But others must subject themselves to demanding and costly tests and treatments like hormone injections, egg retrieval and embryo transfers.

So-called assisted reproductive technologies (ART) almost doubled from 1996 through 2003. Technologies such as gamete intrafallopian transfer (GIFT) and zygote intrafallopian transfer (ZIFT) have also become more widespread, and their live birth rates are steadily improving. With GIFT, the sperm and egg are inserted into the fallopian tubes, where fertilization occurs naturally. For in vitro fertilization (IVF) and ZIFT, fertilization of the eggs by the sperm takes place in the laboratory and the fertilized egg is placed directly into the woman's uterus for IVF, or her fallopian tubes for ZIFT.

Another area that has seen significant progress is in treating male infertility, which accounts for as much as 40 percent of all cases. For example, intracytoplasmic sperm injection (ICSI), which involves injecting a single sperm into an egg, then returning the egg to the uterus, is a technique designed to overcome infertility caused by weak or abnormal sperm. The aggressive procedure has made it possible for men with extremely low sperm counts or defective sperm to become fathers. However, the technique may lead to what is known as inherited infertility, a condition in which newborns develop the same genetic problem that caused their fathers' infertility.

But these high-tech treatments have their limits. There's little evidence that repeating the same procedure more than four to six times increases the likelihood of pregnancy.

When Morning Sickness Comes

It isn't only early in the day. Here are some remedies

Most women experience morning sickness early in their pregnancies. But it does not necessarily strike only in the morning, nor does it always end after the first trimester.

Nausea and vomiting affect 70 to 85 percent of pregnant women, various studies show. Half experience both, and a quarter have nausea only. Some people can be sick through the full nine months. The problem can be so severe that women have to be hospitalized to prevent dehydration and other complications. In fact, severe nausea accompanied by vomiting is the second most common reason, after premature labor, for hospitalization in pregnancy.

Some women suffer such serious psychological and social disturbances as a result of persistent vomiting that they choose to terminate their pregnancies, according to a report from the American College of Obstetricians and Gynecologists. Severe nausea and vomiting, called hyperemesis gravidarum, occurs in up to 2 percent of pregnancies, the association reported in issuing new guidelines for diagnosing and treating the problem.

What can you do to alleviate morning sickness? There are many safe ways to relieve and possibly eliminate the problem. Some suggestions:

Eat frequent small meals, avoiding spicy or fatty foods, eliminating pills with iron, eating bland or dry foods or high-protein snacks, and eating dry crackers in the morning before rising.

Eat ginger, in capsule form (it can also curb motion sickness).

Electrical stimulation of an acupressure point on the inside of the wrists, and round-the-clock use of vitamin B6, particularly when taken with the over-the-counter drug doxylamine, an antihistamine often used as a sleep aid.

Other medications listed as safe and effective are two kinds of prescription antiemetics, phenothiazines and benzamides.

–Jane E. Brody

Quick Delivery? Try Exercise

Pelvic exercices can help women get better control

Finally, there may be a way for pregnant women to try to shorten their labor and delivery: by building up their pelvic-floor muscles in advance.

Women in Norway who took 12 weekly one-hour classes in exercising those muscles between the 20th week of pregnancy and the 36th were less likely than others to spend more than an hour in the pushing stage of labor.

The women who received the training were also encouraged to practice 8 to 12 intensive contractions of the pelvic floor twice a day at home.

The results of the study contradict the assumption that strong pelvic floor muscles—like those developed in women who ride horses or practice gymnastics, for example—make it more dif-

HEALTH

GROWTH OF THE FETUS FROM 8 TO 40 WEEKS

Fetal development has already begun 17 days after conception. While the average pregnancy lasts 280 days from the last menstrual period, it is normal to give birth anywhere from 37 to 42 weeks after the last period.

Week	8	12	16	20	24	28	32	36	40
Length	1 in.	3 in.	6.5 in.	10 in.	13 in.	14.5 in.	16 in.	18 in.	20 in.
Weight	0.07 oz.	0.6 oz.	5 oz.	12 oz.	1.3 lb.	2 lb.	3.5 lb.	5.5 lb.	7.5 lb.

SOURCES: *The American Medical Association Encyclopedia of Medicine* © 1989 by Dorling Kindersley; American Medical Association

ficult to deliver a baby. "This is a myth, because actually quite the opposite thing happens," says Dr. Kjell A. Salvesen, a co-author of the study and a professor of obstetrics and gynecology at Trondheim University Hospital in Saint Olav. "With strong pelvic floor muscles, women maybe get better control in delivery," he says.

The training also seemed to make a difference in the number of women who needed an episiotomy, an incision to enlarge the birth canal. Fifty-six women in the exercise group had them, and 72 in the comparison group.

The study was originally intended to find out whether pelvic floor strengthening could prevent urinary incontinence during and after pregnancy. The researchers found that it did in some women.

–Mary Duenwald

Baby Makes More Than Three
How many should be in the delivery room?

Just a generation after fathers had to beg or even sue for the right to be present, the door to the delivery room has swung wide open. Even the most traditional hospitals now allow multiple guests during labor, transforming birth from a private affair into one that requires a guest list. Like bridesmaids and pallbearers, the invitees are marked as an honored group of intimates.

Though most hospitals allow only a few guests at a time, some have abandoned limits altogether. The newly inclusive approach—despite some awkward and unintended consequences—is a triumph both for hospitals, which have made birth remarkably safe for mother and child, and for the natural childbirth movement, which has long campaigned for more humanized care.

So, what's the magic number? A circle of family and friends in the delivery room, say all concerned, can make a birth even more wondrous than it already is. Hospital personnel say that most guests are beautifully behaved: helpful to husbands during their long bedside vigils, deferential to medical authority and prepared for the indignities of childbirth.

But the most frequent tension arises between various mothers in the room: the mothers-to-be, their own mothers and mothers-in-law. So, it may come as little surprise that an entire discussion thread on BabyCenter.com, a popular parenting Web site, is titled "Don't Want MIL" (meaning mother-in-law) "in the Delivery Room."

—Jodi Kantor

Adopting a Baby or Child
To avoid pitfalls, examine your motivation before you begin

Though the joys of welcoming an adoptive child into your home can be worth any amount of effort, there are considerable challenges involved in meshing the child's needs with those of your existing household. There is also the small but significant risk that your child's birth parents might change their minds during the window of time before the adoption becomes final, and decide to keep their child or baby.

Most adoptive parents, however don't experience that kind of trauma. And though they routinely have to contend with what can seem like long waits and lots of paperwork, particularly in the case of international adoptions, in some ways, that is a useful test of their commitment to completing an adoption. Deb Harder, adoption information supervisor at Children's Home Society & Family Services, has the following advice on how to have a successful adoption.

Examine what's motivating you to adopt. The first step for anyone considering adoption is to make sure you're firmly committed to rearing and nurturing a child. Look very carefully at your skills and strengths as a person, and how they translate to being an effective parent. If you're dealing with infertility, it's important to acknowledge that you're unlikely to bear children. You should see adoption not as a second-best option, but as an alternative way to become a parent and create a family.

Decide what kind of child you can effectively parent. Many families only consider adopting a healthy, same-race infant, and don't think of a child born in another country or a child who has special needs. Some folks are prepared to parent a child with special needs, but not all—assess your strengths and decide what you can manage. In the same way, you must consider whether you can understand the needs of children from other cultural backgrounds. You have to consider if you are willing to honor your child's heritage and how you will incorporate that heritage into your family's day-to-day life.

Learn state laws. Among the first things a family should do is contact their state department of social services and talk to an adoption supervisor to find out what they are legally required to do to complete an adoption in their state.

Choose the type of adoption you're interested in. One of the first decisions is whether you'd like to adopt an older child, in which case you can adopt through a public agency, which primarily works with kids in foster care and group home settings. If you want to adopt an infant or a child from another country, you will work with a private agency. You can also opt for an independent, or private adoption, in which adoptive parents work with a lawyer or other non-agency adoption provider to find a birth parent or child. There are certain risks with private adoptions and more of a safety net with an agency.

Assess the costs. The cost of adopting a child ranges from $5,000 to more than $30,000, depending on the type of adoption. International adoptions tend to be more expensive, because there are additional costs for additional documents and travel. Private adoption has the reputation of being more expensive, because the costs usually aren't set up-front, while some agencies may charge on a sliding scale basis. Different agencies have different fee structures, services and missions. Try to get details about the services they provide, and insist that they assign a service to each fee.

Expect to feel like you're being scrutinized during the adoption process. Most agencies now do open adoptions, meaning that the birth parent(s) choose(s) which prospective adopter(s) they want to adopt their child and the two families make an adoption plan together. The agency staff can and does compile a book of dossiers with biographical information about prospective families for birth

Resources for Adoptive Parents

National Adoption Information Clearinghouse: *For all types of adoption.* Provides summaries of adoption laws, state by state, has excellent fact sheets; contact listings for agencies and public social service agencies, family support groups and more. naic.acf.hhs.gov

Comeunity: *Adoption parenting support for all types of adoption.* Provides information, resources and links to additional resources for families that are just beginning the adoption process to those who are actively parenting. www.comeunity.com

Adoption.com: *For all types of adoption.* Lots and lots of information about all types of adoption and lots of links to additional resources for families. www.adoption.com

Adoptive Families Magazine: *For all types of adoption.* Magazine for all adoptive families and prospective adopters. Excellent Web site with articles and searchable databases. www.adoptivefamilies.com

The National Adoption Center: *For domestic adoption.* 800-TO-ADOPT or www.adopt.org

North American Council on Adoption Children: *Domestic adoption.* An advocacy/education organization focusing primarily on older children and their families who wait for adoption while in U.S. and Canadian foster care; provides excellent resources for families with children who have special needs. www.nacac.org

Karen's Adoption Links: *For international adoption.* A Web site that links families to adoption resources: parent support groups, listservs, books/cultural products and much more. www.karensadoptionlinks.com

U.S. Citizenship and Immigration Services (www.uscis.gov) and the **U.S. Department of State** (www.travel.state.gov/family/adoption.html): *International adoption.* Both sites offer families information and guidance about the processes that they must go through in order to adopt a child from another country.

American Academy of Adoption Attorneys: *For primarily domestic adoption.* An advocacy organization for legal professionals working in adoption; these attorneys (by A.A.A.A. membership requirements) dedicate a certain percentage of their practice to adoption and custody work for families and children. They publish a national directory of adoption attorneys. www.adoptionattorneys.org

Joint Council for International Children's Services: *For international adoption.* An advocacy/education organization made up of international adoption agencies. www.JCICS.org

mothers to review. Some prospective adopters choose international adoption because they feel uncomfortable with openness and/or the feeling of "marketing" themselves. Be honest during the adoption study, also known as a home study. All prospective adoptive parents must undergo an adoption study, a process that helps agency personnel to assess your readiness for adoptive parenting. It's not unlike applying for a mortgage—lots of personal questions to answer that require verification. For example, they assess what's motivating you to adopt, how you were parented and how you plan to discipline the child. They'll also ask for references and look at your finances and psychological stability. If you have a criminal history or a history of psychiatric illnesses, you need to fully disclose these details—don't lie about the situation—or it will cause greater problems than if you're up-front and explain what's what.

Think about the type of child you want to adopt and which program helps you meet that goal. If you want to adopt a domestic newborn, then you need to consider your comfort with an open adoption, because you will likely be working directly with a birth family in making an adoption plan and a plan for ongoing communication after the baby's placement with you. Think not only about your feelings now, but also about how your relationship with your child's birth family might evolve.

Find out how quickly adopted children join their adoptive families. With open adoption and the birth families choosing, agencies have a difficult time estimating how long you will wait. The agency should be able to give you a time line as to what to expect at their agency—how long the adoption study process will take and what are their average wait times. Be flexible, and remember that agencies really act as a family's advocate in the process. Because they work on a child's behalf, they are seeking families that are good matches for the children.

Make sure the people you're working with are reputable. Unless the people you are working with are competent, qualified and ethical, the whole process is jeopardized. If you opt for a private adoption, don't go to a family lawyer unless he or she has experience in adoption. And bear in mind that because a lawyer knows how to complete an adoption according to the letter of the law, it doesn't mean he or she has a background in or understanding of the sociological and psychological aspects of adoption. If you are trying to arrange an international adoption, be aware that what is culturally acceptable in other countries may be counter to our experience or what we may deem acceptable. For example, families report that when they adopted they were asked for gifts that they thought were possibly bribes; a reputable, ethical U.S. agency won't allow gifts other than small customary presents you would take to your host.

The Answer to Colic
Imitate the womb, and the crying will stop

Regard the colicky baby at full throttle. Tiny arms and legs stiffen. Tummy goes hard. Face resembles a beet emitting paroxysmal shrieks. Unbelievably, the crying goes on for one, two, even three hours without pause.

No, nothing is wrong. Studies of infants around the world show that unsoothable colic is a natural phase of early infant development, says Dr. Ronald Barr, a pediatrician and leading authority on colic at the University of British Columbia in Vancouver. Babies typically begin crying at two weeks of age. Colicky crying peaks at six weeks and ends by three to four months. It is not related to weak parental skills, being a single parent, postpartum depression or anything done by adults. Infants in primitive tribes who are held 24 hours a day and breast-feed constantly show the same pattern in peak inconsolable crying.

Dr. Harvey Karp, who has a private practice in Santa Monica, Calif., claims that he has devised a method for calming screaming babies—in minutes. In his book and DVD called *The Happiest Baby on the Block*, Karp shows parents five steps that performed together set off what he calls an infant's innate calming instinct. He says the method can also help infants who do not have colic to sleep an extra hour or two a night.

His solution: re-create for infants sensations in the womb to help them stay calm. In the womb, the soon-to-be-born infant is packed tightly, head down in fetal position, with lots of jiggling and a whooshing sound—blood flowing through the placenta—that is louder than a vacuum cleaner. According to Karp, these conditions put the fetus into a trance.

To calm a baby, Karp sets out five maneuvers that he says will touch off a calming reflex and put the infant to sleep. They must be carried out progressively, as a kind of dance, to work their magic.

- The first is swaddling or snug wrapping that imitates the restrictiveness of the womb for the last two months of pregnancy. But this will not by itself stop the crying.

- The second step is to hold the swaddled infant in one's arms or on one's lap and roll the baby onto its side or stomach.

- Third is a very loud shushing noise delivered directly into the baby's ear. The sound imitates what the fetus hears inside the womb as blood pulses through the placenta. The shushing must be as loud or louder than the infant's cries.

- Next comes the jiggling. A fetus is accustomed to certain motions that can be replicated for the crying infant. Karp recommends supporting the baby's head and neck while delivering tiny energetic movements, like shivering. The movements must be gentle to avoid shaking the baby's vulnerable head.

✔ TIMELY TIPS

What You Can Do to Lessen Toxins in Your Breast Milk

✔ Don't drink much alcohol or caffeine.

✔ Avoid spicy foods, strawberries and cruciferous vegetables, which are believed to cause gas in babies.

✔ Don't smoke.

✔ Be aware of concerns about pesticides and heavy metals, and take precautions. If possible, buy mostly organic food to avoid pesticides. A three-stage reverse-osmosis filter for tap water and ice maker will filter out heavy metals and contaminants.

—Florence Williams

- The last step is non-nutritive sucking. A baby will calm itself if it can suck on a finger.

—Sandra Blakeslee

Serious Face Time With Baby
Talking to your infant makes him smarter

S ome researchers say the number of words an infant hears each day is the single most important predictor of later intelligence, school success and social competence. There is one catch—the words have to come from an attentive, engaged human being. As far as anyone has been able to determine, radio and television do not work.

Dr. William Staso, a school psychologist from Orcutt, Calif., and an expert in neurological development, has written a book called *What Stimulation Your Baby Needs to Become Smart.* Some people think that any interaction with very young children that involves their intelligence must also involve pushing them to excel, he says, but the "curriculum" that most benefits young babies is simply common sense. It does not involve teaching several languages or numerical concepts, but rather carrying out an ongoing dialogue with adult speech. Vocabulary words are a magnet for a child's thinking and reasoning skills. Different kinds of stimulation should be emphasized at different ages, but at all stages, parental interaction and a conversational dialogue with the child are important. Here are some examples:

FIRST MONTH. A low level of stimulation reduces stress and increases the infant's wakefulness and alertness. The brain essentially shuts down the system when there is overstimulation from competing sources. When talking to an infant, for example, filter out distracting noises, like a radio.

MONTHS 1 TO 3. Light/dark contours, like high-contrast pictures or objects, foster development in neural networks that encode vision. The brain also starts to discriminate among acoustic patterns of language, like intonation, lilt and pitch. Speaking to the infant, especially in an animated voice, aids this process.

MONTHS 3 TO 5. The infant relies primarily on vision to acquire information about the world. Make available increasingly complex designs that correspond to real objects in the baby's environment; motion also attracts attention. A large-scale picture of a fork, moved across the field of vision, would offer more stimulation than just an actual fork.

MONTHS 6 TO 7. The infant becomes alert to relationships like cause and effect, the location of objects and the functions of objects. Demonstrate and talk about situations, like how the turning of a doorknob leads to the opening of a door.

MONTHS 7 TO 8. The brain is oriented to make associations between sounds and some meaningful activity or object. For example, parents can deliberately emphasize in conversation that the sound of water running in the bathroom signals an impending bath, or that a doorbell means a visitor.

MONTHS 9 TO 12. Learning adds up to a new level of awareness of the environment and increased interest in exploration; sensory and motor skills coordinate in a more mature fashion. This is the time to let the child turn on a faucet or a light switch, under supervision.

MONTHS 13 TO 18. The brain establishes accelerated and more complex associations, especially if the toddler experiments directly with objects. A rich environment will help the toddler make such associations, understand sequences, differentiate between objects and reason about them.

—Sandra Blakeslee

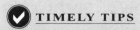 **TIMELY TIPS**

Who's Bringing Up Baby?

It's not who provides the care, but the quality that counts

One of the toughest decisions facing new mothers who return to work is where to look for good child care. Some solid research about the quality of the nation's day care may help allay the fears of parents reluctant to place their babies in the arms of strangers.

A nationwide study conducted by the National Institute of Child Health and Human Development found that child care does not interfere with early childhood development; the quality of care given is more important than who provides the care or how long a child spends in day care.

These findings support earlier research suggesting that for children to thrive in a day-care center, the facility must have a high ratio of staff to children, and the staff must be attentive to each child. "The amount of language that is directed to the child is an important component," says Sarah Friedman, coordinator of the N.I.C.H.D. study. "Language input can predict a child's acquisition of cognitive and language skills, which are the bedrock of school readiness."

The N.I.C.H.D. study also confirmed the conclusions of an earlier study by the same researchers. A key finding in both studies: day care in itself does not harm the mother-child bond. The most important factor influencing a child's development is the home environment, including the mother's psychological well-being and the family's financial situation. The latest study did find, however, that the more hours children spent in day care, the greater the chances that they and their mothers interacted poorly.

Watch Them Grow ... and Grow

Here's how to tell if your child's weight and height are in the normal range

Few processes can be as engrossing to parents as watching their child grow and trying to divine how tall or thin their precious offspring might eventually be. While no one has yet figured out how to predict a child's full adult weight and height, there are plenty of tools, such as the growth charts below, to help you determine if your child's growth is in the normal range.

Infants grow at an incredible pace—doubling their weight in the first four to five months and tripling it by the time they are one. By the end of their first year, their height increases by 50 percent. By age three, a child's head is almost 90 percent of its adult size. Heredity greatly determines a child's ultimate height and weight.

As a rule of thumb, children are considered obese if their weight is 20 percent or more above the expected weight for their height. In between regular pediatric visits, parents can keep tabs on their child's growth rate by using the charts below, which are similar to the ones used in a pediatrician's office.

To plot the child's height, find the vertical line for his or her age at the bottom of the height chart. Locate the horizontal line for the child's stature on the sides of the chart, and mark the point at which the two lines cross. Do the same for the weight chart, using the child's weight and age.

The numbers on the curved lines represent percentiles. For example, if your daughter weighs 125 pounds at age 12, she is about at the 90th percentile. This means that about 90 percent of normal girls weigh less than she does and about 10 percent weigh more.

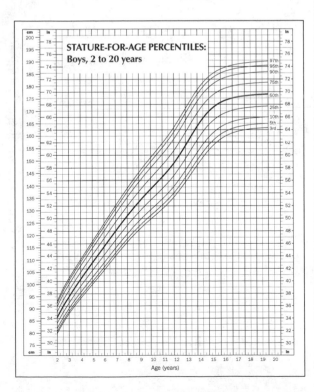

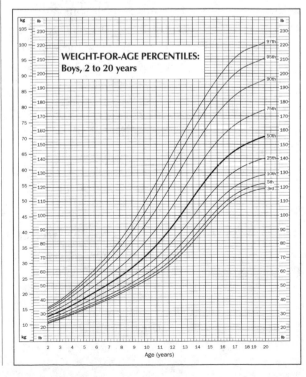

Hello, Mama. Hello, Papa

When should your child begin speaking?

If your 18-month-old speaks fewer than 10 words, your 2-year-old uses no two-word combinations, or your 3-year-old's speech is unintelligible to anyone but the immediate family, should you worry? Is the child merely a slow talker who will eventually catch up to his or her peers, or does the child have a speech or language disorder in need of evaluation and therapy?

Every parent knows that children develop at different rates. There is a very wide range of normal. When children's ability to communicate lags way behind that of their peers, however, there may be reason for concern and a need to attend to the matter. Studies have shown that without any intervention, half of children with delays in the ability to express language at age 2 catch up to their peers by 3, and that another

25 percent have normal speech when they start school. But this leaves 25 percent of late-talking children who do not grow out of their problem before starting school. In such seriously speech-delayed children, intelligible speech may not appear on its own; these children often require professional help if they are to develop with normal social and academic skills.

Speech and language difficulties can have many causes, including an undetected hearing impairment, poor oral muscle tone or coordination, or a neurological disorder like apraxia, a breakdown in the transmission of messages from the brain to the muscles in the jaw, cheeks, lips, tongue and palate.

Too often, when parents express concern to the pediatrician or preschool teacher about what they believe are a child's speech and language problems, they are told to "wait and see." That can result in the loss of precious time, during which

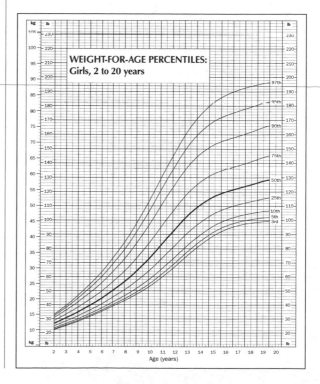

STATURE-FOR-AGE PERCENTILES:
Girls, 2 to 20 years

WEIGHT-FOR-AGE PERCENTILES:
Girls, 2 to 20 years

the child might be receiving therapy. Uncorrected, these problems can lead to learning difficulties and school failure, social ostracism, poor self-image, anxiety disorders and behavioral problems.

The authors of *The Late Talker: What to Do If Your Child Isn't Talking Yet,* Dr. Marilyn C. Agin, Lisa F. Geng and Malcolm J. Nicholl, point out that "speech and language disorders are the No.1 developmental impairment in children under the age of 5." They offer age-appropriate guidelines to help parents detect early warning signs of serious communication gaps and urge parents to act if they find reason for concern. Here, briefly is what they say to look for:

WHAT'S NORMAL

• Typically, by age 2, children use a variety of two-word combinations (more cookie, Mommy work), know at least 50 words and mostly use words to communicate.

• At the age of four, difficulties pronouncing "l" and "th" and frequent failure to string two consonants together ("geen" for "green") is also within the range of normal.

• It is not unusual for a child of 4 or 5 to mispronounce l, s, r, v, z, j, ch, sh and th. A 5- or 6-year-old who says "tiziz" for "scissors" does not have a speech or language disorder.

• All children misarticulate sounds in the course of normal speech development. They may use sound substitutions, like "wady" for "lady." They may omit sounds, saying "baw" instead of "ball." Or they may distort a sound, so that "spaghetti" comes out as "psketti."

One should be concerned, however, when these errors continue beyond the time when a child normally outgrows them—usually by 7 or 8.

REAL PROBLEMS

• Toddlers who have little sound play as infants, who produce a limited number of consonants and make vowel errors

• Toddlers who do not try to imitate word combinations when prompted or fail to use gestures to complement their communicative efforts

• Children who do not show a vocabulary spurt by 30 months

• Children who at 33 months use a limited number of all-purpose verbs—want, go, get, do, make—as in "Me make water down"

• Three-year-olds who often omit consonants at the beginning and end of words, or who substitute consonants most often found at the end of words for front ones, as in "gun" for "done"

ⓘ INSIDE INFO

Body Mass Index for Children

○ Body mass is another means of judging the fitness of an individual.

○ To calculate your body mass, divide your weight by your height squared, and multiply that number by 703.

○ The chart below shows the body mass index (BMI) percentiles for children. (For information about BMI for adults and a table to help you figure your BMI, see page 7.)

	BMI-FOR-AGE
UNDERWEIGHT	< 5th percentile
NORMAL	5th percentile to < 85th percentile
AT RISK OF OVERWEIGHT	85th percentile to < 95th percentile
OVERWEIGHT	> 95th percentile

SOURCE: Centers for Disease Control and Prevention

HAVE YOUR CHILDREN HAD ALL THEIR SHOTS?

The Centers for Disease Control's Advisory Committee on Immunization Practices offers these 2006 recommendations for a schedule of immunizations for children and adolescents:

Vaccine	First dose	Second dose	Third dose	Fourth dose	Fifth dose	Sixth dose
Hepatitis B[1]	At birth	1–2 months	4 months	6–18 months		
Diphtheria, Tetanus, Pertussis (DTaP)[2]	2 months	4 months	6 months	15–18 months	4–6 years	11–16 years
H. influenza (type B)[3]	2 months	4 months	6 months	12–15 months		
Polio	2 months (IPV)	4 months (IPV)	12–18 months (IPV)	4–6 years (IPV)		
Measles, Mumps and Rubella (MMR)	12–15 months	4–6 years or 11–12 years[4]				
Varicella[5]	12–18 months					
Meningococcal[6]	11–12 years					
Pneumococcal[7]	2 months	4 months	6 months	12–15 months		
Influenza[8]	6 months	*Every year thereafter*				
Hepatitis A[9]	12+ months	18+ months				

1. Hepatitis B vaccine (HepB). All infants should receive monovalent HepB at birth. The HepB series should be completed with either monovalent HepB or a combination vaccine containing HepB. It is permissible to administer four doses of HepB (e.g., when combination vaccines are given after the birth dose); however, if monovalent HepB is used, a dose at age 4 months is not needed. Unvaccinated children should receive catch-up immunizations.

2. Diphtheria and tetanus toxoids and acellular pertussis vaccine (DTaP). The fourth dose of DTaP may be administered as early as age 12 months, provided six months have elapsed since the third dose and the child is unlikely to return at age 15 to 18 months. Tetanus and diphtheria toxoids and acellular pertussis vaccine (Tdap – adolescent preparation) is recommended at age 11 to 12 years for those who have completed the recommended childhood DTP/DTaP vaccination series and have not received a Td booster dose. Adolescents 13 to 18 years who missed the 11- to 12-year Td/Tdap booster dose should also receive a single dose of Tdap if they have completed the recommended childhood DTP/DTaP vaccination series. Subsequent tetanus and diphtheria toxoids (Td) are recommended every 10 years.

3. Haemophilus influenzae type B conjugate vaccine (Hib). Three Hib conjugate vaccines are licensed for infant use. If PRP-OMP (PedvaxHIB® or ComVax®) is administered at ages 2 and 4 months, a dose at age 6 months is not required. DTaP/Hib combination products should not be used for primary immunization in infants at ages 2, 4 or 6 months but can be used as boosters after any Hib vaccine.

4. Measles, mumps and rubella vaccine (MMR). The second dose of MMR is recommended routinely at age 4 to 6 years, but may be administered during any visit, provided at least four weeks have elapsed since the first dose and both doses are administered beginning at or after age 12 months. Those who have not previously received the second dose should complete the schedule by age 11 to 12 years.

5. Varicella vaccine. Recommended at any visit at or after age 12 months for susceptible children (i.e., those who lack a reliable history of chickenpox). Susceptible persons aged over 13 years should receive two doses administered at least four weeks apart.

6. Meningococcal vaccine (MCV4) should be given to all children at the 11 to 12 year old visit as well as to unvaccinated adolescents at high school entry (15 years of age). All college freshmen living in dormitories should also be vaccinated, preferably with MCV4, although meningococcal polysaccharide vaccine (MPSV4) is an acceptable alternative.

7. Pneumococcal vaccine. The heptavalent pneumococcal conjugate vaccine (PCV) is recommended for all children aged 2 to 23 months and for certain children aged 24 to 59 months. The final dose in the series should be given at age over 12 months. Pneumococcal polysaccharide vaccine (PPV) is recommended in addition to PCV for certain high-risk groups.

8. Influenza vaccine. Recommended annually for children aged over 6 months with certain risk factors. For healthy persons aged 5 to 49 years, the intranasally administered, live, attenuated influenza vaccine (LAIV) is an acceptable alternative to the intramuscular trivalent inactivated influenza vaccine (TIV). Children aged under 8 years who are receiving influenza vaccine for the first time should receive two doses (separated by at least four weeks for TIV and at least six weeks for LAIV).

9. Hepatitis A vaccine (HepA). Recommended for all children at 1 year of age (i.e., 12 to 23 months). The two doses in the series should be administered at least six months apart.

- Four-year-olds with weak grammar, as in "Her goed home"

- Children who are unable to repeat nonsense words of two or more syllables

For referrals to qualified professionals, contact the American Speech-Language-Hearing Association at 10801 Rockville Pike, Rockville, Md. 20852; 301-897-5700 or 800-638-8255.

—Jane E. Brody

The Knotty Problem of ADHD

To medicate or not, that is the question

To skeptics, a diagnosis of ADHD describes behavior that is only to be expected in children. But to families coping with children who are constantly hyperactive, impulsive and inattentive, learning to recognize and get help for attention deficit hyperactivity disorder is crucial both to the health of the child and the family.

The disorder seems to be anywhere from three to nine times more common in boys than in girls, although that apparent discrepancy could result because boys are likelier to display the clamorous, aggressive behavior that calls attention to their problem, while girls suffer in silence.

Some researchers warn that not all doctors are equipped to diagnose the syndrome properly, and that hyperactivity can serve as what one called a "garbage can" diagnosis, which physicians settle on by default when no other explanation for a child's disturbed behavior can be found. But most agree that hyperactivity is a distinct disorder that can be detected by a well-trained child psychiatrist with access to the most precise diagnostic tests.

In the absence of scientific data, the source of this neurological defect remains obscure. "It appears to run in families, so there is some question about whether there's a genetic contribution," says Dr. Jerry M. Wiener, chairman of the department of Psychiatry at George Washington University. "In some cases, where the pregnancy was difficult, there could have been damage to the fetal brain. Others have raised the possibility of trauma during birth being responsible. Still others have talked about toxins."

For many years, doctors prescribed Ritalin to treat the disorder, a stimulant drug that calms hyperactive children and helps inattentive ones focus. In the past decade, however, other drugs have become widely used as well. In addition to Ritalin, currently the most popular stimulants are Adderall, and Adderall XR and Concerta, the latter two being slow-release versions, which only have to be taken once a day.

In February 2005, the Canadian government suspended sales of Adderall XR, the time-release version of the medication, noting "20 international reports" of sudden deaths, heart-related deaths, and strokes in children and adults. (The standard Adderall is not sold in Canada.) A year later, in February 2006, an advisory panel convened by the U.S. Food and Drug Administration said that stimulants like Ritalin and Adderall could have dangerous effects on the heart, and that federal regulators should require manufacturers to provide written guides to patients and place prominent warnings on drug labels describing the risks. Nevertheless, after the surprise action by the advisory committee, Dr. Thomas Laughren, director of Psychiatry Products at the F.D.A., said "We don't think anything different needs to be done right now," adding that "we think the labeling right now is adequate."

Like other chronic disorders, ADHD is not curable. Some patients have a remission of the disease, and may lead productive adolescent and

EXPERT ANSWERS

If You Suspect a Child Has ADHD

Q. When and where should parents seek help if they suspect that their child may have ADHD?

All children are inattentive, hyperactive, and impulsive to some extent, but the severity has to be great enough to cause impairment. Treatment should be sought when there is notable dysfunctionality, usually a significant disruption at home or school. Schools are often the first to recognize it. After that, parents typically go to their pediatrician or a child psychiatrist or maybe a pediatric neurologist. If there's no interest in treating ADHD with medication, a child psychiatrist might be able to deal with the problem through behavior modification.

What is the best approach to treating ADHD?

Medication has a beneficial effect in 70 percent to 80 percent of children. It's the most well-established treatment. But medication alone probably isn't enough by itself to have long-term impact. School-based intervention and behavioral treatment are the other components to supplement any effect the medication might have, and to make short-term effects persist. Parents are taught to use reinforcement, such as discipline and stimulus control; treatments based on the same principles of behavioral modification are then also used at school.

SOME ONLINE RESOURCES:

- **ADD Resources:** www.addresources.org
- **CHADD (Children and Adults with Hyperactivity Disorder):** www.chadd.org
- **PediatricNeurology.Com:** www.pediatricneurology.com
- **Centers for Disease Control and Prevention:** www.cdc.gov

adult lives. However, approximately 60 percent of children with ADHD will carry their symptoms into adulthood.

—Natalie Angier; Andrew Jacobs; Gardiner Harris

The Real Risks to Children

Parents worry about everything, often needlessly. Here's what should be high on your list

Many parents worry that their children may be harmed by exposure to environmental factors they cannot avoid or control, including pesticide residues on fruits and vegetables, approved food additives, chlorinated drinking water and hormones in milk.

None of these are actual hazards. But even if they were, they are hardly the main threats to the health and lives of fetuses, infants, children and adolescents, says Dr. Robert L. Brent, a professor at Thomas Jefferson University in Philadelphia and a leading expert on what is and is not known about the effects of environmental chemicals and physical agents on developing humans.

In the concluding chapter of a recent report, published as a supplement in the journal *Pediatrics*, Dr. Brent and his co-author, Dr. Michael Weitzman, a pediatrician at the University of Rochester School of Medicine and Dentistry, reviewed what are unquestionably the leading risks to infants, children and adolescents.

Accidents are the leading cause of death in children under 15. Most accidents involving children could be prevented by vigilance. Here are the most important hazards.

Sudden Infant Death Syndrome. Risk is reduced by putting infants to sleep on their backs and providing a nonsmoking environment.

Falls. Infants can suffer head injuries by falling from

HEALTH

strollers, down stairs, off beds or against sharp-pointed furniture. Toddlers and children aged 5 to 9 fall from windows, stairs, trees, roofs and ladders.

Vehicular accidents. Infants and children under 10 should never ride in the front seat, and those under 80 pounds should always ride in a properly installed car seat or booster seat appropriate to the child's age and size.

Outside the car, children under 10 are at risk of death from pedestrian accidents, including being run over by the family car in their own driveway and ignoring safety rules when crossing the street.

For teenagers, reckless driving, impulsive behavior and drunken driving make auto accidents a leading cause of death.

Burns. Infants can suffer burns from kitchen equipment or hot items pulled off the table, as well as hot water in a tub and uncovered radiators. Toddlers should never have access to matches, cigarette lighters, or fuel-filled or flint igniters.

House fires can be started by adults who fall asleep while smoking, faulty wiring, defective heating systems and space heaters. Every home should be equipped with one or more working smoke alarms.

Poisoning. As soon as children can crawl, they are at risk of poisoning from medications, household chemicals (including drain and oven cleaners, alcohol and paint thinner), pesticides and rodent killers. Such items should be stored out of children's reach, in cupboards with childproof locks.

Lead poisoning, though much reduced, is still a risk for millions of children who live in old homes with lead-based paint, plaster or putty, as well as those with old toys, cribs and imported pottery. A child's blood lead level should be checked and elevated levels treated to prevent cognitive deficits.

Drowning. Pools, hot tubs and wading pools must have supervision and be fenced in, locked or covered. The incidence of childhood drownings varies by state according to the number of backyard swimming pools and hot tubs, but is also a problem in bathtubs, bathinettes and kiddie wading pools. An infant or young child in or around water should never be left unattended, not even for a minute. Children relying on flotation devices and those under 4 who can swim are not safe in the water. Children should always swim with another swimmer. When boating, every infant and child—even good swimmers—should wear an approved life jacket.

Choking. Any item that can block a child's airway is a choking hazard. An infant or toddler can aspirate toys with small parts, deflated balloons, and foods like peanuts, raisins, raw carrots and popcorn. In addition to preventing exposure, every caretaker should know how to perform the Heimlich maneuver on infants and small children.

Guns. There are firearms in 40 million American homes. Guns in the home, including the homes of law enforcement officers, are dangers even to infants if there are older children around. Firearms should be stored in locked cabinets separate from their ammunition.

Electrocution. As soon as children can crawl, they are at risk of electrocution from uncovered outlets and frayed or brittle lamp or appliance cords. Older children should be taught what to do when a thunderstorm approaches—get out of the water immediately, and never stand under a tall tree.

Secondhand smoke. Parents or caretakers who smoke in the house or car in the presence of infants or children increase their risk of sudden death, asthma and pneumonia. They also set a terrible example.

How to Raise a Moral Child

Empathy is the key to developing morality

"Children are going to learn morality not from what you tell them, but from how you treat them," says child psychiatrist Stanley Greenspan, whose book, *The Growth of the Mind and Its Endangered Future*, discusses how children develop their sense of morality. The way a child is treated is crucial, says Greenspan, whose research has shown that morality depends on a person's ability to feel empathy for someone else, and to have empathy a child must first develop what Greenspan calls "a sense of shared humanity." That sense of shared humanity, or "buying into the human race," comes from a child experiencing intimacy and warmth in a relationship with another person, whether that figure is the child's parents, relative or other close contact. It's impossible to develop a concern for others, Greenspan argues, unless someone in your life has shown concern for you.

That sense of shared humanity is only the starting point, however, for encouraging morality in children. "You can't empathize with someone else unless you can picture what the other person wants and desires and are able to put yourself in the other's shoes," says Greenspan. "If you can't put yourself in another's shoes, you can't really contemplate how your actions are going to affect them."

Empathy is essential, Greenspan says, because it helps guide children's judgments in cases where there may not be a clear-cut rule to follow, and a child may have to decide how to handle a moral dilemma on his own. If you simply tell a child, "You don't do this, you don't do that," says Greenspan, some children will obey out of a fear of being "a bad person," without really understanding what that means. Such children have what Greenspan calls "a concrete sense of morality, and can just as soon be immoral as moral" if a new authority figure with less savory rules appears. To make moral judgments, stresses Greenspan, "the kind we want in our Supreme Court justices, comes from a sense of empathy."

Sports injuries. Riding a bicycle with an infant, even one in a child carrier and wearing a helmet, is dangerous. A child riding a tricycle, bicycle, scooter or skateboard should always wear a properly fitted helmet, which can reduce the risk of head injury and brain damage by 85 percent in a fall or crash. Cycling by children should be restricted to safe locations in daylight hours only.

Children who play football, baseball, soccer, hockey and lacrosse should always wear protective equipment and be properly supervised.

Power tools. Each year nearly 10,000 children 15 and younger are injured by lawn mowers. A young child should not be nearby when a power mower is in use; children under 12 should not be allowed to operate a walk-behind mower; and children under 14 should not operate a riding mower.

Obesity. Children of all ages in the United States today are getting fatter and fatter, thanks to parents and caretakers who allow them to spend hours a day in front of a television set, who give them access to excessive amounts of snacks and fast foods and to oversize portions, and who do not make sure that they get regular physical activity.

Obesity that begins in childhood becomes a lifelong problem, greatly increasing the risk of a host of health and social problems, including premature death.

—Jane E. Brody

First Aid & Survival

The ABC's of CPR

Every adult should know how to perform CPR

More than 300,000 Americans die of cardiac arrest each year. The American Heart Association estimates that more than 95 percent of them die before they get to the hospital. According to the A.H.A., about 75 percent to 80 percent of all cardiac arrests outside a hospital happen at home, and effective CPR can double a victim's chance of survival.

"The most common reason many people die from cardiac arrest is no one nearby knows CPR," says Dr. Michael Sayre, a professor of emergency medicine at Ohio State University who helped develop the November 2005 guidelines on cardiopulmonary resuscitation for the American Heart Association. For the sake of their family alone, as well as for the community they live in, every adult should learn to properly administer CPR.

 INSIDE INFO

Heart to Heart

○ If CPR is administered within four minutes of collapse, and if defibrillation occurs within 10 minutes of a heart attack, a person has a 40 percent chance of survival.

○ If CPR were performed early enough, 100,000 to 200,000 lives of adults and children could be saved each year.

○ CPR is used not only in the case of heart attacks, but also for other near-death resuscitations, such as near-drowning and electrocution.

SOURCE: American Heart Association

Updating the way everyday people do CPR, the American Heart Association now recommends that rescuers give twice as many chest compressions—30 instead of 15—for every two rescue breaths.

Studies show that the increased number of chest compressions create more blood flow through the heart to the rest of the body, buying time until a defibrillator can be used to shock the heart, or the heart can pump blood on its own. Studies have also shown that blood circulation increases with each chest compression and must be built back up after an interruption, the association says in its online journal *Circulation*.

"When you stop compressions, blood flow stops," says Mary Fran Hazinski, a clinical nurse specialist at Vanderbilt University Medical Center who also helped develop the guidelines. "You have to make up for that lost ground. We think that the fewer the interruptions, the better for blood flow. The bottom line is, we think more people need to learn CPR."

The new guidelines, announced in November 2005, also includes these points:

● Comatose patients should have their body temperature cooled to about 90 degrees Fahrenheit for 12 to 24 hours after resuscitation. Two significant studies have shown that the practice can improve survival and brain function in such patients.

● After giving two rescue breaths, rescuers should not stop to check for signs of circulation before starting compressions.

● Instead of applying defibrillator pads up to three times before beginning CPR, rescuers

A PRIMER ON RESCUE BREATHING

The timing intervals for administering mouth-to-mouth respiration to adults and children are somewhat different, but the mechanics are the same.

If the victim is unable to breathe,

STEP 1: The victim should be on his or her back. You begin by tilting the head slightly back and lifting the chin to move the tongue away from the back of the throat. You should also pinch the patient's nose shut.

STEP 2: Make a tight seal with your mouth around the victim's mouth, breathing slowly into the victim until his chest gently rises. You should give two breaths, each lasting about two seconds. Pause between breaths to let the air flow out.

STEP 3: Check the victim's pulse after the two initial breaths.

If pulse is present, but the person is still not breathing,

STEP 4: For adults, continue giving one breath about every five seconds, or 12 breaths per minute.

For infants and children, continue giving one breath about every three seconds—or 20 breaths per minute.

STEP 5: Recheck the person's pulse every minute.

CONTINUE rescue breathing as long as the pulse is still present, but the person is not breathing.

REMINDER: Call the local emergency number as soon as possible.

---

should give one shock and then do two minutes of CPR, beginning with chest compressions, before trying the defibrillator again.

For more information on how to learn CPR, go to the American Heart Association's Web site: www.americanheart.org.

FOR ADULTS AND CHILDREN

CPR should be given where there is no breathing and no pulse. Tilt the victim's head backward and give two rescue breaths.

STEP 1: Place the heel of your hand on the notch where the ribs meet the lower breastbone.

STEP 2: Place your other hand on top of the first. Using the heel of your bottom hand, apply pressure on the breastbone. Your shoulders should be directly over your hands, and your elbows should be locked. Press the victim's chest down about two inches and then release. Repeat 30 times, keeping a smooth rhythm.

STEP 3: Tilt the victim's head back slightly, lift his chin, place your mouth over his and give two slow breaths.

STEP 4: Do three more sets of 30 compressions and two breaths (Steps 2 and 3). Each set should take about 15 seconds.

STEP 5: Recheck the victim's pulse and breathing. If there is no pulse,

STEP 6: Continue repeating Steps 2 and 3, pausing every couple of minutes to check the victim's pulse

FOR INFANTS

Babies require lighter chest pressure delivered in shorter, more frequent cycles. If the infant is not breathing, give one rescue breath and begin the compressions.

STEP 1: Same as adults, except instead of using your hand, place two fingers on the breastbone just below an imaginary line between the nipples.

STEPS 2 and 3: Same as adults, except give 5 to 10 compressions, about three seconds each.

When giving the baby breaths, place your mouth over the infant's nose and mouth and give one slow breath.

STEP 4: Same as for adults, except do 12 cycles of five compressions and one breath. This should take about one minute. If you haven't yet called the local emergency number, do. Be sure to carry the infant with you so you can continue giving CPR.

STEPS 5 and 6: Same as for adults, except use the shorter, more frequent cycles.

Taking Shock Seriously

When the body shuts down because of injury, immediate care is critical

Shock is the body's way of trying to deal with a bad situation. When a body experiences trauma from a serious injury, it often finds itself unable to maintain proper blood flow to all its organs. Shock is the mechanism that allows the body to ration blood flow so that the most important organs such as the brain, heart, lungs and kidneys get the blood they need, even when that means that less vital parts, such as arms, legs and skin have to make do with less. This natural triage cannot be sustained for very long, however, without causing potentially life-threatening damage to the brain and heart.

CONTROLLING BLEEDING FROM AN OPEN WOUND

Pressure is the key to stopping blood from a serious injury. Bearing down on arterial pressure points may be necessary.

STEP 1: Cover the wound with a sterile dressing or clean cloth and press firmly against the wound with your hand. Don't waste time washing the wound.

STEP 2: Elevate the wound, if possible, above the level of the heart.

STEP 3: Apply a roller bandage over the dressing to keep pressure on the wound. Tie or tape the bandage in place. After applying the bandage, check fingers or toes for warmth, color and feeling. If they are pale and cold, the bandage is too tight and needs to be loosened.

STEP 4: If the bleeding doesn't stop, apply additional dressings. Also find a pressure point where you can squeeze the artery against the bone.

When the emergency that requires your assistance involves heavy bleeding, it's important to protect yourself against the risk of infection—especially if you have a cut, scrape or sore that could allow the victim's blood to mix with yours. One of the easiest ways for an infectious disease such as the AIDS virus or hepatitis B to be transmitted is through direct blood-to-blood exchange. To reduce risk, the American Red Cross advises the following:

- Avoid blood splashes.

- Keep and use disposable latex gloves in emergencies involving bleeding.

- If gloves are unavailable, cover the wound with a dressing or other available barrier such as plastic wrap.

- Avoid any contact in which the victim's blood touches any cuts, scrapes or skin irritations you may have.

- Always wash your hands as soon as possible, whether or not you wore gloves.

Shock, says the Red Cross, "can't be managed effectively by first aid alone. A victim of shock requires advanced medical care as soon as possible."

The early signs of shock include:

- Restlessness or irritability.
- Altered or confused consciousness.
- Pale, cool, moist skin.
- Rapid breathing and rapid pulse.

The proper response to shock is to:

- Stretch the victim out on his or her back.
- Treat any open bleeding.
- Help the injured restore normal body temperature, covering him or her if there is chilling.
- Talk to the victim reassuringly.
- Prop the legs up about a foot unless there are possible head, neck or back injuries, or broken bones in the hips or legs.
- Withhold food or drink, even though the victim probably feels thirsty.
- Call the rescue service immediately.

Saving a Choking Victim

Dr. Heimlich's famous maneuver has saved thousands

Since Dr. Henry Heimlich first published his findings on a technique to rescue choking victims in 1974, many thousands of lives have been saved through its use.

FOR ADULTS

If you see someone who is unable to speak and is choking and turning blue, you need to act immediately. Step behind the person and wrap your arms

DOCTOR'S ADVICE

Dr. Henry Heimlich of Cincinnati recommends:

Seat the infant on the rescuer's lap and use the pads of the index and middle fingers of both hands to press upward—abruptly but gently—just under the diaphragm where the central chest bone (sternum) ends.

Or place the baby faceup on a flat surface and press upward under the diaphragm using the same fingers.

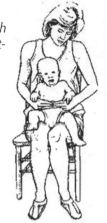

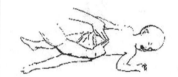

SOURCE: Heimlich Institute

around them. Make a fist and and place the thumb of that hand high up against the person's abdomen, though below the ribcage. Grasp your fist with your other hand and quickly push your fist into the abdomen with an upward thrust. Continue to repeat this motion until the obstruction has been expelled.

FOR INFANTS AND CHILDREN

First, it is important to distinguish between choking that is life-threatening and what people commonly call choking. The time to act immediately to try to dislodge an object obstructing the windpipe is when the child cannot make a sound, cough or cry, or the child's face turns from red to blue.

If a child can cough, then the windpipe is not obstructed, because coughing requires breathing. The situation is unlikely to become dangerous unless you start slapping the child on the back. The slaps can push the object farther down and perhaps obstruct the trachea.

When it comes to treating choking in infants,

Heimlich's advice remains at odds with the American Heart Association, which says a repeated sequence of back blows and chest compressions should be used. But he maintains that could be challenging for a panicked caretaker to execute. Furthermore, Heimlich recommends seating the infant on the rescuer's lap or placing the baby faceup on a flat surface and, using the pads of the index and middle fingers of both hands, pressing upward—abruptly but gently—just under the diaphragm where the central chest bone (the sternum) ends. That compresses the lungs evenly, producing a forceful flow of air that can expel the choking object.

The American Heart Association says this method can damage organs. Instead, it recommends chest compressions, which Heimlich says do not produce the air pressure needed to push out an obstructing object.

For toddlers and older children, Heimlich and the A.H.A. agree that the Heimlich maneuver is the method of choice. It can be done with the child lying faceup or standing or sitting with the rescuer kneeling behind the child.

For a toddler or small child, the rescuer should use the heel of one hand to exert an upward thrust just under the diaphragm. For a larger child, a standard Heimlich can be done, using the fist of one hand with the other hand clasped over it.

Heimlich says the Heimlich maneuver can also dislodge an object like a chicken bone that is stuck in the throat but not completely obstructing the windpipe, because the resulting force of air produces a hurricanelike effect in the airway that can blow out the object.

—Jane E. Brody

Getting Burned

Do's and don'ts for treating a slight singe, to much worse

Burns are classified by the amount of damage done to the skin and other body tissue. Every family member should be able to identify the severity of burns and know how to treat them.

 TIMELY TIPS

What's Dangerous for Babies

Anything bite-size or larger, or any food or object that does not melt or break down easily, can obstruct a baby's windpipe if it is accidentally inhaled instead of swallowed. Thus, Cheerios are safe for babies starting to feed themselves, but raisins are not.

The foods that are hazards for young children include:

✔ **grapes** (remove the skin and quarter the grape for children 4 and under)

✔ **apples and pears** (peel and cook to soften for children under 4, peel and cut small for those 4 to 6)

✔ **raisins** (not for children under 3)

✔ **nuts** (not for children under 6)

✔ **popcorn** (not for those under 4)

✔ **carrots** (purée for children 2 and younger; cook to soften for those 3 and up)

✔ **celery** (never raw for children 4 and under; bite-size for 5- and 6-year-olds)

✔ **hot dogs** (never for children under 3; remove skin and cut into small pieces for older children)

✔ **peanut butter** (not for children under 4; spread thinly on bread for those 4 to 6)

✔ **hard candy** (never for children 4 and under).

—Jane E. Brody

- **First-degree burns** are minor and heal quickly.
  SYMPTOMS: *reddened skin; tender and sore*

- **Second-degree burns** are serious injuries and require immediate first aid and professional medical treatment.
  SYMPTOMS: *blistered skin; very painful*

- **Third-degree burns** are severe injuries and require immediate professional medical treatment.
  SYMPTOMS: *white, brown or charred tissue, often surrounded by blistered areas; little or no pain at first*

If a person has been burned badly by fire, fast action on your part is very important. Have someone call 911. Meanwhile, you must act to begin the cooling process, prevent shock, prevent contamination and control pain.

DO

- **DO** Wet, cover and cool the burn: gently pour water over the burns. Place the cleanest available cloth material over all burned areas, such as sterile gauze, clean sheets or a T-shirt, and gently pour water over them, keeping the material wet. Ensure that the cooling process does not become excessive and cause shivering.

- **DO** Remove smoldering clothing only if it is NOT stuck to the skin.

- **DO** Carefully remove clothing or jewelry that may constrict during swelling.

- **DO** Have the victim lie down. Make certain his head and chest are a little lower than the rest of his body. Raise his legs if possible.

- **DO** Treat for shock: to reduce the risk of shock, keep the victim's body temperature normal. Cover unburned areas with a dry blanket.

- **DO** Get immediate medical help. Call 911.

DO NOT

- **DO NOT** Put ice, burn ointments, butter or grease or anything else besides water on a burn.

- **DO NOT** Remove clothing that is stuck to a burn.

- **DO NOT** Break blisters.

SOURCE: Virginia Department of Fire Programs: www.vdfp. state.va.us/firstaid.htm

When Someone Is Poisoned
How to deal with a variety of toxins

Poison can be inhaled, ingested, injected, or the result of a bite or sting. The more information you have on the cause of the poisoning, the better. Here is what to do:

1. Remain calm.

2. If you have a poison emergency and the victim has collapsed or is not breathing, call 911. If you have a poison exposure and the victim is alert, call 800-222-1222. Try to have the following information ready if possible:

- the person's age and estimated weight

- the container or bottle of the poisonous product, if available

- time that the poison exposure occurred

- your name and phone number

3. Follow the instructions from the emergency operator or the poison control center.

SOURCE: Centers for Disease Control and Prevention

TREATING INSECT BITES

When it comes to emergency treatment for insect bites, unless you do not have one essential ingredient in your first-aid kit, you may be out of luck.

HEALTH

Everyone who has ever had even a mild systemic reaction to an insect bite, or who is suspected of having severe allergies to insect bites should always carry self-injectable epinephrine whenever they venture outside. Guidelines on emergency room treatment call for patients who manifest symptoms of less severe systemic reactions—for example, a sting in one place and a rash or hives in another—to be given immediate treatment with epinephrine, a prescription for self-injectable epinephrine for future prevention and a referral to an allergist. Dr. Carlos A. Camargo, associate professor of medicine and epidemiology at Harvard, says that self-injectable epinephrine is essential equipment for anyone with a history of systemic allergic reactions.

—Nicholas Bakalar

IF A SNAKE STRIKES AND BITES

Follow these three steps:

1. Calm the victim, and wash the bite with soap and water.

2. Keep the bitten area lower than the heart and restrict movement. Remove anything constrictive, as the area may swell.

3. If a victim is unable to reach medical care within 30 minutes, wrap an Ace bandage two to four inches above the bite to help slow the venom's progress toward the heart. Do not use ice. Place a pump suction device over the wound, and remove as much of the venom as possible. Get anti-venom medicine as soon as possible, preferably administered by a doctor.

SOURCE: John Henkel, *FDA Consumer Magazine*

HEROIN OVERDOSES

The sad thing about heroin overdoses is that they are preventable with a simple injection. Heroin is an opioid, just like methadone, OxyContin and Vicodin,

to name a few. Because overdosing kills by slowly stopping a person's breathing, there is a short time in which a person can be injected with an antidote called naloxone, quickly reversing an opioid overdose.

If given early enough, naloxone can prevent damage to the brain caused by lack of oxygen and leave the victim unharmed. According to research by Dr. Sandro Galea of the Center for Urban Epidemiological Studies at the New York Academy of Medicine, at least 75 percent of overdose deaths involve multiple drugs, usually mixtures of heroin and other depressants like alcohol. Removing the opioid from the mix with naloxone is often enough to revive victims.

Naloxone itself is virtually harmless. Its most common side effects are withdrawal symptoms like nausea, shakiness and agitation in those who are physically dependent on opioids. While uncomfortable, these symptoms are not dangerous. Rarely, seizures can occur, but this risk is far lower than the risk to those who are not treated. The drug has no effect on those who haven't taken opioids.

—Maia Szalavitz

How to Alleviate Heatstroke
Cooling the body from the inside out

The thinking used to be that when you were suffering from heatstroke you should cool the outside of the body as quickly as possible. But recently it has been found that these methods are not only an inefficient way for the body to cool down, they can actually be quite dangerous.

Stanford professors Craig Heller and Dennis Grahn have conducted a series of experiments on "exertional hyperthermia" and the methods for combating it. What they found was surprising. Bringing someone suffering from hyperthermia into a cool environment, it turns out, is precisely the wrong thing to do. When warm skin encounters coldness, the blood vessels near the surface of the skin constrict. Heat becomes trapped inside the body and is redirected to the core, which causes a spike in temperature. The better thing to do is to cool the palms of the hand. This thinking is premised on the little-known fact that our palms, along with the soles of our feet and our cheeks, are "natural mammalian radiators," as Heller puts it. When the body is overheated, it naturally increases blood flow to the palms.

Heller and Grahn invented a machine called The Glove. It consists of an airtight, transparent chamber shaped like a giant Dustbuster, inside of which is a metal plate, resting on top of a pool of circulating cool water. A heatstroke victim puts his or her hand into the chamber and places it on the plate, which is usually about 70 degrees Fahrenheit. A mild vacuum pressure further increases

blood flow to the hand. After the blood has been cooled in the person's palm, it returns through the veins directly to the heart, and is then circulated to overheated muscles and organs, cooling the body, according to trials, by more than three degrees in 10 minutes. For those who do not have access to a machine, the next best thing is to submerge a heatstroke victim's hand in cool, not icy, water until medical help can be summoned.

—Joel Lovell

HEALTH

When the Earth Shakes

Some ways to prepare for a temblor and a tsunami

The sheer force of the earth's shifting tectonic plates is tough to imagine. Most people don't realize that 39 states are at risk from earthquakes, and the threat isn't confined to towns on fault lines. Here are some frequently asked questions, and answers, from the geophysicists at the U.S. Geological Survey in Menlo Park, California.

Q **Where are earthquakes most likely to hit?**

California, of course, is the most at risk—the San Francisco Bay area and Los Angeles represent the greatest urban earthquake threats. The U.S. Geological Survey estimated in 2002 a 62 percent chance of a magnitude 6.7 earthquake or larger hitting the Bay area before 2032 along one of seven major earthquake faults. The highest probability—27 percent—is the Hayward fault, which runs along the east side of San Francisco Bay through Oakland and Berkeley, and its extension to the north, the Rodgers Creek fault. The last earthquake there occurred in 1868, estimated at magnitude 7.0 on the Richter scale, and the interval between the last few has been about 135 years. Seattle could also be at risk for a sizable earthquake in the next 10 years. Alaska, too, has had its share of earth-

---

INSIDE INFO

A Handheld Cooling Device

O The Defense Advanced Research Projects Agency, which gave us the Internet, has bankrolled research on a handheld device that essentially cools the body from the inside.

O The device, CoreControl, is a coffee pot–size chamber with a cold metal cone in the center. The user grips the cone and holds it for three to five minutes. Afterward, users report feeling not cooler, but fresher and ready to work again.

O Unlike more common cooling strategies such as cold towels, cooling vests or gel packs, CoreControl focuses special radiatorlike blood vessels in the palm of the hand to take the heated blood that is normally pumped throughout the body during and after exertion and sends cooler blood back to the body core instead.

—Aimée Berg

THE FIRST STEP: A FIRST-AID KIT

Assemble a first-aid kit for your home and one for each car. A first-aid kit should include the following items:

- Sterile adhesive bandages in assorted sizes
- Two-inch and four-inch sterile gauze pads (four to six of each)
- Hypoallergenic adhesive tape
- Triangular bandages (three)
- Two-inch and three-inch sterile roller bandages (three rolls of each)
- Splints: 1/4 inch thick x 3 inches wide x 12 to 15 inches long
- Scissors, tweezers, needle
- Moistened towelettes
- Antiseptic
- Sterile saline solution
- Thermometer
- Tongue blades (two)
- Tube of petroleum jelly or other lubricant
- Assorted sizes of safety pins
- Cleansing agent/soap
- Latex gloves (two pairs)
- Eye goggles
- Sunscreen

NONPRESCRIPTION DRUGS SUCH AS:

- Aspirin or nonaspirin pain reliever (Remember: no aspirin for children!)
- Anti-diarrhea medication
- Antacid (for stomach upset)
- Laxative
- Syrup of Ipecac (use to induce vomiting if advised by the Poison Control Center)
- Activated charcoal (use if advised by the Poison Control Center)
- Self-injectable epinephrine

SOURCE: Centers for Disease Control and Prevention

---

quakes in Fairbanks, Anchorage and the Aleutian Islands. The biggest earthquake in the continental United States, however, was in New Madrid, Missouri, in 1811, causing so much disturbance that the Mississippi River's current ran in another direction. In the early 19th century, Charleston, South Carolina, also got hit hard. There have been some small earthquakes in upstate New York as well, but they're more of a curiosity.

● **What should be done to prepare for an earthquake?**

The collapse of a house isn't very likely, unless the house is located near a ledge where a landslide is possible. Fire as a result of ripping a gas line or shaking water heaters is much more likely. So the first step you should take if you live in an earthquake-prone area is to find and repair faulty electrical wiring, leaky gas and inflexible utility connections. Bolt down water heaters and gas appliances, and put heavy objects on lower shelves, then fasten the shelves to the walls. Store bottled foods, glass and china on low shelves that can be fastened shut. If you live in an apartment built before the 1980's, there are engineering retrofits that can fix "soft" first floors—buildings with garages on the first floor, where the foundation would be most likely to collapse. You may want to check to see if your building has had that done. If you live in a house, make sure you have it anchored to the foundation.

● **Where are the most dangerous places to be in a quake?**

In your home, it's a bad idea to be near anything that can topple over, like tall bookcases and light fixtures. You should also stay away from windows where the glass can shatter, and from fireplaces—the brick or stone could crumble. If you're inside, get under a sturdy desk, table or bench, or hold on to an inside wall. In crowded public places, don't rush for a doorway, since other people will be doing the same thing. Take cover and move away from display shelves and anything else that could fall on you. Stay on the same floor, and don't use elevators. If you're outside, stay there. Move away from buildings, street lights and utility poles and wires. (For more on earthquakes, see "Predicting Earthquakes," page 719.)

How does a tsunami occur and who is at risk?

Tsunamis are caused by earthquakes and other serious disturbances (landslides, volcanoes) of the ocean floor, which set off powerful shock waves. These travel under the ocean's surface at tremendous speeds until they hit land, propelling a giant wall of water, sometimes as high as 100 feet, onto the shore. If you live in a low-lying coastal area and a tsunami warning is issued, you must evacuate immediately inland to higher ground.

Anyone who lives along the Pacific coast is most at risk, though tsunamis have occurred in the Atlantic Ocean, too, hitting the coast of Canada and the Caribbean islands.

Since the devastating 2004 tsunami in South Asia, which killed almost almost 160,000 people, the National Oceanic and Atmospheric Administration (NOAA) has continued to increase the number of deep-ocean sensors that listen for earthquakes on the seafloor, sense the pressure of waves passing over them, and radio their findings to scientists at tsunami early-warning centers in Alaska and Hawaii.

The National Weather Service office disseminates information from there through its early warning systems including, NOAA Weather Radio, weather and other emergency communications systems, and direct connections to state and local emergency response officials. For more information, go to www.tsunamiready.noaa.gov.

SOURCES: U.S. Geological Survey; reporting by Kenneth Chang

HEALTH

TIMELY TIPS

Surviving a Deluge

You can't build an ark, but you can take some precautions

Floods cause more damage nationwide than any other natural disaster. Often the result of hurricanes, floods occur most frequently during the hurricane season, which runs roughly from July through November. Here are some tips from the Federal Emergency Management Agency (FEMA) to help you survive the rising waters and minimize flood damage to your home.

BEFORE THE FLOOD

✔ **Make an itemized list** of your furnishings, clothing and valuables. Photos can help insurance adjusters settle your claims, as well as help you verify uninsured losses, which are tax-deductible.

✔ **Keep your insurance policies** and the inventory of your personal property in a secure place, such as a safe-deposit box.

DURING THE FLOOD

✔ **Have a battery-operated radio on hand** and keep it tuned to a local station for announcements regarding evacuation plans.

✔ **Turn off all utilities at the main switch.** Do not touch electrical equipment unless it is dry, or you are standing on a piece of dry wood and are wearing rubber gloves and rubber footwear.

✔ **Open basement windows** to equalize the water pressure on the foundation and walls.

✔ If you are caught in the house and flood waters are suddenly rising around your house, move to the second floor and, if necessary, to the roof. Take warm clothing, a flashlight and the radio with you. Do not try to swim to safety.

✔ **If you evacuate your home,** avoid areas that are already flooded. Do not attempt to cross any stretch of flood waters on foot if the water is above your knees.

✔ **Do not drive through flooded roads.** Rapidly rising water could carry your car away, possibly trapping you inside. Be careful if you must evacuate at night, when flooded areas are harder to see. If your car stalls, get out and climb to higher ground.

Riding Out a Thunderstorm

Keep away from metal, water and tall structures

All thunderstorms are dangerous because they produce lightning, an electrical discharge that results from the buildup of positive and negative charges within a thunderstorm. When the buildup becomes strong enough, lightning appears as a "bolt." This flash of light usually occurs within the clouds or between the clouds and the ground. A bolt of lightning reaches a temperature approaching 50,000 degrees Fahrenheit in a split second. It is the rapid heating and cooling of the air near the lightning that causes thunder.

In the United States, an average of 300 people are injured and 80 people are killed each year by lightning. Although most victims survive, people struck by lightning often report a variety of long-term, debilitating symptoms.

Other associated dangers of thunderstorms include tornadoes, strong winds, hail and flash

---

 TIMELY TIPS

Preparing for a Hurricane

As victims of Katrina know, you may not ride out the storm

As hurricanes approach the coast, a huge dome of water called a storm surge crashes into the coastline—9 out of 10 people killed in hurricanes are victims of these storm surges. And as any survivor of Hurricane Katrina, the powerful storm that hit the Gulf Coast in 2005, now all too painfully knows, if you live in a coastal area near the ocean, you cannot take the risk of riding out the storm at home.

To be considered a hurricane, a tropical storm must have winds that reach speeds of at least 74 m.p.h. and blow counterclockwise around a center eye. Hurricane winds have been clocked at 175 m.p.h., and the combination of the winds and

torrential rains can spawn tornadoes and cause severe flooding, affecting areas hundreds of miles inland. Some tips from the National Hurricane Center:

✔ **Know how little time a hurricane watch or warning gives you.** If a hurricane watch is issued, you have 24 to 36 hours before the hurricane hits land. A hurricane warning means that hurricane winds and storm tides are expected in a specific coastal area within 24 hours. A NOAA (National Oceanic and Atmospheric Administration) Weather Radio with a warning alarm and battery backup is useful in case the power goes out.

✔ **Ask your local emergency management office about community evacuation plans.** Learn your evacuation routes, and plan a place for your family to meet in case you are separated. As part of this plan, choose an out-of-state contact for everyone to call and say they're O.K.

✔ **Cover your windows.** People who live in Florida, Texas and along the Gulf Coast should have shutters in their homes. If you don't have them, you should cover your windows with 5/8-inch marine plywood, cut to fit and ready to install. Put some sort of slugs in the wall, or lag-bolts, to secure the wood.

✔ **If you live right on the ocean, go far inland.** Fill up your car's gas tank ahead of time if there's a chance you might need to evacuate. Once the storm has arrived, service stations may be closed.

✔ **Know how to shut off your utilities.** It's important that you know where the shut-off devices are for the gas, plumbing and electrical lines in the house. Before leaving your home, turn these systems off.

✔ **Make arrangements for housing your pets.** Many emergency shelters don't allow pets. Call your local humane society for more information.

flooding. Flash flooding is responsible for more fatalities—more than 140 annually—than any other thunderstorm-associated hazard. Here is some advice for what to do in a thunderstorm:

IF INDOORS

- Do not handle any electrical equipment or telephones, because lightning could follow the wire. Television sets are particularly dangerous at this time.
- Avoid bathtubs, water faucets and sinks, because metal pipes can transmit electricity.
- Close all windows.

IF OUTDOORS

- Attempt to get into a building or car.
- If no structure is available, get to an open space and squat low to the ground as quickly as possible. (If in the woods, find an area protected by a low clump of trees—never stand underneath a single large tree in the open.) Be aware of the potential for flooding in low-lying areas.
- Crouch with hands on knees.
- Avoid tall structures such as towers, tall trees, fences, telephone lines or power lines.
- Stay away from natural lightning rods such as golf clubs, tractors, fishing rods, bicycles or camping equipment.
- Stay away from rivers, lakes or other bodies of water. If on the water, get to land if possible.
- If you are isolated in a level field or prairie and you feel your hair stand on end (which indicates that lightning is about to strike), bend forward, putting your hands on your knees. A position with feet together and crouching while removing all metal objects is recommended. Do not lie flat on the ground.

IF IN A CAR

- Pull safely onto the shoulder of the road away from any trees that could fall on the vehicle.
- Stay in the car and turn on the emergency flashers until the heavy rains subside.
- Avoid flooded roadways.

    SOURCE: FEMA

When a Twister Is Approaching

Go to the lowest, innermost room in the building, and crawl under a table away from windows

Tornadoes are nature's most violent and erratic storms. In an average year, around 1,000 tornadoes are reported nationwide, according to the Storm Prediction Center in Norman, Oklahoma, 60 people die and 1,500 are injured as a result of twisters. The most violent of these storms are capable of reaching wind speeds of 250 m.p.h. or more, creating damage paths that can be over a mile wide and 50 miles long. Jennifer Stark, the warning coordination meteorologist for the National Weather Service in Topeka, Kan., in charge of severe weather programs, offers some tips on surviving a tornado:

Plan ahead, no matter where you live. You are at greatest risk for tornadoes if you live in the Midwest, particularly in the plains and the Mississippi Valley, but during the spring and summer, tornadoes have been spotted across the United States. The Northeast is least likely to be hit by tornadoes—Connecticut had 76 between 1953 and 2003, compared to Texas's 7,067. Alaska, with three recorded tornadoes in 50 years, and the District of Columbia, with two, have the fewest tornadoes. But tornadoes do hit major cities: several have occurred in large population centers such as Jacksonville, Fla.; Fort Worth, Tex.; Oklahoma City, Okla.; and Topeka, Kan.

Tornadoes can occur in the mountains, in cities, and over bodies of water.

Know the warning signs. Regardless of where you are, tornadoes rarely arrive unannounced. Before a tornado can develop, first there have to be thunderstorms in the area. There will be thunder, lightning and dark skies. Figure out ahead of time where you would seek shelter if a tornado occurs, and practice this emergency maneuver with your family on a sunny day. Keep a NOAA All Hazards radio plugged in or with fresh batteries. Take it with you if you are outdoors or traveling. This special receiver will be activated when severe weather watches or warnings are issued by the National Weather Service. You'll find stations between 162.400 and 162.550 on the dial. Since this band isn't available on most radios, know where the closest transmitter is, and tune in—this is particularly helpful if you are in a car, or have already sought shelter in a room where television is unavailable and you need a tornado update.

Understand the difference between tornado watches and tornado warnings. The Storm Pre-

diction Center issues tornado watches when the weather is favorable for the formation of severe thunderstorms that will be capable of producing deadly tornadoes. Tornado warnings are issued by the National Weather Service when forecasters have detected a tornado using Doppler radar or when a report of a tornado has been received. Tornadoes can occur without a watch or warning in effect.

Don't open your windows to equalize pressure in the house. This is one of the biggest myths of tornado preparation. Use that time to seek appropriate shelter in a sturdy building, on the lowest floor or innermost room, away from windows. Although houses cannot explode from pressure, the strong winds that accompany severe thunderstorms and tornadoes cause damage to buildings.

Get to the lowest floor of the building you're in. But don't get caught in an elevator trying to do it. If the building has no basement, find an interior room like a bathroom or closet. The pipes in the walls usually reinforce the building structure. Be sure to avoid windows—flying glass is a major cause of tornado injury.

Find a heavy table or workbench to get under. If you have no basement, go to an inside room on the lowest floor, like a closet, hallway or bathroom with no windows. If possible, cover your body with a blanket, sleeping bag or pillows to protect yourself from falling debris. Again, stay away from windows.

Escape to the east if you're in a car and have time. Tornadoes generally move from west to east. If the storm is over a mile away, and you know the area, drive away from it, heading east or south. As it nears, however, do not stay in your car, and do not seek shelter in highway underpasses. High-force winds can easily lift cars—even 18-

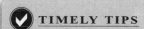

TIMELY TIPS

Disaster Info

Some useful Web sites for disaster information:

✔ **National Weather Service:** www.nws.noaa.gov

✔ **Federal Emergency Management Agency** (FEMA): www.fema.gov

✔ **Centers for Disease Control and Prevention:** www.cdc.gov

✔ **Red Cross:** www.redcross.org

✔ **American Medical Association:** www.ama-assn.org

Safety for Swimmers and Surfers

Lifeguards recommend swimming off sheltered beaches

Swimming is easiest out beyond the breakwaters and away from where the biggest sets of waves are breaking. If you are swimming along the shore, first eyeball how long-shore currents are flowing by watching floating debris or swimmers. Then, swim with the current to limit fatigue and frustration. Water safety experts offer these additional tips:

Body or board surfers get the longest rides on spilling breakers.

These waves commonly occur on relatively flat beaches and are characterized by foam and bubbles that spill down the front of the wave.

Plunging breakers, which are found on moderately steep beaches, can break with great force directly on top of an

unsuspecting surf swimmer. The crests of these waves curl over a pocket of air and result in splash-up. They are generally short-lived waves and as such not the best for surfing.

Surging breakers slide up and down the beach, creating few challenges for surf swimmers.

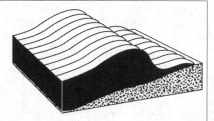

These waves occur on steep beaches and produce little or no bubbles.

Rip currents can endanger even the most experienced swimmer. Remember to swim parallel to the shore to escape the current or to allow it to carry you out to where its strength diminishes.

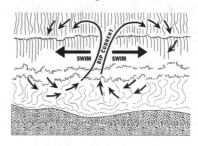

wheelers. The most dangerous place to be during a tornado is in a car. You could be injured by flying debris funneled beneath the bridge.

Find a gully, ditch or low spot on the ground if you are caught outside. Lie flat and put your arms over your head. If possible, cover yourself with a blanket or sweater. Culverts, the drainage pipes that run under roads, are good places to be if you're caught outside. If you are abandoning your vehicle, move a safe distance away from it. Boards and stones lofted at high speeds become quite dangerous. Flying pieces of glass and metal are like razors when they're caught by tornado winds. The winds are unimaginably strong, and

there are many stories of people who were picked up by tornadoes and carried several miles from where they were.

What to Do If You're Mugged

You up the odds of fending off an attacker when you have a plan

One out of three women in America will be attacked in her lifetime, according to the Department of Justice.

It's no wonder that women—and men, too—are anxious about walking to their cars in parking lots, going somewhere by themselves at night or

Basic Moves in Your Own Defense

There are two times when experts say you should fight back physically right away. One is if the attacker has rope or duct tape or another means of tying your hands and feet, which will probably make it impossible for you to escape. The other is if someone wants to take you somewhere else; chances of surviving are lower if you are moved to a second location. Rosalind Wiseman, author of *Defending Ourselves,* describes what moves to make to repel an attacker:

✔ **A FRONTAL ATTACK.** The palm strike has the power of a punch but reduces injury to your hand and fingers. The primary target is the nose, but you can hit the mouth, chin, throat, ear or Adam's apple. The proper hand position is shown at far left.

✔ **CLOSE QUARTERS.** You can use your knee if you are at a close distance to the attacker. The two main targets with the knee are the attacker's groin and his head.

✔ **ATTACKS FROM BEHIND.** If you are attacked from behind or the side, you need to break the attacker's hold and create space between you. When you are touched, immediately yell and round your shoulders to protect your lungs and sternum. Then, look for his closest foot and stomp on it.

even opening their front door at the end of the day. But no one wants to go through life being paranoid, and learning self-defense is a viable way to reach a balanced awareness.

The first step in self-defense is to figure out a plan, whether it is running to safety or delivering a crippling blow. Just as you have a fire escape plan in your house, you should have a plan for physical safety.

Women should be conscious of their body language when they are walking in public places. A confident stride, with eyes up and shoulders down, is preferable. Avoid carrying numerous bags or otherwise showing that you could not immediately fight back.

If a person stops you to ask for directions while you are walking, make sure you can see his feet in your peripheral vision. That means he's a safe distance away. If he asks you for help, volunteer to call the police rather than going anywhere with him.

Carrying Mace or pepper spray can be an effective defense tool, but only if you are both prepared to use it and have practiced. A can of Mace in your purse with a safety latch you've never tried isn't going to do you much good in an emergency.

If someone with a weapon demands your wallet, you should comply—throwing the wallet away from you at a 45-degree angle. When the attacker goes after it, run to safety. Go where other people are—to a neighbor, a store, a gas station, but be sure to think about your destination instead of running blindly. Without a plan, a woman robbed in a parking garage, for example, might run into a stairwell, setting herself up for a second attack.

If you are being followed, use verbal self-defense. State loudly and clearly what you want the person to do, such as, "Go away! Leave me alone!"

Fighting back should only be used as a last resort, but it can be a very powerful tool because it greatly reduces your chances of being raped or otherwise harmed.

If you are a woman fighting back, remember that your lower body is five times stronger than your upper body. When using self-defense techniques, aim for the attacker's eyes, nose, throat, groin, knees or feet. If it seems you can't defend yourself— If the attacker has a knife to your throat, for example—try to lull the assailant into thinking he has control. Convince him he's got you but needs to put down the knife. When he does, strike.

Walking Away From a Crash

An airplane crash survivor shares lessons she learned

Robin Fech was the only flight attendant aboard a 30-seat twin-engine Atlantic Southeast Airlines turboprop on August 21, 1995. That was the day it careened to the ground, crashed and burst into flames on a Georgia hayfield, killing 8 of the 27 people on board. The surviving passengers praised Fech's remarkable composure, crediting her ability to maintain calm and order as the reason they came out of the crash alive. Fech has thought a lot about her ordeal, and here she offers advice on safety measures to take before flying, during a troubled flight and in the aftermath of a crash.

Wear loose-fitting cotton clothing. Jogging pants may not be fashionable, but they allow you ease of movement and removal. And opt for natural fibers. "Synthetic materials are often highly flammable. People who are really concerned about crashing don't wear nail polish, hair spray or perfume, which

are also flammable," Fech explains. Fech would add tennis shoes to that list. In the crash, she spotted a man whose jeans were on fire, but she couldn't remove them because the soles of his shoes had melted and stuck to his feet. She herself was wearing panty hose, which melted on her legs.

Fech recommends comfortable, flat shoes that are easy to slip off, yet offer support to your feet if you need to climb, for example.

As you board a plane, look around. Touch the seats and count them until you reach yours. This helps you to feel your way out in case of darkness or smoke. Locate not only the exit nearest you, but alternates as well. "Our passenger door wouldn't open," Fech recalls, "but in our case, we didn't really need the exit, because the plane had split in half."

Pay close attention during the safety demonstration. "Frequent-flyers are the worst offenders," says Fech. "Some of the survivors on our flight later remembered that they were reading their books instead of paying attention to the safety demonstration." Fortunately, Fech had time to demonstrate the crash position before the plane hit the ground: lean forward, cross your arms on the seat in front of you and place your hands on your arms. If there's room in front of you, grab your ankles, put your chest on your thigh and your head between your knees. The intent is to lean forward as much as possible. Seat belts should be low and tight. Legs should be uncrossed and both feet should be flat on the floor.

Fech also asked passengers to empty their pockets; items there could cause injury upon impact. "Anything in your lap, like a computer, becomes a flying javelin," says Fech. Things like eyeglasses, pens and pencils, should be removed and put in the seat pocket.

Before It All Goes Up in Smoke
Simple precautions can prevent a major bonfire

Recent figures from the U.S. Fire Administration show that residential fires kill more than 3,000 Americans a year. Here are some tips from the U.S.F.A. and Federal Emergency Management Agency to make sure you're never trapped in a burning house, or if you are, how to cope:

Put smoke detectors on every floor of your house. Smoke detectors double your chances of living through a fire. They should be near bedrooms and away from air vents. To ensure that they're not shielded from smoke, keep them at least four to six inches away from walls and corners. Replace batteries at least once a year, at the same time perhaps as you're changing clocks for daylight saving time.

Ask your local fire department to inspect your house for fire safety. Often, local fire houses provide the service. They could help you identify faulty furnaces or stoves, chimneys with buildup and places where home insulation is touching electrical wiring—all potential fire-starters. They can also give you advice on choosing and using fire extinguishers.

Don't overlook basic fire hazards. Be wary of frayed or cracked wiring, and don't put wiring under rugs, over nails or in high traffic areas. Avoid overloading outlets—if you're not sure, check to make certain they're staying cool to the touch. Never fill kerosene heaters with gasoline or camp stove fuel. Plug electric space heaters directly into the wall socket, not into extension cords. For wood-stoves and fireplaces, use only seasoned wood, and always use a protective screen. Don't let old newspapers and magazines accumulate in storage areas.

Plan your escape before the emergency. If you have children, teach them two escape routes from every room. Keep emergency numbers, a whistle, and a flashlight near the phone. Sleeping with doors closed helps delay the spread of fire. If you hear the alarm, feel your door. If it's cool, open it to exit, but crawl to avoid the smoke that rises. Cover your nose and mouth with a moist cloth. Stop, drop and roll if your clothes are on fire—teach it to your kids. Use the stairs, never an elevator during a fire.

If you are trapped. Call the fire department for assistance. If you cannot get to a phone, yell for help out the window. Wave or hang a sheet or other large object to attract attention. Close as many doors as possible between yourself and the fire. Seal your door with rags. Open windows slightly at the top and bottom, but close them if smoke comes in.

If Confronted by a Bear
First decide if he's predatory or defensive

Common wisdom holds that the way to react to a bear, when all else fails, is simple: curl up in a ball and play dead. But that is not always the best idea. Attacks can generally be divided into two groups: predatory and defensive. Each calls for a different strategy.

Black and grizzly bears are capable of both types of attack. Those involving grizzlies tend to be defensive, when the animal feels threatened, according to Stephen Herrero, a bear expert at the University of Calgary and the author of *Bear Attacks: Their Causes and Avoidance.* Playing dead then lets the bear know you're not a threat and can cause it to back off.

Black bears usually flee from humans, but when they do attack, the motive tends to be predatory, and playing dead doesn't work. Neither does running away, since bears are much faster than humans.

Lions and Tigers and Rhinos, Oh My

If you face a wild beast someday, some beast-by-beast advice:

LION: Lions will usually not attack people unless they do not have anything else to eat.

Nevertheless, make sure that you are not alone in an area inhabited by lions.

TIGER: Tigers will usually not attack unless they are able to sneak up on you or you have your back turned. In Nepal, for instance, natives wear a mask with eyes in the back to scare them off. If you do encounter a tiger, act aggressively. Hopefully, this is enough to make the largest predator in the world flee.

RHINO: Rhinos have bad eyesight and only attack if panicked. If you encounter a rhino, make sure that you give it plenty of distance.

GORILLA: When a gorilla attacks you, kneel down and don't look it in the eye.

If the bear is after food, it is best to drop it and back away, Herrero says. If the animal presses, he adds, be aggressive: shout, bang on objects or use pepper spray to scare it off. The National Parks Service and the National Wildlife Federation recommend similar measures.

—Anahad O'Connor

A Post-9/11 Survival Kit

What to do if there is a biological or chemical attack

Ever since the 9/11 terrorist attacks on New York and Washington, D.C., there's been a heightened level of concern about potential future terrorist activities—including biological and chemical attacks. Here are some basic information and advice:

PREPARING FOR A BIOLOGICAL ATTACK

Biological agents are organisms or toxins that can kill or incapacitate people, livestock and crops. The three basic groups of biological agents that would likely be used as weapons are bacteria, viruses and toxins. Most biological agents are difficult to grow and maintain. Many break down quickly when exposed to sunlight and other environmental factors, while others, such as anthrax spores, are very long lived. Biological agents can be dispersed by spraying them into the air, by infecting animals that carry the disease to humans and by contaminating food and water.

Specific information on biological agents is available at the Centers for Disease Control and Prevention's Web site, www.bt.cdc.gov.

Before a Biological Attack: The following are guidelines for what you should do to prepare for a biological threat:

• Check with your doctor to ensure all required or suggested immunizations are up to date. Children and older adults are particularly vulnerable to biological agents.

• Consider installing a High Efficiency Particulate Air (HEPA) filter in your furnace return duct. These filters remove particles in the 0.3-to-10-micron range and will filter out most biological agents that may enter your house. HEPA filters will not filter chemical agents. If you do not have a central heating or cooling system, a stand-alone

portable HEPA filter can be used.

During a Biological Attack: In the event of a biological attack, public health officials may not immediately be able to provide information on what you should do. Watch television, listen to radio or check the Internet for official news and information including signs and symptoms of the disease, areas in danger, if medications or vaccinations are being distributed and where you should seek medical attention if you become ill.

The first evidence of an attack may be when you notice symptoms of the disease caused by exposure to an agent. Be suspicious of any symptoms you notice, but do not assume that any illness is a result of the attack.

If you are exposed to a biological agent:

- Remove and bag your clothes and personal items. Follow official instructions for disposal of contaminated items.

- Wash yourself with soap and water and put on clean clothes.

- Seek medical assistance. You may be advised to stay away from others or even quarantined.

FACING A CHEMICAL ATTACK

The following are guidelines for what you should do to prepare for a chemical threat:

- Check your disaster supplies kit to make sure it includes a roll of duct tape and scissors and plastic for doors, windows and vents for the room in which you will shelter in place. To save critical time during an emergency, premeasure and cut the plastic sheeting for each opening.

- Choose an internal room to shelter, preferably one without windows and on the highest level. Turn off all ventilation, including furnaces, air-conditioners, vents and fans. Seal the room with duct tape and plastic sheeting.

- Listen to a radio for instructions from authorities.

- If you are caught in or near a contaminated area, you should move away immediately in a direction upwind of the source. Find shelter as quickly as possible.

After a Chemical Attack: Decontamination is needed within minutes of exposure to minimize health consequences. Do not leave the safety of a shelter to go outdoors to help others until authorities announce it is safe to do so.

A person affected by a chemical agent requires immediate medical attention from a professional. If medical help is not immediately available, decontaminate yourself and assist in decontaminating others. Decontamination guidelines are as follows:

- Use extreme caution when helping others who have been exposed to chemical agents.

- Remove all clothing and other items in contact with the body. Contaminated clothing normally removed over the head should be cut off to avoid contact with the eyes, nose and mouth. Put contaminated clothing and items into a plastic bag and seal it. Remove eyeglasses or contact lenses. Put glasses in a pan of household bleach to decontaminate them, and then rinse and dry.

- Flush eyes with water. Gently wash face and hair with soap and water before thoroughly rinsing with water.

- Decontaminate other body areas. Blot (do not swab or scrape) with a cloth soaked in soapy water and rinse with clear water, then change into uncontaminated clothes. Clothing stored in drawers or closets is likely to be uncontaminated.

- Proceed to a medical facility for screening and professional treatment.

SOURCES: Centers for Disease Control and Prevention; Federal Emergency Management Agency

CHAPTER **2**

FOOD & DRINK

Diet & Nutrition   **114**

NUTRITION·114: *Are you what you eat?* • *U.S.D.A. food guide* • *Calorie requirements*   **FAT·117:** *The lowdown on low-fat diets* • *The skinny on fat* • *Fat attack*   **VITAMINS·118:** *The home vitamin shelf* • *Don't like the newest diet?* • *More may be too many*   **MINERALS·123:** *The mineral minder* • *Questions about calcium*   **PORTIONS·125:** *The food label at a glance* **HEALTHY EATING·127:** *How fish can help your heart* • *Why olive oil is good for you* • *The almighty yogurt*

In the Kitchen   **130**

RECIPES & UTENSILS·130: *How to evaluate a recipe* • *A barebones kitchen* • *Casting call for pots and pans* • *The sticky issues of Teflon*   **FRESH PRODUCE·133:** *Ripe for the picking* • *Hurry up and ripen* • *Some really delicious apples* • *Where the pesticides are*   **INGREDIENTS·136:** *Think globally, but eat locally* • *How green is your kitchen?*   **BASICS·138:** *Cooking by the book* • *How to carve a turkey* • *How to clean a fish* • *The catch of the day* • *How to grill a fish* • *And now, the perfect sauce*   **GOURMET DINING·143:** *Nigella's midweek dinner* • *The children's menu* • *The many nuances of chocolate* • *Cooking schools* • *How to eat well and stay thin* • *Meeting the Cordon Bleu test*

Wine, etc.   **148**

WINES·148: *Starting a wine collection* • *A worldwide sampler* • *Savoring a good wine* • *Wine by the book* • *Ranking the French élite* • *Matches made in heaven* • *Champagne on the cheap*   **BEERS·157:** *Beyond the basic six-pack*   **SPIRITS·159:** *Mixology 101: Classic cocktails* • *Stocking the liquor cabinet* • *Whisky-sipping secrets* • *Not just any old mint julep* • **COFFEE & TEA·163:** *The perfect cup of espresso* • *A world tour of teas*

FOOD

Diet & Nutrition

You Are What You Eat...or Are You?

The bottom line on healthy eating

Eat this. Avoid that. Take dietary supplements. On second thought, don't. Every week there is another medical study that either touts the benefits of a particular diet or vitamin, or dashes the hopes that some previously favored nutrient can ward off disease and keep you in the pink.

Enthusiasm for the benefits (or drawbacks) of one nutrient or another is not exactly a recent phenomenon. "It's one of the great principles—no, canons—of American culture that what you eat affects your health," says James Morone, a professor of political science at Brown University. "It's this idea that you control your own destiny and that it's never too late to reinvent yourself," he says. "Vice gets punished and virtue gets rewarded. If you eat or drink or inhale the wrong things you get sick. If not, you get healthy."

For decades, many scientists have said, and many members of the public have believed, that what people eat—the composition of the diet—determines how likely they are to get a chronic disease. But that has been hard to prove. Studies of dietary fiber and colon cancer have failed to find that fiber was protective, and studies of vitamins thought to protect against cancer have failed to show an effect. Many cancer researchers have ques-

tioned large parts of the diet-cancer hypothesis, but it has kept a hold on the public imagination.

Two reports—one about low-fat diets and another about calcium (see stories following)—from a huge federal study called the Women's Health Initiative, which were released in February 2006, suggest the possibility that cutting back on fat might not prevent breast cancer, colon cancer or heart disease after all. The calcium report suggests that taking calcium supplements also might not make much of a difference in a woman's health. Recently, the benefits of supplementary doses of vitamin E and C have also been questioned, and supplementation with high doses of vitamin A is now considered inadvisable as well. (See story on page 122).

Barbara V. Howard, an epidemiologist at MedStar Research Institute, a nonprofit hospital group, and a principle investigator in the Women's Health Initiative study, says that people should realize that diet alone is not enough to stay healthy. Many other factors come into play as well. "We are not going to reverse any of the chronic diseases in this country by changing the composition of the diet," Howard says. "People are always thinking it's what they ate. They are not looking at how much they ate or that they smoke or that they are sedentary." Except for not smoking, the advice for a healthy lifestyle is based largely on indirect evidence, Howard says,

> **For folks who are on a low-fat diet, by all means continue. If you're on a high-fat diet, certainly get it down. That's the message we would like to send.**
>
> Dr. Jacques Rossouw, project officer for the Women's Health Initiative

● ● ●

U.S.D.A. FOOD GUIDE

FOOD GROUPS SUBGROUPS	U.S.D.A. Food Guide Amount [b]	Equivalent Amounts [a]
FRUIT GROUP	**2 cups (4 servings)**	½ cup equivalent is: ½ cup fresh, frozen or canned fruit 1 medium fruit ¼ cup dried fruit, ½ cup fruit juice
VEGETABLE GROUP DARK GREEN VEGETABLES ORANGE VEGETABLES LEGUMES (DRY BEANS) STARCHY VEGETABLES OTHER VEGETABLES	**2.5 cups (5 servings)** 3 CUPS/WEEK 2 CUPS/WEEK 3 CUPS/WEEK 3 CUPS/WEEK 6.5 CUPS/WEEK	½ cup equivalent is: ½ cup of cut-up raw or cooked vegetable 1 cup raw leafy vegetable ½ cup vegetable juice
GRAIN GROUP WHOLE GRAINS OTHER GRAINS	**6 ounce-equivalents** 3 OZ-EQUIVALENTS 3 OZ-EQUIVALENTS	1 ounce-equivalent is: 1 slice bread, 1 cup dry cereal ½ cup cooked rice, pasta, cereal
MEAT AND BEANS GROUP	**5.5 ounce-equivalents**	1 ounce-equivalent is: 1 oz of cooked lean meats, poultry, fish 1 egg ¼ cup cooked dry beans or tofu 1 Tbsp peanut butter, ½ oz nuts or seeds
MILK GROUP	**3 cups**	1 cup equivalent is: 1 cup low-fat/fat-free milk, yogurt 1½ oz of low-fat or fat-free natural cheese 2 oz of low-fat or fat-free processed cheese
OILS	**27 grams (6 tsp)**	1 tsp equivalent is: 1 Tbsp low-fat mayo 2 Tbsp light salad dressing 1 tsp vegetable oil
DISCRETIONARY CALORIE ALLOWANCE Example of distribution SOLID FAT [c] ADDED SUGARS	**267 calories** 18 GRAMS 8 TSP	1 Tbsp added sugar equivalent is: ½ oz jelly beans 8 oz lemonade

a All servings are per day unless otherwise noted. U.S.D.A. vegetable subgroup amounts are per week.

b The 2,000-calorie U.S.D.A. Food Guide is appropriate for many sedentary males 51 to 70 years of age, sedentary females 19 to 30 years of age, and for some other gender/age groups who are more physically active. See "Caloric Requirements" table on the next page for information about gender/age/activity levels and appropriate calorie intakes.

c The oils listed in this table are not considered to be part of discretionary calories because they are a major source of the vitamin E and polyunsaturated fatty acids, including the essential fatty acids, in the food pattern. In contrast, solid fats (i.e., saturated and trans fats) are listed separately as a source of discretionary calories.

FOOD

CALORIE REQUIREMENTS

These are estimated amounts of calories needed to maintain energy balance for various gender and age groups at three different levels of physical activity. If you exercise more, you are able to consume more calories. [a]

GENDER	ACTIVITY LEVEL [b,c,d]		
Age (years)	Sedentary [b]	Moderately Active [c]	Active [d]
CHILD			
2-3	1,000	1,000-1,400[e]	1,000-1,400[e]
FEMALE			
4-8	1,200	1,400-1,600	1,400-1,800
9-13	1,600	1,600-2,000	1,800-2,200
14-18	1,800	2,000	2,400
19-30	2,000	2,000-2,200	2,400
31-50	1,800	2,000	2,200
51+	1,600	1,800	2,000-2,200
MALE			
4-8	1,400	1,400-1,600	1,600-2,000
9-13	1,800	1,800-2,200	2,000-2,600
14-18	2,200	2,400-2,800	2,800-3,200
19-30	2,400	2,600-2,800	3,000
31-50	2,200	2,400-2,600	2,800-3,000
51+	2,000	2,200-2,400	2,400-2,800

a These levels are based on Estimated Energy Requirements from the Institute of Medicine (I.O.M.) Dietary Reference Intakes macronutrients report, 2002, calculated by gender, age and activity level for reference-sized individuals. "Reference size," as determined by I.O.M., is based on median height and weight for ages up to age 18 years of age and median height and weight for that height to give a body mass index (BMI) of 21.5 for adult females and 22.5 for adult males.

b Sedentary means a lifestyle that includes only the light physical activity associated with typical day-to-day life.

c Moderately active means a lifestyle that includes physical activity equivalent to walking about 1.5 to 3 miles per day at 3 to 4 miles per hour, in addition to the light physical activity associated with typical day-to-day life.

d Active means a lifestyle that includes physical activity equivalent to walking more than 3 miles per day at 3 to 4 miles per hour, in addition to the light physical activity associated with typical day-to-day life.

e The calorie ranges shown are to accommodate needs of different ages within the group. For children and adolescents, more calories are needed at older ages. For adults, fewer calories are needed at older ages.

SOURCE: U.S.D.A.

but most medical researchers agree that it makes sense to eat well, control weight and get regular exercise. Others caution against being too certain that a particular diet will markedly improve health, and say that whether someone developed a chronic disease might not be entirely under their control—genetics also plays a role.

So, while there are no guarantees about what ensures good health, we have perhaps learned a few things from these multiyear studies and research data. The first is that confidence in the overuse of supplements as either a means of replacing deficiencies in one's diet or warding off disease may be misplaced, or even woefully misguided.

The second is that there is a fair amount of agreement that a balanced and nutritious diet that emphasizes mostly fruits, vegetables and whole grains may help reduce the risk of obesity, a disease that is reaching epidemic proportions in the United States, bringing with it an array of serious secondary diseases, such as hypertension, coronary heart disease, stroke, sleep apnea and other respiratory problems.

Another point of agreement among dietary experts is that Americans have to wean themselves from a dependence on packaged foods, which are often too high in salts, sugars, fats and calories, and overfortified with unnecessary vitamins, while deficient in other valuable nutrients.

One study found that most people think that they eat a more nutritious diet than they really do, and that their intake of fruits, vegetables and whole grains does not begin to meet the guidelines laid out in the most recent U.S.D.A. food pyramid. (See U.S.D.A. Food Guide of recommended food groups at the 2,000 calorie level, the average recommended calorie intake for all age groups on preceding page.)

FOOD

The Skinny on Fat

A primer on fats and trans fats

How much and what kind of fats should you eat? The U.S.D.A. recommends that you limit excess calories, saturated fat, trans fat and dietary cholesterol.

- **Saturated fat** intake should be 7 to 10 percent of calories (or even less).

- **Polyunsaturated fat** intake should be up to 10 percent of calories.

- **Monounsaturated fat** can make up to 15 percent of total calories.

- **Cholesterol** intake should be less than 300 milligrams per day. Dietary cholesterol raises LDL cholesterol levels in the blood.

- **Total fat** intake should be adjusted to caloric needs. Overweight people should consume no more than 30 percent of total calories from fat.

SATURATED FAT INTAKE

The U.S.D.A.'s chart shows you the maximum gram amounts of saturated fat that you should consume to keep your saturated fat intake below 10 percent of total calorie intake recommended for selected calorie levels. A 2,000-calorie example is included so that you can compare it with the amounts shown on food labels, which are based on a 2,000-calorie diet.

1,600	18 g or less
2,000	20 g or less
2,200	24 g or less
2,500	25 g or less
2,800	31 g or less

TRANS-FATTY ACIDS

Trans-fatty acids are formed by the process of hydrogenating vegetable fats. They can be found in shortenings, stick (or hard) margarine, cookies, crackers, snack foods, fried foods, doughnuts, pastries, baked goods and other processed foods made with or fried in partially hydrogenated oils. Consumption of transfat raises LDL cholesterol levels and lowers HDL cholesterol levels, increasing the risk of heart disease and stroke. The U.S.D.A. lists these foods in order of highest to lowest in trans fats.

Cake, cookies, pie, bread, etc.	40
Animal products	21
Margarine	17
Fried potatoes	8
Potato, corn chips, popcorn	5
Household shortening	4
Breakfast cereal, candy, etc.	5

The Lowdown on Low-Fat Diets

A large study says that fat intake does not affect your risk of getting cancer or heart disease

After years of being admonished to cut down on fat intake by nearly every medical professional, the confusion grows for all of us who are trying to eat what is good for us. A study by the Women's Health Initiative, published in the *Journal of the American Medical Association* in February 2006, has provided rigorous evidence that a low-fat diet is not protective against breast cancer or colorectal cancer. The study found that women who were randomly assigned to follow a low-fat diet ate significantly less fat over the next eight years. But they had just as much breast and colon cancer and just as much heart disease. The women were not trying to lose weight, and their weights remained fairly steady. But their experiences with the diets allowed researchers to question some popular notions about diet and obesity.

There is a common belief that Americans get fat because they eat too many carbohydrates. The idea is that a high-carbohydrate, low-fat diet leads to weight gain, higher insulin and blood glucose levels, and more diabetes, even if the calories are the same as in a higher-fat diet.. Others have said the opposite: that low-fat diets enable people to lose weight naturally. But that belief was not supported by this study. As for heart disease risk factors, the only one affected was

LDL cholesterol, which increases heart disease risk. The levels were slightly higher in women eating the higher-fat diet, but not high enough to make a noticeable difference in their risk of heart disease.

Although all the study participants were women, the colon cancer and heart disease results should also apply to men. Critics of the study now say that it was flawed, since it focused on total fat in the diet, rather than on saturated fat, which raises cholesterol levels. Others say that the study made a mistake in aiming for a diet allowing 20 percent of calories as fat. Dietary fat should be even lower, they say, as low as 10 percent. Many medical researchers say that the best dietary advice, for now, is to follow federal guidelines for healthy eating, with less saturated and trans fats, more grains, and more fruits and vegetables.

Some, like Dr. Dean Ornish, a longtime promoter of low-fat diets, said that the women did not reduce their fat to low enough levels or eat enough fruits and vegetables, and that the study, even at eight years, did not give the diets enough time. Others said that diet could still make a difference, at least with heart disease, if people were to eat the so-called Mediterranean diet, low in saturated fats like butter and high in oils like olive oil. The women in the study reduced all kinds of fat. But the Mediterranean diet has not been subjected to a study of this scope, researchers say.

—Gina Kolata

FAT ATTACK

Saturated fat slows down the elimination of cholesterol in your bloodstream, and that can lead to heart disease. Here are some household oils listed by saturated fat content per single tablespoon serving.

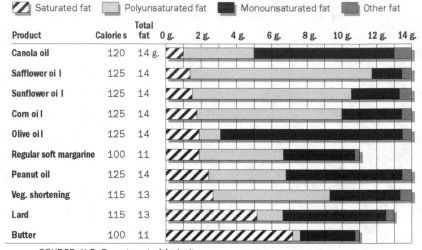

Legend: Saturated fat | Polyunsaturated fat | Monounsaturated fat | Other fat

Product	Calories	Total fat
Canola oil	120	14 g.
Safflower oil	125	14
Sunflower oil	125	14
Corn oil	125	14
Olive oil	125	14
Regular soft margarine	100	11
Peanut oil	125	14
Veg. shortening	115	13
Lard	115	13
Butter	100	11

SOURCE: U.S. Department of Agriculture

The Home Vitamin Shelf
Where to find the most needed vitamins

Your body needs vitamins to form blood cells, build strong bones and regulate the nervous system, but it can't generate most of them on its own. Ideally, all vitamins should be derived from food, not supplements, though that is not always possible. Some limited supplementation is recommended for particular populations, as noted below.

VITAMIN A

DAILY VALUE:	700 micrograms RAE (retinol activity equivalents)
1 scrambled egg:	118 mcg
1 cup nonfat milk:	149 mcg
1 nectarine:	50 mcg
1 piece of watermelon:	27 mcg

WHAT IT DOES: Aids in good vision; helps build and maintain skin, teeth, bones and mucous membranes.

Don't Like the Newest Diet? Wait a While

*G*ood health depends on a good diet. But
which good diet? Experts and pretenders
*have offered countless schemes for salubrity,
from the cabbage regime propounded by Cato
the Elder to the chopped-meat-and-water plan
of the 19th-century physician John Salisbury
(whose name lives on via the Salisbury steak).
Formal theorizing began in the second century,
when Galen codified nutrition as a matter of correctly balanced humors. By the first millennium,
the Byzantine Dietary Calendar advised sipping
aromatic wine in January to avert the dangers of
sweet phlegm. In his book* Terrors of the Table:
The Curious History of Nutrition, *Walter Gratzer,
a biophysicist at King's College, London, says
that today, fear of cholesterol has "supplanted
the Devil as the roaring lion who walketh about,
seeking whom he may devour." The moral of the
story, so far: To eat is basic instinct; how to do it
correctly worries humans more than sex.*

—Jane and Michael Stern

Here's a very short history of diet discoveries
and fads, past and present:

Scurvy was once attributed to everything from
damp sea air to an excess of black bile. The true
cause—lack of ascorbic acid, found in some

fruit juices—was not
widely accepted until
the late 19th century.
In the mid-1800's,
Rose's Lime Juice was
considered a remedy
for scurvy. The version
sold to sailors (called
"limeys" by their
American counterparts)
was spiked with rum
as a preservative.

Sylvester Graham, an 18th-
century Boston clergyman,
argued that chemistry could not
explain the relationship between
health and diet. Long life and
good health, he said, could be
guaranteed by eating bread baked from whole,
unsieved flour. Dubbed "Dr. Sawdust" by skeptics,
Graham's legacy lives on today through Graham
flour and the ubiquitous Graham cracker (now
made with refined wheat flour).

Dr. John Harvey Kellogg
touted a diet based on vegetari-
anism and roughage, ideally
conveyed via "Granula," his
own dried-bean-and-bread bis-
cuits. In 1894, during a milling
experiment gone awry, Kellogg stumbled upon the
corn flake, which gave birth to a cereal empire—
and the modern American breakfast.

Horace Fletcher was an American businessman dogged by ill
health. In 1898, a friend passed
along the wisdom (credited to British Prime Minister William Glad-
stone) that you should chew your
food 32 times, once for each tooth.
Soon he was a star on the lecture circuit, where he
claimed his chew-cure could remedy everything from
anemia and appendicitis to alcoholism and insanity.
Henry James called him "the divine Fletcher"; the less
enchanted dubbed him "the Great Masticator."

In more recent years, nutrition seekers have tried
everything from raw-food diets to radical "breath-
arianism" (the idea that man can live on air alone).
Some have tried more medically based regimens,
such as the Duke University rice diet, the South
Beach Diet and the carbophobic nostrums of Dr.
Atkins. While many scientists are skeptical about
Atkins' ideas, some 30 to 40 million people have
tried the Atkins diet since it was introduced in 1972.

FOOD

Promotes growth and helps keep lining of mouth, nose, throat and digestive tract healthy and resistant to infection. Deficiency can increase susceptibility to infectious disease.

WHAT IT MAY DO: May increase resistance to infection. Excessive supplementation may also cause osteoporosis and increase risk of cancer.

FOOD SOURCES: Milk, eggs, liver, cheese, fish oil. Plus fruits and vegetables that contain beta carotene. You need not consume preformed vitamin A if you eat foods rich in beta carotene.

SUPPLEMENTATION: Not recommended, since toxic in high doses.

VITAMIN B₁ (THIAMIN)

DAILY VALUE:	1.1 milligrams
1 slice enriched white bread:	0.10 mg
3 oz. fried liver:	0.17 mg
1 cup black beans:	0.42 mg
½ cup dry-hull sunflower seeds:	1.65 mg

WHAT IT DOES: Helps convert carbohydrates into energy. Necessary for healthy brain, nerve cells and heart function. Promotes good appetite and digestion.

FOOD SOURCES: Whole grains, enriched grain products, beans, meats, liver, wheat germ, nuts, fish, brewer's yeast.

SUPPLEMENTATION: Not necessary, not recommended.

VITAMIN B₂ (RIBOFLAVIN)

DAILY VALUE:	1.1 milligrams
3 oz. chicken:	0.10 mg
1 bagel:	0.33 mg
1 cup whole milk:	0.4 mg
1 cup cooked spinach:	0.42 mg

WHAT IT DOES: Helps cells use oxygen to release energy from food. Essential for growth, production of red blood cells, and health of skin and eyes.

FOOD SOURCES: Dairy products, liver, meat, chicken, fish, enriched grain products, leafy greens, beans, nuts, eggs and almonds.

SUPPLEMENTATION: Not necessary nor recommended.

VITAMIN B₃ (NIACIN)

DAILY VALUE:	14 milligrams
1 slice bread:	1.0 mg
3 oz. wild atlantic salmon:	8.6 mg
1 oz. dry roasted peanuts:	3.8 mg
½ chicken breast, roasted:	12.5 mg

WHAT IT DOES: Aids in release of energy from foods. Maintains health of skin, tongue, digestive tract and nervous system.

WHAT IT MAY DO: Helps lower blood cholesterol.

FOOD SOURCES: Nuts, meat, fish, chicken, liver, enriched grain products, dairy products, peanut butter, brewer's yeast.

SUPPLEMENTATION: Large doses may be prescribed by doctor to lower blood cholesterol. May cause flushing and gastrointestinal distress.

VITAMIN B₅ (PANTOTHENIC ACID)

DAILY VALUE:	5 milligrams
8 oz. nonfat milk:	0.81 mg
1 large egg:	0.63 mg
8 oz. low-fat fruit-flavored yoghurt:	1.23 mg
3 oz. liver:	3.88 mg

WHAT IT DOES: Necessary for metabolism of fat and helps in the formation of cholesterol and hormones.

FOOD SOURCES: Whole grains, egg yolk, milk, liver.

SUPPLEMENTATION: Not necessary, not recommended. May cause diarrhea.

VITAMIN B₆ (PYROXIDINE)

DAILY VALUE:	1.3 milligrams
1 oat bran muffin:	0.22 mg
1 cup lima beans:	0.14 mg
3 oz. cooked bluefin tuna:	0.45 mg
1 banana:	0.68 mg

WHAT IT DOES: Assists in the metabolism of proteins, carbohydrates and fats. Helps to maintain the health of the skin and red blood cells.

WHAT IT MAY DO: May help to boost immunity in the elderly.

FOOD SOURCES: Whole grains, bananas, lean meats, beans, nuts, wheat germ, brewer's yeast, chicken, fish, liver.

SUPPLEMENTATION: Large doses can cause numbness and other neurological disorders.

VITAMIN B₁₂

DAILY VALUE:	2.4 micrograms
1/2 chicken breast:	0.29 mcg
1 large egg:	0.50 mcg
1 cup nonfat milk:	0.93 mcg
3 oz. lean braised beef flank:	2.81 mcg

WHAT IT DOES: Necessary in the development of normal growth and helps body produce normal red blood cells. Protects against pernicious anemia.

FOOD SOURCES: Liver, beef, pork, poultry, eggs, milk, cheese, yogurt, shellfish, fortified cereals and fortified soy products.

SUPPLEMENTATION: Not usually necessary, but people who are on strict vegetarian diets may need supplementation. Also, some elderly people may be deficient in the vitamin because they lose their ability to absorb it from foods.

VITAMIN C (ASCORBIC ACID)

DAILY VALUE:	75 milligrams
1 orange:	70 mg
1 green pepper (1/2 cup):	56 mg
1 cup raw broccoli:	82 mg
8 oz. tomato juice:	44 mg

WHAT IT DOES: Strengthens blood vessels and hastens healing of wounds and bones. Increases resistance to infections and helps body absorb iron in the diet.

WHAT IT MAY DO: May reduce the risk of lung, esophagus, stomach and bladder cancers, as well as coronary artery disease; may prevent or delay cataracts and slow the aging process.

FOOD SOURCES: Citrus fruits and juices, strawberries, tomatoes, peppers, broccoli, potatoes, kale, cabbage, cauliflower, cantaloupe, brussels sprouts.

SUPPLEMENTATION: 250 to 500 mgs a day for smokers. Larger doses may cause diarrhea.

VITAMIN D

DAILY VALUE:	200 IUs (international units) or .005 milligrams or 5 micrograms
1 oz. Cheddar cheese:	3 IUs or .000075 mg or 0.75 mcg
1 large egg:	27 IUs or .000675 mg or .675 mcg
1 cup nonfat milk:	100 IUs or .0025 mg or 2.5 mcg

WHAT IT DOES: Strengthens bones and teeth by aiding the absorption of calcium. Helps maintain phosphorus in the blood.

WHAT IT MAY DO: May reduce risk of osteoporosis, forestall breast and colon cancers.

FOOD SOURCES: Milk, fish oil, fortified margarine; also produced by exposure to sunlight.

SUPPLEMENTATION: May be necessary for vegetarians, the elderly, those who don't drink milk or get sun exposure. Toxic in high doses.

VITAMIN E

DAILY VALUE:	15 mg ATE (alpha tocopherol equivalent)
1/2 cup boiled brussel sprouts:	0.7 mg
1 cup boiled spinach:	1.7 mg
1 oz. almonds:	7.5 mg

WHAT IT DOES: Active in maintaining the involuntary nervous system, vascular system and involuntary muscles.

WHAT IT MAY DO: May reduce the risk of esophageal or stomach cancers; may prevent or delay cataracts; may boost immunity in the elderly.

FOOD SOURCES: Vegetable oil, nuts, margarine, wheat germ, leafy greens, seeds, almonds, olives and asparagus.

SUPPLEMENTATION: Not recommended.

FOOD

BIOTIN (VITAMIN B)

DAILY VALUE: *30 micrograms*
  1 cup cooked enriched noodles: 4 mcg
  1 large egg: 11 mcg
  1 oz. almonds: 24 mcg

WHAT IT DOES: Important in breakdown of protein, carbohydrates and fats in the body.

FOOD SOURCES: Egg yolk, milk, liver, kidneys, vegetables and fruits (especially bananas, grapefruits, watermelon and strawberries).

SUPPLEMENTATION: Not recommended.

FOLATE (VITAMIN B)
(Also called folacin or folic acid)

DAILY VALUE: *400 micrograms*
  1 navel orange: 47.6 mcg
  1 cup raw spinach: 102.6 mcg
  1 cup homemade baked beans: 121.4 mcg
  $1/2$ cup asparagus, boiled: 131.4 mcg

WHAT IT DOES: Aids in the biochemical reactions of cells in the production of energy. Helps body produce normal red blood cells and reduces the risk of neural tube birth defects in newborns.

WHAT IT MAY DO: May reduce the risk of breast, colon and pancreatic cancer. May be of help to those with high levels of homocysteine in their blood, which may be associated with increased risks of heart disease.

FOOD SOURCES: Leafy greens, wheat germ, liver, beans, whole grains, broccoli, asparagus, citrus fruit juices and enriched flour.

SUPPLEMENTATION: 400 mcg, for all women who may become pregnant, to help prevent birth defects, in addition to the recommended amount of what they should normally consume in a balanced diet. Pregnant women should take a 600 mg supplement.

SOURCES: United States Department of Agriculture—Food and Nutrition; Institute of Medicine; *Bowes and Church's Food Values of Portions Commonly Used*, eighteenth edition, by Jean A. T. Pennington and Judith Spungen Douglass, 2004.

Vitamins: More May Be Too Many

There is usually danger in too many, not too few supplements

As much as 70 percent of the population in America is taking supplements, mostly vitamins, convinced that the pills will make them healthier. But, in fact, some of the vitamins, especially in high doses, may cause serious harm.

"There has been a transition from focusing on minimum needs to the reality that today our problem is excess—excess calories and, yes, excesses of vitamins and minerals as well," says Dr. Benjamin Caballero, a member of the Food and Nutrition Board at the National Academy of Sciences and the director of the Center for Human Nutrition at Johns Hopkins University.

The beneficial aspects of supplements such as vitamins A, C and E, which in earlier studies had shown promise of having a preventive effect

? EXPERT ANSWER

Vitamins Do Not Replace Food

Q. **Are vitamin supplements as effective as vitamins in food?**

If you eat junk food every day, vitamins (in supplement form) are the least of your problems. You cannot replace a healthy diet. We don't know what ingredient in a healthy diet is responsible for which condition. We do know that people who consume five servings or more of fruits and vegetables have less disease. But we don't know which ingredient. We tried beta carotene, vitamin E and antioxidants, and they didn't work. People are looking for the magic bullet. It does not exist.

— Dr. Benjamin Caballero

against cancer and heart disease, have since been discounted; warnings about excess consumption through supplementation and an overenriched diet are now being issued.

With vitamin A in particular, it is easy to step over the edge into a danger zone, says Dr. Joan McGowan, chief of the musculoskeletal diseases branch at the National Institute of Arthritis and Musculoskeletal and Skin Diseases. You can be eating Total cereal, drinking fortified milk, taking a multivitamin. You can get into a situation where you're getting more than you need. Now, she adds, "we may have to rethink the issues." Several recent large studies indicate that people with high levels of vitamin A in their blood have a greater risk for osteoporosis. Two large randomized trials of vitamin A and beta carotene that researchers hoped would show a protective value against cancer found no benefit, and one found that participants who took the supplements had more cancer. Another study, of women with heart disease, found that antioxidant vitamins might actually increase the rate of atherosclerosis.

Similar questions are being raised about other vitamins and minerals, notably iron and vitamins E and C, which are the most popular individual supplements, says Dr. Robert M. Russell, director the Human Nutrition Research Center on Aging at Tufts University, who is head of the Food and Nutrition Board at the National Academy of Sciences. Scientists once thought those vitamins could help prevent ailments like cancer and heart disease, but rigorous studies found no such effects. Vitamin E supplements can increase the risk of heart attacks and strokes, and studies of vitamin C supplements consistently failed to show that it had any beneficial effects. A large study of vitamin E and heart disease found that it did not prevent heart attacks and that people taking it had more strokes. "The two vitamins that are the most not needed are

the ones most often taken," Dr. Russell says.

Excess vitamin C is excreted in the urine, but excesses of some other vitamins are stored in fat, where they can build up. Others warn about overdosing on other vitamins and minerals. Dr. Richard J. Wood, director of the mineral bioavailability laboratory at Tufts, also worries about iron overload, which can increase the risk of heart disease. In a large federal research effort, the Framingham study, Wood found that 12 percent of the elderly participants had worrisome levels. "Hardly anyone had iron deficiency anemia," he says. "But 16 percent were taking iron-containing supplements."

—Gina Kolata

The Mineral Minder

These important nutrients should not be overlooked. Here's where to find them

Minerals help your body form bones, regulate the heart and synthesize enzymes, but experts say too many, or too few, can lead to heart disease, diabetes or even cancer. Here are the F.D.A.'s daily values and where to get them.

CALCIUM

DAILY VALUE:	*1,000 milligrams*
Sardines, Atlantic, 3 oz.	325 mg
1 cup fat-free milk:	301 mg
1 oz. Cheddar cheese:	204 mg
8 oz. nonfat yogurt:	452 mg

WHAT IT DOES: Helps form strong bones and teeth. Helps regulate heartbeat, muscle contractions, nerve function and blood clotting.

FOOD SOURCES: Milk, cheese, butter and margarine, green vegetables, legumes, nuts, soybean products, hard water.

SUPPLEMENTATION: High intakes may cause constipa-

Questions About Calcium

A new study doubts that supplements are beneficial

A large, seven-year study of healthy women over 50 found no broad benefit from calcium and vitamin D supplements in preventing broken bones. The study also found no evidence that the supplements prevented colorectal cancer, and it found an increased risk of kidney stones.

But the study's leaders said there were hints of benefits for some subgroups in the study. The supplements' only positive effect in the overall study population—36,282 normal, healthy women ages 50 to 79—was a 1 percent increase in bone density at the hip.

The $18 million study was part of the Women's Health Initiative, a large federal project whose results have confounded some popular beliefs and raised questions about public health messages that had been addressed to the entire population. Its

results were announced in February 2006 in the *New England Journal of Medicine.*

In the study, the participants were randomly assigned to take 1,000 milligrams of calcium and 400 international units of vitamin D a day, or to take placebos, and were followed for seven years. Researchers looked for effects on bone density, fractures and colorectal cancer. The lack of an effect on colorectal cancer over the seven years was so clear that it has aroused little debate. But the effect on bones is another story.

Osteoporosis specialists said the study was likely to put a dent in what has become a widespread medical practice of recommending that all women take calcium and vitamin D supplements starting at menopause if not sooner, as a sort of insurance policy against osteoporosis. But beyond that there is no agreement on what, if anything, healthy women should do.

—Gina Kolata

tion and increase risk of kidney stones and renal insufficiency. Also, see above.

COPPER

DAILY VALUE:	900 micrograms
2/3 cup seedless raisins:	310 mg
1 oz. dry roasted pistachios:	340 mg
1/2 cup boiled mushrooms:	390 mg

WHAT IT DOES: Helps in formation of red blood cells. Helps keep bones, blood vessels, nerves and immune system healthy.

FOOD SOURCES: Red meat, poultry, liver, fish, seafood, whole-grain cereals and breads, green vegetables, legumes, nuts, raisins, mushrooms.

SUPPLEMENTATION: Not recommended. A balanced diet includes enough copper.

IODINE

DAILY VALUE:	150 micrograms
1 oz. Cheddar cheese:	12 mcg
1 tsp. iodized salt:	400 mcg

WHAT IT DOES: Necessary for proper thyroid gland function and thus normal cell metabolism. Prevents goiter (enlargement of thyroid).

FOOD SOURCES: Milk, cheese, butter and margarine, fish, whole-grain cereals and breads, iodized table salt.

SUPPLEMENTATION: Not recommended. Widely dispersed in the food supply, so even if you eat little iodized salt, you probably get enough iodine.

IRON

DAILY VALUE:	18 milligrams
1 slice whole wheat bread:	1 mg
3 scrambled eggs:	2.19 mg
3 oz. lean sirloin steak, broiled:	2.6 mg
3 oz. fried liver:	5.3 mg
1 packet instant oatmeal:	6.7 mg

WHAT IT DOES: Vital in forming hemoglobin (which carries oxygen in blood) and myoglobin (in muscle).

FOOD SOURCES: Red meat, poultry, liver, eggs, fish,

whole-grain cereals and breads.

SUPPLEMENTATION: Often (but not always) advised for dieters, strict vegetarians. Large doses may damage the heart, liver and pancreas.

MAGNESIUM

DAILY VALUE:	*310 milligrams*
1 tbsp. peanut butter:	28 mg
1 baked potato:	55 mg
¹/₂ cup cooked spinach:	79 mg

WHAT IT DOES: Aids in bone growth, basic metabolic functions and the functioning of nerves and muscles, including the regulation of normal heart rhythm.

FOOD SOURCES: Milk, fish, whole-grain cereals and breads, green vegetables, legumes, nuts and hard water.

SUPPLEMENTATION: Not usually recommended, unless there is a dietary deficiency.

PHOSPHORUS

DAILY VALUE:	*700 milligrams*
6 scallops:	200 mg
1 cup nonfat milk:	250 mg
3 oz. broiled trout:	260 mg
1 cup tuna salad:	280 mg
1 cup low-fat cottage cheese:	340 mg

WHAT IT DOES: Helps form bones, teeth, cell membranes and genetic material. Essential for energy production.

FOOD SOURCES: Nearly all foods, including red meat, poultry, liver, milk, cheese, butter and margarine, eggs, fish, whole-grain cereals and breads, green and root vegetables, legumes, nuts and fruit.

SUPPLEMENTATION: Not recommended. Deficiencies in Americans are virtually unknown. Excessive intake may lower blood calcium level.

POTASSIUM

DAILY VALUE:	*4700 milligrams*
1 cup nonfat milk:	406 mg
1 banana:	422 mg

1 baked potato, with skin:	610 mg
1 cup cooked spinach:	838 mg

WHAT IT DOES: Needed for muscle contraction, nerve impulses, and function of heart and kidneys. Aids in regulation of water balance in cells and blood.

WHAT IT MAY DO: May fight osteoporosis and help lower blood pressure.

FOOD SOURCES: Unprocessed foods such as fruits, vegetables and fresh meats.

SUPPLEMENTATION: Not usually recommended. Take only under a doctor's advice and supervision.

ZINC

DAILY VALUE:	*8 milligrams*
8 oz. low-fat fruit yogurt:	1.52 mg
1 cup boiled lentils:	2.5 mg
3.5 oz. roast turkey, dark:	4.4 mg

WHAT IT DOES: Stimulates enzymes needed for cell division, growth and repair (wound healing). Helps immune system function properly. Also plays a role in acuity of taste and smell.

FOOD SOURCES: Red meat, fish, seafood, eggs, milk, whole-grain cereals and breads, legumes.

SUPPLEMENTATION: Not recommended, except by a doctor for the few Americans who have low zinc levels.

SOURCES: U.S.D.A.; Institute of Medicine; and *Bowes and Church's Food Values of Portions Commonly Used,* eighteenth edition, by Jean A. T. Pennington and Judith Spungen Douglass, 2004.

The Food Label at a Glance

Find out what is in those cookies before you get addicted

The F.D.A.'s food label contains an up-to-date, easy-to-use nutrition information guide, and is required on almost all packaged foods. It serves as an aid in planning a healthy diet for you and your family.

Serving Sizes are standardized to make it easier to compare similar foods; they are provided in familiar units, such as cups or pieces, followed by the metric amount, e.g., the number of grams. Pay attention to the serving size, especially how many servings there are in the food package. For every serving you eat, count the additional number of calories and nutrients/serving.

Calories provide a measure of how much energy you get from a serving of this food. Many Americans consume more calories than they need without meeting recommended intakes for a number of nutrients. Here are simple guidelines for calorie intake:
  —40 calories is low
  —100 calories is moderate
  —400 calories or more is high

Fat Calories are shown on the label to help you meet diet guidelines that recommend you get no more than 30 percent of your calories from fat.

NUTRIENTS

Fat, saturated fat, trans fat, cholesterol or sodium. Americans generally eat these nutrients in adequate amounts, or even too much. Health experts recommend that you keep your percentage intake of them as low as possible as part of a nutritionally balanced diet.

Dietary Fiber, Vitamin A, Vitamin C, Calcium and Iron. Most Americans need to get enough, but not too much, of these in their diets. You can use the Nutrition Facts label not only to help limit those nutrients you want to cut back on, but also to increase those nutrients you need to consume in greater amounts.

THE PERCENT DAILY VALUE

The % DV helps you determine if a serving of food is high or low in a nutrient, and is a frame of reference for how many of your total calories you are consuming in that serving. The % Daily Values are based on the Daily Value recommendations for key nutrients, but only for a 2,000 calorie daily diet—not 2,500 calories.

Nutrients Without a %DV: Note that trans fat, sugars and protein do not list a %DV on the Nutrition Facts label. Experts could not provide a reference value for trans fat nor any other information that F.D.A. believes is sufficient to establish a Daily Value or %DV. A % DV is required to be listed if a claim is made for protein, such as "high in protein." Otherwise, unless the food is meant for use by infants and children under 4 years old, none is needed. Current scientific evidence indicates that protein intake is not a public health concern for adults and children over 4 years of age. No daily reference value has been established for sugars, because no recommendations have been made for the total amount to eat in a day. Keep in mind, the sugars listed on the Nutrition Facts label also include naturally occurring sugars (like those in fruit and milk).

Nutrition Facts	
Serving Size 1 cup	
Servings Per Container 9	

Amount Per Serving	
Calories 110	Calories from Fat 15

	% Daily Value*
Total Fat 2g	**3%**
Saturated Fat 0g	**0%**
Polyunsaturated Fat 0.5g	
Monounsaturated Fat 0.5g	
Cholesterol 0 mg	**0%**
Potassium 95mg	**3%**
Sodium 280 mg	**12%**
Total Carbohydrate 22g	**7%**
Dietary Fiber 3g	**11%**
Soluble Fiber 1g	
Insoluble Fiber 2g	
Sugars 1g	
Protein 3g	

Vitamin A 10%	•	Vitamin C 10%	
Calcium 4%	•	Iron 45%	

* Percent Daily Values are based on a 2,000 calorie diet. Your values may be higher or lower, depending on your calorie needs:

	Calories:	2,000	2,500
Total Fat	Less than	65g	80g
Sat Fat	Less than	20g	25g
Cholesterol	Less than	300mg	300mg
Sodium	Less than	2,400mg	2,400mg
Total Carbohydrate		300g	375g
Dietary Fiber		25g	30g

Calories per gram:
Fat 9 • Carbohydrate 4 • Protein 4

FOOTNOTE TO % DV

The Recommended Daily Values for each nutrient listed in the footnote at the bottom of the label are based on public health experts' advice for recommended levels of intakes. Recommended DV's in the footnote are based on a 2,000 or 2,500 calorie diet.

Upper Daily Limits. The nutrients that have "upper daily limits" are listed first on the footnote of larger labels. Upper limits means it is recommended that you stay below—eat "less than"—the Daily Value nutrient amounts listed per day. For example, the DV for Saturated Fat is 20g or less. This amount is 100% DV for this nutrient. What is the goal or dietary advice? To eat "less than" 20 g or 100% DV for the day.

Lower Limits—Eat "At least"... The DV for Total Carbohydrate is 300g or 375g, both 100% DV respectively for either a 2,000 or 2,500 calorie diet. This is the minimum amount recommended for a balanced daily diet, but can vary, depending on your daily intake of fat and protein.

How Fish Can Help Your Heart

Two servings a week can make a difference

Evidence suggests that eating just two fish meals a week—two three-ounce servings—can make a significant difference in the risk of developing ills like heart attacks and strokes.

Part of the benefit may come simply from eating fish in place of red meat, a supposed cul-

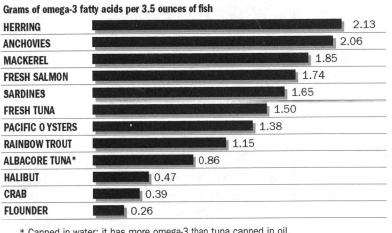

FISH OIL: FROM HERRING TO FLOUNDER

Here's a lineup of the fish and shellfish with the highest concentrations of omega-3 fish oil. Fish caught in the wild generally contain more omega-3 than farm-raised fish.

Grams of omega-3 fatty acids per 3.5 ounces of fish

HERRING	2.13
ANCHOVIES	2.06
MACKEREL	1.85
FRESH SALMON	1.74
SARDINES	1.65
FRESH TUNA	1.50
PACIFIC OYSTERS	1.38
RAINBOW TROUT	1.15
ALBACORE TUNA*	0.86
HALIBUT	0.47
CRAB	0.39
FLOUNDER	0.26

* Canned in water; it has more omega-3 than tuna canned in oil.
SOURCE: University of Washington Cardiovascular Health Research Unit

prit in cardiovascular disease. But another more important part, the evidence suggests, involves the fats found in fish, namely omega-3 fatty acids, which may have a physiological role in preventing cardiovascular disease.

But as with most worthwhile things in life, with fish and shellfish, there's no free lunch. Risks as well as benefits attend eating seafood, although a wise and well-informed consumer can certainly tip the balance in favor of the benefits.

THE BENEFITS

For fish to maintain fluidity in cold water, their fats have to remain liquid, and liquid fats (really oils) are polyunsaturated. But fish oils, rich in omega-3 fatty acids, are chemically different from the polyunsaturated oils in plants like corn and soybeans, and it is that difference that has given fish star billing.

The two omega-3's in fish are eicosapentaenoic

FOOD

Oil That's Really Good for You

As Greeks say, olives are a gift from the gods

Researchers may have pinned down one important reason for the positive effect olive oil appears to have on cardiovascular health: it contains a naturally occurring anti-inflammatory chemical. The substance, which the researchers call oleocanthal, has the same anti-inflammatory effect as drugs like ibuprofen and aspirin, which can inhibit the sometimes harmful effects of enzymes called cox-1 and cox-2.

✔ Scientists have long known that low doses of the cox inhibitors confer various benefits on the people who use them. "There is ample evidence that chronic low-dose anti-inflammatories have multiple health benefits that may range from reducing the risk of heart disease, stroke and certain cancers—breast, lung, colon—to reducing the risk of terminal dementias such as Alzheimer's," says Paul A. S. Breslin, who is a co-author of the report that appeared in *Nature* and a researcher at the Monell Chemical Senses Center in Philadelphia. "Olive oil contains an ibuprofen-like anti-inflammatory that may turn out to convey similar benefits," he continues.

✔ Extra-virgin olive oil has the most benefit, but consumers do not necessarily need to buy the most expensive brands. "What matters is that it is an extra-virgin olive oil that has a good throat sting indicating it has high levels of oleocanthal," Dr. Breslin says. He suggests that the Mediterranean diet—with extra-virgin olive oil used liberally on bread and vegetables and in salad dressing—may be the best way to consume it, "particularly if it substitutes for butter, margarine and creamy dressings."

—Nicholas Bakalar

acid, or EPA, and docosahexaenoic acid, or DHA. They are considered essential fatty acids, although they can be formed in the body from another omega-3, alpha-linolenic acid, or ALA. It is found in plants like flaxseed, spinach, mustard greens, soybeans, canola oil, wheat germ and walnuts, as well as in marine animals that eat plants containing ALA. The conversion rate is poor, however, and you will have to consume large amounts of ALA to obtain a meaningful amount of EPA and DHA. Eating fish is far more efficient.

DHA is a natural ingredient in breast milk, and it is critical to the normal development of the brain and retina. It has been approved as an additive to infant formula. In addition, the omega-3 acids perform many biochemical functions that can benefit the heart and blood vessels. They can inhibit the synthesis of substances that promote inflammation, reduce the tendency of the blood to form clots, stabilize the electrical activity of the heart, lower triglyceride levels, reduce blood pressure moderately and improve the functioning of artery linings.

Most, but not all, studies have found that people who eat fish regularly experience significant reductions in the risk of heart attacks, strokes and deaths from all causes. The benefit has been most clear-cut among people who already have cardiovascular disease, but it has also been found among those who are initially healthy. In one study, of 334 people who had suffered first heart attacks and 493 healthy people matched for age, sex and location, eating just 5.5 grams of omega-3 fatty acids a month was associated with a 50 percent reduction in the risk of cardiac arrest. That amount of omega-3's can come from just four three-ounce servings of Atlantic salmon a month. The omega-3's have proved especially beneficial for people with Type-2 diabetes, who have a greatly increased risk of developing heart disease. Other suggested benefits include an anti-inflammatory effect that can help people with autoimmune diseases like rheumatoid arthritis, psoriasis and ulcerative colitis.

The various findings prompted the American Heart Association to recommend, in October 2000, that everyone strive to consume at least two fish servings a week, especially fatty fish like salmon, sardines, mackerel, herring, lake trout, tuna and anchovies.

THE RISKS

Some fish are contaminated with mercury and other toxic substances introduced as industrial pollutants into their waters. An international research team reporting in the *New England Journal of Medicine* noted that the mercury content of some fish might diminish their cardioprotective effects. Again, not every study has shown this. Mercury at levels experienced by Americans may also cause problems with fine motor control and memory in adults, a study by Dr. Edna M. Yokoo and colleagues at Johns Hopkins says.

Still, mercury is a well-known neurologic and kidney toxin that is best not ingested. The fish most likely to be contaminated are large deep-sea species like swordfish, king mackerel, shark and tilefish and are best avoided, especially by pregnant women. Fish, especially shellfish, can become contaminated by harmful micro-organisms that occur naturally and those that result from sewage pollution.

But raw fish and shellfish are the most common sources of food poisoning. Only ocean-dwelling fish should be used in sushi, sashimi and ceviche, and only from reliable sources that know how to spot contamination by parasites. The filter-feeders—clams, oysters and other mollusks like mussels and scallops—can accumulate waterborne bacteria, viruses or toxins that can cause severe gastrointestinal problems when the shellfish is eaten uncooked. Local health departments periodically issue advisories about contaminated species.

Finally, about 1 percent of adults have clinically proven food allergies, and shellfish are among the most common culprits, so it would be wise for them to avoid all sources. Even kissing someone who just ate shrimp, for example, can cause a reaction in someone allergic to it.

—Jane E. Brody

TIMELY TIPS

The Almighty Yogurt

Bacteria can be good for you

Those elderly people in those yogurt ads some years ago who said, "I'm 110 years old, and I eat yogurt every day," may have been on to something.

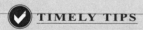 Yogurt has been receiving an increasing amount of attention these days from health-oriented consumers and nutrition scientists because it has been linked to a variety of potential health benefits, from protection against intestinal and vaginal infections and bowel cancer to increased calcium absorption and overall enhancement of the immune system.

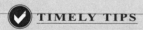 Yogurt is made by adding bacteria to cow's or soy milk, which causes fermentation and creates its distinctive creamy texture and tart taste. The bacteria most often used to prepare yogurts sold in the United States are *Lactobacillus bulgaricus* and *Streptococcus thermophilus*.

Some manufacturers add as many as four others to the two basic bacteria: *Lactobacillus acidophilus, casei* and *reuteri,* and *Bifidobacterium bifidum.*

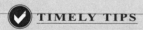 All of these organisms are known as probiotics because, when consumed live and in sufficient quantities, they benefit the consumer through their effects on the intestinal tract. They help to keep illness-causing organisms under control. The best kind of yogurt is low-fat and without sugar.

—Jane E. Brody

In the Kitchen

How to Evaluate a Recipe

Read it through carefully, then make it your own

Looking at a new recipe in a cookbook, a magazine or a newspaper is a little like meeting someone for the first time. Will this be the start of a lovely new relationship, or is it best not to become involved? Like people, recipes can be judged on their physical and sensory qualities.

The first step with any recipe is to read it through. There are a number of parts that all bear scrutiny:

• Does the title suggest an appealing dish?

• Are the ingredients on the list palatable to you, and are they familiar and accessible? Does the recipe include suggestions of sources or substitutions for exotic components?

• Do the techniques required in the directions seem simple and straightforward and, if not, are they clearly explained?

• Do you have the proper equipment?

• And is the yield, or the number of servings, satisfactory for the occasion; if not, does the recipe seem easy to cut in half or to double, or would leftovers be welcome?

A vote of no for any of these elements should be enough to keep you from lighting the stove. There are a million recipes out there, so it makes no sense to take a chance.

But if all these basics appear to be acceptable, then it's time to give the recipe a closer look. Read through the list of ingredients carefully, and check each against the directions to make sure that every ounce, cup or spoonful is accounted for in the preparation. Then ask yourself whether the quantities make sense.

As a rule of thumb, a portion of soup should be one to one and one-half cups. Is the quantity of ingredients enough to supply the servings you will need? Main course servings for stews or casseroles are about two cups. For meat, fish or poultry on the bone, figure a pound of the raw ingredient per person; off the bone, around six ounces should do.

When it comes to dessert, depending on the richness, half a cup to a cup per person is a good average. But for cakes, pies, puddings and the like, you can also measure the capacity of a baking dish and make sure the recipe calls for the correct amount of ingredients for the size of the pan. And do not forget to allow for expansion, especially for cakes.

Finally, before lighting the stove, read through the directions once more, mentally completing each step to see that you understand all the details. And then, as much as a recipe may be a formula, keep your wits about you and your tastebuds on line. Be prepared to vary the timing, depending on how your pots and stove conduct heat. Do not hesitate to make other adjustments, as you go, to the amount of liquid in a sauce, perhaps, or to the seasonings.

Then, when you serve the dish, you will have increased the chances of success, and regardless of who wrote the recipe, you can add it to your repertory and call it your own.

—Florence Fabricant

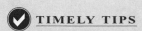

TIMELY TIPS

A Bare-Bones Kitchen

Some absolutely, must-have items for the start-up cook

Like any start-up operation, getting a functioning kitchen up and running requires a capital investment. But depending on where you shop, you can cover the basics for about $1,000 to $1,500, though when it comes to certain items, such as knives and pans, you can easily spend more than double that amount. Try buying your basics from a restaurant supply store. The kitchen items are often more durable and cheaper than what you can find in the specialty kitchen stores, and they often have secondhand items as well.

Spoons

- Measuring spoons in 1/4 tsp, 1/2 tsp, 1 tsp and 1 tbsp sizes
- Cooking spoons, in various lengths and sizes:
  Wooden
  Metal, slotted and regular
  Ladle

Set of Measuring Cups

- Dry Measure
  In 1/4, 1/3, 1/2 and 1 cup sizes. These can be filled to the top and leveled off with your hand or a knife.
- Wet Measure
  Preferably made of glass or some clear material with some kind of a spout.

Knives

- Paring knives, two or three
- Serrated knives, one short one long
- Carving knive
- Chopping knife

Other implements

- Cutting board
- Rubber and metal spatulas
- Tongs
- Whisks
- Parer
- Grater
- Zester
- Garlic press
- Juicer
- Salad spinner
- Wire mesh sieve or colander
- Bottle and can openers

- Coffee filter
- Pepper mill
- Nutmeg grater
- Corkscrew

Pots and pans

- Saucepans in 2 cup, 1 qt., 2qt. and 8 qt. sizes
- Frying pans in 8-inch 10-inch and 12-inch sizes
- Roasting pan
- Casserole dishes in an assortment of sizes

Baking

- Baking sheet
- Cake tins
- Bread and muffin tins
- Pie dish
- Rolling pin
- Bowls of various sizes, for mixing and preparing foods

And if you have any money left over, these are very useful.

- Cuisinart—for chopping and pureeing
- Mixer—for mixing cakes and blending ingredients
- Coffeemaker or espresso machine
- Toaster

Casting Call for Pots and Pans

Forget Teflon, stainless steel or copper, and go with cast iron

When I'm asked for a recommendation for cookware, I reply with an old-fashioned answer: cast iron. As most experienced cooks know, you can't brown food unless you preheat your skillet, and I frequently transfer food from stove top to oven. So cast iron, which can accomplish all these things, is a logical choice, especially in skillets. Furthermore, it is an even distributor of heat, which you will instantly appreciate if switching from stainless steel or aluminum.

Seasoning a cast-iron pan is simple and maintaining it is even simpler. To season a new pan wash it well and dry it. Preheat the oven to 350 degrees Fahrenheit while you warm the pan

The Sticky Issues of Teflon

An empty, overheated Teflon-coated pan poses a risk by releasing toxic fumes, according to the Environmental Working Group, a nonprofit environmental research and advocacy organization. DuPont, which manufactures Teflon, does not dispute that, but there is no agreement between the company and Teflon's critics over what temperature releases the fumes. The Environmental Working Group says 325 degrees, or a medium flame; DuPont says 660 degrees.

Studies have shown that Teflon releases perfluorooctanoic acid, or PFOA, under normal cooking. PFOA causes cancer and other health problems in laboratory animals, and it is under scrutiny by the Environmental Protection Agency and the Food and Drug Administration.

For those who don't want to wait for definitive answers from the government, the Environmental Working Group has some suggestions::

✔ **Use Teflon pans at lower temperatures,** and never put them on the stove to heat without food or liquid inside.

✔ **Greasy food** that is heated in a microwave oven in a cardboard container is a potential source of PFOA; take the food out of the container and heat it in glass or ceramic.

✔ **For popcorn in the microwave,** the group suggests the following: place a quarter-cup of good-quality popcorn in a standard brown paper lunch bag; mix with oil and seasoning; seal the bag with a single staple (one staple does not contain enough metal to cause a spark) and heat for two to three minutes. Alton Brown, who cooks on the Food Network, uses this method.

✔ **Another solution is to cook the old-fashioned way**. If cast iron pans are seasoned and heated properly, very little oil is needed for browning. Chefs generally do not use nonstick pans, because they don't think they do as good a job as cast iron and stainless steel, especially for browning.

—Marian Burros

gently over low heat on top of the stove. Using a brush or a paper towel, spread a tablespoon or so of a fresh, neutral oil like corn or grape seed in the pan; the surface should be evenly covered, with no excess. Put the pan in the oven, bake it for about an hour and let it cool in the oven.

Once the pan is seasoned, routine washing can almost always be done with a scouring pad, not steel wool or anything else that will damage the seasoning (even a little mild soap), although the worst that can happen is that the pan will have to be reseasoned. If rust does appear, scour it off with steel wool or sandpaper, and reseason.

For "grilling" a steak indoors, cast iron can't be beat. Ridged cast-iron "grill pans" are good for two reasons: they raise the meat slightly above the surface, which promotes browning by preventing escaping liquids from contacting the meat, and they leave grill marks, which are attractive if nothing else.

Cast iron is as good at browning as any other cookware, and its mass lets it hold a steady temperature so well that it is perfect for deep- or shallow-frying.

But braising in cast iron, especially with acidic ingredients like tomato or wine, may degrade the seasoning slightly. In extreme cases, you may have to reseason the pan; more likely, you'll just have to treat it to a light coating of oil and a few minutes of warming.

—Mark Bittman

Ripe for the Picking

A grocery shopper's guide to picking fresh fruits and vegetables

There are a few universal truths about choosing the freshest and most flavorful fruits and vegetables: buy seasonally and as close to the source as possible. If you are buying organic or from a local farmer, don't worry about imperfections, including a few insect holes. Perfection and flavor are not necessarily related.

What you don't want are soft, bruised or brown spots, all signs of immediate or impending decay. And you don't want to cause them yourself by squeezing tender fruits, like peaches.

Keep all fruits at room temperature as long as possible, and don't wash them until just before eating. Refrigerate only to prevent overripening or decay. Contrary to popular belief, watermelon thumping, cantaloupe shaking and pineapple leaf plucking are not valid tests for determining ripeness.

Whether melons ripen a little bit at room temperature appears controversial: some authorities say they do; others say no. It may depend more on how much time has elapsed between the time they were picked and the time they reach the customer. Out of season, you should purchase melons cut up to see the color.

CHOOSING FRUITS

Apples: Firm, smooth, shiny skin, good color with no shrivelling; overlarge usually means mealy.

Apricots: Sweetest the moment before they turn from slightly firm to almost soft.

Avocados: Feel heavy for size, yield to pressure when gently pressed; no bruises.

Bing cherries: Darker are the ripest and sweetest.

Bananas: Yellow, with a little browning; no green tinge.

Cantaloupes: Heavy for size; should smell sweet; yield to pressure at indentation.

Grapefruits: Large, firm, fine-grained, heavy for their size.

Grapes: Plump and juicy, firmly attached to stem; no shriveling, soft spots, dried stems.

Honeydews: Heavy for size; characteristic aroma; blossom end should yield to slight pressure.

Kiwis: Plump and fresh, yielding to gentle palm pressure. No bruises, soft spots or shriveling.

Lemons and limes: Heavy for their size; firm with thin skin; bright yellow lemons are more acid than darker yellow; limes should be bright green.

Mangoes: Flesh gives slightly when ripe and is starting to wrinkle. Avoid any with black spots.

Oranges: Firm, heavy for size; don't worry about green on skin.

Papayas: Between green and yellow in color, slightly soft, no bruising or shriveling; no aroma.

Peaches, nectarines and plums: Yield to slight pressure and have a delicate fragrance.

Pears: Yield slightly to finger pressure at stem end; better to ripen fully at home.

Pineapples: Deep green leaves; fresh tropical smell; no skin discoloration or soft spots.

Red raspberries: Lighter berries have more flavor than darker ones.

Strawberries: All red, bright and shiny.

Watermelons: Rind is dull green, side that was on the ground should be creamy yellow, not white.

CHOOSING VEGETABLES

Artichokes: Firm without brown tips, with leaves curling inward.

Arugula: Bright green, no yellowing or limp-

ℹ **INSIDE INFO**

Hurry Up and Ripen

○ To speed the ripening of soft fruits such as avocados, bananas, kiwis, nectarines, peaches, pears, plums and tomatoes, store them in a paper bag with an apple. The apple will boost the partly ripe fruit's exposure to ethylene, a gas required for ripening.

Fruits That Don't Ripen After Harvest:

○ Apples ○ Cherries ○ Grapefruit

○ Grapes ○ Lemons ○ Limes

○ Oranges ○ Pineapples ○ Strawberries

○ Tangerines ○ Tangelos ○ Watermelons

SOURCE: The Produce Marketing Association

ness; the smaller the leaves the better.

Asparagus: No ridges; the diameter is immaterial. The best are standing in water and are firm, the outcroppings close to the spear.

Carrots: Medium to dark orange with no white spots.

Corn: Silky tassels, no dryness in the husk. Pull down a little of husk and stick a fingernail into a kernel. If it bursts easily, corn is fresh; never buy shucked corn.

Cucumbers and summer squashes: Firm, no soft spots or wrinkling (smaller are tastier).

Eggplant: Rich purple color with shiny skin, no wrinkles; the smaller the sweeter.

Fennel: No sign of browning or drying on cut edges; bulb compact, not spread out.

Garlic: Firm and plump.

Green beans: No lumps and when bent should snap.

Lettuces: No wilting, brown or rust spots.

Onion: Firm, no wet spots, no sign of dust.

Peas (all kinds): Pods should be bright green with no dryness.

　　Snow peas: small and flat.
　　Green peas: pods ready to burst.
　　Sugar snaps: plump.

Peppers: Shiny, unblemished skins, without wrinkles or soft spots.

Potatoes: Firm without growth around the eyes and no green spots.

Sweet potatoes: Smooth skin.

Zucchini, yellow summer squash: Firm, not overly large, no soft spots.

—Marian Burros

Some Really Delicious Apples

If you're after flavor, you may have to grow your own

A t one time, each apple-growing region in this country had its local favorites—the Newtown Pippin on northern Long Island, Fameuse along the St. Lawrence River, Willows and Gilpins from West Virginia and York Imperial from Pennsylvania. Today, commercial growers cater to a national or even international market that demands an apple that will appeal to everyone. Yield, pest tolerance and consumer demands for shape, storability and color and other considerations pre-empt what should have always remained most important: flavor.

But it is possible to sidestep this problem by growing your own. Just a little space in the backyard can contain one or more dwarf apple trees,

Which varieties to grow—or search out at a local green market? Here, according to Lee Reich, a horticultural consultant and prolific author, whose most recent book is called *Uncommon Fruits for*

Every Garden, is a list of some apple varieties whose main attribute is excellence of flavor:

Esopus Spitzenburg, or Spitz for short. The apple does not have the appearance needed for today's commercial market but, as William Coxe said in 1817, the Spitz "possesses great beauty, and exquisite flavour." The crisp fruit has a skin of rich yellow covered with a commingling of bright and dark red. Thomas Jefferson preferred Spitzenburg to all other apples.

Cornish Gilliflower was discovered in a cottage garden in Cornwall, England, about 200 years ago. It is an ugly apple, russeted brownish red over an olive base. But its flavor is supreme—a rich sweetness, with a hint of clove.

Cox's Orange Pippin. Orange and red washed with carmine over a yellow background, this fruit has its problems: it is small, yields are low, it sunburns and some years it will crack. But it is full of taste.

Ashmead's Kernel originated more than 200 years ago as a chance seedling in the garden of a Dr. Ashmead in Gloucester, England. The fruit is a russeted golden brown with a reddish bronze cheek where struck by sunlight. Inside is a delicious, crisp yellow flesh. The fruits ripen in late October and keep well.

Calville Blanc d'Hiver, a variety grown over 300 years ago in the garden of King Louis XIII. The fruit, with a smooth, light skin that looks almost like porcelain, is lobed into segments like those of an orange. Its tender, spicy flesh, with just a hint of banana, blends well with cheese for dessert.

Hudson's Golden Gem is an annual, productive bearer of russetted, dull yellow fruits with an intensely attractive taste.

Golden Nugget is a cross of Cox's Orange Pippin with Golden Russet, the latter itself a fine-flavored apple. Golden Nugget fruits are small, do not keep well, and may crack just before ripening in some years. But the aroma is exquisite.

Jonagold is a combination of the sprightly Jonathan and the aromatic Golden Delicious, and has large yellow fruits with a splash of light scarlet.

Spigold is a hybrid of Northern Spy and Golden Delicious, but tastes better than either of them.

Mutsu, a cross of Golden Delicious and Indo, which was introduced from the Aomori Experiment Station in Japan in 1948. Mutsu is a large, round, yellow apple with a delicate spicy flavor. The texture is pleasantly coarse, reminiscent of biting into a snowball.

Melrose is a cross of Red Delicious and Jonathan, with the rich taste of Jonathan and the sweetness of Red Delicious. The trees are productive and begin bearing at a young age.

Gala, from New Zealand, is a cross of Kidd's Orange and Golden Delicious. One of the best of the early apples—juicy and sweet, golden yellow with a pink-orange blush. In contrast to most other early apples, Gala will keep in cold storage until Christmas.

FOOD

 INSIDE INFO

Where the Pesticides Are

○ The lowest pesticide levels are found in asparagus, avocados, bananas, broccoli, cauliflower, sweet corn, kiwi, mangos, onions, papaya, pineapples and sweet peas.

○ The highest pesticide levels are found in apples, bell peppers, celery, cherries, imported grapes, nectarines, peaches, pears, potatoes, red raspberries, spinach and strawberries.

SOURCE: The Environmental Working Group. See www.foodnews.org for a more complete guide.

Think Globally, but Eat Locally

Guess who's coming to dinner: a factory farm chicken or a local bird?

Louella Hill is executive director of Farm Fresh Rhode Island (www.farmfreshri.org), an online organization that links farmers with local eaters and businesses, and one of the leaders of the local food movement that is sweeping the country. Here she offers the arguments for eating locally:

Every time you eat, you are making a choice. For example, consider that chicken you plan to roast for tomorrow night's dinner. When you buy that chicken, you usually have two options: You can buy a chicken that comes from a factory farm 2,000 miles away. The factory farm may house over 20,000 birds. Hormones and antibiotics must be used to help the birds gain weight and fight disease. Tomorrow night's dinner will probably never see sunlight or blue sky, or even have room to move around in its cage. Or you can buy a chicken from a local family-owned poultry farm. The farm where the chicken was raised is probably less than 40 minutes from your house. The chicken spent its life in sunlight and open air. It is an heirloom breed and was raised without the use of hormones or antibotics.

Eating locally means waiting until July for tomatoes or not expecting berries to always be at the grocery store. But the payoff is an enhanced flavor and freshness to all that you eat.

There are many ways to get involved in building a more sustainable food system. Here are a few suggestions:

- Eat with the seasons.
- Shop at farmers' markets, farm stands or at pick-your-own orchards.
- Find groceries that carry locally produced foods.
- Join a C.S.A. (Community Supported Agricul-ture) program in which you prepay for weekly shares of a farm's harvest.
- Ask your waiter which dishes feature locally produced foods the next time you eat out.
- Tell your neighbors, family and friends why that home-grown tomato tasted so good.
- Host a "local flavors" dinner party and highlight as many local ingredients as you can.
- Help a local school district develop their "farm to school" program

More information about farms, farmers' markets or businesses that support local farmers in your area can be found at www.localharvest.com. The Community Food Security Coalition's Web page (www.foodsecurity.org) covers food system policy issues, from community gardens to local foods in hospital cafeterias.

How Green Is Your Kitchen?

It's not only the food you eat, but how you buy it and what you throw away

The shift toward local, seasonal and sustainable agriculture makes sense for the taste buds, the body and the planet. But there's a next step: making home kitchens just as environmentally sound as those pastoral organic farms.

"Once you make the leap into understanding it's better to shop organically and locally, it's a natural step to think about how you store and prepare the food," says Mindy Pennybacker, editor of *The Green Guide*, an online newsletter devoted to environmentally friendly options for the home (thegreenguide.com).

"It's a matter of pleasure," says Annie Berthold-Bond, known as the "Green Heloise" for books like *The Green Kitchen Handbook* and

Better Basics for the Home. "Your enjoyment of life is exponentially improved when the food you eat is wonderful and you don't have a headache from cleaning with chemicals. In the end, it's a much richer, better living experience."

MAKE WISE CHOICES

• Washing fruit and vegetables reduces pesticide residue but does not eliminate it, according to the Environmental Working Group. Peeling works better, but then valuable nutrients in the skin are lost. Lab tests conducted by the organization's team of scientists and engineers have determined some unsettling results, such as nine different pesticides on a single sample.

• Cut down on packaging waste by buying in bulk at health food stores. Bring your favorite display bottles and mason jars into your local health food store, have the cashier weigh and mark them, then turn on the spigots for high-quality olive and canola oil priced by the ounce. The cashier will deduct the weight of the container before totaling the bill.

STARVE THE GARBAGE

• "Remember our rule," Mario Batali, the well-known chef, once told an apprentice while retrieving a handful of greens from the garbage, "We do not make money by buying food and then throwing it away." Find your inner Mario. After you trim the greens off celery, carrots and beets (you want them off because they drain the moisture from the root), freeze them. Over time, add the trimmings of other stock vegetables, including onion and garlic skins and tomato. Parmesan rinds add a wonderful flavor.

• If you make roast chicken for a dinner party, clean the bird after the main course and toss it in a stockpot, adding water and the contents of a couple of freezer bags of trimmings, some salt and a bay leaf. During dessert, a fresh batch of broth will have made itself. It's ready for the freezer by the time the dishes are done.

• Pouring out perfectly good, undrunk wine after a party is a sin. Nigella Lawson says that it can be frozen in Ziploc bags and thawed for stews, ragus and deglazing.

• A household of one or two can also freeze sliced bread, which preserves the quality better than refrigerating it. Pull out a few slices at a time for toast; no thawing necessary. A leftover baguette can be split and cut into 4-to-6-inch lengths and frozen, to be reheated quickly in the oven for a French breakfast with butter and jam. Stale bread, whirred in the food processor, makes perfect, freezable breadcrumbs.

—Julie Besonen and Andrea Kannapell

ℹ️ **INSIDE INFO**

Trash or Black Gold?

○ The average household discards—daily—roughly two pounds of naturally recyclable waste, the raw material for black gold otherwise known as compost, which could be spread around home gardens or community parks or near street trees, according to the New York City Compost Project.

○ You can compost these items: fruits, vegetables, flowers dead plants, coffee grounds, egg shells, nut shells, stale bread, flour, cereal, spices, beans, spoiled juice, food-soiled paper towels, napkins, cardboard, coffee filters, tea bags (staple removed), shredded paper and cornstarch packing peanuts.

○ It takes three to four months for organic material to decompose sufficiently to become compost. Finished compost resembles dark, crumbly topsoil and should bear no resemblance to the original materials. Compost should have a pleasant earthy smell to it.

GERM WARFARE

The right temperatures to keep bacteria at bay

240°	Canning temperatures for low-acid vegetables, meat and poultry in pressure canner.
212°	Canning temperature for fruits, tomatoes and pickles in water-bath canner. Cooking temperatures destroy most bacteria. Time required to kill bacteria is decreased as temperature is increased.
165°	Warming temperatures prevent growth but allow survival of some bacteria.
140°	Some bacterial growth may occur. Many bacteria survive. **DANGER ZONE. Temperatures in this zone allow rapid growth of bacteria and production of toxins by some bacteria.**
60°	Some growth of food-poisoning bacteria may occur. (Do not store meats, poultry or seafoods for more than one week in the refrigerator.)
40°	Cold temperatures permit slow growth of some bacteria that cause spoilage.
32°	Freezing temperatures stop growth of bacteria, but may allow bacteria to survive. (Do not store food above 10° F for more than a few weeks.)

SOURCE: U.S. Department of Agriculture

Cooking by the Book

Intimidated by that rack of lamb? Look no further

Each cut and type of meat has its own method of cooking. Some meats, such as turkey, require more care (such as basting with broth and olive oil or melted butter) as they cook. Others require simply that the temperature and timing be carefully observed.

TO ROAST BEEF *(350° F)*

CUT / WEIGHT	MINS. PER POUND	INTERNAL TEMP (F)
• **Standing rib** / 4 to 8 lbs.		
rare	20 to 25	140°
medium	25 to 30	160°
well done	30 to 35	170°
• **Rolled rib** / 5 to 7 lbs.		
rare	30 to 35	140°
medium	35 to 40	160°
well done	40 to 45	170°
• **Rib eye** / 4 to 6 lbs.		
rare	20	140°
medium	22	160°
well done	24	170°
• **Sirloin tip**	5 to 40	160°
• **Tenderloin** *(roast at 400°)*		
whole / 4 to 6 lbs.	10	140°
half / 2 to 3 lbs.	20	140°

TO BROIL STEAK *1-inch thick, 2 inches from preheated oven broiler.*
If grilling steak, grill 3 inches from fire and cook 1 minute less per side.

• **Sirloin, Porterhouse, T-bone or Rib**	
rare	5 minutes each side
medium	7 minutes each side
well-done	10 minutes each side

• **Filet mignon**, cook 1 minute less per side.

TO ROAST VEAL *(325° F)*

• **Leg** / 5 to 8 lbs.	25 to 30	170°
• **Loin** / 4 to 6 lbs.	30 to 35	170°
• **Rib (rack)** / 3 to 5 lbs.	35 to 40	170°

FOOD

TO ROAST LAMB *(325° F)*

• **Leg** / 5 to 8 lbs.	30 to 35	175° to 180°
• **Shoulder** / 4 to 6 lbs.	30 to 35	175° to 180°
• **Rib (rack)**/ 4 to 5 lbs.	40 to 45	175° to 180°
• **Crown** / 4 to 6 lbs.	40 to 45	175° to 180°

TO ROAST PORK *(325° F)*

• **Loin**, center / 3 to 5 lbs.	40	185°
half / 5 to 7 lbs.	45	185°
rolled / 3 to 5 lbs.	50	185°
• **Sirloin** / 3 to 4 lbs.	50	185°
• **Crown** / 4 to 6 lbs.	45	185°
• **Picnic shoulder** / 5 to 8 lbs.	40	185°
• **Rolled shoulder** / 3 to 5 lbs.	45	185°
• **Spareribs** / 3 lbs.	40	185°
• **Fresh ham (leg)**		
whole / 10 to 14 lbs.	30	185°
half / 5 to 7 lbs.	40	185°

TO ROAST HAM AND OTHER CURED PORK

Temperature should be 325° F. For all boneless meat, allow $^1/_3$ to $^1/_2$ pound per serving; if the meat contains bone, estimate $^1/_2$ to $^3/_4$ pound per serving.

• **Whole ham** / 10 to 14 lbs.		
uncooked	20	160°
fully cooked	15	130°
• **Picnic shoulder** / 5 to 8 lbs.	30	170°
• **Rolled shoulder** / 2 to 4 lbs.	40	170°

TO BROIL PORK

Chops *(3/4- to l-inch thick)*, **shoulder steaks** *($^1/_2$- to 1-inch thick)*, and **patties** *(l-inch thick) should be broiled about 11 minutes on each side.*

TO ROAST DUCK OR GOOSE *(350° F)*
Roast duck or goose about 30 minutes per pound.

TO ROAST CHICKEN *(350° F)*
Chicken weighing between 2 and 4 pounds should be roasted about 30 minutes per pound. Add 15 minutes to the total roasting time if the chicken is stuffed. With bones, estimate about $^1/_2$ pound per serving.

TO ROAST TURKEY *(325° F)*

READY TO COOK WEIGHT	HOURS
4 to 8 lbs.	3 to 4
8 to 12 lbs.	4 to 4 $^1/_2$

HOW TO CARVE A TURKEY

Show off at the table next Thanksgiving dinner. Here's what to do:

1. *Move drumstick and thigh by pulling leg away from body. Joint connecting leg to bone will often snap free or may be severed easily with knife point. Cut dark meat from body by following body* contour carefully with a knife.

2. *Place drumstick and thigh on cutting surface and cut through connecting joint.*

3. *Hold turkey breast firmly on carving surface with fork. Place knife parallel and as close to wing as possible. Make deep cut into breast, cutting toward ribs. This makes a base cut.*

4. *Slice breast by carving downward, ending at the base cut. Keep slices thin and even.*

Source: National Turkey Federation

12 to 16 lbs.	4 1/2 to 5
16 to 20 lbs.	6 to 7 1/2
20 to 24 lbs.	7 1/2 to 9

TO COOK FISH

Cook fish thoroughly or to an internal temperature of 140 degrees Fahrenheit.

For **FIN FISH***, allow 8 to 10 minutes of cooking time for each inch of thickness. Turn the fish over halfway through the cooking time, unless it is less than a half-inch thick. Add 5 minutes to the total cooking time if the fish is wrapped in foil or cooked in sauce.*

METHOD	TIME	TEMP. (F)
Baked	10 minutes	350°
Broiled	15 minutes	500°
Deep-fried	2 minutes	370°
Pan-fried	10 minutes	
Poached or steamed	10 minutes per pound	

TO COOK SHELLFISH

Cooking shellfish thoroughly or to an internal temperature of 140° F is required to help avoid the threat of food poisoning. Boil for three to five minutes after the shells have opened.

Steam shellfish four to nine minutes from the start of steaming. Use small pots for boiling or steaming. If too many shells are cooking in the same pot, it's possible that the ones in the middle won't be thoroughly cooked. Discard any clams, mussels or oysters that do not open during cooking. If the shells remain closed, it may mean they have not received adequate heat.

SIMMER IN BOILING WATER:

SHRIMP	5 minutes
CRAB	20 minutes
LOBSTER	10 to 15 minutes/lobster

Shrimp, scallops, clams and oysters *can be deep-fried at 370° F for about three minutes.*

Shrimp and scallops *can also be sauteed. Other shellfish are best boiled or steamed.*

HOW TO CLEAN A FISH

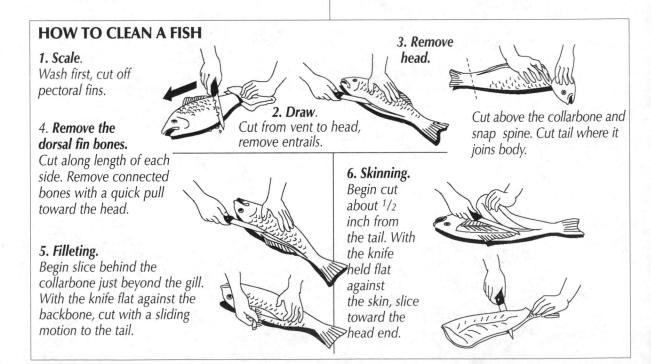

1. Scale.
Wash first, cut off pectoral fins.

2. Draw.
Cut from vent to head, remove entrails.

3. Remove head.
Cut above the collarbone and snap spine. Cut tail where it joins body.

4. Remove the dorsal fin bones.
Cut along length of each side. Remove connected bones with a quick pull toward the head.

5. Filleting.
Begin slice behind the collarbone just beyond the gill. With the knife flat against the backbone, cut with a sliding motion to the tail.

6. Skinning.
Begin cut about 1/2 inch from the tail. With the knife held flat against the skin, slice toward the head end.

THE CATCH OF THE DAY

These days, Americans can get fish caught in waters the world over, in local supermarkets and restaurants. But according to the National Fisheries Institute's study of data collected by the National Marine Fisheries Service, most Americans' idea of fish is still the old standby: canned tuna. If you want to expand your taste horizons, the guide below will help you decide between bluefish and mahi mahi the next time you're in the grocery store or scanning the restaurant menu.

FISH ⇆ Source   🐟 *Type of meat*   ⇆ Flavor

SEA BASS ⇆ Northeast Atlantic coast ⇆ *Dark* ⇆ Light to moderate

STRIPED BASS ⇆ Atlantic and Pacific coastal waters; also farm-raised 🐟 *Light* ⇆ Light to moderate

BLUEFISH ⇆ Atlantic coastal waters ⇆ *Dark* ⇆ Light to moderate

CARP ⇆ Freshwater lakes, ponds worldwide 🐟 *Light* ⇆ Wild carp may taste muddy

FARMED CARP ⇆ Farms worldwide 🐟 *Light* ⇆ Farmed carp is light to moderate

CATFISH ⇆ Lakes, ponds and rivers; also farmed 🐟 *White* ⇆ Wild catfish may taste muddy

FARMED CATFISH ⇆ Farms worldwide 🐟 *White* ⇆ Farmed catfish is light to moderate

COBIA ⇆ Mid-Atlantic from U.S. to Argentina 🐟 *White* ⇆ Light to moderate

COD ⇆ North to mid-Atlantic or North to mid-Pacific, depending on species 🐟 *Light* ⇆ Very light, delicate

FLOUNDER ⇆ Atlantic, Pacific coasts, Asian Pacific coast and Bering Sea 🐟 *White* ⇆ Very light, delicate

GROUPER ⇆ Tropical and subtropical coastal waters and Atlantic coast 🐟 *Light* ⇆ Very light, delicate

HALIBUT ⇆ North Atlantic or Pacific coast, depending on species 🐟 *Light* ⇆ Very light, delicate

LAKE HERRING ⇆ Lakes and rivers in Canada and northern U.S. 🐟 *Light* ⇆ Light to moderate

MACKEREL ⇆ Atlantic or Gulf coast, Pacific, Eur. Atlantic coast, Indian Ocean 🐟 *Light* ⇆ Pronounced flavor

MAHI MAHI ⇆ Off Hawaii and Florida, Gulf Stream, Pacific Calif. to S. America 🐟 *White* ⇆ Light to moderate

MONKFISH ⇆ North to mid-Atlantic 🐟 *Light* ⇆ Light to moderate

ORANGE ROUGHY ⇆ Deep ocean waters off New Zealand and Australia 🐟 *White* ⇆ Very light, delicate

PIKE ⇆ Rivers and streams worldwide 🐟 *Light* ⇆ Light to moderate

POLLOCK ⇆ North Pacific or both sides of North Atlantic and the North Sea 🐟 *Light* ⇆ Light to moderate

RED SNAPPER ⇆ Gulf coast, Atlantic coast from North Carolina to Florida 🐟 *Light* ⇆ Light to moderate

SALMON ⇆ Northern Atlantic or Pacific, rivers when spawning; also farmed 🐟 *Light* ⇆ Light to moderate

SAND SHARK ⇆ Western Atlantic 🐟 *Light* ⇆ Light to moderate

SMELT ⇆ Lakes, rivers, and northern Atlantic and Pacific coasts 🐟 *Light* ⇆ Very light, delicate

SWORDFISH ⇆ Off Calif., New Eng., Hawaii, Spain, Japan, Greece, S. America 🐟 *Light* ⇆ Light to moderate

RAINBOW TROUT ⇆ North American rivers and streams; also farmed 🐟 *Light* ⇆ Very light, delicate

TUNA ⇆ Tropical to temperate waters worldwide ⇆ *Dark* ⇆ Light to moderate

WALLEYE ⇆ Northern North American lakes and rivers 🐟 *Light* ⇆ Very light, delicate

WHITEFISH ⇆ Northern U.S. and Canadian lakes 🐟 *White* ⇆ Light to moderate

SOURCE: National Fisheries Institute

How to Grill a Fish

The secret is not to overcook it

Grilling fish intimidates many people, and not without reason: fish is slippery. More fish has been lost through grill grates than probably any other food. The key is not so much to remember to keep the grill clean, or to oil it—though these are not bad ideas and definitely help—but to choose fish that is most suitable for grilling.

Attempting to grill delicate, ultra-lean fillets—like flounder or sole, or even cod, which is thicker but falls apart almost as soon as you look at it—is an exercise in futility. You can use a grill basket, and this will keep you from losing the fish through the grates, but it will fall apart as you take it out of the basket, ruining your presentation. For these kinds of fish, stick to the broiler (which is really an upside-down grill, anyway) and you'll get good results.

For grilling, it pays to stick to heartier fish.

The safest cut is steak: think swordfish, salmon, tuna, even steaks of halibut and cod (in this instance, the bones will hold it together). Small, firm, whole fish like mackerel, pompano, and red snapper (and, of course, many shellfish) are also practical. Grilling fillets is possible, too, as long as you choose the right ones: salmon, red snapper, catfish, monkfish, striped bass, sea bass, rockfish, tilefish and blackfish are all sturdy enough to grill, as are several others.

Once you've got the right cut, there are some other keys in addition to a clean, oiled grill. Start with a fairly hot fire and, if possible, start grilling the fish with the skin side down. If you let the skin—or the first side you grill—firm up for a couple of minutes before you turn the fish, it will be easier. Once you turn it, remember not to overcook: overcooked fish is dry, and the lack of moisture makes it more likely that the fish will fall apart. Use a sharp knife to peek inside thickest part of fish to judge doneness.

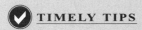 **TIMELY TIPS**

And Now, the Perfect Sauce

However you cook your fish, beurre blanc will work

Any white-fleshed fish—roasted, poached or pan-cooked—will take beautifully to beurre blanc. If you prefer, you can make the sauce first and keep it warm over minimum heat, stirring now and then, for the brief time it takes to cook the fish.

This sauce is easy, foolproof, silken-smooth, impressive, fast and delicious. Start by reducing wine, vinegar and shallots; experienced cooks will recognize that as the first step in making béarnaise sauce. When this is syrupy, stir in butter a bit at a time so that it emulsifies, or combines smoothly with the wine syrup. As long as you take your time and do not stir all the butter in at once, you will succeed on the first try. **TIME:** 10 minutes.

2 tablespoons minced shallots
2 cups white wine
2 tablespoons white wine vinegar
1 stick butter, cut into 6 or 8 pieces
Chopped fresh parsley or chervil for garnish.

1. Combine shallots, wine and vinegar in a small saucepan and turn heat to high. Cook until it is reduced to about ¼ cup, 10 minutes or so.

2. When white wine mixture has reduced, turn heat to very low. Add butter a piece at a time, stirring after each addition until it is incorporated. When all butter has been added, taste and adjust seasoning.

3. Spoon sauce over fish, garnish if you like, and serve.

YIELD: 4 servings.

—Mark Bittman

Most fish are cooked to well done at a rate of about 8 to 10 minutes per inch of thickness. So that's a decent rule of thumb for timing; if you prefer it less well done, remove it from the grill sooner. When done to your liking, about 3 to 5 minutes after you turn, remove it to a platter or serving plates.

—Mark Bittman

Chillin' With Nigella

A "domestic goddess" gives advice on cooking—and planning—ahead

If you are the sort of person who, when catching a train, needs to arrive at the station with time to spare, you will cook in a very different way from someone who habitually boards the train while it is inching away.

Those, like me, who need to arrive on time take comfort from cooking that can be done in advance. It makes us feel safe and relaxed, knowing that not too much frenetic last-minute activity will be necessary. We are not the stir-fry crowd. But even if you are a skin-of-the-teeth type who feels that planning smacks of regimentation, there will be times when you need to get ahead of yourself.

Life, after all, is not always arranged according to our own inclinations. If a crowd is coming for supper at midweek and you work late every night, then it makes sense to find the time on a Sunday afternoon to chop the ingredients and cook the chili.

With the bulk of the work dispatched, the chili can be kept in the refrigerator several days and just heated up in the oven for half an hour when you need to eat it. A little last-minute finessing will be involved before it is reheated, but the effort is minimal: just fork together some buttermilk, eggs, a tiny bit of honey, cinnamon and oil and stir them into some cornmeal and a small amount of flour in a bowl. Spread this wet-sand mixture over the

TIMELY TIPS

The Children's Menu

Don't be afraid to feed your children good food

To test out the theory that children could be educated to eat better, the *New York Times* polled several chefs with young children to see what they fed them and found serious challenges to the notion that small people simply will not brook fresh vegetables, texture or spice.

The fact that chefs' kids eat better than yours or mine isn't surprising. They often bring the little ones to work, where they eat tiny plates of duck confit or buckwheat pasta. Here are some of their rules of the road for getting kids to eat well:

✔ **Have your children eat at the table from a very young age.** Jody Adams, the chef at Rialto in Cambridge, Mass., says her children never had highchairs. "It was really hard, because 2-year-olds throw food. But I saw the benefit in treating the dinner table as something that everyone had to participate in."

✔ **Make them eat what you do, even if you have to purée it.** "If we ate butternut squash and carrots, so did they," Hugo Matheson, a chef at the Kitchen in Boulder, Colo., says, "and sometimes fish." Grant Achatz, the chef and owner of Alinea in Chicago, treated his 4-year-old to a 10-course dinner. "He didn't finish everything, but he tried every course, which included white truffles, crab, bison," he says.

✔ **Pack lunches fashioned from leftovers.** "If we order Thai food," says Naomi Hebberoy, a chef and owner of the Gotham Building Tavern in Portland, Ore., her daughter "takes pad Thai the next day."

✔ **Eschew Goldfish.** "If kids are hungry, they're going to eat," Scott Dolich of Park Kitchen in Portland, Ore. says. "If you fill them up on Bugles, they won't."

—Jennifer Steinhauer (Adapted from *In the Hands of a Chef* by Jody Adams and Ken Rivard)

Nigella's Vegetarian Chili with Corn Bread Topping

Time: *1 hour 35 minutes.*

For the chili:

2 tablespoons olive oil
2 medium onions, finely chopped
2 cloves garlic, minced
3 cups red bell peppers (about 2 large peppers), finely diced
2 teaspoons hot red pepper flakes
1 teaspoon ground coriander
1 teaspoon ground cumin
3 cardamon pods, lightly crushed
1 $^1/_2$ cups red lentils
3 cups canned chopped tomatoes
3 $^1/_2$ cups drained canned kidney beans
$^1/_4$ cup ketchup
$^1/_4$ cup tomato paste
1 tablespoon unsweetened cocoa powder

For the corn bread topping:

1 teaspoon salt
2 cups cornmeal
2 tablespoons flour
3 teaspoons baking powder
1 teaspoon ground cinnamon
1 cup buttermilk
2 large eggs
1 teaspoon honey
2 tablespoons vegetable oil
1 cup coarsely grated Cheddar cheese

For serving:

2 cups sour cream
1 cup chopped cilantro

1. To prepare chili, heat olive oil over medium-low heat in a deep, wide pan with a lid. Add onions, garlic and bell peppers, and sauté until softened, about 5 minutes. Stir in red pepper flakes, coriander, cumin and cardamom pods. Stir in lentils.

2. Add chopped tomatoes, kidney beans, ketchup, tomato paste, cocoa and 3 cups water. Stir well. Cover, and simmer, stirring frequently, until beans are tender, about 45 minutes. (Cover, and refrigerate for up to 3 days, bringing to room temperature before proceeding.)

3. For the corn bread topping, heat oven to 425° F. In a mixing bowl, combine salt, cornmeal, flour, baking powder and cinnamon. In a separate bowl, whisk together buttermilk, eggs, honey and oil. Mix together all ingredients.

4. Pour chili into a baking dish 13 by 9 by 3 inches. Spread topping evenly over chili, and sprinkle with cheese. Bake until topping rises and turns golden brown, about 25 minutes. Add sour cream and cilantro.

Yield: *8 servings.*

chili in its dish and sprinkle lavishly with punchy mature Cheddar.

In cooking, this topping turns into the most fabulous crunchy corn bread—more a crumbly dry biscuit—that you push into the chili as you eat to absorb the hot juices. You need do nothing more to this golden dish than sprinkle freshly chopped cilantro and a dollop of palate-salving sour cream over the top.

—Nigella Lawson, author of *How to Be a Domestic Goddess,* is a regular contributor to the *New York Times.*

The Many Nuances of Chocolate
It's a whole new world of tastemanship

In the new world of chocolate connoisseurship, it is no longer enough to understand the difference between milk and bittersweet. Now the game is all about origin. As with olive oil or coffee, knowing where one's chocolate came from is starting to matter. After all, even the most casual wine drinker can name a preferred varietal, and the neophyte cheese fan understands that Brie is French and good Cheddar comes from England.

Terroir, it turns out, matters in chocolate, too.

Even those who turn cacao pods into artisanal chocolate haven't quite settled on a lexicon for this new way of contemplating chocolate. Maricel E. Presilla, in her book *The New Taste of Chocolate,* refers to it as one broad category—"exclusive-derivation" chocolate. Some chocolatiers use simpler phrases like "single origin," "single bean" or "varietal." Others have gotten more extreme, naming bars after one of the three main varieties of cacao, like the rare criollo, and labeling chocolate made from beans grown on one farm "plantation" or "estate" chocolate.

Harvests believed to be extra special might even be deemed "grand cru," a term borrowed from winemakers.

What is a Valrhona Grand Cru Caraïbe 66 percent dark chocolate supposed to taste like, anyway?

Guittard, the San Francisco specialty chocolate maker; La Maison du Chocolat; Jacques Torres; Pralus, the French chocolate maker known for its intensely aromatic chocolate; and even Trader Joe's, would all be good places to find the materials for a round-the-world chocolate tasting.

HOW TO HOLD A CHOCOLATE TASTING

Sitting in a room with piles of the world's best chocolate might seem like a dream, but you can have too much of a good thing. A successful chocolate-tasting event requires some preparation. For starters, keep the tasting small.

- **Be sure the chocolate is at room temperature.** A temperature of 60° F is perfect for storing chocolate, but you can keep it well wrapped in plastic or a zip-top bag in the refrigerator until an hour or so before you taste.

- **Still water is about all you need**, but a few palate-cleaning tortilla chips nearby help.

- **First, consider the texture.** It should be smooth and shiny. Color can vary from copperish to nearly black.

- **Then, break off a piece and smell it.** Good chocolate should snap cleanly. Rub a finger over the surface to release some aroma. Over-fermented beans can make chocolate smell like rotting fruit. Badly dried beans can be unpleasantly smoky. Cheap chocolate might smell overwhelmingly of vanilla. Good chocolate can smell like caramel, flowers, dried fruit, licorice—even mushrooms or dirt.

- **Next, let it melt in your mouth for 15 to 20 seconds.** Some cacao beans, especially of the forastero variety, contribute an earthy note. Rare criollos or the hybrid trinitario variety offer brighter flavors. Some chocolates taste like dairy, others like fruit. Some produce an astringent feeling in the mouth that comes from tannins like those found in wine or tea. Your preferred flavors will become clear pretty quickly.

—Kim Severson

Cooking With a Foreign Accent
For those who'd like a little on-vacation training

Culinary instruction is available in France and Italy for every type of student, from seasoned chefs to casual cooks. One resource for cooking school vacations is *The Guide to Cooking Schools,* an index of programs throughout the world that ShawGuides publishes annually. The Web site, www.cookforfun.shawguides.com, offers a directory searchable by location and month.

The International Kitchen (800-945-8606 or www.theinternationalkitchen.com) organizes

● **TIMELY TIPS**

Why French Women Don't Get Fat

Eat soup, breath in fresh herbs and know that love is slimming

While close to two-thirds of American adults are either obese or overweight, French women really don't get fat. The reason behind that most enviable difference, says Mireille Guiliano, is that "French women take pleasure in staying thin by eating well, while American women see it as a conflict and obsess over it." Put another way, "French women typically think about good things to eat. American women typically worry about bad things to eat."

✔ Guiliano, the author of the bestseller *French Women Don't Get Fat*, urges us to relax. Walk to the market, breathe in the fresh herbs, cook a good dinner, have a glass of wine or champagne. Just sip it slowly (she makes hers last through a meal). She rejects the "American rule" of "no pain, no gain" and describes exercise machines as a "vestige of Puritanism: instruments of public self-flagellation to make up for private sins of couch riding and overeating." French women make a ritual out of every meal.

✔ She knows we eat portions that are too big and food that is too bland. (Bland food and too much of one kind, a big bowl of pasta for example, breeds boredom, which leads you to alleviate it by eating more.) French women, on the other hand, stress flavor and variety over quantity and, therefore, are more satisfied with less. She knows our tendency to gorge ourselves on Snickers bars rather than savor a single piece of fine, dark chocolate. French women eat slowly and "with all five senses."

✔ She offers no scientific "food plan," just suggestions and seemingly indulgent recipes, including one for fingerling potatoes and caviar. Guiliano reminds us that a half-dozen oysters contain only 60 or 70 calories, that soups fill you up and supply much-needed water to your body ("The theory goes that the French, who eat soup up to five times a week for dinner, eat better and less.")

✔ Guiliano ends her book with a list of more observations about French women. They don't weigh themselves, they don't snack all the time, they eat more fruit but would never give up their bread or other carbs. They dress to take out the garbage, they understand the importance of a good haircut and expensive perfume, they know love is slimming. At the very least, we would all do ourselves a favor to make like Colette, for whom the table was "a date with love and friendship" instead of the root of all evil.

—Julia Reed , a senior writer for *Vogue* and author of *Queen of the Turtle Derby and Other Southern Phenomena*

cooking school vacations to France, Italy and Spain. Options include the Amalfi Coast, Tuscany, Sicily, the Loire Valley, Provence and the French Riviera. All lessons are in English.

A trip to the Walnut Cooking School in Mayenne, Loire, includes a five-night stay at a country farmhouse, five hands-on cooking classes, all meals and excursions, including visits to an 18th-century windmill, a medieval city and a local fromagerie.

An alternative in Italy could be a six-night trip to Chianciano in southern Tuscany, with four cooking lessons and excursions to Siena, Montepulciano, Montalcino, Pienza and Montefollonico.

In addition to vacations exclusively devoted to cooking lessons, Jo-Ann Gaidosz, the owner of Active Gourmet Holidays, (203-732-0771 or www.activegourmetholidays.com), offers holidays for those who want variety or have traveling companions with different interests. For example, a six-night vacation to Sorrento includes five Italian-language lessons, four cooking lessons, all breakfasts and dinners, excursions to Pompeii and Positano and transfers to and from the Naples airport. In France, a vacation could include cooking instruction, wine tasting and bicycle rides in Bordeaux, six nights at a bed-and-breakfast, all meals and wine, four cooking lessons in private homes and all excursions.

—Marjorie Connelly

Meeting the Cordon Bleu Test
How Julia Child passed her final exam

In spring 1951, after memorizing proportions and preparing herself "in every way I could think of," Julia Child took her final examination and earned her diploma from the Cordon Bleu in Paris. It was a near disaster:

"On the big day, I arrived at the school, and they handed me a little typewritten card. I stared at the card in disbelief. Did I remember what an oeuf mollet was? No. How could I miss that? How about the veau "en surprise"? No. Did I remember the exact proportions for caramel custard? No. I was stuck, and had no choice but to make everything up."

Well, being Julia Child, she got her diploma and went on to revolutionize American cooking through her collaboration on *Mastering the Art of French Cooking* and other books, and her appearances on *The French Chef.* She died in 2004 at the age of 91.

A recipe from her exam follows at right.

Crème Renversée au Caramel
(Caramel Custard)

½ cup plus ⅔ cup sugar
2 cups milk
1 ½ teaspoons vanilla extract
2 large eggs
4 large egg yolks

1. Preheat the oven to 350 ° F. In a small saucepan, combine ½ cup sugar with ¼ cup water. Bring to a boil over low heat, stirring to dissolve the sugar. Increase the heat to high and cook, without stirring, until the syrup turns a light caramel color. Remove the saucepan from the heat and dip the bottom into cold water to stop the cooking. Pour the caramel into a 4-cup charlotte mold, and tilt so that it covers the bottoms and sides. Let cool.

2. In a small saucepan, bring the milk and vanilla to a boil. In a heatproof bowl, beat the eggs, egg yolks and cup of sugar until blended. Whisking constantly, pour the hot milk into the egg mixture; let rest for a few minutes, then strain. Pour the custard into the caramel-coated mold.

3. Put the mold in a small but deep baking or roasting pan, and add hot water to come about two-thirds up the sides of the mold. Place the pan on the stove over medium heat, and bring the water to a simmer. Transfer the pan to the oven. (The water should stay at a low simmer at all times; do not let it boil, or the custard will overcook.) Bake until a knife inserted into the center of the custard comes out clean, 40 to 50 minutes. Keep the custard in the baking pan until the water cools. Remove from the pan to finish cooling. To serve, run the tip of a knife around the top of the custard to loosen it. Invert a serving platter over the mold and quickly turn it over again. Carefully remove the mold. Serves 6.

SOURCE: Exerpt and recipe (adapted from *Le Cordon Bleu*) are from *My Life in France* by Julia Child with Alex Prud'homme, published in April 2006.

FOOD

Wine, etc.

Starting a Wine Collection

A delicious assortment for a $1,500 budget

So you want to put together a wine cellar, but you don't want to spend more than $1,500. What kind of wines do you like? If you know, you're on your way. If you don't, here are some good categories—the brand names can change.

1. Champagne. Few wines are as versatile, in terms of mood or food. Serve with sushi, Chinese food or fried chicken. Six bottles of Nicolas Feuillatte Brut should run you about $150.

2. Everyday wines. A case of white and a case of red. For variety's sake let's split each case into three groups of four. Among the whites, one ought to be a racy, always-satisfying sauvignon blanc, like a 2004 Clos Roche Blanche from the Loire for $13 a bottle, or a Patianna 2003 from Mendocino County for $17. We'll want a dry, minerally chardonnay like a 2004 Jean Rijckaert from Arbois in France for $13. Never heard of Arbois? Great value comes from little-known regions. Same with grapes. Gruner Veltliner from Austria is lightly peppery and very refreshing, and best of all, bottles of Hirsch No. 1 from Kamptal can be found for $10 or so apiece.

For the everyday reds, try a juicy Cotes-du-Rhone, like a 2004 St. Cosmé for $13; a 2001 Rioja crianza from Condé de Valdemar, a fine value at $11; and a good 2003 Barbera d'Alba for tomato sauce and pizza from Brovia for $15.

3. Fancier bottles. Two cases. You'll need Bordeaux, six bottles of Pontet-Canet 2001, an excellent Pauillac, for $34 each. Burgundy's trickier and more expensive, but Louis Jadot is always a good value, like a 2002 Nuit St.-Georges Aux Boudots, six bottles for $50 each. For whites, the 2002 Mount Eden chardonnay from the Santa Cruz Mountains is one of the best values in California at $35 a bottle, while a dry 2002 German riesling Gaisbohl Ruppertsberg from Dr. Burklin-Wolf at $52 is one of the world's finest rieslings. Buy six bottles of each.

4. $200 left. How about throwing in two bottles of Bruno Giacosa Barbaresco Santo Stefano at $90 each, one of the world's great wines? Lock 'em away and forget them for 10 years.

—Eric Asimov

TIMELY TIPS

Wine by the Numbers

There are effectively two mega-validators for wines these days. Both use a 100-point scale to rate wines, both report on thousands of wines each year and both have extraordinary influence on what people drink.

✔ **The Wine Spectator,** a magazine and Web site (www.winespectator.com)

✔ **The Wine Advocate,** Robert M. Parker Jr.'s newsletter (www.eRobertParker.com). Also available on the site is the indispensable *The Wine Advocate*'s **Vintage Chart,** ranking hundreds of wines.

—Frank J. Prial

A Worldwide Wine Sampler

Global reports from our expert tasters

For more than a decade, Eric Asimov and Frank J. Prial have been wine critics at the *New York Times,* scouring the world for the best bottles— often with the help of tasting panels consisting of other wine and food reporters at the *Times,* as well as outside experts. What follows are some of their wine selections and comments on vintages ranging from the elegant and serious to the casual and affordable.

FRANCE

BORDEAUX

Premier wines at premier prices

Grapes from the Bordeaux family, like cabernet sauvignon, merlot and cabernet franc, are traditionally blended. Depending on the characteristics of the vintage, producers adjust the blend of grapes each year. In the Médoc area, where many of the great Bordeaux are made, merlot is usually added to cabernet to tame its rough tannins.

Consumers select Bordeaux wines not by the grape, but by the label—a Clerc-Milon, for example, not a cabernet sauvignon. Winemakers for Clerc-Milon use whichever blend makes for the best wine. Mouton-Rothschild, for example, strives for 85 percent cabernet sauvignon, 8 percent merlot and 7 percent cabernet franc. In Saint-Emilion and Pomerol, prestigious wine communities east of Bordeaux, on the other hand, merlot is generally the principal grape, and cabernet sauvignon and/or cabernet franc are added for backbone.

Premier wines fetch astounding prices these days. But there are some bargains, relatively speaking. The 2001 Pontet-Canet from Pauillac, for example, is a great value, as is Cantemerle. Though missing from the area's classification system (see

Savoring a Good Wine

Mind the texture—as well as aroma and flavor

When evaluating a wine, efforts generally focus on aromas and flavors. But another important feature is not detectable by eyes, nose or taste buds. That is texture, the tactile sense of wine on the mouth, tongue and throat.

The idea of texture in a liquid is difficult to describe. You won't find the word "texture" in the encyclopedic *Oxford Companion to Wine,* for example. Instead, you'll find the unwieldy term "mouthfeel" and its constituents: body, density, weight and, for the truly geeky, viscosity.

Whatever you call it, great texture demands that you take another sip because it feels so good. Almost all memorable wines have had beautiful textures, wines such as a '92 Puligny-Montrachet Les Pucelles from Domaine Leflaive, and a '94 Hillside Select cabernet sauvignon from Shafer in the Napa Valley. These are world-class bottles, with three-figure prices, but a wine doesn't have to be expensive to feel great in the mouth. Think of a luscious '02 Austrian riesling from Hirsch in the Kamptal, a minerally '02 Sancerre from Etienne Riffault, and a smoky '98 Tuscan sangiovese from Montevertine.

One way to think of texture is to keep in mind its components—acidity and, especially in red wines, tannins. Most wine drinkers are familiar with tannins. They are the astringent compounds that in a young, tannic red wine—a Barolo, say, or a Bordeaux—can seem to suck all the moisture out of your mouth. Ideally, the tannins soften over time.

Acidity is the juicy, zingy quality. Too much acidity, and a wine can feel harsh and aggressive. Too little, and it feels flabby and shapeless. When you taste a wine, treat it gently. "On first sip, I just let it sit there," says Joshua Wesson, chairman of Best Cellars, "then I push it around with my tongue slowly, ...and get a much better sense of texture."

—Eric Asimov

"Ranking the French Elite," opposite page) some of the wines of Saint-Emilion and Pomerol have long been considered equal in rank to the Bordeaux. Some picks: Chateaux Cheval Blanc and Ausone in Saint-Emilion, and Chateau Petrus in Pomerol.

WHITE BURGUNDY
There's never enough to meet the demand

The best white Burgundys are clearly not simple everyday wines intended for casual sipping. These top-of-the-line wines are lean, dry, profound and virtually demand to be paired with food; they are best matched with seafood and white meats.

Some favorites (from a tasting of 2002's) include the Jadot Corton-Charlemagne, with its incredible depth and elegance; the Chassagne-Montrachet Morgeot, for its developing richness; and the lighter, pleasant Savigny-lès-Beaune, because it represented the best value in our tasting.

The 2001 vintage was difficult in Burgundy, but lucky producers made good wine. Almost everyone there made good, if not great, wine in 2002. But the 2003 vintage whites suffered because of the severe heat wave. So far, the 2004's are promising, especially the premier cru Chablis wines.

✔ TIMELY TIPS

Wine by the Book

Frank J. Prial, the former *New York Times* wine writer, recommends three classic books with staying power:

✔ Hugh Johnson and Jancis Robinson's *World Atlas of Wine*

✔ Kevin Zraly's *Windows on the World Complete Wine Course*

✔ Matt Kramer's *Making Sense of Wine*

BOURGOGNE
The poor man's white Burgundy

A Bourgogne, the lowest level of wine from Burgundy, is no simple chardonnay, though the cost is often far below its Burgundy counterparts. Because of this, it is worth sampling; some treasures are to be found at some surprisingly inexpensive prices.

Les Sétilles, for example, a Bourgogne blanc from Olivier Leflaive, is light and flinty; vintage after vintage, this seafood-oriented chardonnay is a crowd-pleasing aperitif. In another twist on the appellation game, sometimes French marketers declassify a chardonnay qualified to be labeled a Burgundy to the lower-costing Bourgogne label. An example: the 2004 Le Meurger, a chardonnay qualified to be labeled Meursault, which is pricey, was labeled as a Bourgogne, and offered at a lower price.

BEAUJOLAIS
Finding the good stuff gets harder

Over the last 25 years or so the identity of Beaujolais has become muddied, with any number of mediocre, pallid wines giving themselves the name. Once it was clearly an inexpensive, exuberant wine, served by the barrelful in French bistros. Then came the Beaujolais nouveau explosion a few decades back, which turned a quaint local custom of celebrating the new vintage into a worldwide marketing phenomenon. But soon enough the world got over the hype and yawned at yet another proclamation that the Beaujolais "est arrivé."

There was always plenty of bad Beaujolais to go around, of course. But today it takes extra effort to find a good Beaujolais, the kind that makes you happy to have a glassful of wine. One place to start the quest is with the 2003 vintage. Here are some good ones: Château de Chenas Fleurie, which is juicy and balanced with a velvety texture; Michel Tête's Domaine du Clos du Fief Juliénas, light and

INSIDE INFO

Ranking the French Elite

○ Few hierarchies of wine producers have had so long and influential a run as classification of the wines of the Médoc (the peninsula north of the city of Bordeaux), where most of the famous wine estates, like Latour and Lafite-Rothschild, are located.

○ Wine properties are divided into five classes, called growths. For 150 years, this ranking has largely determined how much money the châteaux that are in the classes can charge for their wines. Since then, the rankings have barely changed at all.

○ The five chateaux in the *premier cru*, or first growth, are:
   • Château Lafite-Rothschild, Pauillac
   • Château Latour, Pauillac
   • Château Margaux, Margaux
   • Château Haut-Brion, Pessac, Graves
   • Château Mouton-Rothschild, Pauillac (since 1973)
   (The names Pauillac, Margaux, Pessac and Graves refer to the particular area of the Médoc where the chateaux are located.)

graceful, with persistent mineral, fruit and herbal flavors; and Domaine de la Madone, Beaujolais Villages Le Perreon, dense and earthy with rich, lingering fruit and spice flavors.

RHÔNE WINES

The syrah grape gives these wines their structure

It's too simple, of course, to lump all Rhône wines together. Among Rhône reds, the wines of the northern Rhône, like Hermitage and Côte-Rôtie, are made almost entirely of the syrah grape.

On the other hand, Châteauneuf-du-Pape, from the southern Rhône, and Côtes-du-Rhônes are blended wines. More than a dozen grapes can legally be included in the Châteauneuf mix, but the most important are grenache, mourvèdre and syrah.

The ultimate syrah for most wine lovers is Hermitage itself, made from grapes grown on the famous hill of Hermitage, north of Valence, where producers like Guigal, Chapoutier and Chave make syrah into one of the greatest red wines. Close behind is Côte Rôtie, the renowned "roasted slope" on the west bank of the Rhône at Ampuis, south of Lyon. Some more reasonably priced northern Rhônes to try are J. L. Chave St.-Joseph Estate 2001, Alain Graillot Crozes-Hermitage 2002 and Tardieu-Laurent Crozes-Hermitage Cuvée Coteaux 2001.

MUSCADET

A wine that deserves more respect

More muscadet is produced in France than any other major white wine, yet it receives precious little respect. But when made well by passionate producers, muscadet is a wine of nuance, with a lively freshness, herbal and citrus flavors, and a briny, saline quality that is perfect for oysters. Muscadet should generally be consumed within a few years of the vintage. Yet a good bottle can evolve with age into a wine that combines the racy acidity and aroma of older riesling with enticing nutlike, mineral and honey flavors. And it is still fairly inexpensive.

Basic muscadet is generally to be avoided. The best versions come from three appellations: Muscadet de Sèvre-et-Maine, the largest, followed by Muscadet Côtes de Grand Lieu and Muscadet des Coteaux de la Loire.

ITALY

PIEDMONTESE REDS AND MERLOTS

From the majestic to the easygoing

Some wines reveal themselves slowly, teasing you along with more depth, adding a dimension of flavor, a new aroma. So it goes with Barolos and

FOOD

Barbarescos, the majestic wines of Piedmont in northwestern Italy. They are made from nebbiolo, a grape that seems to flourish only in its home territory. The wine requires time and patience to bloom, but the rewards can be profound. A well-aged example, like the 1978 Barolo Bussia from Prunotto, can be a glorious combination of power and delicacy.

Top Barolos and Barbarescos are expensive, but there are more affordable alternatives made with nebbiolo grapes from less-exalted sites. These "baby Barolos" are often called Nebbiolo d'Alba, but may have other names, too, such as Ghemme, Gattinara, Langhe and Roero. They are less expensive and generally need less aging. Although they can be inconsistent, the best give a clear taste of the potential of nebbiolo.

Merlot, long an important grape in Italy, can be found in 14 of the country's 20 wine regions. Italy has some 75,000 acres of merlot grapes, compared with about 28,000 in the United States.

Millions of gallons of light, fruity, mostly inconsequential merlot are produced every year in the Friuli and Veneto regions. More interesting are those from Trentino-Alto Adige, particularly wines blended with cabernet sauvignon. They are, for the most part, easy-going wines, to be consumed in the Alpine villages where they are made.

In Tuscany, merlot is taken more seriously. Two of the best examples are from Ludovico Antinori's Tenuta dell'Ornellaia estate in Bolgheri: Ornellaia, a blend of cabernet sauvignon, cabernet franc and merlot, and Masseto, which is all merlot. Ornellaia deserves its reputation as one of the super-Tuscans—wines made without traditional Tuscan grapes. It is a balanced, elegant wine with a long, very unmerlot-like finish.

SPAIN

RIOJA AND PRIORAT
Ripe for rediscovery

Rioja, the best-known Spanish region, is ripe for rediscovery. A simple bottle of Conde de Valdemar from Bodegas Valdemar, compared alongside a bottle like the Grandes Añadas from Bodegas Artadi will show you why Riojas are among the best red wine values in the world, offering juicy, balanced pleasures.

White Riojas come in two styles: one crisp and modern, made to be consumed young, and a more traditional version, rich and oaky, with flavors of vanilla, coconut, almond and hazelnut shining through. They are great values. Excellent examples can easily be found for less than $15; even a well-aged version, like a 1981 Gran Reserva, is only $80; not much, considering the cost of other age-worthy whites of similar vintage.

One of the best tales of late-20th-century wine-making is the rebirth of the Priorat region in north-eastern Spain. The area makes intense, concentrated, expensive wines that appeal to globalized tastes without sacrificing their distinctive character.

INSIDE INFO

Wines Have Temperatures, Too

The best temperature for serving a wine varies according to its individual characteristics. Here is a rough guideline:

○ **Sparkling Wines and Champagnes**:
40 to 45° Fahrenheit

○ **White Wines:** 45 to 50° Fahrenheit

○ **Rosé and light reds:**
50 to 55° Fahrenheit

○ **Medium-bodied reds:**
55 to 60° Fahrenheit

○ **Full-bodied reds:** 60 to 65° Fahrenheit

The 2001 Finca la Planeta from Pasanau Germans, for example, could easily be mistaken for a fine Bordeaux, with its deep aromas and flavors of tobacco and berries. It's tannic and acidic, yet also elegant, with earthy, mineral flavors and a whiff of smokiness and a very good value. The 2002 vintage was difficult but, luckily, plenty of Priorat wines from older vintages are still available; any from 1998 to 2001 are preferable.

ARGENTINA AND CHILE

MERLOTS AND MALBECS

Have the Argentinians finally arrived?

Every decade, it seems, Argentina's and Chile's wine industry announces that it has arrived. Maybe this time, it has. After sampling 28 red wines, almost all made from Bordeaux grapes, a *Times* tasting panel was surprised and pleased by the quality of the wines.

The wines included cabernet sauvignons, merlots, malbecs, blends and even one pinot noir. The panel's favorite was a 1999 Montes Alpha "M" from La Finca Estate in Chile; while a 2000 Navarro Correas, a Cabernet Sauvignon from Argentina also was admired. Surprisingly, none of the Argentine wines in the top group was a malbec, Argentina's favorite noble grape. There's no doubt, however, that both countries have the potential to become important sources of fine wine.

AUSTRALIA

CABERNET-SHIRAZ

Or is it shiraz-cabernet? Anything goes Down Under

Those who control French appellations would be aghast at the thought of combining cabernet, the mainstay of Bordeaux, with the northern Rhône's syrah, as shiraz is known elsewhere in the world.

For Summer, Think Pink

Well chilled, rosé is a perfect antidote to 90 degrees in the shade

Rosés range in color from pale salmon to shades that border on red. There are generally two ways to make them. The first is to make a pink wine from red grapes. The depth of shade depends on the strength of pigmentation in the grapes and how long the juice is kept in contact with the skins. A less elegant method is to blend a small amount of finished red wine with a finished white.

Classic rosés come from the South of France, particularly Provence, where dry wines provide relief from the extreme heat of summer. French rosés include cabernet d'Anjou from the western Loire Valley, Tavel and Gigondas from the southern Rhone, and pink wines from Bordeaux. Spain, Italy, Australia, Germany and South Africa can also produce marvelous rosés. An outstanding American example is the iconic Vin Gris de Cigare from Randall Grahm of Bonny Doon Winery in California.

Most rosés aren't built to last and are best drunk within a year of their release. Wine shops generally take delivery on rosés in the mid- to late spring, so that is when you should stock up. If you want to splurge, there is nothing better than a delicious rosy Champagne from Nicholas Feuillatte with sweet-tart notes of cranberry. Spain has delicious rosés, or rosados, as they are called there. Artazuri Navarra, pale red, dry and refreshing, has light berry aromas and a slight effervescence that leave you wanting more. From Napa, try a Saintsbury Vin Gris of Pinot Noir, a clear red with generous aromas of fruit and flowers; a wine of body and substance. Or a Domaine de Nizas Languedoc from France, a dark salmon color, dry, with balanced, persistent fruit and mineral flavors; lively and energizing.

—Eric Asimov

FOOD

But to the freewheeling Aussies, it was a neat solution in the 1960's, when the demand rose for cabernet at the expense of shiraz, but not enough cabernet was available.

For an Australian wine to be called by the name of a single grape, at least 85 percent of the wine must have been composed of that grape. If no grape reaches the 85 percent threshold, then each grape must be named, up to a total of five, providing each is at least 5 percent of the blend. The grapes must be named in order, from highest proportion to lowest. Thus, a cabernet-shiraz would have more cabernet than shiraz, while the reverse would be true of a shiraz-cabernet.

The majority of cabernet-shiraz blends are moderately priced wines that epitomize Australia's skill at making soft, fruity crowd pleasers. They are juicy wines that may offer a lot of pleasure but have little individuality. What these wines offer is a sometimes extraordinary ratio of quality to price. Two to try: Yalumba Signature Barossa 1999, and Oxford Landing Eden Valley 2003.

AUSTRIA

GRUNER VELTLINERS AND RIESLINGS
An adventure for the jaded palette

On those rare occasions when people give any thought to Austrian wines, they most likely think of grüner veltliner. And why not? Austria is the only place on earth that produces these peppery, lively wines. As they have become more popular, grüner veltliner has solidified its place as the semi-pronounceable headliner of Austrian wines.

Total exports of quality Austrian wines amount to fewer than a few million cases of wine, less than

Matches Made in Heaven
Wine and cheese pairings that hit the spot

Max McCalman, a maître fromager, has written an entire book on the subject of which wines go with which cheeses, entitled *Cheese: A Connoisseur's Guide to the World's Best.* Yet even he is sometimes baffled by what works and what does not. "I was reading an article about pairing various American chardonnays with Stilton, and I thought this cannot be," he says. "But I tried it and they were surprisingly good matches."

White wine is almost always a better bet than red, especially whites with lots of lively acidity, like chenin blanc, sauvignon blanc and riesling, which can stand up to dominating cheese flavors. Yet there are exceptions. For instance, a beautifully floral 2002 gewürztraminer, a famously low-acid grape, goes nicely with a fruity aged mimolette.

Even better than acidic dry whites are acidic sweet whites. Coteaux du Layon from the Loire Valley is a great and underappreciated wine. A 2001 from Domaine des Baumard is lovely with a soft, lush Torta de la Merendera, a Spanish goat's milk cheese. It is also wonderful with a creamy, salty Cashel blue cheese from Ireland.

Champagne is often excellent; its effervescence makes a lively contrast to the richness of creamy cheeses. Ales and beers, too, can be particularly delicious matches. And while serving cheese with precious old Bordeaux, Burgundies or other complex and delicate wines is chancy, young reds are another story, especially those with a backbone of lively acidity. A medium-bodied 2002 Napa Valley zinfandel from Alex Sotelo was a neat match for the Irish blue cheese.

McCalman believes that sweet wines work best with a wide range of cheeses; a fallback offering for him is the humble moscato d'Asti, a delicate, lightly fizzy wine from the Piedmont region of Italy that usually tastes like sweet peaches.

—Eric Asimov

some of California's larger wineries. Yet the wines are often well made and a pleasure to drink. Austrian rieslings are almost always bone dry, and are characterized by power and richness. They have great texture, presence and weight, yet are rarely heavy, with wonderful mineral aromas and gentle flavors of peaches and apricots. They resemble rieslings from Alsace, but while the best Alsatian rieslings tend toward austerity, the Austrians are more generous, without losing focus.

CALIFORNIA

SAUVIGNON BLANCS

These pungent, acidic wines are coming into their own

California sauvignon blanc is beginning to assert itself as a wine that is impossible to ignore. For years, it was easy to deride California sauvignon blanc, because its producers either could not or would not make a wine that proclaimed the grape's distinctive identity.

But after the New Zealand wine industry came out of nowhere in the 1980's, California producers began producing a flock of pungent, razor-sharp sauvignon blancs that many people found irresistible. Producers began to take the grape more seriously. They thought hard about the best places to grow it and how to tend the vines. As a general rule when picking California sauvignon blancs, look for the newer vintages.

SYRAH

At home at last in America

Syrah was an insignificant wine in the U.S. until the early 1980's, when a group of young California winemakers, calling themselves the Rhone Rangers, set out to prove that California was more suited to syrah and other Rhône Valley grapes, which can

 **TIMELY TIPS**

Plonk Ain't What It Used to Be

Some $10 wines well worth drinking

Decades ago, when people in wine-producing countries routinely drank a few glasses with every meal, vast amounts of wine were made quickly and cheaply. It was sold for pennies—make that francs, lire and pesetas—to be consumed right away. Most of it was utter swill: thin and sour, or thick, raisiny and volatile.

The wine industry has changed drastically since then. The fact is that today, cheap wine across the board is far superior to what it was 50 years ago. It is not hard to find dry, refreshing, satisfying wines for $10 and under. Here are some good possibilities:

✔ **WHITES**

Steenberg South Africa, Sauvignon Blanc 2004

Veramonte Casablanca Valley, Chile, Sauvignon Blanc 2004

Domaine Duffour, Vin de Pays des Côtes de Gascogne 2003

Bodegas Salentein Mendoza, Argentina, Sauvignon Blanc Finca el Portillo 2004

✔ **REDS**

J. Vidal-Fleury Côtes-du-Rhône 2001

Domaine Lafond Lirac Roc-Épine 2002

Bonny Doon California, Ca'del Solo Big House Red 2003

—Eric Asimov

tolerate hot, dry weather, than cabernet sauvignon and chardonnay, which need more rain.

Wineries like Bonny Doon, Edmunds St. John, Thackrey and Qupé—Rhone Rangers all—have spread the message. Fine syrah is made by Tablas Creek, Ojai Vineyard in Santa Barbara, Joe Phelps

FOOD

and Beaulieu Vineyards in Napa Valley, John Kongsgaard, and Shafer Vineyards.

CALIFORNIA AND OREGON

PINOT NOIRS

Burgundy is the benchmark for these wines

Pinot noirs from Oregon and California are getting better and more distinctive. But as a benchmark for understanding the grape's awe-inspiring combination of beauty, power and finesse, only Burgundy will do. The reasons? California rarely has to endure capricious weather. The grapes there ripen easily, and the wines are often big and alcoholic. But in more marginal grape-growing regions like Burgundy, each year is a struggle to attain enough warmth and sun to ripen the fruit sufficiently, and the wines are often leaner and less fruit-driven than in California. Nonetheless, there are some unusually good pinots to be found in California. From the Russian River Valley, for example. Some of these pinots share a compactness, a core of strength with the best Burgundies, and like good Burgundies, they are pricey.

The Sonoma coast pinot noirs have also shown themselves to be among California's best and most distinctive wines, dense and concentrated without being heavy, full of dark fruit and earth flavors and a singular structure of tightly wound acidity.

In Oregon, winemakers have made the unforgiving pinot noir their signature grape, wrestling it into a wine that is often less flamboyant, less obvious than its California counterpart. Like a top Nuits-St.-Georges Burgundy, a good Oregon pinot, even a light one, can be nuanced and subtle, demanding some thought, even concentration on the drinker's part. From one moment to the next, the aromas and flavors of a good pinot noir can change in the glass, making it difficult to pin down. Some wines to try: Sokol Blosser Willamette Valley 1999; Ken Wright Cellars Willamette Valley Carter Vineyard 2001; J Vineyards Pinot Noir, Russian River Valley 2003.

—Howard G. Goldberg and Alice Gabriel
contributed to these reports

Champagne on the Cheap

Some sage advice on buying your bubbly for $30 and under

Genuine Champagne must be made in the strictly delimited Champagne region of France in a complicated succession of steps known collectively as the *méthode champenoise*.

Producers tend to baby their more expensive vintage Champagnes. Grapes from the best plots—those designated premier cru and grand cru—are generally reserved for the better and more expensive Champagnes.

Basic Champagnes typically receive far less consideration. None of the best wine goes into the blend that will result in the final nonvintage product, which can differ from year to year depending on which wines are available.

Of course, some Champagne houses like Bollinger, Louis Roederer and Billecart-Salmon are among those who still make superb nonvintage Champagnes, and smaller houses like Gosset, Alfred Gratien and Bruno Paillard also make excellent nonvintage Champagnes. But you are not likely to find any of these bottles for less than $30, certainly not anymore.

Included on the list of champagnes below are a couple of blanc de blancs, which are wines made entirely of chardonnay, rather than of the usual Champagne blend of chardonnay, pinot noir and pinot meunier. These blanc de blancs are not necessarily lighter than conventional Champagnes and often have a creamy texture, surprising complexity and precise mineral flavors. Each bottle typically sells for $30 or less.

Lanson Black Label Brut. *Dry and refreshing, with snappy acidity, mineral and citrus flavors.*

Louis de Sacy Brut Grand Cru. *Toasty and full bodied with a creamy texture and long-lasting flavors.*

Paul Goerg Blanc de Blancs. *Yeasty, toasty aromas, with complex floral and fruit flavors.*

Pierre Gimmonet & Fils Brut Blanc de Blancs. *Unusually complex and persistent flavors of apples, minerals and anise.*

Nicolas Feuillatte Brut NV. *Bright, substantial, with citrus and floral flavors; not quite bone dry.*

—Eric Asimov

CHAMPAGNES OF BIBLICAL PROPORTIONS

Many of the largest bottles are named after legendary Biblical kings. Sizes are in liters.

Melchisedec	30 L
Primat	27 L
Salomon	18 L
Nabuchodonosor	15 L
Balthazar	12 L
Salmanazar	9 L
Mathusalem	6 L
Réhoboam	4.5 L
Jéroboam	3 L
Magnum	1.5 L
Liter	1 L
Bottle (Frontignan)	.75 L
Half-bottle	.375 L

Beyond the Basic Six-Pack
Our picks of the best beers and ales

As anyone who has peered into the fridge of a liquor store, supermarket or convenience store lately knows, there are plenty of choices besides Budweiser. For those ready to venture beyond the familiar, here are some picks, along with expert observations from the *New York Times* tasting panels.

PILSNER
The prince of summer is not small beer

Pilsners are a subset of lagers, one of the two main types of beer. Ale, the other main type, is the older style, dating back to ancient Mesopotamia. Lager beers were developed around the 15th century when, before refrigeration, beer could only be brewed in cold weather. To have beer for summer drinking, Bavarian brewers began storing it in frigid alpine caves. Pilsner, a golden lager, is named after the town of Pilsen in Czech Bohemia. It is now the most popular style of beer in the world.

OUR PICKS: Victory Prima Pils, Downingtown, Pa.; Stoudt Pils, Adamstown, Pa.; Dortmunder Gold, Great Lakes Brewing Company, Cleveland, Ohio; Würzburger Hofbräu, Radeberger Pilsner, Germany.

PALE ALES
When they are good, they are complex and stimulating

Pale ale is more complex than a lager. You can discover a host of aromas and flavors in every paradoxically dry, bitter, brisk and refreshing sip. In the 1970's and 1980's, American brewers started using American hops in their pale ales instead

FOOD

of English hops. Far from the restrained aromas and flavors of English hops, American hops are a regular brass band, giving American pale ales their signature raucous aromas of grapefruit, flowers and pine.

OUR PICKS: Oskar Blues Brewery Dale's, Lyons, Colo.; Otter Creek, Middlebury, Vt.; Flying Dog Classic, Denver, Colo.; Southampton Publick House, Southampton, N.Y.

INDIA PALE ALE

A refreshing soldier's brew

This style of beer was developed in Britain in the 18th century, as a way to provide the empire's colonial troops in steamy India with rations of their beloved brew. A brewer named George Hodgson realized that a higher alcohol content would inhibit spoilage, and that bacterial action could be slowed by adding extra doses of hops, which impart bitterness, liveliness and aromatic complexity. The strong ale that resulted had a distinctive backbone of aggressive bitterness that could withstand the journey and still refresh the troops.

OUR PICKS: Smutty Nose Big A, Porstmouth, N.H.; Stone, San Diego, Calif.; Dogfish Head 90 Minute Imperial, Milton, Del.; Harpoon, Boston, Mass.

✔ TIMELY TIPS

The Dos and Don'ts of Drinking

✔ Drinking on an empty stomach gets you intoxicated faster. As soon as alcohol is consumed, the body starts to break it down, but some gets absorbed directly into the bloodstream.

✔ Having food in the stomach—particularly proteins, fats and dense carbohydrates—slows the absorption process.

✔ Carbonated mixers, soda and warm drinks speed up absorption.

—Anahad O'Connor

STOUT

Robust, complex brews that are a meal in themselves

What makes an ale a stout? Primarily it's the dark, almost black color achieved by brewing with barley that has been roasted to the point of charring. This gives stout its characteristic chocolate-coffee flavor as well as a fuller body than other dark beers. Hops lend stout a floral aroma and a little bitterness.

OUR PICKS: Samuel Smith's Imperial Stout, England; Samuel Smith Oatmeal Stout, England; Rogue Shakespeare Stout, Oregon; Brooklyn Brewery Black Chocolate, New York; Young's Oatmeal Stout, England; Rogue Chocolate Stout, Oregon.

TRAPPIST ALES

Heavenly brews with lots of character

The term "Trappist" describes the source of the ales rather than a brewing style. In fact, the beers vary considerably, but they are always strong, ranging in alcohol from about 7 percent to 12 percent.

Only six breweries in the world, all affiliated with Trappist monasteries in Belgium, are permitted to use the hexagonal seal designating each bottle an "Authentic Trappist Product," which guarantees that the beer is brewed in an abbey under the supervision of the religious order, and that most of the income will be used for charitable work.

Dozens of Belgian breweries make excellent versions of Trappist ales. Some of them are even commissioned by monasteries to brew ales or are licensed to use a monastery name. These are known as abbey beers. North American craft brewers, likewise inspired by these beers, have made their own distinctive versions.

OUR PICKS: Westmalle Abbey Triple, Belgium; Unibroue La Fin du Monde, Chambly, Quebec; Affligem Abbey Triple, Belgium; Weyerbacher Quad, Easton, Pa.; Achel Trappist Extra, Belgium.

—Eric Asimov and the Tasting Panel

Mixology 101: Classic Cocktails

From the Bloody Mary to the gimlet

The cocktail's golden age in America lasted from 1870 to 1912, when barmen in white coats were master craftsmen who spent years in apprenticeships and concocted their own bitters, syrups and cordials. Now, a hundred years later, the art of the cocktail is receiving renewed interest. Enterprising bartenders are reaching for off-label brands, while adding homemade touches for new old-fashioned drinks. They are resurrecting such forgotten spirits as pisco, Madeira, Chartreuse herbal liqueur, maraschino liqueur and sloe gin.

In that spirit, here are recipes from some of the finest mixologists in the business:

BLOODY MARY (or the Red Snapper)

Adapted from the St. Regis

The queen of the hangover drinks is the Bloody Mary. But the concoction is notoriously difficult to get right, demanding a balance of strength and flavor, as any cocktail does, plus a degree of spice suited to the drinker, then the real trick, texture.

Dale DeGroff, former head bartender at the Rainbow Room in New York City and an authority on mixology, cautions that too many bartenders overdo the Tabasco and Worcestershire. "They want something that will fry your tonsils, when the beauty of it is the sweetness of the tomato juice," he says. Small cubes melt too fast, so large square cubes only, please.

1 ounce vodka
2 ounces tomato juice
1 dash lemon juice
2 dashes salt
2 dashes black pepper
2 dashes cayenne pepper
3 dashes of Worcestershire sauce

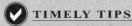

TIMELY TIPS

How to Cure a Hangover

✔ Doctors recommend drinking orange juice or sports drinks that replenish electrolytes, and taking pain relievers like aspirin or ibuprofen. Tylenol is inadvisable because, like alcohol, it is metabolized by the already-overworked liver.

✔ No one advises more alcohol, the "hair of the dog that bit you."

✔ Many experts agree that the best cure for a hangover is to avoid drinking too much in the first place. Dr. Marc K. Siegel, an internist at New York University Medical School, says the best bet is a cup of coffee, a dash of Mylanta and a lot of water. "It's not sexy," Siegel says. "But those things work."

—Alex Williams and Jonathan Glater

Mix all ingredients but vodka. Pour vodka over ice. Add mix. Stir. Do not garnish.

THE CLASSIC MARTINI

John Conti's version

Theories about the origins of the martini are as varied as those concerning the proportion of gin to vermouth. Most people agree, though, that the standard martini is a gin-based drink with a five-to-one ratio of gin to vermouth. A recipe for a dry martini cocktail from 1907 calls for orange bitters, half a jigger of dry vermouth and half a jigger of dry gin. Although vodka has become a frequent substitute for gin in martinis, it is a modern invention.

John Conti, a pupil of master bartender Dale DeGroff, concocted a version that uses a regular premium gin, like Boodles or Tanqueray, not one of the super-premiums like Ten or Wet, which he considers too aromatic for the drink. He uses a long-necked spoon, bent slightly so that it follows the sides of the glass. "You slide the spoon down and twirl, as opposed to agitating, he says.

3 ounces gin
½ ounce dry vermouth
Green olive

Chill a 7-ounce martini glass by filling it with ice and water. Fill a professional bartender's glass, or a tall 16-ounce glass, two-thirds full with ice. Add gin and vermouth to the bartender's glass and stir with a long-necked spoon, keeping the spoon close to the side of the glass as you swirl the ice. Stir until the glass frosts, about 20 seconds. Empty the martini glass and strain the contents of the bartender's glass into it. Garnish with the olive.

THE MANHATTAN

Adapted from Morgan's Bar at Morgan's Hotel

The Manhattan was created in 1874, using rye whiskey, at the Manhattan Club in New York at the behest of Jenny Jerome, a socialite better known in later years as the mother of Winston Churchill. The occasion was an elaborate party celebrating the election of Samuel J. Tilden as governor. Popular tastes have changed the standard Manhattan into a bourbon drink with sweet vermouth, and a cherry or twist of lemon.

One or two dashes Angostura bitters
Maraschino cherry or lemon twist
2 ½ ounces Maker's Mark bourbon (or a rye whiskey, if you prefer)
1 ounce sweet vermouth

Shake one or two dashes of bitters into a cocktail glass, gently twisting the glass from side to side. Shake out the excess, leaving only the residue. Mix bourbon or rye with sweet vermouth in a mixing glass. Add ice. Shake well. Strain the contents into the cocktail glass. Garnish with cherry or lemon.

THE GIMLET

From Fifty Seven Fifty Seven Bar at the Four Seasons Hotel

The gimlet's logic seems clear: gin or vodka, with Rose's Lime Juice and fresh lime juice in equal parts, shaken or stirred until ice cold and served straight up in a stemmed cocktail glass. The garnish—and a gimlet should have it—is a thin crescent moon of lime, floated in the drink invitingly, not perched on the side like a timid swimmer looking at a cold lake. Making a gimlet icy gives it smoothness when sipped. For that reason, it is an excellent summer drink.

Some prefer vodka, for its understatement. Gin talks too much, with its juniper bush-berry accent. And what you want, as everyone knows, is a drinking companion who listens.

4 ounces vodka (or gin if you insist)
½ ounce fresh lime juice
½ ounce Rose's Lime Juice
1 thin lime wedge

Combine liquid ingredients in a cocktail shaker with ice. Shake, and strain into a martini glass. Garnish with lime wedge.

THE MARGARITA

Adapted from Dale DeGroff

The margarita is an American staple, whether in its frozen-slush frat-party style or as a straight-up cocktail that can rival a martini for elegance. It first appeared in the days after the repeal of Prohibition when everyone was creating new cocktails. One widely circulated creation myth credits a bartender who some versions say worked outside Los Angeles and others place near Tijuana. He reportedly concocted the drink for a starlet who could only drink tequila, but didn't like its taste. Her name was Marjorie—Margarita in Spanish.

Lime slice, $^1/_2$ inch thick, for salting glass
Kosher salt
2 ounces silver tequila
1 ounce Cointreau
$^3/_4$ ounce fresh lime juice

1. Rub lime slice around outer rim of cocktail glass. Place salt in a dish. Holding glass parallel to dish, coat only the outside with salt. Place glass in refrigerator.

2. Fill a cocktail shaker with ice and add tequila, Cointreau and lime juice. Shake well. Strain into chilled cocktail glass.

—Frank Prial and William L. Hamilton, with contributions from R. W. Apple Jr., Michael Brick and Christine Muhlke

Stocking the Liquor Cabinet
Our picks for some good basic bottles

Need help choosing bottles for the bar? Here are some recommendations from the tasting panels at the *New York Times*:

VODKA. Most spirits can be made only from certain prescribed ingredients, but vodka can be distilled from just about anything that can be fermented into alcohol: grains, vegetables, even fruits. What sets vodkas apart from one another are essentially the base ingredients used in the distillation and the water. Recommendations:

• Smirnoff (United States) Grain. Pure, clean and ultrasmooth, with pleasing texture and classic vodka aroma.

• Wyborowa (Poland) Single Estate Rye. Elegant and intriguing, with mild flavors and great persistence.

• Belvedere (Poland) Rye. Great smoothness and purity, with good texture and body.

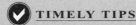 **TIMELY TIPS**

Whiskey-Sipping Secrets

✔ First, says Richard Paterson, a master blender at the Dalmore Distillery in Scotland, $25 is more than enough to spend on a bottle of single malt.

✔ Second, don't make the mistake of serving it on the rocks: ice bruises the flavor. Instead, before drinking, swill a little whiskey around the glass to clean out any lingering odors and then discard. Pour out a small amount and dilute with room-temperature water. Even a teardrop will be enough to activate the chemical reaction that releases whiskey's flavors. If in doubt, add water until the vapors don't sting your eyes when you raise the glass to drink.

✔ Then, follow the years-as-seconds rule: a 12-year-old whiskey, for instance, reveals its complexity after 12 seconds in the mouth.

✔ Pairing a cigar with whiskey is a scam. This affectation simply grew from the tradition of serving them at the end of a meal and helped to provide an excuse for a lingering male-bonding session. Instead, try a morsel of dark chocolate chewed as a chaser to each sip.

—Mark Ellwood

GIN. High-end gins start off as vodka, then are infused with any number of botanicals, mostly juniper berries, but also coriander, anise, lemon and grapefruit zest, cinnamon and many others. While the classic flavor of gin is dominated by juniper, these high-end gins each have their own flavor signatures. Recommendations:

• Boodles and Beefeater make excellent gins, classic yet completely different from each other.

• Bombay Sapphire London Dry, 94 Proof. Elegant; lemon, lavender, coriander and juniper blend deliciously.

FOOD

Not Just Any Old Mint Julep

The original Kentucky Derby recipe—complete with silver cup

The classic julep—first served to Kentucky Derby guests in 1875 by Col. Meriwether Lewis Clark Jr., the founder of Churchill Downs—is made with just four ingredients: finely crushed ice, a little sugar water, fresh spearmint and fine, aged, 90-proof straight Kentucky bourbon. And, of course, the essential silver julep cup.

KENTUCKY DERBY MINT JULEPS
1 cup spring or bottled water
1 cup granulated sugar
$1/2$ cup small spearmint leaves, no stems
Finely crushed or shaved ice, enough to fill the cups completely
High-quality Kentucky bourbon, like Maker's Mark or Woodford Reserve
Sprigs of spearmint

1. The day before serving, or even earlier, put the julep cups in the freezer. Put the water and sugar in a small saucepan, bring to a boil without stirring, and boil for 2 minutes, or until sugar is completely dissolved.

2. Put the mint leaves in a glass jar or cup, pour the slightly cooled syrup over them, let cool, then cover and refrigerate for 12 hours or longer. When ready to use, strain out the mint leaves.

3. Half an hour before serving, pack the julep cups tightly up to the rim with crushed ice and return them to the freezer.

4. For each julep pour 3 ounces of bourbon over the ice, followed by two teaspoons of mint syrup. Do not stir or agitate. Use a cloth to hold each cup by the rim, so as not to disturb the frost. Use a short straw or a chopstick to make a hole in the ice on the side of the cup and insert a sprig of mint. Serve immediately, on a silver tray.

YIELD: Up to 20 juleps.

—Suzanne Hamlin

BOURBON. Deluxe bourbons, with their complex perfumes and amalgams of fruit, sugar and spice flavors, are meant to be drunk slowly. In their rustic quality, they resemble Armagnac, with the flavor of corn, not grapes. By law, bourbon must be distilled at not more than 80 percent alcohol (160 proof) and must contain at least 51 percent corn.

- If you like your alcohol powerful, there is no better choice than Booker's, the only bourbon bottled straight from the barrel.

- A mellowed whisky of great distinction, introduced in the last few years, is Woodford Reserve, produced in Woodford County, Ky. Both should be drunk neat, after dinner.

RUM. Rum can vary greatly, depending on where it is produced and by what method. Like gin and vodka, rum can be made anywhere in the world. Most rums use molasses as their base, but many use sugar cane juice instead, especially rums made in French-speaking areas, which are labeled *rhum agricole*, or agricultural rum. By contrast, molasses-based rums are often referred to as industrial rum, often an unfairly pejorative term. Here are recommendations for white and amber rums:

- 10 Cane Trinidad Light. Neither white nor amber, but pure, smooth and elegant, with luscious sugar-cane flavor and enticing texture.

- Demerara El Dorado. Rich amber color, with aromas of banana and vanilla; pure and subtle.

- St. James Royal Amber. Smooth, rich, floral; lingering flavors, with great personality.

- Cane Louisiana White. Vanilla aroma; smooth, with a thick texture and long, lingering flavors.

- Mount Gay Eclipse. Mellow, pure and smooth, with vanilla and butter aromas.

A Proper Mojito
The technique is simple; the results are heavenly

2 sprigs fresh mint
2 ounces fresh lime juice
1^1/$_2$ ounces white rum
1 teaspoon superfine sugar
Crushed ice
4 ounces club soda

In a mixing glass, muddle the mint leaves with the lime juice in the bottom of a tall cocktail glass. (To muddle, you mash or crush the mint leaves, using the back of a spoon, or a special muddling tool. Muddling releases the oils of the mint into the lime juice.)

Add the rum, sugar, crushed ice and soda. Cover and shake, and uncover, serving with a lime wedge.

Yield: 1 cocktail.

—Dale DeGroff

TEQUILA. Tequila can be called tequila only if it is made in Mexico, from the blue agave plant. The least expensive tequilas need only be distilled from 51 percent blue agave juice. The more expensive, and many say the best, are made from 100 percent blue agave juice, and those words must appear on the label.

After the tequila is produced, it is further classified by how long it has aged. Silver tequila, also called blanco or plata, is bottled immediately after distillation. Reposado is "rested" in wood for at least two months. Añejo tequila is aged in barrels for at least a year. There is also gold tequila, which is unaged but treated with additives to give it an aged effect. Recommendations:

- Chinaco Blanco. Classic agave character and complex mineral and herbal flavors.
- Hacienda del Cristero. Smooth, pure and complex with a great finish, nutty, peppery and vanilla flavors.
- El Tesoro de Don Felipe Silver. Intense mineral and roasted, spicy flavors and a long finish.

—Eric Asimov and Frank J. Prial
with R. W. Apple Jr. on bourbon

The Perfect Cup of Espresso
An insider's tricks to brewing your own tazza

A good cup of espresso can be as close as your kitchen counter. Gerald Baldwin, director of Peet's Tea & Coffee in Berkeley, Calif., a premier coffee company, shares some secrets on preparing a perfect cup:

To enjoy espresso at home, you need a machine that uses steam, says Baldwin. That's because stovetop moka pots and some cheaper espresso machines do not generate enough pressure to produce the intense flavor of espresso.

Start with fresh cold water—never use water from the hot tap, or water that has already boiled. Bottled or filtered water is recommended when old plumbing imparts an unpleasant flavor, or in areas with heavily chlorinated or hard water.

Home grinding is essential, because finely ground coffee goes stale in just a few hours. Precise grinding is crucial in the formation of golden-brown crema, the true sign of a well-made espresso. Crema will not form if the coffee is improperly ground; if it is too coarse, the espresso will come through in less than 15 seconds and there will be too much fluid; if it is too fine, longer than 20 seconds will be required, and there will be only a small amount of bitter fluid. (White crema is another indication that the infusion was too slow.)

If the coffee is fresh, making the appropriate adjustments to the grind should produce the result

FOOD

JAVA JOLTS TO START YOU UP

Shown here are the drinks that contain caffeine—and the number of milligrams in each serving.

you're aiming for—1½ to 2 oz. of rich, brown ambrosia with the desired crema—though you might also try tamping the coffee into the portafilter more or less firmly to slow down or speed up the process.

A World Tour of Teas

Different approaches to an ancient brew

One of the world's most popular beverages, tea is produced everywhere from China to South America. The tea plant, *Camellia sinensis*, is a member of the large family of flowering camellias. The best known is black tea. Other types of tea, such as green, oolong, yellow, white and puerh, are also popular. They differ from one another only in the way they are processed. Once the processing is over, another step is sometimes taken, to add fruit, spice or flower flavorings to create scented teas, such as Earl Grey or orange spice tea.

THE BRITISH CUPPA

British writer George Orwell devoted an entire essay, "A Nice Cup of Tea," to the art of making

tea, with Indian or Ceylon leaves (no tea bags, please). He said the pot should be warmed beforehand, and the water should be poured boiling onto the leaves. Tea should be drunk strong, with milk and no sugar, with many additional cups of tea produced by merely adding more hot water to the pot. Tea should have a bitter taste, like beer, Orwell claimed.

A PURIST'S APPROACH

Roy Fong, owner of The Imperial Tea Court in San Francisco, recommends preparing loose, whole-leaf teas fresh by the cup, steeping them in water for only a minute or two at temperatures not greater than 185 degrees Fahrenheit. The delicate, decidedly nonbitter liquor is then drained from the leaves using a small utility strainer or the lid of a Chinese covered teacup (*gaiwan*) to retain the leaves in the cup. The leaves may be used again for additional infusions with slightly increased water temperature and steeping time, as desired. White, green and yellow teas are prepared this way. For loose red (black), oolong and puerh teas, use a higher water temperature, but for the gourmet palate, never at the boiling point.

THE EUROPEAN WAY

Europeans generally drink their tea with lemon and sugar or honey, and some Russians drink their tea sweetened with fruit jam. Many of them drink tea out of glasses. They tend to favor scented teas as well, but very often add sugar.

MOROCCAN TEA: GARDEN MINT

There is nothing more refreshing to drink than fresh-cut spearmint, steeped in hot water for two minutes. For Moroccan-style mint tea, add several teaspoons of sugar per cup.

CHAPTER 3

MONEY

Personal Finance   166

BUDGETING·166: *You, Inc.* • *Figuring your budget* • *Calculating your net worth* **SAVING·168:** *The best way to save* • *The risks of online banking* • *How to save $100 or more this year* • *How to open a Swiss bank account* • *Want to get rich quick?* **CHILDREN·173:** *What it costs to raise a child* • *Reining in teenage spending* • *Rules for boomerang kids* **CREDIT·177:** *Cards that reward* • *Check your credit rating* **DEBT·178:** *Beyond get-out-of-debt clichés* • *Going bankrupt*

Investing   181

STOCKS & BONDS·181: *Where to put your money* • *The stock or the moment?* • *Bulls vs. bears* • *Amateurs vs. pros* • *Does real estate beat stocks?* • *Staying ahead of the curve* • *Advice from the Oracle of Omaha* **MUTUAL FUNDS·190:** *How to pick a mutual fund* • *Why you can't beat the market* • *Reading a balance sheet* • *Words to watch on Wall Street* • *How to estimate total return* • *Does big mean bad for funds?* • *Beware of mutual fund taxes* **FINANCIAL ADVISORS·197:** *Finding a broker you can trust* **RETIREMENT·199:** *Nurturing your 401 (k)* • *Calculating retirement needs*

Real Estate   202

HOME BUYING·202: *The long view on real estate* • *Better to buy or rent?* **MORTGAGES·207:** *The mortgage minefield* • *Which mortgage is for you?* • *Terms to learn before closing* • *Figuring monthly payments* • *What you can afford* • *Playing the refinancing game* **SECOND HOMES·215:** *A cottage in the country* • *The priciest vacation havens* **OPPORTUNITIES·220:** *Houses on the cheap* • *Bargains abroad* • *Homesick at 64?* • *Beyond houses*

Insurance & Taxes   226

BUYERS' GUIDE·226: *Policies to keep you covered: life, health, disability, homeowners and auto* • *Why bet on long-term care insurance?* • *Coverage you may not need* • *Insurance terms* **TAX PLANNING·237:** *Easily-overlooked deductions* • *Preparing your returns* • *Year-end tax-saving tips* • *The giving circle* • *Charitable contributions* • *What to show your accountant* **AUDITS·243:** *Do you fit the audit profile?* • *If the I.R.S. comes knocking*

MONEY

Personal Finance

You, Inc.

Keeping yourself on track and in the black

Most of us don't think of ourselves as economic units, small business enterprises with inflows and outflows. But, in some sense, of course, we are. Money comes in, hopefully, and we spend it on food, shelter, clothing and various and sundry other things. How are you doing with your inflows and outlays? Here are some ways to keep track.

FIGURING YOUR BUDGET

A budget is the ultimate reality check. It hits you square between the eyes with what you're bringing in and what you're shelling out, no delusions, no fantasies, just the steel-knife economic reality. Start making a budget by tallying up your income and then itemizing your outlays. At the end of the exercise, if your expenses exceed your income, it's time to ask where you can pare down on spending.

If you're spending less than you're bringing home, you have the good fortune of showing a surplus. Note that the "savings" category is on the fixed-expenses side of the ledger. That's because you can develop good habits by thinking of saving as a fixed payment to yourself. If you have a surplus, you might consider giving yourself a raise.

CALCULATING YOUR NET WORTH

An annual checkup on this key household figure is good for your financial health. It's a valuable baseline to see if you're achieving your financial goals—saving for college tuition or retirement, for example, or if you're falling behind. If you find you're

slipping, you may need to consider spending cuts, taking on more work or reassessing that dream.

To calculate how much you're worth, you can turn to the army of personal finance software, internet calculators and tried-but-true financial tomes.

But you still have to plug in the figures. Once you've gathered up the documents and the data (see chart, next page), it's a simple calculation—assets minus liabilities—to arrive at your net worth.

 INSIDE INFO

The Net Worth of a Nation

What's the net worth of the country's households? Here's the latest snapshot from the Census Bureau. (In trillions for 2004)

ASSETS

Tangible assets

Real estate:	$18.75
Durable goods and other:	3.78

Financial assets

Pension funds:	10.12
Stocks:	6.33
Business and farm assets:	6.10
Deposits:	5.59
Mutual funds:	3.73
Credit market instruments:	2.49
Other, including life insurance:	2.14
TOTAL:	**59.03**

LIABILITIES

Mortgages:	$7.55
Credit cards:	2.14
Other types of debt, insurance premiums and bills:	1.01
TOTAL:	**10.70**

NET WORTH:	**$48.33 TRILLION**

FIGURING YOUR BUDGET

INCOME

Salaries (after taxes)	$
Part-time work	$
Child support/Alimony	$
Investment interest, dividends, real estate income	$
Other	$
Total net income	$

EXPENSES

Fixed expenses

Savings	$
Taxes (federal, state and local)	$
Rent or mortgage payments	$
Utilities (gas, electric, water, telephone)	$
Insurance (health, life, disability, house, car)	$
Food	$
Education	$
Personal fixed expenses (i.e., hair care)	$
Transportation	
Total Fixed Expenses	$

Variable expenses

Credit card bills	$
Loans	$
Clothing	$
Gas	
Car maintenance	$
Home improvements	$
Parking, tolls	$
Restaurant meals	$
Entertainment	$
Charitable contributions	$
Gifts	$
Vacations	$
Miscellaneous	$
Total variable expenses:	$
Total fixed and variable expenses:	$
TOTAL NET INCOME:	$

CALCULATING YOUR NET WORTH

ASSETS
Cash and investments

Cash on hand	$
Savings and checking accounts	$
Certificates of deposit	$
Money market funds	$
Common and preferred stock	$
Mutual funds	$
Bonds	$
Brokerage funds	$
Cash value of life insurance	$
Equity in profit-sharing plans	$
Equity in pension plans (401K's)	$
Individual Retirement Accounts (I.R.A.'s)	$
Business and real estate investments	$
Loans owed to you	$
Other	$

Personal Assets (est. market value)

Home or homes and furnishings	$
Cars	$
Boats and other recreational vehicles	$
Furs and jewelry	$
Art, antiques and collectibles	$
Other assets	$
Total assets	$

LIABILITIES

Balance owed on mortgage	$
Outstanding loans:	$
Auto, bank, student or others	$
Home equity credit line	$
Other credit lines	$
Bills due	$
Credit card bills due	$
Outstanding taxes due	$
Other bills	$
Total liabilities	$

TOTAL ASSETS – TOTAL LIABILITIES = NET WORTH

MONEY

WATCHING $100 GROW

Find how much compound interest your original $100 earned at a given rate and time invested.

Rate (annual)	3%	4%	5%	6%	7%	8%	9%	10%
Time (years)								
1	$3	$4	$5	$6	$7	$8	$9	$10
2	6.09	8.16	10.25	12.36	14.49	16.64	18.81	21.00
3	9.27	12.49	15.76	19.10	22.50	25.97	29.50	33.10
4	12.55	16.99	21.55	26.25	31.08	36.05	41.16	46.41
5	15.93	21.67	27.63	33.82	40.26	46.93	53.86	61.05

The Best Way to Save

Simple interest is good, but compounding is so much better

Invest your savings at a simple interest rate and your money will grow, albeit slowly. Simple interest is applied only to the principal amount, not to the accumulated interest. Say you save $100 at 7 percent interest for five years. Your balance will be $135 after five years.

But with compound interest, your savings grow further beyond your initial investment, thanks to interest piling upon interest as well as the principal. That same $100 at 7 percent compound interest for five years will net you $140.26. Now, say you save $100 each month for 5 years at 7 percent. You will have invested $6,000, but your savings will have grown to $7,524.20.

To figure out how long it will take you to double your investment, use the Rule of 72. Take the percentage interest rate you are earning and divide it into 72. The result is approximately the number of years it will take to double your principal without making any other contributions. For example, say you invest at a 7 percent interest rate: 72 divided by 7 = 10.3. It will take just over 10 years for your principal to double.

Know the Risks of Online Banking

It's easy to put your bills on autopilot, but beware of risks

Despite the explosion of online banking and electronic bill paying, growth has been uneven at best. More than 53 million people, or about 44 percent of all Internet users, regularly check their bank statements online, according to a study conducted in 2004 by the Pew Internet and American Life Project. But at large financial institutions like Bank of America and Wells Fargo, fewer than half of customers pay bills online.

Millions of consumers swear by the simplicity and the savings from not using stamps, but millions of others—often older, wealthy and sometimes even technology-savvy—are holding out. Most are concerned with the security of their personal information and the perceived loss of control of paying their bills online.

Financial service companies have been introducing safeguards to their own Web sites, adding extra steps to the sign-in process in an effort to

---

ⓘ **INSIDE INFO**

A Personal Worst for Savings

○ The personal savings rate has been in negative territory only three times in recent history:

○ In 1932 and 1933, when the country was struggling to cope with the Great Depression.

○ In 2005, when consumers depleted savings to buy cars and other big-ticket items.

SOURCE: U.S. Department of Commerce

TIMELY TIPS

How to Save $100 or More This Year

Forget dumpster diving, recycling tin foil and other tacky tightwad tips. Instead, take a systematic look at your spending habits, then apply these suggestions for saving substantial sums.

✔ **1. Pick a bank wisely.** Look for free checking and no A.T.M. or debit card fees. Some banks will waive fees if you have your paycheck deposited directly.

✔ **2. Take advantage of your utility's "load management"** or "off-hours" programs for cheaper electricity bills. You save by allowing the company to switch off your water heater and air conditioner briefly during times of high demand.

✔ **3. Drop telephone calling plans with monthly fees** or minimum usage if you make few toll or long distance calls. Check your bill to see if you have optional calling services you don't use. Each one you drop could save you $40 or more a year.

✔ **4. Forgo stopping at convenience stores,** which often charge the highest prices around. Go to the nearest discount grocery store or drug store instead.

✔ **5. Go grocery shopping with a list and stick to it.** Pay attention to the price per pound or other unit; compare among brands and go with the lowest price per unit.

✔ **6. Buy in bulk,** especially goods like paper towels and diapers. For example, babies use about 2,400 diapers their first year. A 5-cent savings in

the cost of one diaper adds up to $120 a year.

✔ **7. Don't stick to one drug store.** They charge widely differing prices. Shop around and buy generic drugs, when possible. Order prescriptions by mail or through your health plan.

✔ **8. Keep your car engine tuned** and tires inflated to the proper pressure. Doing so can save you up to $100 a year on gas.

✔ **9. Cut round-trip airfare** by up to two-thirds. Buy in advance, include a Saturday-night stayover.

✔ **10. Reconfigure your vacation plans.** Consider alternative travel programs that let you stay free with local families if you host others in your home. (Check out www.exchange-zones.com, for example.)

SOURCES: Consumer Literacy Consortium, Federal Trade Commission

MONEY

reduce fraud. Bank of America, for instance, asks customers to click on a photo assigned to their account in addition to punching in a password.

Perhaps, the biggest risks of online banking and bill payment to consumers are the ones that seem to generate the least concern. "We try to stress that electronic bill payment is not synonymous with instantaneous payment," says Joe Rideout, a spokesman for Consumer Action, a San Francisco–based advocacy and educational group. "You still have to plan your payments well in advance."

Some experts also advise against using automatic bill payment, especially for items like electricity and cellphones where use can vary

substantially month to month. While electronic bill payment reduces desk clutter, it also means that when a mistake is made there is less of a paper trail. Even though federal laws provide the same protections for electronic facsimiles as they do for paper checks, tax experts say hard copies might also be helpful if there is ever a run-in with auditors from the I.R.S.

BEFORE YOU LEAP TO ONLINE BANKING

Online banking and bill payment can be convenient and keep kitchen tables free of clutter. But according to Consumer Action, a San Francisco–based group, there are several things you should consider before you decide to stop writing checks and begin online banking—beginning with a review of your bank's security standards.

Make sure to look for:

- 128-bit encryption technology that offers the maximum protection in scrambling your data.

- A written guarantee to protect account holders from losses from online fraud.

- An automatic lockout if you enter your password wrong more than three or four times.

- An automatic logout if you are not active at the site for a certain amount of time.

Some banks also offer additional safeguards, like picture passwords and security tokens that make account log-in information more difficult for hackers to guess.

WHEN USING YOUR BANK'S WEB SITE

- Choose a unique password that cannot be commonly guessed (not a phone number or mother's maiden name).

- Bookmark the bank's address in your browser rather than typing in the address each time you want to visit. Slight mistakes in entering the address may take you to a "spoofer" site set up by criminals to trick you into entering your account number and password so that they can gain access to your account.

WHEN PAYING BILLS ONLINE

- Enter all account numbers and company names exactly as they appear on your billing statements.

- Plan your payments well in advance.

- Recurring bills of the same amount can be scheduled to be sent automatically. For cellphone or electric bills that can vary each month, enter the amounts in time to avoid a late payment or set up

parameters to pay all bills under a certain amount, but require authorization if they run over.

- Remember that not all companies can accept electronic payments. Your bank must send those businesses a check. This can take up to 10 days. Most sites will advise you of this lag time in advance.

- The funds are withdrawn from your account on the day the bill payment is due to be sent. Update your checkbook register to reflect any payments you have scheduled so that you do not overdraw your account.

—Eric Dash

How to Get a Swiss Bank Account
Worried about keeping your money under the mattress? Here's an alternative

Nearly everyone thinks of Swiss banks as repositories for the tainted funds of Eurotrash and rapacious dictators. Whether that reputation is deserved, only Swiss bankers know for sure. But behind the James Bond–like mystique, Swiss banking is really quite mundane. With a little effort and fewer funds than you might think, you, too, can open a Swiss bank account.

Several Swiss banks have offices in the United States, among them Credit Suisse, UBS AG and Bank Julius Baer & Co., all located in New York. But, U.S. branches offer only investment banking services and asset management for accounts of $200,000 or more. Setting up a retail account requires more effort, if substantially fewer funds. You can set up a retail account with a Swiss bank only through its headquarters in Switzerland. You can find bank names and contact information from the Swiss Bankers Association, online at www.swissbanking.org/en.home.htm.

MONEY

ℹ️ **INSIDE INFO**

Show Me the Money

○ The Bureau of Engraving and Printing is pumping out more colorful currency that's designed to thwart counterfeiters. The new bills have shades of red, yellow and orange added to the traditional green. A transformed $100 bill will make a debut in 2007.

○ Benjamin Franklin still graces the $100 bill, the largest denomination currently issued. Here's the pecking order:

AMOUNT	FRONT	BACK
$1	George Washington	U.S. Seal
$2	Thomas Jefferson	Signers of Declaration
$5	Abraham Lincoln	Lincoln Memorial
$10	Alexander Hamilton	U.S. Treasury
$20	Andrew Jackson	White House
$50	Ulysses Grant	U.S. Capitol
$100	Benjamin Franklin	Independence Hall

○ Martha Washington is the only woman whose portrait has appeared on a U.S. currency note. It appeared on the face of the $1 Silver Certificate of 1886 and 1891, and the back of the $1 Silver Certificate of 1896.

○ The average life span of a $1 bill is about 22 months. A $10 bill survives for about three years.

SOURCE: U.S. Bureau of Printing and Engraving

Once you've picked a bank, you can apply by mail or go directly to the bank's headquarters in Switzerland. The minimum to open a retail account is typically $250. You'll have to go through a fairly rigorous screening process in compliance with the country's strict "know your customer" laws, which are intended to prevent money-laundering. Forms vary among banks, but for a mail application, you will need to send a signature certification form and an authenticated copy of your passport. Whether you apply by mail or in person, you may have to show proof of your address, such as a utility bill, for example, and a copy of a recent credit card statement if you are charging your deposit. In addition, you may be asked for documents to verify your annual income and to prove the "economic origin" of the funds you want to deposit. In other words, how you arrived at the money. That could mean providing a copy of your employment contract, a bill of sale or similar documents.

What happens if your Swiss banking experience turns sour? You have three recourses. First, contact the bank's legal department and file a complaint. If your claim is denied, contact a mediator at www.bankingombudsman.ch/english or call ++41 1213 14 50. Or write to Contact Office for the Swiss Banks, Schweizergasse 21, P.O. Box 1818, CH-8021 Zurich, Switzerland.

If you still get no satisfaction and want to sue, you'll need a Swiss lawyer. Search for one online at www.swisslawyers.com, call the Swiss Bar Association at ++41 31 313 06 06, or write to Swiss Bar Association, Marktgasse 4, P.O. Box 8321, CH-3001, Bern, Switzerland.

The huge appeal of a Swiss bank account is its reputation for privacy. No one is allowed access to your account data, including lawyers or investigators who may want the information for divorce or bankruptcy proceedings, for example. The few exceptions that would force Swiss bankers to "open" your account for scrutiny are cases of suspected criminal activity, such as drug trafficking.

But even that much-vaunted Swiss bank secrecy isn't inviolable. In 2000, the Swiss bank account numbers and data about private transactions of hundreds of people—including James Bond actor Roger Moore—were mistakenly available for view online for one week. Their bank, Credit Suisse, blamed a subcontractor for the technical glitch.

Making Millions by the Book

Here are a few long-time, top-selling books that promise to make you a millionaire. Advice not given: hold seminars and write get-rich books.

THE BOOK	ADVICE GIVEN:	COMMENT
Rich Dad, Poor Dad *Robert Kiyosaki with Sharon L. Lechter* CREDENTIALS: Wealth-building seminar speaker	1. Pay yourself first. 2. Create passive income using, for example, investments in distressed real estate. 3. Skip the formal education and corporate job.	Writes that salting money away each month "blinds" the person from what is really going on, and they miss "major opportunities for much more significant growth of their money." This is advice for people who like to live on the edge.
Secrets of the Millionaire Mind *T. Harv Eker* CREDENTIALS: Motivational seminar speaker	1. Recognize what's keeping you from becoming rich. 2. Change your mind-set. 3. Declare: "I have a millionaire mind."	Suggests a daily affirmation in which you put hand over heart and say, "I am an excellent receiver. I am open and willing to receive massive amounts of money into my life." You then touch your head and say, "I have a millionaire mind!"
The Automatic Millionaire *David Bach* CREDENTIALS: Financial adviser and seminar speaker	1. Stop buying lattes. 2. Use a 401(k) or I.R.A. 3. Pay off your mortgage early.	Makes everything sound as easy as ordering a daily double nonfat latte, which by the way, he advises you should not do. You'll get the same advice reading any number of financial advice columnists at no additional cost.
Cracking the Millionaire Code *Mark Victor Hansen and Robert G. Allen* CREDENTIALS: Co-author of *Chicken Soup for the Soul;* Financial seminar speaker	1. Use "loverage," that is, do what comes naturally. 2. Network. 3. Dream.	Recycles a lot of the language and advice of those hotel ballroom talkathons; namely, you have been conditioned to think like a poor person, but you can remake yourself to think rich.

SOURCE: Nielsen BookScan, publishers

—Damon Darlin

Want to Get Rich Quick?

Write a millionaire book—don't buy one

Socking away that first million used to be so simple. At least it was for people who gave rudimentary advice on how to be a millionaire. Give up that pack-a-day smoking habit, they said, and in 40 years you will have saved almost $250,000 in today's dollars, assuming a conservative 4 percent annual return. Brown-bag your lunch, drop HBO and pay off your mortgage early and gradually, over a lifetime, you will accumulate $1 million in assets. Back then, all you had to do was live below your means and save, save, save.

These days, the money-wasting bad habit that must be broken is the daily $5 Starbucks coffee break. (Savings over 40 years: $173,422.) But giving up the small pleasures in life is no longer the advice given to would-be millionaires, whether they are sipping or puffing.

According to the spate of best-selling self-help books, it is not enough to drive used cars and squirrel money away in the company 401(k). Instead, you have to think like a millionaire.

Gaining millionaire status is still an accomplishment. It's important to note that even though the threshold for making the *Forbes* list of richest Americans is now almost $1 billion, only 7 million out of 100 million American households have net assets of $1 million or more, which includes, of course, the equity built up in most people's biggest asset—their homes. That number has not changed significantly despite all the millions of books sold telling people how to join the club. You have to ask yourself before you buy any of these books, Did my neighbors get rich because they just think differently, or because they use money more wisely?

The bottom line is, save your money by not buying these books. At about $25 a book, buying one every year probably will not decimate your retirement fund. But if you don't, you'll have at least $2,370 more in 40 years.

—Damon Darlin

THE COST OF RAISING A CHILD TO 18*

Family income:	Less than $41,700	$41,700–$70,200	More than $70,200
Housing	$44,580	$61,650	$100,000
Food	$26,490	$31,770	$39,570
Transportation	$18,660	$25,980	$34,860
Clothing	$ 8,660	$9,930	$12,810
Health care	$10,680	$13,830	$15,870
Child care/education	$12,090	$21,180	$33,870
Miscellaneous**	$13,380	$19,980	$32,460
Total:	**$134,370**	**$184,320**	**$269,520**

* Calculated on before-tax income; each child in a two-parent family
** Includes personal care items, entertainment and reading materials
SOURCE: U.S. Department of Agriculture

What It Costs to Raise a Child
A lot, but the rewards can be great, too

Child-rearing is expensive: an average of more than $196,000 from birth until age 18, according to the U.S. Department of Agriculture. Depending on family income, it costs a two-parent family with two children somewhere between $134,370 and $269,520 to raise one child. Raising a single child brings up the cost by a factor of 1.24. It really does get cheaper by the dozen: the expenditure per child drops by .77 in a family with three or more children.

Those lofty sums are mostly for basics like food, clothing, housing and medical care. But as many parents know, raising a child doesn't stop after 17 years. To send a kid to college, parents will have to add to that sum about $30,000 a year, by 2005 estimates, for a four-year private college and $11,000 for an in-state public school.

That particular investment holds a huge promise of future rewards, however: over a 40-year career, a college grad is likely to earn about 73 percent more than a high school graduate, according to the College Board.

ⓘ INSIDE INFO

Your Chances of (Not) Winning the Lottery

○ The odds of winning a pick of six of 42 numbers are one in more than five million. Those odds are the same each week.

○ The chances of winning the California Lotto Jackpot: one in 14 million.

SOURCE: National Coalition Against Legalized Gambling

Can I Have an Allowance?

An expert answers that vexing question

Child psychologists believe that a child learns the concept of trading money for goods as early as age 3 or 4. In that case, it would seem that it's almost never too early to teach your child the value of money and how to manage it. Here, Janet Bodnar, deputy editor at *Kiplinger's Personal Finance* magazine and author of a syndicated column called "Money-Smart Kids," gives her expert advice on the prickly question of allowances.

Q When should you start giving allowances?

It is appropriate to start an allowance around the age of 6 or so, when the child is in the first grade. Age 3 or 4 is a little too early. Children that young think in very concrete terms about money and can't appreciate the abstract idea of managing an allowance. But in first grade children start to learn about money in school, so they know that one dollar equals four quarters or ten dimes and they have an idea how much that will buy.

Q How much should you give?

Start with a weekly base allowance that is equal to one-half the child's age. Most parents I talk to feel comfortable with that figure. And you can adjust it up or down based on the cost of living in your area and what you expect children to pay for with their allowance.

Q At what point during the week should you give your kids their allowance?

Get into the habit of paying them on a regular schedule, preferably a quiet weekday—maybe even on your own payday—instead of during the hectic weekend. You might also consider Sunday night, so the kids aren't tempted to blow the money over the weekend.

Q What should kids be required to pay for with their allowance?

Start small. Put young children in charge of the one thing they most like to spend money on, whether it's stickers, crayons or mini racing cars. Once they're accustomed to making their own purchases, you can expand the allowance as they get older to cover snacks after school, entertainment and clothing.

✔ **TIMELY TIPS**

Teaching Kids to Use Plastic

✔ **Be a role model.** Use your credit cards the way you want your children to use theirs. Let children see you paying bills and hear discussions of how you spend your money. Be honest about spending mistakes of the past.

✔ **Help children learn the limits of their card.** Go through monthly statements. Teach children about interest rates and how they can raise debt.

✔ **If your children receive an allowance, encourage them to budget,** save and spend their money wisely, showing how interest charges, annual fees and bank charges work.

✔ **Set up long-term financial goals.** Guide them to identify how they are spending their money and whether purchases are wise.

✔ **Instruct children what to do if** a card is lost or stolen. Remind your children to keep the 800 number to report lost or stolen cards in a safe place. Urge them to memorize their secret PIN's and tell them not to lend cards.

✔ **Be aware of warning signs of identity theft,** such as preapproved credit card offers arriving in your child's name.

✔ **Check your child's credit report annually** for any unauthorized accounts and requests for credit.

—Jennifer Alsever

Should you pay kids for chores?

I don't recommend that the basic allowance be tied to chores. Children shouldn't be paid to do thing things that they should do as part of the family, such as washing dishes, cleaning up their room, taking out the trash or setting the table. Instead, the basic allowance should be tied to spending responsibilities. You might require kids to pay for their own collectibles, video games and CD's, movie tickets and mall excursions with their friends. To teach them the value of working for pay, have them earn extra cash for jobs such as raking leaves, washing the car or cleaning out the garage. Agree on a wage ahead of time, then pay when you're satisfied with their work. This is also a good way to supplement a basic allowance.

What about baby-sitting for siblings or family members?

It depends on the circumstance. If it's Saturday night and your child could get another baby-sitting job—you should pay, just as you would a baby sitter. It is O.K. to pay less than the going rate as long as you don't take advantage.

Reining in Teenage Spending

How to influence your teen's use of credit and debit cards

Teenagers are a fickle bunch. In a 2000 poll, 34 percent of teens surveyed said they were interested in getting a credit card in their own name. By spring 2005, just 15 percent said so, according to a survey of 2,000 teens.

The portion with credit cards in their name also declined, from 11 percent in 2000 to 9 percent. (Children under the age of 18 cannot legally apply for their own credit cards, but parents can co-sign for them.) The lack of enthusiasm for plastic may

stem in part from other cards in teenagers' wallets, including debit cards, which draw money from banking accounts, and a wealth of prepaid cards that store a certain cash value that can be tapped with a swipe of the card.

Rob Callender, trends director for Teenage Research Unlimited, the market research company that conducted the polls, says, "This group of teens has a great head on their shoulders. They're driven. They're motivated. They're savvy." They are also experienced shoppers. In 2004, the nation's 33 million teenagers, ages 12 to 19, accounted for $169 billion in spending—not including spending on their behalf or family purchases they may have influenced. Much of that money bought clothing, snacks, shoes, CD's, video games, MP3 players, computer equipment and cellphones.

Card companies and banks have noticed. MasterCard has a prepaid card called MyPlash, a reloadable debit card that can be stocked with a limited amount of cash. The card has pictures of music celebrities like Clay Aiken, appealing to young consumers. Visa also has prepaid cards, including a Hilary Duff Visa and the Visa Buxx card tailored to preteenagers.

Card companies emphasize that their cards are not credit cards and so can better prepare youth for the day they sign up for their own credit card. Doling out cash in the form of allowances is becoming antiquated, and given the current climate of repeated data corruption and fears of identity theft, many parents are happy with credit card alternatives. "With debit cards, you are really getting the best of both worlds," says Jenifer Lippincott, author of *7 Things Your Teenager Won't Tell You (And How to Talk About Them Anyway)*. "The teen can have the experience of having a credit card without the liability."

Not everyone views prepaid and debit cards for teens so positively. Critics worry that teens will develop bad habits, especially when it comes to accumulating debt. "The money is just abstract," says James A. Roberts, a marketing professor at Baylor University in Waco, Tex., who has spent 10 years studying credit card behavior.

People who use credit cards tend to spend more, are less price-sensitive and overestimate their wealth, he says. Credit card companies reply that it's up to parents to educate their teens on proper spending habits.

—Jennifer Alsever

Rules for Boomerang Kids

What parents should do when 20-somethings move back in

Young offspring who return to the nest are rising in numbers. The Census Bureau says 50 percent of all 18-to-24-year-olds were living at home in 2003; for 18-to-34-year-olds, it was 27 percent. Chubb Insurance says it has noticed an 11 percent increase in the number of 21-to-25-year-olds on parents' auto insurance.

The main reason for the growing numbers is generally an economic one. In some cases, the offspring, sometimes called boomerangers, may be struggling to pay off college loans or having trouble finding jobs that can cover housing costs. And their parents are often at the peak of their own earning power and can afford to take them back in.

The best of these parent-child relationships are built on some financial rules, or at least on some expectations, that encourage responsibility, such as: A child who is unemployed must try to find work. One who has college debts must strive to pay them off. A graduate student has to hit the books hard. Gainfully employed children should pay rent—or some amount that parents will set aside for them—or invest for their own future.

If you are a parent sharing the nest with a 20-something child, here is some financial advice to consider:

HEALTH INSURANCE Many policies cut off dependents if they have graduated from college or are over 25. If your child has a job that offers no insurance, decide who will pay for it—or run the risk that he or she will be uninsured in the event of illness.

AUTO INSURANCE Multicar discounts usually make it cheaper for a child to stay on his parents' policy, but consider having him pay his share.

FINANCIAL EXPECTATIONS If you require your child to pay rent, you may want to set a lower amount at first, then raise it gradually. If your child is looking for a job, don't let the search become an open-ended excuse for staying in your home.

NEST EGGS Don't assume that by using your own savings to support your adult children, you are guaranteeing that they will support you in the future.

—Dale Buss

 INSIDE INFO

Sex, Beer & Credit Cards

O Nearly 60 percent of those surveyed by *GQ* magazine said they would give up drinking for 12 months if it would eliminate all their credit card debt.

O 39 percent said they would give up sex for a year. Unknown: how many would give up using their credit cards.

—Paul B. Brown

Credit Cards That Reward
Looking that gift horse in the mouth

The hottest segment of the credit card industry today is reward cards. Two-thirds of all cardholders in 2005 had a reward card in their wallets, up from about half of cardholders in 2002. Since then, the number of households using a cash-back card has grown 38 percent, to 32.6 million.

It's time to look this gift horse in the mouth. For starters, why do card issuers do it? Discover, which started the cash-back card, found that if it handed over a little cash to customers, they used the card more. It works. Consumers with cash-reward cards stop using other cards. Industry consultants estimate that cardholders put about 75 percent of their charges on a single reward card, so the benefits to the card issuer are enormous. Surveys showed in 2005 that consumers who used reward cards preferred cash. But credit card companies say air-mile cards are still popular despite many airlines' troubled financial status and the myriad restrictions placed on redemption.

Indeed, cash-reward cards may be one of the most consumer-friendly products the industry has ever marketed. But card issuers don't make it simple to choose a card. Each has different plans offering cash back at various rates depending on where you use your card. So you have to be aware of your habits. Do you spend a lot on restaurants? Do you shop a lot at a specific store? Do you have a house full of teenagers who drive up your grocery and gasoline bills? Here are some tips on going the reward card route.

Pay no fee. If a credit card issuer charges one, find another offer. As for interest rates, if you have to check the rate that is a clear sign you do not need another card. Skip it and start paying down your credit card debt. It makes no sense to borrow money at an interest rate of 12 or 25 percent a year to get 1 percent back.

Taking out another card could affect your credit score. You may not need to worry about it, though, if you are not going to borrow money in the next three to six months. Do not cancel the nonreward card that you hold unless it has an annual fee. That will hurt your credit score by eliminating a source of credit history, the biggest factor influencing your score. Just stop using the card.

Ignore any offer with a low cash-back limit. Citibank's popular Dividend Platinum Select looks like a great card because it pays 5 percent on supermarket, drugstore and gas station purchases instead of the more typical 1 percent rate offered on other cards. The fine print says, however, that the most you can get back in a year is $300. So, anyone putting more than $2,500 a month on his or her card would actually be signing up for a reward card that returns less than 1 percent.

If you use your card a lot, charging more than $500 a month, the best cards offer tiers of rates that rise as you charge more. For instance, the American Express Blue Cash card rewards 1 percent on supermarket, gas station and drugstore

 INSIDE INFO

Credit Gone Bad

○ The Public Interest Research Group found that 70 percent of credit reports they surveyed in 2004 had incorrect information.

○ About 25 percent had errors significant enough to have an adverse effect on a credit decision.

MONEY

Checking Up on Your Credit Rating

If you're planning to take out a loan, be sure to check your credit history first with these major credit bureaus. An inaccuracy could cost you the loan. (See, "Treading the Mortgage Minefield" on page 207.) Even if you're not borrowing, it's wise to check your report for the record. You are entitled by law to one free credit report a year.

Lots of Web sites and television commercials say they will send you a free credit report, but those offers are mostly come-ons to try to get you to purchase other products.

The only legally authorized online source for getting your credit report is www.annual-creditreport.com, the central Web site for the country's three major credit reporting companies (listed at right).

You can get your report by calling or writing:

ANNUAL CREDIT REPORT REQUEST SERVICES
P.O. Box 105281   Atlanta, Ga., 30348-5281
877-322-8228,

For credit questions, other than your free annual report, contact:

EQUIFAX INFORMATION SERVICE CENTER.
P.O. Box 740241   Atlanta, Ga. 30374
800-685-1111

EXPERIAN CONSUMER ASSISTANCE
P.O. Box 2104   Allen, Tex. 75013
800-682-7654

TRANS UNION CORP. CONSUMER DISCLOSURE CENTER
P.O. Box 390   Springfield, Pa. 19064
800-916-8800

purchases and 0.5 percent on everything else for the first $6,500 spent. After that, it pays 5 percent on the everyday purchases and 1.5 percent on the rest. But there is no reward on spending above $50,000.

Look for a co-branded reward card if you are a heavy user at a particular store. Though the Amazon.com Platinum Visa looks like a humdrum 1 percent reward card with its $25 gift certificate award for every 2,500 points, it gives 3 points for every dollar spent at Amazon. If you spend a lot at Amazon, that effectively becomes a 3 percent reward card. Starbucks, Toys "R" Us, eBay and Nascar all offer reward cards.

Go for cash over product. It's usually wiser to stick to cash-reward programs rather than ones that offer products. The products are often available at a discount elsewhere.

Watch for savings plans, the latest marketing wrinkle. One of the most beneficial entries is One from American Express. The card pays 1 percent on

purchases and then automatically sweeps the monthly reward into a savings account paying 3.5 percent.

If you are not finding the card you want in those billions of mail solicitations, go to the Web sites run by the card companies, your bank or card sites like CardWeb.com, Bankrate.com, Credit-Cards.com and CreditRatings.com.

—Damon Darlin

Beyond Get-Out-of-Debt Clichés
Tough-as-nails ways to pay off those credit card balances

Living on borrowed money has never been so easy, but if you're in debt, it's never been so hard to get out. For most people carrying monthly balances, rates are higher, minimum payment requirements are lower and there are hidden penalties, fees and rate increases that kick in for a head-splitting number of reasons.

Credit card companies can be vicious, but consumers who are stuck in the debt maze need to get medieval. Rather than following the old half measures, here's what it takes to be debt-free in today's world:

Know thy debt. Read (yes, read) your statements.

Create an aggressive payback strategy. Use online calculators to determine an affordable monthly payment that will get you out of debt fast. Then, set up an automatic monthly transfer so you can't talk yourself into smaller payments.

Adjust your cost of living. Debt is code for living beyond your means. Figure out what's causing you to be overextended.

Quit using plastic for a while. This is boot camp. By switching to cash for at least a month, you'll know how much money you can afford to spend.

Generate more income. Sorry. Did you think you were going to pull bigger payments from under the bed? Get another job, a raise, a roommate—then sell anything that you can live without and put the profits toward debt. (Finally, a sane use for eBay.)

Save. The only way to get on top of debt is to live on 80 percent of what you earn. At first, the remaining 20 percent will help you climb out of debt—a savings in itself, if your balances carry interest.

From then on it becomes pure savings—and can keep you from ever falling into that hole again.

—M. P. Dunleavey

> ❝
>
> **Debt isn't a problem for everyone. Just over half of Americans either don't use plastic or pay off their balances each month.**
>
> • • •

Going Bankrupt Is Harder to Do
Tougher laws make it less alluring

Few words evoke the specter of financial ruin like "filing for bankruptcy." And laws enacted in 2005 make personal bankruptcy a much tougher proposition.

It's not that filing for bankruptcy was a quick stroll out of the woods, but the new laws impose many hurdles on those hoping to clear away debts. Among them is a lengthy means test to determine the ability to repay what is owed. Depending on the results, some people will be forced to repay debts that would be have been wiped clean under the old laws. Filers are also required to complete a credit counseling course—at their own expense—before bankruptcy is granted.

On the other hand, your retirment savings could be safer under the current bankruptcy law, as well as certain tax-deferred eductional savings plans like 529's and Coverdell accounts, says Henry Sommer, president of the National Association of Consumer Bankruptcy Attorneys. "I.R.A.'s and certain kinds of pension plans were not protected under the old law in some places," Sommer says.

Filing for bankruptcy isn't cheap, and fees vary. But you don't want to skimp on legal advice, especially if your situation is complicated—for example, if you're married but want to file a solo bankruptcy, or if your personal debts are mingled with small-business debts. Avoid cut-rate bankruptcy mills that may make your situation even worse. The American Bankruptcy Institute (www.abi.com) and the National Association of Consumer Bankruptcy Attorneys (www.nacba.com) can make referrals, as can your local bar association.

MONEY

TIMELY TIPS

Choosing a Credit Counselor

Anyone filing for bankruptcy is required by law to get counseling from a government-approved credit counselor. You can find a list of such organizations on the Web site of the office of the Justice Department's Trustee Program, which oversees bankruptcy cases, at www.usdoj.gov/ust.

You can get the counseling in person, by phone or online for a fee of about $50. After you complete counseling, usually a 90-minute session during which your budget is analyzed, you receive a certificate from the organization to present when you file in bankruptcy court.

The Federal Trade Commission suggests you call several of the companies on the list before you chose one. Ask these questions, before deciding on one:

✔ Suppose I only want the credit counseling services and budget analysis required before I can file for bankruptcy, how much does that cost?

✔ What if I cannot afford to pay?

✔ Will you help me develop a plan for avoiding future problems? How much will that cost?

✔ What are the qualifications of your counselors? Are they accredited or certified by an outside organization?

✔ What type of information do you retain about me? Is it confidential and secure?

✔ How will I know that I have the correct certificate to file for bankruptcy? Does the certificate cost extra?

And, if what's holding you back is fear of ruining your credit for the next 10 years—that should be the least of your worries. "The minute, and I mean the literal minute, you file bankruptcy," says Brian Methner, a bankruptcy lawyer in Denver, "you will be inundated with credit card applications, mortgage applications, car loan applications." Paradoxically, lenders see this as a good time to approach consumers who are about to get a fresh record.

The interest rates may be high and the terms may not be ideal, but borrow you can. The bigger question is whether you should. If you're worried about rebuilding your credit rating, a secured card and prompt payments are the best way to go—particularly if the reason for bankruptcy isn't a layoff, illness or divorce, but living above and beyond your means.

For those whose lifestyle was their undoing, experts caution that bankruptcy may ease your debts, but it won't solve your problems. Henry Sommer, president of the National Association of Consumer Bankruptcy Attorneys, offers this advice: "Be more careful about budgeting and not falling prey to predatory lenders. Be more wary of credit in general."

—M. P. Dunleavey

 INSIDE INFO

Filing for Bankruptcy

O You start bankruptcy proceedings by filing a petition at a district court. If you are not using a lawyer, you can get the required forms online at www.uscourts.gov/bkforms/index.html.

O You must state your assets and liabilities and a list of creditors, among other things.

O Filing fees vary depending on the type of bankruptcy case, but the most common type filed by individuals, under Chapter 7 of the bankruptcy code, costs about $275.

Investing

Where to Put Your Money

Don't catch stock mania; it pays to diversify

Nearly every financial market stumbles now and then, costing some investors plenty. Bonds took a dive in the mid-90's; commodity prices fell in the late 90's; and stocks plunged in 2000 into a three-year bear market.

Stumbles and recoveries are inevitable. The lesson for investors: diversifying your portfolio is a very good idea. It increases the chance that part of your portfolio is going up when other portions are going down. In fact, diversification has produced much better results than many investors think. Diversifying doesn't mean simply within a stock,

bond or commodity portfolio. It also means adding what Wall Street calls asset classes, so that your portfolio holds stocks, bonds and commodities.

Diversification among asset classes makes you put your money where you may otherwise fear to go. It also prevents stock mania from distracting you from opportunities in other asset classes.

Stocks are right for the long run, as Jeremy J. Siegel, a professor at the Wharton School of the University of Pennsylvania, has argued for years. But stocks are not the be-all and end-all of a good portfolio, as big gains in commodities in recent years show. Over the recent 3, 5, 10 and 15 years, the usual investment horizons for measuring market performance, only stocks have had a down period. According to Ibbotson

MONEY

WHERE'S YOUR MONEY?

Over the long term, a diversified portfolio of stocks, bonds, commodities and cash has not fared as well as stocks alone. But the diversified portfolio delivered steadier returns, giving investors a smoother ride.

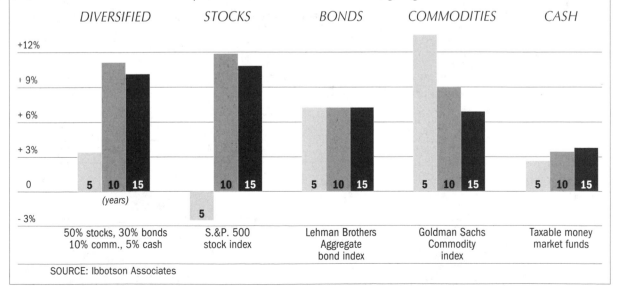

SOURCE: Ibbotson Associates

Associates, in the five years ending in 2004, the average annual total return for the Standard & Poor's 500-stock index was a loss of 2.3 percent. By comparison, bonds had an average annual total return of 7.7 percent over the same period, as measured by the Lehman Brothers aggregate bond index. Commodities were the high flyers, producing annualized returns of nearly 14 percent, as gauged by the total return of the Goldman Sachs Commodity index.

Over the long term, however, equities were the winners, bringing in 12.1 percent average annual returns over 10 years and 10.9 percent over 15 years. By comparison, commodities brought home 9.1 percent a year, on average, over 10 years and 7.1 percent over 15 years; bonds returned 7.7 percent in both periods. Money market funds were far behind the pack: 3.8 percent over 10 years and 4.4 percent over 15 years, according to iMoneyNet.

Diversification is also a benefit, of course, when one big asset class stumbles and another picks up. Looking for such lead changes keeps investors sharp.

What makes diversification unappetizing is that

you would not have racked up the huge returns that stocks alone brought in the late 1990's—or the big gains that commodities brought in 2002 through 2004. But you would have done a lot better with a diversified portfolio than you might have expected. Over the three years through 2004, according to Ibbotson Associates, the average annual return from a portfolio containing all these asset classes was 7 percent, assuming that you held 55 percent stocks, 30 percent bonds, 10 percent commodities and 5 percent cash. That compares with a return of 3.6 percent for a portfolio containing only stocks.

Over five years, the average annual return was 3.4 percent for the diversified portfolio, versus an average annual loss of 2.3 percent for stocks. Over a longer period, a stock-only portfolio fared better, but not by much. The annualized 10-year return for stocks was 12.1 percent, versus 11 percent for the diversified portfolio.Over 15 years, stocks won by only 10.9 percent to 10 percent.

You can live well, and a little less painfully, if you branch out. That makes diversification worth it.

—Jonathan Fuerbringer

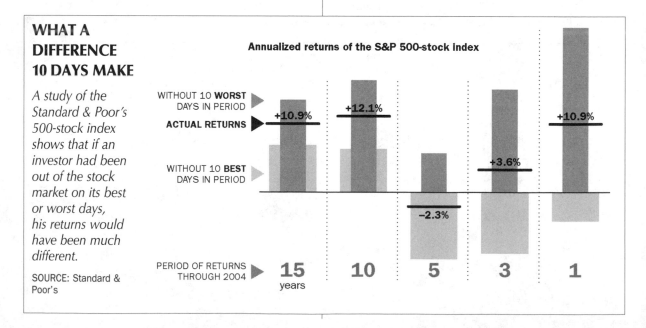

WHAT A DIFFERENCE 10 DAYS MAKE

A study of the Standard & Poor's 500-stock index shows that if an investor had been out of the stock market on its best or worst days, his returns would have been much different.

SOURCE: Standard & Poor's

Annualized returns of the S&P 500-stock index

WITHOUT 10 **WORST** DAYS IN PERIOD

ACTUAL RETURNS

WITHOUT 10 **BEST** DAYS IN PERIOD

+10.9%   +12.1%   +3.6%   +10.9%

−2.3%

PERIOD OF RETURNS THROUGH 2004

15 years   10   5   3   1

Pick the Stock or the Moment?

Timing the market is everything. Or is it?

Fortunes are made on foreseeing swings in the stock market. But a knack for picking the right stocks and holding on through thick and thin has also proved valuable. So does it make sense for ordinary investors to try to predict a market top or bottom?

Opponents of timing point to studies that show how much worse returns would have been, compared to returns from buying and holding, if investors had been out of stocks on certain important dates. What if, for example, an investor stayed out of the market during its best and worst trading days? Standard & Poor's looked at the effect of being on the sidelines during the 10 best trading days in the 10 years through 2004. (See facing page.) The result: an annualized gain of 12.1 percent on the S.&P. 500 index would have shrunk to 6.9 percent.

But anyone who was fully invested on all but the 10 best sessions would be the unluckiest trader alive. What if another trader had the good fortune to have been in the market on all but the 10 worst days in the last decade? The results are very similar, but in reverse. The annualized return would have ballooned to 17.8 percent.

But what are the chances of any investor having such exquisite timing? Not great. In general, says Catherine D. Gordon, head of the investment policy group at the Vanguard fund management firm, market timing is a bad idea because "you have to be right on both sides of the decision, when to move in and when to move out," and picking those right moments is difficult.

There are other difficulties, too, such as the drag on timers' returns in the way of fees and commissions. While you may possibly limit commissions and other charges by using index funds, capital gains on fund sales are taxable. Timers

THE BULLS ARE BEATING THE BEARS

Bull markets have historically lasted longer and moved further than sluggish bear markets. The hottest bull market by far took place during the "Greed Decade"—it started in October 1990 and ended in October 1997. During that period, the Standard & Poor's 500 total return index turned in a stunning 300 percent gain. The latest bull market began in March 2003 and was still upbeat in late-April 2006. The worst bear market in recent years occurred between March and July 2002, when the S.&P. 500 index fell 31 percent.

BULL MARKETS

Beginning Date	Ending Date	No. of Days	Gain in S.&P. 500 Index
10/11/90	10/ 7/97	2,553	300.43%
10/27/97	7/17/98	263	36.98%
8/31/98	7/16/99	319	49.95%
10/15/99	3/24/00	161	23.09%
4/14/00	9/ 1/00	140	12.6%
4/ 4/01	5/21/01	47	19.2%
9/21/01	3/19/02	179	22.01%
7/23/02	8/22/02	30	20.87%
10/ 9/02	11/27/02	49	21.17%
3/11/03	––	1,037*	69.42%*

*As of Jan. 11, 2006

BEAR MARKETS

Beginning Date	Ending Date	No. of Days	Loss in S.&P. 500 Index
7/16/90	10/11/90	87	−19.21%
10/7/97	10/27/97	20	−10.72%
7/17/98	8/31/98	45	−19.19%
7/16/99	10/15/99	91	−11.8%
3/24/00	4/14/00	21	−11.13%
9/1/00	4/4/01	215	−26.93%
5/21/01	9/21/01	123	−26.11%
3/19/02	7/23/02	126	−31.48%
8/22/02	10/9/02	48	−19.12%
11/27/02	3/11/03	104	−14.28%

SOURCE: Ned Davis Research, Inc.

MONEY

argue that if they have capital gains tax to pay, it means that they are achieving capital gains. And while knowing the exact moment to trade would be ideal, they say, just getting close should be good enough to beat a buy-and-hold strategy, and with less risk.

Some experts suggest a middle approach, not quite timing, or buying and holding, either, but allocating assets. A reasonable asset allocation, many advisers say, is 60 percent to stocks and 40 percent to bonds. A number of mutual funds use a similar strategy, providing ways to allocate reasonably and doing it in a disciplined way. That can come in handy, given that markets don't always follow expectations.

—Conrad de Aenlle

As January, So Goes the Year

Why investing clichés are often right

Wall Street is paved with truisms. One favorite is that January is a barometer of the year's market health: if the S.&P. 500 index is up in January, the market average for the year will also rise, and vice versa. Since 1950, according to the Hirsch Organization (www.hirschorg.com), publisher of financial newsletters and the annual investing calendar Stock Trader's Almanac, the indicator has predicted the annual course of the market with a 91 percent accuracy, missing only five times in the past 55 years.

There's no great mystery about why January is such an accurate barometer: January is the month that many major economic and national policy decisions are announced by the government to kick off the new year. Typically, the president delivers his State of the Union message in late January, laying out the year's national goals. And the government's budget also is released. Switch

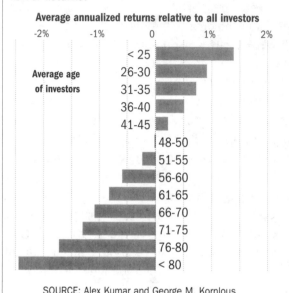

OLDER BUT NO WISER

A study based on more than 75,000 accounts has found that older investors tend to earn lower returns:

Average annualized returns relative to all investors

SOURCE: Alex Kumar and George M. Kornlous

these events to any other month, and chances are the January barometer would switch, too.

Another old chestnut, "sell in May and go away," is also backed by investing wisdom. Research finds remarkable average market gains for each month from November to April, going back to 1950. Hirsh's "best six months" strategy, for example, shows that over a half-century, the Dow gained 9,222 points during these six consecutive months, compared to 1,299 points during the May through October months. The market's sluggish performance through the summer months is generally credited to investors going on vacation, which dampens their appetite for investing.

Also rooted in statistical reality is the notion of a "Santa Claus rally," in which stocks tend to rise during the week after Christmas. Since 1950, this seven-day period has shown an average growth of at least 1.5 percent greater than the S.&P. 500,

Hirsch data show. In fact, the entire fourth quarter is typically the year's strongest: Between 1995 and 2005, the Dow Industrial average suffered a fourth-quarter decline only once (in 1997), according to the *Wall Street Journal.*

One factor driving the rally is that the last quarter of the year is generally a strong one for corporate profits, encouraging investors to buy stock. Another is investor psychology, reflecting the optimism typical of the holiday season.

How Amateurs Might Beat Pros

Join an investment club and you stand a fair chance of beating the market

Afraid to dip into the stock market alone? Then, an investment club, a group of like-minded people who pool their time, skills and money to research and invest in stocks, might be an option. There are nearly 18,000 clubs in the country, with 150,000 members holding an estimated $117 billion in investments. The average club portfolio: $87,000, with some $130 million in new money invested monthly by club members.

On average, investment clubs have generally outperformed market averages, according to BetterInvesting (formerly the National Association of Investors Corp.). During the decade ending April 2005, the average club return was 16 percent compared to 9.5 percent for the Vanguard Total Stock Market Index Fund. The stock-picking credo of investment clubs that are members of BetterInvesting is simple.

1. **Invest a set amount regularly,** once a month, for example, regardless of whether it's a bull or bear market.

2. **Reinvest dividends and capital gains for compound growth.** Don't sell unless the company really sours. One or two down quarters isn't enough to trigger a sell. As long as the company's underlying financials are still healthy, it may still be a good time to buy.

3. **Look for quality growth stocks,** companies with sales and earning that are growing at a faster rate than the industry as a whole.

4. **Diversify your portfolio to spread the risk.** A balanced portfolio includes companies of various sizes from different industries and mutual funds from various categories.

To start your own investment club, find 10 to 15 members who can handle investigating and analyzing securities and making periodic reports. At the first meeting, set a monthly figure, say $10 to $100 per person, that each will invest. Choose an investment strategy, such as, will the club buy stock for long-term gain or current income? Research and pick a broker or a discount brokerage firm. In many cases, you can buy stock directly from companies through dividend reinvestment plans, sidestepping commissions and management fees.

Consider joining BetterInvesting (www.better-investing.org), which provides materials, including guidelines and an investor's manual on stockpicking, maintaining tax records, and other basics.

Does Real Estate Beat Stocks?

Over time, it pays to sleep at home and invest in stocks

Housing booms tend to make homeowners feel like very smart investors. As the value of their real estate skyrockets, owners might conclude that real estate is a safer and better bet than stocks.

To the contrary. Over time, stock prices have risen far more quickly than home values, even in areas where real estate has typically appreciated most. Between 1980 and 2005, for example,

MONEY

INSIDE INFO

Real Estate vs. Stocks

○ Eighty percent of Americans deemed real estate a safer investment than stocks, according to a 2005 NBC News/*Wall Street Journal* poll. Only 13 percent said stocks were safer.

○ The reason: the stock market collapse in 2000 was a more recent memory than the drop in house prices in the early 90's.

money invested in the S.&P. 500 delivered a return of 10 percent a year on average; add dividends and the return rises to 12 percent. Even in the sizzling markets of New York and San Francisco, homes have risen in value only about 7 percent a year over the same span. (See chart to the right.) Says Jeff A. Weiand, executive vice president of RTD Financial Advisors in Philadelphia, "It's very difficult to beat the long-term historical record of stocks."

That's not to say that real estate is a bad investment. It is often an important source of wealth for families. But its main benefit is what it has always been: you can live in the house you own. Despite the fact that home values usually appreciate over time, most of the value of a house actually comes from using it. Unlike stock, which you can cash out of, whenever homeowners sell one house, they pay to live elsewhere, meaning they can never wholly cash out of a home's value.

Another factor is leverage. When home prices are rising, the leverage from a mortgage lifts real estate returns in the short term. Someone putting down $100,000 to buy a $500,000 home can feel as if the investment doubled when told that the house is worth $600,000. But the power of leverage vanishes as homeowners pay off the mortgage. Leverage also creates more short-term risk, especially for those who have stretched to

afford their house. "If the home went down by 30 percent, you'd probably be sitting with a bankruptcy attorney," says Jonathan Golub, U.S. equity strategist at J.P. Morgan Asset Management. "If your I.B.M. stock goes down by 30 percent, it's no big deal. You don't declare bankruptcy; you just don't go out to the movies as much, or you retire a year later."

Beyond the shelter it provides, the biggest advantage of real estate might be that it protects people from their worst investment instincts. Most people do not sell their house out of frustration after a few months of declining values, as they might with a stock. Instead, they are almost forced to be long-run investors who do not try to time the market.

—Motoko Rich and David Leonhardt

INSIDE INFO

Over Time, It's Stocks by Far

○ Although housing prices have risen rapidly in recent years, over longer periods stock prices have risen more. Here are average annual home price increases for selected areas and for the S.&P. 500 since 1980.

○ **Stocks vs. Home Prices**

| | Average annual change | |
	'00-'05	'80-'05
S.&P. 500	-2.7 %	+10.2%
New York	+12.0 %	+7.7 %
Los Angeles	+15.5 %	+6.7 %
Chicago	+7.7 %	+5.5 %

* House price changes are from the first quarter of 1980 to the first quarter of 2005.

**Stock price change is from Jan. 1, 1980, to Jan. 1, 2005.

SOURCES: Office of Federal Housing Enterprise Oversight; Standard & Poor's

—Motoko Rich and David Leonhardt

Staying Ahead of the Curve

Want to know where bonds are headed?
Consult the yield curve

Should you buy a three-month T-bill, a 30-year bond or something in between? A look at the yield curve, found daily in the *New York Times* business pages, may provide the answer. A yield curve is simply a line that plots the interest rate paid by similar bonds with different maturities. The X-axis plots the length of time until the bonds mature. The Y-axis plots the yield of each bond. The average spread between the shortest-term and longest-term Treasuries is usually about two percentage points.

Reading the yield curve can be especially useful for long-term investing. If you have a shorter time frame—say, you'll need to cash in your bond in three years for a child's tuition—you should probably buy a bond that matures within that time period. Keep in mind, too, that interest rates and bond prices move in opposite directions: higher rates mean lower bond prices. Rising interest rates can play havoc on the bond market, when even the highest-quality bond portfolio can lose value as interest rates climb. When rates start heading down, on the other hand, it's usually a good time to buy long-term bonds as a way to lock in current high yields.

A common misconception is that if a bond's yield is going up, the investment is worth more. It's just the opposite: when a bond's yield rises, its price has fallen because the increase in yield comes at the expense of the bond's market value. Conversely, if a bond's yield falls, its market value rises. Another risk: rising inflation, which can cut the worth of a bond's coupon payments and its eventual redemption value.

The yield curve usually slopes upward. That's because longer-term investments carry more risk and pay higher interest rates to compensate. When short- and long-term interest rates are roughly the

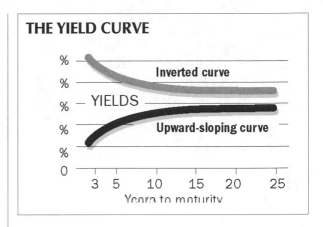

THE YIELD CURVE

%
%
%   — YIELDS —
%
%
0

Inverted curve

Upward-sloping curve

3   5   10   15   20   25
Years to maturity

same, the curve is flat. A thin spread means the market sees little difference between the short-term and long- term risks of inflation. So, buying longer-term bonds gives you only a slight premium.

When short-term yields exceed long-term yields, the curve turns downward or inverts. An inverted curve usually means that a recession is coming. The last time the curve inverted was 2000, signaling the slowdown that led to the 2001 recession. An inverted curve has predicted all recessions since 1950.

Some analysts say inverted curves also signal a buying opportunity for long-term bonds. In other words, when the economy softens and interest rates come down, you want to be in long-term bonds because eventually the curve will normalize and the value of long-term bonds will rise.

From the Oracle of Omaha

A guru expounds on stocks, librarians and
other secrets of success

Warren Buffett, chairman of the Omaha-based holding company Berkshire Hathaway, Inc., is famous both for his spectacular investment acumen and his folksy, commonsense approach to choosing stocks. He is also the second-richest person in the

MONEY

Financial Independence

Many firms offer independent stock research, but relatively few focus on individual investors. Here are some that do:

✔ **MORNINGSTAR**
www.morningstar.com
Companies covered: 1,000
Annual cost: $109
Free information: Stock screens and some stock reports

✔ **NATIONAL ASSOCIATION OF INVESTORS CORPORATION**
www.better-investing.org
Companies covered: 10,000
Annual cost: $39
Free information: Basic corporate information

✔ **STANDARD & POOR'S**
www.spoutlookonline.com
Companies covered: 1,200
Annual cost: $298
Free information: Stock snapshots and top recommended buys and sells*

✔ **VALUE LINE**
www.valueline.com
Companies covered: 8,300
Annual cost: $570
Free information: Reports on the 30 stocks in the Dow industrials

*At www.standardandpoors.com.

—Donna Rosato

nation, worth some $42 billion in 2005, according to *Forbes* magazine. (His good friend Bill Gates, chairman of Microsoft, is first at $50 billion.) With an initial investment of $100,000 at the age of 25, Buffett built a business empire that includes financial companies, insurance giant GEICO and a stable of brands like Fruit of the Loom and Dairy Queen.

Here are some gems of investment wisdom gleaned from published interviews and Buffett's letters to shareholders in Berkshire Hathaway annual reports.

Pick businesses you understand. That means simple, stable companies. No one can predict future cash flows of complex, quickly changing businesses. "What counts for most people in investing is not how much they know, but rather how realistically they define what they don't know. An investor needs to do very few things right as long as he or she avoids big mistakes."

Hang on tight. Hold onto a security as long as "the prospective return on equity capital of the underlying business is satisfactory, management is competent and honest, and the market does not overvalue the business."

Be skeptical of past performance. "If history books were the key to riches, the Forbes 400 would consist of librarians."

Pessimism can be a good thing. It produces low stock prices. "It's optimism that is the enemy of the rational buyer."

Beware of pumped-up, short-term earnings. And of managers who don't deliver for long periods and blame it on their long-term view. "Even Alice, after listening to the queen lecture her about 'jam tomorrow,' finally insisted, 'It must come sometimes to jam today.'"

When index funds make sense. By periodically investing in an index fund, "the know-nothing investor can actually outperform most investment professionals. Paradoxically, when 'dumb' money acknowledges its limitations, it ceases to be dumb."

When diversification makes no sense. An investor

who understands the economics of, say, five or ten reasonably priced companies is better off putting more money into "the businesses he understands best and that present the least risk, along with the greatest profit potential," rather than diversifying.

Forecasting the Future

Where is the economy headed? Check out these everyday signposts

Economists look at thousands of economic statistics, like durable goods orders or jobless numbers, to help divine the state of the economy. Some economists also take notice of more commonplace indicators, clues that might suggest a new way to look at what's happening in the market. Here, four economic observers explain their everyday indicators and the thinking behind them.

HEAVY TRAFFIC
Steven D. Levitt, Professor of economics, University of Chicago and co-author of Freakonomics

HOW IT WORKS: My favorite offbeat indicator of the economy is traffic. The best example, I'm told, is that traffic plunged in Silicon Valley after the Internet bubble burst, but I've even noticed the ebbs and flows in Chicago.

WHAT IT MEANS: When the economy is strong, rush hour traffic tends to be worse.

"FOR SALE" SIGNS
Alan B. Krueger, Professor of economics, Princeton University

HOW IT WORKS: I pay close attention to housing sales and how long it's taking for houses to sell. I look for "for sale" signs. I see how long they're for sale, whether they're being marked down and what they're asking.

WHAT IT MEANS: One of the threats in some areas is that we might be in a bubble and I'm trying to stay attuned to whether it is a bubble. You can get good data from the Energy Department on gas prices, but how hard it is to sell a house—lowering prices, that kind of information—is beneath the kind of data we can get.

"NO VACANCY" SIGNS
Ethan Harris, Chief U.S. economist, Lehman Brothers

HOW IT WORKS: Recently I went on a trip with my son and we couldn't find a hotel room in Hartford. This and other experiences at upscale business hotels in the last year, makes me suspicious that the cost of "lodging away from home" is up only modestly.

WHAT IT MEANS: If hotels are full, prices are rising. Airplanes also seem jam-packed these days, so the corporate sector must be doing great. This seems consistent with the idea that there is a lot of pricing power in business-to-business transactions, but not business-to-consumer.

PAWNSHOP WRENCHES
David Brancaccio. Host of Now on *PBS; former host of* Marketplace.

HOW IT WORKS: In Greenville, Mich., a Rust Belt town where a lot of the jobs have gone elsewhere, there's a pawnshop on the main drag, and in the window is this huge mound of socket-wrench heads. It's clear that people who have used socket-wrenches for a livelihood have gone in and pawned these things.

WHAT IT MEANS: As this mound has gotten bigger or smaller, it has meant something for the economy and jobs in America. It's like that old saw that if your neighbor's out of work, it's a recession; if you're out of work, it's a depression.

—David Leonhardt

How to Pick a Mutual Fund

There's no dearth of information out there. Here's what to focus on

Mutual fund investors can't make perfect choices every time—too many variables are stacked against them: compiling the ideal portfolio, buying into a fund at precisely the right time and bailing out precisely before the wrong time. But investors can stay a step ahead and avoid serious blunders by knowing the basics of analyzing a mutual fund's performance. There are 8,000-odd mutual funds in the United States, with $8.5 trillion in assets. It pays to know what you're getting into. Here are a few basics in evaluating a fund:

RETURN. Many investors obsess over a fund's yield, which tells you the current income distributed annually. But the true test of any fund, even one bought for income, is total return. Total return measures the increases and decreases of your investment over time, assuming the reinvestment of dividends and subtracting the fund's costs. You can find a fund's total return by calling the fund company's toll-free number.

When you compare total returns of several funds, be sure they are from comparable time periods, say January 1 to December 31. Determine, too, whether or not sales charges and other fees have been deducted from total returns. Then, compare the returns annually and, say, over five years or since the fund's inception. If most of the cumulative gains occurred in the most recent years, you're looking at a fund that could burn out.

RISK. It isn't easy to calculate or compare how much risk a mutual fund assumes, but getting an idea of risk is important. A few statistical measures that give an idea of a fund's risk include a fund's alpha, beta and standard deviation. Alpha reports how much the fund's performance deviated from its expected return. A fund with a positive alpha did better than expected. A negative alpha means the fund underperformed.

Beta measures the volatility of a fund's return against an index, such as the S.&P. 500. Aggressive investors prefer funds with a beta above 1.0, which means the fund's returns have moved up and down more than the S.&P. as a whole. A more conservative choice would be a fund with a .75 beta, for example, meaning that the fund is more stable than the market, generally and in the long run.

Academics especially like a risk measure called standard deviation. It gauges how widely a fund's return swings from one time period to another. A fund with volatile returns is supposedly more likely to show a big loss in the future.

INVESTMENT STYLE AND MIX. Two funds can fall under the same general investment category but have different styles that affect their performance. The reason: interpretations of terms such as "aggressive growth" may vary from fund to fund. The prospectus will give you a precise explanation of a fund's strategy and investment objective. (Funds often change their investment style or management team, making past performance an unreliable measure.) Check out a fund's mix of investments, too. Exposure to a vulnerable industry or to volatile foreign stocks can go a

---

ⓘ **INSIDE INFO**

A Poor Knack for Funds

○ Investors seem to have a knack for picking mutual funds poorly. Over the 20 years through 2004, the average stock mutual fund investor earned a reed-thin 3.5 percent, annualized, compared with an average annual gain of 13 percent for the S.&P. 500, according to Boston research firm Dalbar, Inc.

long way toward explaining a fund's performance.

LEVERAGE. Many funds hedge against possible changes in interest rates or currency values with strategies that may be risky. Be sure you're comfortable with a fund's hedging strategy. Can the fund invest in risky derivatives, fill up on Latin American stocks, sell short? Often, the techniques help returns, but just as often they can cause deep losses. Scrutinize the prospectus.

TAXES. Don't ignore the tax implications of buying a particular fund, but don't get carried away by potential tax bills, either. No doubt about it, taxes can take the fun out of a mutual fund gain. If you're shopping for a tax-free fund, avoid those that post most of their income in gains. If you're buying stock funds, find out when the fund posts its annual gains, usually at year-end, and wait until after it has done so to buy in.

But don't pick a fund just for its tax advantages. Studies show that there's not much change in equity-fund rankings on an after-tax basis, so, investors should focus on performance first, not taxes. The tax analysis helps if you're deciding between two similar funds with comparable gross returns.

Why You Can't Beat the Market

A market guru makes the case for index funds

Why search for just the right stock fund or manager when you can do better by investing in an unmanaged index fund? That's the question posed by proponents of index funds, which buy the stocks in the Standard & Poor's 500 to get the same performance as the index. Critics

> **A blindfolded chimpanzee throwing darts at the stock market pages could select a portfolio that would do as well as the experts.**

Burton Malkiel, author of *A Random Walk Down Wall Street* and Princeton University professor of economics

• • •

of index funds ask, Why settle for mediocrity when you could hit a fund that soars?

Princeton University economist Burton Malkiel, author of the classic investment book *A Random Walk Down Wall Street* (the ninth edition is due out in 2007), has long argued that investing in the stock market is like taking a random walk. Here are his views on index funds:

Q Are index funds all they're cracked up to be?

I have argued for over 30 years that an indexing strategy—simply buying and holding the hundreds of stocks making up the broad stock market averages—is probably the most sensible one for individuals and institutional investors. With index funds, investors can buy different types of stocks and get the benefits of stock and bond investing with no effort, minimal expenses, and big tax savings.

Q How have index funds performed"

Over the past 30 years, the Standard & Poor's 500 Index has outperformed about three-quarters of active investment managers. And, they've done well compared to other indexes, too, like the Dow-Wishire 5000 Stock Index.

Q Which index funds do you like?

Indexing isn't simply buying the S.&P. 500. I also like funds that match other indexes such as the broader Dow-Wilshire 5000. Some good values may exist in small-cap stocks, in real estate investment trusts and in foreign equities. Funds that match those indexes have also generally outperformed actively managed funds that invest in similar securities.

MONEY

Q Do index funds simply guarantee mediocrity, as critics say?

Well, you can't boast about the fantastic gains you've made by picking stock market winners. But index fund investors are likely to get better results than those of the typical fund manager, whose huge fees and large portfolio turnover reduce returns. To many, the guarantee of playing at par with the stock market nearly every time is very attractive.

Reading a Balance Sheet

A noted investment authority gives an eloquent short course

John Train is well known as the author of a bounty of business books, including *Money Masters of Our Time,* and is chairman of Montrose Advisors in New York City. In the following explanation, which originally appeared in *Harvard* magazine, Train takes you on a guided tour of a corporate financial statement:

The most important single truth to grasp about investing is that when you buy a share of stock you become a partner in a business. The essence of investing is thus understanding businesses, companies.

Company events are reported in dollar terms. To invest sensibly you therefore need to understand what the company is trying to tell you in its financial statement, which is published in a conveniently stylized form, like a sonnet. Though the elements are fairly simple, I observe that many of my clients have trouble reading one. So here is a simple guide to help get started. A company's financial statement comes in four parts: the balance sheet, the income statement, the cash flow statement and the statement of shareholders' equity:

The balance sheet, the first of these, is in essence a financial snapshot of the company at one moment in time, the end of its fiscal year. It is generally brought up to date each quarter thereafter.

The income (or profit and loss) statement shows how the business did during the period; that is, sales minus costs.

The cash flow statement shows where cash came from and what it was used for. The amounts don't quite match those on the income statement, which includes, for example, purchases or sales on credit, where cash has not yet changed hands.

The statement of shareholders' equity tells how much the company's book value rose or fell during the period, whether because it made or lost money or took in new capital by selling stock. If the company made money, this statement will show how much of the profit was put back into the business and how much was paid out to shareholders.

A company's financial statement ordinarily includes an auditor's opinion. A "qualified" opinion often indicates trouble.

The balance sheet is called that because it is set up to balance, like an equation: there's an implied equal sign between the two parts. On the left (or "asset") side you show all the assets in the company at that moment—what it owns—and on the right (or "liability") side you show all the company's debt—what it owes—plus the money that has been put up by the owners and kept in the business: the "shareholders' equity." If you think about it, the money you have invested in a house—your equity—plus the mortgage—a debt—perforce corresponds to the physical structure: the asset.

Here is an example. Let's suppose the shareholders of a company put up $1 million, which goes to buy a million dollars' worth of gold. A simplified balance sheet would look like this:

ASSETS

Gold:	$1,000,000

LIABILITIES + SHAREHOLDERS' EQUITY

Shareholders' Equity:	$1,000,000

Suppose we now borrow a million dollars from the bank and buy an additional million dollars' worth of gold. Our simplified balance sheet would then look like this:

ASSETS

Gold	$2,000,000
	$2,000,000

LIABILITIES + SHAREHOLDERS' EQUITY

Bank debt	$1,000,000
Shareholders' Equity	$1,000,000
	$2,000,000

In other words, the two sides of the equation still balance.

Good. Now suppose that during our first year of business the price of gold doubles, and we happily sell half our hoard for the original cost of the entire amount. Our simplified income statement now looks like this:

Revenues	$2,000,000
Less: costs of goods sold*	$1,000,000
Profit before tax	$1,000,000
Less: Provision for taxes	$250,000
Net income	**$750,000**

* Sales are ordinarily shown on an accrual basis—that is, what you are committed to—rather than a cash basis (when you actually take in the money).

We can use this $750,000 of free cash to pay down the bank loan, pay ourselves a dividend, build up our shareholders' equity or buy back our own stock. Let's look at the first case. After paying taxes, we pay down the bank loan:

ASSETS

Cash	$1,000,000
Gold (at cost)*	$1,000,000
	$2,000,000

LIABILITIES + SHAREHOLDERS' EQUITY

Bank Debt	250,000
Shareholders' Equity:	
Common stock	$1,000,000
Retained earnings	$750,000

*At market: $2,000,000. Accounting principles require that you show the lower of cost or market value.

"Retained earnings" on the balance sheet is where you put money the company has earned and left in the business, not paid out in dividends.

Footnotes to the financial statements may include information that does not show up in any of the numerical tables, such as pending litigation, company restructuring or prospective mergers. So always read the footnotes.

Perhaps the biggest difference between the way business professionals and nonprofessionals examine financial statements is that if you have actually been in business, you tend to look at the cash and equivalents, and at the cash flow section of the report. If a business is doing well, cash will be building up and can be put to work in useful ways: paying off debt, adding to plant, buying back the company's own shares in the market. If things are going badly, the company will be short of cash, bank and other debt will be rising, and management will be run ragged coping with creditors instead of improving its products. (A hot growth company may also want cash because it has so many opportunities, but that's a more agreeable problem.)

After you have worked with financial statements for a while, you get in the habit of calculating the return on equity, how fast the inventory turns over, the operating profit margin and a hundred other things.

The whole thing is a lot more fun than you might think. And consider this: even if you've only got this far, you're already well ahead of the mass of investors!

Words to Watch on Wall Street

Terms to master before investing in mutual funds

Do you know the difference between a "load" and a "no-load" fund? What's a "growth and income fund" or an "aggressive growth" fund? Terms and interpretations vary within the industry and even from firm to firm; the definitions below are from the Investment Company Institute, the trade association for the mutual fund industry. Before you pick a mutual fund, read the prospectus for a precise explanation of the fund's strategy and investment objective. Here are some terms you're likely to stumble across as you pore over the fine print.

Aggressive growth fund. A fund that seeks maximum capital gains. Current income is not a significant factor. Some may invest in businesses somewhat out of the mainstream, such as fledgling companies, new industries, companies fallen on hard times or industries temporarily out of favor. Or, some may invest in techniques such as short-term trading.

Asset allocation fund. A fund that invests in a variety of different asset classes with the goal of providing diversification and consistent returns.

Back-end load. A sales commission charged when you sell your shares in a mutual fund. Usually ranges from 0.5 to 6.0 percent.

Balanced fund. Generally has a three-part investment objective: to conserve investors' initial principal, to pay current income and to promote long-term growth of both principal and income. Balanced funds mix bonds, preferred stocks and common stocks.

Corporate bond fund. Purchases bonds of corporations for the majority of portfolio. The rest of the portfolio may be in U.S. Treasury bonds or bonds issued by a federal agency.

Derivatives. Financial instruments with values linked to some underlying asset, such as a bond, stock or index.

Emerging market fund. Invests primarily in the equity securities of companies in, or doing business in, emerging countries and markets.

Environmental securities fund. Generally invests in environment-related firms. May include companies involved in hazardous waste treatment, waste recycling and other related areas. Such funds may or may not screen companies to determine whether they also meet specific social objectives.

Flexible portfolio fund. A fund that may be 100 percent invested in stocks, bonds or money-market instruments, depending on market conditions. These funds give the money managers the greatest flexibility in anticipating or responding to economic changes.

Front-end load. A sales commission charged when you buy your shares, usually in the range of 1 to 3 percent of your investment.

Ginnie Mae or G.N.M.A. Fund. Invests in mortgage securities backed by the Government National Mortgage Association (G.N.M.A.). To qualify for this category, the majority of the portfolio must always be invested in mortgage-backed securities.

Global equity fund. Invests in securities traded worldwide, including the United States. Compared to direct investments, global funds offer investors an easier avenue to investing abroad. Professional money managers handle trading and record-keeping details and deal with differences in currencies, languages, time zones, regulations and business customs. In addition to another layer of diversification, global funds add another layer of risk—the exchange rate factor.

Growth and income fund. Invests mainly in the common stock of companies that have had increasing share value, as well as a solid record of paying dividends. Attempts to combine long-term capital growth with a steady stream of income.

High-yield bond fund. Maintains at least two-thirds of its portfolio in lower-rated corporate bonds (Baa or lower by Moody's rating service and BBB or lower by Standard and Poor's rating service). In return for generally higher yield, investors bear a greater degree of risk than for higher-rated bonds.

Income-bond fund. Seeks a high level of current income by investing at all times in a mix of corporate and government bonds.

Income-equity fund. Invests primarily in equity securities of companies with good dividend-paying records.

Income-mixed fund. Invests in income-producing securities, including both equities and debt instruments.

Index funds. Construct portfolios to mirror a specific market index. They are expected to provide a rate of return that will approximate or match, but not exceed, that of the market they are mirroring. Index funds offer a number of investment choices that include various stock market indexes or indexes of international or bond portfolios.

Load. A fee or commission imposed by a mutual fund. Some loads are a flat percentage, others are based on the amount you invest or how long you remain in the fund. A load can be as high as 8.5

MONEY

How to Estimate Total Return

A simple way to figure how much your mutual fund is really making

Following your mutual fund's performance in the newspaper alone won't tell you how you're really doing. The quickest and by far easiest way to learn your fund's total annual return is to call the fund's toll-free number. But, if you'd rather do it yourself, you'll need to know three things to start:

1. The fund's net-asset value per share a year ago.

2. Its NAV now.

3. Distributions per share of dividends and capital gains in the interim.

You should be able to find all this information on your account statement. Here's how to do the calculation:

Say that your fund's net asset value as of the end of last year was $50 per share. A year later, its NAV was $60. During the year, it distributed $5 per share in income and capital gains. Subtract the starting NAV from the ending NAV and add the distributions to that sum. The result—$15—is the total return in dollars.

Now convert this amount to a percentage by dividing the total return by the starting NAV and multiplying by 100.

Example:
$15 divided by $50 X 100 = 30%

Note that this result, while not as precise as one produced by more complicated formulas, is a fairly accurate estimate.

percent. Low loads run between 1 and 3 percent.

Mutual fund. Pools shareholder cash to invest in a variety of securities, including stocks, bonds and money market instruments.

NAV or net asset value. The market value of one share of a mutual fund, calculated at the close of each business day.

No-load fund. Mutual fund that doesn't charge a fee or commision to buy or sell its shares.

Redemption fee. One to 2 percent charge when you sell your shares. Often waived if you hold shares for a given number of years.

Small company growth fund. Seeks aggressive growth of capital by investing primarily in equity securities of small companies—usually in the developing stages of their life cycle—with rapid-growth potential. Shares of such companies are often thinly traded and may be subject to more abrupt market movements than those of larger firms.

Specific social objectives fund. Screens companies for compliance with certain social or ethical criteria, in addition to using traditional measures of financial value when choosing securities for their portfolios.

Taxable money market fund. Invests in the short-term, high-grade securities sold in the money market. Generally the safest, most stable securities available, including Treasury bills, certificates of deposit of large banks and commercial paper (the short-term i.o.u.'s of large U.S. corporations.) Money market funds limit the average maturity of their portfolio to 90 days or less.

Tax-exempt money market fund. Invests in municipal securities with relatively short maturities. Investors who use them seek tax-free investments with minimum risk.

U.S. government income fund. Invests in a variety of government securities, including U.S. Treasury bonds, federally guaranteed mortgage-backed securities and other government notes.

Variable annuities. Insurance products, mainly used for retirement income, that offer investors some advantages of mutual funds, in addition to tax-deferred earnings.

Does Big Mean Bad for Funds?
Fund performance may not suffer as assets swell

Big mutual funds have a reputation as ungainly vehicles that can't keep up with smaller, nimbler competitors. But a close look shows this isn't necessarily so. In fact, for many years, most of the actively managed mutual funds handling the largest pools of money in their investment categories managed to outperform their smaller peers, an

---

NIMBLE DESPITE THEIR SIZE

Many of the largest mutual funds that invest in small-cap stocks have produced above-average results.

FUND	NET ASSET VALUE	RANK*	5 YEARS**
1. Columbia Acorn Z	$15.4 billion	6	14.6%
2. Neuberger Berman Genesis Inv	$10.8	14	16.3%
3. Vanguard Explorer	$10.2	25	7.7%
4. T. Rowe Price Small-Cap Stock	$7.5	61	11.1%
5. DFA U.S. Small Cap Value	$6.7	12	20.2%
6. T. Rowe Price New Horizons	$6.2	22	8.4%
7. Royce Total Return	$5.4	59	14.7%
8. T. Rowe Price Small-Cap Value	$5.2	16	19.1%
9. Baron Growth	$4.9	7	13.8%
10. Fidelity Small Cap Stock	$4.2	63	10.8%

* percentile in their category   **ending Nov. 2005

SOURCE: Morningstar Inc.

analysis of Morningstar fund data shows.

Very successful funds grow larger for two reasons: the value of their holdings appreciates and investors tend to direct their dollars to fund winners. So, when such funds falter, it's easy to say asset growth is a factor. But performance at funds of all sizes can slip for a variety of reasons: a mistake here or there, shifting investor sentiment or simply bad luck. The success of so many large funds suggests that size alone does not dictate subpar performance. Investors must consider factors beyond assets under management, particularly turnover and the size of a fund's positions in individual stocks. Are the holdings so big, for example, that the fund will have difficulty getting out?

–Norm Alster

Beware of Mutual Fund Taxes

Mutual funds seem simple, until it's time to sell

For such a conceptually simple way to invest—people pooling their assets for professionals to manage—mutual funds pose a remarkably complex set of issues for taxpayers. Investors who buy and sell mutual fund shares face an assortment of tax issues. Here are some tax-smart recommendations from financial planners.

• PUT high-tax investments in tax-advantaged accounts.

• REMEMBER that switching funds, even within the same fund family, can have tax consequences. Such a swap outside an individual retirement account or 401(k) is actually a sale and purchase for tax purposes, though commissions are generally waived.

• AVOID buying shares late in the year, so you are not liable for taxes on gains in which you did

not participate; sell before the distribution date. Conversely, sales that are to be minimally taxed should precede this date, which for most funds occurs in the last several weeks of the year.

• CONSIDER taking distributions in cash rather than reinvesting them in new fund shares. That will simplify bookkeeping.

• EVALUATE the various methods of determining the cost basis of shares before making what will be a permanent commitment. One option is to use the average cost of your shares—a method that can be used for mutual fund sales but not for those of individual stocks. Average cost is the most commonly used method, and most fund groups now routinely calculate and provide this figure for you. If you are looking to minimize the tax hit of a sale, however, the best method is the most flexible one: the designation of specific shares. Keeping track of specific lots of shares, of course, requires assiduous bookkeeping.

• KEEP IN MIND the rules governing "wash" sales, which can make reinvestments, as well as repurchases, hazardous. These rules deny a deduction if you sell fund shares at a loss and then buy them back within 30 days. You can avoid this problem by reinvesting your money in a different fund, even one that invests in similar kinds of stocks and bonds.

—Robert D. Hershey Jr.

Finding a Broker You Can Trust

Tips for choosing a good stock picker and what to do if you run into a bad one

You've carefully considered your financial goals. Now, you're ready to pick the broker who will take your money and make it grow. Where do you start?

MONEY

A Broker by Any Other Name...

✔ Only two types of designations are regulated: broker-dealers (stockbrokers) and registered investment advisers (financial planners). Brokers, who facilitate buying and selling stocks and bonds, report to the N.A.S.D., the industry's self-regulating organization. Financial planners, who provide services such as tax and estate planning and advice on building financial plans, report to the Securities and Exchange Commission.

✔ Watch out for "brokers" with baffling titles like C.S.A. (certified senior advisers). Fancy initials could mean little more than that they attended a one-time seminar. To understand the alphabet soup after a financial adviser's name, check the N.A.S.D. Web site (www.nasd.org) for the meanings of professional credentials.

Finding a Financial Planner

Millionaire or not, you can find a financial adviser

✔ The common perception is that financial planners are just for the well-heeled, or "high net-worth individuals," as they are known in the business. Indeed, some planners are reluctant to forgo all-inclusive annual fees for an hourly or flat fee for specific advice, and won't look twice at someone with less than a million to invest. That is quickly changing as financial planners see a wide-open market for small investors.

✔ Web sites of organizations, such as the Certified Financial Planner Board of Standards at www.cfp.net, and the National Association of Personal Financial Advisors at www.napfa.org, provide lists of financial planners across the country.

—Coeli Carr

This advice from Arthur Levitt Jr., a former broker and the longest-serving chairman of the Securities and Exchange Commission, can help. As the nation's top market cop, he made investor protection and education a top priority. After leaving the S.E.C. in 2001, Levitt published the highly acclaimed *Take on the Street*, a hard-hitting analysis of the way Wall Street works.

Here are his tips on finding a good broker and what to do if you encounter an unethical one:

Ask tough questions. The important thing in picking a broker is to look him or her in the eye and ask some tough questions. What is the broker's philosophy on how best to meet your goals? Has the broker ever been disciplined for wrongdoing? Does the broker seem more interested in selling you a stock than getting to know your financial situation and your future financial needs? Ask questions that will help you determine if the chemistry is right and whether the broker will always put your interests first.

Find out how your broker gets paid. Typically, brokers are paid by commissions that reward them for the quantity of business they do, not for the quality. Ask your broker, Do you make more if I buy this mutual fund, for example, than if I buy this stock? Some brokerage firms allow you to pay a flat fee based on the amount of your assets under management. Ask the broker if you would be better off paying a flat fee or a commission.

Determine if your broker is getting you the best price. When your broker quotes you the price at which he'll sell you a stock or bond, ask how much he'd pay to buy it from you. The difference is the spread. You should ask your broker whether you could get a better price for a stock if you place a "limit" order, which specifies a price that falls in the middle of the spread. Also ask your broker if you could get a better price if he routed your order to a particular exchange or another market.

Ask your broker for investment records. Your broker can get key data about the financial health of municipal bond issuers from national or state information centers. For example, your broker can find out if the bond issuer is delinquent on principal or interest payments, if its ratings have been downgraded or if it has lost its tax-exempt status. Be sure to ask for this information.

Check out your broker's personal record. Before you hire a broker, check out his record on the National Association of Securities Dealers Web site at www.nasd.org under "NASD Broker-Check," or contact your state securities regulator (you can find a link at www.nasaa.org). Also, scrutinize your account statements for transactions that you didn't authorize, excessive commissions and delays in executing orders. Complain if you suspect wrongdoing.

What to do if you run into a bad broker. Most stockbrokers are honest, but if you think you've encountered an unethical one, contact the S.E.C. Office of Investor Education and Assistance (202-942-7040; www.sec.gov, click on "Investor Information"). The S.E.C. uses "tips" from investors to keep securities markets free from fraud, and bad brokers and financial planners. Report any problems promptly to the branch officer or the firm's compliance officer as well as to the N.A.S.D.

How to settle a broker dispute. Most investors agree to arbitrate disputes when they sign a customer agreement with a brokerage firm, so arbitration is the main route for settling disputes. You can file for arbitration with the N.A.S.D., or the New York Stock Exchange (212-656-2772 or www.nyse.com), among other exchanges, or the American Arbitration Association (www.adr.org/FileACase).

Nurturing Your 401(k)

Sound advice for a steady road to retirement

For as long as 401(k)'s have been around, more than 25 years, workers in these tax-deferred retirement plans have been encouraged to stay the course.

That's sound advice. Those who have plowed money into their accounts have seen balances recover steadily from bear markets. But there is a big difference between staying the course and simply starting and then forgetting your 401(k) indefinitely—which is what many people do.

A study by Hewitt Associates, the employee benefit research firm, found that from 2000 to 2004, only 40 percent of 401(k) participants touched their accounts even once. In other words, three out of five didn't tweak investment strategies at all; didn't sell out of a single mutual fund or rebalance—a fancy term for resetting your mix of stocks and bonds to ensure that it still conforms to your original plan—during this five-year stretch.

Financial planners say it's important for all investors to rebalance at least every year or two; otherwise, your portfolio will rebalance your investments for you—and not necessarily in a good way. For those who have been neglecting their 401(k) retirement plans, here are some ideas for hitting the reset button:

Keep up with new rules. Thanks to tax law changes, the annual federal limit on 401(k) contributions has been ratcheting higher. In 2006, the government permitted workers to contribute up to $15,000 a year to their 401(k)'s. And those 50 or older were allowed to save an additional $5,000 through so-called catch-up provisions. Some plans have lower contribution limits than the federal maximum, so check with your benefits department.

Save a little more. The beginning of the year is a great time to increase your contribution rate,

MONEY

especially if you received a raise or year-end bonus that allows you to sock away a greater percentage of your salary. Say you put away $500 a month for the next 30 years, earning 8 percent a year. At the end of your working career, you'd have a bit more than $750,000. But if you could put away $1,000 a month for the same period, and earned just 6 percent annually, you would have slightly more than $1 million at retirement.

How much should you be saving? In general, at least 15 percent of your salary, according to many financial planners, if you want to meet your basic retirement goals. Yet research shows that since the late 1990's, the average employee contributed less than 7 percent of his salary.

Diversify. While workers are diversifying across basic asset classes, many 401(k) plan participants often forget about important subclasses of assets, such as large, mid-cap and small-cap stocks, as each category tends to take turns leading the market.

Another glaring area of neglect is international stocks and stock funds. While many planners suggest that investors keep around 20 percent of their equity allocation in foreign shares, 401(k) investors have less than 9 percent of their equity portfolios in overseas stocks and funds. Financial planners are also concerned about the high concentration of company stock held in many 401(k) accounts; the average is nearly 25 percent.

Stay sheltered. If you changed jobs at the end of the year, don't cash out your 401(k). Instead, think about rolling the balance into an individual retirement account. A recent study by Hewitt Associates found that 45 percent of workers who leave their jobs cash out their 401(k)'s when they depart—even though doing so incurs taxes and can lead to a 10 percent penalty for workers younger than 59 1/2.

Because most 401(k) balances are still quite small, it's important that workers keep as much money in the accounts for as long as possible.

Vanguard, the mutual fund company, studied the 401(k) plans it manages and discovered that the average worker had a little more than $65,000 saved in 2004. But the median account balance was less than $24,000.

Try an off-the-shelf mix. If you know that you're not the type of person who will monitor a 401(k) account at least once a year, so-called lifestyle or asset-allocation funds may be for you. These funds invest in a mix of stocks and bonds but also rebalance that mix regularly. And some gradually dial down risk in your portfolio as you age. Ted Benna, an employee benefits specialist regarded by many as the father of the 401(k), calls the rise of these funds, especially those that adjust as you age, "the most noteworthy development" in retirement plans in a number of years.

—Paul J. Lim

Calculating Retirement Needs
Spend more at first, cut back later?

How much can you take out of your retirement nest egg each year without running out of money? Not much, according to the standard, conservative advice of many financial planners. The common maxim is that people who retire at the age of 65 can safely remove only about 4 percent of their portfolios each year, along with adjustments for inflation. On that basis, the initial withdrawal from a portfolio worth $1 million would be just $40,000.

But some experts are suggesting that it may make more sense to withdraw bigger amounts in the early years of retirement. Ty Bernicke, a financial planner in Eau Claire, Wis., for example, says retirees generally spend less as they age, so that it is reasonable for them to spend more when they are in retirement's early stages.

Spending in practically every category, from housing to clothing to entertainment, declines with age, says Bernicke who used data from the Bureau of Labor Statistics' Consumer Expenditure Survey for 2002. The only category in which spending rises with age is health care. People over 75 spent 26 percent less, on average, than those in the 65-to-74 age group. And the greater the age difference, the greater the difference in spending: Those over 75 spent 46 percent less than those aged 55 to 64, and 51 percent less than those aged 45 to 54. "Most retirement planning today assumes that a person retains the same lifestyle throughout their life," Bernicke says. "But as age increases, spending decreases."

Traditional advice that calls for an initial withdrawal of 4 percent is based on compensating for inflation. Someone with a $1 million nest egg could take out $40,000 the first year and $41,200 the next year, for example. And the nest egg would generally be invested at least 50 percent in stocks—as a further hedge against inflation—with the remainder in fixed-income investments and cash. The approach is based on risk-assessment studies using all kinds of hypothetical examples of market returns. The withdrawal rates are intended to leave very little chance of running out of money.

According to Bernicke's calculations, a couple in the first year of retirement at age 55, with expenditures of $60,000, might be able to safely withdraw that much from a portfolio worth $1 million—a 6 percent initial withdrawal rate. They would not run out of money as long as they reduced their spending later. Of course, a 6 percent withdrawal rate could vary because of many factors, including a retiree's spending level and the size of the nest egg.

In order to take out more than 4 percent that first year investors need to follow a few rules, according to Jonathan Guyton, a planner at Cornerstone Wealth Advisors in Minneapolis, writing in a 2004 issue of the *Journal of Financial Planning*. To generate income, they must always sell winning stocks before bonds or losing stocks. They cannot add more than 6 percent a year to their withdrawal even if inflation is higher than that. And no increases are permitted immediately after a year of investment losses.

These notions have their critics, of course. Many planners worry that medical costs may rise so fast that they will undo a well-constructed financial plan. The cost of prescription drugs, for example, has been rising more than three times as fast as inflation, and nursing home costs, meanwhile, have been rising 6 percent a year, according to surveys by Metropolitan Life, an insurance company.

Many planners say people need to save more and withdraw less to hedge against these increases. A more conservative estimate of distribution might be in order. You can't go back and say, "'Oops. You shouldn't have been taking out as much money the last few years' if someone doesn't have enough," says Stephanie Hancock of Hancock Wealth Advisory in Los Angeles. She also questions whether people will cut back on expenses as they shift into retirement. "You have all this time on your hands," she says. "You could actually spend more."

—Ilana Polyak

✔ TIMELY TIPS

Feathering Your Nest

✔ Online retirement calculators abound. For starters, try those on www.dinkytown.com, www.choosetosave.org/ballpark or www.fool.com.

Real Estate

The Long View on Real Estate

What's in store for the housing market?

Robert J. Shiller, a Yale economist, says housing prices are due to end badly, just as they did more than 300 years ago on the Herengracht in Amsterdam. What's Amsterdam got to do with it? More on that later.

Shiller is the same economist who worried about the bubble in the stock market a decade ago, before it later crashed with a thud. In speeches, in television and radio interviews and in a second edition of his prophetic 2000 book, *Irrational Exuberance*, Shiller takes the long view, predicting that housing prices could fall 40 percent in inflation-adjusted terms over the next generation and that the end of the bubble will probably cause a recession at some point. He is the bugaboo of the multibillion-dollar real estate industry. Its executives, like many Wall Street economists, say that low interest rates and a growing population will keep house prices rising, even if future increases are smaller than recent ones.

To Shiller, it is a question of history. Most people have never looked at decades and decades of home prices, because such data have been almost impossible to find. Stock market charts often go back almost a century, while housing charts typically start sometime in the distant decade of the 1970's.

But Shiller came upon some rare worldwide historical housing data, including on houses near the Herengracht canal in Amsterdam more than 300 years ago. The data showed a crash in that market in the 1670's when the prime minister was killed and partially eaten by a mob of angry Dutch. Prices lagged inflation during the Napoleonic wars but surged after William became king in 1814 and the country industrialized. Prices have hardly become more stable over the past few hundred years; in fact, they jumped up and down wildly in the 20th century. Today, the Herengracht is one of the city's finest addresses. Again and again, the cycle repeats itself, he found.

But there is essentially no long-term trend, beyond a general rise in house prices that roughly matches gains in people's incomes. By using a methodology developed from his findings and by

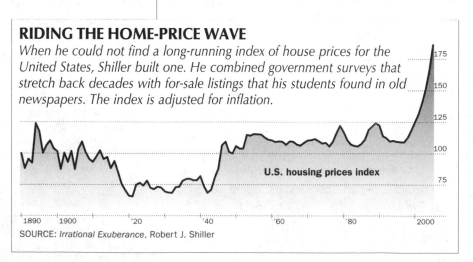

RIDING THE HOME-PRICE WAVE

When he could not find a long-running index of house prices for the United States, Shiller built one. He combined government surveys that stretch back decades with for-sale listings that his students found in old newspapers. The index is adjusted for inflation.

U.S. housing prices index

175
150
125
100
75

1890   1900   '20   '40   '60   '80   2000

SOURCE: *Irrational Exuberance*, Robert J. Shiller

A MEASURE OF THE MARKETS

Over the past 30 years, home prices have risen an average 1.8 percent a year above inflation. Home prices generally reflect the strength of the local economy.

HOTTEST MARKETS

Average annual increase adjusted for inflation 1976-2005

California	4.6%
District of Columbia	3.8%
Massachusetts	3.8%
New Jersey	3.2%
Washington	3.2%
U.S. Average	1.8%

WEAKEST MARKETS

North Dakota	-0.1%
Kansas	-0.1%
Oklahoma	-0.3%
Texas	-0.3%
Mississippi	-0.3%

SOURCE: U.S. Office of Federal Housing Enterprise Oversight

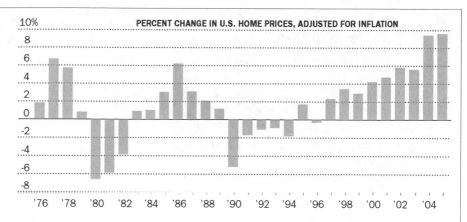

PERCENT CHANGE IN U.S. HOME PRICES, ADJUSTED FOR INFLATION

THE TEN HOTTEST METRO MARKETS

Housing values in these metropolitan areas saw the biggest jump over a 25-year period.

Nassau-Suffolk, N.Y.	9.1%
Boston metro area	8.5%
Salinas, Calif.	8.0%
Essex County, Mass.	7.9%
Cambridge-Newton-Framingham, Mass.	7.9%
New York metro area	7.7%
San Luis Obispo-Paso Robles, Calif.	7.7%
Napa, Calif.	7.7%
Santa Cruz-Watsonville, Calif.	7.6%
Worcester, Mass.	7.5%

—Motoko Rich and David Leonhardt

AVERAGE ANNUAL CHANGE IN REAL HOME PRICES, BY PRESIDENT

Carter	+1.7%
Reagan	+0.8
G.H.W. Bush	-1.7
Clinton	+1.4
G.W. Bush	+7.0

THE POLITICS OF HOME PRICES

The average annual gain in housing prices after inflation during George Bush's years in the White House was 7 percent as of the end of 2005. By contrast, Jimmy Carter's administration posted an annual rise of only 1.7 percent, but still the second highest gain in recent years. During George H. W. Bush's presidency, prices tumbled 1.7 percent.

MONEY

sorting through old classified ads, he was able to fashion a chart for the United States that goes back to the 19th century.

It all points to an unavoidable truth, Shiller says. Every housing boom of the last few centuries has been followed by decades in which home values fell relative to inflation. Over the long term, the portion of income that families spend on their shelter stays about the same. Builders become more efficient, as they are doing today.

Places that were once sleepy hinterlands, like the counties south of San Francisco or a patch of desert in southern Nevada, turn into bustling centers that take pressure off prices elsewhere.

A plausible scenario, says Shiller, is that home-price increases continue for a couple more years, and then "we might have a recession and they continue down into negative territory and languish for a decade." Many economists refute his assessment, contending that interest rates are

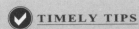

America's Last True Bargains?

Four towns the housing boom forgot

For some people, these cheap markets represent the last true bargains in America. To understand the lure of these overlooked markets, it helps to begin with the median price of an existing home nationally in 2005—$220,000—and see what it buys in these four locations.

1. **In Billings, Mont.,** the cheapest market in the state, you can buy that median house and still have nearly $80,000 left over. Median price: $142,500.

2. **In Spartanburg, S.C.,** housing prices are about half the national median. Median price: $118,700.

3. **In upstate New York,** the cheapest market in the Northeast, $220,000 will get you two houses in Binghamton and leave $40,000 to furnish them. Median price: $93,000.

4. **In Youngstown, Ohio,** you could buy almost three houses. Median price: $82,900.

As with any cheap investment, however, homeowners in these areas risk buying a seed that will never sprout. Houses are inexpensive for a reason. Often, local economies are depressed, the population is aging and shrinking, and the cities are far from cultural and economic hubs.

—Patrick O'Gilfoil Healy

low enough and demand for housing in big urban areas is high enough to keep prices from falling very far. Shiller himself confesses to some doubt. "I don't have any certainty," he says. "I have a lot of humility" about any prediction.

—David Leonhardt

Better to Buy or Rent?

Factors that sometimes make renting a better option

The thought occurs to just about every homeowner during a hot housing market: maybe it's time to cash out. The hard part is figuring out how to do so. Few can pick up their life in, say, California and move it to Nebraska. The other option—renting—has traditionally been derided as the equivalent of throwing money away.

But renting deserves another look. For example, while housing prices doubled in many areas of the country in the hot market of 2000 to 2005, rents barely budged. Add it all up—which the *New York Times* did in a 2005 analysis of the major costs and benefits of owning and renting, including tax breaks—and owning a home can be more expensive than renting in many parts of the country. Renting can be a surprisingly smart option for many people who never gave it a second thought. Here are some of the pros and cons:

Owning a home often ties up hundreds of thousands of dollars that might be invested more safely and more lucratively elsewhere. And while real estate brokers may hate to acknowledge it, home ownership involves its own versions of throwing money away, like property taxes and the costs of borrowing.

There are obvious benefits to home ownership beyond the financial, like peace of mind and a feeling of stability. Owners cannot have their home yanked away by a landlord who has decided to move back in. Owners can also change the color of their living room walls or fix a draft seeping through their windows without asking permission. Combine these benefits with the transaction costs of a house sale, and renting probably doesn't make sense for most people who already own their home and feel settled in it.

But the calculation can look quite different for those who are considering a move anyway or who do not yet own a home. At the very least, renters in boom markets, who often lament that they are wasting money, should know that their choice has as powerful an economic rationale as buying does under certain economic conditions. In the Bay Area of California, a typical family that buys a $1 million house, which is average in some towns, will spend about $5,000 a month to live there, according to the *Times* analysis. The family could rent a similar house for about $2,500, real estate records show, and could pay part of that bill with the interest earned by the money that was not used for a down payment.

When the net costs of owning are less than those of renting—as was the case in Chicago,

> **Just over 69 percent of Americans own their own home. For retirees, the number jumps to nearly 76 percent.**

• • •

Dallas, St. Louis and much of the middle of the country in late 2005 to early 2006—the argument for buying becomes overwhelming. So long as home prices do not fall sharply, home buyers in these places do much better than renters. But when owning is more expensive every month, buyers are betting entirely on price appreciation.

When you look at home appreciation, which is often what makes owning so alluring, the buy-versus-rent debate is a close call. The 10-year break-even point for buyers requires a 25 percent appreciation in home values in New York and 40 percent in California. Such increases have been easily achieved in the past. But some economists predict that price gains will slow; others argue that values will fall, as they did on the coasts in the early 1990's, or be stuck near their current levels for years to come. No matter who is right,

MONEY

More House, Larger Payments

How affordable is housing for a typical home buyer? The National Association of Realtors' composite Housing Affordability Index shows just that—whether the market allows a typical family to qualify for a mortgage loan on a typical single-family home.

When the index measures 100, a family earning the median income has exactly the amount needed to purchase a median-priced resale home, using conventional financing

and a 20 percent down payment.

In 2005, the composite index of 121.5 shows that a family earning the median family income has more than enough

to buy a home with a median price of $206,600. As the chart illustrates, the median price of homes has increased, but so has family income.

COMPOSITE AFFORDABILITY INDEX

YEAR	2005	2004	2003	2002
Median priced home	$206,600	$184,100	$170,000	$158,100
Mortgage rate	5.91	5.72	5.74	6.55
Monthly principle and interest payment	$981	$857	$793	$804
Payment as % of income	20.6%	18.9%	18.1%	18.7
Median family income	$57,214	$54,527	$52,682	$51,680
Qualifying income	$47,088	$41,136	$38,064	$38,592
Composite Affordability Index	121.5	121.1	125.7	131.6

SOURCE: National Association of Realtors

ⓘ **INSIDE INFO**

Men, Homes and Commitment

○ When it comes to buying homes, single women have outpaced single men for more than a decade. A 2005 study by the National Association of Realtors found that single women accounted for 21 percent of home buyers and single men for 9 percent.

○ The compelling question arises, Why are single men half as likely to be home buyers as women? Part of the gap is due to the high numbers of divorced women who have custody of their children and may prefer a home.

○ The consensus among brokers seems to be that single men, even those whose college diplomas are yellowed with age, gravitate to a commitment-free, fraternity-type lifestyle, rife with male companionship. Buying a home, which tethers them to one location, hinders independence.

○ Single women, on the other hand, seem more interested in establishing a sense of security, or "nesting." They see buying a home as an affirmative act of independence and a casting off the timeworn Prince Charming rescue fantasy. As one realtor put it, "They're just not going to wait to live happily ever after anymore."

—Stephanie Rosenbloom

"If you believe you'll be moving in the next four or five years, I'd rent," says Thomas Z. Lys, an accounting professor at the Kellogg School of Management at Northwestern University. "If you're a long-termer, I still would buy."

The single biggest misconception about home ownership, some brokers and economists say, might revolve around tax deductions. Many people seem to believe that buying a home can actually save them money because the interest on their mortgage is tax deductible. But all that deduction does is reduce the cost of borrowing the money—a cost that would not exist if the family were not buying the home. Families spend about six years in a house, on average, according to the National Association of Realtors. In that time, the interest on a $600,000 mortgage would add up to about $120,000, even at low rates and even after the tax deduction, according to National City Corporation, a large lender. Don't buy a house just because you think you're saving on the taxes, specialists say. You may save even more by not buying and renting instead.

Many homeowners also do not receive the full deductions from home ownership. In the Northeast and California, homeowners have so many deductions that some must pay the alternative minimum tax. This tax effectively wipes out part of their property-tax deduction, further cutting into the benefits of home ownership. Other homeowners do not itemize their deductions or, if they do so, end up with total deductions only a little larger than the standard deduction that the government offers to all taxpayers, even renters. "A lot of people hugely overvalue the mortgage deduction," says Dean Baker, co-director of the Center for Economic and Policy Research, a research group in Washington, "because they compare it to no deduction instead of comparing it to the standard deduction."

But to many people, the psychological benefits of buying are almost impossible to overcome. Owning makes them feel that they have achieved the American Dream, or it gives them the secure sense that, if nothing else, they have a tangible asset where they can sleep at night. Those are nice feelings, indeed. The question is, How much are they worth to you?

—David Leonhardt

Treading the Mortgage Minefield

Rules to follow before entering the daunting mortgage market

Rule No.1 for finding the right mortgage is, never jump into a mortgage deal, especially not the first product you're offered, according to Sarah Ludwig, executive director of the Neighborhood Economic Development Advocacy Project, a nonprofit group promoting access to fair credit.

Make a chart of the loan features offered by each potential lender, comparing the term of the loan, the interest rate and adjustable rates, if any; the size of the down payment, whether or not there is a prepayment penalty and the number of points that you will be charged, if any, advises Ludwig. (Points are upfront fees equal to 1 percent of the total loan amount that are used to lower the interest rate.) But before you even start searching for a home, much less a mortgage, take steps to avoid rushed decisions, dead ends and bad choices that you may have to live with for years.

HOW'S YOUR CREDIT?

Determine your credit status. Get your free annual credit report from each of the three major credit bureaus: Equifax, Experian and TransUnion (see "Checking up on Your Credit Rating" on page 178 for contact details). Not all creditors report your account information to all three bureaus, so it's wise to get the report from all three and reconcile the information in all of them, ensuring, for example, that your address and employment records are current, that credit accounts you have closed are recorded as closed and that the information is actually yours, especially if you have a common name.

Fix incorrect entries immediately. If an entry is valid but could have an adverse effect on your credit, you can offer an explanation. But avoid credit repair agencies that promise to correct reports for a fee—you can fix errors on your own. Get your credit score, a computer-calculated number from 300 to 850 based on your credit history that lenders use to determine what loan type and interest rate you can get. (Getting your credit score from the three agencies will cost about $8 each.) Typically, a score of 660 or higher qualifies for a conventional, or "prime" loan; below that, borrowers are considered a higher risk, or "subprime."

WHAT CAN YOU AFFORD?

Some questions to ask yourself: Should I make a larger down payment and deplete my resources? Should I pay points to lower the interest rate? Should I make a smaller down payment and possibly need a private mortgage insurance policy?

Seducing the Buyer

When an open house won't do, dinner parties and sleepovers might

Weekend sea trials are the currency of yacht dealers, lending diamonds is an established jewelry sales tactic, and now it is real estate's turn to be packaged with an experience.

"In the luxury market an open house would be considered a joke," says Dolly Lenz, vice chairman of marketing at Prudential Douglas Elliman in New York. "These buyers expect exclusivity, privacy and special handling."

"People want to understand what a day in a life living at a particular address will feel like," says Toni Alexander, president of InterCommunications, a marketing firm handling condo sales in a complex in Marina del Rey, Calif. The firm's sales agents are encouraged to offer sleepovers in the penthouse, poolside lunches and spa visits to serious clients, and they have sold about half of the units, priced from $500,000 up, since the building shifted from rentals to condos.

—Kimberly Stevens

MONEY

Lenders Want to Know

To get your loan approved, be ready with answers

Requirements may differ among lenders, but generally bringing these documents with you on a loan application interview will speed the process along.

Purchase agreement/sales contract: A signed copy of the agreement outlining the conditions and terms of the sale, along with any amendments; a copy of the listing form for the property; its legal description; and receipts for or down payment deposits.

Your addresses and personal information: All your addresses for the past seven years; your Social Security number and date of birth. The names, addresses and telephone numbers of your employers for the past two years.

Sources of income: Most recent pay stub that shows year-to-date earnings and your W-2 tax forms (original copies sent to you by the I.R.S.) for the past two years.

Current Assets: Account numbers and current balances of checking, savings and other investment accounts, including individual retirement accounts (I.R.A.'s), CD's, stocks, bonds, life insurance, cars, etc. Recent statements should suffice.

Current Debts: Auto loans, student loans, credit cards and other installment debt—provide name and address of each creditor and the monthly payment and total amount due.

Source of down payment: Can be from savings, stocks, investments, sale of other property or life insurance policies; or from relatives, assuming it doesn't have to be repaid.

If you own a home: The property address, current market value, mortgage lender name, mortgage account number, current monthly mortgage payment and outstanding mortgage balance.

If you're renting: The property address, name and address of the landlord, and current monthly rent. If you've lived at your current address for less than two years, bring that information for all previous addresses and landlords.

Source: Fannie Mae

(Private mortgage insurance protects the lender if you default. The premium is based on the terms of the loan and can range from a few dollars to several hundred dollars a month.)

Prequalifying for a mortgage helps to determine how much you can afford. Usually, the real estate agent will run your numbers through a basic prequalification calculation to determine which homes to show you. To get the right loan, consider how long you expect to keep the home and the mortgage; the time periods for the two may not be the same. You will also need to decide how to handle your closing costs. You can pay them at the closing or finance them by taking a larger loan or accepting a higher interest rate.

FINDING A LOAN

Many agencies want your business: banks, credit unions, online lenders, mortgage bankers, mortgage brokers. No size fits all. Choose one based on the products offered and a reputation for good service. Don't accept loan offers that come to you; rather, seek them out after you have looked at ads and gone online to get a sense of prevailing rates and terms. But be wary of giving out your personal information before you have chosen your mortgage. Among the well-known mortgage-comparison sites are www.bankrate.com, www.lendingtree.com and www.eloan.com.

Your first mortgage pitch is likely to come from a mortgage rep in your realtor's office. But be sure to contact other agents as well. First-time buyers should be especially wary of so-called one-stop shops that offer to do it all, from showing you homes to brokering a mortgage to inspecting and appraising the property. Some companies might take advantage of people unfamiliar with the process, says Ludwig.

Verify that your mortgage broker or lender is licensed by the state banking department and has not been the subject of complaints. Get the product description in writing. Read the documents, understand the terms.

Choose a lender who will establish an escrow account to cover property taxes and homeowner's insurance, adding them onto your monthly mortgage payment. That way, you won't be hit by large tax and insurance bills for which you were not prepared.

PICKING A PRODUCT

For most buyers, the best choice probably remains the traditional fully amortizing loan in which the monthly payment covers both the interest and part of the principal (or face value) of the loan, gradually diminishing the balance. (See "Which Mortgage Is For You?" on the next page for descriptions of popular mortgage loans.)

A few new variations on basic products warrant some scrutiny. The 40-year fixed-rate mortgage, for example, lowers the monthly payment but carries higher total interest costs because of the extended term of the loan. Real estate experts caution that since you build equity so slowly, and total interest costs are so much higher compared to a 30-year term, these products are a dubious choice.

Another risky current choice offers a minimum monthly payment based on a very low interest rate that may not even cover all the interest due each month. Over time, that process—called negative amortization—will increase your outstanding loan balance, especially if interest rates rise.

No- or low-down-payment mortgages are also available. "Make sure these features are legitimate," says Ludwig. "Some companies offering these features merely finance your down payment, or part of it, into the principal, adding onto your monthly costs over the life of the loan."

Watch out for so-called interest-only mortgages. Be aware that interest-only really means you pay only interest for a while, typically 5 or 10 years, followed by a sizable jump in monthly payments for the rest of your loan term. Sometimes that jump is into predictable, fully amortizing payments. But, often interest-only loans have adjustable rates that could cause large payment shocks down the road.

SEALING THE DEAL

Don't sign anything you don't understand or anything with a blank space that the broker or lender could fill in later. Don't be afraid to walk away if you're feeling pressured, especially if you are told there are no other options

—Dennis Hevesi

ℹ️ **INSIDE INFO**

Who Needs a Realtor?

○ **Zillow.com** helps consumers get more accurate real estate information. It provides data like previous sales prices and prices of similar properties. It also uses software to offer a free home-value estimate.

○ **Redfin.com,** actually a real estate brokerage company, automates the process of bidding on a house online. It then rebates to the buyer two-thirds of the buyer's agent's commission, which is usually 3 percent.

—Damon Darlin

MONEY

Which Mortgage Is for You?

Brush up on popular options before you make the leap

It's hard to keep track of all the different mutations of mortgages on the market these days, much less choose the one that's the best deal for you. Further, lenders offer endless variations on rates, fees and other terms, making comparison shopping difficult.

Online mortgage shopping tools can help. At www.bankrate.com and www.myfico.com, for example, you'll find tutorials and mortgage calculators. But you'll need to know the basic mortgage options first. Here's an explanation of some of the most popular, along with pros and cons of each:

Adjustable-rate mortgage

Interest rate changes over the life of the loan, resulting in possible changes in your monthly payments, loan term and/or principal. Some plans have rate or payment caps.

Pros. Starting interest rate is slightly below the market. Payment caps prevent wide fluctuations in payments. Rate caps limit amount total debt can expand.

Cons. Payments can increase sharply and frequently if index increases. Payment caps can result in negative amortization.

• TIP: Remember that if your payment-capped loan results in monthly payments that are lower than your interest rate would require, you still owe the difference.

Balloon mortgage

Monthly payments based on fixed interest rate; usually short term; payments may cover inter-est only, with principal due in full at end of term.

Pros. Offers low monthly payments.

Cons. Possibly no equity until loan is fully paid. When due, loan must be paid off in full or refinanced. Refinancing poses high risk if rates rise.

• TIP: Some lenders guarantee refinancing when the balloon payment is due, although they do not guarantee a certain interest rate. Good for homeowners who anticipate selling or refinancing in a few years.

Buy-down

Developer (or other party) provides an interest subsidy that lowers monthly payments during the first few years of the loan. Can have fixed or adjustable interest rate.

Pros. Offers a break from higher payments during the early years. Enables buyer with lower income to qualify.

Cons. With adjustable-rate mortgage, payments may jump substantially at end of subsidy. Developer may increase selling price.

• TIP: Consider what your payments will be after the first few years. They could jump considerably. Also see if the subsidy is part of your contract with the lender or the builder. If it's provided separately with the builder, the lender could still hold you liable for the full interest rate amount.

15-year mortgage

Fixed interest rate. Requires down payment or monthly payments higher than 30-year loan. Loan is fully repaid over 15-year term.

Pros. Frequently offered at slightly reduced interest rate. Offers faster accumulation of equity than traditional fixed-rate mortgage.

Cons. Has higher monthly payments. Involves paying less interest but this may result in fewer tax deductions.

• TIP: If you can afford the higher payments, this plan could save you interest and help you build equity. But, consider if the extra amount you pay is better off invested. (See, "Playing the Refinancing Game," page 213).

Fixed-rate mortgage

Fixed interest rate, usually long term; equal monthly payments of principal and interest until debt is paid.

Pros. Offers stability and long-term tax advantages.

Cons. Interest rates may be higher than other types.

• **TIP:** Can be a good financing method, if you are in a high tax bracket and need the interest deductions.

Graduated-payment mortgage

Lower monthly payments rise gradually (usually up to 10 years), then level off for duration of term. With adjustable interest rates, additional payments changes possible if index changes.

Pros. Easier to qualify for.

Cons. Buyer's income must be able to keep pace with scheduled payment increases. With an adjustable rate, payment increases beyond the graduated payment can result in additional negative amortization.

Growing Equity mortgage

Rapid payoff mortgage. Fixed interest rate but monthly payments may vary according to agreed-upon schedule or index.

Pros. Permits rapid payoff of debt because payment increases reduce principal.

Cons. Buyer's income must keep up with payment increases. Does not offer long-term tax deductions.

Hybrid mortgage

Fixed interest rate for a set number of years at the beginning of the mortgage, after which they become an annual adjustable-rate. Common fixed-rate periods are 3, 5 and 7 years.

Pros. More affordable than fixed-rate mortgages and more stable than A.R.M.'s.

Cons. Do not afford the stability of a fixed rate.

Renogotiable-rate mortgage

Interest rate and monthly payments are constant for several years; changes possible thereafter. Long-term mortgages.

Pros. Less frequent changes in interest rates offer some stability.

Cons. May have to renegotiate when rates are higher.

Reverse-annuity mortgage

Equity conversion. Borrower owns mortgage-free property and needs income. Lender makes monthly payments to borrower, using property as collateral.

Pros. Can provide homeowners with needed cash.

Cons. At end of term, borrower must have money available to avoid selling property or refinancing.

• **TIP:** You can't obtain a reverse mortgage until you have paid off your original mortgage. (See "Beware of the Reverse Mortgage" on page 214.)

Shared-appreciation mortgage

Below-market interest rates and lower monthly payments, in exchange for a share of profits when the property is sold or on a specified date. Many variations.

Pros. Low interest rates and low payments

Cons. If a home appreciates greatly, total cost of loans jumps. If home fails to appreciate, projected increase in value may still be due, requiring refinancing at possibly higher rates.

• **TIP:** You may be liable for the dollar amount of the property's appreciation, even if you do not wish to sell at the agreed upon date. Unless you have the cash available, this could force an early sale of the property.

Wraparound

Seller keeps original low-rate mortgage. Buyer makes payments to seller, who forwards a portion to the lender holding original mortgage.

Pros. Offers lower effective interest rate on total transaction.

Cons. Lender may call in old mortgage and require higher rate. If buyer defaults, seller must take legal action to collect.

• **TIP:** Problems could arise if the original lender or the holder of the original mortgage is not aware of the new mortgage. Some lenders or holders have the right to insist that the old mortgage be paid off immediately.

MONEY

Terms to Learn Before the Closing

How to sound like a real estate pro

Finding your dream house at the right price was the easy part. To help prevent the already-stressful process from turning into a nighmare, here are some basic real estate terms every home-buyer should know:

Amortization. The gradual repayment of the mort-gage through periodic installments over the term of the loan. The scheduled payment minus the interest equals amortization.

Assumable mortgage. A mortgage that can be taken over by the buyer from the seller when a home is sold. Note that many mortgages are no longer legally assumable.

Bridge loan. A short-term loan that allows a buyer to use the proceeds to finance closing on a new house before the current one is sold. Also known as a "swing loan." To qualify for a bridge loan, the borrower must generally have a contract to sell the current house.

Closing costs (settlement costs). Fees and other costs, including down payment, associated with a mort-gage loan, paid generally by the borrower at the time of settlement. These can include attorney fees, loan origination fee, title insurance and other prepaid items, such as escrow deposits for taxes and insurance.

Equity. The owner's interest in a home. To calcu-late, take the home's current fair-market value and subtract the outstanding mortgage amount and any existing liens.

Escrow. Money or other valuables deposited with a third party for safe-keeping and returned once a condition has been fulfilled. Often used for payment of a specified amount of taxes and insurance along with a mortgage payment. Also used to define the process by which a buyer and seller deliver legal documents to a third party who completes the trans-action in accordance with their instructions.

Foreclosure. The legal procedure in which a mort-gaged property whose owner defaults on the loan can be sold by the lender to pay the mortgage debt.

FIGURING YOUR MONTHLY PAYMENTS

This chart shows what you pay on every $1,000 you borrow at different rates over the yearly terms. Here's how to figure other amounts. For example, if you take a $120,000 loan for 30 years at 7 $1/2$ %, divide $120,000 by $1,000 = 120. Then multiply 120 x 6.99 (on chart) = $838.88, your payment, including principal and interest. Or, try one of the ubiq-uitous online mortgage payment calculators, such as the one on www.bankrate.com. Just plug in the numbers to compare different rates and terms.

MONTHLY PAYMENTS FOR $1,000

Rate (%)	30 years	15 years
4 $1/2$	$5.07	$7.65
5	$5.37	$7.91
5 $1/2$	$5.68	$8.17
6	$6.00	$8.44
6 $1/2$	$6.32	$8.71
7	$6.65	$8.99
7 $1/2$	$6.99	$9.27
8	$7.34	$9.56
8 $1/2$	$7.69	$9.85
9	$8.05	$10.14
9 1/2	$8.41	$10.44
10	$8.78	$10.75
10 $1/2$	$9.15	$11.05

Home equity loan. A loan that lets a home owner borrow up to an amount that represents a specified percentage of his or her equity in the prop-erty. Also known as a second mortgage.

Loan origination. The process by which a lender makes a loan, possibly including the loan application, processing and underwriting the applica-tion, and closing the loan. The buyer generally pays a loan origination fee to the lender.

Lock-in. An agreement in which the lender agrees to honor a quoted interest rate for a specified period of time before the closing date.

Origination fee. An upfront fee paid to a lender to cover the administrative costs of processing a loan application. The fee is typically in the form of points: one point is 1 percent of the mortgage amount.

Pre-approval. A process by which a lender approves a borrower's eligibility to receive a mortgage loan of a certain amount before a specific property is identified. The commitment by the lender comes after reviewing the applicant's credit history.

Refinancing. The process of paying off one loan with the proceeds from a new loan on the same property. This is usually done to take advantage of interest rates that have dropped below the rate of the existing loan.

Seller take-back/owner financing. A transaction in which the seller provides all or part of the financing to the buyer for the home purchase.

Settlement/closing. In the sale of a property, this is the process of completing a loan transaction and transferring the house from the seller to the buyer. Mortgage documents are signed and recorded, funds are disbursed and ownership is transferred. Some jurisdictions call this process escrow. In a refinancing, there is no transfer of ownership; the process simply includes repayment of the former lender.

Title search. A check of the public records to ensure that the seller legally owns the property and to identify any potential liens against the property.

Playing the Refinancing Game
When should you trade in your mortgage?

The right answer may be, A lot sooner than you think. Conventional wisdom holds that interest rates have to drop 2 percent to make refinancing attractive. The conventional wisdom may be wrong. In fact, if you're planning to live in your house for many years, refinancing to a lower rate by as little as 1 percent can be profitable.

For a typical mortgage that involves refinancing costs of 1 percent of the total loan, the accounting firm of Ernst & Young figures that, if you can lower your interest rate by a single percentage point, the new loan will put you ahead after just 18 months. Refinancing can give you other opportunities—like switching from a 30-year fixed mortgage to 15 years. The switch usually bumps up your monthly payments, but it

WHAT YOU CAN AFFORD

Here's the maximum monthly amount you could spend for home payments and total monthly credit obligations at a variety of income levels and meet guidelines required by most lenders. As a rule of thumb, no more than 28 percent of your gross monthly income should be used for your mortgage payment (principal, interest, taxes, insurance, condo fees, owners association fee, mortgage insurance premium), and no more than 36 percent of your gross monthly income should be going toward your mortgage payment plus all other monthly credit obligations.

YOUR GROSS ANNUAL INCOME	MONTHLY MORTGAGE PAYMENTS	MAXIMUM CREDIT OBLIGATIONS/MO.
$20,000	$467	$600
$30,000	$700	$900
$40,000	$933	$1,200
$50,000	$1,167	$1,500
$60,000	$1,400	$1,800
$70,000	$1,633	$2,100
$80,000	$1,867	$2,400
$90,000	$2,100	$2,700
$100,000	$2,333	$3,000
$130,000	$3,033	$3,900
$150,000	$3,500	$4,500
$200,000	$4,667	$6,000

SOURCE: Fannie Mae

MONEY

(i) INSIDE INFO

Money in the Bank?

O Payments and savings on a $100,000 mortgage refinanced to 5.5 percent.

Current rate	Current monthly payment	Monthly savings at 5.5%	Annual savings at 5.5%
6%	$600	$32	$384
6.5%	$632	$64	$768
7%	$665	$97	$1,164
7.5%	$699	$131	$1,572
8.0%	$734	$166	$1,892
8.5%	$769	$201	$2,412
9.0%	$805	$237	$2,844
10.0%	$878	$310	$3,720
10.5%	$915	$347	$4,164
11.0%	$952	$384	$4,608

will also reduce the overall cost of your loan, and the interest rate you pay will generally be about a half percentage point lower than a 30-year mortgage.

Another benefit: you build up more equity in your home that you can tap into later. Data show that a third of the holders of 30-year mortgages choose 15-year loans when they refinance. That may not be a good decision, though. For example: If you get a $150,000, 30-year mortgage at 7.3 percent, you will pay $229,208 in interest over the life of the loan. A 15-year mortgage at 6.8 percent would cost less than half that—$89,612. The difference in monthly payments is $304—$1,028 for the 30-year mortgage versus $1,332 for the 15-year mortgage.

But suppose you opt for the 30-year loan and invest the $304 difference in the stock market, where it earns 7 percent after tax. (The historic return on stocks is about 10 percent before taxes.) And suppose you also invest the extra tax savings generated by the longer-term loan. Since the loan amortizes more slowly than a 15-year mortgage, more of your monthly payment is tax-deductible interest. After 10 years, the 30-year loan looks like a much better deal. By the end of 15 years, the holder of the 30-year loan would have earned enough on his investment to pay off the remaining debt on the house and still have some $10,000 left.

After choosing a mortgage, you'll have to decide about refinancing costs: covering them at the outset by paying points or spreading them over the life of the loan by accepting a slightly higher interest rate. In most cases, you should opt for not paying points. By investing the money you would have paid in points, you can build up a tidy nest egg over the life of your mortgage, which should amount to more than you'd save if you paid the points and invested the amount you saved in lower interest costs. The bottom line: the best mortgage for you will be the one whose term most closely matches the time you expect to keep your house.

Beware of the Reverse Mortgage

It's free, except for the thousands of dollars in fees and other costs

Mortgage lending may not be a sexy field, but every now and then a product stops traffic and turns a lot of heads. This appears to be the case with the reverse mortgage, a way for people 62 and older to borrow the equity in their homes—and, in essence, never have to pay back a dime out of their own pockets.

Of course, that basic explanation is rosier than the reality, which is that these loans are annoyingly complicated. Nonetheless, despite breathtaking upfront costs and head-spinning restrictions, reverse mortgages are ever more popular. According to the

Federal Housing Administration, which insures most of these loans, homeowners took out about 43,000 reverse mortgages in the fiscal year that ended last September 2005, up from about 37,829 the year before and only about 7,700 in 2001.

Here's how it works: rather than selling your home or taking out a home equity loan to get access to your equity, a reverse mortgage allows you to take out a loan for a portion of the equity. You can continue to live in your home; and you aren't burdened by monthly payments because when you or your spouse decides to move, or when you die, the proceeds from the sale of the property pay off the loan.

If the property value exceeds the amount of the loan, your heirs inherit that difference. Furthermore, if the bank has lent you more than it receives upon sale of the property, that's the bank's problem. Neither you nor your heirs can be held liable.

Borrowers also can decide whether to take their equity in one lump sum, in monthly payments, in a line of credit—or some combination of the above. The loudly buzzing fly in this ointment is what borrowers must pay for this privilege: a mortgage insurance premium of 2 percent of the loan amount, another 2 percent origination fee and closing costs. Thus, a $300,000 loan would carry a $6,000 insurance fee, a $6,000 origination fee and a few thousand dollars to close. It can cost over $15,000 to take out one of these loans, according to AARP. The fees and a monthly service charge of about $30 are deducted upfront from the total amount of the loan, which is capped at $362,000 in most states under F.H.A. guidelines.

Despite these and myriad other restrictions— some types of dwellings don't qualify; any debt you owe on your home is deducted from the total amount of the loan—some people are beginning to rely on reverse mortgages as a financial tool. While some retirees need the cash for medical and other living expenses, a growing number are taking out reverse mortgages to pay off their original mortgages and relieve themselves of that monthly payment.

As property values have risen, a number of retirees who took out these loans years ago are returning for second and even third reverse mortgages to harvest the additional equity that has built up in their homes. If you don't mind losing a chunk of your equity to fees, these loans have a certain appeal.

But, before you consider a reverse mortgage as a cornerstone of your own financial plans or of your parents' plans, do as much homework as you can. AARP offers reverse mortgage counselors at 1-800-209-8085. Valuable information can also be found on these Web sites: www.aarp.org/money/revmort and www.nrmla.org. Make sure what you get is worth what you pay for it.

—M. P. Dunleavey

A Cottage in the Country
Eight things to consider before you buy

One of the hottest segments of the real estate market is bubbling in seaside towns, rural countrysides and other vacation magnets. Part of the reason is that the typical vacation-home buyer is 55 years old; that is, a member of the huge baby boom generation looking ahead to eventual retirement. Nearly two-thirds of baby boomers own two or more homes, and nearly one out of five second homes will become the owner's primary retirement home, according to the National Association of Realtors. Still, 51 percent of owners say they bought their havens for vacations.

No matter what the lure—relaxation or adventure—consider these factors before you cut the check.

MONEY

1. Have the right attitude. Look at your vacation home as an investment and a consumer durable good, says Karl Case, economics professor at Wellesley College. Buyers often focus on the investment part and forget that the most important part is the actual benefit you get from living in or using the home.

2. Find the right market. Look for a home in an improving market. "Picking markets is like picking stocks," says Case. "The ones we know are good are already expensive." But, occasionally you can find an underpriced market if you're willing to go a bit off the beaten track.

3. Get to know the area. Visit your chosen site at least three times before zeroing in on a home. This could be burdensome if it's not close to home, so it might be beneficial to work with an agent who knows the market—and what you're looking for.

4. Be sure you'll use it. The ideal location for a second home is a spot where you want to spend a lot of time. The biggest mistake buyers make is letting their property sit vacant 10 months of the year. "Letting a vacation home sit idle is like running a factory at less than capacity," says Case.

5. Find the right mortgage. Lenders often view second homes as a higher risk, so you may face a higher interest rate and possibly higher fees than on your primary residence mortgage. Also, lenders generally require a down payment of 20 percent or more.

6. Consider taxes. You can deduct interest on your second home's mortgage as long as the mortgage is secured by your second home. Any profit you make on the property is subject to capital gains tax, unless you sell your first home, move into the second and live there for at least two years before you sell it.

7. Shop for insurance. You may face higher premiums because the house is not occupied daily or because it may be in a remote area, far from services like a firehouse, for example.

8. Make sure you love it. "Love it, use it and take care of it," says Case.

The Priciest Vacation Havens

In some of these hot markets, a cool million won't even buy you a teardown

If housing prices stumble as interest rates rise, those in vacation areas may be hard hit as discretionary spending slows. Investors may also pull out quickly as prospects for big returns start to dim. The most expensive destinations, however, may see less impact, since the wealthiest home buyers often are not deterred by rising interest rates or an economic downturn.

To help identify high-end second-home markets, the *New York Times* enlisted the help of Fidelity National Financial, a real estate title insurer. The study looked at areas with a significant number of such homes and at public sales records of single-family homes. All told, the research examined 358 second-home markets with median single-family home prices of at least $300,000.

Top of the heap? Not surprisingly, it was Aspen, Colo., where the median home price through the end of 2004 was nearly $2.5 million. But even the most jaded real estate hound might be surprised by the fact that some "fractionals" (a fancy name for time shares) in Aspen are now going for $1 million for six weeks.

Town	Zip code	Median home price*
ASPEN, Colo.	81611	$2.47 million

No surprise that this ritzy ski resort is the most

expensive second-home market in the country. The surprising fact: $1 million won't even buy a teardown anymore.

PALM BEACH, Fla.   33480 $2.08 million

Ronald O. Perelman sold his home here for $70 million in 2004. But though prices are high, turnover of high-end homes in this old-line resort can be slow.

NEWPORT BEACH, Calif. 92662 $1.82 million

This zip code belongs to the city of Newport Beach but consists of tiny man-made Balboa Island. It's nestled between the Balboa Peninsula and Pacific Coast Highway and experienced a 40 percent rise in the median home price in 2004.

WATER MILL, N.Y.   11976 $1.58 million

The median home price in this section of the Hamptons climbed 31 percent in 2004. Other Hamptons towns had higher prices but fewer sales.

ℹ **INSIDE INFO**

10 Hot Vacation Markets

These vacation home havens showed a median home-price increase of 91% from 2002 to 2005.

MARKET	3-YEAR GAIN
Florida Keys (Monroe County)	128%
St. Lucie, Fla. (St. Lucie County)	104%
Big Bear, Calif. (San Bernardino County)	103%
Naples, Fla. (Collier County)	95%
Punta Gorda, Fla. (Charlotte County)	92%
Sarasota, Fla. (Sarasota County)	90%
Palm Springs, Calif. (Riverside County)	90%
Daytona Beach (Volusia County)	80%
Fort Lauderdale, Fla. (Broward County)	80%
Cape May, N.J. (Cape May County)	79%

SOURCE: Fiserv CSW, Inc.

MANTOLOKING, N.J.   08738 $1.33 million

Wall Street types arrive by helicopter for weekends on this strip of high-end beach houses on the Jersey Shore. A five-bedroom bayfront house with great views commands a $6.25 million asking price.

NANTUCKET, Mass.   0255 $1.15 million

No shock here. Once a whaling village, this 50-square-mile fishhook-shaped island off Cape Cod is dominated by the hyper-rich.

SULLIVAN'S ISLAND, S.C. 29482 $1.1 million

Edgar Allan Poe's short story "The Gold Bug" is based on Sullivan's Island, which was an Army post through World War II. Median home prices jumped 51 percent in 2004.

HENDERSON, Nev.   89011 $805,000

Including Lake Las Vegas, a 3,592-acre planned resort community just 17 miles from the Strip, this zip code was once a swampy canyon through which flowed sewage from southern Nevada. Now it has an artificial lake and faux-Tuscan villas.

PRINCEVILLE, Hawaii   96722 $715,000

Once open farmland, Princeville is now among the most exclusive planned developments on Kauai. The median price for single-family homes soared 42 percent through the end of 2004.

OXFORD, Md.   21654 $620,000

A wealthy Chesapeake Bay port in the 17th and 18th centuries, Oxford is now a peaceful and sophisticated waterfront town whose residents are seeing sharp increases in the values of homes.

SCOTTSDALE, Ariz.   85262 $528,000

The median home price was up 12 percent in 2004 over the year before in this northern swath of a resort community famed for its desert climate and golf courses.

MONEY

JAMESTOWN, R.I. 02835 $473,000

Better-known Newport is just over the bridge from this island at the mouth of Narragansett Bay. Prices have been rising steadily—these days, even close to $600,000 doesn't guarantee a view of the water.

2004 median home price in each zip code

—Michelle Higgins

Sick of the Suburbs?

Try one of these unusual homesteading opportunities

Some people define a vacation home by its distance from the beach, others by its proximity to cow pastures. Still others, many of them well-heeled, seek out homesteads in unexpected places. Here are some current, unusual real estate options that work as permanent or second homes:

LOVE YOUR HOTEL ROOM? BUY IT

Imagine loving a hotel room so much that you buy it, mortgage and all.

Some investors are doing just that. The definition of a second home continues to stretch, as buyers increasingly invest in rooms in what are called condo hotels. Unlike traditional time shares, which give owners access to properties for defined periods, condo hotel units are fully owned and deeded properties that are rented by a hotel when the owner isn't using them.

The condo hotel concept has been around for more than a decade, but chains like Marriott, Remington, Westin and W Hotels are promoting them more than ever. In 2006, up to 105 condo hotel projects were planned or under construction nationwide. They will eventually produce 29,042 hotel rooms for sale in vacation spots like Las Vegas, Miami and Orlando, Fla., according to

Lodging Econometrics in Portsmouth, N.H.

For maintenance and services like utilities and cable television, some buyers may pay monthly homeowner's association fees. A typical fee may be $350 a month. Other resorts take 1 or 2 percent of rental sales for a reserve account for upgrades, like new carpeting or bedding. The money put into the reserve account cannot be deducted on income taxes until management actually spends the money on specific upgrades. Some hotels charge extra for daily housekeeping, for instance, or for breakfast in the hotel's restaurant.

Condo hotel units tend to sell at a premium, costing $250,000 to $3 million, depending on location and size, while their appreciation tends to stay equivalent to that of traditional condominiums. So getting rich on condo hotels is not guaranteed, or even likely.

—Jennifer Alsever

CRUISING IN YOUR OWN CONDO

If you're very wealthy and have your sea legs then we have three words for you: luxury yacht condo, the R.V. experience for people who love port cities and hate to drive. And have a million or so dollars to plunk down for a one-bedroom.

The concept of the luxury-yacht condo got its start in 1997, when Knut U. Kloster Jr., the billionaire former chairman of Royal Viking Lines and Norwegian Cruise Lines, began noticing that some of his wealthier passengers chose to remain aboard for unusually long periods of time. To capitalize on this observation, he sold spacious furnished suites (with stainless-steel kitchens and laundry service), ranging in price from $1.3 million to $6.3 million on spec, and built a 644-foot, 165-unit ship he humbly christened the World.

The ship made its maiden voyage in 2002, sailing from Oslo, and it now travels the world

TIMELY TIPS

A Piece of the Desert, a Burro to Boot

Those newspaper ads touting sales of cheap public land are come-ons. Homesteading laws were repealed in 1976. Occasionally, though, the Department of the Interior's Bureau of Land Management (202-452-5125; www.blm.gov) sells off parcels of land considered to be "excess" public acreage.

Most of the land is in 10 western states, including Arizona, California, Montana, Utah and Wyoming. You can buy a few acres or a couple hundred, but don't expect dirt cheap prices; the government can't accept offers below fair market value.

✔ **Dreaming of digs in the desert?** You can buy arid or semi-arid land—but you'll have to install an irrigation system, which could run $250,000 or more. Sales are usually held at a site near the property, but you can also send in a sealed bid. After the bid is accepted, it will probably take a year or two before you get title to your property.

✔ **Want your own wild horse or burro?** Some 8,000 mustangs, mules and burros are put up for "adoption" each year by the B.L.M. under its herd-control program. You can adopt a wild horse for about $185, a mule for $160 and a burro for $135 (Feeding and caring for the animal will run $1,000 a year or far more, depending on where you live.) After one year, if you show that you are a responsible caretaker, the B.L.M. will give you title.

To adopt your own mustang or burro, call 800-417-9647 or go to www.blm.gov.

---

constantly, hauling along four restaurants, a full-shot driving range and the planet's only floating House of Graff jewelry store. Its average condo owner is a self-made entrepreneur. The liner has competitors, including the Four Seasons, run by the luxury hotel chain; and the Magellan, where a three-bedroom unit goes for more than $3 million. The ship offers the use of its helipad and on-call Bell 429 jet helicopters. It also sells "fractional ownerships," meaning you can put down $128,000 to reserve a one-month stay every year.

—Elizabeth Weil

DORMS WITH A DIFFERENCE

Baby boomers, who have paved so many ways over the decades, are now making their mark on retirement. And one thing the graying geeks among them want is to bond with people and places that value so-called lifelong learning.

There are more than 50 campus-linked retirement communities in the U.S. so far, many consisting of town houses and apartments clustered near an alma mater. The entrance requirements vary, but most ask that residents be over age 55 and have some link to the school, as an alumnus, a former staff member or a relative of either of the above. (None will ask you for SAT scores.) Some have nursing homes attached; others don't. Some are officially connected to a university; for others the link is merely geographic, the lure of a college town. A few actually require course attendance as a prerequisite of residency, but most do not.

The University Commons, for instance, opened near the University of Michigan a few years ago and has become a model for others around the country. Built on 18 acres of land purchased from the school, the town houses, villas and condo apartments range in cost from $200,000 to $750,000. Even the two-level homes are designed for "main-level living."

Each house has a high-speed Internet hook-up, and each condo owner receives a university e-mail address. Dinner is served twice a week in the Commons dining room—prepared by students from the culinary program at the nearby Washtenaw Community College.

In short, you get everything you loved about college life (a built-in sense of belonging, an intellectual vibe) but none of those you're too old to enjoy—dorm rooms, cafeteria food, beer pong.

—Lisa Belkin

YOUR VERY OWN PRIVATE ISLAND

The rich and powerful have been buying their own islands at least since Caesar Augustus acquired Capri. The average tropical island these days seems to go for $2 million to $6 million, although you could land a four-acre Brazilian island for as little as $25,000. Failing that, you can always rent a slice of a private island.

Not quite four acres, Cayo Espanto in Belize is perhaps the smallest of a number of private island resorts to open in recent years. Some, like the 16-villa, 735-acre Fregate Island (www.clubairtravel.co.uk) in the Seychelles, open since October 1998, are somewhat remote. Others are more like full resorts, like the 58-villa, 1,000-acre Parrot Cay that opened in December 1998 in Turks and Caicos, which has a gym and a spa. The Disney Cruise Line leases Castaway Cay in the Bahamas so passengers can relax on a 1,000-acre island with four beaches (one for adults only), a barbecue area, a few trails and little else. If you like pines instead of palms, you can rent Sleepy Cove Island, Nova Scotia, with its log house by a lake, for $165 a day. For sales or rentals of private islands, check out www.privateislandsonline.com and www.vladi-private-islands.de. For worldwide island rentals, try www.going2travel.com.

—Ray Cormier

Houses on the Cheap
Finding bargains—and headaches—at foreclosure sales

Buying distressed properties—those that are in foreclosure or have a foreclosure pending—is not easy, and it entails considerable risk. Buyers may find that if they have not done their homework, or lack ready cash and an ability to reason with a distraught homeowner, they don't have a prayer of making a profit and could end up in debt themselves. But the rewards can be great, with the most successful investors getting 30 to 40 percent return on their money.

The first hurdle is finding the properties. Defaulting on a mortgage is a matter of public record, so your city or county will have lists including the names of people in arrears, the lenders and the properties' addresses. Sometimes that information is available online, but you often have to go to the courthouse and search a computer database or read posted printouts. Or you could pay $30 to $40 to have the list e-mailed to you by outfits like Foreclosures.com, All-foreclosure.com and Foreclosureworld.net.

The next step is to drive by the property to check on things like structural integrity and whether, for example, there is a toxic waste dump in the area. If the property passes curbside inspection, you will probably want to pay $300 to $400 for a full title search to find out if there are additional liens, or financial claims, against the property.

Announcements of auctions are usually printed in local newspapers; the starting bid is typically only what the lender needs to cover its costs. "Depending on competition from other bidders, you can generally buy properties at public auctions for 25 to 35 percent below market value," says Todd Beitler, founder and president of Real Estate Information Services in Boca Raton, Fla.

Many investors prefer to make offers to property owners before foreclosure, though some distressed owners don't always open doors. Those who do can often be convinced that they might walk away less scathed if they sell to you than if the bank forecloses on them. One benefit is that you bypass the confusion and competition associated with a public auction—and you can inspect the property.

Properties bought at auction are proverbial pigs in a poke: there is often no opportunity even to peek inside before buying, much less get an appraisal. And once you buy the property, you're stuck with it. Forget about warranties or refunds. Furthermore, buyers at auction often have to pay immediately, while buying properties facing foreclosure lets you pay owners a mutually agreed upon amount of "walking money," typically a small portion of their equity. The owners sign over the deed, and the buyer can assume their mortgage or refinance the debt. Buyers holding on to a property for at least a year before selling would save 20 percent on their taxes when they sold because the asset would qualify as a long-term capital gain.

The safest but potentially least profitable way to acquire foreclosed properties is from the lender. Called R.E.O.'s—for real estate owned—these properties usually end up in a bank's possession after they did not fetch desired prices at auction. Buying from the lender ensures that you get clear title, and you do not have to evict anyone. But the 5 to 10 percent discount is far less than you would be likely to get by buying before foreclosure or at auction. R.E.O.'s are generally sold through regular real estate agents.

Regardless of when during the foreclosure process you buy a property, investors say, there's money to be made. But, there's also money to be lost if you aren't aware of all the moving parts. Here's when buyers can jump in:

Pre-foreclosure: At this stage, the property owner is in arrears and the lender is threatening foreclosure. For investors, there is medium risk and medium reward. This may be the most difficult time to buy, because a mutually agreeable deal has to be struck with a distraught and often resistant property owner.

Foreclosure auction: After a property has been seized by the lender, a public auction is held. Investors often get their best deals at auction, but they are also at highest risk: bidders cannot see the interior of the property before purchase, for example, and the winner must usually pay the full amount in cash or by cashier's check on auction day. There are no warranties or refunds, and the winning bidder may have to evict the person who lost the title.

Lender listing : At this stage, the property is known as an R.E.O., for "real estate owned." The lender puts it up for sale usually because it did not receive an acceptable bid at the auction. Investors are at least risk at this point, but they can also expect a smaller discount on the price. Still, they are assured of a clear title and often buy through a real estate agent, so they can tour the property in advance.

—Kate Murphy

Bargains Beyond the Borders

Looking for bang for your real estate buck? Try Bucharest or Buenos Aires

The world is dappled with electric and storied cities. Yet real estate in Manhattan, for example, cost a record-setting $1,002 a square foot on average in 2006, while homes in many cities worldwide remained staggeringly affordable.

Here's a bargain-hunter's tour of the world real estate market:

MONEY

Buenos Aires. This sultry, party-until-the-wee-hours city is known as the Paris of South America. In 2002, the Argentine peso was devalued by the government, resulting in a currency crash. But the city is getting back on its tango-dancing feet.

The enclave of the moment is San Telmo, a hip, urban, ex-pat-friendly community where the arts thrive. The neighborhood is dotted with fine restaurants, bars, boutiques and colonial houses. Property costs between $56 and $93 a square foot. Renting is also affordable. There are furnished studios with weekly maid service for $450 a month at www.buenosaireshousing.com.ar. Real estate is more costly though still reasonable in Recoleta, an elegant downtown tourist magnet. Prices are about $180 to $300 a square foot.

Panama City. Lief Simon, editor of *Global Real Estate Investor,* a newsletter published by International Living, likes Panama City with its high-rise buildings, restaurants and some 80 banks. "It's a first-world city," he says, yet two-bedroom apartments can be had for $60,000 to $80,000.

✓ TIMELY TIPS

Watch Out for Foreign Laws

✔ Many countries welcome foreign buyers. But that doesn't mean the process is devoid of red tape. You can find information about ownership laws in 24 countries on WorldProperties. com. Click on "Country Info," then "Business Practices." Select a country from the drop-down menu. Where it reads "Select Business Practice," choose "Foreign Ownership." That will note any restrictions. In Mexico, for example, foreigners are prohibited from owning residential real estate within 30 miles of any coastline or 60 miles of either border.

—Stephanie Rosenbloom

Mexico City. Recommended by some property experts, the city makes others cringe with its crowded streets and polluted air. Still, lots of young Americans live and work there. Condesa is a chic area where two- and three-bedroom apartments go for about $1,200 to $1,500 a month. Some one-bedrooms in downtown Mexico City are less than $700 a month.

Toronto. Toronto is Canada's financial headquarters, and some of its trendiest neighborhoods are among the most affordable. The Beaches neighborhood has a lively beachfront boardwalk, yet is close to the city's downtown. Buying at the low end of the market in the Beaches is about $260 to $300 a square foot.

Downtown West Queen West is known for its galleries, clubs and shopping, and King West Village for its myriad pubs. New condos in Queen are going for $220 to $330 a square foot and are being snapped up by the young. Loft and one-bedroom rents in both areas are about $870 to $1,130.

Montreal. The "place to be and to be seen" is Plateau Mont-Royal. Property in this area—which is popular with young Canadians because of its cafes, restaurants and nightclubs—is about $220 to $240 a square foot; rentals are about $650 to $1,470 a month. The Gay Village enclave also draws a number of straight people because of its dynamic night life and affordability. Real estate is about $190 a square foot; rentals are about $780 to $1,210.

Quebec city. This Paris of North America is divided into Haute-Ville (the upper town) and Basse-Ville (lower town). Haute-Ville is more expensive than Basse-Ville, which is distinguished by a port (Old Port) along the St. Lawrence River. Warehouses converted into 750- to 2,000-square-foot apartments are about $170,000 to $390,000.

Shanghai. Those doing business in China may want

to work and buy in Shanghai. Adrienne Farrelly, general manager of Shanghai Properties (www. shanghaiprops.com) suggests looking in People's Square, nestled among two of the city's major commercial and retail streets. Nearby is Top of the City, an apartment complex where property is about $350 a square foot, and rentals start at around $700 for a 689-square-foot one-bedroom, probably the best value in town.

Eastern Europe. Property experts agree that the best values are really in Eastern Europe. For example, it costs about $110 a square foot to buy in Bucharest, Romania. Bulgaria is another attractive market, with its magnificent beaches and mountains for skiing.

Paris. The city of Renoir and haute couture is far less expensive than New York and San Francisco, a fact that has escaped many would-be expatriates. "There's a lot that is still way underpriced because it needs renovation and gentrification," says Adrian Leeds, editor of ParlerParis.com, a newsletter about Paris, and FrenchPropertyInsider.com.

Those looking for a deal might try developing arrondissements where the city's bohemians and "bobos" (bourgeois bohemians) flock: the 10th, 18th and 19th. Be wary of the 10th arrondissement, an up-and-coming area, advises Yolanda Robins, a property manager for French Property Insider. The areas along the tree-lined Canal St.-Martin are beautiful, but those near the train station "can be horrible," she says. The average price per square foot: $530 to $670.

The artsy 18th arrondissement, known as Montmartre, is perched on a hilltop. Property costs about $670 a square foot on the west side and about $440 a square foot on the east side, which is undergoing gentrification. Property in the 19th is about $440 to $610 a square foot. Long-term furnished rentals in those areas are about $320 to $430 a month.

—Stephanie Rosenbloom

When You Are Homesick at 64
Retiring abroad sounds appealing, but many ex-pats return home

As more mobile, active and adventuresome baby boomers hit their retirement years, many will be lured overseas by a more affordable cost of living and more temperate weather. Some will want to return to their native countries or to places where they once worked or studied.

Though out-of-country retirement is not the norm, it is likely to become less of an anomaly. An estimated four million Americans live abroad, but there is no data on how many are retired, according to the State Department. The number of Americans 55 and older is expected to grow from 67 million in 2005 to 97 million by 2020. The demand for foreign homes is also expected to grow during that period.

Mexico, Costa Rica and Panama are common retirement havens, but Nicaragua, Honduras, Ecuador and English-speaking Belize are making a push to attract retirees. Various countries in Europe are also viable alternatives, though current exchange rates may make them less attractive.

Retiring to an exotic locale sounds like a good plan, but many expatriates return home. They either miss the grandchildren and lifelong friends too much or find that culture shock was a bit, well, shocking. To increase the chances for success, follow this checklist:

First contacts. Verify your prospective country's stance on home purchases, taxes and residency, and the state of its safety and health care. Contact consulates, because information in books and on the Internet can be outdated. Remember that real estate agents and developers may have a vested interest in your relocation.

Social compatibility. Be sure that you will be able to find the lifestyle you seek. Do you favor museums

MONEY

or nature walks? Do you crave solitude or a full social life (which could prove difficult where you do not speak the language)? Are you likely to become distressed when the phone service or electricity goes down, or can you handle occasional disruptions?

Online research. Read local newspapers. Links to English-language sites are at www.worldnews-papers.com. For advice about living in specific countries: www.internationalliving.com.

Testing it out. Spend a lot of time in your desired location. Some specialists suggest moving there temporarily, perhaps for a year, so you can see if you like it year-round. Contact the local expatriate community for answers to nuts-and bolts questions like availability of domestic help, how to find a contractor, reliability of Internet service and the size of the tarantulas. Check on the ease of traveling back to the United States.

Health care. Medicare is not available abroad, so verify that you are eligible for your new country's health care program. Private insurance is available, but it is more expensive than government care.

Government benefits. Have Social Security checks automatically deposited into your bank account.

—Hillary Chura

Beyond Houses

A primer for branching out into commercial real estate

Almost all home buyers are familiar with the trite but true axiom of real estate and location. But for those who will someday branch out to the commercial side—and as residential markets cool, more people are doing just that—there's another mantra to intone. It's "verify, verify, verify," says Ray Alcorn, a commercial real estate investor and developer from Blacksburg, Va.

Exercising due diligence—a fancy way of saying "do your homework before signing on the dotted line"—will help to assess a property's value, as well as expose potential risks. You will want to be sure, for example, that the seller holds title to that mixed-use property or that an office building is structurally sound. You will want to know of any zoning changes in the pipeline. (And, as always, you have to find the right location.)

How to begin this lofty examination process? A few suggestions from experienced investors:

Learn before you look. Educate yourself. The Wall Street Transcript (www.twst.com), for instance, sponsors three daylong seminars across the country each year on due diligence in commercial real estate.

Real estate investment clubs can also help. The National Real Estate Investors Association Web site, www.nationalreia.com, has club listings by state. Many groups provide educational seminars and guest lecturers on commercial real estate, but more important, they have veteran members who are willing to be mentors to newcomers.

Line up professionals. Experienced investors typically have a group of experts in place, including brokers, engineers, lawyers, accountants and property managers—all of whom specialize in commercial real estate and can be called upon for advice at a moment's notice. If you're unsure about whom to hire, talk to other investors or brokers. Look for leads at your local zoning or building departments. And while you're there, try to familiarize yourself with local zoning regulations.

Set financial goals. Are you looking to make a quick profit with a property that can appreciate in value after improvements? Or, do you want a property that can be leased out, generating a steady monthly cash flow? What do you consider an acceptable capitalization rate—meaning the initial rate of net income from the property? (A cap rate of 6 percent or more is generally considered good.)

But, experienced investors point out that, unless you're an intrepid type who enjoys running the show yourself, you may be better off with bonds or real estate investment trusts, which invest in portfolios of commercial property and disburse most of their income in dividends.

Zero in on property. There are many ways to search. You can work directly with brokers or track down for-sale-by-owner listings and other private sales online and elsewhere. LoopNet.com lists more than 315,000 commercial properties nationwide. You can search property by various criteria, including building type, location, price and size, and can receive demographic reports, maps and market comparisons. The site also provides a directory of real estate professionals.

The most sought after properties on LoopNet are buildings with triple-net leases, in which the tenants agree to pay all the continuing operating expenses like property taxes and insurance premiums. But be warned: they are often difficult to find, specialists say, unless you have a significant amount of money to invest.

Investigate the area. Learn about the demographics of the region where you are buying. What is the average household income? Age? Crime rate? You will also want to know the prevailing vacancy rates, along with rents and property taxes. You can get information from local chambers of commerce and by talking with neighboring business owners.

Deeds, liens and easements, along with zoning maps, can be found in local and county government offices. Many records are accessible online. With a street address, you can determine, among other things, the sale prices and dates of previous sales and the assessed value of the property.

Other helpful Web sites: www.netronline.com, the address for Nationwide Environmental Title Research, a real estate research company; www.naco.org, the National Association of Counties; www.brbpub.com, BRB Publications, a publisher of source books used for finding public records; www.searchsystems.net, run by Pacific Information Resources; and www.realquest.com, run by First American Real Estate Solutions.

Review and verify. Once you settle on an area and go into contract on a property, the heavy lifting begins. In an allotted time, you or your advisers must review and verify the financial data provided by the seller. You will need to have a title search done, peruse a property survey and check the leasing contracts and rent rolls, among other things. Existing tenants should be vetted, particularly their payment histories and credit files.

To evaluate income stream, ask the seller for the most recent historical operating numbers and, in some instances, tax returns. The three biggest expenses you can ascertain on your own: insurance, real estate taxes and utilities. Taxes are public record, and you can get cost estimates from an insurance company or local utility.

Inspect, appraise and confront. Qualified engineers or contractors can help to uncover any hidden problems in a building, whether structural, mechanical or environmental, and many deals are contingent upon their reports. In addition, lenders typically require an appraisal and environmental inspection. Ensure that a building is in compliance with local building, fire or environmental codes and that the seller or previous owners have secured the proper building permits, if necessary.

Whatever shortcomings are discovered should be brought up with the seller, who could decide to fix the problem or to renegotiate the sales price.

—Vivian Marino

MONEY

Insurance & Taxes

Policies to Keep You Covered

It's not easy sorting through insurance policies, but someone has to do it

Buying insurance is right up there with going to the dentist on most folks' list of things they hate to do. And worse, unlike going to the dentist, buying insurance requires some know-how. The insurance industry doesn't make it any easier. Sorting through all the policies offered requires the patience of a crossword puzzle addict and the mathematical skills of an astrophysicist.

Some simple guidelines can help, though. Find a strong, healthy company that tailors policies to the coverage you need, and then focus on getting the best value for your dollar. One thing has become easier: getting quotes on insurance. At www.insure.com, for example, you can get instant quotes from 200 insurance companies on life, auto, health and home insurance.

But before you go comparison shopping, you need to figure out what kind and just how much coverage you really need for the most common varieties of insurance.

LIFE INSURANCE

Life insurance needs vary over the course of your lifetime, peaking as you cope with hefty mortgage payments and big tuition bills for your kids, and falling after you've retired. There's no dearth of insurance companies—more than 2,000, in fact, all ready to sell you a policy. You can also get one from banks and other financial institutions. Whichever route you take, be sure to take out enough coverage. Here are some factors to consider in your assessment.

HOW MUCH YOU NEED: The amount of life insurance you need roughly correlates with your family's annual living expenses for the number of years you'll need the insurance. Add together all your family's expenses for the years you'll need insurance. You should include future college costs, mortgage payments, costs to settle your estate and an emergency fund (typically, three months' salary). Then subtract all family income other than your salary. Be sure to include Social Security and pension payments

---

ⓘ INSIDE INFO

The Span of Life

○ The average American born in 2000 can expect to live more than 30 years longer than his ancestor born in 1900.

○ **LIFE EXPECTANCY IN YEARS**

YEAR BORN	MALE	FEMALE
1900	46.3	48.3
1910	48.6	52.0
1920	54.4	55.6
1930	59.7	63.5
1940	62.1	66.6
1950	65.6	71.1
1960	66.6	73.1
1970	67.1	74.7
1980	70.0	77.4
1990	71.8	78.2
2000	74.3	79.7

SOURCE: Department of Health & Human Services

as well as any income you may receive from your investments. Adjust both your future expenses and income to account for inflation.

The result of this calculation is how much life insurance you need. Some experts suggest an even simpler formula: multiply your annual take-home pay by five. Or, try an online life-insurance calculator, such as on aol.com's money site and others.

YOUR OPTIONS: Term insurance will pay your survivors a death benefit if you die while the contract is in force. It is often called "pure" insurance because it offers a death benefit without a savings component. A term life insurance policy can be locked in for 1 to 20 years. It is often the best and cheapest bet for families who want to provide for the future in the event of the loss of a bread-winner and who want to target the years when their insurance needs will be greatest.

A term insurance policy can often be rolled into a whole life policy later. "Whole life" (also called guaranteed-permanent) insurance provides a death benefit until you reach age 90 or 100, as long as you pay fixed premiums—premiums that cannot have unscheduled increases. Whole life insurance premiums are substantially higher at first than the same amount of term insurance, but term insurance premiums skyrocket as you get older. With whole life, you are betting that you'll be around a while, paying the higher premium at first and then averaging the cost out over a lifetime.

If you are older, the kids have graduated from college and the mortgage is paid off, the fixed premiums of a whole life policy might be more attractive. These policies also offer an investment opportunity. Here, part of your premium payment is invested into a plan where earnings are tax deferred, so that the policy builds "cash value" over the years. At some point, the cash value of the policy should be enough to pay your premiums. "Cash-value"

 INSIDE INFO

Weigh More, Pay More

○ People with medical conditions, like high blood pressure and diabetes, naturally have a harder time trying to buy life insurance. Now, overweight people who are otherwise healthy face a similar difficulty.

○ The fact that an obese person can be denied life insurance is not surprising. Obesity poses a range of health problems. But even those whose weight is significantly above normal compared to their height can be penalized by higher premiums.

○ "If a 40-year-old, 6-foot-tall male is 270 pounds, he will have to pay 15 to 20 percent more than a person of ideal weight. If the person weighs 300 pounds or more, the amount jumps to 30 to 35 percent." says a State Farm senior agent.

SOURCE: Info.insure.com

policies can help build wealth for you, and possibly your heirs—life insurance proceeds are not subject to income tax, or, for the most part, estate tax. However, they still need to be carefully evaluated. You should weigh each policy's returns against those you're getting from your other investments.

WATCH OUT FOR: Remember, the agent's computer models showing the projected returns are estimates, and are by no means guaranteed. Not all policies that appear to provide fixed premiums and cash values are guaranteed-permanent insurance. Universal life, for example, is a form of cash-value insurance that combines term insurance with a "side fund" that is credited with earnings. Instead of making fixed premium payments, you have the flexibility of deciding the size and frequency of your payments to the side fund, which accumulates

MONEY

TIMELY TIPS

Help on Health Insurance

Tap into these sites for information

✔ **National Association of Health Underwriters**
www.nahu.org.
The lowdown on health insurance topics ranging
from high-risk pools to health savings accounts.
You can conduct a search for agents at www.
nahu.org/consumer /termsofuse.htm. If you have
questions, call 703-276-0220 or send them by
e-mail to info@nahu.org.

✔ **U.S. Department of Labor** *www.dol.gov/ebsa/
faqs/faq—consumer—cobra.html*
Find answers about Cobra, the federal rule
that extends medical coverage under certain
circumstances. If you're leaving a job, your
employer's human resources department should
inform you of Cobra provisions. But if you're
getting a divorce or are no longer included on
a parent's policy, you can get details from the
department's toll-free employee and employer
hot line: 866-444-3272.

✔ **National Association of State Comprehensive
Health Insurance Plans** *www.naschip.org*
For information about high-risk insurance pools.
—J. Alex Tarquinio

interest on a tax-deferred basis. You get death-
benefit protection as long as the amount in the side
fund can cover the cost of the insurance.

If you make low payments to the side fund
early on, you will have to make sharply higher
payments later to maintain death-benefit protection. This flexibility means that universal life can
function more like term or guaranteed-permanent
insurance, depending on how you fund it.

Variable life insurance products can be even
riskier. You choose among the investment options
offered by the insurance company—stocks, bonds,

fixed-rate funds, etc. So, you may or may not build
up cash value in the policy, depending on how
the investments perform. Look carefully at the
options the company is offering and be sure they
are balanced and let you invest at a level of risk
you can tolerate.

HEALTH

Employers are not required to provide health
insurance for workers, but most do so for competitive and other business reasons. You're probably covered by group health insurance by your
employer, and should you happen to lose or quit
your job, you are entitled to buy short-term coverage called COBRA from your former employer.
Once that expires, however, you'll have to get
individual coverage, and that comes at a dear price.
Here are your options for health care insurance.

HOW MUCH YOU NEED: At a minimum, you should
buy a catastrophic policy that protects you from
serious and financially disastrous losses that can
result from an illness or injury. You'll have to
factor in how much you must absorb in deductibles
and co-payments.

YOUR OPTIONS: Even if you buy a comprehensive
policy that covers most medical, hospital, surgical
and pharmaceutical bills, it won't cover everything.
You may need additional single-purpose coverage.
You may want a Medicare supplement policy to fill
in the gaps in your Medicare coverage if you are
over 65. Private insurers offer policies specifically to
cover Medicare co-payments and deductibles. Some
also cover outpatient prescription drugs. Hospital
indemnity insurance pays you cash benefits for each
day you are hospitalized, up to a designated number
of days. The money can be used to meet out-of-
pocket medical co-payments or other needs.

Depending on your age and circumstances, you
may want to take a look at long-term-care insurance.

This type of policy covers the cost of custodial care either in a nursing home or in your own home. The Health Insurance Association of America estimates that nursing home care can cost $50,000 a year or more, depending on where you live. Having someone in your home three days a week to care for you runs about $12,000 a year. If those kinds of expenses make you shudder, a long-term-care policy can offer some relief. But remember this: if you arc 65, there's slightly more than a 60 percent chance you'll never collect anything from a long-term-care policy. (See "Why Bet on Long-Term Care?" on page 234.)

WATCH OUT FOR: You can reduce your premiums by opting for a large deductible—you will pay the entire amount due up to a certain limit. You may be able to save more by enrolling in a managed care plan, such as a health maintenance organization (H.M.O.) or a preferred provider organization (P.P.O.). If you have a problem getting insurance because of a pre-existing condition, find out if your state has a risk pool, which provides insurance for people who can't get it elsewhere.

DISABILITY

Disability insurance may be the most important kind of insurance to have. Indeed, during the peak earning years of your career, the possibility of suffering a long-term disability is considerably greater than the possibility of death. The Society of Actuaries says that a 35-year-old is three times more likely to become disabled for three months before reaching 65 than he is to die younger than 65.

HOW MUCH YOU NEED: You can figure out how much disability insurance you need in the same way that you calculated your life insurance needs. Take your annual expenses and subtract your family's annual income without your salary. Buy as much disability insurance up to that level as you can.

Generally, insurers will sell you only enough insurance to replace 60 percent of your income, so that, they say, you will have an incentive to return to work.

How much does it cost? Policies vary greatly, but here are two examples offered by one large insurer, UnumProvident. A 40-year-old man making $250,000 a year will pay about $4,000 a year for a policy that will pay him $10,000 a month until he turns 65. A 40-year-old man who makes $50,000 a year will pay about $1,700 a year for a policy that will pay him $2,900 a month for up to five years.

YOUR OPTIONS: The cost of disability income insurance depends on factors like your age, your profession, the amount of time you've worked or owned your business, whether you smoke and whether

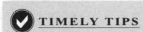

TIMELY TIPS

Ask About Disability Insurance

Because disability policies are full of technical language, it pays to ask questions before signing on the dotted line. Some key questions to ask:

✔ How does the insurance company define a disability: inability to do *any* job or any job that you are trained and qualified for?

✔ What is the monthly benefit?

✔ How long will the company pay benefits?

✔ How long should you expect to wait to receive benefits after filing a claim?

✔ What proof of disability is required?

✔ Must you first qualify for state and/or federal benefits?

✔ What weight will the treating doctor's opinion have?

—Michelle Leder

MONEY

TIMELY TIPS

Save on Homeowner's Insurance

There are plenty of discounts out there, although they do vary by state and insurance company. Do you live near a firehouse? Do you live in a brick house? Are you a non-smoker? Are you 55 years old and retired? Answer yes to any of those questions and you're likely to get a break on your homeowner's policy. Here are other ways to save:

✔ **Insure your house, not the land.** Don't include the value of your land in deciding how much insurance you need. After all, the land is rarely at risk, while your home can be harmed by fire, theft, vandalism, storms, etc.

✔ **Raise your deductible.** A deductible is the amount you pay out of pocket toward a loss before your insurance kicks in. Home insurance deductibles usually start at $250. If you raise it to $500, you cut up to 12 percent off your premiums. Raise it to $1,000 and you save 24 percent; $5,000 gets you up to 37 percent.

✔ **Improve security and safety in your home.** A sophisticated home-security system could save you 15 to 20 percent. But even items such as deadbolt locks, burglar alarms and smoke detectors give you a little break.

✔ **Stick to an insurer.** If you've had coverage with a company for many years, you could qualify for special loyalty treatment. Some insurers will cut premiums by 5 percent if you stay three to five years, and as much as 10 percent after six years.

✔ **Review your policy annually.** Maybe you sold off a valuable item and no longer need the same amount of personal property coverage. (Or, maybe you built a new sun room and need more.)

✔ **Look for group coverage.** Often, insurance companies work out deals with companies, associations, alumni groups and others. Don't simply toss out mail offers you get of this type—check to see if the discount is worth taking them up on.

✔ **Buy your home and auto insurance from the same company.** Many give a multiline discount if you buy both from them.

SOURCE: The Insurance Information Institute

you're a man or a woman. Since women file for disability benefits more often than men, many insurance companies have begun to raise women's rates, while lowering the rates for men.

WATCH OUT FOR: Look for a policy that can't be canceled and has no increase in premium until you are 65. Get a cost-of-living adjustment provision, so that your benefits increase once a year for as long as you are disabled. You should also insist on a provision that allows you to boost your coverage as your income increases.

Pay special attention to the definition of disability. Some insurers say you qualify for benefits if you are unable to do your job, others only if you are unable to do any job. Residual or partial disability benefits can be tacked on to provide a percentage of lost income if you take a lower-paying job because of your disability. Set as long a waiting period as you can afford before the benefits kick in—delaying payments for three months to a year can substantially reduce premiums.

Another tip: You can usually earn substantial premium discounts from insurers simply by doing things such as supplying a copy of your tax return at application time or prepaying a few years' worth of premium up front.

HOMEOWNER'S

The first lesson in buying homeowner's insurance is that it doesn't matter how much you paid for

Underinsured? You're Not Alone

Replacing your home costs more than you think

Updating a home insurance policy is one of those chores that many people secretly hope the insurance elves will handle. Yet, experts say you should update once a year.

Close to two-thirds of homeowners are underinsured, according to Marshall & Swift/Boeckh, which monitors building and insurance costs. Industry professionals advise homeowners to be vigilant, especially in a hot real estate market, when many homeowners invest in home improvements and when construction costs rise. Both can add significantly to the cost of rebuilding a home.

Some policies include an inflation rider, which automatically increases coverage each year by 4 to 6 percent, but if improvements have added to the value of your home, it's your responsibility to tell your insurer. Spending more to be sure you get full coverage may be worth the expense. This is true even in cases where you need to be reimbursed for a repair on just part of your house, say, a portion of the roof, according to the National Association of Insurance Commissioners. If a tree branch destroys part of the roof, you won't get reimbursed unless your home is insured for at least 80 percent of the replacement cost value.

There are many nooks and crannies in home insurance policies, but an important factor is making sure your possessions are also completely covered. What you want is a ''replacement cost content endorsement,'' not an ''actual cash value'' policy. Despite the name, actual cash is what you won't get. A cash-value policy gives you what you paid for an item, minus depreciation, leaving you with little. To get an accurate estimate, walk through your home with a camera and do an inventory.

For a fee, some online tools can help calculate replacement cost. Bluebook International, an insurance data provider, runs the site www.insuretovalue.net. Fill in basic parameters of your property—location, square footage, etc.—and for $19.95 you'll get an estimate of replacement costs. For the same price, www.accucoverage.com, Marshall & Swift/Boeckh's site, provides a similar service based on their data. Local contractors may also be willing to give an estimate.

—M. P. Dunleavey

MONEY

your house. What you need to insure is the cost to rebuild it. The two figures can be wildly different.

HOW MUCH YOU NEED: The conventional formula for gauging how much insurance you need on your home is to figure out how much it would actually cost to rebuild it, then tack on the extras, such as the cost of central air conditioning or a new furnace.

If you can't afford insurance for 100 percent of the house's value, make sure you're covered for at least 80 percent. That way, if you suffer a partial loss—say, a fire destroys your bedroom—an insurer will likely cover the entire cost. If you're less than 80 percent insured, your insurer will only pay that percentage of partial damages.

YOUR OPTIONS: There are three types of homeowner's policies: cash-value, replacement cost and guaranteed replacement cost. Cash-value insurance is the least expensive. It will pay you whatever your valuables would sell for today, which is unlikely to buy you a similar new item.

Replacement cost insurance will replace the item that was lost or damaged with something new, but not necessarily the same as the one you lost, because this type of insurance usually comes with a price cap. You'll be able to replace your furnace, for example, but not necessarily with a top-of-the line model. Guaranteed replacement cost insurance has no cap and offers the best coverage. One thing it might not cover, though, is the cost of upgrading

Getting a Grip on Auto Insurance

Not every driver can save 15 percent on car insurance, as one prominent company promises, but many are finding significant discounts. There are many ways to save on auto insurance premiums, but since each insurer calculates rates differently, you may have to shop around. Here are some tips from the Insurance Information Institute:

✔ **Combine policies.** Compare rate quotes and you may find your best rate is through the company that holds your homeowner's policy. Combining two or more types of insurance from the same company could mean substantial discounts annually on your auto policy. Some insurers also reduce premiums for long-time customers.

✔ **Consider a group policy.** Like health insurance, group auto policies are beginning to be offered by companies, professional organizations and even some enthusiast groups, such as, for example, the Honda Rider's Club of America. You may be eligible to get insurance through a group plan from your employer, or through professional, business and alumni groups or other associations. Group plans often provide substantial discounts. (Members of the American Automobile Association, for example, collectively save more than $27 million a year on car insurance by showing their membership card when they buy a policy.)

✔ **Ask for good behavior discounts.** Most insurance companies reward accident-free drivers with discounts. You may also qualify for a cut if you take a defensive driving course, if you are over 50 and retired, or if a young driver on your policy is a good student, has taken a driver's education course or is away at a college, generally at least 100 miles away. Availability of discounts vary according to state and company.

✔ **Downsize.** Some of the smaller insurance companies offer better rates than larger companies, especially if they are trying to increase business in a certain area.

—Tara Baukus Mello

your house to meet building codes that may have changed since the policy was issued.

Homeowner's insurance also includes a certain amount of liability coverage. If your total assets are more than that amount, you should probably pay a little more and get more coverage. For example, experts counsel that if you have $200,000 to $500,000 in assets, you need about $1 million in liability coverage. The best way to do this is to buy an "umbrella policy" that covers both your home and car. Liability coverage comes fairly cheap. A $300,000 to $1 million umbrella liability policy will cost anywhere from $100 to $400 annually. For another $1 million in coverage, double the price.

WATCH OUT FOR: Cash-value coverage may be a little risky, since an investment you made years ago that is still holding up—such as a good furnace—may now be worth just a fraction of its cost. Replacement-cost coverage usually costs 10 to 20 percent more but is probably worth it. Be sure to find out if there are any caps on what will be reimbursed for individual items, such as jewelry. For example, the policy might say that if all your jewelry is stolen, you can recover a maximum of $1,500. If that amount doesn't begin to cover your jewelry's total value, you may want to buy more insurance by raising the liability or by adding riders to your policy.

Remember that a standard homeowner's policy does not cover flood damage. If you buy a house in a flood-prone zone, you will need to take out a separate policy. The average cost is $400 a year. For more information, check the Federal

Emergency Management Agency website at www. fema.gov. Another exception these days is mold insurance. Insurers are happy to sell you overage for an additional premium. You need to decide whether you really need it.

Another tip: Add coverage when you add on. A rule of thumb is that it costs about $2 a year to add $1,000 in coverage on your homeowner's policy. A typical room addition that cost $50,000 to construct could be covered by an additional $100.

AUTOMOBILE

In most states, drivers are required to have liability insurance for each driver, for accidents and for the other person's car in case of an accident.

HOW MUCH YOU NEED: Generally, insurance experts counsel that you buy as much liability coverage as you're worth. You should also consider an "umbrella policy" described above, that covers both your home and car. Consider getting a higher deductible, which will mean a lower premium. For example, increasing your deductible from $200 to $500 on collision coverage could reduce your premium by as much as 30 percent.

YOUR OPTIONS: Collision and comprehensive coverage accounts for 30 to 45 percent of your premium. If the cost of your collision and comprehensive insurance is more than 10 percent of your car's Blue Book value, you may want to consider dropping it. Remember, though, that if you are in an accident you may find that your car is not worth repairing.

Uninsured or underinsured motorist coverage is sometimes desirable; it is probably cheaper if bought in your home or life policy. You may be able to cut your car insurance by maintaining a safe driving record, or simply by driving a low number of miles each year.

WATCH OUT FOR: If you drive an old jalopy, worth less than $2,000, the premium cost may not be worth what you'd get in case of an accident. The most you might get is the car's Blue Book value—not much if your car is more than five years old.

Another tip: Medical payment, income replacement and rental car insurance can add substantially to your premiums. Check to see if you are already covered for these items elsewhere or if you want to be insured for them outside the policy.

Filing an Auto Insurance Claim

Sooner or later a fender bender is bound to occur. Here's how to deal with your insurance company:

1. Get in touch with your insurer immediately after an accident, regardless of whether you were at fault.

2. Ask your agent what documentation you will need in filing your claim, such as a police report, witness statements, tow-truck receipts, etc. Maintain good records of all conversations, noting times and names.

3. Ask your insurer when a claims adjuster will be assigned to investigate your accident. Keep in regular contact with the insurer and the adjuster to prevent a prolonged process.

4. If your claim is denied and you disagree with the decision, contact your state insurance commission. You can find a directory of state offices at the National Association of Insurance Commissioners website: www.naic.org.

5. Other options for dispute resolutions are to get an arbitrator from the American Arbitration Association (www.adr.org); or, as a final and expensive measure, hire a lawyer to represent your claim.

SOURCE: Insurance Information Institute

MONEY

Why Bet on Long-Term Care?

The insurance is costly, speculative and some don't need it

After more than two decades on the market, long-term-care insurance remains a tough sell. Only 10 percent of people over 65 own policies, with many holdouts saying that they are intimidated by high costs and the bewildering array of benefit levels, deductible periods and other features.

Like most insurance, policies for long-term care protect against improbable events. But unlike homeowner's insurance and auto insurance, this coverage often requires a lifetime commitment to one insurer; premiums can rise sharply if the policyholder switches. And while health insurance covers immediate issues, buyers of long-term-care insurance can pay premiums for decades with no way to predict if their coverage is what they will need.

Consumers who want to protect themselves in the event of the worst-case outcome—many years in a nursing home—can spend at least $10,000 a year on premiums for full coverage. According to a survey by the MetLife Mature Market Institute, the average cost of a year in a private room of a nursing home was $70,080 in 2003, though prices vary greatly by region.

But another study shows that only a small percentage of policyholders need care for long periods—four years or more. So a growing number of specialists recommend more modest policies for which the policyholder pays a bigger share of the costs.

Those who want to hedge their bets can buy a policy to cushion part of the financial blow. They must be prepared to pay for part of their care out of pocket, so they must assess their financial situation and study the many options. Many may need no coverage, including people with few assets and those with substantial assets, specialists say. Those with few assets may be eligible for benefits from state Medicaid programs. And well-off individuals, for example someone with a net worth of $1 million to $1.5 million, not including the family home, could probably pay the cost out of their pocket,

For those in the middle, forgoing some bells and whistles can cut costs considerably. At one insurer, a single 65-year-old who buys a policy with a $200 daily benefit for life with a 30-day deductible can pay $9,936 a year, according to Long-Term Care Quote, an agency in Chandler, Ariz. By comparison, if the daily benefit is lowered to $150 and a 90-day deductible, the cost drops to $2,964 a year.

Buying a policy earlier can lower premiums. A policy that cost a 65-year-old $2,964 a year would cost a 45-year-old $1,584, according to Long-Term Care Quote. Younger applicants are also less likely to be denied coverage for health reasons.

Buyers can also save by opting for a longer deductible. An "elimination period" can be as long as 100 days, during which the policyholder must pay the full cost of care. A policy with a 90-day elimination period costs about 30 percent less than one with a 30-day elimination period. Many

---

ⓘ INSIDE INFO

Investing Premiums Won't Do It

○ Assume the premium for a high-deductible, long-term care policy that pays $65,700 a year for three years is $2,000 a year. If a 55-year-old invested the $2,000 a year at a 6.5% interest rate, he would save $172,750 by age 85.

○ By the time he turned 85, according to Ryan Insurance Strategy Consultants, a single year of care could run $283,951, assuming that costs rose 5 percent a year.

—Susan B. Garland

TIMELY TIPS

Coverage You May Not Need

Consumer advocates say these may not be not worth buying

✔ **Air travel insurance:** It costs too much and pays back only about 10 cents for each dollar of premiums. It is not comprehensive, and you are more likely to die from a heart attack than from an airplane crash.

✔ **Cancer insurance:** What good is a cancer insurance policy if you have a heart attack? To

buy specific illness coverage is like buying toothpaste one squeeze at a time.

✔ **Insurance that pays only if you're hurt or killed in a mugging:** A classic example of "junk" insurance. This risk is covered by good life and health policies.

✔ **Life insurance if you're single:** If you have no dependents, there is no economic reason to buy life insurance since there is no economic catastrophe associated with your death.

✔ **Life insurance if you're married with children and your spouse**

has a good job: If one of you dies, can the other get along on one income? If so, perhaps no life insurance is necessary beyond that which you have at work.

✔ **Mail-order life insurance:** Stay away unless you compare its price to annual renewable term insurance and find it cheaper.

✔ **Rental car insurance:** Your own auto insurance policy probably covers you if you do damage to a rental car. Also, many credit cards cover this.

---

specialists recommend the 90-day version as long as people realize that they may have to pay $12,000 to $25,000 in current dollars out of pocket.

One place not to skimp is inflation protection, insurance specialists say. Only 40 percent of new policyholders buy such protection, says AARP, which estimates that the price of a day in a medium-cost nursing home could more than quintuple by 2035.

If Congress decides to change Medicaid rules, a larger number of elderly people may give long-term-care insurance a second look. A lesser-frills policy, though still costly, may provide the safety net that many risk-averse elderly people need.

One bit of good news is that many policies now cover home care, assisted living, respite care and hospice care; two decades ago, many covered only nursing home care. Policy shoppers should make sure that a plan offers at least home care and assisted-living coverage, and will pay as much for those as for nursing home care.

—Susan B. Garland

Know Your Insurance Terms

It can only help if you know what an agent is talking about

Whether you're in the market for health, auto, home, disability or life insurance, you'll have to familiarize yourself with insurance lingo. Here are some basics to learn before entering the world of annuities, term life and co-payments.

Ancillary care coverage. Some comprehensive insurance policies provide benefits for so-called ancillary care, such as prescription drugs and contacts, for example.

Annuity. Life insurance that pays benefits for a specified period of time—yearly, for example—during the insured's lifetime.

Cobra. Federal law (the Consolidated Omnibus Budget Reconciliation Act) requiring companies to offer employees an extension of their health plan once they leave the company.

INSIDE INFO

Pet Insurance Lovers

Companies may be pulling back from employee health benefits, but they are becoming more generous to their workers' pets.

O Pet insurance was offered by about 10 percent of larger employers in 2005, up from just 1 percent in 2000, according to the Society for Human Resource Management.

O Among the pet-friendly employers: Chipotle, Ford Motor, Google, Hilton and Time Warner.

Collision. Collision insurance generally covers the amount of damage above the deductible amount.

Comprehensive insurance. Provides coverage for auto theft or damage (other than from a collision), as a result of flood, fire, vandalism, etc.

Co-payment. The amount you pay out of pocket when you visit a doctor, often about $20, intended by the insurance company to discourage frequent and unnecessary use of benefits.

Deductible. The amount you pay out of pocket before your insurer pays its share. A larger deductible generally means a smaller premium.

Fee for service. A health insurance plan that allows you to choose your health care providers. You generally pay a percentage of medical costs and the insurance company picks up the rest.

H.M.O. Health maintenance organizations provide medical care to members, who pay a premium. Some H.M.O.'s provide medical services in a given location; others let subscribers get care from specified doctors in their private offices. Some cover prescription medicine and some offer partial coverage of dental care.

Liability insurance. Reimburses you for damages sustained, such as bodily injury, property damage, pain and suffering, etc. A policy usually indicates the maximum amount the insurer will pay.

No-fault insurance. This coverage, available in about one-half the states, pays for medical expenses and damages incurred in a car accident, regardless of who is at fault.

P.P.O. Preferred Provider Organization is a network of health care providers who charge on a fee-for-service basis. Fees are generally discounted at selected providers, but members have the choice of going outside the network.

Premium. Periodic amounts that you pay on an insurance policy.

Property and casualty insurance. Covers damage to and loss of property, both to the insured and to others and their property. This segment of the insurance business includes auto and homeowner's policies. The other sector is life and health.

Term life. Provides death benefits for a specified period of time. Term life has no cash value and can be renewed or converted to whole life.

Umbrella policy. Coverage for losses beyond those in the underlying policy, such as auto or homeowner's insurance.

Universal life. A flexible policy combining benefits for an early death and a savings vehicle that usually earns interest at market rates. Benefits are not fixed and can usually be changed within limits.

Whole life. The classic life insurance policy that combines protection against early death and a savings account. Premiums are fixed and guaranteed throughout the insured's lifetime.

25 Easily Overlooked Deductions

If you can claim any one of these, you can lower your tax bill

Expenses for everything from contact lenses to dry cleaning could help you lower your tax bill. The tax law allows many personal and business expenses to be deducted from your income before you figure your tax liability. The more you can subtract, the more you reduce the amount of your taxable income. Here's a list, from the best-selling *Ernst & Young Tax Guide*, of 25 deductions that are easily overlooked:

1. APPRAISAL FEES: When paid to determine the value of a charitable gift or the extent of a casualty loss.

2. BUSINESS GIFTS: No more than $25 to any one person per year.

3. CELLULAR TELEPHONE: When used in your business, or required by your employer, the cost of the phone, plus phone calls made, may be deductible.

4. CHARITABLE EXPENSES FOR VOLUNTEER WORK: Fourteen cents a mile for use of your car (higher in 2006 if for Hurricane Katrina relief), plus out-of-pocket spending for such items as uniforms and supplies.

5. COMMISSIONS ON SALE OF ASSETS: Brokerage or other fees to complete a sale are taken into account when you figure your profit or loss (generally added to your cost for the asset).

Preparing Tax Returns Right the First Time

Avoid these common tax errors before you sign the tax check

- Are your W-2's and 1099's correct? If not, have them corrected so I.R.S. records agree with the amount shown on your return.

- Be sure you claimed all of your dependents, such as elderly parents who may not live with you.

- If you are single and live with a dependent, see if you qualify for the lower tax rates available to a head of household or surviving spouse with a dependent child.

- Recheck your cost basis in the shares you sold this year, particularly shares of a mutual fund. Income and capital gains dividends that were automatically reinvested in the fund over the years increase your basis in the mutual fund and thus reduce a gain or increase a loss that you must report.

- Fill out Form 8606, Nondeductible I.R.A. Contributions, for your deposits to an I.R.A. account if you don't claim any deductions for the contributions.

- If you worked for more than one employer, be sure to claim the credit for any overpaid Social Security taxes withheld.

- Check last year's return to see if there are any items that carry over to this year, such as capital losses or charitable contributions that exceeded the amount you were previously able to deduct.

- Don't report a state tax refund as income if you didn't claim an itemized deduction for the tax when it was originally paid.

- If you adopted a child, check your eligibility for a tax credit for the adoption, subject to certain limitations.

- People 65 and older who don't itemize deductions should claim a special, higher-than-normal standard deduction.

MONEY

6. CONTACT LENSES: Also include the cost of eyeglasses or cleaning solution.

7. CONTRACEPTIVES: Legitimate medical items include birth control pills, as well as legal abortions.

8. DRUG AND ALCOHOL ABUSE TREATMENT: Includes meals and lodging when staying at a treatment center. Smoking cessation programs if they are considered medically necessary by your physician to reduce health risks can also be deducted.

9. EDUCATIONAL EXPENSES: To improve or keep up your skills at your current job.

10. EMPLOYMENT AGENCY FEES: Whether you get a new job or not; but not if you're looking for your first job or switching occupations. Résumé and travel costs are also deductible.

11. FOREIGN TAX: If you pay tax to another country on income from foreign investments, you can get a deduction or credit for those payments when figuring your U.S. tax.

12. GAMBLING LOSSES: Only up to the amount of reported winnings.

13. LAUNDRY SERVICE ON A BUSINESS TRIP: You needn't pack for an entire trip.

14. MOVING EXPENSES: When changing jobs or starting work for the first time, and only if the new job means a 50-mile-or-longer extra commute if you don't move.

15. PREMIUM ON TAXABLE BONDS: Investors who buy taxable bonds for more than face value can gradually deduct the excess each year they own the bond.

16. MEDICAL TRANSPORTATION: You can claim 18 cents per mile plus tolls and parking in 2006. The amount can change annually.

17. ORTHOEPEDIC SHOES: The extra amount over the cost of normal shoes.

18. PENALTY FOR EARLY WITHDRAWAL OF SAVINGS: When a certificate of deposit is cashed in before maturity, a penalty is deductible as an adjustment to income.

19. POINTS ON A HOME MORTGAGE: Deductible as a lump sum when paid on a loan to buy or remodel a main residence; deductible gradually over the life of the loan when paid to refinance a mortgage.

20. SELF-EMPLOYMENT TAX: Adjustment allows the self-employed to reduce taxable income by half their self-employment Social Security and Medicare tax,

21. SUPPORT FOR SPECIAL SCHOOLING: For the mentally or physically impaired, when the school is primarily to help them deal with their disability.

22. SUPPORT FOR A VISITING STUDENT. Up to $50 per month in housing, food and support for live-in exchange student is deductible, only if you're not reimbursed.

23. TAX PREPARATION: Accountant's fees, legal expenses, tax guides and computer programs.

24. WORK CLOTHES: When required for work, but not suitable for ordinary wear.

25. WORTHLESS STOCK: Claimed as a capital loss in the year it first has no value. (Less than one cent per share generally is considered worthless.)

NOTE: Some deductions are limited. For example, only the portion of total medical expenses exceeding 7.5 percent of your adjusted gross income is deductible. "Miscellaneous" deductions, including most employment-related and investment expenses, are deductible only to the extent they exceed 2 percent of adjusted gross income.

SOURCE: Adapted from the *Ernst & Young Tax Guide*

Six Year-End Tax-Saving Tips

As the year closes, keep your eyes on these strategies

Taxes are among the few obstacles to success that investors can maneuver around. Here are some moves many investors can consider as the year winds down.

Harvest your losers. You cannot will a stock or mutual fund to rise in value as the year comes to a close, but you can extract some benefit from the laggards in your accounts that are not tax-sheltered. When you sell shares of a stock that is trading below your purchase price, those losses can be used to offset capital gains realized elsewhere in your portfolio, thus reducing your tax bill.

Even if you have no gains to offset for the year, you can use still realize losses and use them to reduce ordinary income. Say a stock you bought for $6,000 is now worth half of that. If you took the $3,000 loss, you could reduce your taxable income by $3,000. For investors in the 35 percent bracket, that works out to tax savings of $1,050. So instead of being down $3,000, you're down only $1,950.

What if you book losses of more than $3,000? You can carry forward losses throughout your investing career, which means that today's declines can offset gains in future bull markets.

If you're thinking of dumping shares of a money-losing fund, do so quickly, in case the fund is preparing to present you with a tax bill. Every year, typically near year-end, mutual funds distribute capital gains that they have realized in their portfolios. Even funds that are down at year's end could distribute long-term taxable gains.

A Trust With Pros and Cons

With a little estate planning your house could stay in the family

With homes appreciating in value, many older people may have to worry about their heirs facing estate taxes. Congress raised the estate tax exemption to $3.5 million in 2009 and removed the estate tax entirely in 2010. But the tax relief expires in 2011, which would bring the tax back and scale back the exemption to $1 million if Congress does not act.

What Congress will do about estate taxes over the next couple of years is anyone's guess, but tax planners say it is foolhardy for anyone with sizeable assets to do nothing and hope for the best. The solution could be transferring the home to children via a Qualified Personal Residence Trust. Setting up such a trust is complicated; you'll need a lawyer. Here are a few pros and cons:

PROS

- It removes the appreciated value of a house from a parent's estate for significant estate tax savings.

- The parent continues to live in the house during the term of the trust.

- Paying rent to children is yet another way to transfer wealth to them.

- Residences and vacation homes qualify, and a person can protect two homes, sometimes a third.

CONS

- The cost basis of the house remains the same as it was for the parents, which means higher capital gains tax when it is sold.

- If the parent dies before the term of the trust ends, the children inherit the house at its current value.

- Children become their parents' landlord when the trust expires, and children could evict the parents or raise the rent.

—Damon Darlin

Be mindful of the "wash-sale rule." While it makes sense to sell some losers, it's important not to let those losses alter your asset allocation strategy.

One way to avoid this is to get back into the market immediately. But the I.R.S. says the tax-loss benefit is forfeited if you step back into the same or "substantially identical" investment within 30 days of your sale. This is called the wash-sale rule.

If you are selling shares of a particular stock or of an actively managed mutual fund, for example, a simple way around the rule is to buy a low-cost exchange-traded fund—an index fund, of sorts, whose shares trade like stock on an exchange.

Rebalance with taxes in mind. Year-end is a natural time for many investors to readjust their portfolios, to keep to their long-term asset allocation goals. But if you plan to do so by trimming your stake in holdings that have appreciated significantly, and if you have both taxable and tax-advantaged accounts, consider selling the appreciated stock in your tax-deferred retirement account. That way, you don't create a taxable event.

Give appreciated stock to charity. Year-end is also a good time to consider donating money to a charity, not only for philanthropic purposes, but also for the charitable deduction. But instead of reaching for your checkbook, take a look at your portfolio. By donating appreciated stock, you maximize your gift to the charity while minimizing your taxes. Instead of selling the stock and paying capital gains taxes out of pocket and then sending the cash to the charity, you can donate the appreciated security to the charity, which can then sell the asset on its own without tax consequence. And you can deduct the full market value of the holding at the time of donation.

Give appreciated stock to your children. The same idea for donating appreciated stock works well for paying for a college education. If you're saving money for a child through a custodial account, you can give appreciated shares to the child, instead of selling the asset and funding the account with cash. The child can then sell at his or her lower capital gains tax rate, typically 5 percent instead of 15 percent.

Take full advantage of college savings vehicles. Parents who invest in state-sponsored college savings accounts called 529's can rebalance their investments once a year. Moreover, many 529's offer state tax deductions to residents on at least part of the annual contributions, provided that they use the in-state plan. While there is an annual contribution limit as well as income restrictions on Coverdell education savings accounts, another type of tax-deferred savings plan, there are no such restrictions on 529's. Specific rules vary for each state plan, but contributions into a 529 can be significant.

—Paul J. Lim

The Giving Circle

A novel way to meet, greet and take tax deductions

Instead of just writing checks to their favorite charities, growing numbers of people are joining "giving circles," pooling their money and jointly deciding where to invest. Often, group members are friends who meet periodically over pot-luck dinners and decide where their charitable contributions will go.

A handful of high-tech entrepreneurs pioneered giving circles in the late 1990's, but they have bloomed in recent years. There are some 220 circles in 40 states, according to a study in 2004 by New Ventures in Philanthropy, an organization based in Washington, D.C. Donations range from $100 to $20,000 annually per group; all told, they have donated more than $44 million since 2000.

Circles can be as small as a handful of friends or as large as Social Venture Partners, a group based in Seattle that has 1,500 members in 23 cities in the United States and Canada. Whatever their size, giving circles take time to set up. Founders discover that it takes about a year to recruit members, decide on a focus and to start raising money. Deciding on specific charities requires even more deliberation.

Giving circles can manage their money in different ways, but members often choose to set up a tax-exempt, nonprofit organization or to team up with an established nonprofit or foundation to hold their money. They may also set up a donor-advised fund at some charities, foundations or financial institutions. Donors make irrevocable gifts of stock, money or other investments and can take immediate tax deductions. In such a fund, donors can recommend how and when the money should be used.

—Kristina Shevory

CHARITY BEGINS IN A CIRCLE OF FRIENDS

Want to start your own giving circle? Here are some recommendations. More information can be found through links at www.givingforum.org.

- Decide on the circle's mission, its name and how often it will meet.

- Set contribution amounts for each member.

- Determine how the money will be saved. Members can open a joint banking account, start a foundation, team up with a foundation that can administer the money or write individual checks.

- Focus on specific issues that members are passionate about, and invite specialists in those areas to help educate members.

TIMELY TIPS

The Give-and-Take of Charitable Contributions

✔ When you donate goods, always ask for an itemized receipt, in case the I.R.S. has any questions later on. You can deduct the fair market price of donations; that is, what they would sell for in a secondhand store. Visit a local thrift or consignment store to get a sense of prices.

✔ **When donating furniture,** support your valuation of how much you originally paid with photographs, receipts or canceled checks.

✔ **When contributing a car,** beware that tax laws governing such donations have changed due to I.R.S. concerns that taxpayers were overvaluing their donated cars. As of 2005 tax returns, if you donate a car worth more than $500, you cannot simply deduct the fair market value of the vehicle for taxes. Instead, your deduction will be determined once your car is sold and the charity sends you a receipt of the sale price.

—Alina Tugend

CHECKING UP ON YOUR CHARITY

✔ **The Internal Revenue Service** at 800-829-1040 or www.irs.gov, for information on a charity's tax exempt status.

✔ **Charity Navigator** at www.charitynavigator. org for independent evaluations and ratings of charities.

✔ **GuideStar** at www.guidestar.org for basic information on 1.5 million nonprofit organizations.

✔ **BBB Wise Giving Alliance** www.give.org tracks charities and is affiliated with the Council of Better Business Bureaus.

MONEY

- Delegate tasks so that everyone feels involved.
- Devise a set of guidelines for collecting and donating money.

—Kristina Shevory

What to Show Your Accountant

Leave the shoebox at home, but you'll need brokerage statements and other records

Whether you prepare your own tax return or let an accountant do all the work, the task of gathering up your tax information is unavoidable. In general, you should have documentation that supports all income, deductions and credits that will appear on your return, but supporting documentation can come in many forms, as this listing, adapted from the *Ernst & Young Tax Guide* shows:

Wages and salaries: W-2 forms, usually provided by your employer.

Dividends and interest: Form 1099-DIV and form 1099-INT, usually provided by the bank or company paying the dividend or interest.

Capital gains and losses: Broker's statements for purchase and sale of assets disposed of during the year and form 1099-B, usually provided by the broker who sold the assets.

Business income from sole proprietorships, rents and royalties: Books and records. Form 1099-MISC may also be provided by the payor of the income.

Business income from partnerships, estates, trusts, and S corporations: Schedule K-1, usually provided by the partnership, estate, trust or S corporation.

Unemployment compensation: Form 1099-G, usually provided by the governmental agency paying the unemployment compensation.

Social Security benefits: Form SSA-1099, usually provided by the federal government.

State and local income tax refunds: Form 1099-G; usually provided by the state or locality that refunded the taxes.

Original issue discount: Form 1099-OID, usually provided by the issuer of the long-term debt obligation.

 **TIMELY TIPS**

The Nuts and Bolts of Picking an Accountant

Accountants are in shorter supply these days. Although 54,000 accounting degrees were awarded in 2004, up 20 percent from 2002, that was far short of the peak of 61,000 in 1995, according to the American Institute of Certified Public Accountants in Washington, D.C. Picking from the pack is fairly straightforward.

✔ **First ask for referrals** from friends and associates in similar financial circumstances. Then interview candidates to ensure that they have relevant experience.

✔ **Make sure you understand tax preparers' fee policies,** and don't be afraid to ask how the working relationship will proceed. Some important questions to ask: Who will prepare your return, the accountant you interview, or a junior person? Will the return be outsourced to a site in India? What is the firm's policy on returning phone calls?

✔ **Pick your accountant early in the year.** As filing season nears, most accountants have less time to get to know their clients. What's more, many last-minute chances to save on taxes—like making charitable gifts to maximize deductions—disappear at the close of the calendar year.

—Eryn Brown

All distributions, both total and partial, from pensions, annuities, insurance, contracts, retirement or profit-sharing plans, and individual retirement accounts (I.R.A.): Form 1099-R, usually provided by the trustee for the plan making the distribution.

Barter income: Form 1099-B, usually provided by the barter exchange through which the property or services were exchanged.

Sale of your home: Form 1099-S should be provided by the person who is responsible for the closing of the real estate transaction.

I.R.A. contributions: Form 5498; provided by the trustee or custodian of the I.R.A.

Moving and employee business expenses: Receipts and canceled checks.

Medical expenses: Receipts and canceled checks.

Mortgage interest and points paid on the purchase of a principal residence: Form 1098 or mortgage company statement, usually provided by the mortgage company.

Business and investment interest: Canceled checks and brokers' statements.

Real estate taxes: Canceled checks and mortgage company statements (if they are applicable).

Other taxes: Receipts and canceled checks.

Contributions: Receipts and canceled checks; written acknowledgment from the charitable organization is generally required for contributions of $250 or more. Form 1098-C if you donated a motor vehicle worth more than $500.

WHAT YOUR ACCOUNTANT WON'T NEED:

You don't need to bring all your documentation to your accountant. For example, if you provide a summary of your charitable contributions, just bring the summary to your accountant, rather than the individual documents. Otherwise,

---

ⓘ INSIDE INFO

How Does the I.R.S. Pick Audits?

○ I.R.S. computer programs, using information from forms, such as 1099's and W-2's, spew out returns that don't add up.

○ The agency follows up on outside leads—from newspapers, public records, even tips from individuals.

○ The I.R.S. uses a computer score system to pick audits. After a return is processed, it is assigned a numeric score. The agency says there is a "high potential" that returns with high scores will result in an audit and a higher income tax liability.

Do You Fit the I.R.S. Audit Profile?

A look at individual tax returns audited in 2004 shows that larger estates are most likely to attract Uncle Sam's attention:

TYPE OF RETURN	PERCENTAGE AUDITED
○ **PERSONAL**	
Income under $25,000	1.26%
$25,000 to $50,000	.43%
$50,000 to $100,000	.44%
Over $100,000	1.39%
○ **SELF-EMPLOYED**	
Gross revenue under $25,000	3.15%
$25,000 to $100,000	1.47%
Over $100,000	1.86%
○ **ESTATES**	
Assets under $1 million	4.93%
$1 million to $5 million	6.20%
Over $5 million	26.57%

SOURCE: Internal Revenue Service

your accountant might feel obligated to verify the accuracy of your summaries, which, as you well know, can be a time-consuming and expensive process. You should, of course, be able to provide full documentation on request.

If the I.R.S. Comes Knocking

Chances are you'll end up paying after an audit

A lot of returns do not get audited, but the ones that do must undergo the scrutiny of some annoyingly nosy I.R.S. examiners. Your exam could well go beyond checking the validity of your tax deductions to looking around for income you may have neglected to report.

The I.R.S.'s weapon is what's popularly called a lifestyle audit, in which examiners take a global view of your financial and family affairs to see if your reported income is sufficient to support the lifestyle you're enjoying. Besides asking you for receipts for charitable donations, proof of business

INSIDE INFO

The Price of I.R.S. Advice

Want to ask the I.R.S. whether a wrinkle in rolling money from your 401(k) plan into another retirement account will result in additional taxes? That will cost you plenty.

O   The fees for such a ruling range from $500 to $3,000 as of 2006, compared to $95 the year before. For the top fee, the increase was more than 850 times the inflation rate.

O   Entrepreneurs inquiring whether their simplified employee pension plans are not too complicated face a $9,000 fee, up from $2,750 in 2005. Says one New York accountant: "It sounds like it may be cheaper to mess up than to ask."

—David Cay Johnston

expenses and details of investment transactions, auditors may ask how you can afford that car and a second home on your income. Questions about the amount of your mortgage payment, whether your children work, what appliances you've recently bought, where you went to college and whether you've been divorced are also fair game.

The I.R.S.'s top audit targets are generally upper-income professionals, self-employed people, investors claiming big losses and people with considerable income from tips—but no group is immune. Most audits end up pulling in extra tax for the I.R.S., so emerging unscathed is a long shot.

Audits come in three flavors. Least intimidating is a correspondence audit—usually a letter asking for documentation to back up a single item. More fearsome are office audits in which you go to an I.R.S. office for a face-to-face probe that may cover more topics in greater detail. At the top tier are field audits, which most often involve business-related returns and are conducted by top-trained agents at a taxpayer's home or office. Office audits are most common, partly because budget restraints limit the number of face-to-face encounters the I.R.S. can afford. But exams by mail are also often based on the least solid suspicion of wrongdoing, so they are often the easiest to fight successfully.

When the I.R.S. contacts you, it has usually found at least something suspicious. Generally, it will be up to you to show why any proposed changes are wrong. Mail audits can often be handled on your own, but you may want guidance from an accountant on deeper probes. It's wise not to insist on total victory. Give the auditor a few small wins so the I.R.S. can close your case and move on. And like an elephant, the I.R.S. never forgets: if you have been audited before, the I.R.S. will remember. Don't repeat past mistakes.

SPENDING & SAVING

Consumer Advice 246

SHOPPING ONLINE·246: *The online bazaar • Comparison shopping • Sites for savvy shoppers* **STRATEGIES·248:** *Conspicuous consumption • When to take out your wallet • Tips on tipping • Buying old is new again • Worthless warranties • Bargains in your post office* **IDENTITY THEFT·254:** *How to protect your personal data • Who's vulnerable to identity theft?* **EMERGENCIES·256:** *Preparing for a quick getaway: what to take with you • Cutting funeral costs*

Autos 260

BUYING·260: *What dealers won't tell you • New ways to buy used cars • Plug-in hybrid cars* **DRIVING·265:** *A racer on driving defensively • What it takes to stop in time • Holding your liquor • Helping your child drive safely • When to hang up the keys • Help when you're stranded* **MAINTENANCE·272:** *The manual or the mechanic? • Gas-saving strategies* **CYCLES & R.V.'S·275:** *Taking a cycle for a spin • Make room for scooters • Condos on wheels • Off-road R.V.s • Stopping auto rustlers*

Home Technology 280

COMPUTERS·280: *Networking your home • Desktop vs. laptop • Hard-drive hygiene • Moving data to new computer • Backing up on the go* **ONLINE·290:** *Browsing for browsers • Firewalls* **SERVICE & ENERGY·291:** *Computer doctors • "I vant your vatts"* **AUDIO & VIDEO·293:** *Finding podcasts • Satellite radio at home • Selecting a TV • Big screens on a small budget* **PHONES·296:** *Should your PC be your phone? • Cellphones* **CAMERAS·298:** *Digital cameras*

Collecting 300

ART·300: *A guide for the artless • When beauty and value merge • What to look for in a painting* **ANTIQUES·303:** *How to spot an antique • Going on the Antiques Roadshow • What's your collection worth? • Culling the collectibles* **AUCTIONS·307:** *Bargains at charity auctions • Demystifying eBay • Uncle Sam's attic* **GEMS·312:** *Diamonds: what's in a rock? • Pearls • The price of sparkle* **COLLECTIBLES·314:** *Silver: a lion or a king • Virtual stamp collecting • Consumable assets • On a magic carpet ride • Guitars with nostalgia*

SPENDING

Consumer Advice

The Online Bazaar

How to navigate the giant worldwide flea market

Even Jane Jetson would be amazed at how much easier the Internet has made it to shop for anything, anywhere, at any time. In less than a decade, the curiosity that was online shopping has become an essential, everyday tool that shoppers rely on as unthinkingly as a grocery cart.

But with its giant worldwide flea markets, like the eBay auction site—where the motto is "Whatever it is, you can get it here"—to specialized search sites like Kelkoo.com that list hundreds of overseas online stores, the Internet may engender its own brand of anxiety. There are, for instance, six different international Amazon sites in addition to good old Amazon.com. Where, then, to start?

For browsing, shopping comparison sites, such as Bizrate.com, Shopping.Yahoo.com and Shopping. com, will spit out useful lists of prices and costs of shipping to your zip code of millions of items in categories like computers, jewelry and clothing.

Hobbyists and enthusiasts often offer expert advice on a particular category of merchandise. Visit Watchreport.com before buying a wristwatch, for example, Coffeegeek.com before purchasing anything even vaguely related to caffeine and Spongobongo.com before buying an Oriental rug.

If your search is very specific—if you already know the model number or product name—it may be faster to type in a simple keyword search at Google.com. Follow the results' links to a store that stocks the merchandise.

Is the store unfamiliar? Before purchasing an item online from a merchant you don't know, conduct due diligence by checking merchant ratings at review sites like Epinions.com, at *Consumer Reports'* Consumerwebwatch.org or at the Better Business Bureau's bbb.org.

Protect yourself further by using a credit card to pay; federal law limits your liability for unauthorized charges to $50. For more specifics on how to avoid being swindled online, read about common dot cons at the Federal Trade Commission's consumer site at www.ftc.gov.

—Michelle Slatalla

Comparison Shopping Made Easy

Attention bargain hunters: These Web sites help you find the lowest prices

Finding the lowest prices for goods sold online may seem an easy feat for Web shoppers. Yet how can people be certain they have found the best price, given the ever-expanding universe of Web stores, auction sites and online classified sites?

To help shoppers keep tabs on the rising tide of e-commerce, comparison-shopping engines are adding secondary markets, niche categories and in-browser search tools for more thorough bargain hunting—even including security features that offer warnings about deals too good to be true.

One service, the SquareTrade Sidebar, uses a bit of all these strategies for comparison shopping. The program hides in Internet Explorer, and when it detects that a user is shopping online, it displays a list of alternative prices for the product being searched. SquareTrade presents results from affiliate merchants' sites as well as from sites like eBay and Craigslist, where secondhand items may fetch less.

Users can also type product searches directly into the sidebar—a frame within a browser window—but because the engine's search technology favors comparisons drawn from actual pages, general queries sometimes fall short; where "iPod Nano" yields no results, "iPod Nano black" does.

SquareTrade's main business is verifying eBay merchants and arbitrating disputes, so the toolbar takes precautions against fraud. If a phishing link turns up, an alert offers a warning.

Another large service, Nextag.com, has also turned to toolbars for on-demand price matching, although its toolbar searches only those companies it has deals with.

Vendio's Dealio toolbar (www.dealio.com) will flash its best price for an item when someone visits a product page. People can disregard the box or click to see competing offers, sorted by price.

While many comparison sites stick to popular categories like electronics, others find opportunities in niche categories. LowerMyBills.com compares expenses like phone services, car loans, credit cards and insurance quotes; SimplyHired.com shows job hunters opportunities from newspapers, job boards and corporate Web sites; and the Grocery Saver feature at Cairo.com builds custom shopping lists from sales at neighborhood markets.

Fatlens.com offers comparison shopping for shows and sporting events among traditional ticket agencies, online brokers and individuals on auction sites, and recently expanded into clothing, shoes and jewelry.

Unlike many comparison engines that cull search results only from their retail partners, who pay for the privilege, Fatlens.com is one of the few

TIMELY TIPS

More Sites for Savvy Shoppers

✔ **AddALL.com** No-frills book price comparisons.

✔ **AMusicArea.com** For CD's

✔ **AMovieArea.com** For DVD's

✔ **Amazon.com** The online megastore. Books, music, videos, games, electronics, food, sporting goods—and ever growing.

✔ **Bankrate.com** and **E-loan.com** For finding the best interest rates for a mortgage, auto, credit card or other loan.

✔ **Bizrate.com** Lets you see how fellow consumers rate online merchants and compares prices.

✔ **BizWeb.com** Commercial sites on the Internet by category.

✔ **Buy.com** Good prices and service on electronics, books, music and video.

✔ **Buyer's Index** (www.buyersindex.com) Searches 19,000 Web sites and catalogs for the product you seek.

✔ **ConsumerSearch.com** Reviews of products from a variety of publications.

✔ **DeepDiscountDVD.com** Consistently low DVD prices. **DeepDiscountCD.com** Low CD prices.

✔ **eBay.com** The online auction house and storefront.

✔ **Epinions.com** (part of Shopping.com) Consumer reviews of many products and price comparisons.

✔ **NetMarket.com** Discounts on brand name goods.

✔ **PriceGrabber.com, PriceScan.com** and **Shopping.com** Compare prices for computer hardware and software, electronics, movies, books, other goods.

SPENDING

services trolling the Web for results.

Comparison engines that increase selections by tapping into unconventional sales forums like eBay and Craigslist, however, may end up raising some shoppers' concerns about buying from unknown sellers.

Some companies, like BuySafe, are trying to improve their small-business customers' reputations through comparison searching. BuySafe, which bonds merchants that provide goods and services to help them earn trust, offers a searchable index of its retailers at www.buysafeshopping.com.

—Tim Gnatek

If You've Got It, Flaunt It
The case for conspicuous consumption

Long before Thorstein Veblen coined the term "conspicuous consumption," economists from Adam Smith to Karl Marx had argued that people choose to buy some goods because of what those goods reveal about their standing in society, not because of any intrinsic enjoyment they get from the purchase.

Yet conspicuous consumption remained mainly a theoretical curiosity for more than a century, with little empirical content or support. In 2005, Ori Heffetz, a doctoral student in economics at Princeton University, developed the first broad-gauged index of product visibility. Sure enough, by asking, "When a consumer spends more than average on a product, how visible is that product to others?" he finds that conspicuous items make up a greater share of the consumption budget in wealthier families.

Heffetz looked at 29 types of consumer products and 3,294 households. The visibility ranking that resulted from the survey is quite sensible. Cigarettes, clothing, cars and jewelry are the most visible products, while underwear, home insurance, life insurance and car insurance are the least.

Heffetz's analysis indicates that the higher the visibility of a product, the more likely it is to be a luxury item. For example, spending on cars and jewelry, two highly visible items, rises as a share of a household's budget as its income rises, while spending on home utilities, an inconspicuous category, falls as a share of the budget as income rises.

The relationship is far from perfect, however. Cigarette consumption is greater among lower-income households than among higher-income ones, yet cigarettes are the most noticeable product of all, according to the findings of the study.

Heffetz says he also found support for another of Veblen's pet theories: the notion of "vicarious consumption," meaning the satisfaction someone derives from giving a conspicuous gift or throwing a lavish party. Christmas gifts are 40 percent more visible than the average consumer purchase, Heffetz calculated.

Why give conspicuous presents? One reason is that gift givers wish to signal that they can afford to

ⓘ INSIDE INFO

Spending Habits

Average annual U.S. household spending on selected items:

Rent	$9,224
Cars	$3,020
Home insurance	$619
Books	$447
Haircuts	$307
Cigarettes	$273
Laundry	$128

SOURCE: *Consumption and the Visibility of Consumer Expenditures*, Ori Heffetz, Princeton University

—Alan B. Krueger

be generous. A conspicuous gift transmits that signal to a wider audience than an inconspicuous one.

So, before you return one of those loud ties, that gaudy pair of earrings or other conspicuous gifts, recognize the impact of flaunting the gift on your reputation—and on your benefactor's reputation as well.

—Alan B. Krueger

When to Take Out Your Wallet
Sales are not what they used to be

In these days of lean inventory and fewer deep markdowns, how's a bargain-hunting consumer going to snatch the best price? It will take a little more effort—and knowledge of technology can provide an edge.

There is a rhythm to the introduction of many consumer products. The year-end holiday buying spree, when about 40 percent of all consumer products are purchased, sets that rhythm. New cars, electronics and most other items have to be in stores and ready to go by September.

A few products don't follow the pattern. The big selling season for large kitchen appliances, for example, is an abbreviated period before what the appliance makers call the cooking season. As you might guess, consumers want new appliances in place and ready to go before the Thanksgiving feast.

Sales of air-conditioners are entirely weather related. A mild summer and retailers are stuck with inventory that needs to be cleared out with a big price reduction. Refrigerators tend to break in the heat, so that product has a summer selling season, too.

It used to be that you'd pick up bargains after Christmas. But that is no longer the case. Merchants, who start putting up Christmas decorations at Halloween, extend the season the other direction, well past New Year's Day.

As shoppers use gift cards, the season moves out a few weeks more. It then gets pushed to the Super Bowl, especially for big-screen televisions. The selling season does finally screech to a halt near the end of February.

The big retailers—Wal-Mart, Costco, BestBuy and Circuit City, where Americans now buy the bulk of their gear—rarely get stuck with much unwanted merchandise, so there's no need for a big sale. The inventory has been carefully tracked with something called supply-chain management software, which keeps stocks tight.

So this software is nothing but bad news for the consumer, right? Actually, it has been good news. "There are fewer oh-my-god bargains," says Ron Boire, executive vice president and general merchandise manager for Best Buy, "but now all customers are getting a good price instead of a few customers getting a great price."

So is there still a way to game the system? Yes, but it takes a little more diligence. You have to avoid impulse buying, but still be ready to pounce quickly.

KNOW YOUR PRODUCT. Web sites like Engadget.com and Gizmodo.com are places to gather information on product releases. News.com and Twice.com also track developments that come out of trade shows like the Consumer Electronics Show in January or the Photo Marketing Association conference in late February. Froogle.com and other price-comparison sites allow you to study which reputable dealer is also aggressive on price.

MONITOR THE PRICES. Watch the Sunday circulars or review them at SundaySaver.com. NexTag has a number of useful features to help you track price cuts. It e-mails you when a product finally drops to the price you are willing to pay. The site also lists products that recently had price cuts.

SPENDING

✔ TIMELY TIPS

The Hard Part Is Knowing How Much

Tip jars are everywhere, it seems, even lining counters of self-serve cafeterias and chi-chi cafés. Drop in a few coins if you wish but it's no faux pas to pass. Tipping abroad varies by country and culture, so it's best to consult local guide books.

✔ AIRPORT

Car shuttle driver	$1-$2 per use
Hotel courtesy van	$1-$2
if driver helps with luggage	+$2
Taxi dispatcher	none
Taxi driver	15-20% of fare
Car service	Gratuity included or 15% of bill
Curbside baggage handler	$1-$2 per bag

✔ HOTEL

Doorman: for special services	$1-$2
for help with baggage, depending on number of bags	$1-$2
Bellhop: for taking luggage to room	$1-$2 / bag
for delivering messages or packages	$1-$2 / delivery
Housekeeper	$3-$5 / day
for special service	+$1-$2 / day
Room service waiter	15-20% / bill
(if service is included in the bill)	5% or $1 minimum
Concierge for tickets, etc.	$5 to $10

✔ RESTAURANT

Coffee shop server	15-17% / bill
Maitre d'	
to get a good table	$5 / two
for four or more	$10
(double amounts for five-star restaurants)	
Waiter/waitress	15-20% of bill
(if gratuities are included, an addi-tional tip is warranted for special service)	
Wine steward	15% of wine bill
Bartender	15% of liquor bill
Hat/coat check	$1-$2 / coat or / person
Door attendant	$1-$2 / cab

✔ OTHER

Apartment doorman *(at Christmas)*	$20-$100
Barber	15% ($1 minimum)
Hairdresser	15%
Hair washer	$2 minimum
Manicurist	15%
Parking valet	$1-$2 / use
Rail porter	$1 / bag

✔ 15% TIP TABLE:

CHECK	TIP	CHECK	TIP
$10	**$1.50**	$60	**$9.00**
$20	**$3.00**	$70	**$10.50**
$30	**$4.50**	$80	**$12.00**
$40	**$6.00**	$90	**$13.50**
$50	**$7.50**	$100	**$15.00**

WAIT FOR YOUR PRICE. NexTag also displays price history charts. You can divine a little from those as well. A constantly downward sloping line suggests that the manufacturer has control of inventory and prices are dropping at a natural electronics-just-get-cheaper pace. That means there's not much you can do. Anything you buy will be cheaper a month from now.

But a flat line that also shows some abrupt drops, however small, suggests a struggling product. A need to outflank a competitor with price promotions or trim growing inventories can cause that pattern. If the line is flat for a while, hold off buying. It will drop soon enough. It always does.

—Damon Darlin

Don't Forget the Hotel Maid

Tipping is part of travel, so what about the housekeeper?

Seasoned business travelers always make sure to have a bunch of singles on hand to take care of the parking valet, the bellhop, the doorman and the cabby. But the hotel maid? You know, the woman—and it is virtually always a female worker—who makes the bed, takes out the trash, changes the towels and generally leaves the room looking like something a real estate agent would want to show off.

Perhaps because they were unseen, working in the room when the guest was gone, hotel maids were generally overlooked by many travelers until recently. Yet in most hotels, maids are expected to clean 14 to 16 rooms a shift, a physically daunting task. Consider, too, that today's upscale niches have added luxurious new beds and bedding—some with half a dozen pillows and heavy 300-thread-count sheets. Think of the extra work involved in making those swell beds. That should turn Scrooges into Daddy Warbucks. Here are some tips for tipping the maid on your next domestic trip.

First of all, ignore the laughable advice from the American Society of Travel Agents, frequently reprinted on Internet sites about travel and tipping, stating that $1 a day is standard for the maid. Big spenders, those travel agents. Actually, $3 to $5 a day is more like it. Keep in mind that hotel maids worry about being accused of stealing loose cash, and sometimes will not pick up a tip if they aren't sure it is a tip. So leave the tip on the pillow with a note that clearly indicates what it is. Write "For the housekeeper," or simply "Thanks."

Tipping the housekeeper is a considerate practice, says Amanda Cooper, a spokeswoman for Unite, the union that represents 200,000 workers, including 60,000 housekeepers, among the estimated 1.3 million employees of the hotel industry. Cooper says she always leaves something. Even $5 a day can make a significant impact, she says.

—Joe Sharkey

Buying Old Is New Again

Where to look for deals in the secondhand market

The idea of buying used goods often sounds rather pathetic, as if you are in a real-life version of a Charlie Brown Christmas. Who would want something used?

The answer is, anyone who wants to save money. Now there are robust marketplaces for used products, which are just as good and significantly cheaper than new ones. The movement of used products from a daily newspaper's classified ads to the Web allows the buyer to get better prices because choices are more extensive. While there are some categories you never want to buy used—pillows or toothbrushes—there are enough these days that you won't feel pathetic doing so.

BOOKS. The Internet has created a marketplace for any title, popular or obscure. Amazon.com has jumped into the business in the belief that an active market for used books can stimulate the sale of new books. Services like Alibris.com allow you to search for the unusual book and link you with a buyer or seller.

DVD's. Since the discs take a considerable amount of abuse, grabbing a used one that sells for less than half the price of new movies makes a lot of sense. If you type in the phrase "used DVD" on Google, you'll get scores of online merchants specializing in used goods.

VIDEO GAMES. Thanks to the short attention span of many gamers, stores like EB Games will quickly stock preplayed versions of the latest games. You may have to wait a week to get the hottest game.

EXERCISE EQUIPMENT. You know that Lifecycle in the bedroom? The one you use as a clothes hanger? You're not alone. The problem is that because machines are heavy and bulky, they aren't something one sells on eBay with the greatest of ease. Prices for used equipment can run a wide range so if you are shopping through classified ads, or an online version like Craigslist, it pays to study the market until you get a sense of the average price.

SPENDING

REFURBISHED GOODS. Manufacturers discount refurbished products because they have been returned by an unsatisfied customer and they can't sell an unsealed box as new. (That usually means the customer found the product cheaper someplace else and got his money back, not that it didn't work.) You'll find deals on refurbished products on almost every manufacturer's Web site, sometimes at half the price of new.

—Damon Darlin

Worthless Warranties?

Consumer advocates are dubious about extended warranties—except for a few products

Extended service warranties, or product "accessories," as they are known in the business, are available for everything from $9,000 stoves to $20 DVD's. And they seem like a good idea: products are increasingly complex, with electronic elements that are expensive or impossible to repair. In the past, appliance repairs rarely hit $400, but today, $1,000 repairs are not uncommon. Yet, consumer advocates generally advise against them.

Extended warranties are an estimated $15-billion-a-year business. Retailers view them as a way (and one requiring no shelf space) to lift profits in competitive markets. In electronics, the gross margin for merchandise, or the difference between what a store pays for goods and what it sells them for, is about 25 percent at chains like Best Buy and Circuit City, says Alan Kane, a professor at the Columbia Business School. Extended service contracts, on the other hand, produce a gross margin of 45 percent or more, he says.

Repairing a ruined laptop screen costs about the same as a new machine, or $1,000 for a top-of-the-line model. So a policy that covers repairs or replacement for any reason, including damage

caused by the customer, makes sense. Cellphone coverage, on the other hand, is less easily fathomed. Millions of cellphones disappear or are damaged each year, and some kind of coverage sounds practical. Usually offered by service providers for about $5 a month, the plans seem cheap. If you often lose phones, or if yours is stolen within three months, coverage can save money.

But depending on the company and the fine print, there might be a $50 deductible and limitations. For example, repairs might be covered only if the damage is not the customer's fault. If a phone lasts 23 months before it breaks, the cost of coverage could be $165 ($115 in premiums, $50 for the deductible) on a phone that might sell new for $150 or, with rebates and special offers, might cost nothing.

Consumer Reports generally advises against buying extended service contracts because the cost of repairing could be the same as the warranty cost, in which case it's best to keep that money in your pocket. One *Consumer Reports* survey found that three years after purchase just 5 to 7 percent of televisions needed repair, and 13 percent of vacuums (not counting belt replacements). But 33 percent of laptops had been sent to the shop or the recycle bin.

The consumer group recommends extended service policies on three items: laptops, treadmills (too cumbersome to take to the shop and service calls are expensive) and plasma TV's, because they are so expensive and the technology is relatively new. Some consumers skip extra coverage and choose, when possible, products with long-lasting manufacturer's warranties. Treadmills from Precor USA, for example, include a lifetime warranty on the body, 10 years on moving parts and a year on labor.

—Susan Ferraro

The Bargains in Your Post Office
Except for the lines, it's the next best thing to having a personal assistant

Sure, lines at the local post office are often long and the staff is sometimes surly, but on-time mail delivery rates have soared to over 90 percent, your mail will be held for free if you go on vacation and, if you move, your mail will be forwarded

for up to one year. Here are eight other post office services that will save you time and money:

1. SPECIAL MAIL, SPECIAL RATE. You can send a package that contains books, printed materials, tapes, videos, CD's, diskettes and other such items by using "media mail," otherwise known as the book rate. Media mail is cheaper than parcel post, albeit often a bit slower. A few caveats: you can't include advertising in the package and the item must weigh less than 70 pounds.

2. FAST MAIL. Priority mail lets you send envelopes and boxes (provided free at the post office) that weigh less than 70 pounds at a flat rate. Delivery time is not guaranteed, but usually takes 2 to 3 days on average. The fastest service for packages that weigh less than 50 pounds is express mail. You can choose overnight or second-day delivery. Unlike some private carriers, the post office generally delivers express mail on Sundays and holidays, too. On-time delivery is guaranteed or the postage will be refunded in most cases.

3. ADD-ONS GALORE. For nominal amounts, you can pick and choose from a slew of safety services: track your package, confirm delivery, insure it from loss or damage, get a signature from the recipient, etc. Or, get all those services for $7.50 and up by sending your first class or priority mail as registered mail.

4. STAMPS, ANYWHERE, ANYTIME. More than 44,000 locations—from supermarkets to convenience stores to drugstores—across the country sell stamps at face value. You can also buy stamps from your home by calling 800-STAMP-24, or online at www.usps.com. (There is a nominal shipping charge for phone and online orders.) To ship a package domestically or overseas, find out how much postage you need (www.usps.com), charge it and even print out a shipping label that you affix to the package. For an extra charge, a letter carrier will come to your door to pick it up.

5. SAFE MONEY. For amounts less than $1,000, a money order is a safe alternative to sending cash through the mail. Like a bank check, a money order can only be cashed by the recipient, but because it's prepaid it can't bounce. If it's lost or stolen, show your receipt to get a replacement. To see if a money order is authentic, hold it to the light. You should see a watermark of Ben Franklin on the left side and the letters "USPS" from top to bottom.

6. ZIPPING THROUGH CODES. Need a zip code fast? Online, use the zip code locator at www.usps. com. If you don't have access to a computer, call 800-ASK-USPS for an automated, voice-activated zip code finder.

7. YOUR FACE HERE. Proud dads, brides and narcissists everywhere will love personalized postage stamps that are as good as the real thing. Use any photo that meets certain standards—no pornography or images of infamous people like Hitler, for example. And, no advertising allowed. Go to www.usps.com and follow the links to an approved vendor, such as Endicia, Stamps.com or Zazzle. Pay by credit card—less than $20 for a sheet of 20 stamps—and you'll get your personal stamps in less than one week.

8. STAMP COLLECTORS' HEAVEN. Start or expand a stamp collection. Most post offices stock new issues and mint sets of commemorative stamps, which feature events and people in history, and special stamps, such as the Love and Christmas stamps. These stamps are printed in limited quantities. Work-a-day stamps are called definitive stamps and feature contemporary people, places and causes. They are issued in unlimited quantities and sell for indefinite periods of time.

Protecting Your Personal Data
Be careful. Somebody out there really wants to be you

About 10 million Americans fall victim each year to identity theft, according to the Federal Trade Commission. About one-third of those cases are more than old-fashioned credit card fraud. In full-fledged identity theft, victims' credit card accounts are tapped and private information is used by thieves to open new accounts, secure loans and often to lead parallel lives of luxury. There are some steps to take to protect yourself from becoming an identity or data theft victim. Unfortunately, despite all precautions, there are no guarantees.

Federal agencies and consumer advocates give out well-intentioned advice to victims of identity theft. Some obvious tips are to alert your banks and creditors and to report the crime. Other recommendations sound solid and sensible, but do they help? Here's the lowdown.

WHAT TO DO BEFORE IT HAPPENS

• **Restrict access to your personal data by signing up for the National Do Not Call Registry** (www. donotcall.gov). Remove your name and address from the phone book and reverse directories. Remove your name from the marketing lists of the credit bureaus to reduce credit card solicitations. Go to www.optoutprescreen.com to start.

• **Consider freezing your credit report,** an option available in a growing number of states. Freezing prevents anyone from opening up a new credit file in your name and doesn't otherwise affect your credit rating. (You gain access to it by using a password.)

• **Rein in your Social Security number.** Remove it from your checks, insurance cards and driver's license. Ask your bank not to use it as your identification number. Refuse to give it to merchants and be careful even with medical providers. The only time you are required to give it by law is when a company needs it for government purposes, such as for tax matters and Medicare.

• **Avoid linking your checking to savings.** Use a credit card for purchases rather than a debit card. While individual liability for fraudulent credit card purchases is only $50, it can be higher for debit cards, up to $500 or even all the money in your account in some cases.

• **Do not let your credit cards out of your sight.** Do not let store clerks take away your card on the pretext that there is a "problem." Shred all unneeded documents that contain personal data.

• **Protect your home computer** with virus software and a firewall, especially if you have a high-speed connection.

WHAT TO DO AFTER AN INCIDENT

• **Fraud alerts.** "Place a fraud alert on your credit reports and review your credit reports" is the first tip in the Federal Trade Commission's brochure *Take Charge: Fighting Back Against Identity Theft*, (found on www.ftc.gov). This is one of the most recommended identity theft remedies, but what exactly does a fraud alert do?

"Not enough," says Kerry Smith, a consumer lawyer for the National Association of State Public Interest Groups. Mainly, it means that for 90 days any potential creditor has to take precautions to verify your identity before opening new accounts in your name. Not only is 90 days a short time, but the standards for verifying a consumer's identity are not clearly defined.

An "extended fraud alert," on the other hand, remains on your credit report for seven years. The extended alert requires creditors to contact you if

INSIDE INFO

Who's Vulnerable to Identity Theft?

O Nearly 20 percent of Americans say they've experienced some form of identity theft.

O Odds for the young are higher: 25 percent of those under 30 have been victims, according to a 2005 survey by Experian and the Gallup Organization.

O Geography plays a role. While those in the East (20 percent) and the West (26 percent) are highly vulnerable, the danger drops sharply in the Midwest (12 percent) and South (15 percent).

O Plenty of people are "somewhat" or "very" worried about personal data being stolen: 62 percent fear it happening online, 55 percent in the mail, 53 percent at a store and 47 percent at a restaurant, the survey found.

O Only a paltry 4 percent have checked their credit reports to see if anything's fishy.

—Hubert B. Herring

anyone wants to open an account in your name. That's better and it won't derail your credit. But, it is tough to procure. Consumers need to provide a copy of an official, valid report filed by the consumer with a federal, state or local law enforcement agency, according to the Federal Trade Commission. So, when reporting data theft, don't just call your bank; contact your local police precinct and file a copy with the FTC (877-438-4338).

• **Review your report.** After a data theft incident you are entitled to a free copy of your credit report from each of the three credit agencies: Equifax (800-525-6285), Experian (888-397-3742) and Trans Union (800-680-7289). You can also get one free copy of your credit report per year at www.annualcreditreport.com. Once you get the reports, pore over them

SPENDING

for any suspicious information and report it. In that one in four credit reports contain errors—not fraud, just mistakes—it's worth doing.

• **Freeze your report.** While this step offers the most data protection, so-called security freeze laws are in effect in only a dozen states, with a handful more pending. The beauty of freezing your reports is that only you have the ability to thaw them—and while your access to credit can be delayed for a few days, it's not impaired in any other way.

Some states charge a fee each time you freeze or unfreeze your credit report. Depending on the state, consumers would have to pay those fees (up to $20 in some cases) to each credit bureau.

• **Start fresh?** If your identity has been stolen, you might be tempted to consider starting fresh with a new Social Security number. It doesn't pay. Not only is it difficult to obtain, but your new number is forever linked to the old one, creating even more confusion when employers or banks need to verify your personal data. Better to be aggressive about guarding your current number.

• **Notify the Federal Trade Commission.** E-mail consumerline@ftc.gov, or call the identity theft hotline at 877-IDTHEFT. The FTC has counselors to help victims resolve financial and other problems associated with the crime.

—M. P. Dunleavey

TIMELY TIPS

Maintaining Your Identity

✔ **Privacy Rights Clearinghouse.** (www.privacyrights.org) for preventive measures, fraud watches and privacy tips.

✔ **Identity Theft Resources** (www.idtheftcenter.org) for victim information guides and scam alerts.

Preparing for a Quick Getaway

Forget the family photos, it's the financial and medical records you'll need

If you are like most people, you have documents stashed in various places throughout your home, perhaps some under lock and key. And should danger strike, with your mind racing you won't have the time or wherewithal to figure out which ones you need.

But, new technology is making the tedious task of organizing your records less odious. You can probably secure your records in one afternoon. Even better, doing so has a wonderful side effect: it makes you smarter about how you spend and save money.

First, compile a list of where everything is, such as account numbers and locations of important documents. (See facing page.) The list will help you locate information for the insurance adjuster, for example. This is really the "in case I get hit by a bus" list that financial planners recommend you compile for your heirs. Then, follow these other steps to protect your records and yourself:

RECORD: Once you have made your basic list, save it on a U.S.B. flash drive. A 256-megabyte drive, which you can buy for $20 or less, gives you enough space for that file and all the other suggestions mentioned below.

Several of the big flash-drive makers, like SanDisk and Lexar Media, allow you to encrypt the data, so others cannot read it without knowing the alphanumeric key that unlocks the code. Some are even shock proofed with heavier rubber and plastic coatings. Those will cost about $10 to $20 more, but are certainly worth it when you consider the sensitivity of the data on them. It is also a good idea to copy the contents onto additional drives for backup and for other members of the family.

BONUS: When you are listing the credit cards,

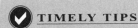
TIMELY TIPS

In Case I Get Hit by a Bus

Keep this list someplace secure, but where family members can get it quickly. Storing it in an encrypted electronic file on a flash drive is a good idea, as long as family members can recall the password for access.

Here are the account numbers for the . . .

✔ **CREDIT CARDS**
  + the toll-free numbers of companies

✔ **BANK ACCOUNTS**
  + PIN numbers or passwords, toll-free numbers

✔ **INVESTMENT ACCOUNTS**
  +online passwords, toll-free numbers

✔ **INSURANCE POLICIES**
  +toll-free numbers

✔ **FAMILY SOCIAL SECURITY NUMBERS**

Here is where the following are stashed . . .

✔ **WILLS**

✔ **LIVING WILL**

✔ **POWER OF ATTORNEY**

✔ **ANY PROPERTY DEEDS**

✔ **INSURANCE POLICIES**

✔ **COMPANY BENEFITS**

✔ **SAFE DEPOSIT BOX KEY**
  and location of box

✔ **LIST (OR PICTURES) OF VALUABLES**
  and their worth

also note the credit limits, so you will know how much you could spend in an emergency. If your credit cards are at their limits now, you are not going to have any cushion to fall back on. So, start paying off balances, beginning with the card carrying the highest interest rate.

SCAN: You will want copies of these documents: tax returns for the last three years (Form 1040 is all you will need in an emergency), a recent pay stub, birth certificates, marriage license, the deed to your home and insurance policy pages that list your coverage. If you do not have a scanner, take the documents to a copy center like Kinko's to scan. Record the image files on the U.S.B. drive.

  BONUS: Check your insurance coverage for potential disasters, like flooding. With homes appreciating in value, you may also find you need to increase coverage.

SHOOT: Some personal finance advisers suggest that you make a spreadsheet listing everything you

own and enter the date and price paid and then file all the receipts, etc. You will never do it. But creating a detailed inventory need not be a major chore if you have a camcorder or digital camera. Walk around each room and take a picture of each item. Then, either store all the photos on a memory card (you can load all the photos on a 256 MB or 512 MB card). Or you can transfer them to the same U.S.B. drive with your other documents.

  Describe each object on the camcorder soundtrack or in the file name of the digital photo. Make an extra copy on another card or drive. For additional protection, you could upload the photos—as well as all your beloved family photos—to one of the free online photo services like Flickr. com, Picasa.com, Snapfish.com or Kodakgallery. com. Anybody you choose can then have access to them from any computer anywhere. (Make sure to set the privacy options, though.)

  BONUS: You are going to discover a lot of stuff you no longer want or need. Sell it or donate it and

SPENDING

take a tax deduction. Intuit, maker of Quicken and TurboTax, sells a $20 program called ItsDeductible that estimates the value of donated items, but Bankrate.com and Salvationarmyusa.org have free valuation guides.

SECURE: Now you can place your health history as well as digitized copies of X-rays, scans and electrocardiograms on the same encrypted flash drive.

Those with serious medical conditions may want to consider a product sold by the nonprofit organization that developed the MedicAlert bracelet 50 years ago. It sells a special U.S.B. flash drive on its Web site (www.medicalert.org) called the E-HealthKey for $85. Pop the flash drive into any computer and a screen flashes with your medical condition to alert emergency room personnel, for instance, to an allergy or your use of a pacemaker. Medical information you enter with the help of a user-friendly program right on the drive is encrypted. For an additional $20-a-year fee, MedicAlert uploads your data to its server, so you have a backup.

Bonus: The E-HealthKey software also plots your weight, cholesterol or anything you regularly record onto a graph. If you are going to run for your life, clutching your flash drive, you had better be healthy.

—Damon Darlin

Going Out Feet First
Here's how to keep funeral costs in check

Every year, Americans arrange funerals for more than two million deceased at an average cost of $6,500 per funeral, not including cemetery costs. Many funerals go for $10,000 and up, ranking in some cases among the most expensive purchases many consumers make. A little research and planning can help keep funeral costs in check. Here are some tips from consumer advocates:

• **Shop around.** Call or visit at least three funeral homes before choosing one. The Federal Trade Commission's Funeral Rule, adopted in 1984, requires funeral directors to give you an itemized price list of their goods and services. Some will try to sell a package deal, but keep in mind that you have the right to buy the items separately. For example, funeral providers cannot refuse to handle a casket you bought elsewhere, nor can they charge you a fee for doing so. They can, however, charge you a "basic services fee," which runs around $1,500 and covers items such as preparing notices, sheltering the remains and coordinating arrangements with the cemetery or crematory.

• **Check out a range of caskets.** At an average price of more than $2,000 for a metal, wood, fiberboard or plastic model, a casket is the single most expensive item in a traditional funeral. Mahogany, bronze or copper models run up to $10,000 or more. Be sure to see a price list and detailed descriptions of all available caskets before you look at actual models. Ask to see lower-priced models, such as those made of pine; chances are they won't be prominently featured.

Metal caskets are often described as having special sealing or protective features that jack up the price. But no casket, regardless of its materials or cost, can permanently keep out water or other natural elements. In fact, federal law prohibits any claim that a casket's features can preserve the remains indefinitely.

• **Clarify plot charges upfront.** Cemetery sites are generally higher in urban areas. A plot runs from $500 to several thousand, but that's just the start. Removing earth and filling it after internment costs from $350 to $1,500, and can double on weekends and holidays. Cemetery operators require a grave liner or vault (average cost, nearly $800) to enclose the casket. A headstone or marker runs from $500 to several thousand, depending on materials and design. Ongoing grave-site care is often included in the price of the site but some cemeteries tack on 10 percent or more for maintaining it. For mausoleum burial, you will need to buy a crypt; costs are comparable to buying a burial plot.

• **Cremation can be cheaper.** Cremation services can be obtained directly from a crematory or cremation society. In some places, a simple cremation goes for as low as $300, not including an urn, which can run from $85 to $1,500 and up, or a crypt or memorial site. All told, the average cremation costs around $1,500. A casket is not required for a direct cremation; a simple unfinished wood box or alternative container will do. Undertakers are required to make such an alternative available.

• **Memorial societies can help.** Memorial or funeral societies are nonprofit organizations run mostly by volunteers. For a onetime membership fee of around $30, your local society can help plan a funeral and suggest a mortuary or crematorium with a good reputation. Members generally spend around $1,000 on a funeral, due to reduced prices on many goods and services. To find a memorial society in your area, call the Funeral Consumers Alliance at 800-765-0107 or go to www.funerals.org.

• **Plan yes, prepay no.** Setting aside money for your funeral and making your wishes known to loved ones is wise, but paying for the arrangements in advance, through so-called pre-need plans, is risky. Consumer advocates say there are too many unknowns: What happens if the funeral home goes under? What if you move out of the area? Or, you decide at the end that you'd rather be cremated? Pre-need plans are often nontransferable, nonrefundable and sometimes carry hidden fees that your survivors may end up having to pay. Further, many states don't offer full protection for pre-need plans. So, if you change your mind, you could lose a bundle.

One way to protect your funeral money, suggests the Funeral Consumers Alliance, is to set up a Totten trust fund, or pay-on-death account, with your bank. Choose your beneficiary, and deposit whatever amount you wish. The trust is portable and accrues interest to your account. When you die, the money goes directly to the beneficiary, who can use it to fulfill your funeral wishes. (For more about creating a will, see "Do I Need A Will?," page 789.)

SPENDING

The Truth About Embalming

Preparing a body for public viewing nearly always involves embalming and cosmetic restoration, processes that can add $600 or more to a funeral bill. Is embalming otherwise necessary or required? Not really.

• **Embalming generally is not necessary** if the body is buried or cremated within a reasonable time after death.

• **Embalming is not required by law** except in certain cases when a body is transported across state lines.

• **Embalming does not preserve the deceased's body indefinitely;** it merely masks the appearance of death and temporarily postpones decomposition.

• **Embalming chemicals are highly toxic.** Embalmers must wear a respirator and full-body covering while performing the procedure.

• **Refrigeration is an alternative to embalming** for maintaining a body intact while awaiting a funeral service. Although not all funeral homes have refrigeration facilities, most hospitals do.

• **Embalming is common only in the United States and Canada.** Orthodox Jews and Muslims consider the procedure a desecration of the body.

SOURCE: Funeral Consumers Alliance

Autos

What Dealers Won't Tell You
With the right data, the salesman will be at your mercy

Most people approach buying a new car with fear and trepidation. But there's no need to feel at the mercy of a car salesman if you've done your homework. Here are some expert tips for gaining control of your buying experience and saving money in the process.

Knock at least 10 percent off the sticker price. For example, if you're interested in a $25,000 car, estimate your monthly payments based on a purchase price of about $22,500. Then search out cars that fit your budget, but stay away from the dealership until you are fully armed with facts. If you do go into a showroom to check out car models, don't engage a salesman. If approached, say you are just looking.

Research the cars on your list using guides such as *Consumer Reports* magazine and *Kiplinger's Personal Finance,* or Web sites like ConsumerReports.org, Edmunds.com and KelleyBlueBook.com. Check a car's reliability, safety, and performance Sometimes you may have to choose between style and reliability. Choosing style alone could mean losing money to depreciation and the repair shop.

Don't begrudge a dealer a modest profit. Books and services provide basic car cost numbers. But the amount a dealer pays for a car varies, sometimes from day to day. Some services track dealer costs on a daily basis. One of them, Fighting Chance (800-288-1134 or www.fightingchance.com) provides a package of data on a car, including factory incentives and other factors that can change a car's price. The service costs $34.95. Once you've determined an accurate dealer's cost, figure in a reasonable amount for profit.

Before going to a showroom, solicit bids by phone. Call a number of local dealers. Tell them that you've done your research and are shopping for the best offer. Describe the car you want, with as much detail as possible, and tell them the names of competing dealers. Notify each of them that if they are interested in selling you a car, they should call you with a price. Chances are you will get bids from interested dealers within a few days. Then, go to the dealer with the best offer.

Consider using an auto-buying service that will do the bidding for you. One example: CarBargains (800-475-7283 or www.checkbook.org), operated by the Center for the Study of Services, a nonprofit group in Washington, D.C., solicits bids from five dealers in your area. You get the dealer quote sheets as well as information on financing, service contracts and the value of your trade-in car. The $190 fee will spare you the hassle of having to tangle directly with dealers yourself.

❝

Seventy-five percent of female car buyers plan to bring a man with them to the dealer to ensure fair treatment.

•••

ALTERNATIVES TO KICKING THE TIRES

You don't have to get yourself covered with grease to tell quickly whether a used car has been well maintained. The following tips for reading a car's history will save you lots of headaches later:

STEERING WHEEL: *There should be no play for power steering when the engine is off, and no more than two inches for manual steering*

INTERIOR: *Resale value as well as comfort will be affected by seats and carpets that look shabby or smell musty.*

FLUID LEAKS: *Checking a car's fluid levels and condition is like taking a person's blood pressure and doing a blood test. They can indicate both present and future problems. Oil spots around the engine or beneath the*

vehicle are obvious signs that something's leaking. Other signs are less obvious: transmission fluids should be pink, not dirty.

BODY CONDITION: *Rust, especially in the rocker panels under the doors, in the trunk or around the wheels is bad news. Sooner rather than later, your car will fall apart.*

TIRES: *Original tires should be good for 25,000 miles. Uneven tire tread can mean an alignment problem, which is easily remedied*

SUSPENSION: *Does the car look lopsided from the side or rear? Bad springs are probably the culprit. Does the car bounce more than a couple times when you push down hard on a corner? The shocks or struts could need replacing. If a front tire can be noticeably lifted by pulling on the top of the tire with both hands, you may have bad bearings or suspension joints.*

BRAKES: *Look for wear on the pads or scars on the rotor disk.*

Be wary of end of model-year deals. The end-of-the-month rule generally holds. Most car salespeople have monthly quotas to meet and may be willing to give you a bargain simply to make the sale. But buying a year-end model at a discount doesn't make up for the depreciation factor: at that point the car has already lost 20 to 25 percent of its value.

Walking out is a good negotiating strategy. The best you have. Keep the process with the salesperson impersonal. Submit an offer and say that if he or she turns you down, you will simply take your business to the competitor. The dealer may let you walk away, but chances are he'll come get you in the parking lot. At that point, you have the upper hand. Say that you will not go back in unless they accept your price.

New Ways to Buy Used Cars
How to get a good deal off the used car lot

Technology has radically changed the way we buy a car. If you walk into a dealership without first downloading the invoice price information on a new car from a site like Consumer Reports (www.consumerreports.org), you are acting foolishly. The availability of information about how much a dealer is paying for a car has actually made the once-dreaded car-buying experience more enjoyable.

That's not the case when buying a used car, however. It's still perilous. Almost everyone has heard that a new car loses an average of 12 percent of its value the moment it is driven off the dealer's lot. Economists tell us this happens not because the new car is losing a premium, but rather that the used car carries a "risk discount." That's because it is hard for a buyer of a used car to trust a seller, who could very well be passing off a lemon he just bought new. So used cars are more heavily discounted for the risk.

Getting a good price boils down to whether you have better information than the seller. One way to even the odds is to check a service like Carfax (www. carfax.com) to trace a car's history. The cost is $19.99 for one vehicle history; $24.99 for unlimited histories. You'll find more than four billion reports on indi-

vidual car histories in their database. Other sources of more general information are consumer groups, which issued warnings after Hurricane Katrina in 2005, for example, about flood-damaged used cars entering the market. A car damaged by water can never be fully repaired, although unscrupulous sellers can use a number of ways to "wash" a car's history. The solution? Find someone you can trust.

Buying a "certified" used car is an increasingly popular option. This concept, popularized by Toyota's Lexus luxury brand, lets you buy a formerly leased or owned car that has been cleaned up, inspected and often sold with a manufacturer's warranty. For those reasons, certified cars command a premium over other used cars. When buying a certified used car, work with a dealer who also sells new cars. He may have more of a reputation to protect.

Also consider that a used luxury car may actually be a better bet than a used economy car. Drivers of luxury cars tend to be a bit more fashion conscious, so they will unload a car for the next new thing long before the car has hit that critical point of things starting to go wrong.

—Damon Darlin

 TIMELY TIPS

Let's Make a Deal

How to assume someone else's lease

Leaseholders who want to escape their multiyear contracts before they expire have some friends on the Internet: Web sites designed to create a secondary market for car leases. Sellers post descriptions of their cars and the terms of their leases on the Web site. Many also offer to pay some amount of cash to induce a buyer to take on the responsibility of making the rest of the payments.

Here's what it costs to assume or escape a car lease at two prominent lease marketplaces on the Internet. These fees are in addition to any charged by finance companies for the legal transfer of the lease, which can run as high as $500.

✔ **LEASETRADER.COM**
  Buyer's fees: $29.95 for contact information on sellers.
  Seller's fees: minimum $39.95 to post vehicle, $149.95 transaction fee.

✔ **SWAPALEASE.COM**
  Buyer's fees: $34.95 to $79.95
  Seller's fees: $99 to $149.95

—Patrick McGeehan

The Car of the Future?

100 M.P.G. plug-in hybrids could be the Hot New Thing

Imagine a passenger car that averaged more than 100 miles per gallon—or, if used only for short trips, 1,000 miles per gallon. What if it could cost the equivalent of only 75 cents a gallon to operate and needed to go to a filling station only every other month?

Well, all that technology exists today, as a handful of demonstration vehicles prove. The cars are known as "plug-in hybrids." They are similar to hybrids like the wildly popular Toyota Prius, but have

Cars Across the Land

Where you live determines what you drive

Geography may be destiny when it comes to which cars consumers are most likely to buy. "If you want to generalize, the East and West Coasts are dominated by imports and specialized, or luxury, brands, while in the center of the country domestic brands still hold sway," says Tom Libby of the Power Information Network, an affiliate of J.D. Power & Associates.

Libby generated some statistics on vehicles sold in 26 major metropolitan markets from Jan. 1 to July 24, 2005. From those figures, it seems that the country rides together in Ford F-150 pickup trucks and Toyota Camrys. Those vehicles appear in the top-10 list in every market but Detroit, where the Camry is out, and in New York, where F-150's are not de rigueur. Otherwise, differences in buying habits around the country fall into these patterns:

PHILADELPHIA—This city seems to be the most eclectic market for vehicles. No brand here sells more than 2.39 percent overall.

DETROIT—It is no surprise that the top-10 cars on the Detroit roster are domestic, but no. 3 is the Chevrolet Impala, not one of the more popular cars nationwide.

OKLAHOMA—If you are not buying a pickup in this market, you are probably out of the loop. The six most popular vehicles, and seven of the top 10, sold in Oklahoma were domestic pickups, totaling 27.25 percent of all vehicles sold. But, notes a spokesman for Edmunds.com: "More than 80 percent of those who buy pickups don't use the bed for anything substantial even once."

NEW YORK METROPOLITAN REGION—The only market without a pickup truck on its top-10 list.

NORTHERN CALIFORNIA AND SEATTLE—With their reputations for environmentalism, it should be no surprise that these markets sell an overwhelming proportion of the Toyota Prius hybrid.

SOUTHERN CALIFORNIA AND MIAMI—Luxury imports are sold mostly in warm-weather climates that have older populations.

MIDWEST—Cadillac DeVilles (the 2006 model has been renamed the DTS) are well liked in this region, selling best in Chicago, Indianapolis and Pittsburgh, but also in Orlando and Tampa, Fla., where many Midwesterners retire or winter.

CALIFORNIA   Over all, Japanese models are the three most popular vehicles in Northern and Southern California.

THE SOUTH—Four decades after its sporty debut, the Ford Mustang still has partisans. Early on, it was a favorite among young suburban buyers, but now its best customers tend to be in the South.

—Robert Strauss

bigger batteries and at night would be plugged into a standard 120-volt outlet to charge the batteries.

They can be built to have a 30-to-50-mile range before the gasoline engine needs to be used at all. So for someone who commutes 15 miles each way to work and rarely takes long drives, a plug-in hybrid usually functions as an electric vehicle and relies on gas only on rare occasions. "If you used it only locally, you would go to a gas station only a couple of times a year," says Felix Kramer, founder of CalCars. org, a nonprofit in Palo Alto, Calif., that converted a regular Prius to a plug-in hybrid.

Estimates of gas mileage with a plug-in tend to be 100 miles per gallon and up, but that depends on how the vehicle is used. People who only putter around their neighborhood could go thousands of miles on a gallon of gas—and a supply of household current. Another advantage is that plug-ins fit easily

Beyond Gasoline

It may well take government incentives before auto companies take the financial risk of mass-producing alternative energy vehicles. Until then, here are some of the gas alternatives out there—what they are, and why some are promising and some less so.

E85:

Blend of corn-based ethanol (grain alcohol) and 15 percent gas. Roughly 4.5 million vehicles on the road can use it instead of gas.

PROS: Comes from the Midwest, not the Mideast.

- Cheaper at the moment by 40 to 50 cents a gallon.
- Lower emissions, most studies show.

CONS: Broad use would mean turning over swaths of farmland to corn production.

- Could drive up food prices.
- Cheaper because of subsidies.

NATURAL GAS:

The same gas used to heat the home used to fuel the car. Honda and G.M. make vehicles modified to run on it.

PROS: Lower emissions.

- People with natural gas heat can refuel at home.

CONS: Prices are rising.

- Might not help energy security much.

HYDROGEN FUEL CELL:

Vehicles combine hydrogen with oxygen from the air to set off a chemical reaction and generate electricity.

PROS: Only tailpipe emission is water vapor.

- Alternative to Mideast oil.

CONS: Substantial technical and cost hurdles.

- Infrastructure hurdles—retrofitting gas stations to carry hydrogen.
- Various ways of producing the hydrogen have environmental and infrastructure ramifications.

ELECTRIC:

Vehicle powered by batteries. Automakers built thousands but have largely abandoned the technology.

PROS: No tailpipe emissions.

- Another domestic alternative to oil.
- Overnight charging beneficial for utilities.

CONS: Various ways of producing the electricity have environmental and infrastructure issues.

- Limited range between charges.
- Charging can take several hours.

BIODIESEL:

Ranges from vehicles running on French-fry grease to vehicles using diesel fuel created from soybeans or vegetable oils. Hobbyists retrofit vehicles to run on used vegetable oil; normal diesel vehicles can use biodiesel blends.

PROS: Can reduce global warming pollution.

- Domestic resource.

CONS: Could worsen or improve smog pollution, depending on several factors.

- Cost hurdles.
- Currently limited availability.

PLUG-IN HYBRID:

Hybrid electric vehicles that can be plugged in to the grid. Just a handful on the road, though enthusiasts are beginning to modify Toyota Priuses to plug in.

PROS: Runs a lot farther on battery.

- More use of domestic energy than regular hybrid.
- Lower emissions.

CONS: Current battery technology might not be durable enough, though there is debate.

- Added cost.
- Lack of enthusiasm from hybrid makers.

—Danny Hakim

into the existing infrastructure, unlike cars fueled by hydrogen. At least at home, the infrastructure is as simple as an extension cord.

While the batteries still aren't perfect, supporters say that plug-in hybrids can be mass-produced today for only about $3,000 more than a conventional hybrid (which already costs $3,000 more than a regular auto). Skeptics say that the additional cost might be greater, up to $15,000 more than a regular gas car—but even that might find a market among car buyers seeking the Hot New Thing.

The higher sticker price is compensated for by lower operating costs, with power from the electrical grid. Indeed, if it is recharged at night when rates drop, a plug-in hybrid could be run for the equivalent of 75 cents a gallon or less.

—Nicholas D. Kristof

A Racer on Driving Defensively

One of the world's greatest drivers shares his tips on the curves ahead

I f avoiding the pesky pothole on your street corner is your biggest daily challenge, try stopping on a dime at over 200 m.p.h. or taking razor sharp curves at speeds that would make your hair stand on end. For premier race car driver, John Andretti, those feats are all in a day's work. The nephew of racing legend Mario Andretti (John's father, Aldo, is Mario's twin), Andretti says he's raced cars "practically since birth." Along the way, he's driven dragsters, midgets, dirt cars, sprint cars, you name it, winning such prestigious races as the 24 Hours of Daytona and becoming a top driver on Nascar's elite Winston Cup circuit. Here

SPENDING

WHAT IT TAKES TO STOP IN TIME

Tailgaters beware: the stopping distance required for a car going 35 m.p.h. is just over half a football field, even when the road is dry. At 65 m.p.h. the distance required is equal to the length of one and a third football fields.

SOURCE: National Highway Traffic Safety Administration

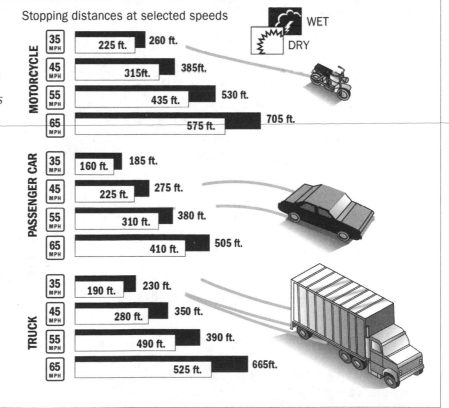

Stopping distances at selected speeds

WET
DRY

MOTORCYCLE
- 35 MPH: 225 ft. / 260 ft.
- 45 MPH: 315ft. / 385ft.
- 55 MPH: 435 ft. / 530 ft.
- 65 MPH: 575 ft. / 705 ft.

PASSENGER CAR
- 35 MPH: 160 ft. / 185 ft.
- 45 MPH: 225 ft. / 275 ft.
- 55 MPH: 310 ft. / 380 ft.
- 65 MPH: 410 ft. / 505 ft.

TRUCK
- 35 MPH: 190 ft. / 230 ft.
- 45 MPH: 280 ft. / 350 ft.
- 55 MPH: 490 ft. / 390 ft.
- 65 MPH: 525 ft. / 665ft.

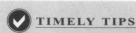

TIMELY TIPS

For Safety, First Buckle Up

Then check these sources to find out how your car will fare in a crash

Road fatality rates are lower than ever, but there are still more than 30,000 deaths a year in cars, minivans, S.U.V.'s and pickup trucks, and many more injuries. When considering safety, these sources can help:

✔ **For free information,** go to the National Highway Traffic Safety Administration at www.safercars.gov, and the Insurance Institute for Highway Safety, a research group financed by auto insurers at www.iihs.org. A database of investigations and complaints is at www.odi.nhtsa.dot.gov/cars/problems/recalls/recallsearch.cfm.

✔ *Consumer Reports* magazine (www.consumer-reports.org) compiles testing results from the government and insurers, runs vehicles through dozens of drive and handling tests and evaluates various design attributes, from blind spots to the difficulty of installing child seats. Looking up a vehicle on its Web site costs $26 a year, or $4.95 monthly.

✔ **To find out how specific car models fared** on government ratings from front and side crashes and rollover tests, go to www.safercars.gov. Click on the listing for each test to bring up a more detailed explanation of the methodology behind the testing. For example, for rollover testing, the star rating is largely computed from a mathematical formula factoring in a vehicle's dimensions; lesser emphasis is put on tests conducted on a track, because most rollovers do not occur on a uniform surface.

—Danny Hakim

---

are Andretti's tips on being a safer driver, off the race track.

Q What is the best way to handle turns and curves?

Always at a safe speed. When the road is dry and it's clear out, if the speed limit says 35 m.p.h., a corner should be quite easily taken at 35. At the same time, you have to be aware that if there's a car coming from the other direction, that car may not be totally under control—it may be coming toward you at a high speed and maybe the driver has lost control of the vehicle. If you're not prepared and don't pull off to the side of the road, for example, it could be a deadly situation for all.

Q What has racing taught you about tailgating and trailing other vehicles?

Appropriate distances between cars vary with the situation. With today's traffic, there are few opportunities to maintain large gaps between cars, therefore, drivers really must pay attention.

My rule is, no matter how fast I'm driving, if someone wants to go faster, they're welcome to pass me. In fact, I try to make it easy for them to get by, which is the opposite of what 90 percent of drivers might do. Most would speed up, or become angry and tailgate. That makes no sense to me. When I'm not on the track, I'm not in a race.

Q What's the best way to change lanes or pass other vehicles?

Many drivers have trouble changing lanes safely. On the highway, for example, you often find the "left-lane hanger," who rides in the left lane no matter what. They make others pass them in the right lane, creating a difficult situation. Often, they speed up as people try to pass, making it worse. There are plenty of open spots in the slow lane. Let others pass you and then get behind them. Most of the time, you don't even have to slow down to allow them to pass.

HOLDING YOUR LIQUOR

Approximate percentage of alcohol in the blood one hour after drinking

EXAMPLES OF ALCOHOLIC DRINKS	AMOUNT OF ALCOHOL (oz.)	BODY WEIGHT (LBS.)					
		100	120	140	160	180	200
Three Dubonnet cocktails	3.0	.252	.208	.176	.152	.134	.119
Four Bloody Marys, Daiquiris, Whiskey Sours	2.8	.234	.193	.163	.141	.124	.110
Three Martinis, Manhattans	2.4	.199	.163	.138	.119	.104	.092
Two Mai Tais, Mint Juleps	2.2	.181	.149	.125	.108	.094	.083
Four Champagne cocktails	2.0	.163	.134	.113	.097	.084	.075
Two Margaritas	1.8	.146	.119	.100	.086	.067	.066
Two Martinis, Manhattans	1.6	.128	.104	.087	.075	.065	.057
Two Highballs, Bloody Marys	1.4	.110	.089	.075	.063	.055	.048
Two 5-oz. glasses table wine	1.1	.075	.063	.054	.047	.042	.038
Two Beers	1.0	.075	.060	.049	.041	.035	.030
One Black Russian	0.8	.057	.045	.037	.030	.025	.021
One Sloe Gin Fizz	0.6	.039	.030	.024	.019	.015	.012
One 1-oz. cordial or liqueur	0.4	.021	.015	.011	.008	.006	.004

THE MEANING OF TIPSY

The bold figures represent the blood alcohol content past which you should not drive:

BLOOD ALCOHOL CONTENT	EFFECTS ON FEELING AND BEHAVIOR	EFFECTS ON DRIVING ABILITY
.40 **.20** **.19** **.18**	**At this point, most people have passed out.**	**Hopefully, driver passed out before trying to get into vehicle.**
.17 **.16** **.15** **.14** **.13**	**Major impairment of all physical and mental functions. Irresponsible behavior. Euphoria. Some difficulty standing, walking and talking**	**Distortion of all perception, judgment. Driving erratic. Driver in a daze.**
.12 **.11** **.10**	**Difficulty performing gross motor skills. Uncoordinated behavior. Definite impairment of mental abilities, judgment and memory.**	**Judgment seriously affected. Physical difficulty in driving a vehicle.**
.09 .08 .07	Feeling of relaxation. Mild sedation. Exaggeration of emotions and behavior. Slight impairment of motor skills. Increase in reaction time.	Drivers take too long to decide and act. Motor skills (such as braking) are impaired. Reaction time is increased.
.06 .05 .02	Absence of observable effects. Mild alteration of feelings, slight intensification of existing moods.	Mild changes. Most drivers seem a bit moody. Bad driving habits slightly pronounced.

SOURCES: National Clearinghouse for Alcohol and Drug Information; National Safety Council

SPENDING

❓ Is a stick shift superior to an automatic transmission in terms of safety?

Both are equally safe in dry and sunny conditions. I find that in very snowy and ice conditions, a stick shift provides more control. Often in an automatic, when you approach a stop sign and the road is icy, if you don't put the car in neutral, you're really fighting the vehicle, because it wants to go forward. In a car with a stick-shift transmission, not only can you switch to a higher gear to get going and avoid wheel-spin, but you can also use the neutral position and the rear tire to slow you down a bit, giving you more control.

❓ How do you alter your driving for various conditions, such as poor visibility, bad weather, etc.?

You should drive within your control. Obviously, that means different things for different people. The conditions I race in are not always ideal. Often, I can hardly see ahead of me and I have to adapt to very difficult situations. On the road, you should drive at whatever speed is necessary for safety. However, if you feel you must drive at a very slow speed, it's important to put on your hazard lights so you won't get hit in the back because drivers can't see you. Extreme conditions require the smart driver to drive within his own means. Again, remember that even though you may be in control of your car, that doesn't mean everyone is, so be constantly aware of other drivers.

❓ If you are approaching an accident or dangerous situation, what is the best way to proceed?

The whole time I drive, I'm always looking for escape routes from potential problems. That's become natural to me. As you go down the road, always be prepared for anything that might confront you. Be aware of the limitations of your car. Understand your car and how it will respond to situations in order to avoid accidents. You could save a life or serious damage to the car by driving defensively.

❓ What other safety advice can you give drivers?

Pay attention. I get more frustrated with drivers who aren't courteous and don't pay attention than with those who drive too fast. I just let the fast drivers pass so that I can see them. Don't get angry at situations that are beyond your control. A car takes more lives every year than guns. It can be a very deadly weapon and should be treated with respect.

ℹ️ **INSIDE INFO**

High Marks for Low Rollover

○ Rollovers only account for about 3 percent of all auto accidents but one third of all fatalities—or more than 10,000 deaths per year nationwide. S.U.V.'s and pickups are particularly vulnerable.

○ The only cars to get top rankings in all government and insurance industry tests in 2005: the Volvo S80 and Honda's Acura RL.

○ Many of the cars that ranked highest have six air bags, two front, two side and two curtain, which form a barrier across the driver-side and passenger windows.

—Danny Hakim

Helping Your Child Drive Safely

Bad things can happen when cars and children come together. How parents can help

Of the three major initiatives taking place nationwide in recent years to reduce accidents among teenage drivers, two involve parents. One requires parents to certify that they have spent a certain minimum amount of time practicing driving with their children. The other trend is the use of "contracts" between parents and new drivers outlining the rules of the road.

The third major initiative, which has become law in a majority of states, is graduated licensing, which requires new drivers to pass a probationary driving period before they can acquire an unrestricted license.

Contracts and supervised driving both focus on building better habits from the beginning—an approach that makes sense, experts say, because the first five months of driving have been found to be the most dangerous. While not regulated by law, contracts are becoming increasingly popular. Some Web sites, like DriveHomeSafe.com, offer detailed advice on setting rules between parents and teenagers. In some states, such as Maine, for example, parents can get sample contracts from the state's Web site, and copies are also provided to driver-education schools for distribution to families.

Contracts cover everything from who is allowed in the car to how late the children can drive and who pays for the gas. It can also avoid conflict down the road, says Maine's secretary of state, Dan A. Gwadosky, when teenagers may try to angle for more freedoms. He says parents tell him, "We sat down. We discussed it. And now we just let the contract do the talking."

Some states have also begun requiring parents to spend a certain number of hours teaching their children how to drive, going beyond driver's education programs. In Maryland, for example, parents must certify that they have spent 40 hours in the car with their children.

Statistics show that increasing restrictions on young drivers are reducing accidents—in part because some teenagers are simply waiting to drive until they are 18, when they qualify for an unrestricted license. And if they don't drive, they don't crash.

—Eric Nagourney

 INSIDE INFO

Permission to Drive

○ In all 50 states, anyone applying for a first driver's license must take tests for vision, knowledge of state driving laws and driving skills.

○ Forty-three states and the District of Columbia require learner's permits before getting a license. In Alaska, Iowa, Kansas and North and South Dakota, the minimum age for getting a permit is 14. In most other states the age is 15. In a handful of states, such as Connecticut, North Carolina and New Jersey, new drivers must wait until 16.

○ In most states, the minimum age for getting a driver's license is 16. A few exceptions include South Dakota, with the lowest minimum of 14 and a half, and New Jersey, with the highest age of 17.

Choosing a Driving School

How to find a driving school that will train your teen well

For teenagers, getting a driver's license is a rite of passage; for parents it can be a source of high anxiety. In fact, young drivers ages 16 to 20 make up only 7 percent of licensed drivers, but suffer 14 percent of the fatalities and are involved in 20 percent of all reported accidents. Inexperience is the main culprit in teen accidents. For many years, parents relied on driver-education courses at public schools to teach teens basic driving skills. But, as budget cuts and liability costs curtail such programs, the solution for many parents is to turn to professional driving schools.

Locating a driving school is the easy part. There are hundreds—from one-man shops to nationwide operations. Here's a quick guide to choosing one that's best for your child and your peace of mind:

SPENDING

EXPERT ANSWER

Saturday Drivers

● **Do holidays, with their heavier traffic, result in more deaths than other weekends?**

No. The number of deaths during a holiday weekend is no greater than during any other weekend, according to the National Highway Traffic Safety Administration.

Even New Year's Eve is not so bad. From 1999 to 2003, the average number of fatalities on Jan. 1 was 149, worse than the average Sunday in those years (132) but not as bad as the average Saturday (151). The average number of deaths on Dec. 31 over those years was 117.

Finding Schools: High schools often provide a list of driving schools. Many local chapters of the Automobile Association of America also operate driving schools (www.aaa.com).

Checking References: Confirm a school's accreditation by asking for the phone number of its accrediting organization, as well as information on its standards. Regulations vary from state to state, and a license does not guarantee a good school, but the most prominent seal of approval comes from the Driving School Association of the Americas (www.thedsaa.org). Members are provided with up-to-date technology and teaching methods. Reputable schools will also offer names of past customers as references.

Reviewing the School: Finalize your selection only after visiting each school on your short list. Check the following points:

- Have instructors successfully completed professional developmental courses? The D.S.A.A., which is the international organization of driving schools and the American Driver and Traffic Safety Education Association are among the most prominent instructional driving associations.

- Classroom lessons should work in tandem with car sessions. A total of 30 classroom hours is average. Beginners learn best with two 45-minute in-car lessons each week, totaling six hours of behind-the-wheel training under varying circumstances and driving environments.

- For the classroom sessions, are textbooks current and in good condition? Each student should also receive a copy of the state's driver's handbook.

- Are instructional vehicles late-model cars in good condition? Some states bar the use of driving-school vehicles more than four years old. Check that the cars have dual-control brakes, power steering and power brakes, along with safety belts and air bags, of course.

When to Hang Up the Keys

When older drivers should find alternative transportation

It's not unusual these days for people in their Medicare years to drive thousands of miles to visit family and friends or escape summer's heat or winter's fury. By 2020, more than 40 million Americans 70 and older will be licensed drivers, and these older drivers are now driving more miles a year, and at older ages than ever before.

Yet, compared with middle-age drivers, older drivers are about three times as likely to be involved in a crash per mile driven. They are also more likely than younger drivers to die as a result of a crash of similar severity. Are older drivers putting themselves and others at risk?

AARP, the advocacy group for older Americans, lists 15 warning signs that should alert drivers to the need to limit driving or stop driving entirely. (For more information on driver safety for older motorists, try www.seniordrivers.org and www.aarp.org/55alive.) If you have just one or two of these signs, you should consider having your driving assessed by a professional, attending a driver refresher course or both.

- Feeling less comfortable and more nervous or fearful while driving
- Having difficulty staying in your lane
- Experiencing more close calls behind the wheel
- Getting more dents or scrapes on your car or on other objects
- Finding it hard to judge gaps in traffic at intersections and on highway entrance and exit ramps
- Having other drivers honk at you more often
- Being told that friends or relatives no longer want to ride with you
- Getting lost more often
- Failing to notice vehicles or pedestrians on the sides of the road while looking straight ahead
- Having trouble paying attention to traffic signals, road signs and pavement markings
- Responding slowly to unexpected situations
- Becoming easily distracted or having difficulty concentrating while driving
- Finding it hard to turn to check over your shoulder when you are backing up or changing lanes
- Getting more traffic tickets or warnings
- Experiencing a worsening of medical conditions or the need to take medications that can impair driving safety

—Jane E. Brody

Help When You're Stranded
Roadside help comes in many guises today

It used to be that when your car broke down on the road, AAA—a name virtually synonymous with roadside help—was the only game in town. Now, consumers have many options from a variety of sources, including car makers, insurers, even cellphone companies.

Most of the big car manufacturers—excluding Honda and Toyota—offer roadside assistance as part of their warranty package for the first three to five years, or 36,000 to 50,000 miles, depending on your deal. With some car brands, such as Mercedes-Benz, you have the assistance as long as you own the car.

Some credit card, insurance and cellphone companies also offer services. Verizon Wireless and Cingular Wireless ($2.99 a month; $35.88 a year) send assistance as long as you have your cellphone with you. They supply the usual tire changes, lockout services, jump-starts and fuel delivery if you have run out of gas. Services differ, so check a plan's rules concerning towing distances, number

SPENDING

ⓘ INSIDE INFO

Licensing Older Drivers

○ Rarely is anything more than a vision test required to renew a senior's driver's license, and renewal cycles vary from state to state. While most states require renewals every 4 or 5 years, in four states it is 8 years, in two states it is 10 years and in one (Arizona) no renewal is required until age 65.

○ Colorado shortens the time between renewals starting at age 61, but Illinois doesn't start until 81. Virginia doesn't require a vision test at renewal until age 80; Illinois and New Hampshire require a road test starting at 75.

—Jane E. Brody

of calls you can make per year and other features. Verizon offers towing in case of mechanical failure or accidents, for example, while Cingular does so only if the breakdown is caused by mechanical problems. Since the plan is attached to the phone, not the car, these services are particularly appealing for someone who does not own a car but wants coverage when renting one.

A heavily advertised assistance system available in many newer General Motors vehicles is OnStar, which uses wireless and global positioning system technology and car battery power to provide live voice assistance. The service provides emergency help, contacts you if your airbags deploy, finds a stolen car and, with the more expensive plan, gives driving directions. OnStar service is free for the first year; afterward, subscriptions range from $16.95 a month ($199 yearly) to $34.95 a month ($399 annually).

The old standby, AAA, with 61 clubs in North America, is still by far the largest provider of roadside assistance in the country. Depending on where you live, membership costs $38 to $80 a year. Aside from standard roadside assistance, membership entitles you to other AAA offerings, such as travel packages and information, insurance and car rentals. AAA Plus, which becomes available in your third year of membership, costs $85 a year. It includes extras, such as up to 100 miles of free towing, up to $100 in locksmith services and free passport photos. Membership also gets you trip interruption reimbursement to cover "reasonable costs" if you are stranded more than 100 miles from home.

Other, smaller companies offer similar services, including GM Motor Club, at $49.95 a year, and Better World Club, "an environmentally friendly auto club" that also offers roadside assistance to bicycle riders for $39.95 a year. If you belong to GM Motor Club, and your car is disabled more than 100 miles from home, the club will reimburse you up to $750 for meals, lodging and transportation within five days of the incident.

It's not necessarily a bad idea to have double coverage, for a number of reasons. For one, with a car warranty package, you may be towed to a dealership, where you may not want to go if you just need a new battery or tires. And roadside assistance plans generally limit the number of miles they tow for free, usually a minimum of 3 to a maximum of 10 miles. If you want your car towed farther, you could end up paying out of pocket; insurance may or may not cover the difference.

A word of caution about being pressured into having your car taken somewhere you do not want it to go, especially after an accident, when you may be dazed and vulnerable. Some tow-truck drivers may work with certain garages to bring in cars, particularly those that have been in accidents and could prove to be lucrative to repair. If a tow-truck driver insists on taking your car to a specific garage, call another service, or complain afterward to the agency that provides your assistance.

Finally, if you're stranded and your roadside assistance provider cannot help you, just dial 911.

—Alina Tugend

The Manual or the Mechanic?

How to tell who knows best

Service practices listed in a car's manual are intended to give cars their best performance and longest life. Yet, take the car to a mechanic, and he's bound to improvise. As a result, many consumers don't know whether to trust the manual or the mechanic.

One problem is that manuals are becoming the size of phone books, as manufacturers try to address every ownership issue to avoid being sued. While independent mechanics may disagree, manufacturers and industry experts generally think that following the manufacturer's guidelines closely is the best way to maintain a vehicle. "The first call is to believe the manual," says Paul A. Eisenstein, editor in chief of TheCarConnection.com, an automotive news Web site. "But reading the manual is not just reading the chart in the back. The subtleties lie within its pages." Unfortunately, even those who read the manual often run into contradictory or unclear advice.

Here are some of the most perplexing maintenance practices and what to do about them:

WHEN TO CHANGE THE OIL. Changing the oil every 3,000 miles, as many quick-lube chains recommend, is usually a waste of money and oil. And cars that use synthetic oils can go much farther without a change.

While it is true that severe driving requires more frequent oil changes, there is no consensus on what constitutes severe driving. "Extreme driving is starting the car, driving 10 miles at low speeds, and then shutting it off," says Don Sherman, technical editor for *Automobile* magazine. "Then why do engines that only receive 15,000-mile oil changes all seize up?" asks Rene Gauch, owner of the German Independent garage in Los Angeles. Gauch recommends a 7,000-mile-change interval with synthetic oil, and a 3,000-to-5,000-mile interval for those who use regular oil. Oil changes, say other auto experts, is the one place where you can err on the side of caution.

PROPER TIRE INFLATION. Few drivers keep their tires inflated to the right pressure, which manufacturers stress is the amount that they have determined based on the tire and the weight of the car. The "maximum tire pressure" embossed on the sidewalls can be more than 20 pounds higher than the pressure that should actually be used. Proper inflation pressures are listed in the manual

INSIDE INFO

Gas Misers

Here are the 10 most fuel-efficient cars sold in the U.S in 2006. Each model was allowed only one appearance on the list. The sole exception is the Honda Civic, which appears twice as a result of being available in both gas-electric hybrid and regular gasoline versions.

○ Honda Insight	60/66
○ Toyota Prius	60/51
○ Honda Civic Hybrid	49/51
○ Volkswagen Golf TD	37/44
○ Volkswagen New Beetle TDI	37/44
○ Volkswagen Jetta TDI	36/41
○ Toyota Corolla	32/41
○ Scion xA	32/37
○ Hyundai Accent	32/35
○ Kia Rio	32/35
○ Honda Civic	30/40*
○ Pontiac Vibe	30/36
○ Toyota Matrix	30/36

NOTE: Rankings are based on the Environmental Protection Agency's miles-per-gallon ratings for city and highway travel. More specifically, Edmunds used the E.P.A.'s combined fuel economy formula: 55 percent of city m.p.g. rating plus 45 percent of highway m.p.g. rating. The rating for each vehicle is expressed in m.p.g. as a city/highway ratio. All ratings apply to base models equipped with a manual transmission, except where indicated otherwise with an asterisk.

SOURCE: Edmunds.com

as well as on a sticker usually located in one of the door sills.

Beginning with the 2005 model year, the manual is the only place to find the right tire pressure for driving in an empty vehicle; the door sticker only lists the proper pressure for a full load.

PROPER GAS GRADE. With high gas prices, many drivers are tempted to use a lower grade

Drinking Soda and Driving

What sticky spills do to your gearshifts

Almost half of drivers eat in their vehicles, according to a 2003 study commissioned by Auto Expressions, a manufacturer of auto accessories like air fresheners and seat covers. That spells a lot of messes. We know that sugar is bad for our waistlines, but is it bad for our car gearshifts, too?

If not properly managed, spills can wreak havoc on a gearshift, says Todd Spaulding, an engineer at Ford Motor Company in Dearborn, Mich. Liquid can drip into the circuitry, which is "not a good thing," he says, causing malfunction.

But Spaulding has found that not all car spills are created equal. His testing shows that the stickier the drink, the more potential for trouble. Coke: bad. Mountain Dew: kind of bad. Coffee: bad, especially with cream and sugar. Red Bull: "maybe even worse," says Spaulding, who adds that is just a hunch, because he has not tested the drink. Best: diet soda, which isn't sticky when it dries.

To prevent major soda malfunctions, car engineers have designed little gutters buried under the gearshift panel that channel the soda away from the electronics and out of the car. "We call it the Coke management strategy," says Spaulding.

—Bonnie Rothman Morris

than the manufacturer recommends. In most cases, that is fine. The fuel requirement listed next to the gas cap "is the worst-case scenario," says Marc Trahan, director of product quality and technical services for Audi of America. Many modern cars have anti-knock sensors, which protect the engine from damage when gas with a lower octane rating is used. General Motors prefers to have customers follow the manual's advice, because many people do not know if their car has anti-knock technology. For cars requiring higher-octane fuel, some mechanics advise staying away from low octane. They agree that an anti-knock sensor could adjust the engine, but the electronics could be affected as the engine tried to compensate.

—Eric A. Taub

Gas-Saving Strategies

Gas is liquid gold these days. Here's how to get better mileage

Whether you're in the market for a hybrid or a traditional gasoline-powered vehicle, you'll have to look beyond the Environmental Protection Agency mileage estimates. Those fuel economy estimates posted on the car window sticker and listed on the E.P.A. Web site warrant skepticism. Consumer Reports tested 69 vehicles this year and found that the E.P.A. figures significantly overstated mileage 90 percent of the time.

For the highway portion of the E.P.A. test, for example, the vehicle's average speed is 48 miles an hour, with the air-conditioner off and no braking for traffic. Not necessarily real-world driving conditions. But the E.P.A. figures can be used to rank the relative fuel efficiency of various models—to determine, say, whether a Dodge Neon gets better mileage than a Toyota Echo.

One way to get better mileage is to pick a smaller, four-cylinder engine rather than the more powerful, heavier and thirstier V-6 or V-8 version. And the savings may be even greater if you choose a diesel engine; diesel fuel contains 10 percent more energy and diesel engines are 30 percent more efficient than regular gas engines. So even if diesel prices spike during the winter or when hurricanes shut down refineries, you are likely to come out ahead.

Vehicles with manual transmissions generally get better fuel economy than those with automatic. An aerodynamic design also improves mileage, but that is hard to discern, says Phillip Reed, co-author of *Strategies for Smart Car Buyers* and consumer advice editor at Edmunds.com. One of the biggest gains in decreasing drag is if the design has a smooth underside, says Reed.

Any vehicle will get better mileage if tires are kept inflated to the manufacturer's specifications. "The majority of people are riding around on underinflated tires," Reed says; fuel efficiency is degraded by 2 percent for every pound per square inch below specifications. Reed recommends buying a digital tire gauge, at $8 to $10, and an electric tire pump, at $45 to $50, to keep tires inflated properly.

Follow the manufacturer's recommendations for replacing spark plugs and air filters, too. Clogged filters and crusty spark plugs, which prevent gas from burning completely, can reduce mileage by up to 12 percent. Use the recommended grade of motor oil; putting 10W-30 oil into an engine intended for 5W-30, for example, will lower mileage by 1 to 2 percent.

Another way to increase mileage: lighten the load by getting rid of unnecessary stuff in the trunk. An extra 100 pounds reduces fuel efficiency by up to 2 percent. And avoid attaching anything to your car, like racks for luggage or bikes; they add weight and create aerodynamic drag.

Still, the biggest factor in your car's gas mileage is how you drive. Aggressive driving that causes you to brake and accelerate often can use up to 33 percent more gas than a more staid style. And speeding can make even the most fuel-efficient engine guzzle gas. The Energy Department says every 5 m.p.h. over 60 cuts gas mileage by 6 percent.

Putting your car into a higher gear whenever possible, to slow engine speed, saves gas and reduces engine wear. And turn off the engine if the car won't be moving for more than 30 seconds—it's a myth that more gas is needed to restart the engine than to let it idle.

—Kate Murphy

Customizing Your Car

INSIDE INFO

- Car customization is a $31 billion business that attracts a variety of consumers and budgets.

- High-end customization goes beyond big wheels to computer and video-game systems, satellite TV's, monogrammed seats, wet bars and more.

- Some owners of dream machines: Eminem, 50 Cent, Yao Ming, Jennifer Capriati, Jennifer Lopez and Marc Anthony.

—Karen Jones

Taking a Cycle for a Spin

Spare yourself a big mistake: learn to ride before you buy

Motorcycle Hall of Fame inductee Ed Youngblood talks about motorcycling as "a spiritual activity, essential for maintaining a healthy mental perspective." The nation's more than six million motorcycle enthusiasts no doubt agree with Youngblood, who spent nearly 20 years as president of the American Motorcyclist Association (www.ama-cycle.org). Since stepping down in 1999, he has written four books on motorcycle history, and through the public-speaking circuit has become one of the great ambassadors of cycling. Youngblood's romance with the motorcycle began more than 45 years ago, when he was just 14 and took the $60 he saved from doing odd

SPENDING

jobs to purchase his first bike, a 1953 Harley-Davidson 165. For anyone tempted to take a cycle for a spin, Youngblood has this advice:

How do you know a motorcycle is right for you?

I don't believe motorcycles are right for everyone. So, before you go out and buy yourself an expensive motorcycle, sign up for a motorcycle training course. The Motorcycle Safety Foundation (800-446-9227), for example, has a referral service for courses. The course will take you through all aspects of motorcycle operation and maintenance. You'll also receive an excellent introduction to motorcycle makes and sizes, so if you do decide to buy a bike, you'll have an idea of the type of bike that fits your personality and needs.

What options are there in motorcycles?

First, you must decide whether you prefer an on-road or off-road motorcycle. In other words, do you plan on riding over dirt trails or on the open highway? If you're in the market for an off-road, you can choose between a total dirt bike and a trail bike made street-legal. The latter comes with turning signals and other requirements of a highway vehicle. If you favor the highway, there

ⓘ INSIDE INFO

Rebels No More

Think of bikers and images of modern-day desperadoes come to mind. In reality, the 264,000 members of the American Motorcyclist Association are established, well educated and financially successful:

○ Average household income: $91,500
○ Post–high school education: 77%
○ Average number of motorcycles owned: 2.8 per member

are essentially three bike types. The sport bike is styled like a high-performance machine; it is light and quick, best suited for short rides. Cruisers are designed for comfort and local riding. These bikes provide an ideal fit for a commuter or the "weekend" rider. Touring bikes are made for the long-distance traveler. They're larger and often have built-in saddlebags for luggage.

Size is also important. Typically, trail bikes have much smaller engines than road bikes. Trail bike sizes usually top out at 600 c.c. (cubic centimeters), while a touring bike can have an engine as large as 1500 c.c.—comparable to a small automobile engine.

Which motorcycle best fits the first-time buyer?

Unlike automobiles, which are typically purchased with practicality in mind, motorcycle selection is determined by personal taste and style. You must remember: the motorcycle is a recreational vehicle. Most A.M.A. members own more than two cycles, and many own more than four.

As far as the leading brands or makes available in the U.S., you have Harley-Davidson, Honda, Kawasaki, Suzuki, Triumph, Yamaha, Ducati, BMW and a variety of smaller manufacturers. Typically, all these manufacturers put out high-quality products. The choice among them usually comes down to brand loyalty. I know people who have driven Harleys for over 20 years and would never try anything else. The same is true for BMW's and most other brands. You can't explain a person's personal taste for motorcycles any more than you can explain a person's clothing selection. It's all up to the individual.

What's the first-time buyer's most common mistake?

First-time buyers often purchase bikes that are too small. Going into the showroom, most first-timers lack confidence, so they choose the smaller bikes, which are easier to handle. After their first month, they're ready for a larger model.

TIMELY TIPS

Make Room for Scooters

These anti-hogs get great mileage and are low on the wimpy factor

Drivers who fear hulking cruisers like Harley-Davidsons, yet want to cut back on gas bills might want to consider a scooter. Just do the math. While the Prius, Toyota's huge-selling hybrid, has a combined city/highway mileage rating of 55 miles a gallon from the Environmental Protection Agency (and users say the real-world average is about 40 to 45 m.p.g.), some scooters can approach 80 miles a gallon.

✔ **A commuter on a motorcycle or scooter faces some hurdles,** of course. The first one is safety.

Motorcycle deaths have been rising, including an 8 percent jump from 2003 to 2004, when 4,008 riders died. The second one is climate. Riding to work in the rain or when it's cold can be more miserable than a Los Angeles freeway jam.

✔ **But the upsides are appealing.** Along with the incredible gas mileage, you can park them almost anywhere. Scooters have also become less wimpy. A new class, maxi-scooters, with engines of about 250 c.c. and higher, has been developed for urban commuters, at prices ranging from $3,000 to $6,000. Most have storage, usually under the seat or in a compartment in the front, can carry two passengers and feature twist-and-go automatic transmissions so you don't need to work a clutch. Some are suitable for short highway trips.

—Brian Alexander

I'm not suggesting every first-time buyer needs a larger bike, but I would recommend some riding experience before going to the dealer.

Q Which, if any, accessories really matter?

This depends upon your cycling plans. If you intend on having a passenger, install a backrest for his or her comfort. A rider taking long trips should consider installing saddlebags. Personally, I prefer a windscreen, simply for the comfort. If you like camping, there are specially made motorcycle trailers, which many people use to haul their outdoor gear.

Q Any other critical advice for first-time cyclists?

A good source for information is a group called Discover Today's Motorcycling (800-833-3995 or www.motorcycles.org). Again, I can't stress how important it is to enlist in motorcycle driving courses before you take to the road. For my first 20 years of riding, no instruction was available and I believed I didn't need any. After participating in my first course, I was horrified to learn of my poor technique and riding habits. I was

so taken by the course that I became an instructor and lifelong advocate. If you don't intend to go through a training course, don't ride.

Condos on Wheels

Baby boomers are behind the wheels of these new kings of the road

Nobody wants a utilitarian camper anymore, it seems. What shoppers of recreational vehicles seem to crave these days is a portable version of their dream home, a roving castle as roomy as a rock star's trailer and as plush as a five-star hotel. And manufacturers are tripping over one another to comply. Spurred on by space-enlarging advances, they are slapping the term "residential style" on any feature that can be supersized.

Ceilings that were once a head-bumping 78 inches have been raised to seven feet and higher. Kitchens that were once limited to hotplates and dorm-style refrigerators have blossomed with four-

SPENDING

burner gas ranges, wine coolers and granite-topped islands. Bathrooms that were once closet-size now have walk-in closets of their own. And the electronics on board, from wireless Internet access to audiophile theaters, rival those of a Silicon Valley bachelor pad.

But just because they look homey doesn't mean that people actually live in them. Unlike the classic Winnebago and its legion of road-trekking retirees, these souped-up R.V.'s are not necessarily being used as primary residences, or even as second homes. Instead, the driving force behind the new R.V.'s are baby boomers looking for quick weekend thrills. Lavish setups—satellite reception, plasma TV—come in handy for Nascar races, outdoor concerts, rodeos, hunting trips, even as a guest suite for visiting relatives.

One downside is that many campgrounds can't accommodate monster motor homes; most are not equipped to handle vehicles longer than 40 feet and also have trouble meeting the electricity demands of the largest R.V.'s, which require 50 amps and can blow the circuitry.

All these luxuries add a certain burden. So-called Class A motor homes, the largest of their kind, were once built to carry up to 17,000 pounds. Today's motor homes, loaded down by generators, slide-outs, marble tiles, granite countertops and air-conditioners, can weigh 50,000 pounds or more.

That added weight means less fuel efficiency, of course. Motor-home owners are lucky if they can squeeze out six miles to a gallon. But despite high fuel prices, high-end motor homes are selling better than ever. In 1992, fewer than 100 such vehicles lumbered off the showroom floor. In 2003, 14,000 motor homes costing more than $200,000 were sold, a 20 percent increase over the year before.

—Denny Lee

On the Horizon: Off-Road R.V.'s

It had to come to this—comfort, style and power in the backcountry

Adventurers who also crave creature comforts can find both in the new four-wheel-drive R.V.'s that let them get into backcountry, unload an A.T.V., go exploring and use the rugged vehicle as a home.

One such hybrid is the EarthRoamer, built by a small Colorado company (www.earthroamer.com). It's a rugged motor home with factory four-wheel drive, designed to take its owner in comfort from the depths of Baja to the wilds of Alaska, and along extreme outback routes like the White Rim Trail in Utah. A customized camper is mounted directly to a pickup frame. The $190,000 to $200,000 vehicle includes amenities like two 50-gallon water tanks, a standup shower and a European-style cassette toilet. Unlike most R.V.'s, which rely on propane, the EarthRoamer taps into its 60 gallons of diesel fuel for cooking, cabin heat and hot water. While driving, hot water is continually supplied through a direct line from the truck's radiator. Solar-charged batteries can power the satellite dish, the hyperefficient Norcold refrigerator and the Sharp air-conditioner for several days, even weeks, without a generator.

Machines like the EarthRoamer occupy a tiny niche in America's total recreational-vehicle market of 370,000 annual unit sales. Off-road R.V.'s are made by just a handful of companies, including

---

 TIMELY TIPS

When You Get a Lemon

✔ You can get an overview of state laws regarding cars that turn out to be lemons at Consumeraffairs.com.

✔ At Autopedia.com you can find lemon-law rights, state laws, attorney links and a free Car-Fax lemon-check link.

Tiger Motorhomes, based in South Carolina. Tiger Motorhomes (www.tigermotorhomes.com) produces fewer than a hundred four-wheel-drive CX models annually, selling mostly via the Internet.

Built on a Chevrolet Silverado 2500 chassis, the Tiger (around $70,000) is lighter than the EarthRoamer and comes in three lengths, 19, 21 and 24 feet. It can be bought with a gasoline or a diesel engine. Equipped with propane appliances, a standard R.V. sewage connection, air-conditioning, an internal generator, ample cabinets, a stand up shower and easy sleeping for four, the Tiger is a much more traditionally equipped Class C vehicle. (Class C means that it is built on a truck chassis with a cab section.) It is also available with solar panels and additional batteries.

—Chris Dixon

Stopping Auto Rustlers

Car thieves will stop at nothing, but there are ways to thwart them

The American infatuation with cars seems to be shared by criminals. A car is stolen every 25.5 seconds, according to the National Insurance Crime Bureau (www.nicb.org). How to foil a car rustler? Aside from obvious theft deterrents, such as locking your car, parking in well-lit areas and never leaving your car running as you hop out for a quick errand, the N.I.C.B. suggests taking a layered approach to protecting your car by using a variety of measures.

Scare thieves away. Have and use a visible or audible alarm. Young thieves in particular are scared off by autos emitting a shrill warning. You can get optional sensors to detect tampering, glass breakage, and towing. Attach a decal to your window indicating that the car is protected by an anti-theft device.

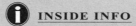

❶ INSIDE INFO

Hot Wheels

This list of the 10 models that thieves liked most in 2004 shows they prefer parts over luxury.

○ **1.** Honda Civic	○ **6.** Ford F150 Series
○ **2.** Toyota Camry	○ **7.** Dodge Ram Pickup
○ **3.** Honda Accord	○ **8.** Acura Integra
○ **4.** Dodge Caravan	○ **9.** Toyota Pickup
○ **5.** Chevrolet Full-size C/K 1500 Pickup	○ **10.** Nissan Sentra

SOURCE: National Insurance Crime Bureau

Immobilize your car. Invest in some low-cost but effective devices, such as a hidden "kill" switch that lets you stop the flow of electricity or gas to a car engine. It can be installed for $10 to $25.

Or invest in a locking device. You can choose from an array, such as floorboard locks that disable the brake pedal, gearshift locks to disable shifting of the transmission, steering-wheel or tire locks to prevent the car from moving, and hood locks that stop thieves from getting access to the battery and security system. A steering-wheel lock, for example, costs $25 to $100. A collar on the steering column can stop a thief from hot-wiring your car. Cost: around $100.

Get smart. Some cars come with "smart keys," containing computer chips or radio frequencies that make it unique to your car. If your car won't start, it won't get stolen.

Partner with the police. On the higher end of high-tech gadgets are tracking devices that can alert you—and law enforcement—the moment an unauthorized user moves your vehicle. LoJack, for example, lets police use a hidden transmitter to find your car. It comes at a big price: $400 to $1,500.

SPENDING

Home Technology

Networking Your Home

Try this and you may never have to leave the couch again

Over 22 million American households have connected their computers and other machines, according to recent research, and they have plenty of motivation to do so.

First, a network can save you money. It allows one cable modem, DSL box or printer to serve all the computers in the house.

Second, a network lets your computers share information. You can copy files from one computer to another. You can sit upstairs at your Windows PC, listening to the iTunes music collection from the Mac in the kitchen. You can check the whole family's calendar from any computer in the house, thanks to networkable calendar programs.

Finally, there's the convenience factor. A network enables a TiVo to display photographs, or a SliMP3 box to play music files, that actually reside on a computer somewhere else in the house. And you can set up networkable computer games to play with other family members.

Plenty of people have set up their own home networks and lived to tell the tale. Others pass out just thinking about it. In between are the legions who wouldn't mind having a home network, but assume that setting one up is, like tuning a car engine, something you hire somebody else to do.

Almost everyone, however, starts out the

same way: overwhelmed. Here it is: your complete Frequently Asked Questions sheet for home networking.

Q **Which kind of network should I set up: wired or wireless?**

In the olden days, people connected their computers using fat wires known as Cat 5 Ethernet cables. This method still has a lot to recommend it. It's supercheap, it moves data superfast, and, compared with wireless networks, it's extremely secure.

All Macs and many Windows computers have built-in Ethernet ports, which look like overweight phone jacks. The idea is to connect all your computers to a small box called a router (each one accommodates as many as four computers). The router lets all of the computers communicate with one another, and with your cable modem or DSL. Most routers also act as firewalls to keep out Internet no-goodniks. The disadvantage of Ethernet is that it means trailing cables along your floors or, worse, snaking them through your walls.

The most promising alternative is the wireless network, also known as Wi-Fi, 802.11 or AirPort. This system works something like a cordless phone: you buy a central base station (also called an access point) that blankets your house with a network signal. A wireless adapter lets each computer receive the signal. Most new laptops have this feature built in; others can be retrofitted with a Wi-Fi card adapter. You can make a desktop computer wireless by adding a U.S.B. Wi-Fi adapter. Now,

> **Microwaving a bag of popcorn can temporarily interfere with your network signal.**
>
> • • •

A NETWORK'S WEAK LINK

A Wi-Fi network can let a household share a high-speed Internet connection wirelessly, as well as linking printers and other devices. But without proper security, it can also enable others with Wi-Fi equipment within range of the signal—typically 200 feet—to share the Internet connection, or even gain access to data on home computers.

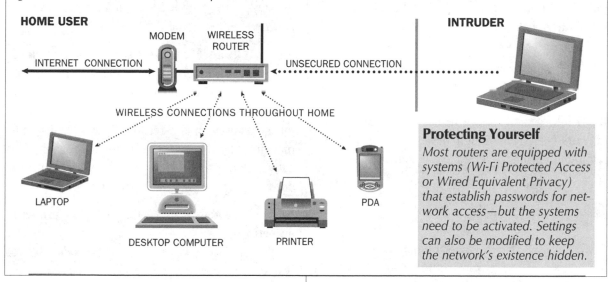

HOME USER

INTRUDER

MODEM   WIRELESS ROUTER

INTERNET CONNECTION

UNSECURED CONNECTION

WIRELESS CONNECTIONS THROUGHOUT HOME

LAPTOP

DESKTOP COMPUTER   PRINTER   PDA

Protecting Yourself

Most routers are equipped with systems (Wi-Fi Protected Access or Wired Equivalent Privacy) that establish passwords for network access—but the systems need to be activated. Settings can also be modified to keep the network's existence hidden.

with very little setup, you've united your computers and cable modem into one glorious, harmonious unit, without drilling a single hole in the walls.

❓ What if I have two desktop computers and two wireless laptops?

In that case, consider buying a combination box called a wireless router. It has jacks for, say, four Ethernet cables, as well as antennas that broadcast a wireless signal to your Wi-Fi laptops.

❓ I've heard that if I use a wireless network, snoopers can rifle through my stuff.

It's theoretically possible for electronic eavesdroppers to intercept text that you send wirelessly, including passwords that you type. On public wireless networks that don't require a password to get online, like the ones in hotel lobbies, there's not much you can do about this risk.

The odds are far smaller that anyone would be

interested in spying on you at home—unless you're some kind of Department of Defense engineer with clever enemies hiding in the bushes outside your house. Still, if you're concerned, you can thwart most of them just by turning on your base station's optional password feature. Most base stations offer something called W.E.P. encryption (much better than nothing); newer ones offer what's called W.P.A. (much better security, fewer problems). The base station's manual explains how to turn these on.

❓ Does that mean I'll have to type in a password every time I want to get online?

Nope. Both Mac OS X and Windows XP can memorize the password for you.

❓ Which kind of wireless gear should I buy?

Every couple of years, the computer industry dreams up another, faster wireless standard for

SPENDING

wireless networking. They go by annoying names like 802.11a, 802.11b and 802.11g.

The "g" variety is faster and has better coverage than the older "a" or "b," yet is compatible with all three. In general, if you're shopping today, you should buy "g" base stations and adapters.

Unless, of course, you want "n."

The next-generation base stations and receivers will be called 802.11n. If all of your gear is "n," your network will be four times as fast as "g" gear.

Here's the funny part: Networking companies like LinkSys and Belkin want to start selling "n" network gear, even though the standard hasn't been completely ironed out by the electronics industry's

technical nerds. So the networking companies are calling their newest products "Pre-N." They work fine, but may not be compatible across brands.

Once the "n" specification is finalized, these manufacturers intend to offer a software update that will turn your Pre-N gear into proper, fully certified "n" equipment.

💬 I can't wait. My Internet connection is so slow!

Well, don't spend a lot of money in the expectation that a faster network means faster Internet speed; it doesn't. Even the slowest home network is already much faster than the real bottleneck, your cable modem or DSL box. A faster network transfers files between your own computers faster, but generally does nothing for your Web or e-mail activity.

💬 Will I be able to connect my old inkjet printer to my network?

Yes, indeed; take your pick of methods. The free way is to connect the printer to one Mac or PC, and then turn on that computer's printer sharing feature. (For instructions, search Mac OS X's or Windows XP's online help for "printer sharing.") The other computers in your house can now send printouts to that printer, as long as the main computer is turned on. If you'd rather not have to worry about the main machine being available, you can also connect the printer to a gadget called a network print server, available in both wireless and wired versions.

One other possibility: if your wireless base station is an Apple AirPort Express, you can plug a printer directly into a U.S.B. jack on the base station. This method saves you both the worry that a certain computer is turned on and the cost of an extra printer-sharing gadget.

💬 I don't know. It still sounds like I'm in for a headache.

Setting up the network can indeed be a slog; consider inviting a neighborhood teenager over to

TIMELY TIPS

A Primer on Networking

Here are some steps toward installing a wireless home network:

✔ Get wireless adapters for all the computers and peripherals you want to include in your network, as well as a base station to transmit your Internet feed.

✔ Make sure that all your equipment operates according to the same 802.11 standard.

✔ Place your equipment for maximum range and clarity. Higher, more central locations are best. Avoid areas with many obstructions or nearby radio-wave devices like cordless phones and baby monitors.

✔ Consider installing access points in your home to act as signal boosters.

✔ Change channel settings to avoid potential interference from other wireless networks or devices.

✔ Activate the equipment's security features.

—Kate Murphy

help. Or, at the very least, visit Google.com and type in "LinkSys wireless Internet sharing" (or whatever problem you're having); the beauty of joining the home-network revolution now is that several million people have been this way before.

But look at the bright side: once your network is in place, it's yours for life. There's no monthly fee, no further learning involved, and no annual upgrades to buy and install. In the world of computers and technology, that makes a home network a valuable investment indeed.

—David Pogue

Many Computers, Many Choices

Desktop or laptop? Bigger hard drive? More memory?

The personal-computer business is like the auto industry: since all cars can go 65 miles an hour on the freeway, car advertisements emphasize the vehicle's off-road abilities or its warranty. Today, all PC's go the bit-crunching equivalent of 65 miles an hour, and they let you surf the Web, check for e-mail messages, download MP3 players and even edit photos. So manufacturers pitch powerful machines for three-dimensional video games or promote protection plans and tech support.

Fortunately, the major computer vendors are hungry for your business. These days, if you know what you want in a computer system—and don't become distracted by the hot rods—you can strike bargains.

LAPTOP OR DESKTOP?

One big quandary is whether to buy a laptop or a desktop computer. The arguments for buying a laptop nowadays are overwhelmingly persuasive. There are plenty to choose from that are under $1,000. Laptops let you gain access to wireless

 TIMELY TIPS

Looking for a Cheaper Mac?
Apple, itself, may give you a discount

This does not mean that a Macintosh is not a sound investment. In fact, being a student or a teacher has its privileges in the Mac world. The Apple Store for Education (www.apple.com/education) sells products up to $300 less than their Apple Store prices. Since Apple controls how much its authorized resellers charge, these discounts are precious indeed.

To qualify, you identify your school (kindergarten through high school or college) from a menu, and agree that you will buy only a total of three computers and one monitor in an academic year. Once you're in, there may be a bonus: a mail-in rebate.

—Wilson Rothman

networks found on campuses and other school grounds and at hangouts like coffee shops. For college and boarding-school students, they are much easier to manage on move-in day. On trips they double as portable DVD players.

But there are many reasons you may not want your children to have access to a portable computer. If your teenager cannot move the family PC around, the chances of its being stolen, smashed or otherwise damaged are greatly reduced. An economic argument for desktop PC's is also worthwhile. Although the prices of laptops have dropped precipitously, desktop prices have also continued to fall.

HOW MUCH COMPUTER DO YOU NEED?

The longer you plan to keep your PC, the bigger your budget must be. If you buy a computer system with more RAM or a bigger hard drive than you had initially planned, you can avoid having to install RAM or add an external hard drive.

SPENDING

284

TIMELY TIPS

A Basic Computer Just for E-Mail

What kind should you get?

E-mail has become a universal application these days, and just about any new computer—whether its operating system is Windows or Macintosh—has the hardware and software you need to get online, like a modem or network card and a Web browser.

Both systems also come with basic e-mail programs that you can use with an existing mail account after you copy the settings from the old computer. (If you happen to use America Online, you can get the current version of the company's software for either Mac or Windows at www.aol.com/downloads.)

E-mail is not as simple as it used to be, however, because of an epidemic of viruses, spam and other mail-borne threats. Installing a good all-around Internet security program and setting it to update itself automatically can keep the machine safer with minimal effort.

✔ **Windows-based computers** are inexpensive and plentiful; a number of companies have full-featured systems for less than $500.

Many viruses and other forms of malicious software can get on your computer by way of e-mail, though. Viruses are typically aimed at Windows-based PC's. If you opt for that, be sure to get an anti-virus program for it.

✔ **A Macintosh computer,** like the one-piece eMac or iMac, is simple to set up, and the Mac operating system is less plagued by virus infections and other forms of malicious code like spyware. The Mac operating system has often been praised for its ease of use, but if you are used to a Windows system, a PC would probably seem like friendly territory.

—J. D. Biersdorfer

Video games may seem like a frivolous reason to buy a more powerful computer. But a student going to design school or to an audio-visual program, say, may need that processing power and graphics acceleration. And you should always check what system your school recommends or requires.

From $300 to $3,000, a PC's basic components vary slightly. Everything still revolves around the processor, the amount of RAM and the size of the hard drive.

A WORD ABOUT WARRANTIES

There are warranties and there are warranties. While Dell typically includes only 90 days of coverage and technical support for systems, its extended warranties are among the most affordable: $60 to $100 for two full years of coverage. Hewlett-Packard automatically provides a limited one-year warranty on every system, but charges $100 for a two-year extended plan. Apple computers come with a one-year hardware and software warranty, but only 90 days of free technical support.

For laptops, there is also accidental-damage protection. Having seen laptops laid low by water, hot tea and wine, it is worthwhile to investigate this option. It can cost $150 to $300, but that often includes an underlying warranty of two or three years.

—Wilson Rothman

Secrets to Hard-Drive Hygiene
To avoid disaster, you must back up your data

Ever-increasing quantities of private and family data are kept on home computers. But until the last few years, there was a gap between the ever-larger hard-disk drives that came with home computers and affordable methods to archive the gigabytes of documents, e-mail messages, home movies and MP3's. That gap has closed as con-

TIMELY TIPS

Moving Data to a New Computer

Moving all your stuff out of an old hard drive and into a new one is a rite of passage when buying a replacement computer, and how you go about it may depend on both the hardware involved and your patience.

There are various ways to move your files and settings, but moving programs can be tricky. If possible, track down the original installation discs (if the software is compatible with your new computer) and have them ready for your new laptop.

✔ One way to move files is to copy to an external hard drive the files you want to move, or burn them to discs, and then transfer the files from the drive or discs onto the new laptop.

✔ It may be possible to link the machines with a network cable (or a FireWire cable, if you are moving between Macs) to create a mini-network that lets you copy files from the old computer to the new one.

✔ Several programs are made to transfer data. Microsoft includes a Files and Settings Transfer Wizard in Windows XP that guides you through moving your files and system settings from an older Windows computer. Many of Apple's Macintosh G5 computers also come with a program that helps you move files and settings from older Mac OS X systems.

✔ Third-party software like PC Relocator from Alohabob (www.alohabob.com) and IntelliMover from Detto Technologies (www.detto.com) also can transfer files from old to new PC's. Detto also has a program called Move2Mac that can move files from an old PC to a new Macintosh.

The easiest option may be hiring a computer professional to move your files. Many stores, like Best Buy, Circuit City, Staples and CompUSA, offer PC data-migration and other services, even if you didn't purchase the new machine there.

—J. D. Biersdorfer

sumer backup software has added features to write archives directly to external hard drives and higher-capacity DVD burners.

WHICH FILES?

All mainstream operating systems comprise a mix of kinds of files. Some are needed by the system itself to manage its hardware and software tasks. Others are programs and their help files and plug-ins, documents you create with those programs and settings for how those programs work. Documents can vary greatly in size from a 500-byte e-mail message to a 10-gigabyte movie you transferred from a digital camcorder.

The most comprehensive way to duplicate a computer's data is to use software that can handle every kind of file, and store the state of those systems as a snapshot in time.

This is a trickier task than it sounds, as some files are hidden or have odd properties. Just dragging a hard-disk icon on the desktop onto a similar hard drive's icon won't work because of these arcane files and obscure aspects of how a hard disk and an operating system talk to each other. (Mac OS, up to version 9, had the unique ability to just copy a drive; it was lost with Apple's switch to Unix underpinnings.)

Picking and choosing which files to back up, like manually copying your document folder to a CD or DVD, allows you to preserve your most critical files—like spreadsheets, photos and word-processing documents. If you use the pick-and-choose method and suffer a complete drive failure, you would have to reinstall your operating system

Making Old Files New Again

Software that converts files between formats can help you tramsfer files in an old format to a new computer.

✔ DataViz makes file-conversion programs for both Windows and Macintosh systems. At www.dataviz.com, you can find the Conversions Plus program that translates many file formats for Windows (and can even open many files created in Macintosh programs); and MacLink Plus Deluxe, which can translate files from older Mac programs and from many Windows applications. A list of the file types each program can convert is posted on the product's Web page.

✔ If you are trying to open image files, several freeware and shareware options are available. XnView (www.xnview.com), a freeware program for Windows, Macintosh and Linux systems, can open 400 image formats. Irfanview for Windows (www.irfanview.com) and Graphic Converter for the Macintosh (www.lemkesoft.de/en/graphcon. htm) are two other image viewer and conversion programs.

J. D. Biersdorfer

and any applications you had separately installed, as well as all upgrades released since the time you purchased the system and software.

WHICH HARDWARE?

For businesses, streaming magnetic digital tape ruled the backup roost through the 1990's, while consumers were stuck with slow and occasionally unreliable diskettes and, later, Zip and Jaz cartridges.

Tape drives are expensive, and tapes run from start to finish: special software is necessary to fast-forward through up to 750 feet of tape to reach a particular file. A modern tape drive with the capac-ity of a home hard drive can cost several hundred dollars. Tapes that hold 25 to 100 gigabytes of data cost much less.

That's why external hard drives have emerged as the backup medium of choice: their low price, high speed and high capacity pairs them neatly with a computer's internal hard drive.

Many users now purchase drives much larger than their internal disk in order to create cumulative archives of files as they change. Backup software creates snapshots so you can choose which version of a file to retrieve, or retrieve the entire data state of your computer at a given point in time. A 200-gigabyte drive for Mac or Windows is available from LaCie USA (www.lacie.com); a terabyte drive (approximately a trillion bytes, or 1,000 gigabytes) is also available.

Both CD and DVD burners are reliable, cost-effective choices for backup, with blank-media costs plummeting. A CD burner can write about 700 megabytes to a single disc. DVD burners can put about 5 gigabytes on one disk, but newer dual-layer recorders can write up to 9 gigabytes. An external dual-layer DVD burner can cost as little as $120.

Some companies offer even simpler hard-drive backups, bundling software and hardware into a single one-button backup option. Install the software, attach the drive and hit a button on devices from Mirra, Seagate, Maxtor and others, and a backup is made with no intervention.

SOFTWARE OPTIONS

The way to good data hygiene is to establish a routine and stick to it. Backup software makes it possible to schedule your archives—preferably at a time you are not also trying to use the computer.

Consumer backup software can write to hard drives and optical media, and often to any kind of media that can be mounted on the desktop.

Software from Microsoft (included in Windows XP) and Apple (included for .Mac online service subscribers) backs up and restores files on a schedule. More sophisticated software from EMC Dantz (Retrospect Desktop, www.dantz.com) and Symantec's Norton division (Norton Ghost, www. symantec.com/sabu/ghost/ghost_personal) offers full disk backup and restore; both packages include CD's that can be used to start up a computer with a failed operating system but a working hard drive to restore from a backup.

The best packages allow you to archive files as well as back them up; that is, to store multiple versions of the same file over time as it changes. But you can choose to store only the latest version of each file, too.

RESTORING DATA

There's often a paradox to restoring data: you need the backup software to restore your backed up files, but it's stored on your dead or damaged drive.

Unlike software you might purchase and download online, it's best to buy physical copies of backup software so that you are sure to have the factory-stamped CD's and other material handy in the event of catastrophe. Don't forget to have that serial number, too, for reinstallation or phone support. (Phone support is quite expensive, while slower e-mail or online support may be free.)

Backup software creates a file that is a catalog or index of the files it has written and when. It is prudent to store the catalog file or similar data on a separate hard drive or on removable media, or by setting up a backup script within your software to copy the catalog separately as a plain file after your main backup has completed.

To recover single files, you typically run the backup software or insert the media that you have used for storing your files and select the ones to retrieve—exercising care to not overwrite folders or directories that you do not want to change.

As with many things, the best time to make a backup is before you experience a crisis.

—Glenn Fleishman

E.R. for Hard Drives

When all else fails and you have to recover your data

If all computer users backed up their hard drives, the data recovery industry would barely exist. But the routine, like flossing teeth, is practiced regularly by few. And as hard drive capacity explodes, the consequences of catastrophic failure mushroom.

Not every hard drive's files can be recovered, but rates are improving. "Eight years ago, 50 percent of our drives could not be restored," says Scott Gaidano, a data recovery specialist in northern California. Now up to 90 percent of the data can

---

❓ **EXPERT ANSWER**

When It Asks Nicely

💬 **Is it necessary to heed the messages that tell you to download a newer version of something like Acrobat Reader or RealPlayer if you already have a version that works?**

Updating this sort of software usually isn't mandatory right away, but it can eventually become necessary when a company makes adjustments to its file formats or adds features that require updated software to function. If you have an outdated version of a media-player program, for example, you may not be able to see or hear a streaming video file that has been created with a new version of the software.

—J. D. Biersdorfer

be salvaged from 85 to 90 percent of drives.

The cost can run to several thousand dollars—the bigger the rush, the higher the price. When nothing can be recovered—typically when drives cannot spin or data has been overwritten—data recovery companies often charge an inspection fee of a couple of hundred dollars.

Once a drive arrives at a data recovery com-

pany, it is typically inspected in a "clean room" to prevent dust contamination. If it got wet, it is submerged in a solvent to remove residue. Because data can be retrieved only from operating drives, many companies will try to get the mechanism running temporarily—often by using components from an inventory of different models.

A copy of the drive's contents is then recorded on a server for protection and another copy is transferred to a functioning hard drive. Using commercial and proprietary software tools, data recovery companies extract the data from that copy. Retrieved files are sent to the customer using DVD's, a new hard drive or Internet file transfer. Generally, companies keep all files confidential, and erase them from their servers shortly after delivery to the customer.

—Eric A. Taub

The Lifespan of a Diskette

Their hard plastic outer cases may give them the look of durability, but those 3.5-inch diskettes, once a common file-storage option, are much more fragile inside. As with television shows recorded on videocassettes, diskette data is recorded onto a magnetic medium that degrades with time and repeated use.

The magnetic material inside a diskette is susceptible to damage from environmental factors like dust and dirt, as well as from extreme heat or cold. The disk's surface can also be scraped inside a drive. The magnetic particles lose strength (and their ability to retain data) over time, and can suffer when placed next to magnetic fields like those that can emanate from computer monitors, speakers and motors.

Some studies have shown that a diskette has an estimated life span of 10 years if stored in a cool, dry place with average care and use. Compact discs, which record data optically with a laser that etches information onto the disc's surface, have a longer estimated life span; tests by some CD makers claim that the data discs can last up to 100 years if stored and maintained properly.

If possible, you might try to see if another drive will read your unresponsive diskettes. If you can get the diskettes to work, copy the files or photos onto your hard drive or burn them to a CD or DVD to give them a more stable storage home.

—J. D. Biersdorfer

Backing Up While On the Go
Keeping your computer and its contents safe

It's hard not to experience anxiety when you're traveling with a laptop: there might occur accidental drops during security screenings, theft from a hotel room, loss in a taxi or restaurant, or hardware failure from too many jolts.

Perhaps the most important safety measure is protecting the information on your computer, so that if it is damaged, lost or stolen, the data remain safe. Travelers now have many backup devices to choose from.

Beside storing your files and data on a removable CD or DVD disk, there is a variety of other portable storage devices. Particularly convenient are flash drives: small key-chain-size plastic devices that weigh only an ounce or so and plug into a computer's U.S.B. port (the port typically used for connecting printers and other peripherals). You can

How Never to Miss an E-mail

Many mail programs allow you to check, send and sort messages from multiple e-mail accounts, but you need to supply the program with the user name, server settings and password for each e-mail address you want to add. If you do not already know this information, ask your Internet service provider.

Once you have all your account information, go to the settings or preferences area for your e-mail program and click on the tab or icon for Accounts; in Outlook Express, for example, you can find Accounts under the Tools menu. Within the Accounts settings, you can add a mail account. For this new account, you'll need to supply the information from the Internet provider, including the Internet address of its incoming and outgoing mail servers, so your software knows where to look for new mail.

After configuring the additional mail account, you can download any waiting messages from all your accounts at once when you click the Check Mail button or when the program automatically checks your mail.

copy your e-mail files, documents, pictures or data files to the U.S.B. flash drive and can then keep the files with you or keep them in the hotel safe.

Lexar makes a U.S.B. memory device, Jump-Drive Secure, with one gigabyte of storage, large enough for lots of documents, photos and e-mail (available at Amazon.com), that includes software that allows only users with a password to download data.

For additional security, there are flash drives with biometric capabilities, like a fingerprint reader that allows access only with a matching fingerprint. For example, ACP makes a U.S.B. memory drive (Security Key Fingerprint Mini Flash Drive, available at www.compusa.com) with one gigabyte of storage.

Other U.S.B. flash drives, like the Relay 512MB (available at Staples) simply provide portable storage without any additional security capabilities.

Alternatively, you might even want to consider storing or backing up your data files on the memory cards that slip into comparably equipped digital cameras or cellular phones. This solution is good for travelers who simply want backup.

Of course, you want to protect the laptop itself, too. A variety of traditional security-oriented devices like cables (just like bicycle locks) for attaching your laptop to something immovable (for example, the Kensington MicroSaver, available at www.kensington.com), or small motion-detecting alarms that are placed in the bag with the laptop (Targus PA400U Defcon 1, available at www.targus.com), help guard against theft.

But there is a range of other, more basic approaches for reducing the risk and stress of taking your computer with you.

There is your hotel, for instance. Before booking a room, security-conscious laptop owners should ask what size room-safe the hotel offers, or if the front desk is willing to store a laptop in the office safe.

You can also insure your notebook by adding it on to your homeowner's or renter's policy. In some cases, your existing homeowner's insurance policy will cover theft of laptops, with your standard deductible, if it's not being used for business purposes. Safeware (www.safeware.com) offers

INSIDE INFO

Internet Access on the Cheap

○ You can find links to free and inexpensive Internet providers around the world at emailaddresses.com/email_internet.htm.

○ Juno has information on its services for Windows and Macintosh users at www.juno.com.

insurance for notebook computers and includes coverage for accidental damage, theft, vandalism and other problems.

If you don't want to travel with a computer but need access to data, files or e-mail while on the road and have the use of a hotel business center or other Internet source, you can arrange to have your computer at home run a remote access program that's included in Windows XP, or through a service like GoToMyPC (www.gotomypc.com) that enables users to gain access remotely to their PC's from any Internet-connected computer. To use a service like GoToMyPC, you register the computer you want to make available on the site, download the remote access host software and install it. To access that computer remotely, you then use a Web-enabled PC to log in to your home PC. You are now able to work as if you were at home.

—David A. Kelly

A Bounty of Browsers
Tired of Internet Explorer? Check out one of these alternatives

It used to be that Internet Explorer, the one-size-fits-all Web browser bundled with every copy of Windows, was enough for most people. It worked well and cost nothing. Who needed anything else?

That attitude is fading as consumers begin to realize that other browsers offer more features, better security and greater freedom. Bells and whistles, perhaps, but some of them can be surprisingly useful.

The number of competitors to Internet Explorer is surprisingly large and diverse. The most commonly mentioned alternatives are Mozilla and its cousin, Firefox 1.0, two browsers descended from Netscape, the early Internet company that is now part of AOL. Firefox is a Web browser pure and simple. Mozilla uses the same basic core (known as

---

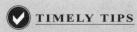 **TIMELY TIPS**

Serene Behind a Firewall

Firewalls—named after the flame-blocking structures designed to keep fires from spreading—are programmed to analyze the network traffic flowing between your computer and the Internet. The firewall compares the information it monitors with a set of rules in its database. If it sees something not allowed, say, another computer trying to connect to one of the machines on your network, the firewall can block and prevent the action.

✔ Most firewall programs let you adjust the rules to allow certain types of data to flow freely back and forth without interference, in cases where you want to do things like stream music or share files with another computer on your network.

✔ Both Windows XP and Mac OS X include basic firewall programs as part of the operating system, and you can find more complex third-party firewall programs from software retailers. Makers of anti-virus software often have a combination package that includes a firewall program and other security software as well, which can help

protect your computer from a variety of Internet threats.

✔ Firewall programs are especially important if you have a high-speed Internet service through a cable modem or DSL, because your computer is typically connected to the Internet for longer periods of time, increasing the exposure to malicious people or programs looking to infect and infiltrate unprotected systems.

And it doesn't take long. A study by a security company found that an unprotected Windows computer was infected within 12 minutes of connecting to the Internet.

—J. D. Biersdorfer

Gecko) and adds tools for reading e-mail, chatting and composing Web pages. Both are open-source tools freely distributed and subject to modification by programmers worldwide.

If you are considering making the leap to a different browser, there are other choices, too. A Norwegian company, Opera, is selling its browser (though a free version that displays advertising is available as well). Apple has Safari, which builds on one called Konqueror, from the world of Linux.

If that's not enough to choose from, there are dozens of browsers out there, like Amaya and Dillo, that cater mainly to people with particular interests (*Star Trek* fans, for example).

There are also hybrids like Netcaptor, Phaseout and Avant that use Internet Explorer's core and add new features. Microsoft encourages software developers to revise and extend Internet Explorer, and maintains a catalog of such offerings at www.windowsmarketplace.com. Some, like Netcaptor, which offers a popular feature called tabbed browsing cost extra, but many are free.

This mix-and-match nature is echoed by Mozilla and Firefox, which also help users create their own features, known as extensions. There is a large collection of extensions at the Mozilla update site (update.mozilla.org), including tools that add weather forecasts to the margins of the Web browser, let you control the music playing in the background or make it easy to look up a word in a dictionary.

In general, all of these browsers display the images and text from Web sites in much the same way. (There are some exceptions, mainly because some Web designers do not test their sites on all browsers. In cases where the layout is mangled or the page simply behaves oddly, the solution may be to use another browser.) Which one is right for you may come down to personality, aesthetics, security concerns and your work environment.

—Peter Wayner

They Make House Calls, Too

Computer doctors may be as close as the local shopping mall

For most of us, setting up the computer, keeping it running smoothly and even figuring out how to add a new printer or network card is one of life's bigger challenges. But what do you do when something really goes wrong—like an operating system stymied by spyware or a DVD drive that won't play your movies?

Although your inclination may be to search for the nearest teenage computer expert or leaf frantically through the Yellow Pages for a PC repair shop nearby, you can often go back where you started: the store. Many major chains now offer their own computer repair departments and, in some cases, will come to your house to fix the problem. Some companies even offer to install, connect and customize your new computer system at your home.

• **Staples,** the office-supply chain store, expanded its Easy Mobile Tech service nationally in 2005 (www.staples.com /easymobiletech). These technicians, who have industry certifications for servicing Windows-based computers, provide technical support and hardware repairs in Staples stores or at customers' homes.

• **Macintosh users** can find help by taking their misbehaving machines to Apple Computer's retail stores around the country. Each Apple store has a Genius Bar, where employees diagnose, advise and repair ailing Macs and other Apple products. A list of Apple stores, each with its own Web page and Genius Bar appointment reservation form, is at www.apple.com/retail.

• **CompUSA** has its own technical support, called Techknowledgist (www.compusa.com/tech_services). The service offers both in-store help and

✓ TIMELY TIPS

Finding Podcasts
Digital audio files are just a few clicks away

Despite the name, which makes it sound as if the shows are broadcast over the airwaves to iPods, podcasts are simply digital audio files, usually created in a common file format like MP3 that just about any digital audio player can handle. Podcasts range from professionally produced radio shows to exuberant homemade rants on a theme that anyone with a computer, a microphone and the right software can create.

Most podcasts on the Web are free. Once you find and download a show you would like to hear, you just transfer the podcast file from your computer to your portable music player, as you would with a music file. News organizations often have podcasts posted on their pages. National Public Radio makes many programs available to download in podcast form at www.npr.org/podcasts/. You can find several programs from the British Broadcasting Corporation at www.bbc.co.uk/radio/downloadtrial.

Searching site by site can be time consuming, but you have plenty of options if you want to browse a lot of podcast offerings at once. Resources like PodCast.net (www.podcast.net), iPodder (www.ipodder.org) and PodCast Alley (www.podcastalley.com) serve as online directories of podcasts and podcasting information. With Apple's iTunes 4.9, you can browse lists of podcasts in the iTunes Music Store and "subscribe" to shows that you would like to download regularly as new installments appear.

Programs like iPodderX, included in Roxio's line of iPod-enhancement software for Mac OS X ($50 at www.roxio.com/en/products/boombox/) can also wrangle podcasts for you.

—J. D. Biersdorfer

next-day appointments for the desperate home or small-business user who needs a personal visit from a technician. The company offers flat rates for both Windows and Macintosh computer service and repairs, as well as installation packages for new computers and networks.

● **Circuit City** operates in-store service centers in many of its outlets where people can drop off their computers for tuneups, cleanups and upgrades. A list of computer repair and upgrade packages is posted under "Services" at www.circuitcity.com.

● **Best Buy's Geek Squad** has 10,500 "agents" dressed in white shirts, black pants and clip-on ties making emergency visits in Volkswagen Beetles to technology-addled homes nationwide, 24 hours a day. Among other things, Geek Squad (www.geeksquad.com) offers specialized missions like setting up online gaming consoles, connecting and configuring a new computer, and linking home-theater components to a network. The technicians also handle more mundane jobs like software glitches and other annoyances that make computing more difficult than it should be.

—J. D. Biersdorfer

I Vant to Drink Your Vatts
All those machines in your house are silently sucking energy—even when they are off

Households across the land are infested with vampires—those gizmos with two sharp teeth that dig into a wall socket and suck juice all night, all day and all year long.

Most people assume that when they turn off the television set it stops drawing power. But that's not how most TV's (and VCR's and other electronic devices) work. They remain ever in standby mode, silently sipping energy to the tune

TIMELY TIPS

Satellite Radio That Follows You Home

With its mostly commercial-free programming and clear signals beaming from the sky, satellite radio found a lot of its early customers among drivers. But with the right hardware and software, you can listen to satellite radio pretty much anywhere you happen to be.

✔ The two main satellite radio providers, Sirius (www.sirius. com) and XM (www.xmradio. com), both sell receivers that can work in the car and in the home audio system, as well as portable players. A list of programs, channels and hardware is posted on each service's Web site.

✔ In addition to having a satellite radio receiver, though, you need a subscription plan to listen to the programs on Sirius and XM. Service contracts are available, and a pay-as-you go plan from either provider costs about $13 a month. Once you subscribe, you can also hear Sirius and XM programs online at each company's site. A free three-day trial is available from each service.

—J. D. Biersdorfer

of 1,000 kilowatt hours a year per household, awaiting the signal to roar into action, drawing more than enough current in the typical house to light a 100-watt light bulb 24/7.

These silent energy users include the chargers for devices that run on batteries, like cellphones, iPods and personal digital assistants, and all the devices around the house that have adapters because they run on direct current, like answering machines. Some have both batteries and steady power use, like cordless phones. Experts call all those adapters "wall warts." Many deliver in direct current only half as much energy as they suck out of the wall; the rest is wasted.

DSL, or cable modems, are also increasingly likely to be left on around the clock. A computer left on continuously can draw nearly as much power as an efficient refrigerator—70 to 250 watts, depending on the model and how it is used.

Among the worst vampires are big-screen televisions, mainly because of satellite and cable boxes, which can draw up to 30 watts when turned off, experts say. It doesn't cost much to make a more efficient device: sometimes just 50 cents

a unit. But consumers don't consider invisible energy use. "There's no labeling of power use in 'standby,'" one expert says, and "no way for people to recognize what a low-standby device is"—making government-imposed energy efficiency the best hope, he says.

The Energy Star program, whose labels on electronics help consumers comparison shop, has announced that it will not rate a product that fails its standby mode requirements (consumers in the market for VCR's, among other things, can see how they rate at www.energystar.gov).

LEAVING IT ON OR SHUTTING IT OFF

The question about whether it is better to shut down your computer at the end of each day or to leave it up and running has been raging for years, with concern for both the computer hardware and saving electricity factoring into the debate.

One older argument for leaving the computer on was that turning it off every night and starting it up again in the morning caused strain on the hard drive—because the magnetic heads that read and write information inside the drive had to start up as well, and could damage delicate parts. But

SPENDING

the hard drives in most modern computers park their heads when the computer is turned off, and starting back up is a much safer process than it used to be. It does take an extra bit of electricity when the computer pops on after being shut down, but the amount of power is less than what would be consumed if the machine was left on continuously.

Leaving the computer on—and linked to the Internet with a high-speed connection—all the time can make it more vulnerable to infection and invasion by intruders. Even if the machine is turned off every night, though, security programs like firewall, anti-virus and anti-spyware software should be installed and updated regularly to help keep the computer safe when on and online.

You obviously save electricity when you shut down the computer after you have finished using it. Turning your machine off at night also clears up items in the computer's memory and gives it a fresh start in the morning, which may make it appear less sluggish if you generally have a lot of programs running over the course of the day.

If you are torn between on and off, consider the third option: setting the machine to hibernate or sleep for the night. The computer uses minimal power in this state, but starts much faster than if it was started up cold in the morning.

—Matthew L. Wald

Where the World Is Really Flat
It's not easy to select the right TV. Here's how

Walk into any electronics retailer and you not only face a wall of screens, you face a barrage of jargon, conflicting standards and an alphabet soup of terminology. How do you cut through the clutter?

There is no easy answer because selecting the right television depends as much on your personal circumstances as on the choice of a plasma, liquid-crystal-display (L.C.D.) or digital-light-processing (D.L.P.) screen. Your finances, as well as the size of your room, the position of the furniture in it or whether the room is wired for cable determines the size and the kind of TV that's best for you.

You can compute the size value by using a tool of the TV marketers: price per diagonal inch. (Digital TV's, like analog models, are measured by the screen

---

✔ TIMELY TIPS

A Big Screen on a Small Budget

How to entertain like a Hollywood mogul

Once reserved for movie moguls and millionaires, the private screening room is coming to more homes, thanks to the emergence of low-cost projectors.

✔ A few years ago, projectors optimized for home theater could easily cost $10,000, but office projectors had begun to fall sharply in price. Many people discovered the potential of digital projectors by taking office models home to watch movies. Eventually, makers of office projectors realized that they were attracting home entertainment buffs as well as business customers, and they began offering so-called crossover models.

✔ Many cite the InFocus X1 as the breakthrough product—a projector with business and video modes, introduced in early 2003. InFocus and several other companies, including Epson, BenQ, Optoma, Panasonic, Sanyo and Sharp, now also make entry-level projectors specifically for home use.

—Sean Captain

diagonal.) Or compute the value more accurately by determining the price per square inch. Either way, you'll see that larger models are generally a better value than small ones. But before you get hung up on what technology is best, let's figure out what you really need by answering a series of questions.

Do I even need a new TV? If your cathode-ray-tube set is working fine, then the answer is most likely no. Digital televisions project a much better picture, but analog sets will continue to work fine until the federal government mandates that all broadcasts must be digital. If you still haven't replaced your set by then, you will have to buy a converter. But even in 2009, 36 percent of households still won't have a high-definition set, analysts predict. So you won't be alone.

Meanwhile, the sets will just get cheaper and better. If, on the other hand, your set is broken or you just have to have a new one, ask yourself:

How much can I afford? Come up with an affordable number, perhaps budgeting more if the set is going into a room where it will be watched by many people. Consider also that the one you buy will most likely last 15 to 20 years. That means you should ignore any unit that says EDTV, standard definition or flat- tube TV. It's old technology.

How much space do I have? The new digitals come in a 16:9 "aspect ratio," much like the dimensions of a theater screen. So if your old 32-inch tube set,

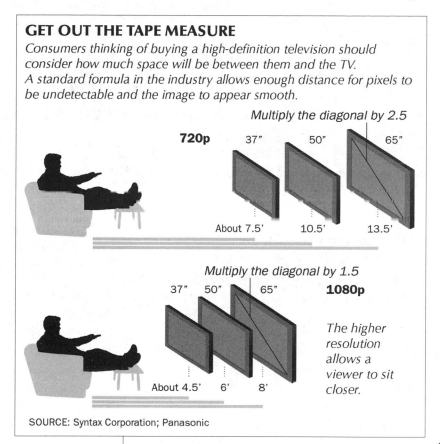

GET OUT THE TAPE MEASURE

Consumers thinking of buying a high-definition television should consider how much space will be between them and the TV. A standard formula in the industry allows enough distance for pixels to be undetectable and the image to appear smooth.

Multiply the diagonal by 2.5

720p   37"   50"   65"

About 7.5'   10.5'   13.5'

Multiply the diagonal by 1.5

37"   50"   65"   **1080p**

About 4.5'   6'   8'

The higher resolution allows a viewer to sit closer.

SOURCE: Syntax Corporation; Panasonic

which has a 4:3 ratio, fits snugly into the living room armoire, a 32-inch HDTV will be about a half foot too wide. (Refresh your knowledge of the Pythagorean theorem to make the measurements, or go to www.1728.com/pythgorn.htm for a calculator.) You might have to go with a 26-inch screen, but account for big frames or speakers that stick out from the sides when you shop.

In general, don't obsess about size. It's high-definition television, after all, which means the picture looks sharper even if the screen isn't as tall.

How far will I sit from the screen? You probably aren't going to be moving your couch, your bed or the kitchen prep island to accommodate the new set. So choose a TV size to fit your viewing habits.

The industry rule for most of the current

HDTV's on the market is to multiply the diagonal by 2.5 to get the distance at which a person with perfect vision can see pixels in the image. The more expensive sets deliver a screen resolution with two million pixels, or twice the resolution of the standard digital TV. That allows you to comfortably sit much closer, about six feet for a 50-inch set. But those models, known as 1080p, cost about twice as much.

Will I hang the TV on the wall? Manufacturers say that the desire to hang the set on the wall like a painting is the leading reason people want a new digital TV. But only about 18 percent of consumers actually do it. The reason? Cords and peripherals. It doesn't look as pretty as a picture when a tangle of cords dangles from the set and a stack of devices, including a cable box, a DVR, an amplifier and maybe a PC or a TiVo-like device sit beneath that handsome new screen.

Should you still want to hang it on the wall, buy an L.C.D. or plasma screen. Even the very thinnest D.L.P. TV's, at about nine inches in depth, are too thick for a wall mounting.

Where and how will I watch it? There are some minor differences in screens. In a sunlit room, L.C.D. has the edge. In a room with less light, plasma wins. If you are watching from a wide angle or from the floor looking up, D.L.P. isn't as good as the other two technologies. For sports or other fast-action viewing, plasma and D.L.P. generally trump L.C.D.

Will I use a set-top box? If there is an easy answer to that question, you can save yourself a lot of money, enough to buy a second set. The set-top box from the cable or satellite company has a digital tuner in it. That means you don't need one

TV's don't die; they just move to another room.

Jeff Cove, vice president for techhnlogy and alliances at Panasonic

● ● ●

in your TV. Here is where it gets a bit confusing. Any set larger than 36 inches without a digital tuner must be labeled as a monitor. Any TV larger than 26 inches is treated the same way. All other HDTV's without tuners are called "HD ready." Those with tuners are described as "HD built in."

If you can keep that straight while shopping, your savings could be significant. But there's just one caveat. If you ever want to move the monitor or HD-ready set to a room that doesn't have a cable box, you have to rent or buy a set-top box from the cable company.

Which screen looks better? In the end, it's a personal preference. Ignore such specifications as contrast ratios and response time if the sales representative starts lobbing those terms at you. Just remember, you stand about four feet away from a TV in a store, while most people at home view a TV from about nine feet. So bring your tape measure along with your wallet.

—Damon Darlin

Making Calls Without a Phone
Phoning via the Internet is the next big thing

Internet telephone service is well on its way into the mainstream. Companies like Vonage, using a technology called voice over Internet protocol, or VoIP, offer cheap long-distance rates and features not found with conventional phone service. Cable giants, too, are taking Internet phones to the masses. And a subset of VoIP services, called PC-to-phone service, is gaining momentum. With these services, users can make calls to and receive calls from regular phones on their PC's as long as they have a broadband connection, VoIP software

TIMELY TIPS

Should Your PC Be Your Phone?

Among the attractions of Internet telephone service, or VoIP for voice over Internet protocol, are inexpensive, often unlimited local and long-distance calling plans and less red tape when compared to conventional phone service.

To establish VoIP service, you need a broadband Internet connection, a standard telephone and a telephone adapter, usually a paperback-size device supplied by the service provider, which connects the telephone to your Internet connection. But while VoIP offers many benefits, there are some negatives:

✔ It is important to understand how a provider's 911 service works before signing on, especially if you are replacing conventional phone service that includes enhanced 911, which automatically provides information to the operator about the location of a caller. Most VoIP providers do not yet offer enhanced 911.

✔ Quality of service can be another drawback. Because the calls often travel across the Internet, packets of data can be lost or delayed, which can cause occasional echo or lag. Such hiccups are usually not disturbing enough to be deal-breakers, and the providers are working on improving the technology.

✔ Another issue is the possibility of a power outage. Even with batteries backing up your broadband modem, router and telephone adapter, the service may not work if you lose power, because your Internet service provider may not guarantee service during outages. This can be important to know during an emergency.

✔ And while in most cases you can tote your telephone adapter with you anywhere, plug it into a broadband connection and resume using your account, with the same phone number and features, it is worth noting the fine print: many providers charge activation and termination fees, and also as much as $1 a call for 411 directory assistance (or do not offer it at all).

✔ With the number of VoIP options expanding, a good strategy is to compare features and then try one or two as a second phone instead of replacing conventional service. Many providers offer free trial periods.

—Thomas J. Fitzgerald

downloaded from the Web and a headset.

One advantage of such services is the ability to make calls through an Internet-connected laptop when cellular service is unreliable. Many people also prefer the convenience of talking while working on a PC; the services can operate while you are doing other tasks on the computer. Another advantage is price. PC-to-phone VoIP rates are less expensive than conventional phone calls and in many cases cheaper than phone-to-phone VoIP services, which route calls through broadband modems to regular phones.

Early versions of these services have been around since the late 1990's, but the rise of Skype, a mostly free VoIP service using file-sharing technology, has increased competition in the field.

Yahoo, America Online and Microsoft have each announced plans to add new phone services to future versions of their instant messaging programs. And Google has introduced Google Talk, a free service that enables users to talk through their computers and could be a first step toward a PC-to-phone service.

PC-to-phone services currently available from companies like Skype (www.skype.com), SIPphone (www.gizmoproject.com), i2Telecom (www.voicestick.com) and Dialpad Communications (www.iconnecthere.com) offer many features like free PC-to-PC calling, conference

TIMELY TIPS

A Cellphone and a Plan

A confusing array of models and contracts

Selecting a cellular service provider is no easy task, either. There are regional carriers and four national companies—Cingular (which acquired AT&T Wireless), T-Mobile, Sprint Nextel and Verizon Wireless.

Most carriers provide coverage maps, but those on T-Mobile's Web site are the most detailed, and are brutally honest. A good resource for all carriers is CellReception.com, where you get access to a map of local cellphone towers and reports from your neighbors about the reception they get.

It is best, however, to try it yourself. Most carriers will let you cancel a new contract and return a phone within the first two weeks, and sometimes longer, with no penalty. (If you currently have a contract with a service you don't like, you may have to spend $150 to $200 to get out of it.)

After you've selected a carrier, choose a calling plan that fits the amount of time you actually talk on the phone, because exceeding your allotted time can mean exorbitant charges—up to 45 cents for each extra minute. You can dig through each carrier's Web site, but it's easier to visit LetsTalk.com, which presents detailed plan information from 19 wireless carriers (national and regional) with side-by-side comparisons. You should also visit stores to ask questions and haggle.

Customer service is a consideration. A reader survey of wireless carriers in the January 2006 issue of *Consumer Reports* magazine found that Cingular was "one of the lower ones" for customer service. Cingular also rated low for reception quality. In general, Verizon was highest in customer satisfaction, followed closely by T-Mobile.

—Sean Captain

calls, voice mail, choice of phone numbers, call forwarding and reduced long-distance rates, especially for international calls. But as with phone-to-phone VoIP services, call quality is not always perfect.

To make free calls to other PC's with Skype, users simply download the software from the Web site; the PC receiving the Skype call also has to be connected to the Skype network. For PC-to-phone calling, the company has added SkypeOut and SkypeIn. Details are available on the Web site.

—Thomas J. Fitzgerald

Have Digital Camera, Will Travel

The good news is you don't need film

While digital cameras can free you from lugging loads of film, they also tend to run out of two things when you're away from home: power and memory. Here are some tips on coping with both.

PACK ENOUGH POWER

Because of their liquid-crystal display screens, automatic focus and flash, some digital cameras can be greedy little pigs when it comes to battery life. Keeping an eye on your battery is important, as you don't want to see a panicky power message in the middle of your bus tour of London.

Many digital cameras run on AA batteries, either the rechargeable type or the disposable cells you can buy at the drugstore. Other digital cameras come with their own rechargeable batteries supplied by the manufacturer.

Alkaline batteries are often the least expensive, but they also have a comparatively short life compared with other battery types—just a couple of hours sometimes in heavy flash situations. Many manufacturers are now making AA-size batteries designed just for power-mad digital cameras, and these could give you more shots between battery changes. Energizer, for example, estimates that its E2 lithium batteries can last seven times as long as ordinary alkaline cells, but they do cost more, around $5 for four AA batteries.

Rechargeable nickel-metal hydride batteries cost more, and you need to buy a charger, but they usually last longer in the camera and cost less over the long run—if you remember to pack the charger, that is.

You will also need to consider plug adapters and possibly voltage converters if you are going places with electrical standards different from those in North America. Check the power adapter or manual that came with your digital camera or battery charger to see what voltage and frequencies it can handle. (There's a chart of international electrical standards at www.travel-island.com/technique_standards/plug_ins.html.)

Plug adapters slip over the prongs of your power cord to make it fit in a foreign socket, but they don't usually convert the voltage. You can buy voltage converters and inexpensive plug adapters in travel stores or electronics shops like Radio Shack. If you're going to several countries, the Kensington Travel Plug Adapter can save suitcase space; the small barrel-shaped device has push-up prongs that fit the outlets in 150 countries.

THANKS FOR THE MEMORY

It's great to get away from the desktop, but sooner or later your camera's memory card is going to fill up. The simplest solution is to buy a few additional memory cards to swap in and out of the camera. Memory cards can be expensive and easy to lose, though. Another option is to find a gadget to serve as an image vault, so you can dump the photos from your memory card for safekeeping.

Several companies make image vaults (also called digital photo viewers), and in addition to copying and storing photographs from a memory card, these tiny hard drives can display your photos, too.

Devices like the Archos AV420 or the SmartDisk FlashTrax typically store 20 or 40 gigabytes of photographs and are much easier on the spine than hauling around a laptop. Prices run from $280 to $500, so it's a considerable investment.

Another photo storage option is the iPod. The color iPod Photo model works with a snap-on widget called the iPod Camera Connector, which lets you connect the camera's U.S.B. cable to the iPod. Then you can copy your images onto its hard drive and even view them on its screen.

You can also copy photos onto a regular iPod if you don't own the fancy Photo model. Belkin makes two different gadgets for transferring pictures to an iPod: the Digital Camera Link and the Media Reader. The Digital Camera Link connects directly to the camera. With the Media Reader, you pop your memory card out of the camera and insert it into the device to transfer the photos onto the iPod. The photos cannot be seen until you connect the iPod to your computer and transfer them.

IF YOU BRING THE LAPTOP

Toting your laptop to stash the photos on your camera's bulging memory card does have some advantages. For one, if you use an online photo-sharing service like Shutterfly or Kodak's Gallery and can find an Internet connection, you can share your vacation photos before you even get home. And e-mailing photos to friends from the hotel gives you the chance to send personalized postcards without having to buy stamps.

—J. D. Biersdorfer

SPENDING

Collecting

A Guide for the Artless

Starting an art collection means dealing with intimidating dealers. Here's how

The art world can be a confusing place for even the most experienced of art buyers. Squishy factors such as "historical interest" or "artistic integrity" will determine whether your purchase is the bargain of a lifetime or just expensive wall-paper. And if you're just starting out, you're at the mercy of often-intimidating dealers.

To even the odds, we asked Alan Bamberger, veteran art consultant, syndicated columnist and author of three art books, including *The Art of Buying Art*, to advise the beginning art collector. Here he gets behind the mystique and offers no-nonsense suggestions:

First of all, be sure that what you want is there to collect. Once you decide, collect the best in the field. Obviously, if you want to collect works by Vincent Van Gogh, you'll have to have a lot of money; otherwise, you'll get the worst of the worst of his work because that's what's most likely to be on the market. To research what's available, talk to dealers and ask them to direct you to other dealers in the same field, place ads in the trade papers, do a thorough online search and turn to international directories of dealers.

Start by collecting an artist's typical works. It's a question of salability down the road—if you want things that will be liquid, you'd be well advised to go with the mainstream. First, find out what the artist is most famous for. Or if you like landscapes of Cape Cod, say, find out what people who collect them like to have in them and, if it also appeals to you, look for that in your pictures.

Don't confuse the work with the environment. Properly lit and displayed, even a sack of trash can look great. You can take anything—a tape measure, a can of soup—put it up on a pedestal, give it good lighting, put it in a gallery and you'll have people walk by and say, "Wow, that's fantastic." But when you get it home, all it is, is a can of soup. Take the piece out of the gallery environment, take it home on approval for a week. Usually you can just leave a deposit, with no commitment to buy.

At the same time, unless you're really experienced, it can be hard to see how beautiful something is. At a garage sale, for example, it may look like a piece of junk, but a collector who knows what he's doing will clean it up and display it properly and it'll look like a million dollars.

Establish as wide of a net of resources as possible. Not only will you see and learn more, but you'll

 INSIDE INFO

Selling to a Dealer

- ○ Expect to get 25 percent to 33 percent of your artwork's retail price if you sell to a dealer. The most a dealer will give is 50 percent, but that's only for the rare item and generally to a known client.

- ○ A dealer might accept to sell your art for you on consignment. Fees range from 35 percent to 50 percent of the sales price. You get the cash after it's sold.

also be able to play the market for the best price and make intelligent price comparisons. But don't purposely play dealers off one another. Just ask intelligent questions. It's a little like comparing cars at auto dealerships. You should ask dealers to explain why you saw something similar somewhere else for a different price.

Don't take bullying. If an art dealer is giving you a hard time, leave. When you hear comments like "The artist is almost dead" or "We sold six of these last month," it's best to exit. If you feel pressure in any way, that's a warning sign that you're in the wrong place.

Work with experts. Avoid galleries with no direction or focus. Such galleries are repositories for pieces that locals happen to find at flea markets and estate sales. Their main focus is to obtain pieces that they can mark up and sell for more. Those galleries have their place, and if you have experience, you can find bargains there. But beginners are better off going with more professional dealers.

Don't ask, don't tell. Forgeries are a touchy area. You don't want to ask one dealer to comment on the authenticity of a painting another dealer is selling. For one thing, you may not get a straight answer, since the second dealer would rather sell you one of his paintings. Rather, educate yourself. As you spend more time collecting, try to meet people—museum people, scholarly types or true collectors who are not overly concerned about the money and who will give you the straight dope. If you suspect a forgery, you may be better off not pointing it out. You might be wrong, you could get entangled in legal problems and you certainly will make enemies fast.

Don't let investment factors weigh too heavily. Art is immediately liquid only if you want to take a severe hit. If you buy and sell stocks and bonds and the like, you normally pay a small percentage in

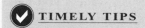

TIMELY TIPS

Brushing Up on Art

Check these sites before starting the quest for your private art collection

✔ **Artcyclopedia.com –** An exhaustive fine art search engine. Links to 180,000 works by 8,200 artists around the world. Features include art news and high-quality scans of famous art. 403-547-9692

✔ **Artnet.com –** The magazine's site, with everything you need to know about the fine arts market. Find the average sales records for 4,000 artists. ($79.99 per report) 212-497-9700

✔ **ArtQuest.com –** This listing service connects collectors and sellers by e-mail, eliminating dealer fees and commissions. The site charges sellers $10 for a six-month listing. To check out available art, click on "Search for Art" and then "Just Browsing." 314-961-2400

✔ **Gallery-Guide.com –** The online version of *Gallery Guide* magazine. A comprehensive source of art gallery and museum exhibits. 908-638-5255

✔ **iCollector.com –** One of the oldest traders of fine art, antiques and collectibles on the Internet. Your portal to the world of live auctions. 866-313-0123

✔ **iTheo.com –** An information resource for the art world. Everything you want to know about 1,000 artists and hundreds of museums and art associations. 404-832-6012

commission; in the art world, you pay a 20 percent commission to buy a work of art and then pay a 20 percent commission when you sell it—and those are very modest commissions in the business. The art has to increase in value 40 percent before you see your first penny of profit.

Don't try to chisel on prices, unless you have a really good argument. Don't worry about letting on that you really like a painting. A poker face won't work anyway. If dealers suspect that you're the type of person who expects to get a deal, they'll bump their price up a bit when they see you coming, and then drop it to the price they wanted in the first place. Or, worse, they will sell you medium-quality art that they would rather have out the door anyway. Sure, they'll flex on the price a little bit, but you're not going to get the good stuff. You have to work for that—you have to fight the competition.

When Beauty and Value Merge

It takes more than a good eye to make a good art investment

What is art? In the ideal, it's beauty—plus a profit. Michael A. Moses, a management professor at New York University, spent four years studying the value of artwork. Together with Jianping Mei, a finance professor at the school, he devised an index that tracks the value of art sold, mainly by the Sotheby's and Christie's auction houses in New York. By their calculations, the value of art has kept pace with the Standard & Poor's 500-stock index over the last 50 years, though art's returns have zigzagged more.

"For people who have a 20-to-30-year horizon, I have no problem talking about

art as an investment," Moses says. The index includes more than 13,000 transactions going back to 1875; a report on the index appeared in a 2002 *American Economic Review.*

Other financial experts are less convinced of art's investment potential. To be sure, art and collectibles can appreciate and command high prices. Witness the $135 million paid in 2006 for a Gustav Klimt portrait of Adele Bloch-Bauer. But they differ from other investments in important ways. They can be hard to sell, and brokerage fees are high, compared with those for, say, an index mutual fund. Plus, they can be costly to store and insure.

Most important, they do not lend themselves to diversification, unless the collector is rich. A company like Microsoft can be divided into shares and sold in tiny pieces, but most works of art can't be split apart. Expertise may also matter more in art than for stocks and bonds. An investor who doesn't want to spend time learning about stocks can choose an index fund. A collector must learn as much as possible—or risk being duped.

What's more, collectors often fool themselves about the value of their beloved collections—and

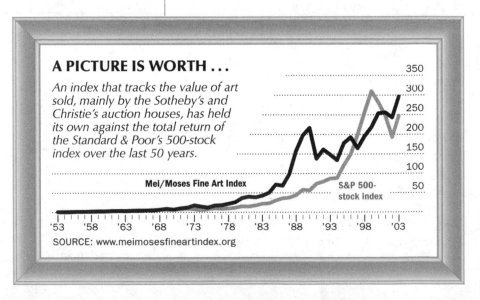

A PICTURE IS WORTH . . .

An index that tracks the value of art sold, mainly by the Sotheby's and Christie's auction houses, has held its own against the total return of the Standard & Poor's 500-stock index over the last 50 years.

Mei/Moses Fine Art Index

S&P 500-stock Index

'53 '58 '63 '68 '73 '78 '83 '88 '93 '98 '03

350
300
250
200
150
100
50

SOURCE: www.meimosesfineartindex.org

What to Look for in a Painting

Roosters sell, sheep and pigs don't

Nearly every dealer knows what sells and what doesn't, or they quickly learn before bankruptcy sets in. Some artistic compositions will never grace the white walls of their galleries: a vertical painting of rough waters, for example, or a dark, church-side cemetery. Here are other well-known secrets of what's taboo in the art world.

WHAT SELLS	WHAT DOESN'T
Horizontal landscapes	Vertical landscapes
Paintings with roosters	Sheep, cows, pigs
Young women, children	Old folks, particularly men
Brightly colored paintings	Dark scenes
Calm waters	Rough seas
Grouse and pheasant	Crows and mallards
Floral still-life	Fruits and vegetables
Roses	Chrysanthemums
Setters, spaniels, terriers	Mongrels, dachshunds
Lions, leopards, elephants	Wolves, wild boars

SOURCE: Chicago Appraisers Association

tend not to be disciplined about selling works when they can get the best price, says Tyler Cowen, economics professor at George Mason University in Fairfax, Va. Therein lies one of the paradoxes of art collecting, he says: to be successful you have to be involved and detached at the same time.

Sometimes, collectors wrongly assume that a dealer's appraised value represents what buyers are willing to pay. "There's always somebody who will value an asset," says Timothy M. Hayes, a financial planner in Pittsford, N.Y., who collects photographs. "But you still can be stuck with something that no one else wants."

—Tim Gray

How to Spot a Real Antique

Examine the finish, hardware, feet and even the smell

How can a casual buyer tell if that attractive antique chest is genuine, a reproduction, a mongrel or a fake? Sam Pennington, publisher of *Maine Antique Digest* (800-752-8521 or www.maineantiquedigest.com), says when you're trying to determine whether an antique is authentic, you should examine several things: finish, backboard, drawers, hardware and feet. "Sometimes, even smell will help," says Pennington. "You shouldn't detect any oil or paint-type odor, which suggests the piece has been recently worked on. Good, early, untouched furniture gives off a wonderful nutty smell from inside the drawers. Once you smell it, you never forget it." Here are Pennington's tips on sizing up an antique chest, bed, mirror and chair from the 18th to early 19th century.

CHEST OF DRAWERS

In American chests, backboards generally tell you a lot. Look at the back carefully. It's usually made of pine and should be well darkened with age and exposure to air and dirt.

The older or earlier the finish, the better. A piece should not be refinished or painted. It should have a uniform patina and age to it.

Pull out the drawers. Dovetails—a special type of tongue-in-groove joint—on drawers are important. They should be hand done. Often cabinet makers would number the drawers in pencil and the numbers are sometimes still visible. There should be no shellac or finish on the inside of the drawers. Glue or black gunk is a sign of repair.

The color of the wood inside the drawers should vary. The bottom drawer should be darker in the front and lighter to the rear. The bottom of the bottom drawer should be darkest of all—it gets more exposure. The middle drawers, which get less exposure to light, shouldn't show as much darkness as the bottom drawer.

Look at the hardware. Is there an extra set of holes? Then the original hardware has probably been replaced. Check out the feet, too. Do they look as old as the chest? If the feet have been replaced, the price of the piece goes way down.

ANTIQUE BED

Tastes in beds have changed over the years and many antique beds have been altered to changing tastes. As a result, beds don't bring a lot of money.

There were no king-size beds 100 years ago, of course, so if the bed's been used, the rails will probably have been lengthened. Another compromise you may have to accept is the addition of box spring holders.

Look at the legs. Most early beds were too high for modern tastes and people have cut off the legs. Beds should be made of all hard woods, such as mahogany, maple, cherry, walnut or birch. The main things to look for in the wood are signs of smeared stain or wood that doesn't match, which suggests that the bed has been altered in some way.

Antique beds should have hand-fashioned bed-bolts holding them together. If it's a tall poster bed, look for the original tester (pronounced "teester"), the framework that holds the cloth canopy over the bed. If there is carving on the bed, be sure it is consistent with the bed's style and period.

ANTIQUE MIRROR

The nicest thing to find in a mirror is a label. Labeled furniture is rare, but you find more labels on mirrors than on any other antique. It's nice to know who made the piece and it helps date it.

If the mirror was made before 1830, the back shouldn't have circular saw marks on it. It should have plane marks instead. Look for major replacements. Curlicues or ears on a mirror often break and get replaced. A number of those round mirrors have eagles or gilded work on them—it's hard to tell if they were made in 1820 or 1920—but you want to look for obvious changes in the finish or breaks in the design. The early ones were made of gesso, plaster with gold leaf rubbed on it.

An early mirror will have wavy glass. You'll see some breaks in the reflectivity. I'd rather have the original glass, if possible.

ANTIQUE CHAIR

A really early chair may have sat in a cellar or on a dirt floor, and part of its feet may have rotted away. Look for replacement of the bottom three or four inches of the legs, which seriously lessens its value.

If the chair is reupholstered, try to see the frame under the upholstery. See if it's the original frame and that no one has put in a bigger wing than was there, for example. Be very careful if it's the original upholstery; that makes the chair worth a lot more. You don't see much original upholstery anymore.

Beware of a chair that has screws in it. The chair will be unstable because screws don't hold well in wood under the stress of a chair.

A Windsor chair with its original paint is more valuable than if it's been stripped down. In a Windsor chair, the legs are generally made of maple or birch, the seat is usually pine, the spindles and back are hickory or ash and the arms might be oak. So, to get a uniform color, Windsor chairs were painted. Collectors are really after a Windsor with the original paint.

HOW TO RECOGNIZE FAMOUS-NAME ANTIQUES

English designers Thomas Chippendale, George Hepplewhite and Thomas Sheraton helped make the 18th century the golden age of furniture.

CHIPPENDALE
1750-1785

CHAIR. *S-shaped curved legs and ball-and-claw feet. Back is fiddle-shaped with decorative carvings.*

CHEST. *Rococco carving often used. Big brass pulls on drawers. Legs curved, ball-and-claw feet common.*

MIRROR. *Frames made of thinly cut mahogany and often feature elaborate, pierced-scroll fretwork.*

HEPPLEWHITE
1785-1810

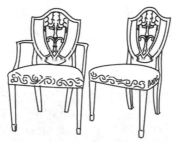

CHAIR. *Distinctive shield-shaped chair backs. Legs are usually tapered, with spade-like feet.*

CHEST. *Usually made of fancy woods, often with inlays. Feet curve outward. Oval brass drawer pulls.*

MIRROR. *Frames are elaborate and heavily gilt. Typical design features a floral urn atop an oval inlay.*

SHERATON
1790-1830

CHAIR. *Thin, tapered legs. Brass castors under feet. Chair backs usually square or rectangular.*

TABLE. *Typically drum-shaped. Curved and fluted legs. Top often covered with leather.*

TESTER CANOPY BED. *Foot and head posts usually lightly tapered. Edge of headboard arched or flat.*

What's Your Collection Worth?

The case against investing in collectibles

Every day, it seems that another collectible is sold for a record price. Consider, for example, the widely publicized sale of Babe Ruth's contract, which sent him from the Red Sox to the Yankees in 1919, that sold for nearly $1 million in mid-2005. A 1913 Liberty Head nickel that went for $4.15 million, up from $3 million a year earlier. And a 1927 gold coin sold by auctioneer Escala Group in early 2006 for $1.9 million, up from $176,000 in 1982.

Are collectibles a sound financial investment? Despite these spectacular sales, if the past is any guide, the answer is no. Historically, collectibles have yielded a much lower return than stocks and carried more risk. The results of exhaustive studies by Benjamin J. Burton of Lehman Brothers and Joyce P. Jacobsen of Wesleyan University estimating the financial return of collectibles were reported in the *Journal of Economic Perspectives* in 1999. They examined the payoff from holding several kinds of collectibles, including art, wine, antiques, ceramics, coins, stamps, books and Beanie Babies.

Measuring the return from investing in collectibles is difficult because items sold each year are not identical, and some items are rarely sold.

Methods to estimate the return involve tracking the prices of objects sold on multiple occasions, following the prices of a portfolio of similar but not identical items each year, and trying to adjust statistically for certain characteristics, such as, for example, a large Picasso should sell for more than a smaller one, other things being equal.

Despite methodological differences, according to Burton and Jacobsen, the results support the same conclusion: "The majority of collectibles yield lower financial returns than stocks, and studies that include a measure of variability over time uniformly find that collectibles embody more risk than most other financial assets." Certainly, there have been periods when artwork and other collectibles yielded a higher return than stocks, but those periods were brief and hard to predict. The resale price of Beanie Babies, for instance, grew at an astonishing rate of 140 percent a year from 1994 to 1999—and has since crashed.

One reason the return on collectibles is inherently volatile is that demand depends mainly on fads and buyers' whims, not on fundamentals. For example, it is true that Babe Ruth was traded to the Yankees for $100,000—which translates to $1.2 million in today's dollars—making the $1 million price tag his contract just fetched sound like a bargain. But the original contract came with Babe Ruth!

Burton and Jacobsen find that, as a whole, collectibles yield a higher return when the stock market does poorly (Beanie Babies notwithstanding). Still, collectibles do not provide as good a hedge against stock market risk as bonds or money market accounts, which may explain why virtually all hedge funds and mutual funds have shied away from investing in collectibles.

So why has the price of some prestigious collectibles surged lately? One possibility is that eye-catching cases gain lots of publicity. Another

---

ⓘ **INSIDE INFO**

Coin of the Realm

○ At least 140 million Americans collect coins, up from 125 million in 2004.

○ A world-famous coin set, called the King of Siam, sold in 2005 for a record $8.5 million. President Andrew Jackson presented it in 1836 to the king of Siam—whose son was immortalized in *The King and I.*

Going on the Antiques Roadshow

Is your great-uncle's musket worth a mint?

Even after a decade of traipsing around America in search of hidden treasures, *Antiques Roadshow* is still the Public Broadcasting System's most-watched TV program. Its premise is addictive. Owners of antique furniture, art, knick-knacks and doodads bring their possessions to the *Roadshow* to have them appraised by experts. The suspense lies in finding out what's trash and what's treasure.

The show tapes in different locations across the land each year; the schedule is listed on www.antiquesroadshow.org. The show's popularity makes getting tickets a challenge. Tickets are free, but you must apply for them online at least three months before the actual show date. Names are randomly selected from among the applications. No one can enter the show without a ticket, and every ticket holder must bring an item for appraisal. Show producers promise that all ticket holders will have their goods appraised by an expert, regardless of whether they are selected to be taped for television.

Once you receive a ticket, you can bring in two items for a free appraisal; a collection of spoons or a tea set, for example, only count as one. The items are appraised by one of the show's 75 onsite experts, who cover more than 20 categories, including silver, old maps, pottery—everything but coins and stamps. If you're thinking of bringing in that huge Hepplewhite sideboard, though, be sure it will fit through standard double doors and that you have help transporting it. Bring along your patience, too: appraisers see about 700 people per hour.

If you'd rather forego the hassle of participating in the *Roadshow* but still want your collectible appraised, check the show's Web site and click on "Appraiser Index." You'll find a list of experts who have appeared on the show, along with contact information. But their appraisal won't be free.

is that given the high price volatility and wide variety of collectibles, some prominent items are bound to rise sharply in value.

It is also possible, however, that we are in one of those infrequent periods when the price of collectibles is surging. Scott Mitchell, a numismatist at Stack's Coins in New York, says that since 2000 there has been an increase in both the sales volume and price of rare coins, because of the attention around sales like the Liberty Head nickel and a desire by investors to move funds from stocks to rare coins.

Still, the average collector would be wise to recognize that collectibles have historically been a poor investment but a good hobby. Presumably, the joy that buyers derive from owning and displaying collectibles is why people buy them despite their poor financial return. That is unlikely to change.

—Alan B. Krueger

Hot Bids, Cold Sweats

How to survive an antiques auction

Owning antiques is a little like being in love. What you don't know won't hurt you. But what you might discover later could hurt you a lot, emotionally and financially. Try thinking about the conditions of sale at an auction—two pages of fine print at the back of the Christie's catalogs and three pages in Sotheby's catalogs—as prenuptial agreements between you and that piece of gilt that just winked at you. Nervous yet?

More than ever, as auctions continue to grow in popularity and the number of sales increase, the buyer must beware. Though the patina of politesse at many of the respected auction rooms can be as venerable as the apparent finish or provenance of the furnishings, it can as quickly prove to be veneer.

SPENDING

And a good tale (Washington slept here—or was it only a power nap?) is best told on paper—as in documentation. Learn more before you prop up your bid card.

Ask for a condition report. At auction, in addition to reading the catalog and examining the lot, a buyer's beware means asking for a condition report, speaking to the department adviser and seeking outside expertise. Obtain as much as you can—previous bills of sale, published references. See whether the story being told is verifiable in scholarly journals and books or through the services of an outside professional appraiser, especially if you're dealing with an item of substantial value.

The more you read, the less is guaranteed. Only the information that is in capitals at the top of an entry is covered by warranty in the conditions of sale. The lower-case phrases after that and the following paragraphs, often with colorful accounts, are generally not. In other words, "The 'story' is always a major sales tool," says Bruce Wolmer, editor in chief of *Art & Auction* magazine. "It reinforces your decision to buy something."

Visit the preview showing shortly before the sale. Often, information is brought to the attention of the house, which will alter the description of a piece—not in the catalog but with a placard on the site, a practice known as gold carding. At an antiques dealer's shop or showroom, it is best to

---

 TIMELY TIPS

Culling the Junk From the Collectibles

When it's time to unload

Downsizing is rarely easy. The first inclination may be to bring in a garbage bin and move on, or maybe hold a yard sale. That could be a costly mistake.

✔ **Hire an appraiser.** Not every dingy piece of furniture is a prized collectible, of course, but one way to know for sure, short of poring through scores of research books yourself, is to hire an appraiser, who can pinpoint items that could be valuable. Appraisal fees run between $60 and $300 an hour. You can find a database of accredited members of the Appraisers Association of America on www.appraisersassoc.org.

✔ **Auction houses** also provide appraisals for varying fees, although they typically do them free if you also allow them to sell the items, as will professional home- or estate-sale organizers. Both work on commissions ranging from 15 to 40 percent and may charge additional fees for services like advertising, cleanup or insurance.

✔ **In an estate or home sale**, usually held on the premises, merchandise is tagged, and buyers are expected to pay that price, or close to it. (They can leave bids for more expensive pieces.) In an auction, everything is sold to the highest bidders, although you can set a "reserve," or price beneath which you won't sell an item.

✔ **Selling to a dealer is another option,** but here again, it's crucial to do some research beforehand. "If you don't know what you have, you've got no bargaining hand," says David Rago, a regular appraiser on the *Antiques Roadshow*. It's important, too, to understand that tastes and interests constantly change. The big sellers of three years ago may be less in demand today.

✔ **You may find that using a variety of selling methods works best.** Maybe a house sale for furnishings and auction or private sales for expensive things like the Navajo rugs. Another option is to donate, for example a sculpture to the local high school, and get a tax deduction.

—Vivian Marino

examine the piece, read any descriptive placard, ask questions, know the terms of sale and come back to visit the antique again with an expert, if it is expensive and cannot be returned.

Know why you're buying it—as a collectible with historical and investment value, or as furnishing. By determining how badly you want it and how much the product claims enter into it, you can determine what you are willing to pay for it. A good antique does not have to be a great antique to be good looking, and a great-looking antique does not have to be good to be worth buying at a price. If you love it, of course, it will always be perfect.

—William Hamilton

Bargains at Charity Auctions

Going, going, gone—for a song?

Charities are increasingly turning to black-tie benefit auctions, using donated items as the fund-raising tool of choice. But, as benefit auctions proliferate—live auction sales climbed to $240 billion in 2005, up 11 percent, according to the National Auctioneers Association in Overland Park, Kan.—and as their offerings turn more elaborate to entice buyers, more bidders are getting a shot at luxury at bargain prices.

For all the glitz and glamour, there is a science and even a formula to charity auctions, according to organizers, auctioneers and veteran bidders. The same types of offerings generally soar: the private dinner prepared by a superstar chef, the coveted bottle of Champagne or—that blockbuster of school auctions—the chance for a child to be principal for a day.

But most items, like a trip to a popular resort, end up selling for about 15 percent off their retail price or fair market value, says Fred Reger, a founder of Benefit Auction Specialists in Manassas, Va.

And in silent auctions, in which bidders place bids on sign-up sheets, the deals can be greater, with luxury listings like Coach bags or skybox sports tickets selling for as much as 35 percent off.

A quick look at an event's format can provide clues to the likelihood of bargains. People seated at dinner tables for an auction almost always bid more aggressively than those sitting in rows, explains Richard Brierley, a Christie's auctioneer. That results not only from the availability of liquor but also from peer pressure from tablemates.

Bargains aren't always just about price. Some charity art auctions give buyers the rare opportunity to get works by hot artists who have waiting-lists of collectors. One tip when buying art at a charity auction: check to see if it has been donated by an artist or by a dealer. Artists tend to donate high-quality works, but also tend to overstate their fair market value. Indeed, a buyer should research the price of any big purchase at auction, since a donor may have a tax incentive to inflate value.

Bargain hunters do better at larger sales, say, of 20 or more items, where interest may flag. Single-theme food or travel auctions of trips with stiff timing restrictions, for example, reduce the number of potential bidders and up the chances of bargains.

Items at private secondary school auctions, where parents do most of the bidding, don't tend to sell at low prices. You do better at auctions for churches and colleges, auctioneers say. And best of all, at least from the perspective of bargain hunters, are auctions that are scheduled to start only after a series of speeches, or after a dinner, when people start streaming out. Bidders who brave it out do well.

For some buyers, the biggest discounts may come in the days after the auction. As many as 10 percent of the buyers at any sale wind up not paying, organizers say. So an item may become available again, this time at a bargain price.

—Alexandra Peers

Demystifying eBay

There's an armada of help for first-time users of the online auction site

First-time sellers can get a gut-wrenching, frustrated feeling trying to learn the ropes for selling on eBay. Well, it turns out there's no need to learn how to post something on eBay—just tap into an entire industry devoted to doing just that. The trade-off for convenience is that the fees you pay for the service could make a serious dent in your profits. Here are some options:

Attend eBay University. For $59, these daylong seminars, held in different locations around the country, introduce you to "Selling Basics" or "Beyond the Basics" in eBay speak. You get tips like creating "eye-catching listings," or, for the more experienced, "bulk selling tools." You can take a similar course online—free for the basics and $19.95 for the more advanced course.

Hire your own trading assistant. These self-styled experts will also post your item for you, then pack and ship it once it's sold. Depending on the person and what you're selling, the trading assistant might pick it up from your house. Their commissions vary, from 5 percent of selling price and up.

You can locate trading assistants on the eBay site; find one near you by typing in your zip code. The criteria are pretty loose: to be included in the Trading Assistant Directory, a person must have sold at least 10 items in the last 90 days; at least 100 different people must have left positive feedback on different transactions, with 97 percent positive feedback or higher; and the eBay account must be in good standing.

Go to a bricks-and-mortar eBay shop. There are thousands of stores around the country where you can drop off items, and let sales personnel do all the work. In exchange, of course, the shop takes a pretty hefty commission, usually around 30 percent. People who run such stores are also considered trading assistants, an eBay spokesperson says, and the company has no more of a relationship with them than with any other trading assistant listed on its site.

The biggest eBay drop-off chain is iSold It, with about 500 branches across the country. These individually owned franchises complete the whole process internally. Typically, its commission is 30 percent of the first $500 and 20 percent of the remaining amount, which includes eBay listing fees.

AuctionDrop shops, another service, are located in some United Parcel Service stores. If your item is worth over $75 and weighs less than 25 pounds, AuctionDrop will box and ship it to a central processing center, where it is photographed and listed. Its commission is 38 percent on the first $200, 30 percent on the next $300, and 20 percent on the remaining amount.

If the item doesn't sell, the store will either give it back or donate it to charity.

—Alina Tugend

Shopping in Uncle Sam's Attic

You might score at a government auction, but there are risks

Some bargain hunters see government auctions as a way to save a bundle on cars, furniture, diamonds and flat-screen televisions. For informed buyers, bidding may yield good investments. But the bang of the gavel can hold risk for novices.

Sponsored by federal, state and local agencies selling seized property, hundreds of auctions are held around the country each year. Depending on the sale, bidding may be done online, by phone or in person. The merchandise is an eclectic mix—from big-ticket items like homes, cars and trucks to products like Rolex watches and Bose speakers. There may also be cartons of air-conditioners, pottery, clothing and shampoo—and even slabs of granite and machine parts.

Many buyers are merchants who conduct business at a low and steady hum, eager to make an eventual profit, but others are individuals looking for that unbelievable bargain. For those interested in shopping at a government auction, specialists offer these pointers.

- Look for auction announcements on Web sites like firstgov.gov/shopping /shopping, for federal sales, and elsewhere for state and local sales.

- Attend several auctions, without bidding, to get an idea of fair prices.

- When you are ready to buy, go to an auction preview and determine your top potential bids. Consider retail prices and past winning bids.

- If you are buying a car, check the blue book value and get a Carfax report. At the preview, ask if you may start the car.

- Be sure you have everything you need to register to bid, such as a photo ID.

- Understand the payment requirements. Some auctions require up to $5,000 on the spot, often by cashier's check or cash.

- Establish a pickup time for the property you purchased.

- Auction items are sold as is, come with no guarantees from the government, and they cannot be returned or exahustively checked out ahead of time. Ask manufacturers whether they will honor warranties.

—Hillary Chura

TIMELY TIPS

Sniffing Out a Fake
Here's how to spot knockoffs on eBay

Counterfeit goods are rampant on the Internet, and buyers using online auction sites like eBay are especially vulnerable. Artwork, jewelry, designer accessories, autographed sports memorabilia and other collectibles are popular among counterfeiters. How can you prevent being taken? A few basics:

✔ **Know your merchandise.** If you learn, for instance, that a certain cookie jar from the 1930's is a rare collectible, and you see someone selling dozens of them at low prices, consider yourself warned that it is probably counterfeit.

✔ **Look at the starting bid price.** If it is low, be suspicious. Prices that seem too enticing are a reason for wariness, according to an eBay spokesman.

✔ **Look for a certificate of authenticity** from a reputable appraiser that has been scanned into the listing.

✔ **Know your seller.** Take the time to look at the details of a seller's feedback. A good sign is a comment from a satisfied buyer who took the extra step to have an item appraised, then reported back on its authenticity.

✔ **If there is any negative feedback on the site, scrutinize it carefully.** To report suspicious listings, hit the "Report This Item" button on each listing.

✔ **If you buy an item that you believe is counterfeit,** and you used PayPal, you are likely to have recourse under the PayPal buyer protection system (pages.ebay.com/paypal/buyer/protection.html).

—Katie Hafner

SPENDING

What's in a Rock?

Solid facts for picking a perfect engagement ring

To the Greeks, diamonds were tears of the gods. To the Romans, they were splinters from falling stars. Today, the glittery chunks of crystallized carbon signify "Forever," as the marketing slogan for the diamond company the De Beers Group, puts it. That hopeful sentiment no doubt drives the fact that three-fourths of first-time brides are proposed to with diamond engagement rings, according to industry figures.

Picking a diamond is fraught with peril, especially for novice buyers, who will have to determine the value of a particular diamond. Fortunately, the Gemological Institute of America (GIA) developed a standard for grading diamonds, referred to as the four C's: the stone's carat weight, its degree of clarity, its color and the skill with which it was cut. Richard Drucker, publisher of an international wholesale price list called *The Guide*, explains what's behind the four C's.

CARAT WEIGHT. Gemstone weight was traditionally measured with carob seeds, which weigh about one-fifth of a gram. Today's standard measure, the carat, sprouted from the carob seed—one carat equals 200 milligrams, or one-fifth of a gram.

CLARITY. Nothing is perfect, but the closer to

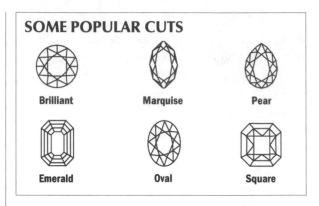

SOME POPULAR CUTS

Brilliant

Marquise

Pear

Emerald

Oval

Square

flawless a stone is, the more valuable. In this case, a flaw refers either to tiny mineral deposits, which are called inclusions, or to fractures in the stone, which are called cleavages. Internal imperfections are graded starting from F, for Flawless or IF for Internally Flawless; then VVS 1 or VVS 2, meaning Very, Very Slightly Included; VS 1 or VS 2, Very Slightly Included; SI 1 or SI 2, Slightly Included; and I 1, I 2, or I 3, Included.

COLOR. Color quality is determined by the stone's actual color (hue), how rich the color is (saturation), and how light or dark it is (tone). This is by far the most important factor affecting price. Slight differences in color may mean great differences in price. Unfortunately for the beginner, judging color is a highly subjective process and one that requires a practiced eye.

Color is graded starting with D as the highest color. D to F are colorless; G to J are nearly colorless; K to M are tinted yellow or brown.

CUT. This factor is the only one determined by the cutter, not by nature. A gemstone is like a tiny prism—the slightest change in the angle of a cut will affect how it refracts light—thus the "fire" in a stone can only be released by a skilled cutter. A well-polished gem will be far more radiant and therefore more valuable.

The GIA began a new cut scale in 2006, rating

 INSIDE INFO

Rules of Engagement

O Nearly 20 percent of couples become engaged during the holiday season, more than any other time of the year, according to a 2004 study by the Condè Nast Bridal Group.

O About 25 percent of all diamond purchases in a year are made during the holiday season.

cuts as Excellent, Very Good, Good, Fair and Poor. Here's how much a round-cut diamond might cost, based on a standard of Very Good.

ROUND	G/VS1	H/VS2	I/SI1	J/SI2
½ carat	$3,300	$2,400	$1,900	$1,600
1 carat	$12,600	$10,200	$7,200	$5,800

Remember that although stores like Tiffany, Winston and Van Cleef & Arpels carry a certain cachet, they don't have a monopoly on fine diamonds. Just be sure to shop at a trustworthy jeweler who will be around if there's a problem. If it's an investment-quality diamond you're after, however, those from the upscale shops signify a high quality of stones and a classic design, thereby retaining their value best.

Only the Oyster Knows for Sure
How to tell a real pearl from a phony

There are two types of pearls these days, the experts say: real ones and fakes. Real pearls come in two varieties: natural and cultured. Natural pearls, which are increasingly rare, are made of layers of nacre, the material that coats an oyster's shell. Cultured pearls are made by introducing a piece of shell into an oyster, which it then combines with tissue to produce the pearl.

Most "natural" pearls found in jewelry stores today are actually cultured pearls. They range in price from the least expensive, freshwater, to the Japanese akoya, the traditional white variety, to the large and often colored pearls of the South Seas.

The Price of Pearls *(Japanese akoya cultured pearl necklace, 16-inch length)*

SIZE	COMMERCIAL	GOOD	FINE	EXTRA FINE
4 ½ to 5 mm	$285	$485	$750	$1,000
5 ½ to 6 mm	$370	$650	$900	$1,100

Fake pearls are made of coated beads, plastic, resin or other artificial material. Sometimes, even jewelers can't tell the real from the fake, so if you suspect granny's inherited strand is made of museum-quality natural pearls, it's best to have it appraised by a certified professional. Otherwise, here's the reliability of some common tests to separate the cultured from the faux.

THE TOOTH TEST. Gently rub the pearl against the edge of your front teeth. Do not scrape the pearl, simply test to see if it feels rough and sandy. Cultured pearls have a grainy feel as a result of the natural buildup of nacre, or layers of crystal. Imitation pearls feel hard and uniformly smooth. This test is more reliable in distinguishing truly natural pearls from imitations, less so in picking phonies from cultured pearls, which have fewer bumps and ridges, and therefore feel smoother.

THE CLASP TEST. A fabulously expensive strand of pearls will have an equally exceptional clasp. It will have a secure closure made of gold, silver or platinum. You can inspect the clasp under a magnifying glass for manufacturer markings. An engraved "M," for example, means the pearls were made by Mikimoto, a high-quality Japanese producer. Good-quality pearl jewelry is generally strung with silk threads and with knots between each pearl.

THE EYE TEST. Real pearls are not as uniformly perfect in appearance. Like anything made naturally, there are variations in size and shape. A series of perfectly round, perfectly white beads is suspect. Look at the drill holes in the pearls. Genuine pearls have tiny holes, drilled from both sides of the pearl. The holes on imitation pearls are generally larger, and may even show some flaking of the lacquer or the bead inside.

THE X-RAY TEST. The only definitive analysis. The lab X-ray shows whether the core of the pearl is naturally produced or is a cheap lacquered bead.

The Price of Sparkle in Your Life

The value of most gemstones is more volatile than many commodities

Gemstone prices rise and fall due to factors such as supply, demand, and changes in treatment and production technology. Prices in these charts were compiled by Richard Drucker, publisher of *The Guide,* an industry pricing standard. They are average retail prices per stone, not per carat, unless otherwise stated, and are accurate as of the beginning of 2006. Remember that these are benchmark prices; you may find prices above or below these at your jeweler.

WEIGHT	COMMERCIAL	GOOD	FINE	EXTRA FINE
Amethyst				
1 carat	$5	$10	$20	$35
3 carat	$15	$40	$85	$150
Aquamarine				
1 carat	$30	$85	$285	$775
3 carat	$135	$315	$885	$2,325
Citrine				
1 carat	$5	$10	$20	$35
3 carats	$15	$35	$80	$120
Emerald				
½ carat	$45	$325	$1,000	2,250
1 carat	$145	$1,000	$3,800	$8,000
Garnet (Rhodolite)				
1 carat	$15	$30	$50	$85
3 carats	$65	$160	$255	$330
Opal (white with play of color)				
1 carat	$10	$40	$100	$300
3 carats	$30	$120	$300	$900

Peridot				
1 carat	$20	$45	$90	$145
3 carats	$60	$135	$270	$435
Ruby				
½ carat	$45	$200	$400	$1,450
1 carat	$205	$1,050	$1,800	$4,400
Sapphire				
½ carat	$25	$95	$320	$650
1 carat	$110	$500	$1,250	$3,200
Tanzanite				
½ carat	$35	$125	$250	$350
1 carats	$165	$375	$650	$875
Turquoise				
8 x 6 mm	$4	$10	$20	$40
10 x 8 mm	$6	$16	$30	$60

SOURCE: Richard Drucker, Publisher, *The Guide*

Silver: Look for a Lion or a King

Silver can be easily altered or imprinted with a phony hallmark

So it pays to know your silver. Sterling silverware is made by mixing pure silver with copper of some other alloy to make it harder and more durable. Three grades of silver are commonly used: sterling, which is 925 parts per 1,000 pure silver; English at 975; and European Continental at 800. To identify silver flatware,  turn the piece over: You may need a magnifying glass to decipher the markings on the back.

Before 1960, American silversmiths marked their wares on the back with their initials or full name. Silver made in America after 1860 is marked with the word "sterling." Sometimes there may also be initials or a silver marker's identification. For example, the markings for American Gorham are a lion, an anchor, a "g" and the word "sterling."

British silver has a complete set of hallmarks, including when and where it was made. Look for a king's or queen's head, a lion or a leopard, among assorted other markings. A lion signifies that the piece is sterling silver. A leopard's head means it was made in London. A king's or queen's head indicates that the piece was made during the reign of the monarch depicted. There are often other marks, as well, which can be identified by referring to one of the many tomes on silver markings, such as *The Book of Old Silver* (Crown Publishers, 1937; available in libraries) by Seymour B. Wyler, the definitive source for silver marks.

The marking on European Continental silver is "800," the designation for Continental-grade silver. Russian pieces are engraved with an

> **It's always best to buy silver on the secondary market, because older silver is heavier and much better crafted than today's silver.**
>
> An editor at
> *Silver* magazine

• • •

"840." Pieces with no markings are either silver plate or some other alloy. Silver plating, which began on a large scale in the 19th century, consists of a metal base with a thin silver coating, usually applied by electroplating. Silver-plated ware sells for about one-third the price of sterling.

Virtual Stamp Collecting
Philatelists are flocking to the Web

Stamp collecting not too long ago required trips to a collectors' convention, or a serendipitous find at a show or shop. "Basically, you were on your own," says Lloyd A. de Vries, president of a site for enthusiasts, the Virtual Stamp Club (www.virtualstampclub.com), and secretary of the American Philatelic Society, the nation's largest stamp collecting organization. Now, collectors use auction sites, catalogs and other Web resources to find stamps to augment collections, which they can then showcase online.

SPENDING

Profiting from Botched-Up Stamps
A printer's mishap can bring big rewards

Botched-up stamps are a rarity, but collectors lucky enough to own one stand to win big. The aristocrat of all botched-up stamps is the invert, or stamp on which the design is mistakenly printed upside down.

And the most famous invert is the Jenny, a 1918 stamp featuring the Curtiss JN-4 biplane in the design. It was the first American issue for air postage; its value was set at 24 cents. But of the roughly two million printed, 100 bore the topsy-turvy center plane and quickly became the stuff of philatelic legend.

In October 2005, a block of four Jennys set a world record for a stamp item: they sold for $2,970,000. The auction house said several factors contributed to the stamps' value: their status as a unique block of a famous error, their excellent condition compared with some other examples of this error stamp, and their colorful ownership history.

The record price for a single stamp belongs to a Swedish stamp, the 3-skilling yellow error of 1857, which sold for $2.2 million in 1996. The most expensive single American stamp is the 1-cent stamp of 1868 with a rare so-called Z-grill, an experimental security waffle pressed into the paper; it sold for $935,000 in 1998.

—Matthew Healey

❓ EXPERT ANSWER

A Consumable Asset

❔ Is wine collecting a good investment?

From an investment perspective, wine and some fragile collectibles, like old manuscripts, can be especially risky. A wine collection can occupy a lot of space, and that space has to be temperature- and humidity-controlled.

Stuart H. Brager, a Baltimore physician and wine collector, spent about $15,000 to convert his basement into a cellar for his 3,500 bottles. If that is not enough to scare away an amateur, Brager points out that even the most cellar-worthy bottle has a finite life. Eventually, it has to be drunk. "And when you pull the cork, the asset's gone," he says. Then again, wine does have a benefit that stocks and bonds lack. "When my WorldCom stock went sour, I didn't have anything but a piece of paper," Brager says. "If the market for wine takes a downturn, I've still got the wine to drink."

—Tim Gray

The lure of meeting other stamp collectors, locating that one elusive stamp for a collection or showcasing entire collections has drawn many philatelists onto the Web. *Linn's Stamp News*, a weekly publication for collectors, found that 44 percent of its subscribers (average age: 65.8) used computers for their collecting in 2003, compared with 34 percent in 1996.

Also gone are the days of cataloging a collection in a tattered spiral notebook. Specialized database software like Stamp Keeper Deluxe, Stamp Collector's Data Base and StampCAT allows philatelists to track their inventory. Some collectors simply turn to commercial databases or spreadsheet applications.

One great challenge for collectors is to identify the lineage of a stamp. Which historical painting was it based on? When was it released, and in what quantity? What variations of the stamp exist, either in denomination or in size? The Web has transformed this arduous research task into one that is usually far more manageable.

"People post images of their stamps and ask others for help to identify the history of a particular stamp," says William F. Sharpe, the secretary of the Philatelic Computing Study Group (www.pcsg.org), an association dedicated to improving the hobby through computer use. Newsgroups are another way to gather this information. Galleries created by individual collectors to help document and preserve the images and history of stamps are also good sources. There are hundreds of exhibits broken down by themes, like stamps of birds, or by region or period. Many philatelists say they would never see the collections were they not displayed on the Web.

Stamp dealers also digitize their collections and post the images online, or provide catalogs on CD's. But collectors often have to search each dealer's Web site for a particular stamp, making it a time-consuming process. Some entrepreneurs are creating searchable databases that include the inventory of as many dealers as are willing to pay to be included. Such portals include Zillions of Stamps, PostBeeld and StampFinder.

Online auctions are increasingly important for buying and selling stamps. While there are many sites that specialize in collectibles, eBay is by far the largest source for stamps, according to stamp enthusiasts. At any given time, there are 40,000 to 50,000 lots of stamps on eBay alone, collectors estimate. Stamps for sale range from garden varieties to rarities in the $6,000 range; auction watchers note seeing some for up to $35,000.

But buying stamps online—especially through auction sites—can be risky. Consumer advocates warn that with stamps, unlike with other valuables, fraud artists need few special tools or skills. Counterfeiting a valuable coin takes special tools and dies; reproducing a painting requires a skilled artist. With stamps, a common ruse is to clean up a used stamp and make it appear new, a step that may drastically increase its value.

Stamp fraud predates the Internet, of course. The main difference now is how quickly con artists can move a large volume of altered stamps over the Internet compared with earlier times. Connoisseurs can also pull a fast one on neophytes who sell stamps without realizing their value. People troll for such bargains on the Internet.

—Sandeep Junnarkar

On a Magic Carpet Ride
How to pick from the glut of Oriental rugs

Oriental rugs have long been valued for their artistry and durability, not to mention their association with taste and gentility. But these days you don't need to be a Brahmin to buy one. There is a glut of affordable Oriental rugs on the market for several reasons. One is the end of a 20-year embargo on Iranian textiles in 2000; another is an expanding range of other floor-covering options.

Discerning quality can be tricky, due to subtleties in materials, design and craftsmanship, but with a few basic guidelines you can find a rug that not only suits your style but is also a sound investment.

Decide first how much you want to spend and where you want to put the rug. If it is destined for the dining room, you'll want it to be bigger than the table, and you may want a dark color that camouflages spills. And just so you don't come across as a rug rube, call the rug a "carpet" only if it is more than six feet long.

✔ **TIMELY TIPS**

Common Senses

When choosing an Oriental rug, use your senses to gauge quality

✔ **SIGHT** – Look for colors that are warm and change hue when viewed from different angles. The colors should not bleed or be darker at the base of the pile.

✔ **TOUCH** – The wool should be soft and springy, like a healthy head of hair. Avoid pile that is frizzy or coarse. You should also feel for uneven or thin areas in the pile—signs of wear or moth damage. These may not be apparent to the eye, because they are often painted over.

✔ **SOUND** – Creaking or cracking noises when the rug is folded back and forth can indicate dry rot.

✔ **SMELL** – Give the rug a whiff. Bad-smelling rugs may indicate poor-quality wool or be a sign of rot or mold.

—Kate Murphy

Your next decision is whether to buy a modern or antique rug. Though there are exceptions, the best-quality rugs are either very old or very new but made in the old tradition, most dealers and collectors say. That's because in recent years there has been a move to make rugs the way they were made a century ago, before the widespread use of chemically treated wool, synthetic dyes and mass production techniques discouraged weavers' creativity.

Historically, the great carpet-making areas have been Iran, Turkey, Turkestan and the Caucasus. But you can also add Afghanistan, Pakistan, Nepal, India and China to the list.

Prices vary according to design, provenance and condition; you can get comparable antique and new room-size Oriental rugs for $2,000 to $10,000. Rare collector's rugs, like a 12-by-14-foot Sultanabad circa 1870, may go for $100,000 to $200,000.

New rugs have the advantage of no wear, but an antique rug that is well made and well maintained will outlast your grandchildren—and hold its value or even appreciate.

When evaluating a rug, look for warm colors that change hue when viewed from different angles. Avoid rugs with brash, one-note colors, like taxicab yellow or mailbox blue, as those can indicate synthetic chemical dyes rather than natural dyes derived from plants and insects. And natural dyes do not run the way some synthetic ones do. Dampen a white handkerchief and rub it over the pile to check for color fastness.

Next, turn the rug over. Don't worry about counting knots per square inch, because the weave's tightness does not always indicate value. More important is that the weave has some irregularity in the knotting. If it's flawless, it may not be handmade; machine-made rugs are anathema to collectors.

Look at the back of the rug to check for repairs—and to see if the rug may have been cut down from a larger size. Tip-offs are lines that look like seams running through the design, or obvious overstitching. Such modifications can reduce the value. Check whether the colors on the back match those on the front. If not, it may have been chemically "aged" to appear antique. You can also check for such aging by separating the pile and looking for dark roots.

The most durable and valuable rugs are usually made of wool and should feel soft, springy and lustrous. If a rug is frizzy or coarse, the wool has probably been scalded and mechanically spun, which strips away its protective fibers and lanolin.

Dealers and appraisers say well-made Oriental rugs increase or at least hold their value over time, and collectors say that some rugs are worth 10 times what they were 20 years ago. But nothing is certain. More important than the potential return on investment, experts agree, is knowing that you enjoy the rug.

—Kate Murphy

Guitars With a Real Twang
Nostalgia is fueling demand among baby boomers

Guitars of the stars are fetching astounding prices, such as the nearly $1 million paid in 2004 for Eric Clapton's Blackie, a 1956-57 composite Fender Stratocaster. But high-priced celebrity guitars aren't the only game in town. Electric guitars, bass guitars and acoustic models, both electric and not, of all price points are changing hands.

A 1965 Fender Jazzmaster sells for about $3,500; the iconic Gibson Flying V, vintage 1958, fetches about $125,000, according to Stanley Jay, a vintage guitar dealer in New York. A Gibson L-50 arch-top acoustic model from the '50s or '60s goes for $1,000 or so. On the other end, you can pay $70,000 for a handcrafted acoustic by John d'Angelico, who worked in the mid-1900's and handcrafted fewer than 1,200 acoustics. By far the most popular and accessible vintage guitars are the American brands Fender, Gibson, Martin and Gretsch, dealers say.

Baby-boomer collectors are driving the market and finding more than nostalgia in vintage guitars: they are proving to be solid investments. "We don't guarantee that everything will go up, but over time they have done as well or better than the stock market," says appraiser George Gruhn, publisher of *Gruhn's Guide to Vintage Guitars.* Gruhn acted as broker for the Carter family on a Gibson owned by Johnny Cash that sold for $131,200 a few years back. Mother Maybelle Carter paid $275 for it in 1928. Still, prices have a way to go to catch up to a rare Stradivarius violin, which can command $2 million or more.

—Claire Wilson

CHAPTER **5**

EDUCATION

Pre-K Through 12   320

PRE-SCHOOL·320: *Lighten up, parents • How children really learn • Identifying a gifted child • Acquiring a second tongue* **LEARNING STRATEGIES·323:** *Does music make you smarter? Chess checkup • How to succeed in science • Phys ed is getting fitter* **TESTING·326:** *Public vs. private school • The child who does too much • Cures for text anxiety • A helping hand at day's end* **TEACHING TECHNIQUES·329:** *Dividing and conquering • Goodbye, class. See you in the fall • Inside the teenage mind* **READING·332:** *Summertime, and the reading is easy • The best books for kids 2001-2005*

College & Beyond   336

GETTING IN·336: *Translating the "new" SAT • Prepping for the SAT's • The truth about rankings • Campus reality tour • The admissions game • From field to dorm • Do A.P. courses help? • Getting credit before you go*

ARTS EDUCATION·346: *What would Picasso have done? • Dancing around the subject* **FINANCIAL AID·348:** *Coping with the cost of college • College grants you don't have to repay* **COURSES OF STUDY·350:** *Life 101 • The two-year option • The student's life • Getting a college degree abroad • Short-term study abroad • No passport required • Harvard at a bargain price • The new face of facebooks • How to win a Rhodes • Other roads to study abroad* **GRAD SCHOOL·358:** *Let Abe Lincoln be your guide • Psst! Apply to law school • Are you a master of the universe? • Beyond the* U.S. News *law school rankings • If you're thinking of med school • Case Study No.1: is B-School worth the big bucks?* **THE REAL WORLD·364:** *Free advice for 20-somethings*

Pre-K Through 12

Lighten Up, Parents

Pushing reading too early is a big mistake

Learning to read early has become one of those indicators—in parents' minds at least—that their child is smart. In fact, reading early has very little to do with whether a child is successful academically. Research over the past few decades has shown that difficulty with reading is often due not to inferior intelligence but to differences in the developmental wiring of each individual child. In some cases, there are neurological problems and developmental lags, many of which, if identified early enough and properly remediated, can be overcome. If children with a language disability can be screened and diagnosed as early as kindergarten or first grade, they can benefit from phonological training at the outset, and will have fewer problems in learning to read at grade level than they might if they are not identified until third grade or later.

Before she died, the late Harvard School of Education professor Jean Chall, author of *Learning to Read: The Great Debate* and other seminal books in the education field, shared her perspective on teaching reading:

At what age should a child learn to read?

Traditionally, American schools teach children at age six, but many schools begin teaching informally in kindergarten and prekindergarten. If parents start too early to encourage reading, and a child does not immediately succeed, the parent has a hard time relaxing and letting the child go at his or her own pace.

Which teaching method works best?

Over the years, research has proved that the use of both the "whole language" method and the "phonic" method is the best way for a child to master reading. While the whole language approach, which includes reading to children and getting them interested in both the activity of reading and the story they are reading, is helpful, phonics must be taught. Children must be taught that one of the squiggles they see on a page is a "p" and another a "b" and that those two letters sound different and are written differently. Getting the print off the page requires a different ability than being able to understand the meaning of what is written. It is very important for normal progress, and especially for children at risk, that both methods be taught.

How do you lay the groundwork for reading in a young child?

You can start developing the skills needed in reading at a very young age without putting any pressure on children. Besides reading to them, parents can start "ear training" their child by playing rhyme games. This develops the child's ability to discern different sounds and to realize that certain words begin to look and sound the same. In reading to children, parents also can point to words as they go, teaching the child that the funny lines on the page are the words you are saying. All of this "early teaching" should not be a serious thing. It should be a fun activity. There is plenty of time for serious learning later.

When should you "get serious"?

Once a child is in school, the learning of reading

is inevitably more serious. If children do not already know how to identify and write letters, and to recognize words, they start to learn it in a systematic way. I am reluctant to tell parents when to teach reading to their children, as they often embark on too serious a task too early for the child.

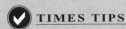 ✔ **TIMES TIPS**

How Children Really Learn

Kids absorb more when they have fun

✔ From John Dewey to Jean Piaget, educators have generally agreed that while didactic teaching has its place, small children learn mainly from interacting and not passive listening, understanding and not memorizing, reading for fun and not simply decoding.

✔ A 2004 study of the Child-Parent Centers, carried out by Arthur Reynolds, a professor of social work, and his colleagues at the University of Wisconsin, reinforces that long-held conclusion. While preschoolers whose teachers used a direct instruction technique did better at the end of kindergarten and had improved test scores in the early grades, the reverse was true later on. Children who were in preschool classrooms that emphasized child-initiated learning had higher eighth-grade reading scores and higher rates of high school graduation

✔ "The good news," says Deborah Stipek, dean of the School of Education at Stanford University, "is that children can be taught basic academic skills—fundamentals of reading, writing and mathematics—in a way that uses, rather than destroys, their natural desire to learn. Vocabulary can be taught by conversation, awareness of print developed through reading and talking about books and mathematics learned with games like a pretend restaurant."

—David L. Kirp

How many children suffer from learning disabilities?

Most schools cite a 10 to 15 percent learning disability rate among their student body; some as high as 20 percent. Many children have some kind of reading difficulty.

What if your child is having difficulty with reading?

You must get a professional diagnosis. While the teacher might say the child is merely disinterested but will get over it, disinterest or poor performance in reading can stem from a number of things, some being very specific learning disabilities that can be identified and worked on. Correcting these early can circumvent a lot of potential problems for the child later in school. Learning disabilities have now been shown to be neurological problems that can be corrected with the proper training. It is very tricky for parents to deal with their own child's learning disabilities and I most certainly do not recommend it.

Identifying a Gifted Child

Their high intelligence is often mistaken for a disorder

Discerning gifted children, long an imperfect science, is even tougher in today's label-prone culture. James T. Webb, a clinical psychologist and author of *Misdiagnosis and Dual Diagnosis of Gifted Children and Adults*, explains what can go wrong.

Parents throw the word "gifted" around. What does it mean, really?

"Gifted" comes in different forms and degrees. Gifted children excel in such areas as general intellectual ability, specific aptitudes like math, creative thinking, visual or performing arts. Most

EDUCATION

have I.Q. scores between 130 and 155. Above that range are the profoundly gifted—a tiny fraction of the group. Over all, the gifted represent about 3 percent of our population.

Q Why would gifted children be tagged as having psychological disorders?

Behaviors of many gifted children can resemble those of, say, attention deficit/hyperactivity disorder. Most teachers, pediatricians and psychologists aren't trained to distinguish between the two. Most gifted kids are very intense, pursuing interests excessively. This often leads to power struggles, perfectionism, impatience, fierce emotions and trouble with peers. Many gifted kids have varied interests, skipping from one to the other—a trait often misinterpreted as A.D.H.D.

Q You write that these misdiagnoses are common.

About a quarter of gifted children have their giftedness misinterpreted as a disorder and aren't recognized as gifted. Even when flagged as gifted, another 20 percent are misdiagnosed. Among children referred to me with a bipolar diagnosis, almost 100 percent have been misdiagnosed, as are 70 percent of those with obsessive-compulsive diagnoses and 55 percent of those with A.D.H.D.

Q What's a parent to do?

Parents should educate themselves about the characteristics of gifted children: intense curiosity, unusually good memory, a remarkable sense of humor, exquisite sensitivity to others and extensive vocabularies. And identify them early. Children's attitudes toward learning get set before age 10. Preschool and the early grades gener-

ally turn off gifted kids: they are told to stop asking so many questions and wait their turn. They need an appropriate learning environment. If not, seeds for underachievement are sown.

—Abigail Sullivan Moore

Acquiring a Second Tongue
If you wait until adolescence, it's too late

English has always been the "American language," but because of the global economy, foreign language ability is increasingly important for Americans. Starting when a child is young is critical, argues Nancy Rhodes, director of the foreign language education division at the Center for Applied Linguistics in Washington, D.C. Rhodes offers this advice on training children to speak foreign tongues:

❝

"Intellectually gifted" may have a variety of definitions. Assuming that people scoring in the top 10 percent of intelligence tests meet the criteria, the country has millions of gifted children.

Julie Bick

•••

Start foreign language training early. After 12 or 13, it is very difficult to learn a language and be able to speak it like a native speaker. Young kids like playing with language and are not embarrassed by making strange sounds, so it's ideal for them to learn a foreign language. If you wait until kids are in adolescence, they are very inhibited and worried about how they appear to their peers.

Don't worry that studying a foreign language will harm a child's native language ability. All of the research shows that studying another language actually enhances your native language abilities. By the time children in foreign language immersion programs get to fifth or sixth grade, they score as well or better in English than their peers who have been studying only in English.

If you have a choice, select a program that integrates foreign language instruction into the rest of the curriculum. About a fifth of the elementary schools in the U.S. teach some type of foreign language. It could be just an introduction, or it could be an immersion experience in which the foreign language is the medium of instruction, so that the students are learning language as well as their content areas through the foreign language. The successful programs are integrated into the school day so that everybody sees foreign language as part of the curriculum.

When a family is multilingual, be as consistent as possible about who speaks what. Children can learn five or six different languages. The important thing is to separate the languages. If the mother speaks English, for example, and the father speaks Spanish, they should try to keep those roles the same. Do not be surprised or alarmed, however, if a young child mixes the languages he or she hears. This is normal and a phase. Do not react with impatience. Remember that by teaching a foreign language early, you are imparting a great gift.

> 66
> **Only the Mozart group of test subjects showed a significantly increased spatial I.Q. score.**
>
> • • •

Does Music Make You Smarter?
Intriguing research suggests it helps develop spatial reasoning

When champions of the liberal arts argue that there's more to education than just reading, writing and arithmetic, music and arts are often cited for their value in stimulating students' creativity and expanding their cultural horizons. Now there is evidence that students who receive formal musical training may enjoy higher standardized test scores and demonstrate greater powers of spatial reasoning than students who do not get this experience.

Two studies by researchers at the Center for the Neurobiology of Learning and Memory at the University of California at Irvine have suggested that there may indeed be a causal link between music and spatial intelligence. Spatial intelligence is the ability to perceive the visual world accurately, to form mental pictures of physical objects and to recognize when objects differ physically. Having well-developed powers of spatial reasoning is considered crucial for excelling at complex mathematics and playing chess, among other things.

In one of the two studies, the U.C. Irvine team led by psychologist Frances Rauscher and neuroscientist Gordon Shaw compared the spatial reasoning abilities of 19 preschool children who took music lessons for eight months with the performance of a demographically comparable group of 15 preschool children who received no music training. The researchers found the first group's spatial reasoning dramatically better. The team also reported that the ability of the music students to do a puzzle designed to measure their spatial reasoning powers rose significantly during the experiment.

A second study, which replicated and expanded on results of an earlier study in the journal *Nature*, found that when college students listened to 10 minutes of Mozart's piano sonata K.448, their spatial I.Q. scores rose more than when these students spent the same amount of time sitting in silence or performing relaxation exercises. Curiously, the researchers observed no improvement in the students' spatial skills after 10 minutes of listening to the avant-garde composer Philip Glass or to a highly rhythmic dance piece, suggesting that hypnotic musical structures do nothing to improve spatial skills.

EDUCATION

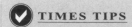

TIMES TIPS

Chess Checkup

It's fun and it improves math skills

In Philadelphia, the seventh-largest school system in the country, 18 of the city's 280 public schools added chess to their curriculums in 2005. The goal: to have all second and third graders receiving chess instruction within a year's time. Why? Paul G. Vallas, chief executive of the school system, said anecdotal evidence showed that chess is a great educational tool. "Chess seems to improve problem-solving skills," he said. "It improves discipline. It improves memory. It certainly seems to improve mathematical skills." Teaching chess, he added, is meant to enrich the curriculum, not replace another subject.

The chess program being used in Philadelphia, the Tampa area, San Diego and Seattle is called First Move and was created by America's Foundation for Chess, a nonprofit organization started in Seattle in 2000. First Move is intended for second and third graders. It uses an interactive DVD and a series of exercises to introduce children to the game. In addition to focusing on rules and basic strategy, the program weaves in the game's origins and includes math exercises based on its geometry.

While teaching chess in the classroom is spreading, it is not a new idea. Chess was added to the curriculum at Hunter College Elementary School in New York in 1981. The Burnsville school district near Minneapolis has had a chess program for 17 years.

For some students, the benefits of learning chess can also include helping to pay for college. The United States Chess Federation lists a number of colleges and universities offering scholarships focused on chess players. For example, some scholarships cover tuition and fees for four years at the University of Texas at Dallas and at the University of Maryland, Baltimore County. The HB Foundation, which runs chess programs for six schools in Minneapolis, also offers college scholarships for students who excel in tournaments.

—Dylan Loeb McClain

How to Succeed in Science

It takes an adult mentor to make it to the top

In 2005, Ward Melville, a suburban Long Island public school, had 12 semifinalist winners out of 300 nationally in the prestigious Intel Science Talent Search, second only to Montgomery Blair High in Silver Spring, Md., which had 13. In the seven years since Intel took over sponsorship from Westinghouse, Ward Melville ranked third nationally, with 68 semifinalists. The only two ahead were Stuyvesant in New York City (94) which requires an exam for admissions; and Montgomery Blair (89) which has a selective-admissions science program.

How does a regular public school do it? Partly, it's because Ward Melville is a well-to-do district with lots of parents who are doctors and other scientists. But there's more to it than that. They've also made scientific research a top priority, naming a former university professor to run the school's science program. In 1999, the school doubled the program's size to 130 students and budgeted for a second full-time teaching slot.

The school subscribes to an online service giving students unlimited access to the latest research papers. The program has its own $4,000 printer that can produce an entire science fair poster board in a single 42-inch-wide sheet, and a large budget to pay travel expenses to nine science fairs a year. Dr. George Baldo, who runs the program, has a large enough staff to make sure all 38 pages of the Intel international science and engineering fair application get filled out correctly by the 25 students going. But none of these is the main reason Ward Melville excels. High school students cannot do research at this level without adult mentors—often a university professor plus a team of grad students—to pick a topic that will break new ground, yet be manageable, and to supervise them at every step.

Ward Melville is so close to the State University at Stony Brook that students can bike to the labs daily. Aditi Ramakrishnan, a semifinalist who researched toxicity of nanoparticles in cosmetics, says she would have no project if it were not for the daily help she received from a team of nearby Stony Brook professors. "I'm only 17," she says. "I didn't have the background to create the experiment. I didn't know how to use the equipment. I couldn't create the hypothesis."

For big-time science fairs, the single most important research students do is finding a willing mentor. Even classroom science teachers—racing to finish prepackaged state and advanced placement curriculums—rarely can oversee serious research.

—Michael Winerip

Phys Ed Is Getting Fitter

The curriculum is moving toward skills for life

Phys ed is making a comeback as a part of the school curriculum, but with a difference. While group sports are still part of the curriculum, the new strategy is to teach skills that are useful beyond gym class. Instead of learning how to dodge a ball or climb a rope, children are taught to lift weights, balance their diets and build cardiovascular endurance. They are graded in part by how long they stay in their target heart rate.

"It's about giving these kids the tools and skills and experience so they can lead a physically active life the rest of their life," says Anne Flannery, the president of PE4life, an advocacy group that sets up the academies and lobbies for federal funds for innovative phys ed programs nationally.

Given that 15 percent of American children 6 to 18 are overweight or obese, advocates say more money and thought must be put into phys ed curriculums. In many cases, that may mean not just replacing the old gym-class model with fitness programs but also starting up phys ed programs because school boards often "put P.E. on the chopping block, cutting it entirely or decreasing" its teachers or the number of days it is offered, says Alicia Moag-Stahlberg, the executive director of Action for Healthy Kids, a nonprofit organization promoting nutrition and physical activity in schools. The disparity in phys ed programs is partly due to the lack of a national standard. "Physical education needs to be part of the core curriculum," she added.

Today only 5.8 percent to 8 percent of schools provide what phys ed advocates recommend—gym classes five times a week—according to the Centers for Disease Control and Prevention.

The wisdom of the new approach has some scientific support. Researchers at the University of Wisconsin have demonstrated how effective the fit-for-life model of gym class can be. They observed how 50 overweight children lost more weight when they cycled, skied cross-country and walked with pedometers than when they played sports. The researchers also found that teaching sports like football resulted in less overall movement, partly because reluctant students were able to sit on the bench. The study was published in the October 2005 issue of the *Archives of Pediatrics & Adolescent Medicine.*

Another problem with exclusively teaching sports in gym class is that only a tiny percentage of students continue playing them after graduating from high school. The new method, advocates say, teaches skills that translate to adulthood.

—Julie Bosman

EDUCATION

Public vs. Private School

In math, public grade schools are tops

When it comes to math, students in regular public schools do as well as or significantly better than comparable students in private schools, according to a large-scale government-financed study. Conducted by Christopher Lubienski and Sarah Theule Lubienski of the University of Illinois at Champaign-Urbana, the study compared fourth- and eighth-grade math scores of more than 340,000 students in 13,000 regular public, charter and private schools on the 2003 National Assessment of Educational Progress. The 2003 test was given to 10 times more students than any previous test, giving researchers a trove of new data.

Though private school students have long scored higher on the national assessment, commonly referred to as "the nation's report card," the new study used advanced statistical techniques to adjust for the effects of income, school and home circumstances. The researchers said they compared math scores, not reading ones, because math was considered a clearer measure of a school's overall effectiveness.

The current study, published in 2006, found that self-described conservative Christian schools, the fastest-growing sector of private schools, fared poorest, with their students falling as much as one year behind their counterparts in public schools, once socioeconomic factors like income, ethnicity and access to books and computers at home were considered.

The report found that among the private schools, Lutheran schools did better than other private schools. Nevertheless, at the fourth-grade level, a 10.7 point lead in math scores evaporated into a 4.2 point lag behind public schools. At the eighth-grade level, a 21-point lead, roughly the equivalent of two grade levels, disappeared after adjusting for differences in student backgrounds.

The exam is scored on a 0-to-500-point scale, with 235 being the average score at fourth grade, and 278 being the average score at eighth grade. A 10-to-11-point difference in test scores is roughly equivalent to one grade level.

The study also found that charter schools, privately operated and publicly financed, did significantly worse than public schools in the fourth grade, once student populations were taken into account. In the eighth grade, it found, students in charters did slightly better than those in public schools, though the sample size was small and the difference was not statistically significant.

—Diana Jean Schemo

ℹ INSIDE INFO

More Tests Coming Soon

- States across the country are administering an expanded testing regimen to comply with the federal No Child Left Behind law.

- Unlike in prior years, when only fourth and eighth graders were tested in two subjects, English and math, exams now run from the third grade on, with additional subjects in various years, and will include essay questions in every grade.

The Child Who Does Too Much

The more activities kids take on, the less enriched their educations are

Every parent knows the exasperation that comes from having a child who "acts up"—whether it be the 5-year-old who is terrorizing other children at nursery school, the 7-year-old who throws a fit every morning before leaving the house, or the 10-year-old who refuses to do her

---

✔ **TIMES TIPS**

Cures for Test Anxiety

If you can keep your wits about you, chances are you'll pass

Test anxiety can mean disaster for a student. Instead of feeling challenged by the prospect of success, they become afraid of failure. This makes them anxious about tests and their own abilities. Ultimately, they become so worked up that they feel incompetent about the subject matter or the test. It does not help to tell the child to relax, to think about something else or stop worrying. But there are ways to reduce test anxiety. Some suggestions from your government:

✔ **Space studying over days or weeks.** (Real learning occurs through studying that takes place over a period of time.) Understand the information and relate it to what is already known. Review it more than once.

✔ **Don't "cram" the night before**—cramming increases anxiety, which interferes with clear thinking. Get a good night's sleep.

✔ **Read the directions carefully** when the teacher hands out the test. If you don't understand them, ask the teacher to explain.

✔ **Look quickly at the entire examination** to see what types of questions are included (multiple choice, matching, true/false, essay) and, if possible, the number of points for each. This will help you pace yourself.

✔ **If you don't know the answer to a question, skip it and go on**. Don't waste time worrying about it. Mark it so you can identify it as unanswered. If you have time at the end of the exam, return to the unanswered question(s).

SOURCE: U.S. Department of Education, Office of Educational Research and Improvement www.ed.gov/pubs/parents/TestTaking/index.html

THE PRIVATE SECTOR CONTRIBUTES ITS 2¢

✔ The Institute of HeartMath sells an interactive CD-ROM called TestEdge, which has strategies for controlling test anxiety for grades 7 through 12. The group plans to create materials for even younger children, as well. (www.heartmath.org)

---

homework. What can a parent do in such cases? Dr. David Elkind, a leading child development expert, shares his views about how to evaluate and cope with your child's behavior. Elkind is professor of child study at Tufts University and author of *The Hurried Child.*

💬 **How can you tell the difference between a child who is acting up because of stress, and one who is precocious and simply wants more stimulation?**

Parents experience very different demands from children depending on what that child is experiencing. For example, a gifted child might demand constant stimulation to try to satisfy his or her voracious appetite for information—a chorus of whys ringing in your ears all day. That's very different from a child who battles for attention and presents parents with strain and power struggles.

You need to look at how many demands there are on a child. Is he having to adapt to too many places and people each day (e.g., school, daycare, baby sitters)? The more changes a child experiences in a day, the more stress he feels. Also, if you are troubled or there is distress in the family, your child's behavior will often mirror it.

💬 **What can be done to relieve stress at school?**

Increasingly, with so many early education programs, educators are assuming that children know their numbers and letters at a younger and younger age. This might not be the case, and it is no reflection on the child's intelligence—different children have different rates of development. If your child has a September or October birthday,

EDUCATION

328

HOMEWORK   EDUCATION

especially for boys, you may want to wait a year before enrolling him. This is much preferred to starting your child and then having him repeat a year. There is such a stigma for kids who are held back that if you are considering holding your child back a year, I recommend allowing him to continue to the next grade, and providing additional tutoring.

How many activities can a child manage adequately?

There is no need for a child to have any organized activity like sports or music before the age of 5 or 6. For school-age children, a sport, a musical instrument, and maybe a "peer activity" like scouts is plenty. These should not take more than a few hours a week. It is very important for a child not to have all his time programmed. Children must learn to manage their own time. I see a lot of new college students who simply do not know how to manage their time because they had such "planned" lives.

> When it comes to homework, more is not necessarily better. Elementary schoolchildren probably spend too much time on homework, and a lot of what they do is busywork.

How do you allow a child to manage his or her own time, yet limit television or video watching?

You can lay down some ground rules. For instance, you allow your child a certain number of hours of video games per week, and the rest must be spent doing other things. You are not saying that he or she can't do something, but you are setting limits on it.

What's the best way to help a child deal with a stress that won't go away, like a death, divorce or a move?

The most important thing is to talk to your child and help him or her deal with his or her feelings. If someone has died, it's very important for the child to talk about that person and to articulate how he or she feels. Similarly, if a child sees something frightening on TV, the child needs to talk about it and be allowed to work through his or her emotions.

When is professional help advisable?

While there are cases where a child needs ther-

A Helping Hand at Day's End

How a parent can aid in after-school work

For parents eager to help their children's learning, getting involved with homework is one of the best methods. Yet all too often, homework becomes a battleground for wars of words between parent and child.

"The relationship [of parent helping the child] is supposed to go on for years," says Dr. Joyce Epstein, who studied homework issues extensively as director of the Johns Hopkins Center on School, Family, and Community Partnerships. "You have to be careful that one night of confrontation doesn't ruin you for 12 years of school."

To develop good family communications, says Epstein, it's important how a parent talks to a child about school. "Many parents are told or advised to ask their child, 'How was school today?' as a way of interacting," says Epstein. "Better to ask: 'Show me something you learned in math today,' because that makes the youngster demonstrate and re-create, rather than comment on nothing." From there, she says, parents can build the kind of interaction that will not only help the child's work but will improve the way the parent and child communicate.

apy, a parent must be very careful. Being sent to see someone can label the child as abnormal and become yet another form of stress. When there is a problem for which a parent wants to seek professional counseling, this should be done as a family. A child does not become emotionally distressed overnight, but in response to the cumulative effect of family behavior patterns. Even when a child is experiencing a physiological problem, such as attention deficit disorder, the parents need counseling as well.

Q **What is the biggest mistake parents make in helping children deal with life's stresses?**

One of the biggest mistakes is to think that bad experiences prepare children for other bad experiences. I believe that the more good experiences parents can give their children—doing things with their children, giving them loving and successful experiences the better they feel about themselves, the better the relationships they have with their parents, the better they are able to cope when something difficult does happen.

Dividing and Conquering

Teaching boys and girls separately in the middle school years

The most challenging time for educators to engage children in learning is generally held to be the middle school years. Hormones are raging, and girls, in particular, are jockeying for position in the social pecking order. Being in a coed environment is a confusing, distracting time for most preadolescents, leaving them little time to focus on their studies, and leaving them often with very poor self-esteem. For

Homework is certainly a good idea in high schools, but a lot of thought has to go into making it worthwhile.

Helen Featherstone, editor of the *Harvard Education Letter*

• • •

that reason, many schools all over the country are opting for a separate-but-equal educational experience for the middle school years.

The Masters School in Dobbs Ferry, New York, formerly an all girls' school, chose this configuration when it went coed in 1996. The Mary Institute and St. Louis Country Day School in St. Louis and the Collegiate School in Richmond, Va., did the same during mergers of girls' and boys' schools in the 1990's. And in England, a similar arrangement is gaining popularity, with three prestigious schools about to join several others that already teach children in single-sex classes between the ages of 11 and 16.

This island of sex segregation takes into account the different learning styles of boys and girls; the uneven pace of their physical, emotional and cognitive development; the hormonal assault at puberty when the part of the brain that governs judgment is still forming; and the effect of a sexualized culture that has made 13 the new 17. It also assumes that if girls gained confidence learning in single-sex math and science classes, popular for the last decade, boys might get a comparable boost in the humanities.

"This is the single most critical time in a child's life, and we are asking them to grow up way too fast," says Dr. Everett J. Wilson, head of the middle school at the Masters School. "This way, the girls get the opportunity to find their voice and the boys get the opportunity to find their voice in an appropriate way. The conventional wisdom is that girls benefit and for boys it's a wash. But we don't buy that here."

Michael Thompson, co-author of *Raising Cain,* says that boys become "angry, resentful and fight back" in middle school because they feel "defective" when compared to girls, who are

Goodbye, Class. See You in the Fall

Having a teacher who gets promoted with you

Having a teacher stay with a class for more than a year—or "looping," as it is known—is on the rise, according to many experts. "As schools try to improve their standardized test scores, this appears to be catching on," says Arthur E. Levine, the former longtime president of Teachers College at Columbia University.

Looping is most common in elementary schools, though some middle schools do it, too. Schools in Colorado Springs have tried looping, as have those in Attleboro, Mass., and Antioch, Ill. In New York City, hundreds of classes stay together for more than a year, most of them in the lower grades. The roots of looping trace back to the one-room rural schoolhouse and to educational innovations in Europe in the early 20th century.

As educational innovations go, it is remarkably simple. So are its benefits, proponents say. Teachers get to know their students, and the students' parents, extremely well. They know each child's strengths and weaknesses, and the children know the teachers' expectations and methods. This familiarity can save a lot of time at the beginning of the school year. Many educators think both lower-income and middle-class children benefit from a more prolonged relationship with teachers.

The potential disadvantages of looping are also clear-cut. If parents think a teacher is inadequate, they would surely oppose having their child spend an additional year in his or her class.

Advocates of looping say options need to be built into any program, so that parents and teachers can decide to place a child in a different class if remaining with a teacher would be detrimental.

Research into looping suggests that it can pay substantial dividends. A school district in East Cleveland, Ohio, experimented with looping from 1993 to 1997. A class in each of four elementary schools stayed with their teachers for three years, generally from kindergarten through second grade. The teachers worked extensively with parents to reinforce lessons in school, and the classes also met for five weeks each summer. After three years, students in the looped classes scored an average of 25 percentage points higher on standardized tests in reading, language arts and math than other students in the school district, says Frederick M. Hampton, an associate professor of education at Cleveland State University who oversaw the research project.

—Alan Finder

"literally out-thinking them." Thompson endorses the separate-but-equal model as a "fascinating, interesting, wonderful experiment" that potentially has more to offer boys than girls.

Carol Gilligan, author of *In a Different Voice,* says she is certain that girls who are "confident at 11 and confused at 16" will more likely be creative thinkers and risk-takers as adults if educated apart from boys in middle school. "It is the most effective moment to stop something from happening that has both personal and cultural costs," she says, referring to the loss of confidence.

—Jane Gross

Inside the Teenage Mind

Daredevils or just poor impulse control?

Remember Farris Hassan? Over the 2005 Christmas holidays, the 16-year-old cut prep school, flew to Kuwait, took a cab to the Iraqi border and, after being turned away, flew to Beruit and on to Baghdad with little more than some cash, an Arabic phrase book and a half-baked plan to see for himself what was going on there.

Hassan arrived home safe and sound a few weeks later, but his was hardly the first or even the most outlandish of risky adolescent stunts.

Remember Mathias Rust, the 19-year-old West German who in 1987 flew a tiny Cessna from Finland to Russia and landed in Red Square, hoping to bring Mikhail S. Gorbachev to terms of peace with the West? Or Keron Thomas, the 16-year-old Brooklyn subway enthusiast who in 1993 borrowed an A train for three hours and carried its 2,000 passengers safely and skillfully to their destinations?

Fiction, too, is full of adventuresome young heroes, from Huckleberry Finn to Holden Caulfield, Harry Potter and even Ferris Bueller. Ferris, unlike Farris, never ventured beyond his own city the day he skipped school but nevertheless spoke to the perpetual teenage urge to push the boundaries of the ordinary with lines like, "Life moves pretty fast. If you don't stop to look around once in a while, you could miss it."

Neither in life nor in fiction do all larks end happily ever after, of course. "Look at the statistics," said Lewis Lipsitt, an emeritus professor of psychology at Brown University. "More young people die of behavioral misadventures than of all diseases combined." So are adolescent adventurers showing only a reckless lack of judgment? Or could they also reflect a healthy imaginative spirit? Maybe a little of both, psychologists say.

"Risk-taking—and thrill-seeking, which is related—is one of the most powerful forces in human nature, the force that created the modern world," says Frank Farley, a Temple University psychologist and former president of the American Psychological Association. "Willingness to enter the unknown, creativity, inventiveness are what brought us out of the caves."

From a developmental point of view, it makes perfect sense that teenagers are drawn to intense feats of derring-do. Exploration and the assertion of independence are basic developmental tasks of adolescence, and the surging hormones of the teenage years contribute to all kinds of impulsive behavior, including dangerous skateboard stunts, binge drinking and sex without contraceptives. And the boys who score highest on tests of sensation-seeking tend to be those with the highest levels of testosterone.

There is, however, "a gap between the development of the systems in the brain that regulate our impulses and the systems that lead to acting out those impulses, which get jolted into a new activation at puberty," says Laurence Steinberg, a psychology professor who directs the MacArthur Foundation Research Network on Adolescent Development and Juvenile Justice. "We find that the ability to anticipate the consequences of what you're doing, to see how one thing might lead to another, is still developing in adolescence, and even until the mid-20's," Steinberg says. "The car-rental agencies have it right when they don't rent to people under 25."

Even though some of the most conspicuous risk-takers act alone, the more common pattern for dangerous adolescent behavior involves groups. Recent research shows just how susceptible adolescents are to peer pressure to put on a brave face. "In one experiment, adolescents, college-age students and adults played a driving video game, with a simulated approach to an intersection where the light was turning yellow," says Steinberg, author of *You and Your Adolescent*. "When individuals did it alone," he says, "there was no difference between the age groups in the chances they took, but when they came back to the lab with two friends, who watched them play, there was a huge increase in risk-taking among adolescents, but adult behavior remained unchanged."

What then do psychologists make of the far less common, carefully planned solo exploits of Farris Hassan and the others? "These solo risk-takers, who haven't really been studied, are probably more interesting than those acting in the context of a group," Farley says. "The solo ones are probably more goal-oriented, more self-confident, more tolerant of ambiguity, more extreme and more self-directed. They could be the kind of people who change human history, like Lindbergh or Einstein."

—Tamar Lewin

Summertime, the Reading Is Easy
But should schools require it?

Eden Ross Lipson, author of *The New York Times Parent's Guide to the Best Book for Children* (3rd edition, revised and updated), convened a discussion of the role of summer reading in children's lives in an age of anxiety over lists, standards and measurable skills. The participants included Clifford Wohl, a former New York City schoolteacher and bookstore owner; Martha Davis Beck, editor of *Riverbank Review*; Molly S. Kinney, the children's consultant to the Georgia Public Libraries; and Jeanette Larson, youth services manager at the Austin Public Library.

LIPSON. Why should children have to practice reading over the summer?

WOHL. I haven't done one of those $100,000 research projects, but we know that when they come back to school in September, kids know less than when they left in June. Children don't realize that they've lost anything. We as teachers know it intuitively. They don't have the same skill that they had when they left.

When you're driving over the summer to different places, listening to some really good children's books on tape is a great way for the family to share that experience.

• • •

LIPSON. You can see the children who have continued to read?

WOHL. Yes. They come in more enthusiastic. Children will come in and talk to you about the books that they read. But more importantly, it's the one time during the course of the year when a child can read just for fun, with no strings attached; no one is looking over your shoulder.

LIPSON. But is it fun if schools are putting a tremendous emphasis on lists of required reading?

KINNEY. I think there are some very, very good reading lists out there, and I think that most of them have been designed by librarians. There are also many teachers who are knowledgeable about the current literature.

LIPSON. What about series and classics?

WOHL. I can't speak for schools in other parts of the country, but I know that in many schools here in New York, in the middle grades, the classics are sort of forgotten. Especially if it's a book that the parent has read as a child, it brings insight for them and they can share it with their children.

LARSON. I'm glad Cliff said something about that, because there are a number of the classic books that are for the whole family to enjoy. One of the things about a lot of the classics, like *The Wind in the Willows,* is that at different ages, including into adulthood, you see different things.

LIPSON. Will children read if their parents don't?

LARSON. I don't think so. If parents are just giving lip service to reading being important, but children never see them read, and their parents never do anything to encourage them to read, say, by taking them to the library and bookstores, then—kids are smart. They're going to do what they see their parents doing.

When you're driving over the summer to different places, listening to some really good children's books on tape is a great way for the family to share that experience. The best nonfiction tells a good story; the story just happens to be true. Have children find books that help them prepare for the vacation.

If you're going to Yellowstone, get some nonfiction books to read up about where you're going.

BECK. There are books that connect to summer activities right out your back door, about stargazing or about bugs or about photography or hopscotch. It's going to be different for each family and each situation. Also, remember books that are good to dip in and out of as opposed to reading straight through. Books of jokes, riddles, puzzles, fairy-tale stories, poems.

The Best Books for Kids 2001-2005

Some great choices for children of all ages

Each year, the editors of the *New York Times Book Review* select the most notable children's books of the year. Here are the editors' picks from for the last five years. (Reviews of most of the titles can be found online at www.nytimes.com.)

2005

ENCYCLOPEDIA PREHISTORICA: DINOSAURS. *Written and illustrated by Robert Sabuda and Matthew Reinhart.* $26.99. (Ages 5 and up) Brilliantly designed and executed pop-ups.

HARRY POTTER AND THE HALF-BLOOD PRINCE. *By J. K. Rowling. Illustrated by Mary GrandPré.* $29.99. (Ages 8 and up) This installment, though darker, has humor, romance and snappy dialogue.

TERRIFIC. *Written and illustrated by Jon Agee.* $15.95. (All ages) Eugene Mudge mutters a sarcastic "Terrific" to everything that befalls him, from winning a free ocean cruise to meeting a talking parrot.

TRACTION MAN IS HERE! *Written and illustrated by Mini Grey.* $15.95. (Ages 4 to 8) The best toys have powerful secret lives, and Traction Man, described as a "generic action figure with dazzle-painted battle pants" on the box he arrives in, is a fine example.

THE OLD COUNTRY. *By Mordicai Gerstein.* $14.95. (Ages 10 and up) The story of a girl who saves her family by becoming the thieving fox she sets out to kill. A reminder that tales of wonder are sometimes history, too.

THE GAME OF SILENCE. *By Louise Erdrich.* Illustrated by the author. $15.99. (Ages 8 to 12) The sequel to *The Birchbark House* picks up the story of Omakayas, a girl growing up in a small Ojibwa community in Minnesota in the mid-19th century.

FLUSH. *By Carl Hiaasen.* $16.95. (Ages 10 and up) The plot involves real threats to Florida's ecosystem, slapstick villains and a boy hiding in the ladies' room.

THE BABY ON THE WAY. *By Karen English. Illustrated by Sean Qualls.* $16. (Ages 3 to 6) In this exquisitely illustrated and beautifully written story, Jamal wonders if his grandmother was ever a baby.

THE LIGHTNING THIEF. *By Rick Riordan.* $17.95. (Ages 12 and up) Percy Jackson's senses "are better than a mortal's" because he is part Greek god. Not bad for a boy who was told he had A.D.H.D.

2004

DREAM OF FREEDOM: The Civil Rights Movement From 1954 to 1968. *By Diane McWhorter.* $19.95. (Ages 12 and up) A young people's history of "America's second Civil War."

EDUCATION

THE PEOPLE COULD FLY: The Picture Book. *By Virginia Hamilton. Illustrated by Leo Dillon and Diane Dillon.* $16.95. (Ages 4 and up) The old story of a "magical African people" who escape plantation hardships by flying away, now beautifully illustrated.

MISS BRIDIE CHOSE A SHOVEL. *By Leslie Connor. Illustrated by Mary Azarian.* $16. (Ages 4 to 8) Miss Bridie travels on a boat to New York, finds a job, rents a room, starts a garden, meets a man, marries him and buys a farm . . . for starters.

CHASING VERMEER. *By Blue Balliett. Illustrated by Brett Helquist.* $16.95. (Ages 10 and up) A first novel "about a stolen Vermeer painting set at the University of Chicago's Laboratory Schools.

POLAR BEAR NIGHT. *By Lauren Thompson. Illustrated by Stephen Savage.* $15.95. (Ages 3 to 5) A comforting bedtime story "to teach children that darkness can be a friend."

MADAM PRESIDENT. *By Catherine Thimmesh. Illustrated by Douglas B. Jones.* $17. (Ages 10 and up) The story of a pigtailed girl who wants to be president introduces first ladies, suffragists, congresswomen and foreign leaders.

KITTEN'S FIRST FULL MOON. *Written and illustrated by Kevin Henkes.* $15.99. (Ages 2 to 5)

A large-format book about "the moon, which doubles as a bowl of milk, and Kitten."

THE BARTIMAEUS TRILOGY, BOOK TWO: The Golem's Eye. *By Jonathan Stroud.* $17.95. (Ages 10 and up) The "top of the class" of the currently popular fantasy series, set in a London governed by magicians.

A CHILD'S CHRISTMAS IN WALES. *By Dylan Thomas. Illustrated by Chris Raschka.* $17.99. (All ages) An artist-musician offers a contemporary take on a Christmas classic.

2003

ALICE'S ADVENTURES IN WONDERLAND: A Pop-Up Adaptation of Lewis Carroll's Original Tale. *Illustrated by Robert Sabuda.* $19.95. (All ages) A faithful adaptation combined with intelligent paper trickery.

ARNIE THE DOUGHNUT. *Written and illustrated by Laurie Keller.* $16.95. (Ages 4 to 8) This book about a wide-eyed young hero with a plain name and decent nature follows the adventures of a doughnut.

A DAY IN THE LIFE OF MURPHY. *Written and illustrated by Alice Provensen.* $16.95. (Ages 3 to 7) "Murphy-Stop-That is my name" yaps from dawn till after dark.

THE DAY THE BABIES CRAWLED AWAY. *Written and illustrated by Peggy Rathmann.* $16.99. (All ages) An enchanting adventure told in verse about babies that crawl away from a party.

THE MAN WHO WALKED BETWEEN THE TOWERS. *By Mordicai Gerstein.* $17.95. (Ages 5 and up) A stunning account of Philippe Petit's stroll between the towers of the World Trade Center.

MORRIS THE ARTIST. *By Lore Segal. Illustrated by Boris Kulikov.* $16. (Ages 4 to 8) Morris is a reluctant guest at another child's birthday party.

THE TREE OF LIFE: A Book Depicting the Life of Charles Darwin, Naturalist, Geologist & Thinker. *Written and illustrated by Peter Sís.* $18. (Ages 8 and up) This work presents the life and work of the great scientist.

WHEN EVERYBODY WORE A HAT. *Written and illustrated by William Steig.* $17.99 (Ages 4 and up) A witty memoir in pictures by the great artist and storyteller.

2002

ACTION JACKSON. *By Jan Greenberg and Sandra Jordan. Illustrated by Robert Andrew Parker.* $16.95. (Ages 8 and up) An account of artist Jackson Pollock's life. Illustrations are brilliantly done.

AMERICA. *By E. R. Frank.* $18. (Ages 12 and up) An absorbing and challenging novel about a teenage boy who has been abandoned, adopted, fostered, abducted and abandoned.

EMILY DICKINSON'S LETTERS TO THE WORLD. *Written and illustrated by Jeanette Winter.* $16. (Ages 5 and up) A rich introduction to the life and work of the poet.

FEED. *By M. T. Anderson.* $16.99. (Ages 12 and up) In this novel about teenagers in a consumerist future, the author imagines an America where people have computer chips implanted in their heads.

HONDO & FABIAN. *Written and illustrated by Peter McCarty.* $16.95. (Ages 2 to 5) Two friends, a dog and cat, spend a perfect day.

I STINK. *By Kate McMullan. Illustrated by Jim McMullan.* $15.95. (Ages 4 to 8) A big urban garbage truck recites a deliciously revolting alphabet of what it devours.

MADLENKA'S DOG. *Written and illustrated by Peter Sis.* $17. (Ages 5 to 9) Madlenka and her imaginary dog on a red leash tour her urban neighborhood in this splendid, witty fantasy.

THE THIEF LORD. *By Cornelia Funke.* $16.95. (Ages 8 and up) A fast-paced German novel about orphan brothers who run away to Venice and join a band of pickpockets.

THE THREE QUESTIONS: Based on a Story by Leo Tolstoy. *Written and illustrated by Jon J. Muth.* $16.95. (Ages 6 and up) A story involving Nikolai and his friends the heron, the monkey and the dog, a wise turtle, and a panda and her baby.

YELLOW UMBRELLA. *Written and illustrated by Jae Soo Liu.* $19.95 (Ages 4 and up) An enchanting wordless account of a rainy day journey, seen mostly from above. Includes a CD.

2001

AMBER WAS BRAVE, ESSIE WAS SMART: The Story of Amber and Essie Told Here in Poems and Pictures. *By Vera B. Williams.* $15.95. (Ages 7 and up) A story of sisters who live hidden in plain sight among adults.

BALONEY (HENRY P.). *By Jon Scieszka. Illustrated by Lane Smith.* $15.99. (Ages 5 and up) Henry, a young green alien, invents an excuse for being late for school.

FAIR WEATHER. *By Richard Peck.* $16.99 (Ages 10 and up) A rich relative asks the Beckett family to the World's Columbian Exposition in Chicago in 1893.

FOUR IN ALL. *By Nina Payne. Illustrated by Adam Payne.* $15.95. (All ages) In a poem using only 56 common nouns, a little girl sets off on a dream journey.

A GIFT FROM ZEUS: Sixteen Favorite Myths. *By Jeanne Steig. Illustrated by William Steig.* $17.95. (All ages) The stories are woven together into one seamless tale.

LOVE THAT DOG. *By Sharon Creech.* $14.95. (Ages 8 to 12) The free-verse journal of a reluctant boy whose teacher is introducing poetry to her class.

MARTIN'S BIG WORDS: The Life of Dr. Martin Luther King, Jr. *By Doreen Rappaport. Illustrated by Bryan Collier.* $15.99. (All ages) Key phrases from King's early life used as markers in telling a simplified story of his life.

OLIVIA SAVES THE CIRCUS. *Written and illustrated by Ian Falconer.* $16. (Ages 3 to 7) The plump piglet tells her classmates how she saved the circus.

A STEP FROM HEAVEN. *By An Na.* $15.95. (Ages 10 and up) A first novel that is a familiar immigrant story with Korean details but universal resonances.

WOODY GUTHRIE: Poet of the People. *Written and illustrated by Bonnie Christensen.* $16.95. (All ages) A beautifully illustrated account of the folk singer and songwriter.

EDUCATION

College & Beyond

Translating the "New" SAT

Now, 2400—not 1600—is the perfect score

The new SAT test, unveiled for the first time in fall 2005, takes a little getting used to. With the addition of a writing section to the traditional sections in math and verbal (now called reading), the longtime perfect score of 1600 has been replaced by 2400. But how do you figure out the equivalent of the old 1200 (the score of yore for midlevel public colleges) or the old 1400 (long held as the Ivy League qualifier)?

Well, you can't. Here's why: 2400 is 50 percent more than 1600, but you can't assess a new score's place in the admissions pecking order just by increasing those 1200 and 1400 benchmarks by 50 percent, says Wayne Camara, vice president of research at the College Board, which administers the SAT. "That is inappropriate to do because you have no idea that the student will score the same on the third test," he says. "In fact, it's unlikely." So the Princeton Review, the test-prep company, plunged in. Its 2006 guides, *The Best 361 Colleges* and *The Complete Book of Colleges*, attempted to convert old benchmarks to new ones—that is, the test

score ranges that 1,776 colleges and universities will accept.

The College Board says the new reading and old verbal scores are comparable, as are the new and old math. The question is how to consider the writing component. By analyzing the results of test-prep clients who took the new exam, the Princeton Review says it found a relationship between the reading scores and the writing scores and "devised an algorithm based on that relationship," explains Robert Franek,

"WILL I GET IN?"

With a new SAT comes a new scoring system. The Princeton Review has tried to calculate what ranges colleges will be looking for. Here are some of their projections.

	MATH	READING	WRITING
Harvard College	700-790	700-800	700-760
Calif. Institute of Tech.	750-800	700-770	700-740
M.I.T.	730-800	680-760	680-740
Washington Univ., St. Louis	690-780	660-740	670-720
Amherst College	680-780	680-770	680-740
Univ. of Pennsylvania	680-760	650-740	670-720
Univ. of Southern California	640-730	620-710	650-700
Univ. of Michigan, Ann Arbor	630-720	580-680	620-680
Univ. of California, Berkeley	620-740	580-710	620-700
Univ. of Virginia	620-720	610-710	640-700
Trinity College, Hartford	620-710	590-700	620-700
U.C.L.A.	610-720	570-690	610-690
New York University	610-710	610-700	640-700
Boston University	610-700	600-690	630-690
SUNY, Binghamton	600-690	570-650	610-670
Univ. of Miami	590-680	570-670	610-680
Syracuse University	580-670	570-650	610-670

—Victoria Goldman

vice president of its publishing department. The Review used the algorithm to convert each college's old verbal range into a writing range. The results are writing score ranges that are similar to verbal ranges.

Camara is skeptical, asserting, "The Review's sample is based on the observation that kids who have high SAT scores in one area more often will have them across the board." Not so, says Franek. Its sample is based "on hard numbers, the scores reported back to us by students who took the actual test." Franek offers this advice: to see how you stack up against a college's expectations, assess each section's score separately. And, when in doubt, apply.

—Victoria Goldman

Prepping for the SAT's

Bone up and you could raise your score by about 150 points

Armed with sharpened number-two pencils, nearly 1.5 million students each year take the College Board's SAT (formerly, Scholastic Aptitude Test), a lengthy multihour assessment, recently revised to produce critical reading, math and writing subscores. As many as 10 percent will have bolstered their test-taking skills with short-term coaching courses. And at least half will have spent hours poring over study manuals or clicking their way through test preparation software programs.

Should every student facing the SAT do some prepping? If so, is a course a better route to honing SAT skills than a guidebook or a software program? Bob Schaeffer, public education director for the National Center for Fair & Open Testing (FairTest), in Cambridge, Mass., says many students require little or no SAT preparation. Others who do not test well should consider taking the other national college admissions test, the ACT, or applying to the more than 730 bachelor-degree-granting schools that do not require test scores before making admissions decisions (lists at www.fairtest.org/optinit.htm).

A student's first step toward gauging how much help may be needed is to take an SAT practice test, available for free from the school guidance office or from the test maker online at www.collegeboard.com. If your score is within the average range at the schools you would like to attend, Schaeffer advises passing up any prep tools. But if your scores are well below par, it's time to explore alternatives.

The range of SAT help tools includes software programs, guidebooks, classroom courses and private tutors. Students who are comfortable on the computer would do well to invest in a software or online program designed for SAT preparation. The self-motivated can probably benefit from using one of the hundreds of SAT guides available in bookstores. Students requiring a more disciplined approach may want to try after-school courses or personalized tutoring.

When it comes to test prep books, some of the best-known publishers are Kaplan, Arco, the Princeton Review and the College Board itself. All their guides are hefty and sell for between $20 and $30. The best way to find one that's right for you is to browse through a few at a library or bookstore. As you do, keep in mind the following questions: Does the book include practice tests that mimic the SAT's format and length? Does it offer explanations or simply provide answers to questions? And does it explain the exam's structure and offer test-taking strategies?

For students searching for a solid SAT preparation course, the leaders in the field are also Kaplan (800-KAP-TEST or www.kaplan.com) and

EDUCATION

The Princeton Review (800-2-REVIEW or www. review.com). Classroom programs typically run six weeks and cost around $900. Both companies offer financial aid to some needy students.

Many good and less expensive local programs can be found, but because the quality of instruction varies, experts advise researching them carefully. Some high schools also offer test prep classes, but again, the caliber of teaching and content can vary enormously among schools.

Does prepping pay off in the end? Absolutely, says Schaeffer, who adds that with good preparation a student's combined SAT scores will rise an average of 150 points on the three-part exam. Of course, how well the preparation works depends on a student's effort.

Whether you prepare or not is your choice, but at the very least, advises Schaeffer, read the SAT registration booklet carefully—it contains vital instructions for the exam along with sample items and test-taking hints. "Anyone who waits to read the directions during the test is wasting time."

The Truth About Rankings

Are they useful or useless? One of the editors who devised the U.S.News *rankings tells all*

Ever since *U.S. News & World Report* started its extensive rankings of colleges—and sub-sequently graduate schools and hospitals—in the late 1980's, they have been the source of endless discussion and controversy. (The rankings are now partially available online for free at www. usnews.com, where you can also purchase all the latest annual data.) To compile its ratings, *U.S. News* groups thousands of colleges, universities and graduate schools into categories of size, geographic whereabouts and educational orientation. It then surveys thousands of college presidents, deans and admissions directors around the country for their assessment of the quality of peer institutions and combines that reputational data with objective information about an institution's selectivity in admissions, faculty resources, graduation rates, alumni satisfaction, among other things, to arrive at rankings for schools in the different categories. (Full disclosure: The writer of this article, while an editor at *U.S. News*, supervised the creation of the Best Colleges, Best Graduate Schools and Best Hospitals lists.)

No ranking system can ever produce a wholly accurate measure of an institution's quality, of course, and a college (or law school or business school) that is appropriate for one student may be a poor match for another, despite their ranking. The *U.S. News* surveys are but one tool in helping students and their families pick the right school for their circumstances.

But just how useful and accurate are the rank-ings? Well, that depends. The lists have certainly made available a lot of data about institutions that was not easily accessible to potential students before; so a student lucky enough to be admitted to Harvard, Princeton, Yale and the University of Pennsylvania—the four top-ranked national universities in 2006—might well find it helpful to look over the list before making his or her decision about what institution to attend. And ultimately, of course, a student does have to make a decision, which may involve a pretty subtle parsing of all the data and factors involved. You can't attend two schools—at least not at the same time!

Critics of the listings point out that the rank-ings themselves are deceptive or misleading or both, and that there is no responsible way to say that this school is No.1 and that one No.2., which has some validity. But the purpose of the rankings is also to provide useful information for readers, and in that way, they are successful. The most

TIMELY TIPS

Campus Reality Tour

Where to find the naked truth about college

Watching an MTV reality show as a freshman at Columbia, Doug Imbruce realized he could create a college video tour based on the same principle. Imbruce's *The U: Uncut,* is a DVD series of behind-the-scenes tours of 50 popular colleges. Now on sale at theu.com, it features 10-minute MTV-style clips gleaned from four-day visits and dozens of interviews at each campus.

Uncut is just one more college-search resource. Blogs, online photo galleries and real-time chats with current students are the high-tech descendants

of "insider" products like the College Prowler guidebooks and Collegiate Choice Walking Tours, student-led videotape tours at 350 campuses.

Online chats, often scheduled on college Web sites near acceptance deadlines, give prospective students a chance to ask questions about academic competitiveness, the social climate on campus or the amount of drinking that goes on. Blogs and photo galleries chronicle what it is like to be a freshman, day by day. Bucknell's Web site, for example, has a Year in the Life section, where students talk about their busy extracurricular lives and the pressures of managing their time.

While colleges don't edit the blogs, they do select the students they want representing

them. So don't expect a glimpse inside a student liquor cabinet. The *Uncut* series flashes glimpses of fraternity parties and interiors of dormitory rooms. Still, the videos do not tell a full story.

For a true sense of campus life, suggests Barmak Nassirian, an official at the American Association of Collegiate Registrars and Admissions Officers, dig into the Web site's section that is meant for current students. Scan student services and the bulletin boards of student organizations. Read the college newspaper. Frequent listservs to see what students care about. "In terms of producing an authentic image of a school," he says, a college's site can be "more telling than any reality-TV interview."

—Lisa Guernsey

---

substantive criticisms have focused on the factors that *U.S. News* considers in calculating its rankings—the factors differ for colleges, law schools, etc. For example, as part of its methodology, *U.S. News* factors in how much a law school spends per student. But just how those costs are calculated, as Alex Wellen reported in an excellent story, "The $8.78 Million Maneuver," published in the *New York Times* on July 31, 2005, "has become a matter of considerable discussion, both in legal education circles and at the American Bar Association." Reports Wellen:

"Consider library costs at the University of Illinois College of Law in Urbana-Champaign. Like all law schools, Illinois pays a

flat rate for unlimited access to LexisNexis and Westlaw's comprehensive online legal databases. Law students troll them for hours, downloading and printing reams of case law. To build user loyalty, the two suppliers charge institutions a total of $75,000 to $100,000 a year, far below per-use rates.

But in what it calls a longstanding practice, Illinois has calculated a fair market value for these online legal resources and submitted that number to *U.S. News.* For the 2005 rankings, the school put that figure at $8.78 million, more than 80 times what LexisNexis and Westlaw actually charge. This inflated expense accounted for 28 percent of the law school's total expenditures on students, according to confidential data filed with *U.S. News* and the bar association and provided to the *New York Times* by legal educators who are critical of rankings and concerned about the accurate reporting of data. These student expenditures affect only 1.5 percent of a school's *U.S. News* ranking, but this is a competition where fractions of a point matter. In the 2006 survey, the magazine ranked Illinois No.26 of 179 accredited law schools.

In addition to student expenditures, there are ways that schools can affect the other "measures of quality" that *U.S. News* uses in assembling its rankings. When they hire their own new graduates as temps, that pumps up their employment figures; when they admit weaker applicants through back-door mechanisms, that makes their admissions standards look stronger.

"Insofar as these polls affect student choices, the notion that I'm losing students because of this is insane," says Larry Kramer, dean of Stanford Law (*U.S. News* 2005 ranking No. 3, behind Yale and Harvard, respectively). "You distort your policies to preserve your ranking, that's the problem," he adds. "These rankings are corrosive to the actual education mean because this poll takes the following 12 criteria and now you have to fetishize them."

Maybe so. But over the years, *U.S. News* has been responsive to specific methodological issues,

> 66
>
> **No ranking system can ever produce a wholly accurate measure of an institution's quality, and a college (or law school or business school) that is appropriate for one student may be a poor match for another.**
>
> • • •

sometimes tweaking the formulas it uses. (For the college rankings, however, the subject reputational survey has remained for years at 25 percent of an institution's score.) And behind the scenes, many schools have spent considerable time and effort gaming the rankings, trying to figure how they might better report certain data to improve their score. As Wellen again reports:

"Playing with numbers, after all, is part of academia. With a higher ranking, a college stands to gain more prestige, competitive students, gifted faculty and alumni donations." "The *U.S. News & World Report* survey truly dominates our lives in ways you couldn't imagine," Paul L. Caron, a law professor at the University of Cincinnati, said in opening remarks at the Next Generation of Law School Rankings symposium in the spring of 2005 in Bloomington, Ind. Attended by 60 professors, deans and students from around the country, the conference was largely devoted to how the survey affects legal education. That is what brought Prof. Cynthia E. Nance from the University of Arkansas School of Law; the charge from her dean, not so unlike that given other attendees: "Find out how we get our rankings up."

Privately, more than one Ivy League president—and not from those whose institutions are at the very top of the *U.S. News* lists—have allowed that the rankings serve a useful educational and institutional purpose and that, more or less, are a fair reflection of a school's standing. Colleges and universities that do well frequently mention the rankings in their marketing materials. And, of course, the students who are most frequently consulting the rankings are, themselves, often in the midst of the admissions process, in which their qualifications are being assessed by a faceless, largely anonymous admissions committee that decides for one reason or another whether they will be accepted or not. It may be some comfort that universities themselves are just as uneasy about such a process when the tables are turned.

—Peter W. Bernstein

NOTE: : This article draws on reporting and writing from "The $8.78 Million Maneuver" by Alex Wellen that appeared in The Education Life supplement of the *New York Times* on July 31, 2005. The views expressed in this article are solely the views of the author.

An additional article about another resource for evaluating law schools appears on page 360.

The Admissions Game

Just how do colleges decide who gets in—and who doesn't?

On what basis do admissions committees anoint the chosen? The question has preoccupied generations of applicants. "There is no magic formula," says Gila Reinstein, a Yale spokeswoman. "It's just not an exact thing." Nonetheless, the College Board's annual survey of colleges and universities does ask them to rank admissions criteria. No surprise: high school academic record is consistently rated "very important," as are standardized test scores (Harvard contends they're only "important"). But what about all that other stuff? Institutions listed here admit the country's best students: 25 percent of their fall 2004 freshman classes scored 700 or more on the math or verbal SAT and placed in the top 10 percent of their high school graduating classes. But academics alone won't get you in. Here's what else matters.

RELATIVE IMPORTANCE OF THESE FACTORS IN ADMISSIONS DECISIONS:

KEY
1 Very important
2 Important
3 Considered
4 Not considered

	Interview	Extracurriculars	Recommendations	Essay	Talent / Ability	Alumni Relations	Minority Status
Amherst (Mass.)	4	1	1	1	1	2	3
Bard (N.Y.)	3	1	1	1	1	3	3
Barnard (N.Y.)	3	2	1	1	2	3	3
Bates (Me.)	1	1	1	1	1	3	3
Beloit (Wis.)	2	3	1	1	3	3	4
Bethel (Kan.)	3	4	3	3	3	3	4
Boston College (Mass.)	4	2	2	2	2	2	3
Boston U. (Mass.)	4	3	2	2	1	3	4
Bowdoin (Me.)	3	1	1	1	1	2	2
Brandeis (Mass.)	3	2	2	2	2	3	3
Brown (R.I.)	3	2	2	2	1	3	3
Bryn Mawr (Pa.)	3	2	1	1	3	4	4
Bucknell (Pa.)	3	2	1	3	1	3	2
Calif. Inst. of Tech.	4	3	1	1	3	4	3
Carleton, (Minn.)	3	2	2	2	2	3	2
Carnegie Mellon (Pa.)	3	2	2	3	2	2	3
Case Western (Pa.)	2	1	2	2	1	2	2
Claremont McKenna (Calif.)	2	2	2	2	4	3	3
Colby (Me.)	2	2	2	2	2	3	2
Colgate (N.Y.)	4	2	1	2	2	3	3
Columbia (N.Y.)	3	2	1	1	2	3	3
Connecticut College	3	1	1	1	2	2	1
Cooper Union (N.Y.)	4	3	3	3	1	4	3
Cornell (N.Y.)	3	1	1	1	1	3	3
Dartmouth (N.H.)	3	1	1	1	2	3	3
Davidson (N.C.)	4	2	1	2	2	4	3
Duke (N.C.)	3	1	1	1	1	3	3
Emory (Ga.)	4	1	1	1	2	2	3
Franklin W. Olin Col. of Engineering (Mass.)	2	1	1	1	1	4	3
Georgetown (D.C.)	2	2	1	1	1	3	3
Georgia Tech.	4	2	4	2	2	4	4
Grinnell (Iowa)	2	1	1	1	1	3	2
Hamilton (N.Y.)	2	2	1	2	3	3	2
Hampshire (Mass.)	3	2	1	1	2	3	3
Harvard (Mass.)	2	1	2	1	1	3	3

RELATIVE IMPORTANCE OF THESE FACTORS IN ADMISSIONS DECISIONS:

KEY

1 Very important
2 Important
3 Considered
4 Not considered

	Interview	Extracurriculars	Recommendations	Essay	Talent / Ability	Alumni Relations	Minority Status
Harvey Mudd (Calif.)	2	2	1	1	2	2	2
Haverford (Pa.)	3	2	1	2	3	3	3
Hendrix (Ark.)	2	2	2	1	3	4	3
Hillsdale (Mich.)	2	2	2	2	3	3	4
Illinois Inst. of Tech.	3	3	2	2	4	3	4
Johns Hopkins (Md.)	3	2	1	1	2	3	3
Kalamazoo (Mich.)	3	1	2	2	1	3	3
Kenyon (Ohio)	2	2	1	1	2	3	3
Knox (Ill.)	3	3	2	2	3	3	3
Lehigh (Pa.)	4	2	1	2	2	3	3
Macalester (Minn.)	3	2	2	2	3	3	3
M.I.T. (Mass.)	2	2	2	3	2	3	3
Middlebury (Vt.)	4	1	2	2	1	3	2
Mt. Holyoke College (Mass.)	2	2	1	1	2	3	3
New College of Florida	3	3	2	1	3	3	4
N.M. Inst. Of Mining &Tech.	3	3	4	4	3	4	4
N.Y.U.	4	2	2	2	2	3	3
Northwestern (Ill.)	3	2	2	1	2	3	3
Notre Dame (Ind.)	4	1	1	1	1	3	3
Oberlin (Ohio)	3	2	2	2	2	1	3
Pomona (Calif.)	1	1	1	1	1	3	3
Princeton (N.J.)	3	1	1	1	1	3	3
Reed (Ore.)	2	3	2	1	3	3	3
Rensselaer Poly (N.Y.)	4	2	3	3	3	3	3
Rice (Texas)	3	1	1	1	1	3	3
Rose-Hulman Inst. of Tech. (Ind.)	3	3	2	4	3	3	2
Sarah Lawrence (N.Y.)	3	2	1	1	2	3	3
Scripps (Calif.)	1	1	1	1	1	1	1
Smith (Mass.)	2	2	1	2	2	3	3
St. John's College (Md.)	1	3	2	1	3	3	3
St. John's College (N.M.)	1	3	2	1	3	3	3
St. Olaf (Minn.)	3	2	2	1	2	3	3
Stanford (Calif.)	4	2	1	1	2	3	3
Stevens Inst. of Tech. (N.J.)	1	2	1	1	2	3	4
Swarthmore (Pa.)	3	2	1	1	3	3	3
Trinity (Conn.)	2	2	2	2	2	3	2
Tufts (Mass.)	3	2	2	2	2	3	3
Thomas Aquinas (Calif.)	3	3	1	1	3	4	4
Tulane (La.)	4	3	2	2	3	3	3
U.S. Air Force Acad. (Col.)	1	1	3	1	1	3	3
U.S. Naval Academy (Md.)	1	1	1	1	2	3	3
U. of Calif., Berkeley	4	2	4	1	2	4	4
U.C.L.A.	4	2	4	1	1	4	4
U. of Calif., San Diego	4	2	4	1	1	4	4
U. of Chicago	3	2	1	1	1	3	3
U. of Illinois, Urbana	3	2	3	1	2	3	3
U. of Md., College Park	4	3	2	2	2	3	3
U. of Mich., Ann Arbor	4	3	2	2	2	3	2
U. of Mo., Kansas City	3	3	3	3	3	4	4
U. of N.C. Chapel Hill	4	1	1	1	1	2	2
U. of Pennsylvania	3	2	1	1	3	3	3
U. of Richmond	4	3	3	2	2	3	3
U. of Rochester	1	3	2	2	2	3	3
U. of Southern Calif.	3	2	1	1	2	3	3
U. of Virginia	4	2	1	2	2	1	3
U. of Wisconsin	3	3	2	3	2	3	3
Vanderbilt (Tenn.)	4	1	1	1	1	3	3
Vassar (N.Y.)	4	3	2	2	3	3	3
Wake Forest (N.C.)	4	2	2	2	2	2	2
Washington & Lee (Va.)	4	1	2	3	3	3	3
Washington U. St Louis	3	1	1	1	1	3	3
Webb Inst. (N.Y.)	1	3	2	4	3	4	3
Wellesley (Mass.)	3	2	1	1	3	3	3
Wesleyan (Conn.)	3	2	2	2	2	2	2
Wheaton (Ill.)	3	3	1	1	2	2	2
Whitman (Wash.)	3	2	2	1	2	3	2
William & Mary (Va.)	4	3	3	2	3	3	3
William Jewell (Mo.)	2	2	2	2	2	3	3
Williams (Mass.)	4	2	1	1	2	3	3
Worcester Poly (Mass.)	3	3	1	2	3	3	3
Yale (Conn.)	3	1	1	1	1	3	3

KEY

1 Very important
2 Important
3 Considered
4 Not considered

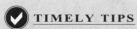

TIMELY TIPS

From Field to Dorm

The straightest line for some is through the locker room

So you think your child has talent? Might even have the fire to play college lacrosse or some other sport? Dave Prossner, a former defenseman for the University of Pennsylvania lacrosse team, a youth coach, certified referee and the author of *High School Athlete Recruiting Guide*, a booklet for lacrosse parents, offers tips on how to leverage that ability.

✔ **Be realistic.** As early as middle school, children with ability begin to shine. But have them play other sports both to develop skills and "to keep it fun," says Prossner, who coached two sons to Division I play and two to Division III. One good indicator is being picked for end-of-season or all-star teams. (Parents, beware: politics may play a part in that selection process.) In high school, ask the coach for an honest assessment.

✔ **Attend camps.** Freshman and sophomore years, seek out skills camps run or frequented by coaches from your favored college campuses. Exposure is invaluable, Prossner says, and the competition will raise your athlete's level of play. After junior year, focus on summer recruiting camps scouted by college coaches.

✔ **Make contact.** Sophomore year, compile a list of 20 colleges and send each coach a one-page sports résumé with a personal letter expressing interest in the athletic program. As seasons and academics change, update and resend it. Junior year, edit the list to eight schools and initiate unofficial visits to coaches and admissions officers. A brief video of best plays on the field should be sent only to coaches who express an interest (say, by writing back).

✔ **Encourage academics.** Coaches always ask about grades. Aim for the university that's going to meet your educational needs. A sport may help get you into college, but your brain is going to get you through life.

—Abigail Sullivan Moore

Do A.P. Courses Help?

It depends, say college admissions officers. But they can't hurt

The Advanced Placement program, administered by the College Board, began 50 years ago as a way to give a select few high school students a jump-start on college work. But in recent decades, it has morphed into something quite different—a mass program that reaches more than a million students each year and is used almost as much to impress college admissions officers and raise a school's reputation as to get college credit. As the admissions race has hit warp speed, Advanced Placement has taken on new importance, and government officials, educators and the College Board itself have united behind a push to broaden access to A.P. courses as a matter of equity in education.

Sixty percent of American high schools now participate in the program, which offers courses in 35 subjects, from macroeconomics to music theory. In 2005, 1.2 million students took 2.1 million A.P. exams, and the number of students taking A.P. courses has increased tenfold since 1980. Newsweek magazine has gone so far as to rank the nation's best public high schools using the number of students who merely show up to take A.P. or International Baccalaureate tests as the sole criterion. (I.B. is another advanced curriculum, though far less common.)

No wonder, then, that more than 3,000 students took seven or more A.P. exams last year. No wonder, either, that some students use the A.P.

EDUCATION

program tactically, knowing that their senior-year A.P. course listings will appear on their transcripts, and be counted in admissions decisions, long before they take the A.P. exam in May—if they ever do. (The A.P. brand is a curious one: students can also take the exams, which run three hours, without taking the courses.) Part of the pressure to take A.P. classes also springs from the fact that most schools weigh A.P. grades more heavily than others—an A in A.P. is often worth five points, while a regular A is worth four—so savvy students know that A.P. courses can raise their G.P.A.'s, one of the most important elements in college admissions.

When all is said and done, how important are A.P. courses in college admissions?

That depends. Certainly, most schools count them in an applicant's favor. One common approach is used at the State University of New York at Geneseo, where admissions officers tally the number of foreign language, math and science courses an applicant has taken, along with the number of A.P. or other advanced courses. Community college courses, often taken by advanced students in districts that lack an A.P. program, count, too, says Kristine Shay, director of undergraduate admissions, but "not exactly on the same basis, since they don't have that known national curriculum."

SUNY Binghamton takes a different tack. Admissions officers look at the grade-point average and SAT scores, circle the number of A.P. and honors courses, consider what coursework was available at the high school and make a non-numeric judgment: "All things being equal, if we had a kid with an 88 average and three A.P.'s, versus a kid with a 90 average and no A.P.'s, we'd probably take the one with the A.P.'s—but make it an 85 average and three A.P.'s and I'm stumped," says Cheryl Brown, director of undergraduate admissions. Almost 100 students arrived on campus for the 2005-6 academic year with enough credits for sophomore standing.

Admissions officers at the most elite colleges say, in almost identical words, that they want students who have taken "the most rigorous program the school offers" (Marlyn McGrath Lewis, Harvard); "the most demanding program they can take at their high school" (Karl Furstenberg, Dartmouth); "courses that challenge them academically" (Jeffrey Brenzel, Yale); and "the most challenging program that's available and that they can handle" (Richard Nesbitt, Williams).

While they acknowledge that taking the most difficult A.P. courses, like Calculus BC, indicates a strong academic background, they take pains to say that there is no magic, no numeric formula—and no penalty for students from schools that do not have an A.P. program. "Sheer A.P. firepower, having 10 A.P.'s, doesn't impress us," says Brenzel. "It's just one factor in evaluating a student's background and preparation."

—Tamar Lewin

❓ EXPERT ANSWER

Last Chance Is Not Least Chance

💬 **What if yours is the very last application to be read?**

Barbara Hall, associate provost for admissions and financial aid at New York University, insists that your chances are no different, even if you're No. 33,683. That's the number of applications, among the most in the country, received for the 2005-6 freshman class. Afterward, Ms. Hall says, the staff does "take a deep breath."

Getting Credit Before You Go

How to take half your college courses while you are still in high school

Earning college credit in high school is becoming increasingly popular, with half of all juniors and seniors taking a college-level course, according to Jobs for the Future, a nonprofit organization that promotes school reform. Some students do it to distinguish themselves at college admissions time; others to opt out of introductory freshman classes, allowing them to save on tuition by compressing the time spent in college or to dive quickly and more deeply into an intended major; still others simply seek a more challenging curriculum.

The granddaddy of programs, of course, is Advanced Placement (see previous story), which offers 35 college-level courses taken, on average, by one in four students (in rural communities, 1 in 10). But there are other ways to earn credit before getting to campus, meant not only for the high achiever but also for those not traditionally tagged for college.

INTERNATIONAL BACCALAUREATE. Taken over the last two years of high school, the I.B. curriculum (www.ibo.org) is intended to provide a classic education and mimics the intensity of the final year of secondary school in much of Europe. Students may take individual I.B. courses, which are more challenging than traditional high school courses, or work toward an I.B. diploma with a package of six courses a year in literature, foreign language, social science, experimental science, math and arts. Many colleges and universities award credit or preferential admissions treatment to students in the program.

About 500 secondary schools in the United States, 90 percent of them public, offer the diploma. Schools are charged an annual flat fee of $8,000,

which is covered either by the school, the district or, in some cases, the state, with an additional $620 per student to cover the costs of the exams. In most cases, this is passed on to the student; many schools make provisions for needy students.

I.B. administrators stress that the program is for motivated rather than gifted students, but each school sets its own standards for enrollment, be they academic cutoff, lottery or student interest.

CONCURRENT ENROLLMENT. High school students take a partner college's courses, taught by approved high school teachers, in the comfort of their own classrooms. Students pay reduced tuition (Syracuse University charges less than 10 percent; Indiana University, 43 percent) or an administrative fee. Generally, courses count toward grade-point average but don't fulfill a graduation requirement.

One major drawback: while many colleges accept credits for these courses, the most selective ones do not. The National Alliance of Concurrent Enrollment Partnerships (nacep.org), housed at Syracuse University, is on a campaign to create a national standard for concurrent enrollment, including accrediting curriculums and defining terms.

Concurrent enrollment, for example, is not to be confused with programs in which students travel to a campus or college faculty members travel to the high school. Such high school–college partnerships are offered in nearly every state, with 1.2 million students taking part, the National Center for Education Statistics says. They are praised in particular for giving students who would not otherwise consider college a taste of postsecondary education and for lowering costs by reducing the time spent in college.

EARLY COLLEGE HIGH SCHOOLS. Jobs for the Future (www.earlycolleges.org or www.jff.org) started this initiative in 2002 with money from

EDUCATION

four foundations. The program, with universities and other partner organizations, establishes small schools where students earn both a high school degree and two years of college credit, either an associate's degree or enough credits to enter a four-year college as a junior.

The initiative's hope is to help students who might not otherwise complete—or begin—college: "first-generation, low-income, English-language learners, and students of color," according to its Web site. There are now 71 early-college high schools in 25 states. The first was Bard High School Early College, one of nine currently operating in New York City. Bard, linked to its namesake college up the Hudson River, is a success story of a different nature: with its stringent entrance requirements, it is one of the city's more selective public schools.

—Cecilia Capuzzi Simon

What Would Picasso Have Done?

Should serious artists choose an art academy or a university?

For any college-bound student, many factors weigh in the decision of which school to select—cost, distance from home, courses. But art students have an additional criterion: should they enroll in an art academy or university? In some ways, the experience is identical. Students at both take a mix of studio and academic courses from professional artists and scholars. But subtle and not-so-subtle differences can be found.

ART SCHOOLS ARE FOR THE ARTSY ONLY

Art schools tend to be small, with fewer than 1,000 students and a student-faculty ratio of nine to one, says Bill Barrett, executive director of the Association of Independent Colleges of Art and Design. On the other hand, art departments of many universities are larger than entire art schools and can still be the smallest department on campus. Syracuse University has 12,000 undergraduates, with 1,119 in its School of Art and Design. Its studio classes have up to 18 students. And all those liberal arts and science majors—"students who really don't want to be there but are just fulfilling a distribution requirement," as Barrett puts it—can slow down a class.

But there's an upside to a large student population. Heterogeneity can expand a studio artist's thinking, and it is the mix of people and ideas that make up what we think of as the university experience. Students with broader interests may find the environment of an academy limiting.

EVERYONE IS A STAR—IN HIGH SCHOOL

Only about half of the freshmen entering an art academy finish within six years, according to surveys by the art college association. There are many reasons students drop out or transfer from any program, but art tends to attract students who are not sure what they want to study.

At a university, students can switch majors, while unhappy students at an art school must apply all over again somewhere else. A student on the fence about the future may find that a university means fewer complications if things don't work out.

MAKING ART WILL BE A JOB

In decades past, institutions like the Yale University School of Art had a reputation for giving their M.F.A. graduates a head start because of faculty members' gallery contacts. But the field has leveled out considerably. Successful artists have emerged from large and small art academies as well as university art programs. Institutions of each type make a point of highlighting the exhibition records of their faculty, and they bring in visiting artists with ties to the contemporary art scene to

Dancing Around the Subject

Choreographer Mark Morris believes dancers should be practicing, not studying

Mark Morris possesses five honorary doctorates. But he did not spend a day in college, rather training for a dance career in what he calls "L'École of Hard Knocks." This consisted of heading to Europe after high school to practice folk dancing in Macedonia, and Spanish dancing in Madrid, while cooking chickens and hanging out at weddings.

No surprise, then, that he dismisses what is almost de rigueur for modern dancers: a college-level education. "Most of it in my opinion is just a big bag of wind," said Morris. Conservatory training fares little better in his view. "I mostly think it ruins people," he said, though Juilliard may be doing something right, given the fact that five of his dancers are graduates.

Nevertheless, college-level dance programs are proliferating. *Dance Magazine*'s 2005 College Guide lists more than 500 such programs, up from 131 in 1966. But stable, paying jobs in the field are hard to find. And the utility of a college degree in dancing is a matter of endless debate.

Not going to college at all gives young dancers a head start on what in many cases is a short career, and it remains the norm for professional ballet dancers. Modern dance is physically more permissive, but also mainly a young person's pursuit. Much of the training of modern dancers still takes place in independent dance studios, not colleges, universities or conservatories. Indeed, conservatories like the Juilliard School and the dance program at New York University's Tisch School of the Arts admit students only by audition, which means most people have some kind of training before they even apply.

Those who rise through the ranks outside academia may be at a disadvantage when it comes to finding teaching jobs after they retire from the stage. "In this climate, if you want to teach, you have to have a master's," said Maile Okamura, who joined the Morris company in 2001, after a career in ballet, and is one of just two of Morris's 17 dancers who lack a college degree.

The dance department at Juilliard, which admits only the very best, estimates that in the last few years some 60 to 70 percent of students have found work as dancers after graduating. Tisch does not maintain graduate employment statistics, but Linda Tarnay, the chairwoman of the dance department, does acknowledge the awkwardness of preprofessional training for a profession with few paid jobs. Nonetheless, Tarnay said that applications to the Tisch dance program increased in 2005 to 450 for 30 slots.

Ultimately, Morris says he does not care what kind of degrees, if any, his dancers have; he cares only that they can dance. His advice to aspiring dancers? "Dance," he said. "Read. Learn music. Look around. Participate in the world."

—Erika Kinetz

bolster networking opportunities.

The University of Texas, Austin, and the University of Illinois, Urbana, have set up career offices for the fine arts. Cornell and the University of Iowa have hired counselors with knowledge of performing and visual arts. But most university career offices focus on general résumé writing and interviewing. The likelihood that a staff member has specific help to offer a B.F.A. student is remote.

The career services office of an art school, however, is tailored more to helping the artist. It may offer courses on topics like finding representation at an art gallery and preparing a portfolio. The School of Visual Arts in Manhattan invites recruiters from design firms to review students' portfolios. The career center at the Moore College of Art and Design in Philadelphia holds seminars on how to price work and install it. *"We want our artists to have information about what's out there,"* says Phyllis Mufson, its director.

YOU'LL STILL BE WRITING TERM PAPERS

The artist Jackson Pollock followed the traditional European model of training: learning how to think about painting and how to paint. Some students think they will never have to read a textbook again. But to earn a baccalaureate, art students take a third to half their classes in academic subjects. The whole idea of the B.F.A. is to combine professional training and a liberal education.

At universities, applicants are first accepted into the institution and then the art department, meaning academics matter more than artistic ability. At art academies, admissions officials and art faculty look over applications together, and some don't even require SAT's. But there is a move to focus more on academic history. *"Students who have done well in high school, even if they haven't had as much art training as other students, are more likely to do well here than students who haven't demonstrated high achievement in high school,"* says Judith Aaron, dean of admissions at the Pratt Institute in Brooklyn. The typical Pratt student, she adds, had a high school grade-point average of at least 3.2.

But providing a variety of liberal arts courses is a challenge, even at large schools like the Rhode Island School of Design, which has a full academic faculty. Some academies have tried to solve the problem by establishing a relationship with an institution nearby. Beginning in their sophomore year, students at the Rhode Island School of Design may cross-register at Brown. Students at the Pennsylvania Academy of Fine Arts can take classes toward a B.F.A. at the University of Pennsylvania's continuing-education arm; and

those at the School of the Museum of Fine Arts in Boston can earn B.F.A.'s from Tufts.

Other considerations abound: most full-time faculty members at universities have doctorates; at art schools they have master's degrees. Art schools, many of which don't offer tenure, might have trouble attracting strong general education teachers but don't pass off instruction on graduate students. And academic expectations do tend to be lower.

—Daniel Grant

Coping With the Cost of College
Borrowing isn't what it used to be

When the last college application gets mailed off, it's time for would-be freshmen and their parents—not to mention returning students—to turn to the subject of financial aid. Increasingly, that quest means selecting a loan from a bewilderingly varied range of offerings.

Student loans recently overtook grants as the leading form of financial aid for undergraduates, a trend likely to accelerate as college costs continue to rise. Two-thirds of students graduate with some debt: the average for a senior in 2004 was $19,200, according to the United States Department of Education, and for a newly minted M.D., $125,800. *"Borrowing, unfortunately, will become the price of postsecondary education,"* says Brett Lief, president of the National Council of Higher Education Loan Programs, which represents private lenders. *"In the future, just about everyone's going to have to borrow."*

Federal loans come in three types: the Perkins, Stafford and PLUS (the Parent Loan for Undergraduate Students). A growing number of borrowers are supplementing these with private loans, whose terms vary widely. For families shopping for loans, here are the choices, in order of most desirable to least:

PERKINS LOANS. For students with exceptional need, the Perkins, has a fixed 5 percent interest rate. But total Perkins borrowing maxes out at $20,000 for an undergraduate's entire college career.

STAFFORD LOANS. With $50 billion to lend, Staffords are the biggest program and come two ways: for those with financial need, the government pays the interest until the student is out of college; unsubsidized loans are available to everyone, and begin to charge interest right away. Low rates have made Staffords especially appealing, but that changed on July 1, 2006, when the rate rose to 6.8 percent. Most students are limited to $23,000 in total Stafford money. For those not supported by parents, the cap doubles, and increases to $138,500 for graduate students.

While the Stafford is federal, only about 25 percent of this money represents direct lending from the government. Most colleges provide Staffords through banks or other private lenders and send students lists of preferred ones. But borrowers are free to hunt around. Many lenders give discounts for prompt repayment or when payments are debited directly from bank accounts. "Look for discounts that are immediate," says Mark Kantrowitz, publisher of the Web site finaid.org, adding that borrowers must pay attention to the terms of the loans: "It's very easy to have one late payment" and forfeit the discount.

PLUS. Parents can borrow up to the total cost of undergraduate education, minus other aid. Under new legislation, interest rates would rise to 8.5 percent. But for the first time, graduate students will be allowed to borrow up to $12,000 annually in their own name. PLUS loans have historically been underused,. Kantrowitz says, perhaps because parents are reluctant to sign for their children and because PLUS traditionally requires borrowers to begin repayment 60 days after disbursement.

PRIVATE LOANS. These loans constitute the business's fastest-growing segment, with an estimated $14 billion now on loan. Most charge much higher rates than Stafford or PLUS and, unlike those loans, set higher rates for applicants with poor credit. In the past, borrowers were often graduate students, for whom PLUS wasn't an option. And with a cap on the amount of federal money that can be borrowed, many students have no choice but to turn to these loans, which have ceilings of $100,000 for undergraduates, $150,000 for graduate students and no limit with a co-signer. Also, parents are often released from their obligation if the student establishes a good repayment

OUT OF POCKET

Some colleges provide a projection of students' expenses (one place to look is the College Board Web site, www.collegeboard.com). Yale estimates $2,700 a year with books. New York University suggests $1,000 for spending money alone.

Average undergraduate expenses, not including tuition, room and board, 2005-2006

	BOOKS AND SUPPLIES	TRANS-PORTATION	OTHER EXPENSES	TOTAL
FOUR-YEAR PUBLIC				
Resident/out of state:	$894	$852	$1,693	**$3,439**
Commuter:	$894	$1,168	$1,962	**$4,024**
FOUR-YEAR PRIVATE				
Resident:	$904	$691	$1,295	**$2,890**

SOURCE: College Board

EDUCATION

College Grants You Don't Have to Repay

From a few hundred dollars to a free ride

✔ **National Merit Scholarships.** The National Merit Scholarship Committee these days gives out 8,200 one-time scholarship awards worth $2,500 each to National Merit finalists based on their PSAT scores, their school record, and their abilities, skills and accomplishments. In addition to this, some corporations and colleges agree to sponsor one or more scholarships for National Merit award winners; these can vary in size from a few hundred dollars to a full ride through college.

✔ **Pell Grants.** A federal Pell Grant, unlike a loan, does not have to be repaid, and is meant to help lower-income families. Generally, Pell Grants are awarded almost exclusively to undergraduate students who have not earned a bachelor's or professional degree. Pell Grants are usually a component of financial aid, to which aid from other federal and nonfederal sources might be added. The maximum Pell grant has been $4,050 for several years, though it may be increased by the time you read this.

✔ For a quick summary of student aid programs available from the U.S. government, go to studentaid.ed.gov.

record. Some lenders, like myrichuncle.com, cut rates for top-performing students who are headed for lucrative careers.

Finaid.org, Kantrowitz's Web site, lists private lenders. For those navigating the loan maze, he advises: *"Live like a student now, so you don't have to after school."*

—Sandra Salmans

Life 101
College's most popular undergraduate course

For parents eager for a sense of what their college-age children's lives are really like, they may as well turn to *I Am Charlotte Simmons*, Tom Wolfe's 2004 campus novel, which does not skimp on either the sex or the drinking. Or they could look at *Binge: What Your College Student Won't Tell You*, by Barrett Seaman, a former editor and bureau chief at *Time* magazine. His book is based on interviews at 12 institutions, ranging from small liberal arts colleges to big state universities.

So what are they doing at college? Having what Michael Moffatt, in his now-famous 1989 Rutgers study calls friendly fun, of course—which these days consists of consuming stupefying amounts of alcohol and then "hooking up" with a partner.

But was it ever very different? Looking back on his Harvard class of 1858 in *The Education of Henry Adams,* Adams wrote that the amount of drinking that went on was so "fantastic" as to make him doubt the veracity of his recollections. And in his new biography of Edmund Wilson, Lewis Dabney says that Wilson had much the same complaint about Princeton in the years before World War I. "Days," Wilson wrote, "of prevalent drunkenness, cheating in examinations, intellectual cowardice and repression, indiscriminate mockery, general ignorance, and the branding as a 'sad bird' of anyone who tried to rise above it." At any point in America's long collegiate history, it seems safe to say, only a tiny percentage of students have been serious scholars, many of them in the hard sciences.

But if college in America has never really been about studying, college life nevertheless used to constitute a kind of distinct subculture: there was, for example, the culture of "manliness" and physical prowess that Teddy Roosevelt urged upon universities at the end of the 19th century, which was succeeded by a more general ethos of "character" and character building in the early part of the last century, which was replaced in turn, in the 50's and 60's, with an ideal of insouciant gentility. Today, college is about being young in a very particular way.

The main subject that college students now master, it turns out, is simply the art of going to college—how to socialize, how to instant-message, how to manage one's time, meet deadlines and sign up for the easiest classes, how to shake mom and dad down for some extra cash and how to "game" the professors, giving them what they want in return for inflated grades and those all-important recommendations.

Seaman, who remains stubbornly optimistic about college in America, suggests that there is a certain practical value in all this; it's preparation for life. What he's too polite to say is that most of us who think we had another kind of college experience, who believe that we actually learned something, would, if we were honest, admit that most of the actual intellectual content of our undergraduate years has long since vanished, leaving only a few half-remembered facts and impressions. What we, too, learned was mostly a code of conduct—how to behave as if we really were educated.

—Charles McGrath

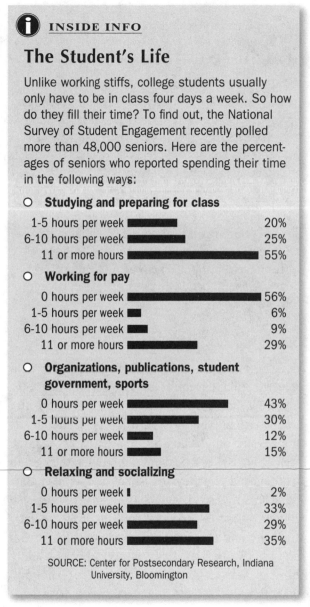

INSIDE INFO

The Student's Life

Unlike working stiffs, college students usually only have to be in class four days a week. So how do they fill their time? To find out, the National Survey of Student Engagement recently polled more than 48,000 seniors. Here are the percentages of seniors who reported spending their time in the following ways:

○ **Studying and preparing for class**

1-5 hours per week	20%
6-10 hours per week	25%
11 or more hours	55%

○ **Working for pay**

0 hours per week	56%
1-5 hours per week	6%
6-10 hours per week	9%
11 or more hours	29%

○ **Organizations, publications, student government, sports**

0 hours per week	43%
1-5 hours per week	30%
6-10 hours per week	12%
11 or more hours	15%

○ **Relaxing and socializing**

0 hours per week	2%
1-5 hours per week	33%
6-10 hours per week	29%
11 or more hours	35%

SOURCE: Center for Postsecondary Research, Indiana University, Bloomington

The Two-Year Option
Community colleges offer lots of choices

Community colleges have been traditionally known as steppingstones: students with dubious academic records, shaky finances or no family tradition of higher education often spend two years at a community college gaining

confidence before transferring to a more glamorous four-year campus. But a lesser-known pool of students head the other way: they start their postsecondary education at a four-year college and switch to a community college.

Some *"reverse transfers,"* as they are known, discover belatedly that four years of semiotics and sociology are not for them and seek practical expertise that can translate into secure jobs; others are foundering academically or socially at a traditional university. For still others, the abrupt transition from the comfort of high school to large survey classes can be daunting. *"Often they get to campus and find they're just not ready,"* says Barbara K. Townsend, author of *Understanding the Impact of Reverse Transfer Students on Community Colleges* and a professor of educational leadership and policy analysis. Community colleges usually limit classes to fewer than 30 students—not 500 which are packed into large lecture courses at state universities. Besides, community colleges cannot relegate teaching to graduate students because there are none, though they often rely on adjuncts. Some students intend to advance no further than the associate degree awarded by two-year colleges; but many expect to return to a four-year institution once they have found their footing in a less pressurized environment.

The rapid rise in university tuition is also pushing students—or parents who pay the bills—to consider a respite at a community college. An analysis by the American Association of Community Colleges using data from the National Postsecondary Student Aid Study of 2003-4, a survey sponsored by the National Center for Education Statistics, found that 32 percent of community college students had previously attended a four-year college. Some say the number is most likely even higher.

Credits are still a tricky issue when transferring between two- and four-year colleges, though. Community colleges honor course work from an accredited college or university, and public universities consider that a student with an associate degree is halfway toward a bachelor's degree. But the attitudes of private colleges vary widely. Some grant a limited number of credits for an associate degree while others scoff at community college credits altogether.

Evan S. Dobelle, who has seen both sides as president of the four-year Trinity College in Hartford and the University of Hawaii and community colleges in Massachusetts and California, says the line is blurring between the two types of institutions. Many community colleges now collaborate with four-year universities to act as satellite campuses, or to offer distance-learning programs for universities.

—David L. Marcus

Getting a College Degree Abroad
Even with air fare, it's a whole lot cheaper

Trinity College, in the heart of Dublin, is Ireland's oldest institution of higher learning, chartered by Queen Elizabeth and home to the illuminated *Book of Kells*, from the year 800. Oscar Wilde studied here; so did Oliver Goldsmith and Jonathan Swift. Trinity is considered the Harvard of Ireland, and at $25,000 in tuition and living expenses, costs far less than a similarly top-ranked institution in the United States.

The price tag may be too steep for families with state-university budgets, but a high-end foreign university will most likely cost the same or less than its American counterpart. Students attending college overseas are eligible for the same federal student loans that are available here, though not Pell grants and National Merit Scholarships.

As domestic tuitions rise yearly and the world grows smaller by the minute, going to an English-language college abroad is an increasing option for superior students. Don't expect to keep bumping into fellow countrymen just yet: the percentage of Americans ranges from 1 percent at Oxford to 10 percent at the University of St. Andrews, on Scotland's east coast.

Admissions criteria overseas range from forgiving to daunting. Trinity and St. Andrews look for a combined SAT math and verbal score of 1300 and B-plus grades. Both colleges say they recognize that American high schools vary greatly in their grading standards so they try to be flexible when reviewing applications. Oxford expects 1400 on the SAT (32 on the ACT), three SAT subject tests at 700 each, top scores on at least two Advanced Placement tests and high school ranking in the top 2 percent. (Good news for weak test takers: Australian universities want a grade-point average of 3.0 to 3.4 but don't always consider the SAT, says Tony Adams, vice chancellor of Macquarie University in Sydney.)

American students who have applied say they like how the admissions process in Europe (and elsewhere) focuses on academic promise rather than considering the other factors that are important in the United States: extracurricular activities, athletic ability, ethnicity, geography or personal connections. At foreign universities, what matters are grades, test scores and class rankings.

Most foreign universities are public—even elite ones like Cambridge and Oxford—and are heavily subsidized by their governments. Homegrown undergraduates pay a small fraction of the true cost of their education, if anything at all. In Ireland, for example, citizens pay a one-time registration fee of about $1,500 and otherwise attend college free. In Australia and Scotland, tuition for citizens is not only low (about $4,000 a year in Scotland and up to $8,000 a year in Australia), but payment is deferred until graduates start earning money. Students from other countries pay full tuition.

HOW TO APPLY

While it may sound intimidating, applying to an English-language college overseas is fairly straightforward.

 INSIDE INFO

Short-Term Study Abroad

○ Many colleges have long had a tradition of foreign study for undergraduates. Large institutions like Stanford and tiny ones like Goucher have encouraged their students to study abroad for decades. At Goucher, foreign study is now a graduation requirement.

○ Now, every college in America is getting on the bandwagon. Harvard recently urged that there be more opportunity for foreign undergraduate study. Yale has even committed to supporting undergraduate study or work abroad regardless of a student's ability to pay.

○ The traditional yearlong stay abroad has been largely replaced (now only 7 percent of all students spend an entire year abroad) by options for summer study, January term or a single semester.

○ For information on study abroad, consult your college's international studies department or go to www.iesabroad.org.

EDUCATION

☑ **TIMELY TIPS**

No Passport Required

Students are increasingly seeking out exchange programs within the U.S.

The idea of spending a junior year—or some other period—abroad is well known and increasingly popular. But many campuses now sponsor domestic exchange programs. "The country is so diverse," says Bette Worley, president of the National Student Exchange, "students can have a variety of academic, cultural and personal experiences right here in their home country."

Some students might be chasing an appealing academic opportunity. Fashion design and technology majors at Buffalo State College can study the textile industry at North Carolina State University, or a marine biology student at the University of Rhode Island can experience the Pacific Ocean at the Hatfield Marine Science Center of Oregon State University, for example. Sometimes students hope one day to work in the exchange city or to do graduate study at the exchange campus. Here's how domestic exchanges typically work.

✔ **WHO GOES.** Mostly juniors, though some domestic exchange programs accept sophomores and seniors.

✔ **CREDITS.** Course work usually transfers back to the home school for full credit. Before signing up, work with an academic adviser to determine which courses will fit into your degree program. Many exchange programs require students to get a written agreement.

✔ **COSTS.** Students usually pay their travel expenses and room and board to the host campus. And because tuition at private universities is higher than at public ones, more often than not domestic exchange students at private colleges go to other private colleges, and students enrolled in public universities go to other public universities. Participants in the mostly public National Student Exchange pay tuition either at their home campus or the host campus at state residency rates. Students usually get to choose where to pay tuition. (The exchange's Web site, www.nse.org, provides details about programs and majors offered by the 177 colleges and universities that participate.)

✔ **FINANCIAL AID.** Federal aid tends to travel with the student, but policies concerning other loans and scholarships vary. Check with your financial aid office to see if you can use them at another college.

—Mary C. Bounds

While you can apply directly to the college of your choice in Britain or Ireland, you can also apply to more than one college or program on a single form from the national offices: the Universities and Colleges Admissions Service in Britain, at ucas.com, or the Central Applications Office in the Republic of Ireland, at www.cao.ie. But you can't apply to both Cambridge and Oxford in the same year.

Most foreign universities ask for a personal statement—usually an essay on why you want to attend the college or pursue a certain field—and an interview, either over the phone or someplace close to home. They accept the same forms of measurement—SAT and ACT, Advanced Placement—common in the United States.

Clear directions are on university Web sites: Trinity (www.tcd.ie), Utrecht (www.uu.nl), St. Andrews (www.st-andrews.ac.uk), Cambridge (www.cam.ac.uk) and Oxford (www.ox.ac.uk). Information about colleges in Australia can be found at this site: studyinaustralia.gov.au.

—Leslie Berger

Harvard at a Bargain Price

For those who will accept nothing less

When Laura Shortill of Buxton, Me., applied to Harvard she, like so many other applicants, knew it was a stretch. And she had a backup: Harvard.

Although Shortill was accepted elsewhere, including Johns Hopkins, when she was rejected by Harvard College, she moved to Cambridge anyway. She enrolled in a bachelor's degree program at Harvard University Extension School—for a fraction of the admissions requirements and a fraction of the cost.

Students Shortill's age make up a small but growing percentage of Harvard Extension School these days, says Michael Shinagel, the dean. While the school does not keep count, he says, the number of bachelor's degrees it gives out (118 in 2005) is double that of 10 years ago, largely because of younger students, at least some of them drawn by the chance to experience Harvard at bargain-basement prices.

Harvard Extension School, with its mission of making a part of Harvard broadly accessible, is unusually inexpensive, charging about $550 per lecture course compared to about $4,000 per course at Harvard College. Students have access to Harvard faculty, even Nobel laureates like Roy J. Glauber, a physicist who has taught extension classes. At least 52 of the 128 credits required for the extension bachelor's degree must come from courses taught by Harvard instructors. And some courses are virtually identical to those at Harvard College, professors say.

There are no requirements to take extension courses; getting into the bachelor's degree program is permitted if students get at least a B minus in three extension courses, including expository writing. What extension students do not get is the experience of living in college dorms, socializing routinely with others their age and having access to all libraries, dining halls and other facilities. They also do not get as much faculty advising.

At Harvard, although extension students must maintain a C average and fulfill language, science and math requirements, they may deal with the perception that they are not full-fledged Harvard citizens. Social life can be challenging because most classmates are older and return home to families. But some students like the mix of ages, and

---

ⓘ INSIDE INFO

The New Face of Facebooks

Facebook.com has become more than a way for young people to stay in touch.

○ Started by Harvard students and now used by millions of students, it is available at most of the country's four-year colleges, and many two-year colleges and high schools.

○ Nearly three-quarters of Facebook users sign on at least once every 24 hours, and the average users sign on six times a day, says a spokesman for the site.

○ Using it is simple: students create online profiles, which they can stock with personal details like sexual preferences, favorite movies and phone contact numbers, with links to photo albums and diaries. The details listed are by no means reliable. Facebook enables users to compile lists of friends whose names and photos are displayed, and to post public comments on other people's profiles. Users can also join or form groups.

○ Despite safeguards placed on access—only those with e-mail addresses ending in edu can register as users, and students can bar specific people from viewing their profiles, though there is concern about cyberstalkers and prospective employers signing on. —Nancy Hass

EDUCATION

that the evening classes allow daytime pursuits. And there is the diploma, a bachelor of liberal arts in extension from Harvard University (that other diploma says bachelor of arts from Harvard College). *"Some people are like, 'What are you exactly?'"* Shortill said. *"But some people are like, 'Oh my goodness, you can do that? Wow, that was really smart of you to figure that out.'"*

As one Harvard professor put it, students getting bachelor degrees from the extension school are *"brilliantly milking the cow of Harvard University."*

—Pam Belluck

How to Win a Rhodes
A postgraduate degree from Oxford for free

A lot has changed since William Jefferson Clinton won his Rhodes from Arkansas in 1968. While the Ivy Leagues, elite private colleges and military academies have long dominated, over the last five years aggressive state universities have begun to make some inroads, and the competition is more intense than ever. Indeed, Harvard may be one of the last places to at least sound nonchalant about the Rhodes. "Nominating for the Rhodes seems to come more or less naturally here," says one Harvard official, although that isn't exactly true. It's just that the machinery has been in place longer. Harvard has a full-time fellowship staff of three, and each of the 13 residence houses has one or two graduate students coaching candidates through the process. (At the University of Arkansas, by contrast, there are two fellowship advisers.) Harvard officials may seem blasé about it, but they actually spend a fair bit of time prepping their students, too.

At 100+ years old, the Rhodes, the granddaddy of all fellowships, is both the most prestigious and the most arduous. To become one of the lucky 32 scholars selected nationwide each December, candidates must be nominated by their university, approved by their state Rhodes committee, pass muster at a cocktail party, interview on the state level and, finally, survive a second cocktail party and interview on the regional level. In sparsely populated states such as Arkansas, maybe one applicant wins a Rhodes. Some years, none does. Here is an idea of what it takes to win the coveted scholarship:

- Maintain as close to a perfect grade-point average as you can.

- Have some extraordinary talents and accomplishments, or extracurricular activities, or leadership roles. One recent winner from Yale had a perfect G.P.A. Another researched female factory workers in Latin America and China and is organizing a national network of student-run tutoring programs for prisoners. She also pursued bachelor's and master's degrees concurrently in anthropology. Another had already had his poetry published in the *New York Times.*

- Get eight recommendations from professors who know you well.

- Travel abroad, not just as a tourist, but in some meaningful endeavor. One candidate traveled extensively in Jordan, worked at an orphanage in Honduras and spent her junior year at Cambridge University in England.

- Meet for three hours every Sunday afternoon during senior year fall semester with your fellowship adviser for coaching on interviews.

- Read daily e-mail messages from advisers crammed with suggested articles to read from the *Economist,* the *New Yorker, Foreign Affairs,* the *New York Times* and the Society for Medical Anthropology, as well as books, poems and the odd tidbit about Cecil Rhodes, the scholarship's founder.

- Undergo numerous mock interviews with faculty members in varied campus settings.

- Write and rewrite your essays.

- Practice answers to questions such as "You have one minute to tell the prime minister of India how to end religious violence. What do you say?"

- Practice your skills at a mock cocktail party to simulate the one with the Rhodes committee.

In their book, *The Founder: Cecil Rhodes and the Pursuit of Power*, authors Miles F. Shore and Robert I. Rotberg point out that Rhodes himself was every bit as odd and eccentric as Rhodes the fellowship. His scholarship to his alma mater, Oxford University, was not to be for bookworms (no "Latin and Greek swots") but instead for, well, young men like Rhodes—outgoing fellows of action. The original formula counted academics four-tenths, athletics two-tenths, character two-tenths and manhood two-tenths. Over time, the formula has been modified (for one thing, women became eligible for the scholarship in 1977) and today, athletics is interpreted to mean personal vigor.

—Michael Winerip

> **The principle of study-abroad programs is that young Americans be introduced to the idea that other people have important things to contribute to societies.**
>
> Sanford J Ungar, President of Goucher College
>
> ● ● ●

who oversaw the economic recovery program to rebuild Europe after World War II. Inaugurated in 1954, the scholarship was conceived as a coeducational alternative to the Rhodes, which until 1977 excluded women and requires study at Oxford University. The Marshall, on the other hand, allows two years of study at any British university. There is no age restriction, but applicants must have earned a bachelor's degree within the previous two years. The program, which covers the entire cost of study abroad, is highly competitive. Generally, at least 40 winners are selected from a nominated pool of more than a thousand applicants. Many applicants have grade point averages of 4.0. Past winners include Ray Dolby, inventor of the eponymous noise reduction system, and Justice Stephen G. Breyer of the Supreme Court. **www. marshallscholarship.org**

GEORGE J. MITCHELL SCHOLARSHIP. George Mitchell, a former senator from Maine, mediated the Northern Ireland peace process from 1996 to 1998. The scholarship, administered by the United States-Ireland Alliance, was established in 1998 to promote exchanges between the two Irelands and the United States. Students spend a year at any institution in Ireland or Northern Ireland and typically earn a master's, but some apply their year toward a degree they have already started, like an M.D. Each class is limited to 12 scholars, who must be no older than 30. The Mitchell, which awards a $12,000 stipend, is financed by the Northern Ireland executive and the Irish and British governments. Because the Mitchell seeks to introduce future American leaders to Ireland, applicants without a connection to Ireland may have an edge, according to Trina Vargo, president of the

Other Roads to Study Abroad

The Rhodes is just one option of many

The Rhodes is just one of a number of international fellowships coveted for their prestige and opportunity. The programs, which pay tuition and a stipend, seek postgraduates who have demonstrated academic excellence and leadership potential in their fields.

MARSHALL SCHOLARSHIP. The British government established the Marshall as a gesture of thanks to the United States and Gen. George C. Marshall,

EDUCATION

United States–Ireland Alliance. But being of Irish descent has no bearing on the selection process. **www.us-irelandalliance.org/scholarships.html**

J. W. FULBRIGHT STUDENT PROGRAM. This flagship program of the American government was inaugurated in 1946 by Senator Fulbright (himself a Rhodes Scholar) to promote international understanding after World War II. Each year, over 1,000 American students—seniors or graduate students—are given full income support for a year to study in a foreign country, many of them uncommon destinations for scholars. In fact, applicants whose proposals entail research in less-sought-after nations (and veterans) may have an advantage in the selection process. On the flip side, 1,300 foreign students study in the United States under the program. Recipients design their own course of inquiry and need not be pursuing a degree. Past recipients include Joseph E. Stiglitz, who shared the 2001 Nobel Memorial Prize in economics; Ruth J. Simmons, president of Brown University; the actor John Lithgow; and the soprano Renée Fleming. **www.iie.org**

HARRY S. TRUMAN SCHOLARSHIP. Recipients are expected to pursue careers in the public sector, including uniformed service, and must have demonstrated such a commitment during college. To prove the point, applicants submit a one-page statement tackling a public policy issue and offering a solution. Truman Scholars are nominated by their university while in their junior year, and get a tenth of their $30,000 stipend in their senior year, the balance during graduate work. Scholars may study at any university or professional school in the United States or abroad, though they typically stay here. Congress established the scholarship in 1975 as the federal memorial to the 33rd president, who had dabbled unsuccessfully in haberdashery, oil wildcatting and banking before entering pub-

lic service. An endowment for the government-financed program is held in trust at the Treasury. Past winners include George Stephanopoulos, ABC political analyst (who went on to win a Rhodes); Janet Napolitano, governor of Arizona; and Jeffrey Toobin, legal affairs writer for the *New Yorker*. **www.truman.gov**

GATES CAMBRIDGE SCHOLARSHIP. In 2001, Cambridge University welcomed its first group of 153 Gates recipients, who can work toward a second bachelor's degree on up to a doctorate. Applications are accepted from any country but Britain, with about a third from the United States. In what was then the biggest single gift to European higher education, the Bill and Melinda Gates Foundation granted $210 million to Cambridge to endow the scholarship, which awards a $15,000 annual stipend. The university had approached Gates, who had shown interest in the city of Cambridge's ambitions to become Britain's Silicon Valley, with its research institutions and start-up technology companies. **www.gates.scholarships.cam.ac.uk**

—Sara Ivry

Let Abe Lincoln Be Your Guide

You can become a lawyer without setting foot in a law school

For some, there is a much cheaper way of becoming a lawyer. A few aspiring lawyers are getting their legal educations in programs that require no law school whatsoever. California, Vermont, Virginia and Washington allow law readers to take bar examinations after three or four years in apprenticeships registered with the state. Three other states—New York, Maine and Wyoming—let those who have not graduated from law schools take bar examinations if they have a

INSIDE INFO

Psst! Apply to Law School

It may a little bit easier to get in these days. It seems that fewer people want to be lawyers.

○ In the 2003-4 admission cycle, the number of law-school applicants hit 100,600, according to the Law School Admission Council. For the entering class of 2006, however, there were approximately 40,000 fewer applications.

○ Admissions officers and career counselors say they are not sure what is causing the drop. Some suggest college students may prefer jobs to law school, or that rising undergraduate debt loads have discouraged them from borrowing still more to pay for a law degree.

○ David E. Kelley, creator and producer of the television show *Boston Legal*, himself a lawyer, has a different explanation: "The more lawyers there are, the more people are out there to encourage others not to go to law school."
                                                                    —Jonathan D. Glater

combination of office study and law school experience. By comparison, more than 140,000 students attend law schools approved by the American Bar Association, and thousands more attend schools not approved by the association.

Despite some challenges, law readers can rise high in the profession. Marilyn Skoglund, for instance, sits on the Vermont Supreme Court, and Gary Blasi is a professor at the University of California, Los Angeles. "I'm really sort of a bizarre case," Professor Blasi says. "The first time I was ever in a law classroom, I was teaching law." The practice was once far more common. For example, Abraham Lincoln and Thomas Jefferson both read law. But it isn't easy. In 2004, only one law reader passed the Virginia bar out

of nine taking the exam. In July 2003, seven law readers took the bar, but only one passed.

The big benefit to law reading is that students get one-on-one instruction from someone who cares about them. Indeed, the supervising lawyers cannot take money for the substantial time they put into training their apprentices. A downside to skipping law school is that a degree can be a job requirement, though in some cases it is possible to get a waiver. Although the bar association maintains rigorous standards for approved law schools, it does not advise against law reading. Some groups see it as a state's right to allow an alternative to law school.

Are You a Master of the Universe?
Choosing the right business school for you depends on your ultimate goals

Learn through case studies or hands-on experience? Generalize or drill down? Stay home or go abroad? These are just a few of the choices facing students who are contemplating a master's in business administration.

With the number of programs proliferating, business schools have been scrambling to woo students—and company recruiters—by trying to distinguish themselves from the rest of the field. Thus, more and more schools are departing from the once-hallowed "case method" established by the Harvard Business School, in which deskbound students analyze the situations of companies, real or fictitious, and make recommendations. Instead, schools are offering opportunities to, say, set up and run actual companies, or take electives in other schools within the university.

"There was a time when the M.B.A. was one size fits all," says John Fernandes, president of the Association to Advance Collegiate Schools

Beyond the *U.S. News* Law School Rankings

The American Bar Association fills in some holes

Prospective law students looking to compare particular law schools may be best served by going to the source—the American Bar Association. Each year, together with the Law School Admissions Council, the association publishes a portion of the information collected for its annual questionnaire in *The Official Guide to A.B.A.- Approved Law Schools*. The guide, $24 at www.ababooks.org, fills in many of the holes in the *U.S. News & World Report* rankings.

After reviewing *U.S. News*, for example, an applicant might consider the University of California, Los Angeles, for its 96.5 percent employment rate within nine months of graduation. But as part of its computation, *U.S. News* removes graduates not seeking employment—39 in the case of U.C.L.A. The 2006 bar association guide shows that these 39 students make up 12 percent of the graduation class—one of the largest proportions in the country—and that the employment rate is closer to 85 percent.

Another student might pick the Columbia School of Law for its student-faculty ratio. What the candidate may not realize is that the 11.2-to-1 ratio reported by *U.S. News* applies only to faculty in fall semesters. The 2006 A.B.A. guide reveals that the ratio is closer to 16 to 1 for the spring. For context, 11.2 to 1 was among *U.S. News*'s top 10 faculty-student ratios, but schools that reported a 16-to-1 student-faculty ratio in the fall were ranked toward the bottom of the top 100. In fact, the guide says, nearly one-third of Columbia's full-time law faculty does not teach in the spring. These are tenured and visiting professors and those with joint appointments at other institutions, says a law school spokesman. The guide discloses that the school accommodates its law students with 32 additional part-time teachers.

The bar association and the admissions council also offer an interactive Web site (http://official-guide.lsac.org/docs/cgi-bin/home.asp) that helps students sort and evaluate different law schools, using criteria like employment rates after graduation, bar passage rate, size of faculty, student body breakdown and tuition. The site includes descriptions, photographs and admissions profiles for all A.B.A.-approved law schools. —Alex Wellen

of Business International, which accredits business schools. "Now, by and large, schools are trying to be very good at fewer specialties and less generic."

In this changing landscape, how does a student find the right educational fit? Of course, time and money often make the choice for you; faced with the cost of tuition and the need to work, nearly 80 percent of M.B.A. candidates attend part time, often subsidized by their employers. Grade-point averages and admissions test scores may also limit your options.

But all else being equal—which it rarely is—here are some programs to consider, depending on what you want to do and who you are.

Are you a specialist or a generalist? Most newly minted business-school graduates begin their careers in a department like product management or finance. But if your goal is to move into general management in 5 to 10 years and ultimately lead an organization, it makes sense to get a strong foundation.

Most of the perennially top-ranked graduate business schools—Stanford, Harvard, Columbia, Kellogg at Northwestern, Wharton at the University of Pennsylvania—still adhere largely to the traditional core curriculum, which is meant to provide an overview of the entire corporation. Students get little or no choice of courses in the

TIMELY TIPS

If You're Thinking of Med School

✔ **Consider attending a public medical school in your own state.** Just about half of the best medical schools in the country are public. Some state medical schools give preference to in-state applicants, and lower tuition as well.

Resources for medical school applicants include the following.

✔ **Medical Students' Resource Guide** (www.studentdoc.com) provides information and strategic advice on a number of topics related to medical school applications.

✔ **Princeton Review** (www.princetonreview.com) has a medical school search tool that allows you to see how your academic record and MCAT scores stack up in comparison to others who have been admitted to particular schools.

✔ **U.S. News** (www.usnews.com) has a comprehensive set of rankings for medical schools around the country, and also information on what sorts of candidates are admitted to each medical school.

first year, typically taking multiple classes in each of some half-dozen categories—strategy, operations, finance, accounting, marketing, leadership and organizational behavior. In the second year, the universe widens to include electives.

"We sometimes describe the first year as the old East Germany and the second as a free market," says Joseph L. Badaracco Jr., chairman of the elective curriculum at the Harvard Business School. "We're very much a general management school. A lot of students come here because they want to run something."

There's an additional advantage to mastering business basics: trendy concentrations can be a blot on one's résumé when a hot market cools. Sharon Hoffman, associate dean and director of Stanford's M.B.A. program, notes that the school was criticized for not focusing on Internet-related business during the dot-com bubble. "But we said, 'The fundamentals remain the fundamentals,'" she recalls.

Do you have a particular passion? Many business schools are adding "tracks" to their curriculum that play to their particular strengths and, they hope, to a marketplace that wants M.B.A.'s prepared to hit the ground running. If you already know that you want to work in a specific field, this could be a good fit.

The specialized curriculum that the Tepper School of Business at Carnegie Mellon rolled out in 2004, for example, includes tracks in biotechnology, computational marketing, technology leadership, operations strategy and management, management of innovation and product development, and wealth and asset management. The idea is to build not scientists and engineers but the people who can manage them. "You can't manage a group of people who think you don't know anything about their field," says Kenneth B. Dunn, Tepper's dean. "We've had a big increase in the number of new firms coming to recruit at Carnegie Mellon as a result of the tracks."

Are you still looking for a field of interest? While all graduate business schools have greatly expanded their lists of electives, some M.B.A. programs make a point of giving students free rein, not only in the business school but in other schools within the university.

The University of Chicago, that champion of free-market economics, boasts on its Web site that "we offer the most flexible curriculum of any top business school in the world," with "very few required courses."

In sweeping changes at the Massachusetts Institute of Technology, the Sloan School of Management in 2004 halved the number of required

ⓘ INSIDE INFO

Continuing Ed

○ In 2000, only 27 percent of students fit the traditional description of enrolling right after high school, attending full-time, being financially supported by parents and either not working or working part-time, according to the National Center for Education Statistics.

○ University of Phoenix, a continuing-education school with 176 campuses, has dropped its rule that students be at least 22. Now 18-to-22-year-olds are nearly 10 percent of its 160,000 undergraduates.

○ At University of Maryland University College, a continuing-education school, students 25 and under seeking bachelor's degrees are the fastest-growing population, tripling to 4,200 in 2004 from 1,400 in 1997.

courses to a half dozen. What's more, M.I.T. has added a number of courses that are only six weeks long and divided the traditional 13-week semester into two sessions, with an "innovation" week in between when professors present their research. This schedule allows students to sample a greater variety of subjects. Compared with the track approach, the M.I.T. program "gives students more opportunity to explore, and also to customize their own curriculum," says Andrew W. Lo, director of the school's Laboratory for Financial Engineering, who was involved in the redesign. "The real benefit is the flexibility."

Do you want to create a business of your own?
If you were the kind of child who couldn't wait to set up a lemonade stand each summer—and maybe took over the neighbor's stand as well—then you may be interested in one of the growing number of hands-on programs for entrepreneurs.

The Henry W. Bloch School of Business and Public Administration at the University of Missouri, Kansas City, which has a strong emphasis on entrepreneurship, is adding a program in January 2006 in which student teams create and run their own companies for six months. At the F.W. Olin School of Business at Babson College, entrepreneurship is embedded in the core curriculum, with yearlong consulting projects for local companies. While only 20 percent of Babson graduates start their own businesses, the rest tend to go into new business development in established concerns.

Are your sights set on the global marketplace?
These days, it's the rare M.B.A. program that doesn't include an opportunity to study abroad. An M.B.A. candidate at one of two dozen Jesuit universities participating in a consortium, including Fordham, Boston College and Loyola University Chicago, can take up to 12 credits at Beijing University. The University of Chicago has a campus in Singapore. The Stern School of Business at New York University lets you spend a couple of weeks in Chile or Denmark. Now, to intensify their international perspective, an increasing number of students are leaving the country altogether to get their M.B.A.'s—in Canada, Britain and elsewhere in Europe.

"In today's global business world, the most sought-after employees know how to work cross-culturally, how to motivate international teams and how to deal with the uncertainty and ambiguity that the global economy throws up," says Julia Tyler, associate dean of the M.B.A. program at the London Business School. Studying with students and faculty representing dozens of nationalities helps prepare M.B.A.'s for doing business internationally, even if based in the United States. If English is your only language, not to worry: generally, M.B.A. classes are taught in English, even in France and Spain.

—Sandra Salmans

Is B-School Worth the Big Bucks?

The degree may not justify the investment

Students at second- or third-tier schools can certainly build successful careers. But given the degree's hefty price tag, deans and corporate recruiters warn that a master's degree in business administration does not necessarily translate into a high-salary job. And the path to a leading investment bank or consulting company runs almost exclusively through a narrow band of elite business schools.

"If you want to be an M.&A. lawyer, investment banker in a top house or a consultant for McKinsey—these elite jobs that everybody seems to want—you're not even going to get an interview unless you go to one of the elite schools," says Robert H. Frank, a Cornell University management professor and co-author of *The Winner-Take-All Society.* "Going to an elite school doesn't guarantee you'll get one of those jobs," he adds, "but for better or worse, you won't even have a shot at it without it."

"Core schools" are those where companies recruit in person year after year. Many have only five or so core schools, some as few as two. At big-time companies, only a few business schools turn up on list after list: Harvard, Northwestern, Stanford, Chicago, University of Pennsylvania, Massachusetts Institute of Technology, Columbia.

A 2004 survey by *Business Week* magazine found that of Citigroup's 164 M.B.A. hires, 23 were from Columbia and 14 from the Wharton School of Finance at the University of Pennsylvania. No other business school placed more than 8 there. Columbia M.B.A.'s took 16 of the 71 M.B.A. jobs at Booz Allen Hamilton, 11 of the 43 at Deutsche Bank and 15 of the 40 at Goldman Sachs.

What do these gold-plated programs bring to the table? Jeffrey Pfeffer, a professor at Stanford's business school, published a study in 2002 based on decades of data to determine what the M.B.A. degree actually did for students. Internal studies by leading consulting firms and investment banks of their M.B.A. and non-M.B.A. employees showed that the degree had no impact beyond helping them get the job. Pfeffer concludes: "There is little evidence that mastery of the knowledge acquired in business schools enhances people's careers, or that even attaining the M.B.A. credential itself has much effect on graduates' salaries or career attainment."

But even critics like Pfeffer say that top business schools do something of value: sort students. People who invest in an M.B.A. are often bright in the first place, and those with the most potential attend business schools from which they can land jobs with important futures. "It wasn't

---

ⓘ **INSIDE INFO**

The New G.R.E.

○ The Educational Testing Service, the maker of the Graduate Record Exam, is delaying its rollout of a revamped test until the fall of 2007.

○ The overhaul is the biggest in the test's history. Although the exam will still include sections on verbal reasoning, quantitative reasoning and analytical writing, every section is being revised, and the test lengthened to about four hours, from two and a half hours.

○ The revamped exam will also change the verbal reasoning section so that it will consist of two 40-minute sections rather than one 30-minute section, and will place less emphasis on vocabulary and more on higher cognitive skills. The quantitative reasoning section will grow from one 45-minute section to two 40-minute sections, with fewer geometry questions and more on interpreting tables and graphs. And the analytical writing measure, which had a 45-minute essay and a 30-minute essay, will now have two 30-minute essays.

EDUCATION

what the students learned, but that you've got this preselected group of people," he says. Roger L. Martin spent 13 years at Monitor, a top consulting company based in Cambridge, Mass., where he was responsible for recruiting. He tended to recruit almost entirely from the Harvard Business School (of which he is a graduate). But, Martin, who went on to become dean of the business school at the University of Toronto, says "If you gave me a choice of recruiting with the admissions list or the graduating list, it would take me a second to decide—I'd go with the admissions list. If people were smart, they would apply to Harvard, get in, and then send their admissions letters out and use that to get jobs." Harvard, he adds, "is a magnificent vehicle for extracting out of the global economy those people who are destined to be great business leaders and motivated and smart." But beyond that, he believes, Harvard adds nothing.

—Scott Jaschik

Free Advice for 20-Somethings

Relax, you're not even an adult yet!

"Emerging adulthood"—a fraught new transitional stage on the path to maturity: the decade between the late teens and the late 20's—is the new moniker favored by the flourishing field of 20-something studies. Jeffrey Jensen Arnett, the psychologist who coined the term, pronounces it a "historically unprecedented period of the life course" that is here to stay.

The optimistic advocates of "emerging adulthood" emphasize the freedom for identity-enriching experimentation. Meanwhile, pessimists focus on possible life-course derailments, and so-called helicopter parents try to micromanage for longer and longer. But the available data suggest that the road to maturity hasn't become as drastically different as people think—or as drawn out, either. It's true that the median age of marriage rose to 25 for women and almost 27 for men in 2000, from 20 and 23, respectively, in 1960, but Americans of all ages have ceased to view starting a family as the major benchmark of grown-up status. When asked to rank the importance of traditional milestones in defining the arrival of adulthood, poll respondents place completing school, finding full-time employment, achieving financial independence and being able to support a family far above actually wedding a spouse or having kids. This new perspective isn't merely an immature swerve into selfishness; postponing those last two steps is good for the future of the whole family.

The magic age that most Americans currently point to as the onset of adulthood, according to a recent survey, is 26. That's not so old, nor is it a radically new marker. Where would literature be without bumpy life journeys well into the 20's? The 28-year-old narrator of Benjamin Kunkel's recent coming-of-age novel, *Indecision*, may be Holden Caulfield's senior by more than a decade, but Goethe's young Werther still agonized after his teens. Tristram Shandy, who broke all records for meandering, was in his 40's. The truth is that restless drift, mixed with drive, is a staple of the American way of growing up.

—Ann Hulbert

Ann Hulbert is the author of *Raising America: Experts, Parents, and a Century of Advice About Children.*

CHAPTER **6**

CAREERS

Getting Started   366

PICKING A PROFESSION·366: *What to be when you grow up: personality tests* **JOB HUNTING·367:** *Networking online • Best Web sites for job seekers • Honing your job-hunting skills* **GETTING HIRED·371:** *What not to do at the interview • 20 terms to avoid on a résumé • A résumé that works* **STRATEGIES·374:** *To get a job, get an internship • Majors with a pragmatic bent* **OCCUPATIONAL OUTLOOK·375:** *Where the best jobs will be • The 30 fastest-growing professions* **SALARIES·379:** *What legends get paid • What 100 jobs pay*

Smart Moves   382

LEADERSHIP·382: *Who gets to the corner office? • Management by the book* **OFFICE POLITICS·385:** *Bully bosses • Disagreeing with the boss • Shushing the office magpie* **JOB TRANSFERS·388:** *A year abroad as a career move • What to know before you go abroad* **STRESS MANAGEMENT·390:** *Ways to beat burnout • Stressful and stressless jobs • The e-mail menace* **MOVING UP·392:** *How to get your next raise • When you get a better offer • How to get your head hunted* **MOVING ON·396:** *When to jump ship • I quit! The exit interview • The womenless workforce* **SECOND CAREERS·400:** *What color is your new career? • Where career switchers go • Want to be your own boss? • The new "retirement" plan*

Getting Started

What to Be When You Grow Up

The clueless might get some clues from a psychological profile

Whatever your age, whatever your career accomplishments, the nagging question remains, Is this what I am best fit to do?

One popular way to try to find out is to take a personality test. The testing business is huge, with annual revenues of about $400 million; some 2,500 tests are on the market today. You can take them on the cheap by using modified versions found in books in the careers section of your local library or bookstore, or on numerous career Web sites (search: "career tests"). But the full-dress tests, administered by career counselors, psychologists or psychiatrists, can cost hundreds of dollars. Do personality tests produce results? The answer is unclear.

The Rorschach test, invented in the 1920's, was the first such test. It is supposed to reveal an individual's underlying personality through his or her reaction to a series of inkblot designs. Today, it is still widely used by psychiatrists, mostly to evaluate prisoners and in child-custody cases. By the 1950's, the Thematic Apperception Test took hold. It asks takers to form stories about a series of drawings. The goal is to ferret out subliminal themes in a person's behavior. Both of these tests have come under criticism and are largely discredited as reliable, other than in determining psychosis.

Two types of tests, the Myers-Briggs Type Indicator and the Strong Interest Inventory, are used by companies hoping to cut down on the expense of hiring a candidate whose personality does not fit the work environment. Increasingly, the tests have gained favor as a way for executives to learn what makes a potential employee tick. Both involve completing a lengthy questionnaire that attempts to gauge an individual's interests and temperament.

Personality tests were once thought to be helpful only for those wanting to change careers in midstream, but they are now administered to people of all ages. Some high schools give them to students to help them with college choices and long-term goals. Some college career centers administer them to seniors before they head into the "real" world. But they are most popular in the workplace: nearly 90 percent of Fortune 100 companies, including AT&T, Exxon and General Electric, use Myers-Briggs, for example, "to identify job applicants whose skills match those of their top performers," according to Annie Murphy Paul, author of *The Cult of Personality*.

Here's a brief assessment of the two most common tests. They are best administered and interpreted by professional counselors. Before shelling out hundreds, check with the career office at a local university; many allow students or alumni to take the tests for free.

MYERS-BRIGGS TYPE INDICATOR. This test categorizes people based on four scales of personal preferences: extroverted or introverted, sensing or intuiting, thinking or feeling, and judging or perceiving. The answers place individuals in one of 16 personality groups. Once M.B.T.I. identifies your type, a counselor provides you with a list of

What's Your Type?

After you take the Myers-Briggs, you are given a score in the form of four letters. These are your personality preferences. They indicate into which 4 of the 16 possible categories you fall. For example, ENTP means you are an extroverted, intuiting, thinking, perceiving personality. Here are some characteristics of the different personality types.

• How you deal with others

E= EXTROVERTED Energized by interacting with others. Act first, think and reflect later. Studies show that about 75 percent of people are extroverted.

I = INTROVERTED Motivated internally. Prefer quiet reflection. Think first, then act. Only 25 percent of people are introverted.

• How you process data

S= SENSING Practical, orderly, use common sense. Good ability to recall details and facts. About 75 percent of people indicate this preference.

N= INTUITING Creative, imaginative, theoretical. Memory emphasizes hazier connections. Only 25 percent indicate this approach.

• How you make decisions

T= THINKING Objective, critical, analytic, logical. About 60 percent of men show this preference.

F= FEELING Use personal feelings to make decisions. Seek consensus. About 60 percent of women indicate this preference.

• How you approach life

J= JUDGING Planned, structured, focus on completing tasks on time. More than half of people have this approach.

P= PERCEIVING Spontaneous, flexible, value freedom. About 45 percent show this preference.

---

job fields best suited for you. One drawback is that it's a personality, not a skills test. Another, say critics, is that it is an unreliable monitor, in that a person can be "introverted" one morning and "extroverted" in the afternoon. Others question its core assumptions, that is, whether the four basic scales actually exist.

STRONG INTEREST INVENTORY. Many counselors recommend taking this test in conjunction with Myers-Briggs. The test collects information about an individual's interests and recommends potential occupations based on work activities involved, the traits of the working environment and personality characteristics that can affect work. Individuals are categorized by one of the six occupational types (realistic, investigative, artistic, social, enterprising and conventional) that correspond with a list of career options. This test works best for college students or individuals with a college degree.

Networking Online

Web sites that can help you get your foot in the door

In your frenzied job hunt, you've sent out truckloads of introductory notes and résumés, and attended too many informational lunches and job groups to count. But the most important step toward landing a new job is clearly networking. Lee Hecht Harrison, an outplacement company, estimates that 80 percent of jobs are found through networking.

Filling the growing need to extend contact lists are Web sites like LinkedIn.com and Ryze.com, which are free to join and are the business equivalents of dating sites like Friendster.com and Match.com. Users create a personal Web page with vital facts like job experience and education, goals, hobbies and sometimes pictures, and are instantaneously hooked into a virtual world of unrealized friends, or a "tribe." Sites like Monster.com and CraigsList.com are also popular for talking shop

CAREERS

Remember Your SAT Scores?

You may need to dredge them up again

SAT scores have been a key factor in college admissions for decades, but like a high school diploma, they could be safely retired to the attic once that acceptance letter arrived. In today's tight job market, however, prospective employers may ask to see the scores of recent—and even not so recent—college graduates.

When you're hiring someone, it's such a crapshoot, says Christopher Wallace, a principal in the Boston office of Towers Perrin, the management consulting firm. Grades depend on what school you went to. SAT scores are the only empirical data. A recent HotJobs.com posting showed several employers and employment agencies asking for SAT scores, along with college grade point averages. Job applicants were expected to have scores well above the norm. Minimum expectations include an overall score of 1350 on the SAT's, stated an advertisement for an entry-level position in investment banking: "You will be required to provide official scores and transcripts, so please do not respond if you do not meet the aforementioned requirements."

Other headhunters specified that they sought SAT scores of 700 or 750 in math. Most employers are filling jobs in engineering, computers or finance.

—Sandra Salmans

and hooking in, but are less organized and more focused on advice and venting.

Since it began in 2003, LinkedIn.com has ballooned to 140,000 members worldwide, and it is growing at the rate of about 1,000 every week, the company says. LinkedIn allows members to search for people in their network within four degrees of separation. However, if users want to communicate with anyone beyond the first degree—mostly immediate friends—they must be referred by a mutual contact.

Ryze.com has 90,000 members and is a lot like a grab bag. A person can search the entire site by signifiers like university, company and state, and contact anyone. Ryze even sponsors mixers for members at local pubs and restaurants nationwide.

It is not only job seekers who interact in this virtual world of networking. As LinkedIn points out, roughly 33,000 of its members are hiring managers from national companies. Some managers are using the Web sites because they have stopped or curtailed advertising available jobs, which makes it all the more urgent for professionals to broaden their contact lists. Steve Tucker, vice president at Z-Tel Communications Inc., an exchange carrier in Tampa, Fla., stopped posting positions on job boards after getting slammed with thousands of responses from a Monster.com listing. "Most of them weren't even qualified,"

✔ TIMELY TIPS

No News Is Not Good News

✔ The most common rejection letter nowadays seems to be silence. Job hunting is like dating, only worse, as you sit by the phone waiting for the suitor who never calls. You got the interview, and another, and another. And then, no call. Well, you're not alone.

✔ People who interview for a living—headhunters, human resource professionals and such—explain that they don't mean to ignore job applicants. It's just that they are very, very busy. "I get up to 100 unsolicited résumés a week," says Deborah Sawyer, who conducts four to six searches at a time for Morgan Howard, an executive search firm.

—Lisa Belkin

Best Web Sites for Job Seekers

Relying on the Internet alone won't land you a job. You'll need to take some warm and fuzzy steps, too, like networking and making personal contact with prospective employers. But the Internet can be valuable for identifying openings, career advice and researching prospective companies. No single site will do it all, however, so surf around. These sites are among the most established and popular on the net.

AfterCollege.com
Jobs, internships and career information for students and recent graduates.

America's Job Bank
www.ajb.org *A database of more than one million, mostly full-time, private-sector jobs nationwide; create and post your résumé online; set up an automated job search.*

America's Career InfoNet
www.acinet.org *Educational, licensing, and certification requirements for different jobs by state. Wages and cost of living; employment trends. Helps identify skills.*

America's Service Locator
www.servicelocator.org *Locate local employment offices and career centers by plugging in your zip code. Free service*

helps you determine if you are "job ready" or require counseling and testing services.

CareerOneStop
877-348-0502 or www.careeronestop.org. *A huge database of jobs, résumés, and career resource tools.*

Career.com
This pioneering recruiting site is still a good source for employment listings, from entry-level to executive employment.

CareerBuilder.com
Database includes several online newspaper classifieds, along with many niche sites.

CraigsList.com
Started in the San Francisco Bay area, now in other major cities. Retains the feel of a community bulletin board. Jobs are easily searched by titles.

Jobs.com
A Monster.com company. Easy to access domestic and international listings.

JobBank USA
www.jobbankusa.com *Jobs in all states; search by state, city, zip code, industry, company. Lots of career tips, such as creating résumés and cover letters.*

Monster.com
Veteran job seeker site. Covers all aspects of career help, from finding educational programs to a résumé service that prom-

ises to create your document in three days or less.

USAJOBS
703-724-1859 or www.usajobs. gov *Search the maze of federal government jobs and then apply directly.*

RÉSUMÉ RESOURCES

CareerLab.com *Struggle no more with cover letters. Peruse 200 for good ideas. Free access.*

CollegeGrad.com *Résumé advice customized for the new graduate with little job experience.*

JobSearch.About.com
Tips from the classic Resumes for Dummies *by Joyce Lain Kennedy (book available at dummies.com).*

ResumeDoctor.com *Professional résumé consulting service. Send them your draft and they will doctor it up for you within three business days. Cost: $199.*

SusanIreland.com *50+ sample résumés from the author of* The Complete Idiot's Guide to the Perfect Resume *and other books. Pick your occupation, career problem you need solved (work gaps, for example) and you'll get a sample that works.*

The Resume Place
www.resume-place.com
Motto says it all: Home of the federal résumé. Learn to do it how the feds want it. Cost: $45 and up.

CAREERS

says Tucker. He says that 80 to 90 percent of his hires are now from networks.

Still, some experts warn job seekers not to do everything online and avoid face-to-face meetings. "It's safer when you do it that way—you won't get hurt as badly when you get rejected," says John A. Challenger, chief executive of Challenger, Gray & Christmas, an executive outplacement firm. "But lots of times you have to be right there for someone to commit to set up a lead. In that way online networking becomes a cheap substitute to effective networking."

—Christopher S. Stewart

Honing Your Skills for the Hunt

How to make a personal connection, project self-confidence and other practical advice

No matter what the state of the economy, job hunting is never simple. Making matters tougher still, plenty of today's job hunters might have problematic résumés, because they have been unemployed, underemployed or employed in positions where they have languished.

What is the most effective way to pursue a job hunt? Stephanie L. Marks, the principal consultant for Human Resources on Call, a firm in Ashland, Mass., that provides executive recruiting and career coaching for job hunters (www.hr-oncall.com), discussed strategies that work.

● How can an applicant stand out from the pack?

No matter what the state of the job market or your résumé, some truths are timeless. Job candidates stand out when they make the extra effort to establish a relationship with the person who's doing the hiring.

I've handled staffing searches for many companies, and I can tell you that the people who make the biggest impressions are those who follow up by phone or e-mail to thank me and to reiterate their strong interest in the job and the company.

It's particularly effective when people manage, in a 20- or 30-second message, to make a connection between something specific in their work experience and key details relating to the job opening. I'm impressed by people who make an effort to stay in touch, even if the original job they applied for wasn't the right one for them.

● Don't such people run the risk of seeming annoyingly persistent or even desperate?

I don't think so. I respect it when a job hunter asks me to keep him or her on my radar screen and works to make that happen. It's a matter of behaving professionally. If someone sends me an e-mail every couple of weeks or telephones me once a month to stay in touch, it's a sign of real interest.

● So many job searches seem to take place on the Internet these days. How can an applicant make that personal connection?

For one thing, you can't just sit at your computer, look for online job postings, e-mail your résumé and wait for something great to happen. Most e-mail résumés just disappear into a black hole. Sometimes the job hunters whom I'm coaching will tell me, "I e-mailed 30 résumés today." My response is, "To whom? What do you know about the company? What's your strategy going to be for following up in a meaningful way?" Job hunting through the Internet can be a waste of time, unless you do it the right way.

● What do you mean by that?

If I'm handling a job search for, say, a marketing position, I might list it on the Internet and receive 300 or more résumés. Who am I going to remember? The person who picks up the phone and calls me to leave a quick voice mail message:

"Hi. I'm John Smith. I saw your ad online, and I'm extremely interested. I've just e-mailed you my résumé." Hopefully, John will end with a quick sentence or two about how he believes he can make an impact on the company.

True, I can't call back, at least not at that stage. But I've heard his name, and I can tell you that I'm going to make a point of looking for his résumé.

Q What about all those job postings that do not list anyone's name? Aren't they really encouraging job hunters to keep their distance?

You've got to work harder in those cases to make that personal connection, but it's every bit as important. The person who stands out will be the one who spends the time to do some due diligence, to research the company and try to find out who in human resources might be involved with the search. Maybe this will take some phone calls or a visit to the corporate Web site.

I encourage job hunters to send e-mails to any Internet user groups or other networks they belong to—maybe someone out there will be able to come up with a contact name or other useful advice about a particular company.

Q What about the fear factor associated with personal contacts, especially when job hunters feel less than confident about their prospects?

I'm the first to admit that job hunting can be frightening. But you've got to take risks. As a coach, I try to help people see this as a time of change and of growth. If you don't come out of your comfort zone, you're probably not going to be able to make something good happen.

Q What's the worst mistake a job hunter can make, besides hiding behind the computer?

Lack of preparation. I warn people, every time you answer the phone, you've got to be ready—it could be a hiring manager on the other end. You've

---

✓ **TIMELY TIPS**

What Not to Do at the Interview

You left the interview believing you'd aced it. But the interviewer never called again. Sure, there are mercurial managers, but maybe you're unknowingly committing some interviewing gaffes. Here are some don'ts from career-consulting professionals.

✔ **Don't let your eyes wander** to the floor, ceiling or walls of the interviewer's office. As basic a tip as it may be, maintaining eye contact with the interviewer is essential.

✔ **Don't forget to research the company.** Know its hot issues before going into an interview. Read the papers and business magazines, and check the Internet for the most up-to-date information about company performance and any breaking news.

✔ **Don't interrupt or answer too quickly.** Listen carefully to questions, and answer each one before elaborating on other points. Be specific and give examples.

✔ **Don't fudge.** Specifically, don't misrepresent salary or benefits. A potential employer may ask you to produce a pay stub or a tax form that shows your former salary. If it shows that you have exaggerated, you will be eliminated immediately.

✔ **Don't forget to maintain your professionalism,** including your e-mail address and home answering machine message. More than one prospective employer has been turned off by a wacky voice mail message.

✔ **Don't forget to say thank you.** Most employers expect a thank-you letter after an interview. Nearly 15 percent of 650 hiring managers surveyed by CareerBuilder.com say they would not hire a candidate who failed to send a follow-up note.

CAREERS

TIMELY TIPS

20 Terms to Avoid on a Résumé

The words below may sound positive, but they will ring hollow unless you back them up with hard facts:

Aggressive	Ambitious
Attention to detail	Capable
Consistent	Effective
Entry level	Hard worker
Knowledgeable	Mature
Original	People person
Qualified	Responsible
Significant	Self-motivated
Special	Stable
Team player	Well-rounded

✔ Rather than stating "effective," indicate your sales growth rate above the previous year, or the number of published articles you've written in a six-month period.

✔ New college grads: refrain from listing "entry level" job as your objective. Why cut your chances of attaining something better?

got to be prepared to communicate effectively, every minute of the day. One good technique is to keep index cards, alphabetically organized, about each job you've applied for. Keep notes on everything connected with your application, as well as what you've learned about the company. Write down a phrase describing how you could make an impact. That way, you'll be ready to make your best case, any time you get the chance.

Q The big risk, of course, is sounding glib, rather than persuasive.

That's why people need to develop what I call a communication strategy for every job application. After all, every job and company is different.

This becomes easier after you perform some due diligence. Let's say you read in a recent article or the latest annual report that the company is diversifying into a certain geographic region or new client base. You might want to prepare a sentence or two that reiterates your expertise in this area.

Q Any words of advice for those who have been either unemployed or underemployed for a long stretch?

It's important for them to take a step back and assess their past job searches. Have they been aggressively networking or just relying on a click-and-send approach? Are their résumés up to speed? Have they been looking for jobs at the wrong level? To some extent, people need to rely on their instincts. The problem may be something permanent within their industry. Or maybe something needs to be changed about the way that they're presenting themselves.

Q Any interview tips you can offer?

I often conduct mock interviews with my clients. When people get nervous, irritating habits might surface. I've seen people who slouch when they're asked questions. One of my clients kept clicking a pen. Another was a foot-tapper. You can change those habits, if you really work at it. It's a question of learning how to project self-confidence and enthusiasm.

Q What other advice can you give job hunters?

Consider whether you need to take some classes to refresh and upgrade your job skills. Maybe you need to work with a career coach to learn some more effective communication techniques. Or maybe you'll figure out that you need to reinvent yourself by finding ways to transfer your skills and interests into a more robust industry or job category.

Q That sounds intimidating.

On the contrary, it's often invigorating and exciting for people to get to the point where they feel they have a positive plan for moving forward. What's frustrating is going around in circles, when all your job searches end in rejection and you don't know how to break the pattern.

—Jill Andresky Fraser

A Résumé That Works

Writing a killer résumé means putting yourself in the employer's shoes

When it comes to job hunting, your résumé does the advance work. Yet the odds facing the document are astounding: for every 200 résumés read, only one interview is granted. Human resource managers say they spend only about 30 seconds to four minutes reading most curriculum vitae, and that's if you're lucky enough to actually have a person read your document. Many companies use electronic scanning programs to pick out key words, making the way you compose your résumé all the more important.

Other trends also affect the way you should present yourself on paper. For one, employers are seeking more information about people they've identified as prospective workers, perhaps because a trend toward smaller staffs means that one person may be required to perform multiple jobs.

Moreover, résumés are no longer the exclusive domain of white-collar workers. Career professionals say they see more blue-collar workers seeking advice about writing a résumé, often for the first time. Many counselors recommend that even union workers and others with seemingly secure jobs put together a résumé. The reason, they say, is that as manufacturing jobs dwindle, the competition for available positions increases, as does the need to market your skills.

To give your résumé the best odds, it needs to be a finely tuned document that gets noticed. There is an abundance of advice on bookshelves and online to walk you through the process of composing your résumé. Tips, such as drop experience older than 10 years, or use buzzwords that will

Now, Let's Go to the Videotape

Video résumés speak and grin, too

One simple way to stand out from the crowd may be the video résumé. The clips range from 20-second presentations of an applicant directly addressing the camera, to four-minute mini-movies replete with graphics and photo montages. Some job seekers spend mere pennies to make simple home videos; a higher-quality video can cost several thousand dollars.

Video résumés can help employers narrow down the application field without wasting time on first interviews. No data exist on the precise number of video résumés in circulation, but a study conducted for Reel Biography, a New York production company that makes them, finds that

they are, so far, used mostly by actors, aspiring news broadcasters and high school athletes applying to colleges, that is, positions that are judged in great measure by appearances.

Job seekers and employers both say the videos save time and travel costs, and can be especially helpful for candidates who don't sparkle on paper but shine in real life. Swapjobs.com in Tampa, Fla., has shot videotapes of nearly 10,000 job hunters in the last few years at more than 30 employment fairs. It then posts the tapes on its Web site along with a candidate's written résumé. A six-month posting costs $89.

Not everyone is optimistic about video résumés, however. Some recruiters say nothing replaces a face-to-face meeting for top-level executives.

—Louise Kramer

CAREERS

Want a Job? Get an Internship First

Employers are relying more and more heavily on interns to fill their entry-level ranks. "In an uneven job market, an internship is, or can be, the deal closer for permanent employment. If you don't have one, you're at a competitive disadvantage," says Mark Oldman, co-founder of Vault Inc., a career counseling company.

✔ About 82 percent of graduating college seniors completed an internship in 2005, either for pay or school credit, according to a Vault survey. "They've moved from résumé enhancer to résumé necessity, and this is reflected in today's frenetic process," says Oldman, one of the authors of *The Vault Guide to Internships*.

✔ The Web makes it easy to go online and zap out résumés, but students shouldn't overlook the importance of personalization. "It's too easy to blast a résumé to 60 places, and the results you often get are proportionate to the work you've put in," says Oldman. "If you cut the number of companies in half and craft those approaches, it really pays off."

✔ At General Electric, where 1,800 students annually are offered internships from a pool of more than 15,000 candidates, Steve Canale, manager of recruiting and staffing, offers similar advice. "It is always beneficial to demonstrate that you know something about the company that you are applying to. It could be the one thing that distinguishes you from the pack," he says. And while referrals or connections might help a candidate, Canale says, they would not guarantee selection. "Each candidate stands on their own merit."

—Marc B. Zawel

attract the attention of electronic scanning programs, abound. But before fussing with cosmetic flourishes, experts say, first focus on mastering details about the job you want.

Don't approach your résumé as your personal history; instead, tailor it by putting yourself in the mind of the employer hiring. Put aside your needs, and zero in on which skills the ideal candidate would possess. Whether or not the job is in your field, talk to others who do the same work, try to meet with employees in the prospective company. Research the company thoroughly. Only after a detailed search can you create a résumé that makes you the outstanding candidate.

Generally, a great résumé has three parts: objective, abilities and successes, and factual evidence. At the top, list the job you intend to get. In the next section, toot your horn as loudly and intriguingly as you can. This is your personal advertisement. Using research you've uncovered about the job opening, craft the ad so that the hiring officer will want to pick up the phone and schedule an interview. The last part backs up your claims by providing education, work, volunteering and other credentials. Then, make the presentation clean, concise, accurate and attractive, and watch the résumé do the legwork.

Majors With a Pragmatic Bent

One of the fastest-growing majors on campuses is health sciences

University officials say the current generation is particularly attuned to selecting majors with strong career possibilities. Add to that the plentiful supply of jobs in the growing health care industry (see "Where the Best Jobs Will Be" on the next page), and one result is that health science programs have been taking off at colleges like the University of Colorado, Stony Brook, Marquette and many others.

Whether called biomedical sciences, as at Marquette, or integrative physiology, at Colorado, the majors give undergraduates a fundamental education in science and health that can lead to careers as optometrists, pharmacists, physical and occupational therapists, radiological technicians, even as doctors. The appeal of helping others and the excitement of scientific advances in diagnosing and treating disease, experts say, is also attracting students.

Some universities developed a health science program after reconsidering the types of undergraduate training to offer students interested in clinical fields like physical therapy, occupational therapy and physician assistant. While these once required only a bachelor's degree, they now generally call for graduate degrees as well.

The programs typically require basic courses in biology, chemistry and math. But unlike students with majors in conventional biology, for example, those in health science do not take many advanced courses in botany or invertebrate biology, concentrating instead on human biology.

So new are the programs that data on the number of students they have attracted is nonexistent. But evidence of their growth is hardly scarce. At Ohio State University, the School of Allied Medical Professions introduced a health science major four years ago. It drew 34 students the first year and now has 250. At Quinnipiac University in Hamden, Conn., where only 10 students majored in health science five years ago, the number is now about 100.

At the University of South Alabama in Mobile, which says it was among the first to create an undergraduate major in biomedical sciences more than two decades ago, about 40 percent of the 40 or so students who graduate from the program each year quickly go on to medical school.

—Alan Finder

Where the Best Jobs Will Be
Service industry jobs will continue to lead the pack

Ask a career counselor what you should do for a living, and more likely than not you'll be told to follow your passion. That's not bad advice, of course. But economists, labor analysts and management consultants who study broad trends shaping the economy and the labor market, will undoubtedly offer a different perspective.

The prism through which they see the world shows an economy that continues its decades-long transformation away from manufacturing and toward service positions. Over the coming decade, demand in services will continue to rise as the population grows and as Americans age in larger numbers. So if your passion puts you at the intersection of the

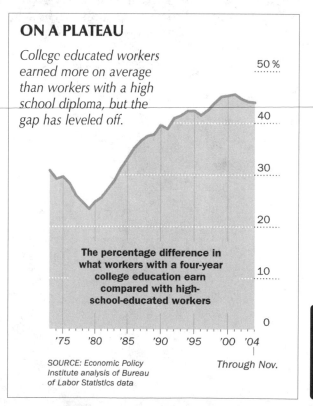

ON A PLATEAU

College educated workers earned more on average than workers with a high school diploma, but the gap has leveled off.

The percentage difference in what workers with a four-year college education earn compared with high-school-educated workers

SOURCE: Economic Policy Institute analysis of Bureau of Labor Statistics data

Through Nov.

high-demand, high-growth service industry, then you are way ahead of the game.

Employment growth is determined by a number of factors, such as changes in demand for goods and services, worker productivity and foreign competition. The total number of jobs in the country came to nearly 146 million in 2004. By 2014, that figure should rise to nearly 165 million, or a growth rate of about 14 percent—about the same rate as during the past decade. That figure includes new jobs created through corporate ingenuity, as well as those required to replace an aging workforce. In fact, more jobs are expected to arise due to replacement needs rather than as a result of the forces of economic growth.

GO WEST, JOB SEEKER

Where will job growth will be hottest over the next decade? Arizona, Idaho, Utah and Nevada will be looking for home health aides, physical therapists and emergency medical technicians, among other medical aides. Nevada will also need financial advisers and loan officers, according to the Bureau of Labor Statistics. Bars show the percentage increase in jobs by 2012.

State	Percentage
Nevada	41%
Utah	31%
Idaho	24%
Arizona	23%
Colorado	23%
Florida	21%
New Mexico	20%
California	19%
Virginia	19%
New Hampshire	18%
Maryland	18%
Texas	18%

SOURCE: Bureau of Labor Statistics

But even within an industry, jobs may grow at different rates, depending on factors such as technological strides and changes in production methods, for example. Replacement jobs also vary by industry. For example, industries with high concentrations of professional and technical positions that require advanced education generally have a lower turnover. More replacement openings occur in fields with greater numbers of lower-paying service and labor jobs.

Some industries will suffer as a whole. In agriculture, for one, consolidation of farm land and greater productivity will continue to result in job losses. And positions in mining, and the oil and gas industry will spiral downward as the country continues to import energy.

Which industries will drive job creation, that is, generate greater than average job openings in the coming decade? Here's a snapshot, based on data compiled by the government's Bureau of Labor Statistics.

Health care. Fueled by population growth and longer life spans, as well as medical advances that increase the numbers of treatable diseases, the health care sector is expected to create the greatest number of new jobs by 2014. Physicians' offices alone will require 760,000 new workers by that time, as more patients are routed to doctors' offices rather than in-patient hospital facilities.

Educational services. The teacher shortage persists. Teachers will be needed at all levels, but especially at the post–high school level, as children of baby boomers continue to reach college age, and as more adults turn to continuing education to enhance or update skills.

Employment services. This field is projected to grow by more than 45 percent over the decade as businesses look for more specialized workers and respond to changing demands in their industries.

THE 30 FASTEST-GROWING PROFESSIONS

The best job opportunities often are not where the most jobs are, but instead where the most growth is. Explosive growth in a relatively small pool indicates an industry in need of a rapid infusion of labor. The following industries are expected to grow at a pace far above average.

Three of the occupations—home health aides, personal and home care aides, and computer software application engineers—are especially hot: they will also have the largest total number of new jobs.

	Jobs, 2004	Anticipated % change	Anticipated no. of new jobs by 2014
Home health aides	624,000	56.0	350,000
Network systems and data communications analysts	231,000	54.6	126,000
Medical assistants	387,000	52.1	202,000
Physician assistants	62,000	49.6	31,000
Computer software engineers, applications	460,000	48.4	222,000
Physical therapist assistants	59,000	44.2	26,000
Dental hygienists	158,000	43.3	68,000
Computer software engineers, systems software	340,000	43.0	146,000
Dental assistants	267,000	42.7	114,000
Personal and home care aides	701,000	4.01	287,000
Network and computer systems administrators	278,000	38.4	107,000
Database administrators	104,000	38.2	40,000
Physical therapists	155,000	36.7	57,000
Forensic science technicians	10,000	36.4	4,000
Veterinary technologists and technicians	60,000	35.3	21,000
Diagnostic medical sonographers	42,000	34.8	15,000
Physical therapist aides	43,000	34.4	15,000
Occupational therapist assistants	21,000	34.1	7,000
Medical scientists, except epidemiologists	72,000	34.1	25,000
Occupational therapists	92,000	33.6	31,000
Preschool teachers, except special education	431,000	33.1	143,000
Cardiovascular technologists and technicians	45,000	32.6	15,000
Postsecondary teachers	1,628,000	32.2	524,000
Hydrologists	8,000	31.6	3,000
Computer systems analysts	487,000	31.4	153,000
Hazardous materials removal workers	38,000	31.2	12,000
Biomedical engineers	10,000	30.7	3,000
Employment, recruitment and placement specialists	182,000	30.5	55,000
Environmental engineers	49,000	30.0	15,000
Paralegals and legal assistants	224,000	29.7	67,000

SOURCE: Bureau of Labor Statistics

CAREERS

SIGNS OF THE TIMES

Are you in a growing or declining occupation? If you're in one of these top 12 industries with growth rates far higher than average, job prospects look good over the coming decade. On the losing end are industries such as textiles and apparel, which will continue to face inroads from foreign imports. The following numbers are for jobs expected to be created or lost between 2004 and 2014.

THE TOP 12 INDUSTRIES FOR JOBS

INDUSTRY	JOBS CREATED
Health care	3,564,000
Educational services	2,123,000
Employment services	1,580,000
Food services	1,451,000
State and local government	895,000
Construction	792,000
Wholesalers	476,000
Management and technical consulting	471,000
Arts, entertainment, recreation	460,000
Computer systems design	453,000
Social assistance (except child care)	445,000
Retailers	423,000

THE 12 WORST INDUSTRIES FOR JOBS

INDUSTRY	JOBS LOST
Textiles and apparel	-321,000
Machinery manufacturing	-146,000
Computer and electronic manufacturing	-94,000
Chemical manufacturing (except drugs)	-86,000
Telecommunications	-68,000
Printing	-65,000
Agriculture, forestry and fishing	-60,000
Banking	-31,000
Mining	-27,000
Steel manufacturing	-21,000
Oil and gas	-19,000
Utilities	-8,000

SOURCE: Bureau of Labor Statistics

Temporary employment agencies and professional employer organizations will grow fastest.

Food and drink industry. Behind the coming growth in these establishments are dual-income families, a growing immigrant population and a general rise in dining sophistication. The increasing popularity of ethnic foods and drinks will create more job openings in places catering to those tastes.

State and local governments. The growth of local populations means a greater need for public services, and more workers to provide them. States will also have job openings as a result of taking on federally funded programs spun off to them by the federal government.

Wholesale trade. Economic growth and a rise in trade will mean more jobs—nearly 500,000 by 2014—especially for sales representatives at the wholesale and production level. Tempering the jobs growth rate in this field, however, is the increasing use of the Internet to conduct business.

ⓘ **INSIDE INFO**

What Legends Get Paid

The past decade has been very, very good to chief executives. To some more than others. In a 2004 study for the *New York Times*, consulting firm Pearl Meyer & Partners calculated the total compensation collected over the 10 previous years by prominent, longtime chief executives.

○ The winner: Sanford I. Weill, chief executive officer of Citigroup, who racked up $979 million in options, salary, bonuses, etc. The yearly average: almost $98 million.

○ Meanwhile, Warren E. Buffett, chairman and C.E.O. of Berkshire Hathaway, was vastly underpaid. His stake is worth about $40 billion, but the legendary investor got a mere $100,000 a year, no bonuses and no options.

—Patrick McGeehan

WHAT 100 JOBS PAY

Below are the salaries of 100 occupations from the Bureau of Labor Statistics' Occupational Outlook Handbook. *In real life, of course, salaries can vary considerably by region, level of experience and other factors. Generally, employees of the federal government earn less than those in the private sector. However, the list provides a good comparison of median incomes.*

TITLE	NO. OF JOBS	STARTING SALARY*	MEDIAN SALARY**	TOP SALARY***
EXECUTIVE, ADMINISTRATIVE AND MANAGERIAL OCCUPATIONS				
ACCOUNTANTS	1.2 million	$32,320	$39,890-$66,900	$88,610
ADVERTISING, MARKETING MANAGERS	646,000	$31,340-$33,873	$89,570	N/A
FUNERAL DIRECTORS	30,000	N/A	$35,880-60,860	$85,910
INSPECTORS	40,000	$30,590	$51,570	$79,530
PERSONNEL MANAGERS	118,880	$36,967	$66,530	$118,880
RETAIL SALES MANAGERS	946,000	N/A	$32,720	$58,400
PROFESSIONAL SPECIALTY OCCUPATIONS				
ACTUARIES	18,000	$52,741	$76,340	N/A
ARCHITECTS	129,000	N/A	$46,690-79,230	N/A
ARCHIVISTS	27,000	N/A	$31,820-$43,620	N/A
ASTRONOMERS & PHYSICISTS	16,000	$56,070	$87,450-$97,320	N/A
BIOLOGICAL SCIENTISTS	77,000	$31,258	$49,430-$88,540	$110,660+
CHEMISTS	90,000	$32,500-$65,000	$41,900-$76,080	$98,010
DANCERS	38,000	N/A	$8.54/hr	$21.59+/hr
DENTISTS	150,000	N/A	$129,920	N/A
DIETITIANS	50,000	N/A	$43,630	$63,760
ECONOMISTS	13,000	N/A	$53,650	$129,170+
ENGINEERS	1,400,000	$43,679-$85,000	$37,680-$140,800	N/A
FINANCIAL ANALYSTS & ADVISORS	355,000	N/A	$61,910-$62,700	$113,490+
HUMAN SERVICES WORKERS	352,000	N/A	$24,270	$39,620
LAWYERS	735,000	$55,000 [1]	$64,620-$143,620	N/A
LIBRARIANS	159,000	N/A	$45,900	$70,200+
MATHEMATICIANS	2,500	N/A	$81,240	120,900+
METEOROLOGISTS	6,600	$27,955-$70,280	$70,100	$106,020
OCCUPATIONAL THERAPISTS	92,000	N/A	$54,660	$81,600+
PHARMACISTS	230,000	N/A	$84,900	$109,850+
PHOTOGRAPHERS	129,000	N/A	$26,080	$54,180
PHYSICIAN ASSISTANTS	62,000	$64,536	$69,410	$94,880
PHYSICIANS & SURGEONS	567,000	N/A	$132,953-$321,686	N/A
PHYSICAL THERAPISTS	155,000	N/A	$60,180	$88,580+
PODIATRISTS	10,000	N/A	$94,400	N/A

Title	No. of jobs	Starting salary*	Median salary**	Top salary***
PSYCHOLOGISTS	179,000	N/A	$54,950	$92,250+
REGISTERED NURSES	2,400,000	N/A	$52,330	$74,760
SCHOOL TEACHERS (K-12)	3,800,000	$31,704 (average)	$41,400-$45,920	$66,240-$71,370
SOCIAL WORKERS	562,000	N/A	$34,820	$57,860
SPEECH-LANGUAGE PATHOLOGISTS	96,000	N/A	$52,410	$82,420+
STATISTICIANS	19,000	$43,448	$56,890	$100,500+
SYSTEMS ANALYSTS	487,000	$61,500-$82,500	$66,460	$99,180+
UNIVERSITY PROFESSORS	1,600,000	N/A	$51,800	$99,980+
VETERINARIANS	61,000	N/A	$66,590	$118,430
WRITERS & EDITORS	320,000	N/A	$44,350	$91,260+

TECHNICIAN AND RELATED SUPPORT OCCUPATIONS

Title	No. of jobs	Starting salary*	Median salary**	Top salary***
AIRCRAFT PILOTS	106,000	N/A	$129,250	N/A
AIR TRAFFIC CONTROLLERS	24,000	N/A	$78,170-$126,260	N/A
COMPUTER PROGRAMMERS	455,000	$50,820	$62,890	$99,610+
EKG TECHNICIANS	45,000	N/A	$38,690	$59,000
EMERGENCY MEDICAL TECHNICIANS	192,000	N/A	$25,310	$43,240
ENGINEERING TECHNICIANS	523,000	N/A	$38,480-$52,500	$67,900+
NUCLEAR MEDICINE TECHNICIANS	18,000	N/A	$56,450	$80,300
PARALEGALS	224,000	N/A	$39,130	$61,390+

MARKETING AND SALES OCCUPATIONS

Title	No. of jobs	Starting salary*	Median salary**	Top salary***
CASHIERS	3,500,000	$5.15/hr	$7.81/hr	$11.30+/hr
COUNTER AND RENTAL CLERKS	451,000	$5.15/hr.	$8.79	$16.79+
INSURANCE AGENTS & BROKERS	400,000	N/A	$41,720	$108,800+
REAL ESTATE AGENTS	460,000	N/A	$35,670	$92,770
SALES REPRESENTATIVES [2]	1,900,000	N/A	$58,580	$114,540+
TRAVEL AGENTS	103,000	N/A	$27,640	$44,090+

ADMINISTRATIVE SUPPORT OCCUPATIONS

Title	No. of jobs	Starting salary*	Median salary**	Top salary***
BANK TELLERS	558,000	N/A	$21,120	$28,100+
COMPUTER OPERATORS	149,000	$27,250-$39,500	$31,070	$48,720+
COURT REPORTERS	18,000	N/A	$42,920	$80,300+
DATA ENTRY KEYERS	525,000	N/A	$28,030	$43,190+
GENERAL OFFICE CLERKS	3,100,000	N/A	$22,770	$35,810+
MAIL CARRIERS	335,000	N/A	$44,450	$54,240+
MEDICAL TRANSCRIPTIONISTS	105,000	N/A	$13.64/hr	$19.11/hr
SECRETARIES/ADMIN.ASSISTANTS	4,100,000	N/A	$34,970	$80,300+
TEACHER AIDES	1,300,000	N/A	$19,410	$29,220+
TELEPHONE OPERATORS	256,000	N/A	$10.38/hr	$15.13+

SERVICE OCCUPATIONS

Title	No. of jobs	Starting salary*	Median salary**	Top salary***
BARTENDERS	474,000	N/A	$7.42/hr	$12.47+/hr
CHEFS & HEAD COOKS	125,000	N/A	$14.75/hr	$26.75/hr
CORRECTIONAL OFFICERS	484,000	$26,747	$33,600	$54,820+
COSMETOLOGISTS	790,000	N/A	$19,800	$35,990

Title	No. of jobs	Starting salary*	Median salary**	Top salary***
DENTAL ASSISTANTS	267,000	N/A	$13.62/hr	$19.97+
FIREFIGHTERS	282,000	N/A	$18.43/hr	$29.21+
FLIGHT ATTENDANTS	102,000	$15,552	$43,440	$95,850
HOME HEALTH AIDES	624,000	N/A	$8.81/hr	$12.32+
HOME APPLIANCE REPAIR	50,000	N/A	$32,180	$49,760+
JANITORS	2,400,000	N/A	$18,790	$31,780+
MAIDS & HOUSEKEEPERS	1,400,000	N/A	$16,900	$25,220+
MEDICAL ASSISTANTS	387,000	N/A	$24,610	$34,650
OCCUPATIONAL THERAPY ASSISTANTS	16,000	N/A	$38,430	$52,700
PHYSICAL THERAPY ASSISTANTS	101,000	N/A	$21,380-$37,890	$52,110+
POLICE OFFICERS	842,000	N/A	$45,210	$68,880+
PRESCHOOL TEACHERS	431,000	N/A	$20,900	N/A
SHORT-ORDER COOKS	783,000	N/A	$8.11	$11.50+
WAITERS/WAITRESSES	2,300,000	N/A	$6.75/hr	$11.27/hr

MECHANICS, INSTALLERS AND REPAIRERS

Title	No. of jobs	Starting salary*	Median salary**	Top salary***
AIRCRAFT MECHANICS	142,000	N/A	$17.82-$27.18/hr	N/A
AUTOMOTIVE BODY REPAIRERS	223,000	N/A	$12.55-$22.04/hr	N/A
ELEVATOR INSTALLERS	22,000	N/A	$28.23/hr	$39.65+/hr
VENDING MACHINE REPAIRERS	46,000	N/A	$13.47/hr	$20.51/hr+

CONSTRUCTION TRADES OCCUPATIONS

Title	No. of jobs	Starting salary*	Median salary**	Top salary***
CARPENTERS	1,300,000	N/A	$16.70/hr	$28.65+/hr
CARPET & FLOOR INSTALLERS	184,000	N/A	$16.39/hr	$29.27+
ELECTRICIANS	656,000	N/A	$20.33/hr	$33.63+/hr
PAINTERS	486,000	N/A	$14.55/hr	$25.11+
PLUMBERS 3	561,000	N/A	$13.68-$19.855/hr	$33.72/hr

PRODUCTION OCCUPATIONS

Title	No. of jobs	Starting salary*	Median salary**	Top salary***
BUS DRIVERS	653,000	N/A	$14.30	$23.53+/hr
BUTCHERS	134,000	N/A	$25,890	$41,980+
JEWELERS	42,000	N/A	$27.400	$49,020+
MACHINISTS	370,000	N/A	$16.33/hr	$24.37/hr
POWER PLANT OPERATORS	47,000	N/A	$52,530	$70,330+
PRINTING PRESS OPERATORS	191,000	N/A	$14.38/hr	$23.06/hr
TOOL & DIE MAKERS	103,000	N/A	$20.55/hr	$31.19+
TREATMENT PLANT OPERATORS	94,000	N/A	$34,960	$53,540
TRUCK DRIVERS	2,800,000	N/A	$16.11/hr	$24.07+/hr

NOTES: * Annual salaries, except as indicated. Salaries are as of May 2004.

** Median salary is the boundary between the highest paid 50 percent of workers in that occupation and the lowest paid 50 percent. So half of workers earn more and half earn less than the median.

***Top salaries are estimates of what the top 10 percent make.

1) Earnings nine months after graduation 2) Sales representatives for manufacturers and wholesaler
3) Includes pipelayers, pipefitters and steamfitters

SOURCE: *Occupational Outlook Handbook*, Spring 2006

CAREERS

Smart Moves

Who Gets to the Corner Office?

Basically, white males. But the times are changing

Today, the corner offices of the nation's largest companies are dominated by white men in a way that few other parts of society still are. As of 2006, only a handful of women held prominent chief executive jobs, while 81 women were in Congress. There were more female senators from Maine (two) than women running Fortune 100 companies (zero).

Yet the full picture is not so simple. In ways less obvious than race and gender, the corporate elite has become less elite and more diverse over the last decade or two, while its counterpart in Washington has become more homogeneous.

C.E.O.'s seem to come from a wider variety of economic backgrounds, though they may all be paid like kings. Growing numbers come from

humble beginnings, and fewer attended Ivy League colleges. Many spent just a few years, or none, at their companies before becoming the boss. Being younger than 50 no longer rules out someone for the top job. "There's much less emphasis on the cosmetic, cultural and refinement aspects, as opposed to the down-and-dirty, get-the-job-done aspect," says Gerard R. Roche, an executive recruiter at Heidrick & Struggles. With the glaring exceptions of sex and skin color, the mold for a big-company C.E.O. has been broken, and there isn't a new one to take its place.

The story is different in Washington, where political leaders are richer, older, more likely to have gone to an expensive college and more likely to have first held another elected office than they were in the past.

The rules for advancement in the political system bear some resemblance to those of the college-application process that many 17-year-olds

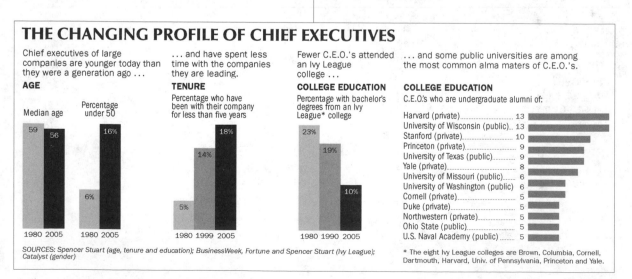

THE CHANGING PROFILE OF CHIEF EXECUTIVES

Chief executives of large companies are younger today than they were a generation ago ...

AGE

Median age

1980: 59
2005: 56

Percentage under 50

1980: 6%
2005: 16%

... and have spent less time with the companies they are leading.

TENURE

Percentage who have been with their company for less than five years

1980: 5%
1999: 14%
2005: 18%

Fewer C.E.O.'s attended an Ivy League college ...

COLLEGE EDUCATION

Percentage with bachelor's degrees from an Ivy League* college

1980: 23%
1990: 19%
2005: 10%

... and some public universities are among the most common alma maters of C.E.O.'s.

COLLEGE EDUCATION

C.E.O.'s who are undergraduate alumni of:

Harvard (private)	13
University of Wisconsin (public)	13
Stanford (private)	10
Princeton (private)	9
University of Texas (public)	9
Yale (private)	8
University of Missouri (public)	6
University of Washington (public)	6
Cornell (private)	5
Duke (private)	5
Northwestern (private)	5
Ohio State (public)	5
U.S. Naval Academy (public)	5

SOURCES: Spencer Stuart (age, tenure and education); BusinessWeek, Fortune and Spencer Stuart (Ivy League); Catalyst (gender)

* The eight Ivy League colleges are Brown, Columbia, Cornell, Dartmouth, Harvard, Univ. of Pennsylvania, Princeton and Yale.

sweat out. Women and minorities, both racial and religious, succeed far more often than they did in the past. The Senate, in 2006, had almost twice as many Catholics—24—as it did in 1980, and more Jews and Mormons, too. (Data on the religious background of C.E.O.'s isn't readily accessible.)

It is almost as if two separate meritocracies have sprung up. In some ways, corporate leaders now mirror the rest of society more closely than elected leaders do. The top of the corporate one remains largely closed to women and minorities. But it also rewards skills—like communication, real-world smarts and a common touch, executives say—that require little in the way of a privileged background.

The changing educational backgrounds of the corporate and political elite may best be summed up in the trends. In 1980, about 23 percent of chief executives at big companies had attended an Ivy League college, while only 13 percent of senators had. The boardroom, not surprisingly, was a more elite place than the halls of democracy. Today, the two groups have switched places. The number of senators educated at an Ivy college has risen to 16. Among C.E.O.'s in the Standard & Poor's 500, the share has fallen by more than half, to 10 percent. The University of Wisconsin and Harvard are tied as the most common alma mater for top executives, according to executive search firm Spencer Stuart.

Yet, students at Ivy colleges have changed relatively little in economic terms over the past few generations. If anything, the percentage from middle-class and working-class households has fallen slightly in recent years, research shows. At Harvard, for instance, the median family income was about $150,000 last year, financial aid forms suggest.

Executives who attended public universities say that these campuses more closely resemble the rest of society than those dominated by the upper middle class, and helped prepare them for the business world. Robert A. Eckert, chief executive of Mattel and a University of Arizona graduate, says, "While private schools have the advantage of smaller classes and the financial wherewithal to attract the world's greatest faculty, the public schools offer the diversity and variety that go along with their size."

High-income students at the Ivies and similar colleges, meanwhile, have been showing less interest in corporate America. Capitalism is more popular on elite campuses now than it once was, but many students do not see corporate jobs as the best match for their skills. Instead, many turn to law, consulting or hedge-fund management, fields that tend to value skills at which the students have long excelled—skills that can often be measured objectively. Minorities have done better in some of these professions than in corporate America. The pay in these fields also tends to be higher for younger employees, and a career rise can happen more quickly.

—David Leonhardt;
Luke Kummer contributed research

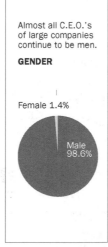

Almost all C.E.O.'s of large companies continue to be men.

GENDER

Female 1.4%

Male 98.6%

Management by the Book

Literary classics for a good read, as well as a few leadership pointers

I f you thought reading Shakespeare was only for English literature students, you're in for a surprise. John K. Clemens, a professor of management at Hartwick College in Oneonta, N.Y., and author (with Scott Dalrymple) of *Time Mastery: How Temporal Intelligence Will Make You a Stronger, More Effective Leader,* uses literature, including

Shakespeare, to teach managerial skills to business students. Clemens, who is founder of the Hartwick Humanities in Management Institute, recommends the following literary classics for managers in search of a good read and a few leadership pointers.

Herman Melville's *Billy Budd*. In this Melville novel, a leader must choose between adhering to a rigid organizational policy or doing what he believes is morally right. The case presents an opportunity to explore the problems that arise when company decisions are based on rules rather than circumstance, and understanding the difference between doing the right thing and doing things right. Also, nearly everyone can relate to the book's primary conflict: the effects of one co-worker's dislike for another.

John Masefield's *The Bird of Dawning*. Observe the birth of a leader, as protagonist Cyril Trewsbury is unexpectedly thrust into a position of power, and must learn through trial and error which leadership techniques work best. The most important lessons here concern recognizing the ways in which one might transform one's vision into reality, and the critical but often unappreciated importance of challenging employees or co-workers to do more than even they thought possible.

Martin Luther King's *Letter from A Birmingham Jail*. This is a classic lesson in how language is a leader's most effective tool. King's masterful oratorical skills come across just as strongly on paper. He also reveals in great clarity his four steps for organizational change. This "recipe" can be used in any social setting, including modern corporations.

Chief Joseph. In his writings, Native American leader Chief Joseph offers an in-depth look at three styles of leadership, the types of organizations they are associated with (bureaucratic, entrepreneurial and integrative), and the problems and benefits unique to each of them. This reading offers one of the big lessons for survival in a changing business environment: A corporation ought to look more like a collection of tribes than a monolithic organization. With "tribalism" comes agility, common beliefs, "local" knowledge and perhaps, most important, respect for the individual.

Shakespeare's *Henry IV* and *Henry V*. Shakespeare's exploration into the lives of these two kings (and their differing leadership styles) offers lessons on the emergence of a leader, important personal and political traits of leaders, and what works and what doesn't. To lead you must first be a follower. Prince Hal was a great follower and, subsequently, as king he was a great leader.

Homer's *Iliad*. This epic poem tells the story of

the anger of the great warrior Achilles and the terrible consequences that his community (the Greek army) endured because of it. Clearly, the major figures in Homer's epic are driven by compelling needs and forces not immediately apparent. Once discovered, however, they help to reveal the inner workings of leadership in any setting.

David Mamet's *Glengarry Glen Ross.* This dark play presents a leader whom most readers will not admire. Yet he is in a difficult position, forced to pursue goals that may be unattainable, using an organization that is often untrustworthy and ineffectual. Analyzing him and the other characters in the play surprisingly reveals human qualities that students can identify with. Readers can evaluate the management strategies used in this organization and decide what, if anything, they have to do with the organization's fate.

William Golding's *Lord of the Flies.* This story portrays leadership development and conflict among a group of boys marooned on a desert island. It also explores the alternative ways a subordinate leader can wrest control of the group from an elected leader. The story clearly demonstrates the importance of collaboration and compromise, rather than competition, in achieving organizational objectives.

Bully Bosses

They tyrannize the workplace. Here's how to escape their clutches

The American workplace can be a brutal place. On any given day, according to Columbia University psychologist Harvey Hornstein, one in five people is abused by a boss. Using questionnaires filled out by nearly 1,000 men and women over an eight-year period, Hornstein estimates that over 90 percent of U.S. workers experience some form of abusive behavior during their working life.

In his study of managerial abuse, *Brutal Bosses and Their Prey*, Hornstein discusses what separates "bully bosses" from those who are merely "tough, but fair" managers. Here he describes brutal bosses and how to deal with them.

Q Are there any places where bully bosses tend to exist more than others?

No, and that's the scary part. By the end of our research, almost all industries were equally represented. Gender was equally represented. Blue-collar workers and white-collar executives were all represented. In some cases, the abuse may have taken different forms—usually verbal or physical—but I don't know that the pain was any less in each case. Abuse occurs in the boardroom as well as on the shop floor. There really are no differences. Some abuse literally occurred in manholes where utility workers were working, as well as on the 68th floor.

Q Which kind of bully bosses are people likely to encounter?

Our evidence suggests conquerors, performers and manipulators (see box on next page for descriptions) are the most common. Power organizations focus you on power. That's the name of the game, that's what the trade is about. Turf and power are the issues. It's what's traded. And the subordinates are the ones made to suffer.

However, I have found dehumanizers, blamers and rationalizers most frequently arise in organizations facing issues such as downsizing, or other measures that are taken in the face of difficult times. Whenever companies are making a transition, these three seem to pop up.

Q What is the most effective way to deal with a bully boss?

From an individual perspective, what works well is to try to find protection within the organization.

A Spotter's Guide to Brutal Bosses

In his book, Harvey Hornstein identifies six different types of brutal bosses. Here's his description of each.

CONQUERORS. Concerned with power and making sure it's not undermined in any way, they use words to bludgeon you. They want to make you feel small. They are the classic schoolyard bullies.

PERFORMERS. These types are threatened by anyone who challenges their competence, or whom they perceive as outperforming them. Rather than take a subordinate's performance as a plus for their camp, they see it as a minus for themselves. Their favorite weapon is to belittle. They are known to put comments in your personnel file without telling you, and criticize your work without giving you a chance to explain or respond. They are also the type to ask for positive comments to affirm their own self-worth. You end up not giving honest feedback, but rather absolute approval.

MANIPULATORS. Concerned with how they are being valued, whether people like them and care about them is what's important. They will attack you personally. Their weapon is to smear your reputation. They take credit for your successes, but will attribute their failures to you, or anyone else who is around. You can't win with these folks.

DEHUMANIZERS. They turn people into numbers. They look at you as simply cogs. They have a machine-like view of human beings and the social world, and that permits them to abuse. It's much easier to abuse someone when the target of your abuse is seen as a "thing," rather than a person.

BLAMERS. They write off their harm by saying that you and the others "deserved it." This is the blame-the-victim attitude. They will say, "I didn't do a bad thing. They deserved what happened to them."

RATIONALIZERS. These brutal bosses don't blame the victim of abuse, but use abuse to justify a greater cause. Rationalizing brutal bosses say things such as, "Just helping out the organization" or "Well, someone had to do it." They use these self-justifying terms to cover up their own feelings about the abuse they have inflicted.

This can usually be found through an ombudsperson, a grievance committee, or even by pursuing legal options. Options do exist, but not always.

One of the reasons I wrote the book was to enable workers to learn the patterns of the predator. What triggers them? What kinds of issues are their major concerns? And how do workers try to avoid them? In many cases, it was quite literally physically avoiding bosses at times when they are at their most volatile. That's how a lot of folks survive working for these kinds of people.

Q What if you can't avoid them?

When you are attacked, it's important to make a good-faith response. Focus on the content of what's being said, not on the curses. Focus on the meaning of the message, not the malevolence. Otherwise, you just inflame them.

Q What about confronting bully bosses when they are being abusive?

That may be the noble thing to do, but it is often the costly thing to do—very costly. Most of the time you pay the price. If you don't lose your job, you certainly get labeled as someone who is a troublemaker. You get pushed into positions that are undesirable. That's the potential downside of taking legal action or invoking other forms of protection. And that's why people are afraid to do it.

The shortcoming of these solutions is that they really don't solve the problem from an organizational perspective. The brutal characters are still there. And even if you get out of their way, and mitigate the harm that's coming your way, they are still free to roam the corridors and beat up on someone else. So the organization hasn't solved the problem.

Q Does senior management need to step in and address the bully boss problem?

Yes, exactly. Ways to do that include introducing progressive management tools such as 360-degree feedback, which gives employees a greater voice and makes them more equal. It gives them access to senior-level management and puts bosses at all levels on notice that their misbehavior will be part of the record and will not go unnoticed.

Disagreeing With the Boss

It's always tricky—especially when he or she is new

After a management change, your new boss reverses some popular policies of your previous boss. What should you do?

If you feel that the new boss is being unfair, it's important to express your frustrations, says Theresa M. Welbourne, president of eePulse, a software company in Ann Arbor, Mich. "Provided you can convey your message in a way that doesn't make the new manager defensive, it's good to set a tone of honesty early on," she says. "Not only will you show the new boss what you're made of, but you also might get what you're looking for."

But it's hard to know which changes are worth

disputing and which are not. In general, experts advise that in the first few weeks of a new regime, employees should be selective about the causes they champion. If the incoming manager eliminates casual Fridays, for example, it is not a good idea to complain loudly. But if the new boss puts an end to something more substantive—tuition reimbursement, for instance, or a policy that damages the fabric of a workplace environment—employees might want to speak up.

Deciding with whom you should share your misgivings is another touchy issue. Generally, you should talk to colleagues you trust, but do it quietly, in a way that the boss cannot construe as gossiping or backbiting. Employees may even want to appoint one of their own to act as a moderator for such discussions. Simma Lieberman, a management consultant in Albany, Calif., says constructive conversations could end up convincing employees that a new policy is palatable.

If that's not the case, should you consider expressing your concerns to the new supervisor? Benjamin Dattner, president of Dattner Consulting in New York, counsels taking a few weeks to observe the new rules in action. Just as employees are sizing up the new boss, Dattner says, the boss is evaluating them, noting who embraces change and who resists it.

"Before you make any arguments to support the status quo, it's important to understand the new boss's mandate and why he or she was brought in," he says. "In order to do this, you need to give the new boss some time to get comfortable." Still, patience should have a limit. Susan Drake, president of Spellbinders, a marketing firm in Memphis, says that if you are still dissatisfied after a few weeks, you might request a meeting with your boss.

If and when you do air your frustrations, you don't want to sound like a complainer. You should be concise, respectful and positive. Hal G.

How to Shush the Office Magpie

Telling a co-worker to shut up may not be the best strategy

One of your co-workers loves to chat, and whenever he isn't dealing with a pressing deadline, he barges into your work space to shoot the breeze. As tempted as you may be to tell him to scram, it's best to approach the situation with tact, says Gini Graham Scott, president of Changemakers, a consulting firm in Oakland, Calif. "Be as diplomatic as possible," says Scott. "But if the person doesn't get the hint, then you have to be firm." Here are some options:

Give nonverbal clues. For example, continue staring at the computer screen in front of you and refuse to make eye contact. Another approach is to check your watch repeatedly.

Cal LeMon, president of Executive Enrichment, a management consulting firm in Springfield, Mo., says more overt gestures include packing your briefcase and putting your hand up, like a policeman stopping traffic. "Open-palmed gestures say to the person that you're trying to wrap things up," LeMon says.

Use technology. Alisa Cohn, president of AC & Associates, an executive coaching company in Brookline, Mass., says she once advised a client to set her Microsoft Outlook calendar program to chime every 10 minutes. When the office chatterbox heard the chime, he assumed that Cohn's client had an appointment.

Confront the chatterbox. If your colleague will not take a hint, then it's time to be more direct. Start with the facts: tally the number of times this person interrupts you throughout the day, note the length of each visit, and then use these statistics in a confrontation about the behavior. Simply outlining the problem may not solve it. Larina Kase, president of Philadelphia firm Performance and Success Coaching, says it's important to have a plan for further action. Ask the talker if you can catch up over lunch. Let him know how to tell whether you have time to talk (for example, if your door is open—if you're lucky enough to have a door).

Keep it civil. Generally, lashing out or yelling in the office is not a great idea. You never know who else may be listening. And shouting is likely to make an unpleasant situation worse. Furthermore, says Don Gabor, president of Conversation Arts Media in Brooklyn, "The chatterbox is annoying, but he might be someone who can help you down the road."

—Matt Villano

Rainey, professor of public administration at the University of Georgia, says it is best to focus on how policy changes would affect the company as a whole. Andrew J. DuBrin, author of *Essentials of Management*, says employees should approach this meeting as if they were presenting a report, providing statistics, facts and figures that support a return to the way things were. "Instead of giving the impression that you're emotionally committed to something," DuBrin says, "present information that makes an objective case for what you want."

—Matt Villano

A Year Abroad as a Career Move

More grads are banking their future on working abroad

Armed with a bachelor's degree and not quite ready for the briefcase or the Brooks Brothers look, an increasing number of college graduates are heading abroad. With an estimated 35,000 young Americans working abroad, whether teaching, bartending, taking care of children, typing or picking grapes, the trend has moved well beyond just trust-fund types.

They are finding that far from being career suicide, it can actually provide a professional boost. Once back in the States, they find their updated résumés more enticing to recruiters, who say that foreign experience demonstrates entrepreneurship, resourcefulness and independence.

Graduates unencumbered by technicalities—like working legally—often branch off on their own with little more than a debit card and confidence. Many depart not knowing how they will earn a living once they hit the ground. With hustle, they often find employment before the jet lag wanes (to the relief of worried parents), according to some who have taken the plunge. Many aspiring expatriates first live at home and work a few months to save money before they leave.

Those working legally tend to earn more, but their stays have a set duration—generally, four months to three years, depending on the country or program. People working illegally may earn less, but can slip under the radar and stay in a country longer. A word of warning: that can result in deportation in extreme circumstances.

Years ago, recent graduates headed for Britain and other parts of Europe. That has changed. "Most students and young people have been to Europe on vacation and seem to be thinking much further afield," says Anna Crew, director of Bunac USA, a group that facilitates the process. Australia and New Zealand are now popular.

The payoffs down the road are genuine. Rosalind Clay Carter, senior vice president for human resources at A&E Television Networks, says people who work and support themselves overseas tend to be inquisitive, flexible and adaptive—valuable skills in today's workplace. "You are interested in that person who can move quickly and is nimble and has an inquiring mind," she says.

—Hillary Chura

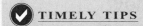

TIMELY TIPS

Know Before You Go

Those who need help in finding work overseas should know that some groups charge hefty placement fees. Determine whether the groups are covering room and board or are charging you just for the paperwork, and which programs require applications a year ahead of time or accept only recent graduates. Following are Web sites for job and volunteer opportunities, and general information:

✔ **Bunac** provides work permits, though not employment, and volunteer opportunities (www.bunac.org).

✔ **Dave's ESL Cafe** lists teaching jobs (www.esl-cafe.com/jobs).

✔ **GoAbroad.com** and Interexchange (www.interexchange.org/) also list foreign jobs.

✔ **Japan Exchange and Teaching Program** calls for a one-year commitment and pays about $32,000 (www.mofa.go.jp/j—info/visit/jet/).

✔ **The National Consortium for Study in Africa** at Michigan State University lists opportunities (www.isp.msu.edu/ncsa/volteer.htm).

✔ **Princeton in Asia** places business, media and nongovernmental fellows in countries like East Timor, Kazakhstan and Hong Kong (webscript.princeton.edu/pia/main/).

✔ **Transitions Abroad** is a travel magazine, but its site offers information about working abroad (www.transitionsabroad.com/listings/work).

✔ **The University of Michigan's** site is open to non-students (www.umich.edu/icenter/overseas/work).

✔ **WorldTeach** dispatches volunteers in developing countries like Costa Rica, China and Poland. Volunteers need not be aspiring teachers (www.worldteach.org).

—Hillary Chura

Ways to Beat Burnout

Smart strategies to deal with that take-this-career-and-shove-it feeling

Millions of Americans report that they are burned out, job-weary, bored, frustrated, overworked or just plain stressed out. Relax, help is just ahead. Cynthia Scott is a clinical psychologist, the author of 10 books on achieving optimal happiness and performance in the workplace, and founding principal of the San Francisco–based firm Changeworks Solutions. Her advice:

Know the burnout signs. The best indication of burnout is your day-to-day relationship with your immediate supervisor. Supervisors who communicate, share information, collaborate and allow some control over how work is done produce less burnout in their co-workers. Research suggests burnout is less related to how much pressure

people feel than to how meaningful they find their work. People who work hard but love what they do don't get burned out—unless they're working around abusive people or doing a job without a clear goal related to it.

Seek balance. If you don't have a lot of control in the workplace, you may need to take on more control at home. Vacuum the rug, clean the house, plant a garden, take up a sport—anything that moves your body, lets the tension out and gives you control. If your work involves long assignments, go home and do things with a quick finishing point. If you're working on real choppy, quick stuff, do something at home that has some longevity, like building a ship in a bottle. If you're isolated all day, go home and talk all night. If you talk to people all day, spend a quiet night reading. Whatever you do, don't get into numbing yourself; that can lead to alcohol and drug abuse, and isn't a real release.

Step back. If things at work are really getting to you, take a day off and get some distance. Ask yourself, "Is the problem short-term stress that will be over soon?" If I'm overloaded with a short-term stressor, I might just go off for an hour and do something nice for myself. If it's a long-term pressure that doesn't stop—like a long commute you have every day—taking an hour off won't do anything. For a chronic pressure like this, you need to ask yourself, "Is it going to get better?" Then see what options might work.

Consult family and friends. I call it bringing together your "board of directors"—the people who know you from different stages of your life. Have a pizza party, bring everyone together, and get their opinions, just as you would in a business meeting. The perspective of others is important, because each has a different view of you and a

---

ⓘ INSIDE INFO

The Long Road to Work

○ Urbanologists call them extreme commuters, and to qualify for that title you have to travel at least 90 minutes each way to work.

○ According to the Census Bureau, 3.4 million American workers fall into this category, an increase of 95 percent since 1990.

○ They travel across state lines—living in New Hampshire, for instance, and commuting to Boston, or living in West Virginia and driving to Pittsburgh. Some even cross time zones.

○ The average national commute is 24.3 minutes.

○ The average commute of people working in New York City, the area with the longest average commute, is 38.3 minutes.

—Lisa Belkin

different time frame. They can often help you deal with some things you thought you could do nothing about.

Learn the truth about your job status. It's better to get laid off than to worry about it. Our worst anxieties come from lack of information. If you know that you will lose your job in three months or three weeks, you can learn coping strategies. If you hear a bunch of "wells" and "maybes," you remain in a perpetual state of anxiety. Approach your boss and ask what's going on; this will release you to take other action. If your boss is not specific, ask for further clarification. The more you know, the better.

Air your work concerns. I'm a fan of not choking on it—of trying to communicate how you feel. Women often have a higher emotional literacy, so they can express their concerns—and don't mind doing so to another person. Try saying to your boss, "Your last comment made me feel devalued. I'm not sure what role I have in this project now. Could we try and work it out?" If a problem is really stressful, and you don't want to deal with it, do something to get yourself centered again. Try deep breathing or taking a walk—just get out of the stressful situation.

Use mental imagery and calming techniques. If you're doing a stressful task, you should envision a place that gives you a sense of ease. People choose lots of different things, such as lying on the couch, going to the beach or sitting in a bathtub.

I encourage people to have one image ready. If you practice this kind of self-care strategy, you can meditate and go to your safe place mentally whenever you want—even as you're being screamed at by your boss. You can have your eyes open and be attempting to listen, but the rest of you is thinking your way into your place of ease.

ⓘ INSIDE INFO

Stressful and Stressless Jobs

○ The National Business Employment Weekly *Jobs Rated Almanac* once evaluated 250 occupations considering factors such as deadlines, confinement, public meetings, hazards, environmental conditions and degree of stamina required. Scores were adjusted to reflect the average number of hours per week a job was likely to entail. These jobs surfaced as most and least stressful.

○ MOST STRESSFUL	LEAST STRESSFUL
1. U.S. president	Med. records technician
2. Firefighter	Janitor
3. Sr. corp. executive	Forklift operator
4. Race car driver (Indy class)	Musical instrument repair person
5. Taxi driver	Florist
6. Surgeon	Actuary
7. Astronaut	Appliance repair person
8. Police officer	Medical secretary
9. N.F.L. football player	Librarian
10. Air-traffic controller	Bookkeeper

Sometimes you need time to unwind to alleviate stress. If you've just left an awful meeting with your boss, take the stairs instead of the elevator. Ease the butterflies in your stomach by breathing in as you take each step to let out tension and get oxygen to your brain.

Judge the stress level of your job. Jobs that are high demand but have low control are the most stressful. It's more about position than occupation. For instance, a nurse working in a clinic has high demand and low control, with no way of knowing how many patients will be coming in each shift.

CAREERS

The New Stressor: E-Mail

Chances are your company reads your e-mail

Not so long ago, e-mail dashed around the world with good cheer, prompting people to race to the keyboard with anticipation. But now that it is an essential form of communication—136 million messages in 2005, up from 5 million in 2000, according to research firm Radicati Group—e-mail is causing as much distress as delight.

Consider the panic that ensues after sending a compromising message to the wrong person, or the unease that festers when a message goes unacknowledged. Even vacation is no longer an automatic escape valve, what with the lure of laptops, Internet cafes, wireless connections, and hand-held devices. Perhaps e-mail's biggest source of stress, though, is the overstuffed in-box. Many employees commonly receive 150 e-mail messages a day. Some high-powered clients can be peppered with 50 an hour.

Dealing with e-mail—filing it, cataloging it, prioritizing it—has added hours of extra work a week, much of it done by people in the late evening and early morning. In a survey by America Online and Opinion Research Corporation, 41 percent of the respondents said they checked their e-mail in the morning before going to work. More than 25 percent said they had never gone more than a few days without checking e-mail, with 60 percent saying they check it on vacation. Four percent looked at e-mail in the bathroom.

E-mail overload is driving an increasing number of employers, bosses and workers to find ways to control or curtail the load. Increasingly commonplace and entirely legal is the practice of corporate snooping. Companies routinely monitor computer use and e-mail to protect proprietary information, like corporate strategies and research; to increase productivity; and to inoculate themselves against prosecutors.

A survey of 850 professionals in 2005 by the American Management Association and ePolicy Institute, a consulting firm, found that 55 percent of the companies "retain and review" their workers' e-mail; a quarter of the companies had fired employees for violating e-mail policies; and 20 percent had their e-mail subpoenaed by courts and regulators. Large companies readily use software to monitor, organize and archive e-mail. Financial institutions are legally required to save e-mail for at least six years.

Some companies preserve e-mail on tapes, CD's and DVD's. To protect themselves and their employees, most companies have adopted an e-mail protocol: no salty language, for example; no discriminatory, derogatory or defamatory remarks; no transfer of company information.

—Lizette Alvarez

How to Get Your Next Raise

The road is paved with a little common sense and a lot of self-confidence

In this era of tight corporate coffers and slow-growing salaries, the last thing anyone wants to do is alienate the boss by asking for a raise. While it's impossible to predict exactly how your boss will react, your chances for a favorable outcome increase by averting a few pitfalls. Here's a roundup of the best advice career counselors have to offer on when to strike, what to say and what to avoid to fatten your take-home pay.

Time it right. A little common sense helps. If your company has just lost a major contract, released poor earning or is downsizing, hold off. Similarly, if your job performance has slipped lately, it's no time to call attention to yourself.

❓ **EXPERT ANSWER**

Don't Ask, Don't Tell

💬 **Should you ever reveal to your boss that you know how much your colleagues make?**

Just because Marvin Gaye crooned about what he heard through the grapevine doesn't mean you should, too. John Lyncheski, a partner at Cohen & Grigsby, a Pittsburgh law firm, says employees should stick to generalities when referring to the salaries of co-workers, because many companies have policies that prohibit employees from discussing salary issues with each other. Mentioning specifics about others' raises may identify you (and your co-workers) as violators of company policy.

Those who openly discuss the salaries of co-workers run another risk: alienating the boss. Evan Shapiro, general manager of the Independent Film Channel in New York, never responds in a positive way to this tactic. "My response to the old 'I know I'm not making as much as so-and-so' complaint is, 'What someone else at this company earns is none of your business,'" he says. "I don't care what industry you're in, it's a terrible negotiating strategy, and it gets you nowhere."

—Matt Villano

When is a good time to strike? If you work for a large organization with a formal human resources policy, the best time is during your performance review. If you work for a small company with no structured policy, approach your boss just after you've made a big sale, brought in a new client, implemented a new computer system or written a blockbuster story, for example.

Another timing tip: Don't hit your boss with it unexpectedly. Make an appointment for an appropriate time, say, after the day's big meetings end.

Research comparable salaries. Be armed with data on comparable salaries in your industry. Such information is readily available. Professional associations publish salary surveys, for example, and state employment services also put out statistics. Check the classified ads for jobs similar to yours to get an idea of salary ranges. Online, try the Bureau of Labor Statistics (www.bls.gov), America's Career Infonet (www.acinet.org) or go to salary comparison calculators at www.salary.com and www.hotjobs.com, among others.

But keep in mind that salaries for the same position can vary by location. So the more localized the information, the better. Remember, too, that salaries will also differ depending on specific responsibilities, years worked and level of expertise.

Never try to find out how much your co-workers are being paid. Many companies are highly secretive about this information, and some prohibit the practice. See "Don't Ask, Don't Tell" on this page.

Accentuate the positive. Don't assume that you deserve a raise just because of seniority or because your colleague got one. You will have to sell yourself. A PowerPoint presentation may be over the top, but you will need to prove specific contributions. Point out the sales growth in your portfolio over the previous year, for example, or itemize changes you made in your department and the resulting savings to the company. Use the industry salary data to prove that you are working for less but producing more.

When you enumerate reasons why you deserve a raise, be sure to focus on your successes, not on sacrifices you may have made.

Ultimatums rarely work. Be assertive and self-confident but not aggressive. Clearly state what you want and why you deserve it. Ask for an amount that's a bit higher—say, a few percentage points—than what you're willing to accept.

You may end up with close to what you want. Or, consider accepting certain perks or increased vacation time instead of a flat raise.

If you use an ultimatum as part of your raise negotiations, be prepared to follow through. Don't threaten to quit unless you are willing to walk out the door. Remember, too, that even if your boss gives in, your reputation may suffer in the end. No one likes to be coerced.

Take the high road. At the end of your pitch, your boss may agree that you deserve a raise, or a few more weeks of vacation, or a more flexible schedule.

But what if your boss turns down your request? Whatever you do, say career counselors, don't lose your cool. Hold in your anger. Focus, instead, on asking about areas that you can improve, then make an appointment to discuss your progress within a few months. Don't forget to keep detailed documentation on your performance until then.

When You Get a Better Offer

If you're lucky enough to be approached by another firm, here's what to do

Out of the blue, a competitor offers you a job for more money than you're earning now. Should you try to use the offer to get a raise from your current employer?

Any attempt to parlay a competitor's interest into more money from your boss is likely to be fraught with peril. Mark Oldman, co-president of employment research firm Vault.com, says that while employees may see this as an opportunity to leverage a raise, employers could view it as a reason to question your commitment to the company. "Playing a game of offer-counteroffer immediately calls your loyalty into question," Oldman says. "There are ways to do this successfully, but to get

what you want without alienating the boss requires you to proceed with caution." Here is some further advice on how to proceed:

● **What should you do first?**

Review the offer thoroughly and be sure you are willing to take it, because if your salary gambit fails, you may have to. Most surprise offers come by telephone, but it's important to meet with the competitor after hours or on a lunch break to discuss the offer. This meeting is also a good opportunity to get information about the job, your prospective colleagues and the corporate culture you might join. "Ideally, by the time you're ready to make up your mind, you will have met 10 or 12 people and will have a solid understanding of what the job will be like." says Peter Bell, president of executive search firm Bell & Associates.

But avoid planning these meetings over company e-mail or your work phone. Also, if you signed a noncompete agreement when you took your current job, any form of employment with a competitor could be prohibited. Check with an attorney before making a mistake that could cost you everything.

● **At what point should you inform your boss of the offer?**

While it may be tempting to get excited about an offer as it develops, Anthony Townsend, associate professor at Iowa State University, says employees should not consider any overtures official until they have received at least a letter outlining specifics like salary, benefits and general responsibilities. "If a firm is committed to the point where they're willing to write it down, it smells more like a contract and you can treat it as such," he says.

● **How do you conduct negotiations with your current boss?**

Explain how the offer came in, outline what aspects of it appeal to you, and enumerate what components of your current job make you want to stay. Deborah Kolb, professor of leadership at Simmons College in Boston, says another strategy is to couch the issue as a collaborative problem-solving discussion, seeking input from your boss rather than demanding answers. "Enlisting your boss in the solution shows that you are not just engaged in an offer-counteroffer game, but that you're interested in getting past this together," she says.

● How much should you reveal about the offer?

It's not necessary to say how much money the competitor is willing to pay you, says Jim Camp, president of Coach 2100, a negotiation training firm in Vero Beach, Fla., but you should outline what kind of salary increase you require to stay. Camp warns that revealing details of a competing offer might put your boss on the defensive.

Don't exaggerate the terms of the offer in an effort to get more out of your current employer. Most senior executives have a solid understanding of the employment market and will know when you're embellishing the truth.

● If your boss counteroffers with a competitive salary, is it time to celebrate?

Not necessarily. A counteroffer could begin a journey to the unemployment line. Katherine E. Simmons, chief executive of NetShare, an online job board in Novato, Calif., says she once capitulated after an employee used an offer from a competitor to leverage a heftier salary. Looking back, Simmons says she felt as if she had a "gun to her head" to increase the employee's pay, but did so because she needed the help. After that, her relationship with the employee fell apart, and the employee resigned four months later. "Once an employee violates the boss's trust, both parties will want to end the relationship quickly," Simmons says.

—Matt Villano

How to Get Your Head Hunted

A top headhunter on what it takes to get on a "most wanted" list

Headhunters prowl the corporate jungle, trying to lure the best and brightest managers and executives from one company to another. So why hasn't your phone rung with a juicy job offer? One of the nation's leading headhunters, Gerard Roche, has spent over 40 years at the New York City executive search firm of Heidrick & Struggles, Inc. His clients have included Disney, Coca-Cola, Office Depot, Starwood Hotels and Resorts, and Home Depot.

● How do you get a headhunter's notice?

Do an extraordinary job at the job you're in, and set a track record where you get recognition. The thing that will get our attention is your current job reputation. Nothing else is nearly as important. If you succeed to a high extent, we'll smoke you out.

One way to get noticed is to be active in your industry—attend association meetings, give a speech, write an article or get a top newsmagazine to quote you. Do whatever you can to be unique and let people know you're a leader. A strong reputation and résumé are mostly gained through individual effort, not public relations departments.

● Say you're ready to move on. Is it wise to approach a headhunter yourself?

This is a networking game. I get hundreds of résumés a week, so just sending a résumé isn't the best move. If you want to approach a top headhunter, try to have someone who knows them to recommend that they pay special attention to you.

● If a headhunter calls, how forthcoming should you be?

It's strictly a matter of whether you're the one pursuing a job, or the one being pursued. If you're secure in a position with an established reputation

TIMELY TIPS

If Your Company Is Sold

Should you sit tight or head for the exits?

Your company's been acquired, and you're waiting for the ax to fall. When do you pursue a new job?

✔ **It's never too early to line up an exit strategy.** Charlie Fleetham, president of Project Innovations, a Detroit consulting firm, says employees should send out résumés immediately upon news of an acquisition. If you interview at other companies, it's acceptable to tell them that the acquisition inspired you to look around. But, don't dwell on it.

"Go in and talk about how you're worried you're going to lose your job and you'll end up with nothing at all," he says. "Instead, mention the transition, but focus on your strengths and talents and how they will fit the new position."

✔ **If you choose to leave, make sure you are not walking away with money on the table.** Marc Karasu, vice president for marketing at Yahoo HotJobs, an Internet-based job board, says many stock options vest immediately in an acquisition, so it pays to check what you have earned. Many companies also offer bonuses for staying through a transition, and these financial incentives can be lucrative if you are willing to endure the uncertainties.

—Matt Villano

and not looking for a job—which is the type of people we normally go after—listen, see what the person has to offer, then respond as you see fit and feel comfortable doing.

If you're looking for a job, never take a headhunter's call raw. Ask if you can call back; this gives you a chance to find out exactly who is calling. Call back when it's convenient for you to talk privately. How forthcoming you are depends on how much you're interested in a new job. Even if you're looking, you should still have a certain amount of detached interest.

◉ Sure, headhunters are hired to search for C.E.O.'s. What if you're a smaller fish in the corporate pond?

It's simple—just do your job. If you excel, we'll pick you up on our radar. If you spend most of your time trying to get our attention, you're probably not going to get it.

When to Jump Ship
What to do if the job isn't as promised

You've been on the job a month, and your responsibilities aren't what the boss said they would be. You may be overwhelmed with unexpected tasks, like overseeing an intern program in addition to performing day-to-day duties. Or you may find yourself outside the circle of power—left out of important meetings and limited in the number of colleagues with whom you are allowed to consult. What should you do?

By all means, speak up, says Francie Dalton, president of Dalton Alliances, a Columbia, Md., consulting firm. "If you don't say anything about your frustration with the situation, you're simply implying your consent," she says. Express your concern to the boss in the context of the business. Marky Stein, president of Parachutes Inc., a management consulting firm in San Jose, Calif., suggests that logging daily work activities for at least two weeks to create a pie chart or bar chart that shows how your time is spent. Stein says the chart should provide detailed proof of how and where your job differs from what was promised.

"You could call this a type of 'time motion'

study with the subject as yourself," she says. "Bosses love visuals, and if you are very detailed about your study, the evidence will be hard to challenge." Such a chart could also help employees ensure they haven't confused their own fantasies with what the boss told them to expect—a common problem that comes with excitement about a new job opportunity.

So, how much time should you give a disappointing job before complaining? Even in the most disappointing jobs, patience can be a virtue. Ellen Ensher, associate professor of management at Loyola Marymount University in Los Angeles, says 90 days is a fair amount of time to assess a new job. Many employers use the first six weeks for training new hires, making that period an unreliable representation of how a job will play out. "The first six weeks are always filled with dreck before it gets better," says Ensher.

Once you've made your position known, there should be some give and take. If your employer shows no interest in improving your situation, it may be time to start circulating your résumé again. "Once you've made an effort to clear things up, if it's not a salvageable situation, you need to move on," says Carol Frohlinger, a partner in the New York consulting firm Shadow Negotiation.

There are ways to prevent this problem from happening in the first place, however. Before you take the job, find out what the new workplace is really like. Some employers offer "realistic job previews"—opportunities to spend some time on the job with current employees, for example, or videos that demonstrate typical workdays. Prospective employees can also ask on their own to spend some time in the office to experience the culture.

More fundamentally, before accepting a new job, ask for a written description of the position, spelling out the specific responsibilities. That could save you grief down the road.

—Matt Villano

I Quit !!!

What to tell the company as you walk out the door

You've resigned from your job, and the human resources department has requested an exit interview. How do you make sure that your last impression is a good one?

Much like an initial job interview, the exit interview requires employees to act with dignity, says Maggie Craddock, president of executive coaching firm Workplace Relationships. "As tempting as it might be to blow it off, the exit interview is not a time to go in and say, 'I'm out

CAREERS

of here,'" Craddock says. "How you leave often is what sticks with people about you after you've gone, so it's critical to handle the exit interview professionally," she says. Some other advice:

Q What purpose do exit interviews serve?

They aren't mandatory, but it's generally a good idea to participate if asked. For employees, the meetings can provide closure for their tenure at a company. For employers, they can help unearth facts about the workplace environment. Beth Carvin, chief executive of Nobscot, a human resources software company in Honolulu, says the best companies use this information to improve the workplace for those who remain. If employees are forthright in exit interviews, what they say will have a bearing on what happens at that company down the road.

Q What questions will be asked?

There's no formula, but three main topics typically will be covered: on-the-job responsibilities, company benefits—including salary—and manager communication. Most of the questions are open-ended, but some interviewers will directly ask employees why they are leaving.

Q How do you prepare for the session?

The more specifics you can provide, the better. It's a good idea to spend a few hours reflecting before the meeting, so you don't fumble when the pressure is on. This will help you remember both highs and lows, and will help contextualize situations so you can give accurate impressions of your experience. "Whatever you do," says Kristin Brown, assistant professor of management at the Rochester Institute of Technology, "make sure that the information you're giving your exit interviewer is organized and clear so that nobody gets the wrong idea."

Q Should you be wary of being too honest?

Honesty is best, but try to avoid too much negativity. "The last thing you want to do is go out griping. Besides, most human resources professionals are trained to read between the lines," says Bernadette Kenny, executive vice president at consulting firm Lee Hecht Harrison.

There is another reason to stay positive: you never know when you may encounter your exit interviewer again. "The exit interview is not the time to burn bridges," says Jim Atkinson, regional vice president at Right Management Consultants. "Most industries are small, and bad behavior is not something you want people remembering about you."

Q Can you decline to answer certain questions in an exit interview?

Certainly, but keeping quiet on particularly sensitive subjects, like your manager's communication skills, might make it seem that you have something to hide. As an alternative, employees should work around uncomfortable inquiries by focusing on something less volatile. "Redirecting questions that could activate land mines is always a safe bet," says Lawler Kang, author of *Passion at Work: How to Find Work You Love and Live the Time of Your Life.* "If you have to rate an area as one for improvement, do so vis-à-vis other strong positive traits."

Q Is it safe to assume that your interview will remain confidential?

The interview may seem like a private meeting, but it's not. Most information or opinions you volunteer can be quoted and distributed around the company. Human resources employees, in most cases, have no legal obligation to keep your comments under wraps.

A notable exception is a discussion of a claim of sexual harassment or discrimination, which must remain confidential until investigated thoroughly. Even under such circumstances, says Robin Bond, president of Transition Strategies in Wayne, Pa., the human resources representative is likely to take copious notes. "When you talk to human resources, everything is on the record," she notes. "Just because you're leaving the company doesn't mean your words won't live there for years to come."

—Matt Villano

The Womenless Workforce

Why are more women staying home? Time, not attitude, is the reason

About 75 percent of women 25 to 34 years old either work or are actively seeking a job, up from around 40 percent in the late 1950's. Since 2000, however, the participation rate for women has declined; it remains far below the 90 percent rate for men in the same age range.

Is this shift evidence that many mothers are deciding to stay home and take care of the children? Maybe, but many researchers are reaching a different conclusion: women are not choosing to stay out of the workplace because of changing attitudes. Rather, the broad reconfiguration of women's lives

 INSIDE INFO

Minority Women and the Glass Ceiling

○ Fewer than 2 percent of Fortune 500 corporate officer and other top-level jobs are held by women of color.

○ Black women hold 1.1 percent of those positions; Asian American women .29 percent; and Latino women .24 percent, according to a study by Catalyst, a New York based research and consulting group.

that allowed most of them to pursue jobs outside the home appears to be hitting some serious limits.

"What happened on the road to gender equality?" asks Suzanne M. Bianchi, a sociologist at the University of Maryland. "A lot of work happened." Bianchi believes that contrary to popular belief, the broad movement of women into the paid labor force did not come at the expense of their children. Not only did fathers spend more time with children, but working mothers, she found, spent an average of 12 hours a week on child care in 2003, an hour more than stay-at-home mothers did in 1975.

"Looking toward the future," says Francine D. Blau, a professor of economics at Cornell University, "one can question how much further increases in women's participation can be had without more reallocation of household work." In other words, working women have hit a ceiling on how many hours they can devote to both work and family, and more are picking the latter.

—Eduardo Porter

UNEQUAL PARTNERS

Nearly half of all law students are women. There are female lawyers aplenty but they aren't making it to the top. Women represent fewer than 20 percent of law firm partners. In some cities, the percentage is even lower.

WOMEN IN LAW SCHOOLS
Percentage of juris doctor enrollment

Year	40%	30	20	10	0
'65 '75 '85 '95 '04					

SOURCES: American Bar Association; NALP

WOMEN IN LAW FIRMS
Percentage who are partners, 2005

National average **17.3%**

HIGHEST	
Miami	23.7%
New Orleans	22.8
Denver	22.3
San Francisco	21.8
LOWEST	
Orange County, Calif.	12.7
Northern Virginia	12.4
Charlotte, N.C.	11.5
Salt Lake City	8.7

CAREERS

Exploiting the Gender Gap

○ Women put a premium on autonomy, flexibility, proximity to home, fulfillment and safety. Nearly 76 percent of men say money is the primary motive for working, according to a Rochester Institute of Technology survey.

○ There are 80 jobs in which women earn more than men, among them financial analyst, speech-language pathologist, radiation therapist, library worker, biological technician and motion picture projectionist.

○ Women who have never been married and are childless earn 17 percent more than their childless male counterparts.

○ Female sales engineers make 43 percent more than their male counterparts; female statisticians earn 35 percent more than men make at the same job, according to Warren Farrell, author of *Why Men Make More: The Startling Truth Behind the Pay Gap.*

What Color Is Your New Career?

A guidance guru's secrets for making a successful switch

The typical American worker can expect to have two or three different careers during his professional life. So, what's the best way to make a smooth transition to a new career? Here's some advice from Richard Bolles, author of the wildly popular *What Color Is Your Parachute?,* a useful guide for first-time job seekers and seasoned career switchers.

💬 **How do I know when I'm ready for a career change, and not just bored in my current job?**

You can determine that by asking yourself the following questions:

1. Do I like my present boss or bosses, and do I enjoy working for them?

2. Do I like my co-workers, and enjoy working with them?

3. Do I like what I do—the tools I work with, the product I produce, the information I disseminate, or the people I am trying to help?

4. Am I using the skills I most love to use?

5. Do I really like the field I am in?

If your answer to either of the first two is no, you should consider changing your job, though not necessarily your career. But if your answer to any of the last three questions is no, you probably need to think about changing careers.

💬 **Let's say I know I want to make a career change but don't know what I want to do.**

There are two ways to solve this common puzzle. First, think about all the people you know or see in a given week. Ask yourself if any of them has a job you would really like to have. If so, what is that job? Second, identify your favorite skills and fields of interest. Your skills are verbs ending in "ing," such as "designing," "writing," "researching," "sewing" and the like. They are transferable from one field to another. Fields of interest are nouns, like "stamps," "computers," "gardens," "design" and "insurance." Your favorite transferable skills, plus your favorite fields of interest will define a new career.

💬 **Once I've decided what I'd like to do, how do I find a job that matches my skills and interests?**

If you know the skills you'd like to use, and the field you'd like to be in, but are not clear as to which career it all points to, there's an easy way to find out. Talk to people in the field. Make use of the Internet and the Yellow Pages to contact them. Ask what kinds of careers in that field require the skills you have identified as your favorites. Keep going, until you find some answers you like.

● **If I want to break into an entirely new field, where and how do I start a job search?**

Once you have identified the career, talk to at least five people who are doing that work. Again, the Yellow Pages can help identify people in that line of work. Also, your local librarian can help you locate the associations of companies in that field, and you can contact them. Do an Internet search to see what turns up in the way of information about that career.

When talking to people in your targeted career, ask these four questions: How did you get your job? What do you like most about it? What do you like least? Who else would you recommend I talk to about this career? Since you're talking to workers and not employers, and you're asking them how they found their job, you'll get plenty of ideas about ways to find work in the field. If your source lives nearby and the career still interests you—and it might not—ask him if you can observe him at work for a day to see what the job involves in detail.

● **What is the most challenging aspect of changing careers?**

Most challenging is taking the time to identify your favorite skills and fields of interest. The process, if done right, takes a full weekend. Next comes taking the time to interview workers in your new career before going job hunting. Most people want to leap over these two essential preliminary steps. Consequently, their career change is often a sort of "out of the frying pan, into the fire" experience.

● **If I'm changing careers at midlife, how do I compete with younger candidates?**

Know your skills better, know the field better and be a harder worker. Come in earlier, stay later, miss fewer days. Finally, you have to be able to tell an employer why you can do the work better than the other candidates, whether they're younger

or older. In short, spend more time preparing for a career change by doing an inventory of yourself and by doing informational interviews, before attempting to launch a new career.

● **Should I work with a career counselor? If so, what should I expect?**

The rule is, Don't rely just on the advice of well-meaning friends. Instead, master the process of changing careers through your own self-study course. Less than $20 for a helpful book may be all you need to spend. But if that doesn't work, look for other low-cost resources—seminars, testing, counseling—available through a community college, library or chamber of commerce.

Only when you have exhausted these resources should you turn to a paid career counselor. When you do, find one who charges by the hour. (Fees are generally the same as those of a competent therapist.) You should not have to sign anything before you begin counseling, and you should be able to end the hourly meetings at any time. The counselor's stated goal should be to teach you how to change careers yourself, rather than trying to do it all for you. Visit at least three counselors before choosing the one you feel is most competent.

● **What about using a headhunter?**

Headhunters generally work for employers, who have hired them. They typically look for candidates who already work for organizations or companies and are tops in their field. A career-changer's chances of being of interest to a headhunter are slim. Still, it can't hurt to send your résumé to a headhunter, as long as it doesn't take too much of your time.

● **What if I identify a dream career but can't find a job in that field?**

Your backup is to pick up your list of favorite skills and fields of interest, each ranked in order

CAREERS

of preference. Show this list to everyone you know and ask them which careers or jobs the list might suggest to them. Then interview workers in the careers that interest you. Your dream may have more than one form, but you should never give up on that dream.

Where Career Switchers Go

The top five choices for those who move on

Restlessness, corporate burnout, the desire for autonomy, the need for flexibility: these are some of the motives driving people toward a career change. And thanks to longer life spans and shifting cultural norms, midcareer transitions are increasingly common.

Here are five of the most popular fields for people making a change—and the skills you'll need to make the transition—according to career consultants and those who track employment trends. But use the list cautiously. Consider first your personal interests, talents, life goals and whether the career makes sense for you. Can you handle the considerable workload demanded for a master's degree, or just juggle a few skill-building courses? Are you willing to take a pay cut? Be low man on the totem pole? As Helen Harkness, author of *Don't Stop the Career Clock*, says: "Look inward first, and then outward to see if there is a marketplace fit."

1. NOT-FOR-PROFITS

Employment in not-for-profit organizations has grown by more than 30 percent in the last decade, according to the Independent Sector in Washington, an industry coalition. Midcareer changers who choose not-for-profit work are typically burned out by the business world, yet still game for professional challenge, despite salaries that are 20 to 50 percent lower than in business or government.

EDUCATION: Follow the money. That means learning grant-proposal writing, fund-raising, and not-for-profit operations and management. The Nonprofit Academic Centers Council (www.nac-council.org) can connect you to schools that offer degree programs and certification courses.

For example, the Association of Fundraising Professionals (www.afpnet.org) offers certification programs in fund-raising techniques and other essentials. The Foundation Center (www.fdncenter.org), offers online tutorials and classes in grant writing, fund-raising and management at five centers across the country. The Grantsmanship Center (www.tgci.com) holds more than 200 workshops a year around the country. Its basic programs teach researching and writing grant proposals and negotiating with financing sources.

2. INFORMATION TECHNOLOGY

Few who lived through the dot-com bust a few years back would have predicted that the technology sector would bounce back. But that's what is happening. Government statistics show that technology is one of the country's fastest-growing industries, with an average salary of $67,900 and some 600,000 new jobs expected by 2012. You'll need a solid grounding in information system basics and a combination of past workplace experience—in areas like management, graphic design, health care, law enforcement—and newly acquired technology skills.

EDUCATION: Computer network security is the hottest thing going, say experts like Brian Reithel, president of the Association of I.T. Professionals. The area promises to get even hotter as national security needs grow, and information systems are increasingly threatened by hackers, identity thieves and even natural disasters. The online I.T. community at www.dice.com provides links to educational opportunities, jobs and industry information.

INSIDE INFO

They'd Rather Switch

O Nearly 60 percent of workers have changed careers—not just jobs—and more than half of those have done so more than once, according to a 2004 survey by the University of Phoenix, whose emphasis is adult education programs.

O "Recareerists" as they are called—are transforming education, leading to all manner of continuing education classes, online universities, certificates and graduate degrees designed to qualify workers to do something completely new. Adults age 25 and older now account for more than a third of those enrolled at degree-granting institutions, according to the National Center for Education Statistics. Enrollment is projected to increase 13 percent among 25-to-29-year-olds and 23 percent among 30-to-34-year-olds by 2014.

O Most workers who set out to change their lives wind up in positions related to the ones they left, according to Right Management Consultants. In a survey of 5,600 displaced workers polled by the company in 2004, 56 percent said they wanted to do something significantly different with their lives. But of the 14,000 people who landed new jobs in 2004 with the company's help, only 5 percent were in different careers.

—Lisa Belkin

3. NURSING

The demand for registered nurses is greater than ever, as is the shortage: more than a million additional nurses will be needed by 2012, according to government figures. Compensation matches the demand: with salaries of $40 to $50 an hour plus overtime, nurses can earn more than $100,000 a year. This would seem to make nursing a good bet for midcareer changers, and in fact, a third of students enrolled in training are 31 to 50 years old, according to the National League for Nursing.

EDUCATION: The most efficient way in for an adult is through an accelerated bachelor's of science in nursing degree—concentrated, rigorous training for those who already hold a bachelor's in another area, but want a quick transition into nursing. More than 160 universities around the country offer accelerated, 11-to-18-month degrees. Lists of programs can be found on the Web site of the American Association of Colleges of Nursing (www.aacn.nche.edu) and at the online guide All Nursing Schools (www.allnursingschools.com).

4. REAL ESTATE

Real estate has historically attracted those in transition, thanks to its ease of entry, flexible hours (15 percent of agents work part time), high earning potential and acceptance of women, who make up 54 percent of the profession. Compensation varies regionally and, since agents work on commission, depends on an agent's activity. The median income in 2004 was $58,700 for those in the business six to ten years. The Department of Labor reports that employment of agents and brokers (who have more training and experience) will grow more slowly than the average for all occupations through 2012. Regardless, half end up leaving the business within three years.

EDUCATION: Efficient development and management, creative financing and urban economics are some of the emerging areas of study at universities under the real estate umbrella, usually in a master of science degree. Some degrees, crafted with midcareer changers in mind, allow part-time study.

For those who simply want to handle residential sales and "work the street," as real estate agents say, making the transition doesn't require a huge investment of time or money. Each state has its own licensing requirements and education hours needed to get a license—from 20 hours in Alaska to 99 in Delaware. The easiest way to get information, and possibly training, is to walk into a real estate office and ask. Some large companies run in-house training in basics like title insurance, zoning regulation and financing.

5. TEACHING

With 375,000 teachers retiring between 1999 and 2009, and the K-12 student population swelling to 55 million by 2010, schools are counting on older workers entering the profession to help fill the gap. The biggest needs are in the West and Northeast, and in urban schools. Career changers are hearing the call: some 70,000 have turned to teaching in the last two years.

EDUCATION: Many career changers, unwilling or unable to invest the time or money needed for a traditional university education degree, take advantage of fast-track training and job placement programs leading to certification. Virtually every state has alternative routes into teaching, some accelerated.

Two ways to find them are through Recruiting New Teachers (www.rnt.org) and the National Center for Alternative Certification (www.teach-now. org). Education departments at local colleges and universities can also provide information on available programs and state licensing requirements.

—Cecilia Capuzzi Simon

Want to Be Your Own Boss?

Learn to minimize the risks before taking the plunge

Entrepreneurs are bursting out all over as workers look for more flexible schedules. The ranks of full- and part-time workers who toil in home offices have swelled. The other side of the picture:

the survival rate for small businesses is a low 30 percent. The fact is, being your own boss isn't easy. So before taking the plunge, keep in mind that self-employment can be financially and emotionally draining, says Jane Applegate, a syndicated newspaper columnist and author of *201 Great Ideas for Your Small Business*. Applegate says that the self-employed need all the agility of a plate spinner at the circus to keep those plates perched on spindly poles from crashing down. Applegate offers the following advice on launching your own business:

● How do I decide which business to go into?

Base the decision on skills you already have. It doesn't make sense to change careers completely, unless you plan to go to school or take special training classes. Figure out if the work you are doing for your current employer is salable and if you can promote those services or goods to former clients and customers after you leave your job. One way to test the market is to conduct your own short survey asking people if they would buy the goods or services you have to offer.

● What research should I do before starting a business?

Before you sink your savings into a business, sign up for classes, attend seminars and consider volunteering in a business similar to the one you have in mind. Meet with other small-business owners—they'll probably tell you more than you ever wanted to know. You can also get free counseling through your local Small Business Development Center. Another program, sponsored by the Small Business Administration, is called SCORE, for the Service Corps of Retired Executives. This team of volunteers will provide answers to many small-business questions.

● How much of my own money should I invest?

That depends on the business you're setting up. If you plan to open a retail store, you will need money to buy merchandise, and pay rent and the staff—all before you make your first sale. A service business usually needs less capital to get started. No matter what sort of business you start, as a general rule, set aside twice as much as you think you'll need. And sock away at least six months' worth of living expenses—it always takes longer to get off the ground than you expect.

How do I attract business investors?

You need more than a dream to share with investors—you need a well-written business plan that will serve as a personal and professional road map. Most major accounting firms offer free business-planning guides, and there are many good planning resources on the market and the Internet.

What are the best sources of financing?

Friends, family, shirttail relatives and colleagues are best. Many entrepreneurs think venture capitalists fund most new businesses, but in reality, they reject about 99 percent of the deals they consider. On the other hand, so-called angel investors—typically professionals looking to invest in a nearby business—put up about $6 out of every $10 invested in very small firms

What about bank loans?

Many banks shun high-risk start-ups, but if you have a substantial net worth or other investments, you can probably get a bank loan for your new business. If you don't qualify, try to get a loan guarantee from the Small Business Administration, which guarantees up to 90 percent of the loan value. Small Business Investment Companies (www.nasbic.org), a group of private companies, offers government-backed loans and equity investments.

When can I expect a profit?

If you are selling a product, you can potentially make money from day one. Other businesses, such as manufacturing or exporting, can take years to pay off. Service businesses may also take longer to build a clientele.

How can I compete with a giant in my industry?

Entrepreneurs competing with a Goliath say the only way to succeed is to figure out a unique way of selling your products. You can't outspend a big corporation, so outsmart it: provide better and faster service, more personal attention, more intelligent sales people or a unique approach.

How much should I pay myself?

There is no magic formula—just be sure that you are able to take something home. Calculate your total living expenses for a few months, and put that in the bank before you open the business. You don't want to sacrifice your family and your home for the business venture.

✔ TIMELY TIPS

A Chair Fit for a Chairman

Chances are you haven't given a lot of thought to what you sit on at the office. But ergonomics experts have. Here are some tips:

✔ **FIT COMES FIRST.** Find a chair that fits your body.

✔ **BEWARE CUSHY SEATS.** You don't want too much weight concentrated on your seat bones.

✔ **AVOID LONG CUSHIONS.** If you can't get against the backrest, you can't get a comfortable, healthy posture.

✔ **KEEP MOVING.** The best way to stay pain-free is to avoid spending hours on end at your desk. Take a break every hour to walk around.

✔ **BACKRESTS AND ARMRESTS.** A chair with good back support gets the spine back into the natural "S curve" equilibrium.

SOURCE: Richard Holbrook, Pasadena, Calif.

Q **What sacrifices will I need to make?**

Be prepared to give up a steady paycheck, a worry-free life, and time for fun and family. You could be sacrificing your company's pension or 401(k) plan, so try to set up an IRA or a small business pension plan to protect yourself when you retire.

Q **What are some benefits?**

You'll enjoy a roller-coaster ride full of adrenaline and the potential to make more money than you ever dreamed of. You can also expect enormous flexibility, a sense of accomplishment and a realization that though you work hard, all the money will come straight back to you and your family.

Your New "Retirement" Plan

For many, going back to work is just the ticket

While many retirees are still focused on leisure activities, a growing number are intent on returning to the workforce.

A recent study by Putnam Investments estimated that seven million previously retired people, or about 10 percent of the workforce over the age of 40, are now back at work or looking for jobs. And among those, the number of older retirees returning to work is growing quickly. Today, nearly one-fourth of all people in the 65-to-74 age group hold jobs, compared with just one in six just two decades earlier, according to the Bureau of Labor Statistics. Putnam's study found that the number of workers in the 65-to-74 group grew three times as fast as the overall workforce last year.

Of course, many Americans find that they have to work in their retirement years to pay the bills. In the Putnam survey, about one-third of those returning to work said they needed the additional income to survive financially. And recent economic research generally indicates that about half of baby boomers are not saving enough to maintain their current living standards in retirement—unless, of course, they supplement their income by taking jobs.

The experience of people now working in retirement can offer valuable clues for those who come next. One important lesson is that the often-heard advice—to save for retirement—may not be enough. Making sure you still have marketable skills as you age may be just as crucial.

—Anna Bernasek

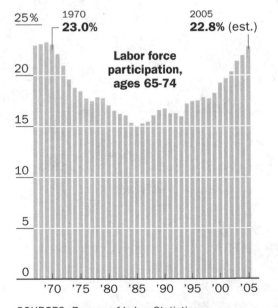

RETURNING TO WORK

Almost a quarter of all 65-to-74-year-olds are in the workforce—the highest percentage since 1970.

25%   1970   2005
       23.0%   **22.8%** (est.)

Labor force participation, ages 65-74

20

15

10

5

0
   '70 '75 '80 '85 '90 '95 '00 '05

SOURCES: Bureau of Labor Statistics, Putnam Investments (estimate for 2005).

CHAPTER **7**

HOUSE & GARDEN

Around the House 408

REMODELING·408: *Picking a contractor • In case things go wrong • The emotional roller coaster • If I had a hammer* **DECORATING·413:** *How to stencil a floor • Taming monster spaces • Living large in small rooms • The secret world of decorators • Ready-to-eat kitchens • Decorative concrete* **STORAGE·419:** *Behind closet doors • Where to stash a flat-screen TV • Shelves for a lifetime* **WALLS & LIGHTING·421:** *The luminous life of paint • Paints aren't equal • Fixing the light fantastic • Track lighting that disappears • Framing pictures* **FURNISHINGS·427:** *Furniture kits • Beds you won't lose sleep on • Pillow talk • Put spring in your sofa • A well-made rug • Ideas for curtains* **MAINTENANCE·431:** *Cut your heating bills • Protect your castle from time • If a house is a hot zone*

In the Garden 440

PLANTING·440: *Figments that turn into flowers • A sower's guide to soil • Dig your garden and you shall reap* **FLOWERS·447:** *Rose gardening • 10 easy roses • Garden scents • How to train a rose • 10 scented roses • Perfect plants for tough places • The 60-second gardener* **VEGETABLES·454:** *Late-season vegetables • Heirloom seeds • A vegetable planting chart • Herbs for all spaces* **PESTS & DISEASES·460:** *Doing battle with blight* **GARDEN TIPSS·462:** *Butterfly gardening • To lure a hummingbird • Plant-pruning advice • Pruners and spades* **TREES·465:** *Tree-planting • Pruning trees* **LAWNS·467:** *The perfect lawn • Greener grass • Shedding light on houseplants • Terrific public gardens*

Pets 474

DOGS & CATS·474: *Picking a canine companion • Congenital defects in dogs • Buying a pedigree pup • Shopping for a doggie online • Shampoo for pooches • How to de-skunk your dog • Dieting—a dog's life • All the cat's meow's • Dog years vs. people years • Smile, say "arf"* **VETS·482:** *When your pet gets sick • Boosting your pet's well-being • A new age in pet care* **BIRDS·486:** *Choosing a bird feeder • Homemade food for wild birds* **GERBILS AND MORE·488:** *Getting a gerbil • Trust funds for pets*

Around the House

How to Pick a Contractor

It may be the most important decision you make in building your dream house

Americans are renovating their homes these days with surprising regularity. Yet in making the most important decision in a major renovation—selecting the contractor who will be charged with turning a drawing into a dream house—many people often rely on third-hand hearsay, personal vibes and a big dose of optimism. Here are some bits of advice on how to successfully renovate.

BEFORE YOU START

Most experts suggest that you start planning what you want and how to finance it a year or more before you hire a contractor.

Your research should include visiting showrooms and decorator house shows to get ideas, developing a clipping file of things you like and surfing the Web—some helpful sites include www.thisoldhouse.com/toh, www.hgtv.com and www.improvenet.com. You also need to learn the contracting lingo.

Unless you are an organizational whiz and know how to obtain permits and variances and schedule workers, you really do need a contractor on most jobs. If you are moving or removing walls, or are redesigning a kitchen, you may also need an architect or a professional designer.

If you are planning just one change, like painting a room or redoing a bathroom, you may want to work directly with one reputable contractor in that trade instead of going through a general contractor.

CHOOSING THE CONTRACTOR

References alone mean next to nothing. It's how you check them that counts. Check not only for raves but also for the presence of repeat customers. Look for gaps. Ask clients not just whether they were happy but, more important, whether the job was done on time and on budget. How did the contractor handle unexpected glitches and changes?

Beyond solid references, look for a contractor who is a good communicator and a good executor. This person should tell you what is going to happen, when it will be messy, how long you will be without lights or water—then draw up a realistic schedule and stick to it.

Competitive bidding will not always result in the best deal. Architectural drawings almost always leave contractors room for interpretation. A good paint job, for instance, is typically described as "patching, priming and two coats of Benjamin Moore or equivalent." But how much sanding is

---

ⓘ **INSIDE INFO**

Smaller Families = Bigger Houses?

○ The size of the average new house built in the United States increased more than 50 percent between 1970 and 2004, even as the size of the average family grew smaller.

○ 83 percent of all new homes built in 2004 had two- or three-car garages, double the number in 1970. The amount of money spent on garage makeovers is expected to rise by 10 percent a year for the rest of the decade.

SOURCE: National Association of Homebuilders

enough: a couple of days or a couple of weeks? How smooth does smooth have to be? In a large apartment, the difference could amount to tens of thousands of dollars and weeks of work.

Contractors will bid on the scope of the work, which should be very specific, including model numbers of window and appliance choices, if possible. The more you can tell a contractor about your project, using blueprints or drawings, specifications, paint chips and hardware preferences, the better.

Beware of low-ballers. If one contractor bids more than 20 percent below the others, you have reason to be suspicious. Has the low bidder really taken a good look at the drawings, or is he just winging it? Is he so desperate for the work that he may not have enough money to carry it out? Some low bidders may count on compensating themselves for lost profits by charging unusually high prices for the inevitable changes. When a hidden pipe turns up in a wall you want to knock down, it's going to cost you.

A bid that goes into great detail is a good sign. Proposals that include quantities and unit prices are better than those that just say "Plumbing: $10,000." An attentive contractor will also ask probing questions and may well suggest ways to save money before the contract has been signed. He may want a small fee for fine-tuning such suggestions. That's O.K. Spending a little extra money and time here can save a lot of both later on.

Once you have checked out the company, do the same for the team assigned to your job. You are well advised to ask for references on the two key figures on your contracting team: the project

> **If you want to make the jump from a tract house but just can't afford to trade up, there is another solution: change the exterior to give it a new architectural stamp.**

manager, who is responsible for your job, and the construction supervisor, who is the day-to-day representative (the one who will be sitting in your kitchen with your keys in his pocket). If you are audacious, you might also ask for the names of dissatisfied customers, to see if the problem was shoddy work or just poor chemistry.

Visits to work sites are of limited use to amateurs. Sure, a neat and organized site is a plus. On the other hand, construction is supposed to be messy.

It would be more helpful to have your contractor arrange visits to several projects, each of them at least a couple of years old, to see how they are holding up. (Or better yet, arrange your own visits through references or friends, since the contractor is likely to send you to only his best work.) Are bathroom tiles loose? Are the moldings cracking? How about the paint job? Any sign of leaks?

A big name does not guarantee good service, especially with interest rates so low that work is plentiful. "All you get with a big company," said Enrico Bonetti, a New York architect, "is a guy in a suit."

The firm should be experienced in your type of renovation, the size of your project and budget, and your kind of apartment building or house.

The company should also be well versed in the permit process, which paralyzes many jobs. A crew of 30 skilled workers can't do much if they are locked out by the super. Nor will it help for the work to be completed on time if the contractor has neglected to arrange for the proper inspections.

Establishing that a contractor has basic competence is easy. Look for a licensed contractor, but

Just in Case Things Go Wrong

Most contractors are reliable and hardworking, insists Thomas Kraeutler, host of the nationally syndicated radio show *The Money Pit*. But to guard against the few who aren't, here he suggests ways to forestall a home improvement disaster.

✔ **Pay the bill in installments.**
A common complaint is that the job takes longer to complete than a contractor estimated. To avoid this, include a "time of essence" clause, which charges the contractor penalties if the work takes too long. The contractor should also set forth a payment schedule. As a general rule, put up a small down payment and space out the remainder. Reserve at least 25 percent of the total amount for a final payment and release it only when you're completely satisfied with the work.

✔ **Check insurance.**
When checking insurance, make sure the contractor provides a "certificate of insurance," which names you as an "additional insured." This guarantees that the contractor's insurance company will attempt to notify you if the policy is canceled for any reason. Also, be sure to check the policy limit of the general comprehensive coverage. A basic policy offers a limit of $50,000. This isn't very much coverage in today's litigious world. For peace of mind, insist on at least $300,000 coverage. In New York City, the average is $1,000,000.

✔ **Keep a written record.**
Good documentation of the job is crucial if something goes wrong later or if disputes arise. Keep written notes of starting and stopping times, how many people are working, and what's getting (or not getting) done. This is especially important if you are paying for the job by the hour. Also, for bigger jobs, keep notes of conversations you've had with contractors about problems, changes, etc.

✔ **Get an outside review.**
If any question arises about the quality of the job, have the work inspected by an independent professional, such as a home inspector. To find a good one in your area, go to the Web site of the American Society of Home Inspectors at www.ashi. org. With all contracts, be sure to have them reviewed by your attorney before signing. The expense of such a review can be well worth it in the event of future problems.

realize that passing the license exam is just the first of many requirements he must meet. You can eliminate deadbeats and fly-by-nights by checking with the Better Business Bureau, www.bbb.org.

AND THEN, THE CONTRACT

You will need to decide between a fixed-price and cost-plus contract. If you know exactly what you want, a fixed-price contract may be your best bet. But be aware that a contractor will pad a fixed-price contract slightly to cover complications. With cost-plus, you pay as you go without a total estimate. You can put a cap on the amount or work out an incentive for meeting a certain price.

Once you get to the contract stage, have a lawyer ensure that the contract is comprehensive, including a start and finish date (with a penalty for not meeting the deadline), a payment schedule and required starting fee, how changes and problems will be handled and a request that the contractor let you know if he changes his insurance, bonding or workers' compensation. The contract should also include a retaining fee—for example, about 10 percent of the total budget—until all the work is finished.

The Emotional Roller Coaster

Anyone who has ever renovated a house knows about the highs and the lows, from the first thrilling moment when the old walls come down to the dark days when the plumber disappears and the carpenter changes his home phone number. But a mood indicator plotted on a timeline? Even a serial renovator might be surprised to learn that for some contractors, monitoring the client's emotional life is just part of the job.

David Lupberger, a contractor who serves as a kind of coach for others in the business, lays it out in a book, *Managing the Emotional Homeowner.*

The graphic below, based on the one in Mr. Lupberger's book, suggests that the typical construction project takes nine months. Any longer, and emotions no doubt run off the charts.

—Marco Pasanella

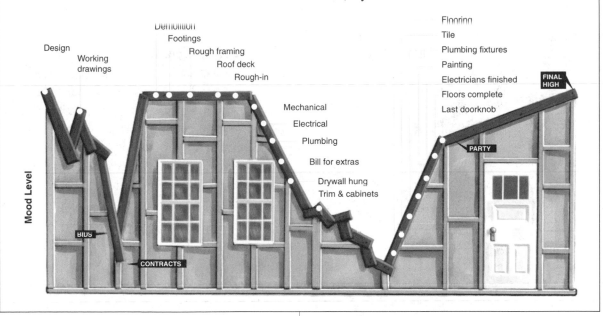

Design

Working drawings

Demolition
Footings
Rough framing
Roof deck
Rough-in

Mechanical
Electrical
Plumbing
Bill for extras
Drywall hung
Trim & cabinets

Flooring
Tile
Plumbing fixtures
Painting
Electricians finished
Floors complete
Last doorknob

FINAL HIGH

PARTY

Mood Level

BIDS

CONTRACTS

Contracts, including the array of those available from the American Institute of Architects, offer substantial protection. But they cannot guarantee a good working relationship any more than a prenuptial agreement ensures a happy marriage. Instead of trying to nail down every contingency at the outset, which tends to set up an adversarial relationship, pick someone you trust and can comfortably talk through the rough spots. Performance clauses may sound appealing, but they are hard to enforce and rarely have the desired effect, partly because they can cause contention in the working relationship.

—Marco Pasanella and Anne Krueger

If I Had a Hammer...

The pros and cons of doing your own remodeling

Steve Thomas, former host of the acclaimed television series *This Old House*, and author of *This Old House Kitchens* and *This Old House Baths,* two very successful books, undertook his first home renovation project in 1974. He has renovated his own 1836 Colonial Revival and 1846 Greek Revival homes, among numerous others. Now pursuing his own projects, he offers us some sage advice on tackling remodeling jobs in any home, no matter how humble.

ⓘ INSIDE INFO

How Long Is a Lifetime?

O *Nothing really lasts forever, of course, but some materials do have greater durability. If you're undecided about whether to put down vinyl or ceramic tiles in your new kitchen, for example, this life-expectancy list can help.*

	YEARS
Slate roof	50 to 100
Wood shingle roof	25
Asphalt shingle roof	15 to 30
Chimney, fireplace, and brick	100
Drywall and plaster	up to 70
Paint	5 to 10
Wallpaper	7
Ceramic tiles	100 or more
Oak or pine floors	100
Carpeting	11
Wood siding	10 to 100
Vinyl siding	50
Aluminum siding	20 to 50
Brick or concrete patio	24
Wood deck	15
Asphalt driveway	10
Swimming Pool	18

SOURCE: *Residential Inspection Guide,* U.S. Dept. of Housing and Urban Development.

◘ Which remodeling jobs can a homeowner take on without too much difficulty?

It really depends on your skill level. If you're willing to put in the time to do a quality job, just about anyone can improve the cosmetic appearance of their home with some fresh paint and new wallpaper, for example. Another type of remodeling job that can be accomplished with few skills but a substantial amount of sweat equity is landscaping. Though many homeowners overlook its importance, landscaping is one of the few renovations that can dramatically increase the value of your home. You should treat landscaping as another renovation project that needs to be well planned and budgeted.

◘ Which jobs are better left to the experts?

Any job that is potentially dangerous or involves meeting building codes should be done by a licensed expert. That would include electrical, plumbing, heating and roofing work. In addition, any job that has to do with critical structural elements, such as load-bearing walls, should be done by a pro.

◘ What's a good starting point for a novice to gain more expertise?

One of the best ways to enhance your level of experience is to specialize in an area of renovation, such as painting or carpentry. Focusing on one aspect will allow you to build upon your experience and over time to acquire more skills and better tools. You should start with a simple project. Building a deck, for example, requires relatively average carpentry skills, but you can learn a tremendous amount about renovation by going through the process. It's a good starting point—from getting the proper permit to creating a good set of plans and buying the right tools.

◘ What are some of the common mistakes that do-it-yourself remodelers make?

For one thing, they generally underestimate the time it's going to take to complete the project. When budgeting, they fail to allow for a contingency of at least 25 percent to cope with unforeseen problems. Difficulties can arise and you may well need to allow time and money to resolve them.

Often, they underestimate the importance of the design process. It's crucial to work with a design professional who can not only help you create the home you want, but also has the foresight to articulate the details of the process from the structural to the ornamental.

How can pitfalls be avoided?

Having a great set of detailed plans will ensure that the work is done in the correct sequence and that the job goes smoothly for all involved. Homeowners who invest a substantial amount of time in the planning phase can potentially save between 20 and 30 percent in the overall cost of their renovation.

When working with a contractor, there is a tendency to take the lowest bid, which may end up costing a homeowner more in the end. It's wise to solicit bids from a number of contractors and compare them carefully. For a successful bid competition, you'll need to provide complete and detailed specifications to ensure that everybody is bidding on exactly the same project. The more decisions you can make about materials, finishes and detailing before asking for bids, the easier it will be to select a contractor and the fewer problems you will have once he begins the job.

Knock, Knock. "Who's There?"
Inviting the past to your doors

Hardware can be the great finishing touch in a renovation project, and for homeowners who are restoring an old house or apartment, the right touch is often a period knob, hinge or door knocker. But a house does not have to be old to be flattered by a period piece. Vintage hardware can also enrich a modern white box.

Charles Lockwood, author of *Bricks and Brownstone,* and a specialist in restoration, points out that "19th-century New Yorkers were very proud of their hardware"—as were other well-to-do homeowners across the country—so there is a rich trove of salvaged fine period hardware or reproductions of them to be found all across the country in specialty hardware houses. Here are a few examples:

• **House of Antique Hardware** in Portland, Ore. (888-223-2545 or www. houseofantiquehardware.

TIMELY TIPS

How to Stencil a Floor
You can find great patterns online

Stenciling a wood floor can be a challenge for novices, as well as time-consuming, so for a beginner, you might want to start with a basic project such as a repeating design as a border along the walls. Greek key patterns and other geometrics are simple to plan, as long as you measure carefully so that the patterns line up and meet correctly. Use masking tape to get the lines straight.

✔ Many stencil patterns are downloadable online for free. Simply transfer the design to thin Mylar and cut it out with an X-Acto knife. If you prefer to buy stencils, check out a craft store or www.stencil-werks.com, which offers more than 3,000 patterns.

✔ To do a proper job, you need to sand the floor and apply a single sealer coat of polyurethane, well-dried and lightly sanded. Then tape your stencil in place, dabbing on or spraying paint or stain and allowing it to dry thoroughly. Now peel

up the stencil and repeat. When the entire stencil design is in place, apply several coats of clear polyurethane. Water-based polyurethane is recommended because oil-based varieties tend to yellow.

✔ If you like the look of the grain of your floor, consider using a thin single coat of artist acrylics to let it show through. Or if you prefer pure color, build up several applications of paint. If you want a truly opaque design, start with a white primer.

—Stephen Treffinger

com). Has original hardware and also does custom reproductions.

• **Historic Houseparts** in Rochester, N.Y. (888-558-2329 or www.historichouseparts.com). Bathroom hardware.

• **Liz's Antique Hardware** in Los Angeles, Calif. (323-939-4403 or www.lahardware.com). Sells doorhandles cast in bronze and based on a 19th-century design, as well as vintage iron doorknobs and plates dating from the early 20th century.

• **Van Dyke's Restorers,** in Woonsocket, S.D. (800-558-1234 or www.vandykes.com). Antique door hardware.

• **Crown City Hardware** in Pasadena, Calif. (800-950-1047 or www.crowncityhardware.com). Victorian-style interior doorknobs and plates, as well as reproductions of 19th-century hinges

—Marianne Rohrlich

Taming Monster Spaces

"McMansions" pose a decorating challenge. Here's how to meet it

The number of large houses (those bigger than 4,500 square feet) built annually has more than doubled in recent years, according to the National Association of Home Builders. The result is an epidemic of vast living areas that often look as cavernous and appealing as airport lounges. It's enough to make a housewife desperate.

Taming the jumbo room is mostly about restoring human scale. Here are a few ways to do it.

Use furniture to define "rooms" within the overall space. For example, if you have a space 20 feet by 60 feet, divide it into three areas: eating, talking and playing games by the fire. Sideboards

---

✔ **TIMELY TIPS**

Living Large in Small Rooms

In more modest-scale rooms, by contrast, the challenge tends to be squeezing in everything you want to do. To live large in tight spaces, try these tricks:

✔ **Use furniture that has more than one function,** like a coffee table that can be raised for eating. Or use the same spot for different tasks at varying times of day. A studio apartment in New York has a bookcase that runs from one end to the next. At night, portions of it swing out on hinges to create a bedroom; by day, they reconfigure to form a designer's workspace.

✔ **Paint the rooms in warm, but not dark colors** to create a cozy feel for small rooms.

✔ **Mirror the walls** to create an illusion of depth where there is none.

---

can be used to separate the dining table from the seating area and the conversation area from the fireside furniture. Rugs are used to further reinforce the groupings

Don't fill an oversize room with oversize furniture. It only pushes people further apart and inhibits conversation. Even if you have a living area the size of a basketball court, massive chairs are not going to make it more comfortable. Your legs and arms are the same length no matter how large your home.

Color can help to tame the scale. Light floors and dark ceilings will bring an intimidating height down to size. A taupe ceiling, for example, will make a study feel cozy. Another way to break down a larger space is to highlight moldings. Paint a picture molding blue-gray to encircle the room.

Or highlight window or door openings with other strong (but not too strong) shades. In a more standard space, 9 feet by 12 feet, you may want to pick just one element, a crown molding for example, and highlight it more gently with a softer tint.

Don't be afraid to consider patterns. A pattern on the walls also helps to break down a jumbo expanse into more pleasing sizes.

You can shrink a room with lamps, making even a cavern seem snug. An impressive chandelier on the ceiling can provide decorative sheen, but the real light, the one by which you read the paper must come from some nearby source. The best of the great rooms have pools of light clustered on furniture groupings and accented by some pretty fixture overhead. Many soft lamps (not brighter than 40 watts) at eye height will bathe guests in a flattering glow.

—Marco Pasanella

The Secret World of Decorators
What you don't know could cost you

Few relationships are more fraught than the one between client and decorator—the only respectable business relationship in which a perfect stranger is in your bedroom within 20 minutes of meeting you, as one designer put it.

The services a decorator renders are often impossible to pin down. There is no right way or wrong way to decorate a room. Nor can a price tag be put on taste, or a so-called good eye.

In today's economy, traditional billing methods are being tested by a savvy new consumer who wants to know what things cost. The old-school approach usually involves a designer's fee plus a markup—usually 25 to 40 percent—on all the furnishings the decorator buys at the to-the-trade price.

> **ⓘ INSIDE INFO**
>
> ## Fun Begins When Children Leave
>
> ○ Nearly a quarter of all spending on home improvement is being done by "zoomers" and "single empty nesters," according to NPD, the market research group, referring to couples and single parents 50 to 64 who have no children under 18 at home.
>
> ○ Projects people undertake: Enlarged, updated kitchens; bathroom complexes with ensuite dressing rooms; deluxe home offices.
>
> —Jane Margolies

Thanks to the easy availability of showroom catalogs and glossy design magazines, and the arrival of eBay and Sotheby's and Christie's online, people have a much better idea what things cost. Designers are trying to figure out how to get reasonable fees for their creative services, which have expanded far beyond furniture procurement.

What's more, stores like ABC Carpet & Home, Crate & Barrel and other retailers have started producing furniture even a picky decorator might purchase. And what client is going to be happy paying a designer markup on something picked up effortlessly in a place like that?

One of the most difficult parts of the design business for the savvy consumer to fathom is the inscrutable relationship between designers and their sources for custom-made furnishings. Custom design is a highly inexact art, with prices fluctuating depending upon many factors, including the availability of fabric and workers, and the due date. Nearly all of the more than a dozen designers interviewed for this article said they had at some point been approached by suppliers and manufacturers more than willing to pad their bills for the decorator.

While many designers defend the old system as the most equitable and most respectful of the designer's talent, a growing number of younger designers are working more on a business school model as consultants, billing by the hour (built-in protection with indecisive clients), charging an agreed-upon lump sum or a day rate and sometimes even using the client's own credit card to pay for purchases directly. More and more designers are spelling out their fees in lengthy contracts.

—Julie V. Iovine

Ready-to-Eat Kitchens

Big home retail stores sell and install whole kitchens, from soup to nuts.

O f the hundreds of thousands of kitchens renovated each year, more than half of such renovations are done by homeowners themselves, and many others by the top-to-bottom services of big retail stores. The stores' popularity is easy to understand. One-stop planning, purchasing and installation cut the annoyances, and eliminating the middleman reduces the price. That's the theory, anyway.

To see what kind of kitchens they deliver, the *Times* asked four companies—Ikea, Boffi, Expo Design Center and the Home Depot to renovate the same 10-by-10-foot kitchen. Each company was given a sheaf of photos, a rough floor plan and a request for a design at their best value. More than $50,000 separated the most expensive plan (Boffi) from the least expensive (Ikea). Here's what we learned:

ADVANTAGES OF GOING OFF-THE-RACK

Beyond the cost advantages, you can expect:

• Hourlong initial design consultations, with courteous, patient service.

• Once you buy their merchandise, the design retainer fee is recouped. Ikea's consultations are free.

• Good quality of design and space planning; all make it easy to envision options.

When we investigated, this is what we found you could expect to get at each price point:

Priciest: Boffi's extra-chunky stainless steel counters are almost twice the standard thickness, and cost roughly twice as much as stainless counters from commercial kitchen supply stores. The finish is nearly as lustrous as sterling silver, rather than the familiar brushed tin. The same level of finish is found in Boffi's luxuriously shiny and indestructible polyester-coated cabinets. Even the utensil drawers have the confident thunk of a Mercedes door.

Mid-price: Expo Design Center renovated the kitchen with cherry cabinets, granite counters, Viking range, G.E. microwave-vent and floor refinishing. The Omega Embassy cabinets selected by Expo were plywood, not the less durable particleboard, with substantial stainless drawer slides. Expo's granite is…well, granite—but the price per square foot installed is competitive with that of specialty stone suppliers.

Mid-price: The Home Depot's package included maple cabinets, Silestone counters, G.E. Profile appliances in stainless steel, a porcelain sink and installation. Their KraftMaid cabinets are also appealing, if a little less solid than Expo's. The Home Depot recommended counters of Silestone, a low-maintenance synthetic that looks fake.

Low-end: Ikea provided cabinets with doors made of gray-stained solid ash and frosted glass; Hi-Macs solid acrylic counters; Frigidaire appliances; Ikea plumbing fixtures and installation. At the low end, Ikea's cabinets are heftier than its furniture,

My Stove Is Bigger Than Your Stove

Just in case 100 people show up for dinner

Based on surveys done in 2005 by *Remodeling Magazine,* the national average for mid-range kitchen renovations these days is $43,862—and that doesn't even buy you any granite. For kitchens of the custom cherry cabinet and granite countertop variety, the national average is $81,552. And numbers upward of $150,000 are possible.

The centerpieces of these kitchens are often Viking six-burner professional gas stovetops, almost inevitably in stainless steel (www.vikingrange.com). These brutish-looking appliances have the same expensive bulky aesthetic as S.U.V.'s—and seem to serve a similar purpose. Just as the average Expedition driver doesn't tool around in the backwoods very often, neither does the average Viking owner often whip up meals for 100.

Having a cool kitchen is as important as having the right car or the right watch. The kitchen-great-room combination has become the center of casual entertaining. So the Viking stovetop is as important a piece of status décor as the Thomasville mahogany dining room set of the 1960's or the Seth Thomas grandfather clock of the 1840's.

Furniture-quality cabinetry is another prime showoff item. Dave Leonard, co-owner of the Kennebec Company in Bath, Me. (207-443-2131 or www.kennebeccompany.com) a purveyor of such work, creates sumptuous kitchens with features that the casual visitor might miss: the 700 Series Sub-Zero (www.subzero.com) refrigerator, for example, hidden, along with a full-size freezer, behind the rich stained wood cabinets. Refrigerators and freezers are not only well hidden now, but spread around the kitchen—a drawer with cold soft drinks over here, a drawer with frozen pork chops somewhere across the room.

Evidence of children and pets is often hidden as well. Children's things go inside individual lockers in the mud room. And definitely no magnets on the refrigerator.   —Debra Galant

and they offer good value, with fully extendable drawers and substantial drawer bottoms, three-eighths of an inch thick. Ikea's hardware may look a little skimpy, but it's easily replaced. Hi-Macs, the acrylic material Ikea recommended for countertops, is durable and stain-resistant.

DISADVANTAGES

Gaining access to a store's expertise can be hard. To meet with a staff designer, who helps you lay out your space and select materials, most of the companies require a retainer.

In some cases, store designers working on commission have incentives to sell customers as much as possible, so they sometimes overload the kitchen. Everyone was quick—overly quick to replace things like a charming old-fashioned stove and two-year-old refrigerator. Each company also called for generous drawers. None of the designers pointed out, for example, that cabinets with drawers are typically 15 percent more expensive than those with doors. None of the designers consulted suggested restoring the moldings. Only some of the designers proposed painting the peeling walls.

Only one of the stores' designers actually saw the kitchen. For that reason, designers may have been hampered because they had only secondhand information, and could not consider the kitchen in relation to other rooms. Some companies do send a measurer who, in turn, conveys the dimensions, and in some cases photographs, to the designer. But the person with the tape measure would rarely take note of where the morning sun comes in or what style furniture is in the living room.

While an individual designer usually sees a renovation through from concept to completion, the store designers generally trade off their completed design to a project manager, who takes over the supervision and completion of the work. When a hollow wall turns out to be solid or a pipe pops up in an unexpected place, the project manager, not the designer adapts the design.

The nuts-and-bolts execution is the stores' biggest challenge. Most store designers hire subcontractors to do the actual work.

Many of the stores may often require full payment up front, rather than in stages, as is the norm when an individual designer supervises the job. So when things do go wrong, customers are left with little leverage.

The construction crew is hired by the companies, which also gives the consumer little or no leverage. Customers may be able to avoid these problems by asking about the specific crew assigned to the job—how many kitchens has it done, and how much experience does it have? Alternatively, customers may want to hire their own contractors.

Despite the range of prices quoted, the four schemes displayed a remarkable uniformity: two rows of boxes set across from each other and a fixation on stainless steel. A store designer is unlikely to offer any radical ideas, like liquid crystal lighting, or even mildly adventurous ones, like open slotted racks for dish storage.

Naturally, the vendors specified only those products carried by their employers. But the best kitchens usually come from a wide and imaginative variety of sources. With a little more flexibility, Ikea's frosted-glass cabinets could be paired with a colorful glass mosaic tile backsplash. Or the Ikea cabinet shells—"carcasses," as they are called in the trade—could be given upgraded doors like solid oiled walnut with nickel-plated flush pulls.

—Marco Pasanella

Concrete Is Oh-So Decorative
It can be more expensive than granite and comes in a rainbow of colors

Decorative concrete, as it is called, took off in the 1990's as designers and consumers discovered its minimalist beauty. It now comes in a rainbow of colors and finishes—mixed with sand, crushed glass and other aggregates—and is used not only for counters but also for bathroom vanities, fireplaces and even beds. At about $80 to $120 a square foot (more in the hands of some artisans), it can be more costly than granite and Corian. And despite its durable image, it can crack and stain. Don't even think about cutting a lemon or spilling red wine on most concrete counters.

But to ease the concerns of fussier consumers, some fabricators have concocted secret recipes, finishes and cleaning methods to keep concrete looking spiffy.

Sonoma Cast Stone, in Petaluma, Calif., entered the field with NuCrete, which is described as stainproof and comes with a money-back guarantee. Just wipe down and wax occasionally. INFORMATION: 877-939-9929 or sonomastone.com.

Another option is Geocrete, made by Cheng Design in Berkeley, Calif. While Geocrete provides a lustrous finish, the company says it is by no means acidproof. The owner, Fu-Tung Cheng, recommends a nontoxic penetrating sealer, wiping up quickly after spills and a light monthly waxing. INFORMATION: 510-849-3272 or www.chengdesign. com.

Stain- and chip-resistant concrete is also made by David Hertz, an architect in Santa Monica, Calif. His product, called Syndecrete, is a cement-based composite that contains minerals and recycled materials like beer bottles and CD's. It comes with an acrylic seal. Some owners wax their Syndecrete daily for a smooth, clean look; others prefer a well-worn surface. INFORMATION: 310-829-9932 or www.syndesisinc.com.

Concrete without a fancy name is still used by custom fabricators like Get Real Surfaces in Poughkeepsie, N.Y. To preserve the concrete's finish, the company applies a solvent-based acrylic sealer and suggests a monthly rubdown with wax. For those with no time to care for their concrete, the company offers a maintenance contract, which includes one service visit by a maintenance person who sands, cleans and polishes the surfaces, which is "like getting an oil change," said Avis Bishop, an owner of Get Real Surfaces. INFORMATION: 845-452-3988 or www.getrealsurfaces.com.

—Ernest Beck

Behind Closed Doors

Advice for going into the closet

Closets, along with kitchens and bathrooms, now form part of a holy trinity of domestic obsession. Americans spend more than $2 billion on closet renovations, according to *Closets*, a magazine devoted to home organization.

A closet by one of the cost-conscious renovation companies can come in at under $1,000, including a free initial consultation. By contrast, a dressing area designed by an architect can easily set you back in the tens of thousands (if you spring for fancy hardware, lots of drawers and few dozen bubinga wood hangers). There are definite cost benefits to using some of the cheaper companies; the trade-off is that you may need time and skill to install the closet components yourself. Although the details of their offerings are prone to change, here is some idea of how some closet companies worked, the last time we checked:

California Closets (800-336-9178 or www.calclosets.com) helps the client envision the fin-

---

☑ TIMELY TIPS

Where to Stash a Flat-Screen TV

These days a television can't be too big or too thin

Buying one of those skinny flat-screen sets is the easy part; finding a place for it is another. Unlike the old graceless, hulking box, best stashed behind closed doors, the svelte new sets seem designed for display.

✔ Some decorators have put them on poles like flags or hung them like art, which can require rewiring and replastering of walls. A competing impulse—to make the flat screen disappear once the show is over—can entail its own logistics. As prices for flat screens drift downward, designers and architects are grappling with other ways to make them look like natural parts of the scenery.

✔ A rising number of smaller flat-screen sets make the job easier. Ten-inch L.C.D. flat-panel sets, for example, can fit virtually anywhere,

✔ Once purchased, a flat screen has to be given a semipermanent place. Flat-screen sets have components that require more space than the screen, which is only inches deep. And then there's the peripheral equipment. VCR's, for example, are still 22 inches deep.

—Amy Goldwasser

---

ished product, by means of a sketch showing the location of every sundress and pair of jeans and gives a price and estimated installation date. Their price included installation.

Another company, Clos-ette (212-337-9771 or www.clos-ette.com) offered a free consultation, but after that it charged a small fee for the design. If you live outside of New York, they give three estimates from custom mill workers in your area to make and install this layout. The customer is allowed to select and pay the contractor.

✓ **TIMELY TIPS**

Closeted Potential

✔ Since your closet is an extension of your bedroom, why not make a virtue of it? Use a dramatic color to brighten it, such as Exotic Red by Benjamin Moore. This fire-engine color is pretty cheering at any time of day.

✔ The small size of most closets means you can often afford to line them with expensive hand blocked wallpapers. Especially appealing are the 18th- and 19th-century reproduction papers from Adelphi Paper Hangings, a small company with headquarters in The Plains, Va., whose reproduction papers hang in the Lincoln Room at the White house and at Colonial Williamsburg (518-284-9066 or www.adelphipaperhangings.com).

—Mitchell Owens

Its typical custom closet ran from $15,000 to $20,000, installed. Clos-ette is unusual, in that light demolition, painting and patching are part of the package.

EasyClosets.com (800-910-0129 or www.easyclosets.com) offered an online design tool that allows you to plan the closet yourself. Assuming you have the right browser, the planner is easy to use. Anticipating that some of us need to talk to a person rather than tap at a keyboard, EasyClosets also gave customers the option of faxing closet dimensions to its designers. They take your measurements and do a design for you for free. The price of the closet may vary widely, depending on what features you choose.

The Container Store (888-266-8246 or www.containerstore.com) closet, uninstalled, can be as low as $500. Customers generally meet with a designer at one of its stores. The designer shared

EasyCloset's long-distance disadvantage because they never see the closet space firsthand.

Installation is as important as design in determining which supplier works best for you. When we investigated, only California Closets was using its own crew, which provided the most streamlined solution. EasyClosets and the Container Store required that you install their shelves and hanging rods, although both companies offered a referral to services that would do it at additional cost. And both companies said that you need little expertise to do it yourself, though EasyClosets required that you cut the metal track and closet rods with a hacksaw, hardly a standard toolbox item.

—Marco Pasanella

Shelves That Last a Lifetime

Why bother with built-ins when you can get these off-the-shelf?

Along with built-ins, which can be expensive, there are many great shelving systems that vary widely in the way they are configured, what the shelves (and tracks) are made of and how they go up. Check your walls (and your lease) before shopping: some systems require strong wallboard and studs while others are free-standing.

The Container Store (800-733-3532 or www.containerstore.com) sells a simple, easy-to-install shelving system called Elfa. Its shelves come in two lengths and four depths, allowing one or more to hold a laptop or an in-basket while the others hold books. Shelf choices include white melamine, beech and walnut veneer. The top track and the hanging standards can be ordered in three lengths or custom cut.

For something with a bit more style, BoConcept, the Danish contemporary furnishings chain, makes shelving that seems to float. Installation involves screwing brackets into wall studs. The solid-looking shelves are two-inch-thick particle board with a white laminate or a wood veneer (wenge, cherry, walnut or maple). They can hold up to 33 pounds. The shelves are 8 ¾ inches deep and come in two widths, 30 ¾ inches and 59 inches. Brackets, free with the shelves, come in sets of two or three.

You can install one set or many, and arrange the shelves however you like: staggered, unevenly spaced, random or one over the other. For store locations: www.boconcept.com.

Moss, the trendy New York City design store (806-888-6677 or www.mossonline.com), sells a high-end system of shelving by Vitsoe, a British company. Called the 606 Universal Shelving System, it was designed in 1960 by Dieter Rams and has been produced ever since with only slight changes along the way.

Materials are basic: anodized aluminum and steel shelves and poles, and lacquered beech or laminated cabinets and shelves. Some of the cabinets have fold-down doors, and others have doors that slide inside. The system starts with vertical posts. They can be free-standing, or wall-supported for heavy loads. They can also be compressed, fitting between ceiling and floor. An "E track" is mounted to the posts or to the wall to give support. There are no brackets: the shelves sit on the E track with the help of small pins.

Components are sold individually and include such options as cabinets, drawers, sloping shelves for magazines or a dictionary, even a workspace. They come in two widths and in several depths.

The system has a look of permanence yet it is easy to take down and pack up. And it is so clean-lined it can fit in almost any interior. Because of the components' variety, you can always modify or expand the configuration.

—Stephen Treffinger

The Luminous Life of Paint

An artist's advice on how to make your home beautiful with paint

Donald Kaufman, a well-known color field painter and architectural color guru, has worked with architects and designers such as I. M. Pei and Philippe Starck. He and his wife, Taffy Dahl, have explored color theory in two books, *Color: Natural Palettes for Painted Rooms* and *Color and Light: Luminous Atmospheres for Painted Rooms*. The Donald Kaufman Color Collection, (www.donaldkaufmancolor.com) his line of paint colors, remains a perennial favorite. Here, Donald Kaufman has some genuinely practical tips for choosing paint for the home.

Start by noticing which colors are already in and around your home. An old rug, a painting, a stone terrace outside the house or even a favorite pair of pants may provide the perfect inspiration. Computers can help turn these colors into paint, but they have limited formulas. Getting a painter to mix the paint often results in more complex colors.

Understand the psychological effects of color. People have different reactions to cool and warm colors. Cool colors—especially blues and violets—tend to create a sense of darkness and depression. They are the most difficult to use successfully because of these unsettling effects. Warm colors—reds, oranges and yellows—are generally more pleasing and fulfill the basic human need for light. For this reason, they account for nearly 90 percent of the paints on store shelves. Warm colors are a safe choice for the dining room and kitchen because they improve the look of food. They also flatter the skin color of guests surrounding the table. If a cool color is a must, use green or a blue that has some yellow in it.

Not All Paints Are Created Equal

Latex paints are getting better, and they are safer than oil-based

In the past, smooth, hard finishes were the decided advantage of oil-based paints. Advances in paint chemistry, however, have improved the performance of latex paints, and they are now preferable for a number of reasons.

Latex paints are water based, and therefore easy to work with, since they can be thinned with water, and paint splatters can be wiped away with a damp sponge before they dry. Latex dries quickly, does not yellow and has less odor. At one time latex paints were more likely to show brush strokes and less able to cover stains, and they were less durable than oil paints as well. Manufacturers point to improvements on all three counts.

All of which is a good thing, because oil-based paints are coming under increasing scrutiny from the Environmental Protection Agency (epa. gov/iaq/voc.html) and others. A variety of health problems, including rising asthma rates in cities like New York and Los Angeles have been linked to the presence of volatile organic compounds (V.O.C.'s) in oil-based paints. V.O.C.'s have also been identified as significant contributors to smog. Though nearly all latex paints emit some V.O.C.'s, they do so at relatively low levels, and there are now several low-V.O.C. latex paints, including Eco Spec by Benjamin Moore (benjaminmoore.com) and Lifemaster 2000, from a company called ICI (icipaintstores.com).

In choosing your paint finish, remember that glossier finishes are harder and more durable. Use them in high-wear or high-humidity areas, such as on woodwork or in kitchens and bathrooms. Low-luster finishes generally have greater hiding power. Use them on walls and ceilings.

—Stephen Treffinger and Danny Hakim

Take the time to test samples. A major complaint about final paint jobs is that they are too bright. Colors on a paint swatch appear twice as bright and twice as light when applied to a wall. Therefore, an adequate mock-up is essential. Paint a five-foot-wide sample swath from floor to ceiling. Block out existing colors with your hand and see how the new colors interact with the room and especially with the color of the floor. Look at the test area at different times of the day to see how it reacts to fluctuations in natural light and to artificial light at night. People who want to paint a brightly colored room a neutral color should prime the entire room before trying samples. Reflected light from strong colors will alter the perceived color of the mock-up.

Brighten rooms. The common solution to a dark room is throwing white paint on the walls to reflect more light. But the lack of light generally makes the white room look washed-out and gray. A better solution is to use a warmer and deeper color, which often can provide the luminosity that is missing from the room. Yellows are particularly effective, because the color value can be kept light enough while still adding warmth.

Enlarge living spaces. If you have light-colored floors, choose a deeper wall color and a light ceiling color to reflect the floor. Walls will appear to recede above the floor. If you have dark floors, keep walls and ceiling light and the same color. Eyes are attracted to contrast, and high contrast between walls and ceiling closes spaces. Some people think they can lift a ceiling by painting it white. That is often the case, because a white ceiling reflects more light. But if there's already plenty of light, similarly colored walls and ceiling can make a room appear more open and atmospheric.

Use the same trim color throughout a number of rooms. The wall color in each room will make the trim appear different. Keep the trim lighter than the walls. Using darker trim colors can be beautiful, but it is much more difficult to pull off.

Think about how the colors of adjoining rooms interact. Colors in abutting rooms tend to reinforce each other—which can have dramatic or unpleasant results. A subtle beige room can appear much stronger if viewed from a subtle blue room, and vice versa. Also, thinking about rooms as a series of colors can make cramped quarters seem roomier. For a three-room apartment, if the kitchen and living room have light, warm colors, a bedroom with stronger and deeper colors can provide a perfect escape.

Address the architecture. Architectural details can be divided into two categories—structural and decorative. Neutral colors work better with structural details such as columns or door frames. Something that looks like it provides support is not the place for a pale peach color. Decorative colors would be more appropriate with friezes and other ornate moldings.

Use top-of-the-line paint from any of the major manufacturers. It lasts the longest and provides the best coverage. Don't overlook regional paint companies. Their top paints are just as good and sometimes better. But preparation is all-important. Clean, smooth surfaces lead to the best results.

And remember, there are no bad colors. Colors change and create different perceptions depending on where and how they are used. A very bright, garish green might seem a bad color for a dining room, but it could be absolutely beautiful as a thin stripe underneath crown molding in a beige living room.

Fixing the Light Fantastic

The right lighting will flatter, accent and fill a home with warmth

For years lighting design has been nearly an afterthought for many residential architects and general contractors. The attitude was, what more could there be than a ceiling-mounted fixture in the center of the room or a homeowner's table lamps? But such light fixtures often tend to call attention to themselves and cast shadows in unflattering ways. Here, lighting designer Randall Whitehead, author of *Residential Lighting: A Practical Guide* and *Lighting Design Sourcebook: 600 Solutions for Residential and Commercial Spaces,* tours the home and offers some advice on lighting.

THE ENTRY. The entrance sets the mood and tone for the rest of the house. In the entryway, lighting can be used to open up the space and provide a welcoming environment for guests. Make sure lights create a warm glow. Avoid harsh shadows by using uplighting instead of recessed downlights.

THE LIVING ROOM. The goal here is to create a soft island of illumination that invites people in to relax and converse. Layering the light creates an environment that is humanizing and dramatic. Wall sconces and torchères can generally provide ambient illumination, which softens shadows on people's faces and fills the room with a soft glow. Recessed adjustable fixtures or track lighting can be utilized to provide the necessary accent light for artwork, plants or tabletops. But be sure not to let accent lighting overpower you or your company.

THE DINING ROOM. This is where dramatic lighting can come into play. Wall sconces are a good source of ambient lighting in this room. A chandelier should only give the illusion of providing

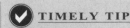

TIMELY TIP

The Right Shade for the Right Lamp

In any given room, shades should be in the same simple style, either white or cream and made of fabric or paper. Simple in style means less visual confusion, and the white or cream color ensures an inviting atmospheric glow.

Trimmings, known as *passementerie* in France, are the most effective way to customize plain shades and the easiest to manage—if you can wield a glue gun. They can be gimp, braid or fringe. If you are unsure about the effect, fix them in place with straight pins, allowing easy substitutions if you want a new look.

The important thing is to keep them simple, avoid trimmings with the kind of operatic effusiveness that might look dated in a few years. As decorator Mark Hampton once noted, nothing ages a room more than a fussy lampshade.

—Mitchell Owens

the lighting in the room, as otherwise it will be too bright or distracting. Using recessed, adjustable fixtures on either side of the chandelier will produce the necessary focal point lighting for the table, without eclipsing the decorative fixture.

THE KITCHEN. With today's open floor plan designs, the kitchen should be as inviting as the rest of the house. Mount fluorescent lights above cabinets, so light is bounced off the walls and ceilings, providing ambient lighting. Lights under cabinets provide good, unobstructed task light for the counters. Pendant-hung fixtures can be used for task light where cabinets are not present. Skylights can provide a cheery feeling during the day, and, through the use of fluorescent fixtures mounted in them, will avoid becoming "black holes" at night. A pot rack over a center island may appear to be

a perfect idea, but how do you light work surfaces without creating shadows by trying to light through pots and pans? If you have sloped ceilings, special care must be taken to select fixtures that don't glare into people's eyes. Also, remember that an all-white kitchen is going to require dramatically less light than a kitchen with dark wood cabinets.

BATHROOMS. Lighting at the mirror is most important. Vertically mounted strip fixtures generally provide the best task light. Wall sconces or fluorescent strip fixtures mounted above cabinets, ledges or beams provide the necessary ambient illumination.

BEDROOMS. It is important that there is good color-corrected light, especially in closets, to aid in the selection of properly color-matched clothes. Aside from the usual ambient light concerns, easily adjustable reading lamps at the bed are a must. A "panic switch" for outside lighting is often a desirable feature.

Track Lighting That Disappears

And can create a soft, indirect glow around you

The phrase "track lighting" once conjured up rows of white cans beaming with searing intensity at unlovely paintings. Great strides have been made since then in the quality, design and versatility of the light fixtures. Some track systems are now honestly quite beautiful.

Lightolier (www.lightolier.com), the company that invented track lighting in 1961, continues to update its fixtures, all compatible with Lightolier's most common residential track, Lytespan. Their fixtures can be adapted with filters to even out spots on the wall, adjustable visors and louvers to hide the bulb, and "snoots," typically cylinders that help focus the light and reduce glare.

For those who don't mind replacing the track

INSIDE INFO

The Right Bulb for the Right Light

○ **FLUORESCENT.** Once derided as cold, unfriendly illumination, new technology has increased its usefulness: there are over 200 color variations, and much greater dimming possibilities. Now people can use energy-efficient fixtures without totally sacrificing the warm glow of more traditional light sources.

○ **INCANDESCENT.** The first light source created, appreciated for its warm, amber illumination, but its color tonality shifts colors within a given space—reds turn orange, whites go yellow, and blues shift to green. Be aware of this when you choose paints and fabrics.

○ **QUARTZ AND TUNGSTEN HALOGEN.** An improvement in incandescent lighting, they provide a whiter source of illumination, so colors are truer. Quartz lamps produce twice as much illumination as standard lamps using less wattage.

○ **H.I.D.** (high intensity discharge). Used mostly in commercial and landscape lighting—e.g., most streetlights. The mercury vapor and metal halide varieties are seeing more use in residential landscape designs.

as well as the fixtures, Kreon (www.kreon.com) combines qualities of recessed and track lighting. This style of track lighting is appealing to some designers because the fixture is almost invisible.

Whichever system you are choosing, keep these points in mind:

Lighting should be layered: ambient for overall liveliness (typically from an overhead fixture) and area for warmth and definition (from table or standing lamps). Track lights can augment or take the place of an overhead fixture.

Pick a style based on the desired effect. When aimed at the ceiling, track lights with a wide beam

create a soft indirect glow, when positioned close to a wall and pointed downward, they can wash it with light, drawing attention to one side of the room. Lights with narrow beams can illuminate a piece of art, a mantelpiece or another element.

Track lights can be suspended from rods, useful when ceilings are high. The rods carry the light closer to its destination, thereby lowering the requisite intensity (light diffuses as it travels). You still want the light to be unobtrusive, so don't position the fixture so low it gets in the way.

—Stephen Treffinger

Frame the World Around You

A picture's display can be the difference between wow! and ho-hum

For millennia, people have understood the importance of using a frame to separate a work of art from its surroundings. Ancient Pompeians framed wall paintings with lines of painted color, while artists in the Middle Ages used wood carved in an ornate Gothic style. Here, Greg O'Halloran (G.O.H.), formerly conservation framer at A.P.F., Inc., in New York; Lou Stovall (L.S.), archival framer and master printer at Workshop, Inc., in Washington, D.C.; and Andrew LaBonte (A.L.), former manager at Haley & Steele in Boston, discuss how to frame art and display it in the home.

THE FRAME

❝ **A good framer will allow the art to make the choice.** If you look at the art, it really can talk to you in terms of what is supposed to surround it. If it is done correctly, you can make a second-rate work of art look like a museum piece. For example, you can't take a scoop molding and put it on an 1850's Bierstadt. A period piece should have a style of frame from the same period. It really has to be a marriage of frame and art." (G.O.H.)

"Aside from aesthetics, the frame has to be sturdy enough to hold the artwork in the glass. A large work requires large moldings. Using a thin frame for a more streamlined look requires extra supports on the back. When it comes to frame styles, the options include gold leaf, burnished frames, ones with antiquing, ornamented styles and plainer models. Generally, people match the frame to the style or period of the art. However, a lot of modern art really works extremely well with antique frames, even very heavily ornamented, gold-leaf frames. It even works well with modern decor." (A.L.)

"You frame for the art. In rare cases, it's okay to frame the art to complement the living environment where the art will be located. Generally speaking, you want the molding to have some sensitivity to the furniture in the room. If you have traditional furniture, you would probably want a traditional frame, such as carved wood. If you have modern or contemporary furniture, you would go for a simple wood, or, most likely, a metal frame. If you have a dining room with brass wall sconces, you might want a brass frame. If you are hanging over wonderful, natural wood paneling, you would probably want a nice maple or cherry frame." (L.S.)

THE MAT

"You always want acid-free, 100 percent cotton mats. You can have single, double or triple mats. Mats set the work back from the glass for protection and give a nice surrounding. I tend to frame with white mats. I don't think much of colored mats, because the art should speak for itself. If the artist required more color around the border, he would have indicated it. But if you are hanging in a dark room painted deep red or forest green, you might consider a colored mat. It softens the blow between the darkness of the room and the art. Mat widths range from 2 $1/2$ to 5 or 6 inches. If something is larger than 36 by 40 inches, chances are you would want a 5 $1/2$ or 6-inch band around it. Anything under 20 inches square, you would want something 2 $1/2$ or 3 inches." (L.S.)

"The bottom border is usually a small increment larger than the top and sides, for visual balance. If you make the margins all the same, the bottom will actually end up looking narrower—it's an ancient principle of proportion. For this reason, columns in Greek architecture are wider at the bottom, and, usually on a chest of drawers, the bottom drawers are wider than the top drawers. A common border size is 3 inches on the top and sides and 3 $1/4$ on the bottom. Instead of using color mats, I paint lines or panels on the mat in the traditional English and French style. Usually, you see this style of mats used on decorative pieces, botanicals, landscapes, things like that. I also wrap mats in pure silks or pure linens. For instance, on Beacon Hill, if someone has watered silk wallpaper, I will do silk mats for their pictures. Silk mats also go well on master drawings." (A.L.)

HANGING THE PICTURE

"With anything large, you want to use Plexiglas because it is light and won't break if the work falls from the wall. With something of value, you want to use UV reflective glass or Plexiglas to diminish the damaging effects of light. Also, you want to place the art on walls washed by light rather than on those with direct light. If you are going to install art lights, you want to place them on the ceiling 30 inches from the wall and at an angle so that light shows brightest on either edge of the frame. You don't want to have the lights on all the time, though. All light takes a toll." (L.S.)

" **One of the largest causes of damage to art and frames is that they fall off the wall.** The wire breaks or mounting screws pull out—so make sure the hardware is top quality. To hang the art on masonry walls, use a masonry screw or drill a hole and insert a lead slug and a lag screw. If you have Sheetrock, traditional hangers will support up to 100 pounds. Anything heavier than that, or if the walls are plaster, I use molly bolts. You should also avoid putting adhesives like glue or tape on the artwork. There are a lot of mechanical mounts that hold the art and work very well." (A.L.)

A Grandfather Clock to Go

Do-it-yourself furniture kits are economical, easy and the quality can surprise

In the 18th century, cabinetmakers spent months crafting furniture for the homes of their well-heeled clients. Today, however, resourceful furniture makers are giving amateurs the opportunity to learn the art of modern furniture-making for themselves.

Furniture kits have become ever more sophisticated in design, with more attention paid to the quality of the woods used in the kits. With many kits, the assembly agony is brief, and the chair doesn't wobble when you are done.

 INSIDE INFO

America's Furniture Mecca

○ More than half of all America's furniture is made in a 200-square-mile region of North Carolina—including the towns of Greensboro, New Bern, High Point and Hickory. There are hundreds of stores and outlets. Some will pay for your lodging if you purchase over a certain amount.

Many companies will sell you their finished pieces for far more than the price of the do-it-yourself kit. But think of the satisfaction you'll get if you put one together yourself. Here are some brief pointers on the assembly:

• Once the kit arrives, check to see that all the pieces are there. Then do what is called a dry-fit assembly: fit all the pieces together before you touch the glue. This step ascertains whether the pieces will assemble as they should.

• Be sure to carefully sand and stain the wood pieces before gluing or fitting them together. Assemble carefully, so as not to mar the stain finish. It may still be necessary to resand and stain.

Here are some sources for furniture kits, and the company's specialties:

Bartley Collection, Denton, Md. Traditional 18th-century-style furniture.
410-479-4480 or www.bartleycollection.com

Shaker Workshops, Concord, Mass. Shaker-style furniture and accessories, and a grandfather clock kit.
800-840-9121 or www.shakerworkshops.com

Wood Classics, Gardiner, N.Y. Teak outdoor furniture. Chairs, tables and swings.
800-385-0030 or www.woodclassics.com

Beds You Won't Lose Sleep On

Almost a third of life is spent sleeping, so take your mattress seriously

Your mattress sags, creaks and wobbles. It's probably time to toss this relic and invest in a new one. Is there any purchase that's more personal? The next time you go mattress shopping, keep these tips in mind from the Better Sleep Council:

A Little Pillow Talk

You will sleep better with the proper headrest

Even if you aren't the Princess and the Pea, you will sleep better with a proper headrest. "Somewhere near 50 percent of the country is sleep deprived" says Dr. James Maas, a professor and sleep researcher at Cornell University, and pillow issues are definitely part of the problem.

The main difference in pillows comes down to down versus synthetic fill, but a good pillow of either stuff should last up to 10 years. You can test your pillow to find out if it's past its prime. You take your pillow and fold it in half. If it doesn't spring forward and open instantly by itself, you've got a dead pillow. Replace it.

Maas says he likes the quality of pillows manufactured by United Feather and Down, an Illinois company whose products, both down and synthetic, sell under various private labels. For instance, United Feather and Down's Insu-loft down and PrimaLoft synthetic-fill pillows are for sale online at thecompanystore.com, Landsend.com, Potterybarn.com and llbean.com.

No matter where you shop, expect to pay from $30 or more for a good synthetic pillow and upwards of $60 for a goose down pillow with a minimum of 550 fill power. Fill power is a measurement of how lofty an ounce of down is and how high it comes up on a beaker after it's compressed. —Michelle Slatalla

SUPPORT: Wear comfortable clothes to your local mattress retailer, so you can lie down on a number of mattresses. The best ones support your body at all points. Pay attention to your shoulders, hips and lower back. Too little support can result in back pain; too much can lead to uncomfortable pressure.

SPACE: Sleepers toss and turn 40 to 60 times a night. If you are constantly fighting your partner for space, it may be time to upgrade to a queen- or king-size bed. Both are several inches longer and wider than the standard double bed.

COIL COUNT: The common innerspring mattress gets its support from tempered steel coils. A full-size version should have more than 300 coils, a queen-size more than 375, and a king-size more than 450.

WIRE GAUGE: The lower the number, the thicker, stronger, and more durable the wire. Stronger coils generally provide better support. Many manufacturers are introducing wire-engineered innersprings that employ lighter wire. They claim these systems make less noise and offer more support. Lie down and shift positions—it's the best way to test these claims and to see which mattress lends your body's curves the most support.

COVER: Look for superior stitching, quality seams and an extra-soft surface. Don't buy a bed based solely on a pretty treatment.

PADDING: Layers of upholstery insulate and cushion the body from the innersprings. Once you've purchased a mattress that meets your comfort needs, remember to flip it regularly from head to toe. This extends mattress life and helps prevent the creation of an uncomfortable impression in the padding.

FOUNDATION: Don't blame a bad night's sleep on the mattress alone. The foundation, or box spring, may also be showing some signs of wear and tear. A mattress and its companion foundation are designed to work as a system. Putting a new mattress on an old foundation can reduce the life and comfort of a mattress.

WARRANTIES: Top brands generally come with 15 years' protection against product defects, but don't let the salesperson sell you a mattress based

Put Some Spring in Your Sofa

If you're in the market for a new sofa, you're probably wondering what makes a hand-made $8,000 sofa any different from one that you can buy for $600 at IKEA. The difference lies in the frame, padding, cushions, springs, fabric and finish.

PADDING: Sofas often wear at the arms because the maker has scrimped on padding. The better sofas have a layer of cotton or polyfiber over a layer of foam. Cheaper sofas have fabric right on top of the foam.

FABRIC: The grade of a fabric determines the price, but is not a measure of the fabric's durability. Grades are based largely on fiber content and on how much waste results from matching the pattern. For durability, consider spending the extra money to treat the sofa with fabric protection.

SPRINGS: Eight-way hand-tied springs used to be a sign of a top-notch sofa. No more. Many less expensive sofas also have them, although they are of inferior quality. A better question: how many rows of springs are used in the seat? The best use four rows.

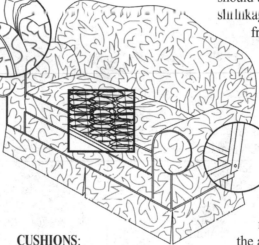

CUSHIONS: Top-quality foam cushions are made from virgin foam with a density of 2.2 pounds per cubic foot. Accept no less than 1.8. Lower-density foam deteriorates more

quickly. If you're looking for a soft down cushion, be sure the cushion has at least 30 percent down feathers in it. Otherwise, you'll be paying for down and getting far less.

FRAME: Maple and other hardwoods that grip nails well make the best frames. The wood should be kiln-dried to prevent shrinkage and warping. The best frames are 1 ½ inches thick. (Experts refer to it as a ⁶/₄ frame.) To keep a sofa from sagging, joints and legs must be firmly attached to the frame. The best joints are double- or triple-doweled at the top corners and firmly attached with reinforcing blocks where the arms meet the seat.

FINISH: Attention to detail makes a difference. In a high-quality sofa, seams are straight, pleats lie flat, corners fill out and cushions have metal zippers.

solely on the warranty. Let comfort and support guide your decision.

FOAM MATTRESSES: Made of a solid core or different types of foam laminated together, these mattresses should come with a minimum density of 2.5 pounds per cubic foot. High-resilience polyurethane and the more traditional latex, or synthetic rubber, mattresses provide the best performance. Memory foam—developed by NASA to cushion

astronauts' bodies during space travel—is another popular (and expensive) component which molds the mattress to the body's curves.

WATERBEDS: Whether you are choosing full motion or waveless, with or without additional lumbar support and memory foam, dual or single mattress systems, make sure the mattress vinyl is a minimum of 20 mil. in thickness, and pay close attention to seam durability.

What's Hidden Under the Rug?

The warp and woof of a well-made carpet

Whether you are looking for basic wall-to-wall carpeting or an oriental masterpiece, picking a good carpet can be a tough job. But you don't need the wisdom of a Confucius or the patience of Job—just a little knowledge of what to look for:

WALL-TO-WALL CARPETS: The first decision is whether to choose wool or a synthetic. Wool is durable and takes color well but it costs a lot more. Polyester used to flatten out with time, but the fibers have been improved and it now holds up pretty well.

The amount of yarn used to make the carpeting is another indication of quality—the more yarn that is used, the more durable the carpet will be. High-traffic areas require a carpet with at least 50 ounces of yarn per square yard. Fibers that have been woven in will last longer than punched-in fibers. Finally, stain protection that has been built in to the carpet is preferable to protection that is sprayed on later.

ORIENTAL CARPETS: They are handmade, usually from wool or silk, in Iran, Pakistan, China, India and Turkey, among other countries. Handmade oriental carpets are almost always better investments than machine-made area rugs. They outlast machine-made carpets by many years and don't cost considerably more. The number of knots per square inch is the usual measure of quality: 100 knots per square inch for a good rug, 300 knots for a better rug, and 600 or more for an exceptional rug. But counting knots can be deceiving. Some rugs, such as lesser-grade Pakistani Bokharas appear to have twice as many knots because the pile yarn is wrapped around the foundation twice.

Wool quality is also important. To test it, scratch the pile. If the rug sheds excessively, don't buy it. Imagine what foot traffic and cleaning will do to it. See, also, "On a Magic Carpet Ride" on page 317.

✔ **TIMELY TIPS**

Out, Out, Damn Spot

Consumer Reports says that these homemade brews will remove stains. For all, blot the spill, then place dry paper towels on the spot. Stand on them a minute, then apply the appropriate series of potions, blotting after each application. End with a cold water rinse and final blotting.

✔ **Pasta sauce or salad dressing** Mix one teaspoon of a clear (not colored) hand dishwashing liquid per one cup of lukewarm water. Hand dishwashing liquid residues can cause rapid resoiling, so rinse thoroughly after using. Note: Never use laundry detergents on upholstery or carpets because they contain optical brighteners that may discolor the fibers or affect light and white colors.

✔ **Wine** Sprinkle fresh stains with club soda. For red wine spills, it might be beneficial to blot; sprinkle on white wine, and blot again. For washable clothing, pouring boiling water through the fabric from a height of 12 inches may help.

✔ **Coffee and tea**
1. Try detergent mixture (see pasta sauce, above).
2. Mix $1/3$ cup of white household vinegar with $2/3$ cup of water. Consumer Union testers also found that Spray 'n Wash stick laundry booster helped remove tea stains.

✔ **Soda, fruits and juices, beer, Kool-aid, chocolate, animal stains**
1. Try the detergent mixture (see salad dressing, above).
2. Mix one tablespoon of household ammonia with $1/2$ cup of water.

SOURCE: *How to Clean Practically Anything,* Consumer Reports Books

Looking Behind the Curtains
*Stitches and strategies that save time
and money*

Few things in the decorating world are more luxurious than dressmaker curtains, the kind that are interlined with bump or domette—thick woven cottons that insulate and block sunlight—and weighted to keep them on the straight and narrow, so to speak. But unless you have unlimited funds or are trying to overcome drafty windows (traditionally made curtains can be thick enough to keep winter's chill at bay), they can seem a bit stodgy.

For a less expensive, 21st-century take on curtains, consider some of the following ideas:

Try sewing together burlap bags in panels of earthy-elegant material to frame the windows of a room with matte paneling the color of driftwood (or walls painted a similar color). Use a cocoa-brown sisal carpet bound in scarlet and some cozy button-tufted furniture upholstered in spicy paisleys, stripes and velvets.

Another great patchwork idea comes from Roger Banks-Pye, a British decorator who died in 1996: cotton gingham napkins in a jaunty blue and white check. You could do something similar by making a grid of old embroidered linen handkerchiefs or colorful thrift-shop scarves.

Artists often have bright ideas when it comes to window dressing. Back in the 1930's the society photographer Cecil Beaton hung the windows of his country house, Ashcombe, with heavy curtains made of hessian, a woven jute speckled with hundreds of white mother-of-pearl buttons sewn in circles, diamonds and stripes.

The elaborate patterns were inspired by the button-bedecked costumes worn by the so-called pearly kings and queens of London parade fame.

(Beaton used the same buttons when he designed the costumes for *My Fair Lady*.) The curtains clicked pleasantly when the windows were left open.

There are also relatively inexpensive ready-made curtains from places like Pottery Barn (888-779-5176 or potterybarn.com). You can jazz them up by attaching wide bands of colorful grosgrain ribbon along the hems with stitching or a glue gun. A heady variety of new and vintage ribbons can be found at Hyman Hendler & Sons, (212-840-8393 or hymanhendler.com).

The famed French textile company Pierre Frey, whose fabrics are typically available in the United States only to the trade, now owns Boussac Fadini and sells its youthful home furnishings in stores. The line includes curtains with large gunmetal grommets that can be threaded onto a hefty wood or metal rod in seconds. For store locations: 212-213-3099.

Don't overlook secondhand curtains at flea markets. They can easily be lengthened with a contrasting band of colored fabric.

—Mitchell Owens

How to Cut Your Heating Bills
Getting a new furnace is expensive, but it might pay off in the end

The frugal American now faces a tough call: the most effective way to cut heating expenses may be to spend thousands of dollars to replace an inefficient furnace.

That one device uses nearly half of the energy piped into your home. Sure, you can save money by tackling the less expensive projects like turning down thermostats, caulking windows and adding insulation. But cost-effective as that is, it has

WEIGHING POTENTIAL SAVINGS FROM A NEW FURNACE

I. FIRST COLLECT THE FOLLOWING INFORMATION:

- ANNUAL HEATING COST— Total winter heating bills, subtracting nonheating energy use, using a bill from May or September as a base.

- EFFICIENCY RATING OF CURRENT FURNACE—Furnaces bought after 1992 should have an annual fuel utilization efficiency (A.F.U.E.) rating. Assume anything older than 15 years is around 65 percent.

- NEW FURNACE AND INSTALLATION COST—Get several estimates for the total cost of installation. Local labor costs, house size and insulation, and extent of new ductwork needed will factor into total cost.

SOURCES: Department of Energy; American Council for an Energy-Efficient Economy

SAVINGS TABLE

EXISTING FURNACE	NEW FURNACE EFFICIENCY RATING (AFUE)								
	55%	60%	65%	70%	75%	80%	85%	90%	95%
50%	$9.09	$16.76	$23.07	$28.57	$33.33	$37.50	$41.24	$44.24	$47.36
55		8.33	15.38	21.42	26.66	31.20	35.29	38.88	42.10
60			7.69	14.28	20.00	25.00	29.41	33.33	37.80
65				7.14	13.33	18.75	23.52	27.77	31.57
70					6.66	12.50	17.64	22.22	26.32
75						6.50	11.76	16.66	21.10
80							5.88	11.11	15.80
85								5.55	10.50
90									5.30

Estimated savings for every $100 currently spent. With fuel costs rising, savings will be greater. Assumes new furnace has the same heat output.

II. THEN ESTIMATE YOUR TOTAL SAVINGS

- YOUR ANNUAL SAVINGS—If your old furnace is A.F.U.E.-rated at 65 percent, your savings per $100 dollars would be $31.57 if you installed a furnace with a 95 percent rating. If your annual fuel bill is $1,500, your annual savings would be 31.57 times 15 or $473.55.

- TIME UNTIL PAYOFF—Divide the investment—say, $4,000—by your annual savings. In this case, it would take more than eight years to break even.

- RETURN ON INVESTMENT— Divide the annual savings by the cost of the installation and multiply that by 100. If the new furnace will cost $4,000, your first year return on investment would be 11.8 percent.

---

its limits. Most new homes are built to be snug, using 22 percent less gas than they did 20 years ago. That leaves you staring at the furnace, which stands between you and several hundred dollars of additional disposable income.

Furnace makers like Carrier or Trane will tell you that you can save as much as 35 percent of your heating bill with a new one. But replacing your old one could cost $2,000 to more than $7,000 depending on its size, type and energy efficiency, as well as local labor rates and the amount of ducting and retrofitting that must be done.

There is no pat answer for this question, but if prices stay high or go even higher, a new furnace could be one of the best investments you will ever make. The problem is that no one can predict the short-term price of natural gas or heating oil, let alone its price in five years. You could stop right here and hope fuel prices drop, but it might be worth running some calculations to see if you would benefit.

Pull out your utility bills to determine how much you spent on heating your home. That is simple with oil because it is used only for heating. With natural gas, take the bills from last winter and subtract what you normally spend in a month like September or May, when you are not running the furnace.

The chart with this article shows you how to calculate your annual savings. The table determines the difference in operating costs between old models and new, fuel-efficient ones. A new furnace can save money because it does not waste as much fuel.

The federal government began requiring in 1992 that furnaces have an annual fuel utilization efficiency, or A.F.U.E., rating of at least 78. With electronic ignitions instead of pilot lights and quiet variable-speed motors, some heaters have ratings as high as 95 percent. You will find, for example, that your new furnace does not need to be as powerful as your old one, because of its greater efficiency. Installing a furnace that is bigger than necessary is a common and costly mistake.

Any good furnace dealer—obtain estimates from several before signing a contract—will help you through these calculations. You may discover, for instance, that you will save as much as $500 a year. If the installation costs $2,000, that means you will recoup your investment in four years.

If you plan to sell your house long before that, you may want to skip this project. Many real estate agents and the furnace dealers themselves say a new furnace does not add much to the resale value of a home. If you plan to keep the house, however, you should look at the expenditure in other ways as well. The American Council for an Energy-Efficient Economy, a Washington advocacy group, suggests consumers use a measure of return on investment. Dividing the annual savings by the cost of the project gives a yield, not unlike a real investment. Using the same numbers as in the example above, you would have an impressive return of 25 percent. It is enough to make you want to start spending to make money.

Figures provided by the federally financed Weatherization Assistance Program Technical Assistance Center suggest that if you can achieve fuel savings of $500 a year over the life of the furnace, an installation cost of up to $5,800 would be cost-effective. Were the annual savings only $250, you might want to draw the line at any project costing more than $3,000.

IF YOU DON'T REPLACE YOUR FURNACE

If the numbers are not convincing, or if your furnace is fine, there are other things you can look into.

Installing new windows usually makes little economic sense. But if you are considering replacing windows for aesthetic reasons, the high cost of fuel will get you a payoff sooner.

Replacing a refrigerator, which typically is responsible for about 6 percent of a home's energy bill, is a consideration. But finding an energy-efficient clothes washer that uses less water might be even smarter because you get to save twice—on the washer's power and on the power used to heat the water.

An old water heater, which accounts for 11 percent of the home energy bill, frequently gets singled out as another money-waster. You can start by insulating the tank and the pipes leading from the tank. Some people are buying tankless water heaters that heat the water only as you need it.

Thermostats that can be programmed to lower the temperature when no one is home can cost less than $100. For every degree you reduce the temperature, you can save 3 percent on heating costs.

As you cost out these projects, do not forget to check the rebates your local utility will offer for these improvements. In addition, the federal Energy Policy Act of 2005 offers tax incentives for homeowners who install new furnaces and water heaters through 2007.

—Damon Darlin

WHEN TO FIX IT, WHEN TO JUNK IT

To help you decide whether to repair or replace an appliance, consult the chart devised by Tom Kraeutler below. In one typical scenario, you're stuck with an air conditioner that dies because the compressor is seven years old. An entirely new system would cost $3,500, but the compressor repair alone would be $950.

According to the chart, a seven-year-old central air conditioner has a low risk of repetitive failure, so it's okay to spend up to 50 percent of the replacement cost on repair. Since the $950 repair cost is 50 percent of the replacement value, go ahead and call for service.

APPLIANCE:	ESTIMATED REPLACEMENT COST[3]	AGE RANGE \ Risk of failure[1] : % REPAIR COST LIMIT[2]		
		Low Risk	Medium Risk	High Risk
FURNACE	$1,500–$3,500	up to 12 years: 30%	12–24 years: 20%	25 years & up: 10%
WATER HEATER	$500–$900	up to 7 years : 30%	7–14 years: 20%	15 years & up: 10%
CENTRAL A/C	$1,800–$4,000	up to 8 years: 50%	8–15 years: 30%	16 years & up: 10%
REFRIGERATOR	$500–$2,200	up to 8 years: 40%	8–15 years: 30%	16 years & up: 20%
KITCHEN RANGE	$500–$1,700	up to 15 years: 30%	15–25 years: 20%	26 years & up: 10%
DISHWASHER	$450–$1,250	up to 10 years: 40%	10–15 years: 30%	16 years & up: 20%
WASHER	$450–$1,500	up to 10 years: 40%	10–15 years: 30%	16 years & up: 20%
DRYER	$450–$1,000	up to 10 years: 50%	10–20 years: 40%	21 years & up: 10%
BUILT-IN MICROWAVE	$350–$1,500	up to 4 years: 20%	4–10 years: 15%	11 years & up: 10%
GARBAGE DISPOSER	$150–$350	up to 1 year[4]:1 year & up: Always replace		—

NOTES: 1. Risk of failure or breakdown increases with age.
2. Percentage indicates minimum cost of repair limit. If cost of repair is greater than percentage of replacement cost shown, then replacement is recommended. If cost of repair is less than percentage of replacement cost show, then repair is likely to be cost-effective.
3. Assumes replacement with like kind and quality as original appliance.
4. Repair disposers only if under manufacturer's warranty. Otherwise, always replace.   © 1995-2005 Squeaky Door Productions, Inc.

Protect Your Castle From Time

From stuck windows to trickling toilets, here's how to fix it yourself

The roof leaks, the basement is damp, and the toilet won't stop running. This scenario represents a homeowner's worst nightmare. But who can afford to call a plumber at the first sign of a leak? Tom Kraeutler, host of The Money Pit Radio Show, and George Pettie, president of the home inspection firm HomeChek Service, have developed the following repair and maintenance guide that will help you protect your number-one investment.

WET BASEMENT

A homeowner once attempted to fix a leaky basement by calling a waterproofing contractor. Quotes ranged from $7,500 to $20,000. Yet he was eventually able to correct his outside drainage and easily fix the problem for under $500. In fact, good gutters and properly sloping soil on a home's exterior can fix 99 percent of wet basement problems.

Start by cleaning out gutters, downspouts and underground drain pipes. A water hose is very useful for flushing out debris. When the accumulated mess in downspouts and drain pipes proves stubborn, rent a power auger to clear a pas-

435

Around the House

MAINTENANCE ●

sageway. If the gutter system doesn't empty into underground pipes, be sure to install downspout extensions that carry water 4 to 6 feet from the foundation. Also, inspect gutters for leaks and sags. Aluminum gutters can be sealed with polyurethane or butyl caulk. Repair sags by removing the spikes that hold the gutter in place, raising the gutter so that it slopes evenly to downspouts, and nailing the gutter back in place.

To keep rainfall from collecting near foundation walls, soil should slope downward 6 inches over the first 4 feet from the foundation wall. Thereafter, it can be graded more gradually. Use clean fill dirt (not topsoil). Tamp the fill dirt down to the correct slope and finish with a layer of topsoil and grass seed, mulch or stone.

LEAKY ROOF

Watch out for unscrupulous contractors who try to sell you a new roof that you don't need. Most roof leaks can be remedied with minor flashing repair. Look for loose or deteriorated flashing around chimneys and vent pipes. Fill any gaps with a good asphalt roof cement. A neatly applied bead of sealant from a caulking gun is better than a thick, troweled-on application.

Loose flashing should be tightened up with masonry nails before resealing. Expect to seal flashing every two years. If sealing doesn't fix the problem, the roof shingles may be in fact worn out. To check your roof for signs of wear and tear, look for cracked, curled or broken shingles. If the worn area is small, it can be repaired by replacing the old shingles or patching with asphalt roof cement. If the entire roof looks this way, replacement is best. Shingles that are allowed to deteriorate can cause major leaks leading to expensive repairs.

EXTERIOR JOINTS AND GAPS

Open joints and gaps in the outside envelope of a house waste energy and provide easy entry for insects and vermin. Gaps often exist where siding meets trim, where electric cables or pipes enter the building, or where the sill of the house meets the foundation. For cracks up to $1/4$ to $5/16$ inches, a smooth, even bead of caulk applied with a caulking gun is best. For wider openings, use an aerosol spray foam insulation. Let the foam expand to fill cracks, and slice away the excess after a day's drying time.

STUCK WINDOWS

Stuck windows are an inconvenience as well as a potential hazard, because they can impede escaping from fire. Most stuck windows are painted shut on the inside, outside or both. With double-hung windows, place the heels of your hands on either end of the sash's top rail and rap sharply upward. Start with light impacts and don't get violent. If the sash doesn't move, cut

WHAT TO LOOK FOR ON A LEAKY ROOF

The source of a leak may not be where you see the leak, so inspect the entire roof. Flashing is material— usually rustproof metal or plastic— used at joints (see right) to keep water from getting into the house. Check for looseness, gaps and holes. Check shingles for rips, curled edges and missing sections.

Vent flashing

Valley flashing

Curled shingle

Chimney flashing

the painted joint between the sash and the window stop or weatherstripping. Repeat the process on the outside. If cutting sash joints fails, work a putty knife deep into the joint between stop and sash. If it still won't budge, you may have to remove the stop. Removing the stop will chip paint and requires careful carpentry skills.

BATHROOM CAULKING AND GROUTING

Neglecting to replace old grout and tired caulking in the bathroom is one of the most common home maintenance failures. It may not seem to be a big problem, but over time, the ceramic tiles loosen, allowing moisture to damage underlying wall materials. To prevent headaches later on, old grout, especially at horizontal tile joints where water penetration is greatest, should be scraped out. Before replacing grout, thoroughly wash tiles and joints with a tub and tile cleaner and then rinse.

Faucet, control and spout joints in the shower or tub also should be well sealed. If they are not, remove the faucet escutcheon plates. Many of these plates have small set screws that must be loosened first. Some plates can be unscrewed after you've removed the faucet handles. Using a putty knife or blade scraper, remove all old caulking, dirt, mildew and soap residue. Finish cleaning with a tub and tile cleaner and then rinse thoroughly. Next, seal all faucet penetrations with a good adhesive caulk. Before reinstalling the escutcheon plates, run a bead of caulk around the plates' mating edges. Tighten the plates against the wall and run another bead of caulk around the outside, where the plates meet the wall.

Don't neglect replacing the worn-out caulk between the tub and the wall tile. Dig out the old caulk to full depth with an old screwdriver or sharp utility knife. Squirt tub and tile cleaner in the joint. Remove all residual caulk, grout, dirt and mildew by working a rag or paper towel with

a putty knife into the gap. Keep working until the towel comes out clean and dry. To seal the gap, run a bead of caulk into the joint. Placing a strip of masking tape along the tile just above the tub results in a neat, crisp edge. The caulk should fill the joint $1/4$- to $3/8$-inch deep. Smooth in the caulk with your finger, wipe away excess from the tub and tile, and then let dry for several hours.

TRICKLING TOILETS

Toilets are one of the most used, yet least understood home appliances. They have two basic moving parts: the flush valve, which lets water out of the tank and down the drain; and the fill valve, which lets the toilet fill up after the flush cycle is complete. Small leaks in either of these valves can waste thousands of gallons of water in the course of a year. Here's how to tell if your valves are leaking:

To test the flush valve, open the top of the tank and pour a small amount of food coloring into the water. After an hour, if there is any colored water in the bowl, the flush valve is leaking and should be replaced.

To test the fill valve, open the top of the tank and find the hollow plastic pipe that sticks up from

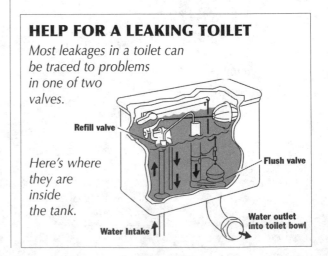

HELP FOR A LEAKING TOILET

Most leakages in a toilet can be traced to problems in one of two valves.

Refill valve

Flush valve

Here's where they are inside the tank.

Water Intake ↑

Water outlet into toilet bowl

the bottom of the tank. The water level should be about an inch below the top of the pipe. If the water level is even with the top, the fill valve may be leaking or improperly adjusted and should be repaired or replaced. Next, flush the toilet and watch the top of the valve. If any water squirts up, you may have a leaky seal, which also means you need a new fill valve.

Both of these parts are easy to replace and cost less than $20. Fluidmaster makes good replacement valves with clear instructions that teach you how to do the job. You can find them at any home center.

If a House Is a Hot Zone

What to do if your house is plagued by environmental hazards

Environmental pollution can be a serious problem even in one's own home. To advise potential homeowners of the environmental hazards that may be present in your home's wall, plumbing and foundations, a group of government agencies and private organizations, including the Environmental Protection Agency (E.P.A.), the Department of Housing and Urban Development, and the National Association of Realtors have joined forces to develop a primer for consumers. Highlights follow:

RADON is a colorless, odorless, tasteless gas that occurs worldwide in the environment as a byproduct of the natural decay of uranium present in the earth. Over time, it breaks down into radioactive particles (called decay products) that remain in the air. Out of doors, this is not a problem, because the gas diffuses in the atmosphere.

THE PROBLEM: When radon gas and its decay products enter your home, they remain in circulation in the enclosed air. As you breath these particles,

they can become trapped in your lungs. As these particles continue to break down, they release bursts of energy (radiation) that can damage lung tissue. This damage can cause lung cancer.

THE SOLUTION: Preliminary screening test kits can be bought over the counter in many hardware, grocery and convenience stores. Tests that measure the amount of radon in water normally require you to send a sample of tap water to a laboratory for analysis. Most homes contain from one to two picocuries of radon per liter of air. If preliminary tests indicate radon levels greater than four picocuries per liter of air in livable areas of the home, the E.P.A. recommends that a follow-up test be conducted. The E.P.A. estimates that the risk of annual radon level of four picocuries is equivalent to the risk from smoking ten cigarettes a day or having 200 chest X-rays a year.

In some cases, homeowners may be able to treat the problem themselves However, radon source diagnosis and mitigation normally require skills, experience and tools not available to the average homeowner.

Installing radon reduction equipment may cost from several hundred dollars to several thousand dollars. If the system chosen involves fans, pumps or other appliances, operating costs for these devices may cause increases in monthly utility bills. When seeking a contractor to assist with a radon problem, ask local, county or state government agencies for a recommendation.

LEAD is a metallic element found worldwide in rocks and soils. Its toxic effects have been known since ancient times. Recent research has shown that lead represents a greater hazard at lower levels of concentration than had been thought. Airborne lead enters the body when an individual breathes lead particles or swallows lead dust. Lead can be present in drinking water, in interior or exterior paint, in the dust within a house and in soil outside.

THE PROBLEM: When ingested, lead accumulates in the blood, bones and soft tissue of the body. High concentrations of lead in the body can cause death or permanent damage to the central nervous system, the brain, the kidneys and red blood cells. Even low levels of lead may increase high blood pressure in adults.

Infants, children, pregnant women and fetuses are more vulnerable to lead exposure than others, because the lead is more easily absorbed into growing bodies. Because of a child's smaller body weight, an equal concentration of lead is more damaging to a child than it would be to an adult.

THE SOLUTION: The only way to determine lead levels

When You Fire the Handyman

Determined to do it yourself, but still need a little help? Try these books on the art of repair and home construction:

HELP, IT'S BROKEN! A Fix-It Bible for the Repair-Impaired.
Arianne Cohen. Three Rivers Press, 2005.
Arianne Cohen tackles household fix-it crises with lucid, easy-to-follow instructions to stop the most ham-handed handyman from hyperventilating.

READYMADE How to Make (Almost) Everything: A Do-It-Yourself Primer.
Shoshana Berger and Grace Hawthorne. Crown, 2005.
The editor and publisher of the magazine *ReadyMade* offer a collection of suggestions for turning detritus into home furnishings, using Marcel Duchamp as their muse.

—Liesl Schillinger

in water is to test a sample of the water. Should you suspect that lead is present in drinking water, or if you wish to have water tested, contact local, county, or state health or environmental departments for information about qualified testing laboratories.

It is best to leave lead-based paint undisturbed if it is in good condition and there is little possibility that it will be eaten by children. Other procedures include covering the paint with wallpaper or some other building material, or completely replacing the painted surface.

Pregnant women and women who plan to become pregnant should not do this work. Professional paint removal is costly, time-consuming and requires everyone not involved in the procedure to leave the premises during removal and cleanup.

ASBESTOS is a fibrous mineral found in rocks and soil throughout the world. It has been used in construction because it is strong, durable, fire retardant and a good insulator.

THE PROBLEM: When ingested, asbestos fibers lodge in the lungs, where they remain in tissue and concentrate as repeated exposures occur. Prolonged work-related exposure can cause cancer of the lungs and other diseases. The health effects of lower exposures in the home are less certain; however, experts are unable to provide assurance that any level of exposure to asbestos fibers is completely safe.

THE SOLUTION: Asbestos is sometimes found around pipes and furnaces in older homes as insulating jackets and sheathing; in some vinyl flooring materials; in ceiling tiles; in exterior roofing, shingles and siding; in some wallboards; mixed with other materials and troweled or sprayed around pipes, ducts and beams; in patching compounds or textured paints; and in door gaskets on stoves, furnaces and ovens.

Generally, if the material is in good condition and is in an area where it is not likely to be disturbed, leave the asbestos-containing material in place. Extreme care should be used in handling, cleaning or working with material suspected of containing asbestos. If it is likely to be banged, rubbed, handled or taken apart—especially during remodeling—you should hire asbestos removal workers who are protected under federal regulations that specify special training, protective clothing and special respirators, and reduce your exposure as much as possible.

FORMALDEHYDE is a colorless, gaseous chemical compound that is generally present at low, variable concentrations in both indoor and outdoor air. It is emitted by many construction materials and consumer products that contain formaldehyde-based glues, resins, preservatives and bonding agents. Formaldehyde also is an ingredient in foam that was used for home insulating until the early 1980's. In homes, the most significant sources of formaldehyde are likely to be in the adhesives used to bond pressed-wood building materials and in plywood used for construction.

THE PROBLEM: Formaldehyde has been shown to cause cancer in animals, and may cause cancer in humans. Higher-than-normal levels of formaldehyde in the home can trigger asthma attacks in those who have this condition. Other symptoms may include skin rashes; watery eyes; burning sensations in the eyes, throat and nasal passages; and breathing difficulties.

Materials containing formaldehyde were used extensively in the construction of certain pre-fabricated and manufactured homes. Although the federal government has curtailed the use of materials containing formaldehyde since 1985, formaldehyde compounds are still widespread in the manufacture of furniture, cabinets and other building materials.

THE SOLUTION: In the case of a new home, you should consult with the builder before you purchase the house if you suspect the presence of materials that emit high levels of formaldehyde. Most builders will be able to tell you if construction materials contain formaldehyde, or they may direct you to manufacturers who can provide information about specific products.

In older homes, formaldehyde- emitting materials may not be apparent and the current owners may not have specific product information. Consider hiring a qualified building inspector to examine the home. Home monitoring kits are also available. If subflooring, walls or foam insulation is the problem's source and increased ventilation is inadequate, removal of the material may be necessary. Such procedures will be costly, time-consuming and temporarily disruptive.

SOURCE: Adapted from *A Home Buyer's Guide to Environmental Hazards*

In the Garden

Figments That Turn Into Flowers

A master gardener reveals her springtime rituals

Anne Raver is the *New York Times* gardening columnist and the author of *Deep in the Green: An Exploration of Country Pleasures* and other books. Here she shares some of the secrets of her rites of spring.

March is the time to plant my kitchen garden, putting seeds of leeks, broccoli rabe, the tiny specks of alpine strawberries in sterile potting soil. They incubate in trays under plastic lids on my concrete floor, which is warmed by water pipes that keep them a cozy 68 degrees.

Many gardeners don't have time to start their own plants. But some mail-order companies will ship interesting well-grown varieties. Burpee, for instance, offers Fairy Tale eggplants, tender little purple and white six-inchers that can be grown in a pot (see contact information below). Seed Savers Exchange grows rare heirlooms like red milkweed, a prairie flower crucial to monarch butterflies (563-382-5990 or www.seedsavers.org). Seeds of Change sells all kinds of peppers, like Corno di Toro, which is delicious roasted (888-762-7333 or www.seedsofchange.com).

Check out local farmers' markets, herb festivals and botanical gardens to discover new plants that you won't have to start from seed. I found some yellow Brandywine tomato plants at Maryland's famous Sheep and Wool Festival (www.sheepand-wool.org) among some of the most beautifully grown organic seedlings I'd ever seen.

Meanwhile, see if your soil is ready for potatoes and peas. If you pick up a handful of soil and squeeze, and it wads into a sticky ball or glistens with water, it's too wet. If it crumbles like damp, rather cool, chocolate cake, get those taters in the ground.

I also like planting Rose Finn Apple, an heirloom fingerling potato I discovered while visiting North

Where Green Thumbs Shop

Some reliable sources for seeds and plants

W. ATLEE BURPEE & CO.
Seeds, bulbs, shrubs and gardening supplies.
800-888-1447 or www.burpee.com

PARK SEED CO.
Seeds, plants and gardening supplies.
800-213-0076 or www.parkseed.com

JACKSON & PERKINS
Wide selection of roses and perennials, also garden accessories.
877-322-2300 or www. jacksonandperkins.com

THOMPSON & MORGAN
English catalog with over 2,500 varieties of flower and vegetable seeds.
800-274-7333 or www.thompson-morgan.com

WAYSIDE GARDENS
Large selection of perennials, trees and shrubs.
800-213-0379 or www.waysidegardens.com

WHITE FLOWER FARM
Perennials, bulbs, trees, shrubs. Excellent catalog with detailed plant and growing instructions.
800-503-9624 or www.whiteflowerfarm.com

Where the Growing Zones Fall

Most plant catalogs specify the regions in which perennial plants thrive. The standard U.S.D.A. zones are defined by the minimum temperatures each region reaches in an average year; the 11 zones are shown.

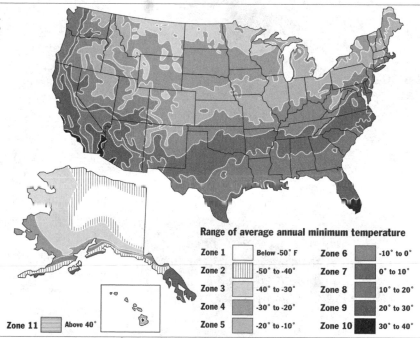

Range of average annual minimum temperature

Zone 1	Below -50° F	Zone 6	-10° to 0°
Zone 2	-50° to -40°	Zone 7	0° to 10°
Zone 3	-40° to -30°	Zone 8	10° to 20°
Zone 4	-30° to -20°	Zone 9	20° to 30°
Zone 5	-20° to -10°	Zone 10	30° to 40°

Zone 11	Above 40°

Hill in Readsboro, Vt., the renowned garden started 30 years ago by Joe Eck and Wayne Winterrowd.

All Blue potatoes are perfect for purple French fries; Red Gold is a highly disease-resistant red potato with yellow flesh; and Yellow Finn is buttery and sweet. I presprouted some of my spuds one spring after reading how to do it in the catalog from Ronniger's, a potato farm in Moyie Springs, Idaho (208-267-7938 or www.ronnigers.com). I just laid them out on a newspaper on the floor in indirect light about a week or two before planting, and stubby sprouts grew from the buds. The plants from these sprouted spuds popped out of the ground quickly, grew into bushy plants with dark green leaves and bore more plentifully than plants that developed from unsprouted potatoes.

As for peas, I like a French petit pois variety from John Scheepers Kitchen Garden Seeds (860-567-6086 or www.kitchengardenseeds.com). I'll plant sugar snaps along the fence and flowering sweet peas to ramble up bamboo tripods set about

the garden. Cupani, a fragrant purple-blue bicolor sweet pea, and Captain of the Blues, a fragrant deep mauve, are only two of the many offered by Select Seeds (800-684-0395 or www.selectseeds. com).

I love to plant nasturtiums like deep red Empress of India on the ends of my raised beds, to spill into the paths, and borage, which has a gray leaf and a gray-blue flower, among blue-green broccoli and kale.

For flowers, zinnias are a must, among them *Z. angustifolia,* the little white daisylike flower with the gold center, and double hybrid forms of *Z. elegans* like Scarlet Splendor and Envy, a chartreuse. I also put a bevy of tall sunflowers outside the kitchen garden fence. Cook's Garden has a knockout deep red sunflower called Moulin Rouge, and Moonwalker, a pale yellow with a dark center (800-457-9703 or www.cooksgarden.com). The cup plant, *Silphium perfoliatum,* looks wonderful against that outer wall of tall annuals. Its delicate canary yellow daisylike blossoms rise above broad

> ✔ **TIMELY TIPS**
>
> ## In the Eye of the Beholder
>
> ✔ *On my list of most useful garden tools, some people might be surprised to find a camera. A camera won't prune a rosebush or dig a hole, but for design help it can be essential. Through its single eye I discover things that are not visible when I walk through my garden: things that can be improved, moved or removed. I can also snap records of successful experiments and other plantings to remember and repeat. And photographs, with dates and notes scribbled on the backs, slip nicely into my garden journal.*
>
> —Ken Druse

green leaves that form little cups where they meet the square stem and capture rainwater.

All the greens thrive in cool weather. I can never grow enough mesclun or arugula, especially the wild self-seeding sylvetta (*Diplotaxis muralis*), which has narrow leaves and a sharper flavor than the regular roquette type (*Eruca vesicaria* var. *sativa*). Tatsoi, kyona mizuna and Osaka purple, a tangy mustard green with a sturdy purple-green leaf, are a few of the many Asian greens on offer.

Unlike a lot of red lettuces, which tend to be bland and soft, Hyper Red Rumple Waved has a savoy-type leaf and plenty of flavor. Jack and Karen Manix, who grow the variety on Walker Farm in Drummerston, Vermont, get the seed from Fedco Seeds (207-873-7333 or www.fedcoseeds. com). Red Rumple looks gorgeous with Australian Yellowleaf, a lime-green lettuce from Seed Savers Exchange. Mr. Manix also talked me into Red Iceberg, another Seed Savers gem.

Purple Dragon, a reddish-purple heirloom car-rot with a yellow-orange core is available through Seed Savers Exchange and Bountiful Gardens (707-459-6410 or www.bountifulgardens.org). Cosmic Purple, a newer hybrid with a plumper, more consistent shape, and Kinbi, a golden yellow, are both offered by Johnny's Selected Seeds (207-861-3900 or www.johnnyseeds.com).

On the tomato front, my favorite is still Brandywine, and Yellow Brandywine, too. I've always sneered at yellow tomatoes as tasteless bland things, but these have a more tangy, if slightly sweeter, taste than the regular reddish pink version. And people like my mother, who have trouble digesting the more acidic types, can eat these with impunity. I found Yellow Brandywine seeds in the Heirloom Seeds catalog (412-384-0852 or www. heirloomseeds.com).

A Sower's Guide to Soil
Germination goes better when the soil is more than backyard earth

S oil pH is just one of several factors that can determine whether a seed develops into a thriving plant or fails to grow at all. Maureen Heffernan, executive director of Coastal Maine Botanical Gardens, and author of *Burpee Seed Starter: A Guide to Growing Flower, Vegetable, and Herb Seeds Indoors and Outdoors,* explains here how a savvy gardener can give seeds a healthy start in life.

💬 **When should I start seed?**

Most seed packages come with full instructions of when to start the seed. As a rule of thumb, however, most annual vegetable and flower seed should be started indoors about six to eight weeks before the average last frost date in your area. See table, page 456-457, for details.

💬 **What is the best soil medium?**

Always use a germination mixture that's been specially formulated for starting seeds. Homemade soil mixtures are easy to make and cheaper than buying premade ones, especially if you start large quantities of seed. One of the best recipes is Cornell Peat-Lite, developed by agronomists at Cornell University. Its ingredients include one bushel of shredded sphagnum peat moss; one bushel of horticultural vermiculite (No. 4-fine); four level tbsp. of ammonium nitrate (a nitrogen source); two level tbsp. of powdered superphosphate (20 percent); and ten level tbsp. of finely ground dolomitic limestone.

Never use as your germination medium soil from the yard or garden because it is often too "heavy" and can cause disease problems since it is not sterile. Homemade or bought, seed starting mixture should be light and almost fluffy even after it is watered.

What is the right temperature for planting?

Most seedlings do best with "warm feet and cool heads." Make sure soil temperatures are at least 70 and no more than 80 degrees F. Air temperature can be about ten degrees cooler at night. Heat cables or heat mats, placed under germination containers, are the best way to insure evenly warm soil temperatures. They are inexpensive and can be found in many gardeners' supply catalogs and most garden centers.

● **How much watering is necessary?**

Water immediately after sowing seeds. Use a spritzer bottle to evenly moisten the surface. The most common mistake is applying too much or too little water. Just keep seeds and seedlings evenly moist and never allow seeds to dry out, even temporarily. A good tip is to premoisten the soil mixture before sowing seeds. This ensures that soil has been thoroughly premoistened from top to bottom. It also prevents seeds being displaced when trying to get the soil thoroughly watered after sowing seeds.

● **How much light do seeds need?**

Some seeds need light to germinate, some need darkness. Check the light requirements on the seed packet. Once germinated, however, all seeds need bright light to develop. Light can come from a sunny window—south is best—or fluorescent lighting. Most seedlings need at least 12 to 16 hours of direct light each day.

If you're using fluorescent light, seedlings need about 15 to 20 watts per square foot of growing area. A double row of fluorescent tubes is enough for a flat up to 16 inches wide. Place the light tubes about three to four inches above the plants. Be sure to raise light tubes as plants grow.

● **When should seedlings be thinned out or transplanted?**

After seedlings have germinated and developed at least two leaves, thin out seedlings by gently pulling them up, being careful not to disturb the root systems of seedlings that will grow on. You can also thin them by cutting them at soil level with scissors so remaining seedlings are one inch apart. If

HOUSE

☑ **TIMELY TIPS**

Sterile *and* Fertile

✔ **Make sure your dirt is clean.** To sterilize a seed medium in an oven or microwave, you can use a medium-size potato as your "sterility gauge." Place the soil medium in the oven at the same depth as you would need to fill a seed flat.

✔ **When the potato is done enough to eat,** the soil should be clean enough for your seeds.

seedlings aren't thinned out, they will get crowded and become thin, weak and disease-prone.

Transplant seedlings to wider and deeper containers after they have developed at least two to four leaves. Transplanting allows seedlings to develop a stronger root system before being planted outdoors.

What kind of soil do seedlings need when they are moved outside?

Good growing soils are fertile, well drained and well aerated. When you pick up a handful of earth, it should have a crumbly texture and, ideally, be filled with organic matter, worms and other enriching organisms. To prepare outside plots for planting, add at least three to four inches of organic matter to your garden beds every spring or fall. Work in the organic matter to a depth of at least 12 inches. If you are working with soil that has a lot of heavy clay or sand, add more organic matter and work it in several inches deeper in both the spring and fall. If your soil is poorly drained, you may need to add sand, build raised beds and/or install drainage pipes.

Is soil pH an important factor?

A soil's pH number indicates the soil's level of acidity (sourness) and alkalinity (sweetness). Numbers below seven indicate more acidic levels and numbers over seven indicate alkaline conditions. The scale is logorhythmic, meaning that a soil pH of five is ten times more acidic than four. The majority of garden plants prefer a slightly acidic soil (pH i.e., 6.2 to 6.5).

How do I know what my soil pH is?

As a general rule, if you live in an area with little rainfall and high temperatures, like the Southwest, you probably have alkaline soil. If you live in

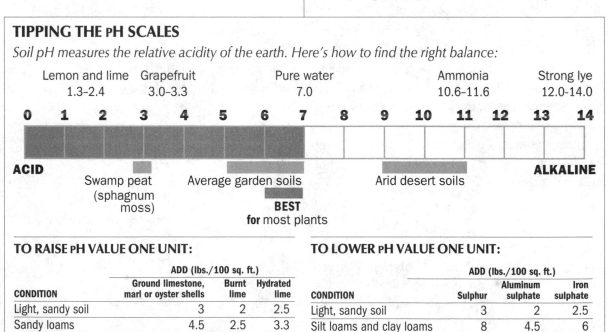

TIPPING THE pH SCALES

Soil pH measures the relative acidity of the earth. Here's how to find the right balance:

| Lemon and lime 1.3–2.4 | Grapefruit 3.0–3.3 | Pure water 7.0 | Ammonia 10.6–11.6 | Strong lye 12.0–14.0 |

0 1 2 3 4 5 6 7 8 9 10 11 12 13 14

ACID   **ALKALINE**

Swamp peat (sphagnum moss)   Average garden soils   Arid desert soils

BEST for most plants

TO RAISE pH VALUE ONE UNIT:

| | ADD (lbs./100 sq. ft.) | | |
CONDITION	Ground limestone, marl or oyster shells	Burnt lime	Hydrated lime
Light, sandy soil	3	2	2.5
Sandy loams	4.5	2.5	3.3
Loams	6.75	3.75	6
Silt loams and clay loams	8	4.5	6

TO LOWER pH VALUE ONE UNIT:

| | ADD (lbs./100 sq. ft.) | | |
CONDITION	Sulphur	Aluminum sulphate	Iron sulphate
Light, sandy soil	3	2	2.5
Silt loams and clay loams	8	4.5	6

NOTE: To raise pH in soils lacking in organic matter, reduce table amounts by 25 percent; for soils with high organic content, double the measurement.

a region with high rainfalls and temperate climate like the Northeast, the soil is probably acidic. To get an exact soil pH reading, you will need to get your soil tested, however.

Most county extension agencies will do such analyses if you bring or mail a sample to them. Be careful to follow the lab's soil-collecting directions carefully to ensure an accurate analysis. They are listed in the blue government services pages of the telephone book. These labs can also analyze your soil's nutrient and organic matter levels and advise if any nutrients or other soil amendments need adding.

🔵 **How reliable are pH home test kits?**

While not as accurate as soil-testing labs, they will give a fairly general pH measurement. You can buy such do-it-yourself soil-testing kits from garden catalogs and centers. Just be sure to carefully follow all directions.

🔵 **If my soil's pH level is off, what should I do about it?**

Soil pH can be lowered (made more acidic) by adding a combination of ground sulfur, aluminum sulphate, iron sulphate and garden gypsum. In addition, pine needles, pine bark and peat moss will slowly bring about slight drops in pH naturally. To raise pH, add agricultural or dolomitic limestone to your soil. See the charts on the previous page for more precise instructions.

Dig and You Shall Reap

Start with a soil test and add a little nutrition

Soil is the foundation for any garden. The effort given to its preparation will largely determine the success of your garden. Soil quality varies widely depending on location, and your local

 TIMELY TIP

Good Gardeners' Secret Weapon

✔ **Compost is the all-purpose answer to everything.** If you have enough of it you won't need much of anything else. Though different crops have different needs, they will be able to serve themselves from the smorgasbord provided by healthy soil with plenty of compost in it. Once you start adding specific fertilizers, you start having to pay close attention to each individual diet. In practice, though, it can be hard to create soil so fertile that no amendment is necessary, especially when growing vegetables in a small space. But before you break out the fertilizer cookbook and start concocting special meals for all the crops you want to grow, make sure the soil is "in good tilth"—well drained and well aerated—and that the pH is between six and seven (the best range for most vegetables).

—Leslie Land

agricultural extension service is likely to be the best information source about the soil in your region. Chris Curless, formerly a horticulturalist at White Flower Farms, offers some tips for getting your garden ready for planting:

1. Test your soil to find out how well it will support plant growth and what you might have to do to improve it. A soil test will show your soil pH and how to adjust it if needed, as well as the levels of specific nutrients to determine fertilizer needs. Agricultural extension services can perform these lab tests on your soil and give you a detailed profile of what you've got in your yard. Most plants prefer a slightly acidic-to-neutral soil. Your soil test will indicate how much lime or sulfur needs adding if adjustment is required. It will also recommend what other nutrients may be needed as supplements.

A BULB LOVER'S FAVORITE CHOICES

They can come back to the same spot for decades, or you can dig them up and move them.

	Height (in.)	Planting depth (in.)	Planting time	Blooming time
● **SPRING-FLOWERING BULBS**				
CROCUS *Crocus* species	3–5	3–4	EARLY FALL	EARLY SPRING
CROWN IMPERIAL *Fritillaria imperialis*	30–48	5	EARLY FALL	MIDSPRING
DAFFODIL *Narcissus* species	12	6	EARLY FALL	MIDSPRING
DUTCH IRIS *Iris xiphium*	24	4	EARLY FALL	LATE SPRING
FLOWERING ONION *Allium giganteum*	48	10	EARLY FALL	LATE SPRING
GRAPE HYACINTH *Muscari botryoides*	6–10	3	EARLY FALL	EARLY SPRING
HYACINTH *Hyacinthus orientalis*	12	6	EARLY FALL	EARLY SPRING
SNOWDROP *Galanthus nivalis*	4-6	4	EARLY FALL	EARLY SPRING
TULIP (early) *Tulipa* species	10–13	6	EARLY FALL	EARLY SPRING
TULIP (Darwin hybrid) *Tulipa* species	28	6	EARLY FALL	MIDSPRING
TULIP (late) *Tulipa* species	36	6	EARLY FALL	LATE SPRING
WINDFLOWER *Anemone blanda*	5	2	EARLY FALL	EARLY SPRING
● **SUMMER-FLOWERING BULBS**				
ANEMONE *Anemone* species	18	2	N: EARLY SPRING S: LATE FALL	LATE SUMMER
BUTTERCUP *Ranunculus*	12	2	SOUTH: LATE FALL	MIDSUMMER
CROCOSMIA *Crocosmia* species	24	4	APRIL–MAY	MID- TO LATE SUMMER
DAHLIA (dwarf varieties) *Dahlia* species	12	4	AFTER LAST FROST	LATE SUMMER
DAHLIA (large varieties) *Dahlia* species	48	4	AFTER LAST FROST	LATE SUMMER
GALTONIA *Galtonia candicans*	40	5	APRIL–MAY	MID- TO LATE SUMMER
GLADIOLUS (large flower) *Gladiolus* species	60	3–4	APRIL–JUNE	MIDSUMMER
GLADIOLUS (small flower) *Gladiolus* species	30	3–4	APRIL–JUNE	MIDSUMMER
LILY *Lilium* species	36–84	8	FALL OR EARLY SPRING	ALL SUMMER
TIGER FLOWER *Tigridia paronia*	16	3	EARLY SPRING	MID- TO LATE SUMMER

● HEIGHT AND DEPTH

A bulb that is planted deep will not necessarily grow tall.

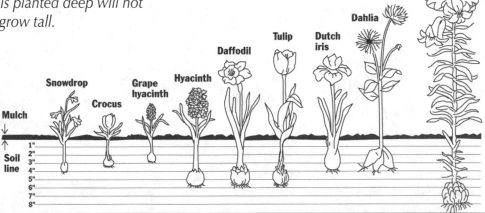

2. Mark the area for your garden before you dig. If it's a simple shape like a rectangle or square, stakes and string are an easy way to do this. For a curved bed, a garden hose will allow you to make smooth bends. Mark the edge of the bed with white spray paint or powdered lime so you know exactly where you want to dig. It's easy to think you know and still get lost in the middle of your digging.

3. Remove existing grass to get to the soil. If you are going to put a border into a lawn, you want to get rid of the turf. If it's a large, relatively flat area, consider renting a sod cutter—a heavy, gas-powered machine. It's not great at corners and awful on a hillside because it weighs about 300 pounds, but for flat areas it is very fast. Smaller mechanical gadgets are also available to cut turf. But the tried-and-true method is to use a sharpened spade to undercut the turf. Since you're removing the top inch or so of soil and a lot of green material, put it in the compost pile so you can use it again in the future.

4. Add a hefty layer of organic matter. Next, spread three to six inches of organic matter on top of the entire area with a rake. Organic matter benefits all kinds of soil, whether it's light and sandy or heavy. In a sandy soil, organic matter improves moisture retention; in a heavy, clay soil it improves the drainage. Remember, if you're planting woody stock or perennials, you have only one chance to work the soil like this, so take advantage of the opportunity. Some good types of organic matter include aged manure, peat moss or leaf mold. In some areas of the South, ground-up pine bark is recommended because it lasts longer in warm, moist soil. If you need to add soil amendments, spread them evenly on top of the organic matter.

5. Thoroughly mix the organic matter and other additions into the soil. The next step is digging. I think turning the soil to a depth of a shovel is enough. Many books recommend double-digging—which means digging twice as deep—but for most people, that's just way too much work.

Start at one corner and work your way backward, so you don't compact the area you have turned. Break up big clods as you go. Digging and incorporating the organic matter and fertilizer creates air spaces in the soil, making it easier for the roots of your plants to get around. The goal of all this is to make it easier for plants to grow.

HOUSE

We Promise You a Rose Garden
Without a ton of chemicals and constant worry

The rose's reputation as an aristocrat is well deserved—it is a regal flower that requires the attention usually reserved for royalty. But rose lovers need not quit their day jobs and sell their silver to grow beautiful roses in their gardens.

Choose disease-resistant varieties. Most varieties of roses become so diseased that they look like they were dunked in weed killer unless bombarded each week with enough chemicals to make Saddam Hussein proud. But a few widely available rose varieties have disease-resistant genes. By choosing healthy varieties, you can pretty much chuck the sprayer. If you look closely, you might notice an insect or two or a nibbled leaf or bloom, but you don't need to get compulsive about your rosebushes. Use organic fertilizers for the most part, and boost only when necessary with a chemical fertilizer. Organic fertilizers are generally better than chemical ones, because they are gentler to the plant, contain many important trace nutrients and contribute to soil health. Nonetheless, an occasional booster of balanced rose food is often helpful, with most experts favoring a balance of heavy nitrogen, light phosphorus and medium

TIMELY TIPS

Out, Out, Black Spot

Black spot is a nasty fungus *(Diplocarpon rosae)* that attacks roses, causing circular black spots with fringed margins to form on the foliage. Infected leaves eventually turn yellow and drop, leaving the plants severely damaged and nearly nude. Because the spores are spread by splashing water, the fungus is worse in periods of rain or high humidity. Preventive sprays like the one below, made from nontoxic ingredients can help quite a bit. You can also try to control the fungus by keeping the foliage dry between rains (water only at the base of the plant), pruning off infected canes and removing all diseased leaves from the soil. Leaf cleanup is especially important in autumn, since the fungus spends the winter on infected leaves and canes, only to rear its ugly head once again in the spring.

HOMEMADE FUNGUS PREVENTION SPRAY:
- 1 gallon unchlorinated water
- 1 tablespoon baking soda
- 1 tablespoon summerweight horticultural oil (optional)
- 1 tablespoon detergent (dishwashing liquid works fine)

✔ This concoction, with an alkaline base of baking soda, prevents the acid conditions necessary for diseases such as black spot and powdery mildew to thrive. Baking soda, being alkaline, neutralizes leaf surfaces and keeps the fungus spores from taking hold.

✔ **Adding a spoonful of detergent helps the soda cling to the leaves.** Adding summerweight horticultural oil increases the fungus-preventive punch while also helping the spray to stick. It's important to have the spray come out as a fine mist, so use a garden sprayer, not an ordinary squeeze bottle.

✔ **Make a fresh batch each time you spray.** Be sure you get the whole plant, including the undersides of the leaves. Spray in the early morning; horticultural oil applied when temperatures are high can damage sensitive plants, and wetting leaves in the evening is counterproductive when you are dealing with black spot.

✔ **Finally, spray often**. The mixture does not last long and its effects are entirely preventive. This isn't a cure, so if you wait until you have problems, you will have waited too long.

—Leslie Land

potassium (18-6-12 and 15-5-13 are typical formulations).

When to feed and how much varies with the quality of the soil and the type of rose, since fast-draining soils need supplementation more often than rich, moisture-retentive loams. If a rose is a repeat bloomer, each bloom cycle should be supported with another meal. In practice, this means one feeding in the early spring for everybody, then follow-up feedings at six-week intervals for heavy bloomers only. It is easiest to start out with dry fertilizer, then follow up (if necessary) with foliar feeding. Many rose growers also give their plants a good shower of seaweed extract in early midseason, and others give their roses vitamin supplements.

Don't forget to water your roses—but don't overwater. Roses do best when they grow in soil that is consistently moist—but not wet—for most of the root zone. In nature, the standard moisture requirement for roses is one inch of rainfall a week, but this ignores important differences between soils. A rose growing in sandy ground that's low in humus might need twice as much water as one growing in rich loam over clay.

To figure out how much your roses need, turn on the watering system you plan to use (drip, sprinkler or hose) and let it run for 10 minutes, then turn it off and do something else for a half hour or so. When the half hour is up, dig a test hole next to the rose, right outside the root zone, and see how far down the water has penetrated. Adjust the watering time as necessary to get moisture all through the root zone, then wait three or four days.

Dig again. The top inch or two of soil may be dry, but things should still be damp farther down. If you are looking at soil that is dry at 3, 4, or 5 inches underneath the surface, get ready for watering twice a week (and get some more organic matter into the soil before you plant any more roses).

10 (Comparatively) Easy Roses
Keep it simple: get disease-resistant varieties

Species roses are tougher than hybrids, and roses on their own roots are more likely to thrive than those that have been grafted. Once-blooming shrub and climbing roses are almost always easier than rebloomers, and everything else in the world of roses is easier than hybrid teas. For maximum grief avoidance, gardeners in zone 5 and further north should concentrate on hardiness; those in zone 6 and further south should bank on disease resistance.

Autumn Sunset (Climber) Very cold hardy and disease resistant. Semidouble, fragrant flowers in apricot-gold or very pale orange.

Betty Prior (Floribunda) The plant is short and the fragrance delicate, but the single, true pink flowers are abundant and charming and well set off by the darker pink of the buds.

Bonica (Shrub) Good foliage and repeated flushes of double pink flowers on a bush that may reach 4 by 5 feet. Lots of small orange hips. Functionally fragrance-free.

Carefree Beauty (Shrub) Large, loosely double pink flowers opening from narrow buds. Moderate fragrance and good cutting stems on a bush large enough to have presence without overwhelming.

Knock Out (Shrub) Phenomenal disease resistance, near constant flowering, and plenty of medium green foliage on a well-rounded, 3-foot bush. Not fragrant, not easy to integrate with other colors; masses of single flowers are a screaming scarlet-magenta euphemized as cherry red.

Rosa rugosa alba (Species) Hardy and disease resistant, with deeply wrinkled foliage and high pink-tinged buds that open to very fragrant single white flowers. Good recurrence, though nothing like the tireless bloom most modern roses strive for. Huge orange hips, and frequently good foliage color in autumn.

Scarlet Meidiland (Shrub) More like a ground cover than an upright bush. Low and wide, and well covered with loosely doubled, clear red flowers borne in large sprays. Small, rather shiny medium green leaves. Negligible fragrance.

The Fairy (Shrub) Very nearly unkillable. The 2½-to-3-foot bushes are covered from early summer to mid fall with large clusters of small, very double, light pink roses that have only a slight fragrance and tend to fade in the sun.

Thérèse Bugnet (Hybrid Rugosa) Huge bush, as much as 6 by 6 feet. Very cold hardy and strongly fragrant. Though described as blooming continuously the very double, medium pink flowers often take breaks between flushes.

William Baffin (Climber) The hardiest repeat-blooming climber, according to most; it's rated to do well without protection as far north as zone 3. The deep pink, semidouble flowers are not fragrant, but you can't have everything.

—Leslie Land

HOUSE

The Scent of a Garden

Ah, the sweet, sweet smell of fragrant flowers

Ken Druse, who writes the "Cuttings" column for the *New York Times,* discusses how to make your garden not only look great but smell great, too.

Smell—the final frontier of the senses—is returning to garden fashion. More nursery catalogs have begun to include lists of fragrant plants on equal footing with categories like hardy vines and ground covers, and breeders are starting to take notice. Still, many fragrant flowers are still not promoted, and many old or overlooked varieties have yet to make a well-deserved comeback, including native azaleas, bearded iris and clethra. Roses, such as Sombreuil, a white climber from the late 19th century, are enjoying a resurgence. Another shrub, the old-fashioned mock orange, smells like orange blossoms. My favorite is the double-flowered *Philadelphus x virginalis* variety. It fills the air with perfume and lasts nearly two weeks as a cut flower.

Scent is invisible, but its placement is crucial. I wouldn't make a planting themed on fragrance, for example, as I would for spring color or dwarf evergreens. I prefer to sprinkle the smells like punctuation. The lily is an exclamation point; the scent of Carolina sweetshrub floats on the evening air like a question mark: "What's that smell?"

Today I plant fragrant flowers under windows and by doors, places where people are most likely to walk or sit. A *Wisteria venusta* climbs a trellis beside the porch door where its early-spring fragrance of honey is intoxicating. I planted tall lilies next to a garden path so beautiful flowers on tall arching stalks would grab passers-by. Immersed in the deep perfume of those lilies, I am reminded of burnt sugar and clove. The yellow primrose hints of linen drying on the clothesline,

with jasmine and a top note of sweet butter.

One of my favorite scents is *Daphne caucasica*; its nearly insignificant flowers remind me of the lily smell with a trace of honey, and a smoky undertone that smells the way a camping lodge does on a rainy day, when memories of crackling fires creep back into the atmosphere.

When the Carolina sweetshrub is in bloom, from May to July, visitors to my garden often debate what the small red-brown flowers smell like. One will say bubble gum, others will say raisins, cider vinegar, pineapple or crushed strawberries.

I love the fragrance of lilacs. The wonderfully fragrant President Lincoln, a variety with about the bluest of lilac flowers, is as lanky as its namesake (great planted under a second-story

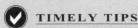

TIMELY TIPS

How to Train a Rose

✔ Training a rose is not hard. It just takes time and patience. The main thing is this: a rose cane that grows straight up will most likely flower at its tip; if forced into a lateral position, it will bloom all along the stem.

✔ Any canes that start growing into the path or start taking over some other plant's space should be trimmed back to three or four inches. The buds on these shortened stems will produce flowers.

✔ To train roses up a stone wall, you could drill into the mortar and insert iron anchors, or use mortar screws. But don't use wire, which cuts into the canes. If you wish to have individual supports for each climbing rose, you can use cedar posts sunk two feet into the ground as vertical supports, and plant a climbing rose at the base of each post. Or a simple tripod can be made with bamboo canes.

—Anne Raver

window). Lilacs come in many colors: one has double snow-white flowers; another's blossoms are cream. There is a double mauve shrub, and one with deep wine-red blossoms. The range of the flower colors are easier to describe than their similarly varied scents.

Free-range flowers worth seeking out include pinks, or dianthus. They have the aroma of clove. The August lily, *Hosta plantaginea*, has giant trumpets that smell like honeysuckle. Heliotrope is one of many plants in which some scent was lost in breeding, but old-fashioned ones can still be found that smell like baby powder haunted by black cherry. *Clematis montana* is an early spring blooming vine that smells like vanilla trailing off to birthday cake.

10 (Absolutely) Scented Roses

One by any of these names will smell so sweet

For many gardeners, it isn't a rose if it doesn't smell sweet, and somehow word has gotten around that only old roses are fragrant. Happily, that isn't true, there are quite a few modern roses with very strong perfumes.

When you listen to rose experts describe fragrance, it's clear that a rose does not always smell like a rose. Some suggest a scent of cloves, many famously of tea, others of lilies or lilacs or fruit. Like fine wines, some roses have faint hints of tobacco or fallen leaves. Therefore, to get what you want, the rule for roses is smell before you buy. But if you are mail-ordering, here are a few which are readily available and are highly reliable in the fragrance department.

Félicité Parmentier (Alba) Very double flowers, almost flat when open; pale pink with silver tones. Spring bloomer.

> **ⓘ INSIDE INFO**
>
> ## Flower Talk
>
> ○ The term **remontant** was brought into the English-speaking rose world from the French in the late 19th century. It refers specifically to roses that bloom at least twice, with distinct rest periods between flowerings.
>
> ○ The term **recurrent** can also be used for those same roses, but it is more commonly applied to roses that bloom in overlapping flushes, with no clearly discernible hiatus between blooming times. —Leslie Land

Madame Isaac Pereire (Bourbon) Enormous, rather floppy, deep pink double flowers; a large shrub where happy. Remontant.

Margaret Merril (Floribunda) Ruffled double flowers of pale pink to white, with golden stamens. Plants are short, but rebloom is good.

New Dawn (Climber) Buds reminiscent of hybrid teas open to somewhat loose double flowers; pale pink, darkening in cold weather. Remontant.

Perfume Delight (Hybrid Tea) Deep pink, classic hybrid teas form on long stems. Recurrent.

Rose de Rescht (Damask) Extremely double, reddish magenta fading to purple pink. Remontant.

Apothecary's Rose (*Rosa gallica officinalis*; Gallica) Semidouble, light red, spring blooming; petals retain fragrance when dried. Remontant.

Sir Thomas Lipton (Hybrid Rugosa) Double white with copper stamens that show when the flower is fully open; bush is large and very thorny. Remontant.

The Prince (Austin) Large, dark, red-magenta flowers that look like cups full of petals. Remontant.

Zéphirine Drouhin (Bourbon) Bright pink, semi-double flowers in spring and fall; a climber, slow to get started but will grow large once established. Remontant.

Perfect Plants for Tough Places

What garden doesn't have problem spots?
Here are some solutions

Nearly every garden has a tough spot, where the sun doesn't shine, or shines too much, or the drainage is poor, or the kids have made it a place to play ball. Instead of altering the nature of those problem spots, it's often easier to find plants that are suitable for the particular condition.

● **Which flowers and foliage plants do you recommend for shady, damp or woodsy areas?**

Moist ground at the edge of the woods is an ideal environment for many plants that do not flourish in the bright heat of a conventional flower garden. Among them are the low growers such as ajuga, creeping blue phlox, moneywort, bunchberry, epimedium, sweet woodruff *(Galium odoratum)* foamflower *(Tiarella cordifolia)*, Virginia bluebells *(Mertensia virginica)* bunchberry *(Cornus canadensis)*, lily-of-the-valley *(Convallaria majalis)*, Canada mayflower *(Maianthemum canadense)* and Jack-in-the-pulpit *(Arisaema triphyllum)*. Taller, showier plants include bleeding heart, columbine, hellebore, celandine poppy *(Stylophorum diphyllum)* Solomon's seal, hardy begonia and astilbe, as well as blue lobelia *(Lobelia siphilitica)* and cardinal flower *(Lobelia cardinalis)*, astilbe, turtlehead *(Chelone glabra)* and black snakeroot *(Cimicifuga racemosa)*. You can also go to town with hostas, which have lovely midsummer flowers, or ferns and moss, which should be very happy in these conditions.

In a really wet spot, you have to make a virtue of it and plant a bog garden, using plants that like their roots in downright wet conditions. Among those are marsh mallow *(Althaea officinalis)*; goatsbeard *(Aruncus dioicus)*; queen-of-the-meadow *(Filipendula ulmaria)*; marsh marigold *(Caltha palustris)*; cattail; Louisiana iris; spider lilies; Japanese iris and yellowflag iris *(Iris ensata* and *Iris pseudocorus)*; bronze-leaf rodgersia *(Rodgersia podophylla)*; meadow rue *(Thalictrum* spp.); and globeflower *(Trollius* spp.).

● **What about plants for really dry locations?**

For very dry and sunny places, you may want to try plants that tolerate drought, and have leaves that are narrow, hairy or silvery (or all three)—strategies to keep evaporation to a minimum. Or they may have the alternative: very thick, succulent leaves that act as water-storage devices. Choices include *Achillea* spp. (yarrow); *Armeria* spp. (thrift, sea pink); *Artemisia* spp. *Aurinia saxatilis* (basket-of-gold); *Catanache caerulea* (Cupid's dart); *Centaurea* (perennial cornflower); *Cerastium tomentosum* (snow-in-summer); *Coreopsis* spp. (tickseed); *Eryngium maritimum* (blue sea holly); *Gaillardia* spp. (blanketflower); *Nepeta* spp. (catmint); *Papaver orientale* (oriental poppy); *Portulaca* spp.; *Santolina chamaecyparissus* (lavender cotton); *Stachys byzantina* (lambs' ears); or *Yucca* spp.

● **Do you have suggestions for really sunny corners of the garden?**

For very sunny places, perennials such as the purple coneflower, rudbeckia, daylily and peonies do very well. Lavender, chrysanthemums, geraniums, zinnias and cosmos also like the sun, too.

● **Kids love to play on the grass. Is there anything besides grass that's tough enough to take the abuse?**

Other plants can be used as lawns: chamomile, for example, and dichondra, which is used mainly in California, but none of them is entirely trouble-free, and all of them, including those just mentioned, aren't a perfect solution for the rough-and-tumble play of energetic children. For really tough areas that defy the possibility of grass, bark mulch works very well, or a rubberized surface, both of which have the added advantage of providing a cushion for falls. Gravel is also an alternative in those absolutely, positively impossible areas where the grass won't grow.

But before you abandon grass altogether, you might first try a tougher variety that is recommended for your part of the country, and specifically for playing fields and high-traffic areas. And once it grows, don't be too fussy about it; the children will be perfectly content if you grow what's called a yachtsman's lawn: "He mows what grows." Just rake off the leaves in fall or, even better, mow them with a mulching mower. In early spring, before the lawn greens up, broadcast a generous sprinkling each of compost and corn gluten (a natural fertilizer that suppresses the sprouting of annual weeds). Repeat the gluten every six weeks or so, stopping at the first sign of frost. Keep your mower sharp, and don't use it too much. Longer grass, a good three inches tall, will cut down on weeds, providing more shade, keeping the grassroots cool and healthy while making it harder for weed seeds to sprout and find the light. And if the grass becomes too compacted because of high-traffic use, you may need to call in the pros to aerate the lawn, or buy a machine and do it yourself. For more tips about grass, see "The Perfect Lawn" on page 467.

How about sloped areas around a house?

If an incline is too steep for mowing a lawn safely, plant a low-upkeep groundcover, like pachysandra, myrtle or ajuga, along with shrubs and understory trees. If the slope is extremely steep, install retaining walls in a series of terraces, and then plant whatever you wish.

What do you recommend for clay soil?

This is a common problem in much of the country. Sometimes, the answer is to install raised planting beds and fill them with well-prepared planting soil. If you are planting directly in clay soil, you should incorporate lots of well-rotted compost. Dig the clay soil eight inches deep and add at least four inches of compost. You can fork or rototill the compost in. You can also treat soil that is too sandy the same way—add lots of well-rotted compost.

What shrubs can I plant by a stream bank without blocking the view? The area gets partial sun and deer are a constant problem.

You are describing an ideal spot for drooping leucothoe. *Leucothoe fontanesiana*, a deer-resistant broad-leafed evergreen with shiny foliage and graceful arches of white flowers. The species form can grow to seven feet, but there are smaller varieties. Nana, the best-known dwarf form, stops around two feet. Rainbow, named for the red and cream streaks on its young leaves, grows to three or four feet. Leucothoes are useful as well as lovely, forming dense thickets that hold the soil on slopes and give the plant its common names of doghobble and fetterbush. And planting them at a distance is wise; the flowers have a strong fragrance that many find unpleasant.

—Leslie Land

The 60-Second Gardener

Some time-saving techniques to keep your garden in shape

As in all areas of their lives, time pressures are transforming the way many backyard gardeners are pursuing their avocation. Shortcuts are in much demand today, giving rise to what one gardening writer recently called "quick-thumb gardening." The object of these new techniques is to keep maintenance low, yet still get beautiful results.

The first principle of quick-thumb gardening is to start out small. Work up to larger gardens and beds once smaller ones are self-sustaining. Careful plant selection also is crucial. Go with plants that are draught tolerant, disease resistant and suited to your climate. More and more gardeners are turning to native plants, because they are likely to thrive in their climate and region without chemical fertilizers and sprays. Your local public garden, agricultural extension agent or state native plant society can tell you which plants are native to your area.

Hurried gardeners should avoid high-maintenance plants such as hybrid roses or fruit trees that require lots of fertilizer, water and spraying to keep them healthy. Plants that need staking and continual deadheading like dahlias, hollyhock and delphinium also are impractical. Select trees and shrubs that don't have fruits or nuts to rake up. If you must grow high-maintenance plants, group them together so that they can be cared for in a single place.

If you don't want to spend time planting and pulling out annuals every spring and fall, hardy perennial flowers are a natural alternative. Although they will need to be divided every three years or so, they still save time and money in the long run.

Probably the most tedious of all gardening jobs is weeding, so all garden beds and pathways should be mulched once or twice a year to keep down weeds and keep soil moist, which also saves time on watering. In addition to organic mulches like compost, pine bark and pine needles, there are new products that can virtually eliminate weeding without harmful chemicals. These synthetic landscape fabrics are spread out in garden beds and completely block weed growth. Unlike regular plastic mulches, they have microscopic holes that permit air and moisture exchange, keeping plants and soil healthy.

To cut down on lawn-maintenance time,

many people are decreasing or even eliminating traditional grass lawns and instead installing low-maintenance plantings such as native trees, shrub borders, hardy ground cover and native perennials and brick, stone or concrete patios.

Watering chores can be reduced by using drip irrigation or soaker hoses instead of watering by hand or relying on overhead sprinklers. Soaker hoses are set down at soil level near plant roots. They save on water because water is emitted directly where it is needed and not lost to evaporation. You can cut down on regular fertilizer feedings of plants by using slow release pellets that last throughout the growing season.

For people with limited space and time, raised bed gardens and container plantings are popular. They are easily planted and watered, and stay virtually weed-free. If you have a sunny, back-door area, plants in containers right outside the door can be easy to water or harvest.

Look for tools and equipment that can save time, too. For example, a mulching lawn mower will save raking lawn clippings, and some new mowers allow you to lime and fertilize as you mow.

For the truly hurried person, there's even a gardening trend called "ungardening," which promotes the idea that weeds, faded flower heads and unpruned shrubs enhance a garden's charm. Nature isn't perfect, so why should your garden be?

Late-Season Vegetables
It's almost never too late to start planting

Early August is the perfect time for planting a fall vegetable garden. Anne Raver, *New York Times gardening columnist*, tells us how to extend the summer pleasures of stepping outside to harvest herbs for dinner well into October.

There is nothing better than September lettuce:

What Makes Them Heirlooms?

Planting the seeds of yesteryear

For years, the only way to grow the vegetables popular in your great-grandmother's day was to get heirloom or open-pollinated vegetable seeds through specialty catalogs devoted to saving a bit of horticultural history. Unlike hybrids, heirlooms can be saved year after year, and passed down to future generations.

But more and more gardeners are recognizing the appeal of antique varieties. Heirlooms offer great flavor and enable gardeners to grow new plants from their seeds. But they offer a lot more than just the freedom from the need to buy seed each year. Heirlooms are the special province of individuals and small, regional seed companies who tend to be better attuned to specific local conditions (drought in the Southwest, humidity in the Southeast, cold in the North) than "one size fits all" hybrids.

Unlike hybrids, each heirloom plant is individual, subtly different from every other. Heirlooms grow and ripen unevenly, so you get a longer harvest period. Also unlike hybrids, which are both identically disease-resistant, but also identically vulnerable to disease, heirlooms react individually to disease. Heirlooms give gardeners a chance to do their part for the preservation of genetic diversity.

The Garden Seed Inventory, available from Seed Savers Exchange, (563-382-5990 or www.seedsavers.org) explains why heirlooms are important, and lists nearly all the open-pollinated (nonhybrid) vegetable seeds available commercially in the United States, along with the names and addresses of the companies that supply them.

Forellenschluss, an heirloom romaine from Austria whose name means "speckled like a trout's back" (888-762-7333 or seedsofchange.com), and lolla rossa, a frilled, magenta loose-leaf lettuce that matures in 55 days if you don't eat all the baby leaves much sooner (Seed Savers Exchange: 563-382-5990 or seedsavers.org).

Unprotected, these lettuces will not last all winter, but they will thrive with cooler weather, through August and September. To determine if a particular lettuce, or any other crop, is a good candidate for fall planting, look at the number of days to maturation listed under the variety in the catalog, and count backward from your first hard frost date. For instance, many spinach varieties, which love cool weather, take only 40 days or so.

Springer spinach is getting a lot of attention lately because it doesn't bolt, or go to seed, or develop brown soft spots in hot weather. It has a very mild, almost buttery flavor, but still a tangy taste. It's available from John Scheepers Kitchen Garden Seeds (860-567-6086 or kitchengardenseeds.com).

Melody hybrid spinach has a dark green, slightly crinkled leaf with loads of flavor. And Tetona, a smooth-leafed variety from Thompson & Morgan (800-274-7333 or thompson-morgan.com), is touted as a good fall producer.

With protection, under a floating row cover like Reemay, a light fabric made of spun polyester, or planted in a cold frame, or covered by a simple Hoop House, these leafy crops will produce long after frost. Such crop extenders, as they are called, are widely available from mail-order companies, including the Gardener's Supply Company (888-833-1412 or gardeners.com) and Johnny's Selected Seeds (800-879-2258 or johnnyseeds.com).

I've grown greens clear through the winter in a wooden cold frame set on the south side of the house and covered with old storm windows. (But

A VEGETABLE FOR EVERY POT

Most vegetables are easily grown from seed. For plants that require a long growing season, you can start the seeds growing indoors during winter months, then transplant the seedlings into your garden after the last frost. Your local agricultural extension service or plant nursery can tell you the best time to plant in your area. As a general rule, plant at a depth four times the seed's diameter.

VEGETABLE When to sow*	Days to germinate	Light	Space between		Days to harvest
			plants (in.)	rows	
ARTICHOKE	7–14	Full sun	36	3 ft.	**90–100 after transplanting**
Start indoors 8 to 10 weeks before last frost, then transplant outdoors					
ARUGULA	7–14	Full sun to partial shade	8–12	18–24 in.	**35–45**
Early spring, as soon as soil can be worked					
ASPARAGUS		Full sun to partial shade	15	3 ft.	**First harvest in second**
Best to start with year-old roots. Plant in spring; comes back every year.					**or third year**
BEANS, bush*	7–14	Full sun	4	2 ft.	**45–60**
BEANS, lima*	7–12	Full sun	6–8	18 in.	**55–75**
BEANS, pole*	7–14	Full sun	36	4 ft.	**45–65**
BEANS, pole lima*	7–12	Full sun	6–8	18 in.	**88–92**
BEETS*	7–14	Full sun	3	15 in.	**49–60**
BROCCOLI	5–10	Full sun	24	30 in.	**50–65**
Start indoors 5 to 7 weeks before last frost, then transplant outdoors					
BRUSSELS SPROUTS	5–10	Full sun	18	2 ft.	**78–100**
Start indoors 5 to 7 weeks before last frost, then transplant outdoors					
CABBAGE, Chinese*	4–10	Full sun to partial shade	12	18 in.	**43–55**
CABBAGE, head	4–10	Full sun to partial shade	18	2 ft.	**50–95 after transplanting**
Start indoors 5 weeks before soil can be worked in spring, then transplant outdoors					
CARROTS	12–17	Full sun	3	14 in.	**60–75**
As soon as soil can be worked in spring					
CAULIFLOWER	5–10	Full sun	18	2 ft.	**45–75 after transplanting**
Start indoors 5 to 7 weeks before soil can be worked in spring, then transplant outdoors					
CELERY	21–28	Full sun	6	2 ft.	**98–105 after transplanting**
Start indoors 10 to 12 weeks before last frost, then transplant outdoors					
CORN, sweet*	7–10	Full sun	10	3 ft.	**66–92**
CUCUMBER	7–10	Full sun	48	6 ft.	**55–62**
After last frost and soil has warmed					
EGGPLANT	7–10	Full sun to partial shade	24	3 ft.	**50–70 after transplanting**
Start indoors 8 to 10 weeks before last frost, then transplant when soil has warmed					
KALE	5–10	Full sun	12–15	2 ft.	**55–65**
As soon as soil can be worked in spring; also in early fall for winter crop					
LEEK	7–12	Full sun	2	1 ft.	**110–145 from planting seed**
Start indoors 6 to 10 weeks before last frost, then transplant outdoors; or sow outdoors 3 weeks before last frost					
LETTUCE, butterhead and romaine (Cos)	7–10	Full sun to partial shade	6	14 in.	**60–75**
As soon as soil can be worked in spring; resow every 2 weeks into fall for continuous harvest					
LETTUCE, crisphead	7–10	Full sun to partial shade	10	14 in.	**56–84**
As soon as soil can be worked in spring; resow every 2 weeks into fall for continuous harvest					

VEGETABLE When to sow*	Days to germinate	Light	Space between plants (in.)	rows	Days to harvest
LETTUCE, leaf	7–10	Full sun to partial shade	6	14 in.	45–50
As soon as soil can be worked in spring; resow every 2 weeks into fall for continuous harvest					
MELONS (cantaloupe/muskmelon, honeydew)	5–10	Full sun	36	6 ft.	68–88 from planting seed
After last frost and the soil has warmed; or, for earlier harvest, start indoors 4–6 weeks before last frost, then transplant outdoors after soil has warmed					
OKRA	7–14	Full sun	10	2–4 ft.	50–60
After last frost and soil has warmed					
ONIONS	10–14	Full sun	2	15 in.	85–120 after transplanting
Start seeds 12 weeks before last frost, then transplant outdoors; or grow from sets instead of seed and plant sets after last frost					
PARSNIPS*	21–28	Full sun	3	18 in.	100–120
PEANUTS*	7–10	Full sun	12	30 in.	120–135
PEAS	7–14	Full sun	8	2 ft.	62–72
As soon as the soil can be worked in spring					
PEPPERS	10–20	Full sun	24	2 ft.	65–75 after transplanting
Start indoors 8 to 10 weeks before last frost, transplant outdoors after soil has warmed					
POTATOES	From tubers	Full sun	12	3 ft.	60–80
As soon as soil can be worked in spring					
PUMPKIN*	7–10	Full sun	60	12 ft.	80–120
RADISH	5–10	Full sun to partial shade	2	14 in.	22–28
As soon as soil can be worked in spring					
SPINACH	7–14	Full sun to partial shade	3	14 in.	39–45
As soon as soil can be worked in spring					
SQUASH, summer	7–14	Full sun	48	3 ft.	45–52
After last frost and soil has warmed					
SQUASH, winter	7–14	Full sun	60	6 ft.	75–110
After last frost and soil has warmed					
SWEET POTATOES	From plants	Full sun	12	3 ft.	90–120
After last frost and soil has warmed					
SWISS CHARD*	7–10	Full sun to partial shade	9	18 in.	60–63
TOMATOES	7–14	Full sun	36	3 ft.	55–85 after transplanting
Start indoors 6 to 8 weeks before last frost; transplant outdoors after soil has warmed					
TURNIPS*	7–14	Full sun	3	15 in.	35–60
WATERMELON	7–14	Full sun	96	8 ft.	65–100
After last frost and soil has warmed					

* Direct sowing in garden after last frost.

HOUSE

don't forget to vent a homemade frame, or the sun will turn it into a sauna.)

If space is a problem, you can plant a fall salad garden in a whiskey half-barrel or two, so long as you don't let the soil dry out.

My favorite greens for fall include sylvetta arugula, which has a sharp, peppery taste and easily self-seeds; claytonia, or miner's lettuce, which tolerates frost and will grow all winter in a cold frame; minutina, another cold-hardy green with a crunchy texture. These three greens alone could get more than a greens-deprived miner through winter.

You might also take a look on the Internet at the long list to choose from, including all the

TIMELY TIPS

Feed Your Plants

Here's when and how to side-dress your vegetable plants

How should you nurture your vegetables to ensure a bountiful harvest? The best way is to give them a fertilizer boost. Most commercial fertilizers contain three major plant nutrients: nitrogen is essential for leafy growth; phosphorus promotes root and fruit development; and potassium encourages vigor. On the package labels you'll find a set of numbers that refers to the percentage of each of the three ingredients in the product. The ingredients are always listed in the same order. For example, a fertilizer labeled 10-15-10 contains 10 percent nitrogen, 15 percent phosphorus, and 10 percent potassium. Here are guidelines for choosing the right fertilizer for your garden.

✔ Granular fertilizers are standard for long-term release of nutrients. Incorporate them into soil before planting. Use liquid fertilizers to give plants a quick boost during the growing season.

✔ Most vegetables benefit from another application of granular fertilizer after they have begun to flower and set fruit. This mid-season boost is called side-dressing. Sprinkle the fertilizer along each row of plants and mix it into the soil. Water well.

✔ For leafy crops, such as spinach and lettuce, use a fertilizer that has a higher ratio of nitrogen. For other vegetables, use a higher ratio of phosphorus.

✔ Chemical fertilizers can't improve soil. To improve the soil, use organic materials, such as leaf mold, peat moss and manure, which provide many nutrients to the soil but perhaps not enough for optimum plant growth.

---

upland cresses, which have the pepper flavor of watercress but thrive on land; and mâche, or corn salad, famous for growing year-round.

As for beets, try Bull's Blood and Chioggia, an old-time variety with red and white rings; and De Milan Rouge, a quick-growing turnip with pink shoulders and white bottoms, best eaten between two and three inches.

Baby turnips are delicious raw, in salads or mashed with potatoes. And I love them in pot roast, with onions and carrots. Hakurei, a white, flat, round turnip, ready in 38 days, is another good one for salads, or lightly cooked (800-213-0076 or www.parkseed.com). And don't forget the radishes: Miyashige, a white Daikon, is ready in 40 days (714-637-5769 or www.evergreenseeds.com); White Icicle, a slender heirloom also known as Lady Fingers, is ready in 30 days (Scheepers and other suppliers).

A member of the cabbage family that deserves more attention is kohlrabi, whose leafy, bulbous stem is as crisp as an apple and more tender than a turnip. Scheepers suggests interplanting Kongo kohlrabi, which is pale green with creamy white flesh, with Kolibri, which is purple on the outside and white on the inside.

Asian greens are another great fall crop. My favorites include Osaka Purple mustard greens, whose rumpled green leaves are tinged with purple, and tatsoi, which forms rosettes of spoon-shaped leaves with a mild but still peppery flavor. A good source for Asian vegetables is www.evergreenseeds.com.

Kale also thrives in the fall. Red Russian is a more tender variety. Its gray-green, purple-veined leaves are delicious, if picked young, in salads. It keels over with the freeze, however. So I plant curly kale, and one of the heirloom Italian Lacinato types, whose narrow, tough, savoyed leaves—best sautéed or simmered in a hearty soup—sweeten after a hard frost or a light snow.

The same is true of carrots, say Barbara Damrosch and Eliot Coleman, who have made an art of growing winter crops under protection at their Four Season Farm in Harborside, Maine. They say the best carrot varieties for winter are Napoli and Adelaide. (Napoli is available at 800-363-7333 or www.veseys.com; Adelaide at Scheepers.) They start them in late August or early September, and harvest carrots until mid-February. They plant the seeds in a cold frame and mulch the young plants with straw. "That's all the covering we need to harvest all winter," Damrosch said.

And if you plant them in late July or early August, the Burpee company (800-888-1447 or www.burpee. com) promises that its hybrid Sunflower Del Sol, a five-footer with long-stemmed flowers with bright yellow petals and deep brown centers, is ready for cutting within 50 days of sowing.

Herbs for All Spaces

Fragrant, tasty and beautiful—outdoors or in

Patches of garden that seem to sprout nothing but weeds should not be written off. "If you can't grow anything else," says gardening and food writer Sally Freeman, "herbs are the answer." Herbs have a long, noble history. They've been used to flavor food, prepare medicinal brews and beautify gardens from at least as far back as, well, the beginning of recorded history.

Growing herbs isn't difficult, as Freeman, author of *Herbs for All Seasons* and *Every Woman's Guide to Natural Home Remedies*, explains.

ESSENTIALS FOR AN HERB GARDEN. Ideally, there are three essentials for an herb garden: good drainage, plenty of sunlight and light soil enriched with compost. Try to keep your garden away from trees; the roots rob soil of moisture and nutrients.

But many herbs will do well without all three. Rosemary doesn't mind some shade. Basil, fennel, dill, Italian parsley and chives do well in soil suitable for growing vegetables. Peppermint doesn't mind wet conditions. Thyme tolerates acid soil, while lavender requires more alkalinity than most herbs.

INDOOR HERB GARDENS. If your windows face south, you should have adequate light for even sun-loving herbs such as dill, coriander, oregano, thyme and marjoram. If your windows face in other directions, you should be able to grow rosemary, sweet woodruff or bay laurel in natural light. You may have to augment natural light with special lighting.

Be sure to place herb containers as far as possible from radiators and other heating appliances, in a room that is cool, moist and well ventilated. On very cold winter days they should be placed away from windows.

GROWING FROM SEED. Most herbs will grow easily from seed, germinating in five to seven days. There are exceptions. Lavender can take up to a month to germinate. Rosemary is best propagated by cuttings and French tarragon, which is more flavorful than the Russian variety and preferable for cooking, must be propagated by root division. Parsley can be very difficult to germinate. Italian parsley is easier to grow than regular parsley and, to my mind, tastes better.

FERTILIZER OF CHOICE. Compost is best because it won't burn the tender roots. Enrich your compost pile by including some weeds, especially dandelion, whose long roots bring up minerals from deep in the soil. A layer of mulch conserves moisture and suppresses weeds in the summer.

WATERING HERBS. Water herbs as soon as the soil feels dry. Rosemary, especially, should never be allowed to dry out. You may need to water every day. Your herbs will also appreciate a daily misting.

HOUSE

Doing Battle With Blight

Stressed-out plants are the most vulnerable to external enemies

Diseases and pests know easy marks when they see them. When fallen fruit and leaves are left too long on garden beds, when plants are placed too close together and diseased vegetation isn't destroyed quickly, it's like hanging out a sign that says, "Unwelcome Visitors, Inquire Within." But pest and disease problems can be greatly minimized if you watch for danger signs and follow good cultivation practices. The first principle of preventive maintenance, says plant pathologist Neil Pelletier, is to keep plants adequately watered, weeded, pruned and fertilized. Plants that are well maintained and healthy will resist most attacks.

Diversifying what you plant, as well as where and when you plant, is also very helpful. By planting a variety of flowers and vegetables, you help ensure that even if one plant species is destroyed by disease or pests, there will still be an abundance of other plants. By rotating vegetable crops to different locations within the garden bed each year, a gardener reduces the risk that insect populations and diseases will infest an area where their favorite plants are most likely to be sited. If you're worried about a particular pest, find out from your local county extension office when that pest will be at its most destructive stage and plant before or after that time.

You can also use nature to repel nature by practicing what gardening writer Louise Riotte calls "companion planting." In this case, you fight fire with fire, or more precisely, odor. For example, many insect pests are repelled by strong-smelling plants such as marigolds, mint, basil, garlic, onions, chives, nasturtiums and savory. Plant these in and around your vegetables and ornamental plants and they'll keep uninvited guests away.

If all this fails to stop incursions, construct barriers around plants to prevent pests from laying eggs nearby or crawling up plant stems. The barriers may include plant collars made of plastic, metal or sticky tape. Why should you provide summer lodging for bad house guests?

THE BEST ORGANIC DISEASE-FIGHTERS

Here's a natural arsenal to defend your turf:

Bacillus Thuringiensis: a natural biological control that is sprayed on plants and soil to control caterpillar pests. Available at most garden centers. Follow package directions.

Bordeaux Mixture: a classic organic spray used for decades in France's wine-growing region. It is effective for preventing most foliage fungal problems on fruits, vegetables, flowers, trees and shrubs (see recipe, facing page).

Liquid Copper: a copper salt mixture used for controlling powdery mildew, bacterial blights and anthracnose problems on vegetables, fruits and ornamental plants.

Diacide: a mixture of diatomaceous earth and Pyrethrum. It will destroy aphids, beetles, leafhoppers, worms, caterpillars and ants.

Diatomaceous Earth: a naturally occurring material with sharp, jagged edges. It is sprinkled around the base of plants to act as a barrier against soft-skinned pests like slugs.

Dormant Oil: a petroleum-based substance which is applied in the fall to smother over-wintering insects. It is very effective against spider mites, scale and aphids. Often used on fruit trees.

Pyrethrum: a dust or spray made from a chrysanthemum species. It kills a wide variety of insects from aphids to caterpillars.

Rotenone and Sabadilla: two botanical insecticides (made from plants) that are used to kill

HOUSE

aphids, worms, beetles, borers, thrips and other hard-to-kill insect pests.

Biodegradable Soaps: composed of nonphosphate liquid soaps. Mixed with water and sprayed on plants, they control a range of insects, including aphids and mealy bugs. Sometimes referred to as insecticidal soap, examples include Safer and Reuter.

Lime Sulphur: useful in preventing fungal outbreaks on fruits, nuts, berries and ornamental plants.

Wettable Dusting Sulphur: a finely ground sulphur; effective against many foliage diseases.

HOMEMADE CURES FOR PESTS AND DISEASES

Organic gardening specialists recommend these do-it-yourself recipes for ridding your garden of unwanted visitors:

Cooking Oil Solution: Effective against eggs and immature insects.

1 cup cooking oil
1 tbsp. liquid dish soap

Mix oil and soap. Use 2½ tsps. per 1 cup of water. Pour into a spray bottle and spray surface and undersides of leaves. Apply once every 2 to 3 weeks until pest is gone.

Potassium Bicarbonate Solution: Effective as an anti-fungal agent, especially against black spot, powdery mildew, brown patch.

4 tsp. potassium bicarbonate
1 gal. water

Combine ingredients. Spray on top and undersides of foliage.

Neem Oil Solution: Interferes with the reproductive cycle of insects.

4 tsp. neem oil
1 tsp. mild dishwashing detergent
1 gal. water

Combine ingredients. Cover

plants with a fine spray. Neem oil is used widely as an organic pesticide in India. It is extracted from neem tree seeds and contains azadirachtin, an effective pest control agent.

Garlic-Pepper Solution: Effective against a wide range of chewing insects and animals.

2 cloves garlic
1 tsp. liquid detergent
2 tsps. cooking oil
1 tbsp. cayenne pepper
2 cups water

Put all the ingredients in a blender and mix until the garlic is thoroughly pureed. Spray solution on affected plants. Reapply as needed.

Bordeaux Mixture: Effective against common fungal disease. Often used on small fruits.

2 heaping tbsps. fresh hydrated spray lime
2 level tsps. copper sulfate crystals
3 gals. water

Dissolve lime in 2 gallons of water. In a separate container, dissolve the copper sulfate in 1 gallon of water. Add the copper sulfate solution to the lime solution. Strain the solution through a cheesecloth directly into a sprayer. Spray to cover foliage. When dry, it forms an insoluble copper precipitate that prevents fungal spores from entering and infecting plants. Begin applications in spring; repeat once every 7 to 14 days through early fall. Don't apply during cool and wet weather.

NATURAL PREDATORS TO FIGHT PESTS

Here are some friendly enforcers, what they can help control and some places to get them:

Assassin Bug: Aphids, caterpillars, leafhoppers and a variety of beetles.

Ladybugs: Aphids, chinch bugs, rootworms, scale, spider mites, weevils, whiteflies.

Praying Mantis: Aphids, beetles, caterpillars, flies, leafhoppers.

Robber, Syrphid and Tachinid Flies: Aphids, Japanese beetles, leafhoppers, mealybugs, scale, caterpillars.

The three top suppliers of predatory insects are Planet Natural (800-289-6656 or www.planet-natural.com); Gempler's (800-382-8473 or www.gemplers.com); and Peaceful Valley (888-784-1722 or www.groworganic.com).

How to Attract Butterflies

The winged beauties will visit if you create an alluring home

Everyone loves butterflies. Every spring, all over the country, public gardens and natural history museums offer seasonal displays, attracting large audiences of all ages. Creating your own garden to attract butterflies is a fairly easy undertaking. Plant what butterflies like to eat, drink and use for resting and laying eggs, and they will likely pay a visit. Here are some essentials for enticing butterflies to your garden:

WHERE TO PLANT THE GARDEN. Most butterflies are sun lovers. Pick a spot that gets at least five to six hours of full sun. Sheltering the garden from the wind with a hedge or vine-covered lattice increases chances that butterflies will settle long enough to lay cggs. You can also attract butterflies to your windowsill, balcony or rooftop by planting some of the flowers recommended below in large containers or window boxes.

WHAT TO PLANT. Groupings of flowers that create large splashes of color are more effective than single plants. Butterflies like brightly colored blossoms with short flower tubes that let them reach the nectar with their probosces. Some butterfly preferences include milkweed, dogbane,

---

TIMELY TIPS

To Lure a Hummingbird

If hummingbirds live in your area you can attract them to your garden. The frenetic little bird—the smallest species is the size of a bumble bee—is fascinating to watch. It hovers like a helicopter, moving forward, sideways or backward at speeds of up to 200 wingbeats per second.

✔ Hummers are attracted to red, tubular flowers. The National Wildlife Federation suggests planting, among others, trumpet honeysuckle, trumpet creeper, cardinal flower, scarlet pentemon, scarlet morning glory, cypress vine, scarlet paintbrush, scarlet salvia, bee balm, fire pink, scarlet petunia, red buckeye, geiger tree, scarlet-brush and coral bells.

✔ You can attract hummers by hanging a red feeder outdoors in the shade, not too close to a window. Fill it with a solution of four parts water to one part sugar. Clean the feeder every three days using a brush and mild soap. Rinse well.

Joe-Pye weed, purple coneflower, thistle, aster, goldenrod, lilac, zinnia, cosmos, strawflower, marigold, verbena and tickseed sunflower.

Some common plants that serve as hosts for caterpillars are Queen Anne's lace, which provides food for the larva of the eastern black swallowtails; milkweed, which feeds monarchs; dill and parsley for various swallowtails; and thistle and hollyhock for painted ladies.

OTHER LURES. Butterflies take in salt and minerals by sipping from mud puddles. Create a shallow puddle in your garden to serve as a drinking hole. Place some flat stones in the garden, which butterflies can use as resting spots. Also, try scattering pieces of rotting peaches or plums and putting out small, flat containers filled with sugar water.

PEST CONTROL. Never use pesticides in or near a butterfly garden. To control pests, try using predatory insects or insecticidal soaps. A healthy butterfly garden will usually attract beneficial insects, such as lady beetles, praying mantis and lacewings, which help the garden care for itself.

Even Plants Need a Haircut

Pruning advice from Tracy Scissorhands

Tracy DiSabato-Aust is an expert pruner with bachelor's and master's degrees in horticulture. After two years interning at botanical gardens in Europe, "Tracy Scissorhands" returned to tend her clients in the Midwest. She is the author of *The Well-Tended Perennial Garden*. Here are her tips:

The lure of pruning is working like a sculptor to form and shape plants. It is a nurturing and gratifying, almost religious experience, bringing me closer to my plants. Sometimes the plants send signals: leggy old growth and fresh new growth at the base of a plant are both red flags. Any outer stems at ground level or panicles at the top are candidates for removal because they tend to shadow their neighbors.

In late spring, try pre-emptive pruning, cutting a tall clump of summer or fall bloomers like bee balm into a slope so that one bloom won't hide another. Crop the plants at the front by half, the middle by a third and the back not at all. The uncut portion blooms on schedule, while the pruned parts are delayed a week or two, extending the overall bloom time.

Pruning can also eliminate the need to stake plants and will yield a more compact plant. Generally, perennials that bloom in summer and fall, with multiple flowers on a single stem, can be halved in late spring when they reach 16 to 24 inches. Candidates include nepeta, asters, garden phlox, balloon flowers, goldenrod and toad lilies. The result is a tidier plant with more (albeit slightly smaller) flowers. (There are exceptions, of course: day lilies refuse to flower the summer they are pruned.)

A clip in time will do wonders for plants like *Eupatorium maculatum,* a Southern favorite that often shoots up to 15 feet. When cut down to a foot or so in early June, it holds its flowering later to a three-foot stem. And if you pinch back the outer stems of a shorter plant, Gateway, you will have a rounded dome and four or more smaller flowers instead of one big one on each stem. But every gardener develops a personal pruning philosophy, and every garden is different: If a 15-foot-tall Eupatorium is your garden's exclamation point, let it be.

Often, spring-blooming perennials look tattered by midsummer, flopping and parting down the middle. You can shorten and shape *Baptisia australis* after flowering to give them structure and substance. Maiden pinks get a crew cut with hedge sheers, and once ribbon grass sports brown tips, cut it to the ground.

By cutting hollyhocks back after blooming, and despite their biennial classification, they return year after year, and their life span increases because they have not been allowed to seed. This sort of pruning can save foxgloves and other biennials as well.

✔ **TIMELY TIPS**

How to Delay Blooming

✔ If you prune the buds on *Chrysopsis villosa,* coneflowers, garden phlox, helliopsis and helianthus, among others, they will hold off blooming for a few weeks. This will allow you to plan a vacation or special event around the prime blooming time of your plants.

—Suzy Bales

Haircuts are followed by watering and a top dressing of compost to hold moisture and quicken growth. Within two weeks, most perennials will look reborn. There are some renegades, though: asters and mums will refuse to rebud.

—Suzy Bales

Pruners and Spades to Die For

Wooden handles cause few blisters; anvil pruners cut most sharply

The gardening rage has brought forth an abundance of top-quality tools, many of them fashioned after classic English tools. But at current prices, equipping yourself fully can be quite an investment, so you must choose wisely.

Materials are important. Metal tools should be made from tempered, heat-treated or forged metal. Stainless steel tools are most expensive, but they are also the strongest and should last you a lifetime.

Choose wooden-handled tools over metal ones whenever possible because they are less likely to cause blisters. Hickory and ash wood make the best handles. Handles made from Douglas fir will be weak and should be avoided. And make sure that there are no cracks or flaws of any kind in the wood before buying. Here is some advice on what to look for in garden tools:

PITCHFORKS: Look for pitchforks with springy stainless steel tines.

HOSES: Those made from rubber or Flexogen last longer than plastic ones.

PRUNERS: Hand pruners that work like scissors make the sharpest cuts.

TROWELS: A narrow-bladed trowel, sometimes known as a rock-garden or transplanting trowel, will also work well for planting bulbs.

SHOVELS: The best shovels and spades have a Y-brace handle to add strength by increasing leverage.

RAKES: Bamboo lawn rakes are the lightest and easiest to handle. They're usually the best for raking leaves. But for raking leaves within flower beds, use a rake that is rubber-tipped. It won't damage the plants.

ROTOTILLERS: Unless you have a large garden, you should probably just rent a rototiller once a year. Look for models that you can easily handle and don't allow you to step on the area just tilled as you move it along the bed. Rear-tined (where the wheels are in front) are best for compacted or rocky soils.

Tool Sources

Where to get a great rake or the best English trowel and other tools that get the job done:

AMES TRUETEMPER INC.
465 Railroad Ave.   Camp Hill, Pa. 17011
800-393-1846 or www.ames-truetemper.com

GRIFFIN GREENHOUSE AND NURSERY SUPPLIES
200 Mountain View Road
P.O. Box 709   Morgantown, Pa. 19543
800-443-4437 or www.griffins.com

SMITH & HAWKEN
25 Corte Madera   Mill Valley, Calif. 94941
800-776-3336 or www.smithandhawken.com

From Root to Branch

Tree-planting is usually a fall pursuit

The selection of trees is one of the largest investments and most important decisions that a homeowner may face in landscaping a property. A well-chosen tree on the right site can transform even the plainest house into a home with visual appeal. Here are some arborist FAQ's and their answers.

Q What factors go into selecting a tree for a landscape?

First of all, you look at ultimate size. You don't want to plant a tree that's going to get too big growing too close to your house. Consider then what type of tree you want—evergreen or deciduous, flowering, or something that may have other attractions, like colored leaves in the autumn, or colored leaves all season. Finding trees that have practically no disease or insect problem is also important.

Q What should you look for at the nursery when buying a tree?

Most of the trees at nurseries are sold in containers nowadays. Look for a tree that has a large enough container so that a pretty decent portion of the root system will be intact. It's very difficult to make any judgments when you are viewing a plant at a nursery, because even a plant with a really tacky root system can look good if it's kept watered. You can't pop it out of the container to see the roots. So you've got to go on the general reputation of the nursery.

Q How about mail-order trees?

Stay away from them. There are some firms with a pretty decent reputation, but there are many horror stories—poor quality, small plants. Specialty items can be an exception, but go to your local nursery first and ask if they can get it for you. They should know where to get the best-quality material.

Q When is the best time for planting?

That depends on where you live. In New England, for example, plant in the spring because fall comes a little fast. Ideally, spring planting is done before growth begins, though with container-grown plants, you can plant a little later. In most of the United States, fall planting is also good. When you plant in the fall, wait until after the buds have set on the tree and growth has ceased, and do not fertilize afterward, which could promote new growth on the tree that sets it up for a killing frost.

Q How should a new tree be planted?

One of the myths people have is that they must fill a planting hole with manure and peat moss to make a nice home for the tree. If the tree is going to survive, the roots have to get out of that hole. In most areas, your home soil is worthless. Generally, you should dig a hole twice the size of the container. When you take the tree out of the container, cut down the roots to promote their growth outward.

PRUNING TREES

Once a tree is established, it will need periodic pruning. The best time to prune deciduous trees is in winter, when trees are dormant—it's also easier to see the problem branches and the general shape of the tree without the leaves. If you're pruning an evergreen tree, wait until spring. Remember to prune with a light hand; overpruning can destroy your tree's look—and your investment.

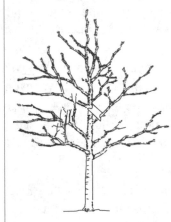

WHAT TO PRUNE

Crossing branches: When branches rub against each other, they may damage the bark and make the tree susceptible to disease and insects.

Dead, diseased or broken branches: Cut back to a healthy branch.

Crowded branches: Thinning weak branches improves the tree's shape and allows better air circulation and light penetration.

HOW TO PRUNE

When pruning a tree, be sure that you cut just above a branch's slightly swollen base at the point where that branch meets another branch. This base consists of plant tissues that help the cut to heal. Leaving too much of a stub creates a conduit for diseases to attack the tree.

If you want to shorten a branch that's too long, make a cut on the branch just above a bud at a 45-degree angle. Pick a bud facing the direction that you want a new branch to grow.

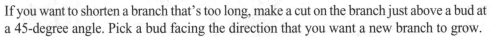

Make enough room in the hole so the roots can escape that bound mess. Otherwise, they will continue to circle. When you backfill the hole, use what you have taken out of the hole—beat it up and put it back. If you have to amend the soil, use some loam or sandy loam. Do not plant the tree too low.

Q **How deep should the hole be?**

If the plant comes in a container, look where the soil level is and plant it just a tad high in the ground. It's going to settle in.

Q **Should the burlap be removed if the roots are covered with it?**

If there are any ties, burlap, plastic wrap or anything, remove it. In the days when burlap was burlap, it might have rotted, but now, with the syn-

thetic things being used, it's just a tragedy to leave them. The roots just can't get out. More trees die because of a lack of planting care than any other factor, although they don't die immediately. At least unwrap the burlap to let those roots get out.

Q **What should you do once a tree has been planted?**

Mulch. It keeps the soil relatively warm; if you are planting in the fall, it might allow more root growth before the cold weather sets in. It also keeps the lawn mower and weeding equipment away from the tree. A two-inch layer of mulch is recommended.

Q **How about watering?**

Absolutely the first thing you have to do is water, and make sure the plant is well seated. Keep the tree watered in times of stress without overwatering.

Should new trees be staked?

The average homeowner is dealing with a tree that has a trunk with a 2- to 2½-inch maximum caliper. If it's well planted, well watered-in originally, and well sited, it's not going to blow over. Just tamp it down.

Should you fertilize your tree?

Most trees do not need fertilization, but if your tree is in your lawn, and you fertilize your lawn, don't worry about it. If you do fertilize, use a slow release fertilizer. A common mistake is when people use lawn fertilizers with weedkillers. This material leaches into the ground and is taken up by the roots. Eventually it's going to get your tree.

Should a newly planted tree be pruned?

Tree growth promotes root growth. The only pruning that should be done on a newly planted tree is if there is a broken branch.

TIMELY TIPS

The Mighty Quince

✔ Quince trees, or *Cydonia oblonga*, grow 12 to 15 feet tall with gnarly shapes that look wonderful against snow. The flowers, pink to white, open a bit later than apple blossoms. Leaves turn bright yellow in autumn, matching the fragrant hard-fleshed fruits. The fruits are delicious and beautiful when cooked. Quinces in a bowl will perfume a whole room.

✔ Quince trees grow best out of the wind in full sun and moist, fertile soil and are winter hardy. They will fruit without cross-pollination, but have better crops when there are at least two trees.

✔ Sources for *Cydonia oblonga* include One Green World, at 877-353-4028 or onegreenworld.com; and Raintree Nursery, at 360-496-6400 or raintreenursery.com.

—Leslie Land

The Perfect Lawn
Hold the chemicals and follow these 12 steps

The most ubiquitous feature of the American-constructed landscape is the lawn of closely mown turfgrass, currently covering more land area than any agricultural crop. In the United States alone, lawns cover upward of 50,000 square miles, more than 80 percent of which is residential land. Clearly, the American lawn is an icon that has more than functional value to the average homeowner. It is an emblem of pride of ownership—and it is unlikely that any alternative treatment for the residential landscape, no matter how attractive or environmentally preferable, will be easily embraced by the American public. So get to work, folks. Keep up with the Joneses.

1. Prepare the soil. Though they are seldom thought of that way, expanses of mown grass are actually very intensive gardens. Loose, fertile soil of the right pH is even more important for good lawns than it is for tasty tomatoes or lavishly blooming shrubs.

2. Invest in the best seed, use enough of it and plant at the right time. The first defense against weeds is a turf that is thick enough to prevent them from getting the light they need to sprout and grow. The grass won't be thick if you're stingy with either quality or quantity, and it won't fill in properly unless you give it a proper start.

3. Think long term. Be sure the seed mixture comprises grasses that will be long lived, such as red fescues and blue grasses. There should be only a very small amount of rye grass, if there is any at all.

Rye grasses grow quickly, helping the lawn to look good fast and preventing the growth of some weeds. But because they are up so quickly, they steal nutrients, water and light from slower-growing but more durable types. As a result, newly established turf has a lot of rye in it. This is fine for a short while. But even perennial rye dies out within a few years, and when it does, it leaves a whole lot of room for weeds to move in.

A sprinkling of rye can be used if you are the impatient type. But you'll have better long-term weed control if you go for the slow stuff and hand-weed for the first year or so while the good grasses are settling in.

4. Adjust the mower to the season. No matter what height you like your lawn, let it get a bit shaggy in summer. Longer grass, a good three inches tall, will cut down on weeds, providing more shade, keeping the grassroots cool and healthy while making it harder for weed seeds to sprout and find the light.

5. Water during the day. After a lawn is established, mow and water it once or twice a week. Watering at night during the summer can invite fungal problems caused by standing water and high humidity. It's better to water during the day. It takes heat stress off the grass and keeps the roots from coming up to the top.

6. Don't water if there's a drought. This may seem counterintuitive, but if you do not have an endless supply of water during a drought and cannot water the lawn thoroughly, you are much better off letting the lawn go dormant than trying to give it just enough to stay alive. Grasses naturally lie low and turn brown during droughts. They aren't dead—they're just sleeping. A small amount of water won't be enough to keep the grasses green, but it will keep the lawn green, because the watered weeds will thrive.

7. Don't throw away the leaves; mulch them. Don't just rake the leaves off your lawn in fall;

mow them with a mulching mower. According to studies done at Michigan State University, the nutritive value of mulching and leaving grass clippings saves 20 to 25 percent of the fertilizer one would ordinarily use.

8. If you have to fertilize, try corn gluten. In early spring, before the lawn greens up, broadcast a generous sprinkling each of compost and corn gluten (a natural fertilizer that suppresses the sprouting of annual weeds). Repeat the gluten every six weeks or so, stopping at the first sign of frost. Keep your mower sharp, and don't use it too much.

9. Aerate your lawn. Lawns should be aerated yearly, and twice yearly is a good idea where the lawn is green year-round. You can do it at any time. There is no rule about the season, and no need to do it all at once. Handheld spiking tools for aeration work fine on small areas. If the lawn is large, a power-driven aerator will make the task easier.

10. Get rid of dead grass at the end of summer. In late August or early September the first year, and every four or five years after that, rent a thatching machine to remove the lower layer of thatch, the dead, dying and decaying organic matter, mostly old turf stems, that accumulates in a layer just above the soil. Then put down some more seed. That should get you ready for winter and a healthy lawn for next spring.

11. Keep your lawn moist after seeding. If you have to reseed a part of the lawn or overseed it, it's very important to keep the seed wet until germination. This takes about two weeks. When the grass is about three inches tall, cut it to two inches. After that, start mowing it to about three inches.

12. Mow with sharp blades, and avoid mowing when the grass is wet with dew or rain. Cutting a living tissue of a grass blade reduces the area of leaf surface, reducing photosynthesis and the ability to take up water. These stresses make the plant weaker and less able to fight off desases, and slow down root growth. When the cut is ragged or torn, the increased surface area open to the air means a 10 to 15 percent additional water loss through evaporation, and a longer time to heal. Diseases find it easier to enter a host with weakened defenses. It is also important to avoid mowing when the grass is wet with dew or rain. Not only are fungal populations higher when it is damp or humid, but the water on the grass impedes the lawn mower blade, leading to a poorer quality cut.

The Grass Is Always Greener

Considering microclimate and foot traffic

To pick the best grass seed for your lawn, take into account the growing region (defined by humidity level and mean temperature), microclimate (how much sun the lawn gets throughout the day), maintenance time and expected foot traffic.

BAIIIAGRASS *Paspalum*   GULF COAST
This wide, coarse-bladed grass is not particularly attractive, but its ruggedness and deep root system make it good for erosion control.

MICROCLIMATE	FOOT TRAFFIC	MAINTENANCE
Sunny to partly shady	High	Low

BENTGRASS *Agrostis*   NORTHERN
Often used on putting greens, this high-maintenance grass should be used only on low-traffic areas or where soft-soled shoes are worn.

MICROCLIMATE	FOOT TRAFFIC	MAINTENANCE
Sunny to partly shady	Low	High

BERMUDAGRASS *Cynodon*   SOUTHERN
Fast-growing, this wide-bladed grass requires frequent edge-trimming, but will tolerate high traffic. Popular in the South for its vigor and density.

MICROCLIMATE	FOOT TRAFFIC	MAINTENANCE
Sunny	High	Medium to high

BUFFALOGRASS *Buchloe*   WEST CENTRAL
Like wheatgrass, a native turf that is thick and rugged, requires low maintenance and will not grow over four or five inches if left unmowed. It is very tolerant of drought.

MICROCLIMATE	FOOT TRAFFIC	MAINTENANCE
Sunny	Medium	Low

CARPETGRASS *Axonopus*   SOUTHERN
Coarse but sensitive to wear, this grass is used primarily on hard-to-mow places because of its low maintenance and slow growth rate.

MICROCLIMATE	FOOT TRAFFIC	MAINTENANCE
Sunny	Low	Low

CENTIPEDEGRASS *Eremochloa*   SOUTHERN
A good "middle-of-the-road" grass—easy to care for, will tolerate some shade and is vigorous and attractive. It requires two seasons to grow.

MICROCLIMATE	FOOT TRAFFIC	MAINTENANCE
Sunny to partly shady	Low	Low

KENTUCKY BLUEGRASS *Poa*   NORTHERN
The most popular of cool-season grasses for its beauty and ruggedness and flexibility. It will excel with minimum maintenance almost anywhere.

MICROCLIMATE	FOOT TRAFFIC	MAINTENANCE
Sunny to partly shady	Medium to heavy	Low to high

PERENNIAL RYEGRASS *Festuca*   NORTHERN
This quick-growing and reasonably hardy grass is used in seed mixes to provide cover and erosion

control while the other seeds take root.

MICROCLIMATE	FOOT TRAFFIC	MAINTENANCE
Sunny to partly shady	Medium	Medium to high

ST. AUGUSTINE GRASS *Stenotaphrum* — SOUTH ATLANTIC

Dense and spongy, this low-growing, coarse-textured grass is prized for its high shade tolerance. Not available in seed form, but usually sold as fairly inexpensive sod.

MICROCLIMATE	FOOT TRAFFIC	MAINTENANCE
Sunny to shady	Medium	Medium to high

TALL FESCUES *Festuca* — NORTHERN

Though it is a cool-season grass, this tough, wide-bladed turf has good heat tolerance and grows well in areas with a steep range of weather. Often used on playgrounds because of its ruggedness.

MICROCLIMATE	FOOT TRAFFIC	MAINTENANCE
Sunny to partly shady	Heavy	Medium

WHEATGRASS *Agropyron* — HIGH PLAINS

Thick and tough, this grass is native to the high plains of the Northwest. It withstands weather extremes and heavy traffic and needs mowing about once a month.

MICROCLIMATE	FOOT TRAFFIC	MAINTENANCE
Sunny	High	Low

ZOYSIA *Zoysia* — SOUTHERN

Takes root very quickly and crowds out other grasses and weeds. It turns a not entirely unattractive straw yellow in cold weather and requires little maintenance in general. Heat- and drought-tolerant.

MICROCLIMATE	FOOT TRAFFIC	MAINTENANCE
Sunny to partly shady	High	Low to medium

SOURCE: Dr. H. A. Turgeon, Pennsylvania State University

Shedding Light on Houseplants

Fluorescent bulbs are best because they don't throw off a lot of heat

Unless you have a sunroom or greenhouse, the biggest dilemma of having plants indoors is providing them with enough light. Even if you have windows, they may be less than ideal if they're facing in a direction that gets little sun, or if they're shaded by a tree or porch overhang. Plants suffering from light deprivation are often lanky, with pale or yellowed leaves. Luckily, you can lend a helping hand with artificial lighting.

The best type of artificial light is fluorescent. Incandescent light doesn't provide the right kind of light for optimal growth, and it produces heat, which can burn plants. Fluorescent lights come in several varieties: the standard ones, which you can find at any hardware store or home improvement center, are fine for growing small plants such as African violets, but for larger plants, go for higher-output fluorescents, which emit much more light and can be found at most well-equipped garden centers or through mail-order gardening supply catalogs. Bear in mind, too:

- When growing plants under artificial light, choose those that prefer low to medium sunlight.

- Keep your plants very close to the light source—no more than 6 to 12 inches away. The intensity of light diminishes drastically the farther away you move from it. To increase intensity, add more fluorescent tubes, grouped together.

- Rearrange your plants regularly around their light source to ensure that they all receive equal exposure. The greatest amount of light is emitted from the center of a fluorescent tube.

- Leave the lights on 14 to 16 hours a day. A couple of hours daily won't suffice. But don't leave them on all the time; plants need darkness to rest.

Location, Location, Location

How to match up a plant's light, temperature and humidity needs to the best window in your house.

NORTH WINDOWS: Receive no direct sun—but, if unobstructed, they do receive good, bright light. Plants grown in a shaded north window during the winter months would appreciate extra light. When choosing plants for a dark window, remember that plants with variegated leaves require more light than ones with strictly green leaves. Consult the key below.

PLANT	WATER	TEMPERATURE	HUMIDITY	FERTILIZER
CAST-IRON PLANT *Aspidistra eliator*	WET/DRY	INTERMEDIATE	MEDIUM	INTERMEDIATE
FERN, BIRD'S NEST *Asplenium nidus*	MOIST	INTERMEDIATE	HIGH	LOW
FIG *Ficus pumila*	MOIST	INTERMEDIATE	HIGH	LOW
PHILODENDRON, VELVET LEAF *Philodendron hederaceum* var. *hederaceum*	WET	INTERMEDIATE	HIGH	LOW
PRAYER PLANT *Maranta leuconeura*	MOIST	WARM	MEDIUM	INTERMEDIATE
SPATHE FLOWER *Spathiphyllum*	MOIST	WARM	MEDIUM	INTERMEDIATE
WANDERING JEW *Zebrina pendula*	MOIST	INT-WARM	MEDIUM	INTERMEDIATE

EAST AND WEST WINDOWS: Both are excellent for growing houseplants. East windows tend to be cooler than west. If you can't grow the following plants in east or west windows, they should do fine in a south window—but add some shading during the day in the summer, especially for ferns.

PLANT	WATER	TEMPERATURE	HUMIDITY	FERTILIZER
BROMELIAD *Bromeliacea*	WET	INTERMEDIATE	MEDIUM	LOW
CAPE PRIMROSE *Streptocarpus*	MOIST	INTERMEDIATE	HIGH	HIGH
FERN, BOSTON *Nephrolepsis exaltata*	MOIST	INTERMEDIATE	HIGH	LOW
IVY, GRAPE *Cissus rhombifolia*	MOIST	INTERMEDIATE	MEDIUM	INTERMEDIATE
LILY, AMAZON *Eucharis grandiflora*	MOIST	INT-WARM	MEDIUM	HIGH
LILY, BUSH *Clivia miniata*	MOIST	INTERMEDIATE	MEDIUM	INTERMEDIATE
LADY PALM *Rhapsis excelsa`*	WET-MOIST	INTERMEDIATE	HIGH	INTERMEDIATE
NORFOLK ISLAND PINE *Araucaria heterophylla*	MOIST	COOL	MEDIUM	LOW
PAINTED BEGONIA *Begonia rex*	MOIST	INTERMEDIATE	HIGH	HIGH
ROSARY VINE *Ceropegia woodii*	MOIST/DRY	INTERMEDIATE	LOW	INTERMEDIATE
RUBBER PLANT *Ficus elastica*	MOIST	WARM	MEDIUM	LOW
SHAMROCK PLANT *Oxalis*	MOIST	INTERMEDIATE	MEDIUM	LOW
FIG, WEEPING *Ficus benjamina*	MOIST	WARM	MEDIUM	LOW
VIOLET, AFRICAN *Saintpaulia*	MOIST	INT-WARM	MEDIUM	HIGH

SOUTH WINDOWS: South windows receive the most light. During the summer months they even can be too bright for many kinds of houseplants—you may need to shade them a bit. All of these plants, while preferring south windows, can also be grown in east or west exposures.

PLANT	WATER	TEMPERATURE	HUMIDITY	FERTILIZER
ALOE *Aloe vera*	WET/DRY	INTERMEDIATE	LOW	LOW
BEGONIA, TRAILING *Cissus discolor*	MOIST	INTERMEDIATE	MEDIUM	INTERMEDIATE
CACTUS *Cactaceae*	WET/DRY	INT-WARM	LOW	LOW
GERANIUM *Pelargonium*	MOIST	INTERMEDIATE	MEDIUM	LOW
GERANIUM, STRAWBERRY *Saxifraga stolonifera*	WET	INTERMEDIATE	MEDIUM	LOW
IVY *Hedera helix*	MOIST	INTERMEDIATE	MEDIUM	INTERMEDIATE
IVY, GERMAN OR PARLOR *Senecio mikanioides*	WET/DRY	INTERMEDIATE	LOW	INTERMEDIATE
JADE PLANT *Crassula argentea*	WET	INTERMEDIATE	LOW	LOW
PASSION FLOWER *Passiflora*	MOIST	INTERMEDIATE	MEDIUM	INTERMEDIATE
POMEGRANATE, DWARF *Punica granatum 'Nana'*	MOIST	INTERMEDIATE	MEDIUM	INTERMEDIATE
SHEFFLERA, HAWAIIAN *Erassaia arboricola*	WET	INTERMEDIATE	LOW	INTERMEDIATE

KEY:

WATER:

WET/DRY:	Water thoroughly, let dry fully before rewatering.
WET:	Water thoroughly but don't let it totally dry out before rewatering.
MOIST:	Keep soil evenly moist, but don't let it stand in water. Top inch of soil should always feel moist.

TEMPERATURE:

COOL:	Cool: 45° nights, 55° to 60° days.
INTERMEDIATE:	50° to 55° nights, 65° to 70° days.
WARM:	Warm: 60° nights, 75° to 80° days.

HUMIDITY:

LOW:	20 to 40 percent.
MEDIUM:	40 to 50 percent.
HIGH:	50 to 80 percent.

FERTILIZER:

HEAVY:	Use balanced fertilizer recommended for frequent feeding, feed each watering.
INTERMEDIATE:	Feed every other week with a balanced fertilizer.
LOW:	Feed about once per month with a balanced fertilizer.

Gardening from A to Z   *For a standard reference guide to gardening, try one of these:*

American Horticultural Society A To Z Encyclopedia of Garden Plants
H. Mark Cathey, Christopher Brickell, ed., Revised edition, 2004
Information on most of the trees, shrubs, flowers and foliage plants grown in American gardens.

Reader's Digest New Illustrated Guide to Gardening
Reader's Digest editors, 2000
If you had no other source, you could develop terrific skills with this book alone. Easy-to-understand and has excellent illustrations.

10 Terrific Public Gardens

Gardeners looking for inspiration may well find it here

The American landscape is scattered with thousands of spectacular public gardens. Here are ten considered to be among the best in the country.

BROOKLYN BOTANIC GARDEN, *Brooklyn, N.Y.* Famous for its systematic collection of plants in a beautifully designed garden setting.
718-622-7200 or www.bbg.org

NEW YORK BOTANICAL GARDEN, *Bronx, N.Y.* Outstanding herb and rose gardens and a wonderful conservatory.
718-817-8700 or www.nybg.org

ATLANTA BOTANICAL GARDEN, *Atlanta, Ga.* Beautiful display of rare and endangered plants; also a gorgeous conservatory.
404-876-5859 or www.atlantabotanicalgarden.org

HUNTINGTON BOTANICAL GARDENS, *San Marino, Calif.* World-class bonsai, succulent and rose gardens.
626-405-2100 or www.huntington.org

CHICAGO BOTANIC GARDEN, *Glencoe, Ill.* Its walled perennial garden is one of the best in the country. Outstanding educational programs.
847-835-5440 or www.chicagobotanic.org

HOLDEN ARBORETUM, *Kirtland, Ohio.* Famous for its woody (trees and shrubs) plant collection
440-946-4400 or www.holdenarb.org

LONGWOOD GARDENS, *Kennett Square, Pa.* Perhaps the most outstanding display garden in the world. Included are 20 theme gardens.
610-388-1000 or www.longwoodgardens.org

UNITED STATES NATIONAL ARBORETUM, *Washington, D.C.* Spectacular display of azaleas and a nearly three-acre herb garden.
202-245-2726 or www.usna.usda.gov

MISSOURI BOTANICAL GARDEN, *St. Louis, Mo.* A geodesic dome houses a full-fledged tropical rain forest.
314-577-5100 or www.mobot.org

SAN FRANCISCO BOTANICAL GARDEN AT STRYBING ARBORETUM , *San Francisco, Calif.* A collection of mediterranean, mild temperate and tropical cloud-forest plants displayed in designed gardens and habitats.
415-564-3239 or www.sfbotanicalgarden.org

 TIMELY TIPS

Beautiful Gardens That Gather Moss

It's not a cinch to grow, but worth the effort

Growing moss can be tricky, unless you are lucky enough to have the right conditions: a shady, moist spot under trees, for example, or a wet spot in the lawn. Moss spreads by spores, not seeds, and thrives on compacted acidic soil or moist bricks and stone.

✔ You can encourage moss that is already growing in your garden by digging up surrounding grass, weeds and woody seedlings, then planting more moss, from other places.

✔ Transplanting chunks of moss and pressing them into bare spots can fail, because birds turn them over, looking for grubs. A better strategy is to make a slurry of moss particles mixed with a solution of seaweed fertilizer, and spread it over the bare spots.

✔ Moss Acres (866-438-6677 or www.mossacres.com), in Honesdale, Pa., ships moss, ferns, soil amendments, misting devices and netting to protect newly planted moss from birds. It also offers a pamphlet, *Gardening With Moss: The Lawn of the Future,* by David E. Benner.

—Anne Raver

HOUSE

Pets

Picking a Canine Companion

A dog's breed is no guarantee that it will act according to the book

Every dog has its own personality. But some breeds are better suited to being jostled by children than others, while the circumstances of other pet lovers may require quite different choices. Here, veterinarian Sheldon L. Gerstenfeld suggests which dogs make good pets for families with children, owners with active lifestyles and people who are older and looking for easy pet companionship. Gerstenfeld is the author of numerous books about pet care, including the *ASPCA Complete Guide to Dogs.*

DOGS FOR CHILDREN

Collie: They're gentle and predictable and won't bite around your kids. They're easy to train and

INSIDE INFO

Fair Weather Friends

A dog may be man's best friend, but for help in coping with stress, a dog's best friend may be another dog.

○ One finding—an owner's efforts to calm a dog had no effect, either positive or negative, on the animal's stress levels during a thunderstorm.

○ Dogs that lived in households with other dogs recovered faster from such stressful situations.

SOURCE: Study by Nancy A. Dreschel and Douglas A. Granger, Pennsylvania State University

—Henry Fountain

really want to please. Adult collies weigh about 50 pounds and their long hair requires grooming. Lassie was a rough-coated collie. The smooth-coated collie is somewhat less popular.

Golden Retriever: Easygoing, active and alert, golden retrievers have the best temperaments. They love to interact with kids and to play ball. The adult female weighs 50 to 60 pounds; the adult male 70 to 90 pounds. They need to be groomed and fed, and that teaches kids about being responsible. The golden retriever is the second most popular breed of the American Kennel Club (A.K.C.).

Labrador Retriever: Black, yellow, and chocolate Labs are known for being even-tempered and friendly. They are always ready to play, and kids can just lie on them. Adult dogs weigh 60 to 70 pounds. They need grooming, so they also teach kids to be responsible. Avoid the Chesapeake Bay retriever, which has a curlier coat. It can be a little nasty and unpredictable and will bite more readily than the others. Labrador retrievers are the most popular A.K.C. breed.

Standard Poodle: A gentle dog that is very intelligent. A standard poodle will let a kid lie on it. You need to groom them, but a fancy haircut is not necessary. Poodles, including miniature and standard, are also one of the most popular breeds in the United States. Because they are so popular, prospective owners have to watch out for puppy-mill degradation. The larger they are, the less active they are and the more exercise they need. Adult standard poodles weigh 50 to 55 pounds.

HOUSE

DOGS FOR THE ACTIVE PERSON

Boxer: Animated, with outgoing personalities, boxers respond readily to playfulness. They are the seventh most popular A.K.C. breed. Prospective owners looking for a dignified dog, however, should be wary of the boxer: They tend to drool and snore.

English Cocker Spaniel: These are sweet dogs, and they haven't been inbred. They're playful and alert at all times and great for children and active people. The English cocker spaniel is a medium-size dog with long hair. An adult usually weighs 23 to 25 pounds, 3 to 11 pounds more than its cousin, the American cocker spaniel. The English cocker is the fifteenth most popular A.K.C. breed.

Greyhound: They are a little aloof, but also very gentle. Most are adopted from the racetrack. Greyhounds have a regal personality and don't slobber with affection like a retriever. They're also very athletic, so they're good for active people. Adult greyhounds weigh 70 to 80 pounds. One caution: they are high-strung and easily upset by sudden movements at times.

Terrier: Terriers start out their morning as if they had eight cups of coffee, so they are good for an active person. I'd recommend the bull terrier, which was bred for pit fighting. They are always ready to frolic and so need firm training, but they are also known for their sweet personalities. The adult bull terrier weighs in at about 50 pounds.

DOGS FOR OLDER PEOPLE

Chihuahua: If they are from a good breeder, they will have a good personality. Chihuahuas have short hair, so they don't need a lot of grooming and so are a good choice for an older person living alone. The Chihuahua is the smallest of all the

---

 INSIDE INFO

Congenital Defects in Dogs

Before selecting a best friend, check this list of the most common potential problems.

○ **COCKER SPANIEL:** Cataracts, kidney disease, hemophilia, spinal deformities, behavior abnormalities

○ **COLLIE:** Deafness, epilepsy, hemophilia, hernia

○ **DACHSHUND:** Bladder stones, diabetes, cleft lips and palate, jaw too long or short, spinal deformities, limbs too short

○ **GERMAN SHEPHERD:** Cataracts, epilepsy, kidney disease, bladder stones, hemophilia, cleft lips and palate, behavior abnormalities

○ **LABRADOR RETRIEVER:** Cataracts, bladder stones, hemophilia

○ **TOY POODLE:** Epilepsy, nervous system defects, collapsed trachea, diabetes, spinal deformities, limbs too short, skin allergies, behavior abnormalities

---

breeds. They can be yappy and clannish at times. An adult Chihuahua weighs about 3 pounds and is the eleventh most popular A.K.C. breed.

Miniature Poodle: These poodles are intelligent, and they're good for older people because they're small and don't shed a lot. They love attention. Again, the poodle is a popular A.K.C. breed (eighth on the 2005 list), so owners have to make sure the dog is not inbred. All poodles are fast learners; generally the smaller they are the faster they learn. The adult miniature poodle weighs in at about 15 pounds.

Toy Poodle: These dogs love to be cuddled and are intelligent. They have to be groomed, but they don't shed, so there's not much hair to clean up. The adult toy poodle weighs less than 10 pounds. It is the brightest of all the toys and will demand its owner's continuous attention. Because of the toy poodle's popularity, inbreeding can be a problem.

Yorkshire Terrier: These dogs are small, easy to care for, and can be picked up. They weigh about 7 pounds and have silky long, draping hair. Their coats require grooming, however, which may not be good for an elderly person who doesn't have the energy, or who has arthritis. The Yorkshire terrier is the third most popular A.K.C. breed.

Buying a Pedigree Pup

When it comes to pure breeds, check both the dog and the breeder

More than 200,000 American households bought puppies online in 2004, according to the American Pet Product Manufacturers Association, a trade group. But not all Internet purchases have a happy ending. There have been more than 30 cases where charges have been filed by consumers who either received sick puppies that later died, or paid upward of $1,000 for a dog and never received it. The American Kennel Club—the largest registry of purebred dogs—says that more people are reporting health problems in dogs bought online.

To help buyers find the right breed and to choose responsible sellers, the A.K.C. has introduced a Web-based service called Breeder Classifieds, found under "Online Services" at www.akc.org. Only breeders in good standing can advertise. The site includes a list of questions to ask of breeders.

Some people mistakenly think that A.K.C. papers alone guarantee that a puppy is healthy and of good quality. They prove only that a puppy is the offspring of a known sire and dam.

Prices for pedigree puppies vary by region, depending on the type of dog, its health-screening tests and whether the parents are champions. In the New York metropolitan area, for example, Rhodesian ridgebacks—large, athletic dogs with permanently raised hair along their backs—sell for around $1,500. In upstate New York, they go for half that price.

In general, buyers can usually expect to pay $500 to $2,000 for a pet-quality pedigree puppy—one that the breeder believes won't be able to compete successfully in dog shows. Pedigree show dogs fetch a much higher price.

Many fans of purebreds say that you know it's a good breeder if you can make sure of the following things:

- They are not in the business solely to make money. For many, it is a hobby, with the goal of improving the breed.

- They often specialize in one breed, and spend time educating buyers about its advantages and disadvantages.

- They raise puppies in a loving home environment, not in a kennel, since socialization to humans occurs between one and 18 weeks.

- They sell only healthy animals and guarantee them for reasonable periods. They have tested a puppy's parents for hereditary diseases, and the puppy's vaccinations should be up to date. They are willing to put you in contact with the veterinarian who has cared for the puppy.

- Their contracts stipulate that if the buyer does not meet specified conditions of care, or becomes unable to keep the puppy, they will take it back. (Most contracts for pet-quality dogs also have a clause that requires spaying or neutering of the dog.)

TIMELY TIPS

How Much Is That Doggie in the Pop-up Window?

If you have bought a puppy online and can't pick it up yourself, here are some expert recommendations:

✔ **GET** the seller's phone number and mailing address. Call the number to verify it.

✔ **CHECK** with people who have bought puppies from the seller and the Better Business Bureau in the seller's area and the Internet to see if any complaints have been lodged.

✔ **HOLD** funds in escrow until the puppy arrives and is checked out by a veterinarian. There are escrow sites available online.

Adopting From an Animal Shelter

There is a growing trend among animal lovers toward adopting dogs—and many other kinds of pets—from animal shelters.

✔ Many animals, pure and mixed breeds, puppies and grown dogs, have been brought to the shelter or rescued from abuse and need homes.

✔ There is, typically, an adoption fee, but it is far less than what one pays for a purebred. For more information, go to www.aspca.org and click on "Adopt" on the topic bar at the top of the home page.

• They are willing to let you meet at least one of the puppy's parents; the appearance and temperament of the parent can provide an idea of how the pup may turn out.

• They have a good reputation at the local breed club.

—Maryann Mott

Smelling Like a Wet Dog

Being bathed and pampered, it turns out, isn't easy for dogs

When it comes to baths, almost all dogs second the notion attributed to Elizabeth I: once a month would be just fine, whether she needs it or not. And most dog owners would subscribe to that view, too, given the fuss their charges make, if it weren't for their habit of lolling in mud puddles and rolling ecstatically over dead fish on the beach.

Slowly, basic dog shampoo is disappearing, replaced by a bewildering array of "pet spa" products with names like Adventure Dog Suds, Earthbath Mediterranean Magic, Polar Pizzazz, Knotty Dog Detangler and Salon Details Tropical Twist.

And that's just the beginning. There are aromatherapy spritzers, between-bath splashes, breath fresheners and even massage oils for the family pooch. None of this surprises Sherril Stone, an expert in human-animal interaction and director of research for family medicine at Oklahoma State University. "Pets provide unconditional love; they're like surrogate children. If we are going to pamper ourselves, we want it for our pets, too."

Some of the newest pet-grooming products come directly from the human beauty industry.

Are all these exotic-sounding products really any better than a basic dog shampoo?

"That depends," said Dr. Heather Peikes, a veterinary dermatologist. A dog with dry skin can benefit from shampoos made with extra fatty acids or oatmeal (which has anti-itch properties and helps moisturize). But pet owners should pay attention to ingredient lists.

"There are products out there that claim to prevent itching, and if you read the label, you'll find they contain steroids," Peikes said. "That's not something we recommend."

In general, because dogs' skin has a pH level different from human skin, it's wise to use a shampoo especially formulated for them. Some human shampoos may dry out their coats. Milder shampoos are usually better, especially for dogs that are bathed frequently. "To be honest, a lot of dogs do just fine with Johnson's Baby Shampoo," Peikes says.

How do the dogs like all these products? Your dog probably doesn't care if the shampoo smells like chamomile or lavender. Most of them would cast their vote by rolling in something dead at the beach.

—Peter Jaret

 TIMELY TIPS

How to De-Skunk Your Dog

This skunk smell remedy is reputed to have been concocted by Paul Krebaum, a chemist and inventor, and has become a widely used remedy:

1 quart 3 percent hydrogen peroxide
¼ cup baking soda
2 tablespoons dishwashing detergent.

Mix the ingredients together. The concoction will foam, as the mixture of hydrogen peroxide and baking soda creates a lot of oxygen. It is important that, once mixed, you should cover your dog, or cat or family member with it as soon as possible, as the oxygen will dissipate almost immediately.

Work the mixture in well to the skin or coat. Krebaum claims that the thiols in the skunk oil which cause the odor are neutralized when they interact with the oxygen. The dish detergent breaks up the oil and makes it easier for it to be rinsed off with water. Rinse thoroughly with warm water. Keep the solution away from the face and eyes.

Dieting—A Dog's Life
Fitness and diet hold the key to a healthy pet

More and more dogs and cats are adopting the habits of their human companions, and like them, they are increasingly overweight. Between 25 percent and 40 percent of America's pets are obese, according to George Fahey, a professor of nutrition at the University of Illinois Animal Sciences Department, a big jump in just the past decade. The proportion of overweight humans is similar; 30 percent of American adults are obese, according to the National Center for Health Statistics.

Psychology aside, there are two basic reasons pets are getting rounder. One is too little exercise. "You've got lots of working dogs out there that live in high-rise buildings and don't have any work to do," Fahey says. The second is too many treats, especially people food. "In our studies, when we've overfed beagles commercial dog food, they put on a little weight," says John E. Bauer, a professor of veterinary nutrition at Texas A&M University, in College Station. "But it wasn't until we added human food that they really began to get fat."

Pets are also suffering the same consequences as overweight people, including joint problems and diabetes, Bauer says. Too many treats may even shorten their lives. A 2002 study compared Labrador retrievers on two eating plans. One group was allowed to gobble as much food as desired during 15-minute daily feedings, and that amount was measured. The other was then given 25 percent less food than that. The dogs on the restricted diet were healthier than the others and lived up to two years longer.

Pet supply companies have begun marketing weight loss supplements, including products like Canine Slim Results and Vetri-Lean. But these don't work any better for pets than they do for people, veterinarians say.

Dozens of companies now sell low-fat or low-calorie pet foods. Researchers in France and Belgium who recently evaluated an Atkins-like high-protein, low-carbohydrate diet for obese dogs found that it worked, but not much better than diets that merely cut back on calories. Many veterinary experts say giving smaller portions of a balanced pet food is a healthier choice for weight loss.

According to Fahey, the best—and simplest—approach is to buy pet food from a reputable manufacturer and follow the directions. "Feeding instructions are very reliable," he says. "If the package says your dog should be eating a cup a day, that's what they should get. A little less if your pet needs to lose weight." Treats like "vanilla woofers" and carob-covered fire hydrants should be reserved for special occasions. Your dog may not like that idea. But the second part of Fahey's prescription—more exercise—should get tails wagging.

—Peter Jaret

All the Cats' Meows

From pharaohs' favorites to loving tabbies, choose your companion

Celebrated for their highly independent nature, cats have been everything from lap companion to religious idol in the pages of human history. Today, over 200 million cats reside in American homes, making them nearly as popular as dogs for household pets. Here's the book on the best, brightest, most elegant and most cuddly cats from which to choose.

Abyssinian: One of the oldest known breeds, their slender, elegant, muscular bodies were often featured in paintings and sculptures in ancient Egyptian art. Abyssinians have arched necks, large ears, almond-shaped eyes, and long, tapered

INSIDE INFO

Dog Years vs. People Years

A popular myth says that household pets—specifically dogs and cats—age seven years for each human year. For example, a dog of age 9 would be said to be 63 in dog years.

○ Technically, there is no direct correspondence between how dogs (or cats) and humans age. But, there is something to the myth.

○ A 1-year-old dog or cat has generally reached its full growth although, like a 14-to-15-year-old human, it still might be lanky and need to fill out.

○ After the second year, a dog or cat has gained the equivalent of another 7-8 years in terms of physical and mental maturity.

○ After that, each year is equivalent to only about four human years. Even these rough guidelines, however, vary tremendously from breed to breed.

tails. The Abyssinian's soft and silky medium-length coat is one of its most unusual features. Each hair has two or three distinct bands of black or dark brown, giving the breed a subtle overall coat color and lustrous sheen. Abyssinians also can have a rich copper-red coat. They are particularly loyal and make good companions.

American Curl: The name comes from the breed's unique curled ears, which curl away from the head to make it look as if this cat is always alert. The American curl is moderately large, with walnut-shaped eyes. Its ears are straight at birth, and curl within 2 to 10 days. A relatively rare breed, the American curl usually weighs 5 to 10 pounds. Curls are short-haired, and their coats come in all colors possible. Even-tempered and intelligent,

HOUSE

with a playful disposition, American curls adore their owners and display affection in a quiet way. They adapt to almost any home, live well with other animals and are very healthy.

American Shorthair: The descendants of house cats and farm cats, American shorthairs are easy to care for and resistant to disease. They have big bones and are docile and even-tempered. The breed is strongly built, with an agile, medium to large body. They have a short, thick coat that ranges in colors from black to white to red to tabby.

American Wirehair: Uniquely American, the breed began as a spontaneous mutation in a litter on a farm in New York in 1966. Its dense, coarse coat is hard to touch and sets these cats apart from any other breed. Some also have curly whiskers. The breed is active and agile and has a keen interest in its surroundings. Although it is quiet and reserved, owners find the breed easy to care for.

Balinese: Related to the Siamese, it has a long silky coat, but unlike most long-haired cats, its coat doesn't mat. Endowed with a long, muscular body, the Balinese can come in several colors, including seal point, blue point and chocolate point. Intelligent, curious and alert, the Balinese is as affectionate and demonstrative as the Siamese, but it isn't as talkative and has a softer voice.

British Shorthair: Perhaps the oldest natural English breed, the British shorthair is enjoying new popularity. These cats tend to be reserved, devoted and good companions. Because of their dense coats, they also are easy to groom.

Burmese: Known as the clown of the cat kingdom, the Burmese thrives on attention and is very gregarious. It has a compact body and a glossy coat. Burmese live well with children and dogs.

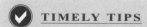

TIMELY TIPS

Smile and Say "Arf"

Pets have their celebrity photographers, too.

In a country where consumers can purchase handbag-shaped Chewy Vuitton plush squeaky toys, diamond-studded dog collars and wrought-iron canopy beds for dogs, there should be little surprise that there is a rapidly growing commercial-photography specialty of pet portraiture.

And the best of them all is Amanda Jones. "Just like there are people who want to be the next Richard Avedon, there are photographers who would give their left arm to be the next Amanda Jones," says Cameron Woo, publisher of *Bark* magazine (www.thebark.com), which *Time* called "the *New Yorker* of pet magazines."

Ms. Jones's studio is in North Adams, Mass., but she shoots mostly on the road. One November, for example, she rented studios in Chicago, Cleveland and London, booking five sessions a day for both a Saturday and Sunday in each location. She does about 150 sittings a year. Ninety percent of her business is dogs; cats make up the rest. A sitting costs about $850.

In addition to doing portraits (her work is online at www.amandajones.com), Ms. Jones has also published three books featuring dog photographs, the last of which was *Dachshunds Short and Long*. Ms. Jones says holiday cards now make up about 10 percent of her business, mostly for clients who don't have children.

—Andrew Adam Newman

They are smart, loyal and devoted. Despite their hefty appetites, they seldom are fat. They are very expensive, though.

Cornish Rex: The Rex has the body of a greyhound, huge ears set high on its head and large eyes. These cats fastidiously groom themselves—and their human companions. If that's not to your liking, choose another cat, since the problem may be impossible to eliminate. The Cornish Rex are excellent choices for people who love cats but dislike cat hair, because they have an undercoat but no outer coat.

Devon Rex: Devons are considered a mutant breed. The mature female averages 6 pounds; the male averages 7.5 pounds. Devons have a full, wavy coat, large eyes, a short muzzle, prominent cheekbones and huge low-set ears. They are very curious and refuse to be left out of anything. People with allergies to cat hair can happily live with a Devon rex because they do not shed.

Exotic Shorthair: Sometimes called the "Teddy Bear" cat, exotic shorthairs have a medium-to-long coat that does not mat. They will jump in your lap to take a nap, but generally prefer cooler places to sleep. They are very quiet but tireless—they will retrieve a toy until you get tired of throwing it.

Japanese Bobtail: The Japanese consider bobtails a symbol of good luck. They are medium-size and muscular with a short tail that resembles a rabbit's. They have high cheekbones, a long nose and large ears. Active, intelligent and talkative, their soft voices have a whole scale of tones. They almost always speak when spoken to. Japanese bobtails are good travelers and good with dogs and children.

Maine Coon Cat: The Maine coon cat was chosen as best cat at the first cat show ever held in America. It is a native American long-hair. Originally a working cat, it is a very good mouser. The Maine coon cat is solid and rugged. It has a smooth, shaggy coat and is known for its loving nature and great intelligence. The breed is especially good with children and dogs.

Oriental Shorthair: The extremely long Oriental shorthair is medium-size and can be a choosy

eater at times. They are easy to care for and make a practical pet. The Cat Fanciers' Association says, "Their innate sensibility verges on psychic. Once communication is established, you'll never need an alarm clock, or wonder where the cat is when you arrive home from work."

 TIMELY TIPS

Jumpy Enough to Chew a Chair? Try DogCatRadio

"Remember, be kind to your mailman," says Jane Harris, a disc jockey. Then she softens her voice until it is a little insinuating: "He only wants to deliver the mail." Harris is a D.J. on DogCatRadio.com, an Internet radio station for pets—live 17 hours a day, 4 a.m. to 9 p.m. Pacific time, and podcast for the rest of the 24 hours.

Those who listen to DogCatRadio will find that there is generally an animal motif to the playlist, like Elvis's " Hound Dog" ("You ain't nothin' but a hound dog, cryin' all the time"). Dionne Warwick is also popular, especially her soothing song "That's What Friends Are For" ("Keep smiling, keep shining, Knowing you can always count on me").

Since many pets are apparently bilingual, DogCatRadio also has a "Spanish Hour" (5 p.m. to 6 p.m. Pacific Time) with Hispanic commentary and music, like Luis Miguel's "No Sé Tú."

Does listening help dogs and cats keep their anxiety, loneliness and restlessness at bay while their owners are out? Dr. Larry Family, who has a talk show program, the Pet Vet, on WROW-AM in Albany, N.Y., recommends the station—especially "for dogs who have behavior problems in the home environment, or separation anxiety issues."

—Dinitia Smith

Persian: The most popular breed, Persians have long, flowing coats that require an indoor, protected environment and regular combing and bathing. They have a massive head and a very round face, as well as short, thick necks and legs and broad, short bodies. Persians have gentle personalities that fare best in serene households.

Russian Blue: Fine-boned, with short hair and a regal appearance, Russian blues are clean, quiet cats that don't shed a lot. They are very intelligent and are well attuned to the moods of their owners. They generally do well in a house full of kids and dogs.

Siamese: Like dogs, Siamese cats will fetch and do tricks, talk a lot and follow their owners around the house. They have blue eyes and a dark, raccoon-like "mask" around them. They have long svelte bodies and short, finely textured coats. Siamese cats have distinctive voices and are intelligent, dependent and affectionate. But because they have been highly inbred, they can be extremely timid, unpredictable or aggressive.

When Your Pet Gets Sick

Some common diseases and their symptoms

Once your pet is weaned, the natural protection it garners from its mother's milk eventually wears off, leaving it prey to a host of opportunistic viruses. As with humans, pets' diseases often are highly contagious and, in cases such as rabies, pose a serious threat to humans as well. Here are some of the ailments our pets may be subject to:

COMMON DISEASES IN CATS AND DOGS

Rabies is a viral disease that can attack the central nervous system of all warm-blooded animals, including humans. It is fatal if not treated. Most states require dog and cat owners to vaccinate their pets against rabies. The disease is transmitted by saliva, which is usually transferred by a bite from an infected animal and is frequently found in wild animals, such as skunks, raccoons and bats.

There are two types of rabies—"dumb" and "furious." Both cause a departure from normal behavior. Animals with furious rabies will have a period immediately prior to death in which they appear to be "mad," frothing at the mouth and biting anything that gets in their way. Dumb rabies differs in that there is no "mad" period. Instead, paralysis, usually of the lower jaw, is the first sign. The paralysis spreads to limbs and vital organs and death quickly follows. Wild animals that are unusually friendly and appear to have no fear of man or domestic animals should be avoided and reported immediately to the police or animal control authorities.

Rabies is almost totally preventable by vaccination. Dogs and cats should receive an initial rabies vaccination by the age of three to four months. Protection lasts from one to three years. Regular boosters are required.

The diseases listed below are those that most commonly affect our pets. Vaccines are available for all of these diseases, but not necessarily recommended for all pets. (See page 484 for recommended vaccinations.)

DOGS ONLY

Canine bordetellosis: Caused by bacteria in the respiratory tracts of many animals, it is the primary cause of kennel cough. Besides the cough, some dogs suffer from a purulent nasal discharge. Transmission usually occurs through contact with other dogs' nasal secretions. Vaccination is generally administered by nasal spray.

Canine distemper virus (CDV): A highly contagious viral disease, canine distemper is transmitted by direct or indirect contact with the discharges from an infected dog's eyes and nose. Early signs are similar to those of a severe cold and often go unrecognized by the pet owner. The respiratory problems may be accompanied by vomiting and diarrhea. A nervous system disorder may also develop. The death rate from canine distemper is greater than 50 percent in adult dogs and even higher in puppies. Even if the dog survives, distemper can cause permanent damage to a dog's nervous system, sense of smell, hearing and sight. Partial or total paralysis is not uncommon.

Canine leptospirosis: A bacterial disease that harms the kidneys and can result in kidney failure. Vomiting, impaired vision and convulsions are all tipoffs. Transmission results from contact with the urine of infected animals, or contact with something tainted by the urine of an infected animal.

Canine parainfluenza: A viral infection of the respiratory tract, it is frequently accompanied by other respiratory viruses and is usually spread through contact with the nasal secretions of other dogs.

Canine parvovirus (CPV): A serious problem because the virus withstands extreme temperature changes and even exposure to most disinfectants. The source of infection is usually dog feces, which can contaminate cages and shoes and can be carried on the feet and hair of infected animals.

CPV attacks the intestinal tract, white blood cells and heart. Symptoms include vomiting, severe diarrhea, a loss of appetite, depression and high fever. Most deaths occur within 48 to 72 hours after the onset of clinical signs. Infected pups may act depressed or collapse, gasping for breath. Death may follow immediately. Pups that survive are likely to have permanently damaged hearts.

Infectious canine hepatitis: Caused by a virus that can infect many tissues, the disease usually attacks the liver, causing hepatitis. In some instances a whiteness or cloudiness of the eye may accompany the disease. Another strain of the same virus can cause respiratory tract infections. These viruses are transmitted by contact with objects that have been contaminated with the urine from infected dogs. Infectious canine hepatitis is different from human hepatitis.

CATS ONLY

Feline panleukopenia: Also known as feline distemper, the disease comes from a virus so resistant that it may remain infectious for over a year at room temperature on inanimate objects. Spread through blood, urine, feces, nasal secretions and fleas from infected cats, the virus causes high fever, dehydration, vomiting and lethargy and destroys a cat's white blood cells. It is 50 to 70 percent fatal, but immunity can be developed through vaccination of kittens and boosters.

Feline leukemia virus: A disease of the immune system that is usually fatal, its symptoms include weight loss, lethargy, recurring or chronic sickness, diarrhea, unusual breathing and yellow coloration around the mouth and the whites of the eyes. Confirmation of the virus requires a blood test. Fortunately, there is a new vaccine that provides protection.

Feline viral rhinotracheitis, feline calicivirus and feline pneumonitis: All three are highly infectious viruses of the respiratory tract, for which vaccinations are available.

HOUSE

Boosting Your Pet's Well-Being

A careful use of vaccines will keep your dog or cat free of many common diseases

By immunizing pets in their early months and bolstering the protection with "booster" vaccinations, you can shield animals from most life-threatening diseases.

However, due to an increased awareness of the dangers of overvaccinating, these days many professionals recognize the difference between the universally necessary, or "core" vaccines, and "noncore" vaccines, those which should be administered only if it seems indicated because of risk of exposure. The American Animal Hospital Association and others recommend that after your puppy or kitten receives the initial series of vaccinations and the appropriate booster, she or he may only need vaccinations in some cases every three years, and may not need to be vaccinated against noncore diseases at all unless there is reason to believe the animal is at risk of exposure. The following are suggested guidelines for canine and feline vaccines listed according to those which are essential (core) or optional (noncore). All others are not recommended.

Vaccinations for Puppies

CORE VACCINES

Core vaccines are recommended for all puppies.

• **Distemper.** There are two types of vaccine recommended: (CDV) (MLV) and recombinant (CDV), which may be used interchangeably. The recombinant version is more likely to immunize puppies against CDV, even in the face of passively acquired maternal antibody.

• **Parvovirus (CPV-2) (MLV)**
• **Adenovirus-2 (CAV-2) (MLV parenteral)**

PROTOCOL: *All these should be given initially at six to eight weeks, the second dose at nine to 11 weeks and a third dose at 12 to 14 weeks. Boosters are given at 1 year, and then every 3 years thereafter. Dogs older than 16 weeks should receive a single dose, and the booster shots.*

• **Rabies.** There are now two vaccines for rabies, both approved for use:

RABIES 1-YEAR (KILLED). *Should be given initially at 12 to 16 weeks, with a booster at one year and revaccinations every year thereafter. Dogs older than 16 weeks should receive a single dose and the booster shot at one year and every three years thereafter.*

RABIES 3-YEAR (KILLED). *Should be given initially at 12 to 16 weeks, with a booster at one year and revaccinations every three years thereafter. Dogs older than 16 weeks should receive a single dose with an initial booster shot at one year*

NONCORE VACCINES

Noncore vaccines should be administered at the discretion of the veterinarian.

• **Bordetella (all types)**
• **Parainfluenza**
• **Lyme vaccine (all types)**
• **Distemper-measles (combined vaccine)**
• **Leptospirosis (all types)**

SOURCE: 2006 American Animal Hospital Association Guidelines

Vaccinations for Kittens

CORE VACCINES

Core vaccines are recommended for all kittens.

• **Feline herpes virus-1 (FHV-1)**
• **Feline calcivirus (FCV)**
• **Feline panleukopenia virus (FPV)**
• **Rabies**

PROTOCOL: *All these should be given initially from seven to eight weeks, and every three to four weeks until 12 weeks of age. Boosters are given at one year, and then every three years thereafter. For cats older than 12 weeks of age, two doses of vaccine are recommended. After a booster at one year, revaccination is suggested every three years thereafter.*

NONCORE VACCINES
Noncore vaccines should be administered at the discretion of the veterinarian.

• **Feline leukemia virus (FELV)**
• **Feline immunodeficieny virus (FIV)**

SOURCE: March 2005 Guidelines, The Veterinary Teaching Hospital at The College of Veterinary Medicine, Ohio State University

A New Age in Pet Care
Medical and high-tech advances are helping vets help pets

These days, pet owners are demanding the same kind of care for their pets as they can get for themselves and their families. The pet care business is responding with medical and technological advances that are helping pets live longer and healthier lives. Because many of these procedures are costly, it may be worth the money to invest in pet insurance.

Farewell to fleas. The most radical changes in veterinary medicine have occurred in flea control. Until recently, pet owners had few choices: use flea powders and collars on their pets and spray the yard with chemicals.

Today, new options include pills and topical spot-on solutions. The pills prevent flea eggs from hatching, and the skin treatments kill fleas on contact for 30 days. Both are available at your vet's office.

New advances in outdoor flea control are available that contain nematodes, live organisms that feed on flea larvae. These products reduce harm to the environment, as well as to humans, animals and insects.

Computer ID. A new way to identify your pet involves implanting a tiny microchip—about $1/4$ to $1/3$ inch long—under the skin of just about any animal. The result is a lifetime ID that can't be lost or removed. The information can be read by scanners now used by animal control centers and humane societies. So if your dog strays and ends up at one of these centers, the scanner reads the identification number that traces the pet back to you.

The chip is injected by a vet with a device that looks like a syringe and needle.

Patching up pain. The new patch technology that's so popular for humans—estrogen patches for women, nicotine patches for smokers—is now being used on animals. If an animal is in pain after an accident, or is having a major dental procedure, a time-release patch can steadily relieve the pain, rather than having to wait until the animal needs another dose of pain killer. Time-release patches are a little bit expensive, but they last several days. At the vet's office, an owner can choose between the patch technology and standard medication. Most owners pick patches because they don't have to get up in the middle of the night or come home from work to redose their pets.

Modifying your pet's behavior. Shelters and humane groups destroy millions of dogs and cats each year because of the animals' behavior problems. That's more than the number killed each year by any disease. But behavior problems like aggression, digging, barking, biting and house-soiling can now be resolved through behavior-counseling programs. The earlier in a puppy or kitten's life that behavior problems are picked up, the greater the success in resolving them. Pets can get behavior counseling at special clinics or through veterinarians or specialists that your vet can recommend. Many counselors will even come to your home.

A pet's behavior can also be modified with drugs. Until a few years ago, information on treating animals with drugs was limited, but now we can treat disorders such as car sickness, aggression and separation anxiety with a combination of behavior training and drug treatments.

Diagnosis and surgery. Ultrasound and endoscopy have been around for humans for many years, but they are now becoming affordable and more routinely used to diagnose and treat animal problems. They have revolutionized exploratory surgery. If an animal has a serious heart problem, or cancer, for example, it can be diagnosed without having to make any incisions. The result is lower costs and less stress for owners.

Pet surgery has also come a long way. Dogs no longer need to go blind from cataracts. Cataracts can be removed surgically and artificial lenses can

be implanted. And pets that suffer from chronic hip or knee deformities can have their joints replaced surgically, just like humans.

Choosing a Bird Feeder
How to get a bird's-eye view of your avian neighbors

The easiest way to attract birds to your yard is to put up a bird feeder. There are many different ones on the market today. Most are made for seeds, but there are also specialty feeders for certain foods, such as sugar solution for hummingbirds, suet or peanuts. Which should you choose? The answer depends on the kinds of birds you want to attract.

The ideal bird feeder is sturdy enough to withstand winter weather, tight enough to keep seeds dry, large enough to avoid constant refilling and easy to assemble and clean. Plastic or metal feeders usually beat wooden ones in meeting all these requirements.

If you want to attract the greatest variety of birds to your yard, you'll want to use several different feeder types offering a variety of foods. Alternatively, you may want to attract certain bird species, but dissuade others. The following information will help you make the correct feeder choice.

TRAY OR PLATFORM FEEDER: *Any flat, raised surface onto which bird food is spread*

Trays attract most species of feeder birds, but they offer no protection against squirrels, chipmunks, rain or snow. Plus the seed can quickly become soiled by droppings because birds stand right on top of it.

Tray feeders placed near the ground are most likely to attract ground-feeding birds such as juncos, doves, jays, blackbirds and sparrows. Tray

TIMELY TIPS

Finding a Boarding Kennel for Fluffy or Fido

Need to go out of town? You wouldn't stay in a hotel that has fleas, nor should you expect your pet to. One way to check out a prospective kennel is to find out if it belongs to the American Boarding Kennels Association, (call 877-570-7788 or send e-mail to info@abka.com), which inspects kennels before it offers accreditation.

feeders work well mounted on deck railings, posts or stumps, and also can be suspended. Some models have a roof to provide some protection from the weather. Be sure your tray feeders have plenty of drainage holes.

HOPPER OR HOUSE FEEDER: *Platform with walls and a roof, forming an enclosed "hopper"*

This type protects seeds fairly well against the weather, but less well against squirrels. It also keeps seed cleaner. Hopper feeders are attractive to most feeder birds, including finches, jays, cardinals, buntings, grosbeaks , sparrows, chickadees and titmice. Most hoppers hold a good quantity of seed. Few are weatherproof, however, so the food may get wet and moldy if it sits for a few days. Hopper feeders can be mounted on a pole or suspended.

WINDOW FEEDER: *Usually made of clear plastic and suction-cupped to a window*

This type of feeder attracts finches, sparrows, chickadees and titmice, allowing close-up views of the birds as they come to feed. Be aware, though, that the birds feed while standing on a pile of seeds inside the feeder, so the food risks becoming soiled.

TUBE FEEDER: *Hollow cylinder, usually of clear plastic, with multiple feeding ports and perches*

Tube feeders keep seed fairly clean and dry, and if they have metal feeding ports they are somewhat squirrel-resistant. The birds attracted depend on the size of the perches under the feeding ports: short perches accomodate small birds such as sparrows, grosbeaks, chickadees, titmice and finches (such as the familiar house finch), but exclude larger birds such as grackles and jays. Styles with perches above the feeding ports are

This Recipe Is for the Birds

Although sunflower seeds are the all-round favorite, particularly for tree-dwelling birds, some birds prefer different foods. Blackbirds relish corn, for instance, whereas doves, like many ground-feeding birds, prefer white millet or red milo. Certain species may even have different food preferences in different parts of their range.

WILD BIRD FOOD RECIPE:

Pour about 25 pounds of black-oil sunflower seed, 10-pounds of white proso millet, and 10 pounds of cracked corn into a clean trash can. Then use a broom handle to mix it up.

SOURCE: Cornell Lab of Ornithology

HOUSE

designed for seed-eating birds that like to feed hanging upside down, such as goldfinches, while dissuading others.

THISTLE FEEDER: *Special tube feeder designed with extra-small openings to dispense tiny thistle seeds*

These feeders attract a variety of small songbirds, especially finches and redpolls. Thistle "socks"— fine-mesh bags to which birds cling to extract the seeds—are also available.

SUET FEEDER: *Wire-mesh cage or plastic-mesh bag, such as an onion bag, which holds suet or suet mixture*

This type of feeder can be nailed or tied to a tree trunk. It can also be suspended. Suet can also be smeared into knotholes.

Suet feeders attract a variety of woodpeckers and nuthatches, as well as chickadees, titmice, jays and starlings. Suet cages that are open only at the bottom are starling-proof; they force birds to hang upside down while feeding, something starlings find difficult.

Caged Birds That Sing

○ Several criteria go into choosing a pet bird. Is it sociable, or does it have a sweet voice? Can it talk? Is it noisy? The answer is that like dogs and cats, and humans themselves, each bird species has its own unique personality. To give you an idea, however, of what kinds of birds have the most universal appeal, here is a listing of the ten most popular birds—and their life expectancy.

		Life expectancy
1.	Cockatiel (38%)	20 yrs.
2.	Parakeet (31%)	12-14 yrs.
3.	Finch (9%)	15 yrs.
4.	Parrot (African Gray) (8%)	50-60 yrs.
5.	Lovebird (7%)	20 yrs.
6.	Conure (6%)	30 yrs.
7.	Amazon (4%)	50 yrs.
8.	Canary (4%)	15 yrs.
9.	Dove (3%)	20 yrs.
10.	Cockatoo (2%)	65 yrs.

SOURCES: 2001-2002 American Pet Products Manufacturers Association National Pet Owners Survey and Lifestyle and Media Study; About.com

You can make your own hummingbird feeder with a bottle, rubber cork and the drinking tube from a pet hamster water bottle. The color red attracts hummingbirds, so paint the feeding port with red nail polish or tie red ribbons to the feeder.

Saucer-shaped hummingbird feeders have feeding ports in the top, making them bee- and wasp-proof. Saucer feeders are better than bottle feeders in direct sunlight. Bottle feeders tend to leak in the sun—air trapped in the top of the bottle expands as it warms and pushes the nectar out. In fact, you should avoid locating your hummingbird feeder in direct sun—it causes the sugar solution to spoil rapidly.

To make sugar solution for hummingbirds, add one part sugar to four parts boiling water (boil the water before measuring, because some water will evaporate away in the process). When the mixture is cool it is ready for use. You can store extra sugar water in your refrigerator for up to one week, but left longer it may become moldy.

SOURCE: Cornell Lab of Ornithology

HUMMINGBIRD FEEDER: *A container to hold artificial nectar or sugar solution; may be bottle or saucer style*

The bottle or tube type of hummingbird feeder is usually made of glass or plastic, often with red plastic flowers and bee-guards (little plastic screens that keep insects away from the sugar solution) on the feeding ports. Saucer types are usually plastic.

Make sure the feeder is easy to take apart and clean, because it should be washed frequently. For example, the fill hole should be large enough for you to reach in while cleaning.

Thinking of Getting a Gerbil?
Some facts to gnaw on

The Mongolian gerbils are the species most commonly kept as household pets. Their great advantage is that they are the descendants of desert rodents, so they make efficient use of food and water, and have little body waste. Consequently, their cages do not need to be cleaned as frequently as those of other rodents.

Gerbils' largest disadvantage is that they are gnawing and scratching animals, so their cages must be made of gnaw-proof material. They are active animals, so a running wheel for exercise is considered an important accessory for the gerbil's well-being.

Gerbils are social. In their ancestral desert habitats, they lived in colonies, and therefore feel most comfortable living with others. So buy a pair, preferably of the same sex (unless you want to breed them) and from the same litter, if possible.

Gerbils can be territorial, so it is important to introduce a newcomer slowly, preferably by dividing the cage in two at first with glass or wire, to get them used to each other. If there is evidence of injury, remove the gerbil who is least injured, as that is certainly the one who is causing the trouble.

SETTING UP A GERBIL'S RESIDENCE:

There are two kinds of recommended gerbil environments. Either a cage with a bottom deep enough to contain a generous layer of nesting material, and a wired upper section which attaches firmly to the bottom, or a large glass aquarium.

- Bedding should be spread thickly over the bottom of the cage. Best materials for this are Aspen wood chips, Carefresh brand or Corncob bedding.

- A nesting box made out of wood serves as the bedroom area of the cage. Torn strips of tissue make the optimum nesting material.

- Gerbils need a source of fresh water, which can be supplied by a self-feeding bottle attached to the side of the cage.

- Food may be placed in a gnaw-proof dish or scattered around the cage. As gerbils are foragers, this act of hunting for food provides stimulation, and is recommended. You can generally find a good, premixed gerbil food at the pet store. It must have protein, minerals, vitamins and bulk, but not too many sunflower seeds, which are fattening.

- A running wheel is also highly recommended, as gerbils need physical activity.

- Place empty toilet paper tubes in the cage for the gerbils to chew on and play with.

HOME MAINTENANCE

- Make sure there is always a supply of clean, fresh water.

- Clean food dish and water bottle regularly and replace bedding and tissue every two to three weeks. Wash down the cage surfaces with very warm water and soap.

SOURCES: The American Gerbil Society (www.agsgerbils.org); National Gerbil Society (www.gerbils.co.uk)

HOUSE

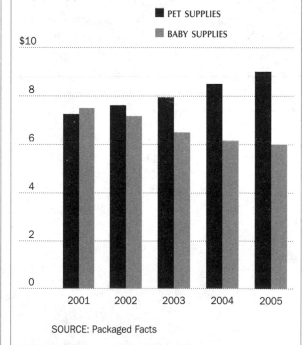

BRINGING UP THE OTHER BABY

If you thought bringing up a child was expensive, take a look at pet expenditures. Retail sales of non-food baby-care supplies are dwarfed by sales of pet supplies (in billions of dollars).

■ PET SUPPLIES
■ BABY SUPPLIES

SOURCE: Packaged Facts

You Can't Take Them With You

Care for your animals when you no longer can

Unlike in ancient Egypt, when a pharoah died, and his pets were buried along with him, pets live on today, sometimes long after their owners die. Yet in many cases, there is no one to properly care for them. Laws in 27 states—including Arizona, Colorado, Florida, New Jersey and New York—now allow owners to establish trusts for pets. These arrangements set aside money for the care of one or more animals in the event of an owner's disability or death.

Leaving money to a pet became legally possible in 1990, when a section validating trusts for domestic animals was added to the Uniform Probate Code. More states may soon allow it. Pet trust legislation is pending in Connecticut, Hawaii, Massachusetts, Oregon, Pennsylvania, Rhode Island and Texas.

Setting up a trust for your pet is, in many ways, similar to creating one for a child.

A trustee and caregiver are named. The trustee is in charge of the money and pays the caregiver a set amount each month for expenses, like food, grooming and veterinary care. At any point, if the caregiver is not doing a good job, the trustee can find a replacement.

Creating a trust can cost as little as $100 if you draw up a will for yourself at the same time or up to a few thousand dollars.

If money is no object, the trust can act like an endowment, experts say, with the interest generated covering expenses. Then, when the pet dies, the remaining balance can go to a charity or family member.

The best way to prevent fraud, trust experts say, is to get a DNA sample from the animal. Then, if the trustee becomes suspicious, a comparison can be made.

Instead of a trust, owners can include a provision for pet care in their will. But William A. Reppy Jr., a professor at Duke Law School in Durham, N.C., says there are some drawbacks to that approach. A will takes effect only upon your death, not if you become ill or incapacitated. And it must go through probate, which can temporarily freeze funds for your pet's care and delay determining the rightful new owner.

The Humane Society of the United States offers a free kit, Providing for Your Pet's Future Without You, complete with a six-page fact sheet, wallet alert cards and caregiver forms (202-452-1100 or send e-mail to petsinwillsrp@hsus.org).

—Maryann Mott

CHAPTER **8**

TRAVEL

Getting There 492

FLYING·492: *Air-fare bargains online • Sites worth a visit • Fly for peanuts • The best vacation packages • Taking the fear out of flying • A cure for jet lag • The safest plane • If you are bumped from a flight • No-fly frequent flier miles* **SAILS & RAILS·501:** *Tall ships sailing • The best cruise ship cabin • Classic rail trips* **LODGING·504:** *The world's most charming inns • Cheap hotels in New York • Rent a house abroad • Swapping houses • Time-out at a monastery* **INCIDENTALS·512:** *Cellphones worldwide • An 11th-hour passport • Call home for less • Trip insurance • Travel guides and blogs*

Hot Spots 519

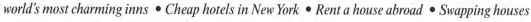

ASIA·519: *Swimming to Cambodia, Laos and Vietnam • Angkor Wat • Eating in Shanghai • Beyond the Taj Mahal* **ISLANDS·523:** *Caribbean gems • Beneath the sea • Forbidden Cuba • Undiscovered Hawaii • For singles only • Less-traveled Greek islands* **FAMILY TRAVEL·533:** *London, Paris, Washington, D.C., and San Francisco • Perfect meals in London and Paris*

Natural Treasures 538

NATIONAL PARKS·538: *America's Crown Jewels • Off-season in the parks • Best undiscovered parks • Classic rustic lodges • Trails across the nation* **WILDLIFE·554** *Big-horn sheep and other wildlife • Watching whales* **WAY SOUTH·556:** *Paddling in the Galápagos • Wet and wild rain forests • Chasing butterflies • The pyramids next door* **SAFARI·561:** *Into the heart of Africa • Where wild things roam*

Adventure 564

TREKKING·564: *Nine classic treks • The magic of G.P.S. devices • Life is better in Bhutan • Nurture and nature hikes in Europe • Hut-to-hut hikes* **BIKING·572:** *Your personal Tour de France* **RIVER TRIPS·573:** *Slow boats through Europe • Renting a canal cruiser • Rafting for the whole family • Whitewater rapids • The ultimate river trip* **PRISTINE PLACES·577:** *Sites for the intrepid traveler*

TRAVEL

Getting There

Fly for Cheap—Online

There are air-fare bargains out there. Here's how to find them

The Internet can be a rat's nest of frustration when it comes to finding air-fare bargains. Nearly every travel Web site boasts a section for "deals" featuring either yawners or true steals that have long since been snapped up. Expedia.com, Travelocity.com and Orbitz.com occasionally turn up good deals, but these sites are built to be ticket sellers, not bargain finders.

SmarterTravel.com, Travelzoo.com, Cheapflights.com, Airfarewatchdog.com and others, however, are havens for good buys. These companies exist primarily to sniff out bargains, consolidate them in one place, and tell consumers exactly where to book them, since the sites never act as booking agents themselves.

While each of the top bargain consolidator sites is worth visiting—and each has specific strengths and weaknesses—SmarterTravel stands out for its ease of use. You might start your search in the "More Air Deals" section, which offers two pull-down menus, "Travel To" and "Last-Minute Web Fares From." The latter, which focuses on deals that are available that week, and organized according to departure point, is especially helpful.

According to Ed Passarella, SmarterTravel.com's editor in chief, the last-minute deals on his site are most likely to be available on Wednesdays, when airlines typically distribute new fares.

Unlike some other bargain sites, like Cheapflights, SmarterTravel does not offer a link that leads directly to a page where customers can book. Still, it offers some information—blackout dates and other restrictions—before visitors start the process of typing in departure and arrival dates to find the fares they want. And while Cheapflights provides a link to the airlines Web site page where the flight could be booked, the site has another drawback. Since airlines can pay to have their fares featured under the "premium position" heading, you must scroll beneath those fares to see all the best bargains.

When it comes to actually booking the flights, the problem is that unless you are among the earliest to discover the fares, too often they are gone quickly. Travelzoo tries to save users the trouble of searching for outdated or sold-out fares by only posting bargains that the company's editors feel will not quickly disappear. Travelzoo publishes a top 20 travel deals section (and e-mail newsletter) each Wednesday, and it also lobbies airlines and hoteliers for more inventory if an offer is selling out quickly.

One significant drawback to using Travelzoo is that it gives users no way to sort through deals by departure city. The best deals are organized according to how good a bargain they are, and you have to scroll through them to find your departure city, if it is even listed at all. In some cases, Travelzoo will not list basic departure information, and users must go to the airline's Web site to find fares from their area.

Another site, Airfarewatchdog.com, is better in this regard. The site lists bargain fares for 36 regions or cities in the United States, with each of the area's airports included. You have to look at each airport's Web site to find the fares, however.

There are other Internet wild cards worth play-

TIMELY TIPS

Online Travel Sites Worth a Visit

There are basically two ways to book flights yourself: either on the airline-specific sites, or on one of the online booking sites. Besides the individual airline sites, here are some other sites worth checking out:

RESERVATIONS

• **Travelocity** (travelocity.com), **Orbitz** (orbitz.com), **Expedia** (Expedia.com) and **CheapTickets** (cheaptickets.com) have airline tickets, car rentals, hotel reservations, travel information.

• **ITA Software** (itasoftware. com/cvg/dispatch/login) Clear, well-organized listings of flights and fares, domestic and international, with booking codes.

• **Hotels.com** Hotels, vacation rentals, packages.

• **Kayak.com** search for travel fares and prices across multiple sites.

• **Quikbook.com** Good rates for selected hotels in major destinations (mostly in the United States).

• **Hotwire.com** can help you find travel bargains if you're flexible.

• **Priceline.com** lets you name your own price for travel (and mortgages) and see if anyone bites.

• **Site59.com** Big discounts on last-minute travel packages.

• **Travelzoo.com** collects special travel offers from many sites.

• **Sidestep.com** See "deals" section.

• **Hertz** (hertz.com), **Avis** (avis. com), **National** (nationalcar. com) and **Budget** (rent.drivebudget.com) will rent you a car.

GUIDES

• **Betterbidding.com** helps you understand what kind of hotel bids succeed on Priceline and Hotwire.

• **Concierge.com** from Conde Nast, publisher of *Traveler*.

• **Fodor's** (fodors.com) Online home of the well known travel books.

• **Forbes.com**'s travel area (forbes.com/lifestyle/travel) has an archive of useful city guides.

• **Frommer's** (frommers. com) Online home of the well-known travel books.

• **Gorp** (gorp.away.com) Guide to adventure travel and outdoor recreation.

• **InfoHub.com** Travel guide organized by specialties.

• **Lonely Planet** (lonelyplanet. com) Online home of the well-known travel books.

• **National Geographic Travel** (nationalgeographic.com/travel)

and its *Traveler* magazine.

• **PlanetRider.com** collects and rates more travel sites than we could list here.

• **Rough Guides Travel** (travel. roughguides.com/default. html) Online version of the travel guides.

• **Savvy Traveler** (savvytraveler. org) from Diana Nyad's NPR show of the same name.

• **This Is Travel** (thisistravel. co.uk) British travel site.

• **Travel+Leisure** (travelandleisure.com) from the American Express magazine.

• **Travelers' Health** (cdc. gov/travel) from the Centers from Disease Control gives health information for your destination.

• **Travelweb.com** Hotel booking from the hotel industry.

• **TripAdvisor.com** Well-organized site, particularly strong for traveler feedback and multisite hotel rate searching.

• **U.S. State Department** (state. gov/travel) Country background papers, passport and visa information, travel warnings and advice.

• **ViaMichelin.com** Travel guides, hotel and restaurant ratings, directions from the venerable Michelin.

—Richard J. Meislin

TRAVEL

ing, if the better-known sites fail to yield bargains. One possibility, ETN (www.etn.nl), actually relies on offline travel agents to deliver online bargains. According to Ad Latjes, ETN's founder and chief executive, the company takes travel requests online and, at no charge, distributes them to roughly 50 agents in the United States.

These agents are consolidators—so called because they buy blocks of tickets for a given des-tination from airlines, and offer them at discounts to customers. One pitfall of buying from these consolidators is that these tickets usually cannot be changed or canceled (terms that have also become fairly common among online bargain-fare sites). The site pledges that requests will be answered quickly within one hour by five agents. Most of the agents who respond to fare requests, Mr. Latjes says, check the online sites first, because they know if they can't quote a lower fare, the customer won't be interested. Most of the time, he says, they'll find the best fare, "although it's hard to guarantee, because there's always some kind of sale going on. But a good agent who specializes in an international destination can still beat the online engines."

—Bob Tedeschi

All's Fair in the Fare Wars

If this week's fare is half of what you paid last week, here's what to do

You've already bought your ticket when you see a ticket online at half the fare for the same route. Getting your ticket rewritten for the lower fare—and pocketing the savings—is not always possible. First, you must meet all the qualifications: it must be the right number of days in advance of your trip; you must have been booked to travel when the fare applies; and there must still be seats available in the cheaper fare category. Even then, you might be charged $50 or so to have your ticket rewritten.

Don't give up if the first airline person who answers tells you your ticket is nonrefundable and nonchangeable, though. Insist on speaking with a supervisor. Also, move fast. The number of seats available at the lower fare is probably limited. Even if you meet all the restrictions, you will not be able to claim one of the cheap seats unless they are still unsold when you call.

A travel agent can give you further assis-tance. Some agents now guarantee you the low-est fare through use of a computer that monitors reservations systems overnight. Your agent may call you when a lower fare pops up. (You certainly won't hear about it from the airline.) If the agent is still holding your tickets, he or she could rewrite your ticket on the spot.

Two Ways to Fly for Peanuts

Charters and couriers are absolutely the cheapest way to go

When *How to Travel without Being Rich* was a hot seller in 1959, a 10-day trip from New York to Paris including airfare, lodging and sight-seeing cost $553. Today, that price would elude even the most serious of cost-cutters. But, it's still possible to get from here to there for less, but don't necessarily expect peanuts (to eat, that is). Here's how:

CHARTER FLIGHTS

Charter flights offer savings that are competi-tive with consolidator tickets, but generally they are only for nonstop routes. Charter companies are able to profit by running less often than regularly scheduled airline flights and by book-ing to complete capacity. On transatlantic flights especially, charter travelers can save a couple of hundred dollars or more and, if they wish, fly

TIMELY TIPS

How to Get an Even Cheaper Fare

Some people just get lucky, others are expert shoppers

When buying airline tickets online, there is a lot you can do to sharpen your shopping skills. Web sites like Expedia.com, Orbitz.com and Travelocity.com are great for comparing fares from multiple airlines, but to root out the best deals, it helps to know a few search (and travel) tricks.

✔ **Travel midweek:** In general, you can often find lower fares by traveling on Tuesday or Wednesday, when planes are less crowded and cheap seats are more likely to be available. When airlines announce sales, the prices are sometimes valid only for travel on certain days—often Tuesday or Wednesday—so you can increase your chances of catching a sale by researching midweek prices.

✔ **Don't overlook low-fare carriers:** Low-fare carriers often don't show up when you search for flights on fare-comparison sites. For instance, the only place airlines like Southwest and Alaska airlines usually sell tickets online is their own Web site, so if you are flying their routes and don't look there you may miss a great deal.

—Susan Stellin

into one city and return from somewhere else. You can even buy one-way tickets.

Charters also are a good alternative for those who like to fly first class but don't want to pay for it, Ed Perkins, author, says, "One of the best values around is the premium-class service on some of the transatlantic charters. First class on charter planes is a third of the price of regular airlines, with many of the same amenities."

But all that does not obscure the drawbacks of charter travel, which are the infrequency of flights and overcrowding of planes. If a charter flight is canceled close to departure, there usually are no other planes available, nor will a charter ticket be honored on another airline. Travelers can often have a lengthy wait for another flight, or worse, will have to pay full fare on a regular airline. Also, despite the aforementioned first-class options, charter flights are not known for luxury service. The meals often come in a brown bag, and you're packed in like the proverbial sardine.

WHERE TO GO: Travel agencies are an excellent source for charter listings. Charter companies also advertise heavily in the travel sections of major newspapers.

AIR COURIERS

This is still usually the cheapest way to fly. In exchange for acting as a "casual courier," accompanying a package or merely an envelope full of documents and giving up some or all of the checked baggage allowance, a passenger can buy a ticket for 50 to 85 percent off the regular fare, depending on time of year and destination. Flights can usually be booked up to three months in advance; the closer to departure, the cheaper, and last-minute tickets can even be free (though that is now much rarer than it used to be). Most tickets are round trip and allow for stays from a few days to six months—and usually passengers can keep the frequent-flier miles. The deal is for one person, so a travel companion must buy an ordinary ticket or, with some of the more regular flights, fly in the next day or two as a courier. (On the return flight, when the passenger is usually not acting as a courier, the two travelers can often fly home together.) The company, not the passenger, is responsible for the goods being shipped, mainly documents or computer-related gadgets, and most companies X-ray all packages before accepting them.

TRAVEL

To qualify, you must be at least 18 (some courier companies stipulate that you be 21) and have a valid passport. It is the traveler's responsibility to obtain any necessary visa. Tickets can be purchased through courier companies themselves or through clearinghouse organizations that charge a fee. Members of these clubs get access to available flights for the next month or so and are then put in touch with the appropriate courier company.

Either way, passengers end up doing business directly with the courier company. It usually works like this: you choose a flight; the company sends you a contract; you fill it out and send it back with a certified check or money order for the agreed amount; you arrive at the airport two to three hours ahead of time and meet an agent from the company; the agent hands you the ticket and helps you check in (the airlines are often well acquainted with these companies and know the drill); you meet another agent at the destination, hand over the baggage ticket and manifest, and go on your way.

COURIER CLUBS

Following are the two most recognized courier clubs that set people up with courier companies. They suggest you agree on return dates and luggage allowance before booking.

The Air Courier Association. Offers members, for a subscription fee, a schedule of courier flights on its Web site. To sign up, call 800-461-8856 or go online at www.aircourier.org. Most tickets are round trips, but ask. Incredibly cheap, even free last-minute flights are posted on the Web site and go to the first taker. ACA also has a service called ACA/Cheaptrips which offers deeply discounted tickets and deals.

International Association of Air Travel Couriers. Charges a yearly fee to link you to the 30 or so courier companies it works with. Tickets are round-trip almost without exception. The Web site offers members a list of last-minute specials. Members also receive a subscription to the association's bimonthly magazine, with courier tales, news and tips. To sign up, go online at www.courier.org. In addition, members can access noncourier flight deals through the Web site's Consolidator Engine, just as they do with the other online consolidators.

—Hope Reeves

Taking the Fear out of Flying

Advice to help get you off the ground

Aviophobia, the fear of flying, is common. Some 64 percent of women and 36 percent of men have it. If you are one of those people, here are a few words of advice:

Get to the airport early. Rushing causes anxiety that won't vanish once you're on board. Plan to arrive at least one hour beforehand for domestic flights and two hours for international flights, giving you enough time to go through security, settle down and walk on board in a relaxed state.

Eat something nutritious. Cut back on caffeine and sugar the day before your flight. Protein and unrefined carbohydrates fortify you best. Have a snack or meal at least every 3½ hours while you are flying.

Try to relax. You can help control your anxiety with relaxation techniques. Try deep-breathing exercises, and listen to the relaxation tapes often available on the airline's audio channels. Or, pick a relaxing scene, such as lying on a beach watching the waves rush in and out. Focus solely on that scene.

Pick the right seat. Many fearful flyers become claustrophobic. Breathing deeply from the diaphragm can help. So can your choice of seats. Choose a forward aisle seat on a wide-body plane, allowing you to move around more freely.

Don't hide your anxiety. Flight attendants will generally go out of their way to help you. Asking

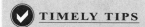

TIMELY TIPS

Getting to the Plane on Time

✔ **An E-ZPass for Frequent Fliers.** Beginning in July 2005, under the federal Registered Traveler Program, frequent fliers have been able to move through security faster than ever before. Fliers submit basic information that enables them to be cleared for expedited screening by the Transportation Security Administration. Once they pass that test, they must pay an annual fee ($79.95 in 2005) and use an identity card encoded with their fingerprints and iris scans to gain access to designated checkpoints.

✔ **Baggage Check.** Airlines have been cracking down on the weight and size of checked baggage. Here's a handy link to a list of the domestic checked-bag rules for over a dozen airlines, from the airline specialist at CheapSeats.com, Terry Trippler. The list of tips is at www.terrytrippler.com/images/video/know_before_you_go.html.

—Joe Sharkey

the crew for a tour of the cockpit can also help put you at ease.

RESOURCES

BOOKS: *The Fearless Flier's Handbook: Learning to Beat the Fear of Flying With the Experts From the Qantas Clinic.*

ONLINE: The Institute for Psychology of Air Travel, at www.fearlessflying.net in Boston, Mass., offers a list of resources and a 10-week course.

COURSES: Some airlines and airports offer courses on how to overcome aviophobia. One such course is a four-day program offered by the Fear of Flying Clinic at San Francisco International Airport, 650-341-1595 or www.fofc.com. Of course, sufferers

TRAVEL

of aviophobia could find it difficult to travel to a workshop. SOAR, or Seminars on Aeroanxiety Relief (800-332-7359 or www.fearofflying.com), is a video program developed by a therapist and retired airline pilot for home use.

MEDICATION: You might want to talk to your doctor about an anti-anxiety medication for a flight. "For a short-term solution, we will sometimes recommend an anxiolytic medication such as Klonopin, which is short-acting, or Xanax, which is a bit longer-acting for longer flights," says Dr. Bradley A. Connor, medical director of the New York Center for Travel and Tropical Medicine.

—Marjorie Connelly

A Cure for Jet Lag?

The jury is still out on whether melatonin works

Some bleary-eyed travelers swear by melatonin as a way to beat jet lag. But experts say research on the hormone's effectiveness is far from clear-cut.

Over the years, more than a dozen studies have tried to determine whether melatonin can ease symptoms of jet lag by adjusting the body's internal clock to new time zones. Some have shown that it helps in small doses; others have

found that it is no better than a placebo.

Dr. Michael Terman, a sleep expert at the New York State Psychiatric Institute who published a study on melatonin and jet lag in 1999, says the split stems from confusion over how jet lag is defined. While taking melatonin has been shown to help reset body rhythms, he says, there is little evidence that it can alleviate symptoms of jet lag that result from the stress of traveling itself—running through busy airports, an altered diet, sudden weather changes, the prospect of meeting new business clients. All of these contribute to exhaustion and sleep disturbances.

"We cannot say that all of the symptoms of jet lag are unequivocally due to circadian rhythm shifting," Terman says. "We see, for example, that some people traveling long distances barely complain of jet lag, even though their internal clocks are undergoing marked change. Overall, the evidence for using melatonin is not strong," he adds.

—Anahad O'Connor

Are You on the Safest Airplane?

If you have a choice, opt for a larger jet

Statistics on airline safety can be elucidating—and sometimes misleading. One airline carrier may have a better safety record than another because its routes are in an area of the country that has generally good weather, while another carrier may fly more frequently in an area where poor weather conditions make flying more dangerous. The picture is less cloudy when it comes to budget and commuter carriers, whose safety records are generally poorer than those of the majors. Says one air safety analyst, "If you have a choice between a small regional airline and a large jet, take the jet."

Safety is directly related to the amount of material and space under your seat to absorb the

INSIDE INFO

Jet Lag Remedies

○ Begin observing mealtimes of your destination as soon as possible on your day of travel.

○ Avoid alcohol while traveling.

○ Avoid caffeine while traveling.

○ Drink a pint of liquids during flight.

○ Sleep according to the schedule of your destination.

energy of the impact, so you have a better chance of surviving a crash if you're on one of the bigger planes, such as the Boeing 757's, 767's, 777's and 787's. Newer planes are preferable to older ones which may suffer from corrosion, wear and stress fractures.

Not all airports are created equal, either. Pilots note that Washington's Reagan airport, New York's LaGuardia airport, and the San Diego airport are surrounded by city neighborhoods and have intersecting runways. Boston's Logan airport is plagued by adverse weather conditions and other runway hazards. Idaho's Sun Valley airport is situated so that a landing plane barely clears a mountain range. Similarly, Alaska's Juneau airport is surrounded by glaciers and mountain peaks.

To learn more, check out the site of the National Transportation Safety Board (www. ntsb. gov), and the F.A.A.'s Internet page (www.faa. gov). All the latest incidents are posted, ranging from crashes to turbulence that results in injury, as well as the types of planes that each airline flies. If you're traveling abroad, call the F.A.A. (800-FAA-SURE), or go online at www.faa.gov to determine if your destination has been cited for failing to meet international safety standards. The International Airline Passengers Association (972-404-9980 or www.iapa.com) provides safety information on most carriers worldwide.

...And in the Safest Seat?

Knowing where to sit could save your life

Since, in most accidents, an aircraft travels with its nose down bumping along the ground for a bit after impact, it stands to reason that sitting in one of the front rows won't increase your chances of survival. But are some seats on a plane really safer than others? Experts usually duck the

TIMELY TIPS

If You Are Bumped From a Flight

It's bumpy out there—and we haven't even left the ground. About 90 passengers per million were bumped against their will in 2005, up from 85 per million in 2004.

✔ **The best-informed travelers reject vouchers** that are good for a free ticket anywhere the airline flies, because often the seats are as difficult to book as frequent-flier seats. Instead, they hold out for denied-boarding certificates with a cash value.

✔ **If there are no volunteers**, an airline will sweeten the offer, adding upgrades or increasing the value of the certificate. Then, if there are still no takers, it starts turning away passengers, which in airline-speak is called "involuntary denied boarding." That is when passengers strike gold: under an airline contract, the holdouts not only get a seat on the next flight, but also cash compensation.

—Christopher Elliott

question since there are so many possible crash scenarios, but here are some precautions you can take when reserving a seat:

Boycott bulkhead rows. Seats that face the bulkheads and interior dividers provide more legroom, but they can also be more hazardous. Serious head injuries resulting when passengers hit their heads on the walls and bulkhead during air turbulence and landings top the list of noncrash injury concerns. The F.A.A., airlines and safety researchers are continuing to look into ways to lessen the danger, such as shoulder belts and airbags. Until an appropriate solution is designed for all aircraft, airline crash injury specialists at the National Institute for Aviation Research advise passengers who are taller than average not to sit in the bulkhead row.

Request a wingside seat. Seats close to the aircraft wings are structurally more sound and have better support.

Look for an exit row. The emergency exit row provides more legroom and allows easier escape from fire and smoke. Wherever you sit, count the number of rows you are from an exit. Then, if the lights go out, you can still find your way out.

More info. For updated air safety information go to AirSafe.com (www.airsafe.com) or the National Transportation Safety Board at www.ntsb.gov/aviation/aviation.htm.

No-Fly Frequent Flier Miles
Or how to stack the credit cards in your favor

For millions of travelers, credit card reward programs are the best way to score free airline tickets and hotel rooms. But with credit card issuers and travel companies ratcheting up the competition for customers in recent months, how do you know which card in your wallet is worth reaching for?

Tim Winship, the publisher of FrequentFlier.com, which focuses on loyalty programs, says that all card offers should be weighed carefully. Too often, consumers sign up for cards that are aligned with a particular travel company, only to find that the marriage doesn't work. "All of these cards have pros and cons, and the trick is to figure out, based on your own travel and consumption behavior, how they work in your case," Mr. Winship says.

Generally, travelers should consider a card that is affiliated with an airline that serves their favorite foreign destinations and offers them the particular advantages that suit their traveling style. American Express Delta SkyPoints does not impose blackout dates, offers double points for many purchases and allows members to transfer

---

✓ **TIMELY TIPS**

Making the Best of a Long Layover

If you are faced with a six-hour layover at, say, the airport in Narita, Japan, there are several things you can do: practice Zen meditation, read *War and Peace* or make a brief escape out into the real world.

✔ Airwise.com and WorldAirportGuide.com provide news, driving directions, contact information and the Web address for each airport. They list the nearest city to each airport and provide brief directions to and from it. For those trying to get into the city and back during a layover, WorldAirportGuide.com's public transport section offers advice on the various options available and how long each will take.

✔ The airports themselves now offer increasingly better information on their own Web sites. BAA.com, the British Airport authority site, for instance, has comprehensive information on what to expect at its airports.

✔ To learn how long it takes to clear airport security at American airports, go to the Transportation Security Administration site, waittime.tsa.dhs.gov, which lists wait times at hundreds of American airports.

—Bob Tedeschi

---

their miles to other airlines. The Diners Club Card allows you to convert points into miles with 25 partners, get tickets on virtually any airline with no blackouts and receive primary rental-car insurance when using the card.

FrequentFlier.com has charts that allow visitors to compare offers on airline- and hotel-related cards, and provides details about bank-specific cards that yield travel rewards

—Bob Tedeschi

Tall Ships Sailing
Navigating like an old salt on the high seas

"Tall Ships" are replicas of old sailing schooners that sail under canvas—with ropes and salt spray and moonlit nights at ocean level. The modern versions of these ships come in two styles: authentic replicas that depend on the sails to get places, and the so-called sail cruise-ships that are largely powered.

DEUTSCHLAND *Peter Deilmann Reederei 800-348-8287 or www.deilmann-cruises.com*

WHERE: All over the world

WHO: Experienced seamen, mature professionals and retirees.

ON BOARD: A beautiful three-masted barkentine (one square-rigged and two schooner-rigged masts). You can assist in sailing the ship. There are candlelit dinners in a handsome dining room with menus featuring international cuisine. You fly to meet the ship at a particular port.

SEA CLOUD *Sea Cloud Cruises 888-732-2568 or www.seacloud.com*

WHERE: East Caribbean in winter and many different itineraries the rest of the year.

WHO: Available for charter with a passenger capacity of 69.

ON BOARD: This may be the most beautiful tall ship afloat—also the oldest. Formerly owned by millionairess Marjorie Merriweather Post. There's handcrafted carved oak paneling, antique furniture and fine original oil paintings. (Note: Sea Cloud Cruises is based in Hamburg, Germany.)

THE POLYNESIA *Windjammer Barefoot Cruises, Ltd. 800-327-2602 or www.windjammer.com*

WHERE: Six-day cruises around the Caribbean (the itinerary depends on the time of year and weather conditions.)

WHO: Singles, retirees, families and young marrieds. A high record of repeat passengers.

ON BOARD: A legendary old fishing schooner. Some cabins are made over into bachelor quarters. Singles and other theme cruises are featured. Life on board is ultra casual—wear shorts and expect no frills.

If Shuffleboard Isn't Your Thing
And you like staring at saltwater, a trip on a freighter may be just the ticket

Freighter travel is still available to the general public today. *Ford's Freighter Travel Guide & Waterways of the World* publishes listings updated quarterly of itineraries for more than a hundred different vessels. But freighter travel isn't for everybody. Christopher Buckley, author of *Steaming to Bamboola,* a first-person account of his trip from South Carolina to the North Sea on a tramp freighter, offers some firsthand counsel:

Those who like shuffleboard, mints on their pillow at night and driving golf balls off the afterdeck, read no further. Freighter travel is not for you. It's also not for people with medical

INSIDE INFO

Cabin Fever

- In the last 10 years, the average age of cruise-takers has dropped from 60 to 50, according to the Cruise Line International Association trade group.

- A record 8.9 million North Americans took cruises in 2004, the group said, compared with about 6.9 million in 2000, and 4.4 million in 1995.

DECK BY DECK

Your cabin's location can have a profound effect on your enjoyment of a cruise.

The first important choice is either an inside or outside cabin. Inside cabins are cheaper, usually quieter and good for sleeping. Outside cabins often have deck access, light and a view. Cruise ships are now bigger and more stabilized, but positioning at the center of the ship still helps prevent seasickness. Cabins should be at least 170 sq. ft. for two people.

AFT: The aft (back end) of a boat pitches less than the bow in high seas, but there can be engine noise.

LOWER: Smaller, cheaper cabins nearer the engine. Some drawbacks: engine vibration, noise and crew traffic.

BRIDGE: Expensive, spacious cabins with more amenities (e.g., whirlpools) and verandas; some rolling and pitching.

UPPER DECKS: Often offer the best value for relative cost if there are no lifeboats blocking the view.

PROMENADE: The most public deck. Can be noisy and the exterior views are mostly of people passing by.

MAIN: The noisiest deck and usually the one with most traffic. Pick a cabin insulated by cabins on as many sides as possible, and do not take a cabin that connects to another cabin, unless it is filled with your relatives.

SOURCES: www.sealetter.com; www.cruisevacations.guide.com; *Frommer's Cruises & Ports of Call*

 TIMELY TIPS

Cruising the World

To find out who's sailing where, when and on what kind of ship, from deluxe cruise lines to barebones freighters, check out these Web sites

✔ **Search2cruise.com.** Comprehensive information about cruises and cruise lines. You can search the site by destination, cruise line or specific ship, several hundred are listed.

✔ **FreighterCruises.com.** Maris Freighter and Specialty Cruises arranges bookings on freighters and other types of specialty ships, including container ships. 800-99-MARIS

✔ **Travltips.com.** TravLtips Cruise & Freighter Travel Organization publishes a small magazine about freighter travel every other month. They will also make reservation arrangements for freighter trips. 800-872-8584

✔ **FreighterWorld.com.** Freighter World Cruises, Inc. offers information on freighters, conventional cruises and expedition cruises. 800-531-7774

conditions, because there's usually no doctor on board. That's why only 12 people are allowed on board at once. But for those who enjoy reading the classics and long, long hours of boring, endless blue saltwater, this is your trip. It's a reader's vacation—or a writer's vacation. Nelson Algren reread all of Hemingway's works while on a freighter from San Francisco to Yokohama, then wrote about the experience in *Diary of a Sea Voyage—or Hemingway All the Way.*

A generation ago, you could go down to the dock, talk to a freighter captain and get a job and berth on board. I arranged to work with the crew to pay my way on a freighter; you can't do that today. But a freighter is still a lot less expensive than traveling on a cruise ship

My first freighter trip came when I was 17 and about to start college; I saw a bit of the world at a young age, and developed a real relationship with the men on board. I only made $20 a week, but felt rich because I could buy cigarettes for $1 a carton and beer for $3 a case at the ship store.

It's like apples and oranges between the way I traveled and a freighter trip today. I doubt someone traveling now would be able to really get to know the crew, or share in their misadventures in quite the same way.

Riding the Rails

Wonderful whistle-stop tours across Europe, North America and much of Asia

❝There isn't a train I wouldn't take, no matter where it's going," wrote Edna St. Vincent Millay. No doubt the poet would have jumped at the chance to purchase a railway pass that guarantees unlimited travel for a set price during a set period. Usually it takes only one or two trips to come out ahead, as compared with a round-trip

ticket. Any inveterate train traveler—and most college students—know about Eurail passes (www.eurail.com), but passes are available the world over from Australia to Canada to India and Japan.

The members and editors of the Society of International Railway Travelers (800-478-4881 or www.irtsociety.com) have been evaluating and organizing train trips around the globe since 1983. We asked Eleanor Hardy, the society's president, to choose five of her favorite train rides.

EUROPE: Venice Simplon-Orient-Express offers the finest service, food and wine on a beautiful and historic antique train. Recommended itinerary is the epic, once-a-year Paris to Istanbul trip, with musical welcomes at every stop, and memorable meals in the Lalique diner.

NORTH AMERICA: The Royal Canadian Pacific. On this continent, it can't be topped: the luxury of the mahogany-lined walls, the burgundy and white china and crested silver, the divinely prepared-on-board meals paired with perfect wines. The fresh-faced Canadian staff serves after-dinner drinks where Winston Churchill smoked his cigars, admiring the mighty snow-peaked Rockies from the open-air rear platform.

RUSSIA: The Trans-Siberian by Private Train is a two-week journey with almost-daily cultural visits. Recommended itinerary is westbound, from Vladivostok to Moscow. This train has good food, great vodka and fascinating off-train tours. It also has large, deluxe ensuite compartments, and makes a stop for a cookout on the shores of Lake Baikal.

SCOTLAND: The Royal Scotsman is like a genteel Scot's country home, with gourmet locally grown food, fantastic matched wines and lovely service. Recommended itinerary: The seven-night Grand North Western, which takes in many of the United Kingdom's most scenic routes. During the trip

DISTANCE BETWEEN SOME MAJOR U.S. CITIES

MILES ☐ / ☐ KILOMETERS	Atlanta, GA	Boston, MA.	Chicago, IL	Denver, CO	Houston, TX	Kansas City, KS	Los Angeles, CA	Minneapolis, MN	Miami, FL	New York, NY	San Francisco, CA	Seattle, WA	Washington, D.C.
Atlanta, GA		1110	715	1405	800	805	2185	1135	665	865	2495	2785	620
Boston, MA	1790		1000	2000	1830	1440	3020	1390	1520	210	3130	3020	450
Chicago, IL	1150	1613		1000	1085	525	2020	410	1380	795	2135	2070	710
Denver, CO	2260	3226	1615		1120	600	1025	915	2065	1780	1270	1335	1620
Houston, TX	1285	2951	1750	1805		795	1550	1230	1190	1635	1930	2450	1370
Kansas City, MO	1295	2302	850	965	1280		1625	440	1470	1195	1865	1900	1040
Los Angeles, CA	3515	4871	3250	1650	2495	2610		1935	2740	2800	385	1140	2650
Minneapolis, MN	1825	2242	665	1470	1980	680	3110		1795	1200	2010	2015	1090
Miami, FL	1070	2451	2220	3320	1915	2365	4405	2885		1280	3115	3365	1060
New York, NY	1390	338	1275	2865	2630	1925	4505	1935	2060		3055	2860	240
San Francisco, CA	4015	5048	3435	2040	3105	3000	615	3240	5015	4915		810	2840
Seattle, WA	4485	4871	3330	2140	3940	3060	1835	2675	5415	4600	1305		2720
Washington, D.C.	1000	725	1145	2613	2209	1677	4274	1753	1709	387	4580	4387	

you can hear Scots music, dance a reel and gaze at the rugged Highlands landscape from the train's open-air rear platform.

SOUTHERN AFRICA: Rovos Rail is one of the most luxurious trains in the world, with the largest compartments of any available, and the Blue Train, with a gold bathtub in some suites, is over the top. Both offer deluxe accommodations and food, friendly yet impeccable service and, with Rovos, visits that range from gold mines to game reserves. Recommended itinerary: Cape Town to Dar es Salaam on Rovos or Rovos and Blue Train with a side trip to Victoria Falls.

Get your tickets on the Web: Two sources for buying international rail tickets online are www.internationaltrainline.com and www.worldtravellers.net

The World's Most Charming Inns
Hard-to-find gems in America and Europe

Small hotels with charm and character can be difficult to find through tourist agencies and guides. But Karen Brown has made that her specialty. She has spent the past three decades evaluating small inns, hotels and bed and breakfasts, and publishing discerning guidebooks of her discoveries (See www.karenbrown.com for titles.) She and her husband, Rick, have also built their own English manor-style hideaway, the Seal Cove Inn in Moss Beach, California, half an hour's drive south of San Francisco. Here are some of her personal choices of the best country inns in the U.S. and Europe. While not necessarily the most luxurious or the best bargains, the hotels are chosen for their charm and most of them offer excellent value.

CALIFORNIA

Whitegate Inn, Mendocino. The inn oozes decadent Victorian charm. 707-937-4892 or www. whitegateinn.com

Oak Knoll Inn, Napa. Surrounded by 600 acres of vineyards, Oak Knoll Inn has an idyllic setting. The guestrooms are luxurious in size. 707 255 2200 or www.oakknollinn.com

MID ATLANTIC

Inn at Whitewing Farm , Kenneth Square, Pennsylvania. Spread over 43 pastoral acres in southern Chester County, it is close to many of the area's attractions, including the adjacent Longwood Gardens and the Winterthur Museum. 610-388-2664 or www.whitewingfarm.com

Morrison House, Alexandria, Virginia. An 18th-century Federal manor in the heart of old-town Alexandria with a staff that provides a level of service that's European in style.The ideal place to stay in the Washington, D.C., area. 703-838-8000 or www.morrisonhouse.com

Inn at Warner Hall, Gloucester, Virginia. Warner Hall dates back to 1642 and the owners have taken this plantation house and re-created a home and a style that will delight the traveler. 804-695-9565 or www.warnerhall.com

NEW ENGLAND

Homestead Inn–Thomas Henkelmann, Greenwich, Connecticut. Only a few inns anywhere in the world can begin to approach the level of accommodation here. 203-869-7500 or www. homesteadinn.com

Maple Leaf Inn, Barnard (near Woodstock), Vermont. Although newly built, this beautiful three-story, gray-and-white inn with wraparound porch has a traditional feel. 802-234-5342 or www. mapleleafinn.com

The 1811 House, Manchester, Vermont. Within the walls of the original building and the adjacent cottage are 13 guestrooms, the most romantic with fireplaces. This property sits right on the main street but has seven acres of land with a pond and gardens. 802 362 1811 or www.1811house.com

PACIFIC NORTHWEST

Channel House, Depoe Bay, Oregon. Many coastal inns lay claim to ocean views—many are prettier—but nothing equals this unique spot for sheer wildness. Channel House is one of our favorites, even compared to much more luxurious alternatives. 541-765-2140 or www.channelhouse.com

Springbrook Hazelnut Farm, Newberg, Oregon. Situated on 70 acres, this enchanting hazelnut farm property is only 20 minutes from Portland, but you'll swear that you are in the Italian countryside. 503-538-4606 or www.nutfarm.com

Run of the River, Leavenworth, Washington. A few miles beyond the charming Bavarian village is an even more fairy-tale place: a log cabin nestled amid pine and aspen trees against a rugged backdrop of mountains. 509-548-7171 or www. runoftheriver.com, info@runoftheriver.com

MEXICO

Dolphin Cove Inn, Manzanillo, Colima. A well-priced, charmingly decorated place to stay with breathtaking views that can't be surpassed anywhere in Mexico, not at any price. 314-334-1692, toll free in Mexico; 800-713-3250 or www.dolphincoveinn.com

TRAVEL

La Casona, Mexico City. A charming, beautifully managed small hotel nestled in a lovely residential area. 55-5286-3001 or www.hotellacasona. com.mx

The Hacienda de los Santos, Alamos, Sonora. If you are anywhere near the colonial village of Alamos, a wonderful old mining town, this hotel is a must. 647-428-0222 or 428-0217 or www. haciendadelossantos.com

AUSTRIA

Landhaus zu Appesbach, Saint Wolfgang. Just outside the popular tourist destination of Saint Wolfgang, the inn borders a lovely, shimmering lake, but escapes the busloads of tourists. 06138-22.09 or www.landhaus-zu-appesbach.com

Schloss Kapfenstein, Kapfenstein. Even among

Austria's superb selection of castle hotels, the Schloss Kapfenstein stands out. 03157-30.03.00 or www.schloss-kapfenstein.at

Gasthof Sänger Blondel, Dürnstein. In the fairytale village of Dürnstein, the Gasthof Sänger Blondel offers pleasant rooms, wonderful food and a great warmth of welcome from the Schendl family who have owned the home since 1730. 02711-253 or www.saengerblondel.at

ENGLAND

The Soho Hotel, London. Central to the attractions of Covent Garden, the British Museum and the National Gallery, the Soho is located on a quiet cul-de-sac. All the rooms are different, sleekly modern, and appointed for the sophisticated traveler. 4 Richmond Mews London W1D 3DH, England. 020-7559-3000 or www.sohohotel.com

Chewton Glen, New Milton, Hampshire. With 58 bedrooms, world-class leisure and sporting facilities, an award winning spa, a Michelin-star restaurant, the hotel has been voted the "Best Small Hotel under 100 Rooms in the World" for two years running. 01425-275341 or www. chewtonglen.com

Bolhays, Salisbury, Wiltshire. An 1899 Victorian townhouse built on church land that is a 10-minute walk from the magnificent cathedral. 01722-320603 or www.bolhays.com

FRANCE

Manoir d'Hautegente, Coly. Down a private drive, the manoir sits idyllically beneath shady trees in a garden. The bedrooms vary greatly in size, but all enjoy river views. 05.53.51.68.03 or www. manoir-hautegente.com

Château de Garrevaques, Garrevaques. The château is lovingly decorated with heirlooms, beauti-

---

 INSIDE INFO

Where the Well-Heeled Stay

The world's top hotels, as ranked by well-heeled readers (in a 2005 annual survey by Institutional Investor magazine):

- **St. Regis** New York
- **Park Hyatt Paris** Vendôme

- **Mandarin Oriental** New York
- **Four Seasons** Milan

- **Four Seasons** Singapore
- **Four Seasons George V** Paris

- **Mandarin Oriental** San Francisco
- **Ritz-Carlton, Millenia** Singapore

- **Peninsula** Hong Kong
- **Four Seasons,** Chicago

- Survey respondents had average annual incomes of $817,000 and spent an average of 62 nights in a hotel within the last year.

—Joe Sharkey

TIMELY TIPS

Taking a Bite of the Big Apple

Hotels that will leave you some money for the rest of the visit

There are two rules to finding an affordable hotel room in Manhattan: do your research and book early. Rates vary wildly, depending on the season and availability. Prices tend to be highest in the fall, when conventioneers converge on the city, and again in December, when holiday shoppers swarm Fifth Avenue.

Don't forget to budget for city, state and occupancy taxes, which come to 13.625 percent, plus $3.50 a night. The hotels below are generally considered moderately priced; rates are quotes for fall 2005, for the least expensive room, single or double.

Affinia Dumont. *From $199.* A business and pet-friendly spot with gym and spa. 150 East 34th Street. 212-481-7600 or www.affinia.com.

Chelsea Hotel. *From $195.* The storied bohemian landmark. 222 West 23rd Street. 212-243-3700 or www.hotelchelsea.com.

Doubletree Metropolitan. *From $159.* A recently renovated landmark. 569 Lexington Avenue. 212-752-7000 or www.metropolitanhotelnyc.com.

Excelsior Hotel. *From $229.* Cozy Upper West Side elegance, steps from Central Park. 45 West 81st Street. 212-362-9200 or www.excelsiorhotelny.com.

Gershwin Hotel. *From $119.* Hotel-cum-hostel popular with young Europeans. 7 East 27th Street. 212-545-8000 or www.gershwinhotel.com.

Hotel QT. *From $125.* A cheap, chic hotel. 125 West 45th Street. 212-354-2323 or www.hotelqt.com.

Hotel Stanford. *From $189.* The staff at this Koreatown hotel speaks Korean, English and Spanish. 43 West 32nd Street. 800-365-1114 or www.hotelstanford.com.

Hudson Hotel. *From $199.* A former Y.W.C.A. redesigned and updated. 356 West 58th Street. 212-554-6000 or www.hudsonhotel.com.

Off SoHo Suites Hotel. *Rooms from $199* (sharing kitchen and bath); *suites from $189.* Euro-style suites between SoHo and the Lower East Side. 11 Rivington Street. 800-633-7646 or www.offsoho.com.

The Time. *From $189.* Another hip, high-concept hotel in Times Square. 224 West 49th Street. 877-846-3692 or www.thetimeny.com.

—Denny Lee

ful antiques. Dinner is a gala event and great fun. 05.63.75.04.54 or www.garrevaques.com

Château-Hôtel André Ziltener, Chambolle-Musigny. In a delightful village nestled among the vineyards in the heart of Burgundy, this is one of the region's most elegant properties. 03.80.62.41.62 or www.chateau-ziltener.com

GERMANY

Gasthof Zum Bären, Meersburg. A picture-perfect 15th-century inn that has been run by the same family for five generations in an absolutely stunning little medieval town hugging the shore of Lake Constance. 07532-43220 or www.baeren-meersburg.de

Louisa's Place, Berlin. A haven within the vibrant, ever-active city of Berlin, many guests come for a month or more. It offers huge, one- to three-bedroom suites complete with kitchens, for a price that is often less than a standard double room at Berlin's deluxe hotels. Excellent restaurant. 03063-103500 or www.louisas-place.de

TIMELY TIPS

Hush-Hush Hotels

These tiny hotels are so private that their name isn't on the door

Ring the unmarked doorbell at 5, rue de Moussy, a small street in the chic Marais district of Paris, and you'll encounter a new breed of luxury accommodation, a concept so new that it has yet to be properly labeled. Minihotel? Lifestyle suite? Haute B&B?

Found in some of Europe's most fashionable neighborhoods, these new hotels are marked by several key characteristics: a striking (often eccentric) style, fewer than eight bedrooms, rarely any signs, nothing that resembles a reception area, a fan base built only by word of mouth and usually owners with a strong, and sometimes famous, personality.

Chic Retreats is a London-based agency with the motto "Small Is Beautiful" representing privately owned luxury hotels with fewer than 30 rooms. You can find more than a few of the properties on the agency's Web site (www.chicretreats.com) that fit within the haute B&B trend. The trend is moving to the States, too. Miami Beach has the five-suite Casa Tua, whose fitting motto is "Privacy Is So Precious." The privacy here is so precious that rooms start at $500.

Antwerp: Miauw Suites Antwerp, Marnixplaats 14. (31-20) 422 0561; www.analik.com/miauwantwerp.html

Madrid: Casa de Madrid, Arrieta, 2. (34-91) 5595791; www.casademadrid.com

Miami Beach: Casa Tua, 1700 James Avenue. 305-673-0973 or www.casatualifestyle.com

Milan: 3Rooms 10 Corso Como, 10 Corso Como. (39-02) 626163 www.3rooms-10corsocomo.com

Ouderkerk aan de Amstel, the Netherlands: Lute Suites, 54-58 Amsteldijk Zuid. 54-58 or 31-20-4722462 or www.lutesuites.com

Paris: 3Rooms 5 Rue de Moussy, 5, rue de Moussy, Fourth Arrondissement. (33-1) 44.78.92.00 or info@3rooms-5ruedemoussy.com

Rome: Residenza Napoleone III; Largo Goldoni, 56. (39-34) 77337098 or www.residenza-napoleone.com

Venice: Charming House DD.724, Dorsoduro 724. (39-041) 2770262 or www.dd.724.it

—Gisela Williams

Schloss Lübbenau, Lübbenau. The Spreewald is an area midway between Dresden and Berlin where the River Spree fans out into a spiderweb of waterways bordered by quaint houses, many accessible only by boat. The Schloss Lübbenau is a large, private estate within walking distance of the boat dock, owned by the same family since 1621. 03542-8730 or www.schloss-luebbenau.de

IRELAND

Ballaghtobin, Callan, County Kilkenny. The town is an excellent location for exploring the counties of Waterford and Kilkenny. Bedrooms are absolutely gorgeous. Breakfast is the only meal served. 056-7725227 or www.ballaghtobin.com

Coopershill, Riverstown, County Silgo. Built in 1774, the house is one of those wonderful places that offers the best of both worlds—the luxury of a country house hotel and the warmth of a home. 071- 91 65108 or www.coopershill.com

Shelburne Lodge, Kenmare, County Kerry. A Georgian farmhouse with attractive grounds, but it is the interior that is outstanding. Scrumptious breakfasts. 064-41013 or shelburne@kenmare.com

ITALY

Albergo Villa Belvedere, Argegno. An enticing

18th-century villa. Only a private terrace separates it from Lake Como. This intimate inn is an incredible value, but the furnishings are simple. 031-82-11-16 or www.villabelvedere-argegno.it

La Frateria di Padre Eligio, Cetona. This 13th century convent (founded by St. Francis), now an enchanting hotel, makes an outstanding base for exploring the beauties of Tuscany and Umbria. 0578-23 82 61 or www.lafrateria.it, info@lafrateria.it

Hotel Flora, Venice. Located down a tiny lane, just off one of the main walkways to St. Mark's Square. Although it is a fairly simple hotel, it is a rare find for those who want a relatively inexpensive place to stay in the heart of Venice. 041-52 05 844 or www.hotelflora.it

SCOTLAND

Summer Isles Hotel, Achiltibuie, Wester Ross. Fifteen miles of winding, single-track road lead you through land and sea lochs in some of Scotland's wildest scenery to Achiltibuie, a few cottages along the road overlooking a broad expanse of bay and the Summer Isles. Just beyond the post office is the hotel. 01854-622282 or www.summerisleshotel.co.uk

Dun na Mara, Benderloch, Oban, Argyll. A lochside location with a private beach and views across the water to the distant Island of Mull, the hotel is a complete oasis of calm. 01631-720233 or www.dunnamara.com

Viewfield House, Portree, Isle of Skye. Viewfield House has always been home to the Macdonald family and there have always been Macdonalds on Skye. At the end of the 19th century, this prosperous family remodeled, adding a huge extension and a baronial tower. Still, this is very much a home stay at a very special house. 01478-612217 or www.viewfieldhouse.com

SPAIN

Posada de San José, Cuenca. Located in the heart of the walled city of Cuenca, just off the Plaza Mayor. Most of the bedrooms have stunning views across the Huecar gorge to the Convento de San Pablo. 969-211-300 or www.posadasanjose.com

Cal Teixidó, Estamariu. Amid the peace of an unspoiled village in the heart of the Pyrenees, the hotel has been cleverly integrated with the old slate-roofed and rough stone-walled farm buildings. 973-36-0121 or www.calteixido.com

Hotel Claris, Barcelona. The rooftop gymnasium and pool offer spectacular views of the city, as does the glass-roofed terrace restaurant. A special, exclusive treat for hotel guests is free access to the owner's private museum. Need wheels but don't want the hassle of a rental car? Borrow the courtesy car available gratis to guests. 93-487-6262 or www.derbyhotels.com

SWITZERLAND

The Rote Rose, Regensberg. This perfect inn, 15 miles from Zurich, has a superb setting on the knoll of a vineyard-laced hill in this beautiful medieval walled village. 044-85 31 013 or www.rote-rose.com

The Landgasthof Ruedihus, Kandersteg. A cozy, flower-laden chalet in a lush meadow backed by mountains, and brimming inside and out with antique charm. Only 10 bedrooms, but an excellent kitchen. 033-675 81 82 or www.doldenhorn-ruedihus.ch

Hotel Tamaro, Ascona. Facing Lake Maggiore, this is a Ticino-style patrician house. Request a lake view. 091-791 02 82 or www.hotel-tamaro.ch/

TRAVEL

Palaces That Could Be Yours

There are unexpected benefits to becoming a temporary chatelaine

The best way to save money on a vacation rental home is to bypass the middleman. You can save 20 to 30 percent by renting directly through the owner. Options include writing the local tourist board or looking through the classified sections of college alumni magazines. Rental agencies, on the other hand, offer the convenience of an experienced pro minding the details. Following are some resources:

RENTAL AGENCIES

If you use a rental agency, try to choose one with a local agent based near the town in which you intend to rent. That way, you'll have someone to contact in case anything goes wrong.

At Home Abroad. Established in 1960, it has years of experience in catering to an upscale market. Villas, castles and apartments in the Caribbean, Europe and Mexico. 212-421-9165, www.athomeabroadinc.com

Barclay International. Specializes in upscale apartment and villa rentals in most of the major cities in Europe. They also have cottage rentals in the U.K. Properties include flats in some luxury hotels. Stay as little as one night or by the week or month. 800-845-6636 or www.barclayweb.com

British Travel International. Properties in France, England, Spain, Portugal, Ireland, Wales, Scotland, and Italy, including over 9,000 country cottages. Linked up with Cottages4you. Also offer advice on hotels throughout Europe. 800-327-6097 or www.britishtravel.com

Creative Leisure International. Private homes and resorts in Hawaii, the Caribbean, Mexico and Tahiti. Will arrange everything from airfare to activities. 800-413-1000 or www.creativeleisure.com

Homes Away. Rentals in the south of France, as well as Umbria and Tuscany in Italy, and in Andalucia and Catalonia in Spain. 800-374-6637 or www.homesaway.com

Interhome. One of the oldest and largest home rental agencies in the world, with over 20,000 listings of apartments, houses and villas in Europe and the U.S 800-882-6864 or www.interhome.us

RENTING BY COUNTRY

FRANCE

Federation Nationale Des Gîtes Ruraux De France: An organization that preserves old country houses and promotes rural tourism. The network consists of over 50,000 houses and modest apartments, or *gîtes*. 59, rue Saint Lazare, 75009 Paris, France. 011-33-1-49-70-75-75 or www.gites-de-france.fr

The French Experience: Has short-term rental apartments. It also handles reservations at small hotels and chateaux, bus/boat tours and various other excursions, with links to Web sites for Italy and the UK. 800-283-7262 or www.frenchexperience.com

ITALY

Villa Vacations: Rents villas throughout Italy (also France and Spain) with or without staff. Prices vary widely according to the size and level of comfort of the home. They focus on the higher end of the rental market. 800-261-4460 or www.villavacations.com

SCANDINAVIA

Scanam World Tours: Rents private homes throughout Scandinavia. Also offers tours throughout Scandanavia. 800-545-2204 or www.scandinaviantravel.com

TIMELY TIPS

Swapping Castles

Save a king's ransom by trading places

A beach house in Carmel, a condo in Captiva, an apartment on the Champs Elysées—imagine vacationing at each and paying little more than the airfare. This may sound too good to be true, but for the thousands of Americans who swap their homes with like-minded travelers, it's no daydream. House swapping is not a difficult undertaking. To get started, list your home with a home exchange agency such as Intervac or HomeLink. It is not expensive to list a home, but you must take care of setting up an exchange with the homeowner in your chosen destination.

The first step is to pick a few preferred destinations, and decide how long you want to visit (the average exchange is two to three weeks). Start planning 9 to 12 months before you intend to travel. When listing with an agency, describe your home in great detail, including amenities, and access to tourist attractions, as well as any pets and include a picture of your home. About 75 percent of home swappers also exchange the use of their cars.

Once your home has been listed, you will be contacted by interested parties, who will also provide information about themselves and their properties. You can also contact people whose properties interest you.

Home Exchange. Usually there is a listing fee, but other arrangements are left to the homeowners. 800-877-8723 or www.homeexchange.com

HomeLink International Extensive listings worldwide and in the continental U.S. and Hawaii. Provide use of a database to members for a fee. Members make their own arrangements. 800-638-3841 or www.homelink-usa.org

Intervac. International and domestic listings for home exchanges in 52 countries. 800-756-4663 or www.intervacusa.com

SCOTLAND

National Trust Scotland. This is the Scottish equivalent of the National Trust in England. 28 Charlotte Square, Edinburgh, Scotland EH2 4ET. +44(0)-131-243-9300 or www.nts.org.uk

UNITED KINGDOM

National Trust Holiday Booking: Determined travelers can find real bargains at this branch of the National Trust (a private charitable organization preserving national landmarks and gardens) in England. They have access to over 300 magnificent historic properties and cottages throughout England, Wales, and Northern Ireland. The National Trust. P.O. Box 39, Warrington WA5 7WD. +44 0870 458 4000 or www.nationaltrust.org.uk (click on the "Visits and Holidays" section for more information on rental properties)

UNITED STATES

Landmark Trust: A charitable trust that has rescued and preserved four beautiful historic landmarks in the U.S. from abandonment and neglect. They offer these restored properties as vacation rentals. All of them are located on many acres of land (one of them sits on 600 acres), and one was even home to Rudyard Kipling. All of their featured properties are quaint, rural and private. Worth a visit if you are looking for peace and quiet and to go back in time within the U.S. 707 Kipling Rd., Dummerston, Vt. 05301. 802-257-7783 or www.landmarktrustusa.org

WEB SITES: These tourist boards also have listings for vacation rentals:

Denmark: www.visitdenmark.com

Finland: www.visitfinland.com
Iceland: www.icelandtouristboard.com
Norway:www.visitnorway.com
Sweden: www.visitsweden.com

Get Thee to a Monastery
Heavenly places to rest body and soul

Christian monasteries have opened their doors to strangers in search of rest and reflection since the sixth century, when St. Benedict, founder of Western monasticism, made it a tenet that guests be received "as Christ himself." Robert Regalbuto, author of *A Guide to Monastic Guest Houses,* has been visiting monasteries and convents across the nation and in Canada since he was in prep school.

Generally, monasteries and convents impose periods of quiet, and often some of the services and parts of the compounds are off-limits to visitors. The rooms are typically spare, but the monastery and its surroundings can be splendid. A day's room and board may cost around $40 to $50 a person at most of these monasteries and convents to defray expenses, but in some cases, there is no fee required. Guest facilities are limited at most of these retreat houses, so make reservations well in advance. Here are some of Regalbuto's favorites:

Abbaye Cistercienne D'Oka *Roman Catholic* Oka, Quebec J0N 1E0, Canada. 450-479-8361 or www.abbayeoka.com

Bay View Villa Guest and Retreat House *Roman Catholic* Saco, Me. 04072 207-286-8762

Incarnation Priory *Episcopal and an order of Roman Catholic monks* Berkeley, Calif. 94709. 510-548-3406 or www.ohcmonks.org

Monastery of St. Mary and St. John *Episcopal* Cambridge, Mass. 02138. 617-876-3037 or www.ssje.org

New Camaldoli Hermitage *Roman Catholic* Big Sur, Calif. 93920. 408-667-2456 or www.contemplation.com

Pecos Benedictine Monastery *Roman Catholic* Pecos, N.M. 87510. 505-757-6415, ext. 254 or www.pecosabbey.org

St. Augustine's House *Lutheran* Oxford, Mich. 48371. 248-628-2604 or www.staugustines-house.org

St. John's Convent *Anglican* Willowdale, Ontario M2N 2J5, Canada. 416-226-2201 ext. 305 or www.ssjd.ca/guest-house.html

St. Leo Abbey *Roman Catholic* Saint Leo, Fla. 33574, 352-588-8182, www.saintleoabbey.org/retreat.htm

Skete of the Resurrection of Christ *Synod of Bishops of the Russian Orthodox Church in Exile* Fridley, Minn. 55432. 763-574-1001 or www.skete.info

Weston Priory *Roman Catholic* Weston, Vt. 05161. 802-824-5409 or www.westonpriory.org

It's a Wireless World
With a G.S.M. phone you can use your cellphone all over the world

American cell phones work fairly well across most of the United States, but what about when you travel to, say, Paris? With newer phones that support international standards, reducing roaming rates and allowing you to take advantage of local rates, it's now easier and cheaper to stay in touch with cellphones when traveling overseas.

The place to start is with a G.S.M. phone. Just as radios operate on different standards (AM vs. FM) and frequencies, so do cell phones. Two of the

TIMELY TIPS

Getting an 11th-Hour Passport

And baby needs one, too

If you're leaving on a foreign trip and discover your passport has expired or that you don't have one, you can get one quickly at one of the 13 passport agencies in the United States. Generally, the agencies serve only travelers who are departing within two weeks and accept applications only by appointment. Addresses and phone numbers can be found at travel.state.gov/passport/about/agencies.html. The necessary forms can also be downloaded from the site. Applicants can also call the National Passport Information Center at 877-487-2778. The agencies are located in the following cities: Boston, Chicago, Honolulu, Houston, Los Angeles, Miami, New Orleans, New York, Norwalk (Connecticut), Philadelphia, San Francisco, Seattle and Washington. (For more information, see page 778.)

✔ If you can't go yourself, try a private expediter. There are about 100 expediters operating in the U.S., many of whom are members of the National Association of Passport and Visa Services, an industry group. Members are listed online at www.napvs.org. Even if you apply in person, the U.S. Passport Agency charges $60 for expedited services. Private expediters generally charge an additional $60 to $200.

✔ Most people who are applying for a child's passport will find that the process is more complicated than ever. In 2004, the government started requiring that children appear in person when they apply for a passport, and that the consent of both parents is documented. There are also new costs and rules that may mean you'll have to make several trips to apply. The State Department's easy-to-navigate travel site, www.travel.state.gov (click on "Passports" and then on the page titled "Minors Under Age 14"), will give you a good start, but the bottom line is this: give yourself plenty of time so you can avoid last-minute panic or expediting fees.

✔ If both parents don't appear with the child at one of the 6,000 "passport acceptance facilities"—go to www.iafdb.travel.state.gov to find the one nearest you—written permission from an absent parent or another documented explanation, like proof of sole custody of a child, an adoption decree or the death certificate of a deceased parent, must be supplied. A sample form letter stating consent is available on the State Department Web site, and it must be notarized. If the form isn't available, a letter with the same information will do. For a regular application, the passport will be issued in six weeks.

—Barry Estabrook and Jeanne B. Pinder

most popular cellular standards are G.S.M. (global system for mobile communications) and C.D.M.A. (code division multiple access), each of which uses different frequencies (think radio stations).

For travelers, G.S.M. is the driving force behind easier roaming, since it's the standard used in most countries (though some like Japan and South Korea use others). G.S.M. is also the main network for American carriers like Cingular and T-Mobile, while others, including Verizon Wireless and Sprint, have recently released hybrid phones that include G.S.M. for roaming. Without a newer hybrid phone, a traveler on a non-G.S.M. network will have limited international roaming options.

Users need a G.S.M. phone with the frequency for the country they're visiting. Sites like www.gsmworld.com (click on "Roaming," then "Coverage Maps") list G.S.M. bands for each country.

Once you have a G.S.M. phone, you need to make sure that it is "unlocked." American carriers usually configure the subsidized phone that you receive when signing a service contract so

✅ TIMELY TIPS

Call Home for Less

A familiar voice is just 37 (or so) digits away

Whether you prefer high-tech options or more conventional landlines, there are affordable ways to call home from abroad, even if you don't carry an internationally-capable cellphone.

✔ PREPAID CALLING CARDS.

Calling cards provide the ultimate in flexibility: they can be used from most locations, including pay phones, cell phones and landlines. But not all calling cards are equal, especially overseas. Compare the rate options associated with different cards, whether you buy them before you travel or on the road. Some charge a per-connection fee as well as a per-minute fee, for example. WHO SHOULD USE THEM: Travelers who don't carry computers; technophobes.

✔ CALLBACK SERVICES.

As the name suggests, these services call you back and then place your call at cheaper rates. You initiate the call by dialing a "trigger" number—a connection to the callback service's computers. Let the call ring once and then hang up. The computer calls you back from the United States using lower international rates and makes the connection after verifying your account number. Often cheaper than direct-dial calls and even some prepaid calling cards, but the services may not work at hotels, where staff may not accept the return calls. WHO SHOULD USE THEM: Those traveling for long periods who plan to make lots of international calls.

✔ VOICE OVER INTERNET PROTOCOL (VoIP).

VoIP works by digitizing your voice and sending it via the Internet to the person you're calling, who hears it on his PC speakers, or by routing it through regular telephone lines to anyone's standard phone line. VoIP services generally work best with a broadband or wireless Internet connection and can be used from hotel rooms, Internet cafés or wireless hot spots if you have a notebook computer. Since most calls use the Internet, and connections into and out of the Internet are typically local calls, the rates are astonishing low. WHO SHOULD USE IT: Travelers who have access to broadband or wireless Internet.

—David A. Kelly

that you can't simply use that phone on another network. Unlocking that configuration allows you to use other carriers' SIM cards—removable chips that determine the phone's network and number—and potentially obtain cheaper rates. Web-based companies like www.unlock123.com will unlock phones for as little as $5.

With an unlocked phone, you can simply walk into any cellphone store in the foreign country you are visiting, purchase a new, local SIM card and some additional air time, pop the SIM card in your phone and start making calls.This new SIM card gives you a local phone number, making local calls inexpensive. Incoming calls (even international) are free in many countries, so you can have friends or associates call you at less expensive United States rates while you can talk free as long as your battery holds out. But your voice mail may or may not work, and you may have to manually dial your voice mail number. Sites like www.telestial.com offer prepaid SIM cards for foreign countries, saving travelers the need to find a store.

Even after you buy a SIM card, you may want to buy a separate prepaid phone card to save money on international calls. Instead of eating up local minutes, you can then call the equivalent of an 800 number and obtain much cheaper rates.

—David A. Kelly

The Case for Trip Insurance

Most health insurance plans do not cover you when you are abroad

Travelers wondering whether it's worthwhile to purchase trip insurance might want to consider these facts:

- Medical care—even in an emergency—is not covered by Medicare or many private health insurance plans when Americans travel overseas.

- Some Medicare supplemental plans include foreign travel emergency coverage, as do some private plans, but they often require notification to qualify for reimbursement of medical expenses (and, often, insurance cards include only toll-free numbers that don't work all over the world).

To get medical insurance coverage when venturing abroad, travelers have several options:

- Package travel policies that also cover things like trip cancellation and lost baggage

- Medical-only policies, which can be bought for a single trip or multiple trips within a year

- Medical transport policies, which primarily cover emergency evacuation (often with exceptions for risky activities like rock climbing).

The price of travel insurance is typically based on the traveler's age, the amount of coverage desired and the cost or length of the trip.

A general guideline is that package travel policies cost 4 to 7 percent of the trip's price (about $200 to $350 to insure a $5,000 trip), while a travel medical policy for a single trip costs roughly $20 to $50 for $50,000 to $100,000 worth of coverage.

Both types of policies generally cover medical evacuation, up to a limit specified in the policy, but you can also buy just a medical evacuation policy for less than $50 a trip.

Most package travel policies also include trip interruption benefits that cover expenses like additional hotel nights or airline ticket change fees, as well as offer reimbursement for the missed portion of a trip.

In general, buying travel insurance doesn't mean you can cancel a trip for any reason and get your money back; policies stipulate acceptable reasons for a cancellation, and there are exclusions for things like existing medical conditions, acts of war and in some cases acts of terrorism. So it's important to read the fine print on a policy to understand what it covers and what's excluded.

Unlike some other types of insurance, travel insurance usually does cover natural disasters—like a tsunami.

Another benefit typically provided by travel insurance involves the worst-case scenario: repatriation of remains—but again, each policy defines specific benefits and limits.

—Susan Stellin

 INSIDE INFO

Travelers' Illnesses

- About 8 percent of travelers to developing countries require medical care during or after travel, according to a study of more than 17,000 people who became ill while traveling from 1996 to 2004.

- Overall, the most common ailment was acute diarrhea, but among travelers to Africa, it was malaria.

- Respiratory illness is second only to gastrointestinal illness as a cause of illness in travelers

SOURCE: GeoSentinel Clinics

A Short Guide to Travel Guides

Picking a guidebook can be more difficult than picking a place to go

Planning a trip involves many difficult decisions, but near the top of many lists is standing in a bookstore trying to choose from a daunting lineup of guidebooks.

Fifteen or 20 years ago, the choice was simpler. Backpackers and budget travelers hit the road with Let's Go, Rough Guides or Lonely Planet. Those taking a break from a job or enjoying retirement packed Fodor's or Frommer's, less adventurous but good for nuts and bolts like museum hours and restaurant addresses. Art and culture connoisseurs carried a Blue Guide, and high fliers relied on Michelin Guides to steer them to Europe's notable hotels and chefs.

To some degree, those characterizations still hold true. But as the budget guides have broadened their focus to retain readers now older and earning a decent salary, and the mainstream guides have tried to become more hip, the lines have blurred. Plus, established publishers have started new books aimed at a wider range of travelers taking different types of trips, and there are the niche guidebooks to consider: titles for hikers, bikers, women, families, gay travelers and people who won't leave home without their pets.

With all these choices, it may be time to branch out from a favorite series and experiment. One trend that's catching on, partly in response to post-Sept. 11 travel patterns, are mini-guides designed for short trips to a single city. The British publisher Dorling Kindersley started its "Top 10" series in 2001, shorter versions of its DK Eyewitness Guides, which are known for glossy pages

The world is a book, and those who do not travel, read only a page.

St. Augustine

• • •

and color photographs. The Top 10 books choose 10 attractions as the best to see or do, plus give additional lists like the top 10 Belgian beers in the Brussels book. Fodor's has introduced a similar "See It" series. The See It guides are nearly 400 pages, compared with 150 to 200 pages for the Top 10 books, but Fodor's also sells a smaller City Pack guide to a city's top 25 sights, plus a foldout map. Both series feature lots of color and pictures. A chapter at the beginning of most Frommer's guidebooks showcases the "best of" a destination. The Frommer's Portable Guides are among the most compact available.

Lonely Planet has introduced a shorter "Best of" series of city pocket guides and another "Road Trip" series focused on weekend road trips, which complement its core lineup of country and regional guides, and its "On a Shoestring" series, still popular with the backpacker set. Not to miss the boat, the Rough Guides introduced a new Directions pocket series, with more color and photos than its other guidebooks. It, too, is designed for shorter trips.

So which guidebook should you choose? Paper quality, the book's weight, the writing style, the size of the type, the number of photos, the quality of the maps and even page layout are all personal preferences—which often vary depending on the trip's length, the destination and who else is traveling. Also, look at the copyright date on any book you're considering; newer is definitely better.

There are dozens of other series; the ones mentioned here barely scratch the surface. Get Lost Travel Books has helpful descriptions of more than 25 series at www.getlostbooks.com. No doubt there will be even more options to consider by the time you read this.

—Susan Stellin

Need Even More Travel Advice?

Blogs from the road take sharing to a new level

Reading an online travel blog will perhaps never have the romance of receiving a dog-eared postcard in the mail, but intrepid travelers armed with digital cameras are finding that keeping a blog on the road can be a compelling and viable way of maintaining contact with friends and family.

A travel blog is a real-time online journal that allows users to post text and photographs to the Internet and share the Web address with whomever they want. As travelers have become more comfortable with the Internet and digital cameras have become more affordable, blogging has become increasingly practical and popular. All over the world, travelers can stop in an Internet cafe, upload their photos and share them with friends and family (and interested strangers) instantly.

The term *blog*, or *Web log*, can refer to almost any personal Web site on the Internet. The travel blogs that can be found on sites like TravelBlog. org, BootsnAll.com and TravelPod.com, however, stand out. Travel blogs often feature beautiful photography and are now beginning to offer video and audio clips. Of course, if one posts anything on the Internet any Web surfer can stumble upon it. Many sites offer password protection to keep interlopers out, but for some bloggers random comments and e-mail from strangers can be a pleasant surprise.

• **TravelPod.com,** one of the original travel blog sites, is easy to navigate. It is simple to join and post photos. No charge; payment of a fee removes all advertising banners from a user's page, and allows users to password-protect their pages. Each page features a map with your destinations and routes highlighted. Users can click on the locations to see entries posted from there. It allows users to embed videos and podcasts.

• **TravelBlog.org** is also quite easy to navigate, and it is easy to post photos and text. Not only is this a good site for people looking to create their own blogs, it is convenient for the user who wants to read about other travelers' experiences and look at photos from various locations. On its main page it offers a world map that allows users to read people's journals by clicking on a particular location. TravelBlog is free and is a good site for the first-time user.

• **Blogger.com,** which is owned by Google, is not designed specifically for travelers, but unlike many of the other offerings, Blogger allows users more freedom with how they post pictures and design their sites. There are a number of design templates to choose from, and getting a blog started is easy. Flickr.com, one of the largest photo Web sites, makes it easy for users to post photos to Blogger

TRAVEL

✔ **TIMELY TIPS**

Onward, Into the Blogosphere

Travel reporter Joe Sharkey's list of more, somewhat specialized blog sites for travelers

✔ www.womenstravelclub.com

✔ www.offbeattravel.com

✔ www.airlinemeals.net

✔ www.hobotraveler.com

✔ www.thetravelinsider.info/blogs/ti

✔ www.tripadvisor.com

✔ www.flyertalk.com

✔ www.joesentme.com

✔ www.aviationplanning.com.

✔ www.johnnyjet.com

✔ www.gadling.com

✔ www.onlinetravelreview.com.

Essential Reading

If you read nothing else in this chapter, read this

I never go anywhere—often not even from room to room in my home—without taking something along to read. It's a lifelong habit, but it became something of a fixation about 15 years ago when I was sent by *Granta* magazine to the town of Hammerfest. Stuck above the Arctic Circle in Norway, in the dead of winter, I ran out of things to read. Hammerfest is the loneliest town in Europe—1,200 miles north of Oslo—and it passes most of the winter in frigid darkness.

I was there to write about the aurora borealis. (I believe the commissioning editor's hope was that I would just go amusingly insane.) I expected to be there for a week. Instead I got more than two weeks of cloud cover with no aurora.

There is little to do in Hammerfest in winter but go for creeping walks in the pitch-blackness, watch the single channel of Norwegian television or read. I read.

By the end of the second week, I had read everything in my possession, including the labels inside my suitcase and every word of the three English-language magazines sold in the local newspaper shop. I reached the point where I was calling in twice a day to find out if the new issue of *Woman's Weekly* had arrived.

Since then I have never ventured abroad without packing more books than is strictly sensible and enough magazines that I can always have one rolled up in a back pocket. More often than not, it is a copy of the *Economist,* which I like very much except sometimes when it reviews my books.

I'm pleased to report that on my 16th day in Hammerfest, the clouds parted and I saw an aurora. It was wonderful—worth the trip. Just as good, the latest issue of the *Lady* arrived at the shop, so I had something to read—and reread and read again—on the 30-hour bus trip back to Oslo.

—Bill Bryson.
Bill Bryson is the author of *A Walk in the Woods, In a Sunburned Country* and *A Short History of Nearly Everything,* among other books.

or other sites by clicking an icon. Since Blogger is not focused on travel blogs, however, there are no forums or easy ways to see what travelers are blogging about or where they are blogging from. Both Blogger and Flickr are free.

• **BootsnAll,** is at tblogs.bootsnall.com, allows for photos and text, but does not offer as many features as some of the other providers. It is free, but your membership must be approved, and that can take 24 hours. There are numerous travel blogs on this site, and the wide array of travel features on the main site make this a good choice for someone looking for inspiration for a trip rather documenting one.

• **MyTripJournal.com** features a convenient itinerary function that is linked to a map that shows the route taken. Unlike the other sites, however, MyTripJournal is free only for a 45-day trial, after which the user must pay a yearly fee, which includes storage of up to 60 photos a month.

• **IgoUgo.com** is owned by Sabre, which also owns Travelocity. It has thousands of members who regularly post detailed journals (with photos) during their worldwide travels. Each member, whether registered under a real name or a nom de web, fills out a personal profile that can be accessed when reading a journal. Four editors regularly read IgoUgo reviews and journals, and work with writers to sharpen them. Each journal is then rated by the editor, and subsequently by readers, on writing quality, accuracy and usefulness. This is a great place to hone travel-writing skills

—Fred Bierman and Joe Sharkey

Hot Spots

Southeast Asia's New Meccas

Why is everyone going to Cambodia? And Laos? And Vietnam?

Suddenly, Cambodia is the world's newest tourist mecca. In 2004, international arrivals to the country topped one million for the first time, a figure reached in only nine months of 2005, according to the Ministry of Tourism. Why Cambodia? For a slew of reasons: gone are the Khmer Rouge, the Vietnamese occupation, the United Nations democracy-restoration period and the era of warring prime ministers. Angkor Wat has been swept clean of land mines, and its streets are generally safe to travel at night.

The country has also undergone another type of revolution, geared toward attracting a new generation of high-end travelers, who not only demand round-the-clock Khmer massages but are also willing to pay $400 a day to hire a luxury car, or more than $1,000 an hour for a helicopter tour.

Cambodia is not alone in its luxury revolution. Since the mid-1990's, the former French colonies of Southeast Asia have made enormous leaps in catering to tourists who prefer plunge pools to bucket showers. From the forests of Laos to the beaches of Vietnam, you can find well-conceived, well-outfitted, well-run hotels that will sleep you in style for hundreds of dollars a night.

Change has come at an amazing pace. Take Luang Prabang in Laos. Less than a decade ago, the few foreigners who climbed the 328 steps of Mount Phousi were usually backpackers who sought guidance from Lonely Planet's *Southeast Asia on a Shoestring*. These days, this tidy hill town feels like a Hollywood set, with painted lamps glowing in French restaurants and brick walkways brightened by a yellow glow emanating from knee-high terra-cotta pots, with a legion of high-end hotels and enough bistros and boutiques to keep a tourist's credit cards on the verge of meltdown. There are spa treatments to succumb to, and Veuve Clicquot to toast with. This town of just 60,000 people has become, almost overnight, a luxury getaway.

Meanwhile, in Vietnam, well-heeled travelers are making pilgrimages to the Evason Hideaway outside Nha Trang, a coastal town 280 miles northeast of Ho Chi Minh City. The Evason, part of Six Senses, a small Bangkok-based chain of resorts, is without question Vietnam's top resort. The villas are enormous, with private plunge pools and wine cellars and free Wi-Fi. Rock-star-style privacy is part of the package: this mountain-backed resort is accessible only by boat.

Vietnam has other outposts of escapism. Along its 2,140 miles of coastline, there's La Résidence in Hue,

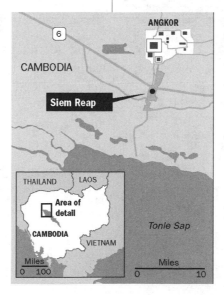

ANGKOR

6

CAMBODIA

Siem Reap

THAILAND   LAOS

Area of detail

CAMBODIA

VIETNAM

Tonle Sap

Miles
0   100

Miles
0   10

the Life Resort in Hoi An and the Furama in Da Nang. You can tour Ha Long Bay in the Emeraude, a replica of a 1920's steamer, or in the Hai Huong, a reproduction of a classic junk. The Victoria chain is setting up four-star hotels in unusual inland spots, such as Can Tho, Chau Doc and Sapa. And the Evason is already at work on a second resort, in the southern hill town of Da Lat.

In Cambodia, you find conceptually and architecturally ambitious hotels in almost every part of the country, from mountainous Ratanakiri, where Terres Rouges Lodge has "the best bar in the middle

INSIDE INFO

Angkor Wat: Temples & Terror

○ During the reign of terror in Cambodia that followed the end of the Vietnam War, the Khmer Rouge killed thousands—if not millions—of their countrymen. However, except for a few bullet holes, the brutal regime left largely intact the ruins of what was once the most magnificent city in Indochina, Angkor.

○ The earliest of the ruins, collectively known as Angkor, date from the ninth century when King Jayavarman II established a capital at Roluos, southeast of the modern town of Siem Reap. At its height, the Khmer empire extended from the coasts of Vietnam to the borders of Burma. Angkor Wat, the most famous of the ruins, as well as one of the better preserved, was built in the 12th century. The walls of Angkor Thom, one of the successive capitals in the area, enclose a space larger than that of any medieval European city.

○ Khmer cities were allegorical representations of the heavens, built around temples constructed atop natural or manmade hills. Most of the architecture combines Hindu and Buddhist symbolism. Angkor Wat boasts the longest bas-relief in existence, extending over 12,000 feet.

of nowhere," according to *Time Asia*, to the south's Kep, where La Villa de Monsieur Thomas, a 1908 oceanfront mansion is being transformed into a French restaurant ringed with bungalows. And then there is Angkor Wat. Foreign visitors are flooding in, and while there are no official figures as to how much each spends in Siem Reap, the nearby town that is the staging area for Angkor expeditions, the dizzying array of luxury hotels is evidence enough that this is no longer Pol Pot's Cambodia.

Still, once outside the compounds of luxury, there's no escaping reminders of the country's wretched history: crumbling roads, frequent floods, implacable heat and tour guides who coolly unload personal tales of the Khmer Rouge horror. Not even a fat wallet can hide the reality of travel in Southeast Asia. The draw for visitors, though, is not just plush beds; it's these countries' uniquely messy histories and the ways all are struggling to move forward.

GETTING AROUND

If the lure of limos, plunge pools and glamorized peasant food leads you to go to Siem Reap, here's what you'll need to know:

The telephone code for Cambodia is 855.

• **The tuk-tuk, or motorized rickshaw** is the most common means of transport, since Siem Reap has no formal taxi service. It offers little protection from rain, dust, noise and heat. Most rides around town cost less than $2 (generally, dollars are preferred to riels).

• **Renting a car is more relaxing.** Your hotel can arrange anything from a four-wheel drive to a vintage limo.

• **To see the temples by helicopter**, contact Angkor Scenic Flights, (12-814-500 or angkorscenicflights. com). It'll cost you.

WHERE TO STAY

More than 100 hotels now serve tourists of all budgets.

• **Raffles Grand Hotel d'Angkor** (63-963-888 or www.raffles.com). The past is on display here: a white-gravel driveway, iron-cage elevator, colonial-style bathroom fixtures and ceiling fans. The restaurant requires men to wear jackets at dinner. Still, it's far from stuffy, with visitors drinking gin and tonics in the Elephant Bar.

• **Hôtel de la Paix** (Sivatha Boulevard, 63-966-000 or www.hoteldelapaixangkor.com) is new, though its roots run back a half-century to an Art Deco hotel that stood on the same spot.

• **The Amansara**, on the road to Angkor (63-760-333 or www.amanresorts.com), is modern rather than classical, intimate rather than sprawling, casual rather than formal. The suites, starting at $650, are big enough to have their own courtyards. Twelve new suites have plunge pools ($850). Two meals a day are included, as well as a car and driver for visiting the temples.

—Matt Gross

Chowing Down in Shanghai

A Times *correspondent with epicurean tastes finds some cheap delights*

Made for trade, Shanghai came into being in the 1800's as a commercial link with the West. British, French, German and American traders settled there, followed by White Russian refugees. They built a metropolis with Asia's first telephones, running water and electric power, a city of drugs, warlords, brothels and legendary riches. And like expatriates everywhere, the settlers brought their culinary tastes with them.

TIMELY TIPS

For Marco Polo Wannabes

Looking for a silversmith in Bali? Dutch Colonial antiques in Sri Lanka? Orchids in Bangkok? *Luxe City Guides*, a series of directories to chic treats in Asia, are fast becoming indispensable for their up-to-date intelligence (each is updated every six months), issued in a cheeky voice. A sample entry on the Metropole in Hanoi: "This grand old Gertie has finally got off her colonial bum and begun an upgrade."

✔ **For more information,** go to www.luxecityguides.com.

To this day, the Shanghainese have an appetite for croissants and French pastry and for Russian borscht (*luo song tang*, or Russian soup, on menus) although many may not know their precise origins.

The old hedonistic culture was gradually submerged in Communist conformity, with gray tunics and shabby state shops supplanting the chic boutiques and throbbing dance halls that gave Shanghai its reputation as "the whore of the Orient." Food, and especially restaurant food, took a backseat to ideology. Today, Shanghai is again a galvanic city, with foreigners now pouring in to seek their fortunes, many of them trying to resurrect the city's glorious culinary tradition.

Renowned chefs and obscure entrepreneurs from Britain, Singapore, Australia, the United States and elsewhere have flocked to Shanghai on the heels of the bankers and brokers, eager to produce Italian, Japanese, Thai, German or Mexican food for you. Foods from afar compete with heaping helpings of first-rate Chinese dishes, from Guangzhou, Sichuan, Hunan and, of course, Shanghai. Local river prawns, slow-cooked pork

TRAVEL

rump, hairy crabs (in season) and above all xiao long bao, the soup dumplings beloved in the United States, are all on offer in classic form.

Shanghai's re-emergence as a prime tourist destination is due to many factors, including the city's refreshing green "lungs"—the many new parks and the thousands of plane trees in the former French Concession—its matchless new art museum, its Art Deco villas and office buildings, and the endless joie de vivre of its people. But for food lovers everywhere, the city's culinary renaissance is perhaps its biggest draw.

Here is a sampler of Shanghai's offerings. If you want to call ahead for reservations, the telephone country code for China is 86, and the city code for Shanghai is 21.

• **Bao Lu,** 2721 Fumin Lu; 6279-2827. As many as 300 people are sometimes jammed into this atmospheric spot early in the evening, but go later and the crush isn't as bad. Classic Shanghainese food, less than $15 a head with beer.

• **Chun,** 124 Jinxian Lu; 6256-0301. Have your hotel concierge reserve well ahead for this tiny

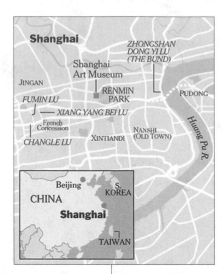

place, and take a Mandarin-speaking friend or guide. Cheap and authentic.

• **Xin Ji Shi,** North Block Xintiandi, Building 9, Number 2, Lane 181; 6336-4746. Try the noodles flavored with scallions.

• **Nan Xiang,** 85 Yuyuan Lu; 6355-4206. Soup-dumpling heaven in the oldest part of the city. All the xiao long bao you can eat for $20.

• **Din Tai Fung,** 12-20 Shuicheng Lu; 6208-4188. It's just a branch of a Taiwanese dumpling house, but who cares? The dumplings and other dishes are first rate.

• **Crystal Jade**, South Block Xintiandi, House 6-7, Lane 123; 6385-8752. Stylish digs and carefully prepared dim sum (including some Shanghai and Beijing items as well as Hong Kong classics) account for long lines.

• **M on the Bund,** 5 Zhongshan Dong Yi Lu; 6350-9988. Great views, excellent wines and competent (if inconsistent) Continental cooking. Eat on the terrace if it's warm.

• **Laris,** 3 Zhongshan Dong Yi Lu; 6321-9922. One of Shanghai's few raw bars, and some of the city's most imaginative house-made chocolates to end. This stuff does not come cheap.

• **Jean-Georges,** 3 Zhongshan Dong Yi Lu, 6321-7733. China's best Western-style restaurant. Polished service, gorgeous room.

• **Whampoa Club,** 3 Zhongshan Dong Yi Lu; 6321-3737. Jereme Leung takes Chinese food out of tourist class and puts it in first, where it belongs.

——R. W. Apple Jr.

Beyond the Taj Mahal

Suddenly, the rest of the subcontinent beckons

Not so long ago, India, a country of one billion people and more than 100 languages, seemed to have just three tourist destinations: Delhi, Mumbai and the Rajasthan-Taj Mahal circuit. Then, almost out of nowhere, Americans got adventurous and discovered Kerala, a lush southwestern state full of rivers, jungles and rich, spicy cuisine. Now, thanks to an aviation agreement between India and the United States, it should become easier to reach far-flung parts of the subcontinent, like the east coast cities of Pondicherry and Chennai.

Pondicherry was France's only possession in India, and it retains some of that Gallic flair (policemen in képis, colonial architecture) with the laid-back air of a university town, albeit one with gorgeous golden beaches. You can stay at the Hôtel de l'Orient, a converted 18th-century mansion (17, rue Romain Rolland, (91-413) 234-3067 or www.neemranahotels.com/pondi) for about 2,000 rupees, or about $46 a night.

Eighty miles up the coast, Chennai (formerly Madras, the first big British settlement in India), has millennium-old temples and a thriving technology industry, zoos and markets where whole streets are devoted to selling single products (from lentils to gray-market digital cameras), cricket grounds and one of the longest beaches in the world. You'll find three high-end properties there, the most opulent and modern of which is the Coromandel, (37 Mahatma Gandhi Road, (91-044) 5500-2827 or www.tajhotels.com). Rooms start at about $250 a night.

You won't necessarily find the newest boutique hotels at these places—yet. But they are major cities with their own distinctive scenes and cuisines, and they are far more exciting than the overly documented, postcard-perfect sights and monuments elsewhere in India.

—Matt Gross

 TIMELY TIPS

Moonlight on the Taj

After more than 20 years, visitors can once again see the Taj Mahal by moonlight, thanks to a 2005 ruling by India's Supreme Court. The white marble mausoleum, in the northern city of Agra, had been closed at night over fears of Sikh separatist attacks.

✔ You can see the Taj Mahal from 8:30 p.m. to 12:30 a.m. from a platform about 350 yards away, on five nights a month—when the moon is full, as well as the two nights before and after.

✔ Only 50 people at a time are allowed, for 30 minutes. You must buy tickets at least 24 hours in advance, at the entrance ticket office or from tour operators in India.

✔ Contact the Government of India Tourist Office, 212-586-4901 or www.incredibleindia.org.

—Marjorie Connelly

The Caribbean's Hidden Gems

Finding your perfect piece of paradise

Cheap airfares have turned Caribbean islands into America's tourist playground. Perennially popular islands, such as Puerto Rico, the American Virgin Islands and even once deserted St. Bart's, are packing in the crowds. Some travelers find all the activity appealing. But those who dream of basking on their own solitary beach can take comfort: there are many yet to be discovered islands in the more than 2,700 scattered within a 2,500-mile-long arc stretching from just south of Florida to the coast of Venezuela. If sun-drenched, bustle-free, natural

TRAVEL

ℹ **INSIDE INFO**

In the Islands

○ The Caribbean islands and the Bahamas together form the West Indies. The islands between the Atlantic and the Caribbean Sea are called the Antilles.

○ Cuba, Jamaica, Haiti and Puerto Rico comprise the Greater Antilles

○ The Lesser Antilles, islands are divided into the Leeward Islands (north of Dominica) and the Windward Islands (all those from Dominica to Trinidad and Tobago).

○ For more information go online to the Caribbean Tourism Organization: www.onecarribean.org.

paradises are your goal, here are some great choices: five tiny, some ultra-exclusive, some off-the-beaten-path Caribbean islands. Don't worry about being too far from civilization, though—the larger islands are just a short plane or boat ride away.

ANEGADA
15 sq. mi.; British Virgin Islands

Twenty miles north of Virgin Gorda's North Sound, Anegada is a flat mass of coral. The most isolated of the British Virgin Islands, it is mostly under the jurisdiction of the B.V.I. National Parks Trust, which oversees sanctuaries for flamingos, herons, ospreys and other birds, as well as a population of 2,000 wild goats, donkeys and cattle. Good bonefishing; great beaches for snorkeling and diving.

INSIDE SCOOP: This is no luxury resort island, although Princess Di and Ted Kennedy both once found their way here. It is peaceful, natural and laid-back. Boating near the surrounding coral reefs can be dangerous; beware of the sunken wrecks.

WHERE TO STAY: The **Anegada Reef Hotel** is a no-luxury affair, with few amenities. 284-495-8002 or www.anegadareef.com

BEQUIA
7 sq. mi.; St. Vincent's and the Grenadines, Windward Isles

This old whaler's island is seemingly little changed by time. Boat building is a major activity. Be sure to visit Paget Farm, an old whaler's village. The yacht basin at Admiralty Bay hosts the annual Easter Regatta. Princess Margaret Beach is recommended for snorkeling. Devil's Table, a site with stupendous fish and coral is a good dive spot.

INSIDE SCOOP: Hope Beach on the Atlantic side is secluded, but the surf is rough. The Bullet at north point has rays, barracuda and nurse sharks.

WHERE TO STAY: Plantation House, with its peach-and-white facade, wraparound porch and lush gardens, overlooks Admiralty Bay. 809-458-3425 or www.hotel-plantation.net

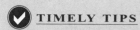

TIMELY TIPS

The Next St. Bart's

Beauty, beaches and bustle, too

Dreaming of crystalline Caribbean water and long, white, empty beaches that seem to exist only in beer ads? Toss in an array of fancy restaurants and a low tackiness quotient, and the answer to your dreams might be in the Turks and Caicos, a British colony of eight inhabited and 40 small and uninhabited keys at the southern tip of the Bahamas, 575 miles southeast of Miami.

On Providenciales, the biggest and most developed island, resorts line the eastern half of Grace Bay, a gentle 12-mile crescent on the island's northern shore. While those resorts might suggest overdevelopment, the island's sheer natural beauty and rugged terrain is actually complemented by the accessibility of fine dining, fresh seafood and excellent diving.

Beaches around the island vary: Grace Bay's sand is fine, white and rock free; more out of the way is Long Bay, on the eastern side of the island, with a rough, windswept beach with conch shells poking through the sand. On the more exclusive southern coast, beachcombers can choose among the warm knee-deep water of the seaward bays, balmy Chalk Sound National Park, an eerily blue lagoon, or Malcolm Beach, located on the far western coast, the least developed part of the island that is home to many natives. Not surprisingly, it is also home to several of its best spots for good, cheap food, including Bugaloo—which could be the best beachside conch shack ever.

—Jesse McKinley

TRAVEL

• **The Frangipani** sits on the waterfront in Port Elizabeth, the island's only town. 784-458-3255 or www.frangipanibequia.com

LES SAINTES, Terre-de-Haut

3 sq. mi.; an archipelago of eight islands; French West Indies (Leewards), Lesser Antilles

Only two of Les Saintes's eight islands are inhabited, Terre-de-Haut and the less developed Terre-de-Bas. Settled by Norman and Breton sailors in the mid-17th century and abounding in Breton architecture, Terre-de-Haut "looks a lot like St. Bart's did before it got glitzed up," says Jonathan Runge, author of the guidebook *Rum & Reggae's French Caribbean*. Like St. Bart's, Terre-de-Haut is relatively hilly, has great beaches, a fort, a town square with bars, good restaurants (though not as many as on St. Bart's) and a small fishing port.

INSIDE SCOOP: Don't miss the tiny fishing village of Bourg, Fort Napoleon, finished in 1867, and the stunning view from Le Chameau, the island's highest point. There are few cars on the island; many tourists rent mopeds or walk. A perfect place for deep-sea diving and snorkeling.

WHERE TO STAY: **Hôtel Bois Joli,** which sits on a long stretch of beach, has 31 rooms and bungalows and a large pool. It is about two miles from Bourg on the west end of Terre-de-Haut, on the shore of the Pain de Sucre bay. (590-590) 99-52-53; fax, (590-590) 99-55-05; www.ifrance.com/boisjoli.

Auberge Les Petits Saints aux Anacardiers has 11 rooms, a restaurant and a pool. This elegant hotel is filled with antiques, and boasts its own art gallery. It's a short walk from Bourg in the former mayoral residence. (590-590) 99-50-99, FAX (590-590) 99-54-51, www.petitssaints.com,

MAYREAU

1.5 sq.mi.; St Vincent and the Grenadines, Windward Isles

Situated halfway between St. Vincent and Grenada, this island is accessible only by boat. No cars

Treasures Beneath the Sea

Sometimes the best spots are underwater

Experienced divers exploring popular Caribbean spots such as Little Cayman's Bloody Bay Wall or the Wreck of the Rhone in the British Virgin Islands know well the telltale sign of underwater traffic jams: circles of dive boats moored at the busiest destinations. Avoiding underwater crowds may require an extra plane connection, but there is a reward: more tranquil wonders above and below water. Here are four lesser-known destinations that should guarantee more fish life than fellow divers:

SABA. Five-square mile Saba (pronounced SAH-buh) in the Netherlands Antilles, is a rain-forest-covered peak of an island, with nary a beach. Underwater, the slope continues, notably in the form of coral-and sponge-encrusted volcanic pinnacles 70 feet and more below the surface. Within the protected Saba Marine Park (www.sabapark. org), the gorgonian and orange elephant ear sponges are vividly healthy, and the marine life gets big: reef sharks, hawksbill turtles and massive tiger groupers.

TOBAGO. The chance to swim with manta rays lures divers to Tobago, Trinidad's smaller, less-developed neighbor. The Orinoco River's nutrient-rich runoff makes Tobago's reef and marine life prolific. The mantas prowl year round, and great hammerheads school in winter. Coral heads grow to super size, including a brain coral that is 16 feet across and growing. Sluicing the underwater scene are gonzo currents, which often run three or four knots, making this a destination for experienced divers.

DOMINICA. Don't go for powdery beaches or fancy resorts: There aren't any. Divers make the trip to aim their lenses at rare small stuff, like sea horses and frog fish. It's also one of the Caribbean's best spots to see dolphins and whales, especially from December through March. Day-Glo reefs bristle with netted barrel sponges and green finger sponges. There's underwater volcanic drama as well, with steep 600-foot walls, gaping craters, tunnel-like swim-throughs and geothermal vents that force up warm freshwater bubbles at the Champagne dive site.

GLOVERS REEF ATOLL, BELIZE. It's tough to go far wrong diving the atolls beyond the world's second-largest barrier reef, off the coast of Belize. Eons of coral growth along giant geological fault lines have produced sheer, 2,000-foot drop-offs. Belize's two major atolls, Turneffe Islands and Lighthouse Reef, have renowned dive sites, among them the 412-foot-deep Blue Hole. But farther south, Glovers is out of reach for day-trippers and, therefore, often all yours to explore. You can stay on 13-acre Long Caye.

—Susan Enfield Esrey

---

or phones—and only one road—create an 18th-century atmosphere. Saline Bay on the leeward coast is lined with sea grapes. Beaches are laden with shells, driftwood and rock crystals. Station Hill, the island's highest point, is where most people live.

INSIDE SCOOP: Salt Whistle Bay has one of the world's most magnificent beaches, featuring powdery white sand shaded by palms and flowering bushes.

WHERE TO STAY: Salt Whistle Bay Club is composed of stone cottages separated from the water by a palm grove. Amenities include diving and boat excursions, water sports and hiking. 784-458-8444 or www.saltwhistlebay.com

Dennis' Hideaway is less expensive, yet offers good food, wonderful views and simple but clean rooms. 01-784-458-8594 or www.dennis-hideaway.com

MUSTIQUE

12 sq. mi.; privately owned; Windward Isles

This island, 18 miles south of St. Vincent, is a retreat for the rich and famous. Its 52 houses are privately owned; some are available for rent. (Mick Jagger rents out his villa.) The island's big attractions are its natural beauty: wooded hills, grassy valleys, and white-sand beaches surrounded by coral reefs. Horseback riding is big.

INSIDE SCOOP: Basil's Bar is *the* watering hole.

WHERE TO STAY: Cotton House, an 18th-century stone-and-coral plantation house with an antique décor is expensive. 800-223-1108 or www.cottonhouseresort.com

Firefly Guest House, the island's only guest house, is intimate, beautiful and also very pricey. 809-456-3414 or www.mustiquefirefly.com

You Can't Get There From Here

Cuba—so near and yet so far

With its magnificent, unspoiled beauty and beautiful beaches, Cuba seduces in many ways. To American tourists, it represents the taste of a forbidden fruit— a land that has been off limits since 1961. But one day soon, and even sooner if you have a reason, you'll be able to go to Cuba.

With a few exceptions, the United States government does not allow Americans to travel to Cuba, just 90 miles from Key West. Among those permitted to travel under a General License (no application necessary) are accredited journalists, research professionals and government officials.

Everyone else must get a permit known as a Specific License, issued by the Foreign Assets Control office in the Department of the Treasury. That includes people traveling for educational or religious activities, or to visit immediate relatives. Though some Americans travel to Cuba from a third country like Mexico or Canada, they risk substantial fines. For more information and travel arrangements, contact Marazul Charters, 4100 Park Avenue, Weehawken, N.J. 07086. 201-319-1054 or www.marazul.com

All licensed travelers must also get a visa from the Cuban government. Visas can be obtained through the Cuban Interests Section, 2630 16th Street N.W., Washington, D.C. 20009: 202 797 8518. The visa fee is $50; consular services, $20.

TRAVEL

✔ TIMELY TIPS

The Pearl of the Atlantic Regains Its Luster

For decades, Punta del Este, a resort town in the southeast corner of Uruguay, was the Hamptons of Latin America, a watering hole for 1960's film icons like Gina Lollabrigida and Yul Brynner. But the "Pearl of the Atlantic" fell out of favor in the 90's with the development of one too many high-rises and the economic breakdown of nearby Argentina. In recent years, however, Americans have rediscovered Punta, a town with miles of beaches and a bohemian mix of people, from New York socialites to musicians to Brazilian models.

✔ About 25 miles north of Punta is **José Ignacio,** the secret epicenter of its bohemian jet set.

✔ For dinner, try **La Huella,** (598-486) 2279 or www.paradorlahuella.com, a rustic beachside spot in José Ignacio that serves grilled fish and sushi.

✔ But the ultimate insider spot is **Marismo**, a restaurant in José Ignacio that supposedly only people with good directions know how to find. O.K., here's the phone number: (598-486) 2273.
—Gisela Williams

Foreign currency must be changed to Cuban convertible pesos; for the best exchange rate, take euros or Canadian dollars.

The best hotel in Havana is Hotel Nacional, Calle O at 21, Vedado, (53-7) 873-3564 or www.hotelnacionaldecuba.com. In the 30's, Hemingway stayed at the Hotel Ambos Mundos, Calle Obispo 153, Old Havana, (53-7) 860-9529, which has undergone a restoration.

There's really only one main attraction in the capital: Old Havana, with museums, cathedrals, plazas, hotels, restaurants and bars. But other areas of Havana—mainly Vedado, Miramar and Siboney—are worth a car tour to get a better view of how the elite live. Outside Havana, the scenic Pinar del Río Province (southwest of Havana) is a three-hour drive on bus tours that leave daily from major Havana hotels. Havanatur, a government tourism agency with offices in major hotels, can arrange your tours: (53-82) 75-0100.

—Luisita Lopez Torregrosa

Beyond Hawaii's Big Island

Three that are just as beautiful but less traveled

Of the eight Hawaiian islands, it's possible to visit only six: Kahoolawe is uninhabited and Niihau is privately owned. The popular islands, Oahu, Maui and Hawaii (known as the Big Island) are still a visitor's paradise but one that must be shared with hordes of other tourists, increasingly marred by gridlock and relentless resort development. Fortunately, there are three other Hawaiian options—paradises that are less-trod and perhaps more inviting. Here's a guide:

KAUAI *533 sq. mi.*

Of all the islands, Kauai has the most beautiful natural scenery, thanks partly to its abundant rainfall. The top of Mt. Waialeale (5,238 ft.) is the rainiest place on earth, and the island's interior is virtually impenetrable

The ancient Hawaiians had two ways to get around the tortuously steep mountains that rise along the Na Pali Coast of Kauai. They either canoed, or they walked, gradually carving out an astonishing 11-mile-long ribbon of red dirt called the Kalalau Trail. Today, as the centerpiece of Na Pali Coast State Park, the rocky trail still snakes its way through some of the most spectacular coastal scenery on earth before ending at the broad strand of Kalalau Beach.

There are two ways to hike the Kalalau Trail: get a hike-camp permit from Hawaii State Parks and continue west past Hanakapi'ai, completing the 11 grueling and occasionally dangerous miles to Kalalau Beach; or complete the nonpermit portion in a day. The Sierra Club rates the full Kalalau Trail a 9 for difficulty on a scale of 10. The guidebook *Kauai Revealed* by Andrew Doughty is a must for any serious visitor

For water sports, head for Nukolii Beach Park or Mahaulepu Beach, with its reef-protected shoreline, pocket beaches and 100-foot sand dunes. Pakala Beach is perfect for all water sports, except swimming. Horseback riding is big, especially in Waimea Canyon. Two great golf courses are the Princeville Makai and the Kiele. The village of Hanalei, the setting for the movie *South Pacific*, is worth a visit.

WHERE TO STAY: **Princeville Resort** is the retreat-of-choice of the wealthy.
800-325-3535 or www.princeville.com

• **Waimea Plantation,** set in a coconut grove, offers cottage-style living.
800-992-4632 or waimea-plantation.com

• **The Rosewood B&B** offers rooms and apartments in private homes and cottage rentals.
808-822-5216 or www.rosewoodkauai.com

• **Keapana Center** is a hilltop B&B with nearby hiking and beach opportunities. 800-822-7968.

—Chris Dixon

MOLOKAI *263 sq. mi.*

Molokai is an island of splendid isolation, offering a nearly complete retreat from tourism and crowds. Its interior is largely privately owned, and has vast stretches of dense wilderness. Kamakou (4,970 ft.), the tallest mountain, is surrounded by jungles and pools.

Hiking trails and rutted dirt roads lead through forests, around volcanic mountains and along a coastline with cliffs soaring thousands of feet out of the ocean. The western end of the island is dry, and the south is flat, with offshore coral reefs. Many beaches are for viewing, not for swimming.

There are no traffic lights on Molokai, no buildings higher than two stories, one elevator, no Starbucks, just a couple of hotels and three gas stations. Nor is there is jet service to the island. The only way to get there is by prop plane or ferry.

The island's most famous institution is a leper colony created in 1865 and still active today. About 30 people, who call themselves residents rather than lepers, live there. To go—and it's definitely a journey worth taking—you must make a reservation. Only a limited number of visitors are allowed to enter each day. Contact the Molokai Mule Ride (808-567-6088 or www.muleride.com) or Damien Tours (808-567-6171 or damientours@aol.com).

Getting to the colony is an adventure in itself. You can take a short flight from the other side of Molokai to a landing strip just outside the colony. Or, ride in a procession of mules that winds its way down the cliff to the shore. Another option is to hike the trail. It is a mule trail that involves navigating a steep decline through 26 switchbacks, slippery with dirt and mule dung. Along the way, you encounter breaks in the foliage that permit views of some of the most inaccessible coastline in the world.

WHERE TO STAY: **The Lodge and Beach Village** at Molokai Ranch in Maunaloa (888-627-8082 or www.molokairanch.com), on the west end of the island, has 40 canvas bungalows (tents) on Kaupoa Beach. The ranch's more traditional Hawaiian Lodge has 22 ocean-view rooms.

• **Hotel Molokai,** on Kamehameha V Highway (Mile Marker 2) (808-553-5347 or www.hotel-molokai.com), is funky if serviceable, though it has seen better days. Ask for a room by the ocean; it's worth the extra cost.

—Adam Nagourney

LANAI *140 sq. mi.*

Don't come to Lanai expecting tiki bars and flashy luaus that go late into the night. This 140-square-mile island welcomes visitors in a laid-back style all its own. Axis deer roam free in the hills, and on a day hike, you're more likely to run into chattering wild turkeys and quail than people. As you cruise around Lanai's southeastern edge on the 45-minute ferry ride from Maui, a series of strikingly high volcanic cliffs rise before you.

One of Lanai's top off-road attractions is the eight-mile Munro Trail, named for George Munro, the New Zealand naturalist who imported the Cook Island pines, planted them to attract rain and hold

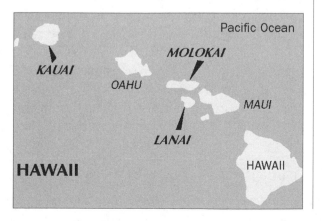

Pacific Ocean

KAUAI

OAHU

MOLOKAI

MAUI

LANAI

HAWAII

HAWAII

TRAVEL

✓ **TIMELY TIPS**

For Singles Only

✔ **Connecting: Solo Travel Network**
It provides practical information for people traveling by themselves, as part of a tour group or independently, and supplies members with lists of singles-friendly cruise and tour companies to help avoid single supplements. Membership costs $30 for one year, $48 for two years. The site includes a calendar of singles-only tours and cruises and a bimonthly newsletter. 800-557-1757 or www.cstn.org

✔ **Meet Market Adventures**
Specializes in weekend getaways, cruises, international tours and local day trips for single men and women, most of whom are in their 30's and 40's. Clients are matched with a roommate to avoid paying the single supplement. 800-239-0542 or www.meetmarketadventures.com

✔ **Singles Travel International**
Organizes activities from weekend getaways to full-length tours to appeal to a wide age range, but it typically provides for clients over 40 and unmarried. The company guarantees a roommate if requested 60 days before departure. 877-765-6874 or www.singlestravelintl.com

the soil, and made them Lanai's signature plant. You can hike or four-wheel-drive the trail as it climbs through heavily forested slopes and gullies to the 3,370-foot Lanai Hale, the island's single volcano and its highest point.

Northwest of Lanai City is the Garden of the Gods, a bizarre area where rocks and boulders are thrown across a Mars-red landscape. Next to it lies the Kanepuu Preserve, a rare dryland forest that has almost 50 native species, including the endangered Hawaiian gardenia and the sandalwood tree.

The island's most accessible and best swimming and snorkeling spot is Hulopoe Beach. The bay is a protected marine preserve, frequented by spinner dolphins and humpback whales. At low tide, shallow lava tide pools along the bay's south shore fill with marine life. Snorkelers in the bay can see vividly blue-green parrotfish, yellow tangs and green sea turtles. A remote beach great for walking is Lopa, near Keomuku Village.

WHERE TO STAY: The Four Seasons Resort Lanai at Manele Bay, 1 Manele Bay Road (808-565-2000) and the Lodge at Koele, 1 Keomoku Highway (808-565-4000) offer high-end accommodations as well as visually stunning, high-level golf courses.

• **The Hotel Lanai,** 828 Lanai Avenue (800-795-7211) at a fraction of the price, remains the island's first and only regular hotel. The main house has a large, airy veranda and a popular Cajun-accented restaurant.

—Bonnie Tsui

So Many Islands, So Little Time
And all of these are just a ferry ride from Athens

The lures of the Greek Islands are many: comparatively inexpensive fares and hotel rates, even during the peak summer months—not to mention near perfect weather and the warm waters of the Aegean Sea. But travelers are confronted with so many options: 220 islands in the Cyclades, a group of islands off the coast of Athens and 163 islands in the Dodecanese (although only 26 of them are currently inhabited) off the southwest coast of Turkey. Don't know where to start? Here are five places the Greeks like:

SERIFOS
Cyclades. Population: 1,200. Area: 70 km

In a testament to the ancient Greeks' sense of irony, the hideous monster Medusa allegedly lived on this stunning island. The approach to Serifos' wide harbor is one of the most beautiful (though least acknowledged) vistas in the archipelago. High above the port, Serifos' main town, Chora, rests on its mountaintop like a crown of white blossoms. The town is a beguiling network of whitewashed houses, bright shutters, clotheslines and steep stone pathways. In summer, Serifos attracts trendy Athenian artists and professionals.

WHAT TO SEE: Rugged rock formations that may or may not be the petrified victims of the Gorgon Medusa. Visit Psili Ammo, the wide beach named for its especially fine sands, or Vaya, a dramatic pebble cove with caves and deep, cool sea. Climb to the top of Chora and visit the 15th-century Venetian castro. Have a drink at Yacht Club in Livadi, the definitive "Serifioti" establishment.

WHERE TO STAY: As the island is largely undeveloped, the most comfortable way to experience Scrifos is from a private boat or rented house. Otherwise, the Asteri Hotel (www.asteri.gr) in Livadi offers clean, air-conditioned rooms.

GETTING THERE: Regular ferries from Piraeus (the port in Athens) and other western Cyclades; 4¹/₂ hours from Athens.

HYDRA

Saronic Gulf. Population: 2,800. Area: 52 km

Hydra's beauty served as a backdrop for the 1957 film *Boy on a Dolphin*, featuring Sophia Loren. The sophisticated jewel of the Saronic Gulf islands, Hydra has a high concentration of elegant neoclassical mansions and artsy cognoscenti (Greek and foreign) who inhabit them. Cars, mopeds, even bicycles are forbidden on the island's cobbled streets.

WHAT TO SEE: Hike 1¹/₂ hours up to the pretty mon-astery of the prophet Ilia. Be prepared to spend some time in a water taxi headed to more remote beaches if you want to enjoy Hydra's beauty in peace; more readily accessible shores are crowded and unspectacular.

WHERE TO STAY: Hotel Bratsera (+ 22980-53-971) is a converted sponge factory with pleasing nautical décor, trellised courtyards and the only swimming pool on the island.

• **Hotel Miranda** (+ 22980-52-230), somewhat cheaper, has nice bay views.

GETTING THERE: Twelve ferries leave from Piraeus daily; 1¹/₂ hours.

FOLEGANDROS

Cyclades. Population: 600. Area: 32 km

People have been hiding in Folegandros for centuries, formerly from pillaging pirates, now from tourists who have trampled many of the larger Cycladic islands. The only tumultuous thing on Folegandros is the wind, which sweeps across the stone terraces that border its steep hills and into the walls of Chora, the elevated, breathtaking town that gazes upon a cobalt horizon. High, cragged cliffs and an inaccessible port make it one of the most innocent destinations in Greece. The few initiated are Greeks and Italians.

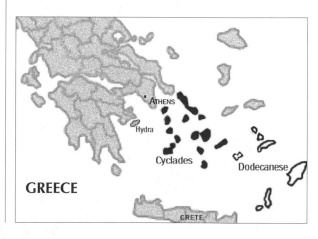

GREECE

ATHENS
Hydra
Cyclades
Dodecanese
CRETE

WHAT TO SEE: In addition to outstanding beaches (Aghios Giorgios and Livadaki), Folegandros's main town, Chora, is a gem, retaining vestiges of a dramatic past, during which nearly 200 families lived in a single cliff-top enclosure called Kastro, built during the Venetian rule after the 13th-century Crusades. The church of Panagia above it on Paleokastro hill is an excellent place to watch the sunset. Get a local fisherman to take you to Chryssospilia, a stalactite cave with traces of ancient occupation.

WHERE TO STAY: Anemomilos Apartments (+30-22860-41309; fax: +30-22860-41407 in season; or during winter: +30-210-6827777; fax: +30-210-6823962)

• **Hotel Castro** (+30-22860-41230; fax: +30-22860-41230 in season; e-mail: ddcastro@otenet.gr)

GETTING THERE: A ferry from Piraeus departs three times a week; 10-hour trip. Also accessible by hydrofoil from other islands.

NAXOS

Cyclades. Population: 17,000. Area: 428 km

Rich in mythological lore, Naxos is the island on which Theseus abandoned his wife, Ariadne. She later took her life on the island's rocky shore. The largest of the Cycladic islands still retains its ancient grace, especially in its quiet mountainous interior.

 INSIDE INFO

Tours for Every Persuasion

○ According to the International Gay and Lesbian Travel Association, a trade group based in Fort Lauderdale, Fla., gay and lesbian travel amounts to a $56-billion-a-year market.

○ Not surprisingly, an increasing number of travel agencies and tour operators are offering specialized trips that cater to single-sex couples and others.

Agriculturally rich, Naxos remains relatively independent of the tourist industry, a stark contrast to the more popular Mykonos and Santorini.

WHAT TO SEE: Apeiranthos, a whitewashed village in central Naxos feels like Greece a century ago. Lord Byron once said he wished to die here. A winding drive has airplane-like views of the Aegean.

WHERE TO STAY: Chateau Zevgoli (028-502-6123; Chateau-Zevgoli@forthnet.gr)

GETTING THERE: Highspeed hydrofoil from Athens (3$^{1}/_{2}$ hours); ferries from other western Cyclades.

PATMOS

Dodecanese. Population: 2,500. Area: 34.6 km

It is said that St. John wrote the Bible's Book of Revelations on leaving this island after a seven-year stint. Patmos is considered the most beautiful island in the Dodecanese archipelago, and possibly all of Greece. Called the "Jerusalem of the Aegean," it remains an important site for Christian pilgrimages. More recently, Patmos attracts well-heeled Greek and French vacationers who enjoy the island's stark, volcanic beauty.

WHAT TO SEE: The monastery of St. John, built in 1088. The impressive fortification, with its frescoes and libraries of rare codices, is open to the (respectfully clothed) public. From the mountain town of Chora, walk the short distance to the Monastery of the Apocalypse, near the grotto where St. John purportedly saw his revelation. Some popular beaches: Psili Ammos for seclusion and sand; Agriolivadi for a rocky cove; and Grikou for a more happening beach scene.

Where to Stay: Galini Hotel (www.galinipatmos.gr); Porto Scoutari (www.portoscoutari.com)

GETTING THERE: Daily ferries from Athens (10 to 12 hrs.) or Rhodes (5 hrs.). Schedules change seasonally.

—Alexa and James Hirschfeld

Beyond Disney World

*Try these real-life theme parks: London, Paris
Washington, D.C., and San Francisco*

The humorist Robert Benchley once famously quipped that the two worst ways to travel were "third-class in Bulgaria" and "with children." But that was a long time ago. These days travel conditions in Bulgaria are better and, while children may or may not be better behaved, family travel has become a mini-industry. Some suggestions for some popular destinations:

LONDON: *Buskers, bunkers, free
museums and a cool maze*

If you can close your eyes to the considerable expense—a decent restaurant meal for a family of four can easily exceed $200—London is the perfect place to take children, combining the unknown and the familiar, the thrills of travel with the comforts of home.

Even the native language is exotically skewed enough to provoke endless familial discussions. While there is weird food—spotted dick, fish and chips—there are also options to satisfy the most ethnocentric American palate. The most cost-efficient way to get around is by subway, a.k.a. the tube. One-day family tickets allow unlimited rides on tubes and buses throughout much of London and are a bargain; www.tfl.gov.uk.

Culture and a bit of history. Maybe you are jaded because, frankly, you know too much about Prince Charles's love life, but children tend to be unreconstructed monarchists. Hampton Court Palace, once the home of Henry VIII, is about 30 minutes by train from Waterloo station. The palace is full of unexpectedly jolly touches—cooks in period costumes, for instance—but the best part is the renovated outdoor maze, half a mile of paths enclosed by seven-foot-tall yew hedges. Information: (44-870) 752-7777 or www.hrp.org.uk.

Historically minded children will love the Cabinet War Rooms, on King Charles Street, a thrillingly claustrophobic labyrinth of tiny offices, bedrooms, telephone rooms, broadcasting studios and kitchens constructed under Whitehall during World War II. Information: (44-20) 7930-6961 or cwr.iwm.org.uk. For an excursion that combines history, architecture, exercise, art and food, start at St. Paul's Cathedral near the City (children love the circular Whispering Gallery, where a quirk in the construction allows murmured remarks at one end to be heard on the opposite side). Then walk across the no longer wobbly Millennium Bridge to the spectacular Tate Modern, with its cathedral-like Turbine Hall. The museum, like most in London, is free. Information: (44-20) 7887-8000 or www.tate.org.uk/modern.

Downtime. Kew Gardens, just southwest of London but easily reachable by subway or train, comprises 300 acres of picnicable land, and houses the world's largest plant collection. Information: (44-20) 8332-5655 or www.rbgkew.org.uk.

The British Library, at 96 Euston Road, has a collection with enough to appeal to both kids and their parents. Here you can look at the original manuscript of Lewis Carroll's *Alice's Adventures Under Ground*, the precursor to *Alice in Wonderland*, electronically turn the pages of a notebook by Leonardo and listen to stirring recordings of Florence Nightingale addressing the old soldiers of Balaclava during the Crimean War. Information: (44-20) 7412-7332 or www.bl.uk.

Outdoors. Covent Garden market is a perfect place to take energetic children. Here there are stores, snack bars, restaurants and buskers, who provide vaudeville-like combinations of magic and music. Information: www.coventgarden.uk.com.
—Sarah Lyall

TRAVEL

Finding the Perfect Meal in London...

These restaurants serve English food the old-fashioned way

Butlers Wharf Chop House, 36e Shad Thames, 011-44-20-7403-3403.

Goring Hotel, 15 Beeston Place, 011-44-20-7396-9000.

The Ivy 1 West Street, Covent Garden, 011-44-20-7836-4751.

Kensington Place, 201-209 Kensington Church Street, Notting Hill Gate, 011-44-20-7727-3184.

J. Sheekey, 28-32 St. Martins Court, Covent Garden, 011-44-20-7240-2565.

St. John, 26 St. John Street, 011-44-20-7251-0848.

Sweetings, 39 Queen Victoria Street, 011-44-20-7248-3062.

Wiltons, 55 Jermyn Street, 011-44-20-7629-9955.

—R. W. Apple Jr.

...And in Paris

At some, you get three-star chefs at one-star prices.

Benoît, 20, rue Saint-Martin, (33-1) 42.72.25.76. Run by Alain Ducassse, the superchef who has nine Michelin stars (three each in Paris, Monte Carlo and New York).

Gaya, 44, rue du Bac, (33-1) 45.44.73.73. Owned and at least partly run by Pierre Gagnaire, the former enfant terrible whose three-star restaurant of the same name is in the Hotel Balzac.

Le Comptoir, Hôtel Relais St.-Germain, 9, carrefour de l'Odéon, (33-1) 44.27.07.97. Prix fixe. One of the toughest reservations in town. Unless you get lucky or are willing to sit outside in chilly weather, you may have to wait three months for a table.

Mon Vieil Ami, 69, rue St.-Louis-en-l'Île, (33-1) 40.46.01.35. A lovely and unusual bistro run by Antoine Westermann.

—Mark Bittman

PARIS: *The City of Light for the Babar bunch*

Though known as a city for lovers, Paris is also an idyllic destination for those traveling with the fruits of their love. Art and culture come to life for children in Paris, and not just because it is the storybook setting for such favorite characters as Madeline and Babar. Artists paint on the banks of the Seine, and jugglers perform to great crowds in Montmartre. Children are welcome everywhere in Paris—be it a fashionable restaurant on the Champs Elysées or a hushed chapel in Sacré-Coeur.

Culture. With so many museums in Paris, a one-, three- or five-day museum pass is the ideal option for families. It allows parents to skip the ticket line (children under 18 are free at most museums) and saves money at the nearly 70 participating museums and monuments. Museum Day Passes, available at www.parismuseumpass.fr, are for one, three or five days respectively; they must be used on consecutive days.

Young imaginations love the Musée d'Orsay, 62, rue de Lille, (33-1) 40.49.48.14 or www.musee-orsay.fr, a former railway station completed in 1900 for the World's Fair, which presents works of art (photography, design, sculpture and painting) from 1848 to 1914. The original archway of the Gare d'Orsay can still be seen, as well as many paintings featuring trains, such as Monet's *La Gare Saint-Lazare.* Young dancers will gravitate to the Degas paintings and sculptures on the upper level.

While most of the intertwined nude statues inside the Rodin Museum, such as *The Kiss*, may result in giggling children, the outdoor sculpture garden with more than two dozen famous Rodin sculptures, including *The Thinker* and *The Gates of Hell,* is fairly G-rated and a sanctuary for the restless. A "garden only" ticket costs just one euro, which is why many Parisian families frequent this gated green art gallery, with two sandboxes hidden in the back behind the circular pool.

Even with a museum pass, entering the Louvre via the glass pyramid can take time because of the crowds. A less dramatic but faster way into the museum is via the Galerie du Carrousel, an indoor shopping mall and food court. Teenagers may beg to be left here (beware, there is a Virgin Megastore), but urge them to venture into the labyrinth of galleries that once housed four centuries of French kings and emperors. For an efficient and educational experience, buy an English-language copy of *Destination Louvre,* available in the children's museum shop.

For families who like to climb, Paris is more challenging than most mountain ranges. There are roughly 300 steps up to the Sacré-Coeur in Montmartre; 704 steps to level two of the Eiffel Tower; 284 steps to the top of the Arc de Triomphe; and 385 steps up to the famous gargoyles at Notre-Dame. Luckily, there is an elevator to all levels of the Eiffel Tower, and a funicular goes up to Montmartre, but the other two are stairs-only.

Downtime. On fair-weather weekends and Wednesday afternoons (when Parisian children have a half day of school), the city's normally serene, manicured parks become lively playgrounds. Most have pony rides, carousels, bumper cars and buvettes—fast-food kiosks that sell croque-monsieur sandwiches, hot dogs and cotton candy—and the Tuileries and Luxembourg Gardens often have toy schooners that children can sail across ponds with the push of a stick.

Both the Luxembourg Gardens and the Champ de Mars have big playgrounds and marionette theaters. Though the puppeteers perform entirely in French, children should have little problem following the plots. The highlight of the 40-minute show is the inevitable appearance of Guignol—the famous French puppet who always enlists the help of the audience as he tries to catch the villain. Marionettes du Champ de Mars, (33-1) 48.56.01.44, hold performances on Wednesday, Saturday and Sunday, at 3:15 and 4:15 p.m. (often daily during school vacations); Marionettes du Luxembourg, (33-1) 43.26.46.47, on Wednesday at 4 p.m., Saturday and Sunday at 11 a.m and 4 p.m..

Tucked away on the northwest side of the Tuileries garden, bordering the rue de Rivoli, are eight trampolines set safely into the ground with long benches on either side. Parents can take in the view of the obelisk towering over the Place de la Concorde while their children jump for joy.

To really see the City of Light, take a bateau-mouche tour on the Seine in the early evening. Children love going beneath the many bridges, their undersides illuminated by the boat's floodlights, and the architecture is even more dramatic at night from the water. Aim to depart at the top of the hour, when hundreds of thousands of small lights flicker on the nearby Eiffel Tower.

Shopping. Rue Vavin is a shopping mecca for stylish mothers. This narrow, quarter-mile-long street near the Luxembourg Gardens has more than a dozen children's clothing boutiques. Make sure to stop in for a gelato at the Paris front-runner in the Italian ice wars, Amorino, 4, rue Vavin (just look for the line). Shopping for food on Rue Cler, a cobbled street in the seventh arrondissement packed with all the necessary small shops for the perfect picnic, is truly a sensory experience. Children will be drawn to the colorful macaroons in the windows of Le Nôtre, as well as the sweet-smelling crêpe stand.

—Jennifer Conlin

Monaco: Not Just for Adults

Monaco will always be known for James Bond, high-stakes casinos, tax-sheltered celebrities and a sizzling night life, but the principality is also becoming more family-friendly. (Beyond the Grimaldi family, that is.)

The Monte Carlo Bay Hotel and Resort now features a 4,300-square-foot junior activity area designed for children ages 6 to 12 that offers supervised games and activities. There is also a 320-foot-long sand-bottomed swimming pool. Information and reservations at 800-595-0898 or www.montecarlobay.com.

The luxurious Hotel Metropole Monte-Carlo, (377) 93.15.15.15 or www.metropole.com, has also started offering a selection of kid-friendly outings. Parents can send up to two of their brood off with a nanny and a driver for a half-day trip to the zoo. Or a family of four can visit the Confiserie Florian candy factory for 500 euros.

For family dining, try Stars 'N' Bars, 6 quai Antoine 1er, (377) 97.97.95.95, a restaurant with a supervised children's playroom.

—Michelle Higgins

WASHINGTON, D.C. *First the museums, then the city*

Like many major tourist destinations, the nation's capital has two faces: there's Washington, place of public lives and public monuments, which is where most visitors venture, and there's D.C. (as residents refer to it), the private city where inhabitants live and work. The ideal Washington weekend borrows a bit from each world.

Culture. The Mall is packed with museums, and they're free, but Washingtonians know that the Mall can be an extremely tiring place and have devised ways to concentrate their visits so that everyone is enriched without being exhausted. The Air and Space Museum may be a perennial must-do for many kids, but the National Gallery (Constitution Avenue between Third and Ninth Streets N.W.; 202-737-4215) makes for an adult-pleasing alternative, and its children's programs are innovative and well thought out (go to www.nga.gov/kids to find out about drop-in workshops, story hours and films).

The Sculpture Garden, at the National Gallery's northern end, offers ice skating in winter and jazz concerts in summer, and the outsize Oldenburg eraser and Scott Burton chairs present great juvenile art history talking points. Try to visit around lunchtime, as the cafeteria's food is above what you'll find at most of the other Mall museums.

Another great lunchtime museum stop is the new National Museum of the American Indian (Fourth Street and Independence Avenue S.W., next to the Air and Space Museum; 202-633-1000), whose collection aims to present objects like cooking baskets and baby bonnets in context, rather than as isolated art objects. The restaurant serves Indian foods from all over the Americas.

A secret to making sense of the abundance of riches on the Mall is to edit well. At the National Museum of Natural History (10th Street and Constitution Avenue N.W.; 202-633-1000), head upstairs to the O. Orkin Insect Zoo to hold live insects in your hand or to see tarantulas being fed. At the National Museum of American History (14th Street and Constitution Avenue N.W.; 202-633-1000), a sure-fire winner is the downstairs transportation exhibition, where kids can see vintage subway and street cars.

For further forays into transportation, consider a visit to the Air and Space Museum's Steven F. Udvar-Hazy Center (14390 Air and Space Museum Parkway, Chantilly, Va.; 202-633-1000) near Dulles Airport. It's centered on a palatial airplane hangar and covers in three-dimensional form the history of aviation from the Wright Brothers era to the space shuttle *Enterprise*.

Outdoors. A bike ride along the placid C&O Canal's towpath will take you far from the bustle of official Washington. The National Park Service offers guided bike rides there, as well as hourlong mule-pulled boat rides; call 202- 653-5190.

For a truly surprising adventure, drive about 15 miles up the Potomac to Great Falls, which can be viewed from either the Virginia or the Maryland side of the river. On the Maryland side, a sturdy wooden walkway takes you out over the water to Olmsted Island, a naturalist's delight. Teenagers with bravado might want to attempt the aptly named Billy Goat Trail nearby.

—Anne Glusker

SAN FRANCISCO: *A mostly adult town with kid appeal*

San Francisco already invites sneaker-footed adult tourists to act childlike: ride a cable car! Gorge on Ghirardelli chocolate! Walk the "crookedest" street in the world! Actual children, however, are statistically in short supply (according to the 2000 census, San Francisco has the lowest percentage of kids among the nation's cities—just 14.5 percent).

The dot-com revolution may have left behind a legacy of kid-friendly technology, like the video arcade at Sony Metreon downtown, but it is the city's unique low-tech thrills—monstrous hills and historic streetcars (free for those under 5; 35 cents for older kids) and cable cars—that they'll chat about on the ride home.

Culture. A visit to the airy, modern Asian Art Museum, at 200 Larkin Street (415-581-3500 or www.asianart.org), doesn't mean tiptoeing past Ming vases. In the AsiaAlive room, visitors can start a self-guided tour or learn to write Persian. Sunday storytelling, video touch screens, multiarmed Hindu deities and Indonesian puppets can buy parents peace in the Contemplative Zen Alcove. Closed on Mondays.

The cellhouse audio tour at Alcatraz (www.nps. gov/alcatraz), featuring the gravelly voiced ex-cons' recollections about life on the Rock, are likely to encourage at least an afternoon's worth of good behavior. Cels of another kind—individual celluloid frames of cartoons—are on view at the Cartoon Art Museum, 655 Mission Street (415-227-8666 or www.cartoonart.org). The collection includes characters like Bugs Bunny and Mickey Mouse.

Kids hunt for Dory and Nemo in the two-story tropical reef tank at Steinhart Aquarium, 875 Howard Street (415-321-8000 or www. calacademy.org/aquarium). Downtown and small as a submarine, the aquarium has two daily penguin feedings. Along with minidonuts and waffle cones, Pier 39 (www.pier39.com), offers a natural attraction: resident sea lions on sun-bleached piers. Kids can learn more at the Gulf of the Farallones National Marine Sanctuary Visitor Center (415-561-6625 or www.gfnms.nos.noaa.gov), on the photogenic west end of Crissy Field.

Outside. Just walking the hills and taking in views will provide plenty of fresh air, but it's worth the 12-mile drive north over the Golden Gate Bridge to stroll beneath the giant redwoods in Muir Woods National Monument (www.nps.gov/muwo). Spur hikes branch off the flat paved loop trail. Rain means banana slugs! Open 8 a.m. to sunset.

Downtime. Vendors charm kids with granola and jam samples at the Ferry Building Farmers Market on Saturday from 8 a.m. to 2 p.m. at the foot of Market Street. Following the trail south along the water leads to the SBC Ballpark, home of the Giants, and a playground behind the left-field bleachers that includes a miniature replica of the stadium. This Coca-Cola Fan Lot is closed on game days.

—Debra Klein

TRAVEL

Natural Treasures

America's Crown Jewels

Folks flock to the 10 most popular national parks for a reason

Italy has Venice. China, the Great Wall. The United States' most remarkable asset is its breathtakingly beautiful national parks, which altogether account for the largest protected wildernesses in the world. Every year, the country's parks draw more visitors. While there are 58 national parks, the 10 most popular account for over half the visitors. It is not uncommon, for instance, to find yourself bumper-to-bumper, or without a parking spot in Yellowstone National Park in its most popular venues.

Unfortunately, the appeal of some parks is proving ruinous to their health. The environmental threat posed by increasing tourism has been met by more Park Service vigilance in protecting areas that do not have road access: backcountry camping is now increasingly regulated by a new permit system.

With a little foresight, you can steer clear of the crowds and parking problems. If you're planning to visit one of the 10 most popular parks during the summer, try to make reservations far in advance. While some campsites are on a first-come, first-served basis, a large number can be reserved through the National Park Service's Destinet system (800–365–2267 or www.reservations.nps.gov) from 10 a.m. to 10 p.m. Eastern Standard Time.

Following are the 10 most popular national parks, ranked by largest numbers of visitors, and a description of the most interesting tracks they have to offer—beaten or otherwise. The visitor totals are the Park Service's official numbers from 2005.

1. GREAT SMOKY MOUNTAINS NATIONAL PARK

Over 9.1 million visitors per year • Largest national park east of the Rockies

A world unto itself, Great Smoky Mountains National Park, located in western North Carolina and eastern Tennessee, has over 1,500 species of flowering plants, 10 percent of which are considered rare, 100 native species of trees and over 100 native species of shrubs—more than in all of Europe. In addition, there are 200 species of birds, about 50 native species of fish, 80 species of reptiles and amphibians, and 66 species of mammals, including wild hogs and black bears.

A hike or drive from mountain base to peak is equivalent to the entire length of the Appalachian Trail from Georgia to Maine in terms of the number of species of trees and plants—every 250 feet of elevation is roughly equivalent to 1,000 miles of distance on the trail. A quarter of the park is virgin forest, the largest one east of the Mississippi.

In addition to its natural attributes, Great Smoky Mountains has farms, churches, cabins and gristmills left by the mountain people who moved away when the park was created in 1934. The park has been designated a United Nations International Biosphere Reserve, as well as a World Historical Site.

Gatlinburg, Tenn. 37738
615-436-1200   www.nps.gov/grsm

Peak season tips: During the summer, in the lower elevations, expect haze, humidity and afternoon temperatures in the 90's—and terrible traffic jams. Cades Cove is generally less crowded.

INSIDE INFO

The Biggest Parks

○ The largest parks cover more ground than some of our smallest states:

Rank	National park or state	Acres
1.	Wrangell–St. Elias, Alaska	13,200,000
2.	Gates of the Arctic, Alaska	8,400,000
	MASSACHUSSETTS	6,755,200
3.	Denali, Alaska	6,028,203
4.	Katmai, Alaska	3,674,530
5.	Death Valley, Calif.	3,367,627
6.	Glacier Bay, Alaska	3,225,284
	CONNECTICUT	3,118,080
7.	Lake Clark, Alaska	2,619,722
8.	Yellowstone, Wyo.	2,219,789
9.	Kobuk Valley, Alaska	1,750,737
10.	Everglades, Fla.	1,399,078
11.	Grand Canyon, Ariz.	1,218,376
12.	Glacier, Mont.	1,400,000
13.	Olympic, Wash.	922,000
14.	Big Bend, Tex.	801,163
15.	Joshua Tree, Calif.	794,000
	RHODE ISLAND	675,200

Camping: Sites at most campgrounds are on a first-come, first-served basis. Camping in the back-country and the campgrounds at Cades Cove and Smokemont are open year-round. Look Rock and Elkmont are closed in the winter.

There is one camping facility, LeConte Lodge, located on the park's third-highest peak, Mt. LeConte (elevation 6,593 feet), a six-hour hike from the main road. Cabins do not have electricity or running water, but do include beds and hot meals. LeConte Lodge is opened from April to mid-November, and reservations must often be booked as far as a year in advance. For information and reservations, call 865–429–5704, fax 865-774-0045, or e-mail reservations@leconte-lodge.com.

Best one-day trip: Entering the park from Gatlinburg, continue on U.S. 441, and stop at the Newfoundland Gap, where there are spectacular views of the mountains. From there, turn onto Clingmans Dome Road (closed in the winter), which ends at a parking lot where there is a strenuous half-mile hike to a lookout tower atop 6,643-foot Clingmans Dome—the highest peak in the park. Back on U.S. 441, continue to the Smokemont Campground, where the easy, two-mile Chasten Creek Falls Trail meanders along a stream through a hardwood forest ending at one of the park's many waterfalls.

Best experience: The Great Smokies is one of the premier places in the East to enjoy magnificent fall foliage. The season lasts from September through October. Peak time: October 15 to October 31.

2. GRAND CANYON NATIONAL PARK

Over 4.4 million visitors per year • The 277-mile canyon is nearly a mile deep in places

A Grand Canyon sunset is glorious, but even during the day, the canyon walls' many layers of stone refract hues of red, yellow, and green light. On a good day, you can see 200 miles across vast mesas, forests and the Colorado River.

The park consists of three different areas: the North Rim, the South Rim and the Inner Canyon, which is accessible only by foot, boat or mule. The North Rim and the South Rim are only 9 miles apart as the eagle flies, but 214 miles by road, taking hikers an average of three days to travel one way.

The different rims are located in entirely different temperate climate zones. The North Rim, on average, is 1,000 feet higher and is heavily forested with blue spruce and alpine vegetation. It is open only from May to late October. The more popular South Rim is closer to population centers and has the juniper bushes and Gambel oak typical of the arid Southwest. The Inner Canyon is desertlike;

temperatures there often exceed 110 degrees in the summer.

Grand Canyon, Ariz. 86023
928-638-7888   www.nps.gov/grca

Peak season tips: The South Rim is crowded all year. To escape the masses, take one of the many trails off East Rim Drive to a private spot overlooking the canyon, or try the North Rim.

Camping: For lodging reservations in the North and South Rims, including Phantom Ranch, 303-297-2757.

Best one-day trip: The West Rim Drive offers wonderful views of the main canyon. In the summer, it is open only to buses, which can be taken from the visitor center. A paved trail runs along the South Rim. All hikes into the canyon are strenuous.

Best experience: A raft ride down the Colorado River is a great way to enjoy the splendor of the canyon. Motorboat trips take 7 to 10 days, raft trips take 10 to 12 days and trips on wooden dories usually last 18 days, though 3- to 8-day partial trips can be arranged. Call the park for a list of outfitters licensed by the National Park Service.

3. YOSEMITE NATIONAL PARK

Over 3.3 million visitors per year • *Home of the giant sequoia*

Yosemite's majestic granite peaks, groves of ancient giant sequoia trees and waterfalls (including Yosemite Falls, which at a height of 2,425 feet is the nation's highest) inspired some of the earliest attempts at conservation in the United States. In 1864, Congress enacted laws protecting the valley. Journalist Horace Greeley noted that he knew of "no single wonder of Nature on earth which can claim a superiority over the Yosemite." And naturalist John Muir, whose efforts led to the park's formation, said

of the valley, "No temple made with hands can compare with Yosemite."

The enormous park occupies an area comparable to Rhode Island, with elevations of up to 13,114 feet.

Yosemite National Park, Calif. 95389
209-372-0200   www.nps.gov/yose

Peak season tips: During the busy summer months, avoid the seven-mile Yosemite Valley, which attracts the hordes.

Camping: Of the 18 campgrounds in Yosemite, the 5 main ones in the valley offer "refugee-style camping"—over 800 campsites crammed into a half-mile of space. For more room and better views, try one of the eight Tioga Road campgrounds. There also are five tent camps on the High Sierra Loop Trail. Campers can obtain meals, showers and cots there. Reservations are advised.

Reservations are required year-round in Yosemite Valley's auto campground and for Hodgdon Meadow, Crane Flat and Tuolumne Meadows campgrounds. Other campgrounds are operated on a first-come, first-served basis. Reservations may be made up to, but no earlier than, eight weeks. Reservable campsites fill up quickly from mid-May to mid-September. Your best bet for snagging a spot is to start calling the Destinet reservation number (800 436-PARK) at 7 a.m. Pacific Standard Time months in advance of the date you want to camp.

Best one-day trip: Avoid the congested route to Yosemite Valley, grab a tour bus and get off at either shuttle stop 7, for an easy half-mile, 20-minute hike to Lower Yosemite Falls, or shuttle bus stop 8, for a strenuous one- to three-hour round-trip hike to Upper Yosemite Falls. Other sites include the Native American Yosemite Village and El Capitan, a 3,000-foot face that is popular with rock climbers.

4. OLYMPIC NATIONAL PARK

Over 3 million visitors per year • *The best example of virgin temperate rain forest in the country*

On a relatively isolated peninsula with no roads traversing it, Olympic is one of the most pristine of the nation's parks. It has been referred to as the "last frontier." It divides into three distinct environments: rugged coastline, virgin temperate rain forest and mountains, at the foot of which is the largest intact strand of coniferous forest in the lower 48 states. The park also has 60 named glaciers.

Port Angeles, Wash. 98362
360-452-4501   www.nps.gov.olym

Peak season tips: Though three-quarters of the precipitation falls from October 1 to March 31, Olympic still receives more rain than any other area in the United States. Always bring rain gear.

Camping: The main coastal campgrounds of Kalaloch and Mora provide privacy and a sense of wilderness. For an even greater sense of solitude, try one of the two smaller campgrounds, Ozette Lake or Ericson's Bay. (The latter is accessible only by canoe.) All of the wilderness campgrounds are available on a first-come, first-served basis.

The Hoh campground is the largest in the rain forest. The smaller campgrounds in that area of the park have more privacy and better wildlife-watching. On the mountain, the Deer Park campground (elevation 5,400 feet) makes an excellent base from which to explore.

Most of the 16 campgrounds in the park are available on a first-come, first-served basis, but in the summer reservations at Kalaloch can be made by calling the reservations number at 800-365-CAMP.

Best one-day trip: On a drive up Route 101, you can take in the park's harbor seals, gigantic driftwood and tide pools teeming with activity along the

 **TIMELY TIPS**

Sure Ways to Beat the Crowds

Travel in the off-season has its own rewards

Traffic on the main roads slows to a crawl, people are everywhere. Morning drive time in New York City? No, it's the summer rush to the nation's most popular national parks. Traffic has gotten so bad at some parks that tourists can spot wildlife simply by looking where other cars have pulled over to the side of the road to gawk.

✔ The surest way to beat the crowds is to visit in the off-season. From June through October, Great Smoky Mountains National Park typically gets well over a million visitors a month, but roughly half that number visit in the months between November and April, when temperatures in the lower elevations average about 50 degrees and occasionally reach into the 70's—perfect hiking weather, in other words.

There are other off-season rewards, too. At Rocky Mountain National Park, the bighorn sheep come down from higher elevations in May to feed on the mud deposits, and wildflowers there are spectacular in the spring. Yosemite National Park's waterfalls rush from the melting winter snows. In the fall, the foliage in many parks is absolutely superb. September is the sunniest month at Rocky Mountain National Park. Grand Teton National Park is open all winter, allowing access to excellent cross-country skiing.

Of course, seasonal difficulties abound. There are, for instance, sudden snowstorms at Yellowstone National Park as early as September. And spring weather at Zion National Park is unpredictable; flash floods are not uncommon.

✔ If such perils are too daunting for you, it is possible to avoid the masses in the summer simply by venturing into the backcountry. Most visitors don't wander very far from their cars.

TRAVEL

coast. On the right, you'll pass a sign for the world's largest cedar tree. Get off onto the spur road to the Hoh Rainforest visitor center. There is a 3/4-mile round-trip hike that winds through the dense rain forest at the end of the road. Back in your car, turn onto the road to the Mora campground, where there are several short scenic trails along the beach.

5. YELLOWSTONE NATIONAL PARK

Over 2.8 million visitors per year • The largest concentration of geysers and hot springs in the world

The center of what is now Yellowstone Park erupted 600,000 years ago. The explosion left behind a 28-by-47-mile crater that contained the world's greatest concentration of geothermal phenomena, including hot springs, fumaroles, steam vents, mud pots and over 300 geysers. Among the geysers is Steam Boat, which shoots columns of water a record 350 feet high.

Yellowstone is the second-largest park in the lower 48 states, encompassing an area larger than the states of Delaware and Rhode Island combined. It is also the oldest park in the country, established in 1872. It has the largest mountain lake (Yellowstone Lake, with 110 miles of shoreline); the biggest elk population in America (30,000 strong); and is the last place in the country where there is a free-ranging herd of bison (3,500 of the woolly beasts).

Yellowstone National Park, Wyo. 82190
307-344-2002   www.nps,gov/yell

Peak season tips: This is one of the coldest parks in the continental United States. Be prepared for winter weather at all times. The park receives half its nearly three million visitors in July and August. To avoid the crowds, head for the backcountry.

Camping: The 12 campgrounds at Yellowstone are available on a first-come, first-served basis except for Bridge Bay, Fishing Bridge, Madison, Grant Village and Canyon Village. Winter camping is available only at Mammoth campground.

Best one-day trip: From the west entrance, drive along Grand Loop Road to the mile-long Upper Geyser Basin, where boardwalks and trails run among the most outstanding geothermal phenomena in the world. Continue on to Yellowstone Lake.

6. ROCKY MOUNTAIN NATIONAL PARK

Over 2.7 million visitors per year • One of the highest regions in the country: 114 mountains above 10,000 feet

On both sides of Rocky Mountain National Park's 44-mile Trail Ridge Road, the highest paved road in America, are craggy snow-capped mountain peaks shrouded in clouds, alpine fields ablaze with wildflowers and crystal-clear mountain lakes. Elk, deer, moose, coyotes, marmots, ptarmigan, and bighorn sheep—the symbol of the park—can often be seen.

Estes Park, Colo. 80517
303-586-1399   www.nps.gov/romo

Peak season tips: The road to Bear Lake is jammed in the summer. Consider spending most of your time on the park's west side; it's less spectacular

---

TIMELY TIPS

For Daredevils...

✔ **Yosemite's** dramatic domes and soaring pinnacles make it one of the best places in the world for rock climbing.

✔ The **Yosemite Mountaineering School and Guide Service** offers beginning through advanced classes from April to mid-October; for information, call: 209-372-8344.

✔ Website: www.yosemitepark.com

but also less crowded, and there are better chances to see wildlife.

Camping: There are five campgrounds in the park, each with a seven-day camping limit. For reservations to Moraine Park and Glacier Basin campgrounds, call the Park reservation service. The other three are available on a first-come, first-served basis. In the summer, Timber Creek, on the west side of the park, is recommended—it doesn't fill up until about 1:30 p.m. Aspenglen and Longs Peak, where one begins the ascent to the summit, are often full by 8 a.m. Privately owned campgrounds also are available.

Best one-day trip: For a sampling of the varied topography, take Old Fall River Road to the Alpine visitors center at Fall River Pass, 11,796 feet above sea level. Drive back along Trail Ridge Road. If time permits, turn off Trail Ridge Road onto Bear Lake Road, which winds past lakes and streams to Bear Lake, where there is an easy 2/3-mile nature walk around the lake and a 1.1-mile hike to Dream Lake. A less crowded trail nearby is the Glacier Gorge Junction Trail to Alberta Falls. Those who are in peak physical condition may want to try Longs Peak Trail, a strenuous 8-mile hike at 14,000 feet.

Best experience: Eighty percent of the park's trails can be ridden on horseback, and there are two historic ranches at the center of the park. Horses can be rented in Glacier Basin and Moraine Park.

7. ZION NATIONAL PARK

Over 2.5 million visitors per year • The 319-foot Kolob Arch is the world's largest sandstone formation

Nineteenth-century Mormons named the main canyon in this park Zion after the Heavenly City and gave religious names to many of the brilliantly colored rock formations.

The park's outstanding features include massive stone arches, such as the Kolob Arch, hanging flower gardens, forested canyons and isolated mesas.

The varied topography and plant life of the canyon have been caused by differences in the amount of water that reaches the various parts of the park. The microenvironments shelter a wide variety of animals, from black bears to lizards.

Springdale, Utah 84767
801-772-3256 www.nps.gov.zion

Peak season tips: Expect traffic jams on summer weekends, when hordes of people visit the park. The west side is less crowded.

Camping: Two campgrounds are open year-round on a first-come, first-served basis. There are picnic areas with fire pits and flush toilets, but there are no hookups for RV's. Campers should arrive before 11:00 a.m. for the best chance at getting a spot.

Best one-day trip: A spectacular stretch of Utah Route 9 descends 2,000 feet in 11 miles into the park. As you enter the half-mile-wide canyon, the road turns into Zion Canyon Scenic Drive and runs north to the Temple of Sinawava. Riverside Walk, an easy 2-mile round-trip and the most popular trail in the park, begins here.

✔ **TIMELY TIPS**

...and Speed Freaks

✔ **Yellowstone** permits the use of snowmobiles (December to mid-March). In addition, snow coaches—buses on skis—are a unique way to travel around the park in the winter.

✔ Call **Xanterra Parks and Resorts** for reservations and rentals: 307–344–7311.

✔ Other outfitters are also listed on the National Park website: www.nps.gov.yose.

8. CUYAHOGA VALLEY NATIONAL PARK

Over 2.5 million visitors per year • *Located along the banks of the winding Cuyahoga River, with 22 miles of steep valley walls*

The valley itself is the product of two unique geographic landscapes—the Appalachian Plateau and the Central Lowlands—giving the park a wide range of different habitats. The park's diverse array of wetland and dry environments offer a wide range of plant and animal life, including 943 species of plants, 20 percent of which are non-native; 194 species of birds, 19 of which are considered endangered, as well as 43 different types of fish; 32 species of mammals; 22 amphibians; and 20 types of reptiles. The most commonly spotted animal is the white-tailed deer. There have also been recent sightings of coyotes and great blue herons.

Located in northeastern Ohio, near Akron and Cleveland, the park has four distinct seasons. The winter brings frequent snowfall, beginning in the late fall. In the spring there is often heavy rainfall. The summertime is usually hot and muggy, accompanied by periodic thunderstorms and foggy skies. Fall is the most popular season to visit. The park is open all year round. Visitors should come prepared for all seasonal conditions, as the weather is often unpredictable.

Brecksville, Ohio 44141   216-524-1497
www.nps.gov/cuva/home

Peak season tips: Although there has been much improvement in the water quality of the park's rivers and streams over the past couple of years, the Cuyahoga River continues to remain unsafe for recreational activities.

Lodging: Cuyahoga Valley National Park does not allow camping. However, there are a variety of hostels and hotels opened year round within the park's perimeters. Cuyahoga Valley lodging is available either at the HI-Stanford Hostel (330-467-8711 or www.stanford hostel.com), or at the Inn at Brandywine Falls (330-467-1812 or www. innatbrandywinefalls.com).

Best one-day trip: When they are too tired to hike, Cuyahoga Valley Scenic Railroad gives visitors the opportunity to tour the park by train. Excursions vary from $1^3/4$ hour round-trip rides to all-day expeditions. 800-468 4070 or www.cvsr.com

9. GRAND TETON NATIONAL PARK

Over 2.4 million visitors per year • *Best part of the beautiful Teton range*

There are not many places in the world where you can literally stand next to a mountain. Imagine then Grand Teton, where the mountains rise out of the relatively flat Jackson Hole Valley like granite skyscrapers.

Another geological oddity formed during the Ice Age, Jackson Hole Valley looks as if some gargantuan infant sculpted it out of Play-Doh. When the valley formed, little driblets from the glaciers formed rocky deposits, called moraines, around the six sparkling mountain lakes that were incongruously punctured into the landscape.

Winding gently through this strange valley is the Snake River, along the banks of which grow willows, cottonwoods and the blue spruces in which bald eagles prefer to nest. Beavers have built dams up and down the river, forming wetlands that have an incredibly dense concentration of wildlife, including bears, elk, moose, trumpeter swans, sandhill cranes and Canada geese.

Moose, Wyo. 83012
307-739-3300   www.nps.gov/grte

Peak season tips: From June through August, the crowds are near Jenny Lake, which has sand beaches and sometimes is warm enough for a quick swim.

Camping: Campgrounds are generally open from late May to October. In summer, Jenny Lake tent

TIMELY TIPS

The Best Park Guides

The National Park Service publishes an excellent series of guides on specific parks with color photos and maps. For more information see below:

IN PRINT

The Essential Guide to Wilderness Camping and Back Packing *Charles Cook, Michael Kesenel Publ. Ltd.*

Provides comprehensive information on all the national parks, with good tips on hiking and backpacking. Includes a good thumbnail guide to camping in national forests and a listing of notable trails.

National Geographic Guide to the National Parks of the United States, *Fifth Edition, revised and updated. National Geographic Society.*

Perfect for the windshield tourist, this book is packed with itineraries, quick hikes and beautiful pictures.

Walking Softly in the Wilderness: The Sierra Club Guide to Backpacking, *Fourth Edition, by John Hart. Sierra Club Books.*

ONLINE

National Park Service Home Page *www.nps.gov*

Offers brief but useful information on the parks and links to the homepages of major parks.

National Parks Electronic Bookstore *www.eparks.com/eparks/*

On this page you can order specialized publications, such as park guides and books about regional flora, fauna and history.

National Parks And Conservation Association *www.npca.org*

A nonprofit citizen group that is dedicated to preserving the Appalachian Trail and the national parks. The site provides information on various activities and provides a link to the latest issue of *National Parks* magazine.

GORP (Great Outdoors Recreation Pages) *www.gorp.com*

This commercial Web site has a vast array of offerings, including detailed reports on national parks, forests, wildlife refuges, etc. You'll also find information on hiking, biking, fishing, skiing, caving, etc., as well as tours of wilderness areas.

---

campground fills the fastest and has a seven-day camping limit—the other five parks have two-week limits. Camping at all five campgrounds is available on a first-come, first-served basis.

Best one-day trip: Beginning at the south entrance on Route 191, stop at Mentor's Ferry and the Chapel of the Transfiguration for a look at the dwellings of some of the area's first pioneers. Then drive north along Teton Park Road to Lupine Meadow and take the spur road to the trailhead, where, if you're in good physical shape, you can try a difficult hike to Amphitheater Lake near the timberline. Head back up Teton Road for a stop at South Jenny Lake, located at the bottom of the tallest Teton peak. An easy six-mile hike there circles the lake and affords spectacular views.

Finally, stop at Colter Bay for a one-mile hike that loops around the wetlands.

Best experience: In winter, horse-drawn sleighs take visitors to see the herd of 7,500 elk that live in the valley.

10. ACADIA NATIONAL PARK

Over 2 million visitors per year. • *Highest coastal mountains on the East Coast*

The park is made of two islands and a peninsula: Mount Desert Island (accessible by a land bridge), Isle au Haut and Schoodic Peninsula.

Artists and writers flocked to Mount Desert Island in the 1850's, attracted by its natural beauty. In the 1890's, wealthy vacationers, inspired by the paintings, came and built opulent "cottages,"

TRAVEL

many of which were destroyed by fire in 1947.

The park's proximity to the ocean gives it a milder climate than that of the mainland, which helps it to sustain more than 500 varieties of wildflowers and makes it one of the best places on the eastern seaboard to take in fall foliage. The park also is known as the Warbler Capital of the United States. Over 275 species of birds, including 26 varieties of warblers and the endangered peregrine falcon, inhabit the park's birch and pine forests.

Bar Harbor, Me. 04609
207-288-3338   www.nps.gov/mtde

Peak season tips: Expect bumper-to-bumper traffic on the Park Loop Road on the east side of Mount Desert Island in the summer. To avoid crowds, try the island's much less crowded western side or take a ferry trip either to Baker Island or to Isle au Haut. June is the best month to see forest birds; August is the best month for sea birds.

Camping: The landscaped Blackwoods campground on the east side of Mount Desert Island has 310 campsites. It is open all year. Reservations are advised.

On the less crowded west side is the 200-site Seawell campground, which is open only during the summer. You have to hike in from a parking lot to reach it, but it's worth the effort. Sites are available on a first-come, first-served basis only. Particularly remote are Isle au Haut's five small lean-to shelters. Here you can escape the cars and crowds without sacrificing convenience. The ferry there lands at a nearby hamlet where you can get provisions.

Best one-day trip: From the visitor center, take Park Loop Road to the 3.5-mile road that leads to Cadillac Mountain, where a short, paved trail winds around the 1,530-foot mountain, the highest coastal mountain in the United States. Back on Park Loop Road, turn around and continue down the East Coast. Stop at Sand Beach for a dip and

the 1.4-mile Great Head Trail for a hike around a rocky, forested peninsula. Continue on Park Loop Road to Route 3 and turn onto Route 198. Look for Hadlock Pond Carriage Road Trail, where there is a 4-mile loop across three granite bridges. This trail goes past the highest waterfall in the park and is one of the best places to enjoy the color of flowering plants in the spring.

Best experience: From mid-June to mid-October, you can take the charming carriage ride through the park that is offered by the Wild Wood Stables (207-276-3622 or www.acadia.net/wildwwood).

If carriages are too tame for you, this also is one of the few national parks where snowmobiles are allowed. The network of carriage roads provides excellent terrain.

Where the Crowds Aren't
Places you've never heard of are just as beautiful as Yellowstone

Getting away from it all is getting more difficult all the time in America's national parks. Increasingly, people are running into the same urban ills that they are trying to escape: traffic jams, pollution and even crime. While most people go for the blockbusters such as Yellowstone and Grand Canyon, there are parks just as magnificent and just as resource-rich with significantly fewer visitors. These lesser-known parks in many cases lie farther from population centers or just don't yet have local T-shirt and calendar industries.

There's a strong argument to be made that the undervisited reserves are the way national parks are meant to be. Without the car horns and camera-toting tourists, they better preserve that sense of yesteryear—and besides, you can grab a campsite at the last minute, instead of having to reserve a year in advance.

Before his death in 2003, Robin Winks, an irrepressible Yale history professor, was the first person to visit all the hundreds of units of the National Parks system. A lover of the outdoors, he devoted much of his career to the study and protection of the world's natural resources, and wrote *The Rise of the National Park Ethic,* a history of the National Park System. Below are some of his favorites of the lesser-known national parks:

CUMBERLAND ISLAND NATIONAL SEASHORE

38,258 visitors per year • 36,415 acres
Nearest big town: *Accessible via the National Park Service ferry, from St. Mary's, Ga., 95 miles from Savannah*

Cumberland Island, the largest of Georgia's Atlantic barrier islands, is also the most unspoiled. The southernmost of Georgia's Golden Isles, it has magnificent beaches, dunes, maritime forests, salt marshes and a number of old estates, as well as, armadillos, wild horses, wild turkeys and loggerhead turtles. The island can be reached only by ferry. Accommodations are available in five campsites on the island.

St. Mary's, Ga. 31558
912-882-4336   www.nps.gov/cuis

VOYAGEURS NATIONAL PARK

249,853 visitors per year • 218,054 acres
Nearest big town: *Duluth, 280 miles*

Much of the park is accessible only by boat (free canoes are available from the Park Service). There is, in fact, only one road. This wilderness is composed of 70,000 acres of dense forest, 30 lakes and 900 islands teeming with wildlife, including a pack of timber wolves. The area has remained relatively unchanged from the days of trappers and explorers.

International Falls, Minn. 56649
218-283-9821   www.nps.gov/voya

GRANT–KOHRS RANCH NATIONAL HISTORIC SITE

29,350 visitors per year • 1,500 acres
Nearest big town: *Butte, 45 miles*

This was one of the largest and best-known ranches in the country at the end of the 19th century. Today, the ranch is almost unchanged: cowboys still gallop by, herds of cattle bellow, and the smells of a working ranch waft through the place. In addition, the site preserves the original log buildings, the main Victorian-style ranch house and an impressive collection of saddles, wagons and other artifacts.

Deer Lodge, Mont. 59722
406-846-2070   www.nps.gov/grko

GREAT BASIN NATIONAL PARK

88,024 visitors per year • 77,180 acres
Nearest big town: *Salt Lake City, 230 miles*

Situated in one of the most rugged and remote parts of the country, this park is reminiscent of the wide open Old West. It has vast stretches of desertlike open country, dramatic tall mountains, including the 13,063-foot Wheeler Peak, which descends to the Great Basin, one of the lowest points in the state. Among the park's attractions are ancient bristlecone pines, which, at 4,000 years

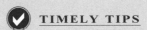

TIMELY TIPS

Shh! Don't Tell Anyone About It

The U.S. Government Printing Office publishes an excellent guide to the less well known, but in many cases no less spectacular, parks called *National Parks: Lesser-Known Areas.* To order a copy:

✔ Contact the G.P.O. at **202-512-1800**, or the Consumer Information Center at **719-544-3142.**

✔ www.nps.gov/pub_aff/lesser.htm

TRAVEL

old, are among the oldest living things in the world; Lehman Cave, one of the largest limestone caves in the country; and remnants of Pleistocene lakes.

Baker, Nev. 89311
775-234-7331   www.nps.gov/grba

NORTH CASCADES NATIONAL PARK

373, 656 visitors per year • 504,780 acres
NEAREST BIG TOWN: *Seattle, 115 miles*

This is one of those hike-all-day-and-not-see-anyone-else parks, largely because Washington's other better-known park, Olympic, is more accessible. Northern Cascades is sometimes called the American Alps because of its numerous immense jagged glaciers —318 in all. This enormous wilderness boasts 248 lakes, 1,700 species of plants, 207 species of birds and 85 species of mammals, including grizzly bears and cougars.

Sedro Woolley, Wash. 98284
360-856-5700   www.nps.gov/noca

CHANNEL ISLANDS NATIONAL PARK

300,000 visitors per year • 249,354 acres
NEAREST BIG TOWN: *Ventura on the coast is about 14 miles away by boat or plane*

Because of the abundant wildlife here, which includes the world's largest creature, the blue whale, biologists often refer to these five tiny islands off the California coast as North America's Galápagos. Among the other animals that can be seen are sea lions, sea otters, pelicans and cormorants. Remains of Spanish farms offer examples of how some of the earliest settlers in California lived.

Ventura, Calif. 93001
805-658-5700   www.nps.gov/chis

LASSEN VOLCANIC NATIONAL PARK

385,489 visitors per year • 106,372 acres
NEAREST BIG TOWN: *Chester, 35 miles*

Before Mount St. Helens erupted in 1980, Lassen Peak was considered the most active volcano in the lower 48 states. The park provides a great vantage point from which to observe volcanic action—fumaroles, bubbling mud pots and hissing hot springs dot the landscape. There are also 150 miles of hiking trails through densely forested areas.

Mineral, Calif. 96063
530-595-4444   www.nps.gov/lavo

ANIAKCHAK NATIONAL MONUMENT

1,193 visitors per year • 117,176 acres in the monument and 465,603 acres in the preserve.
NEAREST BIG TOWN: *Anchorage, 400 miles*

This wilderness is the most remote and difficult to visit in the National Park System. The quickest way to get to the focal point of Aniakchak, which is a giant crater, one of the largest in the world, is to fly into it. However, be forewarned if you're contemplating this feat: For every 10 attempts, only one is successful, because winds are constantly closing the only gap a plane can enter. Inside the crater, Surprise Lake's waters course through the wall of the crater to form the Aniakchak River.

King Salmon, Alaska 99613
907-246-3305   www.nps.gov/ania

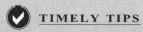

TIMELY TIPS

Into the Wilderness

✔ **WILDERNESS AREAS**—more than 106 million acres—are the most strictly protected lands in the country. "Carry out what you carry in" policies are enforced so that, in the words of the 1964 Wilderness Act, "the imprint of man's works" remains "substantially unnoticeable.." For a complete list of wilderness areas, go to **www.wilderness.net.**

Pick a Park, Any Park

America has designated over 80 million square miles as 58 national parks for the enjoyment of its citizenry and the generations to come. The parks, their claims to fame, principal activities and how to get in touch with them:

ALASKA

Denali • *Mt. McKinley, N. America's highest mountain.* • Dog sledding, cross-country skiing, hiking
907-683-2294   www.nps.gov/dena

Gates of the Arctic • *Greatest wilderness in N. America.* • River running, fishing, mountaineering
907-456-0281   www.nps.gov/gaar

Glacier Bay • *Tidewater glaciers, wild terrain from ice to rainforest* • Sea kayaking, fishing
907-697-2232   www.nps.gov/glba

Katmai • *Alaskan brown bears, the world's largest carnivores* • Sport fishing, kayaking
907-246-3305   www.nps.gov/katm

Kenai Fjords • *300-sq.-mile Harding Ice Field, varied rain forest* • Sea kayaking, charter boats
907-224-3175   www.nps.gov/kefj

Kobuk Valley • *Entirely north of the Arctic Circle* • Canoeing, exploring archaeological sites
907-442-3890   www.nps.gov/kova

Lake Clark • *Headquarters for red salmon spawning* • Charter river trips, fishing
907-271-3751   www.nps.gov/lacl

Wrangell-St. Elias • *Chugach, Wrangell, & St. Elias mnts. meet here* • Rafting, cross-country skiing
907-822-5234   www.nps.gov/wrst

AMERICAN SAMOA
Park of American Samoa • *Paleotropical rain forests, coral reefs* • Bird-watching, sunbathing
011-684-633-7082   www.nps.gov/npsa

ARIZONA
Grand Canyon • *The mile-deep canyon itself* • River rafting, mule rides
520-638-7888   www.nps.gov/grca

Petrified Forest • *Petrified trees, Indian ruins* • Self-guided auto tours, photography
520-524-6228   www.nps.gov/pefo

Saguaro • *Greatest variety of desert life in N. America* • Photography, bird-watching, hiking
520-733-5100   www.nps.gov/sagu

ARKANSAS
Hot Springs • *Some 950,000 gals. of water a day flow through 47 thermal springs* • Hot baths
501-624-3383   www.nps.gov/hosp

CALIFORNIA
Channel Islands • *Seabirds, sea lions and unique plants* • Scuba diving, bird-watching
805-658-5700   www.nps.gov/chis

Death Valley • *Lowest point in Western Hemisphere* • Photography, jeep riding, horseback riding
619-786-2331   www.nps.gov/deva

Joshua Tree • *20- to 40-foot Joshua trees, stunning dunes* • Wildlife-watching, nature walks
619-367-7511   www.nps.gov/jotr

Lassen Volcanic • *Huge lava-flow mountains, sulfur vents* • cross-country, downhill skiing
916-595-4444   www.nps.gov/lavo

Redwood • *Redwood forests and 40 miles of scenic coastline* • Whale-watching, guided kayaking
707-464-6101   www.nps.gov/redw

Sequoia and **Kings Canyon** • *Huge trees, big canyons and wilderness* • Overnight backpacking
209-565-3341   www.nps.gov/seki

Yosemite • *Granite peaks and domes, and the nation's highest waterfall* • Skiing, rock climbing
209-372-0200   www.nps.gov/yose

COLORADO
Black Canyon of the Gunnison • *Spectacular, deep river canyon* • Rock climbing, hiking, fishing
970-641-2337   www.nps.gov/blca

Great Sand Dunes • *North America's tallest dunes* • Hiking, sand castle-building, bird-watching
719-378-6300   www.nps.gov/grsa

Mesa Verde • *Pre-Columbian cliff dwellings and other artifacts* • Guided lectures, exhibits
970-529-4461   www.nps.gov/meve

Rocky Mountain • *Trail Ridge Rd., highest in the lower 48* • Mountain climbing, horseback riding
970-586-1399   www.nps.gov/romo

FLORIDA
Biscayne • *Pristine wilderness, living coral reefs* • Glass-bottom boat tours, snorkeling, scuba
305-230-7275   www.nps.gov/bisc

Dry Tortugas • *Largest all-masonry fort in the west* • Fishing, snorkeling, scuba diving
305-242-7710   www.nps.gov/drto

Everglades • *Largest remaining subtropical wilderness in U.S.* • Backcountry canoeing, fishing
305-242-7710   www.nps.gov/ever

HAWAII
Haleakala • *Inactive volcano, chain of pools linked by a waterfall* • Sunrise- and sunset-watching
808-572-9306   www.nps.gov/hale

Hawaii Volcanoes • *Devastation from volcanic eruptions* • Backpacking, bird-watching
808-985-6000   www.nps.gov/havo

TRAVEL

KENTUCKY
Mammoth Cave · *Longest recorded cave system in the world* · Cave tours, cave boating
502-758-2328   www.nps.gov/maca

MAINE
Acadia · *Cadillac Mountain, highest on East Coast of the U.S.* · Boat tours, skiing
207-288-3338   www.nps.gov/acad

MICHIGAN
Isle Royale · *Largest island in Lake Superior* · Kayaking, hiking
906-482-0986   www.nps.gov/isro

MINNESOTA
Voyageurs · *30 lakes and over 900 islands* · Canoeing, cross-country skiing, ice-skating
218-283-9821   www.nps.gov/voya

MONTANA
Glacier · *Nearly 50 glaciers, lakes* · Excursion-boat cruises, snowshoeing
406-888-7800   www.nps.gov/glba

NEVADA
Great Basin · *Ice field on 13,063-ft. Wheeler Peak, Lehman Caves* · Fishing, climbing, spelunking
702-234-7331   www.nps.gov/grba

NEW MEXICO
Carlsbad Caverns · *U.S.'s deepest cave (1,593 ft.) and largest chambers* · Guided cave tours
505-785-2232   www.nps.gov/cave

NORTH DAKOTA
Theodore Roosevelt · *The arid badlands, Roosevelt's Elkhorn Ranch* · Fishing, photography
701-623-4466   www.nps.gov/thro

OHIO
Cuyahoga Valley · *Rolling floodplain, rugged gorges* · Running, biking, cross-country skiing
216-524-1497   www.nps.gov/cuva

OREGON
Crater Lake · *Deepest lake in the U.S. (1,932 feet)* · Boat tours, snowmobiling, cross-country skiing
541-594-2211   www.nps.gov/crla

SOUTH CAROLINA
Congaree · *Largest contiguous tract of old-growth bottomland hardwoods* · Hiking, fishing, canoeing
803-776-4396   www.nps.gov/cosw

SOUTH DAKOTA
Badlands · *The scenic western badlands* · Hiking, wildlife-watching
605-433-5361   www.nps.gov/badl

Wind Cave · *Beautiful limestone cave and the scenic Black Hills* · Spelunking, cave tours, hiking
605-745-4600   www.nps.gov/wica

TENNESSEE
Great Smoky Mountains · *Loftiest range in the East, diverse plant life* · Hiking, photography
423-436-1200   www.nps.gov/grsm

TEXAS
Big Bend · *Rio Grande passes through canyon walls for 118 miles* · Horseback riding, fishing
915-477-2251   www.nps.gov/bibe

Guadalupe Mountains · *Portions of world's most extensive fossil reef* · Hiking, historic sites
915-828-3251   www.nps.gov/gumo

UTAH
Arches · *Giant arches, pinnacles change color as the sun shifts* · Interpretive walks, auto tours
801-259-8161   www.nps.gov/arch

Bryce Canyon · *Colorful, unusually shaped geologic forms* · Cross-country skiing, snowshoeing
801-834-5322   www.nps.gov/brca

Canyonlands · *Canyons of Green, Colorado rivers* · Mountain biking, country drives, rafting
801-259-3911   www.nps.gov/cany

Capitol Reef · *Waterpocket Fold, a 100-mile-long wrinkle in earth's crust* · Hiking
801-425-3791   www.nps.gov/care

Zion · *Unusual geologic formations–Kolob Arch, world's largest* · Hiking, photography
801-772-3256   www.nps.gov/zion

VIRGINIA
Shenandoah · *The scenic Blue Ridge Mountains* · Skyline Drive, horseback riding, nature walks
540-999-3400   www.nps.gov/shen

VIRGIN ISLANDS
Virgin Islands · *Secluded coves, white beaches fringed by lush hills* · Snorkeling, swimming
809-775-6238   www.nps.gov/viis

WASHINGTON
Mount Rainier · *Greatest single-peak glacial system in U.S.* · Skiing, snowshoeing, climbing
360-569-2211   www.nps.gov/mora

North Cascades · *Half the glaciers in the U.S.; 318 are active* · Backpacking, hiking
360-856-5700   www.nps.gov/noca

Olympic · *One of the biggest temperate rain forests in the world* · Mountain climbing, fishing
360-452-4501   www.nps.gov/olym

WYOMING
Grand Teton · *The flat Jackson Hole Valley and the Teton mountains* · Hiking, climbing, skiing
307-739-3399   www.nps.gov/grte

Yellowstone · *World's largest concentration of geothermal phenomena* · Skiing, snowmobiling
307-344-7381   www.nps.gov/yell

SOURCES: National Park Service; individual parks

Places to Hang Your Hiking Boots

Almost all the comforts of home in the middle of the wilderness

America's national parks contain some of the best-preserved rustic hotels in the United States. These capacious lodges were often built with stones and trees hewn directly from the stunning landscapes they occupy in an attempt to re create the great outdoors indoors. Rates range widely, from under $100 a night per person to five-star hotel prices. Here are some of the best places to stay in the national parks.

AHWAHNEE HOTEL

Yosemite National Park, California. Dating from 1925, this hotel's assymmetrical rock columns and varied levels convey the impression of a mountain range. The floor-to-ceiling stained-glass windows offer splendid views of the soaring walls of Yosemite Valley. Open year-round.

> *866-875-8456 www.nationalparkreservations. com/ahwahnee*

BRYCE CANYON LODGE

Bryce Canyon National Park, Utah. Atop a mesa overlooking the colorfully hued stone walls of Bryce Canyon, the lodge and adjacent cabins are classic examples of rustic architecture. Open April to November. *888-297-2757*

> *www.brycecanyonlodge.com*

EL TOVAR LODGE

Grand Canyon National Park, Arizona. Only 50 feet from the South Rim of the Grand Canyon, it is one of the most luxurious, with first-rate gourmet meals. Open year-round. *888-297-2757*
www.grandcanyonlodges.com/El-Tovar-409.html

LAKE MACDONALD LODGE

Glacier National Park, Montana. The hotel faces out across Lake MacDonald, the largest lake in the park, with views of the magnificent snow-capped mountain beyond. Open May to October.

> *866-875-8456*
> *www.nationalparkreservations.com/glacier.htm*

NORTH RIM LODGE

Grand Canyon National Park, Arizona. Lying on the edge of the North Rim, the lodge offers an inexpensive alternative to El Tovar. Open mid-May to mid-October. *888-297-2757 www.nps.gov/grca/grandcanyon/ north-rim/lodging.htm*

OLD FAITHFUL INN

Yellowstone National Park, Wyoming. Built in 1904, many rooms have views of the world-famous Old Faithful geyser nearby. Open early May to mid-October. *307–344–7311 www.travelyellowstone.com*

OREGON CAVES CHATEAU

Oregon Caves National Monument. This hotel actually spans a small gorge. A stream runs through the dining room. Open May through October—part of the year at "bed and breakfast" rates; the rest of the year as a full-service hotel. Call for a schedule.

> *503–592–3400*
> *www.oregoncavesoutfitters.com/home.asp*

PARADISE INN

Mount Rainier National Park, Washington. One of the earliest ski resorts in the country, the inn lies at an elevation of 5,400 feet. Open mid-May to October.

> *360–569–2275   rainier.guestservices.com/ html/accomodations.html*

WAWONA HOTEL

Yosemite National Park, California. The largest existing Victorian hotel complex within a national park. Open April to November continuously, and intermittently throughout the year.

> *559-253-5635   www.yosemitepark.com*

ROSS LAKE RESORT

Ross Lake National Recreation Area,Washington. The resort consists of 12 rustic cabins and three bunk-houses on floating log rafts along the steep shoreline of the lake. You can hike two miles in or go by boat. Open mid-June to the end of October. Book at least a year in advance.

206–386–4437   www.rosslakeresort.com

Paths Across the Nation

Some no wider than a fat man, all of scenic or historic value

While they may not have hiked it top to bottom, most Americans have heard of the Appalachian Trail. Many are unaware, though, that the Appalachian belongs to a much larger system of trails. In 1968, Congress passed the National Trails Assistance Act to establish a national trail system. The trails fall into two categories: national scenic trails, which are protected scenic corridors for outdoor recreation, and national historic trails, which recognize prominent past routes of exploration, migration and military action and may consist of no more than a series of roadside markers. The entire system includes 19 trails and covers most of the country. Here are eight of the loveliest hikes in America, whatever your stamina.

APPALACHIAN NATIONAL SCENIC TRAIL

LENGTH: 2,174 miles • Beginning in Georgia and ending in Maine, the trail hugs the crest of the Appalachian Mountains and is open only to hikers.

Appalachian Trail Conference,
Harpers Ferry, W.V. 25425
304-535-6278   www.nps.gov/appa

CONTINENTAL DIVIDE NATIONAL SCENIC TRAIL

LENGTH: 3,100 miles • The trail provides spectacular backcountry travel through the Rocky Mountains from Mexico to Canada. The trail is open to hikers, pack and saddle animals and, in some places, off-road motorized vehicles.

Continental Divide Society, Baltimore, Md. 21218
410-235-9610   www.cdtrail.org/page.php

FLORIDA NATIONAL SCENIC TRAIL

LENGTH: 1,300 miles • The Florida Trail extends from Big Cypress National Preserve in south Florida to just west of Pensacola in the northern part of the Florida Panhandle. The trail passes through America's only

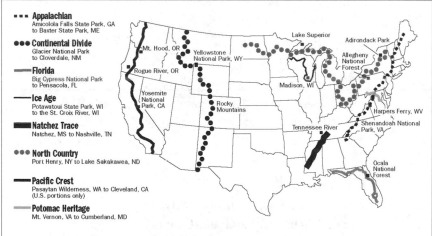

- - - **Appalachian**
Amicolola Falls State Park, GA to Baxter State Park, ME
●●● **Continental Divide**
Glacier National Park to Cloverdale, NM
Florida
Big Cypress National Park to Pensacola, FL
Ice Age
Potawatoui State Park, WI to the St. Croix River, WI
Natchez Trace
Natchez, MS to Nashville, TN
●●● **North Country**
Port Henry, NY to Lake Sakakawea, ND
Pacific Crest
Pasaytan Wilderness, WA to Cleveland, CA (U.S. portions only)
Potomac Heritage
Mt. Vernon, VA to Cumberland, MD

NATIONAL SCENIC TRAILS

Benton MacKaye, the man who created the Appalachian Trail, thought it should be no wider than the space required by the average fat man. The majority of the trails are open to hikers only, although some allow mountain bikes and horses. Many are works in progress and have large sections closed to the public. Call ahead to inquire about available sections, allowable modes of transportation and camping permits.

subtropical landscape, making it popular in winter.

Florida Trail Association, Gainesville, Fla. 32064
352-378-8823
www.florida-trail.org

ICE AGE NATIONAL SCENIC TRAIL

LENGTH: **1,200 miles** • The trail follows a chain of moraine hills zigzaging across Wisconsin from Lake Michigan to the St. Croix River. Almost half the trail is open to the public, and certain sections are sometimes even used for marathons, ski races and ultramarathons.

National Park Service, Madison, Wis. 53711
608-264-5610
www.nps.gov/lat

- **California**
  Independence, MO to Sacramento, CA
- **Iditarod**
  Seward, AK to Nome, AK
- **Juan Bautista de Anza**
  Nogales, AZ to San Francisco, CA
- **Lewis and Clark**
  St. Louis, MO to Astoria, OR
- **Mormon Pioneer**
  Nauvoo, IL to Salt Lake City, UT
- **Nez Perce (Nee-Me-Poo)**
  Wallowa Lake, OR to Chinook, MT
- **Oregon**
  Independence, MO to Oregon City, OR
- **Overmountain Victory**
  Abington, VA to Kings Mountain National Military Park, SC
- **Pony Express**
  St. Joseph, MO to Sacramento, CA
- **Santa Fe**
  Santa Fe, NM to Boonville, MO
- **Trail of Tears**
  Charleston, TN to Tahlequah, OK (northern)
  Chattanooga, TN to Tahlequah, OK (southern)

NATIONAL HISTORIC TRAILS

National historic trails are somewhat more conceptual than national scenic trails. Their objective is to preserve any historic remnants of the trail rather than provide a continuous footpath across its entire length. They are often are no more than a series of roadside signs that direct travelers to historic sites or markers, though foot trails do appear from time to time at the roadside stops. The GORP website has detailed information on each National Historic Trail at gorp.away.com/gorp/resource/us_trail/historic.htm or at www.public.iastate.edu/~sfr/nts/nts.htm.

NATCHEZ TRACE NATIONAL SCENIC TRAIL

LENGTH: **110 miles** • The trail lies within the boundairies the Natchez Trace Parkway, which extends from Natchez, Miss., to Nashville, Tenn., and commemorates an ancient path that began as a series of animal tracks and trails used by Native Americans.

Natchez Trace Parkway, Tupelo, Miss. 38801
800-305-7417   www.nps.gov/natt

NORTH COUNTRY NATIONAL SCENIC TRAIL

LENGTH: **4,000 miles** • Conceived in the mid-1960's, this trail links the Adirondack Mountains with the Missouri River in North Dakota.

National Park Service, Madison, Wis. 53711
608-264-5610   www.nps.gov/noco

PACIFIC CREST NATIONAL SCENIC TRAIL

LENGTH: **2,650 miles** • Running along the spectacular shoulders of the Cascade and Sierra Nevada mountain ranges from Canada to Mexico, the trail is the West Coast counterpart to the Appalachian Trail.

U.S.D.A. Forest Service, Portland, Ore. 97204
503-326-3644   www.fs.fed.us/pct

POTOMAC HERITAGE NATIONAL SCENIC TRAIL

LENGTH: **770 miles** • Commemorates the unique mix of history and recreation along the Potomac River. The last 20 or so miles of the trail along the Chesapeake and Ohio Canal provide a wonderful bicycle ride that ends in the heart of Washington, D.C.

National Park Service National Capital FDO, Washington, D.C. 20242,
202-208-4797   www.nps.gov/pohe

TRAVEL

Catch a Glimpse of a Bighorn
The best places to see magnificent animals

It seems to be an inexorable law that as the human population expands wild animal species decline. Viewing large numbers of wild animals in a relatively pristine habitat is increasingly a rare experience. But it's still possible—even in America.

BIGHORN SHEEP
Georgetown Viewing Site, Georgetown, Colorado

Located along Interstate 70, about halfway between Denver and Vail, the Georgetown Viewing Site is probably the most accessible place for viewing Rocky Mountain bighorn sheep. Between 175 and 200 bighorns occupy the rocky cliffs along the north side of Clear Creek Canyon. Fall and winter are the best times to look for them. (There's a lookout tower shaped like a ram's horns.) An exhibit includes interpretative displays and mounted viewing scopes. 303-297-1192

MANATEES
Crystal River National Wildlife Refuge, Florida

Crystal River N.W.R. is made up of nine small islands totaling little more than 40 acres, but their location in Kings Bay is critical. The headwaters of Crystal River, Kings Bay is fed by fresh water springs at a consistent 72 degrees F. year-round. It is this warm water that attracts the large manatees during cooler weather when temperatures in open water fall. The refuge is critical habitat for 15 to 20 percent of the U.S. manatee population, and is one of six places in Florida with climates unaffected by outside changes.

352-563-2088   www.fws.gov/crystalriver

ROCKY MOUNTAIN ELK
Horseshoe Park, Rocky Mountain National Park, Colorado

During September and October, bull elk bugle as a means to intimidate rival males and as a physical release for tensions of the mating season.. Bugling usually begins an hour before sunset and starts off as a buildup of deep, resonant tones rising quickly to a high-pitched squeal before dropping to a series of grunts. It is this call, or bugle, that gives rise to the term *rut* for mating season.

970-586-1399 www.nps.gov/romo/resources/plantsandanimals/featuredpanda/bighorn.html

WINTERING ELK
National Elk Refuge, Jackson Hole, Wyoming

When snow comes to the high country in the Grand Tetons, elk migrate from their high-elevation summer range to a winter range in the valley. Almost 7,500 elk inhabit the area. Elk arrive in early November and return to the high country in early May. In the winter, visitors can view elk from a horse-drawn sleigh. Sleighs run from late December to March, 10 a.m. to 4 p.m. daily. Tours operate from the National Museum of Wildlife Art, three miles north of Jackson on U.S. Highway 26/191.

307-733-9212 www.fws.gov/nationalelkrefuge

SANDHILL CRANES
Platte River, Nebraska

For about five weeks in early spring (usually starting in March), more than three-quarters of the world's population of sandhill cranes gathers along the Platte River in central Nebraska. More than 500,000 of these stately birds rest and fatten up here on their way back to breeding grounds in the Arctic.

The local chamber of commerce sponsors a three-day program known as "Wings over the Platte," which includes bus tours, seminars and exhibits.

For more information, contact: Field Supervisor, U.S. Fish and Wildlife Service:

308-382-6468   mountain-prairie.fws.gov/es/ Nebraska/GrandIsland.htm

or Grand Island/Hall County Convention and Visitors Bureau, Nebraska:

800-658-3178   www.visitgrandisland.com.

GRAY WHALES

Point Reyes National Seashore, California

Gray whales engage in the longest migration of any mammal in the world, swimming 6,000 miles from feeding grounds in the icy waters north of Alaska to warm breeding lagoons off Baja California, Mexico, and 6,000 back.

Every autumn, the entire gray whale population of more than 18,000 heads south at about the same time. That means that as many as 30 whales an hour may be moving in "pulses" past a particular point during peak weeks. Though other California counties boast worthwhile whale-watching venues, it is the Point Reyes Peninsula that has geography working heavily in its favor. To learn more, contact:

415-464-5100 or www.nps.gov/pore

CALIFORNIA AND STELLER'S SEA LIONS

Sea Lion Caves, Oregon

After descending more than 200 feet in an elevator to Sea Lion Caves on the coast of Oregon, you will find dim light, the hollow sound of waves crashing against cliffs and the echoed barks of hundreds of Steller's sea lions (present year-round) and California sea lions (present from September to April). Sea lions swim and loaf below a cliff-top observation deck.

541-547-3111   www.sealioncaves.com

Where Else to Watch the Whales Around the World

Thar she blows, according to the World Wildlife Fund. Here are the spots where whales are most likely to spout off around the world:

WHERE, Country • *Access* • **Whales** • Peak season

S. OCEAN WHALE SANCTUARY, Antarctica • *Boat access only* • **Humpback, southern right, minke whales** • Summer

SAMANA BAY, Dominican Republic • *Boat and shoreline access* • **Humpback, pilot, Bryde's whales** • Jan.–March

CAMPBELL RIVER, British Columbia • *Shoreline, sailboat access* • **Minke and orcas (killer whales)** • June–Sept.

CAPE COD, Massachusetts • *Boat access only* • **Humpback, fin, northern right, minke, pilot whales** • April–October.

BAJA CALIFORNIA, Mexico • *Shoreline and boat access* • **Gray, blue and humpbacks** • Almost all year around

LOFOTEN ISLANDS, Norway • *Boat access only* • **Sperm, minkes and orcas** • Summer

KAIKKOURA, New Zealand • *Boat, shoreline access* • **Sperm whale, orcas, also Hector's & dusky dolphins.** • Year-round.

WHALE ROUTE, South Africa • *Shoreline access* • **Southern right, humpback, Bryde's whales, orca** • August–Nov.

PATAGONIA, Argentina • *Boat and shoreline access* • **Southern right whale and orcas** • June–Dec.

SHIKOKU, Japan • *Boat access only* • **Bryde's whales** • Year-round

MEXICAN FREE-TAILED BATS

Carlsbad Caverns National Park, New Mexico

On warm summer evenings in the Chihuahuan Desert, thousands of Mexican free-tailed bats exit in a whirling, smokelike column from the natural mouth of Carlsbad Caverns. Research indicates that Mexican free-tailed bats have inhabited the Carlsbad taverns for over 5,000 years, with an estimated 300,000 bats in the caverns. They emerge at dusk to feed on moths; other flights occur in late August and September, when young bats born in June join the evening ritual. Flight Amphitheater, which is located at the mouth of the cavern, seats up to 1,000 people. Park rangers offer programs about the bats from Memorial Day to Labor Day prior to the evening flights. But don't expect to see bats if you visit during the winter—they will have migrated to Mexico.

505-785-2232   www.nps.gov/cave

BALD EAGLES

Skagit River, Mount Baker–Snoqualmie National Forest, Washington

One of the largest concentrations of wintering bald eagles in the lower 48 states occurs at the Skagit River Bald Eagle Natural Area in northern Washington State. More than 300 bald eagles gather along the river's gravel bars between 7 a.m. and 11 a.m. to feed on spawned-out salmon. The eagles feast here between November and early March, with peak numbers occurring in mid-January.

For more information contact: The Nature Conservancy, Washington Field Office:
206-343-4344 nature.org/wherewework/
northamerica/states/washington
or Mount Baker Ranger District, Sedro Woolley, Washington: 360-856-5700
www.fs.fed.us/r6/mbs/maps/nwia.shtml

Galápagos Unbound

Free as a breeze with the blue-footed boobies

It can be tough deciding which wildlife encounters are worthy of pause after only a few days in the Galápagos, those South American islands of evolution cauterized by sun and magma. Nearly any tour that cruises this isolated yet popular chain, 600 miles west of Ecuador, comes packaged with extreme closeups of washer-size tortoises, swimming lizards and crabs the color of rainbows.

Trips to the Galápagos archipelago—nearly all of which is a national park—typically unfold aboard commercial yachts that ply the waters here. From 4 to 100 passengers at a time are whisked around on tightly choreographed schedules between islands. While convenient and comfortable, wildlife encounters are often limited, since passengers must sleep on the boats and disembark only at strictly controlled wildlife viewing sites for short periods.

But now, for the adventurous there's another option: sea kayaking. Unlike yacht-based trips that may offer some kayaking, these excursions are all about melding into the sea and letting the landscape slide by under blue-footed-booby skies. Come evening, paddlers run the kayaks into the sand, pitch tents on the beach and wait for birds to scream in the dawn. The combination is spectacular. Not only do paddlers have the thrill of being among the first tourists to camp in these locations, but along the way, they also nuzzle bow to beak with so much kooky wildlife that stumbling upon sea turtles in the act becomes, well, normal.

An eight-day itinerary offered through ROW International, a division of River Odysseys West (800-451-6034 or www.rowinternational.com), samples 6 of the chain's 18 or so islands and islets and includes a mix of hiking, snorkeling and well-earned rests at an inn.

TIMELY TIPS

A Birdwatcher's Best Friend

Almost 20 million Americans watch birds away from home, according to a 2001 Fish and Wildlife Service survey. And embracing technology, most bird watchers say, is the key to the sport. Today many makers of binoculars have added features that appeal to birders, including image stabilizers and built-in digital cameras. "Now a beginner can capture an image on the spot," notes Greg Butcher, the director of bird conservation at the National Audubon Society.

Marcy Brown-Marsden, an ornithologist, lifelong birder and associate professor of biology at the University of Dallas, recommends what to look for in birding binoculars: a dial to focus, rather than a slide; weightiness to aid in stability; and a compact size that is just big enough to grasp. Here are some of her suggestions for binoculars:

✔ **LEICA ULTRAVID 10x42 BR**
Waterproof and rubber coated, Leica Ultravid are high-end binoculars for serious birders. The focus wheel is calibrated to achieve a crystalline sharpness from 9.7 feet to infinity. www.leica-camera.com

✔ **NIKON STABILEYES 16x32**
Equipped with a built-in image stabilizer, these binoculars are slightly heavy, a boon when you want to hold them steady. A sturdy carrying strap stores the batteries. www.nikonsportoptics.com.

✔ **AUDUBON EQUINOX HP 8x42**
With a wide field of view and 8 times magnification, these binoculars suit beginners. www.audubonbinoculars.com

—Christian De Benedetti

TRAVEL

Tourism is big business in the Galápagos, pouring at least $100 million into the Ecuadorean economy each year, and drawing increasing numbers of workers from the mainland. In 1973, 14 years after the creation of the Galápagos National Park, officials estimated that 12,000 people a year could tour the Galápagos with little impact. About 109,000 visited in 2004, but authorities had already increased the allowed capacity to 150,000 tourists a year.

Though the campsites are spectacular, as a whole the Galápagos are not particularly beautiful, at least not in the way tropical islands often are. There are few palms among uninterrupted stands of haggard salt scrub plants. Some beaches have azure waters and baby-powder sand, but most shorelines are rocky and lapped by dark waves cold enough to warrant a wet suit. "We fancied even that the bushes smelt unpleasantly," Charles Darwin wrote during the voyage of the Beagle, the trip in 1835 that sparked his theory on evolution.

It is the diversity of animals—penguins and flamingos, for example—and their bizarre mutations that bring people here today. After countless generations of not needing to fly, some cormorants can't; the four-eyed blenny fish can crawl on land; iguanas sneeze salt. Most creatures are freakishly unafraid of people. The interaction with wildlife is extraordinary. Sea lions nibble on flippers while others play tug-of-war with a small section of cord. Frigate birds, iguanas, giant tortoises and even a short-eared owl all sit patiently for their portraits.

But it is the slow pace of gliding inches over the water in a kayak that makes this Galápagos experience special. While kayakers can't disembark anywhere they please, the boats are maneuverable enough to ride tidal surges through caves and to cruise rocky shorelines that motorized craft cannot.

—Tim Neville

The Glories of the Wet and Wild

Life thrives more in tropical rain forests

Tropical rain forests occupy only 7 percent of the earth's land surface, yet they contain over half its living organisms. What makes all that life possible is warm weather—averaging 80 degrees—and, of course, rain—lots of it. Tropical rain forests average 100 to 400 inches of rainfall a year, whereas New York City receives 43 inches a year and San Francisco only about 20 inches a year.

In contrast to other places on earth, most of the plant life in rain forests is in the treetops. Below this primary canopy is a secondary one where shrubs and smaller trees grow. Plant life on the forest floor is limited because of the lack of light.

Where should one go to witness the glories of wet and wild habitats up close? Thomas Lovejoy, President of the H. John Heinz III Center for Science, Economics and the Environment, and Russell Mittermeier, president of Conservation International, suggest these South American spots:

Guides for a Rainy Stay

The following groups organize eco-sensitive expeditions to many of the rain forests discussed here.

- **International Expeditions**
  Helena, Ala. 800-633-4734 or
  www.ietravel.com

- **Mountain Travel/Sobek Expeditions**
  El Cerrito, Calif.   800-227-2384 or
  www.mtsobek.com

- **Victor Emanuel Nature Tours**
  Austin, Tex.   800-328-8368 or
  www.ventbird.com

- **Field Guides**
  Austin, Tex. 800-728-4953 or
  www.fieldguides.com

COSTA RICA

Costa Rican rain forests do not have the staggering variety of species or sheer density of plant and animal life of the most significant rain forests in the world, such as those along the eastern Andes. However, they contain about 5 percent of the world's plants and animals.

Parque Nacional Corcovado
On the Peninsula de Osa, about 115 miles southeast of San José

The largest primary lowland rain forest in Costa Rica. Over 400 species of birds live here, including scarlet macaws. The park is also home to pumas, ocelots, tapirs and jaguars, as well as numerous rare butterflies and the almost extinct Harpy eagle.

Monteverde Cloud Forest Reserve *A four-hour drive north of San José*

Situated on a mountain 4,600 feet above sea level, the reserve is a tropical cloud forest where constant low clouds hover in the treetops, creating a highly humid environment. The park contains over 2,000 species of wildlife, including mantled howler monkeys. Also, one of the last remaining nesting sites of the quetzal, reputedly the most beautiful bird in the world.

EASTERN SLOPES OF THE ANDES

This area extends from the southern part of the Colombian Amazon through Ecuador and Peru. Norman Myers, a leading expert on biodiversity, says these rain forests constitute the richest biotic zone on earth.

Yasuni National Park *Oriente region of Ecuador*

The lakes in Yasuni National Park are home to piranhas and caimans (relatives of the crocodile). A number of Indian tribes also live here, including the Waorani, who until recently have avoided contact with outsiders.

INSIDE INFO

Butterflies Are Free

○ From mid-September through early November, about 300 million monarch butterflies flit and flutter from Canada and the northern United States to their winter homes in California and Mexico. Accordingly, the annual spectacle of southbound swarms of orange-and-black-speckled monarchs inspires festivals and butterfly-tagging events across the continent.

○ The tagging is coordinated by Monarch Watch, a research program based at the University of Kansas. Researchers there supply the numbered tags, which look like the stickers used to mark produce at the grocery store. Volunteers at various tagging sites demonstrate how to capture butterflies and affix the stickers to their wings. Then, anyone can track tagged butterflies' progress by checking for sightings on the Monarch Watch Web site (www.monarchwatch.org).

Tambopata-Caudano Reserve area and National Park *About 40 miles south of Puerto Maldonado in the Madre de Dios region of Peru*

This park is contiguous with the Madidi National Park in Peru, and together the two form the largest uninterrupted rain forest on earth. Tambopata-Caudano is also the best place to see butterflies—over 1,100 species live here. In addition, this park has the largest known macaw lick in South America.

Manu National Park *About 75 miles northeast of Cuzco in Peru*

This rain forest is the largest biosphere reserve zone in South America. It has the highest documented diversity of life in the world, containing an estimated 8,000 plant species, 200 animal species and over 900 species of birds.

RAIN FOREST, BRAZIL

This belt of rain forest once extended along the coast of South America; today, only a small portion remains. Up to half of the plant species found here are not found anywhere else. The forest contains the largest variety of primates in South America—over 24 different species.

Itatiaia National Park *Located between Rio de Janeiro and São Paulo near of Itatiaia, Brazil*

This park, with its numerous hiking trails, is very accessible. Over 100 plants found here are endemic to the Atlantic rain forest. Itatiaia National Park is also home to the pale-throated three-toed sloth and the red-breasted toucan.

TRAVEL

The Pyramids Next Door
Mayan ruins are as magnificent as those in Egypt—and a lot closer

Scattered throughout Central America are more ancient cities and ruins than are found in all of Egypt. They are from the Mayan civilization, the most advanced and longest-lived in ancient America. Starting in 300 B.C., the Mayans built metropolises that rivaled those of Rome and Greece—complete with large pyramids, ornate palaces and temples. Mayan civilization was highly developed. Their libraries were legendary, and their calendar proved more accurate than that of the Spanish conquistadors. Their understanding of astronomy enabled them to predict lunar and solar eclipses. But, even before the conquistadores arrived, Mayan civilization began to decline because of war, it is surmised, and diminishing natural resources,

La Ruta Maya, also known as Mundo Maya, is a 1,500-mile route that runs through the lands of the Maya—western Honduras, northern Belize,

Guatemala, El Salvador and the Mexican states of Yucatán, Quintana Roo, Tabasco, Campeche and Chiapas. Mostly paved, the route is a modern creation, dedicated to the preservation of Mayan heritage and wildlife habitats. Below is a list of some of the most significant Mayan cities, which was compiled with the help of Gordon Willey, who was a professor of archaeology at Harvard, and Joyce Kelley, author of *An Archaeological Guide to Northern Central America: Belize, Guatemala, Honduras, and El Salvador*.

CALAKMUL, Campeche, Mexico

Calakmul was one of the largest Mayan cities. It is estimated that over 60,000 people have lived here at one time. One of the oldest Mayan sites, it was established around 1500 B.C. So far, 6,500 structures have been mapped at Calakmul, including a 175-foot-high, 500-square-foot pyramid. From the top of it one can see the Danta Pyramid at El Mirador, another preclassic Mayan city over 20 miles away. Until recently, Calakmul, located in a large jungle reserve, was reachable only by an overgrown jeep path. However, now a road has been built into the site, and travel time from the main road is only several hours.

CHICHÉN ITZÁ, Yucatán, Mexico

Over three million people visit Chichén Itzá each year; it is the most well-known and most extensively excavated Mayan city. Built around A.D. 500, it was the most important city in the late classic period. Between the 11th and 13th centuries, this was where some of the last great Mayan buildings were constructed. Of all the Mayan cities, Chichén Itzá has the most varied architecture and sculpture, due in part to the influence of the Toltec Indian civilization of central Mexico.

UXMAL, Yucatán, Mexico

Uxmal has some of the finest of the restored ruins and is considered by many to be the most beautiful of the Mayan cities. Many important satellite sites such as Kabah, Sayil and Labnó are nearby.

Uxmal is where Mayan civilization reached its apogee in the years between A.D. 800 and 1000. The Governor's Palace is testimony to the Mayan's knowledge of astronomy. The central doorway of this 24-room building is aligned with the path of the planet Venus. At the bright planet's southern solstice, the doorway is suffused with light illuminating the throne in the courtyard, as well as a temple on a hilltop 10 kilometers away.

Several hours' drive away is Mérida. Built by the Spanish in the 16th century, Mérida has fine examples of Spanish colonial architecture, excellent cuisine, a vibrant night-life, and is a good departure point for many day trips to the Gulf Coast.

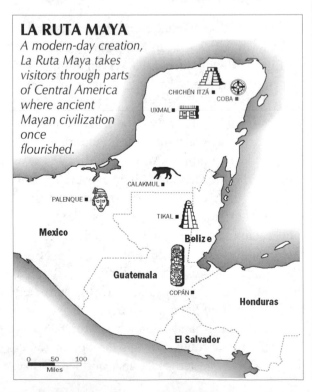

LA RUTA MAYA

A modern-day creation, La Ruta Maya takes visitors through parts of Central America where ancient Mayan civilization once flourished.

CHICHÉN ITZÁ ■
COBA ■
UXMAL ■
CALAKMUL ■
PALENQUE ■
TIKAL ■
Mexico
Belize
Guatemala
COPÁN ■
Honduras
El Salvador

0   50   100
Miles

COBA, Quintana Roo, Mexico

Located in a jungle, the mainly unexcavated ruins of Coba, connected by Mayan limestime causeways, cover an area of 20 square miles. From the 140-foot-high Nohoch Mul pyramid, the views across the jungle and of the other ruins are magnificent. Nearby is Tulum, a Mayan site by the sea, south of which are pristine beaches bordered by verdant jungles.

PALENQUE, Chiapas, Mexico

In 1952, an excavation uncovered the intact tomb of Lord Pacal, one of the greatest Mayan kings, who ruled the city in the seventh century. At winter solstice, the sun enters a doorway, hits the back wall and appears to descend the stairway into a tomb.

TIKAL NATIONAL PARK, Guatemala

Tikal was a great commercial and political power from 100 B.C. to A.D. 900. Plaza Mayor features well-restored buildings dating from 200 B.C. The 212-foot-tall temple is the second-tallest pyramid built by the Mayans. The area known as the Petén is one of the most remote on the Ruta Maya. Eighteen miles from Tikal is Flores, the regional capital of the Petén.

COPÁN, Honduras

The southernmost Mayan city, Copán lies in one of the most remote parts of Honduras. For more than 1,000 years, Copán was a center of culture and learning. The Hieroglyphic Stairway is composed of 2,500 blocks of stone, and records the history of 17 rulers of a single royal dynasty. Fine pottery, jewelry and jade carvings are on display at the Museo Regional de Arqueológica near the site.

Copán Ruinas, one of a number of interesting Spanish colonial villages in the area, is situated a few miles from the ruins. There are some small hotels here that offer simple but comfortable lodgings. About 10 miles from Copán is Agua Caliente, where one can swim in hot springs.

Into the Heart of Africa

There are ever more destinations for today's adventurer into the bush

For years, if you were heading out on a safari, you headed for the game parks of Kenya and Tanzania in East Africa—most notably Serengeti National Park, the Ngorongoro Conservation Area and Masai Mara Natural Reserve—where huge herds of animals still wander across the plains. Nowhere else in Africa could you see such a vast collection of wildlife in its natural habitat.

These days, however, others parts of Africa also beckon. The genocide in Rwanda and the civil war that ravaged Uganda are over, and outsiders are once again starting to visit the region, where gorillas and other primates can be seen. More notably, southern Africa (Namibia, Zimbabwe and Botswana) is increasingly popular.

Instead of the endless savannahs of eastern Africa, immense swamps and forests predominate in southern Africa. In general, safaris to the southern part of the continent offer more options for the active tourist—from walking safaris to expeditions on elephant and horseback. Also, night drives are much more common, an activity prohibited in national parks in eastern Africa. Such forays afford a different perspective on the wild kingdom, since some animals, like leopards, are nocturnal.

Below are some of the game-viewing spots that are not to be missed in Africa. Note: For a successful safari, timing is all. At certain times of the year, the animals you wish to see may be away on migration or dispersed amid thick vegetation during the rainy season, so plan ahead.

EAST AFRICA

KENYA has the highest concentrations of animals and tourists. Its biggest draw is the greatest game migration on the planet, which moves from the Serengeti in Tanzania up to the Masai Mara every year. Over a million wildebeests and hundreds of thousands of zebra can be found here from mid-July to mid-September. The best places to see game are in central Kenya at the national parks—Tsavo, Samburu, Amboseli and Masai Mara (which boasts the largest lion population in Africa).

Kenya is also one of the best places in the world to see birds; over 1,000 species of birds live here in a variety of different habitats. In addition, Kenya has some of the most varied and distinctive tribal cultures in Africa, including the Masai, who still maintain their traditional nomadic life.

TANZANIA has Kenya's game without the crowds. The Serengeti and the Ngorongoro Crater (the largest caldera in the world and the best place to see black rhino in Africa) abound with large herds of zebra and wildebeest. Like Kenya, tourists are restricted to safari vehicles in the national parks. For walking or canoe safaris, head south to the Selous Game Reserve, the largest wildlife preserve in Africa, uninhabited except for a half dozen small tourist camps.

UGANDA. This landlocked country is mostly forested and mountainous, with a terrain reminiscent of Asia—very green, with terraced farming. Having emerged from a time of terror and political instability in the 1980's, Uganda is one of the most exciting places to visit in Africa. It is the best place in Africa to see primates and also the only safe place (safe from warring humans, that is) where one can comfortably see gorillas. Visitors to the primate forests—the most notable of which is the Bwini or Impenetrable Forest—must be ready for hard hikes and prepared for occasional deluges of rain.

SOUTHERN AFRICA

BOTSWANA, one of the most popular safari countries in southern Africa, has incredible wildlife, comfortable isolated safari lodges and good transportation. Botswana has more intimate camps and lodges, which makes it a more expensive place to visit than other African countries. While much of the country is arid and desertlike, the Okavango delta, in the northern part of the country, is like a primordial oasis. The only inland delta in the world, the Okavango is a lush swamp whose numerous rivulets and waterways empty directly into the Kalahari desert; the best way to explore it is by canoe. It's also one of the few bodies of fresh water in Africa where westerners can swim without worrying about parasites. In addition, this wilderness contains more plant species than all the rain forests of West and Central Africa combined. Adjoining the Okavango, the Moremi Reserve and Chobe

Safari Travel Agents

To book lodges, safaris, and tented camps throughout Africa as well as make travel arrangements:

• **Abercrombie & Kent, Inc.**
   1520 Kensington Road, Suite 212
   Oak Brook, Illinois, 60523
   800-554-7016 or www.abercrombiekent.com

• **African Travel**
   1000 East Broadway, Glendale, Calif. 91205
   800–421–8907 or www.africantravel.com

• **Micato Safaris**
   15 West 26th Street, New York, N.Y. 10010
   212 545-7111 or www.micato.com

• **OverSeas Adventure Travel**
   629 Mt. Auburn St. Cambridge, Mass. 02138
   800–221–0814 or www.oattravel.com

• **Uncharted Outposts Inc.**
   9 Village Lane, Santa Fe, N.M. 87505
   888-995-0909 or www.unchartedoutposts.com

WHERE THE WILD THINGS ROAM
Africa's best game-watching parks:

KENYA: **1.** *Sibiloi NP* **2.** *Samburu-Isiolo and Shaba NR* **3.** *Nakuru* **4.** *Meru* **5.** *Masai Mara NR* **6.** *Nairobi NP* **7.** *Tsavo NP* **8.** *Amboseli NP*

TANZANIA: **9.** *Serengeti NP* **10.** *Ngorongoro Cons. Area* **11.** *Tarangire NP* **12.** *Gombe NP* **13.** *Mahale Mts. NP*

UGANDA: **14.** *Kibale FR*

ZAIRE: **15.** *Virunga NP* **16.** *Kahuzi Biega NP*

ZIMBABWE: **17.** *Mana Pools NP* **18.** *Hwange NP* **19.** *Gonarezhou NP*

BOTSWANA: **20.** *Chobe NP*

SOUTH AFRICA: **21**. *Kruger NP* **22.** *Hluhluwe and Umfosoli GR*

NAMIBIA: 23. *Etosha NP*

NOTE: NR = Nature reserve; NP = National park;
GR = Game reserve; FR = Forest reserve.

SOURCE: *The Safari Companion, A Guide to Watching African Mammals*, Richard Estes (Chelsea Green Publishing, 1993)

TRAVEL

National Park have one of the most varied and greatest concentrations of wildlife (including some of the largest elephant herds) in Africa. Botswana is also, together with Namibia, home to the majority of the 60,000 Bushmen in Africa.

ZIMBABWE. This has been one of the all-around best countries to go on a safari. Zimbabwe has traditionally had a good tourist infrastructure, excellent conservation programs and perhaps the widest variety of safari options, including walking, kayaking, houseboat safaris and some of the best white-water rafting in the world. Seven percent of the country is protected, and the national parks, especially Mana Pools, located on the Zambezi river gorge, offer opportunities to see one of the greatest concentrations of wildlife during the dry season. However, due to the deteriorating political situation, safety is now more of a concern.

ZAMBIA. More of a challenge to get to and travel through than other African countries, Zambia rewards the intrepid traveler. The Luangwa Valley is one of the most beautiful places in Africa. Crisscrossed by numerous rivers, the valley is home to many birds, African buffalo, hippos, crocodiles, zebras and elephants. Walking and night safaris are readily available.

MALAWI. There is not much tourism in Malawi, although there are numerous game-watching opportunities. Lake Malawi, which takes up a fifth of the country, contains over 300 varieties of fish, the greatest diversity of tropical freshwater fish of any lake in the world; it's also an excellent snorkeling spot. Zomba plateau, an enormous 8,000-foot plateau that topographically looks like Switzerland—except for the plethora of brilliantly colored orchids, and the leopards and antelope roaming about—can be explored on horseback.

Adventure

A Heck of a Trek
Nine classics not to be missed

Today, trekking has gone mainstream. Companies with glossy brochures offer deluxe trips to every imaginable corner of the globe. You can take your pick from a classic trek in Nepal to a pure wilderness experience in New Zealand. And you can pay Ritz-Carlton prices to sleep in tents under the stars.

The immense popularity of trekking is sparking environmental concerns. Once-pristine environments have become less so as trekkers have passed through. Cultures once isolated from outside influences now experience them with fair regularity.

We asked veteran trekker Robert Strauss, who has trekked on six continents and written numerous books on the subject, including *Adventure Trekking: A Handbook for Independent Travelers*, to pick what he considers to be the world's classic, still relatively pristine treks.

KENYA. A five-day trek to Point Lenana (16,350 feet) in Mt. Kenya National Park (camping or staying in mountain huts en route) can be done with or without porters and guides. Rain forest on the lower slopes gives way to bamboo groves that thin into moorland—and, at higher altitude, the extraordinary giant species of groundsel and lobelia. Wildlife in the area includes elephants, buffalo, monkeys and rock hyrax. Appropriate high-altitude experience and sufficient warm and waterproof gear are essential. Point Lenana is suitable for strong hikers without any climbing experience.

- **Africatours**
  800-23-KENYA or www.africasafaris.com
- **Tusker Trail & Safari Company**
  800-747-2728 or www.tusker.com

PERU. The Inca Trail, a once-secret passage between Cuzco and Machu Picchu, the legendary lost city of the Incas, was rediscovered in 1911. The three-day trek features high passes, forests and ancient ruins. It is strenuous in parts and often crowded, since it is easily the most well-known trekking destination in South America. The best time to go is in September

You can combine this with a second six-day trek, a circuit of Ausangate, the highest peak in the Vilcanota range, which threads its way through high passes with spectacular views, remote llama and alpaca pastures and finishes with a camp near relaxing, natural hot springs. This combo was featured as one of "the 25 trips of a lifetime" by *Outside* magazine in March 2002. Strenuous.

- **Geographic Expeditions**
  415-922-0448 or www.geoex.com
- **International Expeditions**
  800-633-4734 or www.ietravel.com
- **Southwind Adventures** 800-377-WIND or www.southwindadventures.com

VENEZUELA. In the southeast of the country is La Gran Sabana, a region renowned for its many *tepui*, or tablelike mountains of sandstone. The Roraima tepui rises 9,216 feet and is accessible via the village of San Francisco de Yuruaní. The trek itself takes about six days. The trail starts in

 **TIMELY TIPS**

Lost and Found

With a G.P.S., you'll always know where you're going

As Yogi Berra once famously said, "If you don't know where you're going, you're likely to end up somewhere else." That, of course, can often be the case when you are hiking.

Global Positioning System hand-held devices make finding your way effortless. G.P.S. devices use timing signals from a network of 24 satellites to calculate latitude, longitude and altitude and to provide information on how to get to where you want to be.

Restrictions on consumer G.P.S. devices were lifted by the Defense Department, which operates the system, at the turn of the 21st century. As a result, the accuracy of consumer models improved from 330 feet to 30 feet under the best operating conditions. The newest devices can receive signals from the Wide Area Augmentation System, or WAAS, a system designed for airplane guidance, which improve accuracy to within 15 feet.

Navigation companies are now tailoring lightweight hand-held devices to the growing outdoor recreational market. G.P.S. signals are weak and are easily blocked in cities by large buildings and other obstructions—even car roofs and tinted windows. G.P.S. devices need contact with at least three satellites to provide the latitude and longitude of your position; at least four satellites are required for a reading that includes altitude. The devices on the market are designed for a range of outdoor activities including hiking, camping, biking and mountaineering. Models loaded with marine navigation aids can also be used for fishing and boating.

Most top-end G.P.S. hand-held devices have mapping, which allows you to view road and topographical maps while navigating. Using an on-screen map, for example, you can locate your position and follow your progress by marking waypoints. Such a mapping unit will not only guide you during the hike, but also give you driving directions to the trailhead from your front door.

You can get more map data by hooking the G.P.S. device up to a PC and downloading more content. Because road maps lack the detail necessary for outdoor use, hikers will probably want the MapSource U.S. TOPO map, which is similar to United States Geological Survey topographic paper maps, and shows detailed geographic features like elevation contours, as well as hiking trails and campgrounds.

Of course, for many hikers, there is no substitute for a good topographical map and an old-fashioned magnetic compass. Experts advise, in fact, that you always bring maps and a compass along, because they never run out of power. But as long as you keep a spare set of batteries in your pack, a hand-held G.P.S. unit will make it hard to get lost.

—Bonnie Tsui

flat savannah, rises through rain forest, passing waterfalls and streams before the final steep ascent to the stepped plateau. It is strenuous in parts; take warm gear for the cold nights, rain gear and insect repellent. Hiring local guides is advisable. Overnighting en route consists of sleeping under rock overhangs or in caves.

• **Condor Journey and Adventures** +1-318-775 0190 or www.condorjourneys-adventures.com

• **Southwind Adventures** 800-377-WIND or www.southwindadventures.com

TASMANIA. The delightful island state of Tasmania is a bushwalking magnet. Weather can change with amazing speed, so be prepared with cold-weather and wet-weather gear. In the center of the island, the popular 50-mile-long Overland Track in the Cradle Mountain-Lake St. Clair National Park can be covered in a week or less. The trailheads at

Cynthia Bay and Waldheim, at the southern and northern ends of the park respectively, are served by a shuttle bus during the prime summer season. Permits are issued by park offices at both points.

- **Tasman Bush Tours** 011 (03) 6423-2335 or www.tasmanbushtours.com

NEW ZEALAND. Tramping (the New Zealand term for hiking/trekking) has become a passion for the locals. At the southern end of the South Island lie Mt. Aspiring National Park and Fiordland National Park, which are straddled by the Routeburn Track. This very popular three-day tramp has great alpine scenery and passes through valleys covered by rain forest. There is a booking system for huts and campsites on the Routeburn. (Less crowded tracks in the same area are The Greenstone and The Caples.) Information is available from the Department of Conservation (D.O.C.) in Queenstown, which provides a transport base to access the northern end of the trail; Te Anau is the nearest town at the southern end.

- **Down Under Answers**
  800-788-6685 or www.duatravel.com
- **New Zealand Destinations Unlimited**
  011 649 414 1685 or www.holiday.co.nz

GREENLAND. A demanding terrain, lack of trails (for navigation at these latitudes you'll need to adjust your compass) and fickle weather make this destination at the Arctic Circle a challenge even for experienced trekkers. The five- to six-day trek between Qaqortoq, the major town in southern Greenland, and Igaliku offers the scenic variety of icebergs, bays, waterfalls and boulder fields. There are also Norse church ruins dating back to medieval times.

- **Greenland Travel**, Denmark +45-3313-1011; fax: +45-3313-7347 or www.greenlandtravel.com
- **Black Feather**, Canada
  888-849-7668 or www.blackfeather.com

ALASKA. Three-quarters of Alaska is protected wilderness. Backcountry trekking through Denali National Park is regulated through zoning and permit quotas. Free permits are issued a day in advance by the Visitor Access Center. Once you have your permit, a shuttle bus will drop you off at your assigned zone. The park has no marked trails; hikers find their way with topographical maps. Denali, which is dominated by Mount McKinley, America's highest mountain at 20,320 feet, is accessible from Anchorage by car, bus, and rail.

- **Sunlight North Expeditions**, Anchorage 907-346-2027 or www.sunlightnorth.co
- **Alaska Rainforest Tours**, Juneau 907-463-3466 or www.alaskarainforesttours.com

NEPAL. The main gateway for the Annapurna region is the town of Pokhara. The Annapurna Conservation Area Project, based in Pokhara, provides regional support for minimizing impact on the environment. The Annapurna Circuit is a trekking tour de force: it passes through alpine forests to arid semidesert characteristic of Tibet; crosses over the Thorong La pass with dazzling views at 17,650 feet; and drops into the Kali Gandaki gorge, the world's deepest. The full circuit takes around 18 days for seasoned trekkers putting in some seven hours of hiking each day. Be prepared for the effects of high altitude and a possible wait to cross the pass if it's snowbound. The trail has plenty of teahouses and lodges en route.

- **Himalayan High Treks** 800-455-8735 or www.himalayanhightreks.com

PAKISTAN. The northernmost region of Pakistan, where four mountain ranges (Himalaya, Hindu Kush, Pamirs and Karakorum) meet, boasts the largest number of high peaks in the world. The Concordia trek, which passes through this area, is rated as one of the world's best. Because of the travel restrictions here, your best bet is to go on a trip organized through a tour operator. From the trailhead in Askole, the trek takes two weeks or longer, crossing awesome wilderness and glaciers into a natural amphitheater where colossal mountains (K2, Gasherbrum, Chogolisa, Broad Peak and others) soar above you.

- **Snow Lion Expeditions** 800-525-TREK or www.snowlion.com
- **Wilderness Travel** 800-368-2794 or www.wilderness.travel.com

Life Is Better in Bhutan

Magic mountains and Buddhist monasteries mix in a Himalayan kingdom

To Western eyes Bhutan can seem like a precious relic from a lost century. Slightly bigger than Switzerland, and more rugged, it is significantly less populated—some estimates are as low as 700,000 people—and heavily forested. Most Bhutanese own and work small farms. Automobiles are rare; much of the country is connected only by walking trails. There are only two major roads, and they were built in the last 25 years. Journeys by foot of three hours or more between villages are common.

So it was not surprising when Bhutan's health minister, Lyngpo Sangay Ngedup, undertook a 350-mile trek from the eastern town of Tashigang to the Bhutanese capital, Thimphu, along a track over mountain passes more than 13,000 feet high in 2002 to raise money for local health clinics (see map, above). The trek takes about 15 days, with 8 to 10 hours' walking every day, and has no signposts. The majority of it is through the jungle, the habitat of leopards, wild boars, tigers, yeti, bears and snakes, and flora and fauna unrivaled in the Himalayas. (Bhutan's forests, which cover 72 percent of its land, are in fact increasing.)

As in medieval Europe, religion permeates Bhutan, the last remaining independent Buddhist kingdom in the Himalayas. Twelve-foot-tall prayer flags flutter on lonely ridges. Small temples called *chortens* squat beside trails and settlements. Austere *dzongs*, fortress-monasteries, preside over deep valleys.

This pristine country is the new must-see destination in southern Asia. It is attracting those in search of a spiritual journey, a hiking adventure or just a chance to experience a place before the rest of the world gets there. The number of visitors to Bhutan increased to 9,000 in 2004, a third of them Americans. Until 1972, outsiders weren't even allowed into the hermetic kingdom.

Unlike, say, Nepal, Bhutan has taken a cautious approach to tourism. From the start, travelers were required to get visas and book with an authorized tour operator (independent travel in Bhutan is not permitted), and they had to pay a minimum per-day fee ($200 in high season; low-budget backpackers need not apply). Much of the fee goes to the government.

TIMELY TIPS

Into the Tiger's Lair

The Taktsang monastery, perched inside a recess on the face of a dark cliff in the Paro Valley, is at once Bhutan's most imposingly dramatic and holy site. According to myth, Guru Rimpoche, the eighth-century founder of Tibetan Buddhism, transformed his favorite consort into a tiger and flew on her back to this site. Guru Rimpoche meditated in a cave on the same rock face for three months, and when he had finished, descended into the Paro Valley to bring Buddhism to Bhutan. Six centuries later, the first temple was built on the site of the current monastery, which, despite its traditional elegance, has been variously destroyed and rebuilt over the centuries.

✔ Though the ascent to Taktsang Lhakang (the Tiger's Lair) is a strenuous hike at an elevation of 3,000 meters, aesthetic and spiritual rewards abound. Stop at the charming teahouse on the way up for a wonderful view of the monastery and a cup of yak butter tea.

✔ **Geographic Expeditions,** 2627 Lombard Street, San Francisco, Calif. 94123 (800-777-8183 or 415-922-0448; fax: 415-346-5535; e-mail: info@geoex.com) offers a variety of trips to Bhutan.

—James Hirschfeld

Bhutanese guest houses, though they might offer the charm of stenciled walls and handpainted furniture, have been notoriously lacking in hotel amenities (and even, at times, adequate heating). But resorts in the settlement of Paro are upping the ante: one, the Amankora Paro, is the first of six spa-equipped lodges being built in Bhutan by the Singapore-based Amanresorts chain.

At peace with itself and its neighbors, Bhutan isn't marred by political conflict or extreme poverty.

There are no beggars or crime, and one can have friendly contact with the Bhutanese people (their schools teach English). Although they allow satellite TV and cellphones, the government has mandated that women wear the traditional *kira*, a Bhutanese kimono, and men the *gho*, a smocklike wrapper that comes to the knees, in schools and public offices. (They were the first country to ban the sale of tobacco.) Bhutan's traditional culture, which revolves around Buddhism and is preserved in the life of its pastoral hamlets, remains largely intact. This is in large measure due to its revered king, who has instituted a policy of "gross national happiness" as a way to measure progress in his land

—Jane Margolies, Barbara Crossette and Mary Tannen

Hiking All Day, Pampered at Night

If you like nurture with your nature, try exploring Europe by foot

With all due respect to campfires, cowboy coffee and "roughing it," it's hard to beat ending a good day of hiking with a glass of beer, a comfortable bed and a dinner whose preparation doesn't include the direction "just add boiling water." For those who lean toward a little nurture with their nature, Europe is the answer to a hiker's prayers. In almost every old-world country there are civilized multiday hikes sprinkled with lodges, inns or mountain refuges: treks through France's Alps, walks along Hadrian's Wall in England, trips across glaciers in Switzerland—you name it. Here are a few options—classics as well as new destinations—for the traveler who wants to explore Europe on foot:

HADRIAN'S WALL PATH, Britain

In A.D. 122, the Emperor Hadrian ordered a 73-mile-long wall to be built near what is now the border with Scotland to separate northernmost

Roman Britain from the "barbarians" beyond. Those walls and turrets today are a World Heritage Site, a lichen-speckled vestige of Roman domination reaching from Wallsend in the east to Bowness-on-Solway in the west. In 2003, Hadrian's Wall was given another designation, as an 84-mile national trail. Although many people walk the route west, as many guidebooks are written going in that direction, there are decided advantages to walking to the east to keep the prevailing winds (and occasional lashing rains) at your back.

A six-day self-guided hike begins among the salt marshes and peat bogs of the Solway Firth estuary, and soon crosses the pastures and villages of Cumbria. The trip's highlight is a section through Northumberland National Park between Banks and Housesteads, where hikers ramble through rough grazing uplands and rolling moors that are home to some of some of the best preserved sections of the wall. Each day, outfitters move your luggage to your next bed and breakfast destination. Eventually, the trail drops into lowlands again, and hikers walk beside the River Tyne and through the industrial city of Newcastle, and finally end in Wallsend, where Hadrian's legacy disappears under the accretion of centuries of change.

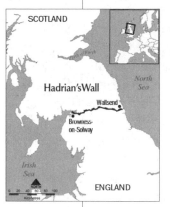

GRUNT FACTOR: Stages are 12 to 15 miles daily for a total of 84 miles, across mostly flat ground, but with some short, steep pitches and steps. For an additional cost, rest days may be added.

SIGNPOST: Trips can be arranged all year. The cost, approximately $620, includes full English breakfast, lodging maps and detailed directions as well as daily luggage transfer. **INFORMATION:** +44 (0) 17684 80451 or www.contours.co.uk

GRAN PARADISO NATIONAL PARK, Italy

Originally a royal hunting reserve, Gran Paradiso became Italy's first national park in 1922. Now this sanctuary of 13,000-foot peaks, plunging valleys, larch forests, ibex herds and wildflower meadows near the French border is the happy hunting ground of waffle-tread-wearing hikers. One recommended itinerary traverses a corner of this 173,000-acre park, from Valgrisenche to Cogne.

Starting at the park's westernmost valley, groups can spend a week crossing high passes and traipsing through alpine meadows of nodding edelweiss and mountain lilies, where golden eagles waver in the thermals overhead. Each afternoon, you arrive either at a rustic, high-mountain hut—usually above tree line—that's run by the Italian Alpine Club or, at midweek, the Albergo Savoia, which is in a valley low enough to offer luxuries like showers—and plenty of good Italian wine and polenta. Those who sign on for a longer journey can pick up crampons and an ice ax near trip's end and climb the 13,323-foot Gran Paradiso; though it is the highest peak in the park, the ascent isn't especially steep (no previous mountaineering experience required) until the last 100 feet. Trips end at the village of Cogne, and a visit to a nearby Alpine botanical garden.

GRUNT FACTOR: Four to seven hours of moderately difficult hiking daily, with 1,500 to 3,000 feet of daily elevation gain.

SIGNPOST: The cost, $1,200 to $1,500, varying with group size (four to eight people) and includes six to eight nights' lodging (depending on group's desires), breakfast and dinner, guide fees and use of any gear. **INFORMATION:** (+1-39-3472) 320106 or www.mountainsandmore.com

TRAVEL

CORSICA

Though it is hardly news to Europeans, Americans have only recently awakened to the hiking opportunity on the rugged Mediterranean island of Corsica, France's "mountain in the sea." Those who don't want to commit to the GR20—the spectacular and arduous 130-mile route that many claim is Europe's best backpacking trail—aren't out of luck. One outfitter—Active Travel, based in Austin, Tex.—offers eight-day self-guided trips that give hikers tastes of the GR20 and other trails, and also lets them experience the comforts of rural village life.

Hikers lace up their boots at Calacuccia, a lakeside town of homes with thick stone walls. Equipped with detailed itineraries and maps, they spend the next several days in pleasant repetition: Each morning they walk out of their inns (several nights are spent in former Franciscan monasteries and former convents) and right into the piney woods, passing through golden countryside with braying donkeys, remote mountain villages and high country where some shepherds still take their flocks to forage during the hot Mediterranean summers. A local tour company representative transfers bags to the next inn, allowing hikers to travel light and at their own pace. The trip concludes by dropping down to the seaside villages of Porto or Piana, where hikers can snorkel in blue waters.

 INSIDE INFO

Meanwhile, in Japan...

○ Mount Fuji, the 12,388-foot volcanic mountain about two hours' drive southwest of Tokyo, is open to climbers during July and August.

○ An estimated 200,000 people make the climb during those months.

GRUNT FACTOR: Mellow to moderate, ranging from four miles of hilly hiking a day to eight miles of flat walking.

SIGNPOST: The cost of $900 a person, based on double occupancy, includes seven nights' lodging on the island, most breakfasts and dinners, luggage transport between towns and other assistance. INFORMATION: 830-868-2502 or www.franceactivetravel.com

BERNESE OBERLAND, Switzerland

Only in Europe, with its grand hotel tradition, could a hiker who's meandering down a glacier so big it would be at home in Alaska encounter a "hut" that sleeps 100, serves hot meals and cold beer, and has a sundeck crowded with card-playing Germans. More than two dozen huts large and small pepper the Bernese Oberland area of Switzerland's Alps, and they're not just for hardcore mountaineers.

One possible itinerary starts from the cog train station at the Jungfraujoch at 11,333 feet. You step out onto the glaciers, and then spend a good chunk of the next few days "on the rocks," wending your way around the crevasses of huge, nearly flat glaciers like the 14-mile-long Great Aletsch Glacier, the longest in the Alps. Hot meals await each night at different huts, like the Finsteraarhorn Hut, on the flanks of the 14,022-foot Finsteraarhorn, the highest peak in the Bernese Oberland. Some outfitters require clients to wear harnesses and ropes, and spiky crampons on their feet for safety, but no previous climbing experience is needed.

GRUNT FACTOR: Four to six hours of mellow walking per day, though at altitudes of 9,000 to 12,000 feet, and sleeping at high elevation can be fitful.

SIGNPOST: Price is $635 a day, at 1.27 Swiss francs to the dollar, for groups of three or four; less expensive

TIMELY TIPS

Hut-to-Hut *en Haut*

Hut-to-hut or inn-to-inn hiking can include guided or self-guided hikes organized by companies that arrange for such lodging, or you can hike on your own where there is a system of huts or inns in place. In the Alps, dormitory-style huts are generally owned by Alpine clubs and leased to individuals who run them, providing blankets and simple meals; snacks and drinks are often sold.

If you prefer to hike on your own, a good source of information on hut systems and trails around the world is the Lonely Planet Walking Guides series, with 22 guides to hiking from Alaska to the Hindu Kush; they may be ordered at www.lonelyplanet.com. Or, you can request information from local tourist offices.

✔ **The Austrian National Tourist Office** (212-944-6880 or www.austria.info) provides a free guide for hiking in the Austrian Alps. One of their listings, Wanderweg Holidays (800-270-2577, or www.wanderwegholidays.com) has four types of programs, including self-guided "hiking without luggage" tours. Hikes are designed for all ages.

✔ **Distant Journeys,** (888-845-5781, www.distantjourneys.com) has been offering guided and self-guided hikes for 18 years in Europe. Self-guided, hut-to-hut hikes described as strenuous include the Mont Blanc Massif (5 to 12 days) and the Dolomites (6 to 9 days).

✔ **Mountain Sobek** (800-227-2384; 888-687-6235 or www.mtsobek.com) offers a strenuous 10-day guided hut-to-hut hike of the classic Haute Route (Chamonix to Zermatt) in the Alps, in addition to treks in many other countries.

—Florence Stickney

TRAVEL

for bigger groups. This does not include $51 per person per day for hut lodging, dinners and breakfasts. INFORMATION: www.swissrockguides.com

JULIAN ALPS, Slovenia

Lovers of the great outdoors are starting to discover the natural beauty that was obscured for decades behind the Iron Curtain. Some trips to Slovenia (which joined the European Union in 2004) explore the limestone massif of the Julian Alps, which straddle that country and northern Italy.

While the Alps here are not so high as in the west, they're perhaps more conducive to high-ridge rambling. From near the lakeside town of Bled, you can ascend into Triglav National Park and spend the next few days traversing a 6,000-foot ridgeline, with views down into green valleys that are rioting with wildflowers. Hikers scramble up rocks, and occasionally cross short but sheer portions of the route using via ferrata (iron way), a popular European form of hiking in which walkers put on harnesses and attach themselves to fixed cables.

At one point, the trail drops into a high, hidden valley of seven lakes, each a different-colored gem in a stark setting, before arriving at the Prehodavci Hut (6,790 feet), one of the wooden, dorm-style mountain huts where most of the trek's nights are spent. The trip reaches its crescendo when hikers awaken early at the Kredarica Hut to climb Mount Triglav, at 9,390 feet the highest peak in Slovenia.

GRUNT FACTOR: Four to eight miles of hiking per day, with moderate elevation gains. Hikers should be comfortable with a little bit of scrambling and some exposure to heights.

SIGNPOST: $1,665 price (plus $85 insurance) includes guide, two nights in hotels, five nights in mountain huts, plus breakfasts and dinners. **INFORMATION:** 800-497-9675 or www.keadventure.com

—Christopher Solomon

Your Personal Tour de France

Bike tours with less haute cuisine, more muscle

Bike tours through Europe used to connote days of gentle exercise followed by nights of gut-busting culinary display at luxury hotels. "People were more obsessed with staying in six-star chateaux than in hotels conducive to better biking," says Cari Gray, a spokeswoman for Butterfield & Robinson. "That trend seems to be waning."

Say farewell to the foie gras. These days, bicycle tour companies are pushing longer and more difficult trips that follow the great cycling races of Europe, fulfilling their clientele's desire to break a sweat and firm up their quadricep muscles even while taking in the French countryside.

Those in the industry call it "the Lance effect." In the wake of Lance Armstrong's seventh Tour de France win in 2005, cycling as a sport is growing more and more popular; and bike tour companies like Butterfield & Robinson, Trek Travel and Backroads are finding that customers are increasingly interested in following in the treads of the greats,

especially people in their 30's, 40's and 50's."

Cyclists who wish to fantasize can do a Tour de France trip in July, which follows the route that the pros will take, albeit at a more leisurely pace. Although Butterfield & Robinson claims to be the first to have offered such a tour, no company is now without one. Trek Travel, the tour company affiliated to Trek Bicycles, which is already associated with Lance Armstrong, says that fully a quarter of its business is now in Tour de France trips. But with the Tour de France route already saturated, companies are expanding their offerings to include other famous (and scenic) European races.

Trek Travel, already the most physically challenging of the bike tour companies, has also added routes that follow the popular European races Giro d'Italia in May and Vuelta a España in September; as well as a route in Girona, Spain, where tour cyclists go to practice in the off season. "It's to capture people who want to ride where the pros ride. They can ride hard in a place that's new to group trips," says Elizabeth Witzke, a Trek spokeswoman.

Even nonprofessional routes are becoming more difficult, thanks to the optional challenge days many bike tour companies are adding to their regular trips. Butterfield & Robinson now offers an optional day when participants can bike 63 miles rather than the normal 25; and Backroads offers a day where avid cyclists can bike up to 100 miles, or on a route with mountain elevations.

To complement the more challenging terrain, tour companies are simultaneously reducing their five-star hotel offerings and replacing them instead with hotels that are slightly more modest but more conveniently located for biking. Similarly, meals that used to require their own kind of endurance have been replaced by lighter fare. Backroads, for example, has added a new category of family-style "casual inns" that are comfortable rather than luxurious.

—Janelle Brown

2005 TOUR DE FRANCE ROUTE

Slow Boats Through Europe

With your craft moving at a snail's pace, you won't miss a thing

In ancient times, before roads, canals and rivers were the major thoroughfares of Europe. Almost all the major cities of Europe were built on the banks of a river. Canals are hardly the avenues of commerce they once were, but they haven't fallen into total disuse. Pleasure boats and refitted barges laden with tourists now ply the waterways. At 8 to 12 mph, the scenery hardly goes whizzing by—and that's the beauty and charm of this antiquated mode of travel. The canals pass through some of the oldest and most picturesque parts of many European towns. It's possible for passengers to disembark for a leisurely walk or bicycle ride. The quarters on board have been modernized. Depending on the barge, the food can be of gourmet standard.

There are several barge options: Hotel barges are the most leisurely way to go; you don't have to maneuver boats into locks, and meals, cocktails and excursions are included. Less pricey are self-driven barges, which accommodate 4 to 10 people. Many of these are converted commercial vessels and can be steered by a beginner, after a minimal amount of instruction. We asked Hugh McKnight, one of the pioneers in the self-drive barge vacation and the author of many books on barges, including *Cruising French Waterways* and *Slow Boat Through Germany*, to recommend the continent's best barge trips.

ENGLAND

Leeds and Liverpool Canal. This early-19th-century waterway in the north of England connects the east and west coasts via the rugged moorland scenery of Yorkshire and Lancashire. The canal features stone-built locks, many manually operated swing bridges and appealing small mill towns.

River Thames. A historic and beautiful river with locks and weirs, crossing southern England from London to Gloucestershire and the Cotswolds. Famous towns and cities include Windsor (an 11th-century royal castle), Henley (Europe's premier rowing regatta) and the university center of Oxford.

SCOTLAND

Caledonian Canal. This early-19th-century engineering feat provides a coast-to-coast navigation through the Scottish Highlands from Fort William to Inverness. Spectacular "staircase" (multiple-chambered) locks and lengths of artificial canal link a series of natural lakes, including Loch Ness, renowned for its elusive monster.

IRELAND

River Shannon. The longest waterway in the British Isles, navigable from the south coast and via lakes large and small to the border of Northern Ireland. A 19th-century canal has been restored to provide a link with the huge island-studded Lough Erne.

FRANCE

Canal du Midi Route. Together with the Canal lateral à la Garonne, the largely 17th-century Canal du Midi provides a navigable link through southern France from the Mediterranean to the Atlantic. Locks, buildings and aqueducts are all over 300 years old.

There is no rushing a river. When you go there, you go at the pace of the water and that pace ties you into a flow that is older than life on this planet.

Jeff Rennicke, author of *River Days*

• • •

TRAVEL

Rent a Canal Cruiser

- **Crown Blue Line Ltd.** *Britain, France, Netherlands, also Erie Canal, U.S.A.*
  888-355-9491 or cblusa@crownblueline.com

- **Hoseasons Holidays** *Britain and France.*
  Sunway House, Lowestoft, Suffolk, NR32 3LT, Great Britain
  +1 44 1 502 502 588 or www.hoseasons.co.uk

- **Andrew Brock Travel Ltd.** *France, Netherlands and Germany.*
  29A Main Street, Lyddington, Oakham, Rutland LE 15 9 LR   +1 44 1 572 821 330 or www.coromandelabt.com

- **Emerald Star Line** *Irish waterways.*
  980 Awald Road, Suite 302, Annapolis, Md. 21403 800-992-0291 or www.emeraldstar.ie

River Meuse. From its upper reaches near the city of Nancy, this canalized river is one of the most beautiful in all Europe, especially as it passes through the Ardennes forests near the border with Belgium.

Waterways of Alsace. The Canal de la Marne au Rhin and associated waterways in the northeastern part of the country have a Germanic character. Radar-operated locks are totally automatic as the route passes through pine forests in the valley of the Zorn River.

GERMANY

River Rhine. The Rhine runs for 640 miles through Europe. The uppermost reaches (Strasbourg to Switzerland) are canalized with giant ship locks. Elsewhere, it flows unimpeded, especially through the castle-filled Rhine Gorge (Bingen to Koblenz). Many large cruise ships ply the river, taking four to five days to cover the best parts.

River Lahn. The Lahn is a Rhine tributary, branching off near Koblenz and terminating in the cathedral city of Limburg. Although the river is only 40 miles long, a return journey can easily fill a week, for every one of the towns and villages en route is well worth exploring.

Mecklenburg Lakes. This is a complicated network of interconnected lakes north of Berlin in former East Germany. The area has been practically untouched by development since the 1930's, though that may be changing.

White Water Runs Through It
Ten rafting journeys for the whole family

White-water rafting isn't for the faint of heart, but it isn't just for daredevils, either. Outfitters all across the country now offer trips for families. Children generally need to be 11 and up, as well as reasonably good swimmers. But those are the only requirements, plus perhaps an ample supply of adrenaline.

We asked Jeff Bennett, author of *The Complete Whitewater Rafter*, for his picks of the 10 best white-water rafting trips for families, along with the best guides.

SOUTH FORK OF THE AMERICAN RIVER
California • 21 miles • Class III
This stretch of California river has dozens of Class II and III rapids, rich gold-era history, and easy access to big cities. Its sunshine and scenic rolling hills makes for the perfect family trip. The big thrills happen at the river's two Class III rapids, Troublemaker and Satan's Cesspool.

- **Beyond Limits Adventures** 800-234-7238 or www.rivertrip.com
- **Tributary Whitewater Tours** 916-346-6812 or www.whitewatertours.com

- **Whitewater Voyages** 800-488-7238 or whitewatervoyages.com

DESCHUTES RIVER

Oregon • 13 to 98 miles • Class III

Running through the heart of Oregon's high-desert country, the Deschutes River provides a bouncy one-day jaunt down the crowded Maupin section, or a two- to five-day canoeing trip down its more remote corridors. Stair-stepped basalt cliffs, grassy meadows and world-class fishing holes add to the experience.

- **Sage Canyon River & Ewing's Whitewater** 800-538-7238 or www.sagecanyonriverco.com
- **High Desert River Outfitters** 800-962-3327 or www.highdesertriver.com

SALMON RIVER, Upper Main

Idaho • up to 35 miles • Classes II to III +

Just 90 minutes north of Sun Valley, the headwaters of the Salmon River cut a path through the Sawtooth National Recreation Area. The Salmon's emerald currents slip past smooth granite boulders and towering pines, occasionally erupting into a series of big roller-coaster waves.

- **The River Company** 800-398-0346 or www.therivercompany.com
- **Triangle C Ranch Whitewater** 800-303-6258 or www.trianglecranch.net
- **White Otter Outdoor Adventures** 208-726-4331 or www.whiteotter.com

SNAKE RIVER (Grand Teton)

Wyoming • 30 miles • Classes I to II

One of the best ways to soak in the breathtaking beauty of Grand Teton National Park is to float the Snake River downstream from Jackson Lake. You can gaze at distant spires or search the banks for moose, bears, otters and a variety of waterfowl.

- **Barker-Ewing Float Trips** 800-365-1800 or barkerewing.com
- **Fort Jackson Float Trips** 800-735-8430

COLORADO RIVER, Glenwood Canyon

Colorado • 10 to 15 miles • Classes II to III

Just three hours from downtown Denver, the Glenwood Canyon section of the Upper Colorado River carves a narrow, cliff-lined gorge alongside Interstate 70. Layers of sandstone, limestone, and granite rise from the riverbed, while cavalcades of big waves accent the toughest rapids.

- **Blue Sky Adventures** 970-945-6605 or www.blueskyadventure.com
- **Timberline Tours** 800-831-1414 or www.timberlinetours.com

 INSIDE INFO

A Quick Guide to Whitewater Rapids

River conditions can vary widely and unpredictably. The following ratings were developed to give those unfamiliar with a river a feel for what they are getting into—before they get into it.

- ○ **CLASS I**: Flat water, some current.
- ○ **CLASS II**: Small waves.
- ○ **CLASS III**: Big waves, requires maneuvering through "hydraulic holes" in which the water breaks back on itself over a rock.
- ○ **CLASS IV**: Big waves, many rocks, and very fast, powerful water. Requires precise maneuverability. Not fun to swim in if you make a mistake.
- ○ **CLASS V**: Pushing the limits of navigability, should be done only by experts. Extremely steep gradient of river: 30- to 40-foot drops. Mistakes or capsizing will result in injury or possibly death.
- ○ **CLASS VI**: Pushing the absurd. Paddlers on the West Coast define it as not runnable. Those on the East Coast recommend it only for experts, lunatics, or both. Injury or death is a distinct possibility.

The Ultimate River-Rafting Trip

Going down the Colorado through the Grand Canyon

A rafting trip through the Grand Canyon, along 226 or 277 (depending on where you get off) unspoiled miles of the Colorado River, is the longest and wildest river trip in the lower 48 states.

Nothing matches the magnitude of the Grand Canyon and the stupendous force that created it. Along the edge of the canyon is writ the geologic history of the last 2 billion years—from the relatively recent Jurassic period, 1.2 million years old, to the bottom layer of Vishnu rock, at approximately 2 billion years, some of the oldest rock in the world.

Three-quarters of the trips down the river are via motorized boats, which whisk though the canyon in about 6 days, but the best way to go is on nonmotorized boats, because they don't interfere with the majestic quiet of the canyon. It takes 12 to 18 days to make the trip that way.

The most common type of nonmotorized craft are oar boats, where one or two river guides control the oars while passengers sit back and take in the scenery. For more adventurous types who want an active participatory experience, a few companies run paddle boats where everyone paddles.

Rafting down the canyon may be the experience of a lifetime, but many people have to wait part of a lifetime to do it. The number of people allowed each year had been limited to around 22,000 per year, but as of 2007, the number of trips allowed will increase to around 24,000. Commercial trips are allowed on the river from May 1 to mid-September. For a commercial trip that averages about 28 passengers, you have to plan at least a year in advance. If you are an experienced rafter, you can apply for a permit, but these days, the average wait for private trips is 12 to 15 years. The best times to go are in the spring and the fall, when it's less crowded, and more temperate. Average summer highs are 106 degrees.

For more information: Call Rivers and Oceans (800-473-4576 or www.rivers-oceans.com) a central booking agency for rafting outfitters and availability for the Grand Canyon.

RIO GRANDE, State Park & Racecourse Sections
New Mexico • 6.5 to 10.8 miles • Classes II to III+

The Rio Grande River rises along the eastern flanks of the southern Colorado Rockies, then flows 1,887 miles south to the Gulf of Mexico. Near Taos, N.M., it enters a spectacular and challenging gorge known as the Taos Box. To catch a taste of the Box, but without the hazards of big rapids, families and the less adventuresome can paddle the Rio Grande's state park and racecourse sections near the quaint town of Pilar.

- **Far Flung Adventures** 800-359-4138 or www.farflung.com
- **New Wave Rafting Company** 505-984-1444 or www.newwaverafting.com

KENNEBEC RIVER
Maine • 6 to12 miles • Classes III to IV+

Controlled releases from the Central Maine Power Company's Harris Station Dam guarantee reliable summertime flows, while memorable rapids like Magic Falls ensure tons of excitement. For a more sedentary experience through the Kennebec wilderness, run the Carry Brook section.

- **New England Outdoor Center** 800-634-7238 or www.neoc.com
- **North Country Rivers** 800-348-8871 or www.ncrivers.com

YOUGHIOGHENY RIVER
Pennsylvania • 7.5 miles • Classes II to IV

The lower Youghiogheny traces a serpentine

path through the Laurel Mountains near Ohiopyle State Park. It alternates between challenging rapids and calm pools. Although scheduled launch times help keep the river traffic in check, plan your trip ahead of time; over 100,000 people run it every year!

- **Mountain Streams & Trails** 800-723-8669 or www.mtstreams.com
- **White Water Adventures** 800-992-7238 or www.wwaraft.com
- **Wilderness Voyageurs** 800-272-4141 or www.wilderness-voyageurs.com

OCOEE RIVER

Tennessee • 4.5 miles • Class III to IV

The Ocoee has long been a favorite among southeastern rafters. A healthy gradient and an endless assortment of boulders combine to form nearly continuous rapids on the section between the Ocoee Diversion Dam and its powerhouse downstream.

- **Nantahala Outdoor Center** 800-232-7238 or www.noc.com
- **Ocoee Outdoors** 800-533-7767 or www.ocoee-outdoors.com
- **Southeastern Expeditions** 800-868-7238 or www.southeasternexpeditions.com

NANTAHALA RIVER

North Carolina • 8 miles • Classes II to III

The Nantahala, just east of Great Smoky Mountains National Park, runs along a valley thick with rhododendron, mountain laurel and princess trees. Nantahala Falls (a sharp Class III+) highlights the trip.

- **Nantahala Outdoor Center** 800-232-7238 or www.noc.com
- **USA Raft** 800-872-7238 or www.usaraft.com/nc.htm
- **Wildwater Ltd.** 800-451-9972 or www.wildwaterrafting.com

Sites for the Intrepid Traveler

Eight emerging destinations

As the well-known traveler Richard Bangs wrote, "adventure across the ages—in style, purpose and destination—has rarely suffered stasis. Almost by definition it is in a constant state of evolution, a complex rolling skein of commerce, geopolitics, faddism and shifting belief systems." This has certainly never been truer than it is today. Here are some more evolved ideas for travel, suggested by *New York Times* travel writers:

Kabul, Afghanistan: *Daring travelers will be rewarded.*

Creating a five-star hotel in a landlocked, war-torn country presents logistical problems, not least of which is maintaining security in a country where Al Qaeda and Taliban supporters still stage attacks on Western interests. Hotels are heavily fortified. The Serena hotel, for instance, is surrounded by a perimeter wall, and the entrance—wide metal tubes filled in with concrete—leads to a thick steel gate guarded by three men with Kalashnikovs.

But the Serena is a symbol of Kabul's new status as an emerging, if risky, destination for daring international travelers. Their interest is marked by the increasing appearance of Afghan travelogues on blogs and travelers' forums like blogs.bootsnall.com and thorntree.lonelyplanet.com.

Whether the Serena will draw high-end visitors remains to be seen. Certainly, ordinary Afghans won't be staying at the hotel, where double rooms start at $230 a night, or about five times the monthly salary of an Afghan government employee. Its location near Zarnegar Park, which was once part of the grounds of a royal palace, has long been a downtown Kabul landmark, but explorations on foot in the area are considered risky.

Yet, for those willing to waive the warnings

for a few moments, a short walk on Kabul's streets can be immensely rewarding. Afghanistan's ethnic diversity—Pashtuns, Hazaras, Tajiks, Uzbeks and others—is visible in the turbans, hats and other ethnic dress. Bazaars are bustling, and despite the dire poverty, evidenced by a large number of enterprising beggars, most people seem warm and good-natured.

On one hillside, a section of the old Kabul wall, which is said to date from the fifth century, designed to repel invaders and now partly in ruins, appears in profile like a row of jagged teeth. And yet so much of Kabul remains defiantly unafraid and gloriously alive.   —Katherine Zoepf

Andorra: *Fois gras and more skiable terrain than Aspen and Vail combined.*

It may not have the glamour of Gstaad or the majesty of Mont Blanc, but little Andorra, once the laughingstock of the Pyrenees, is turning seriously upscale. Two hours north of Barcelona, between Spain and France, this snowball-size nation had been long dismissed as a booze cruise on skis. Lift tickets were cheap, hostels outnumbered five-star hotels (there were none) and the crowd leaned toward beginners, more intent on chugging beers than carving snow.

But over the last several years, some $200 million has been dumped on Andorra, turning it into one of the coolest spots this side of the Alps. There are snazzy new lifts, new hotels with spas and fancy restaurants serving foie gras and baby squid. More important, the skiing has improved dramatically, with the addition of high-tech grooming and snowmaking (see www.skiandorra.ad).

What was once a hodgepodge of rival resorts has merged into two big "ski stations," linked by a high-speed network of 106 lifts and spanning 7,600 acres of skiable terrain, more than Aspen and Vail combined. Vallnord, in the northwest, is the less challenging of the two, with 66 trails, a halfpipe and well-rated ski schools. Grandvalira, closer to France, has 110 trails (one-fifth of them expert), three terrain parks and a vertical drop of about 3,000 feet—not as lofty as St. Moritz, but still more than Gstaad.   —Denny Lee

Bulgaria: *A rare chance to see Europe as it once was.*

Much has changed in Bulgaria since it shook off Soviet domination in 1989. Free elections have been held, and its economic and political capital, Sofia, is thriving. But as it emerges as a tourist destination, mostly in the beach resorts along the Black Sea, Bulgaria is also showing that it is a nation that can celebrate a refreshing lack of progress.

Hidden throughout this big and fertile land, in remote gorges and on craggy hilltops, are dozens of astonishingly intact painted monasteries that are centuries old. They offer visitors a rare chance to see Europe as it once was—before the euro, before World War II, before electricity.

It is a bit like castle-hopping in Tuscany, but without the postcard kiosks and hordes of foreigners who block your photo ops. Of the former nations of the Soviet bloc, Bulgaria has been among the slowest to come in from the cold, which means that much of the country remains off the tourist map. But some luxury tour operators have added Bulgaria to their list of tours. There are also some 600 mineral springs in the country, and a few luxury spa resorts are in the works, not to mention nine Unesco World Heritage Sites and rustic camps from which you can hunt for red stags.   —Denny Lee

Istria, Croatia: *Foodies just might leave Tuscany behind.*

With a bounty of seafood in the surrounding Adriatic waters, and with white truffles in its rolling hills, Istria, a heart-shaped peninsula in

Follow the Silk Road to the Stans

The former Soviet republics aren't for everyone

If Cambodia and Vietnam are today's pearls of the Orient, then the Central Asian countries of Kazakhstan, Uzbekistan, Turkmenistan, Tajikistan and Kyrgyzstan, commonly called "the Stans," are diamonds in the rough. But what these former Soviet republics lack in polish they make up for in historical riches, rugged beauty and, at least for now, few tourists.

Bisected by the Silk Road, the 2,000-year-old trade route that linked Europe to China, the Stans are dotted with museum-quality ruins and architecture from the Middle Ages. Throw in a countryside of canyons, mountain forests and prehistoric glaciers, and the Stans begin to sparkle beneath their raw edges.

Some of the storybook cities of Uzbekistan, with their ornate mosques and citadel walls, are Unesco World Heritage Sites. Tajikistan's crumbling gems include the eerie lost city of Penjikent. And Kyrgyzstan, perhaps the most welcoming of the Stans, has a stunning terrain that includes the Al-Archa National Park (for bird watching, trekking and even glacial skiing), and Lake Issyk-Kul, one of the world's largest alpine bodies of water. Boris Yeltsin has even vacationed there.

The Stans, however, may not be everyone's cup of horse milk. Tourist resources are scarce; rural accommodations may be limited to yurts and tents. But modern-day nomads may find that's reason enough to go.

—Seth Sherwood

northern Croatia, is starting to attract adventurous foodies weary of overpriced and overcrowded tables in Tuscany and Provence.

Lidia Bastianich, chef and author of *La Cucina di Lidia,* grew up outside the town of Pula near the tip of the peninsula, and travels there at least four times a year. Istria is a year-round destination. In early spring, you can forage for wild asparagus; truffle fans might prefer the fall, when generous helpings of white truffles are grated like cheese onto a dish rather than sparingly applied. Coming soon: the Istrian island of Veliki Brijun will be the home of the spa resort complex of Brioni, the fashion company.

—Gisela Williams

Ethiopia: *The Land of the Queen of Sheba is rich in archeological treasures.*

Many Americans have associated Ethiopia with images of crushing poverty, and although poverty still remains, the country is finding something of an economic lifeline in cultural tourism. Indeed, the country holds many of sub-Saharan Africa's most astonishing treasures, like the medieval cave churches at Lalibela, and the 1,700-year-old stone obelisks in the northern town of Axum.

Ethiopia, which calls itself the Land of the Queen of Sheba, also claims title to the Ark of the Covenant, the box of gold and acacia wood that is believed to have once contained the Ten Commandments. Ethiopian Christians say it is somewhere in the Church of St. Mary of Zion in Axum.

Although the country can't compete with Kenya or South Africa when it comes to big game, Ethiopia does have more than a dozen national parks, which are regarded to be among the most beautiful in the sub-Saharan region. The terrain ranges from the plateaus of the Simien highlands to the white-water rapids of the largely uninhabited Omo Valley. There are no luxury tented camps with teak floors and five-course dinners, but several tour operators are offering fly-in safaris into the Rift Valley, Mago National Park and other remote preserves.

Visitors can spend the day spotting leopards and bird-watching, before being whisked back to their hotels in Addis Ababa, the bustling capital with its exotic night life, or Gonder, a slower-paced city invariably referred to as Africa's Camelot because of its many castles.   —Denny Lee

Lithuania: *History buffs will be transported to the Stalin era.*

Now that Estonia has been branded a high-tech wonderland (thanks to Kazaa and Skype) and Latvia has become the next Czech Republic, where does that leave Lithuania, the other Baltic state? Instead of rejecting its Soviet history, Lithuania is embracing it, in a kind of kitschy salute to its Leninist roots.

Gray Soviet-era buildings have been converted into sleek hotels, agitprop statues of Socialist workers have become Kodak moments for amused tourists and trendy restaurants play off the borscht past. NATO, a bar in Vilnius, the capital, for example, was decorated with military hardware, while other bars played old Politburo conferences on their TV's. And in the town of Grutas, there's Grutas Park, better known as Stalin World, styled after a Siberian labor camp, with statues of Marx, Stalin and other Communist icons, a quirky nod to a still-raw chapter—part nostalgia for pre-perestroika innocence, part disaffection with the slow pace of capitalism.

—Denny Lee

Montenegro: *The new playground of the glitterati.*

Montenegro was once an A-list playground for the likes of Elizabeth Taylor and Richard Burton and was called the St.-Tropez of the Adriatic. That is, until war came to the Balkans in the 1990's, and Montenegro, which allied itself with Serbia, suffered NATO air strikes and trade sanctions, crippling its tourism.

Now, this small, craggy republic (it's part of the country of Serbia and Montenegro), with unspoiled beaches, thick pine forests and medieval villages, is poised for a major comeback. The World Travel and Tourism Council, a trade group of business leaders, has highlighted Montenegro as the "fastest growing travel and tourism economy in the world."

Word is that the Singapore-based Amanresorts has plans to restore the Hotel Sveti Stefan—which occupies an entire island of cobblestone streets and terra-cotta-capped cottages. Hip cafes and boutiques have cropped up, and the glitterati are returning again, like couture-wearing refugees after a war. Recent reported sightings include Claudia Schiffer, Jeremy Irons and Sophia Loren.

—Denny Lee

Turkey: *For sybarites, this could be the next St.-Tropez.*

With its white-sand beaches and shop-lined streets, the city of Bodrum has long been the favorite seaside retreat in Turkey. But now this ancient fishing village, set against the blue waters of the Aegean Sea, has crashed the global party circuit.

A glance at the megayachts, some of them straight from the ports of Capri or Monaco, hint at its newfound fame.

In summer, when the population of 50,000 swells tenfold, Bodrum feels a bit like St.-Tropez, except perhaps for the belly dancers.

What's the draw? Gorgeous scenery for one. Situated on Turkey's southwestern coast, the peninsula is a painterly tableau of white-washed stucco homes, purple bougainvilleas and olive-green hillsides. The city is also awash in historical attractions, including the stumpy foundation of the Mausoleum, one of the seven wonders of the ancient world.

Bodrum's night life beckons partiers like a siren's song. Young, well-dressed revelers converge onto Cumhuriyet Caddesi, which visitors call Bar Street, before heading to behemoth discos like Halikarnas, an open-air club that resembles a nearby amphitheater.

—Seth Sherwood

CHAPTER **9**

SPORTS & GAMES

A Fan's Guide — 582

BASEBALL·582: *A guide to major league parks • Winter games • The boys of spring* **TICKETS·588:** *Getting seats for the really big games* **FOOTBALL·591:** *Reading the ref's arms • Get ready for the kickoff •* **BASKETBALL·592:** *A short history of B-ball • Pro hoop teams* **HOCKEY·594:** *The fastest game on ice • Where to watch the puck fly* **BETTING·594:** *Winning the office pool* **AUTO RACING·596:** *Following the racing flags • Track terms to know* **LEGENDS·597:** *How to get to the Hall of Fame*

An Athelete's Guide — 599

GOLF·599: *Get a grip on your game • How handicapping works • The power game* **GAME PLANS·604:** *How to play smart tennis • Hoops for the home court • Growing squash • Hit the softball every time • Turning a Little Leaguer into an all-star • Kids and football* **SUMMER FUN·609:** *Badminton, croquet, horseshoes and more • Ride a raging bull • Buying a bike • Swim like a fish • A mask, fins, and the deep blue* **OUTDOORS·618:** *Finding bigger, meaner fish • Flies that never fail • Night fishing • The call of the hunt • Dick Cheney's hunting lessons • Falconry: sport of sultans • Clinging to the crags* **WINTER GAMES·627:** *Polar chills and thrills • Catching air • It's all downhill • The call of the trail • How long should your skis be? • Building an igloo • Go skijoring • Making it on ice skates* **EXTREME SPORTS·640:** *Radical races • Sports waivers*

Parlor Games — 642

POOL·642: *Cues from a shark* **ONLINE GAMING·644:** *Rules for multiplayer newbies* **BOARD GAMES·645:** *Secrets of Monopoly • A-D-V-I-C-E from a Scrabble master • Go: Chinese "chess" • Mah-jongg: Joining the tile-high club • Where kings and queens reign* **CARD GAMES·653:** *Poker: Texas Hold 'em and more • A guide to poker-table manners • The best of the rest: bridge, pinochle, blackjack, gin, spades • If solitaire's the only game in town • Seduced by sudoku*

SPORTS

A Fan's Guide

Take Me Out to the Ball Game

Where to sit, where to park and what to eat at major league parks

A sweltering summer afternoon and you're at the game watching your favorite team. Of course, you can get peanuts and popcorn and, if you're old enough, beer. But why not try the ribs or kielbasa or sushi? Here's an insider's guide to America's major league parks, including tips on where to park, sit and eat, as well as stadium stats and the last year your team won World Series and League titles.

AMERICAN LEAGUE EAST

Baltimore Orioles

World Series: 1983. League: 1983.

ORIOLE PARK AT CAMDEN YARDS: *48,876 capacity, grass surface, built in 1992. Modern amenities with old-time charm.*

FAN NOTES: Arrive at least 45 minutes early to get a parking spot. Better yet, take public transportation.

 INSIDE INFO

A Gold Medal Event

○ Although baseball is the American pastime, it wasn't an official Olympic sport until the 1992 Summer Games in Barcelona.

○ Since then, Cuba has taken home three gold medals and the United States one.

○ Both baseball and softball are being dropped from the Olympics, starting in 2012.

SOURCES: BaseballLibrary.com; baseball-reference.com; MLB.com

Best seats are along first base. On windy days, avoid top-level seats that have open backs. Former O's first baseman Boog Powell operates a wildly successful barbecue stand in the stadium, near the Eutaw St. entrance. 410-685-9800

Boston Red Sox

World Series: 2004. League: 2004.

FENWAY PARK: *33,871 capacity; grass surface; built in 1912. A baseball classic.*

FAN NOTES: Nearly all seats in the grandstand are good. Best bleacher seat: the red one in row 33, where Ted Williams's 502-foot homer landed in 1946. Fenway franks are a legend, but more for tradition than taste. 617-267-8661

New York Yankees

World Series: 2000. League: 2003.

YANKEE STADIUM: *57,545 capacity, grass surface; built in 1923. The "House that Ruth Built" will be home to the Yankees only until 2008. A new stadium will be built nearby.*

FAN NOTES: Parking is difficult. Views from these seats are obstructed: Rows A-B in all main boxes (210-350) and Sections 1-36 of the reserved tier. Fans walking in aisles block the view. Stadium monuments commemorate the likes of Joe DiMaggio, Lou Gehrig and Babe Ruth. 718-293-4300

Tampa Bay Devil Rays

World Series:— League: —

TROPICANA FIELD: *38,400 capacity, artificial turf surface; opened in 1990. The field went from purely functional to innovative, after a 1996 renovation.*

FAN NOTES: Plenty of amenities, including a cigar bar in the "batter's eye" overlooking center field. Convenient and ample parking, mostly on the park's east side. Seats behind the backstop are as close as they get—only 50 feet from home plate. 727-825-3137

Toronto Blue Jays

World Series: 1993. League: 1993.

ROGERS CENTRE *(formerly SkyDome): 50,516 capacity; artificial turf surface; opened in 1989. It boasts the tallest domed roof, when retracted, but the park lacks atmosphere.*

FAN NOTES: Parking is ample but expensive ($15 to $20 per game); nearby public transportation might be a better bet. The 200-level seats are probably the best. If you're prone to dizziness, avoid seats in the 500 level. 416-341-1111.

AMERICAN LEAGUE CENTRAL

Chicago White Sox

World Series: 2005. League: 2005.

COMISKEY PARK: *44,321 capacity; grass surface; built in 1991. Lacks the charm of the original.*

FAN NOTES: Located in a residential neighborhood, so parking is difficult. Wind shifts wreak havoc with the ball, benefiting hitters. Dirt from the original Comiskey field was recycled here. 312-924-1000.

Cleveland Indians

World Series: 1948. League: 1997.

JACOBS FIELD: *42,400 capacity; grass suface;*

A home run hit 400 feet in Yankee Stadium, which is at sea level, would travel up to 440 feet in Coors Stadium in Denver, the Mile High City

● ● ●

built in 1994. A cozy, urban ballpark.

FAN NOTES: The park helped revitalize downtown. Difficult stadium in which to hit doubles. Offers a smorgasbord of foods (which may help explain the wider than normal seats), including deli, baked goods, sushi and a southwestern menu. 216-420-4200.

Detroit Tigers

World Series: 1984. League: 1984.

COMERICA PARK: *40,000 capacity; grass surface; opened 2000. Built with the hope of revitalizing Detroit's downtown. The Tigers share it with an amusement park and a museum..*

FAN NOTES: No upper-deck outfield seats results in a clear view of the downtown skyline. More home runs go to right field. The air-conditioned lounge at section 330 of the upper concourse has a bar, rest rooms and a seating area—all open to the public. 313-471-2000.

Kansas City Royals

World Series: 1985. League: 1985.

KAUFFMAN STADIUM: *40,625 capacity; grass surface; opened 1973. A good stadium that seems to get better with age.*

FAN NOTES: More than enough parking. Best visibility for hitters in the majors. Only bad seats in the house: the upper-deck where fans could sit in near darkness. Waterfalls and fountains run for 322 feet on the embankment overlooking right center. 816-921-8000.

Minnesota Twins

World Series: 1991. League: 1991.

SPORTS

Baseball's Winter Games

Who says the season's over in October? Try the Caribbean League

The winter months are dark days for baseball fans, The World Series is a distant memory, and the promise of spring training is still months away. But there's no need to fret: the answer is just a plane ride away. Visit the Caribbean winter leagues, home of 28 teams.

Each winter, from November through January, some of baseball's best players head south to play for teams in the Dominican Republic, Mexico, Puerto Rico and Venezuela. The most established players are generally found in the Puerto Rican league; Mexico features the fewest.

The baseball comes cheap (the best tickets are often around $10) and the sideshows are distinctly Caribbean—salsa music between innings, and piña coladas hawked by vendors. For more information, check out www.latinobaseball.com or contact the leagues directly:

DOMINICAN LEAGUE   **809-567-6371**
Estadio Quisqueya, Santo Domingo, Dominican Republic

MEXICAN PACIFIC LEAGUE   **011-67-61-2570**
Av. Insurgentes No. 847, Culiacan, Mexico

PUERTO RICAN LEAGUE   **787-765-6282**
Ave. Munoz Rivera 1056, Rio Piedras, Puerto Rico 00919

VENEZUELAN LEAGUE   **011-58-212-761-4817**
Av. Sorbona No. 25, Edif. Marta-2do. Piso Colinas de Bello Monte, Caracas, Venezuela

HUBERT H. HUMPHREY METRODOME: *55,883 capacity; artificial surface; opened in 1982. Very loud, but keeps out the cold weather.*

FAN NOTES: Arrive early and park on the street using 8-hour meters. Power hitters' park. On May 4, 1984, Dave Kingman hit the ball through the roof. More home runs tend to be hit when the air-conditioning is turned off. 612-375-7444.

AMERICAN LEAGUE WEST

Los Angeles Angels of Anaheim
World Series: 2002. League: 2002.

ANGEL STADIUM OF ANAHEIM: *45,050; grass surface; opened 1966, renovated 1997. Not the prettiest sight in Southern California.*

FAN NOTES: Parking is ample. The cheapest tickets are in the family zone in left field. Nearby geysers shoot water up 90 feet when the Angels hit homers. A power hitter's park. 714-940-2070

Oakland Athletics
World Series: 1989. League: 1990.

MCAFEE COLISEUM *(formerly Oakland-Alameda County Stadium): 48,219 capacity; grass surface; opened in 1966. Neither offensive nor delightful.*

FAN NOTES: Try to arrive at least one-half hour before game time to get a parking spot. Fans can catch home run balls by reaching in front of foul pole screens. Favors pitchers and left-handed batters. Baseball's first appearance of the "wave" took place here in Oct. 1981. 510-638-4627

Seattle Mariners
World Series:— League: —

SAFECO FIELD: *47,116 capacity; grass surface; opened in 1999. Can't beat the views of sunsets over Puget Sound.*

FAN NOTES: Leave early for a game—traffic is heavy in downtown Seattle around the field. Great sightlines, especially behind centerfield fence. Nearby are local food vendors and an open pit barbecue. Smallish seats. Third-deck seating is very steep. 206-346-4001

Texas Rangers
World Series:— League: —

AMERIQUEST FIELD IN ARLINGTON: *49,200 capacity; grass surface; opened in 1994. Still a great ballpark.*

FAN NOTES: Bullpens are just 5 feet above playing level so it's easy to identify pitchers as they warm up. With the right-field foul pole only 325 feet from home plate and the fence only 8 feet high, it pays to be a lefty. Parking is easy. 817-273-5100

NATIONAL LEAGUE EAST

Atlanta Braves
World Series: 1957 (as Milwaukee Braves). League: 1999.

TURNER FIELD: *50,096 capacity; grass surface; opened 1997. Site of the '96 Olympics, retrofitted for baseball.*

FAN NOTES: The parking lot was part of the old Atlanta-Fulton County Stadium; markers show the site of Hank Aaron's record-breaking 715th home run. Air-conditioned concourse. Buy tickets for future games on the suite level. 404-522-7630

Florida Marlins
World Series: 2003. League: 2003.

DOLPHINS STADIUM: *36,331; grass surface; opened 1987. A quirky park, originally designed for football.*

FAN NOTES: Parking is no problem; the lot was built to handle 70,000 football fans. A Fiesta Latina takes place before every Saturday home game at Gate G, featuring Latin food and live music. Some obstructed views from the lower-level seats near foul poles. 305-623-6100

New York Mets
World Series: 1986. League: 2000.

SHEA STADIUM: *55,600; grass surface; opened 1964. Somewhat of an eyesore; planes fly overhead on their way to LaGuardia airport.*

FAN NOTES: Parking is not difficult. Avoid the last two or three rows of the loge and mezzanine levels which have limited or no views of the scoreboard. Worst visibility for hitters in the major leagues. 718-507-TIXX

Philadelphia Phillies
World Series: 1980. League: 1993.

CITIZENS BANK PARK: *43,826; opened 2004. One of the more than a dozen spiffy new ballparks built since 1991.*

FAN NOTES: Ashburn Alley, named for former great Richie Ashburn, opens three hours before weekend games; watch batting practice in a fair atmosphere. Prominent views of the Philly skyline are behind the center field fence. A 50-foot Liberty Bell chimes after a Phillies homer. 215-463-1000

Washington Nationals
World Series: — League:—

RFK STADIUM: *56,000 capacity; grass surface; built in 1961. One of the original cookie-cutter, all-purpose fields has seen better days.*

FAN NOTES: Baseball returned to RFK in 2005 with the Washington Nationals (formerly the Montreal Expos), after 34 years. The stadium literally rocks when masses of fans jump up and down. Sightlines are good; parking is close. A new park along the Anacostia River is scheduled to open in March 2008. 202-675-6287

NATIONAL LEAGUE CENTRAL

Chicago Cubs
World Series: 1908. League: 1945.

WRIGLEY FIELD: *39,538 capacity; grass surface; built in 1914. A Chicago landmark. Fans love it.*

FAN NOTES: Parking is almost nonexistent. Bleacher seats are the most popular; 1,800 more bleachers were added in 2005. After the game a blue flag with a white W or a white flag with a blue L is flown to signify a Cubs win or loss. Strong lake breezes favor pitchers. 773-404-CUBS

Cincinnati Reds
World Series: 1990. League: 1990.

GREAT AMERICAN BALL PARK: *42,059; grass surface; opened in 2003. Plain on the outside but good views of the Ohio River from the inside.*

FAN NOTES: Family-friendly. Clean. A towering smoke stack smokes for home runs and strike-outs. A homey touch but the stack partially obstructs views from some center-field seats. Red seats are a welcome departure from the ubiquitous green. Parking is ample and efficient. 513-765-7600

Houston Astros
World Series: —. League: 2005.

MINUTE MAID PARK: *40,950 capacity; grass surface; opened in 2000. Retro look but big on high-tech features.*

FAN NOTES: The park is wired: 1,400 speaker cabinets get as close to fans as possible; and fans can bring their Wi-Fi compatible devices and surf the Web. Maintains a tradition of $1 tickets for kids 14 and under for seats in the outfield deck. 713-259-8000

Milwaukee Brewers
World Series: —. League: 1982.

MILLER PARK: *41,900 capacity; grass surface; opened in 2001. Distinctive fan-shaped roof.*

FAN NOTES: Retired numbers of Milwaukee legends like Robin Yount hang above the center-field wall. Tailgate facilities overlook the Menomonee River. Grilled kosher dogs and bratwurst are big here. Parking is tight. 414-902-4000

Pittsburgh Pirates
World Series: 1979. League: 1979.

PNC PARK: *38,496 capacity; grass surface; opened in 2001. A classic-style ballpark in the tradition of Forbes Field and Fenway Park.*

FAN NOTES: Easy access from downtown across the Roberto Clemente bridge, named for the great Pirates rightfielder. The bridge is pedestrian-only on game days. The park's highest seat is only 88 feet from the field. Former Pirate Manny Sanguillen runs an outfield barbecue. 412-323-5000

St. Louis Cardinals
World Series: 1982. League: 2004.

BUSCH STADIUM: *50,345 capacity; built in 2005. The Cardinals' first season in the new Busch Stadium was in 2006.*

FAN NOTES: Dramatic views of Gateway Arch and downtown St. Louis skyline. Nearby are the International Bowling Museum, and the St. Louis Cardinals museum, a shrine to legendary Cardinal, Stan "the Man" Musial. See both museums for the price of one ticket. 314-231-6340

NATIONAL LEAGUE WEST
Arizona Diamondbacks
World Series: 2001. League: 2001.

CHASE FIELD: *49,033 capacity; grass surface; opened in 1998. Comfort and amenities reign. Among the best.*

FAN NOTES: The roof and air-conditioning shelter fans from sweltering heat and monsoon storms. Good views from most seats. Fast-food heaven, plus a farmer's market with fresh fruits and veggies. Lots of parking in downtown Phoenix, a short walk from the field. 602-514-8400

Following the Boys of Summer in the Spring

For spring training, fans have two choices: the Grapefruit League in Florida or the Cactus League in Arizona. Here are some places to catch a game before the regular season starts.

GRAPEFRUIT LEAGUE—FLORIDA

Team		Stadium	Information
Atlanta Braves	NATIONAL LEAGUE, EAST	Cracker Jack Stadium, Kissimmee	407-839-3900
Baltimore Orioles	AMERICAN LEAGUE, EAST	Ft. Lauderdale Stadium, Ft. Lauderdale	954-776-1921
Boston Red Sox	AMERICAN LEAGUE, EAST	City of Palms Park, Ft. Myers	239-334-4700
Cincinnati Reds	NATIONAL LEAGUE, CENTRAL	Ed Smith Stadium, Sarasota	941-954-4464
Cleveland Indians	AMERICAN LEAGUE, CENTRAL	Chain of Lakes Park, Winter Haven	863-293-3900
Detroit Tigers	AMERICAN LEAGUE, CENTRAL	Joker Marchant Stadium, Lakeland	813-287-8844
Florida Marlins	NATIONAL LEAGUE, EAST	Roger Dean Stadium, Jupiter	561-630-1828
Houston Astros	NATIONAL LEAGUE, CENTRAL	Osceola Stadium, Kissimmee	321-697-3200
Los Angeles Dodgers	NATIONAL LEAGUE, WEST	Holman Stadium, Vero Beach	777-569-6858
Minnesota Twins	AMERICAN LEAGUE, CENTRAL	Hammond Stadium, Ft. Myers	800-338-9467
New York Mets	NATIONAL LEAGUE, EAST	Tradition Field, Port St. Lucie	772-871-2115
New York Yankees	AMERICAN LEAGUE, EAST	Legends Field, Tampa	813-287-8844
Philadelphia Phillies	NATIONAL LEAGUE, EAST	Bright House Networks Field, Clearwater	727-442-8496
Pittsburgh Pirates	NATIONAL LEAGUE, CENTRAL	McKechnie Field, Bradenton	941-748-4610
St. Louis Cardinals	NATIONAL LEAGUE, CENTRAL	Roger Dean Stadium, Jupiter	561-6301828
Tampa Bay Devil Rays	AMERICAN LEAGUE, EAST	Progress Energy Park, St. Petersburg	727-898-7297
Toronto Blue Jays	AMERICAN LEAGUE, EAST	Knology Park, Dunedin	800-707-8269
Washington Nationals	NATIONAL LEAGUE, EAST	Space Coast Stadium, Viera	321-633-4487

CACTUS LEAGUE—ARIZONA

Team		Stadium	Information
Anaheim Angels	AMERICAN LEAGUE, WEST	Tempe Diablo Stadium, Tempe	602-438-9300
Arizona Diamondbacks	NATIONAL LEAGUE, WEST	Tuscon Electric Park, Tuscon	866-672-1343
Chicago Cubs	NATIONAL LEAGUE, CENTRAL	Hohokam Park, Mesa	480-964-4467
Chicago White Sox	AMERICAN LEAGUE, CENTRAL	Tucson Electric Park, Tuscon	866-672-1343
Colorado Rockies	NATIONAL LEAGUE, WEST	Hi Corbett Field Randolph Park, Tuscon	520-327-9467
Kansas City Royals	AMERICAN LEAGUE, CENTRAL	Surprise Stadium, Surprise	623-594-5600
Milwaukee Brewers	NATIONAL LEAGUE, CENTRAL	Maryvale Baseball Park, Phoenix	623-245-5500
Oakland Athletics	AMERICAN LEAGUE, WEST	Phoenix Municipal Stadium, Phoenix	602-392-0217
San Diego Padres	NATIONAL LEAGUE, WEST	Peoria Sports Stadium, Peoria	800-409-1511
San Francisco Giants	NATIONAL LEAGUE, WEST	Scottsdale Stadium, Scottsdale	480-312-2586
Seattle Mariners	AMERICAN LEAGUE, WEST	Peoria Sports Stadium, Peoria	800-409-1511
Texas Rangers	AMERICAN LEAGUE, WEST	Surprise Stadium, Surprise	623-594-5600

SPORTS

Colorado Rockies
World Series: — League: —

COORS FIELD: *50,445 capacity; grass surface; built in 1995. An all-round good stadium.*

FAN NOTES: Possibly the most spectacular view in baseball; the Rocky Mountains are visible from first base and right field. A hitter's park. Home team has the distinct advantage of being accustomed to Denver's mile-high atmosphere. Limited parking. 303-762-5437

Los Angeles Dodgers
World Series: 1988. League: 1988.

DODGER STADIUM: *56,000 capacity; grass surface; opened in 1962. Doesn't show its age; meticulously maintained.*

FAN NOTES: Parking lots funnel efficiently into nearby freeways. Great views of the San Gabriel mountains but top-deck seats are too far from the action. Dodger Dogs are required eating. A classic pitcher's park. 213-224-1400

San Diego Padres
World Series: —. League: 1998.

PETCO PARK: *42,445 capacity; grass surface; opened 2004. A spanking new stadium with spectacular views.*

FAN NOTES: More than enough parking. Seats have cupholders and lots of legroom. Outstanding sightlines. The Padres are the "Team of the Military;" different branches of the armed forces sometimes take over sections and outchant each other. Big-time pitcher's park. 619-795-5000

San Francisco Giants
World Series: 1954 (as the New York Giants). League: 2002.

AT&T PARK: *41,503 capacity; artificial surface; built in 2000. Urban ballpark with old-time feel.*

FAN NOTES: Nine-foot statue of one of the greatest, Willie Mays, greets visitors at the public entrance. Even from the worst seats you get a view of the Bay Bridge and the marina. Public transportation is abundant and easy. 415-972-2298

Nothing Beats Being There
Watch the game, not the box. Here's how to get a seat for major events

Most couch potatoes' idea of a good seat for the Super Bowl is in front of a wide-screen television. But for real sports fans, nothing beats being there—whether it's the Super Bowl, the World Series, the Masters, or whatever. Getting tickets to some of the nation's sporting events—like the Masters, for example—is next to impossible. But you can get in the door to some of the others if you do some advance planning and are prepared for a little hustle. Here's the lowdown on how and where to get tickets to some of the hottest sporting events.

THE SUPER BOWL   www.nfl.com

Feb. 4, 2007, Miami, Florida
Feb. 3, 2008, Glendale, Arizona
Feb. 1, 2009, Tampa, Florida

Football's biggest game is the world's most watched television event each year; but the Super Bowl itself is not all that hard to see in person, if you're willing to pay the hefty ticket prices (about $600). Season-ticket holders of the participating teams have the best shot; the A.F.C. and N.F.C. champs split 35 percent of the Super Bowl ducats, most of which are made available to their faithful fans. The host team gets another 10 percent of the tickets, and every other N.F.L. team gets hundreds of tickets, which they generally sell to their own ticket holders. The league also distributes 500

Reading the Football Ref's Arms

Nearly everyone knows that a referee with his arms outstretched high above his head means a player has scored a touchdown or field goal. Here's a beginner's guide to football signals.

First down
Arms pointed toward goal

Invalid fair catch
Hand waving above head

Personal foul
One wrist striking the other above the head

Touchdown, field goal or successful try
Both arms extended in air

Holding
Grasping one wrist with clenched fist

No time out; with whistle: time-in
Arm makes circular, clocklike motion

Safety
Palms together above head

Unsportsmanlike behavior
Arms outstretched, palms down

Illegal motion at snap
Horizontal arc made with one hand

Offside, encroachment or free-kick violation
Hands on hips

Time out
Hands crossed above head

Loss of down
Both hands held behind head.

Illegal use of hands
Grasping one wrist with the other hand open and facing forward

Penalty refused, incomplete pass or missed goal
Hands crossing horizontally

Interference with forward pass or fair catch
Hands open and extended forward from shoulders, hands vertical

Illegal forward pass
One hand waved behind back followed by loss of down signal.

SOURCE: www.nfl.com

SPORTS

TIMELY TIPS

Snagging a Seat

A scalper's guide to getting a ticket when the game is sold out

Selling tickets at more than face value is illegal in many places. But it is the scalpers who face arrest, not the ticket buyers. And if a game is completely sold out—or so the newspaper says—buying a scalped ticket can be your best and only way to see the game in person.

Scalping, of course, is somewhat of a covert activity. Reselling tickets at any price on stadium grounds is illegal in some places, so much of the commerce takes place in surrounding areas. You may get a good deal here, but you're probably better off waiting.

✔ **The more scalpers you see, the more patient you should be.** As game time approaches, the prices will drop. If the game is not sold out, or if demand is not high, try to wait until right before the game starts, and you'll discover a buyer's market. Desperate to unload tickets, scalpers will sell them for as little as a third of the price they paid.

✔ **Try to bargain for the best price you can get.** If it's a very big game, the seekers will far outnumber the sellers, and prices may be steep. Scalped tickets at events like the Super Bowl can run $2,000 and up. Most scalpers are trying to do brisk business, so they may take your reasonable offer.

✔ **Before you decide to buy, make sure to get a good look at the tickets.** Fake or expired tickets are often sold and while you may not be able to tell counterfeits, you can at least check the date. Whatever you do, don't buy a press pass; it's probably fake and even if it's not, you're almost sure to get discovered and thrown out.

---

tickets each year through a lottery it conducts. You can enter by sending a self-addressed stamped envelope between February and June to Super Bowl Random Drawing, P.O. Box 16400, Mascoutah, Ill. 62224-6400.

WORLD SERIES   www.mlb.com
Every October

The participating teams control virtually all the tickets to baseball's Fall Classic, so your best bet is to hold season tickets for your favorite team—and hope they make it all the way.

NCAA FINAL FOUR   www.ncaasports.com
Late March, early April

You practically have to jump through hoops to watch the best college basketball teams fight for the national championship each year. Chances of getting a Final Four ticket improved when the NCAA started holding championship games in arenas that seat more than 30,000 but it's still tough. The NCAA begins taking applications just after the previous year's tournament. A random computerized drawing is held during the summer; winners are notified by mid-August.

THE MASTERS   www.masters.org
Final round is held the second Sunday in April

It's almost as hard to watch golf's big event in person as it is to play a round at Augusta National, the Georgia course on which it is played each year. Only the lucky few on Augusta National's "patron' list" are allowed to buy tickets each year. The list is made up primarily of people who had been attending the tournament before 1968 and those who have been added to it off the very long waiting list—which itself was closed to new members shortly after opening in 2000.

Get Ready for the Kickoff

For more information about individual teams, go to www.nfl.com and click on "Teams."

AMERICAN FOOTBALL CONFERENCE

	Team	Last Super Bowl Title	Stadium		Ticket information
EAST	Buffalo Bills	—	Ralph Wilson	716-649-0015	www.buffalobills.com
	Miami Dolphins	1974	Dolphins Stadium	888-FINS-TIX	www.miamidolphins.com
	New England Patriots	2005	Gillette Stadium	800-543-1776	www.patriots.com
	New York Jets	1969	Meadowlands	516-560-8192	www.newyorkjets.com
NORTH	Baltimore Ravens	2001	M&T Bank Stadium	410-261-7283	www.baltimoreravens.com
	Cincinnati Bengals	—	Paul Brown Stadium	513-621-8383	www.bengals.com
	Cleveland Browns	—	Cleveland Browns Stadium	888-891-1999	www.clevelandbrowns.com
	Pittsburgh Steelers	2006	Heinz Field	412-323-1200	www.steelers.com
SOUTH	Houston Texans	—	Reliant Stadium	832-667-2000	www.houstontexans.com
	Indianapolis Colts	1971	RCA Dome (until 2008)	317-299-3663	www.colts.com
	Jacksonville Jaguars	—	Alltel Stadium	904-633-2000	www.jaguars.com
	Tennessee Titans	—	Titans Coliseum	615-565-4200	www.titansonline.com
WEST	Denver Broncos	1999	Invesco Field at Mile High	720-258-3333	www.denverbroncos.com
	Kansas City Chiefs	1970	Arrowhead Stadium	816-920-9400	www.kcchiefs.com
	Oakland Raiders	1984	McAfee Coliseum	888-44-RAIDERS	www.raiders.com
	San Diego Chargers	—	Qualcomm Stadium	877-242-7437	www.chargers.com

NATIONAL FOOTBALL CONFERENCE

	Team	Last Super Bowl Title	Stadium		Ticket information
EAST	Dallas Cowboys	1996	Texas Stadium	214-253-6060	www.dallascowboys.com
	New York Giants	1991	Meadowlands	201-935-8222	www.giants.com
	Philadelphia Eagles	—	Lincoln Financial Field	888-332-2582	www.philadelphiaeagles.com
	Washington Redskins	1992	FedEx Field	301-276-6050	www.redskins.com
NORTH	Chicago Bears	1986	Soldier Field	847-615-2327	www.chicagobears.com
	Detroit Lions	—	Ford Field	313-262-2003	www.detroitlions.com
	Green Bay Packers	1997	Lambeau Field	920-569-7101	www.packers.com
	Minnesota Vikings	—	Metrodome	612-338-4537	www.vikings.com
SOUTH	Atlanta Falcons	—	Georgia Dome	404-223-8000	www.atlantafalcons.com
	Carolina Panthers	—	Bank of America Stadium	704-358-7800	www.panthers.com
	New Orleans Saints	—	Louisiana Superdome	504-731-1700	www.neworleanssaints.com
	Tampa Bay Buccaneers	2003	Raymond James Stadium	800-282-0683	www.buccaneers.com
WEST	Arizona Cardinals	—	Cardinals Stadium	602-379-0102	www.azcardinals.com
	St. Louis Rams	2000	Edward Jones Dome	314-425-8830	www.stlouisrams.com
	San Francisco 49ers	1995	Monster Park Stadium	415-656-4900	www.sf49ers.com
	Seattle Seahawks	—	Qwest Field	888-NFL-HAWK	www.seattleseahawks.com

SPORTS

Your best bet of seeing top golfers play is to go a few days early to watch a practice round. To try to get those tickets, write the club just after the end of the previous year's tournament. Send your name, address, phone and Social Security number to Masters Tournament, Practice Rounds, PO Box 2047, Augusta, Ga. 30903.

INDIANAPOLIS 500   www.indy500.com

Memorial Day weekend. Indianapolis Motor Speedway

Hundreds of thousands of people turn out every year for auto racing's big day, which is also one of the world's biggest parties. Despite the huge number of seats, it's still a tough ticket to land. A huge percentage of the 300,000 seats are filled through renewals—people who attend the race one year and, within a week, request renewals or upgrades for the next year's 500.

To request tickets for the first time, call 800-822-4639; order online at www.indy500.com; or send a check or money order to Indianapolis 500, P.O. Box 24152, Speedway, Ind. 46222. The seats available to first-timers are typically of lesser quality but also cost less: around $40 to $90. If you really want to see the race, despite poor seat quality, the speedway sells general admission, standing-room-only tickets the day of the race. But this is truly partial-view, last-resort seating.

KENTUCKY DERBY www.kentuckyderby.com

First Saturday in May. Churchill Downs, Louisville, Kentucky

The infield is the place to be for the Run of the Roses; more than 80,000 people mill around inside the track oval drinking juleps each year, while about 48,000 sit in the cushier boxes.

Only Churchill Downs season ticket holders and sponsors are guaranteed seats. To sign up for the possibility of getting box seats or infield tickets, you have to set up a Twin Spires Club account and then accumulate points by taking part in other Churchill Downs events. You can sign up online; membership is free. Those who show the most "loyalty," as the company puts it, are invited to buy tickets (cost: about $90). It could take years of showing interest in going to the Derby before you're invited to buy tickets. Applicants find out by the end of November if they can purchase tickets for the race the following May. You can buy a general admission ticket (about $40) on race day but you won't get a view of the racetrack.

A Very Short History of B-ball

The game hasn't changed much since a Canadian invented it

Looking for a vigorous indoor game to keep young men occupied during long New England winters, Dr. James Naismith, a Canadian-born American, invented basketball in December 1891. The first game was played a month later when, as legend has it, he nailed a peach basket to a gym wall. The game hasn't changed much since then. Naismith's original 13 rules have

ⓘ INSIDE INFO

Jumping Through Hoops

- Height of basketball hoop: 10 feet
- Distance between backboard and foul line: 15 feet
- Diameter of basket rim: 18 inches
- Diameter of basketball: 9 inches
- Size of court: 50 feet by 94 feet

A Who's Who of Pro Hoop Teams

For more information on individual teams, go to the N.B.A. Web site at www.nba.com and click on the team's name.

EASTERN CONFERENCE

Division	Team	Last League Title	Arena	Ticket information
ATLANTIC	Boston Celtics	1986	Banknorth Garden	866-4-CELTIX
	New Jersey Nets	—	Continental Airlines Arena	800-7NJ-NETS
	New York Knicks	1973	Madison Square Garden	212-465-JUMP
	Philadelphia 76ers	1983	Wachovia Complex	215-339-7676
	Toronto Raptors	—	Air Canada Centre	416-872-5000
CENTRAL	Chicago Bulls	1998	United Center	312-455-4000
	Cleveland Cavaliers	—	Quicken Loans Arena	800-820-CAVS
	Detroit Pistons	2004	The Palace of Auburn Hills	248-377-0100
	Indiana Pacers	—	Conseco Fieldhouse	317-917-2500
	Milwaukee Bucks	1971	Bradley Center	800-4NBA-TIX
SOUTHEAST	Atlanta Hawks	1958[1]	Philips Arena	866-715-1500
	Charlotte Bobcats	—	Charlotte Bobcats Arena	704-262-2287
	Miami Heat	—	American Airlines Arena	786-777-HOOP
	Orlando Magic	—	TD Waterhouse Centre	407-89-MAGIC
	Washington Wizards	1978	Verizon Center	202-661-5050

WESTERN CONFERENCE

Division	Team	Last League Title	Arena	Ticket information
NORTHWEST	Denver Nuggets	—	Pepsi Center	303-405-1111
	Minnesota Timberwolves	—	Target Center	800-4NBA-TIX
	Portland Trail Blazers	1977	Rose Garden	503-797-9600
	Seattle SuperSonics	1979	Key Arena	206-283-DUNK
	Utah Jazz	—	Delta Center	801-355-DUNK
PACIFIC	Golden State Warriors	1975	The Arena in Oakland	800-GSW-HOOP
	Los Angeles Clippers	—	Staples Center	888-895-8662
	Los Angeles Lakers	2002	Staples Center	310-426-6031
	Phoenix Suns	—	America West Arena	602-379-SUNS
	Sacramento Kings	1951	ARCO Arena	916-928-3650
SOUTHWEST	Dallas Mavericks	—	American Airlines Center	214-747-MAVS
	Houston Rockets	1995	Toyota Center	713-627-DUNK
	Memphis Grizzlies	—	FedEx Forum	901-888-HOOP
	New Orleans/Oklahoma City Hornets	—	Oklahoma City Ford Center [2]	405-208-4600
	San Antonio Spurs	2005	SBC Center	210-444-5050

[1] as St. Louis Hawks

[2] Temporary home of the New Orleans Hornets, who were displaced in 2005 by destruction caused by Hurricane Katrina

SPORTS

TIMELY TIPS

The Odds of Winning the Office Pool

Sports gambling is a losing proposition for all but the savviest—and luckiest—bettors. Russ Culver, former sports book manager at the Mirage hotel in Las Vegas and one of the sharpest handicappers around, can help. Here are his tips on winning the office pool:

✔ **Look for trends.** Statistics aren't as telling as shifts in a team's fortunes and ability.

Knowing that a team goes 8-1 on Thursdays probably isn't important, but knowing that a team hasn't won a road game in ten years may well be.

✔ **Defy the polls.** Associated Press polls of the nation's best college basketball and football teams are like a beauty contest. When you look at the N.C.A.A. tournament bracket in the office pool, bet against the glamour teams when they are playing a strong team that's not as popular.

✔ **Momentum matters.** In baseball, focus on a pitcher's last

five starts. In college hoops look at how a team played down the stretch period before the N.C.A.A. tournament. A team that finished third in its league in the regular season but came on strong to win the conference deserves a good look.

✔ **Seedings mean little in the NCAA tournament.** Seedings are gerrymandered to assure the best matchups for television. The No. 1 and No. 2 ranked teams are accurate but those ranked No. 4 to about 12 are manipulated for TV.

---

been modified over the years, but his basic principles still hold. Some modifications are stylistic maneuvers, like the slam dunk and double pump, which Naismith could hardly have foreseen.

The biggest change came in the mid-50's with the introduction of the clock rule that gives players 24 seconds to either shoot or lose possession of the ball. The 24-second rule instantly transformed the low-scoring, slow-paced game into an exciting, lightening-quick sport. (At about the same time, the orange ball was introduced to make it more visible to players and spectators.)

The game's organization underwent a major change just after the 1948-49 season when the Basketball Association and the National Basketball League merged and the National Basketball Association was born. But it wasn't until the early 80's that the N.B.A. exploded in popularity. Today it's a multimillion-dollar business with 30 franchises across the country and in Canada.

The Fastest Game on Ice

Fans watch the action, while players keep their eyes on the prize: a famous cup

As you might expect of a sport as famous for fighting as for skating skill, there's a dispute over whether hockey was first played on a pond in Nova Scotia using cow dung as a puck or whether it began in Montreal, Quebec. But there's no doubt that the sport, which is played almost exclusively in the northern hemisphere, began in Canada.

Fittingly enough, hockey's top prize, the Stanley Cup, was created in 1893 by Lord Stanley, governor-general of Canada. Since then it has not been awarded only twice. Once, in 1919, when the worldwide Spanish flu epidemic hit Canada and several members of the Montreal Canadiens team had to be hospitalized. One player died and the series was called off for the season. Then, for the second time, in 2005, when as a result of a labor dispute between the N.H.L. and the players' union,

Where to Watch the Puck Fly

Fans can get tickets for favorite teams online at the N.H.L. Web site, www.nhl.com/tickets, through Ticketmaster or by going directly to the arena box office.

EASTERN CONFERENCE

Division	Team	Last Stanley Cup	Arena	Ticket information
ATLANTIC	New Jersey Devils	2003	Continental Airlines Arena at Meadowlands[1]	800-NJ-DEVILS
	New York Islanders	1983	Nassau Coliseum	800-882-ISLES
	New York Rangers	1994	Madison Square Garden	212-465-6741
	Philadelphia Flyers	1975	Wachovia Center	215-218-7825
	Pittsburgh Penguins	1992	Mellon Arena	800-642-PENS
NORTHEAST	Boston Bruins	1972	TD Banknorth Garden	617-931-2222
	Buffalo Sabres	—	HSBC Arena	888-223-6000
	Montreal Canadiens	1993	Bell Centre	514-790-1245
	Ottawa Senators	1927	Corel Centre	613-599-0200
	Toronto Maple Leafs	1967	Air Canada Centre	416-872-5000
SOUTHEAST	Atlanta Thrashers	—	Philips Arena	866-715-1500
	Carolina Hurricanes	—	RBC Center	919-834-4000
	Florida Panthers	—	BankAtlantic Center	954-835-8499
	Tampa Bay Lightning	2004	St. Pete Times Forum	813-301-2500
	Washington Capitals	—	Verizon Center	202-266-2277

WESTERN CONFERENCE

Division	Team	Last Stanley Cup	Arena	Ticket information
CENTRAL	Chicago Blackhawks	1961	United Center	312-943-7000
	Columbus Blue Jackets	—	Nationwide Arena	614-431-3600
	Detroit Red Wings	2002	Joe Louis Arena	313-396-7575
	Nashville Predators	—	Gaylord Center	615-770-7825
	St. Louis Blues	—	Savvis Center	314-421-4400
NORTHWEST	Calgary Flames	1989	Pengrowth Saddledome	403-777-0000
	Colorado Avalanche	2001	Pepsi Center	303-405-1111
	Edmonton Oilers	1990	Rexall Place	780-414-GOAL
	Minnesota Wild	—	Xcel Center	651-222-WILD
	Vancouver Canucks	—	General Motors Place	604-899-7423
PACIFIC	Anaheim Mighty Ducks	—	Arrowhead Pond	877-WILDWING
	Dallas Stars	1999	American Airlines Center	214-GO-STARS
	Los Angeles Kings	—	Staples Center	213-742-7340
	Phoenix Coyotes	—	Glendale Arena	480-563-7825
	San Jose Sharks	—	HP Pavilion at San Jose	800-366-4423

[1] New arena to open in Newark for 2007-2008 season

SPORTS

the entire 2004-2005 season was canceled.

The cup is awarded annually to the winner of the National Hockey League playoffs. Each season, N.H.L. teams play 82 games with the top eight teams in each conference qualifying for the playoffs. Conference winners then vie for the League championship, a best-of-seven series, generally held in the spring.

Over the years, the Montreal Canadiens have won the most Stanley Cups: 24. Though they haven't won one since 1967, the Toronto Maple Leafs come in second with 13 wins. Among the American teams, the Detroit Red Wings have the most—10.

Following the Flags

In auto racing, each one carries a specific message, but the meaning depends on which track

Auto racing is a high-tech affair, dependent as it is these days on computers, radio communication and spotters who do aerial reconnaissance to ensure the safety of the drivers. But one decidedly low-tech tradition has stuck with the sport since the late 1800's: the use of flags to tell drivers and fans what's happening on the track. Each flag carries a specific message, which may vary from one event to the next or even among tracks.

Following are standard auto-racing flags and their meanings.

 Solid green: Signals the start of the race or practice session. Or, when used after a yellow or red flag, means that the track is clear.

 Solid red : Tells the driver to stop racing immediately. No passing allowed.

 Solid black : Directs a driver to stop at his pit. Usually indicates a penalty on the driver or team for a rule violation.

 Solid yellow: Indicates danger. Drivers should slow down, not pass, and be ready to change direction to avoid a hazard on the track.

 Solid white: Signifies that the leader has begun the final lap of the race.

 White with a red cross in center: Signals that medical help is on the course or is needed.

 Black with white cross in center: Warns a driver that he has been disqualified or accused of unsportsmanlike behavior.

 Red with yellow "X": Warns that the pit area is closed.

 Red and yellow vertical stripes: Warns that the track surface is wet or slippery due to oil or water.

 Light blue with yellow diagonal stripe: Cautions to yield to a passing car; or, informs drivers that one lap remains.

 Black and white checkered: Signals the end of the race or practice session; or, the leader has completed the race.

10 TERMS RACE TRACK TROLLERS SHOULD KNOW

Chassis roll. The choppy movement caused by a race car turning a corner at high speeds.

Drafting. Two or more cars running nose-to-tail, almost touching, while racing.

Groove. The best, most efficient or fastest route around a racetrack. Can change depending on the track and weather conditions.

Happy hour. The last official practice before a race, usually the day before the event.

Marbles. Pieces of rubber, dirt, gravel, etc. on the track, which interfere with driving and sometimes cause drivers to lose control.

Pit Road. The area along the straightaway where pit crews service race cars.

Silly season. The period toward the end of a season during which some teams announce driver, crew or sponsor changes.

Stickers. Race track term for new tires; derived from the stickers that tire makers put on new tires.

Superspeedway. The longest type of oval race track. Short tracks are less than one mile long; intermediates are between one and two miles; and superspeedways are two miles or longer.

Victory lane, also called the winner's circle. The place in the track's infield reserved for the winner's car during the victory celebration.

 INSIDE INFO

The Economics of Racing

○ Nascar's 8-year broadcast deal with tv stations will bring track operators, race winners and the Nascar organization $4.5 billion starting in 2007.

○ Top Nascar drivers earn $10 million or more a year.

○ Pit-crew members pull in about $100,000 a year.

○ A spotter makes about $500 to $1,000 per race.

SOURCES: *The Wall St. Journal*; Nascar

How to Get to the Hall of Fame
Practice, practice, practice. But if you need directions, call first

Pick a sport or pastime and, chances are, there's a hall of fame that honors its legends. Baseball, football and basketball have their well-known and popular halls, of course, but so do bodybuilding, show jumping and drag racing. There's even a dog musher's hall of fame in Knik, Alaska, and a jousting hall in Virginia.

Halls of fame are rare elsewhere in the world, but more than 1,000 are spread across America. The vast majority are sports-themed but scores of others feature leading lights in other fields. There's a Barbie Doll Hall of Fame in Palo Alto, California, for instance, and an Aviation Hall of Fame in New Jersey. Here are some good ones:

College Football Hall of Fame, *South Bend, Indiana*: Hall of college-football greats, like Jim Thorpe and Knute Rockne.
   800-440-3263   www.collegefootball.org

International Bowling Museum and Hall of Fame, *St. Louis, Missouri*: "Tenpin Alley" illustrates the 5,000-year history of bowling.
   314-231-6340   www.bowlingmuseum.com

International Boxing Hall of Fame Museum, *Canastota, New York*: Fist castings of boxing legend Jack Demspey.   *315-697-7095*

International Swimming Hall of Fame, *Fort Lauderdale, Florida*: Exhibit on Johnny Weissmuller, "World's Greatest Swimmer" and star of 16 Tarzan films.
   954-462-6536   www.ishof.com

International Tennis Hall of Fame, *Newport, Rhode Island*: Tennis trivia and artifacts

TIMELY TIPS

Must-See Sites for Sports Junkies

✔ **ESPN.com (espn.go.com)** comprehensive sports coverage

✔ **Sportsline.com** from CBS

✔ **CNN/SI.com** from CNN and *Sports Illustrated*

✔ **msn.foxsports.com** Fox Sports

✔ **www.sportingnews.com** Sporting News

✔ **www.sportsnetwork.com** The Sports Network gives up-to-the-minute news and results

✔ **www.allsports.com** Allsports has news, scores, odds, audio feeds and more

✔ **NBA.com** from the N.B.A.

✔ **NFL.com** from the N.F.L.

✔ **MLB.com** from Major League Baseball

✔ **gorpaway.com** GORP, the Great Outdoor Recreation

Pages, has extensive information on parks and outdoor activities of all sorts

✔ **www.bikelane.com** a bit dated, but still offers a good collection of links

✔ **www.tennisserver.com** The Tennis Server has news, schedules, rules and more

✔ **www.golfweb.com** GolfWeb. GolfDigest.com and PGA. com cover the golf world

—Richard J. Meislin

---

galore; spotlights some 200 inductees going back to 1955. *www.tennisfame.com*

Motor Sports Hall of Fame, *Novi, Michigan*: Racers from all over the globe: Indy cars, stock cars, TransAm, dragsters, even snowmobiles.

800-250-7223 *www.mshf.com*

Naismith Memorial Basketball Hall of Fame, *Springfield, Massachusetts*: A big draw: Wilt Chamberlain's uniform from his 100-point game in 1962. *413-781-6500 or 877-4HOOPLA*
www.hoophall.com

National Baseball Hall of Fame and Museum, *Cooperstown, New York*: Mother lode of artifacts.
607-547-7200 www.baseballhalloffame.org

National Cowboy Hall of Fame, *Oklahoma City, Oklahoma*: Display of more than 100 firearms as "functional sculpture." *405-478-2250*
www.nationalcowboymuseum.org

National Fresh Water Fishing Hall of Fame, *Hayward, Wisconsin*: A huge pond surrounds the complex, which is shaped like a giant jumping muskie; its gaping jaw is an observation point that fits 20 people. *715-634-4440*
www.freshwater-fishing.org

National Jousting Hall of Fame, *Mount Solon, Virginia*: Located in a park that also hosts the annual jousting tournament.
434-983-2989 www.nationaljousting.com

National Soccer Hall of Fame and Museum, *Oneonta, New York*: More than 100,000 soccer artifacts, photos and memorabilia, and thousands of photos going back to the late 1800's.
607-432-3351 www.soccerhall.org

Pro-Football Hall of Fame, *Canton, Ohio*: Impressive enshrinement gallery of 229 members; an entire room is dedicated to Super Bowl fanatics.
330-456-8207 www.profootballhof.com

An Athlete's Guide

Get a Grip on Your Golf Game

Everything you need to know to master the green

Golf tournaments haven't quite attained Super Bowl status, but dynamic golfers like Tiger Woods, Annika Sorenstam and Michelle Wie have helped turn a ho-hum sport into one of the coolest games around. Young hotshots draw in younger players to the game, changing its dynamics; golf is not just for billionaires and fat cats anymore. If you're contemplating joining the more than 27 million men and women who tee off each year, read this advice from James Frank, former editor of *Golf* magazine and co-author of *Dave Pelz's Putting Bible*, before you hit the green.

Do I need to join a golf club to play?

No. There are lots of public, daily-fee courses, where you pay per round or for the day. There are about 14,000 golf courses in the country: about 7,000 are daily-fee courses and 2,000 are owned by localities. Private courses account for only about one-third of the total.

How expensive is to play?

Fees at private clubs vary widely but are generally very expensive. At a daily-fee course, the fees are not insignificant. You can find some good ones in the $30 to $50 range and a lot of good ones in the $100 range; fees go up on weekends.

What is the best way to learn the game?

Every newcomer should take some lessons very early on. After you've played a round or two of golf, you pretty much have your swing tendencies in place. Be careful at the outset: once you get into a bad habit, it's difficult to break.

How can I locate golf instructors?

Find a teacher at a course, a driving range, or an adult education program, or go to a golf school—there are thousands around the country, including ones for kids. Many schools advertise in golf magazines, for example. The costs range from a few hundred dollars for a weekend to a few thousand dollars for all-inclusive golf vacations at fancy resorts.

When should I invest in my own set of clubs?

You don't want to buy them right away for a couple of reasons. First, you have to figure out your swing, which you can only do after you've played a few times. Your shape, size and attitude can pretty much tell you what your swing will look like. But all clubs are not the same. If you are short and round, you will need clubs that are constructed differently from those that suit a tall, thin person.

Once you've decided to play seriously and invest in clubs, you should have your clubs fitted. Most pros at clubs and driving ranges can lead you to someone who will watch the way you swing, take measurements and determine what size clubs you need.

If you don't want to buy new equipment, you can buy used clubs at a lot of stores; pros and driving ranges often sell used sets, too. Don't buy any

The chances of making a hole-in-one with any swing are one in 33,000.

•••

equipment until you've tried it out. At the very least, try hitting with the clubs at a driving range.

How do I pick golf clubs?

First, it's important that you like the way the clubs look and that you feel comfortable with the size of the heads. Anyone new to the game, and almost all players who aren't very advanced, should buy game-improvement clubs, or "perimeter-weighted" clubs. The weight of the club is placed around the club head so that even if you don't hit the ball at its "sweet" spot, the clubs will be as forgiving as possible.

How much can I expect to spend on golf clubs?

Very expensive clubs can cost $3,000 for a full set. But you can get good sets for under $200. You can only carry 14 or fewer clubs on the course: 3 woods, a putter, and 10 irons (a 3-iron, a 9-iron, and a few wedges). There's no reason why someone just starting out shouldn't go to a Wal-Mart, or a local sporting goods chain like Sports Authority, and buy a good, adequate set of golf clubs for $150 to $250.

Some good brands in that price range are Wilson, MacGregor and Dunlop. They are not state-of-the-art clubs, but they are perfectly good. And they are of game-improvement design. At the high-end, the good brands are Callaway, Taylor-Made and Cobra. Callaway is the largest company on the high-end; it makes the famous Big Bertha drivers.

Are there any brands to stay away from?

There really aren't a lot of bad clubs out there. One thing to watch out for is shafts made of cheap graphite. Graphite has become a popular replacement for steel because it's lighter than steel, making the head swing faster—and it absorbs the impact of hitting the ball. But graphite can and does break, and cheap graphite breaks easily. Quality graphite clubs should cost more than steel clubs.

How often should a golfer play to see significant improvement?

You cannot improve if you only play once a week, which is what most golfers do. People who are serious practice every day. You should go to

TOUGHING IT OUT ON THE LINKS

Every golf course receives both a course and slope rating by the United States Golf Association. The course rating is established for the scratch golfer; the slope rating evaluates the relative difficulty of a course for players other than scratch. Here are ten of America's toughest courses:

COURSE	MEN/WOMEN	COURSE RATING	SLOPE RATING
Blessings at Clear Creek, *Johnson, Ark.*	M	79.2	155
Butler National, *Oakbrook, Ill.*	M	78.1	152
Concession, *Bradenton, Fla.*	M	77.6	155
Koolau, Kaneoke, *Hawaii*	M/W	78.7	153
Links at Fisher Island, *Fisher Island, Fla.*	W	78.8	155
Los Angeles Country Club, *Los Angeles, Calif.*	W	79.8	153
Ocean Course, Kiawah Island, *Kiawah, S.C.*	M	79.6	155
Pines, The International Golf Club, *Bolton, Mass.*	M	80	155
Riviera Country Club, *Pacific Palisades, Calif.*	W	79.1	152
Trump National, *Westchester, N.Y.*	M	77.8	153

SOURCE: Data from U.S.G.A.

a driving range and work on something every few days. It's easier to have something ingrained in a series of shorter, regular periods than in longer, less frequent periods. A lot of the game is simply learning and mastering the swing.

What can a golfer do to improve his or her swing?

For 95 percent of golfers the solution is to swing slower and not squeeze the grip so hard. You should hold the club just tight enough so that it doesn't fly out of your hands when you swing. When your grip is too tight, your arms and shoulders become tense, making it impossible to swing well. Slow your swing down. And then slow it down more. At some point you will have to see a pro, who can tell you where you need help, teach you some drills and put your swing on videotape so that you can analyze it.

What are some of the frustrations of the game?

Golf is a game of compensation. You have to play your errors. When you mess up, you have to play from where you messed up. You can be out there for six hours, slashing away, and you can hit 140 shots and out of those only one will be a good one. But that's the one that says, "I'll be back next week."

Where's the challenge after you've mastered your swing?

After a while you learn to play the course. That's when it gets to be more fun. One of the clichés is that you aren't playing anyone but yourself and the course. The course is your opponent and playing it intelligently becomes the challenge. You begin to make choices: Should I try to fly it over the stream or lay up short so I have a safer and easier shot? What kind of trouble is over the green? Is there water? Sand? Most novices won't have those experiences for a while, but it all adds to the enjoyment and complexity of the game.

How Handicapping Works
Different strokes for different folks

Golf may be the only sport in which people of differing ability can compete fairly. That's because handicapping allows golfers to shave strokes off their scores depending on the quality of their games and the difficulty of the courses on which they're playing.

In simple terms, your handicap is the number of strokes by which you typically exceed par over 18 holes. But the system now used by the U.S. Golf Association for figuring a handicap is far from simple. Each golfer has a U.S.G.A. handicap index that ranges from +3.4 for outstanding golfers who regularly score under par to 40.4 for players whose scores soar well over 100.

Under U.S.G.A. regulations, a golf club calculates your handicap index. Each course has its own handicap table, based on the course's dif-

---

ⓘ INSIDE INFO

Famous Handicaps

○ **Michael Jordan,** *basketball star*	6
○ **Jimmy Connors,** *tennis star*	11
○ **Robert Redford,** *actor*	12
○ **William Lauder,** *CEO of Estee Lauder*	12
○ **Sandra Day O'Connor,** *former Supreme Court Justice*	12.8
○ **Bill Clinton,** *former President*	13
○ **Sean Connery,** *actor*	15
○ **George W. Bush,** *President*	15
○ **Bill Murray,** *actor*	18
○ **Clint Eastwood,** *actor*	19
○ **George H. W. Bush,** *former President*	20
○ **Warren Buffett,** *investor*	20.8
○ **Newt Gingrich,** *former Speaker of the House*	47

ficulty. By checking where your index falls on the course's handicap table, you can determine how many strokes to subtract from your score in that day's round. The tougher the course, the greater the deduction.

You can estimate your own handicap on sites such as www.usga.org or *Golf* magazine's online handicap estimator at www.golfonline.com. Just plug in the number of rounds you played, your score, the course rating and slope, and you'll see your estimated handicap.

Playing Golf Like a Billionaire

A person's true character comes out during a round on the links

If you're an average golfer, the bad news is that you have no hope of lowering your golf scores beyond a certain point—no matter how much money you have or how much you spend on improving your game. A recent study by the National Golf Foundation, an industry research and consulting service, showed that the average golfer still can't break 100 on an 18-hole round. It has been that way for decades, and it hasn't changed despite the advent of all sorts of high-tech golf clubs and the "juiced up" golf balls that supposedly help you hit longer, straighter shots.

So what's an executive-class golfer who wants to use the game as a tool to succeed in business supposed to do? Forget about improving your golf handicap and start working on your personality handicap. And the best way to improve your personality handicap is to treat your playing partners like they're billionaires even if they're really just country club bums.

In the billionaire golf leagues, as in the billionaire business leagues, discretion is the name of the game. Some billionaire golfers are hookers and some are slicers, but all of them know that the secrets to scoring business and social points lie in loosening up, lightening up and learning to have more fun out on the golf course. Some tips for playing like a billionaire:

SECRET NO. 1: TALK TRASH

Most guides to business golf say you should never try to talk business on the first tee. Better yet, never try to talk business at all. Instead, walk tall and talk trash. If you're playing with a bona fide billionaire, it's likely he's surrounded by sycophants and fawners all day long back at the office. He doesn't need another one out on the links. He wants to be treated like one of the guys for a change. In that regard, remember that good-natured insults are the highest form of flattery. But be prepared to take as good (or as bad) as you give. At all costs, make sure you and your billionaire buddy never take the conversation—or yourselves—too seriously.

SECRET NO. 2: MAKE A BET

Making a wager keeps everyone interested in the outcome of the game, especially if it pits two members of a foursome against the other two. The smaller the wager the better. You can never get the financial edge on a billionaire, so don't even try. Besides, it's not about the money. It's about dealing with one's own strengths and weaknesses, coping with setbacks and adversity, showing patience, persistence and strategic guile. In other words, it's about ego.

SECRET NO. 3: GO AHEAD, GIVE A GOLF TIP

It's wise to avoid giving unsolicited golf tips to playing companions because even well-intended advice can easily backfire if not executed to the letter. But if a billionaire solicits your advice, here's the only golf tip you'll ever need. It comes from Johnny Miller, a former United States Open champion turned television commentator, who says that golfers should time their swing tempo by whispering "Cindy" on their backswings and "Crawford" on their downswings. Angelina Jolie and Julia Roberts also work. Just make sure to stick with names that have four syllables or more.

SECRET NO. 4: TIP THE CADDIE

One of the few ways to make a billionaire feel he is in your debt is to pick up the caddie fees. But just because you play with a billionaire, you don't have to pay like a billionaire. Giving the caddies too much money can be worse than giving them too little because it creates unreasonable expectations for subsequent rounds. It's also kind of tacky. Before you tee off, pull the caddie master aside and ask him to specify the standard fees at that particular course. Add a 20 percent tip if the caddies do even a half-decent job. It never hurts to be in the good graces of someone who carries bags for a billionaire, especially if something valuable happens to shake out.

SECRET NO. 5: HANG AROUND

The time to score business and social points is immediately after the round. Never head straight from the 18th green to the parking lot. Hang around and enjoy the 19th hole. Chances are the billionaire you've played with is also your host, so he will probably feel obliged to buy you a drink. If he wants to talk business, fine. If he doesn't, use the 19th hole to arrange an off-the-course business meeting at some future date. If you really want to surprise him, just say the two magic words that always work with billionaires and country club bums alike—"thank you."

—Harry Hurt

Although golf was originally restricted to wealthy, overweight Protestants, today it's open to anybody who owns hideous clothing.

Dave Barry

● ● ●

The Power Game
It's high, it's far, it's in the rough

Power has become an obsession in golf. A 330-yard drive into the rough, plus a wedge to the green is far more attractive to a player these days than a 280-yard poke and a 5-iron to the pin.

It's all about the equipment and computer analysis, the balls and the Launch Monitor, which, in essence, is a time-lapse X-ray of a swing to determine factors like ball spin and carry distance in order to match a player to the optimum club. "Players are not afraid of missing," says Geoff Shackelford, author of *The Future of Golf: How Golf Lost Its Way and How to Get It Back*. "They're just hitting it as far as they can without worrying about whether they're going to land in the fairway. It's absurd."

One day, ball-shaping and shot-making and strategy may once again come into vogue. But for now, course designers will continue to lengthen and tighten the fairways of the majors in an effort to outdistance the long ball. In 1993, for example, the prestigious Baltusrol Golf Club in Springfield, N.J., added 10 yards to the width of its fairways. "It's a dramatic shift in the way the game is played," says Shackelford. "To anyone who loves the great old golf courses, it's offensive. There used to be an element of strategy, of placement. That is gone now and that is tragic."

It's unfortunate for those who believe accuracy should be rewarded. As it is, power, however errant, is not a hazard. It's the way of the game, unless someone can place a little finesse into the bag of a winner of a major.

—Selena Roberts

SPORTS

How to Play Smart Tennis

Five steps to a better game—mental and physical

Of course, it's important to be physically fit and then to practice, practice, practice. But for people to really enjoy sports, there has to be an element of competitiveness. So, after you get in touch with your inner-winner, say tennis pros, you'll be ready for the following advice:

Step 1: ASSESS YOUR OPPONENT

If you get the chance, watch your opponent play or practice before your next match. Study their movements and strokes; figure out where their weaknesses are. Once you've identified those failings, shape your game to determine how you can maneuver your opponent to take advantage of the weaknesses. For example, if the player has a much weaker backhand than forehand, hit to the weaker side. But don't go so far that you change your own game. If you're primarily a baseline player, and you're playing a hard-core baseliner, switching to become a serve-and-volleyer won't help. But by hitting a lot of deep balls, balls around the court and in corners, you might force mistakes and put yourself in a position to move in and attack.

Step 2: VISUALIZE

Yogi Berra once said that half of baseball is 90 percent mental. Well, you know what he meant, and tennis is, too. Prepare for a match by visualizing your game, playing it out, point by point, in your mind. Close your eyes and picture yourself hitting the strokes exactly the way you want to. Take it to its logical end: make a mental picture of yourself winning.

STEP 3: HAVE A GAME PLAN

Say you've developed a good game plan based on your strengths and your opponent's failings.

But once the match begins, you fall behind five games to one. Do you dump your plan and try something else? Not at all. Stick with the game plan. That doesn't mean that you don't adapt if you find a bigger hole in your challenger's game than the ones you spotted in practice. But if you were thorough and thoughtful going in, you probably picked the right game plan for you, and dumping it probably won't produce a better one.

Step 4: HITTING WINNERS

A lot of tennis players actively try to hit winners: they rear back and try to rip a hole in the opponent's racket, or try desperately to drop a ball daintily over the net. Bad idea. A better strategy is to fully master the basics of tennis first and then concentrate on making your opponent miss. Practice that until you can place the ball so well that your opponent is out of position. That's how to hit winners.

Step 5: RIGHT MENTAL ATTITUDE

Often, players are either over- or underconfident. The overconfident types, believing they are better than they really are, try shots they shouldn't dare try, usually unsuccessfully. The underconfident type of player assumes he'll lose and the assumption is often self-fulfilling. Both mind-sets are damaging to good, smart tennis. The right approach: don't obsess over your opponent's level—just compete as hard as you can, one point at a time.

The Home Court Advantage

How to build the basketball hoop of your dreams

Designing your home court today is not easy or inexpensive. But your options are many, ranging widely in quality, durability and price. Mobility is crucial to playing basketball, and it's also a key

 **TIMELY TIPS**

Picking a Tennis Racket
How to find a good one

You naturally look for an exact fit in shoes, clothes and everything else you buy. Do the same with rackets, individualized instruments that must be chosen carefully. Any racket can be made more or less powerful by adjusting the three systems—handle size and shape, overall weight and balance, and string type and tension. You should plan to adjust the systems of any racket you buy depending on what you want it to do. Warren Bosworth is a racket consultant to stars like Andre Agassi, Monica Seles, Pete Sampras and Lleyton Hewitt, and chairman of Bosworth Tennis (561-241-9966), a company that builds customized rackets. His suggestions:

✔ **BODY.** Wide-body rackets provide power, but at the sacrifice of control. Conventional wisdom suggests that the wider the body, the more power, but the more conventional the racket, the more control. Weight is also a critical factor. Too heavy a racket will strain your wrist, arm, elbow or shoulder, but ultralights have also been a principal cause of injury because they are just too light to overcome the impact of the ball.

✔ **STRING.** Strings are the most important part of the racket in regard to storing energy and influencing the spin of the ball. You have two choices: gut and synthetics. Synthetics, which are much cheaper, are thought to last longer, but you really have to take into account climate and humidity (dry weather is better for strings), surface (clay is

harder on strings), the type of racket (some have grommets, or stringholds, that are harder on strings than others) and the type of player you are (spin players are harder on strings).

✔ **STRING GAUGE.** Gauge, or string thickness, is as critical as string type. Thicker gauges—that is, fatter strings—last longer. The thinner ones provide more feel. Recreational players should expect to get several months out of a set of strings before it loses its flexibility. Tension is another factor. The looser the strings, the more power. Tighter strings may give you more spin control, but also may add shock.

✔ **COST.** Expect to spend $150 to $250 for a standard retail purchase. Look for the previous year's models, which are often just as good as the new ones.

SPORTS

factor in setting up a home court. For gym rats who want to practice on a regulation hoop, however, the traditional 10-foot mounted backboards and pole-secured backboards are still available.

Portable baskets and baskets with adjustable heights are no longer as flimsy as they once were. Players who compete in leagues or gyms should be especially careful in selecting a rim. A springed rim (which gives a little when the ball hits it) will give the shooter a better bounce, but it can cause frustration when the player returns to a real court where tighter steel rims are the rule. To get the ultimate home court advantage, here are your options:

MOUNTED BACKBOARD

PRICE: AROUND $150. The most common of home court hoops can be attached to the house or garage with a few nuts and bolts.

PROS: Very sturdy because it has to be attached to a wall or the side of a building.

CONS: The backboard cannot be moved. The height can't be adjusted, either.

PORTABLE BACKBOARD

PRICE: $200 to $300. Wheels on the base of the basket allow you to move it easily by simply tilting the basket forward. The base should be

Growing Squash

A game with nonstop action now has more gear options

Squash still hasn't hit the mainstream—only 400,000 to 500,000 people play squash across America. But more people are discovering it and finding a squash court is getting easier. In addition to the 3,475 squash courts already in use, another 175 were being built for 2006, according to the United States Squash Racquets Association, to woo more players to the game.

Players also have more options in squash gear. Ten years ago, players could choose from only a handful of rackets; today there are dozens of quality rackets to pick from, says Pat Canavan, a former professional player who runs the New York Athletic Club's squash program. Here are some of the offerings he has tested:

- **Harrow Stealth Racket**
  $250   www.harrowsports.com
  This rigid carbon graphite racket is evenly balanced and has a lightweight head—ideal for experienced players. The sweet spot is smaller than on most rackets, though.

- **Dunlop Jonathon Power Ice Elite Racket**
  $180   www.dunlopsportsonline.com
  This notably light racket is built ultrastiff for accuracy. Ridges on its oversize head add to its sturdiness and give it a soft feel with zero vibration. Deceptively powerful; easy to control.

- **Head Flexpoint 160 Racket**
  $170   www.head.com
  This flexible racket enhances shots with a perfect balance of control and power, says Canavan. But he found the grip too square.
  —Stefani Jackenthal

filled with sand or a combination of water and antifreeze to keep the basket from moving. The height can be adjusted from 7 to the regulation 10 feet. Less expensive portable backboards are made of graphite. The more expensive ones have acrylic backboards that shake less and hold up better in inclement weather.

PROS: The basket can be easily moved to other locations, and the height can be easily adjusted for players of all ages.

CONS: Even with the acrylic backboard, the basket will still shake on hard shots. Because the base is portable, it can at times be wobbly.

IN-GROUND HOOP

PRICE: AROUND $300. The acrylic backboard is attached to a steel pole and inserted in the ground. The height can be adjusted from 7 to 10 feet.

PROS: With an acrylic backboard and base in the ground, this is the sturdiest option.

CONS: It's the most expensive option, and the game cannot be moved.

Hitting the Softball Every Time

Training, batting practice and strategies at the plate can ensure just that

Professional softball players begin with hours of off-season weightlifting and batting practice, but once they get to the plate they can pursue several different approaches. Here's what they do before they get to the on-deck circle and once they're in the batter's box.

TRAINING

Learn to transfer training with weights into hitting with more power. Developing strong leg muscles is important to good hitting, because that's where the spring in your swing comes from. And having a strong lower back is critical to reducing the wear and tear from constant swinging. Work on stomach muscles to keep up with the lower back. For that final burst of power and for building bat speed, work on strengthening your wrists, forearms and biceps.

HITTING THE LONG BALL

Hitting pitches that come in the heart of the plate is easy, but the key to hitting home runs often is knowing how to hit bad pitches hard. Swing to the location of the pitch. If it comes in low, swing with a slight uppercut; for high pitches, swing straight through the ball. The key to hitting any pitch out of the park is to roll the shoulders: turn the hips and transfer weight from the back foot to the front one at the time of contact. Because the pitch floats in slow-pitch softball, the hitter must provide all the momentum. To get even more power on your swing, use a nontraditional grip. A 34-inch bat is the longest permitted by the American Softball Association; hold the bat with your left ring finger on the knob, and then overlap your right hand over the left. The extra length gives you more bat whip and thus more power.

GETTING A HIT EVERY TIME

The hitter should decide where to hit the ball before he sees the pitch. Once he decides where he wants to hit the ball, he should time his swing accordingly. If you want to pull the ball, extend the barrel, the widest part of the bat, in front of your hands at the point of contact. In other words, at the time the bat strikes the ball, the bat barrel is closer to the pitcher than to your hands. If you want to hit the ball up the middle, keep the barrel even with your hands; to hit to the opposite field, point your shoulder in that direction when the bat meets the ball. Use a level swing no matter where the ball is pitched. Any uppercut can lead

to pop outs. The three key factors in hitting are timing the swing, keeping an eye on the ball and transferring your weight at the right moment.

From Little Leaguer to All-Star
Hall-of-Famer Cal Ripken tells you how

With major-league baseball stars signing multimillion-dollar contracts and basking in the spotlight, it's tempting for parents to look at their little athletes and say, "Hmmm. If I just push him a little harder. "Don't do it, says Cal Ripken Jr., who may not be in the spotlight these days (he retired from baseball in 2001) but whose advice is priceless. The former Baltimore Oriole wowed the world with his gritty, gracious pursuit of Lou Gehrig's consecutive-game streak and, as a father of two himself, understands the temptation that parents feel. But he counsels parents to let kids develop an appreciation for baseball and other sports at their own pace. Pushing them won't help, he says. "In order to instill passion for the game, it has to be inside of you. And it's only going to develop if a kid comes to it on his or her own, and if it's fun."

Although Ripken grew up in a baseball family (his dad, Cal Sr., was a longtime coach for the Orioles), he was not pushed into playing the game. Still, his desire to play in the big leagues burned inside him, and from an early age, on the night before his first Little League game each season, he surreptitiously slept in his uniform, his glove by his side. He just wanted to be ready, he said. Here are Ripken's tips for the nearly three million kids who play on Little League teams, and for their parents:

❓ What's the best way to get kids interested in baseball?

The most important thing is to keep it on a fun level. You've got to gear it to whatever makes kids enjoy playing. The worst thing you can see is to go to a Little League game and have parents yelling at the kids. I understand the competitiveness, but too much emphasis on winning saps a lot of the fun out of it. Kids should be encouraged to play any position they want, and to experiment.

● What's the right age to start?

My first competition was as an 8-year-old, which was the age when kids could really play the whole game—hitting, throwing and running. I think it's great you're now shown parts of the game through T-ball and other games like that. Kids can learn how to slide and run a lot earlier than I did.

● A lot of kids love to play but hate to practice. How do you make practice fun?

To learn baseball, like other things, you have to teach fundamentals, and then give kids ample time to practice them. Repetition is key. But it's got a downside: it's boring. The answer is to try to figure out creative ways to make it fun—to find games within the games. Take a game like pepper, and come up with a system where you get points for catches and good throws and make it a competition. All of a sudden the kids won't even realize they've fielded 100 ground balls.

● Is burnout for young pitchers a real threat?

In order to develop your arm you need to develop arm strength, and the way you do that is by throwing straight. Throwing curves doesn't help build up kids' arms. I don't think that you want to not allow them to throw it, but you should make sure that they throw 70 to 80 percent fastballs. You can always teach a kid who has a good arm to throw breaking balls, but if you don't have arm strength, you can't learn to throw a fastball.

● Major leaguers aren't always the best role models; some big stars catch with one hand and violate other

basic fundamentals. **What do you tell a kid who notices that?**

I'll be at a clinic telling kids how important it is to throw overhand, to develop arm strength and accuracy, and a kid will say, "But I saw you on TV and you threw the ball sidearm on a double play." I'll say, "When you get older, you can do some of these things to speed up your throws. But when I was your age, I threw overhand." That's the truth, and it's about all you can say.

Should Kids Play Football?

First weigh the risks and benefits, doctors say

Your 8-year-old comes home one day and proudly announces his intention to try out for the local peewee football team. You've just finished watching another NFL quarterback get carried off the field on a stretcher. It's hard not to picture your son in the same position some day. Do you let him play?

Pediatricians and psychologists see this decision as just one of the many parents confront daily, from what kind of school the kids should attend to whether and when they should drive a car. The first consideration for a child who asks to play football is what are the risks and benefits? Weighing them depends on the child, especially as he gets older. Participating in a sport like football may be more important for kids who need it for self-esteem, psychologists say, because it makes them stand out in high school, for example, or is their ticket to college. Those psychological factors must be considered against the chances of putting their bodies at risk.

How great is that risk? That, too, varies depending on the level of play In general, football has become much safer in recent years as equipment, especially helmets, has improved and rules have been tightened to prevent certain kinds of tackling and blocking. The number of deaths directly related to football has dropped dramatically since 1968, when 26 high school players died, according to the National Center for Catastrophic Sport Injury. Out of some 1.5 million high school and junior high school teens who played football in 2004, four died from injuries directly related to football. Similar declines in the number of permanently disabling head and neck injuries have brought the annual number down to a handful—low numbers but no consolation, of course, if it's your son or daughter.

While catastrophic injuries are relatively rare these days, knee injuries and concussions appear to be on the rise. Knee injuries especially trouble doctors. "If you screw up your knees playing football, they're hurt for the rest of your life," says Dr. Jeffrey L. Brown, chairman of the pediatrics department at New York United Hospital Medical Center. He warns parents to be cautious, but not to discourage kids totally from playing football, especially at younger ages—when the level of play is less intense and knee injuries are generally less severe.

One step parents can take is to get to know the coach and the program he runs. Find out what emergency equipment he keeps on the sidelines and what measures he takes to prevent players from getting heat stroke. (Heat was responsible for three deaths among high school football players in 2004.) Of course, other sports can be as dangerous as football, if not more so. In fact, per capita, the rates of serious injury are higher in ice hockey, gymnastics and pole vaulting. Some parents might now be asking themselves, "Bowling, anyone?"

❝
Cheerleaders age 5 to 18 made some 209,000 trips to the emergency room between 1990 and 2002.

• • •

Sports for a Summer Day
You'd play a lot more if you could remember the rules. Here they are

Baffled about how to keep score in badminton? Not sure how to set up the croquet wickets? Unclear on the difference between a leaner and a ringer in horseshoes? Don't know whether you have to win the serve before getting a point in volleyball?

Here are the basic rules and regulations for four popular pastimes. So, go ahead and dig out the equipment you've stashed away in a musty basement corner and hit the beach or backyard.

BADMINTON

Badminton was popular in England in the 1870's, after being imported from India (where it was called *poona*) by British army officers. The eighth duke of Beaufort introduced the game to English society at his estate, called Badminton, in Gloucester.

Badminton is similar to tennis. The object is to volley, with light rackets, a shuttlecock or bird (a small, hemispheric cork with a tail of 14 to 16 feathers) until it is missed by your opponent or hit out of bounds. The game can be played indoors or outdoors, by two or four people.

• THE RULES. The initial serve goes from the right half of the court to the half diagonally opposite. The serving team continues to serve until losing a rally or committing a fault. A fault occurs if you serve overhand, touch the net or do not serve diagonally across the court. Points may only be scored by the serving team. In doubles, a player serves until his team commits a fault, at which time the teammate gains the serve. Following each game, the players switch sides. The winning side serves first.

SPORTS

• **SCORING.** All doubles and men's singles games are played to 15 or 21 points; women's singles games go to 11 points. The first player or team to win two games wins the match. If a match goes to three games, the players switch sides when the score reaches 8 in a 15-point game and 6 in an 11-point game. In a 15-point game, the team to reach 13 first has the option of extending the game to 18 points if the score becomes tied at 13. In 11-point games, the score may be extended to 12 if the game becomes tied at either 9 or 10. In a one-game match to 21 points, the score may be extended to 24 if there is a tie at 19 or extended to 23 if the game is tied at 20.

BADMINTON: *The basic equipment and layout for a regulation game*

RACKET · Head/Frame · Strings · T-piece · Singles long service line · Ferrule · Grip · Handle · Center line · Butt end · 5'1" high net · 44' · 17' · 20' · 2'6" · Short service line · Singles side line · Doubles side line · Side alley · Doubles long service line · Right service court · SHUTTLECOCK/SHUTTLE/BIRD · Skirt 2¾" · Ribs · Weight: 1/16 OZ. · 1" diameter Button

CROQUET

The game probably originated in France in the 17th century. It became popular in England and Ireland during the 19th century and made its way to the Colonies in about 1870. It was one of the first games in which women and men competed on an even basis. There are three leading modern versions of the game: American lawn croquet, English croquet and roque. Most croquet balls are made of wood, but better balls are made of hard rubber or plastic. The mallet head may be of wood or other material.

• **THE RULES.** There are two courses: nine wickets and two stakes or six wickets and one stake. In the American nine-wicket game, the court is fitted to the area available. The English court has definite boundaries and locations for the six wickets and peg (see diagrams on the facing page). A toss determines who gets which color. These colors are usually painted on the stake, or peg, and control the order of play. Players—two to eight people can play at one time—use balls of the color allocated to them. The first striker hits the ball with his mallet at the balkline or home stake, depending on what course you are playing on. Subsequent players do the same. The course leads through the wickets, or hoops.

Strikers alternate turns. Your turn continues as long as you drive the ball through the proper wicket. If you fail to do so or hit another player's ball, you lose your turn. You also lose your turn if your mallet hits the wicket or the ground but not the ball.

A striker makes a roquet by knocking his ball into an opponent's. If you do so you have three options: (1) You may place your ball against your opponent's and putting your foot on your ball, drive your opponent's ball away; (2) You can drive both

CROQUET: *The basic equipment and layout for a regulation game*

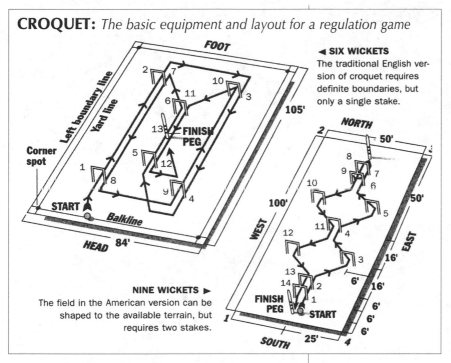

◄ **SIX WICKETS**
The traditional English version of croquet requires definite boundaries, but only a single stake.

NINE WICKETS ►
The field in the American version can be shaped to the available terrain, but requires two stakes.

HORSESHOES

Horseshoe pitching, by some accounts, originated with Greek and Roman soldiers. The more modern version developed in Europe during the 17th century. Today, some 15 million enthusiasts play in tournaments, leagues, parks and backyards across the country and Canada, according to the National Horseshoe Pitchers Association of America (www. horseshoepitching.com).

● THE RULES. The object of the game is to toss a shoe so that it rings the metal stake or comes closer to the stake than your opponent's toss. In singles, both contestants throw from the same side of the course. Shoes are tossed underhanded. Each pitcher is allotted two tosses in an inning. The pitcher who scores in an inning leads off the next.

balls; or (3) you can simply place your ball ahead of your opponent's and take two strokes. Once you hit an opponent's ball, you cannot hit it again until you go through another wicket.

● SCORING. A ball put through the proper wicket in the proper direction scores a point. Winners are decided by the total points scored or by the order in which the course is completed.

● SCORING. Each ringer is worth three points. Each shoe closer than an opponent's is worth one point, but

HORSESHOES: *A regulation course and a look at leaners*

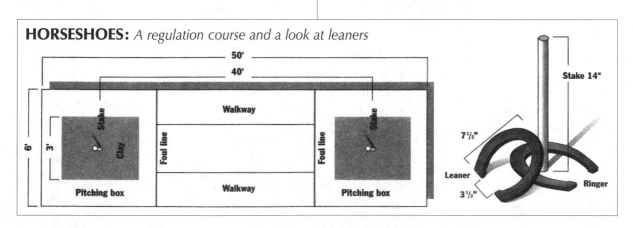

shoes only score when landing within six inches of the stake. If an opponent's shoe knocks a ringer off, it loses value. Two points are awarded if you land two shoes closer than any of your opponents. Leaners, or hobbers, and shoes actually touching the stake count only as close shoes. (In informal games, a leaner can count for two points.) Singles matches are usually played to 50 points, doubles to 21.

VOLLEYBALL

Volleyball was invented by a Y.M.C.A. director in Holyoke, Massachusetts in 1895. It's been modified somewhat since and in 1964 was introduced in the Olympics.

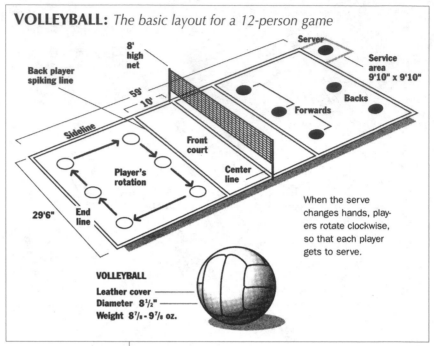

VOLLEYBALL: *The basic layout for a 12-person game*

8' high net

Server

Service area 9'10" x 9'10"

Back player spiking line

59'

10'

Backs

Forwards

Sideline

Front court

Player's rotation

Center line

End line

29'6"

When the serve changes hands, players rotate clockwise, so that each player gets to serve.

VOLLEYBALL
Leather cover
Diameter 8½"
Weight 8⅞ - 9⅞ oz.

• THE RULES. There are six people on each team—usually three forward and three back. The height of the net varies: 8 feet high for men; 7½ feet high for women and sometimes lower for kids. The players can hit the ball to each other before hitting it back over the net. However, the ball can only be hit a maximum of three times on one side of the net. A player may not hit the ball twice in a row.

• SCORING. Points are scored by hitting the ball into the opposing court in a way that the competition cannot return it. The team serving gains one point for doing this and continues serving. If the receiving team does it, it wins the right to serve. A game is 15 points, but it must be won by two points, thus a 14-14 tie continues until either team gains a two-point advantage. When the serve changes hands, players rotate clockwise, so that each player gets to serve.

How to Ride a Raging Bull

Hold on for eight seconds and earn bragging rights for a lifetime

By far the rodeo's most popular attraction is the man-versus-beast sport of bull riding. It's one of the most dangerous sports around, yet the rules couldn't be simpler: ride with only one hand on the bull rope and stay on the bucking bull for a full eight seconds. If you let your free hand touch the bull or yourself, or if the bull tosses you off before eight seconds are up, you are disqualified.

Once the eight-second horn sounds, you must dismount—a process that can be as dangerous as being bucked off. Don't forget, the bulls are bred for their bucking ability and aggressiveness—whether you're on their hump or on the dirt. Stay on for eight seconds and a set of judges assigns you a score; 100 is a perfect score but it is rarely attained. Only one in ten bull riders stay on for eight seconds, and those who do usually score between 50 and 80 points.

GETTING OFF ISN'T EASY, EITHER

Not surprising for a sport that involves climbing on the back of a 2,000-pound twisting mass of muscle, injuries are routine. Bull riders suffer injuries mainly to their arms and shoulders. Mercifully, serious chest injuries have dropped considerably since the 90's, when riders started wearing Kevlar vests to protect the chest and internal organs.

Aside from agility, good bull riders need physical and mental strength. Technique is important, too, of course. Here are some pointers for getting off a raging bull from Professional Bull Riders, Inc: "To dismount, a bull rider reaches down with his free hand, jerks loose his riding hand from his bull rope and flings himself off as the bull is kicking, so that the momentum of the kick will propel the rider as far away from the bull as possible.

When possible, a rider waits until the bull is moving or spinning away from his riding hand, at which time the bull rider dismounts in the direction of his riding hand. For example, a right-handed bull rider waits until the bull spins left, before dismounting from the bull's right side."

BEYOND THE BULL

Bodacious. The name of one of the most feared and famous bulls in bull-riding history. Retired in 1995, Bodacious died a natural death five years later, when he was 12.

Bull rope (or bell). A rope wrapped around the bull's chest that a bull rider hangs on to. A bell at the bottom of the rope pulls the rope down once the rider dismounts or is bucked off.

Down in the well. A dangerous situation in which the bull spins and forcefully pulls down the rider into his swirling movements.

Hooked. A dangerous situation that occurs after a rider is bucked off or dismounts a bull and the animal charges after him, trying to hook him with his horns.

Muley. A hornless bull.

Rank. A bull that is difficult to ride.

SPORTS

Rodeos With a Twist

Where the cowboys and cowgirls are gay

A gay rodeo cowboy might have been a non-concept to most Americans before the movie *Brokeback Mountain*, but the International Gay Rodeo Association (www.igra.com) has more than 4,500 members and is made up of amateur gay rodeo clubs in 33 regions of the United States and Canada. That means you'll almost always find a gay rodeo around the corner.

Generally, a gay rodeo is three days of typical and not-so-typical rodeo events. But, says Barry Luke who represents the Florida Gay Rodeo Association, "the first twist in ours is that men and women are allowed to compete in every category." So events like barrel racing, normally for women, are open to all, as are the macho bull riding, bareback bronco riding, steer riding and calf roping. "Contestants are also allowed to choose what gender they'd like to compete as," Luke says, meaning that folks in the middle of changing from male to female or female to male can pick what best suits them.

Finally, just as traditional rodeos have their own brand of entertainment events, so do gay rodeos. But in this case they're called camp events and include Goat Dressing (a team trying to get a pair of panties onto a goat) and the Wild Drag Race (involving a man, a woman, a drag queen and a wild steer).

—Beth Greenfield

Deals on Wheels
The search for the perfect bike

A stroll into today's bike shop is not for the faint of heart. The days of banana seats and coaster brakes are long gone, replaced by the likes of titanium frames and brakes, and shock-absorbing suspension forks. But don't be intimidated—or fooled. Inside that shop, there is a bike that is exactly what you need, and lots more that you don't need. The following guide through the maze of bike styles and sizes will help you pick one that's perfect for you and your pocketbook. It is compiled from the best advice of biking pros.

❓ What basic types of bikes are there?

There are three types of bikes: road, mountain and hybrid. Each is built for a certain type of riding. A breakdown:

• **Road bikes:** The lightest and fastest of the three bicycle types, these bikes are primarily for people who will be doing distance riding on smooth pavement. The skinny, smooth tires and low handlebars give riders speed and low wind resistance but also make some cyclists feel vulnerable in traffic. Most road bikes weigh between 20 and 30 pounds, but some high-end models can weigh 16 pounds or less. The majority of people riding road bikes today are athletes who use them for training purposes.

• **Mountain bikes:** Created by outdoors enthusiasts in Northern California, they are now the most popular bike in the country. The upright seating, knobby tires and easy gearing make these bikes ideal for off-road riding. But even if you live in the heart of the city and only occasionally hit a trail mountain, bikes offer comfort and stability. If you use your bike only for riding with the kids or short trips around town, a mountain bike might better suit your needs than a road bike.

• **Hybrid bikes:** Hybrids combine the upright seating and shifting of mountain bikes, but offer the thin, smooth tires of road bikes for speed. Many bikers like the versatility of a hybrid; you can ride on some less-challenging trails, and also make better time than you would on a mountain bike. But don't buy a hybrid if you are a serious cyclist: if you want to ride on challenging trails, the hybrid's frame and thin tires can't handle the challenge. And if you want to take it on the open road, you'll be battling wind resistance the whole ride.

❓ How much money should I spend on a bike?

Bikes aren't cheap. You can spend anywhere from several hundred to several thousand dollars for a high-end model. It's hard to purchase a bad bike today, though—you can find a decent bike for $500 to $800. But a less-expensive bike won't perform as well or last as long as a high-end model. Your extra money is buying lighter, sturdier frames, and components (like gears and brakes) that can take a beating and last a long time.

❓ How do I know if my bike fits me?

One of the most common errors is buying a bike that is too large. The best advice is buy the smallest bike that you can comfortably ride. Tests to determine if the size is right for you include straddling the bike frame and lifting the front tire up by the handlebars. There should be several inches of clearance between your crotch and the bike frame, 1 to 2 inches for a road bike, and at least 3 to 4 inches for a mountain bike.

When riding, you should be able to straighten, but not strain, your leg. Adjusting the seat height can help this. Also, especially on road bikes, be sure that you can comfortably reach the handlebars. And on a road bike, make sure

Beyond the Basic Bike

Bike shops are dangerous places for those with an itchy wallet finger. There are hundreds of bike accessories you could purchase, but a much smaller number that you actually need. Here are a few of the basics, and some exotic innovations:

FRAME: They come in all shapes and sizes, but the lightest and fastest are made of titanium and carbon fiber.

SUSPENSION SYSTEMS: Similar to shock absorbers on a motorcycle, the pneumatic or hydraulic forks absorb the impact of big bumps and reduce strain on hands and arms. Popular, but not necessary.

TWIST GRIP SHIFTS: Faster and lighter than traditional Rapid Fire gears.

BAR ENDS: They give you extra leverage when you're up and out of the saddle when climbing. Also, when road riding, they allow a more aerodynamic position and a useful alternate hand position.

TIRES: Can be specialized to fit your riding needs. The spacing and pattern of the knobs affect the tire's performance in sand, mud or hard-packed trails.

TOE CLIPS: Road cyclists may want to investigate toe clips that shoes lock into, while mountain bikers should invest in a pair of toe clips that you slide in and out of. Lock clips give better leverage on climbs, but mountain bikers need to easily put their feet down when navigating tricky trail turns.

your knees are just barely brushing your elbows as you pedal.

❓ There are so many frames to choose from. What's best for me?

Frames vary in price and expense, with the heaviest and least expensive being a steel frame. More expensive and lighter are aluminum, carbon and titanium frames, in that order. One-piece, molded composite frames are the lightest of all but they also carry a price tag in the thousands of dollars. If you are planning on racing, a light frame is a necessity. But for weekend riders, it is just a luxury that will make your ride somewhat more enjoyable.

❓ Which bike brands should I look at?

The surest way to buy a quality bike is to avoid hot gimmicks and new names, and stick with compa-

nies that produce consistently high-quality bikes. For mountain and hybrid bikes, try Trek and Cannondale, which are two of the biggest American companies. Also try GT, Specialized and Schwinn.

For road bikes, Specialized and Trek are reliable. For bikes guaranteed to put a dent in your wallet, look overseas to the Italian-made bikes, such as Pinarello and De Rosa, which some shops carry. They are the most expensive, sometimes as much as $5,000, but not necessarily better than some domestic brands. (For bike trips, see "Your Personal Tour de France," page 572).

❓ What are some easy bike repairs I can do myself?

Everyone should know how to fix a flat tire. Always carry a pump, a patch kit and a spare tire tube. If you get a flat on the road or trail, put on a new

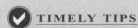
A Superbike at a Super Price

. . . And pedals are extra

Today's bicycles may look like those of yesteryear but the resemblance is largely superficial. Changes in materials and technology have made bikes lighter, stronger, more comfortable—and more expensive. Take the Six13 model, made by Cannondale and ridden by the Lampre-Caffita team in the 2005 Tour de France. It uses aluminum and carbon fiber throughout. At 15.5 pounds, it is much lighter than the 23-pound Rotrax, a state-of-the-art racing model from 1959. Even the finish was designed with weight-saving in mind: using a clear coat instead of paint makes it about an ounce lighter. Amateur cyclists can have a Six13 for about $8,000. But they'll have to pay extra for pedals.　　　　—Ian Austen

SOURCES: Tom Austen, Cannondale Bicycle Corporation; Mike Barry, Bicycle Specialties

tube. If you get a second flat, you can find the hole and patch it. Practice patching a hole at home before you go on a trail. You should always carry a mini tool—the Swiss Army knife of the bike world. It's an all-in-one tool that includes an Allen wrench and spoke wrench, and can be bought at a bike store.

People often forget to keep their bike chains clean and lubricated. If you have a grimy chain, first spray the chain and derailleurs with degreaser, then wet a sponge with warm, soapy water and hold it around the chain as you spin the wheels. Continue until the chain is clean, then dry with rags. Or, buy a chain-cleaning kit that snaps around the chain and cleans and degreases it. Remember to regularly lubricate your chain—lubricants made specifically for bikes can be found at all bike shops. If you ride in the rain, be sure to lubricate your chain every time.

How to Swim Like a Fish

Sure you can stay afloat, but are you an "efficient" swimmer?

Remember those mind-numbing and exhausting laps you were forced to do when you were learning to swim? Unfortunately, many of the swimming techniques you were taught probably won't help you swim better or faster. Terry Laughlin, who runs Total Immersion Swimming in New Paltz, N.Y. (800-609-7946), is a world-class swimming coach. He has dedicated his career to teaching advanced swimming techniques to people who hit the pool for fun and fitness, not for gold medals. Students who attend his seminars know how to swim, but he teaches them to be more efficient swimmers.

Laughlin believes you improve your "stroke efficiency" not with endless laps but by making your body more "slippery," so that it glides through the water by offering less resistance. The formula for swimming speed is this: Velocity = Stroke length (how far you travel with each stroke) x Stroke Rate (how fast you take them). Swimmers are naturally inclined to stroke faster, but the potential for improvement there is limited and the work it takes burns more energy than it's worth.

According to Laughlin, most of the best swimmers in the world actually stroke fewer times than other swimmers: their speed, he argues, comes from increasing the length they travel on each stroke. Your body's tendency is to do that by stroking and kicking harder, but churning your hands and legs won't help much. A better bet, Laughlin says, is to improve your body position in three ways:

1. Balance your body. Many swimmers find that the lower half of their body—the longer, heavier end—lags beneath the surface when they swim, like a lot of excess baggage in a boat. They kick harder—but it won't help. Laughlin calls the solution "pressing your body": push your chest down into the water as you swim, which has the effect of lifting your hips and hence your legs. It takes practice to master this, but it works.

2. Swim taller. Stretch out your body, which will help you glide through the water. As each hand enters the water, reach forward—not downward—before starting your pull. This will be difficult. Your inclination will be to automatically reach for the bottom as your hand hits the water. To fight the tendency, start each stroke as if you're reaching for the wall at the end of a lap. Leave your hand extended for as long as you can before beginning to stroke. It may seem odd to spend more time than you're accustomed to with both arms stretched in front of you, but it will help you glide.

3. Swim on your side. Yachts move more easily through water than barges do. Yet most of us swim more like barges—which lie flat on the water—than like yachts, which are frequently leaning to the side, leaving only a narrow sliver in the water. So when you swim, roll from side to side as you stroke. It's not natural and your body will fight it because you will feel unbalanced. But master it and you'll swim more fluidly with less effort.

...And to Bob Like a Boat

1. Learn to sink evenly, not like a ship with all it's cargo at the stern.

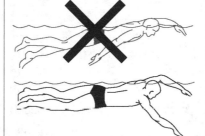

2. Longer boats go faster. Make yourself "taller" by keeping your arms extended in front as much as possible.

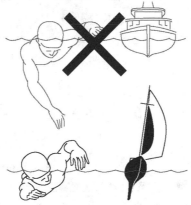

3. Yachts move more easily through the water than barges, which lie flat in the water. So when you swim, roll from side leaving only a narrow sliver in the water.

A Mask, Fins and the Deep Blue
Top spots to get the most out of snorkeling

Jacques Cousteau was best known for scuba diving, a sport he invented. The films he produced made the ocean come alive, revealing the teeming life and vibrancy of the world's waters. But his own eyes were opened not by scuba diving but by snorkeling, when in 1936, he first donned a pair of goggles and floated on the surface of the sea. "Sometimes we are lucky enough to know that our lives have been changed, to discard the old, embrace the new and run headlong down an immutable course," he later wrote. "It happened to me on that summer's day, when my eyes were opened to the sea."

Today scuba diving has largely supplanted snorkeling in the public imagination. But snorkeling still has the power to captivate, and more people snorkel each year than scuba. Partisans say snorkeling offers more freedom than scuba diving, which requires clunky gear and sometimes keeps you tethered to a boat. For snorkeling, all you need are fins, a mask and a snorkel. It's much cheaper and you don't need the certification that scuba diving requires.

Before you hit the water, you'll need to outfit yourself

SPORTS

properly. Most important, pick a mouthpiece and mask that fit comfortably. To test whether a mask fits, hold it to your face, sniff slightly to hold it in place, and let go. If the mask stays on and there are no leaks, the fit is sufficient. Try on as many as five masks with different shapes to see which fits best. Buy fins that cover your entire feet, instead of the open-heeled fins. And buy your equipment in a dive shop, not a discount store. As for destinations, snorkeling pros say the following are among the best:

Bahamas, Out Islands. You won't find the posh hotels and casinos of Freeport on Abaco, Bimini, Eleuthera and the other small islands in the Bahamas but snorkeling sights are luxurious.

BEST TIME: *February-September*

CONTACT: Bahamas Out Island Tourism Adventures, 242-333-3282.

Bonaire Marine Park, Netherlands Antilles. This island off Venezuela's coast, less famous than neighboring Aruba and Curacao, is a diver's paradise. Snorkeling—from its coral gardens to tube sponges as long as a person—is unmatched.

BEST TIME: *Year-round*

CONTACT: Sand Dollar Dive and Photo, 800-288-4773.

Heron Island, Australia. One of about 900 islands that make up the Great Barrier Reef, Heron sits in a protected marine sanctuary, so the diversity of fish life is unparalleled. Park rangers are accessible and knowledgeable, so you learn as you dive.

BEST TIME: *April-July*

CONTACT: P & O Resorts, Ltd., 800-248-824.

Looe Key, Florida. One of dozens of terrific snorkeling spots in the Florida Keys, the most popular diving location in the world. Looe Key features a national marine sanctuary remarkable for fish life and numerous sunken ships that the schoolmasters, snappers and barracuda dart through.

BEST TIME: *Year-round; winds limit visibility in winter.*

CONTACT: Outcast Charters, 305-872-4680.

Finding Bigger, Meaner Fish

Landing a tarpon or a bonefish with a fly rod poses quite a challenge

Fly-fishing has stood the test of time. It's always been popular with serious anglers and, of course, still is. But these days, stream fishing is having to share the limelight with its coastal cousin, saltwater fly-fishing. While fly-fishing on the high seas may lack the bucolic beauty and some of the fly-making artistry of fly-rodding in the streams of Montana, what it offers instead is simple: bigger, meaner fish.

Tarpon, bonefish, striped bass and sailfish are the hard-running and often mammoth quarry of saltwater fly-rodding. Big trout, a primary target of stream fishers, run to 20 pounds; tarpon and sailfish can easily tip the scales at 100 pounds or more. But saltwater fly-fishing isn't just about size; striped bass and bonefish can take your line and tear away from you at dazzling speeds, and the fight to reel them in can give you a workout that'll make a day in the gym look like a walk in the park.

Ocean fly-fishing isn't as accessible as stream fishing, in which you can dabble in most states in the country. And to do some of the best saltwater

Sometimes we are lucky enough to know that our lives have been changed... It happened to me on that summer's day, when my eyes were opened to the sea.

Jacques Cousteau

● ● ●

fly-rodding, you have to travel to exotic locales like the Florida Keys. But you can find good ocean fishing up and down the East Coast, and a few other places besides. (Unfortunately, if you live on the West Coast, most experts say the Pacific Ocean fly-fishing just doesn't measure up.)

It's nice to have an expensive boat that can take you to more far-flung, and less-fished, spots. But shallow water is in many ways the best place to fly-fish, and you can do so successfully off beaches and cliffs, and in and around estuaries.

This is not a sport of kings, but some of the equipment you'll need can cost a princely sum. The specialized gear is much heavier and stronger than for stream fishing, reflecting the bigness and meanness of your foe. The high-end equipment can be outrageously expensive, but you don't have to spend a fortune for quality gear.

For most of the fishing that you'll probably do, you'll need a saltwater-grade graphite rod in the 8/9 or 9/10 weight class, which typically runs anywhere from about $100 to $400. Big-game rods, for going after tarpon or sailfish, say, will run a bit more. The rest of the equipment you'll need—line, leader, flies, etc.—will run a few hundred dollars more.

Flies That Never Fail

Do fish find funny names alluring?

Rule number one for aspiring fly fishermen: never say the word "worm" to another fisherman. Instead, try peppering your conversation with words like "hopper," "nymph" or "woolly bugger" (a few commonly used flies). You'll fit right in.

Fly fishermen fish with imitation insects (flies) instead of worms or minnows, and pride themselves on the intricacy and variety of their flies. To ease your transition into the large and sometimes intimidating world of flies, here is a quick guide to some of the most popular and successful ones, according to fly guru John Bailey. From his fly shop in Livingston, Mont., Bailey has been supplying fly fishermen with his hand-tied flies for decades, and using them to fish the nearby Yellowstone River for more than 40 years. He's also a fly-tier to the stars: he served as a consultant and fly-fishing instructor for the Robert Redford movie *A River Runs Through It.*

Woolly Bugger. One of the most universal flies, the woolly bugger works for both trout and bass on eastern and western waters. The woolly bugger is a streamer fly, which means it replicates minnows that swim below the surface.

Muddler Minnow. Like the woolly bugger, the muddler is a streamer for both trout and bass, but it is more effective on streams than it is on lakes.

Adams. Good for trout fishing, the Adams is a dry fly, which means it floats on top of the surface like an insect.

Royal Wulff. Another dry fly for trout. The white wings on this one allow you to keep an eye on it even in rough or choppy waters.

Hare's Ear Nymph, Prince Nymph, Bitch Creek Nymph and Damsel. Nymph flies imitate aquatic insects in a particular developmental stage. Although nymphs are primarily for trout, the bitch creek nymph is good for both trout and bass, but is rarely used in eastern waters. The damsel is best for catching lake trout.

Elk Hair Caddis. Another good dry fly for trout. This one is made out of real elk hair. Because elk hair is hollow, the fly floats well.

Dave's Hopper. This fly, named for fly-fishing expert Dave Whitlock, replicates a grass hopper, floats on the surface and can be used in most places.

A Little Night Fishing

When there's a moon out, fly-fishing beckons

Some of the best shore-based fly-fishing for striped bass in the Northeast takes place at sundown and after, and it has its special rewards and challenges.

Stripers do a lot of nocturnal feeding. As darkness falls, stripers often move inshore in quest of forage fish like sand eels, within casting range of the shore-based fly-rod angler. Some fly-rod enthusiasts will not fish at night. For them, it is no fun if they cannot see birds working, baitfish skittering along the surface and bass breaking or slashing at a fly. On some still, foggy evenings without a moon, you're lucky to see just the end of the fly-rod. But on clear, starry nights, you can spot surface-feeding bass out to 50 feet or so. And even when they can't be seen, they can be heard.

Night fly-fishing for stripers calls for some special disciplines:

• Since you can't see the line as it unfurls fore and aft, you have to rely on rhythm and feel. Some night casters use a heavier line—a 10-weight on a 9-weight rod, for example—to help them feel when the line has straightened out on the back cast. With the heavier line, there is a bit more of a tug. Still others wrap several turns of monofilament 20 or 30 feet from the end of their line, which warns, when it passes through their fingers on the retrieve, that it is time to make another cast.

• At night, it sometimes helps to shorten the length of your cast. A shorter line is easier to handle. For instance, if you routinely cast 80 feet without special effort, try cutting back to 60 feet. If you do a lot of after-dark casting, you will sense when you are working the right amount of line. Obviously, a longer cast is sometimes needed to reach the fish, and, if you know that to be so, go ahead and try for more distance.

• If you botch your back cast and hit the beach behind you, always inspect the hook. It might have picked up a bit of seaweed or, even worse, gotten its point broken or bent by impact with a stone.

It is a good idea to crush the barbs on your hooks with a pair of pliers. That way hooks can readily be removed from bass that you want to release, and if you keep a tight line this won't cause you to lose any fish.

• If wind and tide have combined to concentrate a line of weed against the beach, you will have to check your fly often. Fish ignore a fly with weed hanging from it, even if it is just a slender tendril of eel grass an inch or two long. If there is a lot of weed in the water, you will simply have to check your fly frequently. At times the weed is in a band—15 to 30 feet wide—against the beach. You can deal with that situation by casting beyond it and, on your retrieve, picking up your fly before it reaches the weed.

• Before setting out for night fishing, stow your gear in your shirt, vest or pack with care. Have a special place for a light—a hat-mounted light is good because it frees your hands to change flies and release fish—knife, pliers, hook sharpener, flies, leader material and close-up glasses (if you need them) for working on leaders and flies. Otherwise, you might wind up kneeling on the beach frantically searching for a key item while stripers are rolling on the surface 50 feet away.

—Nelson Bryant

God never did make a more calm, quiet, innocent recreation than angling.

Izaak Walton, from the 1676 edition of his classic, *The Compleat Angler*

• • •

✔ **TIMELY TIPS**

Rare Books for an Angler's Soul

If you'd like to fish in a wiser man's boots or touch the spirit of angling in the past, now or whenever, pick up one of these :

1. Roland Pertwee's *The River God*, in which a great colonel with side whiskers fans the fishing flame in a young man. When the young man's father admonishes him, saying that he can't always fish, the son responds that he can, and that he has "proved it for 30 years and more."

2. G.E.M. Skues's *Mr. Theodore Castwell*, the tale of a man who dies, goes to "his own place," asks for and then fishes a lovely stretch of a chalk stream that yields a two-and-a-half-pound trout on every cast, fish after fish. Only when he wants to stop does he learn that he's not in heaven but in the other place.

3. Izaak Walton's *The Compleat Angler* embodies a pastoral tradition that fishermen subscribe to every time they choose to fish where trout are wild and there are no crowds. This enduring book abounds in simple truths like "as no man is born an artist, so no man is born an angler" and "be quiet and go a-fishing."

4. Dame Juliana Berners' *The Treatise of Fishing with an Angle*, written in 1496, gives glimpses into a world that could deepen and enrich the piscatorial experience.

5. Frederic M. Halford, in *Dry-Fly Fishing in Theory and Practice,* depicts the dry-fly revolution of the late 19th century. Serious fly-fishers will enjoy shrewd thoughts about major and minor problems in fly-fishing in any work by Skues; and there is no better place to study the origins of the modern American fly-fishing temperament than in the notes and letters of Theodore Gordon.

6. Henry Van Dyke's *A Creelful of Fishing Stories* is an anthology ranging from Plutarch and Theocritus to John Buchan and Lord Grey of Fallodon. Another, fuller anthology, Charles Goodspeed's *A Treasury of Fishing Stories* brings us into the beginning of modern-day fishing.

There are several dozen dealers in used, rare and older fishing books who can help choose, and from whom modestly priced readers' editions can be had—or fine first editions. Among them:

- **Callahan & Company,** Booksellers, Box 505, Peterborough, N.H. 03458 (callahanbooks@cheshire.net).

- Craig Douglass at **Anglers Bookcase,** 148 Walden Brook Way, Aiken, S.C. 29803 (books@anglersbookcase. com).

- **James Cummins Books,** 699 Madison Ave., New York, N.Y. 10021 (cummins@panix.com).

- **Judith Bowman Books,** 98 Pound Ridge Road, Bedford, N.Y. 10506 (jubobo@aol. com).   —Nick Lyons

The Call of the Hunt

Choose your prey, dress warmly and head for the woods

Hunting is a sport of precision, skill, challenge and being outdoors. You have four sports to choose from. You can hunt waterfowl (ducks and geese), upland birds (quail, dove, grouse and pheasant), deer or elk. Each sport has its own seasons, locations, and pros and cons. Dave Petzal, deputy editor of *Field and Stream*, helped compile a beginner's guide to the basics of hunting.

WATERFOWL

Waterfowl are, of course, found near water. Duck hunters spend their time crouched in fields and blinds (structures that hunters erect to conceal them from the ducks) alongside lakes, ponds and marshes. The North American goose population is larger than the duck population. One reason: many geese have adapted to their surroundings and may stay in one spot all year long, rather than migrate. Hunting geese is similar to hunting ducks. The only differences are the seasons and limits. Check with your local fish and wildlife department or a good sporting goods store for local information.

WHERE TO HUNT: There are four principal North American migration routes. So no matter where you live, you're not more than a state or two away from a duck thoroughfare. Much of the best duck hunting land is private. You will need to stick to public land or pay a user's fee for the private land.

WHEN TO HUNT: Early in the morning. You can't shoot until the first daylight, but plan on starting your day about 3 a.m., so you can get set up and ready by sunrise. The best shooting is generally at sunrise and sunset. Duck hunting seasons vary by region, but you can plan on hunting somewhere between November and January, depending on how far south you live. Seasons are set each August by the local fish and wildlife department.

ESSENTIAL GEAR: A license and (in many states) proof of a hunting safety course. The limits on ducks are generally very small and some species are limited or restricted. It's essential to have a license and be within local limits. For information on licenses, check with your local sporting goods store.

- **12-gauge shotgun**—the accepted gun of choice for all duck hunters. Shotguns actually fire hundreds of tiny pellets, which make them ideal for moving targets, but they don't shoot far, so don't

fire at ducks beyond a 40-yard range.

- **Camouflage raingear and hip boots.** Plan on being cold and wet. The best duck hunting is always in the worst weather.

- **A duck call,** very important and worth any investment. A good one costs about $50.

- **Decoys** made of lightweight plastic help lure ducks within range.

- **A good retrieving dog** is crucial. Labrador retrievers are best, followed by golden retrievers.

HUNTING TIP: Don't shoot at anything more than 40 yards away. Wait until the ducks are lured into your decoys, and then pull the trigger as they're descending. Also, the hunting is best on rainy, overcast days.

> ❝
> **There is a passion for hunting something deeply implanted in the human breast.**
>
> Ralph Waldo Emerson
>
> • • •

UPLAND BIRDS

Upland generally refers to the hunting of inland birds. The most popular targets are dove, followed by quail, grouse and pheasant.

WHERE TO HUNT: Upland hunters generally stand around in fields and prairies, near where birds eat, and wait for the birds to descend and take off. Upland hunting is common in all parts of the country, but find out where the private and public lands are.

WHEN TO HUNT: Upland seasons are generally in the fall and early winter months. The bird populations are more dense than waterfowl populations, so seasons are longer and limits are larger. Inland birds feed at all times of day, so you don't necessarily need to be shooting at sunrise or sunset.

ESSENTIAL GEAR: Proper licenses and safety courses, of course. Unlike waterfowl, no calls or decoys are necessary.

Dick Cheney's Hunting Lessons

What the Vice President taught Americans about hunting

The accidental shooting of a hunting partner by Vice President Dick Cheney in early 2006 revealed one thing: what many Americans don't know about hunting could fill a book. Here is some of what they learned.

THE WEAPON. Cheney's shotgun is an Italian-made 28-gauge Perazzi. He was using shells with size 7 1/2 shot. A three-quarter-ounce load of this ammunition contains about 260 lead or steel pellets, each barely the size of a peppercorn. When shot, the pellets scatter in an expanding, cone-shaped path. The size of the cone depends on the gun's choke, which is the diameter of the gun's mouth. With quail hunting, the choke cannot be too tight or too many of the pellets will hit the bird, which could tear it to shreds.

THE DOGS. Two types of dogs, pointers and retrievers, are typically used in quail hunting. Pointers run the field, trying to pick up the scent of the birds, which huddle in coveys of about 10 to 25 in brush. When a pointer finds a covey, the dog freezes until given the order to flush the birds into the air. The hunter shoots and if a bird is hit, the retrievers are sent to find it and bring it back.

THE RULES. Wear blaze orange. If you leave the group, announce yourself upon return. Make sure there is enough daylight to see properly. Above all, never pull the trigger without knowing the location of everyone in your hunting party.

—Ian Urbina

- **Any type of shotgun,** from a 12-gauge to a .410-gauge shotgun, will do.

- **Brush pants** (heavy canvas pants faced with leather or nylon) for trudging through briers and thickets. A jacket of the same material is also essential.

- **A game vest** with multiple pockets provides a handy place to store shells and also a place to stuff the game you shoot.

- **A good dog,** either a pointer (to track down birds), a retriever (to bring back your kill) or a springer (to flush the birds up).

DEER

Two deer species are hunted: the white-tail (the most commonly hunted and found throughout the U.S.) and the mule (only found west of the Mississippi).

WHERE TO HUNT: You can hunt as far south as South Carolina and as far north as Canada. Access to hunting on private land can easily cost several hundred dollars. In some areas, membership in a hunting club grants you access to private areas.

WHEN TO HUNT: Deer hunting seasons tend to be short, simply because the deer can't handle constant hunting pressure. Depending on your latitude, deer season is somewhere between August and January.

ESSENTIAL GEAR: License and proof of hunter-safety course. Safety courses are usually conducted by the local fish and game department at a shooting range.

- **Weapon of choice.** There are three types of weapons to hunt deer, each having its own season. They are rifle, bow and arrow, and muzzle-loading rifle. Proficiency in all three weapons prolongs your hunting season.

- **Camouflage gear** made of soft fabrics. Your clothes must not rustle when you move or bump into trees. The slightest noise can ruin a day of tracking.

- **A bright orange bunting vest** is required in most states.

- **A telescopic scope** on your rifle will help you track your target.

- **A good set of binoculars** is a must. Using your scope exclusively can lead to misfires.

- **Survival kit,** including equipment to start a fire. The woods can be cold, and you may end up spending a full day or night outdoors.

- **Compass.** Don't assume you can find your way back to your car. Trees start to look alike after a while.

HUNTING TIP: Rifles are more precise than shotguns, but you only get one chance. Unlike shotguns, rifles shoot a single, conical-shaped bullet. A careless shot can ruin an entire day of tracking and scare off all deer within earshot, and deer have great ears.

ELK

Hunting elk is similar to hunting deer, but it's harder, you need to travel farther to do it, and you need more expensive stuff.

ESSENTIAL GEAR: Elk are found in the western and Alaskan mountains, so factor in a plane ride if you don't live in the Rocky Mountains or the 49th state.

- **A big-game rifle,** which can cost about $2,000, is essential.

- **An out-of-state elk hunting license,** if you don't live in one of the Rocky Mountain states, which runs about $300 to $500.

- **An access fee.** It's not uncommon to pay $5,000 for prime elk country.

HUNTING TIPS: Hire a guide who knows the area. It's not worth the money to fly out there and spend three days getting the lay of the land.

Falconry: A Sport of Sultans

The road toward having your own raptor is paved with regulations

An ancient field sport favored by kings and sultans is making a modest modern-day comeback of sorts. There are 4,000 or so falconers in the U.S. currently, but their numbers are climbing. Falconers spend years training falcons and red-tailed hawks to respond to commands, hunt prey and then return to their masters. They track down and kill everything from duck and pheasant to rabbits and squirrels. The thrill of the sport, falconers say, is spending time outdoors and the awesome sight of a falcon diving at 200 m.p.h. to attack its prey.

Wannabe falconers must spend several years in training—earning first the title of apprentice, then general, then master falconer—a process that can take seven years or more. You can't just purchase a falcon, you must find a master who is willing to be your sponsor. There are strict state and federal regulations (designed to protect the birds) and multiple levels of examinations to pass. Contact your local game department for information about falconry regulations in your area and a list of potential falconry sponsors. The North American Falconers Association (www.n-a-f-a.org) has lists of local falconers' clubs.

WHERE TO HUNT: Once outlawed in some states, falconry became a legal field sport throughout the United States in 1998. Only in Hawaii is falconry still illegal. State and local rules on falconry are often highly restrictive, however, so it's best to familiarize yourself with local game department regulations.

WHEN TO HUNT: There is no set falconry season. Indeed, if you own a falcon, you must work with, train and care for it every day. You also must first pass a written exam and housing inspection before you can begin training your own bird.

ESSENTIAL GEAR: A falcon or hawk. Apprentice falconers trap wild birds and spend two years training them. Once you are a master or general, you can buy a bred bird.

- **Appropriate housing** for your bird.
- **Classic falconers' bells** alert you to the whereabouts of your bird when it is off hunting.
- **Leather glove** that allows the bird to rest on your arm.
- **Game bag** (sack) to bring home your catch.
- **Lure** to bring your bird back. If properly trained, your falcon will identify the lure with a food-reward and promptly return.

HUNTING TIPS: These birds of prey are not pets. They are working animals and will only return to you because they want to.

Clinging to the Crags
For some, rock climbing is a sheer delight, for others sheer folly

Why do rock climbers risk life and limb to scale craggy heights? Some hope to enjoy what poet Alfred, Lord Tennyson called the "joy in steepness overcome . . . in breathing nearer heaven." Others climb to overcome faintheartedness. But rather than being daredevils, most climbers, in fact, work to reduce the dangers, to have control over their risks.

There are three types of climbing (not counting the ubiquitous wall-climbing), each with its own style and risks. Using "top roping," which uses a block and tackle system, a climber can only slip a few inches before the rope stops the fall. Mountaineering, which combines traditional climbing—in which each climber sets his or her own anchors—and ice climbing on high peaks, can be much more

dangerous, mainly because of uncontrollable risks, such as avalanches and blizzards.

Climbers must always work in pairs, with one "belaying," protecting the other by controlling the rope. And because the belayer literally holds the climber's life in just one hand, it's crucial that climbers have proper training. Rock gyms and many college outdoor clubs offer instruction. The American Mountain Guides Association (303-271-0984 or www.amga.com) and the American Alpine Club (303-384-0110 or www.americanalpineclub.org), are a good place to start for advice and guidance.

Rock climbing is not inexpensive. A beginner's equipment package costs about $400, including $150 for the rope, $100 for the smooth rubber-sole boots, $150 for a harness, nylon slings and the protection system that helps set the rope, the carabiners, nuts, pitons and camming devices. A daylong private lesson with a guide, well worthwhile, runs about $250.

Across the country, there are plenty of cliffs to climb. Brent Bishop has climbed all over the U.S. and the world, including an ascent of Mt. Everest, also conquered by his late father. Bishop is founder of the Sagarmatha Foundation, which is dedicated to cleaning tons of expedition gear off Everest. Here are his favorite climbing spots in the U.S.

YOSEMITE NATIONAL PARK, *California.* A spectacular area with no rival in the U.S. Many climbs demand not only expertise, but also spending nights hanging in a bivouac sack, tied to the rock.

CLASSIC ROUTE: Astroman, possibly the best vertical crack climb in the world for its high degree of difficulty It's well over 1,500 feet long.

OUTFITTER: Yosemite Mountaineering School (209-372-8344 or www.yosemitepark.com)

CITY OF ROCKS, *Idaho.* Scores of granite blocks, many 100 to 120 feet high, cater to every ability

SPORTS

FIVE BASIC KNOTS FOR ROCK CLIMBING

There are nearly 4,000 possible knots. Fortunately you won't need to know them all to rock climb, but these five are essential.

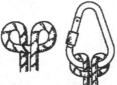

Clove hitch
An easy, versatile knot often used as an anchor knot. Best used with a carabiner.

Double Fisherman
Most often used to construct equipment, but also to join ropes. An alternative to the figure eight.

Tape knot/ring bend
This is an overhand knot used to tie tape or ropes into slings. It is used to secure the sling around an anchor.

Italian hitch
Technically not a knot, this hitch is used for belaying (securing the rope on a rock or other projection) and abseiling (descending).

Figure Eight
Common knot used to attach rope to an anchor and to tie a knot onto a climbing harness, for example.

level and offer awesome traditional crack climbs and hardcore sport routes, most of them safe and user-friendly.

Classic route: Bloody Fingers, a 115-foot-long crack that just fits your fingers.

Outfitter: Exum Mountain Guides (307-733-2297 or www.exumguides.com)

DEVIL'S TOWER, *Wyoming.* Every route up this 365-foot-high core of an ancient volcano requires a sustained crack climb. There's a voluntary hiatus on climbing in June, out of respect for Native Americans who consider this a sacred site.

Classic route: Durrance. Though the climb is rated as moderate in difficulty, it's still an amazing route every foot of the way up.

Outfitter: Jackson Hole Mountain Guides (307-733-4979 or www.jhmg.com)

SENECA ROCKS, *West Virginia.* There are more

than 200 routes here, most of them challenging, up this bizarre slab of quartzite, which looks like two gigantic fins cutting through the forest. The summit is only a dozen feet wide. The cliffs have some good sport climbs and also several easy routes for beginners.

Classic route: Castor and Pollux, two side-by-side cracks, which are steep and scary.

Outfitter: Seneca Rocks Climbing School (304-567-2600 or www.seneca-rocks.com)

SHAWANGUNK MOUNTAINS, *New York.* "The Gunks," as they are better known, are actually four major cliff areas spread over seven miles and offering more than 1,300 different ways up, each topping out between 30 and 200 feet high. Beginners' routes are often next to ones that can defy the proficient, giving everyone a great chance to mingle.

Classic route: Foops, one of the best climbs in the country. It's a tough roof problem, meaning that you climb as if you're hanging on a ceiling.

OUTFITTER: High Angle Adventures (800-777-CLIMB or www.highangle.com)

Polar Chills and Thrills

Who says you have to stay inside in winter? Try curling, for example

It may be winter, but why settle for riding a stationary bike or climbing a fake set of steps in a gym? Skiing isn't the only cold-weather option out there. You may want to try curling, snowshoeing or polar bear swimming. Here's a guide to those and other winter activities that team up well with ice, snow and chilly weather.

CURLING

Curling is a team sport played on ice. Teams of four shove "rocks" down the ice toward a target. Team members slide along the ice with the rock, steering it by sweeping long-handled brooms in front of it. While curling originated in Scotland in the 1500's, it is found mostly in Canada and in the colder northern tier of the country. But there are curling clubs as far west as San Francisco and as far south as Houston. More than 16,000 curling enthusiasts do their stuff all winter long, some of them with dreams of gold: curling debuted as a full-medal sport in the 1998 Olympics.

GEAR: Once you're serious, you'll need Teflon sliders (about $20); a broom and handle ($70 and up); and curling shoes (about $100), although flat-soled athletic shoes will also do. Clubs are also good places to start because many lend equipment to beginners.

TRAINING TIP: Sweeping (the rapid back and forth with the broom in front of the curling rock) is an exhaustive workout for the arms and shoulders.

But don't forget about your quads: curling is done primarily in a squat.

KEEP AN EYE ON: The skip (the "captain" of the four-person team.) The skip is the strategist and controls the flow of the shots and movement.

CONTACT: U.S. Curling Association (715-344-1199; www.goodcurling.net.) Curling is a club-oriented sport. Your first step is to get in touch with one of the more than 135 area clubs. Most clubs also offer instruction for beginners.

SNOWSHOEING

Why is snowshoeing one of winter's fastest-growing recreational sports? Because it is, perhaps, the world's simplest sport: If you can walk, you can snowshoe. The Outdoor Industry Association estimates that of six million snowshoers, about one million are hardcore participants, lured by the woods in winter and the exercise. Many serious athletes now do their winter training on snowshoes and there are annual snowshoe marathons, but you don't need to be an iron man to snowshoe.

GEAR: The snowshoe is a lightweight (about one pound) platform with crampons on the bottom

TIMELY TIPS

Fitting a Snowshoe

✔ The heavier the person and the more powdery the snow, the bigger the ideal snowshoe. But, says Claire Walter, author of *The Snowshoe Experience*, "22 to 25 inches long by 8 or 9 inches wide is the golden mean for size." Women-specific snowshoes are generally narrower.

✔ Beginners may also want to use poles to help with balance.

—Yishane Lee

SPORTS

and a binding system on top that attaches to a shoe or boot, ideally a waterproof hiking boot or a trail-running sneaker. Snowshoes run $150 to $300; poles from $50 to $150. (Many outdoor stores rent them.) A set of poles will give you more balance and stability and also add an upper-body workout. Like cross-country skiers, snowshoers should dress in layers that will keep out the cold but allow you to strip down once you really start sweating—which you will.

TRAINING TIP: Snowshoeing is an excellent cardio-vascular workout. In steep terrain, a snowshoer can burn up to 1,000 calories an hour. A simple way to get in shape for snowshoeing is walking up and down hills. When you first start, you'll feel a burn in the tops of the legs at the hip and groin area from lifting a snow-filled shoe.

KEEP AN EYE ON: The scenery; snowshoeing can take you places you couldn't get to on skis or in boots.

---

① INSIDE INFO

The Dangers of Thin Air

○ **EXTREME COLD:** Can cause hypothermia, which slows the heart and can lead to death. Wear insulated layers of clothing to minimize exposure.

○ **OXYGEN DEPRIVATION.** Summit air can contain just one-third of the oxygen at sea level. Some climbers carry extra oxygen.

○ **IMPAIRED JUDGMENT:** High altitudes can affect the brain, creating confusion and bad judgment. Climb in teams, so members can help each other in crisis.

○ **DRY AIR:** The water content in a climber's blood can drop drastically, increasing the chance of frostbite. Drink plenty of water. Bring stoves to melt snow.

SOURCE: *Newsweek*

But if you're in the mountains, be careful in the backcountry—keep an eye out for avalanches.

CONTACT: The U.S. Snowshoe Association (518-643-8806; www.snowshoeracing.com) has information about races, championships, clubs, equipment makers and more.

ICE HOCKEY

Want to be more than a hockey parent? Want to relive those glory days of Pee Wee hockey? Then strap on your skates and join an amateur hockey league. There are organized hockey leagues all over the country (no checking or blocking an opponent is allowed in older leagues) and the amateur popularity of the sport continues to rise.

GEAR: Hockey requires a fair amount of equipment. You can't play league hockey in your college sweatshirt and a pair of skates; you'll need all the proper body padding (including shoulder pads, shin pads and elbow pads), gloves, a stick and a helmet. Plan on spending anywhere from $400 to $800 or more. You might want to check with used sports stores for good prices on skates and equipment.

TRAINING TIP: Hockey is a grueling cardiovascular workout, so don't hit the ice without some pre-conditioning. Also, although most over-35 leagues outlaw checking, expect to take some knocks and spills and not complain. Before you even think about joining a team, make sure you're confident on your skates—forward, backward and stopping.

KEEP AN EYE ON: The obvious: the puck, your teammates and the opposing team. If you're playing hockey to relieve a little stress and aggression, you may want to throw the occasional hip check. But if you're playing for pure cardiovascular reasons, watch out so you don't end up with your face plastered against the Plexiglas.

CONTACT: USA Hockey (719-599-5500 or www. usahockey.com) is the national governing body for hockey in the United States. USA Hockey can provide information on area leagues. For more information on old-timers' leagues in your areas, check the Yellow Pages for local ice rinks.

SNOWMOBILING

A snowmobile can take you everywhere that a wimpy pair of cross country skis can and make a lot more noise doing it, too. There are nearly 1.5 million registered snowmobiles in the U.S. Tour operators offer everything from half-day to three-to-four-day trips.

GEAR: The average snowmobile costs between $5,000 and $10,000, but used ones can be found for about $2,000. Daily rentals can run from about $100 to several hundred dollars, depending on the package. If you don't own them, you'll also need to rent a snowmobile suit, gloves and a helmet.

TRAINING TIP: Always wear a helmet and follow general safety guidelines. There are a number of snowmobile deaths every year, caused mostly by drunk and reckless driving. Just like cars, snow-mobiles must abide by a set of operating laws. Most operators offer a free lesson on mechanics, handling and safety. Physically, riding a snow-mobile may not seem taxing, but controlling a large machine for several hours at a time wears out anyone. Don't be too ambitious, and be sure to head back before you're beat.

KEEP AN EYE ON: Where you are. Snowmobiling on private land without prior consent could land you in jail. There are over 100,000 miles of groomed, marked snowmobile trails in North America. Always be extra cautious about snowmobiling on frozen lakes. And if you're snowmobiling near a road, don't assume the traffic can see you.

CONTACT: The American Council of Snowmobile Associations (517-351-4362; www.snowmobil-ers.org) is the best place to start. The council can help you organize a trip or direct you to one of 26 state organizations for more region-specific information.

POLAR BEAR SWIMMING

Jump into a body of water in the middle of January and you're considered a fool. Do it with a club and you're called a polar bear swimmer. Polar bears have been gathering on frozen U.S. shores for close to 100 years and today's polar bears claim that the therapeutic benefits of cold-water swimming keep them healthy and happy. It's one of winter's least complicated sports. All you need is a swimsuit, a brisk winter day, a body of water and the determination to walk (or run) into icy cold waves.

GEAR: A swimsuit, goggles, water-proof booties optional, a big warm towel.

TRAINING TIP: Those with heart trouble should check with their physicians before jumping into icy water. The sudden drastic change in temperature could cause problems, but many polar bears are octogenarians who claim the cold water is precisely what keeps them going.

KEEP AN EYE ON: Frolickers. Polar bear swimming is as much about frolicking and splashing in the icy water as it is about exercise. Polar bears swim together because it's fun. If you want a serious, competitive workout, turn down the temperature in the pool and do some laps.

CONTACT: Although you could jump into any old frozen water, it's more fun to do it with members of one the three dozen clubs in the country. The Coney Island Polar Bear Club in New York, N.Y. (founded in 1903), is the nation's oldest club

(718-356-7741 or www.polarbearclub.org). If you're out West, jump in with the Boulder Polar Bear Club, whose motto is "Freezdom for All." For information, call 303-494-3348 or e-mail: infor@boulderpolarbearclub.org.

ICE CLIMBING

Ice climbing was invented by restless rock climbers looking for a way to pass the winter months. It is similar to rock climbing, but climbers scale frozen waterfalls instead of sheer cliffs. Climbers can be found in places where the temperature drops. The mecca for ice climbers is the San Juan Range, near Telluride, Colorado, but East Coasters can find excellent ice climbing outside North Conway, N.H., and midwestern diehards have been known to ice down silos for a good climb. The sport's popularity has soared, due mostly to rock climbing's popularity and to advances in safety equipment.

GEAR: To be properly outfitted, you'll need ice-climbing boots, which are plastic versions of stiff hiking boots and run $200 to $250; crampons, the stiff iron spikes you strap to your boots that cost $125 to $150; two hand tools, basically handles with fancy picks on them that cost about $250; a helmet. Most climbers stick to low climbs, but anything higher requires ropes and harnesses.

TRAINING TIP: Climbing is done with all parts of your body, not just the arms, as many people assume. Women often make excellent climbers because they lack upper body strength, and are forced to use ingenuity instead of brawn.

KEEP AN EYE ON: Melting ice, and avoid it. A sunny, warm day may tempt you outside, but ice climbing is best—and safest—on chilly, cloudy days.

CONTACT: There are no organized ice climbing organizations, but your local out-doors clubs and retail outlets are good sources. In the San Juans, call Ryder Walker Alpine Adventures in Telluride, Colorado (888-586-8365 or www.ryderwalker.com). In New England, call International Mountain Equipment in North Conway, New Hampshire (603-356-7013 or www.ime-usa.com).

Catching Some Air
A head-to-toe guide to snowboarding

Once the domain of 16-year-old grunge boarders, snowboarding is no longer limited to youthful thrill seekers. Today, the sport attracts about 17 million Americans, including middle-aged professional types enticed by the excellent workout and the time spent outdoors. Snowboarding hit the big time when it became an Olympic sport in 1998. Here's a head-to-toe guide to snowboard gear that will get you up and spinning in no time.

THE BOARD: The first thing you'll need is, of course, a board. You can plan on spending about $500 for a board with bindings. There are two styles of boards: freestyle and alpine. Freestyle, with its roots in the skateboard culture, is more common in the U.S. There is no true front or back of a freestyle board, as boarders can ride "fakie"—spin and reverse the direction of the board. Alpine, which is popular in Europe, is done on a thinner board designed to carve the snow and work the board's edges more.

BINDING AND BOOTS: Freestyle boards use boots that are similar to regular snow boots. The binding of the back foot is quickly released, as boarders must skate themselves through the lift line. Boarders either ride regular (left foot forward, right foot skates) or goofy (right foot forward, left foot skates).

Basic Moves

*A*ll you do is work just one edge at a time, heel or toe side. **Traversing 1**, the board will hold a line like a ski when tilted on edge;

Release the edge 2, and the board will sideslip down the fall line.

To make the basic turn, from heel edge to toe edge, say, release the heel edge **3,**

pivot the back foot in the direction of the turn **4,**

engaging and weighting the toe edge **5**. The board's sidecut draws a curve in the snow.

SOURCE: *Men's Journal*

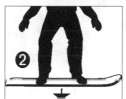

Snowboard Lingo

Air dog. A snowboarder with a preference for aerial tricks.

Bomb. To point the nose of your board straight down the hill to pick up speed.

Butt rocker. (also botwoker) Being on your butt a lot; a novice boarder.

Catching air. The time spent in the air after a jump.

Doing hits. Any kind of move on the snow board.

Fakie. Spin and change the board's direction.

Huckfest. A gathering of snowboarders riding hard and wild.

Laying down an arc. Riding at high speed so far over the board's edges that your body is almost parallel to the ground.

Lip. The top of the jump that is usually the steepest.

Ollie. Lifting the nose and tail of the board into the air at the same time.

Pipe. Short for halfpipe, the area at many mountains where snowboarders can show off their moves.

Pow (or Pow Pow). To hit all powder snow and the jump explodes into a blur of white powder.

$%&#*!!!. Foul language is common and welcome in the snowboard world.

LEGS AND BUTT: Loose-fitting clothing is a necessity on a snowboard. Snowboard pants come with reinforced knees because you'll spend a lot of time on your knees, either after a fall or simply resting. Some snowboard companies sell extra padding for your butt. But no matter how much you pad, beginners will spend a majority of their time falling on their butt and knees and will feel it afterward.

TORSO AND ARMS: Most jackets come with a butt flap that makes sitting on a chilly chairlift more comfortable. Thick gloves with gaiters that come up to the elbows are important, as you will spend much time with your hands on the snow in front of you.

HEAD: Some snowboarders wear elaborate headgear, including long jester hats. Also popular is the plain wool skull cap, but any close fitting hat that covers the ears will do. Snowboarders wear sunglasses and goggles under the same conditions that skiers do, but many boarders opt for sunglasses all the time to add to the total look.

It's All Downhill From Here

Places every skier should go

Skiers are always looking for new terrain and new challenges. The table on the facing page shows the resorts in the western and eastern United States that regularly make the top of ski magazine listings. We asked Chris Davenport, a two-time extreme skiing world champion and one of America's top skiers, according to *Skiing Magazine*, for his choices of the five places every skier should go at least once.

1. TUCKERMAN'S RAVINE. If you're a skier you have to do it before you die. Go spend a sunny, spring day at Tuckerman's with a bunch of friends. That is truly one of the greatest atmospheres and physical locations in the sport of skiing. It's magical up there on the right day. People out West think there's no way that such a place exists in New Hampshire. But it surely exists.

2. HELI-SKIING IN ALASKA. You can go all over Alaska now. Girdwood, Haines, Cordova. It's the best snow and you can ski the steepest stuff more safely than you can the Canadian Rockies. That stuff is totally bomber. I get goose bumps talking about it. It's for advanced skiers but anybody who can ski a black diamond run at their local ski area can ski something like this

3. WHISTLER/BLACKCOMB. I like to take the peak chair at Whistler on a powder morning. Anything off that chair is a great run. At Blackcomb, I like climbing up Spanky's Ladder and that accesses Ruby and Diamond bowls. Those are big, wide open, long and steep powder bowls.

4. ASPEN. Aspen is known as this rich and famous ritzy-ditzy place. In the 1980's, it was totally that: all you saw was people walking around in furs with Gulfstreams at the airport. Aspen reinvented itself in the early 1990's. The terrain parks are world class and so is the on-mountain and off-mountain skiing.

5. THE ALPS. There are more lifts per square mile there than anywhere else in the world. Because it's so big, I'll give you five "must spots" to visits:

- **Chamonix in France** is the birthplace of extreme skiing. It has the longest run in the Alps, 9,000 vertical feet down. Everyone should ride the Aiguille du Midi tram, which goes from the village of Chamonix to this pinnacle of rock, straight up with no lift towers. The ride by itself is a must thing to do. But you have to have a guide—there's big cliffs and glaciers and you can get in trouble.

- **Verbier in Switzerland.** There's easy access to massive terrain. You can ski a week and never ski the same trail twice. Verbier is very sunny with chalets built on a plateau. Idyllic and scenic.

- **St. Anton in Austria.** Different from the others because of the Austrian/German influence.

- **La Grave in France.** Near the Italian border, this is a whole mountain of off-piste runs. It's a wonderful place. Two big trams and no grooming at all.

- **The Monterosa ski region in northern Italy.** It's really unknown, yet it's one of the largest ski resorts in the world. I've spent a lot of time there and have never seen another American. I never wait in line or compete with anyone for powder.

—Bill Pennington

Answering the Call of the Trail

Six ways for cross-country skiers to escape the local loop

There's a tugging romance to the idea of escaping the orbit of the local cross-country ski loop and heading out on a long-distance ski journey. Unfortu-

THE BEST OF THE WEST AND...

Resorts in the western and eastern United States that regularly top ski magazine listings:

Resort	Vertical rise (ft.)	Skiable acres	% Runs that are... EXP	INT	BEG*	Lifts	Snowfall (in./yr.)
Alta, Utah	2,020	2,200	35	40	25	12	500
Aspen, Colo.	3,267	6,310	30	35	35	8	300
Crested Butte, Colo.	3,062	1,154	41	44	15	15	300
Deer Valley, Utah	3,000	1,100	35	50	15	21	300
Jackson Hole, Wyo.	4,139	2,500	50	40	10	11	400
Mammoth Mountain, Calif.	3,100	3,500	30	40	30	20	335
Park City, Utah	3,100	2,000	38	44	18	14	350
Snowbird, Utah.	3,240	2,000	37	38	35	9	500
Snowmass, Colo.	4,406	2,962	34	50	6	22	300
Squaw Valley, Calif.	2,850	4,000	30	45	25	34	450
Steamboat, Colo.	3,668	2,965	31	56	13	20	315
Sun Valley, Idaho	3,400	2,067	22	42	36	19	220
Taos, N.M.	2,612	1,094	51	25	24	12	305
Telluride, Colo.	3,530	1,050	38	38	24	16	309
Vail, Colo.	3,450	5,268	40	32	28	34	346

*Expert, intermediate, beginner

... IN THE EAST

Resort	Vertical drop (feet)	Acres	Trails	Lifts	Contact	
Holiday Valley, N.Y.	1,500	270	53	12	www.holidayvalley.com	716-699-2345
Killington, Vt.	3,050	918	200	33	www.killington.com	800-734-9435
Loon, N.H.	2,100	275	45	10	www.loonmtn.com	603-745-8111
Mont Tremblant, Quebec	2,116	625	94	13	www.tremblant.ca	888-857-8043
Mount Snow, Vt.	1,700	750	104	19	www.mountsnow.com	802-464-3333
Okemo, Ludlow, Vt.	2,200	470	115	18	www.okemo.com	802-228-1780
Smuggler's Notch, Vt.	2,610	250	78	8	www.smuggs.com	800-451-8752
Stowe, Vt.	2,360	485	48	12	www.stowe.com	800-253-4754
Stratton, Vt.	2,003	478	93	8	www.stratton.com	802-297-4211
Sugarbush, Vt.	2,650	500	111	16	www.sugarbush.com	800-53-SUGAR
Sugarloaf, Me.	2,820	1,400	133	15	www.sugarloaf.com	800-THE-LOAF
Sunday River, Me.	2,340	660	128	18	www.sundayriver.com	800-543-2SKI
Whiteface, Lake Placid, N.Y.	3,430	220	74	10	www.whiteface.com	518-946-2223

For lift-ticket prices and other information for all mountains except Alta and Mammoth, call 800-778-8589 or go to www.ski.com. For information on Alta, call 801-359-1078 or go to www.alta.com; for Mammoth Mountain, call 800-MAMMOTH or go to www.mammothmountain.com.

SPORTS

How Long Should Your Skis Be?

It depends on height, expertise and skiing style

Some skis are too big, some are too small, and some are just right. Greenwood's Ski Haus in Boise, Idaho—consistently rated one of the best ski shops in the country by ski magazines—offers these sizing tips:

The first question you need to ask yourself is, What type of skier am I?

- If you are a beginner to intermediate skier, you should probably buy skis about 4 inches taller than yourself

- If you are a more accomplished, aggressive skier, you could go 4 to 8 inches over your head.

- If you are very, very aggressive, you could venture up to 12 inches over your head.

- If you are buying hourglass skis, they may be much shorter.

In general, you should buy skis that are on the long side. In the old days, beginners and intermediates were steered toward very short skis. Not anymore.

The longer the ski, the faster the ride. Add 5 cm. for fast skiing on groomed slopes. Subtract 5 cm. for skiing mostly bumps, or if you are a slow, conservative skier.

Intermediate skiers looking for a basic, all-purpose ski should use the chart below as a general guide.

HEIGHT	SKI LENGTH (cm.)
5'0"–5'1"	158
5'2"–5'3"	168
5'4"–5'5"	178
5'6"–5'7"	183
5'8"–5'9"	188
5'10"–5'11"	193
6'0"–6'1"	198
6'2"–6'3"	201
6'3"+	201

BEGINNER: 4" longer   EXPERIENCED: 4–8" longer   VERY AGGRESSIVE: 12" longer

nately, Nordic skiers have relatively few options for point-to-point adventures unless they're comfortable carrying an anvil-heavy pack in the backcountry and sleeping in a drippy snow cave. But here, with the help of Ron Bergin, editor and publisher of *Cross Country Skier* magazine, are some alternatives that range from easy to challenging, and the amenities can vary from B.Y.O. sleeping bag to feather duvets, post-ski sports massages and tournedos of beef.

10TH MOUNTAIN DIVISION HUT ASSOCIATION, Colorado

The 10th Mountain huts are the closest this continent comes to an extensive mountain hut network like those in the Alps. Most of the 29 huts (the name honors the Army's 10th Mountain Division, whose members trained at Camp Hale in central Colorado during World War II) are at or near timberline, connected to the next by six to eight miles of ungroomed trail.

Almost all the huts along the trail have wood-burning stoves for heating and cooking, propane burners, lighting powered by solar panels, cooking and eating utensils, and mattresses and pillows. Skiers must be their own Sherpas for these huts, however, carrying a sleeping bag, food and toiletries between huts, which sleep about 16 people.

This isn't golf-course Nordic skiing; skiers who aren't familiar with navigation, self-rescue techniques, avalanche training and using metal-edged touring skis and climbing skins should polish skills first with a guide. Rates to stay at a hut on your own can vary, but are usually $28 per person per night. Hut information: 970-925-5775 or www.huts.org.

CATAMOUNT TRAIL, Vermont

The longest ski trail in North America is the 300-mile Catamount Trail, which runs from Readsboro, Vt., on the Massachusetts border, and snakes through the Green Mountains to North Troy, on

Canada's cusp. Though a bit more than half is ungroomed backcountry trail, it links cross-country ski centers as well as inns and lodges like the Trapp Family Lodge in Stowe. Perhaps the best stretch for inn-to-inn skiing lies between Killington and Ripton, about 35 miles in the central part of the state, where at least nine motels, inns and lodges are on or near the trail. Casual skiers can tackle the section in four or five days, skiing 8 to 11 miles a day, and feel confident that there will be a place to stay whenever they have had enough.

Country Inns Along the Trail, 800-838-3301, www.inntoinn.com, creates self-guided ski packages with stays at up to four inns along the route. Trail information: 802-864-5794 or www.catamounttrail.org.

THE BOUNDARY WATERS/GUNFLINT TRAIL, Minnesota

One hundred and fifty miles north of Duluth (the closest airport) and hard by Lake Superior lies a trail network that resembles a mangled barbell. For a four-night trip that covers 28 miles, begin on the right bell, at the Poplar Creek Guest House and go to the Tall Pines Yurt, a Mongolian-style hut with a wood-fired Finnish sauna, which sleeps six to eight people. Gear and food arrive via snowmobile, so skiers can travel light. The next two days skiers traverse the "bar" of the barbell: the Banadad Trail, a narrow 19-mile regularly groomed track through the Boundary Waters Canoe Area Wilderness. At the far end of the Banadad lies another skein of 50 miles of groomed tracks and the Gunflint Lodge. For information: 800-322-8327 or www.boundarycountry.com.

RENDEZVOUS HUTS, Methow Valley, Washington

In the rain shadow of the Cascade Range, about a four-hour winter drive from Seattle, lies

⊘ TIMELY TIPS

Face-Saving Lessons From the North Pole

In Grise Fiord, Northwest Territories, the sun sets in October and doesn't rise again until February, and the winter temperatures rarely rise above 16 below. How do residents protect their skin from the frigid cold? Ray Richer, general manager of the Grise Fiord Inuit Co-op, says he insulates his skin with Dove body lotion. "It's simple, but it works," he says.

✔ In the old days the Inuit did not take baths because they were afraid of washing off the natural oils that protected their faces from frostbite, says Lonnie Dupre, a polar explorer who lives in Grand Marais, Minn., near the Canadian border. "If you can bring yourself to bathe less often, you can keep the natural protective lanolins on your face."

✔ Lips, too, are vulnerable to dry air. "The wind burns your lips and the sun cooks them," says Dupre. When he's out on expeditions, he coats them liberally with Dermatone, made with beeswax and lanolin. It's sold at sporting goods stores like REI and Eastern Mountain Sports.

—Natasha Singer

the Methow Valley, a glacier-scooped landscape carpeted with ponderosa pines of such eye-pleasing beauty that Owen Wister called it "the smiling country." The Methow (pronounced MET-how) is also home to one of North America's largest networks of groomed Nordic trails—130 miles of rarely crowded classic and skate-skiing trails. The least visited are the 27 miles of trails in the Rendezvous area, the highest point of which must be reached by kicking and gliding nearly 1,500 feet up the valley's eastern shoulder. Sprinkled along

Living Like the Inuit

How to build an igloo in five easy steps

Building an igloo, or snowhouse, is a fairly easy process, but making it safe requires some precautions. Choose an area where temperatures won't rise above 32 degrees and where the snow has been windblown and packs easily. Be sure to follow tips for proper ventilation. Without good ventilation, carbon dioxide levels can build up and cause suffocation. Another precaution: do not use stoves in an igloo; they can trap poisonous carbon monoxide inside.

Once your igloo is built, you'll be amazed at how comfortable and well insulated you feel inside.

1. Find an area with dry, hard-packed snow. Using a snow saw or large knife, carve blocks of snow measuring about 3 feet long, 15 inches high, and 8 inches deep.

2. Place the blocks in a circular pattern around the area from which you carved the blocks. This "hole" left in the snow will become the lower half of the igloo. Build up the walls with snow blocks, placing them on top of each other in a spiral formation.

3. Cut a hole under one side of the wall for the entrance and dig a canal for cold air to pass through. (You can also build a roof over the entrance to prevent snow from blowing into the igloo.)

4. From the inside, shape the final block you use to make the igloo roof (this block should be larger than the remaining roof opening), so that it fits tightly between the other blocks. Shape the  entire structure from outside and inside so that it forms a dome.

5. Cut ventilation holes in the walls with an ice ax. Make at least one hole in the roof to ensure there is enough air circulating inside.

---

the trails are five cabins; picture Grizzly Adams's guesthouse. Most cabins are two to three miles apart, not far enough to be a genuine hut-to-hut system, but skiers sometimes move between them if they stay several days. Trail information: 800-257-2452 or www.methow.com/huts.

RONDANE MOUNTAINS, Norway

Norway has more than 400 alpine cabins that are open to the public. But "hut"— a translation of the Norwegian "hytte"— doesn't do these places justice. At many of the lodging options run by the Den Norske Turistforening and private operators, skiers may sleep six people to a room. Yet the inns are inviting, wood-paneled Nordic chalets where a tired skier can find a hot shower, a hearty meal (it helps to be fond of reindeer stew) and Scandinavian hospitality. For general information, see the Norwegian Mountain Touring Association Web site at www.turistforeningen.no.

THE JURA MOUNTAINS, French-Swiss Border

Running parallel to the French-Swiss border northwest of Geneva, the mellow, forested Juras lie in the shadow of the Alps literally and figuratively. The mountain chain remains little visited by Americans in winter, despite its wealth of cross-country skiing opportunities: more than 1,800 miles of groomed tracks and ungroomed trails wrapping around 52 villages. The most famous of these trails is the roughly 125-mile Grande Traversée du Jura. For general information about the area and the Grand Traversée, go to www.gtj.asso.fr.

—Christopher Solomon

Hitch Rover and Go Skijoring

All you need is cross-country skis, some rope—and your dog

Skijoring, a cousin sport to dog sledding, has long been practiced in Alaska and Scandinavia, where sled-dog sports are part of the local culture. But in recent years it has gained momentum in places like Vermont, upstate New York, Michigan, Colorado and Minnesota. Skijoring (pronounced skee-JOAR-ing) now has a following among thousands of recreational skiers and their dogs.

For those who already own a dog and cross-country skiing gear, skijoring is relatively inexpensive. Here's how it's done and what you'll need.

Types of dogs. Many breeds of dogs are fit and strong enough to pull their owners. Pugs and bichon frisés won't qualify, but active healthy dogs that weigh at least 35 pounds can skijor. Arctic sled dogs like Siberian huskies and Alaskan malamutes are popular race breeds. But Labrador retrievers, Rhodesian ridgebacks, Great Danes, and even standard poodles can participate.

How to skijor. Skijoring uses a towline to tether a skier to one or more dogs wearing chest harnesses. The dog runs and pulls; the human skis behind. To maximize speed and preserve the dog's energy on long treks, skiers provide some of the power by striding and pushing off with their poles. Some dogs may need training to run straight down trails rather than in circles around their owner's ankles. To get your dog accustomed to the harness, take him out on short jogs on snowy trails. An experienced canine-human pair can reach speeds of 15 miles an hour or more. Speed is part of the attraction. But skijorers also like the exercise and the camaraderie with the family pet.

Required gear. You'll need a 6-to-10-foot towline, waist belt and dog harness. The equipment is designed and made by small companies like Perry Greene Outfitters, in Waldoboro, Me., which sells

SPORTS

✓ **TIMELY TIPS**

Gear for Warm Toes and Safe Wrists

There is no more unifying fixation in snow sports than the pursuit of toasty toes. Here are some remedies to combat cold feet—and other scourges of the winter sports enthusiast.

✔ Many foot-warmth problems are actually boot problems. When it comes to boot fitting, see a professional in a good ski, snowboard or mountaineering shop. Uncomfortable boots—too small or too big—are always cold boots. While you're there, have them place specially insulated insoles into your boots.

✔ Buy a sport-specific sock. For skiers and boarders that usually means a sock that is a thin, lightweight, modern blend of fabrics that will transport moisture away from the foot. Wearing two pairs won't help; consider wearing an ultralight, thin liner sock, usually made of silk.

✔ Buy a pair of heat-inducing toe warmers (about $2) at the lodge ski shop and take them out of the plastic package at least five minutes before placing them in your boots.

✔ For those who can't get their feet warm any other way, battery-heated socks, which cost about $30, are virtually foolproof. A small battery hooks onto each boot cuff.

✔ The most common serious injury associated with snowboarding is a broken wrist. A revolutionary glove with an integrated wrist guard built in defuses the impact of the usual bone-jarring fall. The Flexmeter, available at www.snowboarsecrets.com, goes for about $100.

—Bill Pennington

the basic waist belt, towline and dog harness for $65 at www.mainely-dogs.com.

Where to skijor. More than 50 ski areas in the United States now allow dogs. Large American ski centers that have skijoring trails include Bretton Woods Mountain Resort in New Hampshire, Okemo in Vermont, Crested Butte Nordic Center in Colorado and Jackson Hole Nordic Center in Wyoming. Skijoring loops are often kept separate from other trails so dogs don't bother regular cross-country skiers. But skijoring can be done in public parks, snowmobile and hiking trails, and even golf courses, though it is easier to get momentum on packed snow.

—Stephen Regenold

TIMELY TIPS

Adventures in Wild Skating

These days, few people skate on nature's ice. Even in the Midwest, where lakes stay hard-frozen for months, estimates are that 90 percent of skaters now learn indoors. But a growing number of skaters are heading outside—helped by European skates just finding their way to this country—for what one enthusiast calls wild skating.

✔ To speed skate on frozen lakes you'll need Nordic skates, a cross between ski boots and kitchen knives. They are available from shops around the country, including the Nordic Skater (326 Main Street, Norwich, Vt.; 866-244-2570 or www.nordicskater.com). Nordic skate blades with bindings are typically $100 to $250. Packages that include plastic insulated boots are about double that amount.

✔ Skaters on untested lakes or ponds should be well-versed on ice conditions and carry ice-testing poles, throw ropes and ice claws. For Nordic skating events go to www.nordicskating.com.

—Diane Daniel

Making It on the Ice
A top coach's tips on teaching kids to figure-skate

What are the odds that the hard work of any given child in America interested in a skating career will pay off with fame, riches and a gold medal? Not great, but also not impossible. What it takes to make it in ice-skating are "Talent, motivation, and a serious interest in the sport," says Audrey Weisinger, an ice-skating coach, judge and former competitor who has spent nearly her entire life in the rink, earning double gold medals in the United States Figure Skating Association in figures and freestyle. Weisinger currently coaches Timothy Goebel, Olympic bronze medal winner and the first skater to land six quads in one competition. Here is Weisinger's advice for budding ice-skaters.

How old should a child be to start learning to figure skate? Anyone can learn to skate and enjoy it as a recreational sport at any age. If you're thinking of a competitive career, though, you have to start young enough to make it feasible—around 6 or 7 for girls, maybe 8 to 10 for boys.

How do you get children interested in the sport?
You can't. If they're not interested in skating on their own, you can't make them interested. You may not want to let your child quit after the first lesson, but be reasonable. If the child has a temper tantrum every day about practicing or going to lessons, it's time to reevaluate continuing.

A parent's role is to be supportive and encouraging—regardless of the skater's ability. Most skaters don't get to the Olympic or "elite" level of competition, but they can still enjoy the benefits of skating recreationally. Parents should facilitate improvement, but not manage it. And they should separate their own goals and desires from their child's. They should provide the opportunities for growth, but not demand it. If your child's not enjoying himself, back off.

● When should you invest in good skates?

A basic pair of beginner skates is perfectly fine to start off with. When and if your child shows an interest in learning new skills, begins skating more than once a week and is motivated to practice to improve, then that's the time to invest in a moderately good pair of skates. Good skates have boots and blades that are mounted separately. They cost about $200 to $400.

● How much time should children spend practicing?

That depends on the child's goals. To learn the basics for recreational skating requires about one hour of lessons per week with another two or three spent practicing. But a beginner who is 10, let's say, and has competitive goals in mind, should practice at least one hour a day with additional time spent on dance and endurance training.

Skaters at the top competitive level devote the majority of their day to becoming a champion—two or three coaching sessions supplemented by hours of practice and one or two daily lessons in ballet or weight training.

No matter what level of competition they reach, children need to take time off. I would suggest at least one day a week off to relax, pursue other interests, and to spend time with family and friends.

● How do you find a good coach?

A good coach is one whose primary interest is in the well-being of the child, not winning medals. The coach should be properly trained as a skater—a future can be ruined by starting off with a poor foundation. And a good coach should teach the child according to the child's agenda, not his or her own.

● What expenses can a competitive skater expect?

Serious recreational skaters can expect to pay about $75 for three lessons per week, and then

INSIDE INFO

Go Figure

○ Ladies' figure skating has the largest fan base of all sports among females 12 and older and does surprisingly well among males, too. Participation is strong also.

○ About 15,000 skaters competed at the regional level between 1999 and 2004.

○ More than 000 skating clubs around the country have 173,000 members.

○ Figure-skating fans are well educated: more than 71 percent have a college degree.

○ They are wealthy: their median household income is $90,000.

SOURCE: U.S. Skating

another $10 a day for practice sessions. At the highest level of competition, though, expenses can reach $50,000 and up a year, including lessons, ice time, costumes, traveling to competitions, etc. The boots alone for custom-made skates can cost $600. For the "elite" class skaters, scholarships and fundraisers may offset some of the costs, but until a skater reaches that level, the family foots the bill.

● What are the benefits of skating for kids who don't reach elite competition?

After every winter Olympics, we see a surge of kids sign up for lessons, and then quit when they realize how much work it takes. But kids who don't reach a high level still learn invaluable life skills. I've seen many skaters who persevered, despite not reaching the top, who then went on to become successful doctors, lawyers and bankers, because they can apply the concentration and drive they learned from skating to other areas of life.

● What advice would you give parents about introducing their kids to the sport?

SPORTS

Anatomy of an Ice Skate

Keys to putting your best foot forward

BOOTS: Should fit more snugly than street shoes, so should be one size smaller. Toes should be close to the front of the skate. You should be able to wiggle your toes, but neither the ball of your foot nor your heel should move when the boot is laced.

BLADES: Always wear plastic or rubber blade guards when off the

ice to protect the blades against scratches and help them remain sharp. But don't store your skates with the guards on—moisture between the guards and blades can cause the blades to

rust. Blades should be sharpened whenever they slip sideways or if the edges are rounded or rough.

LACES: Tie them tightest around the ankle, but not too tight at the top hooks; you must be able to bend your ankle. Laces should be tied in a bow, double knotted, and then tucked between the laces and boot tongue. Always carry an extra pair of laces.

TOE PICK: This row of "teeth" at the front of the blade is used for jumping and spinning—not for stopping.

Go for it! Encourage them to always try to do something a little better, even if it's just for fun. And if your child aspires to climb the competitive ladder, try to find adequate coaching in your own backyard. Keep your family intact and your child in school. If this isn't possible where you live, and if by sixth or seventh grade, your child has shown a lot of promise and determination, then maybe you owe your child the chance to pursue his or her dream.

Radical Races for the Hell-Bent

O.K., tough guy. Let's see how tough you are

Sure, lots of Americans have run a marathon, a 26-mile race. But that's a cakewalk compared to the really tough endurance races out there. Here are seven races that are generally considered the most hell-bent on the face of the earth, taking into account factors such as toughness of the course, rigor of the action and the small percentage of competitors who actually reach the finish line.

BADWATER. *A 135-mile run and walk from Badwater, Calif., the lowest point in the contiguous U.S., to near the top of Mount Whitney, the highest.*

WHERE & WHEN: Death Valley, Calif. July

HOW TOUGH: Temperatures range from 130 degrees in the desert to 30 degrees on the mountaintop. Runners can face everything from sandstorms to ice storms and take anywhere from 26 to 60 hours to finish the course. **www.badwater.com**

IDITAROD SLED DOG RACE. *A 1,100-mile race through Alaskan wilderness that takes the mushers and their dogs 10 to 20 days to finish.*

WHERE & WHEN: Anchorage to Nome, Alaska. March

HOW TOUGH: Like the Ironman, this race has become an icon. The wintry conditions can be brutal, but the race is even tougher on the dogs when it's overly warm. www.iditarod.com

IRONMAN TRIATHLON. *A 2.4-mile ocean swim, followed by 112 miles of cycling and a 26.2-mile marathon.*

WHERE & WHEN: Kailua-Kona, Hawaii. October

HOW TOUGH: The oldest and probably best-known of the endurance events. Eight to nine hours of grueling competition for some of the world's fittest men and women. www.ironmanlive.com

LA TRAVERSEE INTERNATIONALE DU LAC SAINT-JEAN. *A 25-mile swim across a lake in Northern Quebec*

WHERE & WHEN: About 500 miles north of Montreal. July

HOW TOUGH: Three-to four-foot swells make for a rough ride, and no wetsuits are permitted during the nine-plus-hour swim, even though the water temperatures often fall to the low 60's. www.traversee.qc.ca

RACE ACROSS AMERICA. *A 3,000-mile bicycle race in 8 to 10 days.*

WHERE & WHEN: California to a preselected point on the East coast, such as Savannah. Ga., or Atlantic City, N.J. June

HOW TOUGH: The winners cycle about 350 miles a day and sleep little more than an hour. About a third of the entrants finish. www.raceacrossamerica.org

RAID SERIES. *A wilderness endurance race in which five-person teams compete in a long-distance, 5-to-7day adventure race.*

WHERE & WHEN: The site varies from year to year. Event times vary from year to year.

HOW TOUGH: Races have been held over brutal terrain in Patagonia, Argentina, Costa Rica, Oman and Madagascar. Participants may engage in sea-kayaking, mountain biking, white-water canoeing, caving and horseback riding, among other sports.www.theraid.org

VENDEE GLOBE. A four-month solo sailing race around the world.

WHERE & WHEN: From France's Les Sables d'Olonne, past Western Africa, Antarctica, Cape Horn and back. Every four years; latest held Nov. 2004 to March 2005.

HOW TOUGH: Participants can't go ashore or get assistance, so they're totally on their own for four months. www.vendeeglobe.fr/uk

SPORTS

✔ TIMELY TIPS

Waivers: The Fine Print

Trying a new sport? Read this

When faced with a waiver, most people skim the fine print and then sign. But not so fast. Lawyers offer the following suggestions on what to do when confronted with a form:

✔ Read carefully and understand what types of liability you are waiving. A waiver that describes the potential hazards and specifies that the sponsoring company is not liable for injury and property loss may be more likely to be enforced against an adult than one that speaks only in general terms. No matter how well drafted, waivers signed for children may not be enforceable depending on state law.

✔ Ask the proprietor or operator of the company about the maintenance of the equipment.

✔ Ask about recent accidents and your chances of being hurt.

✔ If you are very uncomfortable with the wording of a waiver—if, for example, it is appears to exonerate a business for recklessness—do not sign it. Sometimes the employees will permit you to participate without a completed waiver. If not, walk away.

—Ellen Rosen

Parlor Games

Taking Cues From a Shark

Forget that triple-bank shot until you master these basics

Loree Jon Jones began her pool career at the age of 4 in her father's billiard room. She ran her first rack of balls at age 5 and won her first world championship at 15, setting a record for the young-est world title holder. Jones, nicknamed "Queen of the Hill" because of her penchant for coming from behind to win the final match, is also queen of the tournaments. She holds 8 world titles, 3 U.S. Open championships, 3 National championships, and 5 Player of the Year awards bestowed on her by *Pool & Billiard Magazine*. In 2002, Jones was inducted into the Women's Professional Billiards Association Hall of Fame. Here are some pointers from Jones:

Finding the right cue stick: The most important thing in choosing a stick is comfort. A big key is the material it's made of—especially the shaft (or top) part. Men should use a stick weighing between 19 and 21 ounces, women between 18 and 19 ½. If you're just pulling a stick off the wall to use, make sure it's not too heavy or warped.

Chalking right: This should be done before every shot. Hold the chalk between your thumb, index and middle fingers and stroke downward while turning the middle of the stick. If you hit a ball straight on without chalking, you'll slide off and miscue. Chalk creates a friction to prevent this.

BUILDING BRIDGES

The basic or regular bridge is used for average shots where the cue ball rests in the middle of the table. Place your thumb against your middle finger, put the cue stick between them, then wrap your index finger around the cue stick and touch your thumb. Ring finger and pinkie should be spread out for flex-ibility. Palm and side of hand need to be on the table, and the three locking fingers can be moved to make the bridge tighter or looser.

- **The "rail bridge"** is used when the cue ball is frozen against a rail. Place your palm on the table by the rail, hanging it off the edge if necessary. Keep the cue stick level, curl the index finger underneath, then make a "V" with the thumb and lay the stick against it. The key here is to keep the hand flat.

- **The "near rail" bridge** is used if your cue ball is 1 ½ to 3 inches off the rail; you need more stability than the rail bridge offers. Put the thumb under the hand, place the cue stick on the side of your thumb and rest the cue stick on the felt of the rail. Bring

---

 **TIMELY TIPS**

The Z Factor in the Pool Hall

A warning: if a pool-hall habitué challenges you to a money game, and you notice a "Z" embossed on his cue, run as fast as you can. He's probably brandishing a top-of-the-line Z Shaft.

Lighter and more tapered than other shafts—the skinnier halves of cues—it is intended to minimize what modern players call cue ball deflection. The Z is priced at $245, more than twice the cost of most conventional shafts.

—Brendan I. Koerner

the index finger over the cue stick so the stick sits between your index finger and thumb. The stick should be touching the felt throughout the shot.

- **The "over the ball" bridge** is used when you have a ball sitting directly behind the cue ball—blocking room for a normal bridge. Get on the tips of your fingers as best you can, place them behind the blocking ball and form a "V" by raising your thumb.

- **The "open bridge"** is used to stretch way over the table for a shot. Put your hand flat on the table, stretch out your fingers and raise your hand up to the knuckles. Lay the cue stick over the index finger and raise the thumb for support. If you stroke with your right hand, raise your right leg in the air and stand on your left tiptoe for more stretch.

DEVELOPING A STRONG STANCE

When you see a great player ready to shoot, everything is lined up. If you're a righty, make a bridge with your left hand. As you stand at the table lining up your shot, your right foot should be under the back of the cue stick and the left foot a little more forward and at a 45-degree angle to the right.

Before shooting, lean down and get as low as you can to the ball. When cue stick meets cue ball, the back elbow should be at a 90-degree angle. It's O.K. to adjust for height, moving your hand forward if shorter or backward if taller.

LEARNING YOUR SHOTS

Now you're ready to shoot. Not moving the rest of your body, bring the cue stick back with your stroking arm as you begin eyeing the shot. Making sure your bridge is close enough to the cue ball, draw an imaginary line with your eyes or cue stick going directly from the middle of the cue ball through the object ball and into the pocket. Set

Pool Rules

It helps to know the rules of the game

Pool is one of a number of cue sports—bearing unfortunate names like carom and snooker—within the larger billiards family. The game people commonly refer to as pool, whether played in a dimly lit bar hall or mahogany-paneled parlor, is generally the 8-ball variety. The rules are fairly simple, although variations abound; the challenge is in the execution. Then again, even Minnesota Fats had to start somewhere.

All 15 balls are used for 8-ball. Place the 8-ball in the center of the triangle and the 1-ball in front. Fill the triangle with the remaining balls, alternating the striped and solid colored balls. Flip a coin to determine who will break the ball formation. If the person breaking gets a ball into a pocket and it is a striped ball, for example, he or she must play all the striped balls during the course of the game. The opponent plays the solids.

Players alternate shooting; a player who makes a shot is rewarded with another turn. A player who hits the opponent's ball or who misses a shot, loses a turn. The goal is to shoot all your balls into the table pockets, while avoiding the 8-ball—hence the name of the game.

Only after all your balls are in pockets can you sink the 8-ball. If you pocket the 8-ball before your other balls you automatically lose the game. Once you get your chance to shoot the 8-ball, you must announce which pocket you aim to place it in. If you get it in that pocket, you win. If you miss but it doesn't go into any pocket, then your opponent gets a turn. Once he or she misses a shot, you get another turn.

The first to sink all their balls and the 8-ball wins.

SPORTS

your aim at the start of that line, moving your eyes back and forth between the cue and the object ball. As you bring your stroking arm forward again, think of your body as a pendulum—nothing else moves besides your lower arm.

- **Follow shot.** When you want the cue ball to roll forward after hitting the object ball to set up your next shot, hit the cue ball above its center spot so it spins forward. If you imagine the cue ball as a clock, you should be very high at 12 o'clock. Don't use too much power; it's not power that makes a better roll, it's how high you hit the cue ball.

- **Draw shot.** If you want the cue ball to roll backward after hitting the object ball, strike the cue ball below its center spot at 6 o'clock. To make the shot more effective, snap your stroking wrist back as you make contact with the cue ball.

- **Stop shot.** To make the cue ball stop dead after making contact with the object ball, hit the cue ball just a bit lower at 6 o'clock than on the draw shot.

- **English shot.** This is used to send the cue and object ball to the right or left rather than straight ahead. Try this shot only after you've mastered everything else. If you want the ball to veer to the right, hit it on the right side at 3 o'clock; if you want it to veer to the left, hit it on the left at 9 o'clock. The higher you hit the ball on either side, the less it cuts down an angle shot. The lower you hit it, the wider the angle.

Rules for Multiplayer Newbies

Read this before entering the huge vitual world of cooperative online games

Many people who don't play video games may well think that someone at home tapping a keyboard or wiggling a controller must be a loner

trying to avoid other people.

That might have been true before the advent of the Internet, but no longer. These days, one of the fastest-growing types of gaming is cooperative online play. Rather than isolating players, games in cyberspace let people form teams, make friends, tackle fantastic quests and even sometimes fall in love. Millions of people are being drawn into the pastime because online games are propelled by real people, not inanimate digital constructs.

There are many kinds of Internet games, but the richest and most socially dynamic are known as massively multiplayer online games, or M.M.O.'s. While a strategy or combat game might allow only 16 players at once, in an M.M.O., there are usually thousands of players online at the same time, all spread out through a huge virtual world displayed in rich graphics.

Most M.M.O.'s, like the super-popular World of Warcraft (www.worldofwarcraft.com), are based on classic fantasy archetypes, but there are also science-fiction games like EVE Online (www. eve-online.com) and games like Project Entropia (www.project-entropia.com) that have thriving in-game economies based on real-world money.

Here are some tips for M.M.O. newcomers (or newbies, as they are sometimes known online):

Even though it's a game, treat people with the same respect you do in real life. That's not just out of courtesy, but also self-interest. Your most important asset in an online game is your reputation. It will follow you. Keep in mind that it is usually considered extremely rude to ask someone about their real life (how old they are, where they live) before you know them well in-game.

No matter what kind of game it is, the fastest way to make friends is to create a character that can heal other players. If it's a fantasy game, that means a cleric. If it's a science-fiction game, that means a repair technician. Healing isn't glamorous, but you'll be very popular.

In their immersiveness, M.M.O's become a sort of addiction for some players. Even though the friends you make may be real, remember that it is just a game.

—Seth Schiesel

Secrets of a Monopoly Champ

Don't buy Boardwalk, skimp on hotels, gobble up the orange and more

Roger Craig, a commercial tire salesman from Harrisburg, Ill., reigned as champion of the U.S. National Monopoly Game tournament from 1996 until 1999. Astonishingly, during the beginning of the game that placed him on the throne, he opted not to buy Boardwalk, the game's most expensive property and one highly coveted by lesser players. Craig shares here the rationale behind this action, as well as other secrets of his success.

Craig's strategies are based on the "traditional" game in which each player starts with $1,500 and gives all tax and fine money over to the bank. Nontournament matches often include the "untraditional" $500 bonus pot into which all taxes and fines are placed—a bounty awarded to any player landing directly on Free Parking.

● An important tactical question first. Do you prefer a particular token?

I use the iron. It's the smallest piece on the board and as you're moving it around you can hide it behind hotels and get away without paying rent. It's amazing how much money I've saved over the years using that piece. Once the dice are rolled by two people beyond yourself, you can't be caught for owing money on your last move. In championship finals all moves are announced to the crowd, so I couldn't get away with it.

● What is your strategy in acquiring property?

You buy everything you can, until you get around to the three most expensive sets of properties—the yellow ones (Atlantic, Ventnor, Marvin Gardens), green ones (Pacific, North Carolina, Pennsylvania) and the blue ones (Park Place, Boardwalk). They cost too much to buy, get a monopoly on, then have to improve with houses and hotels. If I get one of the green ones or the yellow ones, that's all I'm interested in. It blocks the other monopolies and it gives me something to trade later in the game.

● Which properties are the best to acquire?

The orange ones—St. James, Tennessee and New York. The two most common numbers rolled on the dice are six and eight—and rolling them just pops you onto the orange ones. You get those three or the red ones—Kentucky, Indiana and Illinois—and you're going to win 75 percent or more of the time unless you roll very poorly. They don't cost too much to build up and they bring in the best return for what you spend.

Knowing that, if you have one of the yellows and two of the greens—or vice-versa—you can trade them for oranges or reds to people who don't know what it takes to win. They see yellows and greens cost more and they're only thinking about how much they'll get when someone lands there—not how much it will cost to build them up. I figure how much cash a player can generate. I would never make such a trade if a guy was sitting there with $1,000 in cash.

● How does your strategy change once you have a monopoly?

If you can get a monopoly of your own without having to trade for it, you ought to have the game in the hand. Then you can spend the rest of your

The Most Landed-on Monopolies

In the 1980's, Parker Brothers, Monopoly's manufacturer, made a list of the most frequently landed-upon monopolies. The list shows the odds of a player landing on one property of a monopoly in one trip around the board.

GO DIRECTLY TO JAIL...

1. **RAILROADS**—B&O, Reading, Short Line Penn	64%
2. **ORANGES**—New York, St. James, Tennessee	50%
3. **REDS**—Illinois, Indiana, Kentucky	49%
4. **YELLOWS**—Marvin Gardens, Atlantic, Ventnor	45%
5. **GREENS**—Pacific, Pennsylvania, N. Carolina	44%
6. **LIGHT PURPLES**—St Charles, States, Virginia	43%
7. **LIGHT BLUES**—Oriental Connecticut, Vermont	39%
8. **UTILITIES**—Water Works, Electric Co.	32%
9. **DARK BLUES**—Boardwalk, Park Place	27%
10. **DARK PURPLES**—Mediterranean, Baltic	24%

DO NOT PASS GO, DO NOT COLLECT $200...

Using a computer, Irvin Hentzel, a mathematics professor at Iowa State University and a frustrated Monopoly player, calculated the 10 spaces you can count on landing on more than others–see list at right. (The most landed-upon space was Jail, but Hentzel deleted that from his list, since a player in Jail had to remain there for three turns or roll doubles to get out.) Upon making his findings in 1973, Hentzel promptly quit playing. "It was no fun anymore," he explained. "I had figured it out."

1. **Illinois Avenue**
2. **Go**
3. **B&O Railroad**
4. **Free Parking**
5. **Tennessee Avenue**
6. **New York Avenue**
7. **Reading Railroad**
8. **St. James Place**
9. **Water Works**
10. **Pennsylvania Railroad**

time blocking everybody else—making a trade that doesn't help any opponent and gets you a piece of property that will block someone else. If you're holding all the single cards to a bunch of monopolies and you've got one monopoly yourself, they can't beat you. The only time I will make a trade that gives someone a monopoly is if I get an outright monopoly itself in exchange.

It usually takes eight or nine times around for everything to be bought up. When all the properties are sold, you start looking around at all the deals you can make. Hardly anybody ever tries to get Boardwalk or Park Place as part of a deal because they cost so much to improve—and at that stage of the game you don't have any money.

Q **How much should you build up your properties with houses and hotels?**

Everybody wants to build up as many houses as they can—as fast as they can. A good rule is to build up to the three-house level, as quickly as possible. Your return on your money from one house to two houses is almost nothing, but once you make the jump to the third house—that's where your real money is made. The jump from the third to the fourth house and the fourth to a hotel isn't that big. So save your money for something else.

The biggest mistake I saw people make during the championships was that as soon as they got a monopoly, they would spend everything in front of them to build land up—without regard to where they or the other players were on the board. You need to leave yourself enough money to cover yourself. If there are several monopolies out, I'll take whatever money I figure I can spend and put it aside, then see where everyone else is on the board. As soon as they get real close to my property, then I'll build on the property and take a chance if they'll land there. I also wait until I pass opposing monopolies before spending cash.

Q What else should players keep in mind?

Don't always go for cash. Say an opponent lands on your property and they owe you $800. See if they can raise that much cash with what they own and by mortgaging properties. It's not always smart to let them do that because if you leave them with three for four mortgaged properties, the next person who lands there is going to be able to get those properties. So a lot of times, I'll take whatever property they have instead of cash.

A-D-V-I-C-E From a Scrabble Master

Seven things you can do to score big

Joe Edley was already a self-admitted games guru when he began playing Scrabble. After two years of "fanatical study," he won the National Scrabble Championship in 1980. Since then he has won two other national titles (1992 and 2000), making him the only three-time winner ever. Edley is an official with the National Scrabble Association, and author of several books on scrabble, including *The Official Scrabble Puzzle Book* ($15, at www. scrabble-assoc.com). The words Edley suggests

They Are, Too, Acceptable Words

These two-letter words may not rack up big points but they will clean up your rack

aa	be	fa	lo	om	ti
ad	bi	go	ma	on	to
ae	bo	ha	me	op	uh
ag	by	he	mi	or	um
ah	da	hi	mm	os	un
ai	de	hm	mo	ow	up
al	do	ho	mu	ox	us
am	ef	id	my	oy	ut
an	eh	if	na	pa	we
ar	el	in	ne	pe	wo
as	em	is	no	pi	xi
at	en	it	nu	re	xu
aw	er	jo	od	sh	ya
ax	es	ka	oe	si	ye
ay	et	la	of	so	
ba	ex	li	oh	ta	

mastering (above) can be found in the *Official Scrabble Players Dictionary*. The fourth edition contains over 100,000 playable words—4,000 more than the third edition—but without the 100 "offensive" words that were removed from the game in 1991.

- Learn the 94 two-letter words.

- Learn the 996 three-letter words.

- Learn the 17 "Q without U" words. Seven of them—Faqir, Qintar, Qanat, Tranq, Qoph, Qaid, Qat—can also be made plural with the addition of an "S" and "Qindar" (an Albanian monetary unit) can become "Qindarka."

- Learn the approximately 1,200 four-and five-letter words containing a J, Q, X or Z.

SPORTS

- Use "vowel dumps"—words containing multiple vowels such as "ourie" (shivering with cold) and "warison" (a battle cry) that get four or more low-scoring vowels out of your rack in one move.

- "S" and "A" are "hook letters" that can often be used to form two words off of one existing word (e.g., "board" can lead to "aboard").

- Learn "bingos"—words that by using all seven of your tiles earn a 50-point bonus. Included in the bingo list are about 200 "six to make seven" words that can be built off just three six-letter words (saltine, satire, retain) and one blank tile.

Go Directly to Go

Chinese "chess" is gaining a following

For the ancient Chinese game of Go, America is pretty much a desert land: only about 20,000 play the game here compared to millions in Asia. But oases are starting to spring up. The American Go Association now counts about 150 members; the game has a cult following in math departments in the U.S. (it made cameo appearances in the films *Pi* and *A Beautiful Mind*); and it is popular among computer scientists interested in artificial intelligence. But millions play it in Asia and it could be catching on in America, as well.

Go has simpler rules than chess, but the endless possibilities of positions on the board make it so complex that no one has devised a computer program that can defeat even a talented amateur. A Go set includes round stones (180 white and 181 black), and a board with a grid pattern of 19 horizontal and 19 vertical lines. The grid contains 361 intersections on which stones are placed. Players use their stones to gain territory on the board by surrounding and capturing their opponent's stones; the white stones invade black territory and vice versa. It generally takes about 200 moves to complete a game.

In China, Go, or *weiqi* was historically considered one of the four arts that a cultured gentleman should master. It was later condemned as bourgeois during the Cultural Revolution, but today there are roughly 30 million Chinese players and two television channels devoted to the game. Millions more play in Japan, the source of the game's name and much of its terminology, and in South Korea, now home of the world's top player, Lee Changho. These three countries are fierce rivals

---

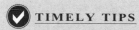 **TIMELY TIPS**

Bored? Looking for Board Games?

Remember the wholesome *Leave It to Beaver* family that played board games like Scrabble and Monopoly at the kitchen table? Online games don't count, we're talking about three-dimensional ones, with boards and pieces and dice, games for multiple players, games that would lure a family back to life.

✔ You can find such games aplenty at online sites such as www.Funagain.com, www.Germangames.com, www.Gamefest.com and www.Areyougame.com. For example, on Funagain.com, owned by a quirky store in Ashland, Ore., you'll find about 2,000 board games from around the world, including cult favorites like Blokus ($24.95) and the Carcassonne series ($19.95 to $24.95), and the Scandinavian edition of Elfenland ($23.95). "All these games take just a few minutes to learn and 45 to 60 minutes to play,' says Funagain.com's Nick Medinger. By and large, the most entertaining board games come from Germany, he says, where board games are family entertainment three or four times a week.

—Michelle Slatalla

on a professional circuit sponsored by banks and newspapers.

Computers have helped to overcome problems of geographical isolation for U.S. players. Those who want to compete can go to Go servers online. A good orientation stop is the American Go Association at www.usgo.com. —Blake Eskin

Joining the Tile-High Club

Mah-jongg uses tiles, instead of cards, and requires practice and patience

Perennially popular in Asia and among women of a certain age in Brooklyn, mah-jongg is seeing a revival, particularly among the young. The ancient Chinese game—a kind of marriage between gin rummy and dominoes—uses tiles instead of cards. Learning the basics of the game won't take long, but mastering its finer points requires practice and patience. The most difficult part is figuring out which rules to adhere to. There are at least 25 variations internationally, and even within China the rules differ between the north and south. Rules for the American version—among the more difficult—are determined by the National Mah Jongg League (www.nationalmahjonggleague.org) and are available in the League's booklet *Mah Jongg Made Easy.*

New players are better off learning basic mah-jongg rules that cut across many game versions before moving on to more complex variations. The game is played by four players at a square table (or online if you prefer to play alone). The object is to be the first to organize your tiles into a pattern of certain combinations that have the highest point values. It is in the variety of tile combinations and scoring that mah-jongg rules differ most.

The game begins with each player building a wall of tiles on the table, using a predetermined number of tiles, usually 34 tiles if four players are in the game. A turn involves a player drawing a tile from the wall and deciding whether to retain it or discard it. Tiles can only be removed from the left to the right edges. A tile that is not on an edge is blocked and cannot be removed. When the player discards a tile, he or she announces the name of the tile discarded. Although tiles are removed clockwise, players take their turns in a counterclockwise direction. A player can take only the most recently discarded tile, and then only if it completes a certain group or hand.

The process of claiming and discarding tiles continues until one player achieves a mah-jongg hand. A complete 14-tile mah-jongg hand, for example, includes four groups (each with three tiles) and a pair. Groups have names like pung, chow and kong, designating whether the tiles are three green dragons, for example, or of the same suit such as three dotted or lined tiles. A pair must be two identical tiles, of any character or suit. Official scoring rules are complicated in mah-jongg and often casual players establish in advance their own values of tiles and groups. Strategy is important but a lot of success in mah-jongg also depends on sheer luck.

SAMPLE MAH-JONGG HAND

This sample mah-jongg hand includes four groups and a pair. They are a pung (three dragons), a chow (three of same suit), a pung (three dotted tiles), a chow (three of same suit) and a pair (two of same suit or character)

Where Kings & Queens Reign

The rules that rule the pieces in checkers, chess and backgammon

The most exciting board games require a unique mix of brains and imaginative brawn. In the best of matches, the rules metamorphose from simple mathematical variations into the physics of a new world in which pawns become warriors and you are the mastermind behind a war in which everything good and decent is at stake. Here are the rules that govern the battlefield.

HOPSCOTCHING THE CHECKER BOARD

Learning to play checkers is child's play, but devising strategies to triumph over a good player takes skill and lots of practice. The winner, of course, is the first player to capture all of an opponent's men or to block them so that they can't move anywhere on the board. To test your mettle, follow these instructions:

• Opponents face each other across the board, which has eight rows of eight squares each, alternately red and black. One player takes the red pieces, or men, and puts them on the black squares in the three horizontal rows nearest him. The opponent places the black checkers on the black squares in the three rows facing him.

• The opponents take turns—black goes first, then red—moving a man forward diagonally toward the opponent's side. Only the black squares are used. With each turn, a player moves one man to an adjacent empty square. When one player's man comes up against an enemy checker and there is an empty space behind it, the player jumps over the enemy, landing on the unoccupied square. The captured checker is removed from the board.

• One man can jump two or more enemy pieces consecutively, by moving diagonally left or right after the first jump, as long as there are empty spaces to land on between each jump. A checker that makes it to any square in the

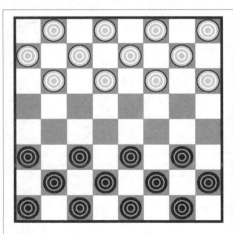

RANK AND FILE: *In both checkers and chess, the rows across are known as ranks; the columns as files. In checkers, only the dark squares are used.*

MANEUVERS: *As shown here, the six chess pieces can move in a variety of ways. The knight, however, is the only one that can move through, or jump over, other pieces. That ability, combined with its unusual L-shaped moving pattern, makes it an end-game linchpin.*

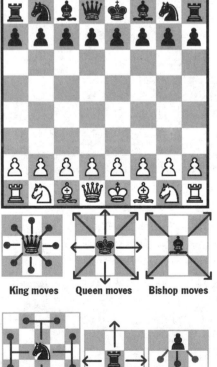

King moves   Queen moves   Bishop moves

Knight moves   Rook moves   Pawn moves

opponent's first row becomes a king—at which time it gets crowned by a man of the same color that is not in play. The king can now move, and jump, forward and backward.

THE MIND FIELDS OF CHESS

When it comes to drama, intrigue and byzantine rules, few games can match chess, which is thought to date back to sixth-century India or China. Odds are you won't become the next Bobby Fischer, who at age 15 was the youngest international grand master in history, but here are the rules that will take you to the endgame: capturing the enemy's king.

• Opponents face each other across the board, which has eight rows of eight squares each, alternately white and black. Each player gets 16 pieces of one color, black or white. From least to most important, the pieces are 8 pawns, 2 knights, 2 bishops, 2 rooks (or castles), 1 queen and 1 king.

• Place the board so that each player has a light square at the nearest right-hand corner. In the row closest to you, place in order from left to right: rook, knight, bishop, queen, king, bishop, knight and rook. Line up the pawns next to each other in the row directly in front of these pieces.

• A piece can move only into a square that's not occupied by another piece owned by the same player. If an enemy piece occupies the square, it is captured. You remove the captured piece from the board and put your piece in its place.

• A pawn moves forward one square at a time, except for its first move when it can go one or two squares. A knight makes an L-shaped move, going two squares forward, backward or sideways, then another square at a right angle. It's the only piece that can jump over another piece. A bishop goes diagonally forward or backward,

but has to stay on the same color. A rook moves forward, backward or sideways, for any distance. The queen is a potent force. She moves forward, backward, sideways and diagonally for any number of squares in one direction. The king's moves are like the queen's except that he moves one square at a time, as long as it's unoccupied or not under attack by an enemy piece.

• When a king is under attack by an enemy piece, the king is in check. The player whose king is in check has several options: to move the king to safety, to capture the attacker or to move another piece to a square between the king and the attacker. If a player can't take any of these moves, the king is captured or "checkmated," and the game is over.

• Pieces capture an opponent's man by moving as they normally do, except for the pawn. It can capture any of its opponent's pieces that are diagonally next to and ahead of it.

• A pawn can also take an enemy pawn "en passant," or in passing. Say an opponent starts by moving his pawn two squares, instead of one, putting it next to one's pawn. You can take that piece by moving diagonally to the square directly behind it. But do it immediately: you can't wait for your next turn.

• Once in each game, in a move called castling, a king gets to move two spaces. Castling is done only if the king is not in check, there are no pieces between the king and a rook, and neither piece has yet made a move. The two-part move is done by moving the king two squares toward the rook and then putting the rook on the square passed over by the king. Castling counts as one move.

THE FINER POINTS OF BACKGAMMON

Backgammon is a game played by two players, each with 15 markers or stones—but these days checkers can be used in a pinch. The object is to be the first player to move all one's markers around the board and then off it.

• To set up, the markers are placed on the board as shown in the diagram below. The board is divided into four "tables" with numbered triangular spaces, or "points." The bar in the middle is also used in the game.

• Each player rolls a die to determine who goes first. The higher one starts. Players then take turns rolling two dice to determine how many spaces to move the stones, with black moving around the board in one direction and white moving in the opposite direction. The numbers on each die can be combined so that one piece moves the total amount indicated. Alternatively, each die's value can be applied separately to a single marker.

• Throwing "doubles" (for example, two 4s), allows a player to move twice as many points as shown on the dice—in this case, either four markers can be moved four spaces each, one can be moved four spaces and one 12 spaces, two can be moved 8 spaces each, or one marker can be moved 16 spaces.

• There is no limit to the number of markers of the same color that may stay on one point, but markers of opposite colors may not occupy the same point. If two or more markers are on a point, the point is closed—a marker of the opposite color can't land there. However, a point that is occupied by only one marker is open and is called a "blot." If an opponent lands on a blot, the other player must move his or her man to the bar between the two halves of the board and can play no other man till the one on the bar re-enters. To do so, the player must make a roll of the dice that corresponds to a space on the other player's inner table that is open or blotted.

• Once all of a player's 15 men have entered his or her "inner table" (the opposite side of the board from which the player began), the player may begin bearing them off the board by rolling the dice and removing any men that occupy spaces indicated by the roll. If a player rolls 5 and 4, for example, he or she may remove one of the men that occupies point 5 and one of the men that occupies point 4. If the number is higher than any of the occupied points, the player may remove a man from the next highest point. Double 6's are an especially good roll at this point. Play continues until one of the players has removed all of his or her men.

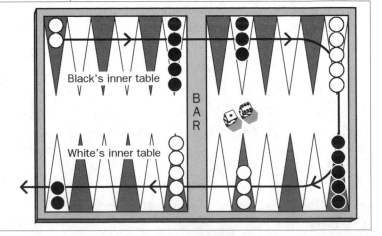

BACKGAMMON: *Board is shown in the starting position. The goal is to move your men from your opponent's inner table to your own inner table on the opposite side of the board. White moves in the direction indicated by the arrows; black moves in the opposite direction. When all of your men reach your inner table, you may begin bearing them off by throwing dice that (hopefully) correspond to the number assigned each point.*

Black's inner table

White's inner table

B A R

Cut the Deck, Please

Know when to hold 'em and when to fold 'em

By some estimates, as many as 80 million people in the United States play poker. And these days, online poker draws about two million people a month. One reason may be because there are so many versions of the game. The current rage: Texas hold 'em and Omaha, which are outshining more traditional stud poker, at least among the young. Here are basic poker rules, some popular variations—and a few tricks for playing them. There's no guarantee, of course, that you'll draw winning cards, but at least you'll be prepared to call the other guy's bet.

POKER (FIVE-CARD DRAW)

Poker pits one player against another; casinos that provide poker tables make their money by taking a percentage of the winnings, or by charging by the hour for the use of the table and dealer. Unless you're an expert, you're better off wagering chips or change in the comfort of your own home.

Hundreds of card games are based on slight modifications of standard poker or "five-card draw." Variations include adding wild cards, changing the way players bet and altering the size of each hand. The goal is always the same: to get a better hand, or selection of cards, than other players.

To play five-card draw, shuffle a regular 52-card deck and deal five cards to each of three to seven players. Typically each player pays a small sum, called an "ante," for the privilege of seeing his or her hand. All best (and antes) are placed in the pot, a pile of money in the center of the table.

Players bet on their cards in a clockwise fashion, starting at the dealer's left. The first player has several betting options:

FOLD: Throwing in the cards and sitting out the rest of the hand. Any time a player folds at this stage, the ante remains in the pot and goes to the winner.

BET: Placing a wager in the pot.

PASS: Choosing not to make a wager and allowing the next player to go.

If the first player doesn't make a bet, then the next player has the same options. Once a player has made a bet, however, other players may no longer pass and are required to do one of the following:

FOLD: And lose your bets and ante.

CALL: Match the other player's bets by placing an equal wager into the pot.

RAISE: Place a higher wager than others have bet into the pot. All other players will need to match this raised bet in order to stay in the game.

After a round of betting, all remaining players are then allowed to exchange up to three of their cards with those from the top of the remaining deck in the same order that the cards were dealt. At this time, the players have a second round of betting. After this round, all remaining players show their cards to each other. The player with the highest hand wins the pot.

Cards are ranked in the following order, from lowest to highest: 2, 3, 4, 5, 6, 7, 8, 9, 10, Jack, Queen, King, Ace. The box on the next page shows the order of winning hands. Each level of the table beats ALL hands below it. For example, even the lowest straight (2, 3, 4, 5, 6) will beat the highest three of a kind (Ace, Ace, Ace, King, Queen). In many games, Aces can be both the highest and lowest card, at the player's discretion.

If two players have the same type of hand, the one who has the higher cards wins the hand. For example, a player with a 9, 9, 9, Jack, 2 (three 9's) beats a player with a 6, 6, 6, Ace, Queen

SPORTS

(three 6's). Extra cards, such as the Ace, Queen, Jack and 2 in this example, only matter when two players have identical winning combinations. For example, a player with a 9, 9, 5, 5, King (two pair, with a King) would beat a player with a 9, 9, 5, 5, Queen (two pair, with a Queen).

LOW-HAND POKER

The rules for this game are identical to poker, except for an interesting 180-degree switch. In low-hand poker, the player with the lowest—not the highest—hand wins. The lowest hand possible is an Ace, 2, 3, 4, 6—known as a "perfect low." The next best low is Ace, 2, 3, 5, 6. In this game, it is common to see players discarding pairs of cards to rid themselves of a beastly hand.

HIGH-LOW POKER

Two players split the pot— the one with the highest hand and the one with the lowest hand. If all but one player folds, then the entire pot goes to the winner.

FIVE-CARD STUD

Unlike draw, five-card stud begins by dealing only two cards to each player. One of these cards is placed facedown and one faceup, in plain view of all players. Each player is allowed to look at his or her facedown card, after which a round of bet-

What Beats What

Hand	Number possible	Odds of obtaining
ROYAL FLUSH The highest straight flush— 10-J-Q-K-A all of the same suit	4	1:649,739
STRAIGHT FLUSH A straight, and all five cards are of the same suit	40	1:64,973
FOUR OF A KIND Four cards of the same value with one extra	624	1:4,164
FULL HOUSE Three cards of one value and two of another	3,744	1:693
FLUSH Five cards of the same suit, such as five spades	5,108	1:508
STRAIGHT Five cards in a sequence of different suits, such as 5-6-7-8-9	10,200	1:254
THREE OF A KIND Three cards of the same value with two extra	54,912	1:46
TWO PAIR Two pairs of cards with one extra	123,552	1:20
ONE PAIR (Two of a kind) Two cards of the same value with three extra	1,098,240	1:1.37
HIGH CARD In a hand with no winning combination of cards, the highest card	1,302,540	1:1

ting ensues. Betting starts with the player showing the highest card. After this round, another card is placed faceup for each player. Now each player has two cards showing and one hidden card. Another round of betting follows. This pattern continues until each player has five cards. At any time during the game, a player can fold and the person with the highest hand at the end wins.

SEVEN-CARD STUD

This lively and often high-stakes game is played much like five-card stud. But the game begins by dealing three cards to each player—two are facedown and one is faceup. Rounds of betting are interspersed with getting additional faceup cards until each player has two facedown and four faceup cards. A final card is then dealt facedown and the final round of betting takes place.

Players can use any of their seven cards to make their best five-card hand. The catch is that the odds are thrown haywire. Having seven cards makes it easier to achieve good hands. It is common to see full houses, straights and flushes.

TEXAS HOLD 'EM

This is by far the most popular form of poker today. Also called simply hold 'em, it is played widely on television tournaments and in card rooms across the country. The game is easy to learn but tough to master. Players make their best five-card poker hands using seven cards: two cards from the dealer and five "community" cards, which are available to all players.

Betting varies; sometimes antes are used, sometimes not. Most games start with the player (or two players) to the left of the dealer putting a predetermined amount of money into the pot before the cards are dealt. That is called "posting the blinds," and ensures that there is an initial amount to get the game started. Each player is dealt two cards, facedown. These are the "hole" or "pocket" cards. After a round of betting, the dealer discards the top card of the deck, or "burn" card, in case a player accidentally saw it.

The dealer then flips the next three cards faceup. These are called the "flop," community cards that everyone can use in combination with their two hole cards to form their poker hand. At this point, another round of betting starts. During all the betting rounds, players can check, call, raise or fold when it's their turn to bet.

After the betting round, the dealer burns another card and flips one more face up on the table. This is called the "turn" card. Following this pattern, the dealer will eventually place five community cards on the table. Players can use any of the community cards and their own two hole cards to form their best possible five-card poker hand. After the fourth and final round of betting, the "showdown" occurs when all remaining players reveal their hands. The player with the best hand wins.

OMAHA

This poker game is similar to Texas hold 'em but differs in that players are dealt four personal or hole cards to start instead of two. Omaha's popularity is partly due to the greater options it gives players. Players form their best possible hands from nine available cards—four hole cards and five flop cards, or community cards. For each five-card hand, a player must use two hole cards and three community cards. Betting is the same as in hold 'em. As in most poker games, at the showdown, remaining players show their hands; the best hand wins the pot. Omaha is often played hi-lo, meaning the player with the highest hand splits the pot with the player holding the lowest hand.

BASEBALL

This variation on the seven-card stud makes chances of getting a high hand fairly easy. The game has wild cards, which can represent any other card in the deck at the player's discretion. All 3's and 9's—the number of strikes and innings in baseball—are wild. But they come with a price; players must either purchase 3's and 9's at a predetermined price if they are dealt them faceup, or they must fold the hand. If a player is dealt a 4 faceup (the number of balls in baseball), the player is immediately dealt another card facedown.

The wild-card feature in this game and the possibility of having more than seven cards if a 4 is dealt, makes it common for a player to get the absurd "five of a kind." For example, a hand of 5, 5, 5, 3, 9, would be five 5's. Five of a kind is the highest hand possible, beating a royal flush.

Be Prepared to Bet the Ranch

The stakes are getting even higher in high-stakes poker

The young studs of poker no longer play very much stud. Today the flop games, those using community cards, have taken over. The variations are endless: pot-limit Omaha; limit, pot-limit and no-limit hold 'em; and, most of all, no-limit hold 'em

ⓘ INSIDE INFO

Online Action

○ More than $60 billion was wagered on more than 200 poker sites in 2005, according to industry research. Most of it lost or won by Americans.

○ PartyPoker.com is the world's busiest card-playing Web site, where tens of thousands of players around the world compete in real time at virtual nine-handed tables. Sportingbet was taking in $530,000 a day from its poker business in 2005.

○ Internet gambling operations are prohibited by federal law. Some American banks refuse to accept transactions processed by Internet casinos.

tournaments. Who's winning the long green these days? In tournaments, at least, about 100 men and half a dozen women have been dramatically more successful than the average player. Most of these players are younger than 35, much like the people who dominate physical sports.

They rely on the fact that their opponent is seldom dealt strong pocket, or hole, cards. Even if you have a big pair, it will seldom be improved by the flop, or community cards shared by all the players. The young guns watch you, not the cards, as the flop hits the board. If they sense disappointment, or anything short of the serene confidence of "flopping the nuts"—gaining the winning hand from the community cards—they make an intimidating bet, even when holding a weak hand themselves. "This is harder to do than it sounds," according to Puggy Pearson, the 1973 world poker champion. The new breed is trading on their opponents' fear of losing, with a relentless assault of raises.

But that doesn't mean that even average Joes and typical Tiffanys don't routinely catch a lucky run of cards and play them with panache and intelligence, winning (or coming close) in a big-money tournament. (Joe Hachem and Tiffany Williamson are only two examples of relatively inexperienced players who broke through in the 2005 World Series of Poker main event.) But as columnist Mike Sexton noted in *Card Player* magazine, mere luck is no longer the greatest equalizer in no-limit hold 'em; the all-in bet is. Sexton's primer, *Shuffle Up and Deal*, introduces novices to the basics of no-limit hold 'em.

More amateurs understand that moving all-in—betting all your chips on one hand—is the most effective way of combating more skillful professionals. All-in bets short-circuit even the toughest pros' ability to outplay you later in the hand—after the board has paired, for example, or made a straight or flush possible. Even so, most players are afraid to reraise all-in without the nuts or close to it, and these hands just don't materialize often. But—if you have the stomach for it—the top-heavy system of payouts of tournaments make an all-in reraise the correct move in a variety of ticklish situations.

This tactic would make "a total novice" no worse than a 2-1 underdog in a heads-up match against the greatest no-limit hold 'em player in the world, Sexton believes. The novice would simply have to move all in on every hand. Sexton predicts that the great player would "fold 8 to 10 times in a row and then make a stand with something like A-10 or a pair of 8's, hands that won't be a big favorite over any other." If the novice wins the hand, he says, it's over. If not, he continues to move all in, building his stack back up.

Yet Sexton and others believe that an over-reliance on all-in bets can make for ugly poker, and he predicts that it will foster a renaissance of pot-limit hold 'em and Omaha, which both require much more ingenuity after the flop.

—James McManus

A Guide to Poker-Table Manners

Mind the clock, respect the dealer and know how to raise properly

Ornery road gamblers keeping one step ahead of cops and robbers, locals whose money they won in illegal stud games—them days are over.

The reality is that most pots these days are contested by polite, unarmed folks in state-sanctioned card rooms. A steely-eyed Marlboro Man may raise you the ranch, but since 2002, smoking has been banned at all major events. Spewing one particular curse word now leaves you suspended for 10 minutes; a second use gets you 20. A third and you're out of the tournament. Subtler guidelines have been around for much longer:

Mind the clock. Unless your whole stack is on the line and you have mind-bending pot odds to calculate, you shouldn't take four minutes to act on your hand. For most decisions 1 to 10 seconds should be plenty of time. To mix up your tempos, occasionally pretending to think for a moment when you have a no-brainer is fine, but don't make a habit of it.

A little class, please. Keep your good luck charms out of your neighbors' space on the felt. Don't get drunk. Don't mock or berate your opponents. Don't whine. Don't slow-roll the nuts (the best possible hand) for dramatic effect.

Moving protocol. When you're moved to another table, carry your chips in a rack, not in one of your pockets. When you arrive at your new seat, restack them by color and place large-denomination chips

A Full House With Harry or Johnny

From Truman to Carson to the cast of Ocean's12, there's nothing like a nightly game of cards

Home poker games are played in every American hamlet and metropolis, and in more than a few other hemispheres. Despite the hundreds of online sites offering a chance to contest pots with strangers from Rio to Seoul any time of day or night, the tradition of sitting down in person with friends also continues to flourish. Most home games keep the stakes low so no player gets hurt financially, though pride can be bruised.

That poker keeps 8 or 10 people elbow to elbow is one reason it has endured for almost 200 years. For Harry Truman, the game was a chance to drop the formality of office and kibbitz with friends. Our 33rd president was reportedly an affable chump who "just couldn't bear to fold." And the wilder the poker, the better. The rules of Truman's favorite game were so goofy that

even regular tablemates couldn't follow them. No matter. A tenth of each pot went into a "poverty bowl," to be redistributed among those who lost their original stake.

Johnny Carson, too, liked his poker longer on camaraderie than cutthroat one-upmanship. He and other well-paid entertainers shared a meal before low-stakes dealer's-choice while shooting the Malibu breeze. The cast of the movie *Ocean's 12* played a nightly hold 'em tournament in Rome but kept the buy-in to 50 euros.

You, too, can host a poker game. Sources like *The Rules of Neighborhood Poker According to Hoyle* and HomePokerTourney.com provide helpful guidelines. To join one already in progress, try the Web for sites that list games within 20 miles of your zip code, with the stakes, game type, age and skill of participants. The younger the players, the more likely they are to favor no-limit hold 'em, with buy-ins ranging from $5 to $100. Stud games are usually rife with AARP cards.

—James McManus

at the front, so opponents can eyeball how expensive it might become if they tangle with you.

Respect the dealer. If the cards are running bad for you, don't call for a deck change. Better to accept that this happens in poker, or politely ask the dealer to give the deck an extra-big scramble.

 INSIDE INFO

Poker Can Make You Rich... or President

O In his 1995 memoir, *The Road Ahead*, Bill Gates recalled marathon dorm sessions during his two years at Harvard that he found at least as productive and intellectually stimulating as his time spent in class. "In poker, a player collects different pieces of information," he wrote, "and then crunches all that data together to devise a plan for his own hand. I got pretty good at this kind of information processing." He also won a significant portion of Microsoft's start-up costs in those games, but it wasn't just dollars being accumulated; it was "the poker strategizing experience."

O "He played poker all through his presidential career for money," William Tecumseh Sherman wrote in 1889 to the president of Harvard about Ulysses S. Grant, who had died four years earlier.

O As a young Navy lieutenant, Richard M. Nixon took home almost $8,000—a genuinely whopping haul in the 1940's—from shipboard games in the Pacific. Once, while holding the ace of diamonds, he drew four cards to make a royal flush, about a 650,000-to-1 shot. "I was naturally excited," he wrote, "But I played it with a true poker face, and won a substantial pot." He later used the $8,000 to finance his first Congressional campaign, in 1946, which he won.

—James McManus

Maintain order. Even more crucial is behavior affecting the outcome of a hand. Always make sure to act in strict clockwise order. Pretending to act out of turn accidentally to get a read on opponents is called shooting an angle and is rightly despised by honest and serious players.

Raise properly. If a player to your right says "raise," and one or more other players have yet to act, don't fold your cards until the raiser has completed her bet, because knowing you will fold may affect how much she raises.

No slapping. Never say or do anything that implies what your hole cards were after you've folded them. If you've wisely folded 7-3, and the flop comes 3-7-7, slap neither the felt nor your forehead.

Collusion is illegal. This obviously includes teaming with partners to raise and reraise other players, while soft-playing each other (not betting strong hands, for example). But even if a friend is short-stacked a few places out of the money, not raising his blind with raise-worthy hole cards is cheating. If you offer opponents a deal, or vice versa, negotiate with the understanding that all deals are voluntary.

—James McManus

The Best of the Rest
Rules for playing some classic card games

Poker may be the rage but some card games call for more than your luck of the draw. Take bridge, for example. "It is an elegant game, full of strategy and tactics. It's part science, part math, part logic, part reason," says Sharon Osberg, a two-time World Champion bridge player. But, as a game played with partners, a huge component of bridge is also very human. It's the combination of those elements, she believes, that sets it apart from many board and card games, making bridge cerebral, creative, unpredictable—and hard to master.

If bridge gets the best of you, try pinochle, blackjack, gin rummy, spades, or the quintessential time-passer, solitaire. Here are the basic rules for each.

THE BASICS OF BRIDGE

It may lack the flash of poker but social bridge maintains a loyal, dedicated, if aging, following. The game's origins date back at least to the early 16th century Brits, who played a similar game called whist. But contract bridge, the version commonly played in the U.S. today, is fairly new; it was refined and popularized by Ely Culberston in the 1920's. Bridge is one of the most orderly card games around today, with clubs, tournaments and championships organized all over the globe.

Contract bridge has a number of variations, but the basic type is called rubber bridge and is played by two teams of two players. Chicago bridge, also known as four-deal bridge has gained in popularity because of its simplicity and greater predictability. Another type, duplicate bridge, is typically played in clubs and tournaments; it requires at least eight players and calls for different sets of players to play the same deals, thereby decreasing the luck factor.

The object of all, however, remains the same: to win as many tricks, or rounds, as possible for the team. The following rules apply to rubber bridge.

Four players sit at a square table. One team member, called North, faces his or her partner, South. Team member East faces partner West. The 52-card deck (minus the jokers) is shuffled and cards are dealt clockwise and facedown to each player. Cards in each suit rank in descending order from Ace, King, Queen, Jack, 10, 9, 8, etc. to 2, which is the lowest.

Bridge is less about card play, though, and more about bidding, and in the opening part of

the game, an auction is held. Each player makes a bid, that is, announces a target number of tricks they expect to win above six. At the same time, the player declares a trump (high-ranking suit) or no trump. For example, "one, spade" is a commitment to take 6+1, or 7 tricks, with spades as the trump suit. A player may choose to increase the bid, or to pass, that is, refrain from bidding. The highest bid becomes the "contract." The goal for the opposing team is to prevent the declarer and his partner from fulfilling the contract.

That's done through a series of 13 tricks, begun by the player to the left of the "declarer." All players must follow suit if possible; the highest suit card, or the highest trump card, wins the trick. When all the tricks are taken, team members combine their scores. Scoring is complicated by factors such as whether the contract was made and by how much. There are also ways to score extra points, such as if a doubled bid was made or if a player receives certain high-ranking cards in the deal. The game ends when one team hits 100 points. The team that wins two out of three games wins a rubber, after which players can choose to change teams and start over.

A PRIMER ON PINOCHLE

This card game was developed in the United States in the mid-19th century and shares many similarities with some old European games, such as the French game bezique. Although not as complex, pinochle is similar to contract bridge—they are both trick games and involve bidding, for example. There are many variations of pinochle, played by two to four players but the most popular form is the four-player double-deck pinochle, described here. The basic object of the game: partners compete, two against two; the first team to score 1,000 points, or some other predetermined total, wins.

Double-deck pinochle is played with an 80-card deck (either two pinochle decks or four regular decks) consisting only of Aces, 10's, Kings, Queens and Jacks in all four suits—spades, hearts, clubs and diamonds. The rankings of the cards descend from Ace to Jack, with the 10 ranking just below the Ace and above the King, as in many European games.

A dealer is chosen randomly for the first hand of the game. For successive hands, dealers rotate clockwise. A double-deck pinochle hand is one set of 20 cards for each player. To start off, the player to the left of the dealer places a card faceup on the table. Other players do the same in rotation. At this point, the person to the left of the dealer begins bidding, which starts at 50. The bid indicates the number of points the player intends to get. Bidding progresses in rotation, skipping anyone who passes. If three people pass, the fourth person has won the bid and chooses the trump suit.

Tricks are won by the highest card played and put aside by the winner to be counted later. The winner of the trick picks the suit that others must follow. If a player does not have the suit, then he must play the predetermined trump suit. One rule in trumping is that if you cannot follow suit and hold a trump card, you must play it, even if you know that the card may be overtaken by a higher trump. (Computer pinochle will stop you from holding on to your trump illegally.)

After all the cards have been played, the cards you take in tricks partly determine the score. There are many methods of scoring tricks, but in the traditional method, an Ace counts as 11 points, ten as 10, King 4, Queen 3 and Jack 2 points. The player who wins the last trick gets an extra 10 points. On top of trick points, players can get points from certain combinations of cards, called melds. These include a King and Queen in the same suit, or marriage; the flush, which is an Ace, 10, King, Queen and Jack in the same suit; groups of cards of the same rank, such as four Aces, four Kings, etc.; and the pinochle—Jacks of diamonds and Queens of spades. The player or team to hit the pre-established number of points wins.

HOW TO PLAY BLACKJACK

The roots of this popular casino game go back to the 1700's, when the French began playing a similar card game they called *vingt-et-un*, or twenty one. The British call their blackjack pontoon. Whatever the name, the object of the game is to have a hand with a point value that is higher than the dealer's. You must do this without going over 21 points, the rule that gives it the alternate name twenty-one. A player or dealer with 22 points or more has busted and automatically loses the hand. All numbered cards are worth their face value. Picture cards—Jacks, Queens, Kings—are worth 10 points each; Aces are worth either 1 or 11—which the player gets to determine. Suits and colors are disregarded in the game.

Before each deal, players make their bets. Two cards are then dealt to everyone including the dealer, who is dealt one card facedown. A player whose first two cards add up to 21, for example, an Ace and a Queen, has a blackjack and is immediately paid 3-2, unless the dealer also has a blackjack. A tie between a dealer and player is know as a "push" and neither one wins the hand.

After the cards have been dealt, players have several options. Your best move depends both on what you have been dealt and on the dealer's exposed card. A player can:

HIT: Take an additional card.

STAND: Take no additional cards.

DOUBLE DOWN: Double the original bet and take only one additional card.

SPLIT: When a player has been dealt two cards of identical value (e.g., two 9's), he can choose to double the original bet and play the two cards as separate hands.

CLAIM INSURANCE: When a dealer is showing an Ace, players are invited to claim insurance that the next dealer's card will be worth 10 (and thus blackjack). Insurance involves risking half the amount of the original bet and pays off at two to one, if the dealer has blackjack.

SURRENDER: Forfeit the hand and lose half of the original bet. This may not be an option in many casinos.

Once all the players are either satisfied with their hands or have busted, the dealer proceeds.

 TIMELY TIPS

Hit or Stand?

Know when to take a card

✔ **Always hit when you have been dealt 8 or less.** You have no chance of busting, and you need to get closer to 21.

✔ **Always stand on hard hands of 17 or more,** regardless of what the dealer is showing. A hard hand is a hand that either has no Aces or has an Ace or Aces that must be worth only one point because to be worth more would mean a bust (e.g., a 6, a Jack and an Ace). If you hit, odds are you will bust.

✔ **Always hit if you have 16 or less and the dealer's card is a 7, 8, 9, 10 or Ace.** These are the best cards and it is likely that the dealer will beat you. Although you have a good chance of busting, it is worth the risk of getting closer to 21.

✔ **Always stand on hard hands of 12 or more if the dealer's first card is a 2, 3, 4, 5 or 6.** These are the worst cards and it is likely that the dealer will bust. But, you don't win if you bust first!

✔ **Always stand on soft 19's and 20's.** A soft hand is one that has an Ace that can still be valued at either 1 or 11. Don't risk losing the good hand.

Unlike the players, who can make choices, the dealer must proceed according to set rules: drawing on any hand that is less than 17 and standing on anything 17 or higher.

GIN RUMMY FOR FUN OR MONEY

Gin rummy (or simply "gin") may have been introduced to this country by Chinese immigrants. Today's version was created in Brooklyn in 1909 and had its heyday in the 40's, when glamorous film stars turned it into a nationwide fad.

All 52 cards are used to play Gin, but suits are not a factor in the game. Face cards are worth 10 points each; numbered cards are worth their face value; Aces are worth one point each. One common variation is to allow Aces to be either high or low. Usually in this case, Aces are worth 15 points instead of one.

The object is to get rid of your cards by creating sets of three or more that can be "melded." Timing is important—the sets are played differently depending on who melds first. The sets can be formed in two ways:

SERIES: Three or more cards form a series in sequential order, such as a 4-5-6-7 or a 10-Jack-Queen.

MATCHING SETS: Cards are in groups of the same value, such as an 8-8-8 or an A-A-A-A.

To play, 10 cards are dealt to two players and the remainder of the deck is placed in a pile between them. The dealer turns over the top card on the pile and places it face up as a discard pile. The second player then has the option of taking this card and switching it with one of the cards in his hand or passing and giving the dealer the same option. If the dealer also passes, the second player takes the card on the top of the pile—so that momentarily there are 11 cards in his hand until

he discards one. The dealer must then either take the card that has been discarded or the next card from the deck. This continues until a player ends the round of play by melding his or her cards to reveal the hand.

The first player to meld or "knock" must have fewer than 10 points in hand that are not part of sets. For example, after several rounds of drawing cards, a player might knock with the following hand: 5-5-5 (a set), 8-9-10-J (another set) and A, 2, 2, K (not a set). This player can discard the King and then meld with the set of 5's, the 8 through Jack sequence, and five points (A+2+2). The second player must meld his or her cards, too. In doing so, the second player has the added advantage of being able to play cards off the first player's hand. For example, the second player might have the following hand: 2-3-4, 9-9-9, 4, 5, 8, Queen. The 2 through 4 sequence and the 9's would be played in their own right. However, the Queen could also be played off the 8 through Jack sequence of the first player; as would the 5 with the three 5's. This would leave the second player with only 12 unused points (4+8). The player who knocked would earn the difference between the two hands, or seven points (12-5).

If a player knocks and then is beaten (or underscored), the second player gets an additional 25 points for the feat. If a player melds an entire hand, with no extra cards, then he is entitled to say "gin" and gets an extra 25 points. The winner of each round deals the next hand. The game continues until one player reaches 100 points (or any score that the players have agreed to before the game).

HOW TO WIN IN SPADES

Once common only in the United States, this card game has taken off internationally over the past decade, thanks to online card rooms. The game can be played by three people, but four is ideal. The goal is to score as many points as possible by collecting tricks.

To begin, deal the 52-card deck evenly to each of the players. If there are four, each player will have 13 cards. The first round is begun by whoever has the 2 of clubs, which is laid in the center of the table. The player to his or her left then lays down any card of the same suit. The next player does likewise, and the next, until each has put down a card. The highest card wins the trick. Aces are played high in spades; 2 is the lowest.

If a player does not have a card in the suit being played, he or she may trump the trick by playing a spade. But if any of the following players in that round also has no cards in the original suit, he or she may "trump the trump" with a higher spade. (No one may open with a spade until spades have been "broken"—that is, played as a trump.) The winner of the book plays the next card, and the round continues until all 13 books have been played.

Each trick is worth 10 points. After a hand is dealt, players must make a bid on how many tricks they expect to get based on the strength of the cards they were dealt. Because each player in a four-person game has 13 cards, there are 13 possible tricks, or 130 points. A player who found among his or her 13 cards a couple of Kings, some Queens and several spades of any value might make a high bid because those cards are all likely to make a trick. The catch: if a player has a strong hand and so bids, say, 6 tricks, that player must make at least those 6. If not, he or she will instead lose 60 points (-10 points for each trick bid).

On the other hand, if the player makes over the amount bid, say 7 tricks instead of the 6 bid, he or she receives only a single point for each extra trick—in this case 61 points. Another catch: if a player gets more than 10 of those extra single points, he or she loses 100 points. This is called "sandbagging."

A player who is behind by more than 100 points may bid "blind six," a bid of six made before the cards are even dealt. If the six are made, the player gets 100 points; if not, the player loses 100 points. Players can play as many hands as they like to a preset score. About 500 points is a good goal for a satisfying evening of spades.

IF SOLITAIRE'S THE ONLY GAME IN TOWN

Solitaire games are programmed into personal digital assistants, cell phones, computers and just about every other electronic gadget. Solitaire has hundreds of variations. The most common in the United States is Klondike, also called Patience, Fascination, Canfield, or simply, "Solitaire."

To play Klondike, deal one card face up from a standard deck. Then deal six additional cards face down to form a row to the right of the first card. Next a card is dealt face up on top of the second card in the row and five more cards are dealt face down on top of the remaining piles to the right. This pattern continues until 28 cards have been used and there are seven piles or columns of cards, ranging from one card in the left column, to seven cards in the right column. The remainder of the deck is placed face down on the table.

Cards can be moved onto the next higher card of a different color to form descending sets that alternate by color. In the example shown, the red 8 of hearts can be placed on top of a black 9 of clubs,

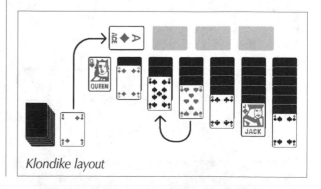

Klondike layout

allowing the card beneath the 8 to be flipped over and brought into play. If a red 10 were to appear, then the 9 and 8 could be moved together on top of the 10, and the player can flip over more cards.

Aces are removed from the layout when they appear, and used as starting points to build ascending sets. These sets follow suit rather than the black-red pattern. In this example, the Ace of diamonds has been set aside. If the two of diamonds appears, it will be placed on top of the Ace, and then the 3 of diamonds, etc. You win if all four Ace piles are built into Ace-through-King sequences.

If one of the seven columns becomes empty because all of its cards have been shifted, any King (and anything stacked on it) can be moved into the empty column, allowing any card under the King to be flipped. After making every possible move on the board, the first card from the remainder of the deck is turned over and played, if possible. When the entire deck has been played, the game is over.

A variation on the game involves flipping the remainder, three cards at a time. If you can play the top card, you can play the next one as well. When you have gone through the pile, turn over the discard pile and go through it again until you call it a loss.

Seduced By Sudoku

Bet you can't do just one!

As humans we seem to have an innate desire to fill up empty spaces. This might explain part of the appeal of sudoku, the international craze which was introduced into the U.S in early 2005. The craze started in England in late 2004, when Wayne Gould, a retired judge from New Zealand, persuaded *The Times* of London to print one of the puzzles.

Sudoku is Japanese for "only single numbers allowed." Nearly all sudoku puzzles are computer generated, using programs that understand all the logical solving strategies, and so can determine mathematically how hard or easy a puzzle is.

Sudoku's major failing is that, if you make a mistake and enter a wrong digit in a square, and then base other reasoning on that mistake, it is practically impossible to localize the problem and undo it. You have to erase the entire puzzle and start over.

The number of possible ways to fill a 9-by-9 sudoku grid is calculated at 6,670,903,752,021,0 72,936,960—and the number of different ways to give starting digits for solving all these combinations is almost unfathomable.

—Will Shortz

Instructions: *Fill the grid with numbers so that every row, every column, and every 3-by-3 box contains the digits 1 to 9, without repeating. This puzzle is rated moderate in difficulty. More sudoku puzzles can be found at www.nytimes. com and elsewhere on the Web.*

	1			2			4	8
			4					
				8			2	3
2	3			7	5	1		
5				8			3	
		2		9			8	7
8	2		6			5		9
	1							4

CHAPTER **10**

ARTS & ENTERTAINMENT

Movies & TV 666

CLASSICS·666: *The very best "Best Movies" list* • *Who is Oscar?*
FAN FUN·671: *Online sites for movie and TV fans* • *Just in case you get invited* **HOME VIDEOS·673:** *The best DVD's you've never seen* • *Films for a very rainy day* **FESTIVALS·677:** *Film festivals worth the journey* • *How to get on a reality TV show* **CHILDREN·679** : *The best 100 movies for kids*

Music 681

CRITICS' PICKS·681: *Discs for a desert island* • *Where classical music thrives* • *What jazzes Wynton Marsalis* **POP & ROCK·686:** *Rock & roll royalty* **OPERA·689:** *Cecilia Bartoli airs her arias* • *A night at the opera—wherever you may be* • *Ballet at its best* **INDIE MUSIC·691:** *The earliest recordings* • *A who's who of music lists* **JAZZ AND R&B·692:** • *For R&B and jazz lovers* • *Sites from the underground* **FESTIVALS·694:** *The best (mostly classical) summer festivals* • *The battle of the bands* • *The world's most remote music festival*

Museums & Books 697

ART MUSEUMS·697: *The world's great modern museums* • *Can't get to the Louvre? Try this* • *Small European gems* **ARCHITECTURE·701:** *Out-of-the-way architectural masterpieces* **GREAT BOOKS·702:** *Time to catch up on your reading: the best books of the 21st century* • *National Book Award and Pulitzer Prize winners, 2000 to 2005* **LIBRARIES·708:** *Getting lost in the stacks: a bibliophile's favorites* • *Beloved American novels*

ARTS

Movies & TV

The Very Best "Best Movies" List

The finest films of the last 30 years, as selected by three eminent authorities

Film fans take endless delight in "best picture" lists. To create this one, we relied on the collected wisdom of three respected sources: the National Film Registry, the film critics of the *New York Times* and the Academy of Motion Picture Arts and Sciences, which, of course, annually presents the Academy Award for best picture.

The National Film Registry was established by Congress in 1989 as a cinematic Noah's ark of sorts—a safe haven for the best that the movies have to offer. The law authorizes the Librarian of Congress and the National Film Preservation Board to select up to 25 films a year for participation in an extensive preservation program. Members of the board tend to be movers and shakers in the film industry, but their recommendations are just that: recommendations.

The ultimate decision rests with the Librarian of Congress, currently James H. Billington. "The selection process should not be seen as the 'People's Choice Awards,'" Billington explains. Instead, he says, he chooses films that "continue to have historic, cultural, or aesthetic significance, and, just as important, represent other films deserving of recognition."

As of December 2005, there were 425 films in the registry. The earliest film, *Blacksmith Scene,* dates from 1893. The most recent film on this list is from 1995, since to be eligible, films must be at least 10 years old; they do not need to be feature-length, however, or have had a theatrical release in order to be considered. A complete list of films in the National Film Registry can be found on the Library of Congress Web site at www.loc.gov/film.

New York Times critics have generally named 10 best films at the end of each year—going back to at least 1931; occasionally, there were more or fewer than 10 if the critics so deemed. From 1991 through 1994, moreover, the "10 Best" designation was dropped in favor of more broad-based year-end roundups. Generally, the "10 Best" list reflects the choices of the paper's chief film critic. But from 2003 to 2005, there was no designated chief film critic, so the choices of all three of the paper's film critics are included. Reviews of more than 15,000 films, including those listed here, can be found at www.nytimes.com.

INSIDE INFO

Who Is Oscar, Anyway?

O We've all seen the ebullient Academy Award winners clutching their gold-plated Oscars as they deliver breathless acceptance speeches. But who is Oscar? The still figure of a man holding a sword and standing atop a reel of film was designed by famed production designer Cedric Gibbons (his credits include *A Night at the Opera* and *An American in Paris*). For many years after the 1927 inception of the awards ceremony, the statue was nameless.

O Then, as Hollywood legend goes, a secretary working at the Academy of Motion Picture Arts and Sciences noticed that the statue's face bore a resemblance to her uncle Oscar, and hence the 13 ½-inch–tall figure was christened.

NOT TO BE MISSED FLICKS 1975-2005

The following films are beloved by three noted authorities: the National Film Registry, the film critics of the *New York Times* or the Academy of Motion Pictures Arts and Sciences. They were selected by the sources as one of the best pictures for the year indicated. For the Academy choices, only the film that won the Academy Award for best picture is listed. Movies are listed under the year when one of the three authorities first put the film on its list.

KEY

- National Film Registry selection
- Academy Award Best Picture Winner
- *New York Times* critics' pick

1975

- *Alice Doesn't Live Here Anymore*
- *Barry Lyndon*
- *The Buffalo Creek Flood: An Act of Man*
- *Distant Thunder*
- *The Godfather, Part II*
- *Hearts and Minds*
- *Jaws*
- *Love and Death*
- *Nashville*
- *One Flew Over the Cuckoo's Nest*
- *The Rocky Horror Picture Show*

- *Shampoo*
- *The Story of Adèle H.*

1976

- *All the President's Men*
- *Chulas Fronteras*
- *Face to Face*
- *Harlan County, U.S.A.*
- *The Memory of Justice*
- *Network*
- *The Outlaw Josey Wales*
- *Seven Beauties*
- *The Seven-Per-Cent Solution*
- *Taxi Driver*
- *To Fly*

1977

- *Annie Hall*
- *Close Encounters of the Third Kind*
- *Effi Briest*
- *The Goalie's Anxiety at the Penalty Kick*
- *Handle with Care*
- *Killer of Sheep*
- *The Late Show*
- *The Man Who Loved Women*
- *Rocky*
- *Star Wars*
- *Stroszek*
- *That Obscure Object of Desire*

1978

- *California Suite*
- *Days of Heaven*
- *The Deer Hunter*
- *Eraserhead*
- *A Geisha*

- *Movie Movie*
- *National Lampoon's Animal House*
- *Perceval le Gallois*
- *Pretty Baby*
- *Powers of Ten*
- *A Slave of Love*
- *Straight Time*
- *Violette*

1979

- *Alien*
- *All That Jazz*
- *Apocalypse Now*
- *The Black Stallion*
- *Breaking Away*
- *Escape from Alcatraz*
- *Fedora*
- *Hair*
- *Kramer v. Kramer*
- *Love on the Run*
- *Manhattan*
- *The Marriage of Maria Braun*
- *10*
- *The Tree of Wooden Clogs*

1980

- *Airplane*
- *Atlantic City*
- *Dressed to Kill*
- *Every Man for Himself*
- *Garlic as Good as Ten Mothers*
- *Kramer vs. Kramer*
- *The Life and Times of Rosie the Riveter*
- *Melvin and Howard*
- *Mon Onclè d'Amerique*
- *Ordinary People*
- *Raging Bull*

ARTS

Return of the Secaucus 7
Stardust Memories
The Third Generation
Wise Blood

1981

Arthur
Body Heat
Four Friends
Pixote
Raiders of the Lost Ark
Reds
Stevie
True Confessions
The Woman Next Door

1982

Le Beau Mariage
Blade Runner
Chan Is Missing
Chariots of Fire
E.T. the Extra-Terrestrial
Fast Times at Ridgemont High
Fitzcarraldo
Gregory's Girl
Lola
Missing
Smash Palace

Tootsie
Victor/Victoria

1983

Berlin Alexanderplatz
Betrayal
The Big Chill
El Norte
Fanny and Alexander
Gandhi
Heart Like a Wheel
The King of Comedy
Koyaanisqatsi
Local Hero
The Right Stuff
Tender Mercies
Zelig

1984

The Bostonians
Broadway Danny Rose
Entre Nous
The Family Game
Greystoke: The Legend of Tarzan, Lord of the Apes
A Love in Germany
A Passage to India
Places in the Heart
Stranger Than Paradise

Terms of Endearment
This Is Spinal Tap

1985

Amadeus
Desperately Seeking Susan
Kiss of the Spider Woman
Prizzi's Honor
The Purple Rose of Cairo
Ran
Secret Honor
7 Up/28 Up
Shoah
The Trip to Bountiful

1986

Blue Velvet
The Color of Money
Down by Law
Hannah and Her Sisters
Hoosiers
Mènage
My Beautiful Laundrette
Out of Africa
Platoon
A Room with a View
Sherman's March
Smooth Talk
Summer

NOTES:

1. From 1991 to 1994, the *Times* did not name the 10 Best Films of the Year. Instead, the paper's critics cited films that impressed them for a variety of reasons.

2. From 2003 to 2005, *New York Times* choices reflect the picks of all three of the paper's film critics. Previous years, the choices shown were of the *Times'* chief movie critic. From 2003 to 2005, there was no chief movie critic.

3. The National Film Registry does not recognize films until a minimum of 10 years after they appear. Therefore, films made since 1995 are not yet eligible for National film Registry recognition.

Typically, new films picked for the National Film Registry are announced each December. The list can be found at www. loc.gov/film.

1987

- Barfly
- The Dead
- Empire of the Sun
- Full Metal Jacket
- House of Games
- Housekeeping
- Radio Days
- Tampopo
- Tin Men
- The Untouchable

1988

- Au Revoir Les Enfants
- Hotel Terminus: The Life and Times of Klaus Barbie
- 1988 The Last Emperor
- Married to the Mob
- Mississippi Burning
- Patty Hearst
- A Taxing Woman
- The Thin Blue Line
- Things Change
- Tin Toy
- Who Framed Roger Rabbit?
- Women on the Verge of a Nervous Breakdown
- Working Girl

1989

- Chocolat
- Crimes and Misdemeanors
- Do the Right Thing
- Enemies, A Love Story
- High Hopes
- Little Vera
- Mystery Train
- 1989 Rain Man
- Roger & Me
- Sex, Lies and Videotape
- True Love

1990

- Akira Kurosawa's Dreams
- Alice
- Dick Tracy
- 1990 Driving Miss Daisy
- Goodfellas
- The Grifters
- Metropolitan
- Mr. and Mrs. Bridge
- My 20th Century
- Reversal of Fortune
- Sweetie

1991[1]

- Barton Fink
- Beauty and the Beast
- Boyz in the Hood
- Cape Fear
- 1991 Dances with Wolves
- Daughters of the Dust
- The Fisher King
- Life Is Sweet
- My Own Private Idaho
- Silence of the Lambs
- Thelma and Louise

1992[1]

- The Crying Game
- A Few Good Men
- Gas Food Lodging
- Howards End
- Malcolm X
- The Match Factory Girl
- One False Move
- Reservoir Dogs
- Savage Nights
- 1992 The Silence of the Lambs
- The Story of Qiu Ju
- 1993 Unforgiven

1993[1]

- Belle Epoque
- Farewell My Concubine
- The Joy Luck Club
- Much Ado About Nothing
- The Piano
- Remains of the Day
- 1994 Schindler's List

1994[1]

- Crumb
- Four Weddings and a Funeral
- Hoop Dreams
- I Like It Like That
- The Madness of King George
- Nobody's Fool
- Il Postino (The Postman)
- Pulp Fiction
- Red
- Vanya on 42nd Street

1995[3]

- Apollo 13
- Before the Rain
- Dead Man Walking
- 1995 Forrest Gump
- Lamerica
- Leaving Las Vegas
- Living in Oblivion
- Persuasion
- To Die For
- Toy Story

1996

- Breaking the Waves
- 1996 Braveheart
- The Crucible
- 1997 The English Patient
- Fargo

ARTS

𝕿 *Flirting with Disaster*
𝕿 *Jerry Maguire*
𝕿 *Lone Star*
𝕿 *Looking for Richard*
𝕿 *The People vs. Larry Flynt*
𝕿 *Secrets and Lies*

1997

𝕿 *The Apostle*
𝕿 *Boogie Nights*
𝕿 *Deconstructing Harry*
𝕿 *In the Company of Men*
𝕿 *L.A. Confidential*
𝕿 *The Pillow Book*
𝕿 *Ponette*
𝕿 *The Sweet Hereafter*
1998 𝕿 *Titanic*
𝕿 *Ulee's Gold*

1998

𝕿 *The Butcher Boy*
𝕿 *The Celebration*
𝕿 *The General*
𝕿 *Happiness*
𝕿 *Henry Fool*
𝕿 *Life Is Beautiful*
𝕿 *The Opposite of Sex*
𝕿 *Saving Private Ryan*
1999 𝕿 *Shakespeare in Love*
𝕿 *A Simple Plan*
𝕿 *The Thin Red Line*

1999

𝕿 *All About My Mother* (Spain)
𝕿 *American Movie*
𝕿 *Being John Malkovich*
𝕿 *Boys Don't Cry*

𝕿 *The Dreamlife of Angels* (France)
𝕿 *Eyes Wide Shut*
𝕿 *The Insider*
𝕿 *The Straight Story*
𝕿 *The Talented Mr. Ripley*
𝕿 *Topsy-Turvy*

2000

2000 *American Beauty*
𝕿 *Beautiful People*
𝕿 *Before Night Falls*
𝕿 *Calle 54*
𝕿 *Chicken Run*
𝕿 *The Decalogue 1987* (Poland)
𝕿 *Hamlet*
𝕿 *Traffic*
𝕿 *Yi Yi: A One and a Two* (China)
𝕿 *You Can Count on Me*

2001

𝕿 *A.I.*
𝕿 *Amores Perros* (Mexico)
2001 *Gladiator*
𝕿 *Ghost World*
𝕿 *The Gleaners and I* (France)
𝕿 *Gosford Park*
𝕿 *In the Bedroom*
𝕿 *The Man Who Wasn't There*
𝕿 *Monsters, Inc.*
𝕿 *Sexy Beast*
𝕿 *Shrek*

2002

𝕿 *About Schmidt*
𝕿 *Adaptation*

2002 *A Beautiful Mind*
𝕿 *Chicago*
𝕿 *Far from Heaven*
𝕿 *The Fast Runner* (Atanarjuat) (Inuit)
𝕿 *Gangs of New York*
𝕿 *The Hours*
𝕿 *The Pianist*
𝕿 *Spirited Away* (Japan)
𝕿 *Talk to Her* (Spain)
𝕿 *Y Tu Mamá También* (Mexico)

2003[2]

𝕿 *American Splendor*
𝕿 *Angels in America*
𝕿 *The Barbarian Invasions*
𝕿 *Bus 174*
𝕿 *Capturing the Friedmans*
2003 *Chicago*
𝕿 *City of God*
𝕿 *Elephant*
𝕿 *Finding Nemo*
𝕿 *The Fog of War*
𝕿 *The Good, the Bad, the Ugly*
𝕿 *House of Sand and Fog*
2004 𝕿 *The Lord of the Rings: The Return of the King*
𝕿 *Lost in Translation*
𝕿 *Master and Commander: The Far Side of the World*
𝕿 *A Mighty Wind*
𝕿 *Mystic River*
𝕿 *Pirates of the Caribbean*
𝕿 *Raising Victor Vargas*
𝕿 *Spellbound*
𝕿 *Thirteen*

℗ *The Triplets of Belleville*
℗ *21 Grams*

2004²

℗ *Bad Education*
℗ *Before Sunset*
℗ *The Big Red One: The Restoration*
℗ *Blind Shaft*
℗ *Bright Leaves*
℗ *Collateral*
℗ *The Door in the Floor*
℗ *Eternal Sunshine of the Spotless Mind*
℗ *Fahrenheit 9/11*
℗ *Ghost in the Shell 2: Innocence*
℗ *Goodbye Dragon Inn*
℗ *The Incredibles*
℗ *Kill Bill Vol. 2*

℗ *Kinsey*
℗ *Maria Full of Grace*
2005 ℗ *Million Dollar Baby*
℗ *Moolaade*
℗ *The Mother*
℗ *Sideways*
℗ *Tarnation*
℗ *Tokyo Godfathers*
℗ *Time of the Wolf*
℗ *Vera Drake*

2005²

℗ *The Aristocrats*
℗ *The Best of Youth*
℗ *Brokeback Mountain*
℗ *Caché*
2006 *Crash*
℗ *Darwin's Nightmare*
℗ *Downfall*
℗ *Funny Ha-Ha*

℗ *Grizzly Man*
℗ *A History of Violence*
℗ *The Holy Girl*
℗ *Junebug*
℗ *Kings and Queens*
℗ *Last Days*
℗ *Look at Me*
℗ *Match Point*
℗ *Munich*
℗ *Mysterious Skin*
℗ *The New World*
℗ *Nine Lives*
℗ *Princess Raccoon*
℗ *Regular Lovers*
℗ *Saraband*
℗ *The Squid and the Whale*
℗ *2046*
℗ *Wallace & Gromit: The Curse of the Were-Rabbitt*

✓ **TIMELY TIPS**

Online Sites for Movie and TV Fans

✔ **Atom Films**
www.atomfilms.com
Offers short films and animations on the Web.

✔ **Internet Movie Database**
www.us.imdb.com
Bills itself as the earth's biggest movie database. Everything you want to know about films.

✔ **Movie Review Query Engine**
www.mrqe.com
Find reviews from all over for the movie of your choice.

✔ **Moviefone** (www.moviefone.com), **MovieTickets.com** (www.movietickets.com) and **Fandango** (www.fandango.com) These three have theater times and advance ticket purchases.

✔ **Ticketmaster**
www.ticketmaster.com
Has information and tickets for music, theater and sporting events.

✔ **Reel.com**
www.reel.com
Helps you find movies it thinks you'll like.

✔ **Rotten Tomatoes**
www.rottentomatoes.com

Popular for its collections of movie reviews, previews and information.

✔ **Sundance Channel**
www.sundancechannel.com
Guide for the Sundance TV channel, which shows movies from past festivals and live coverage during the festival.

✔ **TV Guide**
www.tvguide.com
Now includes an extensive movie database.

✔ **Zap2it**
www.tv.zap2it.com
Provides customized TV listings.

Just in Case You Get Invited
The tribal customs of an Oscar party

Unlike typical cocktail soirees in the rest of America, Oscar parties have rules of behavior that fly in the face of conventional manners. These dos and don'ts are not found in any guidebook to etiquette, but they are just as ironclad as the dictums of Emily Post. To ignore them is to invite ostracism or at least humiliation.

If you're someone's date, don't expect to be introduced. No one cares about spouses, relatives and arm candy at Hollywood parties. You could be a Nobel laureate, but if you're a plus-one during Oscar week, no one will want to meet you. And your significant other probably won't introduce you. Don't take it personally.

If you haven't worked on one of the nominated films, consider staying home. Being at an Oscar party without a nomination is like bleeding in an ocean surrounded by sharks. The safest course is to stay out of the water. "The cool etiquette is don't go if it's not your year," says Cathy Schulman, a producer of *Crash*, the best-picture winner in 2006. "If you want to feel irrelevant in this town, go to a party where you're not what it's all about. It really doesn't matter to anyone how much else you've achieved in your career. Around Oscar time, it's about being part of those nominated films."

Know when to say "when." Oscar parties are known for their filet mignon and Maine lobster, for rare wines and an endless supply of $100 Champagnes. But don't be fooled. There is little eating at these affairs—how else will you fit into your vintage Jean Dessès gown?—and there is not much drinking. Moderation is the word. Your behavior is always being watched, by the industry and by the press.

 INSIDE INFO

The High Cost of Fun

○ The average American spends more on entertainment than on gasoline, household furnishings and clothing and nearly the same amount as spent on dining out, according to the Bureau of Labor Statistics.

○ People in the western part of the country spend about 20 percent more on entertainment than the national average.

○ If you accept statistics that the average American's TV is on eight hours a day, a $100-a-month cable bill is really only a bit more than half a cent for each minute of entertainment.

○ Live opera works out to about 37 cents a minute, for a middling seat in the New York Metropolitan Opera house to hear *Aida*, compared with 7 cents a minute for a movie at the local multiplex. A Gwen Stefani concert in, again, middling seats, is about $1.25 a minute.

—Damon Darlin

Thou shall not pitch. For many, the whole point of attending an Oscar week party is the chance to meet people they can't get on the phone the rest of the year. While subtle pitching is acceptable—as in "Hey, George, can I drop something by next week?"—overt pitching of screenplays and story ideas during an Oscar party is a serious faux pas.

Give your entourage the night off. Yes, traveling with an entourage is a standard way of flaunting power in Hollywood. But this is not the weekend to roll up with a dozen friends from your hometown. In 2001, when Donatella Versace tried to sweep a posse into the V.I.P. lounge of the *InStyle*-Elton John Oscar party, she was turned back for having too many guests. After five minutes of confusion and loud Italian, she decided to proceed with a single guest.

Don't expect to meet your host. Although everywhere else it is considered good manners to seek out your hosts and thank them, in Hollywood the opposite is true.

And if you don't get any invitations at all. For those who live and work in Hollywood and yet for some reason do not show up on any invitation lists, take heart. There is always next year. "If you're not invited to A-list parties, it's a tough night to get through," says Steve Tisch, one of the producers of the Oscar-winner *Forrest Gump.* "I'd recommend three Xanax, a great bottle of cabernet and looking for a new publicist."

—Allison Hope Weiner

The Best DVD's You Haven't Seen

Three Times *critics pick their favorites*

Every year something like 500 new movies make their way to American theaters—sometimes to only a few cities, sometimes only for a short time—and sort themselves into familiar categories. Not just according to the usual video store genres—action, drama, comedy, foreign—but also with respect to more subjective criteria. There are the movies you wanted to see but never got around to, the movies your friends kept telling you not to miss, the movies all your friends hated, the movies you would probably have loved but never heard about, and so on. Here are the selections of favorites from three *New York Times* critics, with the hope that they will ease the anxious quandary you may face wandering up and down the video-store—or Web site—aisles in search of something to watch. For further suggestions, see *The Best DVDs You've Never Seen, Just Missed or Almost Forgotten*, edited by Peter M. Nichols.

A. O. SCOTT

New York Times film critic

THE BARBARIAN INVASIONS

Denys Arcand, 2003. 99 MINUTES. FRENCH WITH ENGLISH SUBTITLES. NO RATING. Rémy Girard, Stéphane Rousseau, Marie-Josée Croze

A broadly humorous, Oscar-winning movie about the reunion of the family and old lovers and pals around Rémy, a 60ish Montreal professor and lifelong lefty who is dying of cancer.

THE FAST RUNNER

Zacharias Kunuk, 2001. 172 MINUTES. INUKTITUT WITH ENGLISH SUBTITLES. NO RATING. Natar Ungalaaq, Sylvia Ivalu, Peter-Henry Arnatsiaq, Lucy Tulugarjuk

A work of superlative narrative sweep and visual beauty that takes place on the Artic ice, where a nomadic tribal society chafes under the pressures of its complex ideas of honor and loyalty.

GEORGE WASHINGTON

David Gordon Green, 2000. 89 MINUTES. NO RATING. Donald Holden, Candace Evanofski, Curtis Cotton III

Green's acclaimed film takes place during a languorous North Carolina summer so green and still and hot that we can feel the humidity and hear the insects. There is trouble here, but like everything else, it's in no hurry in a town that has lost much of its livelihood and slipped into hard times.

THE MAN WITHOUT A PAST

Aki Kaurismäki, 2002. 97 MINUTES. FINNISH WITH ENGLISH SUBTITLES. NO RATING. Markku Peltola, Kati Outinen, Juhani Niemelä

A metalworker is mugged and left for dead on a park bench. Staggering out of a hospital, he collapses and wakes up without his money or his shoes, and with no recollection of his previous life.

ARTS

PUNCH-DRUNK LOVE
Paul Thomas Anderson, 2002. 95 MINUTES. R.
Adam Sandler, Emily Watson, Philip Seymour
Hoffman, Luis Guzmán

A wholesale bathroom-supply salesman, Barry
Egan (Sandler) veers between frightening bursts
of anger and a demeanor of stricken, lobotomized
self-control when the shy, whispery Lena (Watson) decides to fall in love with him.

SEXY BEAST
Jonathan Glazer, 2000. 89 MINUTES. R.
Ben Kingsley, Ray Winstone, Amanda Redman

Logan (Ben Kingsley) has been dispatched to
the sunny Spanish coast to collect a safecracker
named Gal (Winstone) to perform one last job for
his boss, the kingpin Teddy Bass.

SPELLBOUND
A documentary profile of eight contestants at
the 1999 National Spelling Bee, directed by Jeff
Blitz, 2002. 97 MINUTES. G.

Preparations are under way for the first national
spelling bee in Washington, but first the eight
have to survive the state contests. A cliffhanger to
the last syllable.

THE TRIPLETS OF BELLEVILLE
An animated film written and directed by Sylvain
Chomet, 2003. 80 MINUTES. PG-13. The voices of
Jean-Claude Donda, Michel Robin, Monica Viegas

With a perverse pen and a peculiar imagination,
Chomet has created a dense, wonderfully strange
urban world bursting with insouciant whimsy.

WHAT TIME IS IT THERE?
Tsai Ming-Iian, 2001. 116 MINUTES. MANDARIN,
TAIWANESE AND FRENCH WITH ENGLISH SUBTITLES.
NO RATING. Lee Kang-Sheng, Miao Tien, Chen
Shiang-Chyi

After his father's death in a cloud of cigarette

smoke, Hsaio Kang (Lee Kang-Sheng) is stuck in
the house with his distraught mother, who keeps
expecting her husband's resurrection.

YI YI (A ONE AND A TWO)
Edward Yang, 2000. 173 MINUTES. MANDARIN WITH
ENGLISH SUBTITLES. NO RATING.
Wu Nienjen, Jonathan Chang, Kelly Lee

Yang's charming, absorbing film serves up a
bunch of familiar middle-class pickles (well,
some not so familiar), with the major difference
being that this is Taipei and not an American city.

STEPHEN HOLDEN
New York Times film and cabaret critic

ALL ABOUT MY MOTHER
Pedro Almodóvar, 1999. 101 MINUTES. SPANISH
WITH ENGLISH SUBTITLES. NO RATING.
Cecilia Roth, Eloy Azorlin, Marisa Paredes

A story that gets around, to state it mildly, begins
with a mother, Manuela (Roth), who sees her son,
Esteban (Azorin), run down by a car on his 17th
birthday.

AMORES PERROS
Alejandro González Iñárritu, 2000. 153 MINUTES.
SPANISH WITH ENGLISH SUBTITLES. NO RATING. Vanessa
Bauche, Gael Garcia Bernal, Humberto Busto

A film full of criminal riffraff and violence, it is
reminiscent of *Pulp Fiction* in that episodes in
separate segments appear out of sequence, only to
dovetail at the end.

BEAU TRAVAIL
Claire Denis, 1999. 90 MINUTES. FRENCH WITH
ENGLISH SUBTITLES. NO RATING.
Grégoire Colin, Denis Lavant, Michel Subor

Denis moves Melville's *Billy Budd* to a French
Foreign Legion outpost in the East African
enclave of Djibouti.

BEST IN SHOW
Christopher Guest, 2000. 89 MINUTES. PG-13. Christopher Guest, Parker Posey, Michael Hitchcock

Two antagonistic television announcers, the erudite Englishman Trevor Beckwith and the loutish Buck Laughlin, go at it barb-to-barb over the finer points at the Mayflower Kennel Dog Show in Philadelphia.

DANGEROUS LIAISONS
Stephen Frears, 1988. 118 MINUTES. R. Glenn Close, John Malkovich, Michelle Pfeiffer

A witty and entertaining study of decadence, topped by a performance by Close that is as savage as her spurned mistress in *Fatal Attraction.*

ELECTION
Alexander Payne, 1999. 103 MINUTES. R. Reese Witherspoon, Matthew Broderick, Chris Klein

This is one of the two or three finest American comedies of the last 20 years. Tracy Flick (Witherspoon) is running for student-government president at her Omaha high school.

L'HUMANITÉ
Bruno Dumont, 1999. 148 MINUTES. FRENCH WITH ENGLISH SUBTITLES. NO RATING. Emmanuel Schotté, Séverine Caneele, Philippe Tullier

Dumont's flawed masterpiece gives the sense that civilization is really a fragile membrane that barely separates us from our most brutal instincts.

THE SWEET HEREAFTER
Atom Egoyan, 1997. 112 MINUTES. R. Ian Holm, Sarah Polley, Bruce Greenwood

Like Russell Bank's novel, from which it is adapted, Egoyan's film makes a many-faceted moral inquiry into a calamity that has befallen a small Canadian town.

Y TU MAMÁ TAMBIÉN
Alfonso Cuarón, 2001. 105 MINUTES. SPANISH WITH ENGLISH SUBTITLES. NO RATING. Maribel Verdú, Gael Garcia Bernal, Diego Luna

When her husband is unfaithful, the beautiful, sad-eyed Luisa (Verdú) accepts the invitation of two randy teenagers (Garcia Bernal) and Tenoch (Luna), to accompany them to a Mexican beach.

CARYN JAMES
New York Times critic-at-large

THE AGE OF INNOCENCE
Martin Scorsese, 1993. 133 MINUTES. PG. Daniel Day-Lewis, Michelle Pfeiffer, Winona Ryder

Based on Edith Wharton's elegant, wry novel about Old New York society in the late 19th century, this may be one of the most underrated films of the 1990's.

BRIDESHEAD REVISITED
Michael Lindsay-Hogg and Charles Sturridge, 1981. ELEVEN 60-MINUTE EPISODES. NO RATING. Jeremy Irons, Anthony Andrews, Claire Bloom, Laurence Olivier

Quite simply one of the best mini-series ever made, this television adaptation of Evelyn Waugh's novel remains an unparalleled evocation of time and place—from Oxford in the 1920's to World War II and its aftermath—filmed in wonderfully observed detail.

EDDIE IZZARD: DRESS TO KILL
A one-man show with Eddie Izzard, 1999. 110 MINUTES. NO RATING.

Some stand-up routines are so rich and funny that they never seem tired, and this is one of them. Izzard describes himself as "an executive transvestite."

ARTS

THE END OF THE AFFAIR

Neil Jordan, 1999. 102 MINUTES. R.
Ralph Fiennes, Julianne Moore, Stephen Rea

Jordan's intoxicating version of Graham Greene's 1951 novel about illicit romance is a gripping story of passion and renunciation.

LOLITA

Adrian Lyne, 1997. 137 MINUTES. NO RATING.
Jeremy Irons, Dominique Swain, Melanie Griffith, Frank Langella

Lyne's entrancing adaptation of Vladimir Nabokov's novel never reached the big screen but went straight to cable. Irons is Humbert

---

 INSIDE INFO

Films for a Very Rainy Day

Some of the longest movies every made:

○ **Greed** (1924, approximately 9 hours, 30 minutes) Director Erich von Stroheim's silent masterpiece.

○ **Shoah** (1985, 9 hours and thirty minutes) This may be the greatest film made about the Holocaust.

○ **War and Peace** (1968, 6 hours, 13 minutes) Won the Oscar for Best Foreign Film in 1968.

○ **Little Dorrit** (1988, 6 hours) An overly long film of the Dickens classic.

○ **Sleep** (1963, 6 Hours) The film that brought Andy Warhol to prominence.

○ **The Memory of Justice** (1976, 4 hours, 38 minutes) From Marcel Ophuls, an exquisite social commentary about how countries judge their own morality.

○ **The Sorrow and the Pity** (1976, 4 hours, 20 minutes) Ophuls's defining film about the French response during World War II.

○ **Ludwig** (1972, 4 hours, 6 minutes) The film focuses on the Mad King of Bavaria. Stay away.

Humbert, passionately in love with the 12-year-old nymphet Lolita (Swain).

PRIMARY COLORS

Mike Nichols, 1998. 143 MINUTES. R.
John Travolta, Emma Thompson, Billy Bob Thornton, Kathy Bates

Nichol's adaptation of Joe Klein's novel, a fictional version of the Clinton ascendancy, is a shrewd, entertaining and cynical political satire.

SHALLOW GRAVE

Danny Boyle, 1994. 92 MINUTES. R.
Kerry Fox, Ewan McGregor, Keith Allen

Boyle's first film is an uncompromising dark comedy about three Edinburgh roommates who turn into killers after having their heads turned by a pile of money.

SOUTH PARK: BIGGER, LONGER & UNCUT

Trey Parker, 1999. 81 MINUTES. R. The voices of Trey Parker, Matt Stone, Mary Kay Bergman

Infinitely funnier than the TV-series and just as clever, the ambitious film is both a social satire and a brilliant send-up of Hollywood musicals.

TALK TO HER

Pedro Almodóvar, 2002. 112 MINUTES. SPANISH WITH ENGLISH SUBTITLES. NO RATING. Javier Cámara, Dario Grandinetti, Leonor Watling

The story of two physically damaged women and two emotionally tortured men.

WAITING FOR GUFFMAN

Christopher Guest, 1996. 84 MINUTES. R. Christopher Guest, Catherine O'Hara, Parker Posey

This may be the funniest of Christopher Guest's relentlessly clever satires (though some would give that honor to *Best in Show*). Guest plays the artistic and sensitive Corky Sinclair in a spoof of the theater world.

Film Festivals Worth the Journey

Where cinephiles gather around the globe

Not all film festivals are alike, and these days there are more festivals than there are days in the year. Some (like Cannes) are so celebrated that it has become virtually impossible for the public to gain access, and are very much a film professional's festival. Others are far more accessible to the general public and offer just as interesting fare.

Richard Peña is director of the New York Film Festival (www.filmlinc.com), one of the world's premier film festivals showing the newest and most important cinematic works from around the world. The festival, now over 40 years old, is held every September and October in New York City. Beyond his own, we asked Peña to give us his take on the other important and memorable international film festivals worldwide. Here are his picks, and his comments:

Le Festival International du Film

Cannes, France. May. www.festival-cannes.fr

In terms of power and prestige, Cannes is simply in a class of its own. It's actually several simultaneous festivals: the Official Competition, which is the main event; Un Certain Regard, run by the Official Competition for films that for whatever reason weren't invited for the Competition; The Directors' Fortnight, set up after May '68 to feature more "radical" works but now virtually indistinguishable from Un Certain Regard; and the Critics' Week, a small selection of largely first films that often feature a few real discoveries.

Venice Film Festival

Venice, Italy. August/September. www.labiennale.org

Berlin International Film Festival

Berlin, Germany. February. www.berlinale.de

The next level down from Cannes would be these two major European competitive festivals. Venice, the world's oldest continuing festival, has in recent years regained some of its lost luster; Berlin, since moving to its new site in the rebuilt Potsdammer Platz, now has excellent screening conditions, but its official competition section is generally a distant third to those of Cannes or Venice. Both Venice and Berlin, like Cannes, have several simultaneous programs going on, and Berlin's International Forum of Young Film, generally known simply as the Forum, always features a remarkable selection of independent, experimental or just offbeat films from all over the world.

Sundance Film Festival

Park City, Utah. January.
www.festival.sundance.org

Sundance has really become the essential showcase for American independent cinema. Recently, organizers tried to put more emphasis on international films, even creating a competition for their selections but, in truth, few people go to Sundance to see films from abroad—there are simply far too many new American films to see.

Telluride Film Festival

Telluride, Colorado. Labor Day weekend.
www.telluridefilmfestival.org

Held over a long weekend in a former Colorado mining town, the Telluride festival has created in its 30-plus-year history a truly elite reputation. You only discover Telluride's program when you arrive, so people who go there (and it used to be a pretty arduous journey) go on sheer faith that the programmers won't disappoint. They generally don't.

Toronto International Film Festival

Toronto, Canada. September.
www.e.bell.ca/filmfest

ARTS

TIMELY TIPS

How to Get on a Reality TV Show

It takes patience, perseverance, unpredictability

The odds are stiff: for *The Apprentice* alone, for example, a quarter of a million Donald Trump wannabes vie each season for 16 apprentice slots. But if you're persevering and have plenty of time on your hands, here's how to find a reality TV show, get a foot in the door and give the casting staff exactly what they're after.

✔ **The search.** Publications like *Variety* and *Hollywood Reporter* are a good start for casting calls and auditions, whether you want to be the next *American Idol* or just yearn for a walk-on role in a movie. For reality-show leads, check online sites such as realityTVcastingcall.com, www.sirlinksalot.net, www.realityTVlinks.com or www.realityTVworld.com. If you have a particular show in mind, check the network's site. Some shows advertise on local radio and papers, even on Craigslist.com.

✔ **The application.** Each show requires filing an extensive application, often available on the network Web site. Some also request a 10-minute video tape. Those who want to apply for multiple shows can simplify the process by using a service like RTVStar.com. The site posts photos and profiles of members ($24.99 a year); casting agents, the site says, review them regularly. If you become a finalist, you'll have to undergo personality testing, a medical exam, reference checks, and if chosen, will have to sign massive contracts.

✔ **The audition.** Popular audition spots are Chicago, Dallas, Los Angeles, New York, Orlando and Phoenix. Be prepared for long lines and cutthroat competition, especially for the really big shows. From among the hordes, a limited number are given a wristband or number, allowing them to audition.

Once you get this far, the best advice is to show your individuality. Sasha Alpert, vice president for casting for Bunim/Murray Productions, which produces MTV's *The Real World*, says the best candidates are "open, enigmatic and unpredictable." In the minds of producers at least, that makes for good TV.

For many people, the most important North American festival is surely Toronto. It is the template for what might be called the "mega-festival": 300 or so films, many of them scooped up from other international festivals, as well as a healthy dose of films having their world premieres. It has the reputation for being impeccably organized, and is also one of the few festivals to be both a public and professional event.

Festival Internacional Del Nuevo Cine Latinoamericano

Havana, Cuba. December.
www.habanafilmfestival.com

The Havana Film Festival has survived the demise of the Soviet Union (and the loss of Cuba's annual subsidy), and remains perhaps the key Latin American festival. It's truly an event embraced by the city, and you can see an enormous range of work from all over the Hispanic world.

Pusan International Film Festival

Pusan, South Korea. October. www.piff.org/

Hong Kong International Film Festival

Hong Kong, China. April. www.hkiff.org.hk

South Korea's Pusan Film Festival and the Hong Kong International Film Festival are the top Asian festivals. The current explosion in South Korean filmmaking has boosted the importance of Pusan as the place to discover that country's seemingly endless supply of talented new directors. Hong Kong offers not only first-rate Asian and international selections, but also each year mounts major retrospectives on Asian cinema.

Il Cinema Ritrovato
Bologna, Italy. July.
www.cinetecadibologna.it/en/ritrovato

Held every July, this very wonderful specialized festival brings together many works that have been recently discovered and restored by the world's major film archives. All silent films have first-rate musical accompaniment—ranging from piano to symphony orchestras—but the program can feature everything from Italian 60's experimental films to the comedies of Marion Davies. A film lover's version of paradise.

The Pan-African Film and Television Festival
(Fespaco) *Ougadougou, Burkina Faso. February-March. www.fespaco.bf*

Held bi-annually in Ouagadougou, Burkina Faso (the next one is scheduled for late February to early March, 2007), Fespaco is universally recognized as the main showcase for African film.

The Best 100 Movies for Kids
Guaranteed to last for many afternoons

In compiling this list of films—all of which are available on video or DVD—the term "children's movie" is considerably broadened. To be sure, many of these films were made primarily for children, but most of them reach out to a larger family audience. Some—*High Noon, Groundhog Day, Lawrence of Arabia*—don't meet most people's definition of a children's movie at all.

Few of these films are good for simply parking the kids in front of, on a rainy afternoon. They are chosen by film critics to give children up to the age of 12 or so a taste of various genres and eras. All are generally suitable for children, all or most are highly entertaining, but they are also meant to give kids a feel for what the movies have been about over the decades. Many will require some thought and, are better watched with grown-ups on hand to help set the context. Everybody should have some fun in the bargain. A fuller description of the films below can be found in the book *The New York Times Essential Library: Children's Movies, A Critic's Guide to the Best Films Available on Video and DVD.*

- *Abbott and Costello Meet Frankenstein* (1948)
- *The Adventures of Robin Hood* (1938)
- *The African Queen* (1951)
- *Apollo 13* (1995)
- *Babe* (1995)
- *Back to the Future* (1985)
- *The Bad News Bears* (1976)
- *The Bear* (1988)
- *Beauty and the Beast* (1991)
- *Beetlejuice* (1988)
- *Big* (1988)
- *The Black Stallion* (1979)
- *Bound for Glory* (1976)
- *Breaking Away* (1979)
- *Bringing Up Baby* (1938)
- *The Buddy Holly Story* (1978)
- *Butch Cassidy and the Sundance Kid* (1969)
- *Casablanca* (1942)
- *Cat Ballou* (1965)
- *Chariots of Fire* (1981)
- *Chicken Run* (2000)
- *Close Encounters of the Third Kind* (1977)
- *The Day the Earth Stood Still* (1951)
- *Dick Tracy* (1990)
- *Dr. Strangelove or: How I Learned to Stop Worrying and Love the Bomb* (1964)
- *Duck Soup* (1933)
- *Edward Scissorheands* (1990)
- *Emma* (1996)

- *E.T. the Extra-Terrestrial* (1982)
- *Fiddler on the Roof* (1971)
- *Field of Dreams* (1989)
- *Fly Away Home* (1996)
- *Gandhi* (1982)
- *Ghostbusters* (1984)
- *The Gold Rush* (1925)
- *The Great Escape* (1963)
- *Great Expectations* (1946)
- *Groundhog Day* (1993)
- *A Hard Day's Night* (1964)
- *Harry Potter and the Sorcerer's Stone* (2001)
- *High Noon* (1952)
- *The Iron Giant* (1999)
- *It Happened One Night* (1934)
- *James and the Giant Peach* (1996)
- *Jurassic Park* (1993)
- *The King and I* (1956)
- *King Kong* (1933)
- *Lawrence of Arabia* (1962)
- *A League of Their Own* (1992)
- *Lilo & Stitch* (2002)
- *The Lion King* (1994)
- *Little Fugitive* (1953)
- *Little Man Tate* (1991)
- *The Little Mermaid* (1989)
- *A Little Princess* (1995)
- *Little Women* (1994)
- *The Longest Day* (1962)
- *The Lord of the Rings: The Fellowship of the Ring* (2001)
- *Lost Horizon* (1937)
- *The Magnificent Seven* (1960)
- *Mary Poppins* (1964)
- *Monsters, Inc.* (2001)
- *Mr. Smith Goes to Washington* (1939)
- *Mrs. Doubtfire* (1993)
- *The Music Man* (1962)
- *My Fair Lady* (1964)
- *National Velvet* (1944)
- *Never Cry Wolf* (1983)
- *North by Northwest* (1959)
- *Peter Pan* (1953)
- *Pinocchio* (1940)
- *The Princess Bride* (1987)
- *Raiders of the Lost Ark* (1981)
- *Rear Window* (1954)
- *Rocky* (1976)
- *The Rookie* (2002)
- *The Secret Garden* (1993)
- *The Secret of Roan Inish* (1994)
- *Shane* (1953)
- *Shrek* (2001)
- *Singin' in the Rain* (1952)
- *Snow White and the Seven Dwarfs* (1937)
- *Some Like It Hot* (1959)
- *The Sound of Music* (1965)
- *Spirited Away* (2001)
- *Star Wars* (1977)
- *Steamboat Bill, Jr.* (1928)
- *Sullivan's Travels* (1941)
- *Superman* (1978)
- *Swiss Family Robinson* (1960)
- *The Three Musketeers* and *The Four Musketeers* (1974 and 1975)
- *To Kill a Mockingbird* (1962)
- *Toy Story* and *Toy Story 2* (1995 and 1999)
- *20,000 Leagues Under the Sea* (1954)
- *Walkabout* (1971)
- *West Side Story* (1961)
- *Who Framed Roger Rabbitt* (1988)
- *The Winslow Boy* (1999)
- *The Wizard of Oz* (1939)
- *Yellow Submarine* (1968)

—Peter M. Nichols

Music

Picks for a Desert Island

Four New York Times *music critics choose their all-time favorites*

Now that iPods that can hold thousands of songs, the discerning listener, well, doesn't have to be too discerning in responding to the question, What music would you bring along if you were stranded on a desert island? "Personally," notes Allan Kozinn, a *Times* music critic since 1977, "I think the iPod makes the whole desert island question obsolete." Kozinn's iPod currently holds 8,880 songs (with a little room left) and, he adds, "while some come and go, most are there to stay, to be at hand at all times." Nevertheless, we asked four *Times* music critics—Anthony Tommasini, Kozinn, Jon Pareles and Ben Ratliff—to name their personal enduring favorites. The critics oblige, below, supplying their expert commentary as well.

ANTHONY TOMMASINI

Times chief classical music critic and author of *Virgil Thomson: Composer on the Aisle*

VERDI: *Otello*. Herbert von Karajan (conductor), Vienna Philharmonic; with Mario Del Monaco, Renata Tebaldi, Aldo Protti (DECCA, TWO CD's) and *Falstaff*—Georg Solti (conductor), RCA Italiana Opera Orchestra and Chorus; with Geraint Evans, Mirella Freni, Alfredo Kraus, Robert Merrill (DECCA, TWO CD's)

I cannot imagine life without Verdi's final two operas. There are half a dozen classic recordings of Verdi's psychologically astute and affectingly tragic *Otello,* but the one I keep coming back to, from 1961, offers the powerhouse tenor Mario Del Monaco in the title role and the incomparable Renata Tebaldi, my idol as opera-going teenager, singing Desdemona. At nearly 80, Verdi ended his run of bleak, tragic operas with a humane and hilarious comedy, *Falstaff*. Georg Solti conducts this gossamer-like score with zest, clarity and tenderness on his 1963 recording. The cast, headed by Geraint Evans in the title role, is glorious. The young Mirella Freni and Alfredo Kraus as the young sweethearts Nannetta and Fenton have never been topped.

WAGNER: *Die Walküre*. Georg Solti (conductor), Vienna Philharmonic; with Hans Hotter, Birgit Nilsson, James King, Régine Crespin (DECCA, FOUR CD's)

If I could only have one Wagner opera, I'd pick *Die Walküre*. The last 30 minutes, when Wotan, the flawed and self-righteous god, reluctantly punishes his headstrong and devoted daughter, Brünnhilde, is the most movingly sad music ever written. Overall, Solti's recording, with the exciting Birgit Nilsson as Brunnhilde and the noble Hans Hotter as Wotan, is the one to have.

BRITTEN: *Peter Grimes*. Colin Davis (conductor), orchestra and chorus of the Royal Opera. Covent Garden; Jon Vickers, Heather Harper (PHILIPS, TWO CD's)

So let me sneak Jon Vickers, one of my favorite singers, on my list by bringing along Sir Colin Davis's recording of *Peter Grimes,* with Vickers in the title role. Vickers taps into the dangerous and self-destructive emotions simmering below the surface of the character. This is a colossal performance.

Where Classical Music Thrives

The Internet is a boon to Beethoven and his buddies

Hand-wringing is prevalent in the classical music world these days, bemoaning that pop culture and modern technology are threatening the beloved art form. But, in fact, those who thought the Web meant a new future for classical music were right. Classical music is thriving on the Internet. Only, it is not thriving in the form people in recent decades expected it to take.

You want to read about classical music? There are dozens of sites, from ArtsJournal.com, which links to articles in every area of culture, to NewMusicBox.org, which has demonstrated that a serious online music magazine can indeed endure (with, yes, streaming of concerts).

You want to listen to classical music? For opera buffs, Operacast.com has a complete list of broadcasts from around the world that you can hear on your computer. Want a reference? Operabase.com unfailingly tells who is singing what where, and the Metropolitan Opera Archives online database (www.metoperafamily.

org) is a treasure trove for fans. Want to talk about music? There are message boards for almost every aspect of music. Then there are blogs. Many music critics keep blogs in addition to their paying work (like Alex Ross of the *New Yorker* at TheRestIsNoise.com).

But this is still relatively small potatoes. The bigger question is whether classical music can hope to have a wider reach on the Internet. The answer is yes. When the BBC recently mounted a trial Beethoven project that included free downloads of his symphonies, it registered about 1.5 million downloads. And classical music on the Internet sells. By conventional wisdom, classical music accounts for 3 to 4 percent of overall recording industry sales. But on Apple's iTunes, the leading site for music downloads, classical music represents 12 percent of sales.

For violinist Janine Jansen's recording of Vivaldi's *Four Seasons,* 73 percent of its sales were through downloads. And there are more and more places where classical music is sold: subscription sites like eMusic.com, the high-fidelity site MusicGiants.com and MTV's iTunes rival, Urge.com.

—Anne Midgette

SCHUBERT: *Winterreise.* Peter Pears (tenor), Benjamin Britten (piano) (DECCA)

Britten was arguably the greatest all-around musician of the 20th century, not just a towering composer, but a gifted conductor and a very fine pianist. His pianism is exquisite and musically penetrating on a classic recording of Schubert's autumnal song cycle *Winterreise* with Pears, also Britten's lifelong partner.

BACH: *"Goldberg" Variations.* Glenn Gould (piano) (SONY CLASSICAL, TWO CD'S WITH BONUS CD)

With lots of time to kill, I think I'd enjoy hearing a great artist in the throes of an obsession, which describes Glenn Gould playing Bach's *"Goldberg"*

Variations. Gould recorded this work twice: first in 1955, at the beginning of his career, and then in 1981, the year before his death at 50. The early version is impetuous and brilliant; the later version is mellower, yet just as brilliant.

STRAVINSKY: *Symphony in Three Movements, Symphony in C, Symphony of Psalms.* Igor Stravinsky (conductor), Columbia Symphony Orchestra, CBC Symphony Orchestra (SONY CLASSICAL)

Despite their neo-Classical titles, Igor Stravinsky's *Symphony in C* and *Symphony in Three Movements* are as unconventional as his masterpiece for chorus and orchestra, the *Symphony of*

Psalms. But I'd rather have the composer's own recordings of these amazing and compact works on my island than a boxed set of the Beethoven symphonies, which I know so well I could run them through in my head.

BERG: *Wozzeck.* Karl Böhm (conductor), Orchestra of the German Opera, Berlin; Dietrich Fischer-Dieskau, Evelyn Lear (DEUTSCHE GRAMMOPHON, THREE CD'S)

For a break from all the tonal music I've listed so far, my choice would be Berg's searingly beautiful opera *Wozzeck.* On his classic recording, Karl Böhm conducts it like an ingenious extension of the Wagner-Brahms heritage. (The set includes Böhm's recording of Berg's *Lulu*).

BACH: *Mass in B Minor.* Philippe Herreweghe (conductor), Collegium Vocale (HARMONIA MUNDI, TWO CD's)

I would have to have one of the monumental works by Bach, the father of us all. One could argue that the greatest day in music history was the day Bach passed out the parts for the Mass in B Minor. There are many fine recordings, but the lucid and stirring account by Philippe Herreweghe, the insightful Belgian conductor and chorus master, is revelatory.

MARIA CALLAS: *Puccini and Bellini arias.* Maria Callas (soprano), Tullio Serafin (conductor); mostly the Philharmonia Orchestra (EMI)

I could not get by without a Callas recording, and my personal choice would be the collection of arias by Puccini and Bellini released in 1978. Callas's volatile, terrifying and, finally, heartrending account of Turandot's "In Questa Reggia" always moves me.

Now, if I could fudge things and also bring along just one book, the complete plays of Shakespeare in a single volume, between the Bard and my limited trove of recordings I think I'd be O.K.

ALLAN KOZINN
Times classical music critic

MOZART: *Le Nozze di Figaro.* Patrizia Ciofi, Lorenzo Regazzo, Angelika Kirchschlager, Véronique Gens, Simon Keenlyside; Concerto Köln, René Jacobs, conducting (HARMONIA MUNDI)

Comic and lusty, but also a deeply moving study in the power of forgiveness, with magnificently turned arias and fantastic orchestral writing, this is the greatest opera ever written. Among the dozens of fine recordings, this vibrantly played, beautifully sung 2003 period instrument performance gets more directly and vividly to the work's heart than many with starrier casts.

PURCELL: *Dido and Aeneas.* Susan Graham, Ian Bostridge; Le Concert'D'Astrée, Emmanuelle Haïm, conducting (EMI/VIRGIN VERITAS)

Magnificently compact as operas go, at just under an hour, this great English work comes to life in Haïm's freewheeling addition, which includes added winds and ample vocal ornamentation, to say nothing of Susan Graham's and Ian Bostridge's deftly drawn and deeply felt characterizations.

MENDELSSOHN: *Symphony No. 4 in A (Op. 90)* and *Overture and Excerpts from A Midsummer Night's Dream.* Orchestra of the Age of Enlightenment, Sir Charles Mackerras, conducting (EMI/VIRGIN CLASSICS)

These youthful, spirited works bristle with joyful energy under just about any circumstances, but the extraordinarily transparent sound Sir Charles Mackerras draws from this period instrument ensemble gives them a truly magical aura.

BEETHOVEN: *Symphony No. 9 in D minor (Op. 125).* Jane Hobson, Donald Bell, Adele Addison, Richard Lewis; Cleveland Orchestra, George Szell, conducting (SONY ESSENTIAL CLASSICS).

ARTS

Since Szell's entire cycle can be had on an inexpensive 5-CD set, there's no real need to make the difficult choice between the Third, Fifth, Seventh and Ninth Symphonies; but if it's to be just one, the Ninth, with its vigorous Scherzo and fantastic choral finale, has to be it. This remarkably brisk 1961 recording is the one I return to the most.

JOHN WILLIAMS, guitarist, *Virtuoso Variations.* (CBS MASTERWORKS)

An extraordinary collection of variation sets—among them, the Bach Chaconne and Batchelor's "Monsieur's Almaine" and the Paganini Caprice No. 24—played by one of the most eloquent guitarists of our time, this thoroughly satisfying and at times invigorating album has never made the transition from LP to CD. No doubt it will someday, but it's a must-have recording.

DOWLAND: *First Booke of Songes (1597).* The Consort of Musicke, Anthony Rooley, director (L'OISEAU-LYRE)

A perpetual sad sack with a substantial list of grievances, but also a supremely lyrical gift, Dowland pioneered the art of writing angst-inspired music three centuries before Mahler made it his trademark. The songs in this collection are deliciously bittersweet, and the performances by Emma Kirkby and company are irresistible.

BACH: *Brandenburg Concertos.* Il Giardino Armonico (TELDEC, 2 CD's)

Bach made this compilation to demonstrate his compositional fluency with instrumental combinations of all kinds. We take that as a given but, still, this is a remarkable set of works, and Il Giardino Armonico, a young Italian group, plays the six concertos with an explosive energy.

GLASS: *Koyaanisqatsi.* Western Wind Vocal Ensemble, Philip Glass Ensemble (NONESUCH)

In this film score, which plays continuously through Godfrey Reggio's dialogue-free examination of industrial society, Philip Glass made the transition from minimalism to a quasi-Wagnerian Romanticism still driven by the repeating figures and driving rhythms of the minimalist style. It remains some of his most haunting music.

RICHARD THOMPSON: *Across a Crowded Room.* (POLYDOR)

Recorded soon after splitting with his wife and one-time duo partner, Linda Thompson, this 1985 collection raises the breakup song to the level of high art. It also features a good deal of Thompson's brilliant, stinging guitar work, for which he is justifiably revered.

THE BEATLES: *Sgt. Pepper's Lonely Hearts Club Band.* (EMI)

Same problem as the Beethoven symphonies—how can you pick just one? Still, this 1967 classic shows the group at its most brilliantly inventive, with lyrics swatched in colorful imagery, and instrumental textures that take in everything from sitars and harpsichords, to full orchestra and tape loops. Get the slipcased British pressing: the artwork is better and more complete.

THE JIMI HENDRIX EXPERIENCE: *Electric Ladyland.* (MCA)

This third and last Expcricncc album rclcased in 1968 shows Hendrix making his way from being a psychedelic guitar god to—well, unfortunately he didn't live long enough for us to see where he was really headed. But here you have the pure fiery virtuosity of "Come On," "House Burning Down" and "Voodoo Chile (Slight Return)" and brilliantly compact productions. like "All Along the Watchtower," side by side with daring electronic experiments like "1983...(A Merman I Should Turn to Be)" and "Moon, Turn the Tides."

ROLLING STONES: *Exile on Main Street.* (VIRGIN)

The last in the great run of middle-period Stones albums that started with *Beggar's Banquet, Exile* has everything the Stones do best, from the undisguisedly nasty, horn-driven "Rocks Off" and the manically punchy "Rip This Joint" to the more soulfully bluesy "Tumbling Dice" and "Torn and Frayed" and the country-blues tinged "Sweet Virginia" and "Sweet Black Angel," to say nothing of the great Keith Richard's vocal showcase, "Happy."

JON PARELES

Times chief pop music critic

ROBERT JOHNSON: *The Complete Recordings.* (COLUMBIA)

These archetypal blues present a man, his guitar and his world of trouble, where women leave him lonely and the devil won't leave him alone.

CHUCK BERRY: *Gold.* (UNIVERSAL)

In his pioneering mid-1950's singles, Chuck Berry delivered what his label head, Leonard Chess, summed up as "the big beat, cars and young love." But there was even more to it: a succinctly twangy fusion of blues and country and a wisecracking defiance that uses sheer pleasure to bypass authority.

JAMES BROWN: *Star Time.* (POLYDOR, 4 CD'S)

This CD set contains an irresistible overabundance of James Brown: the volcanic R&B belter, the social philosopher, and most of all the genius of funk. The clockwork precision of the grooves is both scientific and sweaty: like a sex machine, absolutely.

ELIS REGINA AND ANTONIO CARLOS JOBIM: *Elis & Tom.* (VERVE)

Brazil's most beloved singer and its most

What Jazzes Wynton Marsalis

The master trumpeter's favorite jazz classics

Jazz, with its mix of bracing intellectuality and moving lyricism, has long been known as America's classical music. Few have done more to foster that reputation than trumpeter Wynton Marsalis, who is renowned both for his classical and his jazz performances. Here, he picks his 10 favorite jazz albums by the greats who inspired him.

LOUIS ARMSTRONG	The Hot Fives (any recording)	Columbia
	The Hot Sevens (any recording)	Columbia
COUNT BASIE	The original American Decca recordings	MCA/Decca
ORNETTTE COLEMAN	The Shape of Jazz to Come	Rhino/Atlantic
JOHN COLTRANE	Crescent	Impulse
MILES DAVIS	Kind of Blue	Columbia
DUKE ELLINGTON	The Far East Suite	RCA
THELONIOUS MONK	It's Monk's Time	Columbia
JELLY ROLL MORTON	The Pearls	RCA
CHARLIE PARKER	The complete Dial recordings	Style/Stash

Rock and Roll Royalty

Who's listed in the Hall of Fame

The Rock and Roll Hall of Fame (www.rockhall.com) began its yearly induction ceremony in 1986, and got many of the biggest, most obvious names out of the way pretty quickly. The first year's haul included Ray Charles, Elvis Presley, Chuck Berry, James Brown, Little Richard, Jerry Lee Lewis and Buddy Holly; by decade's end, the Beatles, the Beach Boys, the Rolling Stones, Bob Dylan and Stevie Wonder had joined them.

These days, what drama there is surrounding the induction ritual concerns the hall's quarter-century rule. According to its Web site, "Artists become eligible for induction 25 years after the release of their first record." Fans can calculate the gap between the year their favorites became eligible and the year they were inducted.

1986

Chuck Berry
James Brown
Ray Charles
Sam Cooke
Fats Domino
The Everly Brothers
Buddy Holly
Jerry Lee Lewis
Elvis Presley
Little Richard

EARLY INFLUENCES
Robert Johnson
Jimmie Rodgers
Jimmy Yancey

1987

The Coasters
Eddie Cochran
Bo Diddley

Aretha Franklin
Marvin Gaye
Bill Haley
B. B. King
Clyde McPhatter
Ricky Nelson
Roy Orbison
Carl Perkins
Smokey Robinson
Big Joe Turner
Muddy Waters
Jackie Wilson

EARLY INFLUENCES
Louis Jordan
T-Bone Walker
Hank Williams

1988

The Beach Boys
The Beatles

The Drifters
Bob Dylan
The Supremes

EARLY INFLUENCES
Woody Guthrie
Lead Belly
Les Paul

1989

Dion
Otis Redding
The Rolling Stones
The Temptations
Stevie Wonder

EARLY INFLUENCES
The Inkspots
Bessie Smith
The Soul Stirrers

1990

Hank Ballard

Bobby Darin
The Four Seasons
The Four Tops
The Kinks
The Platters
Simon & Garfunkel
The Who

EARLY INFLUENCES
Louis Armstrong
Charlie Christian
Ma Rainey

1991

LaVern Baker
The Byrds
John Lee Hooker
The Impressions
Wilson Pickett
Jimmy Reed
Ike and Tina Turner

EARLY INFLUENCES
Howlin' Wolf

1992

Bobby "Blue" Bland
Booker T. & the M.G.'s
Johnny Cash
The Isley Brothers
The Jimi Hendrix Experience
Sam and Dave
The Yardbirds

EARLY INFLUENCES
Elmore James
Professor Longhair

1993

Ruth Brown
Cream
Creedence Clearwater Revival

important bossa nova composer squabbled in the studio while they made an album of surpassing, seductive grace and elegance.

BOB DYLAN: *Highway 61 Revisited.* (COLUMBIA)

Electric in more ways than one, Bob Dylan corralled the apocalypse and backed it with blues-rock. The album is a masterpiece of arrogance, sneering and taunting, and cackling with the certainty that anything from gossip to the Bible is entirely his to transfigure.

ARETHA FRANKLIN: *30 Greatest Hits.* (ATLANTIC)

Gospel and jazz taught Aretha Franklin's voice to soar so spectacularly that it would take more than man trouble to bring it down.

THE ROLLING STONES: *Let It Bleed.* (ABKCO)

As 1960's hopes crumbled, the Rolling Stones dug in. They faced up to the lusts and weaknesses of humanity, using fine-tuned irony and chiseled guitar riffs, demanding "Gimme Shelter" because they knew there was none.

The Doors
Frankie Lymon &
the Teenagers
Etta James
Van Morrison
Sly and the Family
Stone
EARLY INFLUENCES
Dinah Washington

1994
The Animals
The Band
Duane Eddy
The Grateful Dead
Elton John
John Lennon
Bob Marley
Rod Stewart
EARLY INFLUENCES
Willie Dixon

1995
The Allman Brothers
Band
Al Green
Janis Joplin
Led Zeppelin
Martha & the
Vandellas
Neil Young
Frank Zappa

EARLY INFLUENCES
The Orioles

1996
David Bowie
Gladys Knight &
the Pips
Jefferson Airplane
Little Willie John
Pink Floyd
The Shirelles
The Velvet
Underground

EARLY INFLUENCES
Pete Seeger

1997
The (Young)
Rascals
The Bee Gees
Buffalo Springfield
Crosby, Stills &
Nash
The Jackson Five
Joni Mitchell
Parliament-
Funkadelic

EARLY INFLUENCES
Mahalia Jackson
Bill Monroe

1998
The Eagles
Fleetwood Mac

The Mamas & the
Papas
Lloyd Price
Santana
Gene Vincent

EARLY INFLUENCES
Jelly Roll Morton

1999
Billy Joel
Curtis Mayfield
Paul McCartney
Del Shannon
Dusty Springfield
Bruce Springsteen
The Staple Singers

EARLY INFLUENCES
Bob Wills & His
Texas Playboys
Charles Brown

2000
Eric Clapton
Earth, Wind & Fire
Lovin' Spoonful
The Moonglows
Bonnie Raitt
James Taylor

EARLY INFLUENCES
Nat "King" Cole
Billie Holiday

SIDEMEN
Hal Blaine
King Curtis
James Jamerson
Scotty Moore
Earl Palmer

2001
Aerosmith
Solomon Burke
The Flamingos
Michael Jackson
Queen
Paul Simon
Steely Dan
Ritchie Valens
SIDEMEN
James Burton
Johnnie Johnson

2002
Isaac Hayes
Brenda Lee
Tom Petty & the
Heartbreakers
Gene Pitney
Ramones
Talking Heads
SIDEMEN
Chet Atkins

2003
AC/DC

The Clash
Elvis Costello & the
Attractions
The Police
Righteous Brothers
SIDEMEN
Benny Benjamin
Floyd Cramer
Steve Douglas

2004
Jackson Browne
The Dells
George Harrison
Prince
Bob Seger
Traffic
ZZ Top

2005
Buddy Guy
The O'Jays
The Pretenders
Percy Sledge
U2

2006
Black Sabbath
Blondie
Miles Davis
Lynyrd Skynyrd
Sex Pistols
—Kelefa Sanneh

ARTS

STEVE REICH: *Music for 18 Musicians.* (ECM)

The shimmering bell tones echo Indonesian gamelan music, the interlocking xylophones and marimbas suggest West Africa, the orchestral expansiveness hints at Europe and the systematic framework of this symphonic-length piece comes from the classically trained, well-traveled American composer Steve Reich.

BOB MARLEY AND THE WAILERS: *Legend.* (ISLAND)

Reggae's sinuous backbeat became the stoic pulse of righteous resistance once Bob Marley began his ascendance as an icon worldwide. The songs merged protest, spirituality and desire in a ganja haze.

PUBLIC ENEMY: *It Takes a Nation of Millions to Hold Us Back.* (DEF JAM)

Urban density approaches critical mass on this milestone of hip-hop. It's a manifesto punctuated by comedy, a historical montage hurled into the present, an intellectual challenge brandished on the dance floor.

U2: *Achtung, Baby.* (ISLAND)

In a long career of earnest, open-hearted rock anthems, with Achtung Baby U2 stirred some fun and electronics into songs that gave the Irish band a rejuvenating remix.

ARCADE FIRE : *Funeral.* (MERGE)

The music sounds as thrown-together as a backyard musical, but finds precisely the right orchestration for every moment. Constantly teetering between sorrow and hope, the Arcade Fire makes something to hold onto in unstable times.

BEN RATLIFF

Times jazz and pop music critic

JOAO GILBERTO: *Joao Gilberto.* (POLYGRAM*).*

From 1973, and known informally as "the white album," this record presumes that you will have headphones on your desert island: you will want to hear every exhalation, every time a finger hits a string. Gilberto invented bossa nova's guitar rhythm.

DUKE ELLINGTON: *The Okeh Ellington.* (SONY LEGACY)

The best early Ellington reminds you of human possibility: its resourcefulness in melody, harmony and rhythm, arrangement, recording-studio technique, soul, and humor.

JOHN COLTRANE: *Live at the Village Vanguard.* (IMPULSE!)

I have never been sold on the tracks with Eric Dolphy as an added member to Coltrane's quartet—I sometimes find them enervating. But this, his first live album, made at the beginning point of his great quartet, includes "Chasin' the Trane," a 15-minute blues in F with constant fresh improvising.

SARAH VAUGHAN: *Swingin' Easy.* (MERCURY)

I wouldn't call it easy: this is one of the fiercest demonstrations of swing in jazz's entire history. What resonance, what musicality: it was recorded when Vaughan was at her most brilliant.

HECTOR LAVOE: *Hector's Gold.* (FANIA)

The great romantic-rhythmic singer of salsa, Lavoe wasn't just a smooth character: his singing always connoted a slight chaos, intimating that life doesn't always add up. The music, produced by Willie Colon, is brash, brilliant and cinematic at times, amounting to one of the defining sounds of New York City in the last 30 years. It's a best-of collection; if you're allergic to such things, try *La Voz*.

JAMES BROWN: *In the Jungle Groove.* (POLYDOR/UNIVERSAL)

In the late 60's and early 70's, James Brown had some of the most advanced bands in the history of pop music, continually alternating between mesmerizing, jolting, minimalism, maximalism. Some of these tracks reach such a high level of funk that you can't quite believe it exists.

TITO PUENTE: *The Essential Tito Puente.* (RCA/LEGACY)

Mambo makes you feel good to be alive, and Puente's band was one of the genre's best: the rhythms are giant descriptions of graceful motion, and the rhetoric of the solos is entirely based on cutting through the dense curtain of sound. Every time you hear a singer improvising on this anthology of songs recorded between 1949 and 1962—or a brass player or a percussionist for that matter—they're coming fully prepared.

Cecilia Bartoli Airs Her Arias

The Italian diva shares her favorite operas

Cecilia Bartoli is one of the most celebrated classical singers performing today. Highly acclaimed for her concert, opera and recital appearances, she is known to an even wider audience through her immensely popular recordings, which have won numerous awards around the world. Here, the Italian mezzo-soprano known for the warmth and expressiveness of her singing, recommends a list of 10 operas for opera novices and opera lovers alike. She explains:

In trying to compile a list of 10 operas which are my recommendations for seducing people to become opera lovers, I would like to choose only one opera from each of 10 different composers, although each of them has written many other wonderful stage works. They are mentioned here not necessarily in the recommended order for listening.

MOZART'S *LE NOZZE DI FIGARO*

Le Nozze di Figaro is a wonderful marriage of perfect music and a perfect story. Some people will chide me for not choosing *Don Giovanni* or *The Magic Flute* as his most perfect opera. I say, start with *Nozze* and then listen to *all* of Mozart's operas.

ROSSINI'S *LA CENERENTOLA*

La Cenerentola is Rossini's scintillating setting of the Cinderella fairy tale. It also happens to be one of my favorite roles. And if you like the sparkle of *La Cenerentola*, you will find champagne in such other works as his *Barbiere di Siviglia* or *L'Italiana in Algieri*. Eventually, you will find your way also to his serious operas.

PUCCINI'S *LA BOHÈME*

Puccini's *La Bohème* is probably the most directly appealing opera. It's about youth, love, and tragedy in the most realistic terms, set to glorious music. And from *La Bohème* one goes so easily to all the other works of this great composer.

BIZET'S *CARMEN*

Many consider the adventures of the Spanish gypsy to be the perfect opera. This is a timeless story set to timeless music. One could say that it is the first really realistic opera—a path to what later became verismo in opera.

MASCAGNI'S *CAVALLERIA RUSTICANA*

This opera is considered the most important step into the verismo era in music. In verismo, best translated as "stark reality," there are no gods, no mythical beings, no royalty, no deus ex machina—just everyday people in some very realistic, and often violent, circumstances. If it were not for its emotionally charged music, it might be a play or a movie.

VERDI'S *OTELLO*

This is a perfect example of an opera being more powerful than its source. Shakespeare's play is weak in that the jealousy motive built on the missing handkerchief is rather unbelievable. Through Verdi's absolutely glorious music, the story becomes not only completely believable but in the end truly heart-wrenching.

RICHARD STRAUSS'S *ELEKTRA*

Elektra is probably the prime shocker in music and there will be raised eyebrows as to why I have included it in a 10-most-accessible-operas list. This searing score is built on the Sophocles tragedy and it is unsparing in its assault on our senses. But our senses have become accustomed to so much violence in entertainment that *Elektra* may be the very subject matter that has an immediate audience appeal.

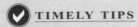

TIMELY TIPS

Opera—Wherever You May Be

True opera buffs cannot be denied. And these days, there is no reason to. Here's how to get tickets at some of the world's leading opera houses.

VIENNA Home of Wolfgang Amadeus Mozart, among others, Vienna is still one of the best places to hear and see opera.

✔ The Vienna Tourist Board, www.vienna.info, includes a listing of concerts and operas, with links to the Web sites of the State Opera and the Volksoper.

✔ To buy tickets directly for either the State Opera or the Volksoper, call (43-1) 513-1513, or go to www.wiener-staatsoper.at or www.volksoper.at.

✔ The easiest way to buy may be to call or visit the Vienna Tourist Board office behind the State Opera, (43-1) 24-555. The staff can put you in touch with the various box offices and other outlets that still have tickets available. The office is on the Albertinaplatz, at the corner of the Maysedergasse.

MILAN After a staff revolt prompted Riccardo Muti's resignation in 2005, his fans predicted that La Scala would never be the same. But the show has gone on under the leadership of a modest 30-year-old Englishman, Daniel Harding, who is getting rave reviews. Behind the scenes, credit is also owed to another man, Stéphane Lissner, a 52-year-old Frenchman, and the first foreigner to head La Scala since its creation more than 200 years ago. He has not only restored calm, but also begun charting a new, more modern and interna-tional, course for the house.

✔ The Web site for the La Scala opera house in Milan is www.teatroallascala.org

PARIS OPERA

✔ To find schedules for both Palais Garnier and the Opera de la Bastille, go to www.operadeparis.fr

LONDON OPERA

✔ **English National Opera** The scrappier younger sibling of the Royal Opera House at Covent Garden, dedicated to presenting opera in English, with an emphasis on innovative productions and nurturing British talent. www.eno.org

✔ **Royal Opera House at Covent Garden** Houses both the Royal Opera and the Royal Ballet, and features more of the traditional repertory. www.royalopera.org

—Ray Cormier and Alan Riding

I've purposely left three of the earliest operas for the end of my list. They are from the early Baroque era, the beginning of the 18th century. Strange as it may seem, to some listeners this early music is the most accessible of all, because of its "logic" in composition. To others it is an acquired taste. My advice is that every listener should do his own experimenting.

HANDEL'S *RINALDO*

Written in 1711, *Rinaldo* is based on the text of Torquato Tasso's *Liberation of Jerusalem.* Although it demands female and male singers capable of extraordinary bravura singing, its music has an almost "healing" quality. If one opens one's heart and ears to this music, it can work like a tonic against the burdens of daily life. Let us not forget that because of the *Messiah,* Handel is no stranger to most of us.

PERGOLESI'S *LA SERVA PADRONA*

La Serva Padrona was written in 1733 and its success, in so many countries in addition to its native Italy, established it as groundbreaking in the area of comic opera—or opera buffa. The music is inventive, charming and often witty. It is extremely easy on the ears, which is a quality to be cherished.

VIVALDI'S *ORLANDO FURIOSO*

Orlando Furioso, which premiered in 1727, is based on Ariosto's epic poem, which was also the inspiration for the three Handel operas *Orlando*, *Ariodante*, and *Alcina*. Like Handel's *Rinaldo*, this is an opera seria—but listen to the differences in composing styles. To my ears, it takes more liberties within the musical boundaries of that era, just like Vivaldi's *The Four Seasons* is looser in concept than Handel's *Water Music* and *Fireworks Music*.

The Earliest Recordings

Thousands are now available—on the Internet

From about 1890 to the mid-1920's, before the advent of electric recording, musicians cut records while crammed cheek-by-jowl-by-trombone around phonograph horns in rackety little studios. Now, the first commercially available recordings

ever produced have become available free of charge to anyone with an Internet connection and some spare bandwidth. In late 2005, the Donald C. Davidson Library at the University of California, Santa Barbara, introduced the Cylinder Digitization and Preservation Project Web site (www.cylinders. library.ucsb.edu), a collection of more than 6,000 cylinders converted to downloadable audio files.

It is an astonishing trove of sounds: opera arias, comic monologues, marching bands, gospel quartets. Above all, there are the pop tunes churned out by Tin Pan Alley at the turn of the century: ragtime ditties, novelty songs, sentimental ballads and a range of dialect numbers performed by vaudeville's blackface comedians and other "ethnic impersonators." For decades, these records languished unheard by all but a few intrepid researchers and enthusiasts.

This mainstream pop music of the early 20th century has been the victim of a variety of prejudices. Some listeners have been put off by the primitive sound of the old records. Pop-song purists have scorned the music as the height of

 TIMELY TIPS

Ballet at Its Best

Dance is a natural human instinct—a primal human activity. It originates from the sexual impulse, from courtship and mating rituals, as well as basic self-expression.

Ballet and modern dance have developed into rich forms, making them some of the most accessible of the arts. A dance performance comes in on many circuits, presenting multiple points of entry—movement,

music, design, expression, color, stage-set and in many cases, drama and narrative.

FIVE GREAT DANCE COMPANIES
Check their Web sites for performance and touring information

✔ **American Ballet Theatre**, New York City: www.abt.org

✔ **The Kirov Ballet**, St. Petersburg, Russia: www.kirov.com

✔ **New York City Ballet**, New York City: www.nycballet.com

✔ **Paris Opera Ballet**, Paris,

France: www.operadeparis.fr

✔ **The Royal Ballet**, London, England: info.royaloperahouse. org/ballet

AND FIVE BALLETS NOT TO BE MISSED

✔ **Giselle** (Choreographers: Jules Perrot and Jean Coralli)

✔ **Swan Lake** (Marius Petipa)

✔ **Serenade** (George Balanchine)

✔ **Revelations** (Alvin Ailey)

✔ **Romeo and Juliet** (Kenneth MacMillan)

—June Schneider

Tin Pan Alley's factory-produced pap. Nearly everybody has been repelled by the content of songs that date from a time when coarse racial caricature was one of America's favorite sources of amusement. But this was roots music in its own right, and deserves a central place in the historical narrative.

TIMELY TIPS

For R&B and Jazz Lovers

Bored by the offerings at your local music store? Try these online sites

✔ **Cadence, The Review of Jazz & Blues**
www.cadencebuilding.com
Online site offerings include more than 12,000 labels. Beyond what you find online, Cadence has a catalog and a magazine. The magazine provides features, extensive artist interviews and dozens of record reviews. Each title is listed in a no-nonsense, phone-book style; over 10,000 titles indexed and alphabetized by record label. Write or call to order a monthly subscription.

✔ **Double Time Jazz** 800-293-8528 (24-hr. order line) or www.doubletimejazz.com
Another well-organized jazz outlet, offering nearly 5,000 titles. All eras of jazz are represented; especially good at locating out-of-print items.

✔ **Rhino Catalog**
888-440-4232 or www.rhino.com
The label bills itself as the top archival record label in the country—and the extensive catalog bears out that claim. It covers music from the 50's to the 90's, with a great selection of funk anthologies and rock compilation albums. Catalogs may feature thick sections devoted to Cajun music, zydeco, New Orleans R&B, folk, world music, country and western, blues, jazz, vocals and a lot more.

The best of these songs were artful, with indelible melodies and flashes of wit, and many have endured: "Give My Regards to Broadway," "Yes, We Have No Bananas," "Shine On, Harvest Moon," "The Darktown Strutters' Ball," "Carolina in the Morning." All can be found on the Web site.

—Jody Rosen

A Who's Who of Music Lists

A critic's guide to where the beat goes on

Beginning sometime after Thanksgiving and extending through Martin Luther King Day, music magazines and Web sites, not to mention newspapers, go list crazy. They rank songs, singers, albums, new releases, the best of a multitude of genres and so on. How much credibility do the rankings merit? Here's one critic's assessment of the various lists:

Rolling Stone: The list isn't attributed to any specific writer or editor. It gives 50 albums an institutional seal of approval.

Blender: *Rolling Stone*'s more playful competitor, it has a quirkier album list that seems to reflect personal obsession as much as institutional approval. *Blender* also prints a list of 100 songs.

Pitchfork: The influential indie-rock Web site (pitchforkmedia.com) publishes a year-end list as carefully compiled as a D.J. set. The Pitchfork list is a group effort. The site's CD reviews come with numerical ratings assigned by the writer, from 0.0 to 10.0. If it's an argument you want, the most productive Pitchfork list is "The 15 Worst Releases of the Year," compiled by one person, the site's editor.

metacritic.com: You can read dozens of top 10's and peruse the site's own calculation of the year's most favorably reviewed albums.

TIMELY TIPS

Sites From the Underground

Independent music online

✔ **Emusic.com:** Has an archive of roughly one million tracks from an array of independent labels, and offers its music in the form of unrestricted MP3 files, unlike Apple's iTunes or Microsoft's MSN Music. Emusic's searchable offerings run from recent independent favorites, like Neko Case and Sufjan Stevens, to the early independent offerings of icons like Johnny Cash and Otis Redding, to current stars like Coldplay and My Chemical Romance. Subscriptions start at $9.99, with the fee acting as a pre-payment for 40 downloads a month.

✔ **Garageband.com:** The site runs as a clearinghouse for independent and unsigned artists who want to post their music. Listeners can search for artists by genre, stream or download MP3 files, and order "physical" CD's from artists who choose to sell them.

✔ **Audiolunchbox:** Founded in 2003, the service offers a wide range of music in MP3 form, including current releases from independent labels and the early music of current major label acts like Queens of the Stone Age. Users can track charts of the most popular albums and songs. The service offers a choice of subscription plans— $9.99 a month for 40 downloads or purchase songs à la carte for 99 cents apiece.

✔ **Download.com:** A division of CNET, Download.com offers tens of thousands of free MP3's from unsigned and independent artists. Besides sorting the offerings by genre or geography, users can place artists they like on a "watch list," and automatically receive e-mail when that artist posts new music.

✔ **Bleep.com:** The U.K.-based service offers a library of independent music, and lets consumers listen to songs in full before deciding to buy them. Like other services focusing on independent labels, it sells unrestricted MP3's. Individual tracks cost $1.35 and albums cost $9.99.

—Jeff Leeds

fimoculous.com: Compiles tons of Top 10's in an impressive range of fields.

The Village Voice: Its indispensable Pazz & Jop poll (not published until January 31) asks some 1,500 critics to list their favorite albums and songs. The resulting list typically confirms the perennial and puzzling fact that music critics across the country love indie-rock more than any other genre.

Only the most gullible reader would consider any of these lists definitive. American lists tend to focus mainly on American releases. (Likewise, mainstream British magazines like *NME, Q* and *Mojo* tend to boost British artists and snub American ones.) English-language lists tend to ignore Latin music. Jazz and classical CD's tend not to appear on pop lists. The woman-centric magazine *Venus* splits its lists in two—one for women and one for men, like a tennis tournament.

Other publications the music-obsessed might want to consult:

• ***Wire:*** A magazine devoted to "adventures in modern music."

• ***Roots:*** The "worldwide roots music" magazine. In 2005, West African artists swept its top four slots—Amadou and Mariam, Ali Farka Touré and Toumani Diabaté, Salif Keita, Thione Seck.

• ***Revolver:*** Its year-end issue offers a smart survey of the year in heavy music.

• ***Decibel:*** A smart and adventurous magazine where heavy metal meets avant-garde.

ARTS

- *DJ:* Emphasizes dance music.
- *Ozone:* A scrappy Southern hip-hop magazine.
- *Spin:* A mainstream music magazine.

—Kelefa Sanneh

The Best Summer Festivals

Where the settings are often as spectacular as the (mostly classical) music

John Rockwell, a cultural critic of the *New York Times,* and founding director of the Lincoln Center Festival, has been one of the most respected voices in the performing arts world for many years. Here, he shares some of his favorite music festivals in Europe and the United States.

EUROPE

Aldeburgh Festival. *Early to late June*
Founded by Benjamin Britten, it offers a repertory of mostly chamber music.
www.aldeburgh.co.uk

Aix-en-Provence Festival. *Early to late July*
This music festival, the most prominent in France, takes place in the historic center of a

---

TIMELY TIPS

Where the Rock Never Stops

Some online resources for rock, dance and other music festivals:

✔ **www.virtual-festivals.com**
International rock and dance festivals

✔ **www.en.wikipedia.org/wiki/Music_festivals** Has a large list of summer festivals.

✔ **www.thefestivalzone.com**
Rock festivals in Europe

---

lovely town not far from the Mediterranean. www.festival-aix.com

Drottningholm Court Theater.
Late May to early September
This pocket-sized theater, the only fully functioning, unimproved Baroque theater in the world, offers charming performances of 18th-century opera on period instruments. During the intermissions, one can walk on the rolling lawns of Sweden's royal palace. www.dtm.se

Edinburgh Festival.
Mid-August to early September
A sprawling, city-wide festival with a bustling fringe. Edinburgh always has interesting offerings. www.eif.co.uk

Glyndebourne Festival Opera.
Late May to late August
Now in a handsome new theater. Interesting in its repertory and productions. Expect to see England's finest in formal wear, but don't worry about stuffiness—the atmosphere is lightened by picnics among contented cows.
www.glyndebourne.com

Lucerne Festival. *August into September*
A classy panoply of symphonic and chamber music. www.e.lucernefestival.ch

Richard Wagner Festival, Bayreuth.
Late July to late August
This festival is not in the finest artistic fettle under the direction of Wolfgang Wagner, and of not much use to anyone who dislikes his grandfather's music, but it is still an extraordinary experience for those who do.
www.bayreuther-festspiele.de

Risor Chamber Music Festival.
Late June and early July
The pianist Leif Ove Andsnes's lively get-

together of first-rate musicians in a small Norwegian town. www.kammermusikkfest.no

Rossini Opera Festival. *Mid- to late August*
A relatively recent addition to the list of major festivals. Pesaro, where the composer was born, offers a familiar and exotic Rossini, with top-flight singers in the midst of Italy's Adriatic coast. www.rossinioperafestival.it

Savonlinna Opera Festival. *Early to late July*
The festival takes place in a brooding medieval castle in the midst of the Finnish lake district. The operas are always very good, and often very innovative. Especially striking is the sunlight which, due to the far-northern latitude, lasts almost until midnight. www.operafestival.fi/en

Salzburg Festival. *Late July to late August*
Salzburg, birthplace of Mozart, is spiritually, if not chronologically, the mother of all festivals. www.salzburgfestival.at

Schubertiade.
Mid-June; and late August-mid-September
Found in the far-western Austrian town of Schwarzenberg in the Vorarlberg Alps, this festival is devoted mostly to Schubert. Nearly every famous lieder singer imaginable appears here annually, along with fine chamber ensembles and solo instrumentalists. If you want a crème de la crème festival, this is the one. www.schubertiade.at

Verbier Festival and Academy. *July-August*
Top-level conductors and instrumentalists mingle with young artists in a spectacular Alpine setting. www.verbierfestival.com

Vienna Festival. *Mid-May to mid-June*
The festival concentrates on avant-garde innovations, but runs concurrently with the gala performances at the Vienna State Opera. www.festwochen.at/wf_servlet/Main

TIMELY TIPS

The Battle of the Bands

If you want to be heard, the South by Southwest Music event is the place

Why would musicians travel halfway across the world to play a 40-minute set through a mediocre sound system for a few dozen people glancing at their cellphones? Because, at the annual South by Southwest music event (www.sxsw.com for dates and details) there's a chance that among those people are the right ones: a booking agent, a manager, a band wanting tourmates, a music supervisor for a video game.

What started in 1987 as a cozy showcase for regional and independent music, with 700 people, has turned into the largest music-business convention in the country. More than 10,000 attended in 2006. There is music of all vintages—from the 1950's rockabilly queen Wanda Jackson to Neil Young to Echo and the Bunnymen to the New Pornographers. And there are newer bands well worth discovering, as well. About 1,400 bands played official showcase sets at the 2006 festival and many more could be heard at parties, in hotel lobbies and on street corners.

Although it includes a little of everything, SXSW has concentrated on rock, while being tentative about the most commercially successful do-it-yourself music of the last 20 years: hip-hop. It serves a dizzying assortment of ambitions. Established musicians (like Norah Jones and Lyle Lovett) play to remind listeners that they're still around, and perhaps to gain a little of the mysterious (and laughable) quality known as "indie cred." Past visitors return for victory laps. Bands from abroad, many subsidized by their governments, arrive to test themselves against American audiences and Texas margaritas. At times, SXSW can be like a musical museum—a good one.

—Jon Pareles

ARTS

White Nights Festival. *June to early July*
The venerable St. Petersburg festival of opera and symphonic music, now revitalized by the conductor Valery Gergiev. www.ticketsofrussia.ru/white-nights

UNITED STATES

Lincoln Center Festival.
Second week of July to end of July
The festival showcases rarely performed or new operas, international dance companies, theatrical extravaganzas and non-Western arts. www.lincolncenter.org

New Orleans Jazz and Heritage Fair.
End of April through first week in May
A wonderful, vital and diverse jambalaya of folk and commercial popular music, a beacon in a beleaguered city. www.nojazzfest.com

Next Wave Festival. *October to mid-December*
A fall festival concentrating on postmodern performance events of all kinds. Held at the Brooklyn Academy of Music, New York.

www.bam.org/events/nextwavefestival.aspx

Ojai Music Festival. *Early to mid-June*
Wonderful performances of challenging contemporary music in a gorgeous southern California setting. www.ojaifestival.org

Ravinia Festival. *June to August*
The summer home of the Chicago Symphony, along with other kinds of music. www.ravinia.org

Santa Fe Opera.
The most diverse, attractive summer opera festival in the United States partly for the opera and partly for the location. www.santafeopera.org

Spoleto Festival *End of May to early June*
A charming, historic city plays host to a festival with a lively and diverse variety of performing arts. www.spoletousa.org

Tanglewood Festival.
Early July to mid-August
Summer performances by the Boston Symphony Orchestra and guest artists in an outdoor theater. www.tanglewood.org

---

 **TIMELY TIPS**

The Most Remote Music Festival

Just a stone's throw from Timbuktu, many arrive on gaily decorated camels

Essakane, an obscure desert oasis a half-day's drive beyond Timbuktu, is the site of what's billed as the "most remote music festival in the world." It's a three-day Afro-pop powwow held by the Tuareg, the traditionally nomadic "blue people" of the Sahara. The Festival au Désert is open to outsiders, including Westerners as well as other tribes.

✔ A predominantly European crowd shows up, along with approximately 6,000 Malians, most of them Tuareg, who arrive on gaily decorated camels. Tradition still rules during the day, but after the sun goes down, the jamboree transforms into an open-air pop concert, complete with a stage, lights and 20-foot-high speaker stacks.

✔ You can fly to Bamako, Mali's capital and then drive more than 500 miles over unpaved or barely paved roads to Timbuktu. Allow six days for the journey. There is no road between Timbuktu and Essakane, just sand. As this book was going to press, the date for the next Festival au Désert (www.festival-au-desert.org), had not been set. Best to check out the Web site before setting out.

—Adam Fisher

Museums & Books

The Most Modern Museums
Minimalist, elegant and Zen in character

For aficionados of modernism, obvious mega-sites like the new Museum of Modern Art (www. moma.org) in New York, which some days can feel as crowded as a suburban shopping mall on Black Friday, or Frank Gehry's titanium-clad Guggenheim in Bilbao, Spain (www.guggenheim-bilbao.es), are must-see places. But they also enhance the appeal of less trafficked spots, such as these lesser-known gems.

The Louisiana Museum (www. louisiana.dk) in the remote town of Humblebaek, Denmark, on the rocky North Zealand coast, is a pilgrimage destination with a smart collection, lively exhibition program and light, airy galleries opening onto sublime views of the sea.

The Menil Collection (www.menil. org), in Houston, Tex., founded by John and Dominique de Menil, mixes Byzantine icons and tribal masks with a refined assortment of French modernist and American postwar art. The collection occupies a wood-and-glass shed designed by Renzo Piano, the building itself is a classic of high modernism.

The Beyeler Foundation (www.beyeler.com/fondation). For Piano, the Menil became a template for the Beyeler, the museum he devised in Riehen,

> ❝
> **Art is never an empty container. Rather, it is a vessel loaded with meaning. There's no longer a general belief that there exists a single canon for art.**
>
> Stephen F. Eisenman, professor of art, Northwestern University

• • •

a suburb of Basel, Switzerland. It's quintessentially Swiss: an immaculate glass temple of serene beauty, 20 perfect white rooms in a long pavilion, housing the superior collection of the blue-chip dealer Ernst Beyeler.

The Chinati Foundation (www.chinati.org). An entirely different class of modernist pilgrimage sites includes this museum in the remote, tumbleweed-tossed, west Texas town of Marfa, where the cantankerous, brainy minimalist sculptor Donald Judd converted a disused army base into a shrine to himself and the few artists he admired. At its center are two barrel-vaulted artillery sheds, their walls removed and turned into windows facing Texas scrub to the horizon, making twin cathedrals for 100 of Judd's austere aluminum boxes.

The Dia Art Foundation (www.diabeacon.org). In that same industrial spirit, the Dia Art Foundation recently turned a former Nabisco factory on the Hudson River in Beacon, N.Y., about an hour north of New York City, into a vast, superbly simple, naturally lighted container for similarly minded minimalists and postminimalists like Judd, Walter de Maria, Dan Flavin, Agnes Martin, Michael Heizer, Robert Smithson, Richard Serra and Gerhard Richter. It is the opposite of the new Modern, a near-Zen experience.

—Michael Kimmelman, chief art critic of the *New York Times*

ARTS

Can't Get to the Louvre? Try This

These days, more people visit the world's great museums online than in person

While nothing can replace standing just feet away from a famous artwork, some museum Web sites give art-curious surfers enormous access, from scholarly treatises to shopping in their stores. Here are highlights:

METROPOLITAN MUSEUM OF ART,
New York   www.metmuseum.org

Fifteen million people a year visit the Web site, more than three times the number who venture inside the museum itself. At the Web site, visitors can learn about the permanent collection, trace a timeline of art history (the site's most popular feature) and log on to activities for children, including learning how to draw like Van Gogh. Shoppers can find everything from a $15.95 box of note cards to a $58,000 sapphire necklace.

TATE, London   www.tate.org.uk

Online visitors can get lost in the Tate's giant Web site as easily as they can visiting the Tate itself. Explore the collections at the Tate's Britain, Modern, Liverpool and St. Ives galleries through links on the left side of the museum's home page. A link on the right leads to free e-cards.

LOUVRE, Paris   www.louvre.fr

There are many virtual halls to explore. For a remarkable lesson on nearly every element of the *Mona Lisa*, click on the Resources tab on the home page, and under that, A Closer Look.

PRADO, Madrid   www.museoprado.mcu.es

You can take a virtual tour of the Prado's 50 most relevant works by clicking on the Visits link on the home page. There is also a link to a monthly featured painting, analyzed in depth.

MUSEUM OF CONTEMPORARY ART,
Los Angeles   www.moca.org

To play around with the museum's fascinating digital artworks, click on the Digital Collection link at the bottom of the home page.

RIJKSMUSEUM, Amsterdam
www.rijksmuseum.nl

Click on the first tab and then Collections to look through the museum's works. Under Explore the Collection, you can sort several ways, including by "art objects," "themes" and "artists." Last year, the museum set up Rijkswidget, a desktop download that offers a new work of art to view every day, including details about the artist and his work.

SAN FRANCISCO MUSEUM OF MODERN ART
www.sfmoma.org

For an in-depth interactive multimedia lesson on 15 of the museum's modern masterpieces, go to www.sfmoma.org/anderson/index.html. A noteworthy online store is also here—Alexander Calder toys include a kangaroo pull-toy for $240.

✓ TIMELY TIPS

Other Art Sites Worth a Click

✔ **www.arts.endow.gov** National Endowment for the Arts.

✔ **www.coudal.com/moom.php** The Museum of Online Museums can guide you to some of the Web's best museum sites.

✔ **www.wwar.com** World Wide Arts Resources. News, links to blogs, galleries and more.

✔ **www.nwhq.net** NWHQ: Independent artists on the Web.

✔ **www.art.net** Art on the Net, an exhibit by 80 artists, and links to other art sites.

POMPIDOU CENTER, Paris

www.centrepompidou.fr

From the home page, click on On-Line Resources. There you will find things like art and biographical videos, access to the Pompidou's collection and a Kandinsky research library. Be sure to click on the Webcam link at the bottom of the page to see the three live shots of Paris.

—Lia Miller and Carol Vogel

Small European Gems

A connoisseur picks some of his favorite smaller museums

One of the greatest pleasures of Europe is the smaller museums formed by individual collectors rather than the intermediaries of the state. They are often idiosyncratic and contain masterpieces in unusual settings, sometimes of great beauty. James Stourton, Deputy Chairman, Europe, of Sotheby's and author of *Great Smaller Museums of Europe,* shares some of the best:

GULBENKIAN MUSEUM, Lisbon, Portugal

www.museu.gulbenkian.pt

In no other museum in Europe do Eastern and Western art sit so happily together. The Gulbenkian is a museum where Iznik plates, Persian manuscripts, Mughal carpets and French bookbindings seem to have been born out of the same desire to transmute the designs of nature into art.

Calouste Gulbenkian, known as Mr. Five Per Cent, was the greatest oil tycoon of his era. He acquired his greatest treasures with skill and patience from the Hermitage, carrying off masterpieces by Rembrandt, Rubens and Houdon as well as great 18th-century French furniture and silks.

KRÖLLER-MÜLLER, Otterlo, The Netherlands

www.kmm.nl

The first surprise of this museum is the location in the middle of an expansive forest known as the Hoge Veluwe, an hour and a half east of Amsterdam, in which Anton Kröller liked to hunt. You are invited (but not obliged) to leave your car and proceed by bicycle into the forest to discover his wife's great museum.

Helene Kröller-Müller started collecting in 1907 and had an extraordinary knack of picking winners. At the center of her collection is Van Gogh—she managed to acquire 92 paintings and 187 drawings. Don't miss the first—and still the best—permanent sculpture garden in Europe.

WALLACE COLLECTION, London, England

www.wallacecollection.org

The Wallace Collection is the supreme example of English francophile taste, and it remains the greatest collection of French art outside France. The main collector, the fourth Marquess of Hertford, was a recluse who lived in Paris and instructed his agent to outbid everybody at auction. His taste was mostly for the ancien regime, superb commodes, paintings by Watteau and Fragonard, Sèvres and snuff boxes. The Long Gallery is the best of its kind in the world, stuffed with masterpieces by Poussin, Velazquez, Rembrandt and, most famously, Frans Hals's *Laughing Cavalier.*

MUSÉE CONDÉ, Chantilly, France

www.chateaudechantilly.com

The glory and spirit of France are seen nowhere, except Versailles, to greater advantage than at Chantilly. The surroundings are spacious and noble, the racecourse, the stables—the most splendid ever conceived—and the landscape marvellously tamed. In the middle of it all the château sits magnificently on its lake. Enter and you discover the finest small museum in France. The most spectacular treasure is

ARTS

Whistler's Mother Unseated

Who's in and who's out in art

Janson's History of Art, a doorstopper first published in 1962, has been a classroom hit ever since Horst Woldemar Janson wrote it while working at New York University. For a generation of baby boomers, it defined what was what and who was who in art, from Angelico (Fra) to Zurbarán (Francisco de). But in recent years it has lost its perch as the best-selling art survey and has been criticized for becoming a scholarly chestnut. So its publisher recruited six scholars from around the country and told them to rewrite as much as they wanted, to cast a critical eye on every reproduction, chapter heading and sacred cow.

The result, at more than 1,100 pages and 1,450 illustrations, undoubtedly has surprised many Janson loyalists. The new edition, published in March 2006, drops not only Whistler's portrait of his mother, but also evicts several other longtime residents. And some permanent fixtures—like the Metropolitan Museum of Art's van Eyck diptych, *The Crucifixion, the Last Judgment*—have been replaced with others seen to be more representative of an artist's work.

The new book adds many more women, and for the first time includes decorative arts. It also uses art much more to discuss race, class and gender.

Joseph Jacobs, a curator and scholar who wrote the modern chapters of the new edition, says he often struggled with the question of what he could dare to take out. But when he decided to replace Whistler's portrait of his mother with his *Symphony in White No. 2,* Jacobs says, he didn't think twice. Of *Symphony in White* he says, "You can just do so much more with it, talking about the Japanese influences on Whistler's work and of things that allow you to see how fantastic a painter he really was."

Jacobs also added some works that have long been cultural superstars, like Grant Wood's *American Gothic*, which surprisingly had never appeared in Janson. This might have been because Wood and Janson once taught together and were said to have disliked each other.

—Randy Kennedy

a book, arguably the most beautiful in the world, the *Très Riches Heures du Duc de Berry*, an extraordinary window into the late Middle Ages. Chantilly is an hour from Paris but worth a day.

GALLERIA BORGHESE, Rome, Italy

www.galleriaborghese.it

Among the prelates in 17th-century Rome who were busy creating the Baroque, none fulfilled his mission more agreeably than Cardinal Scipione Borghese. He created this pleasure pavilion on the Pincio Hill, from 1612 onward, as a home for his collection of antiquities. Today, it houses the cardinal's matchless collection of sculpture by Bernini and paintings by Caravaggio. Upstairs are paintings by Raphael, including *The Deposition,* and Titian's great *Sacred and Profane Love.*

Goethe's father called the villa "the most delicious and remarkable place in the whole of Italy."

OSKAR REINHART COLLECTION, Winterthur, Switzerland

www.roemerholz.ch

Winterthur had more collectors than any other small town in Europe. The greatest of them was Oskar Reinhart, who created two museums, one in his old home, the villa Am Römerholz, for his beloved Impressionist collection. This is one of the most attractive collections of 19th-century painting anywhere, strong on Géricault, Delacroix, Courbet and Daumier, and with superbly chosen examples of Manet, Renoir, Van Gogh and Cezanne. Reinhart devoted his life to the collection, and used to enjoy watching groups of visitors going around while pretending to be the butler.

Sites for Your Eyes

For the truly discerning, these architectural masterpieces are worth a detour

A century ago, landmarks like the Pantheon, Chartres Cathedral and Venice's San Marco's Square were mandatory stops for the educated classes. Today, a similar list might include Frank Gehry's Guggenheim Museum in Bilbao, Spain, and Norman Foster's Gherkin in London. But the most thrilling architectural experiences are apt to occur far from the growing hordes of cultural tourists. Three of them, coincidentally, are in Portugal.

Rem Koolhaas' recently completed Porto concert hall is as potent an expression of contemporary architectural ideas as you are likely to find. Located in Porto, an industrial city in northern Portugal, its chiseled concrete exterior has the hard beauty of a cut diamond. Inside, it is packed with urban energy, its foyers spiraling up to a rooftop belvedere, which offers a sweeping view of the old city.

A short drive north in Braga, **Eduardo Souto de Moura**'s soccer stadium is a sensitive union of natural and man-made forms. The stadium's concrete stands embrace two sides of the field like gently cupped hands. At one end, the stadium is embedded into the side of an abandoned quarry; at the other, it opens up to a view of distant hills.

In the village of Marco de Canavezes, also in Portugal, **Alvaro Siza**'s Santa Maria Church is striking in its simplicity: an unadorned, U-shaped white form resting atop a granite base. But beneath that humble appearance is a work of remarkable subtlety. In front, the tall forms of the baptistery and bell tower frame a small entry court. In back, a cloister leads into a mortuary chapel a level below. An exterior stair joins the two. The sense of being deeply connected to the cycles of life and death—and the humility with which it is conveyed—makes this the most exquisite church built in half a century.

Enric Miralles' Igualada cemetery on the outskirts of Barcelona is equally moving. Built in the shadow of a decrepit industrial neighborhood, the cemetery is conceived as a carefully drawn-out procession that winds its way down into the earth. The path is flanked on either side by heavy concrete retaining walls, their forms embedded with rows of tombs. The descent becomes a haunting metaphor for the relentless march toward death.

In London, **Sir John Soane**'s museum is a more personal kind of mausoleum. Overlooking a lovely London square, the 19th-century house is packed with architectural bric-a-brac the neo-Classical architect collected over the years. The rooms' fragmented pediments and mirrored walls are pictures of architectural eccentricity—the legacy of a fertile creative talent trapped in his own mind.

Finally, two of the most inspiring rooms in America may be the "great work room" in **Frank Lloyd Wright**'s 1936 Johnson Wax building in Racine, Wisconsin, and the interior of **Frank Gehry**'s 2004 Walt Disney Concert Hall in Los Angeles. The slender mushroom-shaped columns, translucent ceiling and vertical bands of glass tubing that envelope Wright's room give it the feel of a gigantic fish tank. Gehry's hall rivals Borromini's Baroque churches in its wonderful play of concave and convex forms. Some visitors have complained about the lack of legroom, but the compactness of the space is part of what makes this an intense social experience—and one of America's greatest public rooms.

—Nicolai Ouroussoff,
chief architecture critic of
the *New York Times*

ARTS

Catching Up on Your Reading

The best books of the 21st century—so far

The century is still young—whether you believe it started in the year 2000 or 2001—so there's still time to read what critics regard as the best fiction and nonfiction of our times. Each year the editors of the *New York Times* select what they regard as the best books of the year—often 10, but in some years fewer. Here are their selections from 2000 to 2005.

In the accompanying boxes you'll find the 📖 NATIONAL BOOK AWARD and ⬤ PULITZER PRIZE winners for the same period. In nonfiction, the N.B.A. honors one nonfiction book; the Pulitzers choose three—one in history, one in biography and autobiography; and one for general non-fiction. In addition, there is an N.B.A. award for Young People's Literature.

2000 FICTION

BEING DEAD *Jim Crace*

Celice and Joseph, both zoologists, are dead in the first paragraph, murdered naked in the midst of sexual fulfillment on a salt dune by the sea. Crace then weaves together three strands of narrative to create a startlingly beautiful vision of life.

BEOWULF: A New Verse Translation *Seamus Heaney.*

Heaney is the most accomplished poet writing in English and a Nobel laureate. In this edition of the translation, Heaney

2000

FICTION
⬤ **Interpreter of Maladies,** *Jhumpa Lahiri*

📖 **In America,** *Susan Sontag*

NONFICTION
⬤ GENERAL NONFICTION
Embracing Defeat: Japan in the Wake of World War II, *John W. Dower*

⬤ HISTORY
Freedom From Fear: The American People in Depression and War, 1929-1945, *David M. Kennedy*

📖 **In the Heart of the Sea: The Tragedy of the Whaleship Essex,** *Nathaniel Philbrick*

⬤ BIOGRAPHY
Vera (Mrs. Vladimir Nabokov), *Stacy Schiff*

POETRY
📖 **Blessing the Boats: New and Selected Poems 1988-2000,** *Lucille Clifton*

⬤ **Repair,** *C. K. Williams*

YOUNG PEOPLE'S LITERATURE
📖 **Homeless Bird,** *Gloria Whelan*

writes an introduction explaining that he decided to give the poem the voice of Northern Irishmen he'd grown up with.

GERTRUDE AND CLAUDIUS *John Updike*

She is too loving and, perhaps more dangerously, too lovable, the young woman in John Updike's novel, whose father offers her, against her wishes, to the older warrior king he admires. But she learns to love her husband, and loves her son too uncritically.

THE HUMAN STAIN *Philip Roth*

Coleman Silk, the central character in Philip Roth's novel, may be the most interesting person Roth has ever invented—a black man of such light hue that he decided simply to pass for white, left his entire family behind and went into the world as a Jew who became a distinguished classicist.

2000 NONFICTION

GENOME: The Autobiography of a Species in 23 Chapters *Matt Ridley*

Ridley's book is a jargon-free excursion of intellectual discovery that will carry any reader along its tour of exciting stories structured to help us understand in everyday terms the revelations about genetic evolution that have come to light in the last few decades.

A HEARTBREAKING WORK OF STAGGERING GENIUS *Dave Eggers*

When Eggers was 21, both of his parents died within 32 days, leaving him the accidental parent of his 8-year-old brother. He sold the family's suburban Chicago home, and the two set out for San Francisco for a life that he says was a "campaign of distraction" and "magic tricks."

ONE PALESTINE, COMPLETE: Jews And Arabs Under The British Mandate *Tom Segev*

Probably the best overall history of the period when Britain ruled the Holy Land under the League of Nations mandate.

RIMBAUD *Graham Robb*

Arthur Rimbaud stopped writing verse before he was 20, and bothered to publish only one volume of his work before he died at 37. Robb has produced the best biography of Rimbaud.

WAY OUT THERE IN THE BLUE: Reagan, Star Wars and the End of the Cold War *Frances FitzGerald*

FitzGerald explains Ronald Reagan's Strategic Defense Initiative (Star Wars) better than anyone ever has. One of her points is that no one ever did understand Star Wars—not its scientific champions, not its Congressional promoters and certainly not Reagan.

2001 FICTION

WHITE TEETH *Zadie Smith*

The story is centered on members of two families, one British and one Bengali, all of whom are

---

2001

FICTION
● The Amazing Adventures of Kavalier & Clay, *Michael Chabon*
📖 The Corrections, *Jonathan Franzen*

NONFICTION
● GENERAL NONFICTION
Hirohito and the Making of Modern Japan, *Herbert P. Bix*
● HISTORY
Founding Brothers: The Revolutionary Generation, *Joseph J. Ellis*
● BIOGRAPHY
W.E.B. Du Bois: The Fight for Equality and the American Century, 1919-1963, *David Levering Lewis*
📖 **The Noonday Demon: An Atlas of Depression,** *Andrew Solomon*

POETRY
📖 **Poems Seven: New and Complete Poetry,** *Alan Dugan*
● **Different Hours,** *Stephen Dunn*

YOUNG PEOPLE'S LITERATURE
📖 **True Believer,** *Virginia Euwer Wolff*

---

a bit ridiculous in their own ways, as are all the other characters who pop up in Smith's magnificent first novel.

AUSTERLITZ *W. G. Sebald*

Memory is moral treachery in the works of W. G. Sebald, and in none is it more threatening than in this one.

THE CORRECTIONS *Jonathan Franzen*

The important thing to know about Franzen's novel is that you can ignore all the literary fireworks and thoroughly enjoy its people.

HATESHIP, FRIENDSHIP, COURTSHIP, LOVESHIP, MARRIAGE: Stories *Alice Munro*

As Alice Munro gets older, the challenges faced by her characters get darker—in this collection cancer, Alzheimer's disease, suicide to escape debilitation, among others.

JOHN HENRY DAYS *Colson Whitehead*

The ambition of Whitehead's second novel is to define the interior crisis of manhood in terms of the entire pop-mad consumer society, and it succeeds.

TRUE HISTORY OF THE KELLY GANG *Peter Carey*

Carey, widely recognized as one of the most engaging historical novelists alive, surpasses himself in this novel about the Australian version of Jesse James.

ARTS

2001 NONFICTION

BORROWED FINERY: A Memoir *Paula Fox*

Paula Fox's children's books have been staples for 35 years, and her adult fiction has had a rousing revival recently. But nothing she has done has prepared her readers for this fragmentary memoir.

JOHN ADAMS *David McCullough*

A gentler, more quiet John Adams. The story of his devotion to his wife, Abigail, and hers to him, is the affecting centerpiece of McCullough's biography.

THE METAPHYSICAL CLUB *Louis Menand*

The club was a short-lived affair begun in Cambridge, Mass., in 1872, but the ideas espoused by three members and one of their disciples became foundations of American thought in the 20th century.

UNCLE TUNGSTEN: Memories of a Chemical Boyhood *Oliver Sacks*

This account of Sack's early years not only recreates a very large extended family of highly individual and eccentric adults who fascinated, repelled and inspired him in Britain in the 1930's and 40's, but focuses on his youthful infatuation with chemistry.

2002 FICTION

ATONEMENT *Ian McEwan*

This novel is shaped as a triptych, each part changing our perspective as it opens up.

2002

FICTION

📖 **Three Junes,** *Julia Glass*

● **Empire Falls,** *Richard Russo*

NONFICTION

📖 **Master of the Senate: The Years of Lyndon Johnson,** *Robert A. Caro*

● BIOGRAPHY

John Adams, *David McCullough*

● GENERAL NONFICTION

Carry Me Home: Birmingham, Alabama, the Climactic Battle of the Civil Rights Revolution, *Diane McWhorter*

● HISTORY

The Metaphysical Club: A Story of Ideas in America, *Louis Menand*

POETRY

● **Practical Gods,** *Carl Dennis*

📖 **In the Next Galaxy,** *Ruth Stone*

YOUNG PEOPLE'S LITERATURE

📖 **The House of the Scorpion,** *Nancy Farmer*

MIDDLESEX *Jeffrey Eugenides*

This story is epic—in spirit, scope and definitely in organization. Jeffrey Eugenides dares to base the plot on genetic theory, so if Homer is a distant ancestor, Darwin is another.

ROSCOE *William Kennedy*

Is this, the seventh novel in William Kennedy's Albany cycle, a valedictory? It has that feeling. Like Roscoe Conway, its protagonist, it is haunted by history.

2002 NONFICTION

ANTHONY BLUNT: His Lives *Miranda Carter*

Carter's biography of Anthony Blunt is more interesting than the man. For three decades the Richelieu of art history in Britain, maker and breaker of reputations, curator of the queen's pictures and the premier teacher of scholars and gallery directors, Blunt was also, for almost 20 years, a Soviet spy

BAD BLOOD *Lorna Sage*

Lorna Sage, in 2001, was a literary critic of such quick psychological penetration that one had to wonder where it came from. Now we know. While her father was at war in the 1940's, she and her mother lived with the mother's parents in a Welsh village.

PARIS 1919: Six Months That Changed the World *Margaret MacMillan*

The history of the 1919 Paris peace talks following World War I is a blueprint of the political and social upheavals bedeviling the planet now.

SEEING IN THE DARK: How Backyard Stargazers Are Probing Deep Space and Guarding Earth from Interplanetary Peril *Timothy Ferris*

In his earlier book *The Whole Shebang,* Ferris gave us an account of the entire range of astronomy and astrophysics. *Seeing in the Dark* is as big a book on the same matter, but more delightful because it celebrates the experiences of a growing army of amateurs.

2003 FICTION

BRICK LANE *Monica Ali*

Leaving home is a journey without end in this novel about Bangladeshi immigrants in London's East End.

DROP CITY *T. Coraghessan Boyle*

The debris left scattered up the entire West Coast of North America in this novel is as frightening and spectacular as any he's ever dropped on his readers.

THE FORTRESS OF SOLITUDE *Jonathan Lethem*

Everyone seeks his own Garden of Eden, but who would think to find it in a single block of Boerum Hill, Brooklyn, in the 1970's, when New York City was going down the tubes.

THE KNOWN WORLD *Edward P. Jones*

What makes this novel so startling is that the situation Jones

---

2003

FICTION
● **Middlesex,** *Jeffrey Eugenides*
📖 **The Great Fire**, *Shirley Hazzard*

NONFICTION
● HISTORY
An Army at Dawn: The War in North Africa, 1942-1943, *Rick Atkinson*
● BIOGRAPHY
Master of the Senate, *Robert A. Caro*
📖 **Waiting for Snow in Havana: Confessions of a Cuban Boy,** *Carlos Eire*
● GENERAL NONFICTION
"A Problem from Hell:" America and the Age of Genocide, *Samantha Power*

POETRY
● **Moy Sand and Gravel,** *Paul Muldoon*
📖 **The Singing**, *C. K. Williams*

YOUNG PEOPLE'S LITERATURE
📖 **The Canning Season,** *Polly Horvath*

---

imagines was reality in parts of this country in the 1850's: there were more than a few black slave owners and a few were pretty well heeled.

2003 NONFICTION

THE BOUNTY: The True Story of the Mutiny on the Bounty *Caroline Alexander*

Alexander's subtitle simply means she sets out to prove that we have never understood the Fletcher Christian who really led a mutiny on the Bounty in 1798, and Captain Bligh and the 18 crewmen who sailed 3,600 miles of the South Pacific after the mutineers tossed them overboard.

KHRUSHCHEV: The Man and His Era *William Taubman*

Taubman presents this sweeping history of the first 47 years of the Communist era, and Khrushchev's explosive, vulgar, warm character, unobtrusively but not without measured judgments.

LIVING TO TELL THE TALE *Gabriel García Márquez. Translated by Edith Grossman*

This memoir takes the author to his early 20's, before he leaves his country as it sinks into violence.

RANDOM FAMILY: Love, Drugs, Trouble and Coming of Age in the Bronx *Adrian Nicole LeBlanc*

LeBlanc focuses on two Puerto Rican girls: one has a baby by one man and twins by his brother before she's 19, and

ARTS

then ties up with a heroin kingpin before going to prison; the other has two babies by the first girl's half brother and three more by three other men.

SAMUEL PEPYS: The Unequalled Self *Claire Tomalin*

Tomalin rescues Pepys from his own diary, and a much larger figure he is outside it.

2004 FICTION

GILEAD *Marilynne Robinson*

This grave, lucid, luminously spiritual novel about fathers and sons reaches back to the abolitionist movement and forward into the 1950's.

THE MASTER *Colm Toibin*

A novel about Henry James, his life and art—beautifully written, deeply pondered, startlingly un-Jamesian.

THE PLOT AGAINST AMERICA *Philip Roth*

An ingenious "anti-historical" novel set during World War II. Charles Lindbergh is elected president on an isolationist platform, and a Jewish family in Newark suffers the consequences.

RUNAWAY *Alice Munro*

Her 11th collection of short stories about people, often women living in rural Ontario, whose vivid, unremarkable lives are rendered with almost Tolstoyan resonance.

2004

FICTION
● **The Known World**, *Edward P. Jones*
📖 **The News from Paraguay**, *Lily Tuck*

NONFICTION
● GENERAL NONFICTION
Gulag: A History, *Anne Applebaum*

📖 **Arc of Justice: A Saga of Race, Civil Rights, and Murder in the Jazz Age**, *Kevin Boyle*

● HISTORY
A Nation Under Our Feet: Black Political Struggles in the Rural South from Slavery to the Great Migration, *Steven Hahn*

● BIOGRAPHY
Khrushchev: The Man and His Era, *William Taubman*

POETRY
📖 **Door in the Mountain: New and Collected Poems, 1965-2003**, *Jean Valentine*
● **Walking to Martha's Vineyard**, *Franz Wright*

YOUNG PEOPLE'S LITERATURE
📖 **Godless**, *Pete Hautman*

SNOW *Orhan Pamuk*

The forces of secular and Islamic Turkey collide in this complex and superbly orchestrated novel, begun before 9/11 and completed shortly thereafter.

WAR TRASH *Ha Jin*

A powerfully apposite moral fable whose suffering hero passes from delusion to clarity as a Chinese P.O.W. in Korea.

2004 NONFICTION

ALEXANDER HAMILTON *Ron Chernow*

An exemplary biography—broad in scope, finely detailed—of the founder who gave America capitalism and nationalism.

CHRONICLES: Volume One *Bob Dylan*

A memoir—idiosyncratic and revelatory—by the peerless singer-songwriter who journeyed from the heartland to conquer the Greenwich Village music scene of the 1960's.

WASHINGTON"S CROSSING *David Hackett Fischer*

An impressively researched narrative about the Revolutionary War that highlights the Battle of Trenton.

WILL IN THE WORLD: How Shakespeare Became Shakespeare *Stephen Greenblatt*

Scholarship, speculation and close reading combine in a lively study that gives shape to the life, and context to the work.

2005 FICTION

KAFKA ON THE SHORE *Haruki Murakami*

This graceful and dreamily cerebral novel, translated from the Japanese, tells two stories—that of a boy fleeing an Oedipal prophecy, and that of a witless old man who can talk to cats—and is the work of a powerfully confident writer.

ON BEAUTY *Zadie Smith*

In her vibrant book, a cultural politics novel set in a place like Harvard, the author brings everything to the table: a crisp intellect, a lovely wit and enormous sympathy for the men, women and children who populate her story.

PREP *Curtis Sittenfeld*

This is a calm and memorably incisive first novel, about a scholarship girl who heads east to attend an elite prep school and has plenty to say about class, race and character.

SATURDAY *Ian McEwan*

This astringent novel traces a day in the life of an English neurosurgeon who comes face to face with senseless violence. It's as carefully constructed as anything McEwan has written.

VERONICA *Mary Gaitskill*

This mesmerizingly dark novel is narrated by a former Paris model who is now sick and poor; her ruminations on beauty and cruelty have clarity and an uncanny bite.

2005

FICTION
● **Gilead,** *Marilynne Robinson*
📖 **Europe Central,** *William T. Vollmann*

NONFICTION
● GENERAL NONFICTION
Ghost Wars, *Steve Coll*
📖 **The Year of Magical Thinking,** *Joan Didion*
● HISTORY
Washington's Crossing, *David Hackett Fischer*
● BIOGRAPHY
De Kooning: An American Master, *Mark Stevens and Annalyn Swan*

POETRY
● **Delights & Shadows,** *Ted Kooser*
📖 **Migration: New and Selected Poems,** *W. S. Merwin*

YOUNG PEOPLE'S LITERATURE
📖 **The Penderwicks: A Summer Tale of Four Sisters, Two Rabbits and a Very Interesting Boy,** *Jeanne Birdsall*

2005 NONFICTION

THE ASSASSINS' GATE: America in Iraq *George Packer*

A comprehensive look at the largest foreign policy gamble in a generation, by a *New Yorker* reporter who traces the full arc of the war, from the pre-invasion debate through the action on the ground.

DE KOONING: An American Master *Mark Stevens and Annalyn Swan*

A sweeping biography, impressively researched and absorbingly written, of the charismatic immigrant who stood at the vortex of mid-20th-century American art.

THE LOST PAINTING *Jonathan Harr*

This gripping narrative, populated with a beguiling cast of scholars, historians, art restorers and aging nobles, records the search for Caravaggio's *Taking of Christ,* painted in 1602 and rediscovered in 1990.

POSTWAR: A History of Europe Since 1945 *Tony Judt*

Judt's massive, learned, brilliantly detailed account of Europe's recovery from the wreckage of World War II.

THE YEAR OF MAGICAL THINKING *Joan Didion*

A prose master's harrowing yet exhilarating memoir of a year riven by sudden death (her husband's) and mortal illness (their only child's).

ARTS

Getting Lost in the Stacks

The favorite libraries of a noted bibliophile

Asking Vartan Gregorian to name his favorite libraries is like asking him to list his favorite colors. "The world is full of a myriad of beautiful hues, and there are hundreds of wonderful libraries," says Gregorian, president of the Carnegie Corporation of New York and former president of Brown University. The following "is not an objective list of great institutions," says Gregorian, who once headed the New York Public Library. "It is more a personal reflection" on some of his favorite libraries. Here are his selections and commentary:

The New York Public Library (www.nypl.org). The N.Y.P.L. is in a class by itself in the sheer size and diversity of its holdings, and because of its writers' room where so many major works of both fiction and nonfiction were written, from Robert Caro's

multivolume biography of Lyndon Johnson to Rachel Carson's *Silent Spring*.

The Library of Congress (www.loc.gov). No country in the world boasts a greater national library, and what a glory it is for a nation barely 200 years old that did not have the patronage of an aristocracy to shape its beginnings.

The British Library (www.bl.uk). This was, is and hopefully will remain one of the great libraries of the world.

The Bibliothèque Nationale (www.bnf.fr). Unlike our Library of Congress, the Bibliothèque Nationale in Paris began as a royal collection as early as the 15th century, and one can hardly imagine the depth and variety of its holdings.

The Vatican Library (bav.vatican.va), with its universal holdings on every possible topic, ranks as one of the great libraries in the world.

University libraries. The greatest university library in the U.S. is **Harvard's Widener Library** (www.harvard.edu), which along with its sister libraries at Harvard, is a universe apart. Some of the public university libraries are also spectacular, such as the one at the **University of Illinois in Urbana** (www.library.uiuc.edu), which is, with about 10 million books, the sixth largest library in the U.S. after the Library of Congress, Harvard, the N.Y.P.L., Yale, and Queens' Borough Public Library. At Oxford is the **Bodleian Library** (www.bodley.ox.ac.uk), and in Cambridge, the **King's College Library** (www.kings.cam.ac.uk/library).

Finally, there are our town and small city libraries. Surely it was one of the greatest philanthropic acts of all time that Andrew Carnegie built some 1,600 public libraries in the U.S. The tradition of making reading and research material available easily and freely continues. One can hardly overestimate their value in the success of this country.

❓ EXPERT ANSWER

Beloved American Novels

Q. What is the best work of American fiction of the last 25 years?

In 2006, the *New York Times Book Review* asked a couple of hundred prominent writers, critics, editors and other literary sages, to identify "the single best work of American fiction published in the last 25 years." The results:

THE WINNER: Beloved, *Toni Morrison* (1987)

THE RUNNERS-UP:

Underworld, *Don DeLillo* (1997)

Blood Meridian, *Cormac McCarthy* (1985)

Rabbit Angstrom: The Four Novels, *John Updike* **Rabbit, Run** (1960) **Rabbit Redux** (1971) **Rabbit Is Rich** (1981) **Rabbit at Rest** (1990)

American Pastoral, *Philip Roth* (1997)

CHAPTER **11**

EVERYDAY SCIENCE

Weather & Geology   710

FORECASTING·710: *Crickets are a poor man's thermometer* •
Weather watching • *Know which way the wind blows* • *Be
your own forecaster* • *Why windchill matters* • *Treating
hypothermia* • *Looking beyond the clouds* **EARTH
SCIENCE·717:** *How to read rocks* • *Common minerals and their uses* • *Predicting
earthquakes* • *Earthquake-prone zones* • *The magnitude of tremors*

Stars & Tides   722

THE STARS & PLANETS·722: *The night sky: stargazing with the naked eye*
• *Stars and constellations* • *Our closest stellar neighbors* • *A portrait of
the planets* • *What's a planet, anyway?* • *Stargazing made easy* **THE SUN
& MOON·731:** *Here comes the sun* • *Solar eclipses* • *Lunar eclipses*
• *Mountains on the Moon* • *Phases of the moon* **STAR TALK·736:** *How to talk like an
astronomer* • *What the stars say about you* **THE TIDES·742** *A beachgoer's guide to the tides*

Times & Dates   744

ABOUT TIME·744: *A very brief history of time* • *A quick glance at the
clock* • *How to tell time like a sailor* **TIME ZONES·746** *Spring ahead, fall
back* • *When it's lunchtime in New York: international zones* **CALENDAR
DATES·748:** *The perpetual calendar* • *Reasons to celebrate: holidays around
the world* • *Why are there leap years?* • *New Year's resolutions* **ANCIENT
TIMES·759:** *Chinese zodiac* • *How to tell geologic time*

Figures & Formulas   762

WEIGHTS & MEASURES·762: *Measurements to fit a king* • *U.S. customary units* • *Temperature
conversions* • *Metric units* • *The long and short of clothing sizes* • *Converting U.S. units to
metric units and vice versa* • *Special weights & measurements* • *Bits, bytes and beyond* •
Household measures **CHEMISTRY & MATH·769:** *The periodic table of elements* • *Placing
math on a timeline* • *Algebra* • *Roman numerals* • *Fractions and decimals* **GEOMETRY·772:**
Understanding angles and triangles • *Quadrilaterals and other polygons* • *Solids*

Weather & Geology

Crickets Are a Poor Man's Thermometer

The science behind farmers' and sailors' maxims

Weather folklore has been passed down through the ages by mariners and farmers who relied on their own observations of astronomical events, animal behaviors and atmospheric changes to predict upcoming weather. Today, while the average person's ability to observe the natural world has declined, much of the folklore still exists, partly because of a psychological yearning to keep in touch with a time when humans seemed more in tune with their environment. Here, senior meteorology lecturer Mark Wysocki of Cornell University helps discern what of today's remaining weather lore is still viable.

 TIMELY TIPS

When to Believe the Weatherman

✔ **Predicting temperature accurately is more difficult in the cool season than in the summer.** That's because weather systems are stronger and move quickly in the winter, leading to greater temperature variability.

✔ **In predicting precipitation, forecasts generally are less accurate when the weather is warm.** Most precipitation in the warm season comes from showers and thunderstorms, which occur randomly, cover small areas, and don't last long. In winter, precipitation usually results from weather systems that cover larger areas and last many hours or days, and thus is easier to predict.

• **Red sky at night, sailors delight. Red sky in the morning, sailors take warning.** Much of the weather folklore based on observations of atmospheric phenomena is a fairly good predictor of short-range weather changes. In the midlatitude regions, the general flow of storm systems follows the jet stream from west to east. The red color at night is due to the reflection of the red colors from the sun as it lowers in the western sky. This signals that the jet stream has pushed the storm systems out of your area. If clouds appear red in the morning, this means that the sun is rising in clear skies to the east with clouds approaching from the west, indicating the storm system is to your west and moving your way.

• **Mackerel clouds in the sky, expect more wet than dry.** This is another good example of accurate weather folklore based on atmospheric observations. Mackerel clouds refer to cirrocumulus clouds that appear pearly white with scaly formations akin to the scales on a fish. Ancient mariners knew that these clouds presaged the approach of a warm front that would produce rain or snow within the next 12 to 18 hours.

• **When there is a halo around the moon, the weather will be cold and rough.** The halo is generated by cirrostratus clouds up to 20,000 feet up in the atmosphere. These clouds cover large areas with a uniform thickness of ice crystals, which are responsible for many optical wonders. A halo around the moon generally means stormy weather within the next 24 hours.

• **If bees stay at home, rain will soon come.** This folklore is comparable to stories that associate

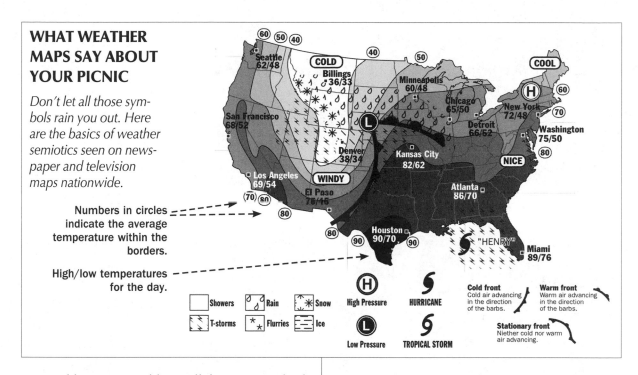

WHAT WEATHER MAPS SAY ABOUT YOUR PICNIC

Don't let all those symbols rain you out. Here are the basics of weather semiotics seen on newspaper and television maps nationwide.

Numbers in circles indicate the average temperature within the borders.

High/low temperatures for the day.

approaching storms with ants lining up to go back to their nest, cows lying down in a field and frogs singing more than usual. These examples are difficult to prove or disprove, because scientists can't isolate what in the environment would be causing these behaviors. But beekeepers swear by the ability of their bees to predict rain. With cows, the question remains, "If 25 cows are lying down in a field and 25 are standing, does this mean there's a 50 percent chance of rain?"

• **Crickets are a poor man's thermometer.** Counting the chirps of a cricket is an accurate way of determining temperatures above 40 degrees Fahrenheit. Below 40 degrees, a cricket's metabolism is too slow. To get the current air temperature within one degree Fahrenheit, count the number of chirps in a 14-second period and then add 40 to this number.

• **When hornets build their nest close to the ground, expect a hard winter.** Folklore that deals with animals and long-term weather forecasts is

generally false. If people observed the hornet's activities over a long period of time, they would find no correlation between the hornet's behavior and seasonal forecasts. The same is true for folklore that links a squirrel's very bushy tail or a large black band on a wooly-bear caterpillar with an upcoming severe winter.

• **When smoke hangs low, a storm is approaching.** The phenomenon of smoke hanging low is attributable to low-pressure systems that cause the atmosphere to be unstable and can signal the approach of stormy weather. However, sometimes near lakes and in valleys, local air circulation can dominate the larger-scale circulation that can give a false reading.

• **The air smells sweet before a storm.** Science definitely has an explanation for this folklore. Before a storm, lower pressure predominates, which causes plants' stomatic openings to enlarge and emit more gases, including aromatic ones.

SCIENCE

INSIDE INFO

WEATHER WATCHING: SUNNY OR COLD? WINDY OR WET?

A breakdown of recent weather patterns in selected major American cities

| City | Average annual sunshine (%) | Mean days below freezing | AVERAGE ANNUAL TEMPERATURE (F) | | Average annual rain (in.) | AVERAGE RELATIVE HUMIDITY (%) | | | | | |
| | | | | | | Annual | | January | | July | |
			High	Low		a.m.	p.m.	a.m.	p.m.	a.m.	p.m.
Albany, N.Y.	52	14.9	58.1	36.6	36.17	79	57	76	63	84	55
Albuquerque, N.M.	76	11.9	70.1	42.2	8.88	60	29	70	40	60	27
Atlanta, Ga.	61	5.3	71.2	51.3	50.77	77	56	74	59	85	60
Atlantic City, N.J.	56	11.0	63.2	42.8	40.29	82	56	76	58	87	57
Baltimore, Md.	57	9.7	65.0	45.2	40.70	75	54	69	57	81	53
Bismarck, N.D.	59	18.6	53.8	29.4	15.47	74	56	75	66	74	46
Boise, Idaho	64	12.4	62.8	39.1	12.11	69	43	81	70	54	21
Boston, Mass.	58	9.8	59.0	43.6	41.51	72	58	65	57	77	56
Buffalo, N.Y.	49	13.2	55.8	39.5	38.58	79	63	77	72	79	55
Burlington, Vt.	49	15.5	54.0	35.2	34.47	77	59	70	63	82	53
Charleston, W.V.	40	10.0	65.8	44.2	42.53	79	56	74	63	90	60
Charlotte, N.C.	63	6.6	70.4	49.7	43.09	76	54	72	56	83	57
Cheyenne, Wyo.	65	17.2	58.0	33.2	14.40	65	44	57	50	70	35
Chicago, Ill.	54	13.3	58.6	39.5	35.82	77	60	75	67	79	56
Cincinnati, Ohio	52	10.8	63.2	43.2	41.33	77	59	75	67	83	57
Cleveland, Ohio	49	12.3	58.7	40.5	36.63	77	62	75	69	81	57
Columbia, S.C.	64	6.0	75.1	50.9	49.91	83	51	78	54	87	54
Columbus, Ohio	49	11.9	61.2	41.6	38.09	77	59	74	67	82	56
Concord, N.H.	54	17.3	57.0	33.1	36.37	82	54	74	58	90	51
Dallas-Fort Worth, Texas	63	4.0	76.3	54.6	33.70	72	56	73	60	67	49
Denver, Colo.	70	15.7	64.2	36.2	15.40	67	40	63	49	68	34
Des Moines, Iowa	59	13.5	59.8	40.0	33.12	75	60	74	67	76	57
Detroit, Mich.	53	13.6	58.1	39.0	32.62	79	60	78	69	81	53
Duluth, Minn.	52	18.5	47.9	29.0	30.0	77	63	74	70	82	59
El Paso, Texas	84	6.5	77.5	49.0	8.81	57	28	66	35	63	30
Great Falls, Mont.	61	15.7	56.4	33.1	15.21	67	45	66	60	66	29
Hartford, Conn.	56	13.5	60.2	39.5	44.14	76	52	69	56	82	51
Honolulu, Hawaii	69	0	84.4	70.0	22.02	76	56	81	61	73	51
Houston, Texas	56	2.1	78.6	57.3	46.07	86	60	82	64	86	58
Indianapolis, Ind.	55	11.8	62.1	42.4	39.94	80	62	78	70	84	59
Jackson, Miss.	60	5.0	76.4	52.0	55.37	87	58	84	65	90	59
Jacksonville, Fla.	63	1.5	78.9	57.1	51.32	86	56	85	57	88	58
Juneau, Alaska	30	14.1	46.9	34.1	54.31	86	73	81	77	87	70
Kansas City, Mo.	62	11.0	63.6	43.7	37.62	74	59	72	63	75	56
Little Rock, Ark.	62	6.0	72.5	51.0	50.86	79	57	76	61	83	56
Los Angeles, Calif.	73	0	70.4	55.5	12.01	79	64	70	59	86	68
Louisville, Ky.	56	8.9	66.0	46.0	44.39	76	58	72	64	81	58
Memphis, Tenn.	64	5.7	72.1	52.4	52.10	76	57	75	63	79	57
Miami, Fla.	72	0	82.8	69.0	55.91	81	61	81	59	82	63
Milwaukee, Wis.	54	14.1	54.3	37.9	32.93	78	64	75	68	80	61
Minn.-St. Paul, Minn.	58	15.6	54.3	35.3	28.32	73	60	72	67	74	54
Mobile, Ala.	59	2.2	77.4	57.4	63.96	83	57	79	61	87	60

City	Average annual sunshine (%)	Mean days below freezing	AVERAGE ANNUAL TEMPERATURE (F)		Average annual rain (in.)	AVERAGE RELATIVE HUMIDITY (%)					
						Annual		January		July	
			High	Low		a.m.	p.m.	a.m.	p.m.	a.m.	p.m.
Nashville, Tenn.	56	7.6	69.8	48.4	47.30	79	57	75	63	85	57
New Orleans, La.	59	1.3	77.6	58.5	61.88	85	63	82	66	89	66
New York, N.Y.	58	7.9	62.3	47.4	47.25	70	56	65	60	74	55
Norfolk, Va.	61	5.4	67.8	50.6	44.64	78	57	72	59	84	59
Oklahoma City, Okla.	NA	7.7	71.1	48.8	33.36	72	54	72	59	70	49
Omaha, Neb.	60	14.1	61.5	39.5	29.86	76	59	75	65	78	57
Peoria, Ill.	57	12.9	60.4	41.0	36.25	79	62	78	68	82	59
Philadelphia, Pa.	56	9.7	63.4	45.1	41.41	76	55	71	59	81	54
Phoenix, Ariz.	86	0.8	85.9	59.3	7.66	51	23	66	32	45	20
Pittsburgh, Pa.	40	12.3	59.9	40.7	30.85	75	57	73	65	80	54
Portland, Maine	57	15.7	54.9	35.8	44.34	82	59	74	60	89	59
Portland, Ore.	48	4.3	62.6	44.5	36.30	86	60	86	75	82	45
Providence, R.I.	58	11.8	59.8	41.0	45.53	76	55	69	56	83	56
Raleigh, N.C.	59	7.8	70.1	48.4	41.43	80	54	73	55	88	58
Reno, Nev.	79	17.4	66.8	34.7	7.53	70	31	79	50	63	18
Richmond, Va.	62	8.5	68.8	46.6	43.16	82	53	77	57	88	56
Sacramento, Calif.	78	1.7	73.5	48.1	17.52	82	45	90	70	76	28
Salt Lake City, Utah	66	12.5	63.6	40.3	16.18	67	43	79	69	52	22
San Diego, Calif.	68	0	70.8	57.6	9.90	76	62	70	56	82	66
San Francisco, Calif.	NA	0.2	65.2	49.0	19.70	84	62	86	66	86	59
San Juan, P.R.	66	0	86.4	74.0	52.34	83	65	82	64	84	67
Sault Ste. Marie, Mich.	47	18.1	49.6	29.8	34.23	85	67	81	75	90	61
Seattle-Tacoma, Wash.	46	3.1	59.4	44.6	37.19	83	62	81	74	82	49
Sioux Falls, S.D.	63	16.8	56.8	34.2	23.86	76	60	75	68	75	53
St. Louis, Mo.	57	10.0	65.4	46.7	37.51	76	59	77	66	77	56
Washington, D.C.	56	7.0	66.9	49.2	38.63	72	53	67	55	77	53
Wichita, Kan.	65	11.1	67.4	45.0	29.33	73	55	76	63	67	48
Wilmington, Del.	NA	10.0	63.6	44.8	40.84	78	55	73	60	83	54

• When human hair becomes limp, rain is near. Human hair—especially blond hair—becomes thicker and longer when exposed to increases in humidity, which sometimes means rain is near. In fact, early hygrometers designed to determine the moisture content of the air relied on measuring the changes in the length of human hair.

• Sinus and joint pain signals stormy weather. This folklore, at least for arthritis sufferers, has been proved to signal rapid changes in the weather. Pressure changes, the cause of the pain, signal the unstable atmospheric conditions that typically precede a storm.

Know Which Way the Wind Blows

Forecast the weather by gauging changes in atmospheric pressure

With a simple aneroid barometer, available at a local hardware store or marine supply center, you can make fairly accurate short-range weather predictions for as little as $20. Generally, when the barometer is high and rising, it means high pressure is approaching. High pressure systems typically are associated with fair weather—light and variable winds, dry air and temperatures below seasonal averages. When the barometer is low and falling, it typically means

SCIENCE

BE YOUR OWN FORECASTER
Basic barometer reading for amateur meteorologists

Barometer reduced to sea level	Wind direction	Character of weather indicated
30.10 to 30.20 and steady	SW→NW	*Fair, slight temperature changes for one to two days.*
30.10 to 30.20 and rising rapidly	SW→NW	*Fair, followed within two days by warmer air and rain.*
30.10 to 30.20 and falling slowly	SW→NW	*Warmer with rain in 24 to 36 hours.*
30.10 to 30.20 and falling rapidly	SW→NW	*Warmer with rain in 18 to 24 hours.*
30.20 and above and stationary	SW→NW	*Continued fair with no decided temperature change.*
30.20 and above and falling slowly	SW→NW	*Slowly rising temperature and fair for two days.*
30.10 to 30.20 and falling slowly	S→SE	*Rain within 24 hours.*
30.10 to 30.20 and falling rapidly	S→SE	*Wind increasing in force with rain within 12 to 24 hrs.*
30.10 to 30.20 and falling slowly	SE→NE	*Increasing wind with rain within 12 hours.*
30.10 and above and falling slowly	E→NE	*In summer with light winds, rain may not fall for several days. In winter, rain within 24 hours.*
30.10 and above and falling rapidly	E→NE	*In summer, rain probable in 12 to 24 hours. In winter rain or snow, increasing winds will often set in.*
30 or below and falling slowly	SE→NE	*Rain will continue one to two days.*
30 or below and falling rapidly	SE→NE	*Rain with high wind, followed within 24 hours by clearing and cooler.*
30 or below and rising slowly	S→SW	*Clearing in a few hours, continued fair for some days.*
29.80 or below and falling rapidly	S→E	*Severe storm of wind and rain or snow imminent, followed within 24 hours by clearing and colder.*
29.80 or below and falling rapidly	E→N	*Severe northeast gales and heavy rain or snow, followed in winter by a cold wave.*
29.80 or below and rising rapidly	Going→W	*Clearing and colder.*

WHEN A FINGER TO THE WIND WON'T WORK
The Beaufort Scale of Wind Force can help you estimate wind speed from simple observations.
It also gives the basis for converting the wind descriptions used in weather reports to wind speed
equivalents, and vice versa.

Wind speed (mph)	Beaufort number	Wind effect on land	Official description
Less than 1	0	*Calm; smoke rises vertically.*	LIGHT
1 to 3	1	*Wind direction is seen in direction of smoke but is not revealed by weather vane.*	LIGHT
4 to 7	2	*Wind can be felt on face; leaves rustle; wind vane moves.*	LIGHT
8 to 12	3	*Leaves, small twigs in motion; wind extends light flag.*	GENTLE
13 to 18	4	*Wind raises dust, loose papers. Small branches move.*	MODERATE
19 to 24	5	*Small trees with leaves begin to sway; crested wavelets appear on inland waters.*	FRESH
25 to 31	6	*Large branches move; telegraph wires whistle; umbrellas become difficult to control.*	STRONG
32 to 38	7	*Whole trees sway; walking into the wind becomes difficult.*	STRONG
39 to 46	8	*Twigs break off trees; cars veer in roads.*	STRONG
47 to 54	9	*Slight structural damage occurs; roof slates may blow away.*	STRONG
55 to 63	10	*Trees uprooted; considerable structural damage caused.*	WHOLE GALE
64 to 72	11	*Widespread damage is caused.*	WHOLE GALE
73 or more	12	*Widespread damage is caused.*	HURRICANE

low pressure is on the way. Low-pressure systems tend to bring inclement weather—strong winds, high humidity clouds and storm fronts.

An aneroid barometer has one pointer, similar to the hand on a clock, which measures atmospheric pressure in inches of mercury and another pointer which is used to reference pressure changes. Rising pressure causes the reading pointer to move clockwise, while falling pressure causes it to move counterclockwise.

Once or twice a day, the reference pointer should be placed to correspond with the reading pointer. Over the course of the day, you can track pressure changes by noting how the reading pointer moves in relation to the reference hand.

To ensure accurate readings, aneroid barometers, and even some electronic ones, occasionally need to be calibrated. A call to the local branch of the Weather Service or listening to the weather report on TV provides the current pressure adjusted to what it would read at sea level. Adjustments should be made on days with settled winds, which usually indicate the pressure is changing slowly.

A useful forecasting tool for amateur meteorologists is the chart on the facing page, which bases its weather predictions on barometric changes and wind direction. However, meteorologists caution that these are general rules that don't hold true for all locations and situations. For example, west winds off the Great Lakes can bring terrible lake-effect snows even when the barometer is high. Similarly, in the Northeast near the Atlantic Ocean, a sea breeze can bring cooler air, clouds, drizzle and fog when the pressure is high.

Why Windchill Matters

Your body loses heat at a faster rate when cold winds blow

Whether you're schussing down the slopes, shoveling the drive or simply walking to work, you know that air temperature is one thing and the temperature it "feels like" out there is another. On cold, blustery days, your body may feel far colder than the mercury warrants. That's because body heat loss is directly proportionate to the amount of body surface that you expose to the environment. So, as

---

 TIMELY TIPS

Hurricanes: Stormy Weather Ahead

It may be time to buy a better raincoat. Ever since Hurricane Katrina devasted New Orleans and much of the Gulf Coast in 2005, forecasters have been warning that a period of intense storms could continue for years to come. The Atlantic Ocean is in a cycle of frenetic hurricane activity that started a decade ago, In 2005, there were more than 26 named storms—more than any other season since the National Oceanic and Atmospheric Administration began keeping records in the mid-1880's.

Jack Beven, a hurricane specialist with the National Hurricane Center in Miami, believes that the active storm period, which is the result of favorable wind patterns, higher sea surface temperatures and other conditions, could last up to 40 years.

Hurricanes do not usually occur until August, even though the season officially begins on June 1. In 2005, however, Tropical Storm Arlene soaked the Gulf Coast in early June and Hurricane Dennis, a Category 3 storm, hit the Florida Panhandle with winds of 120 miles per hour on July 10. The 2005 storm season was so busy, in fact, that forecasters ran through their list of 21 names by October and resorted to the Greek alphabet.

Abby Goodnough

WHAT IT FEELS LIKE OUT THERE

Windchill temperatures can rise by 10 to 18 degrees if the sun is shining brightly.

WIND (MPH) \ TEMPERATURE (°F)	30	25	20	15	10	5	0	-5	-10	-15	-20	-25	-30
5	25	19	13	7	1	-5	-11	-16	-22	-28	-34	-40	-46
10	21	15	9	3	-4	-10	-16	-22	-28	-35	-41	-47	-53
15	19	13	6	0	-7	-13	-19	-26	-32	-39	-45	-51	-58
20	17	11	4	-2	-9	-15	-22	-29	-35	-42	-48	-55	-61
25	16	9	3	-4	-11	-17	-24	-31	-37	-44	-51	-58	-64
30	15	8	1	-5	-12	-19	-26	-33	-39	-46	-53	-60	-67
35	14	7	0	-7	-14	-21	-27	-34	-41	-48	-55	-62	-69
40	13	6	-1	-8	-15	-22	-29	-36	-43	-50	-57	-64	-71
45	12	5	-2	-9	-16	-23	-30	-37	-44	-51	-58	-65	-72
50	12	4	-3	-10	-17	-24	-31	-38	-45	-52	-60	-67	-74
55	11	4	-3	-11	-18	-25	-32	-39	-46	-54	-61	-68	-75
60	10	3	-4	-11	-19	-26	-33	-40	-48	-55	-62	-69	-76

FROSTBITE TIMES: ▨ 30 minutes ▨ 10 minutes ☐ 5 minutes

SOURCE: N.O.A.A. National Weather Service

wind increases, your body cools at a faster rate causing the skin temperature to drop.

The National Weather Service actually calculates windchill temperatures based on the rate of heat loss from exposed skin caused by the effects of wind and cold. When windchill temperatures are potentially hazardous, that is, severe enough to cause frostbite and hypothermia, the agency issues advisories. Frostbite occurs when unprotected parts of the body such as your face or fingers freeze. When body temperature dips below 90 degrees Fahrenheit, the body's shivering ability ceases and it cannot warm itself without outside help. Unless you act quickly, hypothermia can set in. When that happens, the heart rate slows, blood pressure falls, and a person drops into a semicomatose, then comatose state.

Shaded areas in the chart above indicate temperatures that can cause frostbite at exposures of 30 minutes or less.

IN THE EVENT OF HYPOTHERMIA

• **Do not** use a stove, electric blankets or a hot tub to warm someone up. Doing so can cause dangerous physiological changes.

• **Do** get the victim out of the cold and to the hospital quickly. At the hospital, a victim can be warmed using special hypothermia blankets, warmed IV's, and humidified oxygen. In severe cases cardiopulmonary bypass or dialysis can be used to warm the patient from the inside-out, according to cold weather care specialists.

Looking Beyond the Clouds

A clear-eyed look at some nebulous situations

No two clouds are alike, as any child gazing up at a billow-filled blue sky knows. Meteorologists identify three basic types: cumulus, stratus and cirrus, but variations on those types can form in the atmosphere depending on the altitude and temperature of moisture-laden air. Below are the types of clouds that can be found at low, middle and high altitudes.

LOW ALTITUDES (BELOW 6,500 FT.)

Cumulus *(from the Latin "heap")*. Large, white, puffy clouds often resembling huge balls of cotton or heads of cauliflower.

When they turn dark gray and produce rain or hail, they are called **cumulonimbus** clouds. These clouds can span all altitudes, with bases from 1,000 to 5,000 feet and tops sometimes reaching 60,000 feet, and are often accompanied by lightning and thunder.

Stratus *("stretched out")*. Low layers of clouds that cover the entire sky, like sheets of high fog blotting out the sun. Shapeless, dark and dense, these clouds produce gray, overcast days. Low stratus clouds that produce drizzle, rain or snow but are not accompanied by thunder or lightning are called **nimbostratus**.

Stratocumulus. Dark gray, wavelike formations that contain moisture but don't usually produce rain.

MIDDLE ALTITUDES (6,500 to 20,000 ft.)

Altocumulus. Small, gray, patchy clouds composed of water droplets. These clouds create a scalelike pattern in the sky.

Altostratus. Gray midlevel, often opaque clouds. They often contain water droplets that may fall but evaporate before reaching the ground.

HIGH ALTITUDES (20,000 to 40,000 ft.)

Cirrus *("curl")*. Wispy, filament-like clouds made of ice crystals. **Cirrostratus**. White, thin, translucent clouds that could signal an approaching storm.

Cirrocumulus. Small, loosely connected sheets of white clouds that may contain droplets of water or ice. Vertical air currents cause their patchy, scalelike appearance in the sky, often referred to as a "mackerel sky." They can be a sign of stormy weather ahead.

How to Read Rocks

Earth's history is written in stone. A geological primer

Miners in the Middle Ages were the first to realize the need to understand the geological similarities of rocks. It was during that time that the two basic principles of rock formations evolved: first, that sedimentary—or layered rocks—are laid down horizontally, and second, that younger rocks always rest on top of older rocks. A few centuries later, another concept was introduced, stating that geologic processes take place at a similar frequency and magnitude throughout time. Geology moved along apace with the identification of fossils and the discovery in the 1800's that fossils are found in rocks in a very definite chronological order. That tenet led to the development of the geologic time scale, (see page 761), a hierarchical set of time intervals that plot the earth's history.

The earth is made up of rock, from mountain

SCIENCE

24 COMMON MINERALS AND THEIR USES

The earth is home to about 3,000 minerals. Most minerals are chemical compounds but a few, like sulfur and gold, are elements. Minerals crystallize in geometric forms, and along with their chemical compositions, their crystalline structure helps determine properties such as color and hardness. Minerals have numerous practical applications, as the table below shows.

MINERAL	SOURCES	USES
Aluminium	*Guinea, Australia, Jamaica*	Packaging, building
Beryllium	*Brazil, South Africa, U.S.*	Nuclear industry, gemstones
Chromite	*South Africa, Zimbabwe*	Chemicals, metallurgy
Cobalt	*Zaire, Zambia, Canada*	Jet engines, chemicals
Copper	*Chile, U.S., Zambia*	Electronics, chemicals, building
Feldspar	*U.S., Brazil*	Glass, ceramics, bonding agent
Fluorite	*Germany, Mexico, U.S.*	Plastics, ceramics, metallurgy
Gold	*South Africa, U.S., Australia*	Dentistry, electronics, jewelry
Gypsum	*Canada, France, U.K., Mexico*	Building materials, agriculture
Halite	*Worldwide*	Food, chemicals (sodium chloride-salt)
Iron Ore	*U.S., Australia, Brazil*	Metallurgy, chemicals, medicine
Lead	*U.S.*	Electronics, construction, ammunition
Lithium	*U.S., Chile*	Electronics, medicine, lubricants
Manganese	*South Africa, Gabon, Australia*	Iron and steel production
Nickel	*Australia, Canada, Norway*	Chemical, aerospace
Platinum	*Canada, South Africa*	Jewelry, automotive, oil refining
Phosphate	*U.S.*	Agriculture, chemicals
Quartz	*Worldwide*	Electronics, instruments, jewelry
Silica	*Worldwide*	Computers, building, chemicals
Silver	*U.S., Canada, Mexico*	Electronics, jewelry, photography
Sulfur	*Worldwide*	Chemicals, petroleum refining, pharmaceuticals
Titanium	*U.S., U.K., China, Japan*	Jet engines, aerospace
Uranium	*Canada, Australia, Africa*	Electricity, nuclear and defense industries
Zinc	*Worldwide*	Chemical, automotive, electrical

SOURCE: Mineral Information Institute

tops to ocean floor, so clues to its history are plentiful. But even though there are thousands of kinds of rocks and minerals, most rocks are formed from just eight elements: aluminium, calcium, iron, magnesium, oxygen, potassium, silicon and sodium. The combinations of elements that rocks contain, and the wear and tear of wind and water over time, account for the huge variety of rocks on earth. However, geologists have identified three basic rock groups: igneous, sedimentary and meta-morphic. These groups get their names from the major geological processes that formed them and that make them them fairly easy to tell apart.

Pumice

IGNEOUS ROCKS, or fire rocks, form when magma, or melted rock buried deep within the earth, reacts to heat and pressure. It flows upward or is spewed out by an erupting volcano and then cools and solidifies. Magma, which is called lava when it appears above the ground, is made up of a variety of chemicals and cools at different rates, resulting in different types of igneous rocks. But you can easily identify them as igneous because they are typically crystalline or glassy. Obsidian, a common igneous rock, for example, is actually volcanic glass. Pumice, volcanic froth puffed up by gas bubbles, is also a kind of glass and not a mixture of minerals. Another type of igneous rock is granite, a light, coarse-grained rock formed deep in the earth and then exposed by erosion.

Sandstone

SEDIMENTARY ROCKS are formed by natural processes, such as weathering and erosion, which occur mainly under water. These rocks consist of layers, or strata, and are also called stratified rocks. The layers are formed by sediments—mineral grains, mud, sand, pebbles, microscopic organisms and even plant material—washed downstream and deposited on top of each other. In time, these layers press down until the bottom layers turn into rock. Sedimentary rocks are rich in geological history, often containing fossils and showing marks left by water currents or cracks formed by mud. Some examples are sandstone, limestone, shale and gypsum, often used in the building industries.

Gneiss

METAMORPHIC ROCKS started out as igneous or sedimentary rocks but "morphed" due to changes in temperature, pressure, and chemically active liquids. The process transforms them into denser and more compact rocks. Most of the thousands of rare minerals on the earth are found in metamorphic rocks. One type of metamorphic rock, gneiss, may have been granite, an igneous rock, that was changed by tremendous heat and pressure. Look carefully and you'll see mineral layers, or foliation. The mineral grains were flattened and compacted in alternating patterns, giving the rock a striped appearance.

Predicting Earthquakes

The shaky science of determining when and where the next "big one" will strike

After decades of dissecting seismic fault zones, including the long seam between tectonic plates in the bed of the Indian Ocean, scientists have gotten good at describing where large quakes are likely to occur. But predicting with precision exactly when and where the next earthquake will strike remains impossible. Despite their best theories, despite more than $1 billion worth of spending on instruments to examine faults in California and Japan, scientists still cannot give timely warning to people in harm's way.

The best seismologists can do today is predict the probability of an earthquake recurring in the same region. The predictions are typically cast in terms of 10 to 30 years. Such warnings are useful for deciding where to build dams, power stations, roads and pipelines in earthquake regions, says Dr. Lynn Sykes, a geophysicist at the Lamont-Doherty Earth Observatory in Palisades, N.Y., but they do not help ordinary people living in those areas.

The science of earthquake prediction has a long, sorry history, including good ideas that failed, disappointing experiments and an ever-expanding list of goofy claims. In the 1970's, hopes ran high that a so-called seismic gap hypothesis would yield accurate predictions. Long fault zones were divided into smaller segments that were thought to rupture at somewhat regular intervals. By digging trenches along those segments and finding dates for past events, seismologists could infer the timing of future quakes.

But segments of the San Andreas Fault in California are not so well behaved, says Dr. Kerry Sieh, a seismologist at the California Institute of Technology who pioneered the technique. Some sections erupt every 50 to 350 years. " We don't know why," Sieh says. " It may be because so many other faults interact. Or is it something fundamental about individual faults?"

Realizing he would never solve the prediction puzzle in California, Sieh turned his attention a decade ago to faults off the coast of Sumatra. His focus is on a patch of ocean floor shaken by a giant earthquake in December 2004. Both areas are part of a vast subduction zone, where a huge block of the earth's crust slides under the Indonesian archipelago. By dating mortality patterns in coral reefs affected by fault motions and tsunamis, Sieh determined that large earthquakes occur regionally, in pairs, every 230 years or so. In 1797 there was a magnitude 8.2 quake; in 1833 a magnitude 8.7 or bigger quake occurred. There was a cluster in

Aside from setting off devastating tsunamis, the massive 2004 earthquake in the Indian Ocean triggered temblors 7,000 miles from its epicenter.

• • •

the 1500's and one in the 1300's. "We are coming up on the beginning of the next cycle," Sieh says. Since the turn of the new century, he adds, "a number of smaller quakes have been flirting with these larger locked patches."

For example, in June 2000, a quake of magnitude 7.0 was felt in Singapore. A 7.4 temblor in 2002, under Simeulue Island, off the northwestern coast of Sumatra, may have been a foreshock for the big quake in 2004 that unleashed the tsunami that killed hundreds of thousands of people. A second very large earthquake in the same offshore area would not come as a surprise, Sieh says. But it could be decades away.

On land, quake predictions have never proved reliable. On February 4, 1975, the Chinese government said it evacuated the town of Haiching based on earthquake precursors—changes in land elevation, groundwater level, swarms of small quakes and jittery horses, dogs and chickens. A quake of magnitude 7.3 struck two days later, and tens of thousands of lives were saved. But later investigations suggest that the claim was based on ideology, not science. The quake, it turned out, had not been predicted so clearly. Tens of thousands of people were killed or injured. A year later, a 7.6 earthquake struck Tangshan, China, without warning. An estimated 250,000 people died.

Many seismologists say earthquakes can never be predicted because the earth's crust is profoundly heterogeneous. Any small quake has some probability of cascading into a large event. Whether a small one grows into a large one or dissipates depends on myriad fine details of physical conditions in fractured earth.

Dr. John Rundle, a seismologist at the University of California, Davis, says the best hope

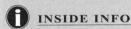

INSIDE INFO

Quaking in Our Boots

○ There are 500,000 detectable earthquakes in the world each year; 100,000 can be felt and 100 cause damage.

○ Depending how big the quake is, aftershocks can last 9 or 10 years.

○ Tsunamis, giant sea waves caused by earthquakes, can travel through the ocean at a speed of 600 mph.

SOURCE: U.S. Geological Survey

for near-term prediction lies in a statistical method that identifies hot spots. Regions of concern are laid out in grids six miles on a side. Instruments pick up areas with frequent small quakes, around magnitude 3. If such activity increases, a quake is more likely within five years. This method predicted the location of 12 out of 14 moderate California quakes over the last five years, Rundle says. Still, he adds, "It only tells you where but not exactly when."

—Sandra Blakeslee (Andres C. Revkin contributed)

Earthquake-Prone Zones

Where the earth shakes, rattles and rumbles most

Earthquakes occur when two tectonic plates, or pieces of the earth's crust under oceans and continents, split, slide or ram into each other. Quakes can happen anywhere on the globe—the earth's surface has seven major tectonic plates and many more minor ones—but history shows that countries along these seismic hot spots are particularly shake-prone:

The circum-Pacific seismic belt. More than 80 percent of the world's largest earthquakes happen along this rim of the Pacific Ocean. Vulnerable areas: the western coast of South America from the tip of Chile northward, Central America, Mexico, and northward from California to Alaska. The belt also extends from the Aleutian Islands to Japan, the Philippines, New Guinea, islands in the Southwest Pacific and New Zealand.

The Alpide belt. This zone accounts for about 17 percent of the world's largest earthquakes, including some of the most destructive. It runs from Java to Sumatra through the Himalayas, the Mediterranean and out into the Atlantic Ocean.

The Magnitude of Tremors

The most widely used measure of an earthquake's intensity is the Richter scale

Developed by American physicist Charles Richter in the mid-1930's, the Richter scale uses a logarithmic scale, ranging from 1 to 9 and higher, in which each whole-number increase in magnitude represents a 10-fold increase in terms of the energy released by the tremor, as measured by seismographs.

Shocks that measure 2 or less are called "microearthquakes" and are usually not felt, although they are tracked by local seismographers. Earthquakes with a magnitude of 4.5 and greater occur at the rate of several thousand each year and are powerful enough to be recorded by instruments worldwide. A quake that measures 5.3, such as the one that shook San Francisco in 1957, would be considered moderate, even though its power was comparable to the explosion of 455 metric tons of dynamite. (The 1989 San Francisco earthquake measured 7 on the Richter scale.)

Earthquakes with a magnitude of about 6.3 and above are major events. The largest recorded earthquake in the United States registered 9.2 and occurred in Alaska on Good Friday in 1964. The largest recorded quake in the world took place in Chile in 1960, measuring 9.5. But the record for the most destructive earthquake in history goes to the shock that hit China's Shaanxi province in 1556. It killed more than 830,000 people.

Which are among the most earthquake-free areas in the United States? Between 1975 and 1995, the only states in the U.S. that had not experienced any earthquakes were Florida, Iowa, North Dakota and Wisconsin. (For tips about how to survive an earthquake, see "When the Earth Shakes" on page 101.)

SCIENCE

Stars & Tides

Stargazing With the Naked Eye

The beauty and majesty of the night sky.
All you have to do is look

In a world of space stations and orbiting telescopes, stargazing with the naked eye may seem a quaint notion. Hardly. "The beauty and majesty of the night sky can only be appreciated by the naked eye," says astronomer Geoff Chester of the U.S. Naval Observatory in Washington, D.C. Even without binoculars and telescopes, it can be quite easy to enjoy some of nature's most extraordinary spectacles—if you know what to look for.

To familiarize yourself with the stars, constellations and other astronomical phenomena, you'll need a celestial map and a red-filtered flashlight to help you read. You can find such maps at planetariums and astronomy clubs, in specialty publications such as *Astronomy* magazine (and in this book on pages 723 to 728). Make a filter by covering your flashlight lens with any porous red paper, or buy a red L.E.D. at Radio Shack. The red filter helps your night vision.

The best locations for viewing the night sky are usually in rural areas, where there is little gazing interference from artificial light and pollution. Begin your celestial search by seeking out the brightest stars. Use the sky's brightest patterns, such as the Summer Triangle (see below), for reference points to the constellations and other celestial objects. The Summer Triangle, found directly overhead in the summer months, is formed by stars in the Vega, Deneb and Altair constellations.

In winter, use the Great Winter Circle, which boasts 9 of the 21 brightest stars in the winter sky. To find it, start with Orion's belt, which lies in the middle of the Circle and points to Sirius. Move clockwise from there to Procyon, Pollux, Castor, Capella, Aldebaran and Rogel.

THE PLANETS

Stars twinkle and planets don't, yet planets, not stars, are generally the brightest objects in the sky. Four planets—Venus, Jupiter, Mars and Saturn—can be seen easily with the naked eye. Venus is the third-brightest object in the sky after

---

TEST PATTERNS IN THE SKY

The Summer Triangle and the Winter Circle will help you find your way in the firmament.

• **THE SUMMER TRIANGLE**
Consists of stars Vega, Deneb and Altair (left).

• **THE GREAT WINTER CIRCLE**
Use Orion's belt to point to Sirius. Then, clockwise, go to Procyon, Pollux, Castor, Capella, Aldeberon and Rigel (right).

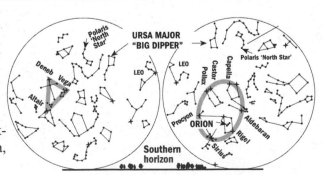

The Night Sky in January

The Night Sky in February

the sun and moon and displays a milky white glow. Jupiter, usually the fourth-brightest object, appears creamy or yellow. Mars follows Jupiter in visibility and is the only planet whose color, a pinkish hue, represents its surface color and not its atmosphere. Saturn is the faintest of the naked-eye planets and is yellowish.

Mercury can also be seen if you're skilled, but doing so is difficult because of its proximity to the sun. Most astronomers believe Copernicus, the grandfather of modern astronomy, never spotted Mercury.

SHOOTING STARS AND COMETS

Ever seen a shooting star? Think of what you viewed as a grain of sand hitting the earth's atmosphere at tremendous speed and bursting into flames. A meteor shower occurs when such debris, usually from a comet, enters the earth's atmosphere.

A really bright shooting star is called a fireball. It's not uncommon for such a phenomenon to illuminate an entire state. Comets, like meteors,

are random visitors to our world. But comets can remain in view from a few days to several months. The Hale-Bopp comet, the brightest comet in the twentieth century, was visible from March until the beginning of May 1997.

ECLIPSES

A total solar eclipse is one of the most spectacular sights in the natural world. It owes its occurrence to the fact that the moon is 400 times smaller than the sun, but 400 times closer to earth—hence the moon and the sun appear to have equal diameters. So when the moon comes between the sun and earth, we are left with an awe-inspiring sight of a pearly halo around a black disc.

Total lunar eclipses may not be as impressive, but they more than reward the small effort required to see one. At least once a year the moon passes into the earth's shadow and completely disappears from the night sky. Unlike a solar eclipse, a lunar eclipse can be enjoyed across an entire hemisphere.

SCIENCE

The Night Sky in March

The Night Sky in April

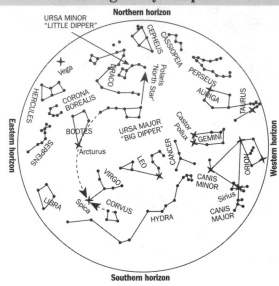

Stars and Constellations

The explosion that created the universe gave birth to trillions of stars

Only about 5,000 stars are visible to the naked eye. Since only half the sky can be seen at any one time, that means only 2,500 stars will be in your field of vision on the next clear night. Constellations are groups of stars whose patterns have reminded stargazers through history of familiar shapes. In 1929, astronomers officially adopted 88 constellations, listed here with their names and meanings.

Andromeda	Chained Maiden	**Camelopardalis**	Giraffe
Antila	Air Pump	**Cancer**	Crab
Apus	Bird of Paradise	**Canes Venatici**	Hunting Dogs
Aquarius	Water Bearer	**Canis Major**	Great Dog
Aquila	Eagle	**Canis Minor**	Little Dog
Ara	Altar	**Capricornus**	Sea-goat
Aries	Ram	**Carina**	Keel
Auriga	Charioteer	**Cassiopeia**	Queen
Bootes	Herdsman	**Centaurus**	Centaur
Caelum	Chisel	**Cepheus**	King

Cetus	Whale	**Hydrus**	Water Snake (male)
Chamaeleon	Chameleon	**Indus**	Indian
Circinus	Compasses (art)	**Lacerta**	Lizard
Columba	Dove	**Leo**	Lion
Coma Berenices	Bernice's Hair	**Leo Minor**	Little Lion
Corona Australis	Southern Crown	**Lepus**	Hare
Corona Borealis	Northern Crown	**Libra**	Balance
Corvus	Crow	**Lupus**	Wolf
Crater	Cup	**Lynx**	Lynx
Crux	Cross (southern)	**Lyra**	Lyre
Cygnus	Swan	**Mensa**	Table Mountain
Delphinus	Dolphin	**Microscopium**	Microscope
Dorado	Goldfish	**Monoceros**	Unicorn
Draco	Dragon	**Musca**	Fly
Equuieus	Little Horse	**Norma**	Square (rule)
Eridanus	River	**Octans**	Octant
Fomax	Furnace	**Ophiuchus**	Serpent Bearer
Gemini	Twins	**Orion**	Hunter
Grus	Crane (bird)	**Pavo**	Peacock
Hercules	Hercules	**Pegasus**	Flying Horse
Horologium	Clock	**Perseus**	Hero
Hydra	Water Snake (female)	**Phoenix**	Phoenix
		Pictor	Painter
		Pisces	Fishes

The Night Sky in May

The Night Sky in June

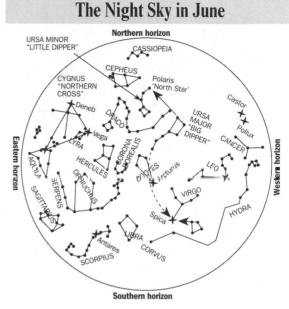

Piscis Austrinius	Southern Fish
Puppis	Stern (deck)
Pyxis	Compass (sea)
Reticulum	Reticle
Sagitta	Arrow
Sagittarius	Archer
Scorpius	Scorpion
Sculptor	Sculptor
Scutum	Shield
Serpens	Serpent
Sextans	Sextant
Taurus	Bull
Telescopium	Telescope
Triangulum	Triangle
Triangulum Australe	Southern Triangle
Tucana	Toucan
Ursa Major	Great Bear
Ursa Minor	Little Bear
Vela	Sail
Virgo	Maiden
Volans	Flying Fish
Vulpecula	Fox

Our 12 Closest Stellar Neighbors

Astronomers are discovering nearby stars at an astonishing rate by using increasingly sensitive detectors. The closest star is the sun, of course; next comes Proxima Centauri, among the dimmest in the firmament. Sirius, also known as the Dog Star, shines brightest after the sun. Another close star, Barnard's, is thought to have planets orbiting around it. Stars are far apart from each other—many light-years separate the stars below. Many stars occur in multiple-star systems, shown here by the suffixes A and B.

NAME	DISTANCE FROM THE SUN (light-years)*	CONSTELLATION
Proxima Centauri	4.3	*Centaurus*
Rigil Kentaurus	4.3	*Centaurus*
Barnard's Star	5.9	*Ophiuchus*
Wolf 359	7.6	*Leo*
Lalande 21185	8.1	*Ursa Major*
Sirius [A & B]	8.6	*Canis Major*
Luyten 726-8[A & B]	8.9	*Cetus*
Ross 154	9.4	*Sagittarius*
Ross 248	10.3	*Andromeda*
Epsilon Eridani	10.7	*Eridanus*
Luyten 789-6	10.8	*Aquarius*
Ross 128	10.8	*Virgo*

*A light-year is the distance light travels in a year, equal to 5.88 trillion miles or 9.46 trillion kilometers.

SCIENCE

The Night Sky in July

The Night Sky in August

A Portrait of the Planets
Getting to know our fellow orbiteers

Of the nine planets in the solar system, only four besides the Earth are visible to the naked eye: Venus, Mars, Jupiter and Saturn.

MERCURY. The smallest of the planets is Mercury. Its diameter is less than half the Earth's. Named for the winged messenger of the gods, it is the planet closest to the sun and has no satellites. It is believed that Mercury always turns the same side toward the sun and that the sunlit part of Mercury has a temperature hotter than 600 degrees Fahrenheit. By contrast, the temperature on the side away from the sun is thought to be -460 degrees Fahrenheit.

VENUS. Named for the goddess of love and beauty, Venus is almost the same size as Earth and is often called Earth's sister planet. The brightest of all the planets in the night sky, Venus is shadowed only by the sun and the moon. It is the first "star" to appear in the evening sky and the last to disappear in the morning. At its brightest, Venus may even be visible during the day. Many astronomers believe that the core of Venus is largely metallic, mostly iron and nickel. Because of the dense carbon dioxide clouds enveloping the planet, the surface of Venus can't be seen.

EARTH. This is the third-closest planet to the sun—they are only 93 million miles apart. Seen from space, the planet appears as a blue ocean sphere with brown and green areas marking the location of its continents. Its diameter at the equator is 7,900 miles, and its atmosphere contains 78 percent nitrogen and 21 percent oxygen, in addition to traces of water in gaseous form, carbon dioxide and other gases. By measuring the radioactive decay of elements in the earth's crust, scientists estimate that the planet is about 4.5 billion years old.

MARS. Like Earth, Mars has four seasons, but its diameter is just about half that of Earth's, and its mass is only about a tenth of ours. Named for the god of war, Mars takes 687 days to complete

The Night Sky in September

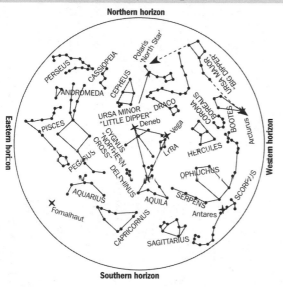

The Night Sky in October

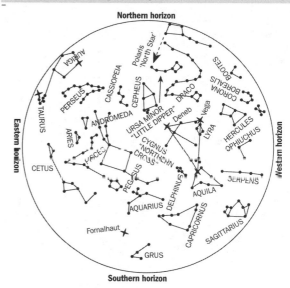

one revolution of the sun. About 80 percent of the planet's atmosphere is carbon dioxide. The white caps that cover its poles increase in size during the Martian winter and shrink during the summer. Martian seasons are about twice as long as Earth's.

JUPITER. Next to the sun, Jupiter is the largest and most massive object in the solar system. Named for the leader of the gods, Jupiter has a mass more than twice that of all other planets combined. A body on the surface of Jupiter would weigh 2.64 times its weight on Earth. Jupiter completes a revolution every 10 hours, giving it the shortest day in the solar system. It has 12 satellites, the largest number of any planet in the solar system. It is perhaps most famous for its Great Red Spot, which scientists believe is a storm that has been going on for 300 years.

SATURN. The second-largest planet in the solar system, Saturn is named for Titan, the father of Jupiter and the god of sowing. It is best known

for its system of concentric rings, which are not visible to the naked eye. The rings are probably composed of debris from a shattered satellite. Saturn is the least dense of all the planets but one of the brightest.

URANUS. Visible by the naked eye on a dark, clear night, Uranus is unique because its axis of rotation lies almost in the plane of its orbit. The planet was discovered by the German-English astronomer William Herschel in 1781. Herschel proposed to name the planet Georgium Sidu, in honor of England's King George III. But in keeping with the tradition of naming planets after Greek gods, it was eventually named after the father of Titan and the grandfather of Jupiter. Uranus has five known satellites and a mass over 14 times that of Earth. Its temperature is thought to be below -300 degrees Fahrenheit.

NEPTUNE. Named for the god of the sea, Neptune takes 165 years to complete one revolution of the sun. Its atmosphere is made of methane,

The Night Sky in November

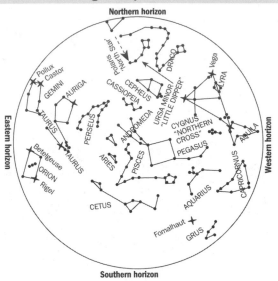

The Night Sky in December

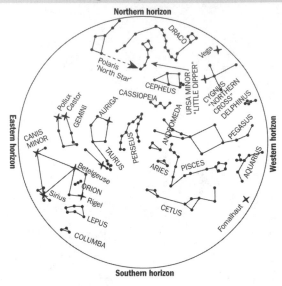

hydrogen, ammonia and helium, and its mass is about 17 times that of Earth. The planet was discovered as a result of a mathematical prediction. Two mathematicians, John Couch Adams and Urbain Leverrier, calculated that there must be an unknown planet more distant from the sun than Uranus because they could detect the gravitational pull on Uranus.

PLUTO. There is probably little or no atmosphere on Pluto because of its extreme temperature, which is nearly -400 degrees Fahrenheit. From Pluto the sun would only appear as a bright star. Named for the god of the underworld, the planet's first two letters are also the initials of Percival Lowell, whose research on gravitational forces led him to predict the planet's existence. However, Pluto wasn't discovered until after Lowell's death. Recent discoveries of an object larger than Pluto and three times its distance from the sun bring into doubt whether Pluto is indeed a planet. (See, "What's a Planet, Anyway?" next.)

What's a Planet, Anyway?

Add another planet or two to the solar system, or possibly subtract one

The solar system is a much more complicated place these days than in 1930 when Clyde Tombaugh added Pluto to the inventory of wandering lights circling the sun. In addition to Earth, Mars, Venus, Jupiter, Saturn, Mercury, Neptune, Uranus and Pluto, schoolchildren now learn that there are also comets and asteroids bumping about in the night. But there are also the Oort cloud, a hypothesized halo of cometary bits hibernating in deep, deep space, and the Kuiper Belt, a ring of icy bodies beyond Neptune's orbit. Not to mention the dozens of moons circling the planets.

But Pluto is the big problem. Is it a planet or not? Some astronomers have long argued that its small size, less than one-fifth the diameter of Earth, and a weird tilted orbit that takes it inside Neptune's orbit every couple of hundred years make Pluto more like a Kuiper Belt body than a full-fledged planet. The controversy became more desperate in mid-2005 when astronomers discovered a new object larger than Pluto orbiting in the Kuiper Belt at a distance of nine billion miles from the sun. Michael E. Brown of the California Institute of Technology, its discoverer, says it would be fine with him if Pluto is demoted to a minor planet, but, he argues, if Pluto is a planet, so is the new object—temporarily dubbed 2003 UB313 but nicknamed Xena by Brown. Xena, then, should be the tenth planet. The further discovery that Xena has a tiny moon makes it seem even more planetlike.

Some astronomers suggest changing the taxonomy and calling both Pluto and Brown's Xena minor planets. Or, maybe the definition of a planet should change, so that only those larger than 2,000 kilometers (or about 1,250 miles) in diameter (Pluto is about 1,500 miles) qualify. Or, maybe it's time to retire the term *planet* altogether in favor of words like "terrestrials" for balls of dirt and rock like Earth; "Jovians" for giant gaseous planets like Jupiter and Saturn; and so forth.

Still others say the criterion of planethood should be roundness—a body big enough for gravity to have conquered geological and mechanical forces. That would include in the roll call of planets not only Pluto, but dozens of objects likely to be discovered out in the Kuiper Belt.

Being limited to making observations in the pursuit of their science, astronomers tend to characterize and classify new phenomena by their appearances: their colors, for example. Objects that resemble one another then get lumped together under the name of their progenitor until enough differences accumulate to start a new category. So it was that a starlike object known as BL Lacertae, the progenitor of a kind of exploding galaxy, was eventually said to not be a good example of a BL Lacertae object.

Whatever name is finally given to 2003 UB313, a.k.a Xena, it's clear that the fate of oddball Pluto, and the controversy over what constitutes a planet will not be resolved anytime soon—particularly as new objects are discovered in the Kuiper Belt and beyond.

—Dennis Overbye

The Question of Comets
Dirty ice balls or icy dirt balls?

For scientists who study dusty comets, the big question is, Just what is inside—and outside—of a comet? In 2005, NASA's Deep Impact mission spacecraft slammed an 800-pound, copper-tipped probe into the comet Tempel 1. The explosion created a spectacular display of fireworks on July 4, and was recorded by instruments in space and around the world. A team of researchers studied the data and came up with a surprising discovery: the comet is covered with tiny traces of water ice.

Comets are small sun-orbiters, believed to be left over from the formation of the solar system. The discovery of ice on Tempel 1 is the first definitive evidence of surface ice on any comet, according to Jessica Sunshine, chief scientist and lead author of an article on the subject in a February 2006 online edition of *Science* magazine. "Understanding a comet's water cycle and supply is critical to understanding these bodies as a system and as a possible source that delivered water to Earth."

The surface of Tempel 1 is roughly 45 square miles. The three pockets of ice that were discovered are tiny, comprising only about 300,000 square feet. Further, less than 10 percent of that area is pure water ice. The remainder is mostly dust. The research team believes that the surface ice used to be inside the comet, along with an abundance of organic matter, and that it became exposed over time. They also concluded that the comet most likely originated from the part of the solar system now occupied by Uranus and Neptune.

SCIENCE

Stargazing Made Easy

Computer-assisted telescopes find the stars. All you have to do is look

Backyard stargazers know that a simple way to find Polaris, the North Star, is to look for the Big Dipper. The two stars that make up the front edge of the dipper's cup point straight at Polaris.

A growing number of amateur astronomers, however, don't need tricks like this to find a particular star or anything else in the heavens. They rely instead on computer-assisted motorized telescopes that in a few seconds can find any object among thousands listed in a database.

Since the late 1990's, prices of these "go to" telescopes, as they are known, have declined, and the technology, at least in its most basic form, is now available on scopes costing as little as $250. For hobbyists who value learning about the sky almost as much as they do looking at it, that development has brought with it controversy. "Some people thought that this is an evil thing, buying your way into the sky," says Dave Eicher, the editor of *Astronomy* magazine. "The lingering disappointment for old-timers is that this diminishes the hobby to something that is akin to beer can collecting."

Still, the initial resistance to go-to technology from experienced amateur astronomers is waning. And no one disputes that the technology can help novice stargazers avoid disappointment.

Computerized controls that steer consumer telescopes to specific objects in the sky have been around since the mid-1980's, although the early models found relatively few buyers. Early computerized systems could store the celestial

---

 **TIMELY TIPS**

A Match Made in Heaven

Hook a computer up to a telescope to catch a lucky star

These days, even the most casual of backyard stargazers have found their hobby touched by computers. Many of the simplest and least-expensive telescopes available for hobbyists now contain processors, keypads and motors that allow them to be automatically pointed at stars, planets and other objects in the sky just by punching in a number (see story above).

All these developments mean that more amateur astronomers have more sophisticated equipment that they can do a lot more with.

✔ **Software packages for home computers** that map thousands of celestial objects and serve as interactive desktop planetariums have replaced printed star charts that filled volumes. Digital cameras now allow amateurs with relatively modest equipment to capture space images easily.

✔ **Star charting** was one of the first aspects of amateur astronomy to be touched by computers. Today several Internet sites, including one operated by *Sky & Telescope* (www.skyandtelescope.com), have free online systems that can generate charts for any point on earth at any time over a span of centuries.

✔ **Astronomy software packages** like Starry Night Pro and Red Shift go even further. Starry Night Pro, for example, produced by a Toronto-based subsidiary of Space.com, has a database of 19 million stars that users can turn into animations showing celestial activity over time. Many astronomy software packages can connect to motorized telescopes. Such connections allow users to select a specific star or planet and then have the computer direct the telescope to the precise location of that object in the sky

—Ian Austen

coordinates of only a relatively small number of planets, stars and other objects. But that wasn't their only limitation. Early systems required users to level the telescope, point it toward the North Star, and enter some information in the telescope's computer, including location (in degrees of latitude and longitude) as well as the date and exact time. Even after that, early systems often just pointed the telescope in the general vicinity of an object. It was up to observers to zero in manually on what they were seeking.

These days, most smaller telescopes—those with lenses or mirrors that are six inches in diameter or less—still require the user to enter location and time by hand. But some larger scopes costing $2,000 and up have eliminated even those steps by including circuitry that can pick up signals from Global Positioning System satellites. All users have to do is turn the telescope on, punch up an object from the database by using a hand-held controller and wait. The computer, which knows the scope's latitude and longitude and the exact time because of the G.P.S. signals, does the rest, controlling small drive motors so that the telescope mirror points to the proper position in the sky. Meade Instruments Corporation and Celestron are the two main manufacturers of high-quality computerized telescopes.

A growing numbers of experienced astronomers are using go-to systems. "If you have a go-to drive on your telescope you don't have to waste an hour hunting for objects," says Bon Gent, president of the Astronomical League, an alliance of amateur astronomers' groups, "you can spend the time observing them." Still, newcomers will find stargazing more fulfilling with some advance study. "Get some beginning astronomy books, subscribe to one or two magazines, learn a little and then get a telescope," Gent counsels.

—Ian Austen

Here Comes the Sun

Catching a total eclipse of the sun can be a jaw-dropping event

A solar eclipse takes place when the earth, moon and sun are in alignment. During a total eclipse, all the light of the sun is blocked because of the moon's position. But never stare at the sun with an unprotected eye or you risk serious eye damage. Just a quick glimpse—even when the sun seems dim—is dangerous. Use filtered telescopes or binoculars to protect your eyes.

20 YEARS OF SOLAR ECLIPSES
2000-2020

DATE	TIME (U.T.)[1]	TYPE
2000 Feb 5	12:48	Partial
2000 July 1	19:32	Partial
2000 July 31	2:13	Partial
2000 Dec 25	17:35	Partial
2001 June 21	12:03	Total
2001 Dec 14	20:52	Annular
2002 June 10	23:43	Annular
2002 Dec 4	7:30	Total
2003 May 31	4:07	Annular
2003 Nov 23	22:49	Total
2004 April 19	13:33	Partial
2004 Oct 14	2:59	Partial
2005 April 8	20:36	Hybrid
2005 Oct 3	10:31	Annular
2006 March 29	10:10	Total
2006 Sep 22	11:39	Annular
2007 March 19	2:32	Partial
2007 Sep 11	12:31	Partial
2008 Feb 7	3:55	Annular
2008 Aug 1	10:20	Total
2009 Jan 26	7:59	Annular
2009 July 22	2:35	Total
2010 Jan 15	7:06	Annular
2010 Jul 11	19:33	Total
2011 Jan 4	8:49	Partial
2011 Jun 1	21:15	Partial
2011 July 1	8:38	Partial

2011 Nov 25	6:20	Partial
2012 May 20	23:52	Annular
2012 Nov 13	22:12	Total
2013 May 10	0:24	Annular
2013 Nov 3	12:46	Partial
2014 April 29	6:02	Annular
2014 Oct 23	21:44	Partial
2015 Mar 20	9:45	Total
2015 Sept 13	6:54	Partial
2016 Mar 9	1:57	Total
2016 Sept 1	9:07	Annular
2017 Feb 26	14:52	Annular
2017 Aug 21	18:24	Total
2018 Feb 15	20:50	Partial
2018 July 13	3:00	Partial
2018 Aug 11	9:45	Partial
2019 Jan 6	1:41	Partial
2019 July 2	19:22	Total
2019 Dec 26	5:16	Annular
2020 June 21	6:40	Annular
2020 Dec 14	16:33	Total

2030 Nov 25	06:50	3m 44s
2033 Mar 30	18:01	2m 37s
2034 Mar 20	10:17	4m 09s
2035 Sep 02	01:55	2m 54s
2037 Jul 13	02:39	3m 58s
2038 Dec 26	00:58	2m 18s
2039 Dec 15	16:22	1m 51s
2041 Apr 30	11:51	1m 51s
2042 Apr 20	02:16	4m 51s
2043 Apr 09	18:56	—
2044 Aug 23	01:15	2m 04s
2045 Aug 12	17:41	6m 06s
2046 Aug 02	10:19	4m 51s
2048 Dec 05	15:34	3m 28s
2052 March 30	18:30	4m 08s
2053 Sept 12	9:32	3m 04s
2055 July 24	9:56	3m 17s

NOTES:

[1] Universal Time (U.T.) is an astronomical standard that is five hours ahead of Eastern Standard Time.

[2] No total solar eclipse took place in 2000.

SOURCE: Eclipse prediction data by Fred Espenak, NASA/GSFC

A HALF CENTURY OF TOTAL ECLIPSES[2]

DATE	TIME (Of greatest eclipse in U.T.)	DURATION (Mins. and secs.)
2001 Jun 21	12:04	4m 57s
2002 Dec 04	07:31	2m 04s
2003 Nov 23	22:49	1m 57s
2006 Mar 29	10:11	4m 07s
2008 Aug 01	10:21	2m 27s
2009 Jul 22	02:35	6m 39s
2010 Jul 11	19:34	5m 20s
2012 Nov 13	22:12	4m 02s
2015 Mar 20	09:46	2m 47s
2016 Mar 09	01:57	4m 09s
2017 Aug 21	18:25	2m 40s
2019 Jul 02	19:23	4m 33s
2020 Dec 14	16:13	2m 10s
2021 Dec 04	07:33	1m 54s
2024 Apr 08	18:17	4m 28s
2026 Aug 12	17:46	2m 18s
2027 Aug 02	10:06	6m 23s
2028 Jul 22	02:55	5m 10s

Shadows of the Moon

A lunar eclipse occurs only during a full moon

An eclipse occurs when a celestial body, such as the earth or the moon, casts a shadow so that another celestial body seems to disappear. A lunar eclipse occurs when the sun, earth and moon are aligned so that the moon is in the shadow of the earth.

20 YEARS OF LUNAR ECLIPSES 2000-2020

DATE	TIME (U.T.)	TYPE
2000 Jan 21	4:42	Total
2000 July 16	13:56	Total
2001 Jan 9	20:20	Total
2001 July 5	14:54	Partial
2001 Dec 30	10:29	Penumbral
2002 May 26	12:02	Penumbral
2002 Jun 24	21:26	Penumbral
2002 Nov 20	1:45	Penumbral

2003 May 16	3:40	Total
2003 Nov 9	1:18	Total
2004 May 4	20:29	Total
2004 Oct 28	3:03	Total
2005 April 24	9:55	Penumbral
2005 Oct 17	12:02	Partial
2006 March 14	23:47	Penumbral
2006 Sep 7	18:50	Partial
2007 March 3	23:20	Total
2007 Aug 28	10:37	Total
2008 Feb 21	3:25	Total
2008 Aug 16	21:10	Partial
2009 Feb 9	14:38	Penumbral
2009 July 7	9:38	Penumbral
2009 August 6	0:39	Penumbral
2009 Dec 31	19:23	Partial
2010 June 26	11:38	Partial
2010 Dec 21	8:17	Total
2011 June 15	20:12	Total
2011 Dec 10	14:32	Total
2012 June 4	11:03	Partial
2012 Nov 28	14:33	Penumbral
2013 April 25	20:07	Partial
2013 May 25	4:10	Penumbral
2013 Oct 18	23:50	Penumbral
2014 April 15	7:45	Total
2014 Oct 8	10:54	Total
2015 April 4	12:00	Total
2015 Sep 28	2:47	Total
2016 March 23	11:47	Penumbral
2016 Sept 16	18:54	Penumbral
2017 Feb 11	0:44	Penumbral
2017 Aug 7	18:20	Partial
2018 Jan 31	13:30	Total
2018 July 27	20:22	Total
2019 Jan 21	5:12	Total
2019 July 16	21:31	Partial
2020 Jan 10	19:10	Penumbral
2020 June 5	19:25	Penumbral
2020 July 5	4:30	Penumbral
2020 Nov 30	9:43	Penumbral

SOURCE: Eclipse prediction data by Fred Espenak, NASA/GSFC

Mountains on the Moon
The man in the moon is made of frozen lava

The moon is earth's only natural satellite and was probably created in the same cosmic event that created the earth. The leading theory on how the moon was formed is known as the Great Impact, or informally as the Big Whack. It holds that while earth was very young, an object the size of Mars hit it, spewing debris into space that coalesced into the moon. Such a large impact would have released a lot of energy, so along with the Big Whack, planetary scientists say, came the Big Melt.

The moon is only 238,860 miles away, making it an object of endless human fascination—and superstition. Although its only light is reflected from the sun, it is the brightest object in our nighttime sky. In size it is slightly more than a quarter the diameter of the Earth. Temperatures can be as high as 273 degrees Fahrenheit on the bright side and as low as -274 degrees Fahrenheit on the dark side.

There is no air, and thus no liquid water on the lunar surface. That means the moon has no clouds, winds, rain or snow. Without air and water to cause erosion, the moon's features are nearly permanent—they include towering mountain ranges and seas of hardened lava. The astronomer Galileo was the first to study many of these features with a telescope he built in the early 1600's.

The lunar surface has also been pitted with craters from crashing meteorites—over 30,000 can be seen from earth. The circular depressions range in size from less than a mile to over 100 miles across. As intriguing as all of these features are, however, none of them can compare with the fact that the pull of the moon's gravity on the earth's oceans plays a huge role in creating our daily tides. (See "A Beachgoer's Guide to the Tides," page 742.)

NEW MOON

WAXING CRESCENT

FIRST QUARTER

WAXING GIBBOUS

FULL MOON

WANING GIBBOUS

LAST QUARTER

WANING CRESCENT

The Phases of the Moon

The science behind the lunar calendar

The moon takes slightly longer than 27 days to complete its elipticl orbit around the earth, but because the earth also moves around the sun, it takes 29 days, 12 hours, 44 minutes and 3 seconds to go from one new moon to the next. At the start of each orbit, the moon is directly between the earth and the sun, and thus invisible because its dark side is toward us. Gradually, a crescent appears and waxes toward the full moon, and then wanes again to invisibility.

The moon has no light of its own; it merely reflects the light of the sun. If the moon did not rotate as it revolves around the earth, we would see all its sides; as it is, we always see the same side.

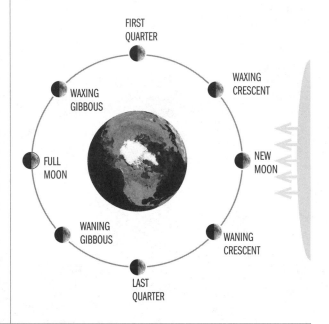

MOONLIGHT SONATA

Here's a month-to-month calendar for the moon's phases from 2007 to early 2011. Times are expressed in Universal Time (U.T.), an astronomical standard that is five hours ahead of Eastern Standard Time.

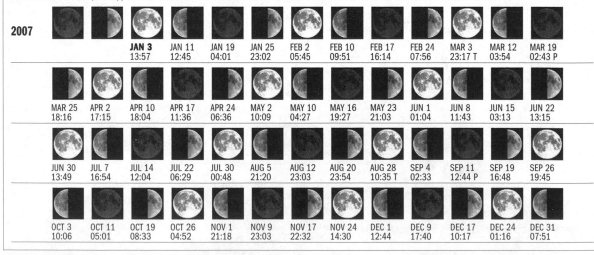

2007

	JAN 3 13:57	JAN 11 12:45	JAN 19 04:01	JAN 25 23:02	FEB 2 05:45	FEB 10 09:51	FEB 17 16:14	FEB 24 07:56	MAR 3 23:17 T	MAR 12 03:54	MAR 19 02:43 P
MAR 25 18:16	APR 2 17:15	APR 10 18:04	APR 17 11:36	APR 24 06:36	MAY 2 10:09	MAY 10 04:27	MAY 16 19:27	MAY 23 21:03	JUN 1 01:04	JUN 8 11:43	JUN 15 03:13	JUN 22 13:15
JUN 30 13:49	JUL 7 16:54	JUL 14 12:04	JUL 22 06:29	JUL 30 00:48	AUG 5 21:20	AUG 12 23:03	AUG 20 23:54	AUG 28 10:35 T	SEP 4 02:33	SEP 11 12:44 P	SEP 19 16:48	SEP 26 19:45
OCT 3 10:06	OCT 11 05:01	OCT 19 08:33	OCT 26 04:52	NOV 1 21:18	NOV 9 23:03	NOV 17 22:32	NOV 24 14:30	DEC 1 12:44	DEC 9 17:40	DEC 17 10:17	DEC 24 01:16	DEC 31 07:51

2008

JAN 8 11:37	JAN 15 19:46	JAN 22 13:35	JAN 30 05:03	FEB 7 03:44 A	FEB 14 03:34	FEB 21 03:31 T	FEB 29 02:18	MAR 7 17:14	MAR 14 10:46	MAR 21 18:40	MAR 29 21:47	APR 6 03:55
APR 12 18:32	APR 20 10:25	APR 28 14:12	MAY 5 12:18	MAY 12 03:47	MAY 20 02:11	MAY 28 02:57	JUN 3 19:23	JUN 10 15:04	JUN 18 17:30	JUN 26 12:10	JUL 3 02:19	JUL 10 04:35
JUL 18 07:59	JUL 25 18:42	AUG 1 10:13 T	AUG 8 20:20	AUG 16 21:16 P	AUG 23 23:50	AUG 30 19:58	SEP 7 14:04	SEP 15 09:13	SEP 22 05:04	SEP 29 08:12	OCT 7 09:04	OCT 14 20:00

2009

OCT 21 11:55	OCT 28 23:14	NOV 6 04:04	NOV 13 06:17	NOV 19 21:31	NOV 27 16:55	DEC 5 21:26	DEC 12 16:37	DEC 19 10:29	DEC 27 12:23	JAN 4 11:56	JAN 11 03:27	JAN 18 02:46
JAN 26 07:55 A	FEB 2 23:13	FEB 9 14:49 N	FEB 16 21:37	FEB 25 01:35	MAR 4 07:46	MAR 11 02:38	MAR 18 17:47	MAR 26 16:06	APR 2 14:34	APR 9 14:56	APR 17 13:36	APR 25 03:23
MAY 1 20:44	MAY 9 04:01	MAY 17 07:26	MAY 24 12:11	MAY 31 03:22	JUN 7 18:12	JUN 15 22:15	JUN 22 19:35	JUN 29 11:28	JUL 7 09:21 N	JUL 15 09:53	JUL 22 02:35 T	JUL 28 22:00
AUG 6 00:55 N	AUG 13 18:55	AUG 20 10:01	AUG 27 11:42	SEP 4 16:03	SEP 12 02:16	SEP 18 18:44	SEP 26 04:50	OCT 4 06:10	OCT 11 08:56	OCT 18 05:33	OCT 26 00:42	NOV 2 19:14

2010

NOV 9 15:56	NOV 16 19:14	NOV 24 21:39	DEC 2 07:30	DEC 9 00:13	DEC 16 12:02	DEC 24 17:36	DEC 31 19:13 P	JAN 7 10:40	JAN 15 07:11 A	JAN 23 10:53	JAN 30 06:18	FEB 5 23:49
FEB 14 02:51	FEB 22 00:42	FEB 28 16:38	MAR 7 15:42	MAR 15 21:01	MAR 23 11:00	MAR 30 02:25	APR 6 09:37	APR 14 12:29	APR 21 18:20	APR 28 12:18	MAY 6 04:15	MAY 14 01:04
MAY 20 23:43	MAY 27 23:07	JUN 4 22:13	JUN 12 11:15	JUN 19 04:30	JUN 26 11:30 P	JUL 4 14:35	JUL 11 19:40 T	JUL 18 10:11	JUL 26 01:37	AUG 3 04:59	AUG 108 03:08	AUG 16 18:14
AUG 24 17:05	SEP 1 17:22	SEP 8 10:30	SEP 15 05:50	SEP 23 09:17	OCT 1 03:52	OCT 7 18:44	OCT 14 21:27	OCT 23 01:36	OCT 30 12:46	NOV 6 04:52	NOV 13 16:39	NOV 21 17:27

2011

NOV 28 20:36	DEC 5 17:36	DEC 13 13:59	DEC 21 08:13 T	DEC 28 04:18	JAN 4 9:03	JAN 12 11:31	JAN 19 21 21	JAN 26 12:57	FEB 3 2:31	FEB 11 7:18	FEB 18 8:36	FEB 24 23:26

 **TIMELY TIPS**

To the Moon, Alice!

(Use the Internet, Dear)

Imagine soaring over the surface of the moon, dipping into a crater and seeing rock slides on its slopes and boulders piled up at the bottom. You don't have to wait for a spaceship or even the night sky to get such a close-up view of the moon. You can visit it with a PC and a broadband Internet connection, courtesy of a free public-access program developed by the National Aeronautics and Space Administration's Ames Research Center in California.

The moon views—detailed and three-dimensional—are an extension of NASA's World Wind computer program that has allowed computer users to see almost any place on earth by tapping into databases of satellite information. Using the system's Blue Planet data set, you can see the entire earth down to a resolution of 50 feet and the entire United States to a resolution of about 3 feet. Data for about 30 urban areas lets you see objects one foot wide, good enough resolution to recognize houses and cars.

Programmers expanded this view to the moon by incorporating 1.8 million pictures and other data about its surface acquired by the *Clementine*, which orbited it for two months in the mid-90's. After downloading the World Wind program, users of computers running Microsoft's Windows operating system can tap into the lunar data set. From a vantage point in space, you can see the moon and virtually control its movements. Zoom in and slowly soar over the surface, dip into craters and valleys. You must have a high-speed, broadband Internet connection and a computer running Windows 2000 or XP; programmers are working on a version for Apple and Linux operating systems.

World Wind can be downloaded at www.worldwind.arc. nasa.gov. Some program users have produced a Web site that provides instructions and help, as well as applications that use the World Wind data, such as an add-on program that makes it easier to find spots like the Apollo landing sites. These features and help are online at www.worldwindcentral.com.

—Warren E. Leary

How to Talk Like an Astronomer

Key terms to help you navigate the universe

Even amateur astronomers know the difference between a "blue moon" and a "white dwarf." Here are other astronomy terms to master.

ACCRETION. A process in which matter that revolves around a celestial body is gradually pulled in and added to the body's mass. The process is thought to be responsible for the formation of planets and satellites.

APHELION. The point in time and distance at which an object orbiting the sun is farthest from the sun.

ASTEROID. Rocky object that orbits the sun, mostly in the asteroid belt between Mars and Jupiter. Asteroids are thought to be debris from the formation of the solar system or from collisions between larger planetary bodies. There are an estimated 100,000 asteroids. The largest, Ceres, has a diameter of 580 miles; the smallest detected asteroids have diameters of several hundred feet.

ASTRONOMICAL UNIT. An astronomical unit (A.U.) is 93 million miles, or the distance from the earth to the sun.

BIG BANG THEORY. The belief that a massive explosion of a dense mass of matter started the universe. After the explosion, the universe was splattered with energy and atomic particles, followed by lower density and lower temperatures. Space itself was thought to expand after the big bang, and continues to expand, according to the theory.

BINARY STAR. A system of two stars revolving around a common center and linked by a mutual gravitational pull.

BLUE MOON. The second full moon that occurs within one calendar month.

BLACK DWARF. A star that has used up its energy sources and can no longer emit light. In theory, the universe is too young to have yet produced a black dwarf.

BLACK HOLE. A theoretical region in space thought to contain a body with such a strong gravitational field that no matter or energy can resist the pull. The theory states that even light cannot escape from it, explaining why black holes can never be seen.

COMET. Small objects that orbit the sun independently in an elliptical orbit. Astronomers have theorized that comets have three identifying components: the nucleus, made up of rock and ice; the coma, its gaseous atmosphere; and the tail, made up of gases and atomic dust. But recent studies question whether comets are largely dusty ice balls or icy dust balls.

CORONA. The outer layer and hottest part of the sun's atmosphere. During a solar eclipse, the corona is sometimes visible around the moon's periphery.

DARK MATTER. Undetected matter in the universe, presumed to exist because of gravitational effects. Astronomers believe it comprises a large part of the universe's mass but have not yet observed it directly.

DECLINATION. The system for measuring the altitude of a celestial body. It is expressed in degrees, minutes and seconds of arc north or south of the celestial equator.

DOPPLER EFFECT. A change in the frequency of a wave (of sound or light) as the distance between the source and the observer changes. The shifts are used to determine the direction and velocity of a distant object.

EQUINOX. A crossing of the celestial equator by the sun. There are two annual equinoxes—vernal (around March 21) and autumnal (around September 23). On these days, the lengths of day and night are approximately equal everywhere on earth.

FIREBALL. An exceptionally bright meteor sometimes visible during the day.

LIGHT-YEAR. The distance light travels in one year, equal to 5.88 trillion miles, 9.46 trillion kilometers or 63,240 astronomical units.

MAGNITUDE. A measure used to describe the brightness of a celestial object. The smaller the number, the brighter the object. The brightest star, Sirius, shines at a magnitude of -1.5. A full moon measures -13, and the sun blazes at almost -26. Apparent magnitude of a star is its luminosity measured from the earth; absolute magnitude is the measurement of its intrinsic brightness.

METEOR. Small rocky, icy particles that produce a streak of light in the sky as they burn up in the earth's atmosphere. Meteors are often called shooting or falling stars because they travel across the sky in short bursts. Meteor showers, it is thought, are produced by debris left by comets as they orbit the sun.

METEORITE. A piece of fallen rock from outer space that has reached the surface of the earth, often creating a crater on

The first time that the thin, waxing crescent moon is visible after a new moon (low in the evening sky just after sunset) marks the beginning of a month in the Islamic calendar.

• • •

SCIENCE

impact. The largest meteorite to date weighed 60-tons; it landed in Namibia, Africa, in 1920.

MILKY WAY. The spiral galaxy to which the earth and its solar system belong. Parts of it appear as a faint band of light in a clear night sky. The Milky Way is made up of billions of stars, is about 12 billion years old and has a diameter of 100,000 light-years.

NEBULA. A cloud of interstellar gases and dust in the galaxy that appears as a hazy, fuzzy or dark patch.

NOVA. A star that suddenly flares in brightness by more than 10 magnitudes and then slowly fades to its original luminosity. The burst of brightness may be caused by the fusion reaction that occurs when one star mass collides with another. Novas appear every few years; supernovas are a rare occurrence.

PENUMBRA. Faint outer shadow of the moon; partial eclipses are seen from within this shadow.

PERIGEE. The point in the orbit of a moon or planet in which it comes closest to the earth.

PERIHELION. The point in which a celestial body in orbit comes closest to the sun.

PLANETESIMALS. Rocky celestial bodies thought to have orbited the sun in the early solar system. Astronomers believe the objects coalesced to form the cores of planets.

PLASMA. Hot ionized gas found in the sun and stars, as well as in fusion reactors.

PULSARS. Generally thought to be rapidly rotating neutron stars, pulsars emit brief, intense bursts of radio waves, radiation and X-rays in specific directions. The word comes from a contraction of "pulsating stars."

QUASARS. The most distant celestial objects known. These compact objects emit massive amounts of energy, sometimes equal to many times more than the energy output of an entire galaxy. The name is a contraction of "quasi-stellar radio source."

SOLSTICE. The point at which the sun is farthest away from the celestial equator. It signals the beginning of summer in the Northern Hemisphere and the beginning of winter in the Southern Hemisphere.

SUPERNOVA. A massive explosion of a large star in the final stages of stellar life that creates a short but intense light that is up to 100 million times the brightness of the sun. The gases produced by the blast spew into space and the core collapses into a neutron star or perhaps into a black hole.

SYZYGY. The straight-line formation or opposition of three celestial bodies. Syzygy takes place during lunar and solar eclipses, for example, when the sun, earth and moon are aligned.

UMBRA. Dark inner shadow of the moon; total eclipses are seen from within this shadow.

WHITE DWARF. A dim, dense star that has collapsed on itself and is near the end of its stellar life. A white dwarf is about the size of the earth and has a high surface temperature. An example of a white dwarf is Sirius's companion star in the Canis Major constellation.

ZENITH. The point directly overhead in the sky, or 90 degrees above the horizon. The highest point reached by a celestial body.

ZODIACAL LIGHT. A faint glow of light in the sky visible before sunrise to the east and after sunset to the west. The light is caused by interplanetary dust reflected in the sunlight.

What the Stars Say About You

Clues to your personality from palm-reading the heavens

Astrology, the practice of predicting the future based on movements in the cosmos, has deep and tangled roots in astronomy. The two, in fact, were intertwined well into the 1500's, when Copernicus quietly proposed that the earth revolved around the sun rather than vice versa. When Galileo later strongly embraced the theory, the scientific world went into a tailspin, and the two disciplines diverged.

Most horoscope readings today are based on sun sign astrology, which takes into account only one's birth date. Genethliac astrology factors in an array of other information, including a person's time and place of birth, the location of the sun, moon, planets and some asteroids, and the path of the moon's orbit around the earth. What does your sign say about you? Here's a beginner's guide to what astrologers say is written in the heavens.

 **ARIES**

March 21 – April 19 The Ram

Aries, the first sign of the zodiac, represents birth. As such, the ram is like a baby—very self-absorbed. And like a baby, Aries puts his or her needs first. The Ram is fearless, extremely honest and direct, and shows unbridled enthusiasm. Arians often possess a ferocious temper, but after a fight, do not hold grudges. With all the energy they expend, you have to wonder when they relax. But they can be calm too. They find their soul mates in Sagittarius, Scorpio and Cancer.

 **TAURUS**

April 20 – May 20 The Bull

Taurus is a rocky coast that's been beaten by the elements for centuries. Those born under this sign are strong and stubborn with a quiet demeanor. Taureans are steady, speak sparingly and possess an inner strength, but don't like change. They are outstanding workers who are willing to take orders without resentment. Their hearts and pockets are open to a friend in distress, but they may have trouble expressing their own feelings. Cancer, Leo and Capricorn are most compatible with Taureans.

 **GEMINI**

May 21 – June 20 The Twins

Being born under the sign of the Twins means you never know when you might switch your looks, house, job or spouse on an impulse. Geminis can never get enough money, fame or love. They live by their own rules and do what they want; they have little patience for indecisive people and can be very rude, selfish and immature. The Gemini woman has a hard time committing herself to one man at a time, and the Gemini man may shower a love interest with flowers but he's unlikely to reveal his innermost core. Still, Gemini will be drawn to Leo, Capricorn and Aquarius.

 CANCER

June 21 – July 22 The Crab

The Cancer person is full of laughter and loves a good joke. But at other times Cancer's moods are blacker than the darkest cavern. Yet people from under this sign also are sweet and gentle and will find a way to rise above adversity when the moon changes. Cancerans are sentimental about their roots and their family. They have vulnerable hearts and sensitive feelings. In love, the Cancer person can be so dependent it can border on obsession. Virgo, Leo, and Aquarius are the most compatible.

LEO
July 23 – Aug. 22 The Lion

Leo is the leader of the jungle, a dignified, stately presence, lying luxuriously in the sun for all to see. Leos have strong personalities and can be vain. But they also are loveable, seldom waste energy on fruitless tasks and are good organizers. The regal ways of the sun sign make them great hosts or hostesses. Leos like royal treatment and spend money freely, but they also give money to just about anyone. They play hard, work hard, rest hard and live hard. Leo will want to meet Pisces, Aries and Gemini.

VIRGO
Aug 23 – Sept. 22 The Virgin

These perfectionists are dependable, industrious, practical, cool and sincere. They are blessed with great curiosity and are mentally very active, excelling in the written and spoken word. They can endure and thrive on intense work longer than most. But they can also destroy relationships by being too critical, analytic and irritable. If you're in a jam, however, Virgo natives will gladly roll up their sleeves and help. Capricorn, Aries and Pisces are best matches for a Virgo.

LIBRA
Sept 23 – Oct 22 The Scales

With the scales as a sign, Libra is a natural balancer. Librans are good listeners but are also inveterate talkers. They are intelligent but naïve at the same time. They love people, but detest crowds. They are gracious, caring and calm, but when the weight of the scales changes they can be stubborn, annoying and depressed. Librans dislike arguments, and, with their desire to please, can make an ideal mates. Gemini and Taurus stand the best chance of benefiting from the Libra disposition.

SCORPIO
Oct 23 – Nov 21 The Scorpion

The most passionate people in the zodiac, Scorpios are nocturnal creatures. They have hypnotic, intense eyes that make others feel nervous. Scorpios have strong emotions that are deeply hidden. They can be sarcastic, stubborn and even cruel at times to those close to them. They are difficult to get to know and understand and must test a person before showing their true selves. Scorpions are fascinated with death and the spiritual. Scorpio will appreciate Cancer and Aquarius the most.

SAGITTARIUS
Nov 22 – Dec 21 The Archer

When you start a new job, the first person to walk up to you with a smile, shake your hand and welcome you aboard will be a Sagittarian. They mean well but often put a foot in their mouth. They make friends easily, are optimists and refuse to take life seriously. But they can show violent tempers, and are unlikely to keep a secret. They have a terrific memory but can't remember where they left their keys. Pisces, Cancer and Leo will be most understanding.

CAPRICORN
Dec 22 – Jan 19 The Goat

Like the goat, the Capricorn looks and acts harmless but is tough as nails. Capricorns are steady, serious and sensible, and never let obstacles or disappointments block their way to the top of the mountain. They are gentle and persuasive, and though they are sometimes labeled as snobbish, that charge is unfair. The Capricorn person is trustworthy and makes a good provider. Leo, Aries and Virgo are Capricorn's favorites.

TIMELY TIPS

The Stars They Are A-Changin'

Astrologers are studying the effect of cramming another celestial body into cosmic charts

Astronomers aren't the only ones excited about the discovery of a possible new planet (See "What's a Planet, Anyway?" on page 728). Their mystical cousins, astrologers, have also been jolted; they are speculating about what it might mean for their cosmic readings and prophecies. After all, they, too, are students of the solar system.

Astrologers often use the maxim "As above, so below." Now suddenly what is "above" may be radically changed. If 2003 UB313 is a tenth planet, astrologers say it may have a profound influence over people's lives, and thus on the forecasts astrologers make. But its potency cannot be discerned until perhaps several years after the astronomical debate is settled, when astronomers have had time to chart its orbit. For now, astrologers are not inclined to do anything hasty. There will be no tearing up of charts, no hurriedly penciling in a new planet and certainly no crossing out of Pluto, a body that many astrologers hold near and dear.

On the contrary, astrologers seem to have reached an unspoken consensus to take a wait-and-see approach. Wait and see if there is a tenth planet. Then wait and observe its influence on human life. Throughout history, when faced with the addition of a new planet, many astrologers have duly figured out how to use it in their calculations. In any case, Pluto, the most recently discovered planet, is so tightly woven into astrological charts that it would be unthinkable to lose it. Because Pluto is an outer planet, it operates on a level that affects humanity as a whole as well as individuals, astrologers say. (The farther out a planet is, theoretically, the more global its effects.) Named for the Greek god of the underworld, Pluto is thought to bring about unexpected changes. It's usually dark, suggesting huge upheaval in a person's life, astrologers say. That upheaval—in a person's health, family or career—is generally followed by a rebuilding, a resurrection, they add.

—Stephanie Rosenbloom

AQUARIUS
Jan 20 – Feb 18 The Water Bearer

Freedom-loving Aquarians are unpredictable and secretly delight in shocking others with their erratic behavior. They are natural rebels with a dreamy gleam in their eyes. The Aquarian seeks the security of crowds and then demands to be left alone. When it comes to friends, they seek quantity, rather than quality. Trusting people isn't natural for Aquarians, but they love to network. Sagittarius, Taurus and Libra will be most in sync with Aquarius.

PISCES
Feb 19 – March 20 The Fish

Pisces natives dislike being in the same spot for too long, as their fish sign suggests. They prefer to swim from one spot of light to another. They are the most spiritual of all signs; they are often mystical, impressionable and intuitive. Pisces people are also creative, clever, sarcastic, and never answer a question directly. Yet no sign is more sensitive to human suffering. They are compassionate and love to help. Pisces will find Virgo, Gemini and Scorpio to their liking.

SCIENCE

A Beachgoer's Guide to the Tides

Read this to know more about tidal effects than most fishermen

Some ancient myth-makers held that the earth's pulse or breathing caused the tides. The Greeks began to notice the moon's influence when they started to venture out of the relatively tideless Mediterranean. Our modern understanding of the tides is based on Sir Isaac Newton's equilibrium theory of tides, which described the gravitational attractions of the sun and moon on the earth's waters. Today, tides can be predicted with astronomical precision and need no longer be a mystery. Here's what landlubbers will find when they are at the beach:

If you live on the East Coast, expect the tides to be semidiurnal. That's when high and low tides occur twice per lunar day, and the heights of both the first and second set of tides are roughly the same. A lunar day is 50 minutes longer than a day on earth, which is why in many places high and low tides occur about 50 minutes later than the corresponding tides of the previous day.

If you live on the West Coast, expect mixed tides. The tides on America's left coast rise and fall twice per lunar day, but the heights of the second set of tides differ from the first. The different tides each day are termed high water, lower high water, high-low water and lower low water. The order of occurrence varies over the course of the month and from place to place.

Along the Gulf of Mexico, the tides are diurnal. Here, high and low tides appear only once every day.

About twice a month, near the time of the new and full moon the tidal range between high and low tides is usually 20 percent above average. These tides, known as spring tides, occur when the sun and moon are in a straight line with the earth. When the sun and moon are at right angles to each other with respect to the earth, tidal ranges between high and low tides are about 20 percent less than average. These tides, known as neap tides, occur around the time of the first and third quarters of the moon.

For another big swing in height between high and low tide, wait until the moon is at perigee. That's when the moon is at its closest point to the earth each month. That's also when the tidal range between high and low tide is greatest. Roughly two weeks later the moon is at apogee, which is its farthest point from the earth for the month. At

---

THE MOON AND TIDES

The tide is the rise and fall of water throughout the earth's oceans. Occurring every 12 hours and 26 minutes, tides are created primarily by the moon's pull of gravity on the water.

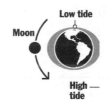

HIGH TIDES are produced when the earth is nearer the moon and water is pulled toward the moon. This happens on the opposite side of the earth at the same time.

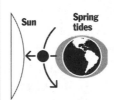

SPRING TIDES occur when the sun and the moon are directly in line. The moon is either in front of or behind the earth. This produces a very high tide twice a month.

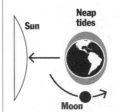

NEAP TIDES do not rise as high as normal because the moon is at right angles to the sun. A neap tide occurs twice a month.

that point, the moon's influence is at a minimum.

During the course of the month, daily inequities between successive high or low tides also can occur. This happens as the moon moves from about 28 degrees north of the equator to 28 degrees south. When the moon is at one of these extremes, the difference in height between morning and evening tides is greatest. When the moon is at the equator, tides are roughly equal.

The tidal range also increases in January. That's when the earth's elliptical orbit around the sun brings the planet closest to the sun, in what astronomers call the state of perihelion. In July, when the earth is farthest from the sun in what astronomers refer to as the state of aphelion, the tidal range decreases.

The shape and depth of ocean basins change tidal ranges, too. The smallest differences in the heights between high and low tides occur along open coasts. For example, spring tidal ranges (near the time of the new and full moon) vary from about 2 feet on the Gulf Coast to as much as 8 or 9 feet on the California coast. The largest tidal ranges are found in tidal inlets, estuaries and salt marshes. The Bay of Fundy in Canada has the greatest difference in the world between high and low tide. There, the funnel-like opening of the bay concentrates the energy and increases the height of the incoming tide, resulting in average tidal ranges of about 45 feet.

Meteorological conditions can also disrupt normal tide patterns. While the tide tables provide accurate times and heights of high and low tide,

> 66
> **Ancient sea-dwellers held that a child could be born only during an incoming tide and a dying person could not expire until the tide went out.**
>
> ● ● ●

strong and persistent winds and the low atmospheric pressure associated with storm systems can alter the time and height of high or low tide. If you are planning to go clamming or to collect seashells at low tide and there is a strong onshore breeze, you may want to delay for as long as an hour after the predicted time of low tide.

Horizontal water movements, known as tidal currents, are generally strongest midway between high and low tide. When the tide rises and water flows in to fill estuaries and inlets, the water is called a flood current. When the tide goes out and water drains from these coastal areas, the flow is called an ebb current. Slack currents are found around the time of both high and low tide.

Surf fishing is best done when tidal currents are strongest. Strong flood currents force bait fish up closer to the beach and cause them to school up tighter and hide behind features such as rocks or jetties. Game fish such as bluefish or striped bass take advantage of these conditions, and so should knowledgeable surf fishermen. Game fish lie in wait for the bait fish to be swept in and out of inlets, estuaries and bays by flood and ebb currents. Slack water is usually the worst time to fish.

Boaters shouldn't rely on the tidal charts in coastal newspapers. While most coastal newspapers list the times and heights of high and low tide, boaters need more tidal information than the papers provide in order to ensure safety over the ocean floor and to know where to anchor. They should consult the tide and tidal current tables published each year by the government.

SCIENCE

Times & Dates

A Very Brief History of Time

What makes 24 hours a day?

Great minds have pondered the elusive concept of time for centuries. "What then is time?" asked St. Augustine in the mid-300's. "If no one asks me, I know what it is. If I wish to explain it, I do not know."

More easily explainable is how we arrived at a concrete division of time into a 24-hour day, 60-minute hour and 60-second minute. Man's efforts to harness and measure time over the ages were rewarded by gazing at natural phenomena, especially the stars and sun. One way to define a day is to measure the time that it takes the earth to rotate 360 degrees compared to the position of the stars. The length of the "sidereal day" (*sider* is Latin for star) is 23 hours, 56 minutes and 4 seconds. Another measure is the solar day or the time it takes for the sun to cross the same point in the sky two times. The length of the true solar day is 24 hours. (The slight difference between the sidereal day and the solar day comes from the fact that the earth travels nearly a degree farther on its yearly trek around the sun.)

But, over the course of a year, the length of a true solar day—also defined as the time it takes the earth to make one revolution around the sun—varies because of the earth's elliptical orbit and the angle of the equator. So, some days may be longer, some shorter. The average length of the true solar day over one year is 24 hours.

Ancient cultures arrived at a 24-hour day but the starting and ending points varied with the culture. Ancient Egyptians and Babylonians (in today's Iraq), for example, began their day at dawn. Jews and Muslims started their day at dusk; Romans at midnight; and Greeks at moonrise.

History books generally credit the Sumarians, who lived some 4,000 years ago, for giving us the mathematical system based around the number 60 and, thus, the notion of dividing hours and minutes into 60 parts. But the need to measure hours, minutes and seconds precisely didn't arise until the late Middle Ages with the invention of mechanical clocks. It was after this period that the modern-day system of time-telling, using smaller units of uniform length was adopted on a general scale.

As for the more elusive definition of time, Albert Einstein went a long way toward trying to pin it down. Before Einstein, time was considered absolute, that is, it had an immutable frame of reference, apart from factors like speed. Einstein found that time is not absolute but relative; only the speed of light does not vary. As he famously observed, "When a man sits with a pretty girl for an hour, it seems like a minute. But let him sit on a hot stove for a minute—then it's longer than any hour. That's relativity!"

A Quick Glance at the Clock

Does anybody really know what time it is?

The oldest clocks date back to the ancient Egyptians and Mesopotamians, who measured time by checking the position of a shadow created by the sun on a sundial. The Greeks, Romans and Chinese used water clocks to calculate the passage of time by observing the level of water flowing from a container.

But neither method, although greatly refined over the years, ensured great precision. Sundials couldn't be used at night, for example, and it was difficult to regulate the flow of water within a vessel.

At the basis of clock-making are two functions: a repetitive process to mark off the passage of time and a way to keep track and display the result. Clock-making has always been about finding ever more consistent actions to regulate the rate of a clock to get increasingly precise results. The introduction of the pendulum advanced the process significantly. During the mid-1600's, Dutch scientist Christiaan Huygens used a pendulum's motion to turn wheels that controlled the hands of the clock. Pendulum clocks proved accurate to within one minute per day. The next major advance came in the 1927 with the introduction of the quartz crystal, the most commonly used device today. Electricity applied to the crystal causes it to vibrate at a constant rate, making the clock's hands move precisely. But even quartz watches can have their drawbacks. Factors like humidity, for example, can impair their accuracy.

The most precise timepiece around, and the basis of modern timekeeping today is the atomic clock, which was developed in 1949. It uses the vibration of certain atoms to regulate time with great precision; the latest version is accurate to within less than one second in 30 million years. But atomic clocks are large, power-hungry, and expensive to build. That, too, is about to change. A miniscule atomic clock, developed by the Commerce Department's National Institute of Standards and Technology (N.I.S.T.) in 2004 is believed to be 100 times smaller than any atomic clock; its inner workings are about the size of a grain of rice. This chip-scale atomic clock opens the door to atomically precise timekeeping in portable, battery-powered clocks for use in cell phones, for example, or in navigation systems.

 INSIDE INFO

How to Tell Time Like a Sailor

○ Long before sailors wore wristwatches and the chronometer measured time at sea, it fell to a junior crewmember to watch sand trickle through a half-hour glass. When the sand ran out, he turned the glass over and rang a bell, letting the crew know that one half-hour had passed. Thus was born the tradition of ships' bells as time signals.

○ Why are time intervals so vital? When a ship is at sea, all of its essential stations, such as the navigation bridge and engine room, must be manned round the clock. To divvy up the duty, the day is divided into four-hour periods called watches. Crew members stand two four-hour watches a day. The hours between 4 p.m. and 8 p.m. are further divided into two two-hour watches, called "dog watches," to allow those on duty to go to dinner.

○ The age-old practice of sounding the ship's bell on the hour and half-hour lives on in the U.S. Navy, regulating daily routine just as it did centuries ago. Today, mechanical bell clocks do the work on many ships. But all ships must comply with maritime law requiring them to carry an efficient bell for emergencies, such as fog. The ship's bell can also be used to ring in the New Year: 16 peals—8 for the old year and 8 for the new. Here's how to decode a ship's bells:

Assume a watch begins at noon:

8 bells	Noon	1 bell	12:30
2 bells	1:00	3 bells	1:30
4 bells	2:00	5 bells	2:30
6 bells	3:00	7 bells	3:30
8 bells	4:00 (The next watch begins.)		
1 bell	4:30 (The pattern starts over.)		

Note that an odd number of bells denotes a half hour and an even number one hour.

In the meantime, you can set your clocks to the N.I.S.T.'s atomic clock time by going to the agency's Web site at nist.time.gov. You can also synchronize your computer clock through the internet. For instructions, go to tf.nist.gov.

Spring Ahead, Fall Back

More daylight for merchants, consumers and goblins, too

Ben Franklin, as minister to France in the late 1700's, first proposed to the French that shops could save on the cost of lighting by opening and closing earlier. Franklin's *bonne idée* was taken a step further in the early 1900's by a British builder who pushed for advancing clocks in the spring and turning them back in the fall. The plan took hold during the two World Wars as a fuel-conservation measure. Localities across the United States, however, adopted the practice willy-nilly, wreaking havoc on airline, railroad and broadcasting schedules. President Lyndon Johnson eliminated the chaos in 1966 by signing Public Law 89-387, creating a uniform starting and ending daylight saving time.

So, in the spring move your clocks ahead by one hour; in the fall, turn them back, thereby shifting an hour of daylight from the morning to the evening. (Consumer safety advocates advise also changing smoke-alarm batteries twice a year, at the start and end of daylight saving time.) Starting in 2007, daylight saving time will start at 2 a.m. on March 10, the second Sunday in March; and it will extend until 2 a.m. on November 3, the first Sunday in November. In 2006, daylight saving time started in April and ended in late October but Congress changed that. Those who stand to benefit: energy-saving consumers and young trick-or-treaters who will get a little more daylight on Halloween night.

Travelers should keep in mind that some states and territories—generally those in warmer climates and those split by time zones—don't observe daylight saving time. These currently include Arizona, Hawaii, Puerto Rico and parts of Indiana. And, in most Western European countries, daylight saving time begins the last Sunday in March and ends on the last Sunday in October.

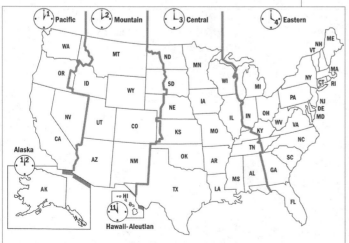

U.S. TIME ZONES AND DAYLIGHT SAVING TIME Note that Arizona and parts of Indiana do not observe daylight saving time.

EUROPEAN TIME ZONES:

When It's Lunchtime in New York...

The standard time in 65 major foreign cities, assuming it is noon in the Eastern Standard Time zone

CITY, COUNTRY	TIME
Addis Ababa, Ethiopia	8 pm
Algiers, Algeria	5 pm
Amman, Jordan	8 pm
Amsterdam, Netherlands*	6 pm
Athens, Greece*	7 pm
Bagdad, Iraq*	8 pm
Bangkok, Thailand	12 midnight
Beijing, China	1am**
Beirut, Lebanon*	7 pm
Berlin, Germany*	6 pm
Bogota, Colombia	12 noon
Brussels, Belgium*	6 pm
Bucharest, Romania*	7 pm
Budapest, Hungary*	6 pm
Buenos Aires, Argentina	2 pm
Cairo, Egypt*	7 pm
Caracas, Venezuela	1 pm
Casablanca, Morocco	5 pm
Copenhagen, Denmark*	6 pm
Dublin, Ireland*	5 pm
Frankfurt, Germany*	6 pm
Geneva, Switzerland*	6 pm
Hanoi, Vietnam	1 am**
Havana, Cuba*	12 noon
Helsinki, Finland*	7 pm
Hong Kong, P.R. of China	1 am**
Istanbul, Turkey*	7 pm
Jakarta, Indonesia	12 midnight
Jerusalem, Israel*	7 pm
Johannesburg, South Africa	7 pm
Kabul, Afghanistan	8:30 pm
Karachi, Pakistan	10 pm
Kuala Lumpur, Malaysia	1 am**
Kuwait City, Kuwait	7 pm
Lagos, Nigeria	6 pm
Lima, Peru	12 noon
Lisbon, Portugal*	6 pm

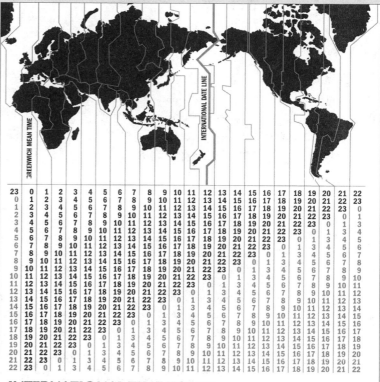

INTERNATIONAL TIME ZONES

The 24 time zones are figured in relation to their distance from the prime meridian, which is the longitudinal position of the Royal Observatory in Greenwich, England. Anyone crossing the International Date Line going west should move the calendar ahead one day; if the line is crossed going east, the date moves back one day.

London, England*	5 pm	Seoul, Korea	2 am**
Madrid, Spain*	6 pm	Singapore, Singapore	1 am**
Manila, Philippines	1 am**	Stockholm, Sweden*	6 pm
Mexico City, Mexico*	11 am	Sydney, Australia	4 am**
Moscow, Russia*	8 pm	Taipei, Taiwan	1 am**
Nairobi, Kenya	7 pm	Teheran, Iran*	8:30 pm
New Dehli, India	10:30 pm	Tel Aviv, Israel	7 pm
Oslo, Norway*	6 pm	Tokyo, Japan	2 am**
Ottawa, Canada*	12 noon	Toronto, Canada*	12 noon
Paris, France*	6 pm	Vienna, Austria*	6 pm
Prague, Czech Republic*	6 pm	Warsaw, Poland*	6 pm
Rio de Janeiro, Brazil	2 pm	Zagreb, Croatia*	6 pm
Riyadh, Saudi Arabia	8 pm	Zurich, Switzerland*	6 pm
Rome, Italy*	6 pm		
Santiago, Chile	1 pm		

* Cities observe Daylight Saving Time
* * The following day

SCIENCE

The Perpetual Calendar: 1820-2080

Datebooks must reflect changing times

By definition, New Year's Day has always marked the start of a new calendar year, but that calendar year hasn't always been in January. Until the 16th century in Western Europe, New Year's Day was rung in on the vernal equinox, the start of spring in the northern hemisphere. But other, non-Christian cultures have always had festivals to celebrate the birth of the sun around the time of the winter solstice in the dead of December. In 1582, Pope Gregory XIII rearranged the calendar, which is now universally used, and decreed that the Christian New Year should commence on January 1.

On which day of the week will New Year's fall next year, or in 2010? Or, in case it's slipped your mind, which day of the week were you born? With the perpetual calendar on the following pages, the answers are at your fingertips. The letter shown for each year indicates which calendar to use.

THE PERPETUAL CALENDAR LEGEND

Year		Year		Year		Year		Year		Year		Year		Year	
1820	J	1854	K	1888	D	1920	H	1952	F	1984	D	2016	I	2050	C
1821	L	1855	L	1889	M	1921	C	1953	A	1985	M	2017	K	2051	K
1822	M	1856	F	1890	N	1922	K	1954	B	1986	N	2018	L	2052	E
1823	N	1857	A	1891	A	1923	L	1955	C	1987	A	2019	M	2053	N
1824	H	1858	B	1892	I	1924	F	1956	D	1988	I	2020	G	2054	A
1825	C	1859	C	1893	K	1925	A	1957	M	1989	K	2021	B	2055	B
1826	K	1860	D	1894	L	1926	B	1958	N	1990	L	2022	C	2056	J
1827	L	1861	M	1895	M	1927	C	1959	A	1991	M	2023	K	2057	L
1828	F	1862	N	1896	G	1928	D	1960	I	1992	G	2024	E	2058	M
1829	A	1863	A	1897	B	1929	M	1961	K	1993	B	2025	N	2059	N
1830	B	1864	I	1898	C	1930	N	1962	L	1994	C	2026	A	2060	H
1831	C	1865	K	1899	K	1931	A	1963	M	1995	K	2027	B	2061	C
1832	D	1866	L	1900	L	1932	I	1964	G	1996	E	2028	J	2062	K
1833	M	1867	M	1901	M	1933	K	1965	B	1997	N	2029	L	2063	L
1834	N	1868	G	1902	N	1934	L	1966	C	1998	A	2030	M	2064	F
1835	A	1869	B	1903	A	1935	M	1967	K	1999	B	2031	N	2065	A
1836	I	1870	C	1904	I	1936	G	1968	E	2000	J	2032	H	2066	B
1837	K	1871	K	1905	K	1937	B	1969	N	2001	L	2033	C	2067	C
1838	L	1872	E	1906	L	1938	C	1970	A	2002	M	2034	K	2068	D
1839	M	1873	N	1907	M	1939	K	1971	B	2003	N	2035	L	2069	M
1840	G	1874	A	1908	G	1940	E	1972	J	2004	H	2036	F	2070	N
1841	B	1875	B	1909	B	1941	N	1973	L	2005	C	2037	A	2071	A
1842	C	1876	J	1910	C	1942	A	1974	M	2006	K	2038	B	2072	I
1843	K	1877	L	1911	K	1943	B	1975	N	2007	L	2039	C	2073	K
1844	E	1878	M	1912	E	1944	J	1976	H	2008	F	2040	D	2074	L
1845	N	1879	N	1913	N	1945	L	1977	C	2009	A	2041	M	2075	M
1846	A	1880	H	1914	A	1946	M	1978	K	2010	B	2042	N	2076	G
1847	B	1881	C	1915	B	1947	N	1979	L	2011	C	2043	A	2077	B
1848	J	1882	K	1916	J	1948	H	1980	F	2012	D	2044	I	2078	C
1849	L	1883	L	1917	L	1949	C	1981	A	2013	M	2045	K	2079	K
1850	M	1884	F	1918	M	1950	K	1982	B	2014	N	2046	L	2080	E
1851	N	1885	A	1919	N	1951	L	1983	C	2015	A	2047	M		
1852	H	1886	B									2048	G		
1853	C	1887	C									2049	B		

A 2009, 1998

JANUARY
S	M	T	W	T	F	S
				1	2	3
4	5	6	7	8	9	10
11	12	13	14	15	16	17
18	19	20	21	22	23	24
25	26	27	28	29	30	31

FEBRUARY
S	M	T	W	T	F	S
1	2	3	4	5	6	7
8	9	10	11	12	13	14
15	16	17	18	19	20	21
22	23	24	25	26	27	28

MARCH
S	M	T	W	T	F	S
1	2	3	4	5	6	7
8	9	10	11	12	13	14
15	16	17	18	19	20	21
22	23	24	25	26	27	28
29	30	31				

APRIL
S	M	T	W	T	F	S
			1	2	3	4
5	6	7	8	9	10	11
12	13	14	15	16	17	18
19	20	21	22	23	24	25
26	27	28	29	30		

MAY
S	M	T	W	T	F	S
					1	2
3	4	5	6	7	8	9
10	11	12	13	14	15	16
17	18	19	20	21	22	23
24	25	26	27	28	29	30
31						

JUNE
S	M	T	W	T	F	S
	1	2	3	4	5	6
7	8	9	10	11	12	13
14	15	16	17	18	19	20
21	22	23	24	25	26	27
28	29	30				

JULY
S	M	T	W	T	F	S
			1	2	3	4
5	6	7	8	9	10	11
12	13	14	15	16	17	18
19	20	21	22	23	24	25
26	27	28	29	30	31	

AUGUST
S	M	T	W	T	F	S
						1
2	3	4	5	6	7	8
9	10	11	12	13	14	15
16	17	18	19	20	21	22
23	24	25	26	27	28	29
30	31					

SEPTEMBER
S	M	T	W	T	F	S
		1	2	3	4	5
6	7	8	9	10	11	12
13	14	15	16	17	18	19
20	21	22	23	24	25	26
27	28	29	30			

OCTOBER
S	M	T	W	T	F	S
				1	2	3
4	5	6	7	8	9	10
11	12	13	14	15	16	17
18	19	20	21	22	23	24
25	26	27	28	29	30	31

NOVEMBER
S	M	T	W	T	F	S
1	2	3	4	5	6	7
8	9	10	11	12	13	14
15	16	17	18	19	20	21
22	23	24	25	26	27	28
29	30					

DECEMBER
S	M	T	W	T	F	S
		1	2	3	4	5
6	7	8	9	10	11	12
13	14	15	16	17	18	19
20	21	22	23	24	25	26
27	28	29	30	31		

B 2010, 1999

JANUARY
S	M	T	W	T	F	S
					1	2
3	4	5	6	7	8	9
10	11	12	13	14	15	16
17	18	19	20	21	22	23
24	25	26	27	28	29	30
31						

FEBRUARY
S	M	T	W	T	F	S
	1	2	3	4	5	6
7	8	9	10	11	12	13
14	15	16	17	18	19	20
21	22	23	24	25	26	27
28						

MARCH
S	M	T	W	T	F	S
	1	2	3	4	5	6
7	8	9	10	11	12	13
14	15	16	17	18	19	20
21	22	23	24	25	26	27
28	29	30	31			

APRIL
S	M	T	W	T	F	S
				1	2	3
4	5	6	7	8	9	10
11	12	13	14	15	16	17
18	19	20	21	22	23	24
25	26	27	28	29	30	

MAY
S	M	T	W	T	F	S
						1
2	3	4	5	6	7	8
9	10	11	12	13	14	15
16	17	18	19	20	21	22
23	24	25	26	27	28	29
30	31					

JUNE
S	M	T	W	T	F	S
		1	2	3	4	5
6	7	8	9	10	11	12
13	14	15	16	17	18	19
20	21	22	23	24	25	26
27	28	29	30			

JULY
S	M	T	W	T	F	S
				1	2	3
4	5	6	7	8	9	10
11	12	13	14	15	16	17
18	19	20	21	22	23	24
25	26	27	28	29	30	31

AUGUST
S	M	T	W	T	F	S
1	2	3	4	5	6	7
8	9	10	11	12	13	14
15	16	17	18	19	20	21
22	23	24	25	26	27	28
29	30	31				

SEPTEMBER
S	M	T	W	T	F	S
			1	2	3	4
5	6	7	8	9	10	11
12	13	14	15	16	17	18
19	20	21	22	23	24	25
26	27	28	29	30		

OCTOBER
S	M	T	W	T	F	S
					1	2
3	4	5	6	7	8	9
10	11	12	13	14	15	16
17	18	19	20	21	22	23
24	25	26	27	28	29	30
31						

NOVEMBER
S	M	T	W	T	F	S
	1	2	3	4	5	6
7	8	9	10	11	12	13
14	15	16	17	18	19	20
21	22	23	24	25	26	27
28	29	30				

DECEMBER
S	M	T	W	T	F	S
			1	2	3	4
5	6	7	8	9	10	11
12	13	14	15	16	17	18
19	20	21	22	23	24	25
26	27	28	29	30	31	

A Multitude of Reasons to Celebrate

Every day is a holiday— somewhere

Merchants like holidays, when gift-happy consumers make cash registers ring. The religious faithful take their holy days very seriously. And those who simply need a break cheer at the prospect of a day free of the normal routine. Whatever your reason to celebrate, here are the dates of major holidays, in the United States and abroad.

MAJOR AMERICAN HOLIDAYS

Dates marked with an asterisk (*) are officially designated national holidays. Federal government offices nationwide, and schools, banks and offices in Washington, D.C., are closed.

*New Year's Day, *Jan. 1.* Roman mythology says two-faced Janus, the god of beginnings for whom our first month is named, looked back on the old year and ahead to the new. In the U.S., we ring out the old year at midnight with champagne and a few bars of that cryptic Scottish melody, *Auld Lang Syne* ("The Good Old Days").

*Dr. Martin Luther King Jr. Birthday, *third Monday in Jan.* The civil rights activist, minister, and advocate of nonviolent protest

SCIENCE

was born on January 15, 1929. A bill to make his birthday a federal holiday was first introduced in 1968, the year King was assassinated. President Ronald Reagan signed the bill in 1983.

Groundhog Day, *Feb. 2.* Rumor has it that if a groundhog comes out of his hole on this day and sees his shadow, winter will last for six more weeks. But if the sky is overcast and the groundhog is shadowless, mild weather is on the way. Pennsylvania's Punxsutawney Phil is the country's most famous rodent meteorologist. Since 1887, the Punxsutawney Groundhog Club has gone to Gobbler's Knob to watch successive generations of Phils offer their predictions.

Valentine's Day, *Feb. 14.* The origin of this romantic holiday is uncertain, but it may have been inspired by the martyrdom of St. Valentine in A.D. 270. The first commercial Valentine's Day cards in the U.S. hit the shops in the 1840's; in the early 1900's, when risqué cards were "common," the Chicago postal service refused to deliver 25,000 valentines it deemed unfit to be mailed.

＊President's Day, *third Monday in Feb.* Honors two of our most famous presidents, George Washington (born Feb. 22, 1732) and Abraham Lincoln (born Feb. 12, 1809), whose birthdays used to be celebrated separately. These larger-than-life figures

---

C — 2011, 2005

JANUARY
S	M	T	W	T	F	S
						1
2	3	4	5	6	7	8
9	10	11	12	13	14	15
16	17	18	19	20	21	22
23	24	25	26	27	28	29
30	31					

FEBRUARY
S	M	T	W	T	F	S
		1	2	3	4	5
6	7	8	9	10	11	12
13	14	15	16	17	18	19
20	21	22	23	24	25	26
27	28					

MARCH
S	M	T	W	T	F	S
		1	2	3	4	5
6	7	8	9	10	11	12
13	14	15	16	17	18	19
20	21	22	23	24	25	26
27	28	29	30	31		

APRIL
S	M	T	W	T	F	S
					1	2
3	4	5	6	7	8	9
10	11	12	13	14	15	16
17	18	19	20	21	22	23
24	25	26	27	28	29	30

MAY
S	M	T	W	T	F	S
1	2	3	4	5	6	7
8	9	10	11	12	13	14
15	16	17	18	19	20	21
22	23	24	25	26	27	28
29	30	31				

JUNE
S	M	T	W	T	F	S
			1	2	3	4
5	6	7	8	9	10	11
12	13	14	15	16	17	18
19	20	21	22	23	24	25
26	27	28	29	30		

JULY
S	M	T	W	T	F	S
					1	2
3	4	5	6	7	8	9
10	11	12	13	14	15	16
17	18	19	20	21	22	23
24	25	26	27	28	29	30
31						

AUGUST
S	M	T	W	T	F	S
	1	2	3	4	5	6
7	8	9	10	11	12	13
14	15	16	17	18	19	20
21	22	23	24	25	26	27
28	29	30	31			

SEPTEMBER
S	M	T	W	T	F	S
				1	2	3
4	5	6	7	8	9	10
11	12	13	14	15	16	17
18	19	20	21	22	23	24
25	26	27	28	29	30	

OCTOBER
S	M	T	W	T	F	S
						1
2	3	4	5	6	7	8
9	10	11	12	13	14	15
16	17	18	19	20	21	22
23	24	25	26	27	28	29
30	31					

NOVEMBER
S	M	T	W	T	F	S
		1	2	3	4	5
6	7	8	9	10	11	12
13	14	15	16	17	18	19
20	21	22	23	24	25	26
27	28	29	30			

DECEMBER
S	M	T	W	T	F	S
				1	2	3
4	5	6	7	8	9	10
11	12	13	14	15	16	17
18	19	20	21	22	23	24
25	26	27	28	29	30	31

D — 2012, 1984

JANUARY
S	M	T	W	T	F	S
1	2	3	4	5	6	7
8	9	10	11	12	13	14
15	16	17	18	19	20	21
22	23	24	25	26	27	28
29	30	31				

FEBRUARY
S	M	T	W	T	F	S
			1	2	3	4
5	6	7	8	9	10	11
12	13	14	15	16	17	18
19	20	21	22	23	24	25
26	27	28	29			

MARCH
S	M	T	W	T	F	S
				1	2	3
4	5	6	7	8	9	10
11	12	13	14	15	16	17
18	19	20	21	22	23	24
25	26	27	28	29	30	31

APRIL
S	M	T	W	T	F	S
1	2	3	4	5	6	7
8	9	10	11	12	13	14
15	16	17	18	19	20	21
22	23	24	25	26	27	28
29	30					

MAY
S	M	T	W	T	F	S
		1	2	3	4	5
6	7	8	9	10	11	12
13	14	15	16	17	18	19
20	21	22	23	24	25	26
27	28	29	30	31		

JUNE
S	M	T	W	T	F	S
					1	2
3	4	5	6	7	8	9
10	11	12	13	14	15	16
17	18	19	20	21	22	23
24	25	26	27	28	29	30

JULY
S	M	T	W	T	F	S
1	2	3	4	5	6	7
8	9	10	11	12	13	14
15	16	17	18	19	20	21
22	23	24	25	26	27	28
29	30	31				

AUGUST
S	M	T	W	T	F	S
			1	2	3	4
5	6	7	8	9	10	11
12	13	14	15	16	17	18
19	20	21	22	23	24	25
26	27	28	29	30	31	

SEPTEMBER
S	M	T	W	T	F	S
						1
2	3	4	5	6	7	8
9	10	11	12	13	14	15
16	17	18	19	20	21	22
23	24	25	26	27	28	29
30						

OCTOBER
S	M	T	W	T	F	S
	1	2	3	4	5	6
7	8	9	10	11	12	13
14	15	16	17	18	19	20
21	22	23	24	25	26	27
28	29	30	31			

NOVEMBER
S	M	T	W	T	F	S
				1	2	3
4	5	6	7	8	9	10
11	12	13	14	15	16	17
18	19	20	21	22	23	24
25	26	27	28	29	30	

DECEMBER
S	M	T	W	T	F	S
						1
2	3	4	5	6	7	8
9	10	11	12	13	14	15
16	17	18	19	20	21	22
23	24	25	26	27	28	29
30	31					

E — 2024, 1996

```
         JANUARY                      MAY                    SEPTEMBER
S  M  T  W  T  F  S        S  M  T  W  T  F  S        S  M  T  W  T  F  S
      1  2  3  4  5  6                 1  2  3  4     1  2  3  4  5  6  7
 7  8  9 10 11 12 13        5  6  7  8  9 10 11        8  9 10 11 12 13 14
14 15 16 17 18 19 20       12 13 14 15 16 17 18       15 16 17 18 19 20 21
21 22 23 24 25 26 27       19 20 21 22 23 24 25       22 23 24 25 26 27 28
28 29 30 31                26 27 28 29 30 31          29 30

         FEBRUARY                     JUNE                    OCTOBER
S  M  T  W  T  F  S        S  M  T  W  T  F  S        S  M  T  W  T  F  S
            1  2  3                          1              1  2  3  4  5
 4  5  6  7  8  9 10        2  3  4  5  6  7  8        6  7  8  9 10 11 12
11 12 13 14 15 16 17        9 10 11 12 13 14 15       13 14 15 16 17 18 19
18 19 20 21 22 23 24       16 17 18 19 20 21 22       20 21 22 23 24 25 26
25 26 27 28 29             23 24 25 26 27 28 29       27 28 29 30 31
                           30

         MARCH                        JULY                    NOVEMBER
S  M  T  W  T  F  S        S  M  T  W  T  F  S        S  M  T  W  T  F  S
               1  2              1  2  3  4  5  6                    1  2
 3  4  5  6  7  8  9        7  8  9 10 11 12 13        3  4  5  6  7  8  9
10 11 12 13 14 15 16       14 15 16 17 18 19 20       10 11 12 13 14 15 16
17 18 19 20 21 22 23       21 22 23 24 25 26 27       17 18 19 20 21 22 23
24 25 26 27 28 29 30       28 29 30 31                24 25 26 27 28 29 30
31

         APRIL                        AUGUST                  DECEMBER
S  M  T  W  T  F  S        S  M  T  W  T  F  S        S  M  T  W  T  F  S
      1  2  3  4  5  6                  1  2  3        1  2  3  4  5  6  7
 7  8  9 10 11 12 13        4  5  6  7  8  9 10        8  9 10 11 12 13 14
14 15 16 17 18 19 20       11 12 13 14 15 16 17       15 16 17 18 19 20 21
21 22 23 24 25 26 27       18 19 20 21 22 23 24       22 23 24 25 26 27 28
28 29 30                   25 26 27 28 29 30 31       29 30 31
```

F — 2008, 1980

```
         JANUARY                      MAY                    SEPTEMBER
S  M  T  W  T  F  S        S  M  T  W  T  F  S        S  M  T  W  T  F  S
         1  2  3  4  5                    1  2  3           1  2  3  4  5  6
 6  7  8  9 10 11 12        4  5  6  7  8  9 10        7  8  9 10 11 12 13
13 14 15 16 17 18 19       11 12 13 14 15 16 17       14 15 16 17 18 19 20
20 21 22 23 24 25 26       18 19 20 21 22 23 24       21 22 23 24 25 26 27
27 28 29 30 31             25 26 27 28 29 30 31       28 29 30

         FEBRUARY                     JUNE                    OCTOBER
S  M  T  W  T  F  S        S  M  T  W  T  F  S        S  M  T  W  T  F  S
                  1  2      1  2  3  4  5  6  7                    1  2  3  4
 3  4  5  6  7  8  9        8  9 10 11 12 13 14        5  6  7  8  9 10 11
10 11 12 13 14 15 16       15 16 17 18 19 20 21       12 13 14 15 16 17 18
17 18 19 20 21 22 23       22 23 24 25 26 27 28       19 20 21 22 23 24 25
24 25 26 27 28 29          29 30                      26 27 28 29 30 31

         MARCH                        JULY                    NOVEMBER
S  M  T  W  T  F  S        S  M  T  W  T  F  S        S  M  T  W  T  F  S
                     1              1  2  3  4  5                       1
 2  3  4  5  6  7  8        6  7  8  9 10 11 12        2  3  4  5  6  7  8
 9 10 11 12 13 14 15       13 14 15 16 17 18 19        9 10 11 12 13 14 15
16 17 18 19 20 21 22       20 21 22 23 24 25 26       16 17 18 19 20 21 22
23 24 25 26 27 28 29       27 28 29 30 31             23 24 25 26 27 28 29
30 31                                                 30

         APRIL                        AUGUST                  DECEMBER
S  M  T  W  T  F  S        S  M  T  W  T  F  S        S  M  T  W  T  F  S
      1  2  3  4  5                       1  2        1  2  3  4  5  6
 6  7  8  9 10 11 12        3  4  5  6  7  8  9        7  8  9 10 11 12 13
13 14 15 16 17 18 19       10 11 12 13 14 15 16       14 15 16 17 18 19 20
20 21 22 23 24 25 26       17 18 19 20 21 22 23       21 22 23 24 25 26 27
27 28 29 30               24 25 26 27 28 29 30       28 29 30 31
                           31
```

stood out in the crowd even by today's standards: Washington was 6 feet tall, and lanky Lincoln was 6 feet 4 inches.

St. Patrick's Day, *March 17.* The patron saint of Ireland was born in England around A.D. 389 and immigrants who came to America from the Emerald Isle brought this holiday with them. So many of George Washington's troops were Irish that the secret password during one Revolutionary War battle was "Saint Patrick."

Vernal Equinox, around *March 21.* Day and night are equally long on this first day of spring.

April Fools' Day, *April 1.* No one is sure when or why the first of April turned into a day for making friends look like fools, but the tradition dates back at least to the early 18th century. April fools are labeled "gowks" (cuckoos) in Scotland, and "gobs" or "noddies" in England; the French call April 1 pranks "poisson d'avril," or April fish.

Earth Day, *April 22.* In 1970, the Environmental Protection Agency first asked us to "Give Earth a Chance." Congress has passed laws that protect our natural resources, and curbside recycling is now common. But the E.P.A. reports that we still produce more solid waste per person every day than any other nation—4.4 pounds.

SCIENCE

Mother's Day, second Sunday in May. Julia Ward Howe, author of "Battle Hymn of the Republic," first floated the idea of a national holiday to honor mothers in 1872. But Philadelphian Anna Jarvis, whose mother had wanted such a day to comfort families after the Civil War, launched the campaign that made it a reality. President Woodrow Wilson officially established the holiday in 1914.

✱Memorial Day, last Monday in May. The government bowed in 1868 to the campaign of a Union veterans group that wanted to honor soldiers who died in the Civil War. The holiday has now become a tribute to all fallen soldiers and deceased loved ones.

Flag Day, June 14. The Second Continental Congress adopted the official flag design on June 14, 1777. Protocol dictates that the American flag may not touch the ground, nor may it be dipped to anyone or anything while being carried in a parade. The star-spangled banner Francis Scott Key saw by the dawn's early light was hit by 11 bullets as it flew above Baltimore's Fort McHenry; it is preserved at the Smithsonian Institution.

Father's Day, third Sunday in June. The daughter of a Civil War veteran (whose wife died giving birth to their sixth child) persuaded her church in Spokane, Wash., to conduct a special

G — 2020, 1992

JANUARY
S	M	T	W	T	F	S
			1	2	3	4
5	6	7	8	9	10	11
12	13	14	15	16	17	18
19	20	21	22	23	24	25
26	27	28	29	30	31	

FEBRUARY
S	M	T	W	T	F	S
						1
2	3	4	5	6	7	8
9	10	11	12	13	14	15
16	17	18	19	20	21	22
23	24	25	26	27	28	29

MARCH
S	M	T	W	T	F	S
1	2	3	4	5	6	7
8	9	10	11	12	13	14
15	16	17	18	19	20	21
22	23	24	25	26	27	28
29	30	31				

APRIL
S	M	T	W	T	F	S
			1	2	3	4
5	6	7	8	9	10	11
12	13	14	15	16	17	18
19	20	21	22	23	24	25
26	27	28	29	30		

MAY
S	M	T	W	T	F	S
					1	2
3	4	5	6	7	8	9
10	11	12	13	14	15	16
17	18	19	20	21	22	23
24	25	26	27	28	29	30
31						

JUNE
S	M	T	W	T	F	S
	1	2	3	4	5	6
7	8	9	10	11	12	13
14	15	16	17	18	19	20
21	22	23	24	25	26	27
28	29	30				

JULY
S	M	T	W	T	F	S
			1	2	3	4
5	6	7	8	9	10	11
12	13	14	15	16	17	18
19	20	21	22	23	24	25
26	27	28	29	30	31	

AUGUST
S	M	T	W	T	F	S
						1
2	3	4	5	6	7	8
9	10	11	12	13	14	15
16	17	18	19	20	21	22
23	24	25	26	27	28	29
30	31					

SEPTEMBER
S	M	T	W	T	F	S
		1	2	3	4	5
6	7	8	9	10	11	12
13	14	15	16	17	18	19
20	21	22	23	24	25	26
27	28	29	30			

OCTOBER
S	M	T	W	T	F	S
				1	2	3
4	5	6	7	8	9	10
11	12	13	14	15	16	17
18	19	20	21	22	23	24
25	26	27	28	29	30	31

NOVEMBER
S	M	T	W	T	F	S
1	2	3	4	5	6	7
8	9	10	11	12	13	14
15	16	17	18	19	20	21
22	23	24	25	26	27	28
29	30					

DECEMBER
S	M	T	W	T	F	S
		1	2	3	4	5
6	7	8	9	10	11	12
13	14	15	16	17	18	19
20	21	22	23	24	25	26
27	28	29	30	31		

H — 2032, 2004

JANUARY
S	M	T	W	T	F	S
				1	2	3
4	5	6	7	8	9	10
11	12	13	14	15	16	17
18	19	20	21	22	23	24
25	26	27	28	29	30	31

FEBRUARY
S	M	T	W	T	F	S
1	2	3	4	5	6	7
8	9	10	11	12	13	14
15	16	17	18	19	20	21
22	23	24	25	26	27	28
29						

MARCH
S	M	T	W	T	F	S
	1	2	3	4	5	6
7	8	9	10	11	12	13
14	15	16	17	18	19	20
21	22	23	24	25	26	27
28	29	30	31			

APRIL
S	M	T	W	T	F	S
				1	2	3
4	5	6	7	8	9	10
11	12	13	14	15	16	17
18	19	20	21	22	23	24
25	26	27	28	29	30	

MAY
S	M	T	W	T	F	S
						1
2	3	4	5	6	7	8
9	10	11	12	13	14	15
16	17	18	19	20	21	22
23	24	25	26	27	28	29
30	31					

JUNE
S	M	T	W	T	F	S
		1	2	3	4	5
6	7	8	9	10	11	12
13	14	15	16	17	18	19
20	21	22	23	24	25	26
27	28	29	30			

JULY
S	M	T	W	T	F	S
				1	2	3
4	5	6	7	8	9	10
11	12	13	14	15	16	17
18	19	20	21	22	23	24
25	26	27	28	29	30	31

AUGUST
S	M	T	W	T	F	S
1	2	3	4	5	6	7
8	9	10	11	12	13	14
15	16	17	18	19	20	21
22	23	24	25	26	27	28
29	30	31				

SEPTEMBER
S	M	T	W	T	F	S
			1	2	3	4
5	6	7	8	9	10	11
12	13	14	15	16	17	18
19	20	21	22	23	24	25
26	27	28	29	30		

OCTOBER
S	M	T	W	T	F	S
					1	2
3	4	5	6	7	8	9
10	11	12	13	14	15	16
17	18	19	20	21	22	23
24	25	26	27	28	29	30
31						

NOVEMBER
S	M	T	W	T	F	S
	1	2	3	4	5	6
7	8	9	10	11	12	13
14	15	16	17	18	19	20
21	22	23	24	25	26	27
28	29	30				

DECEMBER
S	M	T	W	T	F	S
			1	2	3	4
5	6	7	8	9	10	11
12	13	14	15	16	17	18
19	20	21	22	23	24	25
26	27	28	29	30	31	

I   2016, 1988

```
        JANUARY                      MAY                    SEPTEMBER
 S  M  T  W  T  F  S      S  M  T  W  T  F  S      S  M  T  W  T  F  S
             1  2         1  2  3  4  5  6  7                  1  2  3
 3  4  5  6  7  8  9      8  9 10 11 12 13 14      4  5  6  7  8  9 10
10 11 12 13 14 15 16     15 16 17 18 19 20 21     11 12 13 14 15 16 17
17 18 19 20 21 22 23     22 23 24 25 26 27 28     18 19 20 21 22 23 24
24 25 26 27 28 29 30     29 30 31                 25 26 27 28 29 30
31

        FEBRUARY                     JUNE                    OCTOBER
 S  M  T  W  T  F  S      S  M  T  W  T  F  S      S  M  T  W  T  F  S
    1  2  3  4  5  6            1  2  3  4                           1
 7  8  9 10 11 12 13      5 66  7  8  9 10 11      2  3  4  5  6  7  8
14 15 16 17 18 19 20     12 13 14 15 16 17 18      9 10 11 12 13 14 15
21 22 23 24 25 26 27     19 20 21 22 23 24 25     16 17 18 19 20 21 22
20 29                    20 27 28 29 30           23 24 25 26 27 28 29
                                                  30 31

        MARCH                        JULY                    NOVEMBER
 S  M  T  W  T  F  S      S  M  T  W  T  F  S      S  M  T  W  T  F  S
       1  2  3  4  5                     1  2            1  2  3  4  5
 6  7  8  9 10 11 12      3  4  5  6  7  8  9      6  7  8  9 10 11 12
13 14 15 16 17 18 19     10 11 12 13 14 15 16     13 14 15 16 17 18 19
20 21 22 23 24 25 26     17 18 19 20 21 22 23     20 21 22 23 24 25 26
27 28 29 30 31           24 25 26 27 28 29 30     27 28 29 30
                         31

        APRIL                        AUGUST                  DECEMBER
 S  M  T  W  T  F  S      S  M  T  W  T  F  S      S  M  T  W  T  F  S
                1  2         1  2  3  4  5  6                     1  2  3
 3  4  5  6  7  8  9      7  8  9 10 11 12 13      4  5  6  7  8  9 10
10 11 12 13 14 15 16     14 15 16 17 18 19 20     11 12 13 14 15 16 17
17 18 19 20 21 22 23     21 22 23 24 25 26 27     18 19 20 21 22 23 24
24 25 26 27 28 29 30     28 29 30 31              25 26 27 28 29 30 31
```

J   2028, 2000

```
        JANUARY                      MAY                    SEPTEMBER
 S  M  T  W  T  F  S      S  M  T  W  T  F  S      S  M  T  W  T  F  S
                   1         1  2  3  4  5  6                     1  2
 2  3  4  5  6  7  8      7  8  9 10 11 12 13      3  4  5  6  7  8  9
 9 10 11 12 13 14 15     14 15 16 17 18 19 20     10 11 12 13 14 15 16
16 17 18 19 20 21 22     21 22 23 24 25 26 27     17 18 19 20 21 22 23
23 24 25 26 27 28 29     28 29 30 31              24 25 26 27 28 29 30
30 31

        FEBRUARY                     JUNE                    OCTOBER
 S  M  T  W  T  F  S      S  M  T  W  T  F  S      S  M  T  W  T  F  S
       1  2  3  4  5               1  2  3         1  2  3  4  5  6  7
 6  7  8  9 10 11 12      4  5  6  7  8  9 10      8  9 10 11 12 13 14
13 14 15 16 17 18 19     11 12 13 14 15 16 17     15 16 17 18 19 20 21
20 21 22 23 24 25 26     18 19 20 21 22 23 24     22 23 24 25 26 27 28
27 28 29                 25 26 27 28 29 30        29 30 31

        MARCH                        JULY                    NOVEMBER
 S  M  T  W  T  F  S      S  M  T  W  T  F  S      S  M  T  W  T  F  S
          1  2  3  4                        1            1  2  3  4
 5  6  7  8  9 10 11      2  3  4  5  6  7  8      5  6  7  8  9 10 11
12 13 14 15 16 17 18      9 10 11 12 13 14 15     12 13 14 15 16 17 18
19 20 21 22 23 24 25     16 17 18 19 20 21 22     19 20 21 22 23 24 25
26 27 28 29 30 31        23 24 25 26 27 28 29     26 27 28 29 30
                         30 31

        APRIL                        AUGUST                  DECEMBER
 S  M  T  W  T  F  S      S  M  T  W  T  F  S      S  M  T  W  T  F  S
                   1         1  2  3  4  5                        1  2
 2  3  4  5  6  7  8      6  7  8  9 10 11 12      3  4  5  6  7  8  9
 9 10 11 12 13 14 15     13 14 15 16 17 18 19     10 11 12 13 14 15 16
16 17 18 19 20 21 22     20 21 22 23 24 25 26     17 18 19 20 21 22 23
23 24 25 26 27 28 29     27 28 29 30 31           24 25 26 27 28 29 30
30                                                31
```

service in honor of fathers. That was in 1910, and though the idea soon became popular around the nation, it wasn't made an official holiday until 1966.

Summer Solstice, around June 21. The first day of summer; the year's longest day.

✳Independence Day, July 4. Fireworks and fanfare generally mark Fourth of July festivities commemorating the 1776 signing of the Declaration of Independence. Two of the signers were loyal to it even in death: On July 4, 1826, John Adams, the second president, died at age 90, and Thomas Jefferson, president number three, died at age 83.

Women's Equality Day, Aug. 26. The 19th Amendment to the Constitution was passed on this day in 1920, giving women the right to vote. In Tennessee's House of Representatives, the last vote needed to ratify the amendment was cast by 24-year-old Harry Burns, who, though his district opposed the measure, promised his mother he would vote for it to break a tie.

✳Labor Day, first Monday in Sept. During the Industrial Revolution, a bad time for laborers, union leader Peter McGuire drummed up support for a day to pay homage to America's workers. He chose early September for its pleasant weather, and because no other legal holiday

SCIENCE

broke up the stretch between Independence Day and Thanksgiving. It's always been thought of as the end of summer vacation, although many schools now resume in late August.

Autumnal Equinox, around Sept. 21. The first day of fall.

*Columbus Day, Second Monday in Oct. Christopher Columbus and his entourage first touched American soil on October 12, 1492, probably on Samana Cay in the Bahamas. At sea, Columbus kept an accurate private log of the miles traveled each day, but subtracted miles for the ship's official log. He did so to avoid mutinies caused by sailors who didn't want to be so far from home, and to make sure his directions to Asia, which turned out to be wildly inaccurate, wouldn't fall into the wrong hands.

United Nations Day, Oct. 24. When the United Nations was founded in 1945, it had 51 member countries. Now it has more than 190. Its six official languages are Arabic, Chinese, English, French, Russian and Spanish.

Halloween, Oct. 31. The attendant ghouls and goblins stem from the myths of the ancient Celts, who thought witches, ghosts and the souls of the dead wandered about on the last night of their harvest season. The name comes from the Catholic Church, which in the ninth cen-

---

K   2017, 2006

JANUARY

S	M	T	W	T	F	S
1	2	3	4	5	6	7
8	9	10	11	12	13	14
15	16	17	18	19	20	21
22	23	24	25	26	27	28
29	30	31				

FEBRUARY

S	M	T	W	T	F	S
			1	2	3	4
5	6	7	8	9	10	11
12	13	14	15	16	17	18
19	20	21	22	23	24	25
26	27	28				

MARCH

S	M	T	W	T	F	S
			1	2	3	4
5	6	7	8	9	10	11
12	13	14	15	16	17	18
19	20	21	22	23	24	25
26	27	28	29	30	31	

APRIL

S	M	T	W	T	F	S
						1
2	3	4	5	6	7	8
9	10	11	12	13	14	15
16	17	18	19	20	21	22
23	24	25	26	27	28	29
30						

MAY

S	M	T	W	T	F	S
	1	2	3	4	5	6
7	8	9	10	11	12	13
14	15	16	17	18	19	20
21	22	23	24	25	26	27
28	29	30	31			

JUNE

S	M	T	W	T	F	S
				1	2	3
4	5	6	7	8	9	10
11	12	13	14	15	16	17
18	19	20	21	22	23	24
25	26	27	28	29	30	

JULY

S	M	T	W	T	F	S
						1
2	3	4	5	6	7	8
9	10	11	12	13	14	15
16	17	18	19	20	21	22
23	24	25	26	27	28	29
30	31					

AUGUST

S	M	T	W	T	F	S
		1	2	3	4	5
6	7	8	9	10	11	12
13	14	15	16	17	18	19
20	21	22	23	24	25	26
27	28	29	30	31		

SEPTEMBER

S	M	T	W	T	F	S
					1	2
3	4	5	6	7	8	9
10	11	12	13	14	15	16
17	18	19	20	21	22	23
24	25	26	27	28	29	30

OCTOBER

S	M	T	W	T	F	S
1	2	3	4	5	6	7
8	9	10	11	12	13	14
15	16	17	18	19	20	21
22	23	24	25	26	27	28
29	30	31				

NOVEMBER

S	M	T	W	T	F	S
			1	2	3	4
5	6	7	8	9	10	11
12	13	14	15	16	17	18
19	20	21	22	23	24	25
26	27	28	29	30		

DECEMBER

S	M	T	W	T	F	S
					1	2
3	4	5	6	7	8	9
10	11	12	13	14	15	16
17	18	19	20	21	22	23
24	25	26	27	28	29	30
31						

L   2007, 2001

JANUARY

S	M	T	W	T	F	S
	1	2	3	4	5	6
7	8	9	10	11	12	13
14	15	16	17	18	19	20
21	22	23	24	25	26	27
28	29	30	31			

FEBRUARY

S	M	T	W	T	F	S
				1	2	3
4	5	6	7	8	9	10
11	12	13	14	15	16	17
18	19	20	21	22	23	24
25	26	27	28			

MARCH

S	M	T	W	T	F	S
				1	2	3
4	5	6	7	8	9	10
11	12	13	14	15	16	17
18	19	20	21	22	23	24
25	26	27	28	29	30	31

APRIL

S	M	T	W	T	F	S
1	2	3	4	5	6	7
8	9	10	11	12	13	14
15	16	17	18	19	20	21
22	23	24	25	26	27	28
29	30					

MAY

S	M	T	W	T	F	S
		1	2	3	4	5
6	7	8	9	10	11	12
13	14	15	16	17	18	19
20	21	22	23	24	25	26
27	28	29	30	31		

JUNE

S	M	T	W	T	F	S
					1	2
3	4	5	6	7	8	9
10	11	12	13	14	15	16
17	18	19	20	21	22	23
24	25	26	27	28	29	30

JULY

S	M	T	W	T	F	S
1	2	3	4	5	6	7
8	9	10	11	12	13	14
15	16	17	18	19	20	21
22	23	24	25	26	27	28
29	30	31				

AUGUST

S	M	T	W	T	F	S
			1	2	3	4
5	6	7	8	9	10	11
12	13	14	15	16	17	18
19	20	21	22	23	24	25
26	27	28	20	30	31	

SEPTEMBER

S	M	T	W	T	F	S
						1
2	3	4	5	6	7	8
9	10	11	12	13	14	15
16	17	18	19	20	21	22
23	24	25	26	27	28	29
30						

OCTOBER

S	M	T	W	T	F	S
	1	2	3	4	5	6
7	8	9	10	11	12	13
14	15	16	17	18	19	20
21	22	23	24	25	26	27
28	29	30	31			

NOVEMBER

S	M	T	W	T	F	S
				1	2	3
4	5	6	7	8	9	10
11	12	13	14	15	16	17
18	19	20	21	22	23	24
25	26	27	28	29	30	

DECEMBER

S	M	T	W	T	F	S
						1
2	3	4	5	6	7	8
9	10	11	12	13	14	15
16	17	18	19	20	21	22
23	24	25	26	27	28	29
30	31					

M — 2013, 2002

JANUARY
S	M	T	W	T	F	S
		1	2	3	4	5
6	7	8	9	10	11	12
13	14	15	16	17	18	19
20	21	22	23	24	25	26
27	28	29	30	31		

FEBRUARY
S	M	T	W	T	F	S
					1	2
3	4	5	6	7	8	9
10	11	12	13	14	15	16
17	18	19	20	21	22	23
24	25	26	27	28		

MARCH
S	M	T	W	T	F	S
					1	2
3	4	5	6	7	8	9
10	11	12	13	14	15	16
17	18	19	20	21	22	23
24	25	26	27	28	29	30
31						

APRIL
S	M	T	W	T	F	S
	1	2	3	4	5	6
7	8	9	10	11	12	13
14	15	16	17	18	19	20
21	22	23	24	25	26	27
28	29	30				

MAY
S	M	T	W	T	F	S
			1	2	3	4
5	6	7	8	9	10	11
12	13	14	15	16	17	18
19	20	21	22	23	24	25
26	27	28	29	30	31	

JUNE
S	M	T	W	T	F	S
						1
2	3	4	5	6	7	8
9	10	11	12	13	14	15
16	17	18	19	20	21	22
23	24	25	26	27	28	29
30						

JULY
S	M	T	W	T	F	S
	1	2	3	4	5	6
7	8	9	10	11	12	13
14	15	16	17	18	19	20
21	22	23	24	25	26	27
28	29	30	31			

AUGUST
S	M	T	W	T	F	S
				1	2	3
4	5	6	7	8	9	10
11	12	13	14	15	16	17
18	19	20	21	22	23	24
25	26	27	28	29	30	31

SEPTEMBER
S	M	T	W	T	F	S
1	2	3	4	5	6	7
8	9	10	11	12	13	14
15	16	17	18	19	20	21
22	23	24	25	26	27	28
29	30					

OCTOBER
S	M	T	W	T	F	S
		1	2	3	4	5
6	7	8	9	10	11	12
13	14	15	16	17	18	19
20	21	22	23	24	25	26
27	28	29	30	31		

NOVEMBER
S	M	T	W	T	F	S
					1	2
3	4	5	6	7	8	9
10	11	12	13	14	15	16
17	18	19	20	21	22	23
24	25	26	27	28	29	30

DECEMBER
S	M	T	W	T	F	S
1	2	3	4	5	6	7
8	9	10	11	12	13	14
15	16	17	18	19	20	21
22	23	24	25	26	27	28
29	30	31				

N — 2003, 1997

JANUARY
S	M	T	W	T	F	S
			1	2	3	4
5	6	7	8	9	10	11
12	13	14	15	16	17	18
19	20	21	22	23	24	25
26	27	28	29	30	31	

FEBRUARY
S	M	T	W	T	F	S
						1
2	3	4	5	6	7	8
9	10	11	12	13	14	15
16	17	18	19	20	21	22
23	24	25	26	27	28	

MARCH
S	M	T	W	T	F	S
						1
2	3	4	5	6	7	8
9	10	11	12	13	14	15
16	17	18	19	20	21	22
23	24	25	26	27	28	29
30	31					

APRIL
S	M	T	W	T	F	S
		1	2	3	4	5
6	7	8	9	10	11	12
13	14	15	16	17	18	19
20	21	22	23	24	25	26
27	28	29	30			

MAY
S	M	T	W	T	F	S
				1	2	3
4	5	6	7	8	9	10
11	12	13	14	15	16	17
18	19	20	21	22	23	24
25	26	27	28	29	30	31

JUNE
S	M	T	W	T	F	S
1	2	3	4	5	6	7
8	9	10	11	12	13	14
15	16	17	18	19	20	21
22	23	24	25	26	27	28
29	30					

JULY
S	M	T	W	T	F	S
		1	2	3	4	5
6	7	8	9	10	11	12
13	14	15	16	17	18	19
20	21	22	23	24	25	26
27	28	29	30	31		

AUGUST
S	M	T	W	T	F	S
					1	2
3	4	5	6	7	8	9
10	11	12	13	14	15	16
17	18	19	20	21	22	23
24	25	26	27	28	29	30
31						

SEPTEMBER
S	M	T	W	T	F	S
	1	2	3	4	5	6
7	8	9	10	11	12	13
14	15	16	17	18	19	20
21	22	23	24	25	26	27
28	29	30				

OCTOBER
S	M	T	W	T	F	S
			1	2	3	4
5	6	7	8	9	10	11
12	13	14	15	16	17	18
19	20	21	22	23	24	25
26	27	28	29	30	31	

NOVEMBER
S	M	T	W	T	F	S
						1
2	3	4	5	6	7	8
9	10	11	12	13	14	15
16	17	18	19	20	21	22
23	24	25	26	27	28	29
30						

DECEMBER
S	M	T	W	T	F	S
	1	2	3	4	5	6
7	8	9	10	11	12	13
14	15	16	17	18	19	20
21	22	23	24	25	26	27
28	29	30	31			

tury declared the first of November All Saints' Day and called the previous evening All Hallows Eve. Candy-loving children benefit from the combination of influences, as does UNICEF, which has earned more than $119 million since 1950 from its Halloween fundraising campaign.

✻**Veterans Day,** *Nov. 11.* Formerly called Armistice Day, it commemorated the end of World War 1 and honored those who had died fighting it. The holiday was renamed in 1954 and its scope widened to include all who have served in the U.S. armed forces. For a short time in the 1970's, the date was changed to the fourth Monday in November to add another three-day weekend to the calendar. But many Americans thought making the observance moveable was disrespectful, and the date was changed back in 1978.

✻**Thanksgiving Day,** *third Thursday in Nov.* The first Thanksgiving feast was cooked up around 1621 when pilgrims and Native Americans sat down together to enjoy the fruits of harvest. Formerly scheduled for the last Thursday in November (which usually turns out to be the fourth), Thanksgiving was moved up in 1939 by Franklin D. Roosevelt, who wanted to help the economy by extending the Christmas shopping season.

Winter Solstice, *around Dec.*

SCIENCE

21. First day of winter; shortest day of the year.

❋ Christmas, *Dec. 25.* Now a widespread secular celebration notable for turkey dinners, holiday cheer and mass gift-exchanging, Christmas has long and complex roots. Biblical historians believe Jesus of Nazareth was born around 6 B.C., but most likely not on December 25. A 6th-century monk suggested that date to commemorate Jesus' birthday and it stuck through the ages. (See "Selected Religious Holidays" on facing page.)

Kwanzaa, *Dec. 26 to Jan. 1.* The name means "first fruits" in Swahili, and the holiday is based on African harvest festivals. Brought to America in the mid-60's by Maulana Karenga, a civil rights leader who wanted black Americans to learn about their ancestors' cultures, Kwanzaa celebrates the history and culture of African Americans.

SELECTED INTERNATIONAL HOLIDAYS

New Year, CHINA
Second new moon after winter solstice.
Families gather on New Year's Eve for a sumptuous banquet (the fish dish served last is not eaten, symbolizing the hope that there will be food left at the end of the year) and children awaken the next morning to find red envelopes filled with money under their pillows. Chinese tradition says babies are one year old at birth, and everyone's birthday is New Year's Day. So a child born at 11:59 p.m. on New Year's Eve hits the terrible twos in under three minutes.

Cinco de Mayo, MEXICO
May 5.
Parades, parties, bullfights and beauty pageants commemorate the 1862 Battle of Puebla, when Mexican soldiers beat the odds and the French. France finally conquered Mexico in 1864, but lost the country just three years later. A monument of the town of Puebla honors the soldiers of both armies who died there.

Canada Day, CANADA
July 1.
In honor of the nation's confederation in 1867, fireworks (heavy on the red and white) light up the skies and "O Canada" echoes through the capital city of Ottawa, which hosts an annual concert on Parliament Hill. Across the country, Canadians trot out their flags and firecrackers.

Why Are There Leap Years?
We have a pope to thank for fixing the glitch

Our calendar has 365 days, but the earth actually takes 365 days, 5 hours, 48 minutes and 46 seconds to travel around the sun. With an extra quarter-day each year, in 120 years the calendar would be ahead by a month. New Year's Eve would arrive somewhere around Thanksgiving. Luckily, we have a built-in safeguard: the occasional February 29. To avoid the chaos that would ensue should our seasons fall out of sync, every fourth year an extra day is added to keep the calendar consistent with the sun.

Julius Caesar introduced the leap year in 46 B.C., but despite his admirable mathematic and administrative efforts, the calendar was 10 days ahead by 1582. Enter Pope Gregory XIII, creator of the calendar we use today. He got the months back on track by dropping 10 days from October 1582. He also rescheduled leap year to fall every fourth year except in the case of century years that are not evenly divisible by 4. So, the year 2000 was a leap year but 3000, the next century year, will not be.

Most of Europe adopted the Gregorian calendar right away, but England and its American colonies held out until 1752. At that point, they had accumulated 11 extra days. To make up for gained time, September 2, 1752, was followed immediately by September 14.

Obon Festival, JAPAN
July 13-15 or Aug. 13-15. (varies by region)

The souls of the dead are said to return for a visit during this festival, so the Japanese go to cemeteries and decorate their ancestors' graves in anticipation. Drummers and kimono-clad folk dancers perform, and lanterns and bonfires are lit to comfort the spiritual guests.

Bastille Day, FRANCE
July 14.

A Parisian mob stormed the famous fortress and prison in 1789, not satisfied to eat just cake and hell-bent on releasing the political prisoners they thought were held there. They freed seven inmates, none of whom was actually a political prisoner, but the action marked the lower classes' entry into the French Revolution. Today, the Bastille is gone and Parisians are more restrained: they light firecrackers, decorate their neighborhoods with paper lanterns and waltz in the streets to accordion music.

Sinter Klaas, THE NETHERLANDS
Dec. 5.

St. Nicholas is the patron saint of children, so the Dutch celebrate his birthday to please them. Legend says he wears a red cape, rides a white horse and delivers presents via chimneys. Children leave their shoes out overnight (as well as carrots for the horse) and find them filled with trinkets in the morning.

Santa Lucia, SWEDEN
Dec. 13.

St. Lucia wore a crown of candles to bring light during the darkest day of the bleak Swedish winter. At dawn in homes across the country, one girl dons a wreath topped with burning white candles (electric ones are available for wobbly Lucias) and a long white dress with red sash. She and her white-clad siblings bring coffee and saffron bread to their parents, singing carols as they go. Students often organize "Lucia trains" and visit the homes of their teachers as well.

Boxing Day, UNITED KINGDOM
Dec. 26.

Churches used to open their collection boxes the day after Christmas and distribute the contents to the poor. Now Britons use the occasion to give gifts to the people who have helped them throughout the year—those who deliver mail, newspapers and milk bottles are the big winners.

SELECTED RELIGIOUS HOLIDAYS

Ramadan, ISLAMIC.
Varies. (ninth month of the lunar-based Islamic calendar)

The fourth of the five pillars of Islam is to keep the fast of Ramadan, which celebrates Muhammad's reception of the divine revelations recorded in the Koran. During the month-long fast, Muslims (except sol-diers and the sick) may not eat between sunrise and sunset.

Ash Wednesday, CHRISTIAN.
Forty days before Easter.

This day marks the beginning of Lent, a period of fasting that begins 40 days before Easter. The ashes that are smudged on the foreheads of the faithful symbolize penitence and mortality. The Tuesday before Ash Wednesday, or Mardi Gras, which literally means "Fat Tuesday" in French, is a day of raucous celebration in some parts of the world. The celebration marks the last hurrah before the solemn season of Lent begins at midnight.

Passover, JEWISH. *Generally March or April. (Hebrew month of Nissan)*

The eight-day holiday reminds Jews that Moses led the Israelites from Egypt, where they had been slaves under the Pharoah. At special dinners called seders, everyone takes part in reading the Israelites' story and tasting foods that symbolize aspects of their journey.

Easter, CHRISTIAN. *Spring. (the first Sunday after the first full moon of spring)*

The Christian religion's most important holiday, Easter celebrates the resurrection of Jesus Christ after his death on a cross. It is the last day of Holy Week, which includes Palm Sunday, Maundy Thursday, and Good Friday, and marks the end of

SCIENCE

✔ **TIMELY TIPS**

Keeping New Year's Resolutions

Tips from a Nobel Prize winner

Why do we make New Year's resolutions? Because they help us cope with some of the most difficult conflicts human beings face. So argues one of the world's greatest experts on conflict, Thomas C. Schelling, who shared the 2005 Nobel Prize in economics. In the early 1980's, Schelling sought to develop what he called "strategic egonomics, consciously coping with one's own behavior, especially one's conscious behavior."

The problem, he says, is that pretty much everybody suffers from a split personality. One self desperately wants to lose weight or quit smoking or run two miles a day, and the other wants dessert or a cigarette or hates to exercise. Both selves are equally valid and rational about pursuing their desires. But they do not exist at the same time. New Year's resolutions help the earlier self overrule the later one by raising the cost of straying. But, as many a broken resolution demonstrates, the consequences of straying are not a big enough deterrent. Schelling's work suggests a few additional strategies to make success more likely:

✔ **Setting bright-line rules, which make it harder to cheat through clever reinterpretation.** For example, many people find it easier to eliminate whole categories of food, like carbohydrates, rather than simply to cut back on calories.

✔ **Making a mild precommitment,** such as not keeping sweets or tobacco in the house, for instance. At the very least, this step forces you to delay indulgence until you can go to the store, allowing you time to recover your resolve.

✔ **Giving yourself permission to indulge later.** Instead of deciding to go without eternally, you allow yourself to smoke or drink or eat chocolate cake within a specified time, say, three hours, after deciding to go off the wagon. Like having to go out to buy supplies, this strategy allows you time once again to resolve not to indulge.

✔ **Letting a third "self" mediate between the two in conflict** by enforcing a prearranged deal, such as the chance to sleep late at the price of skipping TV at night, for instance, or a new dress in exchange for losing 10 pounds. This works only if two conditions are met: one, if the incentives are strong enough; and, two, as Schelling writes, "the 'someone' who wants to turn off his alarm with his eyes closed has to believe that another 'somebody' will later have the fortitude to administer the punishment or deny the reward, when 'they' are really all the same person."

—Virginia Postrel

Lent. The traditional Easter eggs are thought to represent new life and immortality.

Baisakhi, HINDU. *April 13.* Hindus bathe in the Ganges River or in other holy waters during the celebration of this beginning of the New Year. Charitable acts performed throughout the following month are considered especially good, so people give generously to the poor during this time.

Rosh Hashanah, JEWISH. *Sept./ Oct. (Hebrew month of Tishri)* The start of the Jewish New Year is the first of 10 High Holy Days, during which Jews reflect on their sins of the past year and seek forgiveness for them. A hollowed out ram's horn, called the shofar, is sounded in syna-gogue to remind people of the trumpets of Judgment Day.

Yom Kippur, JEWISH. *Sept./Oct. (Hebrew month of Tishri)* This Day of Atonement ends the 10 High Holy Days that begin on Rosh Hashanah and is the most important part of the Jewish year. It is a day of fasting and prayer, repentance and forgiveness.

Dewali, HINDU.
Late Oct./early Nov.
The five-day festival of lights celebrates the human desire to move toward truth and light from ignorance and darkness. The streets are strewn with festive lamps and homes are decorated with flowers and colored paper. Festivities include fireworks, parties, and gift giving.

Hanukkah, JEWISH. *Late Nov./late Dec. (Hebrew month of Kislev)*
After a group of Jews recaptured a temple in Jerusalem that had been seized by Syrian-Greeks, they had enough oil to light the temple's lamp for a day. But the lamp burned for eight days, and Jews celebrate this miracle by lighting candles in the menorah (a special candelabra), adding one each night until all eight candles are lit.

Christmas Day, CHRISTIAN.
Dec. 25.
Christians celebrate the birth of Jesus Christ by attending religious services and displaying "crèches," or nativity scenes depicting Jesus, Mary, and Joseph in a manger. The tradition of gift-giving reenacts the story of the Three Kings who brought gifts to the newborn Jesus. Many other familiar traditions of the season originate from pagan beliefs. The ancient Druids, for example, worshiped holly and mistletoe, and Norsemen burned yule logs in the winter to scare off demons.

Chinese Zodiac: What Are You?

You may be faithful as a dog, witty as a monkey or wise as a snake

The Chinese zodiac is based on a 12-year cycle, with each year of the cycle represented by a different animal. There is also a cycle of the elements—wood, fire, earth, metal and water—connected with the animal sign of the year you were born. So, you could be an Earth Monkey or a Golden Rat, for example. Ancient Chinese used the signs to match couples, according to the interaction among the five elements and the personality traits of the animals. For example, a Water Dog is compatible with a Wood Pig but dominates a Fire Pig because water helps wood but controls fire.

If the ancient Chinese were right about the traits they ascribed to their calendrical animals, then Leonardo da Vinci, born in the year of the Monkey, was charismatic and witty. Confucius, on the other hand, would have been a pleasing fellow, though perhaps a trifle too sentimental since his birthdate in 551 B.C. would have made him a Rabbit. Oprah Winfrey, one of the world's richest women, may have achieved her riches from the wisdom, charm and caution with money that come from being a Snake. For clues to understanding Joan of Arc, Picasso, Osama Bin Laden and Madonna, read on.

RAT
- *FIRE: 1936, 1996* • *EARTH: 1948, 2008*
- *METAL: 1960* • *WATER: 1972*
- *WOOD: 1984*

Traits: Imaginative, generous, quick-tempered, overly critical, opportunist. **Some Rats:** Shakespeare, Truman Capote, Prince Charles, Antonio Banderas, Gwyneth Paltrow

BUFFALO (OR OX)
- *WOOD: 1925, 1985* • *FIRE: 1937, 1997*
- *EARTH: 1949, 2009* • *METAL: 1961*
- *WATER: 1973*

Traits: A born leader, conservative, methodical, chauvinistic and demanding. **Some Buffaloes:** Napoleon, Adolf Hitler, Princess Di, B. B. King

SCIENCE

TIGER

- *FIRE: 1926, 1986* • *EARTH: 1938, 1998*
- *METAL: 1950, 2010* • *WATER: 1962*
- *WOOD: 1974*

Traits: Sensitive, emotional, stubborn, rebellious. **Some Tigers:** Marco Polo, Oscar Wilde, Marilyn Monroe, Jay Leno

RABBIT

- *FIRE: 1927, 1987* • *EARTH: 1939, 1999*
- *METAL: 1951, 2011* • *WATER: 1963*
- *WOOD: 1975*

Traits: Affectionate, obliging, cautious, conservative, overly sentimental. **Some Rabbits:** Confucius, Albert Einstein, Fidel Castro, Frank Sinatra, Angelina Jolie

DRAGON

- *EARTH: 1928, 1988* • *METAL: 1940, 2000*
- *WATER: 1952, 2012* • *WOOD: 1964*
- *FIRE: 1976*

Traits: Enthusiastic, energetic, perfectionist, foolhardy, demanding. **Some Dragons**: Joan of Arc, Martin Luther King Jr., John Lennon

SNAKE

- *EARTH: 1929, 1989* • *METAL: 1941, 2001*
- *WATER: 1953, 2013* • *WOOD: 1965*
- *FIRE: 1977*

Traits: Wise, charming, romantic, intuitive, procrastinator, cautious with money. **Some Snakes:** Edgar Allan Poe, James Joyce, Pablo Picasso, Bob Dylan, Oprah Winfrey

HORSE

- *METAL: 1930, 1990*
- *WATER: 1942, 2002* • *WOOD: 1954, 2014*
- *FIRE: 1966* • *EARTH: 1978*
- *WATER: 1983*

Traits: Hard working, independent, intelligent, cunning, egotistical. **Some Horses:** Rembrandt, Teddy Roosevelt, Clint Eastwood, Paul McCartney

GOAT

- *METAL: 1931, 1991*
- *WATER: 1943, 2003* • *WOOD: 1955, 2015*
- *FIRE: 1967* • *EARTH: 1979*

Traits: Charming, elegant, artistic, pessimistic, materialistic. **Some Goats:** Michelangelo, Mark Twain, Mel Gibson, Bill Gates

MONKEY

- *WATER: 1932, 1992*
- *WOOD: 1944, 2004* • *FIRE: 1956, 2016*
- *EARTH: 1968* • *METAL: 1980*

Traits: Clever wit, well-liked, opportunistic, distrustful. **Some Monkeys:** Julius Caesar, Leonardo da Vinci, Elizabeth Taylor, Pope John Paul II, Tom Hanks

ROOSTER

- *WATER: 1933, 1993*
- *WOOD: 1945, 2005* • *FIRE: 1957, 2017*
- *EARTH: 1969* • *METAL: 1981*

Traits: Shrewd, straight-talker, boastful, extravagant. **Some Roosters:** Rudyard Kipling, Yoko Ono, Osama Bin Laden, Rod Stewart, Britney Spears

DOG

- *WOOD: 1934, 1994* • *FIRE: 1946, 2006*
- *EARTH: 1958, 2018* • *METAL: 1970*
- *WATER: 1982*

Traits: Loyal, honest, sharp-tongued, fault finder. **Some Dogs:** Socrates, Elvis Presley, Bill Clinton, George W. Bush, Madonna, Donald Trump

PIG

- *WOOD: 1935, 1995* • *FIRE: 1947, 2007*
- *EARTH: 1959, 2019* • *METAL: 1971*
- *WATER: 1983*

Traits: Good companion, sincere, tolerant, honest, naïve, materialistic. **Some Pigs:** Thomas Jefferson, Humphrey Bogart, Ronald Reagan, Elton John

How to Tell Geologic Time

Geologists use a timeline of the Earth that divides the planet's history into a series of intervals, each defined by significant events that occurred during those divisions. As the geologic time scale below shows, the four eras, the Cenozoic, Mesozoic, Paleozoic and Precambrian, are subdivided into periods. Some of the major events that took place during the different periods, as well as representative animal life are used to identify the particular periods.

AGE (in millions of years before the present)	ERA	PERIOD	ANIMAL AND PLANT LIFE
65 to present	**Cenozoic** *(Age of mammals)*	QUATERNARY	Modern man, modern seed plants
		TERTIARY	Primitive man, gorillas, elephants, whales, apes, horses, modern birds
250 to 65	**Mesozoic** *(Age of dinosaurs)**	CRETACEOUS	Birds, snakes, fish. Flowering plants appeared; sequoia trees prominent
		JURASSIC	Flying reptiles; modern insects. Conifers, ginkos, tree ferns
		TRIASSIC	Vertebrates, aquatic reptiles such as ichthyosaurs
550 to 250	**Paleozoic** *(Age of fishes)**	PERMIAN	Small reptiles; ammonites
		CARBONIFEROUS	Amphibians, large insects. Primitive conifers; first seed plants
		DEVONIAN	Starfish, primitive land vertebrates. Ferns, mosses, primitive evergreens
		SILURIAN	Sea scorpions, mollusks, corals
		ORDOVICIAN	Gastropods, clams, snails; first primitive fishlike vertebrates
		CAMBRIAN	Protozoans, first shells. Lichens in some regions
4,500 to 550	**Precambrian** *The time between the birth of the planet and the appearance of complex life forms*		Jellyfish, amoebas, worms, sponges, algae

*These designations are popular, but they are somewhat broad. For example, animal life during the Mesozoic era was not limited to dinosaurs; mammals, turtles, crocodiles and many varieties of insects also inhabited the earth.

SOURCE: U.S. Geological Survey

SCIENCE

Figures & Formulas

Measurements to Fit a King

How to measure the world around you, from round holes to square pegs

Weights and measures have been a matter for pharaohs, emperors and kings to establish and for practical men and women to follow for thousands of years. The Egyptians based their system of measurement on the human body: the little finger to the thumb tip was considered a span, and two spans were the equivalent of one cubit, which was the distance from a person's fingertips to the elbow. The mile was a roman unit of measure: it came from the word, "mille," which stood for "1,000 paces."

There are several legends to explain where the English unit of measure, the yard, originated. One is that it was the same length as King Henry I's arm. Another is that it represented the distance from the tip of Henry's nose to the end of his thumb. Yet another version suggests that it was inspired by the length of the arrows used by the king's archers. In any case, the state's role in setting standards has never been in doubt. For many centuries the weights and measures that Americans inherited from Britain were referred to as "the king's standard."

Americans have moved a fair way, however, from the Queen's English and what has come to be known as the British Imperial System of weights and measures. In the United States today, weights and measures are usually referred to by the name "U.S. Customary System."

Most of the rest of the world, of course, follows the International (or Metric) System, which is a decimal system in which units of measurement increase by multiples of 10. First developed by ancient Hindu mathematicians and then embraced by the Arabs in the 10th century, the Metric System came into gradual use in Europe after 1100, and was officially adopted by the French in the late 1700's, about the time Louis XVI and Marie Antoinette faced the guillotine.

Led by the government agencies and the scientific and engineering communities, metrics are gradually winning wider acceptance in U.S. industry. Still far off, however, is the day when the rulebook states that the proper height of a basketball hoop is 3.048 meters—rather than 10 in feet.

 TIMELY TIPS

Making Do Without a Ruler

A little ingenuity can go a long way when you need a quick measurement, albeit an approximate one. Knowing the dimensions of a few common objects can help.

✔ **Need the dimensions of a room?** It helps to know that most floor tile is 9 x 9 or 12 x 12 inches.

✔ **At a flea market with no tape measure?** Use a dollar bill (or any denomination). A bill is 6 $1/18$ inches long.

✔ **For measuring smaller areas, use a coin.** A quarter is approximately 1 inch in diameter; a penny is $3/4$ inches in diameter.

✔ **It pays to know** that a credit card is 3 $3/28$ by 2 $1/8$ inches; a business card is generally 3 $5/8$ x 2 inches.

U.S. Customary Units

• LENGTH

Use to measure lines and distances

12 inches =	1 foot
3 feet =	1 yard
1,760 yards =	1 statute mile
5 1/2 yards =	1 rod
40 rods = 1 furlong =	220 yards
8 furlongs = 5,280 feet =	1 statute mile

• AREA

Multiply length by width in units of the same denomination to find surface area.

144 square inches =	1 square foot
9 square feet =	1 square yard
30 1/4 square yards =	2 square rods
160 square rods =	1 acre
640 acres =	1 square mile

• VOLUME

Multiply length by breadth by thickness to find cubic content or volume.

1,728 cubic inches =	1 cubic foot
27 cubic feet =	1 cubic yard

• LIQUID CAPACITY

Use to measure a container's capacity to hold liquids.

1 gill =	4 fluid ounces
4 gills = 2 cups =	1 pint
1 pint =	16 fluid ounces
2 pints =	1 quart
4 quarts =	1 gallon
31 1/2 gallons =	1 barrel
2 barrels =	1 hogshead

• DRY CAPACITY

Use to measure a container's capacity to hold solids such as flour.

2 pints =	1 quart
4 quarts =	1 gallon

TEMPERATURE CONVERSIONS

To convert temperatures from Fahrenheit to Celsius, subtract 32 degrees and multiply by 5, then divide by 9. To go from Celsius to Fahrenheit, multiply by 9, divide by 5, then add 32 degrees.

Celsius = Fahrenheit	Fahrenheit = Celsius
−45 = −49	−45 = −42.8
−40 = −40	−40 = −40.0
−35 = −31	−35 = −37.2
−30 = −13	−30 = −34.4
−25 = −8.5	−25 = −31.7
−20 = −4	−20 = −28.9
−15 = 5	−15 = −26.1
−10 = 14	−10 = −23.3
−5 = 23	−5 = −20.6
0 = 32	0 = −17.8
5 = 41	5 = −15.0
10 = 50	10 = −12.2
15 = 59	15 = −9.4
20 = 68	20 = −6.7
25 = 77	25 = −3.9
30 = 86	30 = −1.1
35 = 95	32 = 0.0
40 = 104	35 = 1.7
45 = 113	40 = 4.4
50 = 122	45 = 7.2
55 = 131	50 = 10.0
60 = 140	55 = 12.8
65 = 149	60 = 15.6
70 = 158	65 = 18.3
75 = 167	70 = 21.1
80 = 176	75 = 23.9
85 = 185	80 = 26.7
90 = 194	85 = 29.4
95 = 203	90 = 32.2
100 = 212	95 = 35.0
125 = 257	100 = 37.8
150 = 302	105 = 40.6
175 = 347	110 = 43.3
200 = 392	212 = 100.0
225 = 437	225 = 107.2
250 = 482	250 = 121.1
275 = 527	275 = 135.0
300 = 572	300 = 148.9
325 = 617	325 = 162.8
350 = 662	350 = 176.7
375 = 707	375 = 190.6
400 = 752	400 = 204.4
425 = 797	425 = 218.3
450 = 842	450 = 232.2

SCIENCE

8 quarts =	1 peck
4 pecks =	1 bushel

• AVOIRDUPOIS (MASS) WEIGHT

Use for weighing heavy articles such as grain and groceries.

27.344 grains =	1 dram
16 drams =	1 ounce
16 ounces =	1 pound
100 pounds =	1 short hundredweight
20 short hundredweight =	1 short ton

Metric Units

• LENGTH

10 millimeters (mm) =	1 centimeter (cm)
10 centimeters =	1 decimeter (dm)
10 decimeters =	1 meter (m)
10 meters =	1 decameter (dam)
10 decameters =	1 hectometer (hm)
10 hectometers =	1 kilometer (km)

• AREA

100 square millimeters =	1 square centimeter
100 square centimeters =	1 square decimeter
100 square decimeters =	1 square meter
100 square meters =	1 square decameter
=	1 are (a)
100 ares =	1 hectare (ha)
100 square decameters =	1 square hectometer
100 square hectometers =	1 square kilometer
100 hectares =	1 square kilometer

• VOLUME

1,000 cubic millimeters =	1 cubic centimeter
1,000 cubic centimeters =	1 cubic decimeter
1,000 cubic decimeters =	1 cubic meter

• DRY AND LIQUID CAPACITY

10 milliliters (ml) =	1 centiliter (cl)
10 centiliters =	1 deciliter (dl)
10 deciliters =	1 liter (l)

ⓘ INSIDE INFO

Of Aglets and Eyelets

○ How long a shoelace do you need? That depends mainly on your shoe type. But, other, more subtle factors also influence shoelace length, including how many pairs of holes—or eyelets—your shoes have, the distance between the holes, the elasticity of the laces, how tightly you tie the laces and which of the dozen or so lacing methods you use.

○ The following rough guide is for an average shoe, using the standard style of lacing, a symmetrical crisscross pattern.

○

	Shoelace length
2 hole pairs	18 inches
3 hole pairs	18 or 24 inches
4 hole pairs	24 inches
5 hole pairs	30 inches
6 hole pairs	36 or 45 inches

○ The plastic or metal tip on each end of a shoelace is called an "aglet," derived from the Latin word for needle

---

10 liters =	1 decaliter (dal)
10 decaliters =	1 hectoliter (hl)
10 hectoliters =	1 kiloliter (kl)

• MASS

Use to measure weights and both dry and liquid capacities.

10 milligrams (mg) =	1 centigram (cg)
10 centigrams =	1 decigram (dg)
10 decigrams =	1 gram (g)
10 grams =	1 decagram (dag)
10 decagrams =	1 hectogram (hg)
10 hectograms =	1 kilogram (kg)
100 kilograms =	1 quintal
1,000 kilograms =	1 metric ton (t)
10 quintals =	1 metric ton (t)

The Long and the Short of Clothing Sizes

Men in Europe don't have huge heads or exceptionally large feet—they just have a different system for sizing hats and shoes. A look at how clothing sizes compare:

WOMEN

BLOUSES AND SWEATERS

U.S.	32	34	36	38	40	42	44
British	34	36	38	40	42	44	46
Continental	40	42	44	46	48	50	52

COATS AND DRESSES

U.S.	8	10	12	14	16	18	20
British	30	32	34	36	38	40	42
Continental	36	38	40	42	44	46	48

STOCKINGS

U.S. & British	8	8½	9	9½	10	10½
Continental	0	1	2	3	4	5

SHOES

U.S.		5–5½	6–6½	7–7½	8–8½	9
British		3½–4	4½–5	5½–6	6½–7	7½
Continental		36	37	38	39	40

MEN

SUITS AND COATS

U.S. & British		34	36	38	40	42	44	46
Continental		44	46	48	50	52	54	56

HATS

U.S.	6⅝	6¾	6⅞	7	7⅛	7¼	7⅜	7½
British	6½	6⅝	6¾	6⅞	7	7⅛	7¼	7⅜
Continental	53	54	55	56	57	58	59	60

SHIRTS

U.S. & British		14	14½	15	15½	16	16½	17
Continental		36	37	38	39	41	42	43

SHOES

U.S.	7	7½	8	8½	9	9½	10	10½	11
British	6½	7	7½	8	8½	9	9½	10	10½
Continental	39	40	41	42	43	43	44	44	45

SOCKS

U.S. & British	9½	10	10½	11	11½	12	12½
Continental	39	40	41	42	43	44	45

CONVERTING U.S. CUSTOMARY UNITS TO METRIC UNITS

• LENGTH

1 inch = 2.54 centimeters
= 0.025 meter

1 foot = 30.48 centimeters
= 0.305 meter

1 yard = 91.44 centimeters
= 0.914 meter

1 statute mile = 1,609.3 meters
= 1.609 kilometers

• AREA

1 square inch = 6.452 square centimeters
1 square foot = 929.03 square centimeters

SCIENCE

	=	0.093 square meter
1 square yard =		8,361.274 square centimeters
	=	0.836 square meter
1 acre =		4,046.856 square meters
	=	0.405 square hectometer
1 square mile =		2,589,988.11 square meters
	=	258.999 square hectometer
	=	2.589 square kilometers

• LIQUIDS

1 fluid ounce =		29.574 milliliters
	=	0.029 liter
1 cup =		236.588 milliliters
	=	0.237 liter
1 pint =		473.176 milliliters
	=	0.473 liter
1 quart =		946.353 milliliters
	=	0.946 liter
1 gallon =		3,785.41 milliliters
	=	3.785 liters

• MASS

1 ounce =		28.349 grams
1 pound =		453.59grams
	=	0.454 kilogram
1 short ton =		907.18 kilograms
	=	0.907 metric ton

CONVERTING METRIC UNITS TO U.S. CUSTOMARY UNITS

• LENGTH

1 centimeter =	0.394 inch
1 meter =	3.281 feet = 1.094 yards
1 kilometer =	0.622 mile

• AREA

1 square centimeter =	0.155 square inch

HOW FAR IS THAT IN MILES?

Miles to	kilometers	Miles to	kilometers
1.6	1	1	0.6
3.2	2	2	1.2
4.8	3	3	1.9
6.4	4	4	2.5
8.0	5	5	3.1
9.7	6	6	3.7
11.3	7	7	4.3
12.9	8	8	5.6
14.5	9	9	5.6
16.1	10	10	6.2
160.9	100	100	62.1
1,609.3	1,000	1,000	621.4

1 square meter =		1,550.003 square inches
	=	10.764 square feet
	=	1.196 square yards
1 hectare =		107,639.1 square feet
	=	11,959.90 square yards
	=	2.471 acres
	=	0.004 square mile
1 square kilometer =		247.105 acres
	=	0.386 square mile

• LIQUIDS

1 milliliter =		0.034 fluid ounces
1 liter =		33.814 fluid ounces
	=	4.227 cups = 2.113 pints
	=	1.057 quarts = 0.264 gallons

• MASS

1 milligram =	0.000035 ounce
1 gram =	0.03527 ounce
1 kilogram =	35.27 ounces = 2.205 pounds
1 metric ton =	2,204.6 pounds
=	1.102 short tons

Bits, Bytes & Beyond

Computers code information using the binary numeral system, which uses the digits 0 and 1 in combination to represent various values.

- ○ A BIT (short for binary digit) is the tiniest unit of information; the number 011, for example, is 3 bits long.

- ○ A BYTE is a collection of 8 bits; it is a basic unit in modern computers.

- ○ A KILOBYTE, roughly 1,000 bytes, is about the size of a short e-mail.

- ○ A MEGABYTE is about 1 million bytes; a megabyte of storage can hold around one minute of an MP3

music file, for example.

- ○ A GIGABYTE is a billion bytes. The storage of most hard drives nowadays is 100 to 200 gigabytes.

- ○ TERRABYTE. As the technology advances, expect to hear about hard drive storage in the terabyte, or the 1 trillion byte, range.

What's a Pixel, Anyway?

- ○ A PIXEL (a contraction of picture and element) is a tiny, basic unit of an image on a display screen, such as a computer monitor or a television.

- ○ A MEGAPIXEL is 1 million pixels. It usually refers to the resolution capability of

a digital camera; the more pixels, the more realistic the image.

- ○ A COMPUTER SCREEN is divided into a matrix of thousands or millions of pixels. You can try to see pixels on your screen by setting your monitor to a low resolution, say, 640 x 480 (that's a matrix of 640 x 480 pixels, or a total of 307,2000 pixels). You may be able to see the separate dots, or pixels, that make up the image on your screen.

- ○ IN COLOR DISPLAYS, each pixel is made up of red, blue and green subpixels, or rays of light of varying intensity.

Special Weights & Measures

• ANGLES AND CIRCLES

Use in surveying, navigating, astronomy, geography, figuring latitude and longitude, and computing differences in time.

60 seconds =	1 minute
60 minutes =	1 degree
30 degrees =	1 sign
45 degrees =	1 octant
60 degrees =	1 sextant
90 degrees =	1 quadrant = 1 right angle
180 degrees =	1 straight angle = 1 semicircle
360 degrees =	1 circle

• APOTHECARIES' FLUID MEASURE

Use in mixing medicines.

60 minims =	1 fluid dram
8 fluid drams =	1 fluid ounce
16 fluid ounces =	1 pint
2 pints =	1 quart
4 quarts =	1 gallon

• APOTHECARIES' WEIGHT

For weighing medicines for prescriptions.

20 grains =	1 scruple
3 scruples =	1 dram
8 drams =	1 ounce
12 ounces =	1 pound

• MARINERS' MEASURE

To measure distance depth, or speed at sea.

6 feet =	1 fathom
1,000 fathoms =	1 nautical mile (approx.)

SCIENCE

FORMULAS FOR KEY HOUSEHOLD CONVERSIONS

○ Ounces x 28.349 = **grams**

○ Grams x 0.032 = **ounces**

○ Pounds x 453.592 = **grams**

○ Pounds x 0.453 = **kilograms**

○ Cups x 0.24 = **liters**

○ Gallons x 3.785 = **liters**

1 nautical mile =	1.15 statute miles
3 nautical miles =	1 league
60 nautical miles =	1 degree
1 knot =	1 nautical mile per hour

• SURVEYORS' MEASURE
Use to measure the borders and dimensions of a tract of land.

7.92 inches =	1 link
100 links =	1 chain
1 chain =	4 rods = 66 feet
80 chains =	1 survey mile = 5,280 feet

• SURVEYORS' SQUARE MEASURE
Multiply length by breadth to find surface area of land.

272 1/4 square feet =	1 square rod
16 square rods =	1 square chain
160 square rods =	10 square chains
=	1 acre
640 acres =	1 square mile
=	1 section
36 square miles =	36 sections
=	1 township

• TROY WEIGHT
Use in weighing gold, silver and jewels.

24 grains =	1 pennyweight
20 pennyweights =	1 ounce
12 ounces =	1 pound

• WOOD MEASURE
Use to measure the volume of a pile of wood.

16 cubic feet =	1 cord foot
	= a wood pile that is 4 feet high by 4 feet wide by 1 foot long
8 cord feet =	1 cord
	= a wood pile 8 feet long by 4 feet wide by 4 feet high

• TIME MEASURE
Use to measure the passage of time.

60 seconds =	1 minute
60 minutes =	1 hour
24 hours =	1 day
7 days =	1 week
4 weeks (28 to 31 days) =	1 month
12 months (365 or 366 days) =	1 year
100 years =	1 century

• COMMON HOUSEHOLD MEASURES
Use to measure ingredients for cooking.

3 teaspoons =	1 tablespoon
1 tablespoon =	1/18 cup
=	0.5 fluid ounce
4 tablespoons =	1/4 cup
5 tablespoons =	1/2 cup + 1 teaspoon
6 tablespoons =	3/8 cup
8 tablespoons =	1/2 cup
10 tablespoons =	2/3 cup + 2 teaspoons
12 tablespoons =	3/4 cup
16 tablespoons =	1 cup
32 tablespoons =	2 cups
48 teaspoons =	1 cup
1 cup =	8 fluid ounces
2 cups =	1 pint
4 cups =	1 quart
2 pints =	1 quart
4 quarts =	1 gallon

Chemistry: It's Elemental

The periodic table of elements includes all the building blocks of matter

The periodic table of the elements was first devised in the 19th century to show the atomic weights of the elements and to group them by similar properties. The discovery of protons and electrons in atoms in the early 20th century gave rise to a new and more accurate arrangement of the elements in a periodic table. This new arrangement is based on the atomic number, which is the number of protons (positively charged particles) present in the atomic nucleus of an element.

The table lists the elements in horizontal rows (or periods), according to their atomic numbers. Each vertical column (except hydrogen in the first column) groups elements that have related properties and are likely to behave similarly in chemical reactions. Except for hydrogen, the elements on the left side of the table are metals while those in the last six columns are predominantly nonmetals. In those columns, a heavier, stepped boundary line separates the metals from the nonmetals.

Hydrogen is the lightest and simplest element in the table but it has many unique properties. For example, in chemical reactions, it can give up or acquire an electron from other elements that are incapable of transferring electrons both ways.

Aside from the atomic number, the periodic table also lists each element's name, chemical symbol and atomic weight (or atomic mass). Atomic weight is the mass of an atom relative to the mass of an atom of carbon-12, which is arbitrarily assigned an atomic weight of 12 by an international convention.

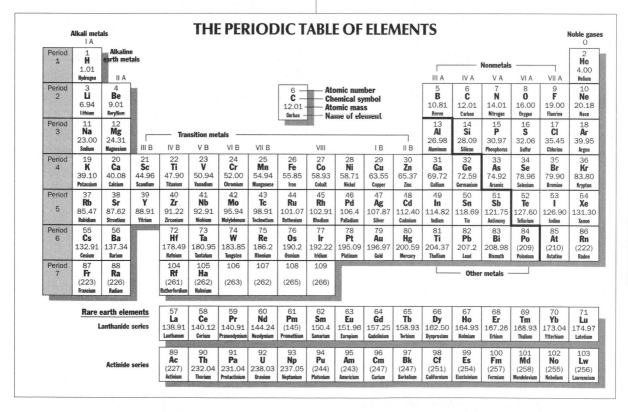

THE PERIODIC TABLE OF ELEMENTS

SCIENCE

Placing Math on a Timeline

The study of numbers has been both practical and sublime for millennia

Without numbers it would be impossible to set a clock, keep score or create a symphony. If numbers had not been needed, the civilizations of ancient Mesopotamia, Egypt and China would not have felt it necessary to invent counting systems, which they then applied to their commerce and government. An early appreciation for the principles of geometry helped the Egyptians construct the pyramids and accurately record their boundaries.

By the sixth century B.C., the Greeks took the practical math that they had learned from the Babylonians and Egyptians and ventured into more abstract investigations. The Greek philosopher Pythagoras and his disciples proposed a theorem, for instance, that showed the mathematical relationship among the three sides of a right triangle (see page 773). Another Greek, Euclid, was the first to suggest that geometry possessed a single set of logical rules. Archimedes laid the conceptual groundwork for integral calculus in the third century, B.C., and the celebrated astronomer Ptolemy played a leading role in developing trigonometry.

The Romans largely contented themselves with the use of math in solving practical problems, but the more ethereal inquiries into the nature of numbers championed by the Greeks were taken up by Islamic thinkers in the 9th and 10th centuries. One of them, an astronomer named Muhammad ibn Musa al-Khwarizmi, laid many of the foundations for algebra.

Beginning in the 11th century, Islamic advances in mathematics gradually made their way to Europe. But it was not until the Renaissance in the 15th century that Europeans contributed to the breakthroughs, with astronomers such as Nicolaus Copernicus, Galileo Galilei and Johannes Kepler making major contributions. Working independently, Sir Isaac Newton, an Englishman, and Baron Gottfried Wilhem von Leibniz invented calculus in the 1680's, effectively ushering in the modern age of mathematics.

Following is a ready reference to many of the most commonly used mathematical concepts and operations.

READING THE SIGNS

No science is more elegant at explaining the world around us than mathematics. In examining the properties, relations and measurement of quantities, it relies on a system of mathematical signs, or directions. The most commonly used:

+ plus or positive	≤ less than or equal to
– minus or negative	>> much greater than
± plus or minus, positive or negative	<< much less than
· multiplied by	√ square root
÷ or / divided by	∞ infinity
= equal to	∝ proportional to
≠ not equal to	∑ sum of
≈ approximately equal to	∏ product of
~ of the order of or similar to	Δ difference
	∴ therefore
> greater than	∠ angle
< less than	‖ parallel to
≥ greater than or equal to	: is to (ratio)

ALGEBRA

Algebra is based on the five fundamental laws that govern the operations of addition, subtraction, multiplication and division. Each of the laws is expressed in letter variables. Where variables *a, b* and *c* are all real numbers, any number can be substituted for a variable without conflicting with the way the rule works.

THE COMMUTATIVE LAW OF ADDITION

$$a + b = b + a$$

Under this law, the order in which two numbers are added has no bearing on the sum derived. Thus,

$6 + 7 = 7 + 6$, or $(-10)+(-2) = (-2)+(-10)$

THE ASSOCIATIVE LAW OF ADDITION

$a + (b+c) = (a+b) + c$

Under this law, it does not matter which combination of numbers is added first, the sum remains the same. Thus,

$1 + (8+2) = (1+8) + 2$

THE COMMUTATIVE LAW OF MULTIPLICATION

$ab = ba$

Under this law, it does not matter which order numbers are multiplied in, the product is the same. Thus,

6 times 7 = 7 times 6

THE ASSOCIATIVE LAW OF MULTIPLICATION

a times $(bc) + (ab)$ times c

Under this law, numbers can be multiplied in any sequence without affecting the final product. Thus,

5 times (4 times 3) = (5 times 4) times 3

THE DISTRIBUTIVE LAW OF MULTIPLICATION OVER ADDITION

$a(b+c) = ab + ac$

Under this law, if a number multiplies a sum, the total is the same as the sum of the separate products of the multiplier and each of the addends represented by b and c. Thus,

3 times (2+9) = 3 times 2 + 3 times 9

A Roman Innovation
Numbers that outlived the empire

The Roman system of recording numbers lasted considerably longer than the Roman Empire. As recently as 500 years ago, Roman numerals were still being used for addition and subtraction throughout Europe. But the Roman approach to numbers didn't translate well to higher math, and by the late 1500's Arabic numbers were being adopted in the West.

The Roman system uses only seven symbols, individually or in combination. When more than one symbol is used to form a number, the value of each symbol generally is added together, reading from left to right.

To multiply a numeral by 1,000, place a bar over the symbol like a long vowel sound. For instance, X with a bar across its top would stand for 10,000.

1	I	50	L	1000	M
2	II	60	LX	1500	MD
3	III	70	LXX	1900	MCM or
4	IV	80	LXXX		MDCCCC
5	V	90	XC	1910	MCMX
6	VI	100	C	1940	MCMXL
7	VII	150	CL	1950	MCML
8	VIII	200	CC	1960	MCMLX
9	IX	300	CCC	1990	MCMXC
10	X	400	CD	2000	MM
15	XV	500	D	3000	MMM
20	XX	600	DC	5000	$\overline{V}$
25	XXV	700	DCC	10,000	$\overline{X}$
30	XXX	800	DCCC	100,000	$\overline{C}$
40	XL	900	CM	1,000,000	$\overline{M}$

THE QUADRATIC EQUATION

A key algebraic equation is the quadratic equation, in which the highest power to which the unknown quantity is raised is the second. Assuming a, b and c are real numbers, and a does not

SCIENCE

equal zero, the formula is as follows:

If: $ax^2 + bx + c = 0$

Then: $x = \dfrac{-b \pm \sqrt{b^2 - 4ac}}{2a}$

Thus, if $a=1$, $b=4$ and $c=3$, and we know that $1x^2 + 4x + 3 = 0$, then we can find the value of x as follows:

$x = \dfrac{-4 \pm \sqrt{4^2 - (4 \cdot 1 \cdot 3)}}{2 \cdot 1} = (-1, -3)$

GEOMETRY

This branch of mathematics deals with points, line, planes and figures and their properties, measurement and spatial relationships.

ANGLES. *Angles are expressed in degrees, which are fractions of a circle. A circle has 360 degrees.*

FRACTIONS AND THEIR DECIMAL EQUIVALENTS

Rounded to the nearest four decimals

½	.5	2/11	.1818	5/16	.3125
⅓	.3333	¾	.75	6/7	.8571
¼	.25	⅗	.6	⅞	.875
⅕	.2	3/7	.4286	7/9	.7778
⅙	.1667	⅜	.375	7/10	.7
1/7	.1429	3/10	.3	7/11	.6364
⅛	.125	3/11	.2727	7/12	.5833
1/9	.1111	3/16	.1875	7/16	.4375
1/10	.1	⅘	.8	8/9	.8889
1/11	.0909	4/7	.5714	8/11	.7273
1/12	.0833	4/9	.4444	9/10	.9
1/16	.0625	4/11	.3636	9/11	.8182
1/32	.0313	⅚	.8333	9/16	.5625
1/64	.0156	5/7	.7143	10/11	.9091
⅔	.6667	⅝	.625	11/12	.9167
⅖	.4	5/9	.5556	11/16	.6875
2/7	.2857	5/11	.4545	13/16	.8125
2/9	.2222	5/12	.4167	15/16	.9375

 An **acute angle** is greater than zero degrees and less than 90.

 A **right angle** has 90 degrees. The lines forming the angle run perpendicular to each other.

 An **obtuse angle** has more than 90 degrees but less than 180 degrees.

 A **straight angle** has 180 degrees and forms a straight line.

 Complementary angles exist when two angles total 90 degrees.

 Supplementary angles occur when two angles add up to 180 degrees.

 Conjugate angles add up to 360 degrees when combined.

TRIANGLES. *The sum of the internal angles of a triangle is always 180 degrees.*

 An **equilateral triangle** has sides that are of equal length and internal angles that are all 60 degrees.

 An **isosceles triangle** has two sides that are of equal length and two equal angles.

 A **scalene triangle** has no sides and no angles of equal size.

 A **right triangle** has one internal angle of 90 degrees.

An **obtuse triangle** has one obtuse angle, which is an angle greater than 90 degrees but less than 180 degrees.

 An **acute-angle triangle** has three acute angles, meaning that all are under 90 degrees.

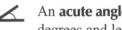

To calculate the area of a triangle, multiply the base by the height by one-half:

 $A = (1/2)bh$

QUADRILATERALS. *A quadrilateral is a four-sided polygon.*

 A **square** has four equal sides and four right angles. To calculate the area of a square, square the length of one side:
$A = a^2$

 A **rectangle** has equal opposite sides and all right angles. To calculate a rectangle's area, multiply base by height:
$A = bh$

 A **rhombus** has equal sides and no right angles. To calculate its area, multiply base by height:
$A = bh$

 A **parallelogram** has opposite sides that are parallel to each other and are the same length. To calculate the area of a parallelogram, multiply the base by the height:
$A = bh$

OTHER POLYGONS

 A **pentagon** is a five-sided polygon. To calculate the approximate area of a pentagon, multiply the square of the length of one side by 1.721:
$A = 1.721a^2$

 A **hexagon** is a six-sided polygon. To calculate the approximate area of

The Right Way to View Right Triangles

The relationships between the angles of a right triangle and its sides have been studied by mathematicians for millennia. Among the important trigonometric concepts are:

SINE: In a right triangle, the ratio of the opposite side of a given acute angle to the hypotenuse is known as the sine of that angle.

Sine of angle A = a÷c

COSINE: In a right triangle, the ratio of the adjacent side of an acute angle to the hypotenuse is known as the cosine of that angle.

Cosine of angle A = b÷c

TANGENT: In a right triangle, the ratio of the opposite to the adjacent side of an acute angle is known as the angle's tangent.

Tangent of A = a÷b

COTANGENT: In a right triangle, the ratio of the adjacent side of an acute angle to the opposite side is known as the angle's cotangent.

Cotangent of angle A = b÷a

THE PYTHAGOREAN THEOREM:

In a right triangle the square of the hypotenuse is equal to the sum of the square of the other two sides.

$$c^2 = a^2 + b^2$$

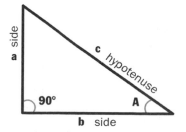

SCIENCE

a hexagon, multiply the square of the length of one side by 2.598:

$$A = 2.598a^2$$

An **octagon** is an eight-sided polygon. To calculate the approximate area of an equilateral octagon: multiply the square of the length of one side by 4.828:

$$A = 4.828a^2$$

A **circle** is a figure in which every point on its boundary is equidistant from the center. The radius is that distance to the center. The diameter is twice the radius, or the longest distance across the circle. The circumference is the total distance around the boundary of the circle. To calculate the area, multiply the square of the radius by pi (3.1416 …):

$$A = \pi r^2$$

To calculate the circumference of a circle, multiply radius of the circle by 2 and by pi (3.1416 …):

$$C = 2\pi r$$

SOLIDS. *Solids are three-dimensional geometric objects that exist in space.*

A **cube** is a solid with six equal, square sides. To calculate a cube's surface area, multiply the square of the length of a side by 6:

$$S = 6a^2$$

To calculate the volume of a cube, cube the length of one side:

$$V = s^3$$

A **sphere** is a body whose surface is equally distant from the center at all points. To calculate the surface area, multiply 4 by pi by the square of the radius:

$$S = 4 \pi r^2$$

To calculate the volume of a sphere, multiply the cube of the radius by pi by $^4/_3$:

$$V = (^4/_3) \pi r^3$$

A **pyramid** has a square base and four sloping triangular sides meeting at the top. To calculate the surface area, multiply base by length, and multiply 2 by the base and the height. Add the results:

$$S = bl+2bh$$

To calculate a pyramid's volume, multiply the base's area by height and by $^1/_3$:

$$V = (^1/_3)bh$$

A **cylinder** is a solid described by a line that always has a point in common with a given closed curve. The surface area of a right, circular cylinder: multiply 2 by pi by radius by height:

$$S = 2 \pi rh$$

To calculate a cylinder's volume, multiply the square of the radius of the base by pi by height:

$$V = \pi r2h$$

A **cone** is a flat-based, single-pointed solid formed by a rotating straight line that traces out a base from a fixed vertex point. To calculate the surface area of a cone, multiply pi by the radius of the base by the slant height (s):

$$S = \pi rs$$

To calculate the volume of a cube, multiply the square of the radius of the base by pi by height by $^1/_3$.

$$V = (^1/_3) \pi r2h$$

LAW & MORES

Legal Guide   776

CITIZENSHIP·776: *How to become a U.S. citizen* • *How the electoral college works* • *Registering to vote* • *How a bill becomes law* • *Getting a passport* • *Obtaining a Social Security number* • *Registering for the draft* **POLITICS·780:** *How to make campaign contributions* • *Deciphering a poll* • *For the good of the nation: AmeriCorps* **LEGALITIES·783:** *The truth about jury duty* • *Having your day in small claims court* • *The ABC's of legalese* • *How to read your F.B.I. file* • *Divorce on the cheap* • *How to change your name* • *When a child needs a guardian* • *Do you need a will?* • *Living wills*

Manners & Miscellany   791

ETIQUETTE·791: *High-tech manners* • *If the queen drops by* • *Women's issues* • *Personal ad abbreviations* • *Relationship rules* • *Handling social predicaments* • *Entertaining with children* • *Putting the R. in R.S.V.P.* • *The lost art of letter writing* • *Thank-you notes* • *Multicultural manners* **WEDDINGS·798:** *Weddings ring a new bell* • *More wedding planning tips* • *Looking for Mr. Right* • *Raising a glass* • *All the nuptials fit to print* • *Gems for special occasions* **GENEALOGY·803:** *Tracing your family tree* • *Finding ancestors through DNA* **WORDS·804:** *How to solve the* New York Times *crossword puzzle* • *Grammar mistakes to avoid* **RESEARCH·806:** *Your personal reference desk*

Signs & Symbols   807

VISUAL AIDS·807: *Negotiating a road map* • *Map symbols and international road signs* **CODES·808:** • *Symbols of distress* • *Tracking signs* • *Secrets of the semaphore code* • *Morse code* **WITHOUT WORDS·810:** *Musical notations for budding Beethovens* • *Proofreaders' marks* • *Second that emoticon* • *The Braille system*

Legal Guide

Proud to Be an American

How to become a citizen, get a passport, register to vote or for the draft

Being an American can be a time-consuming endeavor. You get to vote in federal, state and local elections. You are eligible for Social Security. All citizens and noncitizens who are residents of the U.S. are required to pay taxes. You can volunteer to serve in the U.S. armed forces. Whether or not you volunteer, all males at 18 years old have to register for the military. American citizens also have the duty of serving on jury duty. Here's a guide to being a law-abiding citizen.

HOW TO BECOME A U.S. CITIZEN
The road to citizenship can be rigorous

What does it take to become American? For many, just a little luck at birth. If your parents are not Americans but you were born on American soil, you can claim citizenship. Even if you were not born on U.S. soil but one of your parents is an American citizen, you are entitled to claim American citizenship. Otherwise, the process of applying for citizenship can be a long and tortuous road. But it's not impossible: between 1994 and 2004, more than 6.5 million immigrants became U.S. citizens.

To become a U.S. citizen an immigrant must meet several criteria: live in the U.S. as a permanent resident for five years (three years for spouses of U.S. citizens), be conversant in English and have a general knowledge of the principles of American government. Application forms are available at local offices of the U.S. Citizenship and Immigration Services (U.S.C.I.S.) or online at uscis.gov. You can also order forms by calling 800-870-3676.

But becoming a permanent resident is not easy. A relative or an employer must sponsor you, or you must be lucky enough to win one of the 50,000 slots in the annual visa lottery. (For more information about the lottery, go to travel.state.gov/visa.) Once you become a permanent resident, you will be issued a "green card," officially known as the Alien Registration Receipt Card. The cards are valid for 10 years. Legal immigrants must present them when applying for jobs, for state and federal entitlements, and when they re-enter the U.S. after a trip abroad. Curiously, the color of green cards changed to pink in 1996.

After legal immigrants have lived in the U.S. for a minimum of five years (without being jailed for over 180 days, or convicted of an aggravated felony or murder), they are eligible to take the citizenship test. People over age 50 who have been permanent residents of the U.S. for 20 years are exempt from being tested on their English skills. However, everyone must pass the citizenship exam. You can take the test as many times as you need to. The test includes questions on the three branches of government and voting requirements.

There are prep courses for the test through public schools, community and private groups, as well as by mail. The federal government also publishes citizenship study guides containing all of the information that appears on the citizenship test. They are available from the Superintendent of Documents, Government Printing Office, Washington, D.C. 20402.

HOW THE ELECTORAL COLLEGE WORKS

It's a complex system to simplify the way we elect a president

The authors of the Constitution devised the Electoral College to act as a kind of buffer between the masses and the ultimate process of selecting a president. The voters would choose electors for their state on a predetermined election day and then those individuals, along with elec-tors from other states, would take it upon themselves to choose the president.

Today, the Electoral College is a body of 538 people. Each state receives a number of electoral votes equal to the number of senators and representatives in its congressional delegation, and Washington, D.C., which has no Congressional representation, gets three votes. A candidate needs 270 electoral votes, slightly more than a majority, to be elected president. The candidate who wins a majority of a state's popular vote wins all of its electoral votes. As a result, the electoral vote tends to exaggerate the popular support of the winner.

If no candidate receives a majority of the votes of the Electoral College, the election will be decided by the House of Representatives. This has only happened once, so far, when in 1824 Andrew Jackson won the popular vote in a four-way race, but John Quincy Adams was elected president by the House. In 1876, Rutherford B. Hayes lost the popular vote but won the presidency by a single electoral vote.

Electoral college votes, by state

Once you have passed the citizenship test and interviewed with the U.S.C.I.S. officer, there is a further 30-day wait before you can officially become a citizen. If your application is approved, you will be invited to participate in one of many annual nationwide ceremonies for new citizens. Usually held around the 4th of July, citizens-to-be take the Oath of Allegiance, agreeing to defend the Constitution and fight in wars if necessary.

HOW TO REGISTER TO VOTE

Making your voice heard

Registering to vote couldn't be easier these days, thanks to "get-the-vote" groups tripping over themselves to lasso in new voters.

The first step is to get a registration form. Check your phone book for the number of your local election office, usually under the county clerk's office or municipal election board.

Or if you'd rather have your mouse do the work, use one of several online voting registration tools, such as the one on the League of Women Voters Web site at www.lwv.org. You can fill out the form online, but you'll still need to print it out and mail it to your local election office.

What qualifications do voters need? You must be a U.S. citizen and at least 18 years old. Some states disqualify anyone who has been convicted of a felony or is mentally incapacitated.

A few weeks after filing the form, you can expect a letter of confirmation, along with the address of where you must go to vote on election

HOW A BILL BECOMES A LAW

The law of the land and how it comes to pass

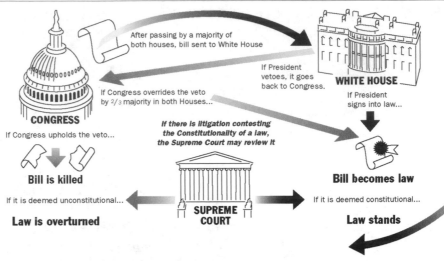

After passing by a majority of both houses, bill sent to White House

If President vetoes, it goes back to Congress.

WHITE HOUSE

If President signs into law...

If Congress overrides the veto by 2/3 majority in both Houses...

CONGRESS

If Congress upholds the veto...

If there is litigation contesting the Constitutionality of a law, the Supreme Court may review it

Bill is killed

If it is deemed unconstitutional...

Law is overturned

SUPREME COURT

If it is deemed constitutional...

Bill becomes law

Law stands

We all learned it in grade school, but for those of us who passed the civics test much too long ago, here's a refresher course on how laws are made:

- The Senate and the House of Representatives have equal voice in making laws, although revenue bills originate in the House.

- Differences in a piece of legislation between the two houses are reconciled by a joint committee that includes members of both chambers.

- A presidential veto of congressional legislation can be overrriden by a two-thirds vote in each chamber.

day. If you move locally, be sure to update your registration and find out where your new polling place will be. If you move outside your old jurisdiction, you must reregister in your new area. If you change your name, use your state's form to submit the name change, or make the change online at sites such as www.lwv.org.

When you go to the polls, be sure to bring a photo identification that also shows your address, such as a driver's license. If for some reason, your name is not on the registration list, don't panic. You will generally be permitted to cast a provisional ballot that will be counted after election officials have double-checked your registration. For those who are housebound or will be out of their district on voting day, absentee ballots are available from your local election office.

HOW TO GET OR RENEW A PASSPORT
Don't leave home without it

It is illegal to leave or enter the country without a valid passport, and getting a passport is so time-consuming that it's best to apply several months before your departure. Also, some countries require that your passport be valid at least six months beyond the date of your stay. Check with the country's nearest embassy or consulate before you plan your trip.

If you have never had a passport, apply in person at one of 1,000 authorized post offices, or make an appointment before going to one of 13 passport agencies across the country. Complete the DS-11 application form (but do not sign the form until the passport official asks you to do so) and bring proof of U.S. citizenship, such as a certified copy of your birth certificate or a Certificate of Naturalization, if you are a naturalized citizen.

You must also bring two 2x2-inch color photographs taken within the past six months. The photos must have a plain, white background and show a frontal view of your face. Also bring a picture ID, including a valid driver's license, government or military ID, or previous passport. The fee is $97 for a 10-year passport. Forms of payment vary, depending on the location: some accept cash, checks, money orders and credit cards; some take only cash. Be sure to ask in advance.

If you are renewing an expired passport, the process is easier. You may apply by mail if your passport was issued within the past 15 years and you were at least 16 when you received it. You can get an application form (DS-82) from a post office or online at www.travel.state.gov. Attach your most recent passport, two identical passport photos and a $67 check (payable to the U.S. Department of State) or money order, and mail to National Passport Center, P.O. Box 371971, Pittsburgh, Pa. 15250-7971. The National Passport Information Center at 877-487-2778 can answer all passport related questions.

HOW TO GET A SOCIAL SECURITY CARD
They've got your number

The Social Security Administration only came into existence in 1935, in the midst of the Great Depression. But the cards have become indispens-

---

ⓘ INSIDE INFO

The Power of Many

○ Does someone else get your Social Security number when you die? No. More than 420 million numbers have been issued so far (around 5½ million each year), but enough new numbers remain to last several generations.

○ What do the numbers mean? The first three digits represent the area where you lived when you got the card. People on the East Coast have lower numbers than those on the West Coast. The remaining six digits are issued randomly.

○ Members of Congress, the Vice President and the President are covered under Social Security. They have been paying into the system since 1984.

SOURCE: Social Security Administration

---

able: you need one to open a bank account, get a credit card or apply for most government services for yourself or your child. Legal immigrants are also entitled to Social Security payments and need a number to collect benefits.

Since 1985, any child you claim as a dependant on your income tax return must have a Social Security number. The easiest way for a child to get a number is at birth. When your hospital asks for the information needed to complete your newborn's birth certificate, ask to have your state's vital statistics office share that information with the Social Security Administration. A Social Security card will be mailed to you directly.

If you decide to wait or your child does not yet have a number, you can get one by contacting the nearest Social Security field office (You can find it online at www.ssa.gov.) You will be asked to fill out a form SS-5 and provide evidence that you are the child's parent or legal guardian, and furnish a birth certificate with proof of your child's age, identity and citizenship.

To replace a lost Social Security card, to change the name on your card or request a new card, call Social Security at 800-772-1213 for an appointment with an agent at your local office. Or start by downloading an application online at www.socialsecurity.gov/online/ss-5.html.

HOW TO REGISTER FOR THE DRAFT
Calling all 18-year-old men

The draft technically ended in 1973, when the country converted to an all-volunteer military, but that doesn't mean young men are totally off the hook. Within 30 days of their 18th birthday, they must register with the Selective Service System. In the event that a national draft returns, a lottery system based on birthdates would go into effect to provide the additional soldiers needed to fight wars.

 TIMELY TIPS

Politics on the Web

✔ **Project Vote Smart** (www.vote-smart.org), a guide to candidates and issues

✔ **Federal Election Commission** (www.fec.gov) data on campaign contributions

✔ **PoliticalMoneyLine** (www.tray.com/fecinfo) Federal Election Commission and other campaign money and lobbying information in a useful format

✔ **The Living Room Candidate** (www.livingroom-candidate.movingimage.us/index.php) Presidential campaign commercials from 1952 to 2000

✔ **Politics Navigator** (www.nytimes.com/ref/politics/POLI_NAV.html), from the *New York Times* on the Web, has many more political links.

The first to be called would be those whose 20th birthday falls on the date drawn in the lottery. They would be followed by those ages 21 through 25, as needed. Men remain on the list until they turn 26.

Registration forms are available at local post offices and high schools. If you are applying for Federal Student Financial Aid, you can register at the same time by checking "yes" on Box 29 of the form; the Education Department will send the information to the Selective Service System. But the quickest and easiest way to register is online at: www.sss.gov.

You should receive acknowledgement of your registration within 90 days. If you don't, it is your responsibility to contact the Selective Service System (847-688-6888). The penalty for not registering: a fine of up to $250,000 or five years in jail.

HOW TO MAKE A CAMPAIGN CONTRIBUTION
Putting your money where your vote is

Money seems to amplify the voice of the electorate substantially, so you may want to consider supporting the candidate who supports your views. But before you write a check to your favorite candidate or political party, be aware of the federal election laws.

Individuals may give no more than as follows: $2,100 to each candidate or candidate committee in an election (primaries and general elections count separately); $26,700 to a national party committee per calendar year; and $5,000 to any other political committee per calendar year. Some contribution limits are linked to the inflation rate and may change. For more information, contact the Federal Election Commission at 800-424-9530 or go online to www.fec.gov. Foreign nationals are prohibited from donating to campaigns in the United States.

HOW TO DECIPHER A POLL
Ah, the fickleness of public opinion. A pollster tells all

Polls putatively take the pulse of public opinion. But do they really tell us what we think? Well, yes and no. How reliable a gauge any poll is often depends on how large the sample size was, how the poll was taken and, of course, precisely how the questions were asked.

Peter D. Hart has been taking and analyzing polls for more than 30 years. He has been a pollster for NBC News and the *Wall St. Journal*, among other organizations, and is a regular commentator on television and radio public-policy programs. Here are his tips for reading a poll:

Take a look at how the poll was conducted. One big problem in the polling business is that the word "survey" refers to anytime you to talk to the American people. But questionnaires through the mail or phone-in surveys are self-selecting—anyone who calls a 900-number is a certain kind of person, and it won't make for an evenly distributed survey. Telephone surveys are probably the most accurate, and we do random-digit dialing to make sure we reach people with unlisted numbers, because they make up a segment of the population that has definite opinions about some issues.

Find out the purpose of the poll, and who is doing the polling. Is the pollster a news organization, an academic group or a politician? And why are they doing the poll? Do they have an agenda? News organizations are one of the best sources for surveys.

When you see a person described as a Democratic or Republican pollster, it means that they are specialists. It doesn't mean their polls are going to be biased—because their client wants a very accurate picture of where they stand.

Wiring Into Washington
How you can speak truth to power

Your official representatives may be out of touch, but that doesn't mean they're out of reach. The Web sites here will help you find out who they are, what they're up to and how to make your views known. After all, they work for you.

• **U.S. House of Representatives.** Provides access to your individual House members' home pages, as well as indexed Congressional Records updates. www.house.gov

• **U.S. Senate**. A virtual tour of the Capitol, along with senators' bios and committee listings www.senate.gov

• **White House.** Features access to all of the Cabinet level sites and to an archive, updated daily, of more than 4,000 White House speeches, briefs and reports. You can also get information on White House tours and other events at the mansion and send a message to the President. www.whitehouse.gov

• **Courts.** The Federal Judicial Center offers general information about the court system. www.uscourts.gov and www.fjc.gov

Look for bias in the poll. Look at the choice of answers that respondents were given. Are there four answers in one direction and really only one choice for an answer if you feel differently? Also look at the order of questions. Questions should go from general to specific. The order changes how you think about questions; the previous question always influences the later question.

Look at when the poll was done. Maybe a candidate does a burst of media advertising, and I conduct a poll right after that blitz. The poll might show very favorable results that might be a temporary result of the media push. Also,

For the Good of the Nation

How to join the "domestic Peace Corps"

AmeriCorps is a national service organization that lets volunteers earn an army of benefits while doing good in the larger community. Since the program started in 1994, more than 400,000 men and women have helped millions of Americans. In exchange for service, members receive financial support, learn new skills and reap the psychic rewards that volunteering can bring. For more information, log on to www.americorps.org.

• Members serve with more than 3,000 nonprofit groups, public agencies and religious and community organizations nationwide, including Habitat for Humanity, the American Red Cross and the New York Police Department. In exchange for a year of service, members receive a modest living allowance, health coverage and free education awards.

• Any American citizen or permanent resident of the United States, who is 17 years (18 for some programs) or older is eligible, regardless of income.Competition is fairly tough. In a recent five-year period, AmeriCorps received four applications for every available slot. Generally, applicants learn within two months if they have been accepted, rejected or put on a waiting list.

• Members who complete a full year of service can get an education award of $4,725. (The amount is prorated for part-time service.) Students can use this amount within seven years of completing service to help pay for college, graduate school or vocational training, or to repay a prior educational loan. Some members have received college credit for their service, but that decision rests with the individual school.

• The application procedures vary with each program, but generally there are two deadline dates: March 15 for the fall cycle, and July 15 for the winter cycle. Selection is continuous, so applicants should file early since a program could fill up even before the deadline date.

• Volunteers receive a variety of training, depending on the service project. Members who help build houses, for example, are taught building fundamentals, such as framing a house and putting up sheetrock. Those who work with children in schools will learn tutoring techniques. Members also get CPR/First Aid and Disaster Relief certification from the Red Cross. In addition, training sessions for conflict management and leadership, team and community building are given.

sometimes polls are done before a major event, but not released until afterward. It's important to know when the poll was conducted and to consider what has happened in the interim.

The size of the sample, not the size of the universe determines the accuracy of the poll. If you poll 500 people in Nevada and 500 in California, which poll is more accurate? They're both equally accurate. A good analogy is if you have a 300-pound linebacker and an 80-pound kid and you need blood samples from both—there will be no difference in the sampling.

Look at a poll's accuracy rate. A poll with an accuracy of plus or minus 3 percent means that if I tell you 50 percent of people favor welfare reform, that number could be between 53 and 47 percent. The more people you survey, the more accurate the poll. To get an accuracy of plus or minus 1 percent, you have to interview 9,000 people. I tell clients that an accuracy rate of plus or minus 4 percent is fine for most decisions you're going to make.

Jury Duty: The Whole Truth

Revealing the ins and outs of serving on a jury

To meet your civic responsibility when you get a summons for jury duty, work and family schedules often need to be revised. But many say the rewards of serving on a jury duty often more than compensate for the inconvenience. What should you expect when you receive a summons? Jury consultant Jo-Ellan Dimitrius, who has advised legal teams on many high-profile trials, including O.J. Simpson's criminal defense team, shares her insights here.

💬 **What should people know when they show up for jury duty?**

Jurors have the right to ask questions: what days will we have off, will I be sequestered, will I remain anonymous? Also, if you anticipate legitimate conflicts, like a long-planned family vacation, the court may be able to work around them.

💬 **Who make the best jurors for criminal and civil cases?**

For a defendant in a criminal trial, or a plaintiff in a civil trial, you look for jurors who are liberal. Someone who is a member of the Sierra Club or PETA (People for the Ethical Treatment of Animals), for example, or church members and minorities. For defendants in civil cases, or pros-

> ℹ️ **INSIDE INFO**
>
> ## A Jury of Your Peers
>
> ○ Potential jurors are chosen randomly from lists of voters and licensed drivers.
>
> ○ People over 70, anyone who served on a jury within the past two years, and volunteer firefighters and members of a rescue squad or ambulance crew may be excused from serving.
>
> ○ Members of the armed forces on active duty, and professional firefighters and police are usually exempt from serving on jury duty.
>
> ○ Jurors are paid—usually about $40 a day. (Don't forget to declare it when you file your tax return.) Your employer can choose to continue to pay your salary during all or part of your jury duty but is not required to do so. However, employers cannot legally fire you for the absence.

ecutors in criminal cases, you look for the more conservative, older jurors, perhaps someone who had been the victim of a crime.

In all cases, you want to have one or two firm, authoritarian types who will lead in your direction during the deliberation process. And for the rest, you want followers who will listen.

💬 **What is the best way to get excused from jury duty?**

It raises red flags anytime a juror walks in with sunglasses on, anytime anyone's hiding their eyes. I avoid jurors who give very brief answers on the questionnaire and during the oral questioning. It makes me wonder what they are trying to hide. I look at body language—there have been times when jurors are giving me a positive response, but shaking their heads no. Also, the way they talk about the defendant. During the O.J. trial, for example, a juror was referring to Simpson as "the incarcerated," not a good sign.

Finally, I'll avoid a person who clearly doesn't

> **INSIDE INFO**
>
> ## America's Most Wanted
>
> Think you might have seen a suspicious-looking person at the supermarket? Check out one of these two sites:
>
> ○ **The F.B.I.'s Most Wanted** (www.fbi.gov/ mostwant/fugitive/fpphome.htmand
>
> ○ **The F.B.I's Most Wanted Terrorists** (www.fbi. gov/mostwant/fugitives.htm)

want to be there. People make up weak excuses, like their dog is sick. When it's clear they don't want to be there, the last thing I want to do is to put that person in the jury box.

Having Your Day in Court

When compromise fails, you can make your case in small claims court

Before filing a suit in small claims court, you need to answer two questions. First: Do you have a case? "There is a big difference between having something bad happen to you and actually having grounds for a lawsuit," says Ralph Warner, author of *Everybody's Guide to Small Claims Court*. "You have to know exactly how and why the other party is the author of your misfortune."

The second question: If you win, can you col-

The ABC's of Legalese

Arraignment. A court proceeding during which a defendant is formally charged with a crime and asked to plead guilty or not guilty.

Defendant. The person or organization being sued in a civil case; the person accused of a crime in a criminal case.

Grand jury. A panel of citizens who hear evidence of criminal allegations and decide whether there are grounds for a criminal prosecution.

Plaintiff. The person who files the complaint in a civil lawsuit.

Subpoena. A court-ordered command that a person appear at a specified time and place to testify under penalty of law.

Voir dire. French term meaning "to speak the truth;" describes the questioning process used by judges and lawyers to pick a jury from potential jurors.

lect? "The biggest mistake people make is suing deadbeats," says Warner. "If they don't have two nickels to their name, don't waste your time."

If you answered yes to both questions, Warner suggests that the next step is to write to the other party. Calmly describe what went wrong and why that party is responsible. Propose a remedy. If the other party is a business, you can contact the Better Business Bureau or local consumer affairs department, which might be able to exert some pressure. If you fail to get satisfaction, it is time to go to court.

The key to victory is doing your homework. States put a cap on the maximum amount you can sue for, so find out your state's limit. The average national cap is $5,000, but some states like Tennessee have a $15,000 to $20,000 maximum. Most cases boil down to he-said, she-said tussles, but you can gain an edge by gathering corroborating evidence. Log all contacts and keep all receipts and gather every shred of documentation you can. You must file your case at a court near the defendant's home or place of business. You pay a nominal fee and fill out a brief form, stating the claim and providing the defendant's address. A case index number and court date are assigned. If the day is inconvenient, you can ask for an adjournment.

When the day arrives, several things can happen. If the defendant does not show up, you present your case and your odds of winning are enhanced. If the other party is there, you can make a last attempt to settle: an imminent trial can often make even the more unreasonable people reasonable. If you still can't resolve the matter, you go to arbitration, mediation or trial. Most people choose arbitration or mediation, because making an argument and introducing evidence are much more informal than at a trial and resolution is faster.

Even if you opt for a trial and win, your troubles may not be over. Typically, 25 percent of defendants

Where to Go When the Stakes Are Low

Mad as hell at your neighbor who mistakenly cut down one of the trees on your property? Furious at the mechanic who did everything but fix your car? Disputes like these, where the anger quotient is high and the dollar value relatively small, usually end up in small claims court. The filing fee is nominal, often around $25, and most cases be settled within two months. Although you can hire a lawyer to present your case, in most states, representation isn't necessary. Many states send cases to mediators, who help the parties reach a compromise, and arbitrators, whose decisions are binding. The following are state-by-state guidelines from the National Center for State Courts in Williamsburg, Va.

STATE	MAXIMUM DOLLAR AMOUNT	JURY TRIALS	LAWYERS PERMITTED
Alabama	$3,000	No	Optional
Alaska	$7,500	No	Yes
Arizona	$2,500	No	No
Arkansas	$5,000	No	No
California	$5,000	No	No
Colorado	$7,500	No	No
Connecticut	$2,500	No	Yes
Delaware	$15,000	No	Yes
District of Columbia	$5,000	Yes	Yes
Florida	$5,000	Yes	Yes
Georgia	$25,000[1]	Yes[2]	Yes
Hawaii	$3,500[3]	No	Yes
Idaho	$4,000	No	No
Illinois	$2,500	Yes	Yes
Indiana	$3,000	No	Yes
Iowa	$5,000	No	Yes
Kansas	$1,800	No	No
Kentucky	$1,500	No	Yes
Louisiana	$2,000	No	Yes
Maine	$4,500	No	Yes
Maryland	$2,500	No	Yes
Massachusetts	$2,000	Yes[4]	Yes
Michigan	$3,000	No	No
Minnesota	$7,500	No	Yes
Mississippi	N/A	N/A	N/A
Missouri	$3,000	No	Yes
Montana	$3,000	No	No
Nebraska	$2,100	No	No
Nevada	$5,000	No	Yes
New Hampshire	$5,000	No	Yes
New Jersey	$5,000[5]	No	Yes
New Mexico	N/A	N/A	N/A
New York	$3,000	N/A	Yes
North Carolina	$4,000	No	Yes
North Dakota	$5,000	No	Yes
Ohio	$2,000	No	Yes
Oklahoma	$3,000	Yes	Yes
Oregon	$5,000[6]	No	No
Pennsylvania	$8,000	No	Yes
Rhode Island	$1,500	No	Yes
South Carolina	$7,500	Yes	Yes
South Dakota	$8,000	No	Yes
Tennessee	$15,000–$20,000	No	Yes
Texas	$5,000	Yes	Yes
Utah	$7,500	No	Yes
Vermont	$3,500	Yes	Yes
Virginia	N/A	N/A	N/A
Washington	$4,000	No	No
West Virginia	N/A	N/A	N/A
Wisconsin	$5,000	Yes	Yes
Wyoming	$3,000	No	Yes

NOTES:

N/A=Information not available

Maximum dollar amount=maximum amount of suit

1 (Civil Court); $5,000 (Magistrate Court); $15,000 (Municipal Court)

2 Except Magistrate Court

3 Except in residential security deposit cases

4 Except for Superior Court

5 $15,000 for security deposit demand cases

6 $2,500 in Justice Court

do not pay up. If this happens, you must go back to court to get a default judgment. You can then seek help from the local sheriff's or marshal's office, which can garnish the defendant's wages or put a lien on his bank account.

– J. Peder Zane

How to Read Your F.B.I. File

Find out if you're among the ranks of the rich, famous and nefarious

Frank Sinatra's racy parties with John F. Kennedy, the Beach Boys' penchant for psychedelic drugs, Liberace's fondness for gambling—all are well-known morsels from F.B.I. files. The bureau won't say how many files it has, but estimates are they number more than six million. Lucille Ball, Marilyn Monroe—even Albert Einstein—were checked out by the bureau as potential Communists. Some files are longer than others: Andy Warhol's film company gets 38 pages; Elvis's shenanigans merit 600; and what the government knows about U.F.O.'s fills 1,600 pages.

The F.B.I. maintains that it no longer spies on individuals for political purposes, and hasn't done so since Director J. Edgar Hoover's death in 1972. Some civil liberty groups may doubt that assertion, but despite its reputation, the fact is the F.B.I. does not keep a file on every American man, woman and child. However, if you suspect that you have come under the F.B.I. radar—or if you're just curious about a long-dead ancestor—you are entitled to read the file.

Lennon appears to be radically orientated, however he does not give the impression he is a true revolutionist since he is constantly under the influence of narcotics.

From the F.B.I. file on late former Beatle "John Winston Lennon"

• • •

For access to your personal report, you must file a request under the Privacy Act and the Freedom of Information Act. For information about another individual, an organization or a business, file a request under the Freedom of Information Act alone. For a Privacy Act request, send your complete name, address, date and place of birth, Social Security number and former addresses. If you're asking about a specific incident—F.B.I. agents stormed your house one night, for example—provide as much information as possible about the event. Sign the request and have it notarized.

If your request is for the file of a person who is dead, provide all the pertinent information and send proof that he or she is deceased, such as a published obituary, for example. Mail all requests to F.B.I., Record Information/ Dissemination Section, Service Request Unit, Room 6359, 935 Pennsylvania Ave., N.W., Washington, D.C, 20535. In some cases, you can file online at www.foia.F.B.I..gov.

Even if you don't have an F.B.I. file, chances are that you have a bureau "rap sheet." That's a roster of data on individuals that the F.B.I. gets from fingerprint cards filed by federal government workers, naturalized citizens, members of the military or people who are arrested. You can get a copy of your rap sheet by sending the F.B.I. a letter of request, including proof of your identity and a set of rolled-ink fingerprint impressions, such as those taken at a police station. The fee is $18, payable by certified check or money order to the Treasury of the United States. Send the payment, letter and documents to: F.B.I., CJIS Division,

Attention: SCU, Mod. D-2, 1000 Custer Hollow Rd., Clarksburg, West Virginia 26306.

As for what fills those 1,600 pages on U.F.O.'s— see for yourself by visiting the F.B.I.'s Electronic Reading Room at foia.fbi.gov

Divorce on the Cheap

With no kids, few assets and an amenable spouse, a do-it-yourself divorce may be for you

The statistics are dismally familiar: half of marriages end in divorce. More than a million couples a year call it quits. A full-blown divorce trial can take years of wrangling in court and cost from $60,000 to $100,000 or more, according to HALT, a Washington, D.C., organization that pushes for legal reform. Even an amicable divorce case with no children involved can run about $3,000. By comparison, a self-help divorce could cost less than $300. The downside: some do-it-yourselfers end up paying for it in legwork and frustration.

You may have no choice but to retain a lawyer if your spouse contests any aspect of the divorce: spousal support, splitting up assets, custody of children, for example. These issues are too contentious and generally require a third party to help resolve. But if you expect a peaceful divorce, have no children and are tenacious, then the cheaper, do-it-yourself route is wide open.

Bookstores and the Internet are rife with divorce software, which costs anywhere from $24.99 for a bare-bones kit to several hundred or more for a package that includes some legal consultation. You get general divorce forms and some specific to your state, but you may not necessarily get all the forms you need for your specific locality. To be safe, contact your circuit clerk's office or family court clerk's office (numbers are found in your phone directory) for the list of documents you need. They may have your missing documents available. Once you've prepared the documents, file them with the court (filing fees are usually around $250) and ask for a hearing. Once a court date is set, ask the clerk exactly which documents you'll need to bring to the hearing. Then show up on time, with your paperwork in hand.

Don't be surprised if you encounter resistance on the part of clerks and judges during this process. Although attitudes are softening toward those who represent themselves, some courts try to discourage self-helpers, who often come to court unprepared, taking up more court time than a lawyer would. But if all goes well, your divorce will be granted, the judge will sign the decree and you will have saved thousands.

ⓘ **INSIDE INFO**

The Great Divide

When divvying up a divorcing couple's assets, most states take many factors into account, including length of marriage, a partner's age, marketable skills, lifestyle and needs. In the following community-property states, however, most assets acquired during a marriage belong to both spouses, while assets brought into the marriage by one spouse remain his or her property. These states split assets equally between spouses.

- Alaska*
- Arizona
- California
- Idaho
- Louisiana
- Nevada
- New Mexico
- Texas
- Washington
- Wisconsin

*Married couples in Alaska can choose to have assets treated as community property by written agreement.

- A woman's standard of living drops by as much as 27 percent after a divorce, while for men it rises about 10 percent, according to the Marriage Project at Rutgers University. Single mothers, many of them divorced, suffer some of the highest bankruptcy rates.

The Name Game

Change it from Mary to Sue if you so desire

"What name to call thee by?" asked 14th-century poet Petrarch in a poem to his beloved. But the same question can be asked of the more than three million Americans who legally change their names every year. As part of your right to freedom of expression, you can opt for a new name for just about any reason: religious, social, aesthetic or just because you want to—called "desire" in legal lingo. There are limits, however: you can't use a new identity in a fraudulent way, such as to evade debtors; and pornographic or racially insulting names won't pass muster with the court.

Many name changes are simply a result of marriage or divorce. In those cases, changes are made almost automatically. A bride who takes on her husband's name—or less frequently a groom who takes his wife's—simply indicates the desired name on the marriage license. A divorced woman who wants to revert to her maiden name can easily make the change in the divorce documents.

But for those who want a fresh persona for other reasons, the process is more complicated. First, you have to figure out what documents your state requires and in which court you need to file the petition. Your county clerk's office (the number can be found in your local phone directory or on your county's Web site) can tell you the requirements and how to get requisite forms. Be prepared in some courts to provide a list of the names and addresses of all your creditors. You pay a nominal court fee and are given a docket number. A judge reviews your petition and either approves it, or requests a court hearing, which may be routine in some states. The final step, after court approval, is to place an ad in a specified newspaper announcing the name change. The court will then inform you that your new identity is legal.

The process can be done without a lawyer, but for those who need some guidance, name-change kits (from $20 to $150) are available online. Or you can get a lawyer to do the leg-work at a cost of between $500 and more than $2,000, depending on whether children are also involved. Once you are officially rechristened, be sure to let all interested parties in on your new name. Notify employers, banks, credit card companies, the I.R.S, the motor vehicle department, Social Security Administration, etc. Remember to revisit your will, your grandpa's will, retirement plans, contracts and real estate deeds. Alas, in some cases, your old identity will never die. Your passport, for example, may very well state your original name with an a.k.a., "also known as," and your new moniker.

When a Child Needs a Guardian

What-if decisions that need to be made

A quick way to cast a pall over a conversation is to ask parents if they've appointed a guardian for their children in the event that, God forbid, both of them should die. "It's not at the top of everyone's to-do list," says Richard S. Finkelstein of the New Jersey law firm Berkowitz, Lichtstein, Kuritsky, Giasullo & Gross. Finkelstein has worked for 20 years in trusts and estates.

The sobering truth is that if parents don't state who they want as guardians in their will, and they both die, a judge will make that decision. The basic issue parents worry about is finding a relative—and parents overwhelmingly choose a relative—with similar religious and educational backgrounds. Other concerns to resolve before naming a guardian are, for example: Is the person physically up to the job? Does he or she have the time? Does the family have children close to the same age as yours? Would your children have to move? Do you and the potential guardian share the same moral beliefs and parenting style?

A big issue is wealth. Most parents make sure that if they were to die, their children would be taken care of financially, but what if the family the children go to is not as well off? One way to address this discrepancy, Finkelstein suggests, is to leave money from the estate directly to the guardian, which may help the guardian's children and narrow the gap.

It is important to realize that the person you appoint as guardian does not need to be the same person who controls the finances. It is possible, and some lawyers recommend, naming a guardian, and then naming a separate person as trustee of the financial assets or co-trustee with the guardian. Finkelstein believes naming a different person as a trustee is a good option because it offers a check and balance, and "puts a second head in the process," that is, it doesn't place the entire decision-making burden on one person.

Often trusts are structured so that the child receives the money in stages—one-third at age 25, for example, one-third at 30 and one-third at 35, rather than receiving a lump sum at 18. And make sure you understand where your money is going. You may have your assets, such as proceeds from the sale of your house, for example, going to your children's trust if anything happens to you, but what about your 401(k), your individual retirement account and your life insurance?

So being a guardian is a serious job, a fiduciary responsibility, for which you can get sued if you do a poor job. For that reason, think carefully about who you ask to take care of your offspring. The same is true when agreeing to care for someone else's children. Still, as hard as it may be to pick one guardian, many lawyers advise selecting one or even two backups, in case, when the time comes, the chosen person is not in a position to take the

children. Also, as families and children evolve, you may want to rethink guardianships down the line and reflect those changes in your will.

You may not need a lawyer to complete the paperwork; companies like Nolo (www.nolo.com) offer books, software and forms for do-it-yourself legal solutions.

—Alina Tugend

Do You Need a Will?

The answer is probably yes. Here's why and what it should include

More than half of American adults do not have wills. What are the potential consequences of not planning for the disposition of your estate? Boston attorney Alexander Bove, a frequent lecturer on estate planning, taxes and trusts, provided the following expert responses to why you (and your heirs) might be better off drawing up a will.

Q What happens if I don't have a will?

If you have no will, your estate will end up in probate court and important decisions will be out of your hands. Normally, you name an executor, a trusted friend or family member who is responsible for determining taxes, assets, bills and debts to be paid on your estate. Without a will, the court becomes the executor and your estate is divided under state laws.

Q What are the important components of a will?

As a rule, wills are broken up into two parts. Bequests include specified property, such as amounts of money, real estate and stocks that are left to a designated beneficiary. The residue is everything else, or everything not specifically defined, and will normally go to the primary beneficiary of the estate, usually a

Whose Life Is It Anyway?

Living wills give you control and give your family peace of mind

Fewer than 30 percent of Americans have filled out living wills or appointed someone to make medical decisions for them if they become incapacitated.

Living wills describe a person's wishes regarding medical treatment. Another type of document, called a health care power of attorney or health care proxy, names someone else, usually a relative or a friend, to make decisions when a patient can no longer do so. Such written instructions, also called advance directives, can be used in every state. They are backed by either law or precedents set in court cases, and a federal law requires that hospitals and nursing homes inform patients that they have the right to fill out the documents. Details vary from state to state; in some places no official form is needed, and patients can draw up their own statements. Two witnesses are usually needed. The details should be discussed with family members and doctors, who should also be given copies. A copy should also be included in the medical chart if the person is hospitalized.

Living wills give people a chance to say how far doctors should go in hopeless situations. Patients can specify whether they would want treatments like respirators, feeding tubes, resuscitation, transfusions or kidney dialysis.

A Web site for a nonprofit group, www. medicaldirective.org, offers documents for $15 along with detailed work sheets describing possible medical situations for patients and families to consider.

But it is nearly impossible to anticipate every situation that will arise during an illness. Therefore, some experts say it is more important to have a proxy than a living will, someone who knows the patient and can make decisions if the unexpected occurs. Picking a backup proxy is also recommended. But patients must discuss their wishes in detail with proxies, and make sure that doctors and relatives know who the proxy is.

—Denise Grady

---

spouse, children, or both. Only property in your name at the time of your death can be passed on to your heirs.

● How often should I update my will?

Whenever there is a major change in the tax laws, or if there is a change in your family or your family's finances, you should reflect that in your will.

● How can I provide for minor children?

If you have minor children, you should be sure to name a trusted relative or friend as the guardian who will be responsible for the "person and property" of the minors.

● How are a will and a living trust different?

A living trust is a legal document that you create while you are alive; you can transfer assets to the trust while you are alive and the trust governs the assets. You may be your own trustee. Whatever is in the trust does not have to pass through probate. Whatever you do not put into the trust goes into a will.

A living trust—including a will, durable power of attorney and health care proxy—and a living will are the typical documents in a modern estate plan.

● How much should I pay to have a will drawn?

That depends on the complexity of the estate. The process of drawing up a will can range between $50 and $5,000 or more, depending on how complicated it is. Often the amount of property is not as important a factor as the family circumstances.

Manners & Miscellany

Etiquette for the 21st Century

Savoir-faire today means faring with newfangled devices and families

The day when rules of etiquette were etched in parchment and folks adhered to them blindly is long gone. Etiquette buffs wax nostalgic for those simpler times, when married women took their husband's last name, second marriages were rare and third marriages almost unheard of. The etiquette game is made even murkier these days with high-tech gadgetry and services—cellphones, personal digital assistants, texting and the like—that test the limits of polite interaction with society.

How to navigate this new age of etiquette confusion? For those trying to keep up with changing mores, here's a primer on some of the more contentious issues on the etiquette beat.

HIGH-TECH MANNERS

Call waiting. The best advice is not to succumb to the rudeness of this service at all. But if you must, and your conversation is interrupted by another call on your line, apologize to the person with whom you are talking. Switch to the other caller and tell him or her that you'll call back. Then return to the original conversation and apologize again.

Caller ID. If you have this service and you know who is calling, do you still answer as if you don't know who is on the line? Yes, say etiquette experts.

Avoid greeting callers by using their names. Wait until they say hello and identify themselves.

Cellphones, etc. If you get a call when you are in a meeting, at a dinner party, show or other social event, turn off your cell or BlackBerry immediately and then politely excuse yourself to make the call. When you return you do not need to reveal the nature of the call, unless it is an emergency and you must leave the event immediately. And remember, no cellphone conversation is completely private—your conversation may be picked up on another phone.

Unknown calls. A sticky situation arises when a number shows up on your cell that you don't recognize. Say you call back and get a strange voice. What do you say without revealing your identity? The proper protocol, according to etiquette experts, is to say: "Hello, this is (your phone number). I noticed you called and wondered if there is anything I can help you with?" It may well have been a wrong number, but you don't want to miss out on opportunities either.

> **Whenever two people come together, and their behavior affects one another, you have etiquette.**
>
> Emily Post
>
> •••

E-mail. When you send an e-mail, make the header specific so recipients know immediately whether the message is important. It is acceptable to acknowledge an impromptu missive, such as "Congratulations on your new job," with an e-mail note of thanks, according to manners guru Judith Martin. E-mail is not confidential,

IF THE QUEEN DROPS BY

Bow or curtsey and address her as "Your Majesty" when you run into a queen. Here is the correct form of address for various personages:

PERSON	SPOKEN GREETING
President of the U.S.	*Mr.* or *Madam President*
Former President	*Mr.* or *Mrs., Ms.* [Jones]
Senator	*Senator* [Jones]
General	*General* [Jones]
FOREIGN HEAD OF STATE	
Premier or President of a republic	*Your Excellency*
Prime Minister	*Mr.* or *Madam Prime Minister*
The Pope	*Your Holiness* or *Most Holy Father*
Cardinal	*Your Eminence* or *Cardinal* [Jones]
Priest	*Father* [Jones]
Protestant Clergy	*Reverend* [Jones]
Rabbi	*Rabbi* [Jones]
King or Queen	*Your Majesty* or *Sir* or *Madam*
Duke/Duchess	*Your Grace* or *Duke/Duchess*
Knight	*Sir* [John]
Wife of knight	*Lady* [Jones]

however, so personal or controversial messages have no place in office e-mail.

Fax machines. Use the fax only for communicating business or nonconfidential information quickly. Never use the fax to send a thank-you note after a job interview.

Speaker phones. Use speaker phones as infrequently as possible, because they tend to make the person who is not in the room feel uncomfortable. Always apologize for having to use the speaker phone and be sure to end the call with your handset.

Voice mail. Keep your outgoing message clear and brief, and update it regularly, especially if you travel frequently. When leaving a message on an answering machine, follow the same rule: clearly and briefly leave the information requested in the outgoing message. Jot down a few points that you want to make before you call. Try not to hold a prolonged one-way conversation unless you really don't want the person to call you back. Never eat or chew gum while on the phone.

WOMEN'S ISSUES

Never-married woman. Steer clear of the antiquated "Miss." Today it's used mainly to address girls younger than 18. Even when addressing formal invitations to adult single women, Miss is no longer used, etiquette experts say. Unmarried adult women, and married or divorced women who prefer not to use their husband's name, are addressed as "Ms."

Married woman. Formally, a woman who takes her husband's name is addressed as *Mrs. Richard Saunders.* Some women prefer to keep their middle name and drop their maiden name: *Ms. Sarah Marie Saunders.*

Although commonly done, a married woman is not addressed as Mrs. with her own first name and married name. Traditionally, that combination is reserved for divorced women.

Mail to the couple is addressed to *Mr. and Mrs. Richard Saunders* or, alternately to *Mr. Richard Saunders and Ms. Sarah Saunders.* If the woman keeps her maiden name, address correspondence to both *Mr. Richard Saunders and Ms. Sarah Smith,* on the same line.

A woman who uses her maiden name at work and husband's name socially, is addressed as Ms. for business, and either Ms. or Mrs. socially. For formal correspondence, use *Mr. Richard Saunders and Ms. Sarah Smith*; informally, use the traditional *Mr. and Mrs. Richard Saunders.*

When writing to a woman who uses a hyphenated name, her name goes first: *Sarah Smith-Saunders.* For a couple, both names are used, *Mr. Richard Saunders and Ms. Sarah Smith-Saunders.*

Divorced woman. A divorced woman often reverts to her maiden name. But when children are involved, it can get confusing. A divorced woman with children, who keeps her married name, is addressed as *Mrs. Sarah Saunders,* without her husband's first name. That identifies her as divorced and as the children's parent.

Widow. Until she remarries, a widow keeps her husband's name, and is addressed the same way as a married woman, *Mrs. Richard Saunders* or *Ms. Sarah Saunders.* If she remarries, she can use either her former husband's last name or her maiden name as a middle name, *Sarah Saunders Franklin* or *Sarah Smith Franklin.*

---

① **INSIDE INFO**

Personal Ad Abbreviations

ANI	age not important
DTE	down to earth
GSOH	good sense of humor
ISO	in search of
LTR	long-term relationship
NMM	no married men
NLP	no losers, please
NUMP	no ugly men, please
OHAC	own house and car
VGL	very good looking
WTT	willing to travel

RELATIONSHIP RULES

Living together. When addressing mail to an unmarried couple that lives together, each name should be on a separate line; the names should not be joined by the word "and," say the rules of etiquette.

When introducing couples who live together, most labels—boyfriend, girlfriend, significant other, date, lover—sound awkward, so it is best to forgo the explanation and simply introduce each person by name.

Divorced. A divorced couple does not return wedding gifts. A divorced woman should not wear her engagement ring on her wedding band finger, etiquette authorities hold. Often, the stone is reset into a bracelet or necklace or kept for her children's future use.

Friends of a newly divorced couple should not pry for details of the breakup. A friend's goal should be to help the person get through the difficult time. If children are involved, both sides of the family should respect the other side's efforts to see the children. Also vital: one parent should not criticize the other in front of their children, even if the impulse is nearly irresistible.

If You Only Knew What to Do

How to handle some common— but excruciating—social predicaments

Who hasn't had an embarrassing moment? Incited an argument at a dinner party. Met someone and then promptly forgotten his or her name. Entered a room and panicked at not recognizing a soul. Agonized over whom to invite with whom, or whether to invite either at all. The list of potentially embarrassing social scenarios is endless. Here are three fairly common yet awkward

TIMELY TIPS

The Dos and Don'ts of Entertaining With Children

No matter how well-behaved, kids are not always welcome

The proper protocol is ever changing in the world of parties and kids. Here are a few ironclad rules regarding whether to lug the kids along or leave them home with the babysitter.

✔ **If the invitation does not specify that it is a family event or that children are invited,** you should not ask to bring them to a party. Some invitations are quite explicit, with notes such as, "Nobody under 4½ feet tall, even though we love them" or "Book your babysitters early." Do not ignore those messages.

✔ **If both you and the hostess have little kids,** and you assume that she assumes you will bring your kid to her 5 p.m. Sunday event, it is O.K. to call and ask, and you probably should. Anyway, the hostess can always say no.

✔ **If children are invited,** remember it's the host's duty to provide entertainment for the kids. A good hostess also provides kid-friendly food. And if your little guest announces, "I hate chicken fingers," no need to panic. Pasta and butter seems to meet with universal approval. Plus, everything grown-ups liked when they were kids, kids still like. Except peanut butter, which is a big allergy food.

—Joyce Wadler

situations and how to emerge from them graciously, cordially and with your dignity intact.

Q What to do when you remember him but he doesn't remember you.

How to deal with the cold, punishing smack of not being remembered at a party? There's liquor, of course. Or you can always be Zen about it and reintroduce yourself for the third or fourth time. Manner mavens suggest that a quick self-effacing remark like "Oh that's O.K., I forget people all the time" will ease any awkwardness. That's nice advice for the self-effacing, but not for socially obsessed high schoolers, who are a lot more like all of us than we would like to think.

Is it silly to care about any of this? If it's any comfort, some big shots feel just as bad as the rest of us for forgetting faces. Joan Rivers, the comedian, for example, blanks all the time. "I have two ways to deal," she says. "Either I touch the person's chest and look like I'm concentrating and say, 'Yes, I do remember you, but from where?' If that doesn't work, I tell them they look 20 years younger, and ask if they've had work done."

Ultimately, not caring who knows you or whom you should know may be the only way to have fun at a party. Or think about it this way: people who don't need people are the luckiest people in the world.

Q If someone invites you over, do you have to invite them back?

In this quid pro quo culture, people hit one another up for their own charitable causes all the time, just as they play a tennis-like game of returning business favors. You scratch my back, I'll scratch yours. It's part of both the social and the socialite's contract.

Etiquette suggests that you should reciprocate, of course, but in any way that works for you. If you don't want to make a dinner party for hosts who have entertained you lavishly, taking them out is acceptable, just as it is for houseguests who want to give their hosts a break from cooking.

But what if you can't keep yourself from attending the show-stopping parties of the same great hosts year after year, without being able to imagine returning their hospitality? Isn't that completely unacceptable?

Well, maybe reciprocity doesn't have to be the point. There will always be those who want to be more generous than others, whether as philanthropists or hosts. That's all any good host or guest needs to know, along with the simple idea that doing something nice for others doesn't necessarily mean those who have done something nice for you. And without great guests, how could great hosts be great hosts?

● Should you argue about politics, or shut up?

"Fighting about politics is like doing drugs," says author Jay McInerney. "You know you shouldn't get involved, but once you start, you lose all control."

Perhaps that's why etiquette and protocol arbiters have always recommended staying clear of the topic with tactics like changing the subject. Garrison Keillor, radio host and author, argues, however, that "the hottest place in hell is reserved for those who remain neutral in times of crisis."

So how do we proceed? "Calm, cool, collected," suggests Pat Buckley, the socialite married to William F. Buckley, adding that she often finds her "blood boiling" over what she hears at dinner parties. "I'll listen for a while, then I'll speak up," she says. "But I'll always do it in a civilized way. You don't want to frighten the horses."

Don Gabor, author of *Words That Win: What to Say to Get What You Want,* says, "My advice is, don't even pick up the gauntlet when it's thrown down. Most political arguments don't do any good at all." The only time to get into one, Gabor says, is if you are with someone who hasn't made up his mind. Even then, proceed with caution, and follow some rules: Don't be disagreeable when you disagree. Don't interrupt or argue one point to death. Don't expect someone to agree with you just because you think you're

Flummoxed by Finger Bowls?

A veteran of New York dinner parties dips into uncharted waters

An embossed sterling silver bowl sitting on a plate, flanked with a knife and spoon. I, deluded soul, had assumed it was about to be filled with dessert. After all, a waiter hovered behind me with a silver tray, and after making a few guttural noises, after poking the bowl once or twice, which he seemed to hope would nudge my memory, give me an "Aha!" moment to do what, exactly? Well, that's when the scolding began. "Move it. Just move it," he said. Because I, veteran of hundreds of New York dinner parties (it only feels like thousands) did not recognize a finger bowl.

Well, once I figured out my transgression, I glanced around the table to see what the other guests had done. Yes, there the bowls were, tucked off to the side, right as rain. My mistake, of course, was not looking straight to the hostess for guidance. Then again, the host must have moved his, and it could only have been my utter absorption in his conversation that derailed me.

That and the lack of a doily. Because on the rare occasion when I have encountered a finger bowl, I vaguely remember its being set upon a doily. When your dainty ablutions are done, you're supposed to pick up the doily and the bowl and move them together off the dessert plate. And if you don't believe me, so it is written in Letitia Baldrige's *New Manners for New Times: A Complete Guide to Etiquette.* But these bowls had no doilies. Or lemon peels or flowers or any of the other floating detritus that passes for finger bowl accessories.

After that dinner, I spoke with the best hostess I know in New York. She assured me that she had never seen silver finger bowls, only glass—and since she has also entertained extensively in Europe, I felt somewhat vindicated.

—Alex Witchel

right. And don't assume that you and the other person disagree on all issues.

In such a loudly opinionated, powder-keg culture, maybe the best way to promote peace is by not saying what's on your mind at all. Or as Calvin Coolidge once said: "Nobody ever listened himself out of a job."

—Bob Morris

Putting the "R" Back in R.S.V.P.

When some response—even an e-mail—is expected

A new indifference to the old-fashioned protocol of invitations is turning entertaining into a guessing game, say hostesses, party planners and etiquette authorities. Nobody seems to bother to R.S.V.P. anymore. Even requests to attend seemingly monumental events like weddings, 40th-birthday parties and Christmas dinners routinely go unanswered. Whether it is a result of a more casual attitude toward socializing or an overabundance of nonevents that generate a kind of lavish junk mail of their own, hosts—and not guests—are now the ones feeling left out in the cold.

Extiquette experts fear the practice is giving so many people heartburn, they aren't entertaining anymore. Proper manners, experts say, call for a response to an invitation within 48 hours.

Joy Lewis, the president of Mrs. John L. Strong, a society stationer, explains that *répondez s'il vous plaît* became a chic addition to invitations in the late 1800's. At one time, a wedding invitation never asked for a response. "Getting an important invitation was the highest honor that could be bestowed, and it was expected that you would respond in the same degree of formality," she says. That meant sitting down and writing a letter.

ⓘ INSIDE INFO

The Lost Art of Letter-Writing

○ While most people send and receive only two to five thank-you notes a year, according to research by the American Greetings Corporation, half of those questioned would like to receive more.

○ Part of the problem is that note writers are unsure about how to begin. Etiquette experts who offer letter-writing classes for children note that the basics—like the salutation and its place on the page—are news to most. Women in focus groups conducted by Hallmark said they had difficulty figuring out what to say.

○ The Postal Service acknowledges that the personal letter appears to be going the way of the telegram. In a 2004 study, it found that personal mail has dropped off by about a third in the past 25 years, to about 1.1 pieces a week per household. The Postal Service noted the "continuing shift in household preference toward electronic alternatives to mail."

○ Even soldiers in the field don't appear to be getting the letters they used to. "It is far different now than during the Persian Gulf war in 1991," says a spokeswoman for Hallmark, citing a trend toward letter writing then because "that was the only way to contact military people." Today, soldiers in Iraq, for example, routinely check their e-mail queues.

—Elizabeth Olson

Lewis is quick to note, though, that it is important to keep up with the times and, though some may disagree, she sees nothing improper with an e-mail reply to an engraved request for the honor of your company at a black-tie wedding reception. "I think the point is to respond, whether it happens on a nice handwritten note or with a quick e-mail," she says.

THE ART OF THE THANK-YOU NOTE

Expressing appreciation need not be a chore The only imperative when it comes to thank-yous is to send them.

Drew Souza, a New York City stationer, suggests you write at least three sentences, avoid clichés—an anecdote specific to the evening or gift is thoughtful—and do it preferably by hand.

For Christmas presents in particular, he advises waiting until January to send holiday-related thanks: "If it arrives on Dec. 22, no one will have time to open it."

—Kimberly Stevens and Mark Ellwood

Minding Multicultural Manners

Never give yellow flowers to a friend from Iran, and other gaffes to avoid

More than ever before, a new neighbor, classmate or business associate is apt to be a recent immigrant whose social traditions are unfamiliar to most Americans. Today's changing demographics call for new rules that will preclude cross-cultural misunderstandings. As a folklorist, Norine Dresser studies the customs, rituals and beliefs of different cultures. Author of *Multicultural Manners: Essential Rules of Etiquette for the 21st Century,* Dresser offers her dos and don'ts for avoiding cultural faux pas.

Q **What are some of the biggest multicultural gaffes Americans make?**

Our major problems are that we get too friendly and too informal, too fast. Our use of first names when we first meet someone, for example, is very offensive to most people in other parts of the world. It is interpreted as disrespectful. Americans also have a habit of getting right down to business. If you're dealing with Asian and Latin American cultures, you don't march in with your product and expect an order after a sales spiel. First, you establish rapport by introducing yourself and your company, then you leave a token, such as a company pen or calendar. Finally, you follow up with a phone call later in the week.

Q **Can you give us some examples of communications blunders?**

Americans should avoid asking questions that require direct yes or no responses. For example, we often say when asking for something, "Please feel free to say no, but would you . . ." In many cultures, responding no directly to a request is unheard of, so the newcomer becomes confused. Another point is that newcomers might be too embarrassed to say they don't understand because of language differences. Rather than ask, "Do you understand what I mean?" Say, "Please tell me what you don't understand."

Q **Would a recent immigrant really be offended by American blunders, knowing that customs are different here?**

Sure, the newcomers are being acculturated, but your efforts to pay attention to what's important to them show that you respect them. For example, you should never send yellow flowers to an Iranian. In that culture yellow flowers mean "I hate you and wish you were dead." One Iranian woman I know was given yellow flowers by a guest. She politely excused herself, threw the flowers on the floor, and cried.

Yellow also has bad connotations for many Peruvians and Mexicans. On the other hand, yellow flowers say "I miss you" in the Armenian culture.

Q **Are there other colors to avoid?**

Most Asian cultures respond negatively to white, which has death connotations. It would be safer not to give white flowers as a gift to an Asian friend. Guests to an Indian wedding should avoid wearing white. It is thought to bring bad luck, even death, to the bride and groom. Many Chinese people believe wedding guests shouldn't wear black or white, which both represent death in their culture.

❓ What are some other customs that Americans should be aware of?

Removing shoes before you enter the home of a Japanese person is well known. Less known is the fact that when you remove your shoes in a Japanese house, you should place the shoes so that the toes face the door. Removing shoes is also a tradition among some Koreans, Filipinos, Thais, Iranians and Indian Buddhists.

Sometimes what you wear can be misunderstood. For example, jewelry made of bright cobalt blue ceramic beads from the Middle East were fashionable at one time in the U. S. But an Iranian would laugh at the thought of women wearing such jewelry—in Iran, peddlers decorate their donkeys with the necklaces, known as donkey beads.

❓ Are there foods that should not be served to guests from certain cultures?

Most people know that eating pork is taboo for religious Jews and Muslims, but fewer people are aware that orthodox Jews and Muslims also don't eat shellfish, or any fish without fins. Hindus don't eat beef and Seventh Day Adventists don't eat meat. Muslims, Hindus and Mormons, of course, do not drink alcoholic beverages.

❓ What's the best way to approach an unfamiliar multicultural situation?

It helps to be very observant. When in doubt, ask. It's best to ask someone of your own sex, so that it's less awkward for both of you in situ-

ations where there are significant male-female differences. Age matters too; young people may feel reluctant to tell older people what to do. It all gets back to the main point: making an effort to understand, and showing others that you're trying to learn from them.

Weddings Ring a New Bell
For one thing, the bride's family doesn't always foot the bill

Weddings are hard work. Just ask Diane Forden, editor in chief of *Bridal Guide* magazine. "Planning a wedding is probably the best training for marriage," she says. "You have to talk things out, to spot each other's hot buttons, to compromise." For starters, all those rules you learned growing up are now as obsolete as dowries. Here are some examples:

OLD RULE: White gowns are a symbol of bridal purity.

MODERN PRACTICE: Anything goes, including red on a first-time bride or white on a serial spouse. "Queen Victoria got married in an ivory gown; that's the only reason the style took off," Forden says. "Before then, all brides got married in their Sunday best."

OLD RULE: The bride's parents pay for the wedding, while the groom's parents pay for the flowers and the music.

MODERN PRACTICE: Nearly half of couples pay for their whole wedding, and the vast majority pick up a large share of the cost. "Money is control, and couples want to call the shots on what kind of wedding they'll have," Forden says.

OLD RULE—Couples register for china, silver and other household items.

MODERN PRACTICE: Many couples already have well-stocked linen closets and silverware drawers—and little need to discard his and hers in favor of ours. Increasingly, they are registering at sporting goods stores, electronics shops and even travel Web sites. "It's perfectly O.K. to want luggage for the honeymoon, or a monetary contribution to the honeymoon itself," she says. But it is also perfectly fine for a guest to give nothing at all. "The bridal shower is the only time you really have to give a gift," she says. Play it safe and give at least enough to cover the cost of your meal—in many metro areas that's probably upward of $100.

MORE WEDDING PLANNING TIPS

Don't think that ancillary celebrations are just for first-timers. Second-time brides deserve a shower, and couples who have lived together for years deserve an engagement party, but invita-

> ❝
> **By the time you swear you're his, shivering and sighing, and he vows his passion is infinite, undying— Lady, make a note of this: One of you is lying.**
>
> Dorothy Parker
>
> ● ● ●

tions should probably specify that while presence is requested, presents are not. "Parties acknowledge that a wedding is special, and that every wedding is as special as the first," she says.

Don't be constrained by gender when assembling your wedding party. There is no reason that brides must be attended by women, grooms by men. "It's about who you want to honor, who you feel close to," Forden says. You can also have more than one maid or man of honor, so you don't have to choose between sister and best friend, or mother and stepmother, or brother and father.

Gay weddings are no different from straight weddings. A gay couple can have a joint shower, register for gifts and throw a wedding, intimate or huge. It's easy to make invitations gender-neutral and to sidestep any parental discomfort. "There's

Looking for Mr. Right
And often finding Mr. Wrong

Anyone looking for a mate these days knows that there are scores of online dating services—from Match.com to eHarmony.com to JDate, each with its own distinct personality. One newly single, 40-something user of the services characterizes JDate as "the Jewish equivalent of safe sex, with a platinum card." Nerve.com is "much edgier," and eHarmony, she says, has "a geezer/Republican feel to its marketing," along with a rule disqualifying separated people from using the site. You can go to any search engine, like Google, and find a long list of online dating services and judge for yourself.

Whatever the opportunities, however, Internet dating is not without its issues. Unearthing a potential mate's cheating, thieving, maybe even psychotic ways during the early stages of courtship has always been tricky business. But it is particularly difficult today, when millions are searching for dates online and finding it far easier to lie to a computer than to someone's face.

But the Internet is offering up an antidote, as well. Web sites like DontDateHimGirl.com, ManHaters.com and TrueDater.com are dedicated to outing bad apples or just identifying people who may not be totally rotten, but whose dating profiles are rife with fiction.

—Lizette Alvarez

LAW & MORES

Raising a Glass

Ah, the eloquence of a good toast. Mark Brown, once voted best speaker in the world by Toastmasters International, offers a few tips on how to give terrific toasts anytime

✔ First of all, a toast and a roast are not to be confused, though they often are. A roast pokes fun. A toast is sweetness and light and never, ever rude.

✔ A good toast should leave a "good feeling," he says. "It leaves a positive taste in the mouth. It should always contain good wishes, warm feelings and convey love and happiness."

✔ Brevity is good. "There is an old adage that says you stand up, you speak up, and then you shut up," says Brown.

✔ Toastmasters International (949-858-8255 or www.toastmasters.org) offers a few other pointers. Pick a subject that is personal and appropriate. Use humor only if the occasion warrants. Dress your best—if you look good, you'll feel more confident. And practice, practice, practice, using family and friends as sounding boards.

nothing wrong with a wedding invitation that says 'John Smith and Joe Brown invite you to celebrate their wedding with them,'" says Forden.

A pregnant bride can choose a long wedding gown or a maternity dress in white or another light color, depending on how comfortable she is with her condition. Traditionally, a bridal veil is a symbol of virginity, so she may want to opt against it. When announcements are sent by the bride's parents, it shows that they support the couple's decision to marry.

If your betrothed really wants a big wedding, give in. You can have hundreds of intimate dinners and parties during a marriage, so why deprive someone of a celebration he or she may have been dreaming about since childhood?

Stand your ground with parents—to a point. "If you want roses, don't get peonies because mom likes them better," Forden says. "But compromise on hot-button issues." For an interfaith marriage, consider having clergy members of both faiths present. Or if parents want a much bigger party than you do, suggest that they have a second reception after your honeymoon.

Set up a wedding Web site. It's a good place to list details about rehearsal dinners, day-after brunches, hotel rates and your gift registries.

Find ways to save money without looking chintzy. Buy your own flower vases, and supplement costly flowers with greenery and candles. Ask the guitarist from the wedding band to play at the cocktail reception; it will cost less than hiring a separate pianist. A designer dress in white for a bridesmaid is a lot cheaper than a wedding dress, and often just as elegant. A small ornate wedding cake is symbol enough: while you are cutting that first slice, the staff can be unobtrusively slicing up a cheaper, unadorned version to feed the guests.

Use the occasion to reach out to others. Donate centerpieces to a nursing home or hospital; your guests don't really need them. Instead of tossing the bouquet, give it to the grandmother whose marriage has lasted the longest. Some brides donate their dresses to a consignment store. "The 'grateful' bride and groom has turned into a nice humanitarian trend," Forden says.

Attend your own wedding, for goodness' sake. "So many brides say the wedding went by

801

801**Manners & Miscellany**   **WEDDINGS** ●

in a blur," she says. "Visit the tables, dance with your siblings, make the guests feel wanted, eat the food you've spent so much on. In the end, the best weddings are the ones where the bride and groom really enjoy themselves."

—Claudia H. Deutsch

All the Nuptials Fit to Print

What it takes to get your wedding announced in the New York Times

Overachieving couples everywhere drool at the prospect of having their wedding announced in the Sunday Styles section of the *New York Times*. The free news items have long chronicled the nuptials of Carnegies, Rockefellers, Vanderbilts and their offspring. In recent years, the ranks have become more egalitarian. But what are the chances for the average Joe and Jane to have their announcement chosen to

be printed for free? Slim, but not impossible. Part of the problem: too many applicants vying for too little space, so editors pick the most newsworthy.

To give it a shot, couples should follow the paper's rules to a tee. Send in all the following details at least six weeks before the event: your full names, addresses, and date, time and location of the event, and the officiant's name. Mention your alma maters, current occupations, noteworthy awards, special achievements and charitable activities. Do the same for both sets of parents. (Dropping the names of a few illustrious ancestors can't hurt.) Everyone loves "how we met" stories, so go ahead and include your own.

Send in a horizontal photo, (5x7 or 8x10 inches," formal or informal, color or black and white), of the two of you. Be sure your eyebrows are on exactly the same level and your heads are fairly close together. Print contact information and the photographer credit on the back of the photo.

Send the application by mail or courier to (note: in 2007 the *Times* is moving to a new address): The New York Times
Society News, 5th floor
229 West 43rd St., NY, NY. 10036
By fax: 212-556-7689
Or by e-mail: society@nytimes.com

Then wring your hands and hold your breath.

Actually, that last step may not be necessary. There is now an almost foolproof way to announce your wedding in the paper: buy an ad. Your paid wedding announcement will run in the Sunday Styles section near the free wedding news items. To place your ad in this section, call the New York Times at 212-556-3900.

The cost: a minimum of about $200.

LAW & MORES

Ways to Remember a Big Day

Easy, yet meaningful gifts for every month of the year

The origins of ancient birthstone designations are lost to history, but we know how modern birthstones were designated: not by a poet in love or a qualified stone interpreter, but by a jeweler's association. One consideration the jewelers may have had was the limited availability of some gems. Not surprisingly, assigning flowers to birth months evolved in the same way: by the availability of certain blooms.

MONTH	STONE COLOR	SOURCE	FLOWER
January	GARNET *Dark red*	Brazil, India Sri Lanka	Carnation snowdrop
February	AMETHYST *Purple*	Brazil Uruguay	Violet iris
March	AQUAMARINE *Pale blue*	Brazil, Nigeria Zambia	Jonquil daffodil
April	DIAMOND *White*	South Africa, Congo	Sweet Pea daisy
May	EMERALD *Green*	Colombia, Brazil, Pakistan	Lily of the valley
June	PEARL *Cream*	Japan, China Australia	Rose
July	RUBY *Red*	Myanmar* Tanzania, Kenya	Larkspur
August	PERIDOT *Pale green*	Myanmar Pakistan, U.S.	Gladiola
September	SAPPHIRE *Pale to dark blue*	Austrialia, Madagascar SE Asia, U.S.	Aster
October	OPAL *Variegated*	Australia, Mexico, U.S.	Calendula
November	CITRINE *Yellow*	Brazil, Nigeria	Mum
December	BLUE TOPAZ *Sky blue*	Brazil, Sri Lanka Nigeria	Narcissus

AFTER THE FIRST DIAMOND
Everyone knows it's silver for a 25th anniversary. But for a 9th? Try leather

YEAR	TRADITIONAL GIFT	MODERN GIFT
1	Paper	Clock
2	Cotton	China
3	Leather	Crystal or glass
4	Fruit or flowers	Appliances
5	Wood	Silverware
6	Candy or ironware	Wood
7	Copper or wool	Pens, desk sets
8	Pottery or bronze	Linens or laces
9	Pottery or willow	Leather
10	Aluminum or tin	Diamond jewelry
11	Steel	Fashion jewelry
12	Silk or linen	Pearls or gems
13	Lace	Textiles
14	Ivory	Gold jewelry
15	Crystal	Watches
16	Silver hollowware	
17	Furniture	
18	Porcelain	
19	Bronze	
20	China	Platinum
25**	Silver	Silver
30	Pearl	Diamond
35	Coral	Jade
40	Ruby	Ruby
45	Sapphire	Sapphire
50**	Gold	Gold
55	Emerald	Emerald
60**	Diamond	Diamond
75**	Diamond	Diamond

* Formerly called Burma

* * Indicates jubilee anniversary

SOURCES: Jewelers of America; Leading Jewelers Guild, Inc.

Stepping Out, Gingerly

Practice can help relieve the pressure of hitting the dance floor

Bridal couples preparing for the traditional first dance, and anyone who wants to avoid the all-too-familiar "clutch and sway," can now tap online dance masters and learn to dance like stars.

Learntodance.com, for one, walks you through steps for learning the tango, swing, salsa, even ballet. The site, and others like DanceVision.com and Dancetv.com, will also sell you instructional videos for just about any dance imaginable. At Learntodance.com you'll find 30 different ballroom-dance videos alone. And, if virtual dance lessons don't appeal, you can also locate a bricks-and-mortar dance studio on the site. Just plug in your zip code and nearby options appear.

Whatever method you choose, learning the rudimentaries isn't difficult. Several dances have a basic box step as their foundation. Master this dance figure and you're on your way to learning the waltz, fox trot and rumba, at least in their American guises.

The box step is so called because the steps form a box or square with your feet resting on the corners as you move. Here's how it's done:

The leader starts by moving his left foot forward, then sliding the right foot up to meet the left. The right foot then moves to the right and the left foot meets it. That's the first half of the box. Now, the right foot steps back and the left foot slides to meet it. The left foot then moves to the left and the right foot slides over to meet it. That completes the box. The steps are repeated, with the pace and rhythm changing—and other flourishes added—depending on the specific dance.

FINDING YOUR FRED OR GINGER

Locating a spry and compatible dance partner is no easy feat, but online sites like DancePartner.com and 1greatdancesite.com can help. Prospective partners post their profiles and hope a suitable match gets in touch.

Tracing Your Family Tree

Oh, the things you can learn about your ancestors if you just look

Haunted by your past? Finding answers about your ancestors can be a long and arduous process, but there is an armada of resources ready to help. Here's how to conduct the search:

1. Interview family members. Scour through memorabilia, keeping detailed notes. Documents to look for: birth, death and marriage certificates; baptism and christening records; family bibles, diaries, letters, as well as school records, scrapbooks, military discharge papers, naturalization records and passports.

2. With clues in hand, consult libraries and genealogical societies. The huge collection of the Church of Jesus Christ of Latter-day Saints (or the Mormon church) in Salt Lake City, Utah, is open to all. You can also visit them online at Familysearch.org, a free site. To find a society near you, try the *Directory of Historical Societies and Agencies in the United States and Canada.* At Genealogy.com you can get subscription access to genealogical records.

FOX TROT BOX STEP: MAN'S PART / WOMAN'S PART

LAW & MORES

Finding Grandma, the DNA Way

Bypass the hassle of a genealogical search

DNA testing has added a new twist to genealogy: using genetic data to uncover details about your heritage.

More than a dozen companies, like Family Tree DNA in Houston, Relative Genetics in Salt Lake City and African Ancestry in Washington, D.C. sell home DNA tests; priced from $100 to $900. Here's how the tests typically work: Order the test online and you get a kit with toothbrush-like scrapers, collection tubes and instructions on how to take a swab from inside the cheek. The samples are mailed to a lab, where scientists analyze DNA markers, or genetic traits. You get test results in two to eight weeks, depending on the type of test and the company.

The broad array of tests and the accompanying jargon may be confusing. Tutorials on company Web sites, online discussion forums and newsletters dedicated to "genetic genealogy" can help. Or hire a genealogy consultant, for about $50 an hour, to muddle through the process for you.

—Jennifer Alsever

Check U.S. Census records at the National Archives in Washington, D.C. (866-272-6272 or www.archives.gov), which has records from 1790 to 1930, and at some libraries. The online site Ancestry.com has two billion records from thousands of sources, including the Census.

3. Search passenger arrival records for immigrant ancestors. The National Archives and some regional libraries have passenger and arrival records dating back to 1817. To find when your ancestor arrived, or the ship's name, try P. William Filby and Mary K. Meyer's *Passenger and Immigration Lists Index.* Ellisisland.org lets you search the records of anyone who entered the country through Ellis Island.

4. To organize your search, genealogical database programs can help. One popular software program is Family Tree Maker ($20 to $100). One free program, Gramps (gramps.sourceforge.net), lets you enter data, store results, and produce charts and Web pages. For reviews of genealogy software packages, go to genealogy-software-review.com.

5. To skip the labor-intensive process, hire a genealogical sleuth. For a list of certified genealogists in your area, go to the Web site of the Board for Certification of Genealogists at www.bcgcertification.org.

Puzzled by Crosswords?

A little help–but not much–from the New York Times *puzzlemaster himself*

A perfect puzzle may put up lots of resistance. It may, in fact, seem impossible at first. Ideally, though, in the end the solver should triumph and think, Oh, how clever I am!

The perfect level of difficulty, of course, differs from person to person. This is why, as editor, I vary the weekday *Times* crossword difficulty from easy-medium on Monday, up to what the actor and puzzle aficionado Paul Sorvino calls "the bitch mother of all crosswords" on Saturday. (He said this as a compliment.) the Sunday *Times* puzzle, while larger than its weekday counterpart, averages only Thursday-plus in difficulty.

Step 1 in solving any crossword is to begin with the answers you're surest of. Fill-in-the-blank clues are easy to spot and often the easiest to solve. Focus on the three-, four- and five-letter words, because the English language has relatively few of these, and they tend to repeat a lot. This is especially so for vowel-heavy words like alee, eel, oreo, etc. Watch for celebrity names (Uma, Erte, Agee) and geographical names (Ada, Ames, Elon).

Don't be afraid to guess. At the same time, don't be afraid to erase an answer that isn't working out. Don't assume that because you have a few crossing letters that your answer is necessarily correct. And if nothing seems to cross the answer you have filled in, be very wary.

Let your mind wander. The clue "Present time" might suggest nowadays, but in a different sense it might lead to the answer yuletide. Similarly, "Life sentences" could be obit, "Inside shot" is x-ray and my all-time favorite clue, "It turns into a different story" (15 letters), results in the phrase "spiral staircase." Be on your toes for multiword answers. One answer that always seems to trip solvers up is r-a-n-d-r, which was clued as "Leave time?"

A question mark at the end of a clue can mean "This clue is tricky! Be careful!" It can also indicate that the answer only loosely fits the clue. When question marks appear at the ends of the clues for all the long answers, usually the marks are signals for related puns.

No matter how tricky or misleading the clues, they always follow a fairly strict set of rules. Most important, a clue and its answer are always expressed in the same part of speech and must be interchangeable in a sentence, with the same meaning each way.

If a crossword answer is not a standard English word, the clue will signal this fact. Thus, a slangy answer will have a slangy clue. The clue for an abbreviated answer will contain the tag "Abbr." or else a word that is not usually abbreviated ("Entrepreneur's deg." = M.B.A.).

If you get stuck on a puzzle, a time-honored technique is to put it aside and return later. A fresh look at a tough puzzle almost always brings new answers.

—Will Shortz

Grammar in a Jiffy
Common mistakes that can be easily corrected

For many people, knowing that the grammar police may be lurking in their midst is an unsettling situation. If you were absent the day your teacher covered sticky grammar rules in class, here are a few pointers on gaffes to avoid.

- **Nouns following prepositions (even when they are compound) are always objects.**

She gave the message *to me*.　　　(not *to I*)

Tim lied *to Jane and me*.　(not *to Jane and I*)

I gave it *to Sue and them*. (not *to Sue and they*)

- **Any word that is a contraction is actually a shortening of two words, and does NOT imply possession.**

EXAMPLES:

CONTRACTION	POSSESSIVE ADJECTIVE
IT IS: *It's* a sunny day.	France has *its* wines.
THEY ARE: *They're* here.	*Their* dog barks.
YOU ARE: *You're* right.	I took *your* pen.
WHO IS: *Who's* that?	*Whose* hat is this?

- **Do not confuse the use of simple past verbs with past participles.**

CORRECT		INCORRECT
She *sang* the song.	NOT	She *sung* the song.
She *has sung* the song.		
Tom *spoke* to us.	NOT	Tom *has spoke* to us.
Tom *has spoken* to us.		

- **The subject of a dependent clause stays a subject, even after a preposition.**

That's *for whoever* needs it.　NOT　That's *for whomever* needs it.

- **Use the subjunctive tense for statements contrary to fact.**

If she *were* a rocket scientist...　NOT　If she *was* a rocket scientist...

- **Don't use adjectives to modify a verb.**

She did *really* well.　NOT　She did *real* well.

He sang *beautifully*.　NOT　He sang *beautiful*.

Your Personal Reference Desk

Web sites where you'll find answers to practically everything

Queries that used to send you tromping off to the nearest library can now, of course, be answered online. Here are some of the best sites for your reference needs:

GENERAL REFERENCE

Research It (www.itools.com/research-it): An all-in-one reference desk: dictionary, quotes, translators and more.

LibrarySpot.com: An extensive guide to online reference works.

YourDictionary.com and **Onelook** (www.onelooki.com): Access to hundreds of dictionaries, specialized and general.

Encyclopedia Britannica (www.britannica.com): The one and only (now with a fee for full articles).

Refdesk.com: Leads you to a world of reference materials.

Answers.com: Gives answers on an array of topics.

Wikipedia.org: The Web's popular (but not uniformly accurate) user-maintained encyclopedia.

Roget's Internet Thesaurus (www.thesaurus): Help finding a better word.

Information Please Almanac (www.infoplease.com): Almanac, dictionary and the full Columbia Encyclopedia.

Biography.com: Offers brief, cross-referenced biographies of more than 25,000 notables.

Travlang (dictionairies.travelang.com): Language-to-language translation dictionaries.

Babel Fish (world/altavista.com) and FreeTranslation.com: Basic (and sometimes amusing) translations of Web pages or text. (The latter offers human translation at a price.)

The Elements of Style (www.bartleby.com/141/index.html): The 1918 version of the classic handbook for conscientious writers.

C.I.A. World Factbook (odci.gov/cia/publications/factbook/index.html): Info on every country in the world.

Library of Congress (www.loc.gov): Including Marvel and Locis.

The New York Public Library (www.nypl.org)

The World Wide Web Virtual Library (vlib.org/Overview.html)

Ingenta.com: Free citations from 26,000 publications; charges for full articles (formerly Carl Uncover).

The Merck Manual (www.merck.com/pubs): Guide to diseases.

RxList: The Internet Drug Index (www.rxlist.com): Extensive information on prescription and over-the-counter drugs.

Law Guru (www.lawguru.com): Access to hundreds of legal search engines and the Internet Law Library.

Lawoffice.com. From West's Legal Directory and Martindale-Hubbell's Lawyer Locator (wwwo.martindale.com/locator/home.html).

The Bible Gateway (bible.gospelcom.net): Replaces the Bible Browser, which is defunct.

I.R.S. (www.irs.gov): For information and publications. For more tax sites, try taxsites.com.

National Geographic's Map Machine (plasma.nationalgeographic.com/mapmachine)

Mapquest.com, Yahoo! Maps (maps.yahoo.com) and **MSN Maps** (www.mapblast.com): Give street-level maps and directions for U.S. addresses.

Social Security death index (ssdi.genealogy.rootsweb.com)

Currency converter (www.oando.com/converter/classic): From Olsen & Associates converts from any currency to another.

ConvertIt.com: Converts measurements, currencies, timezones and more.

Cost-of-living calculator (www.newengin.com/NewsEngin.nsf/JumpOffPoints/Free+Tools): Also includes other useful tools.

TELEPHONE AND E-MAIL DIRECTORIES

Anywho.com: From AT&T, has fast, clear directory service, and a reverse directory.

Switchboard.com and InfoSpace.com: Offer nationwide telephone, address and reverse directory.

Superpages.com: National business yellow pages and residential listings from Verizon.

Zip Code and Zip+4 Finder (www.semaphore.com/cgi/form.html): Simple and efficient, but sometimes busy. Also try the U.S.Postal Service (usps.gov/zip4).

—Richard J. Meislin

Signs & Symbols

Negotiating Highways & Byways

What you need to know to get from here to there

Whether you're trying to decipher a national, state or local map, the visual vocabulary is fairly standard. Although there are minor stylistic differences among map makers—for example, the use of different colors to differentiate highways and toll roads—the basics generally don't vary. A star signifies a capital, solid lines signify main roads and thinner lines suggest a more scenic route.

There are other similarities nationwide. You can identify an interstate highway, four- to eight-lane roads that link the country, by the sign that has a blue and red shield with the highway number inside. Smaller, older routes known as U.S. Routes (formerly called federal highways because funding used to come from Congress), are two or four lanes wide. In many states, they are often lined with motels, strip malls, amusement parks and other vestiges of Americana. State routes are smaller, slower paced roads, identifiable by a number within a plain white rectangle or circle. These roads less traveled often offer the greatest scenic rewards.

If you're traveling on the autostrada or the autobahn, however, you'll need to learn the language of the international road signs below.

MAP SYMBOLS

BOUNDARIES AND HIGHWAYS

International	State	County	Town	Village

Capital	Urban area	City	Town	Interstate highway	U.S. highway	State highway

INTERNATIONAL ROAD SIGNS

Caution, danger	Curve ahead	Intersection	Pedestrian crossing	Road narrows	Road work	Slippery road	Tunnel ahead

No entry	No left turn	No U-turn	No passing	Speed limit	Stop	Yield	Restrictions end

LAW & MORES

If You Are Lost in the Woods

How to signal your distress

Whether you're lost in the woods or on a tropical island, these ground-to-air communications are a stranded survivor's bible. You can use materials like tree branches, drift wood, large stones or strips of parachute, for example, to cobble together the symbols. Similarly, sticks and stones can be used to form tracking codes, if you have lost your way on a hiking trail, for example.

The best known symbol of distress is the SOS, of course. You can transmit an SOS by forming 3 short, 3 long and 3 short signals, and then repeating the pattern. The signal can be constructed with rocks and logs or by reflecting the sun on a mirror. At night, use a flashlight to send the signal.

The most effective means of signaling for help in the woods is a camp fire. During the day, the smoke is visible for long distances, and at night the flames are easily spotted from the air.

The internationally recognized distress signal is to build three fires. You can arrange them in a triangle or in a straight line. Leave about 100 feet (30 meters) between the fires.

SYMBOLS OF DISTRESS

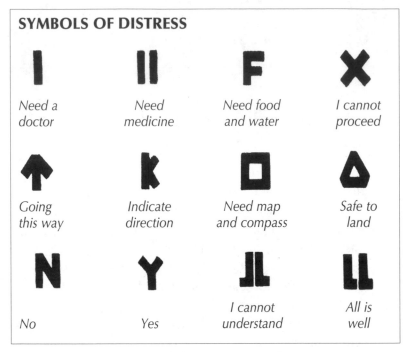

Need a doctor

Need medicine

Need food and water

I cannot proceed

Going this way

Indicate direction

Need map and compass

Safe to land

No

Yes

I cannot understand

All is well

TRACKING CODES

Proceed in this direction

Turn left

Turn right

Do not proceed this way

Find water in this direction

Go this way over an obstacle

There is a message in this direction

The group has divided

Hike is over

Secrets in Code

Any Boy or Girl Scout worth their badges is familiar with the semaphore flag signaling system

This method of sending messages over long distances uses hand-held flags that are moved to form letters of the alphabet. The flags are generally square, with red in the top diagonal and yellow in the lower. The system is fast, but can be used only during the day and at short distances. It is mostly used to communicate at sea and was established in 1901 as the International Code of Signals, evolving out of an earlier British system. Shown here are the flag positions that form each letter of the alphabet.

DOTS AND DASHES

There are many ways to send the Morse code, a standardized worldwide system of dashes and dots that represent letters and numbers. A ship's whistle or foghorn can transmit it, as can a signal flag that's raised for a longer interval for dashes than dots.

The Morse code was originally developed for use in the electric telegraph, invented by Samuel Morse, a Yale-educated, itinerant artist. The first message transmitted by telegraph asked "What hath God wrought?" Morse chose the words, which were sent from the U.S. Capitol to the railroad station in Baltimore in 1844.

Modern technologies have made the code nearly obsolete. It is now used mainly by the tens of thousands of amateur radio operators.

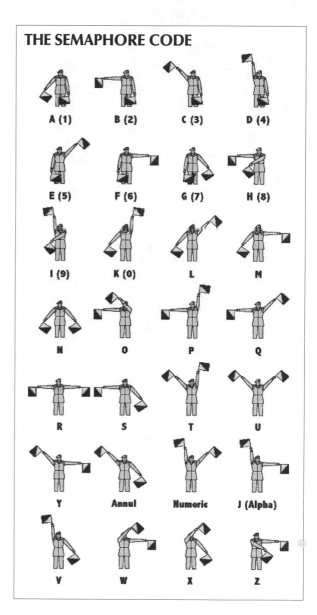

THE SEMAPHORE CODE

A (1) B (2) C (3) D (4)
E (5) F (6) G (7) H (8)
I (9) K (0) L M
N O P Q
R S T U
Y Annul Numeric J (Alpha)
V W X Z

THE MORSE CODE									
		• • — •	F	— •	N	• • • —	V	• • • — —	3
		— — •	G	— — —	O	• — —	W	• • • • —	4
		• • • •	H	• — — •	P	— • • —	X	• • • • •	5
• —	A	• •	I	— — • —	Q	— • — —	Y	— • • • •	6
— • • •	B	• — — —	J	• — •	R	— — • •	Z	— — • • •	7
— • — •	C	— • —	K	• • •	S			— — — • •	8
— • •	D	• — • •	L	—	T	• — — — —	1	— — — — •	9
•	E	— —	M	• • —	U	• • — — —	2	— — — — —	0

For Budding Beethovens
Modern musical symbols

The father of our system of musical notation is thought to be Roman philosopher and statesman Boethius, who lived in the early 6th century. Boethius used letters of the alphabet to signify the notes of the two-octave range that was used at the time. The system of adding the letters A to G in each octave was introduced later, followed by the addition of the five notes of the chromatic scale, or the black keys on the piano.

Guido of Arezzo in the Medieval era is credited with perfecting the staff and developing notations to indicate pitch. A Benedictine monk, he also gets credit for coming up with the familiar "do-re-mi" scale.

Over time, other formulations evolved, such as those to denote pitch, and when to rest or repeat. The terminology for musical dynamics, or how softly or loudly a musical piece is played, is said to derive from Italian Renaissance composer Giovanni Gabrieli. But it wasn't until the late 18th century that use of musical dynamics became popular. Following are essential symbols for learning to read music or play an instrument.

NOTE VALUES OR DURATION

Whole note

Half note

Dotted half note

Quarter note

Eighth note

Sixteenth note

Thirty-second note

Sixty-fourth note

Tie

RESTS

Whole rest

Half rest

Quarter rest

Eighth rest

Sixteenth rest

Thirty-second rest

Sixty-fourth rest

METER

3/4 3/4 time

4/4 4/4 time

2/2 2/2 time

6/8 6/8 time

PITCH-RELATED

Sharp

Double sharp

Flat

Double flat

Natural

Bass, or F, clef

Treble, or G, clef

STAFF SYMBOLS

Staff

Measure

Final bar

Repeat measure

D.C. (da capo) Repeat from the beginning

DYNAMICS

p   Piano (soft)

mp   Mezzo piano (med. soft)

pp   Pianissimo (very soft)

f   Forte (loud)

mf   Mezzo forte (med. loud)

ff   Fortissimo (very loud)

<   Crescendo

>   Decrescendo

PROOFREADER'S MARKS

These symbols are generally used to correct manuscripts and papers. Every symbol used in the text requires a corresponding symbol or notation in the margin of the text.

✄	Delete
◡	Close up (delete space)
⌒	Delete and close up
∧	Caret (add material)
#	Add a space
⊙	Add a period
⌃	Add a comma
:/	Add a colon
;/	Add a semicolon
❡ ❡	Add a quotation mark
❡	Add single quotation mark
?	Add a question mark
⌄	Add apostrophe
⎮·⎮·⎮·⎮	Add ellipses
⎮=⎮	Add hyphen
⊥̄	Add a one-em dash
⊥̄	Add a one-en dash
(/)	Add parenthesis
[/]	Add square bracket
ln #	Add a space between words
stet	Let stand. Restore deleted material. Use dots to indicate material to be restored
ⓢⓟ	Spell out circled text
wf	Wrong font
lc	Lowercase letter
cap	Capitalize letter
s.c.	Set in small caps
rom	Set in roman type
bf	Set in boldface type
ital	Set in italic type
tr	Transpose letters or words
⌐	Move copy right
⌐	Move copy left
⊓	Move up
⊔	Move down
⟧⟦	Center
‖	Align vertically
=	Align horizontally
¶	Begin a new paragraph
no ¶	No paragraph here; run sentences together

SECOND THAT EMOTICON

An emotional shorthand used to express yourself online:

:)	Smile, happy
: (	Frown, sadness
:-I	Can't decide how to feel; no feelings either way
:-O	Yelling or completely shocked
:-()	Can't (or won't) stop talking
:-&	Tongue-tied
:-X	Lips are sealed
I-O	Yawning or snoring
%-(	Confused, unhappy
:'-(	Crying
:'-)	Crying happy tears
:-} or :-]	Sarcastic smile
:-D	Big, delighted grin
{} or []	Hug
*	Kiss
}:[	Frustration
I-I	Boredom, asleep
:-#	Lips are sealed
:-\	Undecided
;-)	Winking

FREQUENTLY USED ABBREVIATIONS

AFKB	Away from keyboard
BRB	Be right back
BTW	By the way
f2f	Face to face, used when you're referring to meeting an online friend in person, or when you'd like to
FAQ	Frequently asked questions
IMHO	In my humble opinion
IMNSHO	In my not so humble opinion
IRL	In real life
ITRW	In the real world
LOL	Laughing out loud
MorF?	Male or female? Used when your online name is gender-neutral
OTF	On the floor (laughing)

How to Sign

*Learn this to communicate
with the deaf*

Thomas Gallaudet, a 19th-century educator of the deaf, gets the credit for developing American Sign Language (A.S.L.), which uses hand movements and symbols to express words and ideas. Gallaudet built on the earlier work of the French, who had formulated a sign system for the deaf in the 1700's. A.S.L. is similar to spoken languages in that it has an extensive vocabulary and specific rules of grammar. And like spoken languages, it is subject to regional dialects and the occasional new colloquialism.

Another method of communicating is through the American manual alphabet, used by many deaf people along with A.S.L. and lip reading.

Here are the finger positions that correspond to numbers and alphabet letters, used to spell out words.

THE BRAILLE SYSTEM

Named after its creator, Louis Braille, this system of characters or cells is used by the blind to read and write.

Each Braille cell has six dot positions (see left, top). Dots are arranged in each cell to make letters and numbers.

To make a capital letter, a dot in position 6 is placed just before a letter.

Braille is not a language in itself but rather another way to read English or any other language.

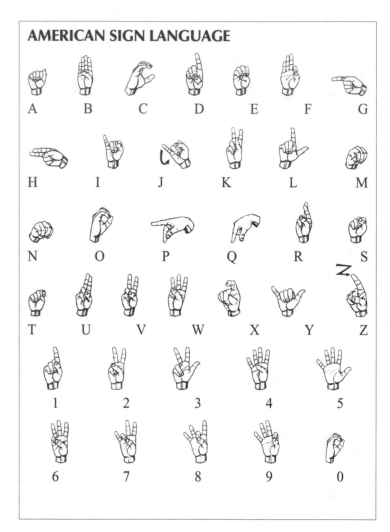

AMERICAN SIGN LANGUAGE

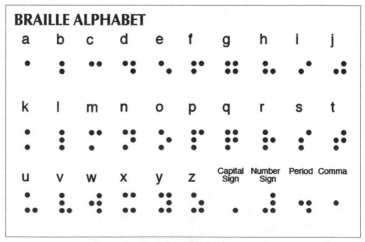

BRAILLE ALPHABET

INDEX

A

AAA (Automobile Association of America), 271, 272
AARP, 235, 271
A.P. (Advance Placement program), 343-44, 345
Aaron, Judith, 348
abortion, 46-47
  facts and figures, 46
  morning after options, 47
abstinence as contraception, 39
Academy of Motion Picture Arts and Sciences, 666
  See also Oscar
Acadia National Park, 545-46
accountant, picking, 242
Achatz, Grant, 143
Achtung, Baby (U2), 688
Across a Crowded Room (Thompson), 684
Action Jackson (Greenberg/Jordan), 334
Action for Healthy Kids, 325
Adams, Henry, 350
Adams, Jody, 143
Adams, John, 753
Adams, John Couch, 728
Adams, John Quincy, 777
Adams, Tony, 353
Adderall, 90
Adelphi Paper Hangings, 420
ADHD (Attention Deficit Hyperactivity Disorder), 90-91
  misdiagnoses, 322
  resources, 91
  treatment, 91
adjustable-rate mortgage, 210
administrative personnel
  changing profile of, 382
  salaries, 379, 380
  women and minorities, 382-83, 330
  See also leadership; office politics; stress management
adoption, 80-83
  resources, 82
adventure, 564-80
  biking, 572
  pristine places, 577-80
  river trips, 573-77

trekking, 564-71
  See also traveling; travel destinations; vacation hot spots
Agee, Jon, 333
Agin, Dr. Marilyn C., 88
aging, 23-26
  anti-aging makeup, 24
  hands and, 33
  hormones and, 37-38
AIDS. *See* HIV/AIDS
Air and Space Museum's Steven F. Udvar-Hazy Center, 536
Air Courier Association, 496
air couriers, 495-96
  courier clubs, 496-97
air-cushioned-sole shoes, 22
air travel insurance, 235
Airfarewatchdog.com, 492
airplane crash
  surviving, 109
airports
  safety of, 499
  tipping at, 250
AirSafe.com, 500
Airwise.com, 500
Aix-en-Provence Festival, 694
Alaska
  trekking in, 566
Alcatraz (San Francisco), 537
Alchemy of Love and Lust, The (Crenshaw), 36
alcohol
  bourbon, 162
  and driving, 267
  gin, 161
  rum, 162
  Scotch, 161
  tequila, 163
  vodka, 161
  See also beer; cocktails; wine
Alcorn, Ray, 224
Aldeburgh Festival, 694
Alexander Hamilton (Chernow), 706
Alexander, Caroline, 705
Alexander, Toni, 207
Alfred, Lord Tennyson, 625
algebra, 770-71
Ali, Monica, 705
Alice's Adventure in Wonderland (Carroll/Sabuda), 334

Alito, Samuel A., Jr., 384
Allen, Robert G., 172
Alpert, Sasha, 678
alprostadil, 42
Alsatian riesling wines, 156
alternative energy vehicles, 204
  biodiesel, 164
  E85, 264
  electric, 264
  hydrogen fuel cells, 264
  natural gas, 264
  plug-in hybrids, 262-65
alternative medicine, 64-68
  alternative therapies, 66
  artificial light and depression, 65
  foot massage, 67
  hypnosis, 64
aluminum siding
  durability of, 412
Amazon.com, 246, 247
Amber Was Brave, Essie Was Smart (Williams), 335
America (Frank), 335
America Online, 392
America's Foundation for Chess, 324
America's most wanted
  Web sites, 783
American Academy of Sleep Medicine, 69
American Alpine Club, 625
American Animal Hospital Association, 484
American Arbitration Association, 199
American Association of Community Colleges, 352
American Ballet Theatre, 691
American Bar Association, 361
American Boarding Kennels Association, 486
American Cancer Society, 57, 60, 61
American College of Cardiology, 54
American College of Obstetricians and Gynecologists, 72, 79
American College of Sports Medicine, 12

American Council for an Energy-Efficient Economy, 433
American Council of Snowmobile Associations, 629
American Driver and Traffic Safety Education Association, 270
American Economic Review, 302
American Football Conference
  Baltimore Ravens, 591
  Buffalo Bills, 591
  Cincinnati Bengals, 591
  Cleveland Browns, 591
  Denver Broncos, 591
  Houston Texans, 591
  Indianapolis Colts, 591
  Jackson Jaguars, 591
  Kansas City Chiefs, 591
  Miami Dolphins, 591
  New England Patriots, 591
  Oakland Raiders, 591
  Pittsburgh Steelers, 591
  San Diego Chargers, 591
  Tennessee Titans, 591
American Go Association, 648
American Gothic (Wood), 700
American Greetings Corporation, 796
American Heart Association, 54, 94, 99
American holidays, 749-56
  April Fools' Day, 751
  Autumnal Equinox, 754
  Christmas Day, 756
  Columbus Day, 754
  Dr. Martin Luther King Jr. Birthday, 749-50
  Earth Day, 751
  Father's Day, 752-53
  Flag Day, 752
  Groundhog Day, 750
  Halloween, 754-55
  Independence Day (July 4), 753
  Kwanzaa, 756
  Labor Day, 753-54
  Memorial Day, 752
  Mother's Day, 752
  New Year's Day, 749
  President's Day, 750-51

St. Patrick's Day, 751
Summer Solstice, 753
Thanksgiving Day, 755
United Nations Day, 754
Valentine's Day, 750
Vernal Equinox, 751
Veterans Day, 755
Winter Solstice, 755-56
Women's Equality Day, 753
American Horticultural Society A to Z Encyclopedia, 472
American Institute of Architects, 411
American Journal of Public Health, 71
American Kennel Club, 476
American League Central
  Chicago White Sox, 583
  Cleveland Indians, 583
  Detroit Tigers, 583
  Kansas City Royals, 583
  Minnesota Twins, 583-84
American League East
  Baltimore Orioles, 582
  Boston Red Sox, 582
  New York Yankees, 582
  Tampa Bay Devil Rays, 582-83
  Toronto Blue Jays, 583
American League West
  Los Angeles Angels of Anaheim, 584
  Oakland Athletics, 584
  Seattle Mariners, 584-85
  Texas Rangers, 585
American Management Association, 392
American Motorcycle Association, 276
American Mountain Guides Association, 625
American Pet Product Manufacturers Association, 476
American Red Cross, 97
American River (CA)
  white-water rafting, 574-75
American Sign Language, 812
American Society of Home Inspectors, 410
American Society of Plastic Surgeons, 32

American Softball Association, 607

AmeriCorps, 782

Ames Research Center (NASA), 736

Ames Truetemper Inc. (garden tools), 464

amniocentesis, 76

An Na, 335

Anaheim Mighty Ducks, 595

Anderson, M. T., 335

Andes
rain forests in, 558-59

Andorra
as travel destination, 578

Andretti, Mario, 265-68

Anegada
as travel destination, 524

Angkor Wat, 520
lodging, 521
transportation, 520

angles, 772
and circles, 767

Aniakchak National Monument, 548

animal attacks
bears, confronting, 110-11
surviving, 111

ankle injuries, 20

Annals of Internal Medicine, 3

anniversary gifts, 802

Anthony Blunt: His Lives (Carter), 704

antiques, 303-7
beds, 304, 305
chairs, 304, 305
chests of drawers, 303-4, 305
collectibles as investment, 306-7
mirrors, 304, 305
tables, 305
See also auctions

Antiques Roadshow, 307

anxiety, 62-64

Anxiety Disorders Association of America, 63

apartment doorman
tipping, 250

apothecaries' fluid measure, 767

apothecaries' weight, 767

Appalachian National Scenic Trail, 552

appearance, 23-35
beauty aids, 27-30
cosmetic enhancements, 31-33
hair loss, 33-35
hands and aging, 33
skin damage, 23-26
tooth whitening, 35

See also children; doctors and medicine; first aid and survival; fitness; sexuality

Apple's iTunes, 682

Applegate, Jane, 404-6

apples, 134-35

appliances
energy use and, 292-94

appraisers, 308

Appraisers Association of America, 308

April Fools' Day, 751

arboretum. **See** botanical gardens

Arcade Fire, 688

Archimedes, 770

Archives of Internal Medication, 69

Archives of Pediatrics & Adolescent Medicine, 325

Arco, 337-38

Argentina
wine industry in, 153

Arizona Cardinals, 591

Arizona Diamondbacks, 586

Armstrong, Lance, 572

Armstrong, Louis, 685

Arnie the Doughnut (Keller), 334

art (collecting), 300-303
dealers, 300-302
information resources, 301
as investment, 302-3

Art of Buying Art, The (Bamberger), 300

Art on the Net, 698

arts and entertainment, 665-708
architecture, 701
books and libraries, 702-8
movies and TV, 666-80
museums, 697-700

arts education, 346-48

ArtsJournal.com, 682

asbestos, 438-39

ascorbic acid (vitamin C), 121

Ash Wednesday, 757-58

Ashmead, Dr., 135

Asia (as travel destination), 519-23
Angkor Wat, 520
Cambodia, 519, 520
guide books, 521
Laos, 519
Shanghai, 521-22
Southeast Asia, 519-21
Taj Mahal, 523
Vietnam, 519-20

Asian Art Museum (San Francisco), 537

Asimov, Eric, 149

asphalt durability
driveway, 412
roof shingles, 412

Assassin's Gate: America in Iraq, The (Packer), 707

Association of American Publishers, 708

Association of Fundraising Professionals, 402

astrological signs
Aquarius, 740
Aries, 739
Cancer, 739
Capricorn, 740
Gemini, 739
Leo, 740
Libra, 740
Pisces, 740
Sagittarius, 740
Scorpio, 740
Taurus, 739
Virgo, 740

astrology, 739-41
Chinese zodiac, 759-60

astronomy, 722-43
stars and planets, 722-31
sun and moon, 731-36
terminology, 736-38
tides, 742-43

Astronomy magazine, 722

Atkins diet, 119-20

Atkinson, Jim, 398

Atlanta Botanical Garden, 473

Atlanta Braves, 585

Atlanta Falcons, 591

Atlanta Hawks, 593

Atlanta Thrashers, 595

atmospheric pressure
and weather, 713, 715

Atonement (McEwan), 704

auctions, 307-11
antiques auctions, 307-9
charity auctions, 309
collection, culling, 308
counterfeits, 311
eBay, 247, 310
government auctions, 310-11
See also antiques; art

audio and video, 292-96

Audiolunchbox, 693

Austerlitz (Sebald), 703

Australian wine, 153-54

Austrian National Tourist Office, 571

Austrian wine, 154-55

Auto Expression, 274

auto insurance, 233
boomerang kids and, 176
filing a claim, 233
saving on, 232

auto maintenance, 272-75
gas-saving strategies, 274-75
gearshifts, sticky spills and, 274
manuals vs. mechanics, 272-74

auto racing, 596-97
economics of, 597
flags, 596
Indianapolis 500, 592
Motor Sports Hall of Fame, 598
terminology, 596-97

Automatic Millionaire, The (Bach), 172

Automobile Association of America, 270

Automobile magazine, 273

autos, 260-79
alternative energy vehicles, 264
buying, 260-65
car leases, 262
car theft, 279
customizing, 275
cycles and RV's, 275-79
driving, 265-72
fuel-efficient, 273
gas grade, 273-74
lemons, 278
maintenance, 272-75
oil changes, 273
plug-in hybrids, 262-65
tire inflation, 273
See also collecting; consumer info; driving; home technology; used cars

Autumnal Equinox, 754

aviophobia (fear of flying), 497-98

B

Babson College
F.W. Olin School of Business, 362

Baby on the Way, The (English), 333

Bach, David, 172

Bach, Johann Sebastian, 682, 683, 684

back injuries, 19

back pain
exercising away, 68

backgammon, 651-52

Backroads (bike tours), 572

bacterial vaginosis, 44

Bad Blood (Sage), 704

Badaracco, Joseph L., Jr., 361

badminton, 609-10

Badwater, 640

baggage check, 497

Bahamas (Out Islands), 618

Bailey, John, 619

Baker, Dean, 206

bald eagles, 556

Baldo, Dr. George, 324

Baldrige, Letitia, 795, 801

Baldwin, Gerald, 163

ballet
principle companies, 691
recommended, 691

Balliett, Blue, 334

Balloon mortgages, 210

Baloney (Henry P.) (Scieszka), 335

Baltimore Orioles, 582

Baltimore Ravens, 591

Bamberger, Alan, 300

Bangs, Richard, 577

Bank magazine, 480

bankruptcy, 179-80
filing, 180

Banks-Pye, Roger, 431

Barbarescos (Piedmontese wines), 151-52

barber, tipping, 250

bargains, 249-50
post office, 253-54

Barolos (Piedmontese wines), 151-52

barometer reading, 714

Barr, Dr. Ronald, 83

Barrow, Mary Mills, 27

bartenders, tipping, 250

Bartimaeus Trilogy Book Two: The Golem's Eye, The (Stroud), 334

Bartley Collection (furniture kits), 427

Bartoli, Cecilia, 689-91

baseball, 582-88
American League Central, 583-84
American League East, 582-83
American League West, 584-85
Cactus League (Arizona), 587
Dominican League, 584
and kids, 607-8
Grapefruit League (Florida), 587
Mexican League, 584
National Baseball Hall of Fame and Museum, 598
National League Central, 585-86
National League East, 585
National League West, 586, 588
as an Olympic sport, 582
Puerto Rican League, 584

Venezuelan League, 584

World Series, 590

See also auto racing; basketball; betting; football; hockey; tickets

basements

fixing wet, 434-35

Basie, Count, 685

basketball, 604-6

home court, designing, 605-6

basketball (professional), 592-93

Eastern Conference, 593

history of, 592, 594

miscellaneous facts, 592

Naismith Memorial Basketball Hall of Fame, 598

NCAA Final Four, 590

Western Conference, 593

See also auto racing; baseball; betting; football; hockey; tickets

basketball shoes, 22

Bastianich, Lidia, 579

Bastille Day (France), 757

Batali, Mario, 137

bathroom

caulking and grouting, 436

lighting, 424

Bauer, John E., 478

Bauman, Dr. Alan J., 34

BBB Wise Giving Alliance, 241

Beatles, The, 684

Bear Attacks: Their Causes and Avoidance (Herrero), 110

Beaton, Cecil, 431

Beaufort Scale of Wind Force, 714

Beaujolais wines, 150-51

beauty aids, 27-30

facial peels, 30-31

foundation primers, 28

makeup tips, 29-30

moisturizer, 27-28

skin luminizers, 30

Beck, Martha Davis, 332-33

bedroom lighting, 424

beds, 427-29

beef

roasting and broiling, 138

beers, 157-58

drinking dos and don'ts, 158

India pale ale, 158

pale ales, 157-58

Pilsner, 157

stout, 158

Trappist ales, 158

Beethoven, Ludwig von, 682, 683-84

Being Dead (Crace), 702

Belize

as travel destination, 526

Bell, Peter, 394

Bellini, Vincenzo, 683

Benchley, Robert, 533

Benjamin Moore paints, 420, 422

Benner, David E., 473

Bennett, Jeff, 574-77

Beowulf: A New Verse Translation (Heaney), 702

Bequia

as travel destination, 524-25

Berg, Alban, 683

Berger, Shoshana, 438

Bergfeld, Dr. Wilma, 23, 24, 25

Berlin International Film Festival, 677

Bernese Oberland (Switzerland)

hiking, 570

Bernicke, Ty, 200-201

Berry, Chuck, 685

Berthold-Bond, Annie, 136-37

Best Buy, 249, 292

Best DVDs You've Never Seen, Just Missed or Almost Forgotten, The (Nichols, ed.), 673

Better Business Bureau, 410

Better Sleep Council, 427

Better World Club, 272

BetterInvesting, 185

betting on sports, 594

Beven, Jack, 715

beverages, 148-64

beers, 157-58

coffee and tea, 163-64

spirits, 159-63

wines, 148-57

See also cooking; diet and nutrition

Beyeler Foundation, 697

Bhutan, trekking in, 567-68

Bianchi, Suzanne M., 399

Bibliothèque Nationale (Paris), 708

bicep curls, 15

Bick, Julie, 322

bighorn sheep, 554

biking, 614-16

in France, 572

Bill and Melinda Gates Foundation, 45, 358

Billington, James H., 666

Billy Budd (Melville), 384

Binge: What Your College Student Won't Tell You (Seaman), 350

binoculars, 557

biodiesel

as alternative energy, 164

biological attacks

preparing for, 111-12

surviving, 112

biotin (vitamin B), 122

Bird of Dawning, The (Masefield), 384

bird-watching binoculars, 557

birds

caged birds, 488

choosing a feeder, 486-88

wild bird food, 487

birthstone designations, 802

Bishop, Avis, 419

Bishop, Brent, 625

Bizet, Georges, 689

black spot, 448

blackjack, 661-62

Blasi, Gary, 359

Blau, Francine D., 399

bleeding from open wound

controlling, 96

Bleep.com, 693

Blender magazine, 692

blight, 460

blog sites

for travelers, 517-18

See also Web sites

Blogger.com, 517-18

Bloody Mary recipe, 159

Bluman, David, 18

board games, 645-52

backgammon, 651-52

checkers, 650-51

chess, 651

Go, 648-49

Mah-jongg, 649

Monopoly, 645-47

online sites, 648

Scrabble, 647-48

See also card games

Bobbi Brown Beauty: The Ultimate Beauty Resource (Brown), 29

BoConcept (furnishings), 420-21

Bodleian Library (Oxford), 708

Bodnar, Janet, 174

body mass index (BMI), 7

body sculpting, 13-18

DVD/video cardio classes, 18

exercises, 15-16

pulse rate, checking, 17

tai chi and yoga, 17-18

weight lifting and weight loss, 16-17

See also exercise

Boethius, 810

Boffi

and kitchen renovation, 416-18

Bohème, La (Puccini), 689

Bolles, Richard, 400-402

Bonaire Marine Park (Netherlands Antilles), 618

Bond, Robin, 398-99

bonds. *See* stocks and bonds

Book of Old Silver, The (Wyler), 315

books

National Book Award (2000-2005), 702-7

Pulitzer Prize for literature (2000-2005), 702-7

secondhand, 251

21st century's best books, 702-7

See also libraries

BootsnAll, 518

Bordeaux wines, 149-50

Borrowed Finery: A Memoir (Fox), 704

Boston Bruins, 595

Boston Celtics, 593

Boston Red Sox, 582

Bosworth, Warren, 605

botanical gardens

Atlanta Botanical Garden, 473

Brooklyn Botanic Garden, 473

Chicago Botanic Garden, 473

Holden Arboretum, 473

Huntington Botanical Gardens, 473

Longwood Gardens, 473

Missouri Botanical Garden, 473

New York Botanical Garden, 473

San Francisco Botanical Garden at Strybing Arboretum, 473

United States National Arboretum, 473

Botox injections, 32

Botswana, safaris in, 562-63

Boulder Polar Bear Club, 630

Boundary Waters/Gunflint Trail (Minnesota), 635

Bountiful Gardens (seed company), 442

Bounty: The True Story of the Mutiny on the Bounty, The (Alexander), 705

bourbon, 162

Bourgogne wines, 150

Boussac Fadini, 431

Bove, Alexander, 789

boxers, 475

Boxing Day (United Kingdom), 757

Boyle, T. Coraghessan, 705

Brager, Stuart H., 316

Braille, Louis, 812

Braille system, 812

Brancaccio, David, 189

Brandenburg Concertos (Bach), 684

Brandt, Dr. Frederic, 33

Brazil

rain forests in, 559

breast cancer, 57-59

mammograms, 58

a primer, 57

self examinations, 57-59

breast enlargement, 31-32

Brent, Dr. Robert L., 91

Brenzel, Jeffrey, 344

Breslin, Paul A. S., 128

Breyer, Stephen G., 357

Brick Lane (Ali), 705

Bricks and Brownstone (Lockwood), 413

bridge, 659-60

Brierly, Richard, 309

British Broadcasting Corporation, 292

British Library (London), 533, 708

Britten, Benjamin, 681

Brooklyn Botanic Garden, 473

Brown, Alton, 132

Brown, Bobbi, 29

Brown, Cheryl, 344

Brown, James, 685, 688

Brown, Dr. Jeffrey L., 609

Brown, Karen and Rick, 504

Brown, Kristin, 398

Brown, Mark, 800

Brown, Michael E., 729

Bruner, Dr. Denise, 4

Brutal Bosses and Their Prey (Hornstein), 385-87

Bryson, Bill, 518

Bucharest

real estate values in, 223

Buckley, Christopher, 501

Buckley, Pat, 795

budgeting, 166-67

net worth, calculating, 167

personal budget, 167

U.S. households, net worth of, 166

Buenos Aires

real estate values in, 222

Buffalo Bills, 591

Buffalo Sabres, 595

Buffett, Warren, 187-89, 378, 659
building materials
  durability of, 412
bulbs, 446
Bulgaria
  as travel destination, 578
bull markets, 183
bull riding, 612-13
bully bosses, 385-87
  guide to, 386
bumped airline passengers, 499
Bureau of Labor Statistics, 406
Burger, Warren, 384
burnout, 390-91
burns, 98-99
  and children, 92
  treating, 99
Burns, Harry, 753
Burpee Seed Starter: A Guide to Growing Flower, Vegetable, and Herb Seeds Indoors and Outdoors (Heffernan), 442-45
Burton, Benjamin J., 306
business school
  choosing, 359-62
  cost of, 363
  entrepreneurism, 362, 404-6
  global marketplace, 362
  and high-salary employment, 363-64
  specialized curriculum, 361
Business Week magazine, 363
Butterfield & Robinson (bike tours), 572
butterflies
  attracting, 462-63
  monarch migration, 559
buy-down mortgages, 210
Byrne, Leslie, 778
Byzantine Dietary Calendar, 119

C

Caballero, Dr. Benjamin, 122
cabernet-shiraz (Australia), 153-54
Cactus League (Arizona), 587
Cadence, The Review of Jazz & Blues, 692
Caesar, Julius, 756, 757
caffeine content in beverages, 164
calcium, 123-24
  questions about, 124
calendars, 744-62
American holidays, 749-56
international holidays, 756-57
leap year, 756
New Year's resolutions, 758
perpetual calendar, 748-56
religious holidays, 757-59
See also time
Calder, Alexander, 698
Calgary Flames, 595
California
  housing market, 204-6
California and Steller's sealions, 555
California Closets, 419, 420
California wines
  pinot noirs, 156
  sauvignon blanc wines, 155
  syrah wines, 155-56
Callas, Maria, 683
Callender, Rob, 175
calorie requirements, 116
Camara, Wayne, 336-37
Camargo, Dr. Carlos A., 100
Cambodia
  as travel destination, 519, 520
Cambridge, 353
cameras
  digital, 298-99
  as gardening tool, 442
Camp, Jim, 395
campaign contributions, 780
Canada Day, 756
Canale, Steve, 374
Canavan, Pat, 606
cancer. *See* breast cancer; prostate cancer
cancer insurance, 235
Canine Slim Results (pet diet supplement), 478
car theft, 279
CarBargains (auto-buying service), 260
card games, 653-64
  blackjack, 661-62
  bridge, 659-60
  gin rummy, 662-63
  pinochle, 660
  poker, 653-58
  solitaire, 663
  spades, 663
  See also board games
Card Player magazine, 656
careers, 365-406
  entrepreneurism, 362, 404-6
  getting hired, 373-74
  job hunting, 367-73
  job transfers, 388-89
leadership, 382-85
moving on, 396-99
moving up, 392-96
occupational outlook, 375-78
office politics, 385-88
picking a profession, 366-67
salaries, 378-82
second careers, 400-406
strategies, 374-75
stress management, 390-92
Carey, Peter, 703
Carfax (research service), 262
Caribbean, 523-27
  Anegada, 524
  Bequia, 524-25
  Les Saintes, 525
  Mayreau, 525-26
  Mustique, 527
  Turks and Caicos, 525
  underwater dive sites, 526
Carmen (Bizet), 689
Carnegie, Andrew, 708
Carnegie libraries, 708
Carnegie Mellon
  Tepper School of Business, 361
Carolina Hurricanes, 595
Carolina Panthers, 591
Caron, Paul L., 340
carpets
  oriental, 430
  wall-to-wall, 430
Carroll, Lewis, 334
Carson, Johnny, 657
Carter, Miranda, 704
Carter, Mother Maybelle, 318
Carter, Rosalind Clay, 389
Carvin, Beth, 398
cast iron skillets, 132-33
cat breeds, 479-82
  Abyssinians, 479
  American curl, 479-80
  American shorthair, 480
  American wirehair, 480
  Balinese, 480
  British shorthair, 480
  Burmese, 480
  Cornish Rex, 480-81
  Devon Rex, 481
  exotic shorthair, 481
  Japanese bobtail, 481
  Maine coon cat, 481
  Oriental short hair, 481
cat diseases and treatment
  diagnosis and surgery, 486
  feline calicivirus, 483
  feline leukemia virus, 483
feline panleukopenia, 483
feline pneumonitis, 483
feline viral rhinotracheitis, 483
vaccinations for, 484-85
Catamount Trail (Vermont), 634-35
Cato the Elder, 119
cats, 479-82
  behavior modification, 485-86
  boarding kennels, 486
  dieting, 478
  DogCatRadio, 481
  fleas, 485
caulking and grouting, 436
Cavalleria Rusticana (Mascagni), 689
cellphones
  models and contracts, 298
  and roadside assistance, 271-72
  warranties, 252-53
Cenerentola, La (Rossini), 689
Centers for Disease Control and Prevention, 12, 45, 55, 111, 325
ceramic tiles
  durability of, 412
chair
  choosing for the office, 405
Chall, Jean, 320
Challenger, John A., 370
Champagne, 156-57
  naming bottles, 157
Channel Islands National Park, 548
charitable contributions, 241
  giving circles, 240-42
charities
  checking on, 241
Charity Navigator, 241
Charlotte Bobcats, 593
charter flights, 494-95
ChaseFreedom, 5
Chasing Vermeer (Balliett), 334
Cheapflights.com, 492
checkers, 650-51
cheese
  and wine pairings, 154
Cheese: A Connoisseur's Guide to the World's Best (McCalman), 154
chemical attacks, 112
  preparing for, 112
  surviving, 112
chemical peels, 30-31
chemistry, 769
  periodic table of elements, 769
Cheney, Dick, 623
Cheng, Fu-Tung, 418
Cheng Design, 418
Chernow, Ron, 706
chess, 651
  and math skills, 324
Chester, Geoff, 722
Chicago Bears, 591
Chicago Blackhawks, 595
Chicago Botanic Garden, 473
Chicago Bulls, 593
Chicago Cubs, 585-86
Chicago White Sox, 583
chicken, roasting, 139
Chihuahuas, 475
Child, Julia, 147
Child's Christmas in Wales, A (Thomas), 334
child development and parenting, 83-93
  ADHD, 90-91, 322
  body mass index for children, 88
  colic, 83-84
  empathy and morality, 93
  immunizations, 89
  quality of care, 85
  real risks, 91-93
  serious face time with baby, 84-65
  speech and language difficulties, 87-90
  toxins in breast milk, 84
  weight and height charts, 86, 87
child guardianship, 788-89
Child-Parent Centers, 321
child-rearing, 173-76
  allowances, 174-75
  boomerang kids, 176
  cost of raising, 173
  credit cards, 174
  teaching to drive, 268-69
  teenage spending, 175-76
children, 70-93
  adoption, 80-83
  child development and parenting, 83-93
  conception, 70-72
  entertaining with, 794
  and gourmet food, 143
  pregnancy, 72-80
  See also doctors and medicine; first aid and survival; fitness; infants
children's movies
  New York Times guide to, 679-80
Chile
  wine industry in, 153
chili, 143-44

Nigella's Vegetarian Chili with Corn Bread Topping, 144
Chinati Foundation, 697
Chinese New Year, 756
Chinese zodiac signs, 759-60
Buffalo (or Ox), 759
Dog, 760
Dragon, 760
Goat, 760
Horse, 760
Monkey, 760
Pig, 760
Rabbit, 760
Rat, 759
Rooster, 760
Snake, 760
Tiger, 760
Chippendale furniture, 305
chlamydia, 44
chocolate, 144-45
tasting, 145
choking and children, 92
choking victim, 97-98
cholesterol, 117, 118
chorionic villus sampling (CVS), 76
Christ, Jesus, 756, 757, 759
Christensen, Bonnie, 335
Christmas Day, 756, 759
Chronicles: Volume One (Dylan), 706
Churchill, Winston, 503
Cialis, 42-44
Cincinnati Bengals, 591
Cincinnati Reds, 586
Cinema Ritrovato, Il (Italy), 679
Cingular, 298
Circuit City, 249, 292
Circulation (medical journal), 52, 94
citizenship, 776-80
draft registration, 780
electoral college, 777
legislation, 778
passport renewal, 778-79
social security card, 779-80
U.S. citizenship, 776-77
voter registration, 777-78
City of Rocks (Idaho)
rock climbing at, 625-26
Clapton, Eric, 318
classical music
festivals, 694-96
online sites, 682
recommended, 681-83, 683-85
See also opera
Clemens, John K., 383-84
Cleopatra, 30

Cleveland Browns, 591
Cleveland Cavaliers, 593
Cleveland Indians, 583
Clinton, Bill, 356
clocks, 744-46
Clos-ette, 419-20
closets, 419-20
wallpapering, 420
Closets magazine, 419
clothing
and ultraviolet rays, 27
clothing sizes, 765
clouds, 717
altocumulus, 717
altostratus, 717
cirrocumulus, 717
cirrostratus, 717
cirrus, 717
cumulonimbus, 717
cumulus, 717
stratocumulus, 717
stratus, 717
cocktails, 159-61
Bloody Mary, 159
gimlet, 160
Kentucky Derby mint juleps, 162
margarita, 160-61
martini, 159-60
mojito, 163
See also alcohol
coffee and tea, 163-64
caffeine content, 164
espresso 163-64
world teas, 164
Cohen, Arianne, 438
Cohn, Alisa, 388
coin collecting, 306
Cole, Roger, 18
Coleman, Eliot, 458-59
Coleman, Ornette, 685
colic, 83-84
collagen injections, 32
collecting, 300-318
antiques, 303-7
appraisers, 308
art, 300-303
auctions, 307-11
gems, etc., 312-18
See also autos; consumer info; home technology
college and grad school, 336-64
admission, 336-46
arts education, 346-48
athletic considerations, 343
courses of study, 350-58
domestic exchange programs, 354
financial aid, 348-50
grad school, 358-64
real world, 364

See also K through 12
college and grad school (financial aid), 348-50
federal loans, 348-49
Gates Cambridge Scholarship, 358
George J. Mitchell Scholarship, 357-58
Harry S. Truman Scholarship, 358
J. W. Fulbright Student Program, 358
Marshall Scholarship, 357
National Merit Scholarships, 350
Pell Grants, 350
Perkins loans, 349
PLUS loans, 349
private loans, 349-50
Rhodes scholarship, 356-57
Stafford loans, 349
College Board, 336, 337-38, 341
See also SAT
college credits
in high school, 345-46
College Football Hall of Fame, 597
colleges
admissions considerations, 341-42
campus reality tours, 339
rankings, 338-41
SAT requirements, 336
collies, 474
congenital defects, 475
Color: Natural Palettes for Painted Rooms (Starck/Dahl), 421
Color and Light: Luminous Atmospheres for Painted Rooms (Starck/Dahl), 421
Colorado Avalanche, 595
Colorado River (CO)
white-water rafting, 575
Colorado Rockies, 588
Coltrane, John, 685, 688
Columbus, Christopher, 754
Columbus Blue Jackets, 595
Columbus Day, 754
comets, 723, 729
commercial real estate, 224-25
community colleges, 351-52
Community Food Security Coalition, 136
commuting, stress from, 390
comparison shopping
online, 246-48
Compleat Angler, The (Walton), 620

Complete Recordings, The (Johnson), 685
Complete Whitewater Rafter, The (Bennett), 574-77
compost, 137, 445
food waste into, 137
compounding interest, 168
CompUSA, 291-92
computer programs
updating, 287
computer servicing, 291-92
computerized telescopes, 730-31
computers, 280-90
bits and bytes, 767
choosing, 283-84
data backup, 284-87
data recovery, 287-88
diskettes, lifespan of, 288
e-mail, 284, 289
energy use and, 293-94
flash drives, 56
hard drives and RAM, 283-84
laptop vs. desktop, 283
laptops, 288-90
Macintosh discounts, 283
networking, 280-83
pixels, 767
viruses, 284
warranties, 284
See also online
conception, 70-72
best day to try, 70-72
facts, 71
pre-conception, 70
concrete
decorative, 418-19
durability of, 412
concurrent enrollment, 345
condoms, 38-39
HIV/AIDS and, 45-46
Condor Journey and Adventures, 565
condos
hotels, 218
yachts, 218-19
Coney Island Polar Bear Club, 629-30
Connecting: Solo Travel Network, 530
Connelly, Jennifer, 30
Connor, Dr. Bradley A., 498
Connor, Leslie, 334
conspicuous consumption, 248-49
construction trades salaries, 381
Consumer Action, 169-70
consumer info, 246-59
emergencies, 256-59
identity theft, 254-56

shopping online, 246-48
strategies, 248-54
See also autos; collecting; home technology
Consumer Reports, 246, 253, 260, 261, 298, 430
Container Store, 420
Conti, John, 159
Continental Divide National Scenic Trail, 552
contraception, 38-39
contraceptive injection, 39
contractors (home remodeling)
choosing, 408-10
contracts, 410-11
disasters, forestalling, 410
Cook, Charles, 545
Cook's Garden (seed company), 441
cooking, 130-48
basics, 138-43
fresh produce and ingredients, 133-38
gourmet dining, 143-47
recipes and utensils, 130-32
See also beverages; diet and nutrition
cooking basics, 138-43
bacteria, temperature and, 138
beurre blanc sauce, 142
cooking temperature and timing, 138-40
fish, 141-43
turkey, carving a, 139
Coolidge, Calvin, 796
Copernicus, Nicolaus, 739, 770
copper, 124
Cordon Bleu test, 147
Corrections, The (Franzen), 703
Corsica, hiking, 570
cosmetic enhancements, 31-33
breast enlargement, 31-32
eyelid surgery, 32
hands and aging, 33
injections, 31, 32
liposuction, 31
nose reshaping, 31
surgical procedures, 31-32
tummy tucks, 32
cosmetic injections, 31, 32
cosmetic surgical procedures, 31-32
Costa Rica
rain forests in, 558
Costco, 249

couch potatoes, cure for, 20
counterfeit goods, 311
court, 784, 786
Cousteau, Jacques, 617, 618
Covent Garden (London), 533
Cowen, Tyler, 303
Coxe, William, 135
Coyle, Edward F., 13
CPR, 94-96
    adults and children, 95
    facts, 94
    infants, 95-9
    rescue breathing, primer on, 95
crab, cooking, 140
crabs (venereal), 44
Crace, Jim, 702
Cracking the Millionaire Code (Hansen/Allen), 172
Craddock, Maggie, 397-98
Craig, Roger, 645-47
credit, 177-78
    bankruptcy, 179-80
    bankruptcy, filing, 180
    credit counselors, 180
    credit rating, checking, 178
    See also debt
credit cards, 176, 177-78
    children and, 174
    identity theft and, 255
    reward cards, 177
credit reports, 177, 179
    identity theft and, 254
Creech, Sharon, 335
Crème Renversée au Caramel, 147
Crenshaw, Dr. Theresa, 36, 37
Crew, Anna, 389
croquet, 610-11
cross-trainers, 22
crossword puzzles, 804-5
Crown City Hardware, 413
cruise ships, 502
cruises, 502
    single-friendly, 530
Cruising French Waterways (McKnight), 573
Cuba
    as travel destination, 427-28
Culberston, Ely, 659
Cult of Personality, The (Paul), 366
Culver, Russ, 594
Cumberland Island National Seashore, 547
Curless, Chris, 445, 447
curling, 627
currency design, 171
curtains, 431

Cuyahoga National Park, 544
CyberDiet, 5
Cylinder Digitization and Preservation Project, 691

D

d'Angelico, John, 318
Dabney, Lewis, 350
dachshunds
    congenital defects, 475
Dahl, Taffy, 421
Dalbar, Inc., 190
Dallas Cowboys, 591
Dallas Mavericks, 593
Dallas Stars, 595
Dalrymple, Scott, 383
Dalton, Francie, 396
Damrosch, Barbara, 458-59
dance education, 347
Darwin, Charles, 557
data (computer)
    backup, 284-87
    recovery, 287-88
Dattner, Benjamin, 387
Dave Pelz's Putting Bible (Pelz/Frank), 599
Davenport, Chris, 632
Davern, Dr. Tim, 54
Davis, Miles, 685
Day in the Life of Murphy, A (Provensen), 334
Day the Babies Crawled Away, The (Rathmann), 334
daylight saving time, 746
De Kooning: An American Master (Stevens/Swan), 707
de Maria, Walter, 697
de Menil, John and Dominique, 697
de Moura, Eduardo Souto, 701
de Vries, Lloyd A., 315
debit card
    identity theft and, 255
debt, 178-80
    credit counselors, 180
    See also credit
Decibel magazine, 693
decorating. **See** home decorating
decorative concrete, 418-19
decorators, 415-16
Deep in the Green: An Exploration of Country Pleasures (Raver), 440
Defending Ourselves (Wiseman), 108
Defense Advanced Research Projects Agency, 101
DeGroff, Dale, 159
Delitto, Anthony, 68
Denver Broncos, 591

Denver Nuggets, 593
depression, 62-63
    artificial light and, 65
Deschutes River (OR)
    white-water rafting, 575
Detroit Lions, 591
Detroit Pistons, 593
Detroit Red wings, 595
Detroit Tigers, 583
Deutschland (tall ship), 501
Devil's Tower (Wyoming)
    rock climbing at, 626
Dewali, 759
Dewey, John, 321
Dia Art Foundation, 697
diabetes, 55-57
diamonds
    choosing, 312-13
    popular cuts, 312
Diary of a Voyage—or Hemingway All the Way (Algren), 503
Didion, Joan, 707
Dido and Aeneas (Purcell), 683
diet and nutrition, 114-29
    fat, 117-18
    healthy eating, 125-29
    minerals, 123-25
    nutrition, 114-16
    vitamins, 118-23
    See also beverages; cooking
diet plan, customizing, 4
diet pills, 8-9
diets, 119
DietTalk, 5
digital cameras, 298-99
    batteries, 298-99
    laptops and, 299
    memory cards, 299
Dimitrius, Jo-Ellan, 783-84
dining room lighting, 423-24
DiSabato-Aust, Tracy, 463
disability insurance, 229-30
    questions to ask, 229
disasters, 101-7
    earthquakes, 101-3
    floods, 103
    hurricanes, preparing for, 104
    information sources, 106
    swimming and surfing safety, 107
    thunderstorms, 104-5
    tornadoes, 105
    tsunamis, 103
Discover Today's Motorcycling, 277
diskettes (computer)
    lifespan of, 288
Distant Journeys, 571
Ditre, Dr. Cherie, 23, 24

divorce, 787
DJ magazine, 694
DNA testing, 804
Dobelle, Evan S., 352
doctors
    finding, 48-50
    health, education and income and, 50
    online, 49
    personal attention, 48
    talking with, 50-52
doctors and medicine, 48-69
    alternative medicine, 64-68
    back pain, 68
    breast cancer, 57-59
    diabetes, 55-57
    heart disease (male and female), 52-55
    mental health, 61-64
    prostate cancer, 60-61
    sleep, 68-69
    See also appearance; children; first aid and survival; fitness; sexuality
documents and records, organizing, 156-58
dog breeds (for active people)
    boxers, 475
    English cocker spaniels, 475
    greyhounds, 475
    terriers, 475
dog breeds (for children)
    collies, 474
    golden retrievers, 474
    Labrador retrievers, 474
    standard poodles, 474
dog breeds (for older people)
    Chihuahuas, 475
    miniature poodles, 475
    toy poodles, 475-76
    Yorkshire terriers, 476
dog diseases and treatment, 482-83
    canine bordetellosis, 482
    canine distemper virus (CDV), 483
    canine leptospirosis, 483
    canine parainfluenza, 483
    canine parvovirus (CPV), 483
    congenital defect in, 475
    diagnosis and surgery, 486
    infectious canine hepatitis, 483
    vaccinations for, 484
DogCatRadio, 481
dogs, 474-79
    animal shelter, adopting from, 477

bathing, 477-78
behavior modification, 485-86
boarding kennels, 486
buying online, 477
and companion dogs, 474
de-skunking, 478
dieting, 478-79
dog vs. people years, 479
DogCatRadio, 481
fleas, 485
for older people, 475-76
pedigree pup, buying, 476-77
Dolby, Ray, 357
Dole, Bob, 384
Dolich, Scott, 143
Dominica
    as travel destination, 526
Dominican League, 584
Don't Stop the Career Clock (Harkness), 402
Donald Kaufman Color Collection, 421
Donnelly, Joseph, 16
Dorling Kindersley, 516
Double Time Jazz, 692
Doughty, Andrew, 528
Dover, Dr. Jeffrey, 28
Dow-Wilshire 5000, 191
Dowland, John, 684
Download.com, 693
Dr. Martin Luther King Jr. Birthday, 749-50
draft registration, 780
Drake, Susan, 387
Dream of Freedom: The Civil Rights Movement From 1954 to 1968 (McWhorter), 333
Dresser, Norine, 797-98
drink industry employment, 378
drinking dos and don'ts, 158
driver's licence, 269
    and older drivers, 271
driving, 265-72
    age and, 270-71
    alcohol and, 267
    car safety, checking, 266
    defensive driving, 265-68
    roadside help, 271-72
    rollovers, 268
    tailgating, 265
Driving School Association of the Americas, 270
driving schools, 269-70
Drop City (Boyle), 705
Drottningholm Court Theater, 694
drowning and children, 92
Drucker, Richard, 312, 314
drug companies
    guideline authors and, 55

Druse, Ken, 450-51
drywall
durability of, 412
DuBrin, Andrew J., 388
Dubroff, Patti, 30
duck, roasting, 139
Duke University rice diet, 119
dumbbell flies, 15
Dunn, Kenneth B., 361
Dupre, Lonnie, 635
DVD/video cardio classes, 18
DVD's
list of best, 673-76
secondhand, 251
Dylan, Bob, 686, 706

E

e-mail, 284, 289
cheap access, 289
and stress management, 392
and viruses, 284
See also online
E85
as alternative energy, 264
early-college high school, 345-46
Earth, 726
closet stellar neighbors, 725
See also astronomy
Earth Day, 751
earthquakes, 719-21
Alpide belt, 721
circum-Pacific seismic belt, 721
Richter scale, 721
surviving, 101-3
EarthRoamer (off-road R.V.), 278-79
Easter, 757
Eastern Conference (basketball)
Atlanta Hawks, 593
Boston Celtics, 593
Charlotte Bobcats, 593
Chicago Bulls, 593
Cleveland Cavaliers, 593
Detroit Pistons, 593
Indiana Pacers, 593
Miami Heat, 593
Milwaukee Bucks, 593
New York Knicks, 593
New Jersey Nets, 593
Orlando Magic, 593
Philadelphia 76ers, 593
Toronto Raptors, 593
Washington Wizards, 593
See also Western Conference (basketball)
Eastern Conference (hockey)
Atlanta Thrashers, 595

Boston Bruins, 595
Buffalo Sabres, 595
Carolina Hurricanes, 595
Florida Panthers, 595
Montreal Canadiens, 595, 596
New Jersey Devils, 595
New York Islanders, 595
New York Rangers, 595
Ottawa Senators, 595
Philadelphia Flyers, 595
Pittsburgh Penguins, 595
Tampa Bay Lightning, 595
Toronto Maple Leafs, 595
Washington Capitals, 595
See also Western Conference (hockey)
Eastern Europe
real estate values in, 223
EasyClosets, 420
eating locally, 136
Eating Thin for Life: Food Secrets and Recipes From People Who Have Lost Weight & Kept It Off (Fletcher), 4
eBay, 247, 310
Eck, Joe, 441
Eckert, Robert A., 383
eDiets, 5
Edinburgh Festival, 694
Edley, Joe, 647-48
Edmonton Oilers, 595
education, 319-64
K through 12, 220-35
college and grad school, 336-64
Education of Henry Adams, The (Adams), 350
educational services, 379
educational strategies (K through 12), 323-25
chess and math skills, 324
music and spatial intelligence, 323
phys ed, 325
science, succeeding in, 324
See also pre-school; reading; teaching techniques; testing
Eggers, Dave, 702-3
Eicher, Dave, 730
Eisenstein, Paul A., 273
Eker, T. Harv, 172
elbow injuries, 20-21
Electoral College, 777
Electric Ladyland (Jimi Hendrix Experience), 684
electricity
as alternative energy, 264
electrocution
and children, 92

Elektra (Strauss), 689
Elis & Tom (Regina/Jobim), 685-86
elk
hunting, 624
Rocky Mountain elk, 554
wintering elk, 554
Elkind, Dr. David, 327
Ellington, Duke, 685, 688
elliptical trainers, 14
embalming, 259
emergencies, 256-59
documents and records, organizing, 156-58
funeral costs, 258-59
Emerson, Ralph Waldo, 622
Emily Dickinson's Letters to the World (Winter), 335
emoticon, 811
employment services, 378, 379
eMusic.com, 682, 693
Encyclopedia Prehistorica (Sabuda/Reinhart), 333
energy bill
appliances and, 433
heating, 431-33
thermostats, 433
water heaters, 433
windows and, 433

Energy Star program, 293
energy use
appliances and, 292-94
engagement rings
choosing, 312-13
England
river trips, 573
English, Karen, 333
English Opera (London), 690
Ensher, Ellen, 397
entrepreneurism, 362, 404-6
entryway lighting, 423
environmental hazards, 437-39
asbestos, 438-39
formaldehyde, 439
lead, 437-38
radon, 437
Environmental Protection Agency (EPA), 274, 277, 422, 437
Environmental Working Group, 132, 137
Epstein, Dr. Joyce, 328
Equifax (credit bureau), 207
Erdrich, Louise, 333
erectile dysfunction, 41-44
treatment, 42-44
Ernst & Young Tax Guide, 237, 242
Espresso, 163-64

Essential Tito Puente, The (Puente), 688
Essential Guide to Wilderness Camping and Back Packing, The (Cook), 545
Essentials of Management (DuBrin), 388
Ethiopia
as travel destination, 579-80
etiquette, 791-98
correct forms of address, 792
entertaining with children, 794
finger bowls, 795
high-tech manners, 791-92
letter-writing, 796
multicultural manners, 797-98
R.S.V.P., 796
relationship rules, 793
social predicaments, 793-95
thank-you notes, 797
women's issues, 792-93
Euclid, 770
Eugenides, Jeffrey, 704
Europe, rail travel in, 503
Ever Green Seeds, 458
Every Woman's Guide to Natural Home Remedies (Freeman), 459
Everybody's Guide to Small Claims Court (Warner), 784
executives
changing profile of, 382
salaries, 379
women and minorities, 382-83, 399
See also leadership; office politics; stress management
exercise, 9-13
benefits at a glance, 10-11
cardio machines, 13-14
excessive, 22
home gym, 9
integrative, 12-13
and lackluster skin, 29
schedule, 9
and weight loss, 4-5
See also body sculpting
exercise equipment, secondhand, 251
exercise shoes, 21-22
exfoliation, 30-31
Exile on Main Street (Rolling Stones), 685
Expedia.com, 492, 495, 496
Experian (credit bureau), 207

Expo Design Center
and kitchen renovation, 416-18
extended service warranties, 252-53, 284
exterior joints and gaps, fixing, 435
eyelid surgery, 32

F

F.B.I. files
accessing, 786-87
F.D.A. food label 125-27
Facebook.com, 355
facial peels, 30-31
Fahey, George, 478, 479
Fair Weather (Peck), 335
Falconer, Ian, 335
falconry, 624-25
falls and children, 91-92
Falstaff (Verdi), 681
Family, Dr. Larry, 481
family travel, 533-37
London, 533, 534
Monaco, 536
Paris, 534-35
San Francisco, 537
Washington, D.C., 536-37
Farley, Frank, 331, 332
Farrell, Warren, 385
Farrelly, Adrienne, 223
fat, 117-18
facts and information, 117
low fat diets, 117
saturated fat, 118
fat injections, 32
Father's Day, 752-53
Fear of Flying Clinic (San Francisco International Airport), 497
Fearless Flier's Handbook: Learning to Beat the Fear of Flying With the Experts From the Qantas Clinic, 497
Featherstone, Helen, 329
Fedco Seeds, 442
Federal Election Commission, 780
Federal Emergency Management Agency, 110, 232-33
Federal Housing Administration, 215
Federal Trade Commission, 254, 255, 256, 258
Feed (Anderson), 335
feet and joints
protecting, 21
Fernandes, John, 359-60
Ferris, Timothy, 705
fertility facts, 71
fertilization

terminology and acronyms, 77
fertilizer, 458
Festival au Désert (Afro-pop), 696
Festival International Del Nuevo Cine Latino-americano (Cuba), 678
Festival International du Film, Le (Cannes), 677
Fidelity National Financial, 216
15-year mortgages, 210
Fighting Chance, 260
Filby, P. William, 804
film festivals, 677-79
fimoculous.com, 693
finance. See personal finance
financial advisors
   financial planners, 198
   finding a broker, 197-99
finger bowls, 795
Finkelstein, Richard S., 788
fire precautions, 110
Firefox (Web browser), 290-91
fireplace and chimney
   durability of, 412
firewall programs, 290
first aid, 94-101
   burns, 98-99
   choking victim, 97-98
   CPR, 94-96
   first aid kit, 102
   food hazardous to children, 98
   heatstroke, 100-101
   open wound, controlling bleeding from, 96
   shock, 96-97
   poisonings, 99-100
first aid (and survival), 94-112
   disasters, 101-7
   first aid, 94-101
   self-defense, 107-9
   survival strategies, 109-12
   See also appearance; children; doctors and medicine; fitness; sexuality
First Booke of Songes (Dowland), 684
First Move, 324
Fischer, David Hackett, 706
fish, 141
   beurre blanc sauce, 142
   cleaning, 140
   grilling, 142-43
   and heart health, 127-29
   See also shellfish
fish oil, 127
Fisher, Helen, 36

fishing, 618-21
   books on, 621
   flies, 619
   night fishing, 620
fitness, 3-22
   avoiding injuries, 18-22
   body sculpting, 13-18
   exercise, 9-13
   weight loss, 3-9
   See also appearance; children; doctors and medicine; first aid & survival; health and fitness; sexuality
FitzGerald, Francis, 703
fix-it-yourself, 434-37, 438
   bathroom caulking and grouting, 436
   exterior joints and gaps, 435
   leaky roof, 435
   stuck windows, 435-36
   trickling toilets, 436-37
   wet basement, 434-35
fixed-rate mortgages, 210-11
Flag Day, 752
flat-screen TV
   concealing, 419
Flavin, Dan, 697
Fleetham, Charlie, 396
Fleming, Renée, 358
Fletcher, Anne, 4, 5
Fletcher, Horace, 119
floods, surviving, 103
floor stenciling, 413
flooring materials durability of, 412
Florida Marlins, 585
Florida National Scenic Trail, 552-53
Florida Panthers, 595
flowers, 446, 447-54
   black spot, 448
   bulbs, 446
   delaying blooming, 463
   for problem areas, 452-53
   roses, 447-49, 449
   roses, training, 450
   and scent, 450-51, 451-52
   time-saving techniques, 453-54
   See also garden diseases and pests; lawns; planting; pruning; trees; vegetables
fluorescent light bulbs, 425
Flush (Hiaasen), 333
flying, 492-500
   air couriers, 495-96
   aviophobia (fear of flying), 497-98
   baggage check, 497

bumped passengers, 499
charter flights, 494-95
courier clubs, 496-97
fare wars, 494
frequent flier miles, 500
jet lag, 498
long layovers, 500
online fares, 492-94
Registered Traveler Program, 497
safest airplane, 498-99
safest seat, 499-500
   See also rail travel; sailing
foam mattresses, 429
Fodor's Travel Guides, 516
folate (vitamin B), 122
Folegandros, 531-32
Fong, Roy, 164
food and drink, 114-64
   beverages, 148-64
   cooking, 130-48
   diet and nutrition, 114-29
food hazardous to children, 98
food industry employment, 378
food waste into compost, 137
foot massages (reflexology), 67
football, 589, 591
   American Football Conference, 591
   College Football Hall of Fame, 597
   and kids, 608-9
   National Football Conference, 591
   Pro-Football Hall of Fame, 598
   signals, 589
   Super Bowl, 588, 590
   See also auto racing; baseball; basketball; betting; hockey; tickets
foot-warmth, 637
Forbes magazine, 188
Ford, Gerald R., 384
Ford's Freighter Travel Guide & Waterways of the World, 501
Forden, Diane, 798
formaldehyde, 439
forms of address, 792
Foster, Norman, 701
Fortress of Solitude, The (Lethem), 705
Foundation Center, 402
foundation primers, 28
Founder: Cecil Rhodes and the Pursuit of Power, The (Shore/Rotberg), 357
Four in All (Payne), 335
Four Seasons (Vivaldi), 681

401(k), 199-200, 244
Fox, Paula, 704
fractions and decimal equivalents, 772
France
   biking in, 572
   river trips, 573-74
Franek, Robert, 336-37
Frank, E. R., 335
Frank, James, 599-601
Frank, Robert H., 363
Frankel, Dr. Richard, 51
Franklin, Aretha, 686
Franklin, Benjamin, 746
Franzen, Jonathan, 703
Free Trees and Plants, 465
Freeman, Sally, 459
freighter travel, 501, 503
FreighterCruises.com, 502
FreighterWorld.com, 502
French wines, 149-51
   Champagne, 156-57

   ranking, 151
French women and diet, 146
frequent flier miles, 500
Friedman, Sarah, 85
Frohlinger, Carol, 397
Frommer's Travel Guides, 516
fruits
   choosing, 133-24
   pesticides and, 135
   ripening, 134
   See also vegetables
Fulbright, J. W., 358
Funeral (Arcade Fire), 688
Funeral Consumers Alliance, 259
funeral costs, 258-59
   embalming, 259
fungus prevention spray, 448
Funke, Cornelia, 335
furnishing. See home furnishing
furniture kits, 427
furniture manufacture
   North Carolina and, 427
Furstenberg, Karl, 344
Future of Golf: How Golf Lost Its Way and How to Get It Back, The (Shackelford), 603

G

G.S.M. phones, 512-14
Gabrieli, Giovanni, 810
Gaitskill, Mary, 707
Gaidano, Scott, 287
Gaidosz, Jo-Ann, 146-47
Galápagos, 556-57
Galea, Dr. Sandro, 100

Galileo Galilei, 733, 739, 770
Gallagher, Dympna, 17
Gallaudet, Thomas, 812
Galleria Borghese (Rome), 700
Game of Silence, The (Erdrich), 333
games, 642-64
   board games, 645-52
   card games, 653-64
   online gaming, 644-45
   pool, 642-44
Garageband.com, 693
Garbor, Don, 388, 795-96
Garden, Dr. Jerome M., 26
garden diseases and pests, 460-63
   black spot, 448
   blight, 460
   homemade fungus preventions spray, 448
   natural predators, 461-62
   organic disease-fighters, 460-62
   See also flowers; pruning; lawns; planting; trees; vegetables
Garden Seed Inventory, The (Seed Savers Exchange), 455
Gardener's Supply Company, 455
gardening, 440-73
   butterflies, attracting, 462-63
   diseases and pests, 460-63
   flowers, 446, 447-54
   houseplants, 470-72
   hummingbirds, attracting, 462
   lawns, 467-70
   moss, growing, 473
   planting, 440-47
   pruning, 463-64
   public gardens, 473
   trees, 465-67
   vegetables, 454-59
gardening tools
   hoses, 464
   pitchforks, 464
   pruners, 464
   racks, 464
   rototillers, 464
   shovels, 464
   tool sources, 464
   trowels, 464
Gardening With Moss: The Lawn of the Future (Benner), 473
Gates, Bill, 188, 658
Gates Cambridge Scholarship, 358
Gauch, Rene, 273

gay rodeos, 613
gays and lesbians
    travel, 532
    weddings, 799-800
Geek Squad (Best Buy), 292
Gehry, Frank, 697, 701
Gemological Institute of
    America, 312
gems
    diamonds, 312-13
    gemstones, value of, 314
    pearls, 313-14
    popular cuts, 312
gender gap, exploiting, 400
genealogy, 803-4
    DNA testing and, 804
general references, 806
Geng, Lisa F., 88
genital herpes, 43
*Genome: The Autobiography
    of a Species in 23
    Chapters* (Ridley), 702
Geocrete (decorative con-
    crete), 418
geologic time, 761
geology, 717-21
    common minerals, 718
    earthquakes, 719-21
    geological primer, 717-19
geometry, 772-74
    angles, 772
    polygons, 773-74
    Pythagorean theorem,
        773
    quadrilaterals, 773
    right triangles, 773
    solids, 774
    triangles, 772-73
George J. Mitchell Scholar-
    ship, 357-58
gerbils, 488-89
German shepherds
    congenital defects, 475
Germany
    river trips, 574
Gerstein, Mordicai, 333, 334
Gerstenfeld, Sheldon L., 474
Gertrude and Claudius
    (Updike), 702
Get Lost Travel Books, 516
Get Real Surfaces, 419
Gherkin (London), 701
Gift From Zeus, A (Steig),
    335
gifted children, identifying,
    321-22
Gilberto, Joao, 688
Gilead (Robinson), 706
Gilligan, Carol, 330
gimlet recipe, 160
gin, 161
gin rummy, 662
Ginsburg, Ruth Bader, 384

Glass, Philip, 323, 684
Glauber, Roy J., 355
Glengarry Glen Ross
    (Mamet), 385
global marketplace, 362
GM Motor Club, 272
Go (Chinese board game),
    648-49
Goebel, Timothy, 638-40
Gold (Berry), 685
"Goldberg" Variations (Bach),
    682
golden retrievers, 474
Golden State Warriors, 593
Golding, William, 385
Goldsmith, Oliver, 352
golf, 599-603
    etiquette, 602-3
    famous handicaps, 601
    handicapping, 601-2
    the Masters, 590, 592
    power game, 603
    ten toughest courses,
        600
Golf magazine, 602
gonorrhea, 44
goose, roasting, 139
Gordon, Catherine D., 183
Gordon, Dr. James, 64
gorilla attacks, 111
Gorman, Dr. Jack, 64
GORP (Great Outdoors Recre-
    ation Pages), 545
Gould, Wayne, 664
gourmet dining, 143-47
    children's menu, 143
    chili, 143-44
    Cordon Bleu test, 147
    chocolate, 144-45
    Crème Renversée au
        Caramel, 147
    French women and diet,
        146
    vacation, culinary instruc-
        tion during, 145-47
    Vegetarian Chili with Corn
        Bread Topping, 144
government contact informa-
    tion, 781
grad schools
    admissions consider-
        ations, 341-42
    rankings, 338-41
    SAT requirements, 336
Graduate Record Exam
    (Educational Testing
    Service), 363
graduated-payment mort-
    gages, 211
Graham, Sylvester, 119
Grahn, Dennis, 100-101
grammar, 805
Gran Paradiso National Park
    (Italy)

hiking, 569
Grand Canyon National Park,
    539-40
    white-water rafting, 576
Grand Teton National Park,
    541, 544-45
Grant-Kohrs Ranch National
    Historic Site, 547
Grantsmanship Center, 402
Grapefruit League (Florida),
    587
grasses
    microclimate, foot traffic
        and maintenance,
        469-70
Gratzer, Walter, 119
Gray, Cari, 572
gray whales, 555
Great Basin National Park,
    547-48
*Great Smaller Museums of
    Europe* (Stourton),
    699
Great Smoky Mountains,
    538-39, 541
Greaves, April, 30
Greek Islands, 530-32
    Folegandros, 531-32
    Hydra, 531
    Naxos, 532
    Patmos, 532
    Serifos, 530-31
Green Guide, The (Penny-
    backer), 136
Greenberg, Jan, 334
Greenblatt, Stephen, 706
Greenland
    trekking in, 566
Greenspan, Stanley, 93
Gregorian, Vartan, 708
Gregory XIII, Pope, 748, 756
Grey, Mini, 333
greyhounds, 475
    congenital defects, 475
Griffin Greenhouse and Nurs-
    ery Supplies, 464
Groundhog Day, 750
growing equity mortgages,
    211
growing zones, 441
*Growth of the Mind and Its
    Endangered Future,
    The* (Greenspan), 93
Gruhn, George, 318
grüner veltliner wines,
    154-55
Guatemala, pyramids in, 561
Guerry, Dr. DuPont, IV, 25
Guggenheim Museum (Bil-
    bao), 697, 701
*Guide to Monastic Guest
    Houses, A* (Regalbuto),
    512
GuideStar, 241
Guido of Arezzo, 810

Guiliano, Mireille, 146
Gulbenkian, Calouste, 699
Gulbenkian Museum (Lis-
    bon), 699
Gulf of the Farallones
    National Marine Sanc-
    tuary (San Francisco),
    537
guitars, collecting, 318
guns and children, 92
Guyton, Jonathan, 201
Gwadosky, Dan A., 269

H

H.I.D. (high intensity dis-
    charge) light bulbs,
    425
Ha Jin, 706
Hadrian's Wall (Britain)
    hiking, 568-69
hair loss, 33-35
    hairpiece, choosing, 34
    Rogaine, 34-35
hair washer, tipping, 250
hairdresser, tipping, 250
Hall, Barbara, 344
Halloween, 754-55
ham, roasting, 139
Hamilton, Virginia, 334
Hampton, Frederick M., 330
Hampton, Mark, 424
Hampton Court Palace (Eng-
    land), 533
Hancock, Stephanie, 201
Handel, George Frederic, 690
hands and aging, 33
hangover cures, 159
Hansen, Mark Victor, 172
Harr, Jonathan, 707
Hanukkah, 759
*Happiest Baby on the Block,
    The* (Karp), 83-84
hard drives (computer),
    283-84
Harder, Deb, 81
Harding, Daniel, 690
hardware, antique, 413-14
Harkness, Helen, 402
Harris, Ethan, 189
Harris, Jane, 481
*Harry Potter and the Half-
    Blood Prince* (Rowling),
    333
Harry S. Truman Scholarship,
    358
Hart, John, 545
Hart, Peter D., 781-82
Hassan, Farris, 330, 331
Harvard, 341, 353, 356
Harvard Extension School,
    355-56
Harvard Magazine, 192

*Hateship, Friendship, Court-
    ship, Loveship, Mar-
    riage: Stories* (Munro),
    703
Hawaiian islands, 528-30
    Kauai, 528-29
    Lanai, 529-30
    Molokai, 529
Hawthorne, Grace, 438
Hayes, Rutherford B., 777
Hayes, Timothy M., 303
Haywood, Dr. Van B., 35
Hazinski, Mary Fran, 94
headhunters, 395-96
health, 3-112
    appearance, 23-35
    children, 70-93
    doctors and medicine, 48-
        69
    first aid and survival, 94-
        112
    fitness, 3-22
    sexuality, 36-47
health care employment, 376
health insurance, 228-29
    boomerang kids and, 176
    Web sites for, 228
healthy eating, 125-29
    F.D.A. food label 125-27
    fish and heart health,
        127-29
    fish oil, 127
    olive oil, 128
    yogurt, 129
Heaney, Seamus, 702
heart disease
    acetaminophen and, 54
    fish and, 127-29
    male and female, 52-55
    mini-stroke, handicapping,
        53
    mini-strokes, 53-54
    patient beware, 55
    statins, 54-55
    time, importance of, 52
*Heartbreaking Work of Stag-
    gering Genius* (Eggers),
    702-3
heating bills, 431-33
    new furnace, savings
        from, 432
heatstroke, 100-101
Hebberoy, Naomi, 143
Hector's Gold (Lavoe), 688
Heffernan, Maureen, 442-45
Heffetz, Ori, 248
height and weight chart, 4
Heimlich, Dr. Henry, 97-98
Heimlich maneuver, 97-98
Heirloom Seeds, 442
Heizer, Michael, 697
Heller, Craig, 100-101

Help, It's Broken! A Fix-It Bible for the Repair-Impaired (Cohen), 438

Hendrix, Jimi, 684

Henkes, Kevin, 334

Henry IV/Henry V (Shakespeare), 384

HEPA filters, 111-12

Hepatology, 54

Hepplewhite furniture, 305

herb gardens
  essentials, 459
  fertilizer of choice, 459
  growing from seed, 459
  indoor, 459
  watering, 459

Herbs for All Seasons (Freeman), 459

heroin overdoses, 100

Heron Island (Australia), 618

Herrero, Stephen, 110

Herschel, William, 727

Hertz, Davis, 418-19

Hewitt Associates, 199

Hiaasen, Carl, 333

high-tech manners, 791-92

Highway 61 Revisited (Dylan), 686

hiking
  Bernese Oberland (Switzerland), 570
  Corsica, 570
  Gran Paradiso National Park (Italy), 569
  Hadrian's Wall path, 568-69
  Julian Alps (Slovenia), 571
  Mount Fuji (Japan), 570
  See also biking; trekking

Hill, Louella, 136

Hill, Dr. J. Edward, 64

Hirsch Organization, 184, 185

Hirschfeld, Alexa and James, 532

Historic Houseparts, 413

HIV/AIDS, 43
  blood-to-blood exchange, 96
  PrEP (pre-exposure prophylaxis), 45
  protecting yourself from, 44-46
  Sculptra injections, 32
  transmission, 44-45
  toll in U.S., 44
  vaccine, search for, 45

hockey, 594-96
  Eastern Conference, 595
  Stanley Cup, 594, 596
  Western Conference, 595

See also auto racing; baseball; basketball; betting; football; tickets

Hodgson, George, 158

Hoffman, Sharon, 361

Holden, Stephen, 674-75

Holden Arboretum, 473

holidays (American), 749-56
  April Fools' Day, 751
  Autumnal Equinox, 754
  Christmas Day, 756
  Columbus Day, 754
  Dr. Martin Luther King Jr. Birthday, 749-50
  Earth Day, 751
  Father's Day, 752-53
  Flag Day, 752
  Groundhog Day, 750
  Halloween, 754-55
  Independence Day (July 4), 753
  Kwanzaa, 756
  Labor Day, 753-54
  Memorial Day, 752
  Mother's Day, 752
  New Year's Day, 749
  President's Day, 750-51
  St. Patrick's Day, 751
  Summer Solstice, 753
  Thanksgiving Day, 755
  United Nations Day, 754
  Valentine's Day, 750
  Vernal Equinox, 751
  Veterans Day, 755
  Winter Solstice, 755-56
  Women's Equality Day, 753

holidays (international), 756-57
  Bastille Day (France), 757
  Boxing Day (United Kingdom), 757
  Canada Day, 756
  Chinese New Year, 756
  Obon Festival (Japan), 757
  Santa Lucia (Sweden), 757
  Sinter Klass (The Netherlands), 757

holidays (religious)
  Ash Wednesday (Christian), 757-58
  Christmas Day (Christian), 759
  Dewali (Hindu), 759
  Easter (Christian), 757
  Hanukkah (Jewish), 759
  Passover (Jewish), 757
  Ramadan (Islamic), 757
  Rosh Hashanah (Jewish), 757
  Yom Kippur (Jewish), 757

holistic medicine, 64-65

Hollywood Reporter, 678

home, 408-39
  decorating, 413-27
  furnishing, 427-31
  maintenance, 431-39
  remodeling, 408-13

home buying, 202-6
  bargains, 204
  buying vs. renting, 204-7
  composite affordability index, 205
  the long view, 202-4
  markets, measure of, 203
  men vs. women, 206
  real estate vs. stocks, 185-86
  See also mortgages; real estate opportunities; second homes

home decorating, 413-27
  closets, 419-20
  closets, wallpapering, 420
  decorative concrete, 418-19
  decorators, 415-16
  flat-screen TV, hiding, 419
  hardware, 413-14
  kitchen renovations, cost of, 417
  kitchens, 416-18
  lamp shades, 424
  large spaces, dealing with, 414-15
  lighting, 423-24
  paint, 421-23
  paint, oil-based vs. latex, 422
  picture frames, 425-27
  shelves, 420-21
  small spaces, dealing with, 414
  stenciling a floor, 413
  track lighting, 424-25
  when the children leave, 415

Home Depot
  and kitchen renovation, 416-18

home furnishing, 427-31
  beds, 427-29
  carpets, 430
  curtains, 431
  furniture kits, 427
  pillows, 428
  sofas, 429
  stain remover, homemade, 430

home maintenance, 431-39
  appliances, fixing vs. replacing, 434
  environmental hazards, 437-39

heating bills, 431-33
  fix-it-yourself, 434-37, 438

home remodeling, 408-13
  contractor, choosing, 408-10
  contracts, 410-11
  disasters, forestalling, 410
  house size, growth in, 408
  remodeling and emotions, 411
  remodeling pros and cons, 411

home technology, 280-99
  audio and video, 292-96
  cameras, 298-99
  computers, 280-90
  online, 290-91
  phones, 296-98
  service and energy, 291-92
  See also autos; collecting; consumer info

homemade fungus prevention spray, 448

homeowner's insurance, 230-33
  saving on, 230
  underinsured, 231

HomePokerTourney.com, 657

Homer, 384-85

Hondo & Fabian (McCarty), 335

Honduras, pyramids in, 561

Hong Kong International Film Festival, 678-79

Hoover, J. Edgar, 786

Hope in a Jar (Peiss), 27

hormones, 36-38
  and aging, 37-38
  sex effects, 37
  sexual and reproduction activity, 36

Hornstein, Harvey, 385-87

horseshoes, 611-12

hotel tipping, 250
  maids, 250-51

House of Antique Hardware, 413-14

household measures, 768

houseplants
  fluorescent light and, 470
  window location, 471-72

Houston Astros, 586

Houston Rockets, 593

Houston Texans, 591

Howard, Barbara V., 114

Howe, Julia Ward, 752

human papilloma virus (HPV), 44

Human Stain, The (Roth), 702

Humane Society of the United States, 490

hummingbirds
  attracting, 462
  feeder for, 488

hunting, 621-24
  Dick Cheney and, 623
  deer, 623-24
  upland birds, 622-23
  waterfowl, 621-22

Huntington Botanical Gardens, 473

hurricanes, 715
  preparing for, 104

Hurried Child, The (Elkind), 327

Huygens, Christiaan, 745

hybrid mortgages, 211

Hydra, 531

hydrogen fuel cells
  as alternative energy, 264

Hyman Hendler & Sons, 431

hypnosis, 64

hypothermia, 716

I

I Am Charlotte Simmons (Wolfe), 350

I Stink (McMullan), 335

I.R.S. audits, 243, 244

Ibbotson Associates, 182

Ice Age National Scenic Trail, 553

ice climbing, 630

ice hockey, 628-28

ICI (icipaintstores.com), 422

identity theft, 254-56
  credit cards vs. debit card, 255
  credit report, freezing, 254
  home computer, protecting, 255
  National Do Not Call Registry, 254
  Social Security number and, 254-55
  vulnerability, 255
  Web sites, 256

Identity Theft Resources, 256

Iditarod Sled Dog Race, 640

igloo building, 636

igneous rocks, 718-19

IgoUgo.com, 518

Ikea
  and kitchen renovation, 416-18

Iliad (Homer), 384-85

Imbruce, Doug, 339

immunizations for children and adolescents, 89

iMoneyNet, 182

In a Different Voice (Gilligan), 330

In the Jungle Groove (Brown), 688

incandescent light bulbs, 425

Indecision (Kunkel), 364

Independence Day (July 4), 753

India pale ale, 158

Indiana Pacers, 593

Indianapolis Colts, 591

Indianapolis 500, 592

indie music
online sites, 693

infants
Heimlich maneuver and, 97-98
See also children

information technology sector
employment in, 402

injuries, avoiding, 18-22
ankle injuries, 20
back injuries, 19
children and, 19
couch potatoes, cure for, 20
elbow injuries, 20-21
exercise, excessive, 22
exercise shoes, 21-22
feet and joints, protecting, 21
knee injuries, 20
neck injuries, 19
shoulder injuries, 20

inns, 504-12
Austria, 506
California, 505
England, 506
France, 506-7
Germany, 507-8
Ireland, 508
Italy, 508-9
Mexico, 505-6
mid-Atlantic, 505
New England, 505
Pacific Northwest, 505
Scotland, 509
Spain, 509
Switzerland, 509

insect bites, 99-100

insomnia, 69

installers' salaries, 381

Institute for Psychology of Air Travel, 497

Institute of HeartMath, 327

insurance, 226-36
auto insurance, 176, 232, 233
buyers guide, 226-36
disability insurance, 229-30
health insurance, 176, 228-29

homeowner's insurance, 230-33
life insurance, 226-28
long-term care insurance, 234-35
pet insurance, 236
terminology, 235-36
unnecessary insurance, 235
See also investing; personal finance; real estate; tax audits; tax planning

Internal Revenue Service, 241

International Association of Air Travel Couriers, 496

International Baccalaureate, 345

International Boxing Hall of Fame Museum, 597

International Gay and Lesbian Travel Association, 532

International Gay Rodeo Association, 613

international holidays, 756-57
Bastille Day (France), 757
Boxing Day (United Kingdom), 757
Canada Day, 756
Chinese New Year, 756
Obon Festival (Japan), 757
Santa Lucia (Sweden), 757
Sinter Klaas (The Netherlands), 757

International Mountain Equipment, 630

international road signs, 807

International Swimming Hall of Fame, 597

International Tennis Hall of Fame, 597-98

international time zones, 747

Internet
voice over internet protocol (VoIP), 514
See also online; Web sites

Internet phone service, 296-98

investing, 181-201
financial advisors, 197-99
mutual funds, 190-97
retirement, 199-201
stocks and bonds, 181-89
See also insurance; personal finance; real estate; tax audits; tax planning

island travel destinations, 523-32
Caribbean, 523-27

Cuba, 427-28
dive sites, 526
Greek Islands, 530-32
Hawaiian islands, 528-30
Punta del Este, 527
single-friendly cruises, 530

investment clubs, 185

iodine, 124

Ireland
river trips in, 573

iron, 124-25

Ironman Triathlon, 640-41

Irrational Exuberance (Shiller), 202

Istria (Croatia)
as travel destination, 578-79

It Takes a Nation of Millions to Hold Us Back (Public Enemy), 687-88

Italian wines, 151-52

IUD (intrauterine device), 39

J

J. W. Fulbright Student Program, 358

Jackson & Perkins (seed company), 440

Jackson, Phil, 18

Jackson Jaguars, 591

Jacobs, Joseph, 700

Jacobsen, Joyce P., 306

James, Caryn, 675-76

James, Henry, 119

Janson, Horst Woldemar, 700

Janson's History of Art, 700

Jarvis, Anna, 752

jazz and R&B
"best of" lists, 692-94
online sites, 692
recommended, 685, 688

Jefferson, Thomas, 359, 753

Jerome, Jenny, 160

jet lag, 498

Jimi Hendrix Experience, 684

Joao Gilberto (Gilberto), 688

job hunting, 367-73
best and worst industries for jobs, 378
health science majors, 374-75
honing skills, 370-73
internships, 374
networking online, 367-70
rejection, 368
SAT scores and, 368
service industry jobs, 375-79
Web sites for, 369

job interviews, 373-74

résumé terms to avoid, 372
résumés that work, 373-74
what not to do, 371

job transfers, 388-89
abroad, 388-89
better offer, 394-95
dismissal, 397
exit strategy, 396
headhunters, 395-96
resigning, 397-99
Web sites, 389

Jobim, Antonio Carlos, 685-86

Jobs for the Future, 345, 345-46

Jobs Rated Almanac (National Business Employment Weekly), 391

John Adams (McCullough), 704

John Henry Days (Whitehead), 703

John Scheepers Kitchen Garden Seeds, 455, 458

Johnny's Selected Seeds, 442, 455

Johnson, Hugh, 150

Johnson, Lyndon B., 746

Johnson, Robert, 685

Johnson Wax building, 701

Jones, Amanda, 480

Jones, Edward P., 705

Jones, Loree Jon, 642

Jordan, Sandra, 334

Joseph, Chief, 384

Journal of Economic Perspectives, 306

Journal of Endocrinology, 36

Journal of Financial Planning, 201

Journal of the American Dietetic Association, 8

Journal of the American Medical Association, 25, 117

Journal of Woman's Health, 40

Judd, Donald, 697

Judt, Tony, 707

Juilliard, 347

Julian Alps (Slovenia)
hiking, 571

Jupiter, 727

Jura Mountains (French-Swiss border), 636

jury duty, 783-84

K

Kabul (Afghanistan)
as travel destination, 577-78

Kafka On the Shore (Murakami), 707

Kang, Lawler, 398

Kansas City Chiefs, 591

Kansas City Royals, 583

Kantrowitz, Mark, 349

Kaplan, 337-38

Karasu, Marc, 396

Karenga, Maulana, 756

Karp, Dr. Harvey, 83-84

Kase, Larina, 388

Kauai
as travel destination, 528-29

Kauai Revealed (Doughty), 528

Kaufman, Donald, 421

Kaufman, Dr. Howard L., 25

Kazakhstan
as travel destination, 579

Keillor, Garrison, 795

Keller, Laurie, 334

Kelley, David E., 359

Kellogg, Dr. John Harvey, 119

Kennebec Company, 417

Kennebec River (ME)
white-water rafting, 576

Kennedy, John F., 778

Kennedy, William, 704

Kenny, Bernadette, 398

Kentucky Derby, 592

Kentucky Derby Mint Juleps, 162

Kenya
safaris in, 461-62
trekking in, 564

Key, Francis Scott, 752

Khwarizmi, Muhammad ibn Musa al-, 770

Khrushchev: The Man and His Era (Taubman), 705

King, Martin Luther, Jr., 384, 749-50

King's College Library (Cambridge), 708

Kinney, Molly S., 332

Kinsey, Alfred, 36

Kiplinger's Personal Finance, 260

Kirov Ballet, 691

kitchen utensils. *See* recipes and utensils

kitchens
lighting, 424
renovations, 416-18
renovations, cost of, 417
stovetops, 417

Kitten's First Full Moon (Henkes), 334

Kiyosaki, Robert, 172

Kligman, Dr. Albert, 27-28

Klimt, Gustav, 302

Kloster, Knut U., Jr., 218

knee injuries, 20
Known World, The (Jones), 705
Kolb, Deborah, 395
Koolhaas, Rem, 701
Koop, C. Everett, 50
Koyaanisqatsi (Glass), 684
Kozinn, Allan, 681, 683-85
Kraemer, William, 17
Kraeutler, Thomas, 410, 434
Kramer, Felix, 263
Kramer, Larry, 340
Kramer, Matt, 150
Kreon (track lighting), 425
Kröller, Anton, 699
Kröller-Müller (Otterlo, The Netherlands), 699
Kröller-Müller, Helene, 699
Krueger, Alan B., 189
Krumholz, Dr. Harlan M., 52
Kunkel, Benjamin, 364
Kwanzaa, 756
Kyrgyzstan
  as travel destination, 579

L

La Cucina di Lidia (Bastianich), 579
La Ruta Maya (Mundo Maya), 559-60
La Traversée Internationale du Lac Saint-Jean, 641
LaBonte, Andrew, 425-27
Labor Day, 753-54
Labrador retrievers, 474
  congenital defects, 475
lamb, roasting and broiling, 139
lampshades
  trimming, 424
Lanai
  as travel destination, 529-30
Lancet magazine, 53
Laos
  as travel destination, 519
laptops
  data backup, 288-90
  vs. desktop, 283
  digital cameras and, 299
  warranties, 252, 253
Larson, Jeanette, 332-33
Lassen Volcanic National Park, 548
Late Talker: What to Do If Your Child Isn't Talking Yet, The (Agin/Geng/Nicholl), 88
Latjes, Ad, 494
Laughlin, Terry, 616
Laughren, Dr. Thomas, 90
Laumann, Edward O., 40
Lavoe, Hector, 688

law school
  admissions, 359
  rankings, 360
Law School Admissions Council, 361
lawns, 467-70
  microclimate, foot traffic and maintenance, 469-70
  without chemicals, 467-69
  See also flowers; garden diseases and pests; planting; pruning; trees; vegetables
Lawson, Nigella, 137
lead, 437-38
leadership, 382-85
  books on, 383-84
  See also executives; office politics; stress management
leaky roof, fixing, 435
leap years, 756
Learning to Read: The Great Debate (Chall), 320
LeBlanc, Adrian Nicole, 705-6
Lechter, Sharon L., 172
Leeds, Adrian, 223
leg raises, 16
legal system, 783-90
  child guardianship, 788-89
  court, 784, 786
  divorce, 787
  F.B.I. files, 786-87
  jury duty, 783-84
  legal terminology, 784
  living wills, 790
  most wanted Web sites, 783
  name, legally changing, 788
  small claims, 785
  wills, 789-90
legal terminology, 784
Legend (Marley), 687
legislation, 778
Leibniz, Baron Gottfried Wilhem von, 770
Leitch, Marilyn, 57-59
LeMon, Cal, 388
lemon-law rights, 278
Lennon, John, 786
Lenz, Dolly, 207
Leonard, Dave, 417
Les Saintes
  as travel destination, 525
Let It Bleed (Rolling Stones), 686
Lethem, Jonathan, 705
Letter from A Birmingham Jail (King, Jr.), 384
letter-writing, 796

Leverrier, Urbain, 728
Levine, Arthur E., 330
Levitra, 42-44
Levitt, Arthur, Jr., 198
Levitt, Steven D., 189
Lewis, Amy B., 24
Lewis, Joy, 796
Lewis, Marlyn McGrath, 344
Libby, Tom, 262
libraries, 708
  See also books
Library of Congress, 708
Lieberman, Simma, 387
Lief, Brett, 348
life expectancy, 226
life insurance, 226-28
  health and, 227
  life expectancy in U.S., 226
  mail-order, 235
  for singles, 235
light bulbs
  fluorescent, 425
  H.I.D. (high intensity discharge), 425
  incandescent, 425
  quartz and tungsten halogen, 425
Lightning Thief, The (Riordan), 333
lighting, 423-24
  bathroom, 424
  bedroom, 424
  dining room, 423-24
  entryway, 423
  kitchen, 424
  lamp shades, 424
  living room, 423
  track lighting, 424-25
Lighting Design Sourcebook: 600 Solutions for Residential and Commercial Spaces (Whitehead), 423
Lightolier (track lighting), 424
Lincoln, Abraham, 359, 750-51
Linn's Stamp News, 316
lion attacks, 111
liposuction, 31
Lippincott, Jenifer, 175
Lipsitt, Lewis, 331
Lipson, Eden Ross, 332
liquor. *See* spirits
liquor cabinet, stocking, 161-63
Lissner, Stéphane, 690
Lithgow, John, 358
Lithuania
  as travel destination, 580
Liu, Jae Soo, 335
Live at the Village Vanguard (Coltrane), 688
living room lighting, 423

Living to Tell the Tale (Márquez), 705
living wills, 790
Liz's Antique Hardware, 413
Lo, Andrew W., 362
lobster, cooking, 140
local government
  employment with, 378
Lockwood, Charles, 413
lodging, 504-12
  Manhattan hotels, 507
  monasteries, 512
  most charming inns, 504-12
  private hotels, 508
  top hotels, 506
  vacation rental agencies, 510-12
London
  dining, 534
  family travel and, 533
Lonely Planet Guides, 516, 519, 571
long-term care insurance, 234-35
Longwood Gardens, 473
Looe Keys (Florida), 618
looping (teacher promotion), 330
Lord of the Flies (Golding), 385
Los Angeles Angels of Anaheim, 584
Los Angeles Clippers, 593
Los Angeles Dodgers, 588
Los Angeles Kings, 595
Los Angeles Lakers, 593
Lost Painting, The (Harr), 707
lottery odds, 173
Louisiana Museum (Denmark), 697
Louvre (Paris), 535, 698
Love That Dog (Creech), 335
Lovejoy, Thomas, 558
low fat diets, 117
Lowell, Percival, 728
Lubienski, Christopher, 326
Lubienski, Sarah Theule, 326
Lucerne Festival, 694
Ludwig, Sarah, 207, 209
lunar eclipse, 723, 732-33
lunges, 16
Lupberger, David, 411
Luxe City Guides, 521
Lyncheski, John, 393
Lys, Thomas Z., 206

M

M.M.O.'s (massively multiplayer online games), 644-45
Macintosh computers, 284

backup software, 286-87
  discounts, 283
  repair, 291
  software that converts file formats, 286
  See also computers; Windows-based computers
MacMillan, Margaret, 704-5
McCalman, Max, 154
McCarty, Peter, 335
McCullough, David, 704
McEwan, Ian, 704, 707
McGowan, Dr. Joan, 123
McGuire, Peter, 753
McInerney, Jay, 795
McKnight, Hugh, 573
McMullan, Kate, 335
McWhorter, Diane, 333
Madam President (Thimmesh), 334
Madlenka's Dog (Sis), 335
magnesium, 125
mah-jongg, 649
Mah Jongg Made Easy, 649
maintenance. *See* home maintenance
makeup, anti-aging, 24
makeup tips, 29-30
Making Sense of Wine (Kramer), 150
Malawi, safaris in, 563
Malkiel, Burton, 191
Mamet, David, 385
mammograms, 58-59
Man Who Walked Between the Towers, The, 334
managerial personnel
  changing profile of, 382
  salaries, 379
  women and minorities, 382-83, 399
  See also leadership; office politics; stress management
Managing the Emotional Homeowner (Lupberger), 411
manatees, 554
manicurist, tipping, 250
Manix, Jack and Karen, 442
map symbols, 807
margarita recipe, 160-61
mariners' measure, 767-68
marketing salaries, 380
Marks, Stephanie L., 370-73
Marley, Bob, 687
Márquez, Gabriel García, 705
Mars, 726-27
Marsalis, Wynton, 685
Marshall, George C., 357
Marshall & Swift/Boeckh, 231
Marshall Scholarship, 357
Martin, Agnes, 697

Martin, Roger L., 264
Martin's Big Words: The Life of Dr. Martin Luther King, Jr. (Rappaport), 335
martini recipe, 159-60
Marx, Karl, 248
Mascagni, Pietro, 689
Masefield, John, 384
Mass in B Minor (Bach), 683
Massachusetts Institute of Technology
    Sloan School of Management, 361-62
Master, The (Toibin), 706
Masters, the, 590, 592
Masters and Johnson, 36
Masters School (Dobbs Ferry), 329
math education
    public vs. private schools, 326
mathematical signs, 770
mathematics, 70-72
    algebra, 770-71
    fractions and decimal equivalents, 772
    geometry, 772-74
    mathematical signs, 770
    Roman numerals, 771
Matheson, Hugo, 143
Matis, Dr. Bruce A., 35
mattresses
    coil count, 428
    cover, 428
    foam mattresses, 429
    foundation, 428
    padding, 428
    space, 428
    support, 428
    warranties, 428-28
    waterbeds, 429
    wire gauge, 428
Mayreau
    as travel destination, 525-26
measuring without ruler, 762
mechanics, salaries of, 381
media mail, 253
medical school
    applicant resources, 361
Medical Students' Resource Guide, 361
medicine. *See* doctors and medicine
Medicine & Science in Sports & Exercise, 17
Meet Market Adventures, 530
Melanoma (Poole/Guerry), 25
Melanoma Book, The (Kaufman), 25
melanomas, checking for, 25

Melanson, Edward, 16
Melville, Herman, 384
Memorial Day, 752
men
    and heart disease, 52-55
    and home buying, 206
Menand, Louis, 704
Mendelssohn, Felix, 683
Menil Collection (TX), 697
menopause, 38-40
    sex life changes and, 40
mental health, 61-64
    depression, real nature of, 63
    depression and anxiety, relief from, 61-64
    holiday depression, 62
Mercury, 726
merlot wines
    Italian, 152
    South American, 153
metacritic.com, 692
metamorphic rocks, 719
Metaphysical Club, The (Menand), 704
Methner, Brian, 180
MetLife Mature Market Institute, 234
metric units, 764
    converting to U.S. customary units, 766-67
Metropolitan Museum of Art (NYC), 698
Mexican free-tailed bats, 556
Mexican League, 584
Mexico
    pyramids in, 560-61
Mexico City
    real estate values in, 222
Meyer, Mary K., 804
Miami Dolphins, 591
Miami Heat, 593
Micheli, Dr. Lyle J., 68
Michelin Guides, 516
microdermabrasion, 30-31
Middlesex (Eugenides), 704
miles to kilometers, 766
Millay, Edna St. Vincent, 503
Milwaukee Brewers, 586
Milwaukee Bucks, 593
minerals, 123-25
    calcium 123-24
    common, 718
    copper, 124
    iodine, 124
    iron, 124-25
    magnesium, 125
    phosphorus, 125
    potassium, 125
    zinc, 125
Minnesota Timberwolves, 593
Minnesota Twins, 583-84

Minnesota Vikings, 591
Minnesota Wild, 595
mini-strokes, 53-54
    handicapping, 53
Miralles, Enric, 701
Misdiagnosis and Dual Diagnosis of Gifted Children and Adults (Webb), 321
Miss Bridie Chose a Shovel (Connor), 334
Missouri Botanical Garden, 473
Mitchell, Scott, 307
Mittermeier, Russell, 558
Moag-Stahlberg, Alicia, 325
Moffatt, Michael, 350
moisturizer, 27-28
mojito cocktail recipe, 163
moles, 25
Molokai
    as travel destination, 529
Monaco
    family travel and, 536
monarch butterfly migration, 559
money, 166-244
    insurance, 226-36
    investing, 181-201
    personal finance, 166-80
    real estate, 202-24
    tax audits, 243, 244
    tax planning, 237-44
Money Masters of Our Time (Train), 192
money orders, 254
Money Pit, The (radio show), 410
Monk, Thelonious, 685
Monopoly, 645-47
monounsaturated fat, 117
Montenegro
    as travel destination, 580
Montreal
    real estate values in, 222
Montreal Canadiens, 595, 596
moon, 733
    lunar eclipses, 723, 732-33
    phases of, 734-35
    tides, 742-43
    See also astronomy
Moore College of Art and Design (Philadelphia), 347-48
Moos, Dr. Merry-K., 70
Moreno, David, 18
morning after pills, 47
Morningstar, 188
Morone, James, 114
Morris, Mark, 347
Morris the Artist (Segal), 334
Morse, Samuel, 809

Morse code, 809
mortgages, 207-15
    monthly payments, 212, 213
    mortgage market, entering, 207-9
    mortgage options, 210-11
    refinancing, 213-14
    required information, 208
    reverse mortgages, 214-15
    terminology, 212-13
    See also home buying; real estate; opportunities; second homes
Morton, Jelly Roll, 685
Moses, 757
Moses, Michael A., 302
Moss (design store), 421
moss, growing, 473
Moss Acres, 473
Mother's Day, 752
motor homes, 277-78
Motor Sports Hall of Fame, 598
Motorcycle Safety Foundation, 276
motorcycles, 275-77
Mount Fuji (Japan)
    hiking, 570
Mountain Sobek, 571
movies and TV, 666-80
    best DVD's, 673-76
    best movies, 666-71
    best movies for kids, 679-80
    cost of producing, 672
    film festivals, 677-79
    long movies, 676
    online sites, 671
    Oscar parties, 672-73
    Oscar's name, 666
    reality TV shows, 678
Moyers, Susan B., 8
Mozart, Wolfgang Amadeus, 323, 683, 689
Mozilla (Web browser), 290-91
Mufson, Phyllis, 348
muggings
    fending off, 107-9
    insurance and, 235
Muhammad, 757
Muir Woods National Monument (San Francisco), 537
multicultural manners, 797-98
Multicultural Manners: Essential Rules of Etiquette for the 21st Century (Dresser), 797
Munro, Alice, 703, 706
Murakami, Haruki, 707

muscadet wines, 151
Musée Condé (Chantilly, France), 699-700
Musée d'Orsay (Paris), 534
Museum of Contemporary Art (L.A.), 698
Museum of Modern Art (NYC), 697
Museum of Online Museums, 698
museums, 697-700
    modern art, 697-99
    online sites, 698-99
    small European gems, 699-700
music
    and spatial intelligence, 323
music festivals (classical)
    Aix-en-Provence Festival, 694
    Aldeburgh Festival, 694
    Lucerne Festival, 694
    Ojai Music Festival, 696
    Ravinia Festival, 696
    Risor Chamber Music Festival, 694-95
    Salzburg Festival, 695
    Schubertiade Festival, 695
    Tanglewood Festival, 696
    Verbier Festival and Academy, 695
music festivals (general)
    Edinburgh Festival, 694
music festivals (opera)
    Drottningholm Court Theater, 694
    Richard Wagner Festival, Bayreuth, 694
    Rossini Opera Festival, 695
    Santa Fe Opera, 696
    Savonlinna Opera Festival, 695
    Vienna Festival, 695
music festivals (pop & rock)
    Festival au Désert (Afro-pop), 696
    South by Southwest Music event, 695
Music for 18 Musicians (Reich), 687
musical notations, 810
MusicGiants.com, 682
Mustique
    as travel destination, 527
Muth, Jon J., 335
mutual funds, 190-97
    big mutual funds, 196-97
    and the market, 191-92
    mutual fund taxes, 197
    picking, 190-91
    balance sheet, reading, 192-94

terminology, 194-96
total return, estimating, 195
My Food Diary, 5
Myers-Briggs Type Indicator, 366-67
MyTripJournal.com, 518

N

Naegele, Franz Karl, 73
Naismith, Dr. James, 592, 594
Naismith Memorial Basketball Hall of Fame, 598
name, legally changing, 788
Nance, Cynthia E., 340
Nantahala River (NC)
white-water rafting, 577
Napolitano, Janet, 358
Naral Pro-Choice America, 46
Nashville Predators, 595
Nassirian, Barmak, 339
Natchez Trace National Scenic Trail, 553
National Alliance of Concurrent Enrollment Partnerships, 345
National Assessment of Educational Progress, 326
National Association of Counties, 225
National Association of Health Underwriters, 228
National Association of Home Builders, 414
National Association of Insurance Commissioners, 233
National Association of Investors Corporation, 188
National Association of Realtors, 205, 437
National Association of Securities Dealers, 199
National Association of State Comprehensive Health Insurance Plans, 228
National Auctioneers Association, 309
National Baseball Hall of Fame and Museum, 598
National Book Award winners (2000-2005), 702-7
National Center for Alternative Certification, 404
National Center for Catastrophic Sport Injury, 609
National Center for Education Statistics, 345, 352, 362, 403
National Center for Health Statistics, 478

National Center for State Courts, 785
National City Corporation, 206
National Cowboy Hall of Fame, 598
National Do Not Call Registry, 254
National Endowment for the Arts, 698
National Environmental Title Research, 225
National Film Registry, 666, 668
National Football Conference
Arizona Cardinals, 591
Atlanta Falcons, 591
Carolina Panthers, 591
Chicago Bears, 591
Dallas Cowboys, 591
Detroit Lions, 591
Minnesota Vikings, 591
New Orleans Saints, 591
New York Giants, 591
Philadelphia Eagles, 591
St. Louis Rams, 591
San Francisco 49ers, 591
Seattle Seahawks, 591
Tampa Bay Buccaneers, 591
Washington Redskins, 591
National Fresh Water Fishing Hall of Fame, 598
National Gallery, 536
National Geographic Guide to National Parks of the United States, 545
National Institute for Aviation Research, 499
National Institute of Child Health and Human Development, 62
National Institute of Environmental Health, 70
National Institute of Mental Health, 62
National Institute of Standards and Technology, 745-46
National Institutes of Health, 45, 45, 54, 64
National Insurance Crime Bureau, 279
National Jousting Hall of Fame, 598
National League Central
Chicago Cubs, 585-86
Cincinnati Reds, 586
Houston Astros, 586
Milwaukee Brewers, 586
Pittsburgh Pirates, 586
St. Louis Cardinals, 586
National League East
Atlanta Braves, 585

Florida Marlins, 585
New York Mets, 585
Philadelphia Phillies, 585
Washington Nationals, 585
National League West
Arizona Diamondbacks, 586
Colorado Rockies, 588
Los Angeles Dodgers, 588
San Diego Padres, 588
San Francisco Giants, 588
National Mah Jongg League, 649
National Merit Scholarships, 350
National Museum of American History, 536
National Museum of the American Indian, 536
National Museum of Natural History, 536
National Oceanic and Atmospheric Administration, 103, 715
NOAA Weather Radio, 103, 104, 106
National Park Service, 527
Home Page, 545
national parks, 538-53
Acadia National Park, 545-46
Aniakchak National Monument, 548
by state, 549-50
Channel Islands National Park, 548
Cumberland Island National Seashore, 547
Cuyahoga National Park, 544
Grand Canyon National Park, 539-40
Grand Teton National Park, 541, 544-45
Grant-Kohrs Ranch National Historic Site, 547
Great Basin National Park, 547-48
Great Smoky Mountains, 538-39, 541
guides and online sites, 545, 547
Lassen Volcanic National Park, 548
North Cascades National Park, 548
Olympic National Park, 541, 542-43
ranked by size, 539
Rocky Mountain National Park, 541, 542
rustic hotels in, 551-52

trails in, 552-53
Voyageurs National Park, 547
Yellowstone National Park, 541, 542
Yosemite National Park, 540, 542, 625
Zion National Park, 541, 543
See also wildlife
National Parks and Conservation Association, 545
National Parks Electronic Bookstore, 545
National Passport Center, 779
National Postsecondary Student Aid Study of 2003-4, 352
National Public Radio, 292
National Real Estate Investors Association, 224
national scenic trails, 552
National Soccer Hall of Fame and Museum, 598
National Transportation Safety Board, 499
National Weather Service, 103, 106, 716
National Wildlife Federation, 464
natural gas
as alternative energy, 264
Nature, 55, 128, 323
naval time, 745
Naxos, 532
NCAA Final Four, 590
neck injuries, 19
Nepal, trekking in, 566
Neptune, 727-28
Nesbitt, Richard, 344
net worth, calculating, 167
networking (computer), 280-83
firewall programs, 290
New England Journal of Medicine, 70, 78, 124, 129
New England Patriots, 591
New Jersey Devils, 595
New Jersey Nets, 593
New Manners for New Times: A Complete Guide to Etiquette (Baldrige), 795
New Orleans Saints, 591
New Orleans/Oklahoma City Hornets, 593
New Taste of Chocolate, The (Presilla), 145
New Year's Day, 749
New Year's Eve resolutions, 758
New York Botanical Garden, 473
New York City

real estate values in, 221
New York City Compost Project, 137
New York Giants, 591
New York Islanders, 595
New York Knicks, 593
New York Mets, 585
New York Public Library, 708
New York Rangers, 595
New York Stock Exchange, 199
New York Times, 13, 143, 149, 161, 187, 204, 216, 340, 356, 378, 416, 440, 450, 666, 681, 702
crossword puzzle, 804-5
film critics' picks (1975-2005), 667-71
guide to children's movies, 679-80
wedding announcements in, 801
New York Times Book Review, 333, 708
New York Times Parent's Guide to the Best Book for Children (Lipson), 332
New York Yankees, 582
New Zealand
trekking in, 566
NewMusicBox.org, 682
Newsweek magazine, 343
Newton, Sir Isaac, 742, 770
Nextag.com, 247
niacin (vitamin B_3), 120
Nicholl, Malcolm J., 88
Nichols, Peter M., 673
Nigella's Vegetarian Chili with Corn Bread Topping, 144
Nixon, Richard M., 658
nongonococcal urethritis, 43
Nonprofit Academic Centers Council, 402
Nordic Skater, 638
North America
rail travel in, 503
North American Falconers Association, 624
North Carolina
furniture manufacture in, 427
North Cascades National Park, 548
North Country National Scenic Trail, 553
nose reshaping, 31
not-for-profit organizations
employment in, 402
novels, beloved American, 708
Nozze di Figaro, Le (Mozart), 683, 689

NuCrete (decorative concrete), 418
Nurses' Health Study, 39, 40
nursing
employment in, 403
nutrition, 114-16
calorie requirements, 116
diets, 119
U.S.D.A. food guide, 115
See diet and nutrition
NWHQ (Independent artists on the Web), 698

O

O'Connor Dr. Francis, 68
O'Halloran, Greg, 425-26
Oakland Athletics, 584
Oakland Raiders, 591
obesity
and children, 93
in the U.S., 3
Obon Festival (Japan), 757
occupational outlook, 375-78
best and worst industries for jobs, 378
educational services, 379
employment services, 379, 378
food and drink industry, 378
health care, 376
fasting-growing professions, 377
regional job growth, 376
state and local governments, 378
wholesale trade, 378
Ocoee River (TN)
white-water rafting, 577
Official Scrabble Players Dictionary, 647
Official Scrabble Puzzle Book, The (Edley), 647
office politics, 385-88
boss, disagreeing with, 387-88
bully bosses, 385-87
office magpie, dealing with, 388
Ojai Music Festival, 696
Okamura, Maile, 347
Okeh Ellington, The (Ellington), 688
Old Country, The (Gerstein), 333
Oldman, Mark, 374, 394
olive oil, 128
Olivia Saves the Circus (Falconer), 335
Olympic National Park, 541, 542-43
On Beauty (Smith), 707
One Green World, 467

One Palestine Complete: Jews and Arabs Under the British Mandate (Segev), 703
online, 290-91
air-fare bargains, 492-94
browser alternatives, 290-91
cheap access, 289
eBay, 247, 310
e-mail, 284, 289
firewall programs, 290
identity theft and, 255
Internet phone service, 296-98
job hunting, 367-70
M.M.O.'s (massively multi-player online games), 644-45
movie information, 671
museums, 698-99
podcasts, 292
viruses, 284
VoIP (voice over Internet protocol), 297
See also Internet; Web sites
online banking, 168-70
online dating services, 799
online gaming, 644-45
online shopping, 246-48
bargain hunting, 246
consumer advice, 246
counterfeit goods, 311
price comparison, 246-48
sites for savvy shoppers, 247
See also Web sites
OnStar (global positioning), 272
open wounds
controlling bleeding, 96
opera
festivals, 694-96
online sites, 682
opera houses, 690
recommended, 681-83, 683-85, 689-91
See also classical music
Opera (Web browser), 291
Opera de la Bastille (Paris), 690
Operabase.com, 682
Operacast.com, 682
Operative Dentistry, 35
Opinion Research Corporation, 392
oral contraception, 38
Orbitz.com, 492, 495, 496
Oregon wines
pinot noirs, 156
Oriental rugs, 430
choosing, 317-18
Orlando Furioso (Vivaldi), 691

Orlando Magic, 593
Ornish, Dr. Dean, 118
Orwell, George, 164
Oscar
Oscar's name, 666
parties, 672-73
Oskar Reinhart Collection (Winterhur, Switzerland), 700
Otello (Verdi), 681, 689
Ottawa Senators, 595
Outdoor Industry Association, 627
outdoor travel, 538-63
national parks, 538-53
safaris, 561-63
south-of-the-border, 556-61
wildlife, 554-56
See also adventure; vacation hot spots; traveling
Overture and Excerpts from A Midsummer Dream (Mendelssohn), 683
Oxford, 353
percentage of American students at, 353
Ozone magazine, 694

P

Pacific Crest National Scenic Trail, 553
Packer, George, 707
paint, 421-23
durability of, 412
oil-based vs. latex, 422
Pakistan
trekking in, 566-67
Palais Garnier (Paris), 690
pale ales, 157-58
Pamuk, Orhan, 706
Pan-American Film and Television Festival (Fespaco), 679
Panama City
real estate values in, 222
pantothenic acid (vitamin B5), 120
Pareles, Jon, 685-88
Paris
dining, 534
family travel and, 534-35
real estate values in, 223
Paris 1919: Six Months That Changed the World (MacMillan), 704-05
Paris Opera Ballet, 691
Park Seed Co., 440
Parker, Charlie, 685
parking valet, tipping, 250
Parron, Jose, 28

Passenger and Immigration Lists Index (Filby/Meyer), 804
Passover, 757
passport renewal, 778-79
last minute, 513
Paterson, Richard, 161
Patmos, 532
Paul, Annie Murphy, 366
Payne, Nina, 335
peas, seeds for, 441
pearls, 313-14
clasp test, 313
eye test, 313
tooth test, 313
X-ray test, 314
Peck, Richard, 335
PeerTrainer, 5
Pei, I. M., 421
Peikes, Dr. Heather, 477
Peiss, Kathy, 27
Pell Grants, 350
pelvic inflammatory disease (PID), 43
Pennington, Sam, 303
Pennsylvania Academy of Fine Arts, 348
Pennybacker, Mindy, 136
Peña, Richard, 677
People Could Fly, The (Hamilton), 334
Pergolesi, Giovanni, 690-91
periodic table of elements, 769
Perkins, Ed, 495
Perkins loans, 349
perpetual calendar, 748-56
personal ad abbreviations, 793
personal budget
figuring, 167
personal finance, 166-80
budgeting, 166-67
children, 173-76
credit, 177-78
debt, 178-80
saving, 168-73
See also insurance; investing; real estate; tax audits; tax planning
Peru, trekking in, 564
pesticides, 135
pet diseases and treatment, 482-86
behavior modification, 485-86
cats, 483
diagnosis and surgery, 486
dogs, 482-83

fleas, 485
pain, patch technology and, 485
vaccinations, 484-85
pet insurance, 236
Peter Grimes (Britten), 681
Petratos, Dr. Marinos, 33
pets, 474-90
birds, 486-99
boarding kennels, 486
cats, 479-82
computer ID, 495
dieting, 478
diseases and treatment, 482-86
DogCatRadio, 481
dogs, 474-79
gerbils, 488-89
pet portraiture, 480
pet supplies, cost of, 489
trusts, establishing for, 490
Petzal, Dave, 621
Pew Internet and American Life Project, 168
Pfeffer, Jeffrey, 263-64
Philadelphia Eagles, 591
Philadelphia Flyers, 595
Philadelphia Phillies, 585
Philadelphia 76ers, 593
Phoenix Coyotes, 595
Phoenix Suns, 593
phones, 296-98
callback services, 514
cellphones, 298
Internet phone service, 296-98
prepaid calling cards, 515
voice over internet protocol (VoIP), 514
phosphorus, 125
phys ed (physical education), 325
Piaget, Jean, 321
Piano, Renzo, 697
pictures
frames, 425-26
hanging, 426-17
mats, 426
Pierre Frey, 431
pillows, 428
Pilsner, 157
pinochle, 660
pinot noirs, 156
Pitchfork, 692
Pittsburgh Penguins, 595
Pittsburgh Pirates, 586
Pittsburgh Steelers, 591
planting, 440-47
cameras as tool, 442
compost, 137, 445
growing zones, 441
seeds and plants, 440

soil and seeding, 442-45, 445, 447
soil pH, 442, 444
springtime rituals, 440-42
See also flowers; garden pests; pruning; lawns; trees; vegetables
plaster
durability of, 412
Plot Against America, The (Roth), 706
plug-in hybrids
as alternative energy vehicles, 262-65
PLUS loans, 349
Pluto, 728, 741
podcasts, 292
Poe, Edgar Allan, 63
poisonings, 99-100
and children, 92
heroin overdoses, 100
insect bites, 99-100
snake bites, 100
poker, 653-58
baseball, 655
five-card stud, 654
high-low poker, 654
high-stakes poker, 655-56
low-hand poker, 654
Omaha, 655
online, 656
poker (five-card draw), 653-54
poker-table manners, 657-58
seven-card stud, 654
Texas hold 'em, 654-55
what beats what, 654
polar bear swimming, 629-30
Polar Bear Night (Thompson), 334
political polls deciphering, 781-82
politics, 780-82
AmeriCorps, 782
campaign contributions, 780
government, contacting, 781
polls, deciphering, 781-82
Web sites, 780
Pollock, Jackson, 348
polygons, 773-74
Polynesia (tall ship), 501
polyunsaturated fat, 117
Pompidou Center (Paris), 699
poodles
congenital defects, 475
miniature poodles, 475
standard poodles, 474
toy poodles, 475-76
pool, 642-44
rules, 643
Z Shafts, 642

Pool & Billiard Magazine, 642
Poole, Catherine M., 25
pop music
"best of" lists, 692-94
recommended, 684-85, 685-88
popcorn, making at home, 132
pork, roasting, 139
Portland Trail Blazers, 593
Post, Emily, 791
post office, 253-54
add-ons, 253
media mail, 253
money orders, 254
priority mail, 253
stamp collecting, 254
stamps, 253-54
stamps, personalized, 254
zip codes, finding, 254
Postwar: A History of Europe Since 1945 (Judt), 707
potassium, 125
potatoes, seeds for, 440-41
Potomac Heritage National Scenic Trail, 553
Pottery Barn, 431
power tools and children, 93
Prado (Madrid), 698
Pratt Institute (Brooklyn), 348
pregnancy, 72-80
deliveries in the afternoon, pain and, 80
delivery room invitees, 80
drugs that can cause problems, 74
due date, figuring, 73
exercise and quick delivery, 79-80
fertilization, 77
fetus growth (8 to 40 weeks), 79
infertility, 77-78
medical checks in womb, 72-76
miscarriage, avoiding another, 76
morning sickness, 78-79
Web sites for a safe pregnancy, 72
preimplantation genetic diagnosis (PGD), 76
Prep (Sittenfeld), 707
pre-school, 320-23
gifted children, identifying, 321-22
how children learn, 321
reading, 320-21
a second language, 322-23
Ptolemy, 770
Public Enemy, 687-88
public gardens, 473
Puccini, Giacomo, 683, 689
Puente, Tito, 688
Puerto Rican League, 584
Pulitzer Prize

See also educational strategies; reading; teaching techniques; testing
President's Day, 750-51
Presilla, Maricel E., 145
Prial, Frank J., 149, 150
Princeton Review, 336-37, 361
Priorat wines, 152-53
priority mail, 253
Privacy Rights Clearinghouse, 256
Pro-Football Hall of Fame, 598
produce and ingredients, 133-38
apples, 134-35
eating locally, 136
environmental considerations, 136-37
fruits, ripening, 134
fruits and vegetables, choosing, 133-24
pesticides, 135
waste into compost, 137
production occupations
salaries of, 381
profession (choosing), 366-67
fastest-growing, 377
Myers-Briggs Type Indicator, 366-67
psychological profiles and, 366
salaries of, 379-80
strong interest inventory, 367
proofreader's marks, 811
prostate cancer, 60-61
diagnosis and treatment, 60-61
fitness and prostate, 60
tomatoes and, 61
prosthesis implantation and erectile dysfunction, 42
Provensen, Alice, 334
pruning, 463-64
delaying blooming, 463
tool sources, 464
tools, 464
trees, 466
See also flowers; garden diseases and pests; lawns; planting; trees; vegetables

winners for literature (2000-2005), 702-7
pulse rate, checking, 17
Punta del Este, 527
Punxsutawney Phil, 750
Purcell, Henry, 683
Pusan International Film Festival (Korea), 678
Putnam Investments, 406
pyramids, 559-61
Guatemala, 561
Honduras, 561
Mexico, 560-61
pyroxidine (vitamin B6), 120-21
Pythagoras, 770
Pythagorean theorem, 773

Q

quadrilaterals, 773
quartz and tungsten halogen light bulbs, 425
Quebec City
real estate values in, 222
Quesnel, Dr. Nadia-Marie, 26

R

R.S.V.P., 796
R.V.'s, 277-79
four-wheel-drive, 278-79
Race Across America, 641
radical races, 640-41
Badwater, 640
Iditarod Sled Dog Race, 640
Ironman Triathlon, 640-41
La Traversée Internationale du Lac Saint-Jean, 641
Race Across America, 641
Raid Series, 641
Vendee Globe, 641
Radicati Group, 392
Radiesse injections, 32
radon, 437
Rago, David, 308
Raid Series, 641
rail porter, tipping, 250
rail travel, 501-4
Europe, 503
North America, 503
Russia, 503
Scotland, 503-4
Southern Africa, 503
tickets on the Web, 504
See also flying; sailing
rain forests, 558-59
Andes, 558-59
Brazil, 559
Costa Rica, 558

eco-sensitive expeditions, 558
Rainey, Hal G., 387-88
Raintree Nursery, 467
Rainville, Dr. James, 68
Raising Cain (Thompson), 329
RAM (computer), 283-84
Ramadan, 757
Ramakrishnan, Aditi, 325
Random Family: Love, Drugs, Trouble and Coming of Age in the Bronx (LeBlanc), 705-6
Random Walk Down Wall Street, A (Malkiel), 191
Rappaport, Doreen, 335
Rathmann, Peggy, 334
Ratliff, Ben, 688
Rauscher, Frances, 323
Raver, Anne, 440, 454-55, 457-59
Ravinia Festival, 696
Reader's Digest New Illustrated Guide to Gardening, 472
reading
best books, 333-35
K through 12, 332-35
pre-school, 320-21
summertime, 331-33
See also books; educational strategies; preschool; teaching techniques; testing
ReadyMade magazine, 438
ReadyMade How to Make (Almost) Everything: A Do-It-Yourself Primer (Berger/Hawthorne), 438
Reagan, Ronald, 750
real estate, 202-24
home buying, 202-6
mortgages, 207-15
opportunities, 220-25
second homes, 215-20
See also insurance; investing; personal finance; tax audits; tax planning
real estate opportunities, 220-25
commercial real estate, 224-25
foreclosure sales, 220-21
foreign laws and, 222
international market, 221-23
out-of-country retirement, 223-24
See also home buying; mortgages; second homes
real estate sales

employment in, 403-4
reality TV shows, 678
recipes and utensils, 130-32
cast iron, 132-33
essential utensils, 131
recipes, evaluating, 130
Teflon, 132
Recruiting New Teachers, 404
Reed, Phillip, 275
Reel Biography, 373
reflexology (foot massages), 67
refurbished goods, 252
Regalbuto, Robert, 512
Roger, Fred, 300
Regina, Elis, 685-86
Registered Traveler Program, 497
Reich, Lee, 134-35
Reich, Steve, 687
Reinhart, Matthew, 333
Reinhart, Oskar, 700
Reinstein, Gila, 341
Reithel, Brian, 402
relationship rules, 793
religious holidays (selected)
Ash Wednesday (Christian), 757-58
Christmas Day (Christian), 759
Dewali (Hindu), 759
Easter (Christian), 757
Hanukkah (Jewish), 759
Passover (Jewish), 757
Ramadan (Islamic), 757
Rosh Hashanah (Jewish), 757
Yom Kippur (Jewish), 757
remodeling
emotional reacting to, 411
kitchens, 416-18
pros and cons, 411
stovetops, 417
See also home remodeling
Remodeling Magazine, 417
Rendezvous Huts (Methow Valley, Washington), 635-36
renegotiable-rate mortgages, 211
Renova, 24
rental car insurance, 235
repairers, salaries of, 381
Reppy, William, A., Jr., 490
rescue breathing, 95
Residential Lighting: A Practical Guide (Whitehead), 423
Resnik, Dr. Barry, 35
restaurant tipping, 250
Restylane injections, 32
résumés, 373-74

terms to avoid, 372
videotaping, 373
Retin-A, 27
retinol, 27
retirement, 199-201
calculating needs, 200-201
401(k), 199-200
out-of-country, 223-24
retrievers
golden retrievers, 474
Labrador retrievers, 474
reverse-annuity mortgage, 211
Revolver magazine, 693
Reynolds, Arthur, 321
rhino attacks, 111
Rhino Catalog, 692
Rhode Island School of Design, 348
Rhodes, Cecil, 356-57
Rhodes, Nancy, 322
Rhodes fellowship, 356-57
Rhône wines, 151
riboflavin (vitamin B2), 120
Rich Dad, Poor Dad (Kiyosaki/Lechter), 172
Richard Wagner Festival, Bayreuth, 694
Richer, Ray, 635
Richter, Charles, 721
Richter, Gerhard, 697
Richter scale, 721
Ridley, Matt, 702
Right Management Consultants, 403
right triangles, 773
Rijksmuseum (Amsterdam), 698
Rimbaud (Robb), 703
Rinaldo (Handel), 690
Rio Grande (NM)
white-water rafting, 576
Rioja wines, 152
Riordan, Rick, 333
Riotte, Louise, 460
Ripken, Cal, Jr., 607-8
Risor Chamber Music Festival, 694-95
Ritalin, 90
river trips, 573-77
canal cruisers, renting, 574
England, 573
France, 573-74
Germany, 574
Ireland, 573
Scotland, 573
Road Ahead, The (Gates), 658
Robb, Graham, 703
Roberts, James A., 176
Roberts, Dr. Janet L., 34

Robins, Yolanda, 223
Robinson, Jancis, 150
Robinson, Marilynne, 706
Roche, Gerard R., 382, 395-96
Rochester Institute of Technology, 400
rock and roll festivals, 694
Rock and Roll Hall of Fame, 686-87
rock climbing, 625-27
basic knots, 626
rocks, 717-19
igneous rocks, 718-19
metamorphic rocks, 719
sedimentary rocks, 719
Rockwell, John, 694
Rocky Mountain National Park, 541, 542
Rocky Mountain elk, 554
Rodin Museum (Paris), 534
Rogaine, 34-35
Rolling Stone, 692
Rolling Stones, 685, 686
Roman numerals, 771
Rondane Mountains (Norway), 636
Ronniger's (potato farm), 441
roof
fixing leaky, 435
roofing materials
durability of, 412
Roosevelt, Franklin D., 755
Roosevelt, Theodore, 351
Roots magazine, 693
Roscoe (Kennedy), 704
rosé wines, 153
roses
disease-resistant varieties, 449
growing, 447-49
homemade fungus preventions spray, 448
scented, 451-52
terminology, 451
training, 450
Rosh Hashanah, 757
Ross, Alex, 682
Rossini, Gioacchino, 689
Rossini Opera Festival, 695
Rossouw, Dr. Jacques, 114
Rotberg, Robert I., 357
Roth, Philip, 702, 706
Rounds, Michael, 46-47
Rovos Rail, 504
ROW International, 556
rowing machines, 14
Rowling, J. K., 333
Royal Ballet, 691
Royal Canadian Pacific, 503
Royal Opera House at Covent Garden (London), 690

Royal Scotsman, 503-4
Rules of Neighborhood Poker According to Hoyle, The, 657
rum, 162
mojito cocktail, 163
Rum & Reggae's French Caribbean (Runge), 525
Runaway (Munro), 706
Rundle, Dr. John, 720-21
Runge, Jonathan, 525
running shoes, 21
Russell, Dr. Robert M., 123
Russia
rail travel in, 503
Rust, Mathias, 331
Ruth, Babe, 306
Ryder Walker Alpine Adventures, 630

S

Saba
as travel destination, 526
Sabuda, Robert, 333, 334
Sacks, Oliver, 704
Sacramento Kings, 593
Sacred Hoops: Spiritual Lessons of a Hardwood Warrior (Jackson), 18
Safari (Web browser), 291
safari travel agents, 562
safaris, 561-63
best game-watching, 563
Botswana, 562-63
Kenya, 461-62
Malawi, 563
Tanzania, 562
Uganda, 562
Zambia, 563
Zimbabwe, 563
Sage, Lorna, 704
sailing
cruises, 502
freighter travel, 501, 503
tall ships, 501
See also flying; rail travel
St. Augustine, 744
St. Louis Blues, 595
St. Louis Cardinals, 586
St. Louis Rams, 591
St. Lucia, 757
St. Nicholas, 757
St. Patrick, 751
St. Patrick's Day, 751
St. Valentine, 750
salaries, 378-82
administrative support, 380
construction trades, 381
executive, administrative and managerial, 379
marketing and sales, 380

mechanics, installers and repairers, 381
production, 381
professional specialty, 379-80
raises, 393-94
service occupations, 380-81
technicians, 380
sales
as occupation, 249-50
sales personnel
salaries of, 380
Salisbury, John, 119
Salmon River (ID)
white-water rafting, 575
Salvesen, Dr. Kjell A., 80
Salzburg Festival, 695
Samuel Pepys: The Unequalled Self (Tomalin), 706
San Antonio Spurs, 593
San Diego Chargers, 591
San Diego Padres, 588
San Francisco
family travel and, 537
San Francisco Botanical Garden at Strybing Arboretum, 473
San Francisco 49ers, 591
San Francisco Giants, 588
San Francisco Museum of Modern Art, 698
San Jose Sharks, 595
sandhill cranes, 554-55
Santa Fe Opera, 696
Santa Lucia (Sweden), 757
SAT (Scholastic Aptitude Test)
and job hunting, 368
new scoring system, 336
perfect score, 336-37
preparation for, 337-38
See also College Board
satellite radio, 293
saturated fat, 117, 118
Saturday (McEwan), 707
Saturn, 727
sauvignon blancs from California, 155
saving, 168-73
books on, 172
compounding interest, 168
currency design, 171
getting rich quick, 172-73
lottery odds, 173
online banking, 168-70
personal savings rate, 168
Swiss bank accounts, 170-71
Savonlinna Opera Festival, 695

Sawyer, Deborah, 368
Sayre, Dr. Michael, 94
scabies, 43
scallops, cooking, 140
scalpers, 590
Schaeffer, Bob, 337, 338
Schelling, Thomas C., 758
Schneider, June, 691
School of the Museum of
    Fine Arts (Boston),
    348
School of Visual Arts (NYC),
    347
schooling (K through 12),
    220-35
    college credits in high
        school, 345-46
    pre-school, 320-23
    reading, 332-35
    strategies, 323-25
    teaching techniques, 329-
        32
    testing, 326-29
    See also college and grad
        school
Schubert, Franz, 682
Schubertiade Festival, 695
Schulman, Cathy, 672
science, 709-74
    astronomy, 722-43
    chemistry and math, 769-
        72
    geology, 717-21
    geometry, 772-74
    time and dates, 744-62
    weather forecasting, 710-
        17
    weights and measures,
        762-68
science, succeeding in, 324
Science magazine, 729
Scieszka, Jon, 335
scooters, 277
SCORE (Service Corps of
    Retired Executives),
    404
Scotch, 161
Scotland
    rail travel in, 503-4
    river trips, 573
Scott, A. O., 673-74
Scott, Cynthia, 390
Scott, Gini Graham, 388
Scrabble, 647-48
Sculptra injections, 32
scurvy, 119
Sea Cloud (tall ship), 501
Seaman, Barrett, 350
Search2cruise.com, 502
Seattle Seahawks, 591
Seattle SuperSonics, 593
Sebald, W. G., 703
second careers, 400-406

retirees and, 406
self-employment, 404-6
top five choices, 402-4
second homes, 215-20
    homesteading, 218-20
    priciest vacation homes,
        216-18
    See also home buying;
        mortgages; real
        estate; opportunities
second languages
    children learning, 322-23
secondhand market, 251-52
    books, 251, 708
    DVD's, 251
    exercise equipment, 251
    refurbished goods, 252
    video games, 251
secondhand smoke
    and children, 92
Secrets of the Millionaire
    Mind (Eker), 172
sedimentary rocks, 719
Seed Savers Exchange, 440,
    442, 455
seeds and plants, 440
    heirloom seeds, 455
Seeds of Change, 440
Seeing in the Dark: How
    Backyard Stargazers
    Are Probing Deep
    Space and Guarding
    Earth from Interplan-
    etary Peril (Ferris),
    705
Segal, Lore, 334
Segev, Tom, 703
Selective Service System,
    780
self defense, 107-9
    basic moves, 108
    muggings, fending off,
        107-9
semaphore code, 809
Seneca Rocks (West Virginia)
    rock climbing at, 626
Serifos, 530-31
Serra, Richard, 697
Serva Padrona, La (Per-
    golesi), 690-91
service industry, 375-79
    educational services, 379
    employment services,
        379, 378
    food and drink industry,
        378
    health care, 376
    salaries of, 380-81
    state and local govern-
        ments, 378
    wholesale trade, 378
service warranties, 252-53,
    284

7 Things Your Teenager Won't
    Tell You (And How to
    Talk About Them Any-
    way) (Lippincott), 175
Sexton, Mike, 656
sexuality, 36-47
    abortion, 46-47
    contraception, 38-39
    erectile dysfunction, 41-
        44
    hormones, 36-38
    menopause, 38-40
    sexual diseases, 42-46
    See also appearance;
        children; doctors and
        medicine; first aid and
        survival; fitness
sexually transmitted disease
    (STD), 42-46
    See also HIV/AIDS
Sgt. Pepper's Lonely Hearts
    Club Band (Beatles),
    684
Shackelford, Geoff, 603
Shaker Workshops (furniture
    kits), 427
Shakespeare, William, 384
Shanghai, 521-22
    real estate values in,
        222-23
    restaurants, 522
Shapiro, Evan, 393
shared-appreciation mort-
    gages, 211
Sharkey, Joe, 517
Sharpe, William F., 316
Shaw, Gordon, 323
Shawangunk Mountains (New
    York)
    rock climbing at, 626-37
Shay, Kristine, 344
Shayne, Cameron, 18
shellfish
    cooking, 140
    See also fish
shelves, 420-21
Sheraton furniture, 305
Sherman, Don, 273
Sherman, William Tecumseh,
    658
Shiller, Robert J., 202-4
Shinagel, Michael, 355
ships. See sailing
shock, 96-97
shooting stars, 723
shopping, 248-54
    conspicuous consump-
        tion, 248-49
    post office bargains, 253-
        54
    sales and bargains, 249-
        50
    secondhand market, 251-
        52
    spending habits, 248

tipping, 250-51
    warranties, 252-53
    See also online shopping
Shore, Miles F., 357
Shortill, Laura, 355
shoulder injuries, 20
shrimp, cooking, 140
Shuffle Up and Deal (Sexton),
    656
siding durability
    aluminum, 412
    vinyl, 412
    wood, 412
Siegel, Jeremy J., 181
Siegel, Dr. Marc K., 159
Sieh, Dr. Kerry, 720
signs and symbols, 807
    American sign language,
        812
    Braille system, 812
    emoticon, 811
    international road signs,
        807
    map symbols, 807
    Morse code, 809
    musical notations, 810
    proofreader's marks, 811
    semaphore code, 809
    symbols of distress, 808
    tracking codes, 808
silver hallmarks, 314-15
Simmons, Katherine E., 395
Simmons, Ruth J., 358
single-sex school, 329-30
Singles Travel International,
    530
Sinter Klass (The Nether-
    lands), 757
Sis, Peter, 334, 335
Sittenfeld, Curtis, 707
Siza, Alvaro, 701
skating, 638-40
    boots and blades, 640
    figure skating, 638-40
    wild skating, 638
skiing, 632-36
    cross-country, 632, 634-
        36
    resorts, 633
    skis, buying, 634
skiing (top choices)
    Alaska, 632
    Alps, 632
    Aspen, 632
    Tuckerman's Ravine (New
        Hampshire, 632
    Whistler/Blackcomb, 632
Skiing Magazine, 632
skijoring, 637-38
skin damage, 23-26
    aging wars, 23-25
    anti-aging makeup, 24

clothing and ultraviolet
    rays, 27
    moles, 25
    sunscreens, 26-27
skin luminizers, 30
skin protection, 635
Skoglund, Marilyn, 359
Sky & Telescope, 730
slate roofs
    durability of, 412
Slow Boat Through Germany
    (McKnight), 573
Small Business Development
    Center, 404
small claims court, 785
Smart Bells, 12
SmarterTravel.com, 492
Smith, Adam, 248
Smith, Kerry, 255
Smith, Zadie, 703, 707
Smith & Hawken (garden
    tools), 464
Smithson, Robert, 697
smoking
    and aging, 23
    and children, 92
snake bites, 100
Snake River (WY)
    white-water rafting, 575
snoring, 68-69
snorkeling, 617-18
Snow (Pamuk), 706
snowboarding, 630-31
    terminology, 631
snowmobiling, 629
Snowshoe Experience, The
    (Walter), 627
snowshoeing, 627-28
Soane, Sir John, 701
SOAR (Seminars on Aeroanxi-
    ety Relief), 497
social predicaments, 793-96
Social Security Administra-
    tion, 779-80
Social Security card, 779-80
Social Security number
    identity theft and, 254-55
Social Venture Partners, 241
Society of International Rail-
    way Travelers, 503
sofas, 429
softball, 606-7
soil and seeding, 442-45,
    445, 447
    soil pH, 442, 444
solar eclipse, 723, 731-32
    total, 732
solar system, 722-23,
    726-28
    Earth, 726
    Jupiter, 727
    Kuiper Belt, 728-29
    Mars, 726-27

Mercury, 726
Neptune, 727-28
new discoveries, 728-29
Pluto, 728, 741
Saturn, 727
Uranus, 727
Venus, 726
Xena (2003 UB313), 729, 741
See also astronomy
solids, 774
solitaire, 663-64
Sommer, Henry, 180
Sonoma Cast Stone, 418
Sorvino, Paul, 804
South America
wine industry in, 153
South Beach Diet, 119
South by Southwest Music event, 695
Southeast Asia
as travel destination, 519-21
Southern Africa
rail travel in, 503
Southwind Adventures, 565
Souza, Drew, 797
spades, 662-63
spaniels
congenital defects, 475
English cocker spaniels, 475
Spanish wines, 152-53
SparkPeople, 5
Spaulding, Todd, 274
spending and saving, 246-318
autos, 260-79
collecting, 300-318
consumer info, 246-59
home technology, 280-99
U.S. and, 248
Spin magazine, 694
spirits, 159-63
classic cocktails, 159-61
drinking dos and don'ts, 158
hangover cures, 159
Kentucky Derby Mint Juleps, 162
liquor cabinet, stocking, 161-63
mojito, 163
whiskey-sipping secrets, 161
sports (athlete's guide), 599-641
badminton, 609-10
baseball, 607-8
basketball, 604-6
biking, 614-16
bull riding, 612-13
croquet, 610-11

falconry, 624-25
fishing, 618-21
football, 608-9
golf, 599-603
horseshoes, 611-12
hunting, 621-24
radical races, 640
rock climbing, 625-27
snorkeling, 617-18
softball, 606-7
squash, 606
swimming, 616-17
tennis, 604-5
volleyball, 612
walvers, 641
See also games; winter sports
sports (fan's guide), 582-98
auto racing, 596-97
baseball, 582-88
basketball, 592-93
betting, 594
football, 589, 591
halls of fame, 597-98
hockey, 594-96
tickets, 588-90
Web sites for, 598
sports injuries
and children, 93
Sprint Nextel, 298
SquareTrade Sidebar, 246-47
squash, 606
Stafford loans, 349
stain remover, homemade, 430
stair climbers, 14
stamp collecting
counterfeiting, 316-17
errors and value, 315
the Post Office and, 254
the Web and, 315-17
stamps, 253-54
personalized, 254
Standard & Poor's, 183, 188, 190, 191
Staples, 291
Star Time (Brown), 685
stars
constellations, 724-25
earth, closest stellar neighbors to, 725
Great Winter Circle, 722
Summer Triangle, 722
See also astronomy
Starck, Philippe, 421
stars (night skies)
January, 723
February, 723
March, 724
April, 724
May, 725
June, 725

July, 726
August, 726
September, 727
October, 727
November, 728
December, 728
Staso, Dr. William, 84
state government
employment with, 378
stationary bikes, 14
steak, broiling, 138
Steaming to Bamboola (Buckley), 501
Steig, Jeanne, 335
Steig, William, 334
Stein, Marky, 396-97
Steinberg, Laurence, 331
Steinhart Aquarium (San Francisco), 537
stenciling a floor, 413
Step From Heaven, A (An Na), 335
step-ups, 16
Stephanopoulos, George, 358
Stevens, Mark, 707
Stewart, Martha, 397
Stiglitz, Joseph E., 358
Stipek, Deborah, 321
stocks and bonds, 181-89
age and investing, 184
Warren Buffett on, 187-89
bull markets, 183
diversification, 181-82
economic forecasting, 189
independent stock research, 188
investment clubs, 185
January as barometer, 184-85
real estate vs. stocks, 185-86
10-day difference, 182
timing, 183-84
yield curve, staying ahead of, 187
Stone, Sherril, 477
Storm Prediction Center, 105
Stourton, James, 699
stout, 158
Stovall, Lou, 425-26
Strategies for Smart Car Buyers (Edmunds/Reed), 275
Strauss, Richard, 689
Stravinsky, Igor, 682-83
stress management, 390-92
burnout, 390-91
and commuting, 390
and e-mail, 392
stressful and stressless jobs, 391

strokes
mini-stroke, handicapping, 53
mini-strokes, 53-54
Strong Interest Inventory, 367
Stroud, Jonathan, 334
stuck windows, fixing, 435-36
students (college)
campus reality tours, 339
Facebook.com, 355
partying, 350-51
studying abroad, 352-54
time management, 351-52
study courses (college), 350-58
health science majors, 374-75
law school admissions, 359
studying abroad, 352-54
partying, 350-51
studying abroad, 352-54
costs, 354
credits, 354
financial aid, 354
Rhodes fellowship, 356-57
short-term, 353
Sudden Infant Death Syndrome, 91
sudoku, 664
Summer Solstice, 753
sun
solar eclipses, 723, 731-32
See also astronomy
Sun Protection for Life (Barrow), 27
Sundance Film Festival (Utah), 677
sunscreens, 26-27
Sunshine, Jessica, 729
Super Bowl, 588, 590
surveyor's measure, 768
surveyor's square measure, 768
survival. *See* first aid and survival
survival strategies, 109-12
airplane crash, 109
animal attacks, 111
bears, confronting, 110-11
biological attacks, 111-12
chemical attacks, 112
fire precautions, 110
See also first aid and survival
Swan, Annalyn, 707
Swift, Jonathan, 352
Swingin' Easy (Vaughan), 688

swimming, 616-17
International Swimming Hall of Fame, 597
swimming and surfing safety, 107
swimming pools
durability of, 412
Swiss bank accounts, 170-71
Swiss Bankers Association, 170
Sykes, Dr. Lynn, 719
symbols of distress, 808
Symphony in C (Stravinsky), 682-83
Symphony in Three Movements (Stravinsky), 682-83
Symphony in White No. 2 (Whistler), 700
Symphony No. 4 in A (Mendelssohn), 683
Symphony No. 9 in D minor (Beethoven), 683-84
Symphony of Psalms (Stravinsky), 682-83
Syndecrete (decorative concrete), 418-19
syphilis, 43
Syracuse University
arts education at, 346
syrah wines from California, 155-56

T

T-Mobile, 298
tai chi, 17-18
Taj Mahal, 523
by moonlight, 523
Tajikistan
as travel destination, 579
Take Charge: Fighting Back Against Identity Theft (FTC), 255
Take on the Street (Levitt, Jr.), 198
tall ships, 501
Tampa Bay Buccaneers, 591
Tampa Bay Devil Rays, 582-83
Tampa Bay Lightning, 595
Tanglewood Festival, 696
Tanzania, safaris in, 562
Tarnay, Linda, 347
Tasmania
trekking in, 565-66
Tate Art Gallery (London), 533, 698
Taubman, William, 705
tax audits, 243, 244
See also insurance; investing; personal finance; real estate; tax planning
tax planning, 237-44

accountant, picking, 242
charitable contributions, 241
documentation, 242-44
estate planning, 239
giving circles, 240-42
overlooked deductions, 237-38
tax returns, common errors, 237
tax-saving tips, 239-40
See also insurance; investing; personal finance; real estate; tax planning
Taylor, Dr. Susan C., 34
tea. *See* coffee and tea
teaching
as employment, 404
teaching techniques (K through 12), 329-32
looping (teacher promotion), 330
single-sex school, 329-30
teenage risk-taking, 330-32
See also educational strategies; pre-school; reading; testing
Teatro alla Scala, 690
technicians
salaries of, 380
technology, 280-99
audio and video, 292-96
cameras, 298-99
computers, 280-90
online, 290-91
phones, 296-98
service and energy, 291-92
See also home technology
teenagers
risk-taking, 330-32
spending, 175-76
Teflon, 132
telephone and e-mail directories, 806
Telluride Film Festival (Colorado), 677
temperature conversions, 763
Tennessee Titans, 591
tennis, 604-5
picking a racket, 605
playing smart, 604
tennis shoes, 22
10th Mountain Division Hut Association (Colorado), 634
tequila, 163
Terman, Dr. Michael, 498
terriers, 475
Yorkshire terriers, 476
Terrific (Agee), 333

Terrors of the Table: The Curious History of Nutrition (Gratzer), 119
testing (K through 12), 326-29
expanded testing regimen, 326
homework, helping with, 328
over-active children, 326-29
test anxiety, cures for, 327
See also educational strategies; pre-school; reading; teaching techniques
Texas Rangers, 585
thank-you notes, 797
Thanksgiving Day, 755
thiamin (vitamin B1), 120
Thief Lord, The (Funke), 335
Thimmesh, Catherine, 334
thin air, dangers of, 628
Thomas, Dylan, 334
Thomas, Keron, 331
Thomas, Steve, 411-13
Thompson, Lauren, 334
Thompson, Michael, 329-30
Thompson, Paul D., 14
Thompson, Richard, 684
Thompson, Walter, 12
Thompson & Morgan (seed company), 440, 455
Three Questions, The (Tolstoy/Muth), 335
thunderstorms
surviving, 104-5
tickets, 588-90
Indianapolis 500, 592
Kentucky Derby, 592
the Masters, 590, 592
NCAA Final Four, 590
scalpers, 590
Super Bowl, 588, 590
World Series, 590
tides, 742-43
tiger attacks, 111
Tiger Motorhomes (off-road R.V.), 278-79
Tilden, Samuel J., 160
time, 744-47
brief history of, 744
clocks, 744-46
daylight saving time, 746
geologic time, 761
international time zones, 747
naval time, 745
See also calendars
Time Asia, 520
Time magazine, 480

Time Mastery: How Temporal Intelligence Will Make You a Stronger, More Effective Leader (Clemens/Dalrymple), 383
time measure, 768
Times of London, 664
tipping, 250
hotel maids, 250-51
Tisch School of the Arts (NYU), 347
Tisch, Steve, 673
toast, making a, 800
Toastmasters International, 800
Tobago
as travel destination, 526
Toibin, Colm, 706
toilets
fixing trickling, 436-37
Tokyo Free Guide, 522
Tolstoy, Leo, 335
Tomalin, Claire, 706
tomatoes
and prostate cancer, 61
Tombaugh, Clyde, 728
Tommasini, Anthony, 681-83
Toobin, Jeffrey, 358
tooth whitening, 35
Topol, Dr. Eric, 55
tornadoes, surviving, 105
Toronto
real estate values in, 222
Toronto Blue Jays, 583
Toronto International Film Festival, 677-78
Toronto Maple Leafs, 595
Toronto Raptors, 593
Townsend, Anthony, 394
Townsend, Barbara K., 352
toxins in breast milk, 84
Toyota Prius hybrid, 262-63, 277
tracking codes, 808
Traction Man Is Here! (Grey), 333
Trahan, Marc, 274
Train, John, 192
trans-fatty acids, 117
Trans-Siberian by Private Train, 503
TransUnion (credit bureau), 207
Trappist ales, 158
travel, 492-580
adventure, 564-80
getting there, 492-518
hot spots, 519-38
national treasures, 538-63
travel blogs, 517-18
travel guides, 516
travel incidentals, 512-18
calling home, 514

essential reading, 518
G.S.M. phones, 512-14
Last-minute passports, 513
travelers' illnesses, 515
trip insurance, 515
TravelBlog.org, 517
travelers' illnesses, 515
traveling, 492-518
flying, 492-500
lodging, 504-12
sails and rails, 501-4
See also adventure; travel destinations; vacation hot spots
Travelocity.com, 492, 493, 495, 496
TravelPod.com, 517
Travelzoo.com, 492, 493
Travltips.com, 502
treadmills, 14
Tree of Life, The (Sis), 334
trees, 465-67
adopting, 465
planting, 465-67
pruning, 466
quince trees, 467
See also flowers; garden diseases and pests; lawns; planting; pruning; vegetables
Trek Travel (bike tours), 572
trekking, 564-71
Alaska, 566
Bhutan, 567-68
Greenland, 566
Kenya, 564
Nepal, 566
New Zealand, 566
Pakistan, 566-67
Peru, 564
Tasmania, 565-66
Venezuela, 564-65
See also biking; hiking
triangles, 772-73
trichomoniasis, 43
trickling toilets, fixing, 436-37
Trinity College (Dublin), 352
trip insurance, 515
Trippler, Terry, 497
tropical islands, purchasing, 220
troy weight, 768
True History of the Kelly Gang (Carey), 703
Truman, Harry S., 358, 657
Trump, Donald, 397
tsunamis, 720
surviving, 103
tubal ligation (contraception), 38
Tucker, Steve, 368, 370
tummy tucks, 32

Turkey
as travel destination, 580
turkey (fowl)
carving, 139
roasting, 139
Turkmenistan
as travel destination, 579
Turks and Caicos
as travel destination, 525
TV's
big screen, 294
energy use and, 292-93
selecting, 294-96
201 Great Ideas for Your Small Business (Applegate), 404
Tylenol and liver problems, 54
Tyler, Julia, 362

U

U: Uncut, The (DVD series), 339
U2, 688
Uganda, safaris in, 562
ultrasound, 74-75
ultraviolet radiation, 26-27
clothing and, 27
Uncle Tungsten: Memories of a Chemical Boyhood (Sacks), 704
Uncommon Fruits for Every Garden (Reich), 134-35
Understanding the Impact of Reverse Transfer Students on Community Colleges (Townsend), 352
underwater dive sites
Belize, 526
Dominica, 526
Saba, 526
Tobago, 526
United Nations Day, 754
United States
cities, distance between, 504
citizenship, 776-77
households, net worth of, 166
life expectancy, 226
spending habits, 248
U.S. Bureau of Engraving and Printing, 171
U.S. Census, 804
United States Chess Federation, 324
U.S. citizenship, 776-77
U.S. Curling Association, 627
U.S. customary units, 763-64
converting to metric units, 765-66

U.S. Department of Education, 348
U.S. Department of Labor, 228, 403
U.S. Department of Housing and Urban Development, 437
U.S. Department of Justice, 107
U.S. Department of State, 513
U.S. Fire Administrations, 110
U.S. Geological Survey, 101
United States Golf Association, 600-602
  Web site, 602
United States National Arboretum, 473
U.S. News & World Report, 338-40, 361
U.S. Snowshoe Association, 628
United States Squash Racquets Association, 606
USA Hockey, 629
U.S.D.A. Food Guide, 114, 115, 116
University Commons, 219-20
University of Chicago, 361
University of Illinois in Urbana library, 708
University of Missouri
  Henry W. Bloch School of Business and Public Administration, 362
University of St. Andrews (Scotland)
  percentage of American students at, 353
universities
  admissions considerations, 341-42
  rankings, 338-41
  SAT requirements, 336
UnumProvident, 229
Updike, John, 702
Uranus, 727
used cars
  buying, 261, 261-62
  car leases, 262
  checking, 261
Utah Jazz, 593
Uzbekistan
  as travel destination, 579

V

vacation
  culinary instruction during, 145-47
vacation hot spots, 519-38
  Asia, 519-23
  islands, 523-32
  family travel, 533-37

See also adventure; travel destinations; traveling
vacation rental agencies, 510-12
  France, 510
  Italy, 510
  Scandinavia, 510
  Scotland, 511
  United Kingdom, 511
  United States, 511
  Web sites, 511-12
vacuum constrictor devices and erectile dysfunction, 42
Valentine's Day, 750
Vallao, Paul G., 324
Value Line, 188
Van Dyke's Restorers, 413
Van Gogh, Vincent, 62
Vancouver Canucks, 595
Vanguard Total Stock Market Index Fund, 185
Vargo, Trina, 357-58
Variety, 678
vasectomy, 39
Vatican Library, 708
Vaughan, Sarah, 688
VCR's
  energy use and, 292-93
veal, roasting, 138
vegetables
  choosing, 133-34
  pesticides and, 135
  ripening, 134
  See also fruits
vegetables (growing), 454-59
  fertilizing, 458
  herbs, 459
  growing from seed, 456-57
  heirloom seeds, 455
  late-season, 454-59
  See also flowers; garden pests; lawns; planting; pruning; trees
Vegetarian Chili with Corn Bread Topping, 144
vehicular accidents and children, 92
Vendee Globe, 641
Venezuela
  trekking in, 564-65
Venezuelan League, 584
Venice Film Festival, 677
Venice Simplon-Orient-Express, 503
Venus, 726
Verbier Festival and Academy, 695
Verdi, Giuseppe, 681, 689
Verizon Wireless, 298
Vernal Equinox, 751
Veronica (Gaitskill), 707
Versace, Donatella, 672

Veterans Day, 755
Vetri-Lean (pet diet supplement), 478
Viagra, 42-44
video games, secondhand, 251
Vienna Festival, 695
Vienna State Opera, 690
Vietnam
  as travel destination, 519-20
Village Voice, 693
vinyl siding
  durability of, 412
Virtuoso Variations (various), 684
viruses (computer), 284
vitamins, 118-23
  biotin (vitamin B), 122
  folate (vitamin B), 122
  supplements, 114, 122-23
  supplements vs. food, 122
  vitamin A, 118, 119
  vitamin B1 (thiamin), 120
  vitamin B2 (riboflavin), 120
  vitamin B3 (niacin), 120
  vitamin B5 (pantothenic acid), 120
  vitamin B6 (pyroxine), 120-21
  vitamin B12, 121
  vitamin C (ascorbic acid), 121
  vitamin D, 121
  vitamin E, 121
Vivaldi, Antonio, 681, 691
vodka, 161
VoIP (voice over Internet protocol), 297, 514
volleyball, 612
Vonage (online phone service), 296
voter registration, 777-78
Voyageurs National Park, 547

W

W. Atlee Burpee & Co. (seed company), 440
Wagner, Richard, 681
waist-to-hip ratio, 6
waiters, tipping, 250
Wal-Mart, 249
walking shoes, 22
Walking Softly in the Wilderness: The Sierra Club Guide to Backpacking (Hart), 545
Walküre, Die (Wagner), 681
Wall Street Journal, 185
wall-to-wall carpets, 430
Wallace, Christopher, 368

Wallace Collection (London), 699
wallpaper
  durability of, 412
  hand-blocked, 420
Walt Disney Concert Hall (L.A.), 701
Walter, Claire, 627
Walton, Izaak, 620
War Trash (Ha Jin), 706
Ward Melville (public school), 324-25
Warner, Ralph, 784, 785
warranties, 252-53, 284
Washington, D.C.
  family travel and, 536-37
Washington, George, 750-51
Washington Capitals, 595
Washington Nationals, 585
Washington Redskins, 591
Washington Wizards, 593
Washington's Crossing (Fischer), 706
waterbeds, 429
Watts, Naomi, 30
Way Out There in the Blue: Reagan, Star Wars and the End of the Cold War (FitzGerald), 703
Wayside Gardens (seed company), 440
weather forecasting, 710-17
  accurate predictions, 710
  atmospheric pressure and, 713, 715
  basic barometer reading, 714
  Beaufort Scale of Wind Force, 714
  clouds, 717
  folklore, 710-13
  hurricanes, 715
  hypothermia, 716
  weather maps, reading, 711
  weather patterns in selected cities, 712-13
  windchill, 715-16
weather forecasting (and folklore), 710-13
  bees and rain, 710-11
  crickets as thermometer, 710
  halo around the moon, 710
  hornets and winter, 710
  human hair and rain, 713
  low-hanging smoke, 710
  mackerel clouds, 710
  red sky at night, 710
  sinus and joint pain, 713
  sweet-smelling air and storms, 710

Weatherization Assistance Program Technical Assistance Center, 433
Web sites (selected)
  ADHD, 91
  air-fare bargains, 493
  art collecting, 301
  Centers for Disease Control and Prevention, 111
  credit reports, 179
  disaster information, 106
  financial planners, 198
  foreign retirement, 224
  health insurance, 228
  job hunting, 367-68, 369
  job transfers abroad, 389
  identity theft, 256
  international cooking schools, 145
  local food resources, 136
  movie and TV, 671
  PC-to-phone services, 297-98
  rail travel, 504
  real estate, 209
  real estate (commercial), 224, 225
  safe pregnancy, 72
  shopping, 247
  stamp collecting, 315-17
  stock research, 188
  vacation rentals, 510-12
  weight loss, 5
  wine ratings, 148
  See also blog sites; Internet; online; online shopping
Webb, James T., 321-22
weddings, 798-803
  anniversary gifts, 802
  birthstones and flowers, 802
  first dance, 803
  how to cancel, 801
  New York Times wedding announcements, 801
  old vs. new practices, 798-99
  toasts, 800
wedding planning, 799-801
Weiand, Jeff A., 186
weight lifting
  genetics and, 17
  and weight loss, 16-17
weight loss, 3-9
  body mass index (BMI), 7
  diet pills, 8-9
  diet plan, customizing, 4
  exercise and, 4-5
  focus and, 5
  general height and weight chart, 4

obesity and children, 93
portion control, 4
quick fixes, 3
waist-to-hip ratio, 6
Web sites and, 5
weights and measures, 762-68
 angles and circles, 767
 apothecaries' fluid measure, 767
 apothecaries' weight, 767
 clothing sizes, 765
 household measures, 768
 mariners' measure, 767-68
 measuring without a ruler, 762
 metric units, 764, 766-67
 miles to kilometers, 766
 surveyor's measure, 768
 surveyor's square measure, 768
 temperature conversions, 763
 time measure, 768
 troy weight, 768
 U.S. customary units, 763-64, 765-66
 wood measure, 768
Weill, Sanford I., 378
Weinkle, Dr. Susan H., 27
Weinstein, Dr. James N., 68
Weitzman, Dr. Michael, 91
Welbourne, Theresa M., 387
Well-Tended Perennial Garden, The (DiSabato-Aust), 463
Wellen, Alex, 339-40
Wesson, Joshua, 149
Western Conference (basketball)
 Dallas Mavericks, 593
 Denver Nuggets, 593
 Golden State Warriors, 593
 Houston Rockets, 593
 Los Angeles Clippers, 593
 Los Angeles Lakers, 593
 Minnesota Timberwolves, 593
 New Orleans/Oklahoma City Hornets, 593
 Phoenix Suns, 593
 Portland Trail Blazers, 593
 Sacramento Kings, 593
 San Antonio Spurs, 593
 Seattle SuperSonics, 593
 Utah Jazz, 593
 See also Eastern Conference (basketball)
Western Conference (hockey)

Anaheim Mighty Ducks, 595
Calgary Flames, 595
Chicago Blackhawks, 595
Colorado Avalanche, 595
Columbus Blue Jackets, 595
Dallas Stars, 595
Detroit Red wings, 595
Edmonton Oilers, 595
Los Angeles Kings, 595
Minnesota Wild, 595
Nashville Predators, 595
Phoenix Coyotes, 595
St. Louis Blues, 595
San Jose Sharks, 595
Vancouver Canucks, 595
 See also Eastern Conference (hockey)
Westerterp, Klaas, 12
wet basement, fixing, 434-35
whale watching, 555
What Color Is Your Parachute? (Bolles), 400
What Stimulation Your Baby Needs to Become Smart (Staso), 84
When Everybody Wore a Hat (Steig), 334
whiskey-sipping secrets, 161
Whistler, James McNeill, 700
white Burgundy wines, 150
White Flower Farm (seed company), 440
White Teeth (Smith), 703
white-water rafting, 574-77
 American River (CA), 574-75
 Colorado River (CO), 575
 Deschutes River (OR), 575
 Grand Canyon, 576
 Kennebec River (ME), 576
 Nantahala River (NC), 577
 Ocoee Tiver (TN), 577
 Rio Grande (NM), 576
 Salmon River (ID), 575
 Snake River (WY), 575
 Youghiogheny River (PA), 576-77
Whitehead, Colson, 703
Whitehead, Randall, 423
wholesale trade employment, 378
Why Men Make More: The Startling Truth Behind the Pay Gap (Farrell), 400
Why We Love (Fisher), 36
Widener Library (Harvard), 708
Wilde, Oscar, 352
wilderness areas, 548
wildlife, 554-56

California and Steller's sea lions, 555
 bald eagles, 556
 bighorn sheep, 554
 gray whales, 555
 manatees, 554
 Mexican free-tailed bats, 556
 Rocky Mountain elk, 554
 sandhill cranes, 554-55
 wintering elk, 554
 See also safaris
Will in the World: How Shakespeare Became Shakespeare (Greenblatt), 706
Williams, Vera B., 335
wills, 789-90
Wilson, Edmund, 350
Wilson, Dr. Everett J., 329
windows
 fixing stuck, 435-36
Windows-based computers, 284
 backup software, 286-87
 software that converts file formats, 286
 See also computers; Macintosh computers
Windows on the World Complete Wine Course (Zraly), 150
wines, 148-57
 Australian wines, 153-54
 Austrian wines, 154-55
 books on, 150
 Californian wines, 155-56
 Champagne, 156-57
 Champagne bottles, 157
 drinking dos and don'ts, 158
 evaluating, 149
 French wines, 149-51
 as investment, 316
 Italian wines, 151-52
 Oregonian wines, 156
 ratings, 148
 rosés, 153
 serving temperatures, 152
 South American wines, 153
 Spanish wines, 152-53
 starting a cellar, 148
 wine and cheese pairings, 154
Winner-Take-All-Society, The (Frank/Cook), 363
Winship, Tim, 500
Winter, Jeanette, 335
Winter Solstice, 755-56
winter sports
 curling, 627
 dangers, 628

foot-warmth, 637
ice climbing, 630
ice hockey, 628-28
igloo building, 636
polar bear swimming, 629-30
skating, 638-40
skiing, 632-36
skijoring, 637-38
skin protection, 635
snowboarding, 630-31
snowmobiling, 629
snowshoeing, 627-28
 See also games; sports
wintering elk, 554
Winterreise (Schubert), 682
Winterrowd, Wayne, 441
Wire magazine, 693
Wiseman, Rosalind, 108
Wister, Owen, 635
Wohl, Clifford, 332
Wolfe, Tom, 350
Wolmer, Bruce, 308
Woman's Health Initiative, 39, 40, 114
women
 and calcium, 124
 as executives, 382-83
 gender gap, exploiting, 400
 and heart disease, 52-55
 and home buying, 206
 self-defense, 108-9
 in the workforce, 399
Women's Equality Day, 753
women's issues, 792-93
Woo, Cameron, 480
wood (durability of)
 shingles, 412
 siding, 412
wood measure, 768
Wood, Grant, 700
Wood, Dr. Richard J., 123
Wood Classics (furniture kits), 427
Woody Guthrie: Poet of the People (Christensen), 335
words, 804
 crossword puzzles, 804-5
 grammar, 805
Words That Win: What to Say to Get What You Want (Garbor), 795
Work: How to Find Work You Love and Live the Time of Your Life (Kang), 398
workforce, women in, 399
World Atlas of Wine (Johnson/Robinson), 150
World Series, 590
World Wide Arts Resources, 698

WorldAirportGuide.com, 500
Worley, Bette, 354
Wozzeck (Berg), 683
wraparound mortgages, 211
Wright, Frank Lloyd, 701
Wyler, Seymour B., 315
Wysocki, Mark, 710-13

X
Xena (2003 UB313), 729, 741

Y
Yale, 353
 arts education, 346
Year of Magical Thinking, The (Didion), 707
Yellow Umbrella (Liu), 335
Yellowstone National Park, 541, 542
 snowmobiles in, 543
yoga, 17-18
yogurt, 129
Yom Kippur, 757
Yosemite National Park, 540
 rock climbing, 542, 625
You and Your Adolescent (Steinberg), 331
Youghiogheny River (PA)
 white-water rafting, 576-77
Youngblood, Ed, 275-77

Z
Zambia, safaris in, 563
Zelickson, Dr. Brian D., 26
Zimbabwe, safaris in, 563
zinc, 125
Zion National Park, 541, 543
zip codes, finding, 254
zodiac signs
 Aquarius, 740
 Aries, 739
 Cancer, 739
 Capricorn, 740
 Gemini, 739
 Leo, 740
 Libra, 740
 Pisces, 740
 Sagittarius, 740
 Scorpio, 740
 Taurus, 739
 Virgo, 740
Zraly, Kevin, 150